Microsoft

MCSE

Exam
70-224

Microsoft® Exchange 2000 Server Implementation and Administration

Training Kit

Microsoft Corporation and Kay Unkroth

IT Resource Library

PUBLISHED BY
Microsoft Press
A Division of Microsoft Corporation
One Microsoft Way
Redmond, Washington 98052-6399

Library of Congress Cataloging-in-Publication Data
Unkroth, Kay.
    MCSE Training Kit: Microsoft Exchange 2000 Server Implementation and
    Administration / Kay Unkroth.
        p. cm.
    Includes index.
      ISBN 0-7356-1028-2
      1. Electronic data processing personnel--Certification. 2. Microsoft
software--Examinations--Study guides. 3. Microsoft Windows server.   I. Microsoft
Corporation. II. Title.

    QA76.3 .U54   2000
    005.7'13769--dc21   00-046053

Printed and bound in the United States of America.

1 2 3 4 5 6 7 8 9   QWT   6 5 4 3 2 1

Distributed in Canada by Penguin Books Canada Limited.

A CIP catalogue record for this book is available from the British Library.

Microsoft Press books are available through booksellers and distributors worldwide. For further information about international editions, contact your local Microsoft Corporation office or contact Microsoft Press International directly at fax (425) 936-7329. Visit our Web site at mspress.microsoft.com. Send comments to *tkinput@microsoft.com*.

Acquisitions Editor: Thomas Pohlmann
Project Editor: Michael Bolinger

Author: Kay Unkroth

Contents

Acknowledgments

The current work is the successor to *Microsoft Exchange Server 5.5 Training Kit*, which was an extremely successful book project. It received the Excellence Award of the Society for Technical Communication (SCT) in 1998, and I would like to take the opportunity to mention that all of us that were involved in producing this book are very thankful and proud of this high recognition. Very positive feedback also came from numerous readers. Among other things, the depth of technical detail, the accuracy of information, and the practical exercises were generally recognized as outstanding positive features. Yet, there was critical feedback as well. Many readers found the outline of the old Training Kit, especially the repetition of concepts and facts, difficult to handle. This repetition of information was indeed intentional, but I had to learn that this was not an optimal approach to transfer knowledge. In other words, there was plenty of room for improvement. I hope that you will find the new Training Kit crisper, more to the point, less repetitive, and, therefore, easier to read.

The current Training Kit is written for computer specialists that want to gain a high level of professionalism in Microsoft Exchange 2000 Server. Knowledge of earlier versions of Exchange Server is not a prerequisite. This Training Kit is the right source for those who want to become Exchange 2000 Server experts, do their jobs better, go forward in their careers, and advance to new job opportunities. Our Training Kit allows you to thoroughly prepare for the Microsoft Certified Professional exam 70-224, "Installing, Configuring, and Administering Microsoft Exchange 2000 Server."

I love writing computer books, but I'm a very slow writer. My best score is seven pages per day; often I only get five pages done, and sometimes zero—those are the hard days, when nothing works. It took ages to get this manuscript to the publisher, but a manuscript is not a book. It takes a whole team of highly professional editors and artists and support from many sources to bring a book project to a successful completion. Please let me introduce to you all the people that had an important influence.

Before anybody else, I want to mention and thank Jeff Madden for his support and tremendous help. He was my Acquisition Editor at the time when we settled the project plan. Without him this book would not have come true. I also would like to thank Anne Hamilton, who helped to get the project on schedule during the early stages and who allowed me to have it 100% my way—yes! Later on, Thomas Pohlmann became my Acquisition Editor. That is a funny coincidence because Thomas and I had worked together on a few projects in Munich,

Germany, before. So here we were again, this time in Redmond, WA (it's only half-way around the world).

I also want to mention Stuart Stuple for his great support when I needed it the most. He brought me in touch with a brilliant support specialist for Exchange 2000 Server, Jeff Wilkes, who supported the early adopters for Microsoft since the initial stages of Platinum. Jeff gave me answers to many questions that nobody else could answer, and he referred me to Michael Lee, Microsoft's disaster recovery expert, who gave me very deep insights into the disaster recovery concepts of Exchange 2000 Server. I want to point out that Jeff and Michael helped me even though their own workload was enormous during the last weeks before the product shipped.

Now it's high time I introduced to you the actual editorial team working on this Exchange 2000 Server Training Kit. Michael Bolinger, the Project Editor, was my direct communication partner for the past nine months. Michael is a very experienced coordinator. He has been working in technical publishing for the past five years, spending much of his time working on MCSE Training Kits. His latest guess at the number of books he has contributed to constitutes some 60 titles. Michael, I really enjoyed working with you. I'm going to miss the large amounts of e-mail messages from you.

My Technical Editor, Tony Northrup, is likewise an old hand (MCSE and Compaq ASE). Tony has worked as a consultant at some of the largest corporations in the United States. He is the author of *Introducing Windows 2000 Server* and *NT Network Plumbing*, co-author of *Networking Essentials Unleashed*, and he is the Technical Editor for *Microsoft Windows 2000 TCIP/IP Protocol and Services Technical Reference* and *MCSE Training Kit—Microsoft Windows 2000 Network Infrastructure Administration*. It's obvious that his work is excellent. He caught me on many inaccuracies and fuzzy statements. It was very impressive to see how persistently Tony worked through 29 chapters with a constant level of highest precision.

The nontechnical editing of the manuscript was also in very good hands. Just give it a try—open this book somewhere in the middle, read a few sentences, and then look at the artwork. You must admit that our editing team did an excellent job. That is the work of Sarah Kimnach Hains, Project Manager, and her team of worker bees Theresa Horton, Copy Editor; Lucia Colella, Page Layout and Art; Mary Beth McDaniel, Page Layout and Art; Joanna Zito, Page Layout; Tara Lynn Murray, Art; Rebecca Merz, Proofchecker; Sarah Campbell, Proofreader. Sarah Kimnach Hains is responsible for managing publications and online projects at nSight, Inc., of Cambridge, MA. She is one of the "Resident Experts" at nSight concerning the production of Microsoft books, such as Pocket Consultants, Training Kits, and Technical References. She and her team enjoy the challenge of producing complicated books while maintaining the highest standard of quality.

Nobody can write a book without support from family, business partners, and friends. Perhaps this is the reason many authors dedicate their work to their wives, husbands, or other family members. The constant support of my wife, Jean (my wonderful Buggy-Darling), is one basis of my success in business. Jean, Scott, Kelly, I love you with all my heart. Another important person in my life is my business partner, Fergus Strachan. Book writing is a full-time job that does not leave much room to manage a company. Fergus understood, silently gave in, and managed our company in London, England, alone, for more than nine months while I followed my writing ambitions. In addition to that, he took an active part in compiling the Glossary for me. Thanks for everything, Ferg. I owe you more than a single malt. And there's one more person who I would like to mention—my colleague Carl John. He spent many extra hours setting up test environments for me so that I would not lose precious time from my writing.

It's the great help of so many people that make me feel very special. I can't mention all of them. Personal friends at IBM/Lotus, Novell, Microsoft, many self-employed colleagues, and even customers of ours were eager to assist. I hope that I was able to pass their help further on to you to help you master the challenges of Exchange 2000 Server.

London, 17th of October, 2000
Kay Unkroth
Director Corporate OnSite Ltd.

About This Book

Welcome to the MCSE Training Kit—Microsoft Exchange 2000 Server Implementation and Administration.

Note   For more information on becoming a Microsoft Certified Systems Engineer, see the section titled "The Microsoft Certified Professional Program," later in this introduction.

Each chapter in this book is divided into lessons. Most lessons include hands-on procedures that allow you to practice or demonstrate a particular concept or skill. Each chapter ends with a short summary of all chapter lessons and a set of review questions to test your knowledge of the chapter material.

The "Getting Started" section of this introduction provides important setup instructions that describe the hardware and software requirements to complete the procedures in this course. It also provides information about the networking configuration necessary to complete some of the hands-on procedures. Read through this section thoroughly before you start the lessons.

Intended Audience

This book was developed for information technology (IT) professionals who need to design, plan, implement, and support Microsoft Exchange 2000 Server or who plan to take the related Microsoft Certified Professional exam 70-224, "Installing, Configuring, and Administering Microsoft Exchange 2000 Server."

Prerequisites

This course requires that students meet the following prerequisites:

- Have a general understanding of Microsoft Windows 2000 Server networking technologies and the TCP/IP protocol suite.

- Be familiar with the concepts and administration of the Active Directory directory service.

Reference Materials

You might find the following reference materials useful:

- Planning and Installation Guide from the Microsoft Exchange 2000 Server Online Documentation for detailed information about Exchange 2000 Server.

- *Microsoft Windows 2000 Server Online Documentation* for detailed information about Windows 2000 management utilities and their usage.

- *Microsoft Windows 2000 Resource Kit* for complete information regarding Windows 2000 components and technologies leveraged in Exchange 2000 Server.

- *Microsoft Platform Software Development Kit (SDK)* for a concise discussion about the architecture of Microsoft Management Console (MMC) snap-ins.

- *Microsoft Exchange Software Development Kit (EDK)* for details about the development of custom workgroup and workflow solutions.

- *Microsoft Exchange 2000 Server White Papers* published by Microsoft Product Support Services (PSS) on the Internet and also available on the Microsoft TechNet CD.

About the CD-ROM

The Supplemental Course Materials CD contains a variety of informational aids that may be used throughout this book. This includes multimedia demonstrations, sample utilities, and files used in hands-on exercises. For more information regarding the contents of this CD, see the section titled "Getting Started," later in this introduction.

A complete version of this book is also available online with a variety of viewing options available. For information about using the online book, see the section titled "The Online Book," later in this introduction. (The other CD contains a copy of the Microsoft Exchange 2000 Server, 120-day Evaluation Edition, software.)

Features of This Book

Each chapter opens with a "Before You Begin" section, which prepares you for completing the chapter.

▶   The chapters are then broken into lessons. Whenever possible, lessons contain practices that give you an opportunity to use the skills being presented or explore the part of the application being described. All practices offer step-by-step procedures that are identified with a bullet symbol like the one to the left of this paragraph.

The "Review" section at the end of the chapter allows you to test what you have learned in the chapter's lessons.

Appendix A, "Questions and Answers," contains all of the book's questions and corresponding answers.

Notes

Several types of Notes appear throughout the lessons.

- Notes marked **Tip** contain explanations of possible results or alternative methods.
- Notes marked **Important** contain information that is essential to completing a task.
- Notes marked **Note** contain supplemental information.
- Notes marked **Caution** contain warnings about possible loss of data.

Conventions

The following conventions are used throughout this book.

Notational Conventions

- Characters or commands that you type appear in **bold lowercase** type.
- <Angle brackets> in syntax statements indicate placeholders for variable information.
- *Italic* is used for book titles and Web addresses.
- Names of files and folders appear in Title Caps, except when you are to type them directly. Unless otherwise indicated, you can use all lowercase letters when you type a file name in a dialog box or at a command prompt.
- File name extensions appear in all lowercase.
- Acronyms appear in all uppercase.
- `Monospace` type represents code samples, examples of screen text, or entries that you might type at a command prompt or in initialization files.
- Square brackets [ ] are used in syntax statements to enclose optional items. For example, [*filename*] in command syntax indicates that you can choose to type a file name with the command. Type only the information within the brackets, not the brackets themselves.
- Braces { } are used in syntax statements to enclose required items. Type only the information within the braces, not the braces themselves.

▪ Icons represent specific sections in the book as follows:

Icon	Represents
	A file that can be found on the Supplemental Course Materials CD.
	A hands-on practice. You should perform the practice to give yourself an opportunity to use the skills being presented in the lesson.
	Chapter review questions. These questions at the end of each chapter allow you to test what you have learned in the lessons. You will find the answers to the review questions in Appendix A, "Questions and Answers," at the end of the book.

Keyboard Conventions

▪ A plus sign (+) between two key names means that you must press those keys at the same time. For example, "Press ALT+TAB" means that you hold down ALT while you press TAB.

▪ A comma (,) between two or more key names means that you must press each of the keys consecutively, not together. For example, "Press ALT, F, X" means that you press and release each key in sequence. "Press ALT+W, L" means that you first press ALT and W together, and then release them and press L.

▪ You can choose menu commands with the keyboard. Press the ALT key to activate the menu bar, and then sequentially press the keys that correspond to the highlighted or underlined letter of the menu name and the command name. For some commands, you can also press a key combination listed in the menu.

▪ You can select or clear check boxes or option buttons in dialog boxes with the keyboard. Press the ALT key, and then press the key that corresponds to the underlined letter of the option name. Or you can press TAB until the option is highlighted, and then press the spacebar to select or clear the check box or option button.

▪ You can cancel the display of a dialog box by pressing the ESC key.

Chapter and Appendix Overview

This self-paced training course combines notes, hands-on procedures, multimedia presentations, and review questions to teach you Microsoft Exchange 2000 Server Implementation and Administration. It is designed to be completed from beginning to end, but you can choose a customized track and complete only the sections that interest you. (See the next section, "Finding the Best Starting Point for You," for more information.) If you choose the customized track option, see the "Before You Begin" section in each chapter. Any hands-on procedures that require preliminary work from preceding chapters refer to the appropriate chapters.

The book is divided into the following chapters:

- The "About This Book" section contains a self-paced training overview and introduces the components of this training. Read this section thoroughly to get the greatest educational value from this self-paced training and to plan which lessons you will complete.

- Chapter 1, "Introduction to Microsoft Exchange 2000 Server," discusses basic messaging features and describes Microsoft's design goals for Exchange 2000 Server. It also briefly covers Exchange 2000 Server's support for industry messaging standards and interoperability issues.

- Chapter 2, "Integration with Microsoft Windows 2000," provides you with an overview of how Exchange 2000 Server is built into Windows 2000 and utilizes the Active Directory directory service. The chapter also examines important networking components Exchange 2000 Server relies on for its own communication.

- Chapter 3, "Microsoft Exchange 2000 Server Architecture," addresses the architecture of Exchange 2000 Server, the interaction of its components, and the server-to-server communication. You will find a concise description of the essential Exchange 2000 Server elements, the communication paths among the various server components, and the message flow as handled by Exchange 2000 Server.

- Chapter 4, "Planning the Microsoft Exchange 2000 Server Installation," explains the prerequisites and some of the most important considerations for a successful deployment of Exchange 2000 Server. You can read about various deployment options, necessary preparations of Windows 2000 Server and Active Directory, the hardware and software requirements, and security and maintenance.

- Chapter 5, "Installing Microsoft Exchange 2000 Server," deals with the Setup program of Exchange 2000 Server and various postinstallation considerations. This chapter covers, in detail, the installation types, available setup options, and issues you should consider after a setup procedure is completed successfully.

- Chapter 6, "Coexistence with Previous Microsoft Exchange Server Versions," covers, in detail, the important tasks you face when upgrading or migrating an existing Microsoft Exchange Server 5.5 organization to Exchange 2000 Server. It demonstrates how to integrate Exchange Server 5.5 with Active Directory, deals with the actual upgrade procedures, and concludes with a discussion of postupgrade tasks. This chapter contains five optional exercises that you may want to follow if you have an Exchange Server 5.5 CD available. You can run multimedia demonstrations that illustrate how to perform the procedures from the \Exercise_Information\Chapter6 folder on the Supplemental Course Materials CD.

- Chapter 7, "Microsoft Exchange 2000 Server in Clustered Environments," focuses on the installation of Exchange 2000 Server in a clustered Windows 2000 environment. It covers important concepts, such as active/active clustering and failover procedures, with an eye on the actual installation of Exchange 2000 Server into server clusters that consist of up to four nodes. This chapter contains three optional exercises that you may want to follow if you have a server cluster available. You can run multimedia demonstrations that illustrate how to perform the procedures from the \Exercise_Information \Chapter7 folder on the Supplemental Course Materials CD.

- Chapter 8, "Microsoft Outlook 2000 Deployment," focuses on the installation and configuration of Outlook 2000 in an Exchange 2000 Server environment. This chapter covers the various installation types and valuable setup utilities, and examines Exchange-specific configuration settings.

- Chapter 9, "MAPI-Based Clients," introduces the client family of MAPI-based applications and then concentrates on the creation and configuration of messaging profiles and the most important MAPI information services. This chapter also discusses advanced configuration topics, such as configurations for roaming users and for remote users working disconnected from the network.

- Chapter 10, "MAPI-Based Clients in a Novell NetWare Environment," addresses the main aspects of combining Windows 2000 Server and NetWare and then covers the client-side requirements for establishing remote procedure call (RPC) connections to an Exchange 2000 server. This chapter also explains how to troubleshoot client connectivity problems.

- Chapter 11, "Internet-Based Client Access," deals with popular Internet messaging protocols and their implementation in Exchange 2000 Server. Among other things, this chapter explains how to configure virtual servers for access to mailboxes and public folders across the Internet.

- Chapter 12, "Management Tools for Microsoft Exchange 2000 Server," introduces various Windows 2000 and Exchange 2000 snap-ins that are important for managing Exchange 2000 resources. This chapter provides a general feature overview.

- Chapter 13, "Creating and Managing Recipients," concentrates on the management of recipient objects in Active Directory. Available recipient objects and their characteristics are introduced and resource management tasks are discussed.

- Chapter 14, "Managing the Server Configuration," focuses on the management of Exchange 2000 resources using Exchange System Manager. It covers important configuration issues at the server, administrative group, and organization levels.

- Chapter 15, "SMTP Transport Configuration," deals with the configuration of Simple Mail Transfer Protocol (SMTP) virtual servers and the customization of the SMTP service. This chapter provides information about how to connect an Exchange 2000 server to the Internet without deploying an SMTP Connector.

- Chapter 16, "Message Routing Administration," discusses the design of routing topologies in Exchange 2000 organizations. This chapter explains how multiple routing groups are managed to optimize message transfer and covers how routing and link state information are propagated between servers.

- Chapter 17, "Public Folder Management," addresses the management of public folders that reside on a single Exchange 2000 server. This chapter discusses public folder concepts and the administration of public stores.

- Chapter 18, "Public Folder Replication," covers the various aspects of public folder replication, including advantages, granularity, and configuration. This chapter discusses the various methods of collecting and delivering public folder instances from and to other servers and the replication process in detail.

- Chapter 19, "Implementing Advanced Security," covers in detail how Exchange 2000 Server integrates into the Windows 2000 security architecture and then focuses on advanced security services based on the X.509 industry standard recommended by the Public Key Infrastructure (PKI) working group of the Internet Engineering Task Force (IETF).

- Chapter 20, "Microsoft Exchange 2000 Server Maintenance and Troubleshooting," focuses on important maintenance features that can ease the task of system management and addresses backing up and restoring Exchange 2000 Server. This chapter includes in-depth explanations of how to recover information store databases in various situations.

- Chapter 21, "Microsoft Outlook Forms Environment," covers the development, installation, and use of Outlook forms and related workgroup solutions at a basic level. This chapter also explains the management of electronic forms libraries.

- Chapter 22, "Microsoft Outlook Web Access," deals with Outlook Web Access (OWA) of Exchange 2000 Server. This chapter covers the OWA architecture and then approaches this client from a more practical point of view, discussing the various methods of resource access as well as backward compatibility issues.

- Chapter 23, "Microsoft Exchange 2000 Web Storage System," concentrates on an introduction to the Web Storage System. This chapter provides essential information for administrators and briefly discusses how to use the features of the Web Storage System to build customized enterprise applications.

- Chapter 24, "Workgroup and Workflow Technologies," concentrates on the new Collaboration Data Objects (CDO) technologies for Exchange 2000 Server and illustrates how to use them to implement messaging capabilities, manage an Exchange 2000 server, and design workflow processes.

- Chapter 25, "Real-Time Collaboration," addresses the features of Exchange 2000 Server for instant communication and real-time collaboration. This chapter covers the architecture and implementation of Instant Messaging and

Exchange 2000 Chat and introduces Microsoft Exchange 2000 Conferencing Server.

- Chapter 26, "Connecting to Microsoft Mail and Schedule+," covers the Microsoft Mail Connector, directory synchronization with MS Mail (Dirsync), and the Microsoft Schedule+ Free/Busy Connector.

- Chapter 27, "Connecting to Lotus cc:Mail," addresses the installation and configuration of the Connector for Lotus cc:Mail for e-mail message transfer and propagation of address information. This chapter focuses on environments with Lotus cc:Mail DB8.

- Chapter 28, "Connecting to Lotus Notes," focuses on the architecture and administration of the Connector for Lotus Notes. This chapter explains how to provide messaging connectivity and directory synchronization between Exchange 2000 Server and Lotus Domino/Notes R5.

- Chapter 29, "Connecting to Novell GroupWise," introduces the Connector for Novell GroupWise and explains how to use this connector for messaging connectivity and directory synchronization with Novell GroupWise 5.5.

- Appendix A, "Questions and Answers," lists all of the review questions from the book and the suggested answers.

- The Glossary contains the definitions of important terms used in this book.

Finding the Best Starting Point for You

Because this book is self-paced, you can skip some lessons and revisit them later. Note, however, that you must set up a test environment, as described later in this section, before you can perform procedures in any of the chapters. Use the following table to find the best starting point for you:

If You	Follow This Learning Path
Are preparing to take the Microsoft Certified Professional exam 70-224, "Installing, Configuring, and Administering Microsoft Exchange 2000 Server."	Read the "Getting Started" section. Then work through Chapters 1 through 5. Work through the remaining chapters in any order.
Want to review information about specific topics from the exam.	Use the "Where to Find Specific Skills in This Book" section that follows this table.

Where to Find Specific Skills in This Book

The following tables provide a list of the skills measured on certification exam 70-224, "Installing, Configuring, and Administering Microsoft Exchange 2000 Server." The table provides the skill and where in this book you will find the lesson relating to that skill.

Note   Exam skills are subject to change without prior notice and at the sole discretion of Microsoft.

Installing and Upgrading Exchange 2000 Server

Skill Being Measured	Location in Book
Install Exchange 2000 Server on a server computer	Chapters 4, 5, 6, and 7
Diagnose and resolve failed installations	Chapters 4, 5, and 6
Upgrade or migrate to Exchange 2000 Server from Exchange Server 5.5	Chapter 6
Diagnose and resolve problems involving the upgrade process	Chapter 6
Manage coexistence with Exchange Server 5.5	
■ Maintain common user lists	Chapter 6
■ Maintain existing connectors	Chapters 6 and 16
■ Move users from Exchange 5.5 to Exchange 2000	Chapter 6
■ Configure the Exchange 2000 Active Directory Connector to replicate directory information	Chapter 6
Diagnose and resolve Exchange 2000 Active Directory Connector problems	Chapters 3 and 6
Perform client deployments	
■ Microsoft Outlook 2000	Chapters 8, 9, and 10
■ Outlook Web Access, POP3, IMAP4	Chapters 11 and 22
■ Internet Relay Chat	Chapter 25
■ Configure Outlook Web Access	Chapter 22
■ Configure client access protocols	Chapter 11

Configuring Exchange 2000 Server

Skill Being Measured	Location In Book
Configure mailbox stores	Chapters 12, 14, and 20
Configure public folders	Chapters 12, 17, 18, and 20
Configure connectors and gateways	Chapters 12, 15, 16, 26, 27, 28, and 29
Configure virtual servers	Chapter 11
Configure Chat	Chapter 25
Configure Instant Messaging	Chapter 25

Configuring Exchange 2000 Server *(continued)*

Skill Being Measured	Location In Book
Configure server objects for messaging and collaboration to support the assigned server role	
■ Configure information store objects	Chapters 12, 14, and 20
■ Configure multiple storage groups for data partitioning	Chapter 20
■ Configure multiple databases within a single storage group	Chapter 20
■ Configure virtual servers to support Internet protocols	Chapters 11, 22, and 25
■ Configure Exchange 2000 Server information in Windows 2000 Active Directory	Chapters 2, 3, 4, 5, 13, 26, 27, 28, and 29
■ Configure Instant Messaging objects	Chapter 25
■ Configure Chat objects	Chapter 25
Create and manage administrative groups	Chapters 4, 5, 6, and 14
Configure separate Exchange 2000 Server resources for high-volume access. Configure stores, logs, and separate RAID arrays	Chapters 7 and 20
Diagnose and resolve Exchange 2000 availability and performance problems	
■ Diagnose and resolve server resource constraints (resources include processor, memory, and hard disk)	Chapters 12 and 20
■ Diagnose and resolve server-specific performance problems	Chapter 20
Configure Exchange 2000 Server for high security	
■ Configure Exchange 2000 Server to issue v.3 certificates	Chapter 19
■ Enable digest authentication for Instant Messaging	Chapter 25
■ Configure certificate trust lists	Chapter 19
■ Configure virtual servers to limit access through firewalls	Chapters 11 and 19
■ Configure Key Management server (KM server) to issue digital signatures	Chapter 19
Create, configure, and manage a public folder solution	
■ Configure the Active Directory object attributes of a public folder	Chapter 17
■ Configure the store attributes of a public folder	Chapter 17
■ Configure multiple public folder trees	Chapters 17 and 18
Configure and manage system folders	Chapters 17 and 18

Managing Recipient Objects

Skill Being Measured	Location In Book
Configure and manage mailbox-enabled recipients	Chapter 14
Configure and manage mail-enabled recipients	Chapter 14
Configure a user object for messaging	
■ Configure a user object for e-mail	Chapter 14
■ Configure a user object for Instant Messaging	Chapter 25
■ Configure a user object for Chat	Chapter 25
Manage user and information store association	
■ Configure user information stores	Chapters 14 and 20
Diagnose and resolve problems that involve user and information store placement	
■ Diagnose and resolve security problems	Chapters 11 and 19
■ Diagnose and resolve performance problems	Chapters 4, 5, 11, 14, 20, and 22
■ Perform a disaster recovery	Chapter 20
Create and manage address lists	
■ Create security groups	Chapter 14
■ Create distribution groups	Chapter 14
Diagnose and resolve Recipient Update Service problems	Chapters 13 and 14

Monitoring and Managing Messaging Connectivity

Skill Being Measured	Location In Book
Monitor messaging connectivity	Chapters 12 and 20
Manage messaging connectivity	Chapters 15, 16, 26, 27, 28, and 29
Manage and troubleshoot messaging connectivity	
■ Manage Exchange 2000 Server messaging connectivity	Chapters 15, 16, 26, 27, 28, and 29
■ Manage connectivity to foreign mail systems	Chapters 26, 27, 28, and 29
■ Manage X.400, SMTP, and Internet messaging connectivity	Chapters 15 and 16
■ Diagnose and resolve routing problems	Chapters 16 and 20
■ Diagnose and resolve problems reported by nondelivery report messages	Chapter 16
Manage messaging queues for multiple protocols	Chapter 20

Monitoring and Managing Messaging Connectivity *(continued)*
Skill Being Measured

Monitor link status	
■ Monitor messages between Exchange 2000 Server computers	Chapter 20
■ Monitor messages between Exchange 2000 systems and foreign systems	Chapters 20, 26, 27, 28, and 29
Configure and monitor client connectivity	
■ Configure and monitor Outlook 2000	Chapters 8, 9, and 10
■ Configure and monitor Outlook Web Access	Chapters 11 and 22
■ Configure and monitor POP3 and IMAP4 clients	Chapter 11
■ Configure and monitor Internet Relay Chat (IRC) clients	Chapter 25
Diagnose and resolve client connectivity problems	
■ Diagnose and resolve DNS problems	Chapters 11, 15, and 16
■ Diagnose and resolve problems with a server publishing structure	Chapters 11, 13, 17, 22, 23, and 24
■ Diagnose and resolve DSProxy/DSAccess problems	Chapter 3
■ Diagnose and resolve problems with address resolution	Chapters 3 and 14
■ Diagnose and resolve problems with Instant Messaging clients	Chapter 25
■ Diagnose and resolve problems with various connection protocols	Chapters 11, 15, 16, and 22
■ Diagnose and resolve problems with non-Windows 2000 environments	Chapters 10, 27, 28, and 29
Manage public folder connectivity	
■ Configure and monitor public folder replication	Chapter 18
■ Diagnose and resolve public folder replication problems	Chapters 17 and 18

Managing Exchange 2000 Server Growth

Skill Being Measured	Location In Book
Load balancing through server clusters	Chapter 7
Load balancing through front end/back end configurations	Chapters 11, 19, and 22
Improve server scalability	Chapter 20

Skill Being Measured	Location In Book
Monitor services use	
■ Monitor Chat	Chapter 25
■ Monitor public folder access	Chapter 17
■ Monitor the Information Store service	Chapters 3, 12, 13, 14, and 20
■ Monitor server use by configuring server monitors	Chapters 12 and 20
■ Monitor Instant Messaging by using System Monitor	Chapter 25
Manage growth of public and private message store databases	Chapters 12, 14, and 20
Manage growth of user population and message traffic	Chapters 12, 13, 16, and 20
Monitor the growth of client use. Clients include Outlook 2000, Outlook Web Access, POP3, IMAP4, and IRC	Chapters 8, 9, 10, 11, 12, 14, 20, and 22
Manage recipient and server policies	Chapters 13 and 14
Diagnose and resolve problems that involve recipient and server policies	Chapters 13 and 14
Optimize public folder and mailbox searching	
■ Configure the store for full-text indexing	Chapter 14
■ Perform full-text indexing	Chapter 14

Restoring System Functionality and User Data

Skill Being Measured	Location In Book
Apply a backup and restore plan	
■ Design a backup and restore plan	Chapter 20
■ Restore system functionality and user data	Chapter 20
Diagnose and resolve backup and restore problems	Chapter 20
Restore user data and system state data	
■ Recover deleted mailboxes	Chapter 20
■ Recover deleted items	Chapter 20
Restore information stores	Chapter 20
Configure a server for disaster recovery (configurations include circular logging, backup, and restore)	Chapter 20
Diagnose and resolve security problems that involve user keys	Chapter 19

Getting Started

This self-paced training course contains hands-on procedures to help you learn about Exchange 2000 Server. To complete some of these procedures, you must have access to three networked computers. It may be possible to perform the procedures in this book with two computers when installing Outlook 2000 on an Exchange 2000 server. However, this configuration is not supported due to possible version conflicts related to MAPI32.DLL. All computers must be capable of running Microsoft Windows 2000 Server with Service Pack 1.

Caution   Several exercises may require you to make changes to your servers. This may have undesirable results if you are connected to a larger network. Check with your network administrator before attempting these exercises. It is highly recommended that you use two or three dedicated test machines that are not connected to a production environment.

Hardware Requirements

Each computer must have the following minimum configuration. All hardware should be on the Microsoft Windows 2000 Server Hardware Compatibility List.

- 128 to 256 megabytes (MB) of RAM
- 2 gigabytes (GB) of available disk space on the drive for Exchange 2000 Server
- 500 MB on the system drive
- CD-ROM drive
- Intel Pentium or compatible at 300 megahertz (MHz) or faster
- Microsoft Mouse or compatible pointing device
- Paging file set to twice the amount of RAM or larger
- VGA-compatible display adapter

Software Requirements

The following software is required to complete the procedures in this course.

- Microsoft Windows 2000 Server with Service Pack 1
- Microsoft Exchange 2000 Server (120-day Evaluation Edition included on CD in this kit.)
- Microsoft Outlook 2000 (120-day Evaluation Edition included on CD in this kit.)
- If available, Microsoft Windows NT Server 4.0 with Service Pack 6 and Microsoft Exchange Server 5.5 to follow the optional exercises in Chapter 6.

Caution   The 120-day Evaluation Editions provided with this training are not the full retail product and are provided only for the purposes of training and evaluation. Microsoft Technical Support does not support these editions. For additional support information regarding this book and the CDs (including answers to commonly asked questions about installation and use), visit the Microsoft Press Technical Support Web site at *http://mspress.microsoft.com/support/*. You can also email TKINPUT@MICROSOFT.COM, or send a letter to Microsoft Press, Attn: Microsoft Press Technical Support, One Microsoft Way, Redmond, WA 98502-6399.

Setup Instructions

Set up your computers according to the manufacturer's instructions. Because the exercises require networked computers, you need to make sure the computers can communicate with each other. Two computers will be configured as domain controllers and will be assigned the computer account names BLUESKY-SRV1 and BLUESKY-SRV2 with the domain names BLUESKY-INC-10.COM and CA.BLUESKY-INC-10.COM.

The third computer will act as workstation for most of the procedures in this course. This computer will be assigned the computer account name BLUESKY-WKSTA. If you are limited to two computers, you may use BLUESKY-SRV1 for all exercises that name BLUESKY-WKSTA.

In Chapter 6, two additional computers called BLUESKY-PDC and BLUESKY-BDC are required. Chapter 7 presupposes that you have a Windows 2000 server cluster available. The cluster nodes are called BLUESKY-ND1 and BLUESKY-ND2. However, the exercises of Chapters 6 and 7 can be considered optional if required hardware and software are unavailable.

Caution   If your computers are part of a larger network, you *must* verify with your network administrator that the computer names, domain names, IP addresses, and other information used in setting up Microsoft Exchange 2000 Server as described in this section and Chapters 4, 5, 6, and 7 do not conflict with network operations. If they do conflict, ask your network administrator to provide alternative values and use those values throughout the exercises in this book.

Installation of Windows 2000 Server

Follow these steps to install the Windows 2000 Server software on your computers. It is assumed that you are working with the 120-day Evaluation Edition of Microsoft Windows 2000 Advanced Server. Windows 2000 Service Pack 1 is also required.

▶ **To install Windows 2000 Server**

1. Insert the Windows 2000 Advanced Server CD into your CD-ROM drive and reboot the system from CD. Alternatively, use the Windows 2000 installation disks to begin the installation.

2. After Windows 2000 Setup has loaded its system files, a Setup Notification will be displayed informing you that you are installing an Evaluation version of Windows 2000, which contains a time-limited expiration. Press ENTER to continue the installation.

3. A Welcome To Setup notification is displayed. Press ENTER to set up Windows 2000 now.

4. The Windows 2000 Licensing Agreement is displayed next. Read the agreement carefully and, if you agree, press F8 to continue the installation.

5. If you have installed Windows 2000 Server previously on your test machine, a Windows 2000 Server Setup screen is now displayed asking you whether to repair the existing installation. In this case, press ESC to install a fresh version of the operating system.

6. A Windows 2000 Server Setup screen is displayed informing you about existing partitions. Make sure your test computer doesn't contain any important data, erase the existing partition scheme, and then configure two partitions, C and D, both with at least 2 GB of disk space.

7. As soon as you have partitioned your hard disk appropriately, select the partition C and press ENTER to install Windows 2000 on it.

8. You will be asked which file system to use. Select Format The Partition Using The NTFS File System and then press ENTER to continue.

9. Your hard disk will now be formatted, which might take up to several minutes depending on your hardware. After the formatting and conversion to NTFS is complete, Windows 2000 will boot automatically. Make sure that your system doesn't boot from CD-ROM (which would reset the procedure to Step 1).

10. The Windows 2000 Setup will continue in Windows mode. As soon as the Windows 2000 Setup Wizard appears, click Next to continue the installation (or wait a number of seconds until the wizard continues automatically).

11. Windows 2000 Server Setup is now detecting and installing devices. After that, the Regional Settings wizard screen is displayed. Make sure the system locale and keyboard layout match your configuration, and then click Next.

12. The Personalize Your Software wizard screen is displayed next. Under Name, type **Administrator** and, under Organization, type **Blue Sky Airlines** before you click Next to continue.

13. The Your Product Key wizard screen is displayed where you need to type the product key specified on your CD jewel case. After that, click Next to continue.

14. On the Licensing Modes wizard screen, select Per Seat, and then click Next to continue.

15. On the Computer Name And Administrator Password wizard screen, under Computer Name, type **BLUESKY-SRV1**, or **BLUESKY-SRV2**, **BLUESKY-ND1**, **BLUESKY-ND2**, or **BLUESKY-WKSTA**, depending on which computer you are installing. Under Administrator Password and Confirm Password type **password**. Click Next to continue.

16. On the Windows 2000 Components wizard screen, from the list of components, select Internet Information Services (IIS) and then click on the Details button. In the Internet Information Services (IIS) dialog box, select the NNTP Service check box and make sure the SMTP Service is selected as well. Click OK and then Next to continue the installation.

17. On the Date And Time Settings wizard screen, make sure Date & Time as well as Time Zone correspond to your location and then click Next to continue.

18. In case a Windows 2000 Server Setup dialog box appears asking you whether to use typical or custom settings, select Custom Settings, and then click Next to continue and configure the TCP/IP protocol.

19. In the Networking Components dialog box, select Internet Protocol (TCP/IP), and then click Properties.

20. In the Internet Protocol (TCP/IP) Properties dialog box, select Use The Following IP Address, and then specify the IP Address information according to the computer you are installing:

Computer	IP Address
BLUESKY-SRV1	192.168.1.22
BLUESKY-SRV2	192.168.1.23
BLUESKY-ND1	192.168.1.24
BLUESKY-ND2	192.168.1.25
BLUESKY-WKSTA	192.168.1.50

21. Under Subnet Mask, type **255.255.255.0** and then click OK.

22. In the Networking Components dialog box, click Next to continue the installation.

23. In case a Windows 2000 Server Setup dialog box appears asking you whether your computer is connected to a network, make sure the option No, This Computer Is Not On A Network, Or Is On A Network Without A Domain is selected, and then click Next to continue.

24. Windows 2000 Setup is now installing the networking and other components and completes the final set of tasks. After that, the Completing The Windows 2000 Setup Wizard screen is displayed, where you need to click Finish to finalize the installation.

25. Windows 2000 Advanced Server will reboot the computer and after that log on to the system using the Administrator account and a password of "password". Verify that you can access resources on the network.

▶ **To install Windows 2000 Service Pack 1**

1. Insert the Windows 2000 Service Pack 1 CD into your CD-ROM drive and start UPDATE.EXE (usually from the \i386\Update directory).

2. In the Windows 2000 Service Pack Setup dialog box, select the Accept The License Agreement (Must Accept Before Installing The Service Pack) check box, and then click Install.

3. In the final Windows 2000 Service Pack Setup dialog box, click Restart to reboot the system and complete the update.

Configuration of the Windows 2000 Active Directory Environment

Follow these steps to promote the computer BLUESKY-SRV1 to a domain controller in the domain BlueSky-inc-10.com. You also need to add BLUESKY-SRV2, BLUESKY-ND1, BLUESKY-ND2, and BLUESKY-WKSTA as members to this domain.

▶ **To promote BLUESKY-SRV1 to a domain controller**

1. Make sure you are logged on to BLUESKY-SRV1 as Administrator.

2. Click Start and select Run. In the Run dialog box type **dcpromo** and then click OK.

3. The Active Directory Installation Wizard is launched, displaying its welcome screen, where you need to click Next to continue.

4. On the Domain Controller Type wizard screen, make sure Domain Controller For A New Domain is selected, and then click Next.

5. On the Create Tree Or Child Domain wizard screen, make sure Create A New Domain Tree is selected, and then click Next.

6. On the Create Or Join Forest wizard screen, make sure Create A New Forest Of Domain Trees is selected, and then click Next.

7. On the New Domain Name wizard screen, under Full DNS Name For New Domain, type **BlueSky-inc-10.com**, and then click Next.

8. On the NetBIOS Domain Name wizard screen, under Domain NetBIOS Name, make sure BLUESKY-INC-10 is displayed, and then click Next.

9. On the Database And Log Locations wizard screen, accept the default settings, and then click Next.

10. On the Shared System Folder wizard screen, accept the default settings, and then click Next.

11. A dialog box will be displayed informing you that a DNS server could not be contacted. Click OK to configure the DNS server on this computer.

12. On the Configure DNS wizard screen, accept the setting Yes, Install And Configure DNS On This Computer (Recommended), and then click Next.

13. On the Permissions wizard screen, make sure Permissions Compatible With Pre-Windows 2000 Servers is selected, and then click Next.

14. On the Directory Services Restore Mode Administrator Password wizard screen, under Password and under Confirm Password, type **password**, and then click Next.

15. On the Summary wizard screen, make sure the settings are correct, and then click Next to start the configuration of your Active Directory forest.

16. If an Insert Disk dialog box appears asking you for the Windows 2000 Service Pack 1 CD, make sure this CD is in the CD-ROM drive, and then click OK.

17. If an Insert Disk dialog box appears asking you for the Windows 2000 Server CD, insert this CD in the CD-ROM drive, and then click OK.

18. On the final wizard screen, click Finish to complete the configuration procedure. A dialog box will be displayed prompting you to restart the computer. Click Restart Now to perform the required reboot.

▶ **To allow dynamic DNS updates**

1. Log on to BLUESKY-SRV1 as Administrator.

2. Click Start, point to Programs, point to Administrative Tools, and then click DNS.

3. In the console tree, expand BLUESKY-SRV1, expand Forward Lookup Zones, select Bluesky-inc-10.com, and then right-click on it and select Properties.

4. In the Bluesky-inc-10.com Properties dialog box, under Allow Dynamic Updates, select Yes, and then click OK.

5. Close the DNS snap-in.

▶ **To configure DNS and add computers to the BlueSky-inc-10.com domain**

1. Make sure you are logged on as Administrator.

2. On the desktop, right-click My Network Places, and then select Properties.

3. Right-click Local Area Connection, select Properties, select Internet Protocol (TCP/IP), and then select Properties again.

4. In the Internet Protocol (TCP/IP) Properties dialog box, under Preferred DNS Server, type **192.168.1.22**, and then click OK twice to close all dialog boxes. Close the Network And Dial-Up Connections window.

5. On the desktop, right-click My Computer, and then select Properties.

6. Click on the Network Identification tab, and then click Properties.

7. In the Identification Changes dialog box, under Member Of, select Domain, and then, in the Domain box, type **Bluesky-inc-10.com**. Click OK.

8. In the Domain Username And Password dialog box, under Name, type **Administrator**. Under Password, type **password**, and then click OK.

9. In the Network Identification message box that welcomes you to the Bluesky-inc-10.com domain, click OK.

10. Click OK twice, and then click Yes to reboot the computer.

Installation of Exchange 2000 Server and Microsoft Outlook 2000 for Chapters 1 Through 4

Follow these steps to install Exchange 2000 Server on BLUESKY-SRV1, as required to perform the procedures in Chapters 1 through 4. You will also need to install Microsoft Outlook 2000 on BLUESKY-WKSTA and create a mailbox and distribution group.

▶ **To install Exchange 2000 Server on BLUESKY-SRV1**

1. Make sure you are logged on to BLUESKY-SRV1 as Administrator@Bluesky-inc-10.com.

2. Insert the Exchange 2000 Server, Enterprise Edition, evaluation software installation CD in the CD-ROM drive and start the Setup program from the CD's \Setup\i386 directory.

3. A Welcome To The Microsoft Exchange 2000 Installation Wizard screen appears. Click Next to begin the installation.

4. On the End-User License Agreement wizard screen, select I Agree, and then click Next to continue.

5. On the Product Identification wizard screen, under CD Key, enter the CD key of your Exchange 2000 Server version, and then click Next.

6. On the Component Selection wizard screen, under Action, verify that Typical is selected for Microsoft Exchange 2000. Leave all other settings at their defaults, and then click Next.

7. On the Installation Type wizard screen, accept the default setting of Create A New Exchange Organization, and then click Next.

8. On the Organization Name wizard screen, type **Blue Sky Airlines**, and then click Next.

9. On the Licensing Agreement wizard screen, select I Agree That: I Have Read And Agree To Be Bound By The License Agreements For This Product, and then click Next.

10. On the Component Summary wizard screen, verify that the configuration settings are correct, and then click Next to configure the system and complete the installation.

11. A Microsoft Exchange 2000 Installation Wizard dialog box appears, informing you that the domain Bluesky-inc-10.com has been identified as an insecure domain. Click OK.

12. On the final wizard screen, click Finish to complete the configuration procedure, and, in the initial auto-start application, click Exit.

▶ **To create a mailbox-enabled user account**

1. Make sure you are logged on to BLUESKY-SRV1 as Administrator, and then, from the Microsoft Exchange program group, start Active Directory Users and Computers.

2. Expand the console tree, right-click on the Users container, point to New, and then select User. In the New Object – User dialog box, type the following information:

   First Name   Carl

   Last Name   Titmouse

   Full Name   Carl Titmouse

   User Logon Name   CarlT

3. Click Next.

4. On the next wizard screen, under Password and Confirm Password, type **password**, and then click Next.

5. On the next wizard screen, make sure the Create An Exchange Mailbox check box is selected. Accept the default settings and click Next.

6. Click Finish and then verify that the new user Carl Titmouse is listed in the details pane.

▶ **To create a mail-enabled distribution group**

1. It is assumed that you are logged on to BLUESKY-SRV1 as Administrator and currently working with Active Directory Users and Computers.

2. Right-click the Users container, point to New, and then select Group. In the New Object – Group dialog box, define the following information:

   Group Name   All Test Users

   Group Name (pre-Windows 2000)   All Test Users

   Group Type   Distribution

   Group Scope   Universal

3. Click Next.

4. On the next wizard screen, make sure that the Create An Exchange E-Mail Address check box is selected, and that an Alias of AllTestUsers is specified. Click Next and then click Finish.

5. Verify that the new group is created successfully, double-click on it to display the All Test Users Properties dialog box, and then click on the Members tab.

6. Click the Add button to add Administrator and Carl Titmouse to the group. Close all dialog boxes by clicking OK twice, and then close Active Directory Users and Computers.

▶   **To install Outlook 2000 on BLUESKY-WKSTA**

1. Make sure you are logged on to BLUESKY-WKSTA as Administrator.

2. Insert the Outlook 2000 CD in the CD-ROM drive, and then start the Setup program from the CD's root directory.

3. On the Welcome To Microsoft Outlook 2000 wizard screen, verify that the information matches your environment, type your CD key under CD Key, and then click Next.

4. On the Microsoft Outlook 2000 License And Support Information screen, select I Accept The Terms In The License Agreement, and then click Next.

5. On the third wizard screen, click Install Now to finish the installation.

6. On the desktop, double-click Outlook 2000, and, in the Outlook Startup dialog box, click Next.

7. In the E-Mail Service Options dialog box, select Corporate Or Workgroup, and then click Next.

8. On the Microsoft Outlook Setup wizard screen, select Microsoft Exchange Server, and then click Next.

9. On the Microsoft Exchange Server wizard screen, type BLUESKY-SRV1 under Microsoft Exchange Server, and make sure Administrator is displayed under Mailbox. Click Next.

10. On the next wizard screen, accept the defaults by clicking Next, and then click Finish.

11. If a User Name dialog box appears, verify that the personal information is correct, and then click Next.

12. If a Microsoft Outlook dialog box appears asking you whether you want to register Outlook as the default manager, click Yes.

13. In the Office Assistant, click Start Using Microsoft Outlook. Verify that you are logged on to the Administrator mailbox successfully, and then close Outlook 2000.

Installation of Exchange 2000 Server for Chapters 5 and Higher

Follow these steps to prepare the test environment as required to perform the procedures in Chapters 5 and higher. Essentially, the environment relies on two domain controllers, BLUESKY-SRV1 and BLUESKY-SRV2, both running Exchange 2000 Server.

Note   BLUESKY-SRV2 is not required prior to Chapter 12, "Management Tools for Microsoft Exchange 2000 Server."

▶ **To prepare the test environment**

1. Install Windows 2000 Server and Windows 2000 Service Pack 1 on BLUESKY-SRV1, BLUESKY-SRV2, and BLUESKY-WKSTA, as described earlier in this section.

2. Install Exchange 2000 Server on BLUESKY-SRV1, as outlined in Exercise 1 of Chapter 5, "Installing Exchange 2000 Server," or use the procedure described earlier if you do not want to perform the exercise.

3. Create an account for Carl Titmouse and a distribution group called All Test Users, as outlined earlier.

4. Install Outlook 2000 on BLUESKY-WKSTA, as outlined earlier, if you do not plan to follow the exercises in Chapter 8, "Microsoft Outlook 2000 Deployment."

5. For Chapters 12 and higher, configure BLUESKY-SRV2 as an additional domain controller in the Bluesky-inc-10.com domain, and install Exchange 2000 Server on this computer (as explained in the following).

▶ **To configure BLUESKY-SRV2 as an additional domain controller in the Bluesky-inc-10.com domain**

1. Make sure you are logged on to BLUESKY-SRV2 as Administrator, that BLUESKY-SRV2 is a member of the Bluesky-inc-10.com domain, and that it uses BLUESKY-SRV1 as the DNS server.

2. Click Start and select Run. In the Run dialog box type **dcpromo** and then click OK.

3. On the welcome screen of the Active Directory Installation Wizard, click Next.

4. On the Domain Controller Type wizard screen, select Additional Domain Controller For An Existing Domain, and then click Next.

5. On the Network Credentials wizard screen, under User Name, type **Administrator**. Under Password, type **password**, and make sure Bluesky-inc-10.com is displayed under Domain. Click Next.

6. On the Additional Domain Controller wizard screen, make sure Bluesky-inc-10.com is displayed under Domain Name, and then click Next.

7. On the Database And Log Locations wizard screen, accept the default settings, and then click Next.

8. On the Shared System Folder wizard screen, accept the default settings, and then click Next.

9. On the Directory Services Restore Mode Administrator Password wizard screen, under Password and Confirm Password, type **password**, and then click Next.

10. On the Summary wizard screen, verify that the configuration parameters are correct, and then click Next to start the promotion.

11. On the final wizard screen, click Finish.

▶ **To install Exchange 2000 Server on BLUESKY-SRV2**

1. Make sure BLUESKY-SRV1, running Exchange 2000 Server, is operational and available in the network. Log on to BLUESKY-SRV2 as Administrator@Bluesky-inc-10.com.

2. Insert the Exchange 2000 Server CD in the CD-ROM drive and start the Setup program from the CD's \Setup\i386 directory.

3. A Welcome To The Microsoft Exchange 2000 Installation Wizard screen appears. Click Next to begin the installation.

4. On the End-User License Agreement wizard screen, select I Agree, and then click Next to continue.

5. On the Product Identification wizard screen, under CD Key, enter the CD key of your Exchange 2000 Server version, and then click Next.

6. On the Component Selection wizard screen, under Action, verify that Typical is selected for Microsoft Exchange 2000. Leave all other settings at their defaults, and then click Next.

7. On the Licensing Agreement wizard screen, select I Agree That: I Have Read And Agree To Be Bound By The License Agreements For This Product, and then click Next.

8. On the Component Summary wizard screen, verify that the configuration settings are correct, and then click Next to configure the system and complete the installation.

9. If a Microsoft Exchange 2000 Installation Wizard dialog box appears informing you that the domain Bluesky-inc-10.com has been identified as an insecure domain, click OK.

10. On the final wizard screen, click Finish to complete the configuration procedure, and, in the initial auto-start application, click Exit.

Installation of Microsoft Windows NT 4.0 and Microsoft Exchange Server 5.5 for Chapter 6, "Coexistence with Previous Microsoft Exchange Server Versions."

Follow these steps to configure the computers BLUESKY-PDC and BLUESKY-BDC for Exchange Server 5.5. This installation is only required if you want to perform the optional exercises of Chapter 6. The software required to prepare the Exchange Server 5.5 environment is not provided with this book.

▶ **To install Windows NT Server 4.0 on BLUESKY-PDC**

1. Insert the Windows NT Server 4.0 installation CD in the CD-ROM drive and use the three Windows NT Server installation disks to boot the server and begin the installation. Alternatively, if your computer supports bootable CDs, you can simply boot from the Windows NT Server 4.0 CD.

2. On the Windows NT Server welcome screen, press ENTER to continue. Press ENTER again to detect mass storage devices.

3. On the Windows NT Server Setup screen that lists the devices in your computer, press ENTER.

4. On the Windows NT Licensing Agreement screen, use the PAGE DOWN key to scroll to the end of the agreement, and then press F8 to agree and continue the installation.

5. On the Windows NT Server Setup screen listing the computer configuration, verify that the settings match your hardware and then press ENTER to continue.

6. On the Windows NT Server Setup screen listing existing partitions, delete all partitions, and then press C to create a new partition.

7. On the next Windows NT Server Setup screen, specify a partition size of 2048 MB, and then press ENTER to create the partition.

8. In the list of existing partitions, select Unpartitioned Space, and press C.

9. Accept the suggested size and press ENTER.

10. Make sure the C partition is selected, and then press ENTER to install Windows NT Server on this drive.

11. On the next Windows NT Server Setup screen, select Format The Partition Using The NTFS File System, and then press ENTER to continue.

12. After the C drive is formatted using NTFS, on the next Windows NT Server Setup screen, accept the default installation directory (that is, \WINNT), and press ENTER to continue.

13. On the next Windows NT Server Setup screen, press ENTER to check the hard drives of your server.

14. After that, Setup will copy installation files to your hard disk. On the next Windows NT Server Setup screen, press ENTER to restart your computer.

15. The Windows NT Setup program will reboot your computer, check the current hard disk format, and convert the file system to NTFS. After that, the computer is restarted automatically.

16. After the second reboot, Windows NT Setup is launched in graphical mode. In the first Windows NT Server Setup dialog box, click Next.

17. In the Name And Organization dialog box, under Name, type **Administrator**. Under Organization, type **Blue Sky Airlines**, and then click Next.

18. In the Registration dialog box, type the CD key of your Windows NT Server version, and then click Next.

19. In the Licensing Modes dialog box, select Per Seat, and click Next.

20. In the Computer Name dialog box, under Name, type **BLUESKY-PDC**, and then click Next.

21. In the Server Type dialog box, make sure Primary Domain Controller is selected, and then click Next.

22. In the Administrator Account dialog box, under Password and Confirm Password, type **password**, and then click Next.

23. In the Emergency Repair Disk dialog box, select No, Do Not Create An Emergency Repair Disk, and then click Next.

24. In the Select Components dialog box, accept the defaults, and then click Next.

25. In the Windows NT Setup dialog box, click Next.

26. In the next dialog box, make sure the Wired To The Network check box is selected, and then click Next.

27. In the next dialog box, deselect the Install Microsoft Internet Information Server check box, and then click Next.

28. In the next dialog box, click the Start Search button to detect your network adapter automatically. If your network adapter is not detected, click Select From List, and install your adapter from the manufacturer's floppy disk.

29. As soon as the correct adapter is listed, click Next to continue the installation.

30. In the next dialog box, in the Network Protocols list, deselect NWLink IPX/SPX Compatible Transport, make sure TCP/IP Protocol is selected, and then click Next.

31. In the following dialog box, click Next to accept the default Network Services list.

32. Click Next again to install the networking components.

33. A TCP/IP Setup dialog box appears, asking you whether you would like to use DHCP. Click No.

34. In the Microsoft TCP/IP Properties dialog box, under IP Address, type **192.168.1.222**. Under Subnet Mask, type **255.255.255.0**, and then click OK.

35. In the next Windows NT Server Setup dialog box showing service bindings, click Next.

36. Click Next one more time to start the networking components.

37. In the next Windows NT Server Setup dialog box, under Domain, type **BLUESKY-OLD-10**, and then click Next.

38. In the final Windows NT Setup dialog box, click Finish.

39. In the Date/Time Properties dialog box, make sure that the date, time, and time zone information is correct, and then click Close.

40. In the Detect Display dialog box, click OK.

41. Click Test, and, in the Testing Mode dialog box, click OK.

42. If you were able to see the test screen, click Yes in the Testing Mode dialog box.

43. In the Display Settings dialog box, click OK, and then, in the Display Properties dialog box, click OK one more time.

44. Windows NT Server Setup is now copying program files to your computer's hard disk. After that, configuration and security settings are saved, and then a Windows NT Setup dialog box appears, in which you need to click Restart Computer.

▶   **To install Windows NT Server 4.0 on BLUESKY-BDC**

1. Insert the Windows NT Server 4.0 installation CD in the CD-ROM drive and use the three Windows NT Server installation disks to boot the server and begin the installation.

2. On the Windows NT Server welcome screen, press ENTER to continue, and then press ENTER again to detect mass storage devices. If you receive any warnings, press ENTER to bypass them.

3. On the Windows NT Server Setup screen that lists the devices in your computer, press ENTER.

4. On the Windows NT Licensing Agreement screen, use the PAGE DOWN key to scroll to the end of the agreement, and then press F8 to agree and continue the installation.

5. On the Windows NT Server Setup screen listing the computer configuration, verify that the settings match your hardware, and then press ENTER to continue.

6. On the Windows NT Server Setup screen listing existing partitions, delete all partitions, and then press C to create a new partition.

7. On the next Windows NT Server Setup screen, specify a partition size of 2048 MB, and then press ENTER to create the partition.

8. In the list of existing partitions, select Unpartitioned Space, and press C.

9. Accept the suggested size and press ENTER.

10. Make sure the C partition is selected, and then press ENTER to install Windows NT Server on this drive.

11. On the next Windows NT Server Setup screen, select Format The Partition Using The NTFS File System, and then press ENTER to continue.

12. After the C drive is formatted using NTFS, on the next Windows NT Server Setup screen, accept the default installation directory (that is, \WINNT), and press ENTER to continue.

13. On the next Windows NT Server Setup screen, press ENTER to check the hard drives of your server.

14. After that, Setup will copy installation files to your hard disk. On the next Windows NT Server Setup screen, press ENTER to restart your computer.

15. The Windows NT Setup program will reboot your computer. Check the current hard disk format, and convert the file system to NTFS. After that, the computer is restarted automatically.

16. After the second reboot, Windows NT Setup is launched in graphical mode. In the first Windows NT Server Setup dialog box, click Next.

17. In the Name And Organization dialog box, under Name, type **Administrator**. Under Organization, type **Blue Sky Airlines**, and then click Next.

18. In the Registration dialog box, type the CD key of your Windows NT Server version, and then click Next.

19. In the Licensing Modes dialog box, select Per Seat, and then click Next.

20. In the Computer Name dialog box, under Name, type **BLUESKY-BDC**, and then click Next.

21. In the Server Type dialog box, make sure Backup Domain Controller is selected, and then click Next.

22. In the Emergency Repair Disk dialog box, select No, Do Not Create An Emergency Repair Disk, and then click Next.

23. In the Select Components dialog box, accept the defaults, and then click Next.

24. In the Windows NT Setup dialog box, click Next.

25. In the next dialog box, make sure the Wired To The Network check box is selected, and then click Next.

26. In the next dialog box, deselect the Install Microsoft Internet Information Server check box, and then click Next.

27. In the next dialog box, click the Start Search button to detect your network adapter automatically. If your network adapter is not detected, click Select From List, and install your adapter from the manufacturer's floppy disk.

28. As soon as the correct adapter is listed, click Next to continue the installation.

29. In the next dialog box, in the Network Protocols list, deselect NWLink IPX/ SPX Compatible Transport, make sure TCP/IP Protocol is selected, and then click Next.

30. In the next dialog box, click Next to accept the default Network Services list.

31. Click Next again to install the networking components.

32. A TCP/IP Setup dialog box appears asking you whether you would like to use DHCP. Click No.

33. In the Microsoft TCP/IP Properties dialog box, under IP Address, type **192.168.1.223**. Under Subnet Mask, type **255.255.255.0**, and then click OK.

34. In the next Windows NT Server Setup dialog box showing service bindings, click Next.

35. Click Next one more time to start the networking components.

36. In the next Windows NT Server Setup dialog box, under Domain, type **BLUESKY-OLD-10**, under Administrator Name, type **Administrator** and under Administrator Password, type **password**. Click Next.

37. In the final Windows NT Setup dialog box, click Finish.

38. In the Date/Time Properties dialog box, make sure that the date, time, and time zone information is correct, and then click Close.

39. In the Detect Display dialog box, click OK.

40. Click Test, and, in the Testing Mode dialog box, click OK.

41. If you were able to see the test screen, click Yes in the Testing Mode dialog box.

42. In the Display Settings dialog box, click OK. In the Display Properties dialog box, click OK one more time.

43. Windows NT Server Setup is now copying program files to your computer's hard disk. After that, configuration and security settings are saved, and then a Windows NT Setup dialog box appears in which you need to click Restart Computer.

▶   **To install Windows NT Service Pack 6 and the Microsoft Windows NT Option Pack 4 on BLUESKY-PDC and BLUESKY-BDC**

1. Log on to Windows NT Server as Administrator (Password: password).

2. Insert the Windows NT 4.0 Service Pack 6 CD into your CD-ROM drive to update the installation with Service Pack 6. The update program is launched automatically.

3. In the Windows NT Service Pack Setup dialog box, select the Accept The License Agreement (Must Accept Before Installing The Service Pack) check box, and then click Install.

4. The Windows NT Service Pack Setup will back up the system files. Afterward, the installation is updated. In the final Windows NT Service Pack Setup dialog box, click Restart.

5. Log on to Windows NT Server as Administrator again.

6. Insert the Windows NT Option Pack 4 CD into the CD-ROM drive.

7. Launch the IE4Setup program from the \Ie401\X86 directory on your Option Pack 4 CD.

8. On the Internet Explorer 4.01 SP1 wizard screen, click Next.

9. On the License Agreement wizard screen, select I Accept The Agreement, and then click Next.

10. On the Installation Option wizard screen, select Standard Installation, and then click Next.

11. On the Windows Desktop Update wizard screen, select No, and then click Next.

12. On the Active Channel Selection wizard screen, select (None), and then click Next.

13. In the Destination Folder dialog box, accept the defaults, and then click Next.

14. The installation of Internet Explorer version 4.01 will be started at this point. After that, in the Internet Explorer 4.01 SP1 Active Setup dialog box, click OK.

15. In the final Internet Explorer 4.01 SP1 Active Setup dialog box, click OK to restart the computer.

16. Log on to Windows NT Server as Administrator again.

17. With the Windows NT Option Pack CD, from the \Ntoptpak\En\X86\WINNT.SRV directory, launch the Setup program.

18. In the Setup dialog box warning you that SP4 or greater is installed, click Yes to proceed.

19. On the Windows NT 4.0 Option Pack welcome screen, click Next.

20. On the End-User Licensing Agreement wizard screen, click Accept.

21. On the following wizard screen, click Custom.

22. On the Select Components wizard screen, select Internet Information Server (IIS), and then click Show Subcomponents.

23. Select the Internet NNTP Service check box, then click OK. On the Select Components wizard screen, click Next.

24. Accept the default directories on the next wizard screen, and then click Next.

25. Accept the default settings for Microsoft Transaction Server 2.0 and then click Next.

26. Click Next four more times to begin the installation.

27. On the final wizard screen, click Finish.

28. In the System Settings Change dialog box, click Yes to restart the computer now.

▶ **To install Exchange Server 5.5 and Exchange Server 5.5 Service Pack 3 on BLUESKY-PDC**

1. Log on as Administrator to BLUESKY-PDC. Insert the Microsoft Exchange Server 5.5 Enterprise Edition installation CD into the CD-ROM drive, and launch Setup from the \Server\Setup\i386 directory.

2. In the Microsoft Exchange Server Setup dialog box displaying the End-User License Agreement, click Accept. In the next dialog box, click Complete/Custom.

3. In the Microsoft Exchange Server Setup – Complete/Custom dialog box, make sure Microsoft Exchange Server is selected, and then click Change Option.

4. Deselect all check boxes with the exception of Microsoft Exchange Event Service. (You don't need any connector components for the exercises in Chapter 6.) Click OK.

5. In the Microsoft Exchange Server Setup – Complete/Custom dialog box, click Continue.

6. In the Microsoft Exchange Server Setup dialog box, informing you that the IIS must be stopped, click OK.

7. In the Microsoft Exchange Server Setup dialog box, type the CD key for your installation CD, and then click OK twice to continue.

8. In the Licensing dialog box, select I Agree That…, and click Continue.

9. In the Organization And Site dialog box, accept the suggestions, and then click OK.

10. In the Microsoft Exchange Server Setup dialog box, click Yes.

11. In the Site Services Account tab, under Account Name, accept BLUESKY-OLD-10\Administrator. Under Account Password, type **password**, and then click OK. (Although it is generally not advisable to specify the Administrator account as the site services account, it is sufficient for the purposes of the exercises in Chapter 6.)

12. In the Microsoft Exchange Server Setup dialog box informing you that the Administrator has been granted additional rights, click OK.

13. The Setup program is now installing Exchange Server 5.5 on your computer.

14. In the final Microsoft Exchange Server Setup dialog box, click Exit Setup. (It is not necessary to optimize the installation.)

15. Insert the Exchange Server 5.5 Service Pack 3 CD into the CD-ROM drive.

16. From the \Eng\Server\Setup\i386\ directory on this CD, launch Update.

17. In the Microsoft Exchange Server Setup dialog box informing you that Setup is going to update the installation, click OK.

18. In the Microsoft Exchange Server Setup dialog box informing you that the IIS will be stopped temporarily, click OK.

19. In the Microsoft Exchange Server Setup dialog box informing you that existing Outlook Web Access files will be backed up, click OK.

20. In the Microsoft Exchange Server Setup dialog box informing you that existing databases are preserved, click OK.

21. The current Exchange Server installation will now be updated. In the final Microsoft Exchange Server Setup dialog box, click OK.

▶ **To install Exchange Server 5.5 and Exchange Server 5.5 Service Pack 3 on BLUESKY-BDC**

1. Log on as Administrator to BLUESKY-BDC. Insert the Microsoft Exchange Server 5.5 Enterprise Edition installation CD into the CD-ROM drive, and launch Setup from the \Server\Setup\i386 directory.

2. In the Microsoft Exchange Server Setup dialog box displaying the End-User License Agreement, click Accept. In the next dialog box, click Complete/Custom.

3. In the Microsoft Exchange Server Setup – Complete/Custom dialog box, make sure Microsoft Exchange Server is selected, and then click Change Option.

4. Deselect all check boxes with the exception of Microsoft Exchange Event Service, and then click OK.

5. In the Microsoft Exchange Server Setup – Complete/Custom dialog box, click Continue.

6. In the Microsoft Exchange Server Setup dialog box informing you that the IIS must be stopped, click OK.

7. In the Licensing dialog box, select I Agree That…, and click Continue.

8. In the Organization And Site dialog box, select Join An Existing Site, and, under Existing Server, type **BLUESKY-PDC**. Click OK.

9. In the Confirm Exchange Site And Organization dialog box, verify that the information is correct, and click Yes.

10. In the Site Services Account tab, under Account Password, type **password**, and then click OK.

11. The Setup program is now installing Exchange Server 5.5 on BLUESKY-BDC and replicating the directory.

12. A Microsoft Exchange Server Setup dialog box will appear informing you that the directory replication is not an immediate process. Click OK.

13. In the final Microsoft Exchange Server Setup dialog box, click Exit Setup to skip the optimization of the installation.

14. Insert the Exchange Server 5.5 Service Pack 3 CD into the CD-ROM drive.

15. From the \Eng\Server\Setup\i386\ directory on this CD, launch Update.

16. In the Microsoft Exchange Server Setup dialog box informing you that Setup is going to update the installation, click OK.

17. In the Microsoft Exchange Server Setup dialog box informing you that the IIS will be stopped temporarily, click OK.

18. In the Microsoft Exchange Server Setup dialog box informing you that existing Outlook Web Access files will be backed up, click OK.

19. In the Microsoft Exchange Server Setup dialog box informing you that existing databases are preserved, click OK.

20. The current Exchange Server installation will now be updated. In the final Microsoft Exchange Server Setup dialog box, click OK.

▶ **To create several test users in the Exchange Server 5.5 organization**

1. Log on as Administrator to BLUESKY-PDC.

2. Click Start, point to Programs, point to Microsoft Exchange, and then select Microsoft Exchange Administrator.

3. If a Connect To Server dialog box appears, type BLUESKY-PDC, and then click OK.

4. In the Exchange Administrator program, open the File menu, and select New Mailbox.

5. If a dialog box appears explaining that recipients cannot be created in the selected container, click OK to go to the Recipients container.

6. A Properties dialog box appears. Type **Veronica** in the First box, and **Magpie** in the Last box. The Display and Alias fields will be inserted automatically.

7. Click on the Primary Windows NT Account button at the bottom, select Select An Existing Windows NT Account, and then click OK.

8. Assign the Administrator account to the mailbox either by scrolling down to the Administrator account or typing **Administrator** in the Add Name box. In the Add Users Or Group dialog box, click OK.

9. Click on the Advanced tab and, under Home Server, select BLUESKY-BDC. It is important to create the mailboxes on this server to perform the procedures outlined in Exercise 5 of Chapter 6.

10. In the Veronica Magpie Properties dialog box, click OK, and then repeat these steps for four additional mailboxes, such as Greta Gannet, Hank Hawk, Phil Puffin, and Josephine Eagle. Always specify the Administrator account as the primary Windows NT account to avoid the creation of additional user accounts in the domain.

Installation of Windows 2000 Cluster Services

Follow these steps to install Windows 2000 Cluster service. It is assumed that you have installed the 120-day Evaluation Edition of Microsoft Windows 2000 Advanced Server and Windows 2000 Service Pack 1 on BLUESKY-ND1 and BLUESKY-ND2, as described earlier in this section under "Installation of Windows 2000 Server."

Note   This installation and configuration of Windows 2000 Cluster service is only required if you want to perform the optional exercises in Chapter 7, "Microsoft Exchange 2000 Server in Clustered Environments."

► **To configure the shared hard disks for the server cluster**

1. Power on the external cluster disks then switch on BLUESKY-ND2 and press the PAUSE key while it is in the BIOS stage of the boot process to stop it before booting Windows 2000 Server.

2. Power on BLUESKY-ND1 and let it boot Windows 2000 Server. Make sure the Small Computer System Interface (SCSI) adapter detects all external SCSI drives. (Your cluster requires at a minimum two separate, shared hard disks.)

3. When Windows 2000 Server starts, log on using the Administrator account. On the desktop, right-click My Computer, and select Manage.

4. Select Disk Management under Storage to display all of the hard disk devices currently attached to the server. Create a partition on each of the two external disks by right-clicking them and selecting Create Partition.

5. In the Create Partition Wizard, click Next, and then select Primary Partition and click Next again.

6. In the Specify Partition Size dialog box, select the largest size (as default), and then click Next.

7. On the next screen, assign drive letter S for the first disk. (This has to be assigned the same letter on each node. It is a good idea to note which disk is which.)

8. In the Format Partition dialog box, select Format This Partition With The Following Settings, select NTFS for the File System, Default for Allocation Size, and a Volume Label of S. Select the Perform A Quick Format check box to reduce the time required to format the drive. Click Next and then click Finish to create the partition.

9. Follow the same procedures for the second shared disk, and allocate drive letter T to this volume.

10. Close the Computer Management console.

11. Use Windows Explorer to verify that the new drives are available. After that, shut down and power off BLUESKY-ND1.

12. Power on BLUESKY-ND1 and stop the boot process at the same stage as described for BLUESKY-ND2 in Step 1.

13. Go to BLUESKY-ND2 and continue to boot this server.

14. Follow Steps 3 through 9 for BLUESKY-ND2, except that there is no need to format the disks again. Make sure the drive letters correspond to the correct disks. If required, reboot BLUESKY-ND2 for the drive mappings to take effect.

► **To install Windows Cluster service**

1. Click Start, point to Settings, and then click Control Panel.

2. Double-click Add/Remove Programs, and then click Remove Program Components. Select the Cluster Service check box, and then click Next.

3. If prompted, insert the Windows 2000 Advanced Server CD in the CD-ROM drive.

4. The Cluster Service Configuration Wizard appears. Click Next, and then click on the I Understand button to proceed to the next wizard screen.

5. On the Create Or Join A Cluster wizard screen, select The First Node In The Cluster, and then click Next.

6. On the Cluster Name wizard screen, type **BLUESKY-CLUST** as the name of the cluster and click Next.

7. On the Select An Account wizard screen, type **Administrator** under User Name and **password** under Password. Make sure that BLUESKY-INC-10 is displayed under Domain, and then click Next.

8. If the external disks are not displayed under Managed Disks, select them and click Add. Click Next.

9. On the Cluster File Storage wizard screen, specify disk S under Disks, and then click Next. Click Next again.

10. On the Network Connections wizard screen, select both the Enable This Network For Cluster Use and All Communications check boxes if BLUESKY-ND1 and BLUESKY-ND2 only have one network card each for both public and private network use. Click Next to use the network for data and for cluster communication.

11. Under Cluster IP Address, type **192.168.1.140** as the cluster IP address, with a Subnet Mask of **255.255.255.0,** and then click Next.

12. To complete the Cluster service setup, click Finish.

13. A Cluster Service Configuration Wizard message box appears informing you that the Cluster service has started successfully. Click OK to let the Windows Components Wizard finish setting up the components. Click Finish one more time.

14. Start Cluster Administrator from the Administrative Tools program group. In the Cluster Administrator window, open the Groups container. Verify that two resource groups exist, one for each physical disk.

15. Un-pause BLUESKY-ND1 to boot Windows 2000 Server. Log on as Administrator and verify that the shared disks are recognized.

16. Click Start, point to Settings, and then click Control Panel. Double-click Add/Remove Programs, and then click on Remove Programs Components. Select the Cluster Service check box, and then click Next. If prompted, insert the Windows 2000 Advanced Server CD in the CD-ROM drive.

17. On the welcome screen of the Cluster Service Configuration Wizard, click Next, click on the I Understand button, and then click Next again.

18. On the Create Or Join Cluster wizard screen, select The Second Or Next Node In The Cluster, and then click Next.

19. When prompted, type **BLUESKY-CLUSTER** as the cluster name, and then click Next.

20. If you have only one network card, a message box will appear to inform you about the configuration. Click OK. After that, on the Select An Account wizard screen, under Password, type **password**, and then click Next.

21. A message box appears, informing you that you have successfully completed the Cluster Service Configuration Wizard. Click Finish and wait for the system to configure the resources.

22. While the Cluster service is being configured, the Cluster Administrator program on BLUESKY-ND2 will show the addition and starting of BLUESKY-ND1 within the cluster.

23. In the dialog box detailing how to administer the cluster, click OK.

24. When the Windows Components Wizard has finished its processing, click Finish.

The Online Book

The CD also includes an online version of the book that you can view on-screen using Microsoft Internet Explorer 4.01 or later.

▶ **To use the online version of this book**

1. Insert the Supplemental Course Materials CD into your CD-ROM drive.

2. From the Start menu on your desktop, select Run, and type **D:\Ebook\Setup.exe** (where D is the name of your CD-ROM drive).

    This will install an icon to for the online book to your Start menu.

3. Click OK to exit the Installation Wizard.

Note You must have the Supplemental Course Materials CD inserted in your CD-ROM drive to run the online book.

The Microsoft Certified Professional Program

The Microsoft Certified Professional (MCP) program provides the best method to prove your command of current Microsoft products and technologies. Microsoft, an industry leader in certification, is at the forefront of testing methodology. Our exams and corresponding certifications are developed to validate your mastery of critical competencies as you design and develop, or implement and support, solutions with Microsoft products and technologies. Computer professionals who become Microsoft certified are recognized as experts and are sought after industrywide.

The Microsoft Certified Professional program offers eight certifications based on specific areas of technical expertise:

- *Microsoft Certified Professional (MCP)*. Demonstrated in-depth knowledge of at least one Microsoft operating system. Candidates may pass additional Microsoft certification exams to further qualify their skills with Microsoft BackOffice products, development tools, or desktop programs.

- *Microsoft Certified Professional + Internet*. MCPs with a specialty in the Internet are qualified to plan security, install and configure server products, manage server resources, extend servers to run scripts, monitor and analyze performance, and troubleshoot problems.

- *Microsoft Certified Professional + Site Building*. MCPs with this certification have demonstrated what it takes to plan, build, maintain, and manage Web sites using Microsoft technologies and products.

- *Microsoft Certified Systems Engineer (MCSE)*. Those with this certification are qualified to effectively plan, implement, maintain, and support information systems in a wide range of computing environments with Microsoft Windows NT Server and the Microsoft BackOffice integrated family of server software.

- *Microsoft Certified Systems Engineer + Internet*. These MCSEs have an advanced qualification to enhance, deploy, and manage sophisticated intranet and Internet solutions that include a browser, proxy server, host servers, database, and messaging and commerce components. In addition, an MCSE + Internet certified professional is able to manage and analyze Web sites.

- *Microsoft Certified Database Administrator (MCDBA)*. These individuals derive physical database designs, develop logical data models, create physical databases, create data services by using Transact-SQL, manage and maintain databases, configure and manage security, monitor and optimize databases, and install and configure Microsoft SQL Server.

- *Microsoft Certified Solution Developer (MCSD)*. These professionals are qualified to design and develop custom business solutions with Microsoft development tools, technologies, and platforms, including Microsoft Office and Microsoft BackOffice.

- *Microsoft Certified Trainer (MCT)*. MCTs are instructionally and technically qualified to deliver Microsoft Official Curriculum through a Microsoft Certified Technical Education Center (CTEC).

Microsoft Certification Benefits

Microsoft certification, one of the most comprehensive certification programs available for assessing and maintaining software-related skills, is a valuable measure of an individual's knowledge and expertise. Microsoft certification is awarded to individuals who have successfully demonstrated their ability to perform specific tasks and implement solutions with Microsoft products. Not only does this provide an objective measure for employers to consider; it also provides guidance for what an individual should know to be proficient. As with any skills-assessment and benchmarking measure, certification brings a variety of benefits: to the individual, and to employers and organizations.

Microsoft Certification Benefits for Individuals

As a Microsoft Certified Professional, you receive many benefits:

- Industry recognition of your knowledge and proficiency with Microsoft products and technologies.
- Access to technical and product information directly from Microsoft through a secured area of the MCP Web Site.
- MSDN Online Certified Membership that helps you tap into the best technical resources, connect to the MCP community, and gain access to valuable resources and services. (Some MSDN Online benefits may be available in English only or may not be available in all countries.) See the MSDN Web site for a growing list of certified member benefits.
- Logos to enable you to identify your Microsoft Certified Professional status to colleagues or clients.
- Invitations to Microsoft conferences, technical training sessions, and special events.
- A Microsoft Certified Professional certificate.
- Subscription to *Microsoft Certified Professional Magazine* (North America only), a career and professional development magazine.

Additional benefits, depending on your certification and geography, include:

- A complimentary one-year subscription to the Microsoft TechNet Technical Plus, providing valuable information on monthly CD-ROMs.
- A one-year subscription to the Microsoft Beta Evaluation program. This benefit provides you with up to 12 free monthly CD-ROMs containing beta software (English only) for many of Microsoft's newest software products.

Microsoft Certification Benefits for Employers and Organizations

Through certification, computer professionals can maximize the return on investment in Microsoft technology. Research shows that Microsoft certification provides organizations with:

- Excellent return on training and certification investments by providing a standard method of determining training needs and measuring results.
- Increased customer satisfaction and decreased support costs through improved service, increased productivity, and greater technical self-sufficiency.

- Reliable benchmark for hiring, promoting, and career planning.

- Recognition and rewards for productive employees by validating their expertise.

- Retraining options for existing employees so they can work effectively with new technologies.

- Assurance of quality when outsourcing computer services.

To learn more about how certification can help your company, see the backgrounders, white papers, and case studies available at *http:// www.microsoft.com/mcp/mktg/bus_bene.htm*:

- Financial Benefits to Supporters of Microsoft Professional Certification, IDC white paper (1998WPIDC.DOC 1608K)

- Prudential Case Study (PRUDENTL.EXE 70K self-extracting file)

- A white paper (MCSDWP.DOC 158K) that evaluates the Microsoft Certified Solution Developer certification.

- A white paper (MCSESTUD.DOC 161K) that evaluates the Microsoft Certified Systems Engineer certification.

- Lyondel Case Study (LYONDEL.DOC 21K)

- Stellcom Case Study (STELLCOM.DOC 132K)

Requirements for Becoming a Microsoft Certified Professional

The certification requirements differ for each certification and are specific to the products and job functions addressed by the certification.

To become a Microsoft Certified Professional, you must pass rigorous certification exams that provide a valid and reliable measure of technical proficiency and expertise. These exams are designed to test your expertise and ability to perform a role or task with a product, and are developed with the input of professionals in the industry. Questions in the exams reflect how Microsoft products are used in actual organizations, giving them real-world relevance.

Microsoft Certified Product Specialists are required to pass one operating system exam. Candidates may pass additional Microsoft certification exams to further qualify their skills with Microsoft BackOffice products, development tools, or desktop applications.

Microsoft Certified Professional + Internet specialists are required to pass the prescribed Microsoft Windows NT Server 4.0, TCP/IP, and Microsoft Internet Information System exam series.

Microsoft Certified Professionals with a specialty in site building are required to pass two exams covering Microsoft FrontPage, Microsoft Site Server, and

Microsoft Visual InterDev technologies to provide a valid and reliable measure of technical proficiency and expertise.

Microsoft Certified Systems Engineers are required to pass a series of core Microsoft Windows operating system and networking exams and BackOffice technology elective exams.

Microsoft Certified Systems Engineers + Internet specialists are required to pass seven operating system exams and two elective exams that provide a valid and reliable measure of technical proficiency and expertise.

Microsoft Certified Database Administrators are required to pass three core exams and one elective exam that provide a valid and reliable measure of technical proficiency and expertise.

Microsoft Certified Solution Developers are required to pass two core Microsoft Windows operating system technology exams and two BackOffice technology elective exams.

Microsoft Certified Trainers are required to meet instructional and technical requirements specific to each Microsoft Official Curriculum course they are certified to deliver. In the United States and Canada, call Microsoft at (800) 636-7544 for more information on becoming a Microsoft Certified Trainer or visit *http://www.microsoft.com/train_cert/mct/*. Outside the United States and Canada, contact your local Microsoft subsidiary.

Technical Training for Computer Professionals

Technical training is available in a variety of ways, with self-paced training, online instruction, or instructor-led classes available at thousands of locations worldwide.

Self-Paced Training

For motivated learners who are ready for the challenge, self-paced instruction is the most flexible, cost-effective way to increase your knowledge and skills.

A full line of self-paced print and computer-based training materials is available direct from the source—Microsoft Press. Microsoft Official Curriculum courseware kits from Microsoft Press are designed for advanced computer system professionals and are available from Microsoft Press and the Microsoft Developer Division. Self-paced training kits from Microsoft Press feature print-based instructional materials, along with CD-ROM–based product software, multimedia presentations, lab exercises, and practice files. The Mastering Series provides in-depth, interactive training on CD-ROM for experienced developers. Both are great ways to prepare for MCP exams.

Online Training

For a more flexible alternative to instructor-led classes, turn to online instruction. It's as near as the Internet and it's ready whenever you are. Learn at your own pace and on your own schedule in a virtual classroom, often with easy access to an online instructor. Without ever leaving your desk, you can gain the expertise you need. Online instruction covers a variety of Microsoft products and technologies. It includes options ranging from Microsoft Official Curriculum to choices available nowhere else. It's training on demand, with access to learning resources 24 hours a day. Online training is available through Microsoft Certified Technical Education Centers.

Microsoft Certified Technical Education Centers

Microsoft Certified Technical Education Centers (CTECs) are the best source for instructor-led training that can help you prepare to become a Microsoft Certified Professional. The Microsoft CTEC program is a worldwide network of qualified technical training organizations that provide authorized delivery of Microsoft Official Curriculum courses by Microsoft Certified Trainers to computer professionals.

For a listing of CTEC locations in the United States and Canada, visit *http://www.microsoft.com/CTEC/default.htm*.

Technical Support

Every effort has been made to ensure the accuracy of this book and the contents of the companion disc. If you have comments, questions, or ideas regarding this book or the CD, please send them to Microsoft Press using either of the following methods:

E-mail:

TKINPUT@MICROSOFT.COM

Postal Mail:

Microsoft Press
Attn: MCSE Training Kit—Microsoft Exchange 2000 Server Implementation and Administration Editor
One Microsoft Way
Redmond, WA 98052-6399

Microsoft Press provides corrections for books through the World Wide Web at the following address:

http://mspress.microsoft.com/support/

Please note that product support is not offered through the above mail addresses. For further information regarding Microsoft software support options, please connect to *http://www.microsoft.com/support/* or call Microsoft Support Network Sales at (800) 936-3500.

Evaluation Edition Software Support

The Evaluation Edition of Microsoft Exchange 2000 Server included with this book is unsupported by both Microsoft and Microsoft Press, and should not be used on a primary work computer. For online support information relating to the full version of Microsoft Exchange 2000 Server that might also apply to the Evaluation Edition, you can connect to

http://support.microsoft.com/

For information about ordering the full version of any Microsoft software, please call Microsoft Sales at (800) 426-9400 or visit *www.microsoft.com.* Information about any issues relating to the use of this Evaluation Edition with this training kit is posted to the Support section of the Microsoft Press Web site (*http://mspress.microsoft.com/support/*).

C H A P T E R   1

Introduction to Microsoft Exchange 2000 Server

About This Chapter

Almost a decade ago, Microsoft began its development of a powerful enterprise messaging system, which years later became known as Microsoft Exchange Server. The first Visual Basic demo of the Exchange Administrator program was shown at computer fairs in 1994. However, the market had to wait until July 1996, when Microsoft finally released Exchange Server version 4.0, which relied on a full-featured X.400 (88) message transfer agent. In the early 1990s the X.400 standard was widely recognized as the framework for global messaging.

Today, the Internet is the single most important global messaging environment, so Microsoft Exchange 2000 Server focuses entirely on Internet technologies. It is Microsoft's most recent answer to the demand for a high-end, Internet-aware messaging and collaboration system. When you take a closer look, you will find that Exchange 2000 Server opens new avenues for exciting technologies and eliminates some of the limitations of earlier Exchange Server versions.

This chapter discusses basic messaging features and describes Microsoft's design goals for Exchange 2000 Server. It also covers in brief Exchange 2000 Server's support for industry messaging standards and interoperability issues.

Before You Begin

To complete this chapter:

- Prepare your test environment according to the descriptions given in the "Getting Started" section of "About This Book."
- Understand Windows 2000 Server networking technologies and the TCP/IP protocol suite.
- Be familiar with the concepts of the Active Directory directory services.

Lesson 1: General Overview of Messaging Systems

A new messaging system cannot expect to find an uncultivated market segment. Messaging is one of the most popular network applications, available virtually everywhere. Why should your organization, which most likely has a messaging solution in place, consider Exchange 2000 Server?

This lesson provides basic guidelines for evaluating messaging systems. It will help you if you are considering Exchange 2000 Server. If you have decided to use Exchange 2000 Server, this lesson will give you the confidence that you have made the right choice.

At the end of this lesson, you will be able to:

- Describe the differences between a shared-file and a client/server messaging system.
- Identify the characteristics of modern collaboration systems.

Estimated time to complete this section: 75 minutes

Shared-File Messaging Systems

Shared-file messaging systems maintain a structure of directories and files at a centralized location—usually on a file server. These centralized structures are often called *post offices*. Every user who wants access to e-mail messaging needs to access a *mailbox* within a post office. The post office serves as the mailbox repository for multiple users. Typical messaging systems that use shared-file post offices are Microsoft Mail for PC networks and Lotus cc:Mail.

Client Sending and Polling

To send messages, users must write their data into the directories (mailboxes) of the post office. The users on the receiving end recognize the written data as incoming messages. The post office itself is a passive file structure, meaning that the client programs must perform all processing of sending and receiving themselves. To check for new messages, clients must poll the post office at regular intervals (see Figure 1.1).

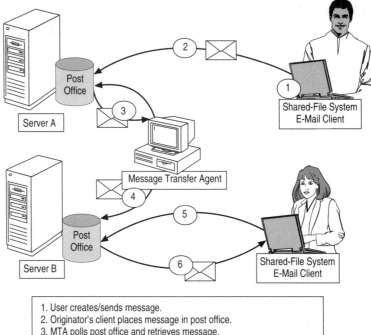

1. User creates/sends message.
2. Originator's client places message in post office.
3. MTA polls post office and retrieves message.
4. MTA stores message in the recipient's post office.
5. Recipient's client polls post office for new messages.
6. Recipient's client receives (downloads) new messages.

Figure 1.1   A shared-file messaging system

File Locking

When one client opens common files for writing, these files must be locked to prevent accidents. All other clients must wait until one client has completed its write operation. The more clients that access the same post office, the more often these common files will be locked and all other clients will have to wait. This effect can be worsened if the underlying network operating system is not optimized for fast input/output operations. It is not advisable to create a very large number of mailboxes on one server. Microsoft Mail post offices, for instance, are limited to 500 users.

Table 1.1 lists the general advantages and disadvantages of shared-file messaging systems.

Table 1.1   **Advantages and Disadvantages of Shared-File Messaging Systems**

Advantages of Shared-File Messaging Systems	Disadvantages of Shared-File Messaging Systems
Messaging systems are independent of the underlying network operating system as long as read-write access to the post office is guaranteed.	The client must perform all the work to download messages. Client polling generates a high volume of network traffic.

Table 1.1   Advantages and Disadvantages of Shared-File Messaging Systems
(continued)

Advantages of Shared-File Messaging Systems	Disadvantages of Shared-File Messaging Systems
A shared-file–based e-mail system doesn't need a very powerful machine on the server side because all processing is accomplished at the client side.	The passive character of the post office does not support processing of mailbox rules (such as out-of-office notifications).
Shared-file–based e-mail systems are easy to install. The administrator must simply grant read-write access for the post office data structure to all users who have mailboxes.	A shared-file–based e-mail system provides only limited scalability. It is not advisable to create numerous mailboxes (more than 500) on one server, for instance, because each polling client is a drain on system resources.
	The direct read-write access to and within the post office allows users to damage the internal structure of a post office by deleting files either inadvertently or intentionally.

Exercise 1: A Simulated Shared-File Messaging System

In this exercise you will evaluate the characteristics of a client sending and polling for e-mail messages. You can simulate client polling when configuring Microsoft Outlook 2000 for offline and remote use. For this purpose, you need to configure a personal folder store (.pst) file, which requires some advanced configuration steps. Follow the steps outlined here; Chapter 8, "Microsoft Outlook 2000 Deployment," and Chapter 9, "MAPI-Based Clients," contain more information about Outlook 2000 and the configuration of messaging services.

To view a multimedia demonstration that displays how to perform this procedure, run the EX1CH1.AVI file from the Exercise_Information\Chapter1 folder on the Supplemental Course Materials CD.

Prerequisites

- Make sure your test environment is prepared according to the descriptions given in the "Getting Started" section of "About This Book."

- Ensure that Exchange 2000 Server is operational and running on BLUESKY-SRV1.

- Log on as Administrator to BLUESKY-WKSTA and make sure you can use Outlook 2000 to work with your mailbox.

▶   **To simulate client polling with Microsoft Outlook 2000**

1. In Outlook, double-click the Tools menu to display all available menu options, then select Services.

2. In the Services dialog box, click Add to display the Add Service To Profile dialog box.

3. Within this dialog box, from the Available Information Services list, select Personal Folders, and then click OK.

4. In the Create/Open Personal Folders File dialog box, under File Name, type **personal.pst**, and then click Open.

5. In the Create Microsoft Personal Folders dialog box, click OK to accept the default settings.

6. Switch to the Delivery property page and under Deliver New Mail To The Following Location, select Personal Folders. Outlook 2000 will now work primarily with the newly configured personal folder store and download incoming messages from the Exchange 2000 Server.

7. Switch back to the Services property page, select Microsoft Exchange Server, and then click Properties.

8. In the Microsoft Exchange Server dialog box, select Manually Control Connection State, as shown in Figure 1.2. Under Default Connection State, select Work Offline And Use Dial-Up Networking.

9. Switch to the Dial-Up Networking tab and select Do Not Dial, Use Existing Connection.

10. Click OK twice to close the dialog boxes.

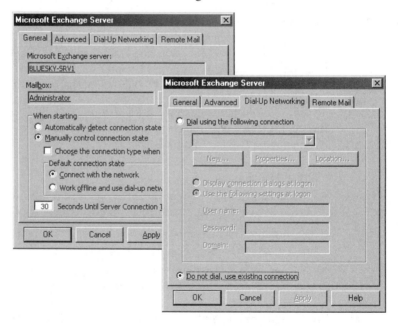

Figure 1.2   Configuring Outlook 2000 for offline usage

11. In Outlook, from the File menu, select Exit And Log Off.

    At this point you have successfully configured Outlook 2000 for offline usage.

12. Start Outlook 2000 again. The client will start offline and a notification message may be displayed, informing you that the location messages are delivered to has changed, in which case you need to click No to prevent the removal of your shortcuts.

13. Create a new message and type **Recipient@Domain-Not-Valid.com** as the recipient address.

14. Specify a subject line and enter some message text, then click Send.

    At this point, notice that your test message remains in your Outbox and is not sent to the server, as shown in Figure 1.3.

15. Because you did not configure a polling interval, messages will not leave your Outbox until you manually connect to the server. You can accomplish this using Send on the Tools menu.

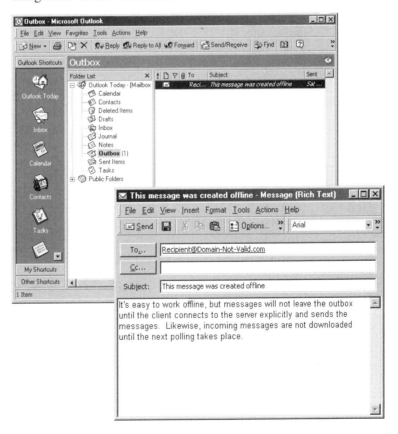

Figure 1.3 Messages remain in Outbox until Outlook 2000 works online

16. The recipient address specified does not exist; therefore, the system should return a nondelivery notification. However, you are not aware that a new message is awaiting your attention, because new messages are not discovered automatically.

17. To poll for new messages, from the Tools menu, point to Send/Receive, and then select Microsoft Exchange Server.

    At this point, Outlook checks for new messages and downloads the nondelivery report that was generated automatically as a response to your test message sent to a nonexistent recipient, as shown in Figure 1.4. This indicates that messages are only received after the next polling interval.

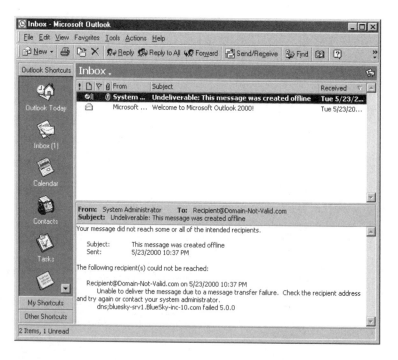

Figure 1.4   Messages are received after the next polling interval

Exercise Summary

The preceding experiment illustrates one of the most important disadvantages of shared-file messaging systems. Messages may be waiting, yet the recipients will not be aware of them until the clients are polling their message repositories. Even system processes, such as message transfer agents, which transfer messages between post offices, can be seen completely as clients (see Figure 1.1). These systems also do not recognize new messages until they perform their next polling. Consequently, message delivery in shared-file messaging systems is generally slow. To increase delivery performance, you would have to decrease the polling interval on all client systems, which in turn increases the network load. To make matters worse, polling always happens at regular intervals, even if there are no new messages to retrieve.

Client/Server Messaging Systems

Overcoming the limits of the passive post office structure requires active server components or services. These active services interact with the clients and will process the client requests to return the results only (see Figure 1.5). The client program only has to inform the server, "Here is a message for you. Please deliver it to Paul," and the server services will take care of that request. After completion, the server services return only the result to the client: "Done. Looking forward to servicing you again soon." The client does not need to perform the actual server-side processing, access any file server resources directly, or poll the server anymore because the active server services are able to contact the client themselves when new messages arrive: "Hey, aren't you Paul's Outlook client? Here's a new message for you."

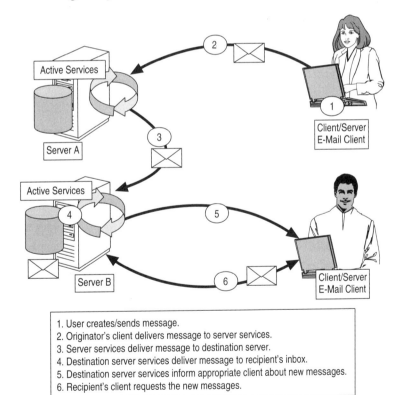

1. User creates/sends message.
2. Originator's client delivers message to server services.
3. Server services deliver message to destination server.
4. Destination server services deliver message to recipient's inbox.
5. Destination server services inform appropriate client about new messages.
6. Recipient's client requests the new messages.

Figure 1.5   A client/server messaging system

Hardware Resources

In a client/server messaging system, the bulk of the work is shifted to the active server. This requires more powerful and expensive server hardware than what is needed by a shared-file–based messaging system. To give an example, it is very common to install Exchange 2000 Server on dual-processor machines, with at least 256 MB of RAM and a well-designed high-performance Small Computer System Interface (SCSI) disk system. You might go along with less, yet the more the better.

Table 1.2 lists the advantages and disadvantages of client/server messaging systems.

Table 1.2   Advantages and Disadvantages of Client/Server Messaging Systems

Advantages of Client/Server Messaging Systems	Disadvantages of Client/Server Messaging Systems
Higher security, because the client does not need read-write permission in a post office. The server services are the actual components that write messages into and read messages from the server's messaging databases. No other components require direct read-write access.	The need for powerful server hardware, which is required due to the amount of processing performed by the server.
Reduced network traffic, because the active server can inform the client about the arrival of new messages (making polling unnecessary).	Increased complexity that may be excessive for small organizations.
Improved scalability, which makes client/server messaging systems suitable for the needs of large and quickly growing organizations. Clients do not poll the active messaging server and files will not be opened directly by any messaging client.	

Exercise 2: Testing the Performance of a Client/Server Messaging System

In this exercise you will use Outlook 2000 online and compare the resulting performance to the outcome of Exercise 1. This will emphasize the reasons to decide in favor of a powerful client/server messaging system, such as Exchange 2000 Server, for your environment.

To view a multimedia demonstration that displays how to perform this procedure, run the EX2CH1.AVI file from the \Exercise_Information\Chapter1 folder on the Supplemental Course Materials CD.

Prerequisites

- Complete Exercise 1, in the previous lesson.

- Outlook 2000 is started and you are currently working offline according to the resulting configuration of Exercise 1.

▶ **To configure Microsoft Outlook 2000 for online usage and compare the results with the outcome of Exercise 1**

1. From the Tools menu, select Services.

2. In the Services dialog box, from the list of installed services, select Personal Folders, and click Remove.

3. A message box appears telling you that you are about to remove the default message store. Click Yes.

4. Select the Microsoft Exchange Server service from the list of installed services, and then click Properties.

5. In the dialog box that appears, under Default Connection State, select Connect With The Network, as shown in Figure 1.6.

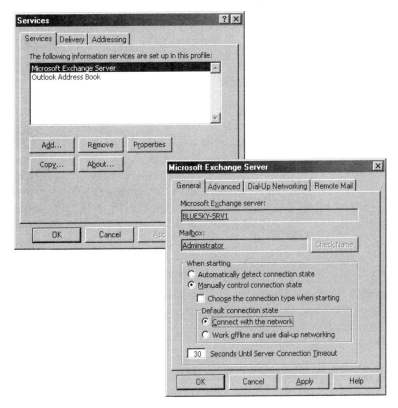

Figure 1.6 Configuring Outlook 2000 for online operation

6. Click OK twice to close the Services dialog box.

7. From the File menu, click Exit And Log Off to close Outlook 2000. It is necessary to reconnect to Exchange 2000 Server explicitly.

8. Start Outlook 2000 again. Your Outlook 2000 client should be switched back to the normal, online connection mode.

9. From the Tools menu, select Services to display the Services dialog box.

10. Select the Delivery property page and, under Deliver New Mail To The Following Location, select Mailbox - <User Name>.

11. Click OK to close the Services dialog box.

12. From the File menu, select Exit And Log Off (it is necessary to close Outlook to activate the new location for messages).

13. Start Outlook 2000 again and create a new message.

14. Type **Recipient@Domain-Not-Valid.com** as the recipient address.

15. Specify a subject line and enter some message text, then click Send.

At this point, you should notice that the message leaves your Outbox immediately and that a nondelivery report is returned in a relatively short period of time, as shown in Figure 1.7.

Figure 1.7   Sending and receiving messages takes only seconds

Exercise Summary

Exchange 2000 Server is strictly a Windows 2000 Server system comprising various active Windows 2000 services, which are typically launched when the operating system starts. Examples are the Microsoft Exchange System Attendant and the Microsoft Exchange Information Store. It is the Information Store that handles message processing on behalf of client programs. This service assists the clients in sending and receiving messages and accessing public folders. You can read more about the purpose and tasks of the Exchange 2000 Server services in Chapter 3, "Microsoft Exchange 2000 Server Architecture."

Collaboration/Groupware Systems

Your future messaging system should have capabilities beyond plain messaging. It should provide you with powerful workgroup and workflow capabilities. It should be a collaboration or groupware system that allows your users to interact efficiently, find and share information conveniently, publish information quickly, and track how information is used. Even better, automated processes on the active server can deliver information to you when the system determines it may be helpful or relevant.

Collaboration Solutions

Outlook 2000 provides numerous items you can customize easily (Appointments, Tasks, Journal, and Contacts). Basically, you only need to place the desired standard module in a public folder and your work is done. It is really that easy. In Chapter 21, "Microsoft Outlook Forms Environment," you will learn how to customize Outlook's standard modules.

The following are types of collaboration solutions based on Exchange 2000 Server and Outlook 2000:

- **Discussion groups.**   The repository of a discussion group is a public folder, where users can post and share information using a standard or customized post form. It is also possible to post responses to existing contributions in the public folder. A threaded conversation view allows users to view the history of responses to a particular discussion.

- **Instant collaboration.**   Solutions of this type rely on built-in Outlook 2000 modules to realize collaboration solutions with minimal configuration and development effort.

- **Reference systems.**   A reference system stores unstructured data of any kind, such as e-mail messages, graphic images, URLs, voice mail messages, and Microsoft Office or other documents. A user manual consisting of numerous Microsoft Word documents placed together in a public folder is a good example of a reference system. Exchange 2000 Server includes built-in content indexing for high-speed, accurate full-text searches, which makes this system an ideal document management platform.

- **Routing systems.**   Routing solutions pass information to individual users in sequence or to a group of users simultaneously. Exercise 3 illustrates a simple routing scenario. Exchange 2000 Server's extensive routing engine and capabilities are covered in more detail in Chapter 24, "Workgroup and Workflow Technologies."

- **Tracking systems.**   Tracking solutions keep a history of the usage of information and are most useful for data that is constantly updated. Using a tracking solution, for instance, you can track who currently is reviewing a particular document, who reviewed the document already, and whether the reviewer(s) approved or made changes to the document. Tracking systems are often implemented in conjunction with workflow solutions.

- **Real-time collaboration.**   Real-time collaboration provides services that enable you to schedule, create, administer, join, and track online sessions and conferences. Exchange 2000 Conferencing Server supports data and video conferencing and Exchange 2000 Server's Instant Messaging platform allows you to detect the presence of other users on the network and communicate with them in real time. In addition, Exchange 2000 supports multiuser chat environments, where users can interact with each other using chat conversation channels.

- **Microsoft Web Storage System.**   Web Storage System solutions represent a new and exciting technology that combines data repositories of various types, such as the folder system of Exchange 2000 Server, the file system of Windows 2000 Server, and Web-based resources, and presents them as a single place for storing information. You can access all information through URLs in any Web browser, in Outlook, or any Internet-based e-mail client, as well as Windows Explorer.

Exercise 3: Setting Up a Corporate Phone Book for Business Contacts

In this exercise you will take a first glance at the extensive collaboration capabilities of Exchange 2000 Server. The following procedure suggests a public phone book for business contacts. You will set up the repository as a moderated resource according to the process illustrated in Figure 1.8.

To view a multimedia demonstration that displays how to perform this procedure, run the EX3CH1.AVI file from the \Exercise_Information\Chapter1 folder on the Supplemental Course Materials CD.

Prerequisites

- Make sure you have completed Exercise 2 and Outlook 2000 is working online.

- Perform the following steps on BLUESKY-WKSTA.

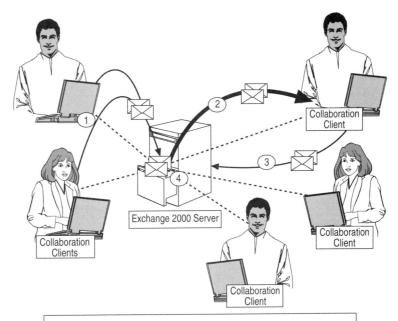

1. One or many users contribute new information to a collaboration system.
2. Active server services forward any new items to an assigned moderator.
3. Moderator approves contributed information and places it back in repository.
4. The information is now available to all users in the organization.

Figure 1.8   A collaboration example using a moderated public folder

▶ To set up a public phone book for business contacts

1. In Outlook 2000, from the File menu, point to Folder, and then select New Folder to display the Create New Folder dialog box.

2. In the Create New Folder dialog box, under Name, type **Business Contacts**.

3. Under Folder Contains, select Contact Items.

4. Under Select Where To Place The Folder, expand the Public Folders tree, select All Public Folders, and then click OK.

5. If a dialog box appears asking you whether you want to create a shortcut on your Outlook Bar, click Yes.

6. On the Outlook Bar, click My Shortcuts to display the list of your shortcuts, which also shows an icon named Business Contacts.

7. Right-click Business Contacts, and then select Properties.

8. Switch to the Administration property page, and then click Moderated Folder.

9. Activate the Set Folder Up As A Moderated Folder check box, and then click To to select Carl Titmouse as the folder moderator.

10. Activate the Reply To New Items With check box.

11. Under Moderators, click Add, and specify the user selected in Step 9 again (Carl Titmouse).

12. Click OK twice.

At this point, you have set up the public contact repository and specified a folder moderator, as shown in Figure 1.9.

Figure 1.9   Specifying a folder moderator

13. Open the public folder Business Contacts by clicking on its shortcut using the left mouse button.

14. Double-click in the empty right pane to create a new contact object.

15. Type a contact name (for instance, **Mr. Frederick Fly**) and a telephone number, and then click Save And Close.

16. When you are entering the phone number, a Location Information dialog box may appear asking you for information regarding the country/region system settings. Enter the information according to your location. If, subsequently, a Modem Properties dialog box appears, click OK again.

17. A Check Phone Number dialog box will appear asking you for country information and an area code for the phone number specified. Verify the information, and then click OK.

At this point, the new object does not appear in your public folder yet. Instead you have received a standard notification that your submission has been received and is reviewed. Open your inbox to read the response from Business Contacts, as shown in Figure 1.10.

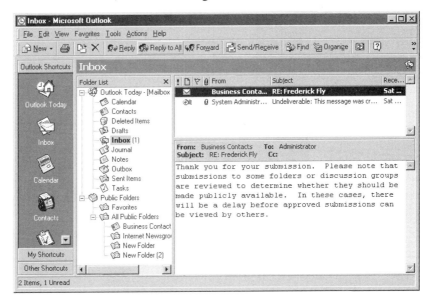

Figure 1.10   A standard response from the Business Contacts folder

18. Log off from Outlook 2000 and Windows 2000 and then log on as Carl Titmouse (the public folder moderator). Then, start Outlook 2000 and connect to the mailbox of Carl Titmouse. Note that the object created during the previous steps is awaiting your attention.

19. Double-click on the object, verify the correctness of the information, and then from the File menu, select Move To Folder.

20. In the Move Item To dialog box, open the Public Folders tree, then All Public Folders, and then double-click Business Contacts to move the object back into the public folder. If another item is opened automatically, close it again.

21. In the right Outlook pane, click Inbox (the button available on the top-left of the list of messages), open Public Folders, then open All Public Folders, and then select Business Contacts.

At this point, your contact object is publicly available. Optionally, you may log off and back on as Administrator to verify the result, as shown in Figure 1.11.

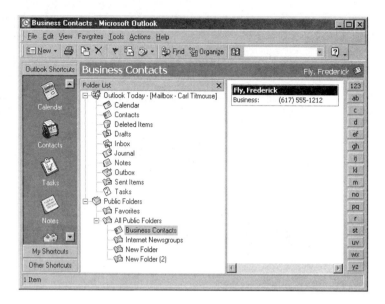

Figure 1.11   Moving an item into a public folder

Exercise Summary

Exchange 2000 Server provides an excellent set of workgroup and workflow features. Following the steps just outlined, you created an instant collaboration solution with basic routing capabilities in which users contribute new information, which is then forwarded automatically to a central moderator for approval. After approval, the information is made available to all users in the organization. A moderator can guarantee that only valid information is published. You can read more about public folders and their configuration in Chapter 17, "Public Folder Management."

Lesson 2: Exchange 2000 Server Design Goals

Microsoft's customer-driven software design process relies on direct customer responses, usability testing, and field studies. Customer responses are gathered from sources such as Microsoft Product Support Services and discussion forums on the Internet, as well as direct design requests, which come primarily from developers, solutions providers, independent software vendors, and IT managers. Usability testing is the process of verifying the implementation and design of certain product features until they pass specific usability standards, which is performed in usability labs at Microsoft. Field studies are conducted to observe how customers apply the software in their own environments. Early adopters, for instance, used Exchange 2000 Server in their production environments during the beta phase and provided valuable feedback that helped to guarantee a high quality standard for the released software.

This lesson highlights the three major design goals Microsoft defined for its development of Exchange 2000 Server, which address customer demand for increased performance and scalability, new technologies for collaboration and Web integration, and support of emerging technologies, such as teleconferencing.

At the end of this lesson, you will be able to:

- List the most important design goals for Exchange 2000 Server.

- Describe system improvements in respect to earlier versions of Exchange Server.

Estimated time to complete this lesson: 75 minutes

Powerful Infrastructure for Messaging and Collaboration

Each organization has a unique environment and a unique set of requirements. A small company might plan to use Exchange 2000 Server for only 80 users. Their requirements will differ from Internet service providers (ISPs) and application service providers that may plan to use Exchange 2000 Server to provide outsource messaging and collaboration services for millions of users. To best support the former, Exchange 2000 Server must be easy to maintain and administer; to support the latter, the system must provide excellent scalability.

Distributed Security Services

You can ensure a secure messaging and collaboration environment for your organization because Exchange 2000 Server takes advantage of Windows 2000 Server's flexible and comprehensive security architecture. This includes Kerberos and Secure Sockets Layer (SSL), which allow seamless access to all authorized network, messaging, and collaboration resources on the basis of a single authentication that is performed during the initial logon to the network. You can read more about the Windows 2000 security integration in Chapter 19, "Implementing Advanced Security."

Distributed Server Configurations

With Exchange 2000 Server, you can partition services across multiple servers to implement front-end/back-end server configurations. You can read more about front-end/back-end server configurations in Chapter 4, "Planning the Microsoft Exchange 2000 Server Installation."

Integration with Active Directory Directory Services

Trouble-free administration and maintainability is achieved through seamless integration with Windows 2000, particularly with Microsoft's Active Directory. Active Directory enables you to build an organization-wide directory that contains information about user accounts and mailboxes as well as the configuration of messaging components, such as connectors and gateways. You can read more about the integration with Active Directory in Chapter 2, "Integration with Microsoft Windows 2000."

Internet Mail Integration

Seamless integration with Windows 2000 is also a key factor in Exchange 2000 Server's improved performance and scalability, which is achieved through increased integration with Internet-based message transport protocols. For instance, Exchange 2000 uses and extends the Simple Mail Transfer Protocol (SMTP) service of Windows 2000 for all native server-to-server communication, which results in a flexible routing scheme. Advanced routing algorithms relying on link state information can ensure message delivery even if network problems occur. You can read more about SMTP-based routing in Exchange 2000 Server in Chapter 16, "Message Routing Administration."

Likewise, Exchange 2000 Server provides the best performance for Internet-based e-mail clients through its capability of storing and retrieving message objects encoded with Multiple Internet Mail Extensions (MIME). Format conversion takes place on demand when Messaging Application Programming Interface (MAPI)-based messaging clients, such as Outlook 2000, are accessing the same objects. In addition, Exchange 2000 Server supports X.509 V3 certificates and certificate trust lists (CTLs), which enable Secure/MIME (S/MIME) compatible e-mail clients to send S/MIME encrypted and signed e-mail. You can read more about the support of Internet-based messaging clients in Chapter 11, "Internet-Based Client Access."

Microsoft Management Console (MMC) Integration

Exchange 2000 Server supports the MMC-based management environment of Windows 2000. Utilizing MMC's features, you can create customized management tools and assign them to your administrators to let them focus on specific management tasks, such as mailbox and public folder maintenance. You can read more about MMC integration in Chapter 2, "Integration with Microsoft Windows 2000."

Multimaster Clustering

Windows 2000 Advanced Server supports multimaster clustering. Clustering with multiple active nodes and Exchange 2000 Server can benefit from these advanced configurations. Cluster configurations are often used to increase system availability and performance. You can read more about the installation of Exchange 2000 Server in a clustered environment in Chapter 7, "Microsoft Exchange 2000 Server in Clustered Environments."

Multiple Storage Groups

With Exchange 2000 you can split your mailbox and public folder resources across multiple message databases. This allows you to perform backup and restore operations for subsets of messaging resources independently. For instance, you can place the mailboxes of senior management in a separate storage group and perform backups more frequently than for ordinary users. If you need to restore a storage group, other storage groups can remain online. Splitting mailbox and public folder resources across multiple storage groups increases reliability, results in fewer lost work hours in the event of system failure, and reduces the time required to restore a system. You can read more about storage groups in Chapter 20, "Microsoft Exchange 2000 Server Maintenance and Troubleshooting."

Support for Collaborative Business Solutions

When specialists get excited about a particular software solution, they sometimes refer to it as a "killer app." The installable file system of Exchange 2000 Server, which relies on the Web Storage System, is such a solution because it allows you to access your mailbox and public folder resources using virtually any application you want. You can access your mailbox directly from within Microsoft Windows Explorer, any Web browser, Microsoft Word, a similar office application, or any other standard application. Have you ever tried a DIR command to list all your messages at the command prompt?

Knowledge Workers Without Limits

The Web Storage System combines the features and functionality of a file server, a Web server, and a collaboration server. Using a Web browser, for instance, you can access all items through URLs and it establishes a platform for information management that includes consistent search and data categorization. Exchange 2000 Server's built-in content indexing and search capabilities can make your organization more productive through better access to information. You can learn more about the Web Storage in Chapter 23, "Microsoft Exchange 2000 Web Storage System."

Exercise 4: Cross-Platform Collaboration

In this exercise you will examine how standard office programs can read and write items from and to your mailbox and public folders. Because the test environment does not include a full Microsoft Office installation, you will use WordPad.

To view a multimedia demonstration that displays how to perform this procedure, run the EX4CH1.AVI file from the \Exercise_Information\Chapter1 folder on the Supplemental Course Materials CD.

Prerequisites

- Make sure your test environment is prepared according to the descriptions given in the "Getting Started" section of "About This Book."
- Log on as Administrator to BLUESKY-SRV1.

▶ **To work with mailbox resources in Wordpad**

1. Click Start, point to Programs, point to Accessories, and then click on Wordpad.

2. In Wordpad, from the File menu, select Open.

3. In the Open dialog box, from the Look In list box, select M:\BLUESKY-INC-10.COM\MBX\Administrator\Inbox and, under Files Of Type, select All Documents (*.*). You should be able to see a list of test messages generated using the CDOStress utility used in the previous procedure.

4. Open one of the test messages and note the HTML-based formatting structures following the line <!DOCTYPE HTML PUBLIC "-//W3C//DTD HTML 3.2//EN">.

5. Open the File menu again, and select Save As to display the Save As dialog box.

6. From the Save In list box, select M:\BLUESKY-INC-10.COM\PUBLIC FOLDERS.

7. Right-click in the window area displaying subfolders and, from the shortcut menu, point to New and select New Folder.

8. Accept the suggested name of the new folder and save the opened message document in this folder by clicking Save. If a Wordpad dialog box appears informing you that you are about to save the document in text-only format, click Yes.

9. Close Wordpad.

   At this point, you can switch to Outlook 2000 to open the new public folder called New Folder from the public folders tree. You will then be able to verify that a message object exists and that it is indeed a message, as shown in Figure 1.12.

Exercise Summary

Office 2000 users will benefit from the features of the Web Storage System because it allows working with files and folders directly from within the

Figure 1.12 Saving documents directly into a public folder

applications. For instance, you have the option to use Microsoft Word 2000 to share documents easily. Just save your documents directly into a public folder. This public folder may then trigger additional workflow processes, as illustrated in Exercise 3.

Collaboration and Communication Without Limits

For most organizations, it is crucial to invest in future-oriented technologies, especially when entire business processes must rely on it (such as, the communication infrastructure). With Exchange 2000 Server, you can be confident that your decision is as future-oriented as possible. There is no doubt about it; the future of Exchange 2000-based messaging and collaboration will be exciting. When reading the following words from Bill Gates, keep in mind that Exchange 2000 Server is one of the most important parts of Microsoft's initiative to help knowledge workers overcome the physical and technical limits that often affect their productivity.

"We'll have smart TVs. We'll have cell phones that connect up to the Web and give you the latest information. All the information you care about—your schedule, your address book, your files—will automatically be available. And as you travel, you'll be able to book an appointment or look at your stock portfolio wherever you go. Wherever you are, you'll be able to access your own digital dashboard—the set of information that you care about on any screen, from a PC to that small pocket device. Microsoft and thousands of other companies are advancing the software that makes this possible. We'll spend next year about $3 billion on research and development." —Bill Gates, June 15, 1999

Outlook Web Access

Outlook Web Access is an application that works in conjunction with Internet Information Services (IIS). Using Outlook Web Access, you can access your mailbox, public folders, calendar and appointment items, and contact information using any standard browser that supports script languages and frames. Both anonymous and validated access are possible. Outlook Web Access for Exchange 2000 Server has been significantly improved in terms of performance, scalability, and ease of use. You can read more about Outlook Web Access in Chapter 22, "Microsoft Outlook Web Access."

Online Conferencing

Exchange 2000 Conferencing Server supports two forms of online conferencing—data conferencing and video conferencing. Data conferencing services rely on the T.120 standard, which supports document authoring with client software such as Microsoft NetMeeting. Video conferencing, on the other hand, offers integrated scheduling and management services for multicast video conferencing based on the H.323 protocol suite. You can read more about online conferencing in Chapter 25, "Real-Time Collaboration."

Instant Messaging and Presence Information

Instant Messaging allows you to see who is online (similar to the "buddy lists" of various Internet online services) and send instant messages to online users. It is also possible to invite multiple online users to join your instant messaging conversation. You can read more about instant messaging in Chapter 25, "Real-Time Collaboration."

Unified Messaging

Unified messaging is a synonym for the convergence of voice and data systems. Exchange 2000 Server includes support for the Voice Profile for Internet Mail standard that facilitates interoperability and compatibility among voice and messaging systems and built-in voice forms.

Chat Services

Chat services allow you to create a chat server network for real-time one-to-one, one-to-many, and many-to-many conversations. Chat Service in Exchange 2000 Server can be scaled up to 20,000 users per server. Integration with Active Directory simplifies the configuration of chat rooms and other settings. You can read more about the support of chat services in Chapter 25, "Real-Time Collaboration."

Lesson 3: Backward Compatibility and Interoperability

Messaging systems are typical computer network applications: They don't make much sense if they are used as a stand-alone application on a single computer. The larger the computer network, the more heterogeneous the installed system base will be. The Internet, for instance, combines all kinds of computer systems. For this reason, protocol standards have been developed to allow different computer systems to communicate with each other. Exchange 2000 Server supports the relevant messaging standards, making it a tremendously flexible platform.

This lesson provides a brief overview of available options for integrating Exchange 2000 Server into an existing messaging network. It covers integration into an environment relying on earlier Exchange Server versions as well as options for coexistence with other messaging systems.

At the end of this lesson, you will be able to:

- List the components that facilitate the integration of Exchange 2000 Server into an existing Exchange Server environment.
- Describe available options for connecting Exchange 2000 Server to foreign messaging systems.

Estimated time to complete this lesson: 45 minutes

Coexisting with Earlier Versions of Exchange Server

Exchange 2000 Server and previous versions are not alike. The system architecture has changed significantly in that the new version integrates tightly with Windows 2000 Server, whereas previous versions maintain their resources separately.

Account and Mailbox Information

As Figure 1.13 indicates, Active Directory architecture holds the directory attributes typically required for Windows 2000 as well as Exchange 2000– specific attributes. In contrast, Exchange Server 5.5 maintains its own directory information separately from Windows NT security information. Here, an association between Windows NT accounts and Exchange Server resources must be configured explicitly.

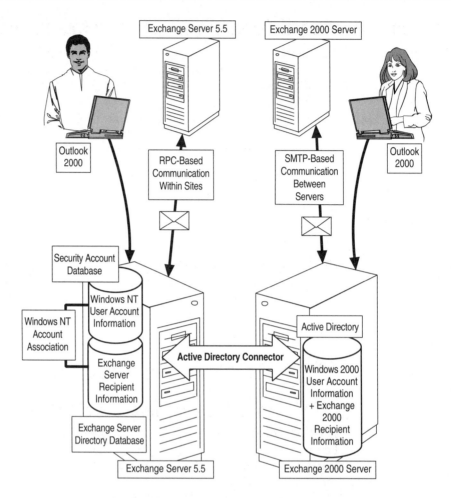

Figure 1.13 Differences between Exchange Server 5.5 and Exchange 2000 Server

Server-to-Server Communication

Computers running Exchange Server 5.5 at a single site communicate with each other using remote procedure calls (RPCs). Exchange 2000 servers, on the other hand, use SMTP as their native server-to server transport protocol. The latter increases system flexibility because it doesn't require a high-speed permanent network connection. You can read more about the integration of Exchange 2000 into Windows 2000 in Chapter 2, "Integration with Microsoft Windows 2000."

Mixed Mode Operation

Exchange 2000 Server supports a specific operation mode called *mixed mode* to facilitate coexistence with previous Exchange Server versions and it provides all required components for directory replication with previous versions (Active

Directory Connector [ADC] and Site Replication Service [SRS]). Exchange 2000 operates in mixed mode by default. You can read more about it and its counterpart, the native mode, in Chapter 4, "Planning the Microsoft Exchange 2000 Server Installation."

Note   If you need to connect your Exchange 2000 Server environment to previous versions in the future, continue to operate your organization in mixed mode for full backward compatibility.

Active Directory Directory Services Integration

Integration with Active Directory represents a significant task when planning your system coexistence. Using the ADC, earlier Exchange Server versions are able to replicate their directory information with Active Directory. This guarantees a consistent global address list across the entire organization. Detailed information about the ADC is provided in Chapter 6, "Coexistence with Previous Microsoft Exchange Server Versions."

Coexistence with Other Messaging Systems

Direct connections to Microsoft Mail, Lotus cc:Mail, Lotus Notes, and Novell GroupWise are supported. These connections are introduced in detail in Chapters 26 through 29.

Coexistence Through Messaging Standards

Exchange 2000 does not provide connectors to further messaging systems, which is an issue if you plan to connect Exchange 2000 Server to an environment currently utilizing Professional Office Systems (PROFS), System Network Architecture Distributed Systems (SNADS), or any other system not mentioned previously. In these situations, use one of the well-established messaging standards (SMTP or X.400) to build the e-mail bridge. Contact your remote administrator to determine which standard to utilize, and then configure the connection accordingly. Generally, it is advisable to use the SMTP transport because it is native to Exchange 2000 and provides the most powerful routing capabilities.

Coexistence via Earlier Exchange Server Versions

Alternatively, you may use connectors installed on computers running Exchange Server 5.5, provided you operate your Exchange 2000 organization in mixed mode. In this way, you have the option to use the PROFS/OV connector or the SNADS connector of Exchange Server 5.5 to provide connectivity to PROFS or SNADS, or third-party gateways for systems, such as DEC ALL-IN-1, MEMO, or MHS (see Figure 1.14).

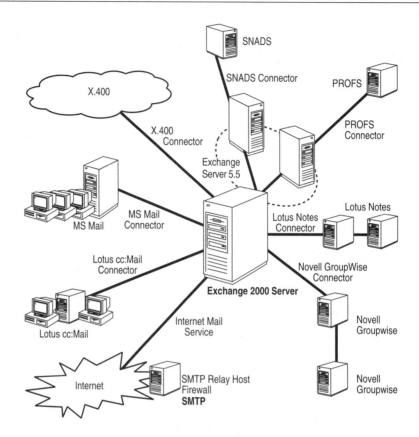

Figure 1.14 Native Exchange 2000 connectors and other messaging connections

---

Note Connectors to foreign messaging systems are included in both the Standard and the Enterprise Server edition of Exchange 2000 Server.

Windows 2000 Network Components

Exchange 2000 provides various connectors and relies on Windows 2000 protocols to support its integration into a heterogeneous environment. UNIX-based messaging systems, for instance, can easily be connected to a computer running Windows 2000 Server and Exchange 2000 using TCP/IP and SMTP. Lotus cc:Mail and Lotus Notes can operate over a variety of local area network (LAN) protocols, such as TCP/IP or Internetwork Packet Exchange/Sequenced Packet Exchange (IPX/SPX), all of which are supported by Windows 2000 Server. Thus, it is easy to integrate Exchange 2000 with these systems as well. Exchange 2000 also benefits from the powerful capabilities of Windows 2000 Server if you want to integrate this system into a Novell GroupWise or MS Mail environment, where the same protocols are used. More information about integration with a Novell NetWare environment is provided in Chapter 10, "MAPI-Based Clients in a Novell NetWare Environment."

Supported Client Platforms

Because of its implementation of popular messaging standards, Exchange 2000 Server supports a wide variety of messaging clients. It is possible to divide the available messaging clients into two primary categories—MAPI-based clients and Internet-based clients (see Figure 1.15).

Figure 1.15 MAPI-based clients and Internet-based clients

Messaging Application Programming Interface

MAPI is more than a single protocol; it's a description of a messaging architecture. It defines the interfaces for both the client and the underlying messaging system. Native Exchange clients, such as Outlook 2000, rely on MAPI for communication with Exchange 2000 Server. Many different vendors of messaging systems now provide MAPI drivers for standardizing access to their messaging servers as well. For more information about MAPI, its components, and its configuration, read Chapter 9, "MAPI-Based Clients."

Internet-Based Messaging Standards

The most popular Internet-based messaging standards supported by Exchange 2000 Server are POP3, IMAP4, HTTP, and Network News Transfer Protocol (NNTP). Several other Internet standards and protocols, such as MIME, are likewise implemented. For instance, you can use POP3 client software regardless of your operating system to download messages from a computer running Exchange

2000. In fact, the POP3 client doesn't know that it is communicating to a host that is specifically an Exchange 2000 server. The Internet-based client protocols are covered in detail in Chapter 11, "Internet-Based Client Access."

Exercise 5: Verifying Options for Internet-Based Client Connectivity

In this exercise you will verify Exchange 2000 Server's support for Internet client protocols, such as POP3, IMAP4, NNTP, and HTTP. Although not a specific messaging protocol, HTTP is supported via the Web Storage System and Outlook Web Access. You will check TCP ports available on a typical Exchange 2000 server and take a glance at Outlook Web Access.

To view a multimedia demonstration that displays how to perform this procedure, run the EX5CH1.AVI file from the \Exercise_Information\Chapter1 folder on the Supplemental Course Materials CD.

Note   If you are experiencing problems logging on to your mailbox using Outlook Web Access, it may be a good idea to reboot BLUESKY-SRV1 to successfully initialize the Web Storage System.

Prerequisites

- Verify that a mailbox exists for the Administrator account on BLUESKY-SRV1.

- Log on as Administrator to BLUESKY-SRV1.

▶   **To examine Exchange 2000 Server's support for Internet protocols**

1. Click Start, and then click Run.

2. In the Run dialog box, under Open, type **telnet.exe**, and then click OK. You will use Telnet to connect to the individual POP3, IMAP4, and NNTP ports. Note that the Windows 2000 Telnet client is a command-line application, which will be familiar to users of UNIX-based Telnet clients.

3. At the Microsoft Telnet command prompt, type **Set LOCAL_ECHO** and then press ENTER to activate the echo of entered characters. Otherwise you might not be able to see what you type.

4. At the Microsoft Telnet command prompt, type **Open Bluesky-SRV1 110** and then press ENTER to connect to your server's TCP/IP port 110. Note the reply from the Microsoft Exchange 2000 POP3 Server Version, which indicates that POP3 support is currently enabled.

5. Type **Quit** and then press ENTER to disconnect from your server. Press any key to return to the Microsoft Telnet command prompt.

6. At the Microsoft Telnet command prompt, type **Open Bluesky-SRV1 143** and then press ENTER to connect to your server's TCP/IP port 143. Note the

reply from the Microsoft Exchange 2000 IMAP4rev1 Server Version, which indicates that IMAP4 support is currently enabled.

7. Type **0000 Logout,** press ENTER to disconnect from your server, and then press any key to return to the Microsoft Telnet command prompt.

8. At the Microsoft Telnet command prompt, type **Open Bluesky-SRV1 119** and then press ENTER to connect to your server's TCP/IP port 119. Note the reply from the NNTP Service 5.00.0984 Version: 5.0.2195.1608, which indicates that this is the NNTP service of Windows 2000.

9. Type **Quit** and then press ENTER to disconnect from your server. Press any key to return to the Microsoft Telnet command prompt.

10. Type **Quit** and then press ENTER to close the Telnet client program.

11. Click Start, and then click Run. In the Run dialog box, under Open, type **http://Bluesky-SRV1/Exchange**, and then click OK.

12. If the Internet Connection Wizard appears, select the I Want To Set Up My Internet Connection Manually option, and then click Next.

13. On the next wizard screen, select I Connect Through A Local Area Network (LAN), and then click Next.

14. On the next wizard screen, leave all settings as defaults and click Next.

15. On the next wizard screen, under Do You Want To Set Up An Internet Mail Account, select No and click Next. On the next wizard screen, click Finish.

    At this point, you should be able to verify that you are logged on to the Administrator's mailbox using Microsoft Internet Explorer and Outlook Web Access, which indicate that HTTP-based access to your mailbox is possible, as shown in Figure 1.16.

16. Close Microsoft Internet Explorer.

Exercise Summary

You can use Outlook 2000 or any available Internet client to work with Exchange 2000 resources. Hence, you should determine if your users want all the available features at their disposal, as in Outlook 2000; if they are able to manage with only some of the features, as in Outlook Web Access or an IMAP4rev1-compliant client; or if they can get along with just the basics, as provided by a POP3 client. Deploy your client software accordingly. Outlook client software is available for many operating systems including MS-DOS, OS/2, Windows 3.1 and Windows for Workgroups 3.11, Windows 95 and Windows 98, Windows NT, and Windows 2000, as well as Apple Macintosh. UNIX users are only supported through POP3, IMAP4, HTTP, and NNTP protocols. Of course, you can use Internet-based protocols in Windows environments as well.

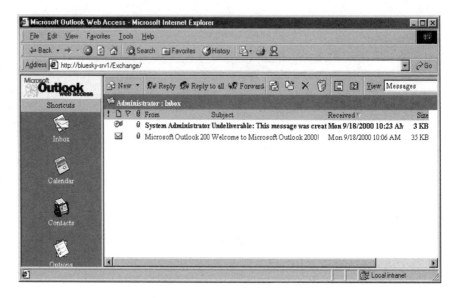

Figure 1.16   Internet-based client access to Exchange 2000 resources

Chapter Summary

Exchange 2000 Server relies heavily on Internet technologies and integrates tightly with Windows 2000 Server. Integration with Active Directory opens options for single-seat administration even in complex environments. Attributes and settings for Exchange 2000 are maintained in the Active Directory architecture along with ordinary Windows 2000 attributes. Compared to earlier versions, Exchange 2000 has been completely redesigned, making it one of the most powerful messaging and collaboration systems today.

Beyond simple e-mail messaging, Exchange 2000 provides extensive workgroup and workflow capabilities. For instance, little or no programming experience is required to configure discussion groups, reference or routing systems, Web solutions, information tracking applications, instant collaboration solutions, and simple workflow. Likewise, Exchange 2000 introduces powerful components for collaboration in real time, such as video and data conferencing, instant messaging, and chat services.

Exchange 2000 is easy to integrate in heterogeneous environments. It supports seamless mixing with earlier Exchange Server versions. It also provides all required components for coexistence with MS Mail, Lotus cc:Mail, Lotus Notes, and Novell GroupWise. Connectivity to other messaging systems must be established via Exchange Server 5 connectors, such as for PROFS or SNADS, or via common messaging standards, such as SMTP and X.400.

Review

The following review questions can help you determine if you have sufficiently familiarized yourself with the material covered in this chapter. You can find the answers to these questions at the end of this book in Appendix A, "Questions and Answers."

1. Why would you prefer a client/server messaging system to a shared-file messaging system?

2. What is the most significant difference between Exchange Server 5.5 and Exchange 2000 Server?

3. Exchange 2000 Server supports a variety of Internet protocols. What clients can be used to access e-mail–related information on the server?

4. You are planning to utilize Exchange 2000 Server's powerful collaboration solutions; however, workgroup and workflow applications are new to your administrators. Which type of collaboration solutions allows you to implement workgroup applications with minimal configuration and development effort?

5. Your organization is currently using Exchange Server 5.5 for messaging and collaboration. A PROFS connector is installed to provide a messaging path between PROFS and Exchange. You are planning an upgrade to Exchange 2000 Server. How can you provide connectivity to PROFS in the future Exchange 2000 Server environment?

C H A P T E R   2

Integration with Microsoft Windows 2000

About This Chapter

Microsoft Exchange 2000 Server takes full advantage of the features of Microsoft Windows 2000 such as the network architecture, security features, and directory services. In fact, Microsoft's new messaging and collaboration platform integrates so tightly with the operating system that it appears to be a Windows 2000 extension rather than a separate server platform. That is why a thorough understanding of Windows 2000 is an essential prerequisite for effective Exchange 2000 Server administration.

At first glance, you might find the new management tools of Windows 2000 puzzling because they rely thoroughly on Microsoft Management Console (MMC). It seems that nothing is where it once was in Windows NT. However, you will soon appreciate the new tools because they give you powerful capabilities for managing your network resources—this includes Exchange 2000 Server—via Active Directory directory service.

This chapter provides you with an overview of how Exchange 2000 Server is built into Windows 2000. You will read about the MMC framework and customized management tools. That is followed by an introduction to how Exchange 2000 Server utilizes Active Directory. The last lesson examines important networking components Exchange 2000 Server relies on for its own communication.

Before You Begin

To complete this chapter:

- Prepare your test environment according to the descriptions given in the "Getting Started" section of "About This Book."
- Understand Windows 2000 Server networking technologies and the TCP/IP protocol suite.
- Be familiar with the concepts of Active Directory.

Lesson 1: Integration with Microsoft Management Console

MMC is a Windows-based multiple-document interface (MDI) application representing a framework for Windows 2000 management tools. The Windows Administration Development Team originally designed the MMC for its own utilities, but because of its valuable features, it soon became publicly available as part of the Microsoft Platform Software Development Kit (SDK). Microsoft encourages all independent software vendors to provide MMC-based management applications for their systems to support a common administrative interface for Windows 2000 across all platforms. A common interface can simplify system administration. You have the option of combining various management applications to create individual tools for specific tasks and delegating these tools to the members of your workforce.

This lesson provides an overview of standard Windows 2000 and extended Exchange 2000 MMC components. You will learn how to utilize MMC features, such as taskpads, and create your own Exchange 2000 management tools to accomplish your work more conveniently.

At the end of this lesson, you will be able to:

- Describe the purpose and concept of the MMC.
- Combine administrative components to create powerful MMC tools for Exchange 2000 administration.

Estimated time to complete this lesson: 45 minutes

Microsoft Management Console Overview

Contrary to its name, the Microsoft Management Console has no management features itself. It is more of a framework for system developers and administrators. System developers write administrative applications for MMC, called snap-ins, and administrators then snap these management applications into the MMC and use them for their system administration.

Common MMC Elements

The MMC host application heavily utilizes Internet technologies, but it is up to the various snap-ins to perform the actual work. Because all snap-ins rely on MMC, a common set of user interface elements is generally available to all of them, such as the main menu, the action bar (the area that contains the Action, View, and Favorites menus), standard toolbars, a console tree (the child window's left pane), and a details pane (the child window's right pane). In fact, this is the primary function of MMC: It is meant to provide a common look and feel for all administrative utilities (see Figure 2.1).

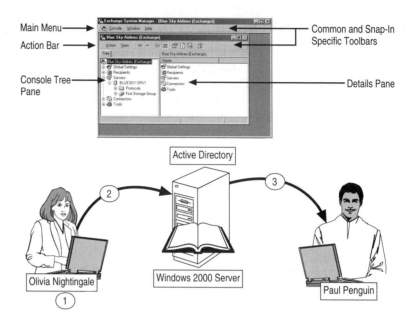

Main Menu
Action Bar
Console Tree Pane
Common and Snap-In Specific Toolbars
Details Pane

1. Olivia Nightingale, an experienced administrator, configures an MMC tool for system administration.
2. Olivia distributes the MMC tool via e-mail or Active Directory to Paul.
3. Paul Penguin, a less experienced administrator, uses the preconfigured management tool to perform his management tasks.

Figure 2.1   MMC user interface elements of management tools

Taskpads

Taskpad views represent a very interesting alternative to plain list views. A taskpad is a dynamic HTML (DHTML) page that allows you to combine a details pane displayed as a vertical or horizontal list with shortcuts to available commands. Using shortcuts to define important tasks and provide additional descriptions will help you simplify system administration.

User Mode MMC Tools

You have the option to assign MMC tools saved as .msc files to other administrators. Distribute your tools manually, through e-mail messages, or via Active Directory (by using the Group Policy snap-in's Software Installation extension). To prevent the modification of management tools, save your .msc files in User Mode (in contrast to Author Mode, which allows full access to all MMC functionality). To save a tool in user mode, open the Console menu, select Options, and then in the Options dialog box, under Console Mode, select one of the following three options:

- **User Mode - Full Access.**   The user can take advantage of all functionality of the management tool, but it is not possible to add or remove other snap-ins or to save changes to the .msc file.

- **User Mode - Limited Access, Multiple Windows.**   It is not possible to add or remove snap-ins or to save changes to the .msc file. In addition, it is not possible to close those windows that were open when you saved the .msc file. However, the administrator has the ability to open additional child windows.

- **User Mode - Limited Access, Single Window.**   Same as User Mode - Limited Access, Multiple Windows, with the exception that additional child windows cannot be opened. The administrator can only work with those windows that were open when you saved the console.

MMC Snap-Ins and Exchange 2000 Server

Numerous snap-ins come with Windows 2000, but they do not cover all aspects of Exchange 2000 Server administration. Therefore, the Setup program of Exchange 2000 Server registers additional snap-ins during the installation of Exchange 2000 Server's management utilities.

Exchange 2000 Snap-Ins

Exchange 2000 registers its snap-ins in the Windows 2000 Registry under the following key:

```
HKEY_LOCAL_MACHINE

  \SOFTWARE

   \Microsoft

    \MMC

     \SnapIns
```

The following MMC-based management utilities are included in Exchange 2000 Server:

- **Active Directory Users and Computers.**   This snap-in replaces the standard Windows 2000 Active Directory Users and Computers snap-in to allow management of user accounts and associated mailboxes as explained in Chapter 13, "Creating and Managing Recipients."

- **Exchange Advanced Security.**   This snap-in allows you to enable the users of your Exchange 2000 organization to use Advanced Security as explained in Chapter 19, "Implementing Advanced Security."

- **Exchange Conferencing Services.**   This snap-in is only available as part of Exchange 2000 Conferencing Server. It allows you to configure resource accounts for scheduling online conferences as explained in Chapter 25, "Real-Time Collaboration."

- **Exchange Folders.**   This snap-in allows you to configure configuration settings and permissions for public folders as explained in Chapter 17, "Public Folder Management."

- **Exchange Message Tracking Center.**   This snap-in allows you to track messages sent through your Exchange 2000 organization provided you enabled the message tracking feature as explained in Chapter 20, "Microsoft Exchange 2000 Server Maintenance and Troubleshooting."

- **Exchange System.**   This snap-in allows you to configure an entire Exchange 2000 organization. This is the primary management utility of the Exchange 2000 administrator.

Exercise 1: The MMC and Exchange 2000 Administration

In this exercise you will create a management tool that includes the Active Directory Users and Computers as well as the Exchange System snap-in in one management tool. This universal management tool will provide you with a complete set of management functions to maintain recipient information and Exchange 2000 Server resources from a single utility.

To view a multimedia demonstration that displays how to perform this procedure, run the EX1CH2.AVI files from the \Exercise_Information\Chapter2 folder on the Supplemental Course Materials CD.

Prerequisites

- Log on as Administrator to BLUESKY-SRV1 running Exchange 2000 Server.

▶   **To create a customized MMC Tool for Exchange 2000 administration**

1. Click Start, click Run, and then under Open, type **mmc**. Click OK to start the Management Console.

2. In the management console, open the Console menu, and then select Add/ Remove Snap-In.

3. In the Add/Remove Snap-In dialog box, click Add to display the Add Standalone Snap-In dialog box.

4. From the Available Standalone Snap-Ins list, select Exchange System, then click Add. Click OK to accept the default settings, and then click Close to close the dialog box.

5. In the Add/Remove Snap-In dialog box, under Snap-Ins Added To, double-click Blue Sky Airlines (Exchange), then click Add again and add the Active Directory Users and Computers snap-in to the management console.

6. Close the Add Standalone Snap-In dialog box by clicking Close and then, in the Add/Remove Snap-In dialog box, under Snap-Ins Added To, select Console Root.

7. Click on the Extensions tab.

8. From the Snap-Ins That Can Be Extended list, select the available entries one at a time and make sure the Add All Extensions check box is selected for all of them. Note the various extensions available for this standalone snap-in (such as Exchange Protocols, Exchange Servers, or Exchange X.400). Click OK to close the dialog box.

   At this point, the Exchange 2000 snap-ins are displayed in the console tree, as shown in Figure 2.2.

9. Save the changes to your .msc file with a name of your choosing.

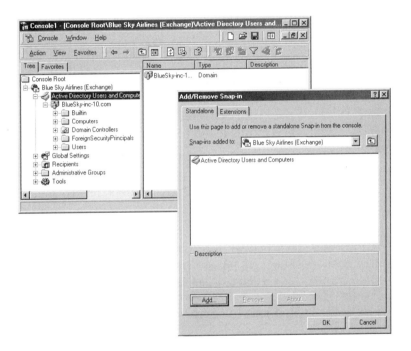

Figure 2.2   Adding Exchange 2000 snap-ins to create a custom console

Exercise Summary

Snap-ins are either stand-alone snap-ins or extension snap-ins. Stand-alone snap-ins, as the name implies, don't require support from other snap-ins. You can add them to any of your management tools at any time. Extension snap-ins, on the other hand, require a parent snap-in, which they extend in terms of functionality. Extension snap-ins typically depend on stand-alone snap-ins and may display items below the parent in the console tree. However, extension snap-ins are not required to provide viewable elements. They might simply extend a stand-alone snap-in by adding shortcut menu items, toolbars, property pages, wizards, or Help features. For more information about the structures, options, and features of the MMC, see the Microsoft Platform Software Development Kit.

Lesson 2: Active Directory Directory Service Integration

Are you administering a messaging environment already? Then you are most likely forced to accomplish the same or similar steps multiple times using dissimilar utilities. For example, in a Windows NT/Exchange Server 5.5 environment, you need to maintain user accounts in a Windows NT domain and associated mailboxes in an Exchange Server directory. The integration of Exchange 2000 Server with Active Directory overcomes the duplication of similar information in multiple directory repositories and will help reduce your system maintenance overhead. With Exchange 2000 Server, the quality of your messaging administration depends on the quality of the Active Directory design.

This lesson covers in more detail how Exchange 2000 Server uses Active Directory. You are introduced to directory extensions for Exchange 2000 Server and various aspects important to successfully maintaining your Exchange 2000 organization.

At the end of this lesson, you will be able to:

- Describe the physical and logical structure of Active Directory in general terms.
- Display and configure Exchange 2000-related directory object attributes.
- Identify important issues regarding directory replication and Exchange 2000 administration.
- Explain how Exchange 2000 Server supports Messaging Application Programming Interface (MAPI)-based clients, such as Microsoft Exchange Client 4.0 and 5.0, and Outlook 97, 98, and 2000.

Estimated time to complete this lesson: 2 hours

Physical and Logical Structure

When designing your Active Directory hierarchy, you typically need to reflect the physical and logical structure of your resources. The physical structure is based on sites, and the logical structure is comprised of the individual directory objects, organizational units (OUs), domains, trees, and forests.

Sites, Domains, OUs, and Directory Objects

Sites are combinations of IP subnets connected to each other via high-speed network links. They are used to optimize the directory replication (see "Active Directory Replication" later in this lesson). A Windows 2000 domain, on the other hand, is the core unit of the logical structure. Domains contain OUs and are arranged in a tree and a forest. OUs can contain other OUs as well as directory objects. Every individual directory object, maintained in an OU, represents a distinct set of attributes (display name, e-mail address, title, etc.) for a network resource, such as a user account, workstation, server, printer, shares, files, and so on. For detailed information about Active Directory see the *Microsoft Windows 2000 Server Resource Kit*, especially the *Windows 2000 Server Distributed Systems Guide*.

Moving Users Between OUs

Using the Active Directory Users and Computers Snap-In, you can create additional OUs in a domain. It is easy to move directory objects between OUs. Just right-click the desired directory object, such as Administrator, and then, from the shortcut menu, select Move. In the Move dialog box, select the desired target OU, and then click OK to move the account into the specified OU. This can provide a high level of convenience, for instance, if a user moves between departments in an environment where departments are mapped to OUs in the Active Directory architecture. Instead of deleting and re-creating the user account and mailbox, move the corresponding directory object to its new location and the job is done. If you have administered a previous version of Exchange Server, you will especially appreciate this convenience. You can read more about the management of directory objects and the configuration of security settings and group policies in Chapter 13, "Creating and Managing Recipients."

Domains and Namespaces

Less complex environments will find a single domain environment sufficient. Windows 2000 domains include one or more domain controllers and define the security boundary for all network resources they contain. Domain controllers authenticate users and hold a complete replica of their own domain information as well as configuration and schema information from other domains that may exist in the same forest. In complex environments with numerous users, domains are used to physically organize domain account objects (such as user, group, computer, and printer accounts).

Domain Controllers and Access Control Lists

Use the DCPROMO.EXE utility to promote a computer running Windows 2000 Server to a domain controller. The same utility can also be used to demote domain controllers. Access control lists (ACLs) define the permissions associated with directory objects. ACLs control user or group access to particular objects, as outlined in more detail in Chapter 19, "Implementing Advanced Security."

Note Plan your domain environment carefully and keep in mind that Active Directory domains cannot be renamed. This functionality may be available in future versions of Windows 2000.

Parent–Child Relationships

Complex environments might require a more involved domain architecture, such as the one shown in Figure 2.3, especially if very granular network management is desired. You can arrange multiple domains in a hierarchical manner to establish a parent–child relationship between these domains. An arrangement of parent and child domains is known as a domain tree.

Figure 2.3 shows an arrangement of multiple domain trees. This structure is called a forest. It is worth noting that a particular Active Directory database can only hold the configuration and schema information from a single forest. This information is replicated to all domain controllers in every domain of the forest.

Note   It is advisable to deploy a single Active Directory forest to enable a common security model and to be able to replicate configuration and schema information across your organization. A single Exchange 2000 organization cannot span multiple forests, but it is possible to spawn multiple domains of a single forest.

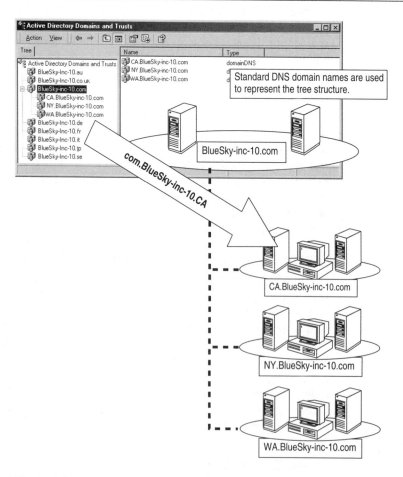

Figure 2.3   Multiple domain trees in a forest

Continuous and Disjointed Namespaces

Every DNS name of a child domain in the hierarchy contains the name of the parent domain. For instance, the subdomain CA.BlueSky-inc-10.com contains BlueSky-inc-10.com (see Figure 2.3), which is exactly the name of the first domain in the forest. Both domains form a domain tree and, because the child object contains the name of the parent object, they also form a continuous namespace.

The domain BlueSky-inc-10.fr, on the other hand, does not form a continuous namespace with BlueSky-inc-10.com because BlueSky-inc-10.com is not included in BlueSky-inc-10.fr. Consequently, both domains are not part of the same tree, yet they are still interrelated because they are part of the same forest and share configuration and schema information. Objects that do not share a common naming structure but are interrelated (such as multiple trees in a forest) form a disjointed namespace.

Exercise 2: Creating a Domain Tree in the Test Environment

In this exercise you will create a continuous namespace spanning two domains by adding a child domain to BlueSky-Inc-10.com. Completing the following procedure is a prerequisite for other exercises in subsequent sections and chapters.

To view a multimedia demonstration that displays how to perform this procedure, run the EX2CH2*.AVI files from the \Exercise_Information\Chapter2 folder on the Supplemental Course Materials CD.

Prerequisites

- Log on as Administrator to BLUESKY-SRV2, which is not running Exchange 2000 Server.
- Use the DNS Manager on BLUESKY-SRV1 to configure the existing forward lookup zones to accept dynamic updates. Under the Forward Lookup Zones tree, right-click on Bluesky-inc-10.com and select Properties. In the General tab, set Allow Dynamic Updates to Yes.

▶ **To create a single domain tree of two domains**

1. Click Start and then click Run.
2. In the Run dialog box, under Open, type **dcpromo**, and then click OK to start the Active Directory Installation Wizard.
3. On the first Active Directory Installation Wizard screen, click Next.
4. On the Domain Controller Type wizard screen, accept the default selection Domain Controller For A New Domain, and then click Next.
5. On the Create Tree Or Child Domain wizard screen, select Create A New Child Domain In An Existing Domain Tree, and then click Next.

6. On the Network Credentials wizard screen, enter the following information, and then click Next to continue:

User Name	Administrator
Password	password
Domain	BlueSky-inc-10

7. On the Child Domain Installation wizard screen, under Parent Domain, type **BlueSky-inc-10.com** (or use Browse to conveniently select the correct domain from the Browse For Domain dialog box). Under Child Domain, type **CA,** and then click Next to continue.

8. On the NetBIOS Domain Name wizard screen, accept the suggested Domain NetBIOS Name of CA and click Next.

9. On the Database And Log Locations wizard screen, accept the default settings and click Next.

10. On the Shared System Volume wizard screen, accept the default settings and click Next to continue.

11. On the Permissions wizard screen, make sure the default option Permissions Compatible With Pre-Windows 2000 Server is selected, and then click Next to continue.

12. On the Directory Services Restore Mode Administrator Password wizard screen, under Password and Confirm Password, type **password**, and then click Next to continue.

13. On the Summary wizard screen, displaying a summary of all configuration changes, click Next to complete the configuration of Active Directory. This process might take several minutes until you reach the final wizard screen where you click Finish to complete the configuration.

14. In the final Active Directory Installation Wizard message box, click Restart Now to immediately have the changes take effect.

15. Log on again as Administrator, click Start, point to Programs, point to Administrative Tools, and then click Active Directory Domains And Trusts to start the Active Directory Domains and Trusts snap-in.

16. In the console tree, verify that the domain CA.BlueSky-inc-10.com is displayed as a child domain under BlueSky-inc-10.com. All Active Directory domains are identified by a DNS name that includes the complete name of the parent domain.

17. Right-click the CA.BlueSky-inc-10.com domain object and then, in the shortcut menu, click Manage, which will start the Active Directory Users and Computers snap-in.

18. Open the Domain Controllers OU and, in the details pane, right-click on the BLUESKY-SRV2 computer object and, in the shortcut menu, select Properties.

19. Verify that the DNS Name is Bluesky-srv2.CA.BlueSky-inc-10.com.

    At this point, you should be able to verify that BLUESKY-SRV2 is a host in
    the child domain CA.BlueSky-inc-10.com, which contains the parent tree
    BlueSky-inc-10.com in its domain name (see Figure 2.4).

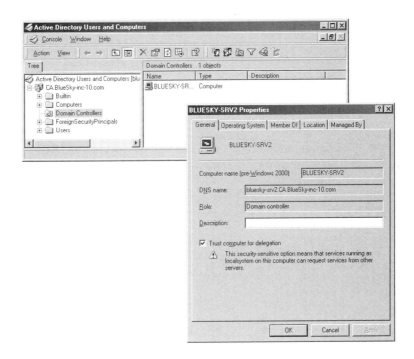

Figure 2.4 A child domain's DNS name

Exercise Summary

It is relatively easy to create multiple domains in a domain tree, provided DNS is
configured properly and you have the required permissions. Start the
DCPROMO.EXE utility (which resides in the \Winnt\System32 directory) and
make sure you choose the Create A New Child Domain In An Existing Domain
Tree option. At this point, you need to specify the parent domain. You may
specify the first domain installed in the forest or another subdomain that already
exists. It is not possible, however, to use DCPROMO.EXE for creation of parent
domains (domains above the first domain or above a sublevel domain). You may,
however, use DCPROMO.EXE to remove a sublevel domain from the domain
tree by demoting the domain controller(s) to member server(s).

Active Directory Replication

Active Directory includes a replication feature that ensures that changes to a
domain controller, including changes made to your Exchange 2000 organization,
are passed along to all other domain controllers in the same domain.

Replication can be performed via IP, synchronous remote procedure call (RPC) communication, or via Simple Mail Transfer Protocol (SMTP; e-mail messages). IP-based and synchronous RPC communication works best over fast and reliable network connections (such as a local area network [LAN]). SMTP-based communication via e-mail, on the other hand, is an alternative if network connections are unreliable, slow, or if data transfer generates costs (such as a wide area network [WAN]). The physical structure of your Active Directory environment determines the communication mechanism used for replication.

Windows 2000 Sites

Only replication links between sites need to be configured manually. Sites can contain computers from a single domain and from multiple domains (see Figure 2.5). Multiple Windows 2000 sites may also exist within a single domain. The configuration of sites and site links is covered in detail in the *Windows 2000 Server Distributed Systems Guide* of the *Microsoft Windows 2000 Server Resource Kit.*

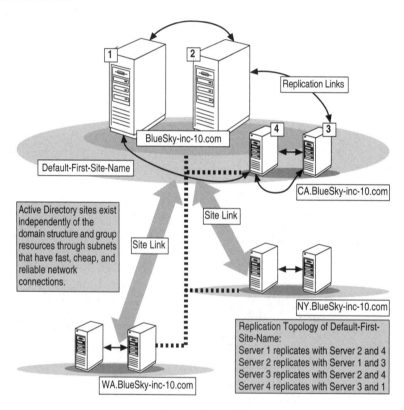

Figure 2.5   Active Directory sites and directory replication

> **Note** Windows 2000 sites are only used to identify regions in the network where fast and reliable connections are present. They do not serve any purpose for Exchange 2000 administration. Here, you will use administrative and routing groups instead, which are covered in Chapter 4, "Planning the Microsoft Exchange 2000 Server Installation."

Exchange 2000 Attributes in the Active Directory Directory Service

When you install Exchange 2000 Server, the setup routine automatically extends the Active Directory forest. To demonstrate this, log on to your test computer BLUESKY-SRV1 (where Exchange 2000 Server is installed), start the Active Domain Users And Computers utility, and display the properties of the Administrator object. You will discover Exchange 2000-related property pages, such as Exchange General, which provides you with information about the Mailbox Store and the Alias name and gives you the option to set Delivery Restrictions, Delivery Options, and Storage Limits. This information did not exist before the installation of Exchange 2000 because it isn't relevant to standard Windows 2000 administration.

First Server Installation

During the installation of the very first Exchange 2000 server in an organization, the Setup program will take an extended period of time to extend the forestwide Active Directory schema (see Figure 2.6). You may have noticed this when installing Exchange 2000 on BLUESKY-SRV1 in your test environment. Schema extensions are required to provide you with the ability to manage Exchange 2000 resources.

Active Directory Schema

The schema consists of numerous classes that represent the various instances of directory objects (user, computer, connector, etc.) and specifies the relationships between classes. Classes are sets of object attributes (user name, logon name, alias, etc.), and attributes are governed by syntaxes (single value, multiple value, data type, etc.). Exchange 2000 adds new classes to the schema as well as new attributes to existing object classes. Likewise, existing attributes are modified to replicate them to the Global Catalog. You can find detailed information about the Active Directory schema in the *Windows 2000 Server Distributed Systems Guide* of the *Windows 2000 Server Resource Kit*, specifically in Chapter 4, "Active Directory Schema."

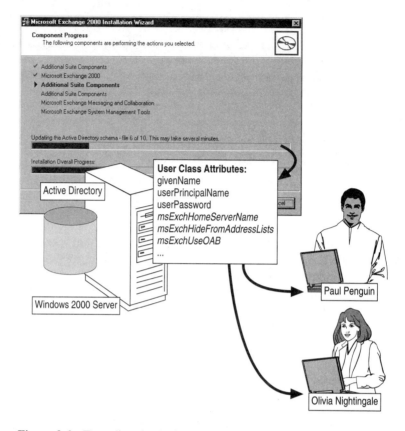

Figure 2.6   Extending the Active Directory schema

Exercise 3: Verifying Exchange 2000 Extensions to the Active Directory Directory Service

In this exercise you will examine the Active Directory schema extensions for Exchange 2000. For this purpose, you need to install a specific Windows 2000 snap-in called Active Directory Schema, which allows you to display the individual object classes and attributes.

To view a multimedia demonstration that displays how to perform this procedure, run the EX3CH2.AVI files from the \Exercise_Information\Chapter2 folder on the Supplemental Course Materials CD.

Prerequisites

- Log on as Administrator to BLUESKY-SRV2, where Exchange 2000 and Exchange 2000 MMC snap-ins are not installed. This emphasizes that the schema extensions are replicated to all domain controllers in the forest after the first Exchange 2000 server is installed.

- The Active Directory Schema snap-in is not yet installed on BLUESKY-SRV2. To install this specific snap-in, run the Windows 2000 Administration Tools Setup Wizard, which is available on the Windows 2000 Server CD, in the folder \I386 (named ADMINPAK.MSI). Most likely, ADMINPAK.MSI exists in your \Winnt\System32 directory as well. Alternatively, you can enable this snap-in via the regsvr32 SCHMMGMT.DLL command.

▶ **To verify the presence of Exchange 2000 schema extensions**

1. Click Start and then click Run. In the Run dialog box type **mmc**. Click OK to start the Management Console.

2. Open the Console menu and select Add/Remove Snap-In.

3. Click Add, and then, in the Add Standalone Snap-In dialog box, double-click the Active Directory Schema Snap-In, then click Close and subsequently OK to close all dialog boxes.

4. Maximize the MMC and the child window, and then, in the console tree, open the node called Active Directory Schema and select Classes.

5. In the details pane, scroll down through the objects until you see items that begin with msExch. Exchange 2000 Server adds several of these object classes to the Active Directory schema.

   At this point, scroll down to the class named msExchPFTree, as shown in Figure 2.7. Double-click on this object to display its properties. Switch to the Attributes property page and check the list of optional attributes that form this class, then click OK to close the dialog box.

6. In the console tree, select Attributes and, in the details pane, scroll down to the attributes that have a description starting with msExch. Note that although Exchange 2000 Server is not installed in the subdomain CA.BlueSky-inc-10.com, the schema information is replicated to BLUESKY-SRV2 from BLUESKY-SRV1, which runs Exchange 2000 Server.

7. Exchange 2000 Server also modifies existing attributes. To demonstrate this, search for the attribute givenName (which describes the first name of a user object) and note that the Index This Attribute In The Active Directory, Ambiguous Name Resolution (ANR), and Replicate This Attribute To The Global Catalog check boxes are selected. The Exchange 2000 Setup program activated these options to optimize the address name resolution as well as address book searches in Outlook 2000.

8. Close the MMC without saving the console settings.

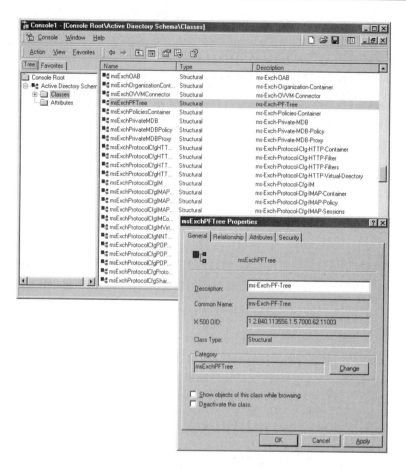

Figure 2.7   Exchange 2000 object classes and attributes

Exercise Summary

Descriptions of Exchange 2000–specific attributes begin with msExch. They are added to Active Directory as part of the first Exchange 2000 installation and are replicated to all domain controllers in the forest. Permissions of a schema admin (member of the Windows 2000 group Schema Admins) are required to change the configuration. Should those permissions be missing, settings are displayed in read-only mode. Attribute settings may be changed manually or automatically (for instance, through the Exchange 2000 Setup program) to include, for example, specific attributes for Global Catalog replication, address name resolution, and address book searches.

Active Directory Integration and Outlook Clients

When you use Outlook to connect to your server-based mailbox and open the address book to look up recipient information from your Exchange 2000 organization, this information does not come from your Exchange 2000 server at all; instead it is retrieved from the Windows 2000 Global Catalog server. However, Outlook and other previous MAPI-based clients, such as the legacy Exchange Client, are typically not aware of the Global Catalog and expect to communicate with an Exchange directory service. Earlier versions of Exchange Server provided their own directory service.

DSProxy Feature

To support MAPI-based clients, Exchange 2000 Server provides a feature known as DSProxy. DSProxy forwards directory lookups of MAPI-based clients straight to a Global Catalog server. MAPI-based clients obtain access to Active Directory by using the Name Service Provider Interface (NSPI). DSProxy also keeps a reference of connections between clients and servers, ensuring that the response from the Global Catalog is passed to the correct client (see Figure 2.8).

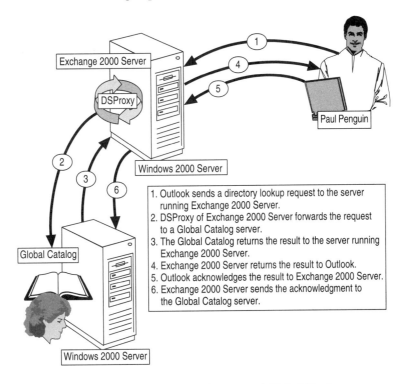

Figure 2.8   Directory lookups via DSProxy and Global Catalog

Note   DSProxy requires TCP/IP, Internetwork Packet Exchange (IPX), or the AppleTalk protocol. NetBEUI is not supported.

DSProxy Implementation Details

The DSProxy process is part of the Microsoft Exchange System Attendant service, and is implemented in DSPROXY.DLL, which resides in the \Program Files\Exchsrvr\bin folder. You can verify its activities in the Windows 2000 Event Log, although you probably do not yet have any such event logged. Start the Event Viewer from the Administrative Tools program folder and filter the details of the Application Log; under Event Source select MSExchangeSA and under Category select NSPI Proxy (this stands for Name Service Provider Interface). You can read more about the System Attendant and other important Exchange 2000 services in Chapter 3, "Microsoft Exchange 2000 Server Architecture."

Global Catalog Servers

Global Catalog servers are specific domain controllers that support forestwide directory lookups. By default, only the first domain controller in the forest is a Global Catalog server, but you can add one or more to increase the fault tolerance. When you start Exchange 2000 Server, the System Attendant service detects the Global Catalog servers to be used by DSProxy. You also have the ability to statically reference a Global Catalog by adjusting the parameters of the System Attendant in the Registry. Add the value NSPI Target Server (type **REG_SZ**) under

```
HKEY_LOCAL_MACHINE

  \System\

  \CurrentControlSet

  \Services

  \MSExchangeSA

  \Parameters
```

and set it to the name of the desired Global Catalog server.

Note   Setting the NSPI Target Server manually via the NSPI Target Server Registry parameter may be necessary in some situations; however, this decreases system resilience. The Registry setting overrides the list of automatically detected catalog servers. If the Global Catalog specified is not available for any reason, MAPI-based clients cannot log on to their mailboxes.

Diversion of Smart MAPI Clients

DXProxy, especially its Director Service Referral (RFR) Interface, also has the ability to divert so-called smart MAPI clients (such as Outlook 2000) to the Global Catalog directly. Windows 2000 domain controllers support MAPI as well as Lightweight Directory Access Protocol (LDAP), and can therefore communicate with Outlook 2000 without proxying. Outlook 2000 only needs to learn that it should contact a Global Catalog. To cause DSProxy to divert Outlook 2000 and other smart clients, set the registry parameter RFR Target Server (type **REG_SZ**) on the server to the name of the desired Global Catalog server under

```
HKEY_LOCAL_MACHINE

 \System

  \CurrentControlSet

   \Services

    \MSExchangeSA

     \Parameters
```

MAPI Profile Settings

Outlook 2000 stores the Global Catalog server name received from DSProxy in its MAPI profile and uses it for all subsequent directory access. Consequently, diverting Outlook 2000 to the Global Catalog can reduce the load on the Exchange 2000 server and the latency for address book lookups. You can read more about MAPI and the configuration of MAPI profiles in Chapter 9, "MAPI-Based Clients."

DNS Records for Global Catalog Servers

Global Catalog servers must be registered through service (SRV) records in DNS. If your DNS server supports dynamic updates, Windows 2000 registers the required information automatically. In the test environment, use the DNS snap-in to find the corresponding _gc records, for instance, under DNS\BLUESKY-SRV1\Forward Lookup Zones\Bluesky-inc-10.com_msdcs\gc_tcp. The name of the record will be _ldap.

Global Catalog Load-Balancing

MAPI-based clients communicate with the Exchange directory service in many situations, such as for client logon, displaying the address book, resolving recipient information, and so forth. Consequently, the Global Catalog is heavily utilized in an Exchange 2000 environment and can become bottlenecked. Configure multiple Global Catalog servers if possible. This is accomplished quickly using the Active Directory Sites and Services snap-in. In the console tree, open Sites, then Default-First-Site-Name, then Servers, and then the desired server, such as BLUESKY-SRV2. Right-click NTDS Settings, and then select Properties. In the General property page, select the Global Catalog check box, and then click OK.

Exchange 2000 Server can balance the generated workload between the available Global Catalog servers. For scalability and resilience, at least two Global Catalog servers should exist per Active Directory site; if your site spans multiple domains, configure at least one Global Catalog in each domain.

Lesson 3: Windows 2000 Protocols and Services Integration

TCP/IP is Microsoft's strategic network transport protocol. Exchange 2000 Server integrates tightly with Active Directory, and Active Directory requires DNS, which in turn requires TCP/IP. Therefore, you may consider Exchange 2000 primarily a TCP/IP-based system, although it can also use other networking protocols (such as Internetwork Packet Exchange/Sequenced Packet Exchange [IPX/SPX], AppleTalk, Banyan Vines protocol). In fact, focusing on TCP/IP makes it easy to integrate Exchange 2000 into any PC-based environment. In addition, Windows 2000 Server protocols and services, such as IP Security (IPSec) and Kerberos, allow you to operate securely over TCP/IP networks. Windows 2000 also provides application layer components, such as the SMTP and Network News Transfer Protocol (NNTP) services, which the Exchange 2000 Setup program extends to provide the functionality required for an enterprise-class messaging and collaboration system.

In this lesson, you will read about the network infrastructure of Windows 2000 that Exchange 2000 relies on for its own communication purposes. This lesson focuses on those aspects relevant to the communication between Outlook 2000 and Exchange 2000 Server and the communication between Exchange 2000 servers themselves.

At the end of this lesson, you will be able to:

- Describe how Outlook 2000 and Exchange 2000 utilize the Windows 2000 network infrastructure.
- Identify information services of Windows 2000 used for Exchange 2000 server-to-server communication.
- Describe extensions added to Windows 2000 information services for Exchange 2000 server-to-server communication.

Estimated time to complete this lesson: 60 minutes

Windows 2000 Network Architecture

Messaging systems rely heavily on the underlying communication infrastructure for client-to-server and server-to-server data transfer. Exchange 2000 Server is no exception and utilizes a number of high-level interfaces to access network resources, such as RPCs and Windows Sockets. You can find further information about RPCs and Windows Sockets in Chapter 3, "Microsoft Exchange 2000 Server Architecture."

TCP/IP Protocol Suite

The Internet has proven that the TCP/IP protocol suite is the right choice for computer networks of any size and purpose. Choose TCP/IP and don't deploy any other network protocol if you don't have to. Most, if not all, modern network systems support TCP/IP. It is advisable to configure your workstations and servers for only one protocol stack because this minimizes configuration overhead and resource consumption and maximizes network performance.

MAPI-Based Clients

MAPI-based clients, such as Outlook 2000, depend on synchronous RPCs. In a TCP/IP-only environment, the Outlook client attempts to connect to the Exchange 2000 server via TCP/IP and the RPC-based communication is handled via Windows Sockets (see Figure 2.9). You can read more about RPCs in respect to non-TCP/IP environments in Chapter 10, "MAPI-Based Clients in a Novell NetWare Environment."

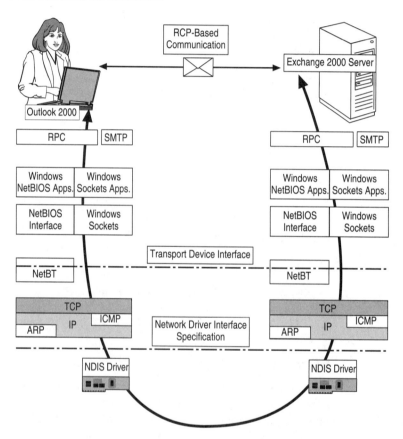

Figure 2.9 RPC-based communication

Server-to-Server Communication

Windows Sockets is also utilized for server-to-server communication. Servers running Exchange 2000 Server transfer messages preferably via SMTP, which requires the Windows Sockets interface (see Figure 2.10).

Unlike earlier versions of Exchange Server, which used synchronous RPCs for server-to-server communication within sites, Exchange 2000 Server does not rely on RPCs between servers. Instead, SMTP is used. As an asynchronous transport protocol, SMTP allows Exchange 2000 Server to operate well under high- and low-bandwidth network conditions. RPC-based server-to-server communication, on the other hand, is only important when connecting Exchange 2000 Server to previous Exchange Server versions as outlined in Chapter 6, "Coexistence with Previous Microsoft Exchange Server Versions."

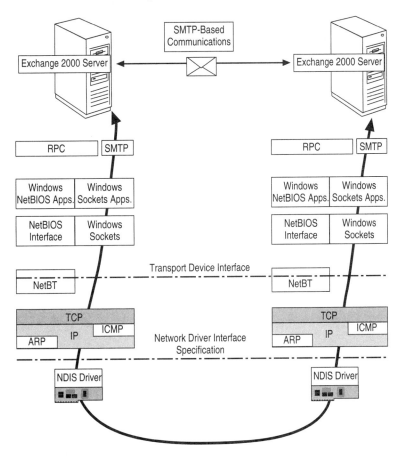

Figure 2.10   SMTP-based communication

Internet Information Services 5.0

Exchange 2000 Server takes advantage of the SMTP and NNTP services that ship with Internet Information Services (IIS) 5.0. IIS 5.0 is installed by default as a networking service of Windows 2000 Server. Exchange 2000 extends the SMTP and NNTP services to implement Exchange-specific functionality. You can read more about the extension of the IIS in the later section, "Exchange 2000 Server Extensions."

Native Message Transport Protocol

SMTP is Exchange 2000 Server's native messaging transport protocol. If two or more Exchange 2000 servers exist in your environment, they will detect each other via Active Directory and route messages to one another directly using SMTP (see Figure 2.11).

Exchange 2000 uses the SMTP service to perform the following functions:

1. Accept messages from SMTP-based messaging systems (and Internet-based clients) for transfer and delivery to one or more recipients in the Exchange 2000 organization.

2. Determine whether any recipients reside on the local Exchange 2000 server and, if so, deliver the messages to each recipient's mailbox.

3. Relay messages for recipients on other servers on the network to the appropriate SMTP service according to the routing plan.

4. Relay messages for recipients outside the Exchange 2000 organization to the appropriate service or gateway queue so that the messages are eventually delivered to the appropriate recipients.

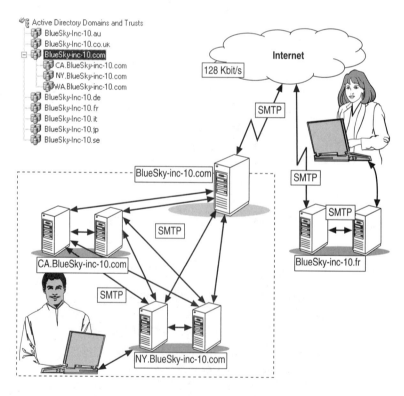

Figure 2.11   Native message transfer between Exchange 2000 servers

Exercise 4: Checking the SMTP Service

In this exercise you will verify the version of the SMTP service running on an Exchange 2000 computer and the specific SMTP verbs it supports. This emphasizes that Exchange 2000 does not provide its own SMTP transfer service for its native communication but relies on the component that actually comes with Windows 2000.

To view a multimedia demonstration that displays how to perform this procedure, run the EX4CH2.AVI files from the \Exercise_Information\ Chapter2 folder on the Supplemental Course Materials CD.

Prerequisites

- Ensure that Exchange 2000 Server is operational and running on BLUESKY-SRV1.
- Log on as Administrator to BLUESKY-WKSTA.

▶ **To establish a connection with the SMTP service**

1. Click Start and then click Run.

2. In the Run dialog box, under Open, type **TELNET.EXE,** and then click OK to start the Windows 2000 Telnet client.

3. At the Microsoft Telnet command prompt, type **Set LOCAL_ECHO,** and then press ENTER to activate the echo of characters entered so that you are able to see what you type.

4. At the Microsoft Telnet command prompt, type **Open Bluesky-SRV1 25,** and then press ENTER to connect to your server's TCP port 25.

    At this point, you should be able to note the reply "220 bluesky-srv1.BlueSky-inc-10.com Microsoft ESMTP Mail Service Version: 5.0.2195.1600," which indicates that this is the Windows 2000 SMTP service (Version: 5.0.2195.1600 refers to Microsoft Windows NT 5.0 with Service Pack 1 [see Figure 2.12]).

5. Type **ehlo** and then press ENTER to communicate with the SMTP service. Verify that the server responds with a hello message as well.

6. Type **help** and then press ENTER to see a list of commands the SMTP service supports.

7. Type **quit** and then press ENTER to terminate the connection, and then press any key to return to Telnet.

8. Type **Q** and then press ENTER to close the Telnet client.

Figure 2.12   Telnet to the Windows 2000 SMTP service

Exercise Summary

Exchange 2000 servers don't need to communicate using synchronous RPCs anymore, which require a relatively high network bandwidth and reliable connections. Instead, they use SMTP as the native transfer protocol, which supports server-to-server communication over low-bandwidth and high-latency networks as well as high-bandwidth connections. Hence, especially when compared with previous Exchange Server versions, Exchange 2000 Server offers very flexible routing capabilities. The SMTP transport allows you to focus on administrative issues when designing your environment, rather than on the physical network structure.

Exchange 2000 Server Extensions

It is important to note that the SMTP transport supports service extensions via protocol and event sinks. A sink is a way for one process to notify another process when specific criteria are met. Exchange 2000 Server utilizes these sinks to extend the SMTP features. Similarly, Exchange 2000 Server also extends the NNTP service for Exchange-aware newsgroup and newsfeed functionality. For now, we focus on the SMTP extension because in Exchange 2000 Server the

SMTP service represents an essential messaging service. The SMTP service is discussed in detail in Chapter 15, "SMTP Transport Configuration," and NNTP is covered in Chapter 11, "Internet-Based Client Access."

SMTP Command Extensions

Among other things, Exchange 2000 Services uses protocol sinks to implement various SMTP command extensions. These extensions, handled by Exchange 2000 Server exclusively, enhance the standard set of SMTP protocol commands. If you review the procedure of Exercise 5, you will find verbs, such as X-EXPS, X-LINK2STATE, and XEXCH50, that are not part of the basic SMTP command set. The new Exchange 2000 commands are especially important for optimal communication between computers running Exchange 2000. For example, the X-LINK2STATE command verb is used to support link state information, which is important for message routing decisions. You can read more about Exchange 2000 message routing in Chapter 16, "Message Routing Administration."

Exchange 2000 Store Driver

By default, the SMTP service uses a simple mail drop directory on the file system to "deliver" messages categorized for local delivery (such as the \Mailroot directory, which is moved to the \Exchsrvr directory after the Exchange 2000 installation). To fully integrate the SMTP service, Exchange 2000 Server registers event sinks to implement an extremely advanced Exchange 2000–specific mail store driver, which allows the SMTP service to interact with the information store. The new mail store relies on events of the SMTP service to pick up, relay, and drop off messages from Exchange 2000 message queues.

Enhanced Routing Capabilities

Without a doubt, complex Exchange 2000 organizations require enhanced routing capabilities to maximize the throughput and reliability of SMTP message delivery. Exchange 2000 Server registers a number of event sinks to enhance the default SMTP routing behavior. The advanced routing engine of Exchange 2000 Server provides efficient message routing based on the current conditions within the network (such as link state information).

Advanced Queuing Engine

Finally, Exchange 2000 Server also extends SMTP message queuing by implementing its advanced queuing engine. This engine asynchronously performs actions based on the individual properties of the messages. For instance, when a local user sends a message, the engine parses the message header and performs specific actions accordingly, such as handing the message over to the categorizer, to custom event sinks, and to the router to process and send the message. You can read more about the advanced queuing engine, store driver, and router in Chapter 3, "Microsoft Exchange 2000 Server Architecture."

Chapter Summary

The configuration of Exchange 2000 resources relies primarily on the Active Directory and MMC snap-ins. Snap-ins for Exchange 2000 Server are added to the standard console when you install the Exchange 2000 Management utilities. Exchange 2000 also changes the Active Directory schema definition to include new classes and attributes, extend existing classes, and modify existing attribute definitions to support the configuration of the messaging system.

Exchange 2000 Server modifies a variety of directory attributes to include them in Global Catalog replication, such as the user class's givenName attribute. This is necessary to provide similar address book information to Outlook users, as in Exchange Server 5.5. For address list lookups, Outlook users connect to the computer running Exchange 2000 Server, where a specific process known as DSProxy intercepts the request and forwards it without modification to the Global Catalog server. DSProxy returns the results from the Global Catalog to the Outlook client as well. Smart MAPI-based clients, such as Outlook 2000, can store referral information received from DSProxy in their messaging profile to subsequently contact the Global Catalog directly without the help of DSProxy.

MAPI-based clients communicate with Exchange 2000 Server using synchronous RPCs that can be carried over a variety of network protocols. In a Windows 2000/Active Directory/Exchange 2000 environment, communication via TCP/IP and Windows Sockets is preferred. Server-to-server communication, on the other hand, relies primarily on SMTP. Unlike previous versions of Exchange Server, Exchange 2000 Server does not utilize RPCs for server-to-server communication. Asynchronous SMTP offers more flexibility and independence from the underlying network than RPCs. Exchange 2000 Server extends the SMTP and NNTP services that ship with IIS 5.0 through event sinks to implement the required functionality for a top-class enterprise messaging and collaboration solution.

Review

The following review questions can help you determine if you have sufficiently familiarized yourself with the material covered in this chapter. You can find the answers to these questions at the end of this book in Appendix A, "Questions and Answers."

1. After the installation of Exchange 2000 Server, you want to create new mailboxes for your user accounts. Which MMC snap-in would you use?

2. Recently, you have installed Exchange 2000 Server in your organization. Your organization is comprised of multiple domain trees arranged in a single forest. You intend to configure your mailbox resources from one of your computers. However, when you open the Active Directory Users and Computers snap-in, most of the Exchange-related property pages are not available. What do you have to install on the computer to configure mailboxes successfully?

3. Your organization has deployed Active Directory and organized its resources in OUs according to the structure of the enterprise. Names of OUs reflect the names of departments. Frequently, users move between departments. Consequently, it is necessary to move user accounts to the appropriate OUs as well. Do you need to delete the old user accounts and create new ones to reflect the organizational changes in Active Directory?

4. Active Directory holds all of the address information, such as the Global Address List, of Exchange 2000 Server. How does Exchange 2000 Server support MAPI-based client programs that are expecting to connect to an Exchange-based directory service?

5. In the past, your organization deployed Outlook 2000 successfully. Now you are installing Exchange 2000 Server. You wish to redirect your Outlook 2000 clients to a Global Catalog server. Outlook 2000 should contact the Global Catalog directly and without proxying. What do you have to configure on the computer running Exchange 2000 to achieve the desired result?

6. You plan to install Exchange 2000 Server in two locations connected to each other via a slow dial-up telephone connection. Do you need to upgrade the existing link to a permanent connection?

C H A P T E R   3

Microsoft Exchange 2000 Server Architecture

About This Chapter

Microsoft Exchange 2000 Server is a complex, component-oriented client/server messaging and collaboration system. Active modules running on the server machine perform dedicated tasks, such as storing e-mail messages, routing messages to the correct destinations, and so forth. To fulfill their particular tasks, these components have to communicate with each other and with services provided by Windows 2000, such as the Active Directory directory service and the extended Simple Mail Transfer Protocol (SMTP) service.

Depending on your specific situation, you need to install and configure more or fewer Exchange 2000 Server components. For instance, it might be necessary to connect Exchange 2000 Server to a foreign mail system, in which case you have to configure an appropriate gateway. You can go without various components and save precious server resources if connectivity to a foreign mail platform or other specific functionality is not needed. However, the basic functionality of a messaging and workgroup platform will exist no matter how you configure your system. By default, users can send e-mail messages and share information through public folders.

This chapter examines the architecture of Exchange 2000 Server, the interaction of its components, and the server-to-server communication in more detail. In the first lesson you will find a concise description of the essential Exchange 2000 Server elements. The following lesson then addresses the communication paths among the various server components and covers the message flow as handled by Exchange 2000 Server.

Before You Begin

To complete this chapter:

- Prepare your test environment according to the descriptions given in the "Getting Started" section of "About This Book."

- Have a general understanding of Windows 2000 Server networking technologies and the TCP/IP protocol suite.

Lesson 1: Exchange 2000 Server Components

To make the best use of Exchange 2000 Server's capabilities, a general understanding of the essential services and their interaction is absolutely necessary. The essential components in conjunction with various Windows 2000 services provide the basic messaging facilities. In plain English, if an essential component is not operating properly, you will experience a major system problem. You should also understand optional components. They provide alternative connectivity and add valuable functionality to the standard server. Without an awareness of the various components, you will not be able to properly address configuration and maintenance issues.

This lesson provides a brief summary of the components that ship with Exchange 2000 Enterprise Server edition. It also covers the additional elements that are part of Exchange 2000 Conference Server. You will learn about the particular responsibilities of each component and their dependencies.

At the end of this lesson, you will be able to:

- Describe the responsibilities of the System Attendant.
- Explain the purpose of the Information Store.
- List the various optional components and describe their features.

Estimated time to complete this lesson: 75 minutes

Essential Components for Exchange 2000 Server

Exchange 2000 Server comes with numerous services. If you start the Services tool from the Administrative Tools program group on a fully installed Exchange 2000 Conferencing server, you can find 17 services that have names starting with Microsoft Exchange: Microsoft Exchange Chat, Microsoft Exchange Conferencing, Microsoft Exchange Connectivity Controller, Microsoft Exchange Connector for Lotus cc:Mail, Microsoft Exchange Connector for Lotus Notes, Microsoft Exchange Connector for Novell GroupWise, Microsoft Exchange Directory Synchronization, Microsoft Exchange Event, Microsoft Exchange IMAP4, Microsoft Exchange Information Store, Microsoft Exchange MTA Stacks, Microsoft Exchange POP3, Microsoft Exchange Router for Novell GroupWise, Microsoft Exchange Routing Engine, Microsoft Exchange Site Replication Service, Microsoft Exchange System Attendant, and Microsoft Exchange T.120 Minimum Coded Units (MCU) Conferencing. Additional services with names that don't start with Microsoft Exchange, such as the MS Mail Connector Interchange, also belong to the Exchange 2000 Server installation, and there are several standard Windows 2000 services, such as SMTP and Network News Transport Protocol (NNTP) service, which are relevant in respect to Exchange 2000 Server as well. The number of Windows 2000 and Exchange 2000 Server components involved in messaging can seem overwhelming.

SMTP Service

Unlike previous versions of Exchange Server, Exchange 2000 Server always requires message processing through the SMTP transport. This is demonstrated in Exercise 1. Specifically, the advanced queuing engine within the SMTP transport assumes the role of a central information controller. All messages submitted to Exchange 2000 Server must pass through this engine. You can read about the flow of messages through an Exchange 2000 server in Lesson 2, "Communication Between Essential Server Components." The actual configuration of the SMTP transport is covered in Chapter 15, "SMTP Transport Configuration."

Information Store

You can consider the Information Store service and its databases the most important Exchange 2000 Server component because it maintains the structured repository of all server-based user data, such as e-mail messages. The executable file of the Information Store is STORE.EXE, which resides in a default installation in the \Program Files\Exchsrvr\Bin directory.

Mailbox and Public Stores

The Information Store service divides user data into two categories: private and public. Private messages are maintained in private mailboxes, and public data can be shared among users through public folders. Hence, the information store is split into two general types, the mailbox store and the public store. Both maintain their database files separately from each other. All database files together form a complete server repository (see Figure 3.1). You can read about mailbox and public server configurations in Chapter 14, "Managing Server Configuration."

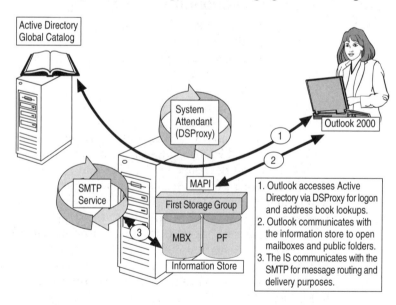

Figure 3.1   Essential services for a single-server Exchange 2000 Server environment

The two components of the information store are as follows:

- **Public store.**   Maintains information stored in public folders
- **Mailbox store.**   Maintains all messages sent to an individual or a selected group of addresses in private folders

---

Note   When Information Store and Active Directory are in an operational state, users can gain access to their messages and other data stored in mailboxes and public folders using a Messaging Application Programming Interface (MAPI)-based client, such as Outlook 2000.

Storage Groups

The information store is organized in storage groups, which in turn can hold mailbox stores, public stores, or both. A storage group is a set of individual databases that share the same set of transaction log files. You can manage up to four individual storage groups on a single computer running Exchange 2000 Enterprise Server, and each storage group is capable of holding up to five individual stores. This allows you to create a maximum of 20 physical message stores and spread them across your server's hard disk system. You can read more about information store databases and advanced configurations using multiple storage groups in Chapter 20, "Microsoft Exchange 2000 Server Maintenance and Troubleshooting."

System Attendant

The Information Store depends on the System Attendant (SA), which is likewise implemented as a Windows 2000 service. The executable file is MAD.EXE located in the \Program Files\Exchsrvr\Bin directory. This component performs regular maintenance tasks, such as the monitoring of server services and messaging connectors. The SA starts the defragmentation routines of the Information Store and handles the DSProxy process to forward MAPI-based address lookups to a Global Catalog server, as explained in Chapter 2, "Integration with Microsoft Windows 2000."

System Attendant Responsibilities

You can get hints about the responsibilities of the SA service by looking at the various categories the SA may use to write events into the Windows 2000 application event log. Start the Event Viewer from the Administrative Tools program group on an Exchange 2000 server, select the Application Log, and then click View in the toolbar to select the Find command. In the Find In Local Application Log dialog box, under Event Source, select MSExchangeSA, and then open the Category list box. Many of the categories are self-explanatory, such as (system) Monitoring, E-Mail Address Generation, Move Mailbox, Routing Table Generation, and so forth. RFR Interface and NSPI Proxy relate to the DSProxy process that was introduced in Chapter 2, "Integration with Microsoft Windows 2000."

Note   The Microsoft Exchange SA must be running before several other Exchange 2000 Server services can start. If you start an Exchange 2000 Server service, such as the Information Store, when the SA is stopped, the SA will be started automatically.

Exchange 2000 Server Shutdown

The SA can assist you in the task of shutting down Exchange 2000 Server, which might be necessary if you want to perform an offline backup or accomplish other maintenance tasks. You will use this feature in Exercise 1 to shut down all Exchange 2000 Server services without affecting the standard Windows 2000 components, such as the Internet Information Services (IIS) Admin Service or the SMTP service.

Note   Shutting down the Exchange 2000 Server services via SA does not stop the SMTP service, the NNTP service, or the IIS process (INETINFO.EXE).

Exchange 2000 Server Startup

However, you can't start the server services via the SA the same way you stopped them. You need to start every component manually through the Services utility or reboot your server. An easier way to restart all those services stopped via the SA is to write a small batch file. For example, you can use the following batch to restart the essential Exchange 2000 Server services using a single command (EMSSTART.BAT):

```
REM ******************************************

REM This Batch starts only the core services

REM of the Microsoft Exchange Server

REM EMSSTART.BAT

REM ******************************************

net start MSExchangeSA

net start MSExchangeIS

net start MSExchangeMTA

net start IMAP4Svc

net start POP3Svc

REM *********** server activated ***********
```

If you want to start additional components, such as the SMTP service or the Routing Engine, you need to enhance this batch file accordingly. Required keywords can be found in the Registry under the following key:

```
HKEY_LOCAL_MACHINE

\System

 \CurrentControlSet

  \Services
```

Each installed service is registered via a corresponding sub-key. The name of each sub-key refers to the keyword that you need to specify (such as MSExchangeIS, IMAP4Svc, SMTPSvc, etc.).

Note   Instead of keywords, you can also specify full-service names in the net start command. To give an example, net start MSExchangeSA will start the System Attendant, as does net start "Microsoft Exchange System Attendant."

Exercise 1: Reducing Exchange 2000 Server to the Minimum

In this exercise you will examine the services of Exchange 2000 Server and find out which of them are essential for message handling. You will stop the relevant Windows 2000 and Exchange 2000 Server services and check the behavior of Outlook 2000 in response to that.

To view a multimedia demonstration that displays how to perform this procedure, run the EX1CH3*.AVI files from the \Exercise_Information\Chapter3 folder on the Supplemental Course Materials CD.

Prerequisites

- Ensure Exchange 2000 Server is operational and running on BLUESKY-SRV1.

- Log on as Administrator to BLUESKY-SRV1 and BLUESKY-WKSTA, and make sure you can use Outlook 2000 on BLUESKY-WKSTA to log on to your mailbox. Leave Outlook 2000 running as you start this exercise.

▶ **To examine the responsibilities of essential Exchange 2000 Server services**

1. On BLUESKY-SRV1, start the Services management tool from the Administrative Tools program group.

2. In the details pane, select Microsoft Exchange System Attendant, and right-click on it. From the shortcut menu, select Stop.

3. A Stop Other Services dialog box appears listing the POP3, IMAP4, MTA, and Information Store services, which will be stopped as well. Click Yes to essentially stop the entire Exchange 2000 Server.

4. Select the IIS Admin Service, right-click on it, and, from the shortcut menu, select Stop.

5. A Stop Other Services dialog box appears listing the Exchange Routing Engine, as well as the SMTP, NNTP, and the Web Publishing service. Click Yes to stop these services.

6. Switch to BLUESKY-WKSTA and try to work with Outlook 2000. You will be informed that the connection to the Exchange Server computer was lost. Close Outlook 2000.

7. On BLUESKY-SRV1, in the Services utility, right-click on Microsoft Exchange Information Store and, from the shortcut menu, select Start. Note that Microsoft Exchange System Attendant and IIS Admin Service are started automatically. This is because the Information Store depends on these services.

8. Switch to BLUESKY-WKSTA and try to start Outlook 2000. You will be able to log on to your mailbox. Create two new messages. Send the first to the Administrator account and the second to the All Test Users distribution list. Note that you don't receive any messages. Both messages remained in your Outbox.

9. On BLUESKY-SRV1, in the Services utility, start the Simple Mail Transfer Protocol (SMTP) service.

   At this point, you should be able to see that both test messages are delivered to your Inbox, as in Figure 3.2. All outgoing messages, including those addressed to recipients on the same server, are routed through the SMTP service.

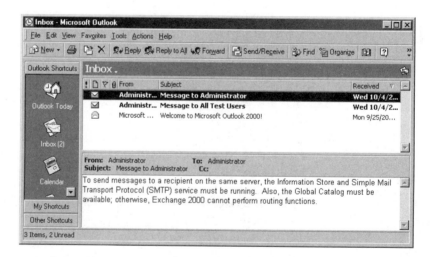

Figure 3.2   Essential Exchange 2000 services and Outlook 2000

Exercise Summary

Although Exchange 2000 Server impresses with an overwhelming number of services, only very few (such as Information Store and SMTP service) are required to provide the basic messaging functionality to Outlook users. Information Store and SMTP service depend on further services (such as the SA and the IIS Admin Service). Of course, Active Directory must be operational also. Interdependencies with Windows 2000 services were introduced in Chapter 2, "Integration with Microsoft Windows 2000."

Internet Information Services for Exchange 2000 Server

Exchange 2000 Server is seamlessly integrated with IIS 5.0 to support SMTP, NNTP, IMAP4, POP3, and HTTP/Web Distributed Authoring and Versioning (WebDAV). SMTP allows sending and receiving of Internet mail messages. NNTP provides newsreaders and newsfeeds with access to public folder resources presented as newsgroups. IMAP4 is a modern mail access protocol that allows you to work with your mailbox or public folders. POP3 provides simple services to download messages from your Inbox. Finally, HTTP/WebDAV is a solution that gives you the ability to work with mailboxes and public folders using almost any Web browser. WebDAV is an extension to HTTP 1.1. See Chapter 11, "Internet-Based Client Access," for a discussion of the Internet client access protocols.

IIS Process and Internet-Based Client Access

Integrating Internet-based client access protocols with the IIS process offers the advantages of providing best performance and allowing you to control all Internet access protocols via IIS 5.0. For instance, you have the option to design Exchange 2000 Server subsystems based on virtual servers. In Chapter 4, "Planning the Microsoft Exchange 2000 Server Installation," you can read about front end/back end server arrangements that take full advantage of the new features to support hosted environments with potentially enormous amounts of users. Figure 3.3 shows the various Internet services running in the context of the IIS process.

IIS Service Dependencies

You can check all components that depend on the IIS process using the Services utility. View the properties for the IIS Admin Service and click on the Dependencies tab. Under These Services Depend On "IIS Admin Service," you will see a listing of other services that cannot be run without first starting IIS, including the IMAP4 service, NNTP service, POP3 service, the Exchange Routing Engine, SMTP service, and the Web Publishing service.

IIS Metabase

When you check the Windows 2000 Registry for advanced IIS configuration settings, you will be disappointed. The keys in the Registry are used primarily to initialize the IIS services, but the important configuration settings are not stored here. The IIS maintains its configuration mainly in a separate repository known as the IIS metabase, which is smaller, faster, more flexible, and more expandable than the Registry. You configure many of the metabase parameters implicitly when using the Internet Service Manager or the Exchange System Manager. The section "Introduction to the IIS Metabase," in the IIS 5.0 online documentation, provides more information about the metabase.

Metabase Update Service

Exchange 2000 Server stores its configuration information primarily in Active Directory, relies on the SMTP service, and may use additional Internet services to extend its functionality. Hence, it is also desirable to manage the IIS the same way. However, IIS 5.0 does not integrate with Active Directory as tightly as Exchange 2000 Server. In fact, IIS 5.0 is designed to operate independently of Active Directory. So how can you configure an IIS on an Exchange server installed in the middle of the desert without having a permanent network connection?

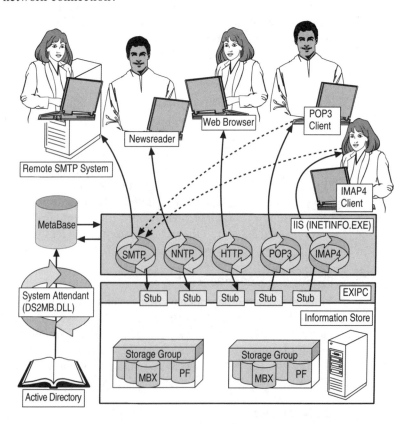

Figure 3.3   IIS integration with Exchange 2000 Server

Surprisingly, Exchange 2000 Server stores IIS-related configuration in Active Directory! Any changes that need to find their way into a remote IIS metabase are replicated to the IIS as part of the normal Active Directory replication. At the destination the changes need to be incorporated into the metabase. This is performed by the SA that is running on the destination IIS as part of the Exchange 2000 Server services. The SA hosts a process known as the Metabase Update service implemented in DS2MB.DLL (see Figure 3.3). DS2MB.DLL resides in the \Program Files\Exchsrvr\Bin directory by default.

Note IIS configuration changes are only replicated in one direction—from Active Directory to the IIS metabase.

Exchange Interprocess Communications Layer

All Internet transport and access protocol engines need to communicate with the Information Store service to access and store messaging-related information in mailbox and public stores. Separate processes, however, need to use the mechanisms provided by the operating system for their interprocess communication. This usually involves additional processing and resource consumption.

For best performance, Exchange 2000 Server implements a dedicated queuing layer known as Exchange Interprocess Communications Layer (ExIPC). ExIPC is part of the Information Store service and is also implemented in a DLL named EPOXY.DLL, located in the \Program Files\Exchrvr\Bin directory. The Exchange Routing Engine, IMAP4, POP3, and Exchange 2000 Server–specific SMTP and NNTP service extensions use EPOXY.DLL to rapidly exchange data directly with the Information Store service through the computer's memory rather than through remote procedure calls (RPCs) or another communication method (see Figure 3.3).

IIS Restart

You can benefit from various IIS management features, such as the reliable restart feature of IIS 5.0, which allows you to restart the Internet Information Services of Exchange 2000 Server together with the standard IIS services conveniently without rebooting the computer or restarting the services manually.

▶ **To accomplish the services, restart locally or remotely**

1. Start the Internet Services Manager from the Administrative Tools program group. In the IIS management tool, right-click the container object that represents your server, and, from the shortcut menu, select Restart IIS.

2. In the Stop/Start/Reboot dialog box that appears, make sure that Restart Internet Services On Bluesky-srv1 is selected, and then click OK.

3. A Shutting Down dialog box appears informing you that the Internet services will be stopped. When this dialog box disappears, the Internet-related services are automatically started again. The Stop/Start/Reboot dialog box gives you

the option to selectively start, stop, and restart the Internet services on the selected computer and to reboot the entire server machine. Stopping the Internet services stops the IIS Admin Service, Microsoft Exchange IMAP4, Microsoft Exchange POP3, Microsoft Exchange Routing Engine, Network News Transport Protocol (NNTP), World Wide Web Publishing Service, and Simple Mail Transfer Protocol (SMTP). Stopping the Internet services a second time stops the Microsoft Exchange Information Store service and the Microsoft Exchange MTA Stacks in addition. Starting or restarting the Internet services starts all these services in one cycle.

Alternatively, you can use the command-line utility IISRESET.EXE to restart the IIS. The command iisreset /restart /status, for instance, restarts the services and provides status information at the command prompt. Use the command line iisreset /? for additional help regarding all available options.

Examining Metabase Settings for Internet-Based Exchange 2000 Services

You can examine the IIS metabase in regard to Exchange 2000 Server components and extensions, by using the MetaEdit 2.0 utility available on the Windows 2000 Resource Kit companion CD. The metabase resides on the local hard disk of each IIS server in a file named METABASE.BIN, which is located in the \Winnt\System32\Inetsrv directory, by default. The metabase is loaded into memory when the IIS process starts.

▶ **To check Exchange-related metabase entries**

1. Click Start, point to Programs, and then select MetaEdit 2.0 to launch the Metabase Editor.

2. In the left pane, open the LM node and note the existence of the IMAP4SVC and POP3SVC keys, in addition to the keys of standard services, such as NNTPSVC and SMTPSVC. Exchange 2000 Server registers the IMAP4SVC and POP3SVC keys and various parameters for these services, such as the application type, maximum number of connections, and so forth.

3. Open the key SMTPSVC, then the key named 1, then EventManager, and then EventTypes. When you examine the registered event types, you will find numerous references to Exchange 2000 Server components, such as the Exchange Router, Exchange Store Driver, and Exchange Categorizer. These components are explained later in this chapter.

4. Notice the top-level node Resvc, which provides access to one key called 1 (which refers to the default virtual server), containing a value named ServerBindings. This value indicates the port number used by the Microsoft Exchange Routing Engine (RESVC.DLL) to receive routing information from other servers. Message routing is covered in detail in Chapter 16, "Message Routing Administration."

5. Open the Schema node, and then open Classes. Verify that several classes exist whose names begin with IisIMAP and IisPOP3, which indicate class definitions for the IMAP4 and POP3 services of Exchange 2000 Server.

6. Make sure you don't change the configuration and close the Metabase Editor.

Note Using the MetaEdit 2.0 utility allows you to configure properties in the metabase. Configuring the metabase incorrectly can cause problems and may damage the IIS. Edit the metabase properties using MetaEdit directly only if you cannot adjust the settings in the Internet Service Manager, System Manager, or other user interface.

Additional Components for Exchange 2000 Server

Additional components can be used to connect to previous Exchange Server versions or foreign mail systems, or to implement extra features such as advanced security or online conferencing. These components don't usually need to be running on every Exchange 2000 server in your organization (see Figure 3.4). The

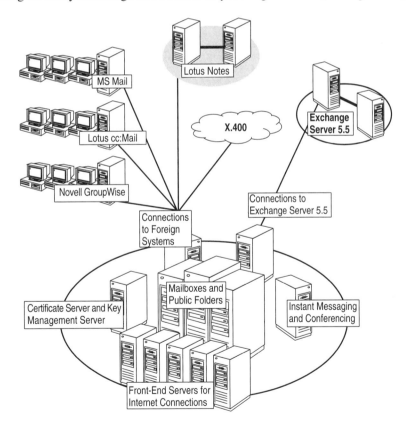

Figure 3.4 Separate servers for individual services

Key Management server, in fact, must not be running on more than one server in a particular administrative group. You can read more about Key Management server in Chapter 19, "Implementing Advanced Security."

Installing Optional Components

In a typical Exchange 2000 Server installation, some additional components are installed for backward compatibility: Exchange Event Service, Site Replication Service (SRS), and for connectivity to foreign mail systems, the Message Transfer Agent (MTA). Numerous other components, such as gateway connectors or conferencing services, may be installed in addition, but you would need to select them manually during setup. The various installation options are covered in Chapter 5, "Installing Microsoft Exchange 2000 Server."

Message Transfer Agent

Seen from the perspective of previous Exchange Server versions, the MTA has traded its role with the SMTP transport. It has given up the responsibilities of the central routing engine and assumed the role of an additional component connecting Exchange 2000 Server to foreign systems. This doesn't mean that the MTA has given up all routing functions. The MTA is still responsible for the routing of messages through X.400 and gateway connectors to foreign environments. This service maintains its own specific message queues outside the Information Store service in the \Program Files\Exchsrvr\Mtadata directory.

The MTA is a real X.400 system that conforms to the 1984 and 1988 CCITT (International Telecommunication Union) X.400 standards. In addition to transmitting messages, the MTA is responsible for message conversion between the Exchange format and the native X.400 format. The MTA of Exchange 2000 Server supports RFC 2156 MIME Internet X.400 Enhanced Relay interoperability.

Note   You can use the MTA to configure X.400-based connections to other computers running Exchange 2000 Server or previous Exchange Server versions, but the SMTP transport is the better choice because it offers more flexible routing capabilities.

Event Service

The Event Service supports server-based scripting agents developed for Exchange Server 5.5. The Event Service can process message items and other data in public folders and mailboxes on an event-driven basis (valid events include new message creation, message deletion, etc.). In Exchange 2000 Server, event sinks can replace the former event scripts. Event sinks are covered in Chapter 24, "Workgroup and Workflow Technologies."

Site Replication Service and Active Directory Connector

SRS and Active Directory Connector (ADC) provide directory interoperability between Exchange 2000 Server and Exchange Server 5.5. If you need to integrate Exchange 2000 Server with an environment running previous versions of Exchange Server, you need to configure and use these services to handle directory replication with the legacy Exchange directory service. The ADC uses the Lightweight Directory Access Protocol (LDAP) to communicate with Active Directory and SRS. SRS, on the other hand, communicates with the directory service of Exchange Server 5.5 through RPCs or e-mail messages. You can find more information about these components in Chapter 6, "Coexistence with Previous Microsoft Exchange Server Versions."

MS Mail Connector

The MS Mail Connector provides connectivity to MS Mail postoffices. The MS Mail Connector itself basically consists of the MS Mail Connector Interchange component, one or more MS Mail MTA services, and an MS Mail Connector Postoffice. The Connector Postoffice provides the native MS Mail interface for the MS Mail messaging network. To transfer messages back and forth to MS Mail systems, the MS Mail Connector must communicate with the MTA on the Exchange 2000 server side. Its architecture and configuration will be explained in detail in Chapter 26, "Connecting to Microsoft Mail and Schedule+."

Directory Synchronization with MS Mail

Directory Synchronization service (DXA) is the active component that exchanges address information between Exchange 2000 Server and MS Mail by using the MS Mail DirSync protocol. During a Dirsync cycle, address list changes will be sent from the MS Mail postoffices and Active Directory to a Dirsync server. This server collects and processes all the changes it receives during the cycle and returns the updated master address list to the requesting postoffices and Active Directory. Once an entire Dirsync cycle is complete, all postoffices and Active Directory are synchronized with each other, and each will contain a complete global address list. The MS Mail addresses are maintained as mail-enabled contact objects in Active Directory as usual. Chapter 26, "Connecting to Microsoft Mail and Schedule+," provides more information about the configuration of the DXA.

Microsoft Schedule+ Free/Busy Connector

When you connect your organization to an MS Mail network, you might also want to exchange Schedule+ Free/Busy information between both systems. To do this, configure the Schedule+ Free/Busy Connector, which exchanges calendar free and busy information between users working on Exchange 2000 Server and users working on MS Mail postoffices. The Schedule+ Free/Busy Connector configuration is covered in Chapter 26, "Connecting to Microsoft Mail and Schedule+."

Connector for Lotus cc:Mail

If you plan to integrate Exchange 2000 Server in a Lotus cc:Mail messaging network, use the Connector for Lotus cc:Mail. This connector allows you to send messages between both systems, but it can connect to only one cc:Mail post office directly. Messages destined for other Lotus cc:Mail post offices must be routed within the Lotus cc:Mail messaging network.

The connector for Lotus cc:Mail supports directory synchronization between Active Directory and the Lotus cc:Mail post office so that you can import and export e-mail addresses automatically. The connector performs directory synchronization based on the Lotus Import/Export programs. In fact, the process of exchanging addresses is less complex than the MS Mail Dirsync. The configuration and usage of the connector for Lotus cc:Mail is explained in Chapter 27, "Connecting to Lotus cc:Mail."

Connector for Lotus Notes

The Connector for Lotus Notes provides connectivity to a Lotus Notes network by means of message transfer and directory synchronization. This Connector also supports various calendar functions such as meeting invitations. It relies on Lotus Notes client software, which must be installed on the server that will run the Connector service. The installation, configuration, and usage of the Connector for Lotus Notes are covered in Chapter 28, "Connecting to Lotus Notes."

Connector for Novell GroupWise

The Connector for Novell GroupWise is a complete messaging solution for connecting Exchange 2000 Server and Novell GroupWise environments. The Connector for Novell GroupWise supports message transfer, directory synchronization, and the exchange of calendar information. The Connector relies on the Router for Novell GroupWise service and the Novell GroupWise API gateway to build the messaging path. The Connector for Novell GroupWise is covered in Chapter 29, "Connecting to Novell GroupWise."

Key Management Server

The Key Management server offers advanced security features at the application layer for e-mail messages, such as encryption and digital signatures. The Key Management server operates in conjunction with Microsoft Certificate Server to maintain X.509 version 3 certificates and encryption keys. Once this component has been installed in your organization, you can allow your users to sign and seal messages. A signed message provides verification of whether someone has tampered with this message on its way to the destination mailbox. A sealed message, on the other hand, is completely encrypted and prevents unauthorized persons from reading the information. You can read more about security issues in Chapter 19, "Implementing Advanced Security."

Outlook Web Access

Outlook Web Access (OWA) is installed as part of the default setup of Exchange 2000 Server and supports HTTP-based access to mailbox and public folder resources. This component includes various DLLs, Web pages, and script files involved in displaying Exchange 2000 Server resources in a Web browser. OWA requires Windows 2000 and the Web Publishing service of IIS 5.0. You can read more about OWA in Chapter 22, "Microsoft Outlook Web Access."

Exchange Chat

Exchange Chat Service allows you to configure chat rooms on your server to support real-time collaboration using any standard Internet Relay Chat (IRC) or Extended IRC (IRCX) client. In a chat community, users can communicate online (synchronously) with each other in chat rooms, which provide text-based collaboration between users. Multiple chat communities can be hosted on the same server, or separate instances can be hosted on multiple servers. You need not install Exchange Chat Service on the computer running Exchange 2000 Server, but Exchange 2000 Server must be installed on a server in the same domain. More information about Exchange Chat Service is found in Chapter 25, "Real-Time Collaboration."

Instant Messaging

Instant Messaging integrates with the IIS 5.0 Web Publishing service. This feature provides one-to-one communication, similar to a normal telephone conversation. Instant Messaging also provides presence information, which means that you can see whether other users are working online, in which case you can send them your instant messages. As a user yourself, you can control to whom to provide your presence information (such as Online, Busy, Be Right Back, Away, On The Phone, Out To Lunch, Offline) and to control who can contact you. You can learn more about the Instant Messaging feature of Exchange 2000 Server in Chapter 25, "Real-Time Collaboration."

Video and Data Conferencing

Conferencing Server of Exchange 2000 Server is primarily a centralized reservation system that allows your users to schedule and join meetings from Outlook or a Web browser. Using the conferencing facilities of Exchange 2000 Server, you have the option to schedule online video and audio meetings and share application data. In addition to Exchange 2000 Server, you need a data conferencing program such as Microsoft NetMeeting or another T.120 standard client program and, for video conferencing, an appropriate third-party software solution that allows you to see and hear all other meeting participants simultaneously. The video and data conferencing technologies implemented in Exchange 2000 Server are introduced in Chapter 25, "Real-Time Collaboration."

Lesson 2: Communication Between Essential Server Components

Active Directory maintains all of the address lists and most of the Exchange 2000 Server configuration information in its directory database. The Information Store is responsible for the mailbox and public folder stores. The IIS process and its information services pull configuration information primarily from their metabase. The MTA keeps its data in its own specific message queues outside the Information Store. Other components, such as MS Mail Dirsync and Key Management server, might add additional data repositories, such as the Dirsync and Key Management databases. Following the object-oriented programming model, only that particular component has direct access to a repository that is responsible for its maintenance. All remaining server elements must communicate with this repository service through an appropriate communication mechanism to obtain the desired information. Well-defined communication paths have been implemented, and knowledge of these paths can help you understand the functionality of Exchange 2000 Server.

This lesson addresses the communication between server-based components and the paths between these components and Outlook 2000 and the Exchange System Manager utility. The communication between optional components and essential components is also discussed. At the end of this lesson, you can read about the flow of messages through an Exchange 2000 server system.

At the end of this lesson, you will be able to:

- Describe the communication between Outlook 2000 and the components running on the server.
- Describe the communication between the Exchange System Manager utility and the components running on the server.
- Describe the communication between the most important components involved in message processing.
- Describe the communication between the essential and additional components.
- Understand the Exchange 2000 Server message-handling process.

Estimated time to complete this lesson: 90 minutes

Interprocess Communication Mechanisms

The components of Exchange 2000 Server can communicate with each other using various interprocess communication mechanisms. They rely on lightweight remote procedure calls (LRPCs) and simultaneously support Windows Sockets. LRPCs are the local version of RPCs used between the information store and those components that depend on MAPI and related APIs for communication. Regular RPCs, on the other hand, are used when the server components need to

communicate with MAPI-based programs, such as Outlook 2000 or the
Exchange System Manager, over the network. The Exchange 2000 Server components themselves prefer SMTP and e-mail messages for their network communication, a new feature in Exchange 2000 Server.

Exchange 2000 Server also utilizes new communication mechanisms, such as the
ExIPC layer, which allows shuttling data between the IIS services and the Information Store quickly using shared memory (see Figure 3.5). In some cases, processes also share data via ordinary files on the file system. For instance, the
internal modules of the connector for Lotus cc:Mail place temporary scratch files
into the \CCMCData directory when transferring messages between the two systems, which is explained in Chapter 27, "Connecting to Lotus cc:Mail."

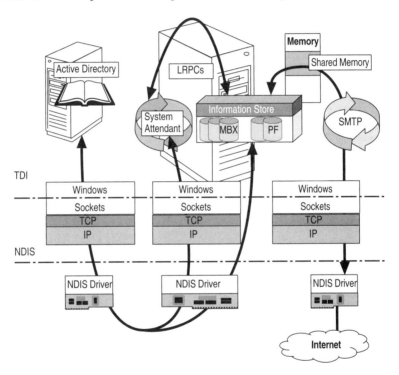

Figure 3.5   Essential components and interprocess communication mechanisms

Windows Sockets

Windows Sockets is Microsoft's implementation of a network communication
mechanism known as Sockets, which was first popularized by Berkeley Software
Distribution UNIX. Sockets is a de facto standard for accessing datagram and
session services over TCP/IP. Windows Sockets, however, is not limited to TCP/
IP. Windows Sockets 2 provides a protocol-independent interface supported over
both TCP/IP and Internetwork Packet Exchange/Sequenced Packet Exchange
(IPX/SPX). It is important to note that Windows Sockets is not a protocol in

itself; it is only an interface utilized to access the underlying network protocol. Because it is not a protocol, it does not add any protocol overhead to the network packet. Exchange 2000 Server components written to the Windows Sockets interface include the IIS modules but also the Information Store, MTA, SA, and others. Basically, every Exchange 2000 Server service supports communication over Windows Sockets.

Windows Sockets is a protocol-independent networking API offering the following advantages:

- Familiar networking API to programmers using Windows or UNIX
- Binary compatibility between Windows-based TCP/IP stacks and utilities from different vendors
- Support of connection-oriented and connectionless protocols (such as TCP and User Datagram Protocol [UDP])
- No protocol overhead added to the data packet (NetBIOS interface and mapping layers are not required)
- Supported on workstations running only TCP/IP without NetBIOS support

If you are interested in further information about Windows Sockets, refer to the Microsoft Software Development Kit and the Microsoft Developer Network.

Remote Procedure Calls

Microsoft RPCs are compatible with the Open Software Foundation Distributed Computing Environment specification for RPCs. RPCs are an application-layer communication mechanism, which means that RPCs use other interprocess communication mechanisms, such as NetBIOS, named pipes, or Windows Sockets, to establish the communication path. With RPCs, essential program logic and related procedure code exist in different executable modules possibly running on different computers, which is important for distributed applications. In other words, RPCs enable applications to call functions remotely. This makes interprocess communication as easy as calling a function in a program, which is why some programmers prefer this form of interprocess communication. However, RPCs have several disadvantages, including the following:

- RPC client and server components are tightly coupled and communication is synchronous (such as the client program execution stops until the server function returns results).
- Because of their synchronous nature, RPCs require a reliable, high-speed network connection.
- RPCs involve further interfaces for network communication, such as Windows Sockets, and add significant overhead to the network packet.

Shared Memory, Files, and E-Mail Messages

Exchange 2000 Server processes can share information through shared memory, files, and e-mail messages. The principle is always the same: One process writes the data into a file-based repository, and the component that is supposed to receive the information retrieves it from there. Shared memory can only be used on the local computer, files are used primarily for interprocess communication on the local machine, and e-mail messages are used for communication over unreliable network links. Many Exchange 2000 Server components, such as the Public Folder Replication Agent, rely on e-mail messages for server-to-server communication. Shared memory, on the other hand, works similar to ordinary files on the file system. You can think of shared memory as a file that is held in memory instead of the disk.

Clients and Administrative Interfaces

Messaging clients and administrative utilities communicate with various server components to perform their tasks. Clients prefer RPCs and management utilities rely primarily on LDAP to communicate with Windows 2000 Server's directory service, although RPCs are also used when necessary.

Messaging Clients

Client-based communication is straightforward and less complex than communication through administrative interfaces. This is not astonishing because clients serve one primary purpose: They provide users with access to personal mailboxes and public folders, which together are maintained by the information store. Hence, the Information Store service is the client's most important communication partner.

Outlook 2000 and other MAPI-based clients also need to communicate with Active Directory to log on to mailboxes and retrieve recipient information from address lists, which is often accomplished using the DSProxy component of the SA service. Therefore, MAPI-based clients communicate unknowingly with SA as well (see Figure 3.6). Internet-based clients, on the other hand, don't access the Information Store directly. They use their respective intermediate services, which are covered in more detail in Chapter 11, "Internet-Based Client Access."

Administrative Tools

You will start administrative utilities, such as the Exchange System Manager utility, whenever you want to inspect or change the configuration of Exchange 2000 Server components. The Exchange System Manager allows you to manage most aspects of the server configuration, so it must communicate with many server components.

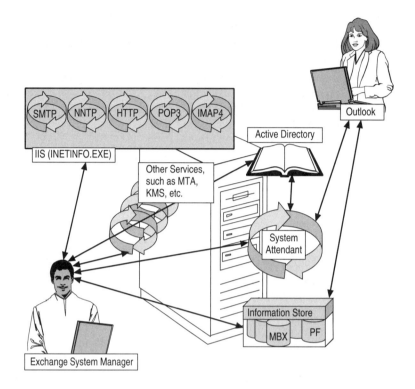

Figure 3.6   Outlook and Exchange System Manager communication

Active Directory Directory Service

When you administer Exchange 2000 Server, the Exchange System Manager communicates with the nearest Active Directory (a domain controller) via LDAP. When you change the configuration of any objects within Active Directory, these modifications are replicated automatically to all existing domain controllers in your forest. This was covered in Chapter 2, "Integration with Microsoft Windows 2000."

Information Store

The Information Store service the Exchange System Manager's communication partner. Using the Exchange System Manager, you can specify which public folders your server will maintain. You can also configure the Exchange 2000 server to become a dedicated public or mailbox server by removing all mailbox or public stores, and you can configure multiple storage groups. The configuration of the information store is covered in more detail in Chapter 17, "Public Folder Management," and Chapter 18, "Public Folder Replication."

System Attendant

The SA service is contacted in the event you attempt to examine dynamic information maintained by the SA service, such as the Domain Controller Used By Services On This Server (which can be found on the General property page of each server object).

Transport Components

To view messages awaiting delivery in the message queues of the SMTP service, the MTA, or installed connectors, communication with the corresponding service is required. Otherwise, you will not be able to open the Queues tree in the System Manager (found under Servers/BLUESKY-SRV1/Protocols/SMTP/Default SMTP Virtual Server/Queues). You can read more about message queues later in this chapter and in Chapter 20, "Microsoft Exchange 2000 Server Maintenance and Troubleshooting."

Additional Components

The Exchange System Manager also communicates with other components when they are installed, configured, and active, for instance, to display status information, such as information about current user sessions. The Key Management server will be contacted if you want to enable users with advanced security features. Note that the Key Management Service (KMS) must be accessible through RPCs if you want to create security tokens or designate additional security administrators. The administration of Key Management server is covered in detail in Chapter 19, "Implementing Advanced Security."

Exercise 2: Communication Partners of the Exchange System Manager

In this exercise you will find out when and why the Exchange System Manager is communicating with Exchange 2000 Server components. The Exchange System Manager is introduced in more detail in Chapter 12, "Management Tools for Microsoft Exchange 2000 Server."

To view a multimedia demonstration that displays how to perform this procedure, run the EX2CH3*.AVI files from the \Exercise_Information\Chapter3 folder on the Supplemental Course Materials CD.

Prerequisites

- Log on as Administrator to BLUESKY-SRV1.

▶ **To verify the Exchange System Manager communication**

1. Click Start, select Run, and in the Run dialog box, type **cmd**, then click OK to open the command prompt window.

2. Type the command **iisreset /stop**, and press ENTER to stop all IIS services.

3. Type the command **net stop msexchangesa /y**, and press ENTER to stop all Exchange 2000 Server services.

4. Click Start, point to Programs, point to Microsoft Exchange, and then select System Manager to start the Exchange System Manager.

   At this point, you are able to start the System Manager successfully and display the configuration of your environment (see Figure 3.7) because the configuration is stored in Active Directory, which is still active and can be accessed.

5. In the console tree, iterate through the nodes under Global Settings and Recipients. You can select all containers without problems because Active Directory provides this information.

6. Open the Servers container, then BLUESKY-SRV1, then Protocols, then SMTP, for instance, and then open the container Default SMTP Virtual Server. A red indicator will inform you that communication with IIS is not possible at this time.

7. Under Default SMTP Virtual Server, select Current Sessions. In the SMTP Configuration dialog box, informing you that the SMTP service is not running, click OK.

8. Under Default SMTP Virtual Server, select Queues. An Exchange System Manager warning pops up informing you that the Queue Viewer is unable to retrieve an interface to the queues.

9. Under Protocols, select the container First Storage Group. In the Exchange System Manager dialog box, informing you that the Microsoft Exchange Information Store service needs to be running, click OK. You will be unable to examine the status of mailbox and public folder resources on this server until you restart the Information Store.

10. Attempt to open the Public Folders container under Folders, and note the Exchange System Manager error message that an operation failed. Without an active Microsoft Web Storage System, you cannot configure public folder resources; click OK.

11. Right-click the node named BLUESKY-SRV1 and choose Properties to display yet another Exchange System Manager warning message informing you that the communication with the SA service is impossible. Click OK and, in the BLUESKY-SRV1 Properties dialog box, note that the field Domain Controller Used By Services On This Server remains empty. Click OK to close the Properties dialog box.

12. Close the Exchange System Manager, switch back to the command prompt, type **iisreset /start** to start all services again, and then optionally repeat Steps 4 to 11.

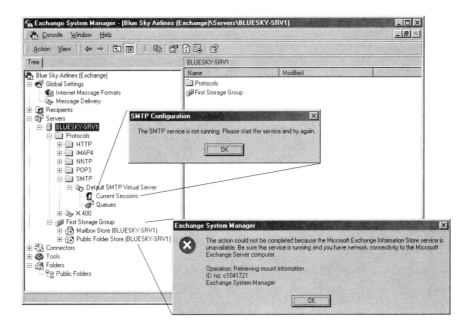

Figure 3.7   Error messages in Exchange System Manager

Exercise Summary

The Exchange System Manager must be able to communicate with all essential components and additional components, if they are installed. This application communicates with Active Directory through LDAP, but also uses RPCs to communicate directly with other server components, such as the information store for mailbox and public folder statistics. This communication takes place through LRPCs when you run this application directly on the server computer, or RPCs when communicating over the network.

Component-to-Component Communication

Which is the busiest component in any Exchange 2000 Server environment? As Figure 3.8 suggests, almost every Exchange 2000 Server component retrieves information from Active Directory, such as configuration information or information about recipients, or at least communicates with Active Directory for validation of access permissions. Some components, such as the MS Mail directory synchronization, may also want to place information in Active Directory. The only component this doesn't apply to is the Event Service implemented to provide backward compatibility with event scripts written for Exchange Server 5.5. The Event Service doesn't need to retrieve information from Active Directory because it only awaits notifications from the Information Store service.

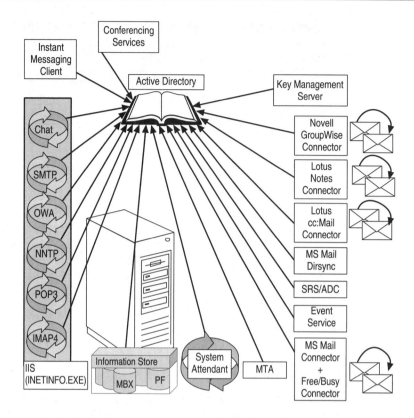

Figure 3.8   Exchange 2000 Server components and Active Directory

Active Directory Directory Service

With so many components, plus MAPI-based clients and the administrative utilities accessing directory information, Exchange 2000 Server has the potential for
monopolizing Active Directory. The Global Catalog represents an especially precious resource. By default, only the first domain controller installed in a forest is
a Global Catalog server, so you should manually configure additional Global
Catalogs in each site and monitor their workload carefully. At least one Global
Catalog should be available in each domain.

Exchange 2000 Server helps reduce the load on Active Directory through its
directory access cache (DSAccess). As shown in Figure 3.9, DSAccess is used to
cache directory information on the Exchange 2000 server. The IIS process, SA,
Information Store, MTA, and other components perform directory lookups
through DSAccess, which returns the information directly without contacting
Active Directory if the information is available in the cache. This greatly
increases the performance of both Exchange 2000 Server and Active Directory.

Note   With the exception of address book lookups from MAPI-based programs
and the SMTP routing process, all directory access goes through DSAccess.

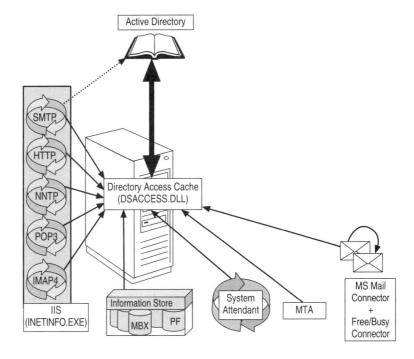

Figure 3.9   Caching Active Directory information

System Attendant

Active Directory is not the only component involved in component-to-component communication. The System Attendant (SA), for instance, contacts the Information Store and the KMS if installed. The SA also has to deal with the IIS process to update the IIS metabase with information from Active Directory, as explained earlier in this lesson.

According to Figure 3.10, the SA contacts several server components for the following reasons:

- **Active Directory.**   The SA communicates with Active Directory to build routing tables and generate proxy e-mail addresses for newly created recipient objects. The DSProxy component, which forwards directory lookups on behalf of MAPI-based clients, is also a component of the SA service.

- **Information Store.**   The SA service communicates with the Information Store whenever you configure a monitor to check the conditions of server services and messaging links. The SA owns a hidden mailbox in the Information Store to send the monitor messages. This mailbox is also used for KMS-related messages during the process of enabling advanced security as explained in Chapter 20, "Microsoft Exchange 2000 Server Maintenance and Troubleshooting."

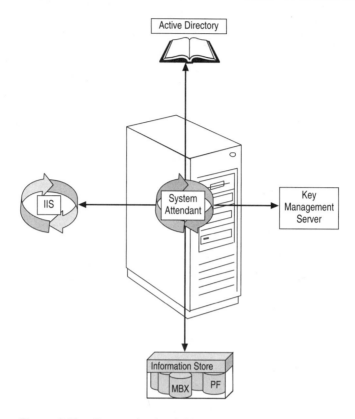

Figure 3.10   Communication initiated by the SA

- **IIS process.**   The SA service communicates with the IIS to update the IIS metabase. The SA retrieves the information from Active Directory and hands it over to the IIS Admin Service. Internet information services retrieve their information from the metabase, as explained previously in this lesson under "Internet Information Services for Microsoft Exchange 2000 Server."

- **KMS.**   The SA service performs important tasks in the background if the KMS has been installed in your organization. The SA receives the requests of users in the form of e-mail messages from the Information Store to enable the advanced security that the administrator has configured for them. First the SA has to "unwrap" the e-mail messages to retrieve the requests. It then communicates with the Exchange KMS to take over the users' security keys and X.509 certificates. KMS is covered in Chapter 19, "Implementing Advanced Security."

Information Store

The Information Store works primarily with the messaging clients, the SMTP service, and the SA as messages are sent and delivered within an organization.

The SA, for instance, is notified about link monitor test messages and replies coming in from other SAs. The Information Store also provides delivery-related data to the SA, which is necessary if you want to maintain tracking log information that can be used to verify whether and when a particular message has arrived at its destination mailbox. Tracking logs are explained in Chapter 20, "Microsoft Exchange 2000 Server Maintenance and Troubleshooting."

As shown in Figure 3.11, the Information Store communicates with the following components:

- **Active Directory.**   The Information Store communicates with Active Directory to retrieve security-related information (such as access permissions) and information about the configuration of its resources.

- **Connectors for Lotus cc:Mail, Lotus Notes, and Novell GroupWise.** The Information Store communicates with gateways to foreign systems to announce the presence of new mail awaiting transfer in message queues.

- **MAPI-based clients.**   The Information Store communicates with MAPI-based clients to notify them that new messages have arrived.

- **MTA.**   The Information Store communicates with the MTA to announce the presence of new mail awaiting transfer through X.400 connectors or connectors to foreign messaging systems.

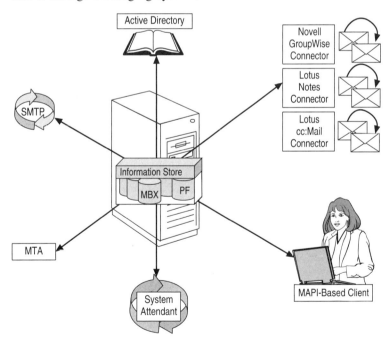

Figure 3.11   Communication initiated by the Information Store

- **SA.** The Information Store communicates with the SA to request the creation of and provide information for tracking log files to be used by the message tracking center. The Information Store also submits link monitor test messages and advanced security-related messages of MAPI-based clients to the SA.

- **SMTP transport.** The Information Store communicates with the SMTP transport to submit messages for delivery. The SMTP transport also expands distribution lists to perform routing for every recipient.

- **Third-party gateways and connectors.** The Information Store communicates with third-party gateways in much the same way as with the connectors for Lotus cc:Mail, Lotus Notes, and Novell GroupWise to announce the presence of new mail awaiting transfer.

SMTP Transport Service

The SMTP service has to process all messages sent by users on an Exchange 2000 server. In other words, the SMTP service receives every individual message from the Information Store to determine whether the recipients reside on the local computer or on remote systems (see Exercise 1 in Lesson 1). When distribution lists are specified, the SMTP service can expand these lists to perform the operation for each individual distribution list member.

Note   In a native Exchange 2000 Server environment, the SMTP service is the only component directly communicating with its counterparts on remote Exchange 2000 servers. All other Exchange 2000 Server components rely on the SMTP message transport for their server-to-server communication.

As shown in Figure 3.12, the SMTP service communicates with the following components:

- **Active Directory.** The SMTP service communicates with Active Directory to look up address information to resolve recipients and expand distribution groups.

- **Information Store.** The SMTP service communicates with the Information Store to obtain messages from and place messages into the Information Store.

- **Remote SMTP services.** The SMTP service communicates with other SMTP services over the network to transfer e-mail messages.

MTA and Messaging Gateways

It is important to note that the SMTP service does not directly communicate with the MTA or any gateways installed on the local computer. If a message is sent to

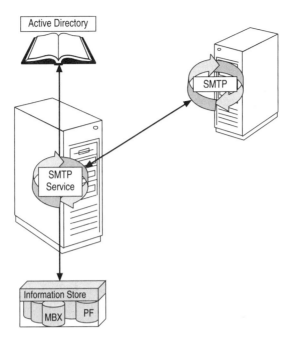

Figure 3.12   Communication initiated by the SMTP transport

a foreign X.400 system, for instance, the SMTP service uses the MTA by means of the Information Store to transfer the message. The MTA receives its messages from the Information Store and can establish connections to remote systems via X.400 connectors. The MTA is also directly involved in the communication through the MS Mail Connector, as explained in Chapter 26, "Connecting to Microsoft Mail and Schedule+."

All MAPI-based messaging connectors, such as the connectors for Lotus cc:Mail, Lotus Notes, and Novell GroupWise, are not accessed by the MTA because they communicate directly with the Information Store where their message queues reside (see Chapters 27–29). However, the MTA performs the message routing to foreign systems and has to deliver the messages to the message queues of these gateway connectors by means of the Information Store.

Other Components

Table 3.1 gives a brief overview of which additional components may initiate communication with other components.

**Table 3.1   Additional Components That May
Initiate Communication with Other Components**

Component	Contacted Components
Conference Management Service (CMS)	**Information Store**. To coordinate the conference bookings via Outlook meeting requests sent to a conferencing mailbox. (The CMS supports the Microsoft Exchange Conferencing service for video conferences and the T.120 MCU Conferencing service for data conferences, which both don't initiate any communication with Exchange 2000 Server components.)
Connector for Lotus cc:Mail	**Active Directory**. To perform directory synchronization
	Information Store. To process messages from and to Lotus cc:Mail post offices
	SA. To process Address Book information from Active Directory via DSProxy
Connector for Lotus Notes	**Active Directory**. To perform directory synchronization
	Information Store. To process messages from and to Lotus Notes
	SA. To process Address Book information from Active Directory via DSProxy
Event Service	**Information Store**. To track and process events and data
Exchange Chat	Does not initiate any communication with Exchange 2000 Server components but integrates with Active Director and IIS
Instant Messaging	Does not initiate any communication with Exchange 2000 Server components itself but integrates with Active Directory
Key Management Server	Does not initiate any communication with Exchange 2000 Server components itself
MS Mail Connector	**SA**. To resolve recipient addresses from Active Directory via DSProxy and convert them into Exchange or MS Mail formats, respectively
	MTA. To transfer mail from and to MS Mail and StarNine/MS Mail (AppleTalk)
	SA. To enable message tracking for messages transferred through the MS Mail connector
MS Mail Directory Synchronization	**Active Directory**. To create, modify, or delete user definitions from remote systems and to check for modifications in the Exchange address list that need to be distributed to foreign systems
	MTA. To receive and submit Dirsync-related messages from and to foreign systems

**Table 3.1   Additional Components That May
Initiate Communication with Other Components** *(continued)*

Component	Contacted Components
MTA	**Active Directory**. To retrieve configuration information, perform routing to foreign systems, and to resolve remote distribution lists locally
	Information Store. To deliver and retrieve messages
	MS Mail connector. To exchange mail with MS Mail and StarNine/MS Mail (AppleTalk) users
	X.400 connectors. To send messages to other Exchange servers and foreign X.400 systems
NNTP Service	**Information Store**. To process messages in public folders
Outlook Web Access	**Active Directory**. To resolve address information and check user privileges
	Information Store. To process messages in mailboxes and public folders
Schedule+ Free/Busy Connector	**Information Store**. To receive and store schedule information from MS Mail postoffices and to send schedule information from Exchange Server to MS Mail
	SA. To retrieve Address Book information from Active Directory using DSProxy
SRS and ADC	**Active Directory**. To transfer directory-related information between the SRS database and Active Directory using connection agreements
	Information Store. To generate and receive directory replication messages to integrate Exchange 2000 Server seamlessly with previous Exchange Server versions

Exchange 2000 Server Message Handling

The central control station of all native Exchange 2000 Server message transfer is the SMTP service—the Exchange 2000 Server extensions of the SMTP service, to be exact. Exercise 1 in this chapter is a proof of it. However, getting a message on its way to the destination is not a trivial task. For instance, a message may be addressed to a distribution list of hundreds of people including users on the local server, remote Exchange 2000 servers, and a variety of foreign messaging systems.

SMTP Transport and the MTA

If your environment contains connections to the Internet, X.400 systems, MS Mail, Lotus cc:Mail, Lotus Notes, Novell GroupWise, a legacy PROFS connection through a computer running Exchange Server 5.5, a popular fax gateway, and not to forget an exotic pager gateway, then a distribution group called *Cosmopolitan* may contain recipients from all these environments. By simply selecting *Cosmopolitan* from the address book and sending your e-mail message, you are giving your messaging system a huge job to accomplish. To get your message to all those recipients, the SMTP transport works in conjunction with the MTA. The SMTP service is responsible for delivery to local recipients as well as recipients on remote Exchange 2000 servers and the Internet. The MTA, on the other hand, takes care of the routing to foreign messaging systems.

SMTP Transport Components

Several SMTP components are involved in message handling and transfer (see Figure 3.13). The store driver, for instance, allows the SMTP transport to directly interact with the Information Store. As soon as the Information Store indicates to the store that new mail has arrived, the store driver informs the advanced queuing engine that a message must be routed. After parsing the message header, the engine passes the message to the categorizer, possibly to custom event sinks, and to the message router if the message needs to be transferred to remote SMTP-based systems. Each of these components processes the message and passes it back to the queuing engine.

Message Handling

The advanced queuing engine is the central control station of the entire SMTP-based message handling process in Exchange 2000 Server.

Exchange 2000 Server handles messages as follows:

1. A remote SMTP system connects to the local SMTP service and transfers a message.
2. The SMTP service creates a temporary file for each incoming message on the file system (in the \Program Files\Exchsrvr\Mailroot directory) and streams the message into this file. After that, it confirms message reception and informs the advanced queuing engine that a new message requires processing.

Alternatively:

1. Outlook users on the local server send messages, which are placed in the information store first. Figure 3.13 also shows a path for messages that arrive through the MTA (for example, via an X.400 connector) that are directly transferred to the Information Store service.
2. For each message, the message store driver informs the advanced queuing engine that a new message requires processing.

In both cases:

3. The advanced queuing engine needs to pass the incoming messages to the categorizer to determine how to process the messages further. For this reason, it places the messages in a specific queue known as the precategorizer queue.

4. The categorizer takes the messages from the precategorizer queue, processes them, and then places individual message copies in the appropriate delivery queues for delivery through the SMTP service (destination-domain queues) or the Information Store (local delivery queue).

5. The advanced queuing engine now allows any custom event sinks installed on the server to process the message.

6. Messages in the destination-domain queues are passed to the routing engine, which returns a next-hop identifier for each message destination. The next-hop identifier informs the SMTP service where to transfer the message next.

7. The store driver informs the Information Store and the Information Store retrieves the messages from the local delivery queue to deliver them to local recipients or the MTA for further processing.

8. The SMTP service transfers the messages from the destination-domain queues to the next hop in the routing infrastructure.

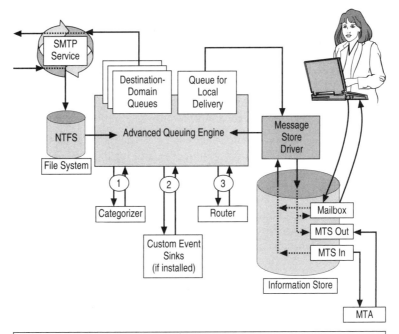

Figure 3.13 Exchange 2000 Server message handling

Message Categorization

Each recipient may require specific message handling. For instance, a message may be addressed to a local recipient, a recipient on another Exchange 2000 server, and a recipient on the Internet. Consequently, multiple copies of the same message must be generated; one copy must be delivered locally, one needs to be transferred across the intranet to the remote Exchange 2000 server, and one copy needs to go to the Internet domain. It is the task of the categorizer to classify each recipient and create multiple message copies if required.

The Exchange 2000 Categorizer performs the following steps:

1. Attempts to resolve the originator address using Active Directory.

2. Expands any distribution groups to determine all recipients, provided that local group expansion is allowed on this server. If expansion is prohibited for a group, the Categorizer analyzes the group's Home-VSI (Virtual Server Instance) attribute to determine the expansion server.

3. Resolves all recipients that exist in Active Directory and marks the remaining recipients as unknown.

4. Checks if delivery restrictions and other limits exist for the originator and recipients. Users with restrictions are marked for individual processing according to the restrictions.

5. Creates multiple copies of the message if recipients require separate processing, such as local and remote recipients, or recipients with restrictions.

6. Places the individual copies of the message in the appropriate delivery queues (destination-domain queues and local delivery queue).

7. Informs the advanced queuing engine that the message categorization is complete.

The Exchange 2000 Categorizer is implemented in PHATCAT.DLL, which resides in the \Program Files\Exchsrvr\Bin directory. You can read more about the SMTP service in Chapter 15, "SMTP Transport Configuration."

Chapter Summary

Exchange 2000 Server is a complex, component-oriented client/server messaging and collaboration system that includes active Windows 2000 services. These services communicate with each other using LRPCs, RPCs, Windows Sockets, ExIPC, regular files, and e-mail messages. With the exception of the Event Service, all components have to communicate with Active Directory.

Information Store and SMTP service, in conjunction with SA, Active Directory, and IIS Admin Service, are required to provide basic messaging functionality to Outlook users. Exchange 2000 Server maintains mailboxes and public folders in the information store and always requires message processing through the SMTP transport. Active Directory hosts the address books and provides recipient information to clients and system components. The SA, again, takes care of the Exchange 2000 Server system and the IIS Admin Service controls the SMTP transport. When Information Store and Active Directory are in operational states, users can gain access to their messages and other data stored in mailboxes and public folders, but without the SMTP service, there is no message transfer.

The Exchange 2000 Server–specific SMTP and NNTP service extensions, as well as the Exchange Routing Engine, IMAP4, and POP3, use ExIPC to rapidly exchange data directly with the Information Store through memory rather than through RPCs or other communication methods. This provides the best performance and reduces overhead required for interprocess communication. Exchange 2000 Server implements an advanced queuing engine for the SMTP transport, which processes every message sent through the server and determines how to reach each recipient.

Review

The following review questions can help you determine if you have sufficiently familiarized yourself with the material covered in this chapter. You can find the answers to these questions at the end of this book in Appendix A, "Questions and Answers."

1. What are the essential Exchange 2000 Server components required to deliver messages in a single-server environment?

2. To perform an offline backup, you want to shut down the IIS and the Exchange 2000 Server services without rebooting the entire server. Which of the components must be stopped directly to stop all other server components as well?

3. You have stopped the MTA service. How does this affect the behavior of connected Outlook clients?

4. As an administrator you have stopped the Microsoft Exchange Information Store service. How does this affect Outlook clients?

5. To satisfy growing messaging demand, you decide to install a second Exchange 2000 server. Which components communicate directly with each other between servers?

6. List the two general types of information stores an Exchange 2000 server can maintain.

7. How many storage groups can you configure on a particular Exchange 2000 server, and how many information store databases can each storage group contain?

8. As a user using Outlook 2000, you can happily send messages to all other users in your environment. After lunch, however, the situation changes. All of a sudden, your messages don't seem to leave the Outbox anymore. Other users with mailboxes on your server report the same problem. What is most likely the cause of this dilemma?

C H A P T E R   4

Planning the Microsoft Exchange 2000 Server Installation

About This Chapter

The installation of Microsoft Exchange 2000 Server on a single computer is not a very complex task. After a few mouse clicks and some configuration parameters, the first server is running. You just did this to prepare your test environment. Unfortunately, many Exchange environments begin their evolution this way. They are meant to be test environments, then the administrator puts on some test mailboxes, and soon the test users discover the benefits of the new system, get excited, and immediately start using the test installation as their production environment. At this stage, it is often too late for a fresh and more optimal implementation or major structural changes, so the test environment manifests itself irreversibly as the production system. With the benefit of hindsight the administrator looks back, wishing the environment had a better design.

It is generally advisable to put some thought into planning before embarking on the task of implementing Exchange 2000 Server. Even if you are only responsible for a handful of people, you're doing more than just installing a server; you're launching a new messaging and collaboration network. Several irrevocable decisions regarding the network configuration must be made at this point. This becomes especially clear as you add new resources to the network, as you will need to install them in a context that has been predefined by that time. Thus, if you need to change the fundamental parameters of your network at a later date, you will have to engage in a much more complex task than it would have been in the beginning. Forethought can help avoid unnecessary work and costs during the rollout and afterward.

This chapter explains the prerequisites and some of the most important aspects you might want to consider to ensure a successful deployment of Exchange 2000 Server. You will read about various deployment considerations, necessary preparations of Microsoft Windows 2000 and the Active Directory directory service, the hardware and software requirements, and security and maintenance. Lesson 1 is focused primarily on theoretical aspects. Lesson 2 then addresses the installation preparation from a more practical point of view.

Before You Begin

To complete this chapter:

- Prepare your test environment according to the descriptions given in the "Getting Started" section of "About This Book."
- Have a general understanding of Windows 2000 networking technologies, Active Directory, and the delegation of administrative permissions in an Active Directory forest.
- Have an understanding of the essential Exchange 2000 components, as covered in Chapter 3, "Microsoft Exchange 2000 Server Architecture."

Lesson 1: Deployment Considerations

Exchange 2000 Server is enormously flexible and offers numerous mutually exclusive deployment options. You have to decide what is best for your organization. Would you prefer centralized or decentralized system administration? Centralized management is usually preferable, but not always appropriate. Therefore, it is important to define a suitable deployment plan designed around your infrastructure needs. This will give you a clear direction for your Exchange 2000 environment. It also benefits your users because it ensures that Exchange 2000 Server will meet their requirements. Finally, a deployment plan benefits your organization's management because it outlines business goals, time frames, and necessary investments.

This lesson discusses aspects that you should take into consideration when planning your Exchange 2000 infrastructure. Even if your environment concentrates all its resources in one location and is easy to manage, give some thought to administrative dependencies and infrastructure.

At the end of this lesson, you will be able to:

- Identify the advantages and disadvantages of centralized and decentralized management structures.

- Describe the purpose of administrative and routing groups.

- Explain the restrictions that apply to mixed-mode environments in comparison to native-mode organizations.

Estimated time to complete this lesson: 75 minutes

Distributed Versus Centralized Management

The dynamics of distributed PC-based networks are challenging to the people in charge of their maintenance: You simply can't be in more than one place at the same time. Because of this, distributed configurations have a higher total cost of ownership than their centralized counterparts. Directory services offer the ability to centralize administration and provide a simplified, faster, and more coordinated organization (see Figure 4.1). That is why Microsoft, Novell, and Banyan have each developed their own directory services.

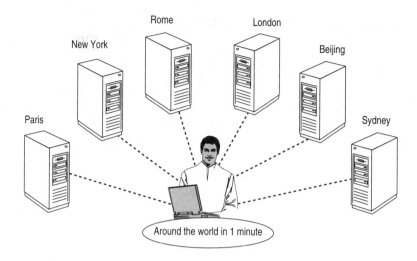

Figure 4.1   Benefits of centralized administration

Windows 2000 Permissions

In a standard Windows 2000 domain environment, only the administrator of the top-level domain has the required permissions to install Exchange 2000 Server. In other words, no sublevel domain administrator can just set up Exchange 2000 Server in your domain environment without prior coordination. This restriction applies no matter how complicated your domain forest. If you are the administrator of the top-level domain, you are in total control. You may assign other administrators the required permissions or perform the installation tasks yourself.

To first install Exchange 2000 Server, you need to use an account that is a member of one of the following Windows 2000 security groups:

- Domain Admins
- Enterprise Admins
- Schema Admins

Schema Admins membership is only required for the installation of the first Exchange 2000 server in a forest.

Note   To install Exchange 2000 Server successfully, you need to run the Setup program in an Active Directory environment on Windows 2000 Server, Windows 2000 Advanced Server, or Windows 2000 Datacenter Server. The installation must be updated with Windows 2000 Service Pack 1.

Exchange 2000 Server Permissions

In addition to Windows 2000 requirements, you need explicit administrative permissions in Exchange 2000 if you want to add another server to an existing organization. You will set the required permissions in Lesson 2 of this chapter to prepare a subsequent Exchange 2000 Server installation.

Windows 2000 Server and Exchange 2000 Administration

If you are working in a single domain environment as the only administrator for both Windows 2000 Server and Exchange 2000 Server, you don't need to delegate authority to any additional accounts. Just install Exchange 2000 Server using the default Administrator account. If you are working in a more complex environment, however, consider the following aspects of Windows 2000 before installing Exchange 2000 Server:

- Consolidate multiple existing domains into fewer Windows 2000 Server domains if possible to simplify the environment prior to the installation of Exchange 2000 Server.

- Create individual security groups for each administrative role in your environment, such as administrators for user accounts and mailboxes and administrators for system configuration. Add members to those groups accordingly and assign them the required permissions.

- Form a deployment team with members of both messaging administrators and administrators managing Active Directory. If your enterprise has a separate team for each platform, careful coordination is essential. Assign at least one administrator the permissions to manage both Windows 2000 Server and Exchange 2000 Server.

- Review your Windows 2000 Active Directory design prior to the installation of Exchange 2000 Server. As outlined in Chapter 2, "Integration with Microsoft Windows 2000," the load on the Global Catalog will increase due to address lookups of Messaging Application Programming Interface (MAPI)-based clients and other messaging components.

Exercise 1: Centralized Exchange 2000 Administration

In this exercise you will verify that only the administrator of the top-level domain BlueSky-inc-10.com is allowed to manage and add Exchange 2000 resources to your test environment. In other words, you will check whether the administrator from the subdomain CA.BlueSky-inc-10.com has the ability to install Exchange 2000 Server.

To view a multimedia demonstration that displays how to perform this procedure, run the EX1CH4.AVI files from the \Exercise_Information\Chapter4 folder on the Supplemental Course Materials CD.

Prerequisites

- Restart BLUESKY-SRV1 and BLUESKY-SRV2 to bring the test environment into a standard operational state.

- Log on as Administrator@CA.Bluesky-inc-10.com to the computer BLUESKY-SRV2 running Windows 2000 Advanced Server without Exchange 2000 Server.

- Insert the Exchange 2000 Enterprise Server CD into the CD-ROM drive (E drive) of BLUESKY-SRV2.

▶ **To verify required permissions for setting up Exchange 2000 Server**

1. Start the Exchange 2000 Setup program from the \Setup\i386 directory on the installation CD.

2. The Welcome To The Microsoft Exchange 2000 Installation Wizard screen appears. Click Next to start the installation.

3. In the End-User License Agreement dialog box, click I Agree, and then click Next to continue the installation successfully.

4. In the Product Identification page, under CD Key, enter your CD key, and then click Next.

5. In the Component Selection page, under Action, in the first row for Microsoft Exchange 2000, select Minimum. Verify that a Microsoft Exchange 2000 Installation Wizard dialog box appears.

   At this point, you will be informed that you don't have the required permission to set up Exchange 2000 Server (see Figure 4.2). Although you are using an administrator account fully capable of managing the sublevel domain (decentralized), you are unable to install Exchange 2000 Server because this enterprisewide messaging and collaboration system favors a centralized management by default.

6. Click OK to close the dialog box, and then click Cancel to abort the installation.

7. In the final Microsoft Exchange 2000 Installation Wizard dialog box asking you whether you are sure you want to cancel, click Yes.

Exercise Summary

Exchange 2000 Server administration is bound to Windows 2000 administration because both use Active Directory to store configuration and security-related information. Someone who plans to set up Exchange 2000 Server on any given network must have access to update Active Directory.

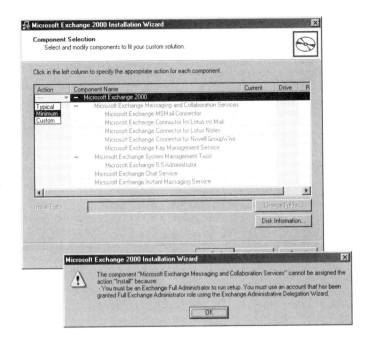

Figure 4.2   An unsuccessful Exchange 2000 installation attempt

Exchange 2000 Hierarchy

Although desirable, it is not always practical to enforce a centralized administrative model, for instance, if you are in charge of a large computer network with server resources in different geographic locations. User account administration, however, should not be affected by physical system arrangements.

Note   Exchange 2000 Server allows you to design the system administration independently of physical network links and server arrangements and can be adapted to both centralized and decentralized infrastructures.

Exchange 2000 Boundaries

There are three separate boundaries you need to take into consideration when planning your Exchange 2000 infrastructure. These are namespace, administrative groups, and routing groups (see Figure 4.3). The namespace is your

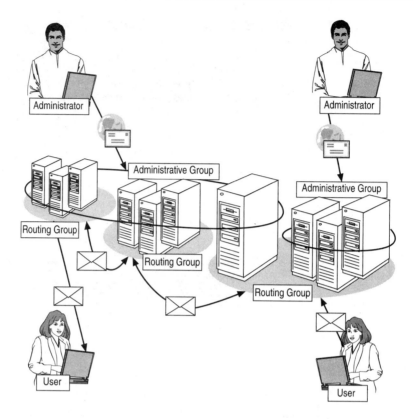

Figure 4.3   Administrative groups and routing groups

Active Directory forest, which contains all of the directory information for your Exchange 2000 environment. To subdivide the management of resources within a particular namespace, use administrative groups. It's often applicable to define your administrative topology according to departments or divisions. The physical network topology should dictate the configuration of routing groups because they define how messages are actually transferred across the network. They also help you to optimize access to public folder resources. Servers are set in routing groups, and routing groups are typically collected into administrative groups, although you can split a routing group across multiple administrative groups (see Figure 4.3).

Note   The relationship between routing groups and administrative groups is not necessarily hierarchical.

Exchange 2000 Namespace

The namespace represents the core of the Exchange 2000 hierarchy. It exists in Active Directory in the form of a domain forest and contains directory information about all of the Exchange 2000 resources, for instance, to map user accounts to their corresponding mailboxes. Hence, within the namespace, user accounts can be resolved to their corresponding mailboxes.

Note   All Exchange 2000 resources must exist in the same namespace (such as the Active Directory forest). Consequently, Exchange 2000 organizations cannot span multiple namespaces (such as multiple forests).

Administrative Groups

Use administrative groups to define the management topology of your organization. Administrative groups help to simplify system management, for instance, to define groups of administrators separately responsible for servers in different departments. In another scenario, you may group dedicated servers, such as public folder servers, together in an administrative group and assign them a group of administrators specifically responsible for public folder maintenance. You can read more about public folder management in Chapter 17, "Public Folder Management."

Routing Groups

Similar to Windows 2000 sites, you should define routing groups primarily to describe regions of high-speed connections within your network. For instance, if your enterprise is located in one physical location relying on one high-speed local area network (LAN), you don't need to configure routing groups at all. Placing all servers in the first routing group that is automatically created by Exchange 2000 Server guarantees simple and fast delivery of messages. Messages sent between servers in the same routing group are transferred directly and immediately using the Simple Mail Transfer Protocol (SMTP) transport service.

Manual administration becomes necessary only when you need to connect two or more routing groups or when you need to install connectors to foreign messaging systems. You can use a Routing Group Connector, X.400 connector, or an SMTP Connector to provide a message path between Exchange 2000 routing groups.

Grouping of Servers

When installing the very first server, you are automatically creating an administrative group and a routing group (see Exercise 2). You are not prompted for their creation. However, when you install subsequent Exchange 2000 servers, you need to specify an administrative and a routing group in which to add the server. Every server in your organization must belong to an administrative and a routing group. After installation, you can move servers between groups, which might be advisable if management or physical conditions in your network have changed.

Exercise 2: Default Administrative and Routing Group Configuration

In this exercise you will examine the hierarchal structure of your test environment. Specifically, you will look for administrative and routing groups, which are hidden by default. You can easily make them visible with the Exchange System Manager utility.

To view a multimedia demonstration that displays how to perform this procedure, run the EX2CH4.AVI files from the \Exercise_Information\Chapter4 folder on the Supplemental Course Materials CD.

Prerequisites

- Log on as Administrator to BLUESKY-SRV1 running Exchange 2000 Server.

▶ **To configure System Manager to display routing and administrative groups**

1. Start the System Manager from the Microsoft Exchange program group.

2. Right-click the top-level node Blue Sky Airlines (Exchange), and, from the shortcut menu, select Properties.

3. In the Blue Sky Airlines (Exchange) Properties dialog box, select the Display Routing Groups and Display Administrative Groups check boxes, and then click OK. In the message box informing you that you need to restart the System Manager, click OK and restart the System Manager.

4. At this point, you should be able to find a container called Administrative Groups in the console tree. Most of the other nodes are now placed underneath this node for better orientation. Expand all the nodes. By selecting the Members container within the First Routing Group object, you will see that the server BLUESKY-SRV1 is the Master server in the First Routing Group, which you can find under Routing Groups (see Figure 4.4).

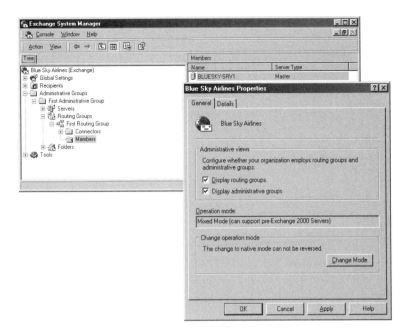

Figure 4.4   Identifying the Master Server

Exercise Summary

If your situation permits a centralized administration, use a single administrative group containing all server resources, which may then be split across a number of routing groups. This allows you complete control over Exchange 2000 Server with minimal coordination overhead for administration tasks. The centralized model is most suitable for small- and medium-sized organizations.

If your environment has several departments independently maintaining their own server resources and user accounts, configure multiple administrative groups with the Exchange System Manager—one or more for each department or division—and assign permissions to establish a decentralized administrative model. Each of the departments and divisions is then able to define its own routing group topology. This model is suitable for large companies in which a central information technology bureau may be responsible for managing standards and guidelines but not for daily system administration. You can read more about the management of administrative groups in Chapter 14, "Managing Server Configuration."

Mixed Mode and Native Mode

If you have administered previous versions of Exchange Server, you will find many of the structural elements in Exchange 2000 Server familiar, especially if you operate in mixed mode for backward compatibility. For example, you will be limited to a 1:1 relationship between administrative and routing groups in regard to Exchange Server sites.

If you are not using an earlier version of Exchange Server and are not planning to connect your Exchange 2000 environment to a server running Exchange Server 5.5 in the future, don't worry about mixed mode and native mode. Go to Exercise 3 and switch the environment into native mode to gain the full flexibility of Exchange 2000 Server.

Mixed Mode

In mixed mode, administrative groups map directly to sites in an Exchange Server 5.5 organization. This means that Exchange Server sites replicated to Active Directory appear as administrative groups and administrative groups replicated to the Exchange Server directory appear as sites. For backward compatibility reasons, the mixed mode limits Exchange 2000 Server to constraints imposed by earlier software releases.

The following limitations apply in mixed mode:

- Administrative groups are handled similar to Exchange Server 5.5 sites.
- It is impossible to move mailboxes between servers in different administrative groups.
- Routing groups can only contain servers from the same administrative group. Although one administrative group may contain multiple routing groups, routing groups cannot span multiple administrative groups (see Figure 4.5).

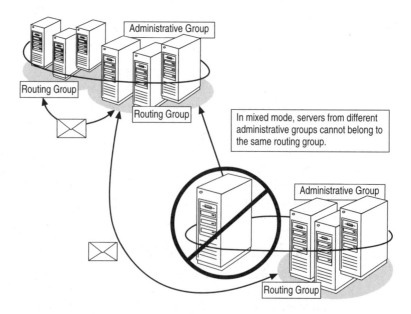

Figure 4.5   Exchange 2000 Server routing in mixed mode

However, it is possible to move servers between routing groups in the same administrative group.

Note   By default, Exchange 2000 Server operates in mixed mode to ensure maximal interoperability with previous Exchange Server versions.

Native Mode

You can switch Exchange 2000 Server to native mode if you don't plan to use previous versions of Exchange Server or as soon as you have upgraded all of your servers. In native mode, earlier release restrictions, which limit the flexibility of routing groups, don't apply. Hence, routing groups can contain servers from multiple administrative groups, and you gain the ability to create administrative groups independently of the routing infrastructure for your organization. It is also possible to move servers between administrative groups should the underlying infrastructure require this kind of change.

Note   Keep in mind that switching to native mode is an irreversible process; you cannot go back to mixed mode. It is likewise impossible to install earlier versions of Exchange Server into a native mode organization.

Exercise 3: Checking the Mixed/Native Mode Attribute

In this exercise you will check whether your organization operates in mixed mode. If it does, you will switch it to native mode. You will use the Active Directory Services Interface (ADSI) Edit tool to check where the Exchange System Manager keeps track of the mode of your organization.

To view a multimedia demonstration that displays how to perform this procedure, run the EX3CH4.AVI files from the \Exercise_Information\Chapter4 folder on the Supplemental Course Materials CD.

Note   You should use the ADSI Edit utility to view the settings, but generally use the Exchange System Manager to configure your system. Using ADSI Edit incorrectly can seriously damage your Active Directory information and may require you to reinstall your entire test environment.

Prerequisites

- Install the support tools from the Windows 2000 Server installation CD (\Support\Tools directory) on BLUESKY-SRV1 using the default installation options. If the software is not at hand, skip the steps that require ADSI Edit, yet make sure you follow the procedure to switch the organization into native mode using Exchange System Manager.

- Log on as Administrator to BLUESKY-SRV1 running Exchange 2000 Server.

▶   **To change from mixed mode to native mode**

1. Click Start, point to Programs, then to Windows 2000 Support Tools, then Tools, and then select ADSI Edit.

2. Open the Configuration container [Bluesky-srv1.Bluesky-inc-10.com], then the container labeled CN=Configuration,DC=Bluesky-inc-10,DC=com, then the container named CN=Services, then CN=Microsoft Exchange, and right-click on CN=Blue Sky Airlines.

3. From the shortcut menu, select Properties to display the CN=BlueSky Airlines Properties dialog box.

4. On the Attributes property page, in the Select Which Properties To View list box, make sure Optional is displayed, and then, under Select A Property To View, select msExchMixedMode. Verify that the Attribute Value is set to True, which indicates mixed mode operation. Click OK.

5. Start the System Manager snap-in from the Microsoft Exchange program group.

6. Right-click the top-level node Blue Sky Airlines (Exchange), and from the shortcut menu, select Properties.

7. In the Blue Sky Airlines Properties dialog box, in the General tab, click Change Mode.

8. An Exchange System Manager warning message will be displayed, informing you that this operation is irreversible. Click Yes to confirm that you want to switch your organization to native mode.

9. In the Blue Sky Airlines Properties dialog box, click OK.

   At this point, you should switch back to the ADSI Edit utility and repeat Steps 2 through 4. Note that the msExchMixedMode attribute is now set to False, indicating that the organization is operating in native mode (see Figure 4.6).

10. Close ADSI Edit and the Exchange System Manager.

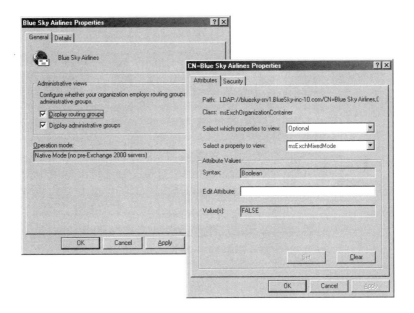

Figure 4.6 Switching to native mode

Exercise Summary

The msExchMixedMode attribute in Active Directory defines the mode of your Exchange 2000 Server organization as mixed mode or native mode. Using the ADSI Edit utility, you can verify that your organization is operating in native mode. However, you should not set the msExchMixedMode attribute back to True manually to attempt to switch your organization back into mixed mode. This only switches back the display in the Exchange System Manager. Do not manipulate the msExchMixedMode attribute in ADSI Edit to avoid configuration inconsistencies.

Lesson 2: Preparing the Server Installation

System requirements for a successful server installation will vary. You will need to address architectural issues, server roles, requirements for system performance, and questions regarding system maintenance. You need to decide between single-server and multiserver environments, and it might be advantageous to consider advanced configurations for load balancing and fault tolerance.

This lesson covers important tasks that demand your attention prior to installing Exchange 2000 Server. These include various dependencies, the delegation of administrative permissions for subsequent installations, and advanced configurations for hosted environments intended to support thousands of users.

At the end of this lesson, you will be able to:

- Describe the hardware requirements for a successful installation of Exchange 2000 Server.
- Identify important tasks that need to be accomplished before running the Setup program.
- Explain how to install and configure Exchange 2000 Server in large hosted environments.
- Describe the requirements for installing Exchange 2000 Server in a clustered system.

Estimated time to complete this lesson: 90 minutes

Exchange 2000 Requirements

During the setup of the first server, you need to define the organization name. This name cannot be changed later. Subsequent installations, on the other hand, introduce new questions. You must decide whether to add the server to the default administrative and default routing group or to new groups that you created with the Exchange System Manager. Several other necessities, such as software and hardware requirements, must also be met.

Hardware Requirements

The actual hardware requirements for Exchange 2000 Server are difficult to ascertain. Although minimum requirements can be determined quickly, they are seldom sufficient for a server that must cope with real-world demands. Nevertheless, if you check the product documentation, you will not find much discussion about detailed sample configurations—the flexibility of this system is simply too enormous to calculate the actual hardware requirements for every possible scenario beforehand.

Microsoft recommends, at a minimum, a Pentium 300 or faster processor and 128 or 256 megabytes (MB) of random access memory (RAM). This is appropriate for small- to medium-sized organizations, but does not achieve best system performance. For better performance, consider more powerful and sophisticated hardware configurations such as multiprocessor computers, 512 megabytes of RAM, and caching disk array controllers. It may seem that the minimum recommendation is fine to start with because you have the option to add further hardware, such as more memory or more processors, at a later time. Keep in mind, however, that the hardware industry is quickly introducing new systems. If you start with a single-processor system today and plan to add new hardware in the future, you may find that your processor type or memory bank is no longer available.

Microsoft recommends the following equipment for a typical computer running Exchange 2000 Server:

- 128 to 256 MB of RAM
- 2 gigabytes (GB) of available disk space on the drive for Exchange 2000 Server
- 500 MB on the system drive
- CD-ROM drive
- Intel Pentium or compatible at 300 Megahertz (MHz) or faster
- Paging file set to twice the amount of RAM or larger
- VGA-compatible display adapter

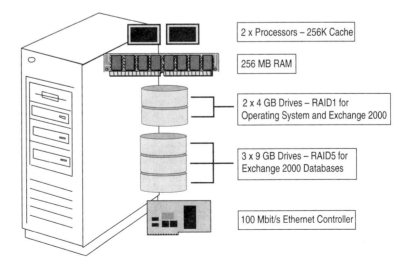

Figure 4.7   Exchange 2000 Server hardware configuration
for small- to medium-sized environments

In addition, consider the two reference configurations shown in Figure 4.7 and Figure 4.8 when planning your server hardware. It is also a good idea to build a test system to simulate any number of users sending and receiving messages and working with public folders.

You can find a discussion about advanced hard disk arrangements and their purposes in Chapter 20, "Microsoft Exchange 2000 Server Maintenance and Troubleshooting."

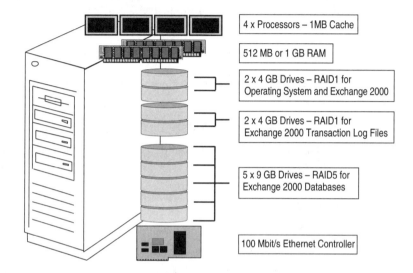

4 x Processors – 1MB Cache

512 MB or 1 GB RAM

2 x 4 GB Drives – RAID1 for Operating System and Exchange 2000

2 x 4 GB Drives – RAID1 for Exchange 2000 Transaction Log Files

5 x 9 GB Drives – RAID5 for Exchange 2000 Databases

100 Mbit/s Ethernet Controller

Figure 4.8   Exchange 2000 Server hardware configuration for medium- to large-sized environments

Software Requirements

Exchange 2000 Server can be installed on Microsoft Windows 2000 Server, Windows 2000 Advanced Server, or Windows 2000 Datacenter Server with Service Pack 1. It is important to note that the Internet Information Services (IIS) 5.0 with SMTP and Network News Transfer Protocol (NNTP) service must be installed prior to launching the Exchange 2000 Setup program. During the installation of Windows 2000, you will need to add the NNTP service manually. The SMTP service is part of the default installation.

Note   You need to install Exchange 2000 Server on an NT file system (NTFS) partition.

Exchange 2000 Server supports Windows 2000 clustering. To benefit from such a configuration, however, you need to install the Advanced Server or Datacenter Server edition of Windows 2000.

Active Directory Dependencies

You need to prepare Active Directory and the underlying Windows 2000 domain structure of your organization. This is important because you must have administrative permissions on the computer on which you will install Exchange 2000 Server. The computer needs to be located in your own domain or in a domain that trusts your domain. If this is not the case—if you cannot access the computer using your account—you will not be able to install or manage the Exchange 2000 computer. A single Exchange 2000 organization cannot span multiple Active Directory forests.

Licensing

Licensing is an important issue, but Microsoft's licensing agreements are not always easy to understand. You need to exercise care not to violate the software copyright. Finding the best options for you can help to maximize your financial investments. To give an example, if you are responsible for an educational institution, you may find appropriate options through Microsoft's special educational licensing program. Companies in the private business sector, in turn, may be eligible for a variety of different discounts through Microsoft's volume licensing, depending on the number of licenses obtained. Small companies with five or more PCs will find the Microsoft Open License Program attractive, and large organizations with hundreds of PCs are better off with the Select License Program.

Note   If you have any doubts, go to *http://www.microsoft.com/* and search on the word "license" for the product you're looking for.

Installation Preparation

If you are planning to install Exchange 2000 Server in an environment with multiple domains in a forest, it might be advantageous to import the Exchange-specific schema extensions prior to the actual installation. This eliminates the need to be a Windows 2000 Schema Admin when installing Exchange 2000 Server at a later time. The Setup program of Exchange 2000 Server offers two specific modes for the purpose of preparing Active Directory, which you can launch through the command line switches /ForestPrep and /DomainPrep.

Preparing the Active Directory Forest

If you are responsible for messaging administration and have forestwide permissions to mange Active Directory, no special preparation is required. Make sure you have the permissions mentioned in Lesson 1, start the Exchange 2000 Setup program, and install the first server. All of the required forest modifications are then performed automatically.

Note   You need to install the first instance of Exchange 2000 Server into the domain where the schema master resides. By default, this is the first Windows 2000 domain controller installed in your forest. Only one domain controller in the forest can be the schema master.

However, should your messaging management be separated from Windows 2000 administration, you need to ask the Active Directory administrators to prepare the forest for you by launching ForestPrep. To run ForestPrep successfully, you need to be a member of the Enterprise Admins and Schema Admins groups and you need to be a member of the local Administrators group on the computer where you are running ForestPrep. Launch the Setup program from the \Setup\i386 directory on your Exchange 2000 installation CD using the command **setup /ForestPrep**. Accept the welcome page and end-user license agreement, enter your product key on the third wizard screen, and then, on the Component Selection page, make sure that the action next to Exchange 2000 Server is set to ForestPrep. Click Next, and on the Installation Type wizard screen, select Create An Exchange 2000 Organization. Subsequently, you need to specify the name of your new organization and the name of the administrator account or group responsible for installing Exchange 2000 Server. After that, ForestPrep is ready to go and prompts you a last time to verify the schema update. Click OK to start the processing.

Launched using the /ForestPrep switch, the Setup program extends the Active Directory Schema to add Exchange-specific classes and attributes as outlined in Chapter 2. These extensions affect the entire forest and may take a considerable amount of time to replicate throughout the forest. ForestPrep also creates the container object for the Exchange 2000 organization in Active Directory and assigns to the account that you specified Exchange Full Administrative permissions to the organization object. This account then has the authority to install and manage Exchange 2000 Server throughout the forest, and it has the authority to assign further administrators Exchange Full Administrative permissions once the first server is installed.

Preparing Windows 2000 Domains

To simplify the deployment of Exchange 2000 in your forest, run Setup with the option /DomainPrep in each domain including the domain where you ran ForestPrep to add further Exchange-specific configuration information to Active Directory. You need to be a member of the Domain Admins group for the domain that you want to prepare, and you also need to have administrative permissions on the computer from which you are running DomainPrep.

Launch Setup from the \Setup\i386 directory on your Exchange 2000 installation CD using the command **setup /DomainPrep**. Again, accept the welcome page and end-user license agreement, enter your product key on the third wizard screen, and then, on the Component Selection page, make sure that the action next to Exchange 2000 Server is set to DomainPrep. Click Next and complete the domain preparation. The server on which you run DomainPrep will become your domain's Recipient Update Server (RUS). This is especially important if you do not plan to fully deploy Exchange 2000 Server in the domain (the Exchange 2000 server for your users resides in another domain). You can read more about the management of recipients and the Recipient Update Service in Chapter 13, "Creating and Managing Recipients."

Note   When installing Exchange 2000 at a later time, you should install it on the server where DomainPrep was performed.

Exchange 2000 Roles and Permissions

Although an Exchange 2000 administrator is typically a Windows 2000 administrator, the reverse is not necessarily true. By default, only the administrator who has installed the first server or was specified during the preparation of the domain forest receives explicit administrative privileges at the Exchange level. Members of the Enterprise Admins and local Domain Admins groups inherit administrative permissions. They remain able to manage the entire domain environment as well as e-mail addresses and mailbox resources for Windows 2000 user accounts. Permissions for additional users must be granted manually to selected Windows 2000 accounts. Once this is done, these accounts can start the Exchange System Manager to accomplish configuration tasks or perform subsequent Exchange 2000 Server installations.

The Exchange System Manager includes a tool called the Exchange Administration Delegation Wizard that simplifies permission management. Similar to its Windows 2000 counterpart, used to delegate administrative control for OUs to individual administrators, the Exchange Administration Delegation Wizard simplifies permission management for Exchange administrators. You will use the Exchange Administration Delegation Wizard in Exercise 4 to prepare a subsequent Exchange 2000 Server installation.

Using the Administration Delegation Wizard, you can assign the following roles to your Exchange 2000 Server administrators (and security groups):

- **Exchange Full Administrator.**   Can administer the Exchange organization and modify permissions on Exchange configuration objects.
- **Exchange Administrator.**   Can administer the Exchange organization, yet does not have the ability to modify permissions on Exchange configuration objects.
- **Exchange View-Only Administrator.**   Can only display the Exchange configuration information in read-only mode.

Microsoft recommends running the Exchange Administration Delegation Wizard after the first Exchange 2000 Server installation and before any subsequent installations. You cannot utilize this utility until the first Exchange 2000 server is installed.

Note Enterprise and domain administrators that have been granted the role Exchange View-Only Administrator will remain fully capable of managing the Exchange 2000 organization due to permissions inherited from the Enterprise Admins or Domain Admins security groups. The Exchange Administration Delegation Wizard will list those accounts with the Exchange View-Only Administrator role although they are full administrators.

Exercise 4: Preparing and Performing a Subsequent Installation in a Subdomain

In this exercise you will prepare the domain CA.BlueSky-inc-10.com for Exchange 2000 Server. You will assign the administrator of CA.BlueSky-inc-10.com the responsibility to maintain the Exchange 2000 resources in CA.BlueSky-inc-10.com. You don't need to run Setup in ForestPrep mode because you already installed Exchange 2000 Server on BLUESKY-SRV1 in BlueSky-inc-10.com, which took care of the forest preparation.

To view a multimedia demonstration that displays how to perform this procedure, run the EX4CH4*.AVI files from the \Exercise_Information\Chapter4 folder on the Supplemental Course Materials CD.

Prerequisites

- Make sure BLUESKY-SRV1 and BLUESKY-SRV2 are up and running.
- Log on as Administrator to BLUESKY-SRV1 running Exchange 2000 Server.
- Insert the Exchange 2000 Enterprise Server CD into the CD-ROM drive (E drive) of BLUESKY-SRV2.

▶ **To change the Active Directory forest to native mode and install Exchange 2000 Server in a sublevel domain**

1. To switch the domain BlueSky-inc-10.com into native mode, on BLUESKY-SRV1, start the Active Directory Domains and Trusts utility from the Administrative Tools program group.

2. In the console tree, expand all nodes, and then right-click on BlueSky-inc-10.com.

3. From the shortcut menu, select Properties to display the BlueSky-inc-10.com Properties dialog box.

4. Click Change Mode. An Active Directory warning message appears informing you that this is an irreversible process. Click Yes.

5. In the BlueSky-inc-10.com Properties dialog box, click OK.

6. In the Active Directory dialog box that appears to inform you that the configuration change was completed successfully and may take up to 15 minutes for replication to all domain controllers, click OK.

7. Repeat Steps 1 through 6 for the domain CA.BlueSky-inc-10.com.

    At this point, all your Windows 2000 domains operate in native mode (see Figure 4.9). This gives you more control over the forest and the ability to manage universal groups.

8. To add the Administrator account from CA.BlueSky-inc-10.com to the Enterprise Admins group, start the Active Directory Users and Computers utility by right-clicking on BlueSky-inc-10.com and selecting Manage.

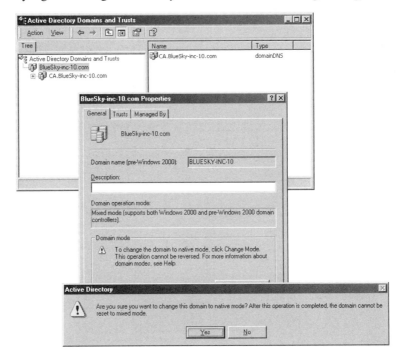

Figure 4.9   Switching Active Directory to native mode

9. Make sure the Users container is selected in the Active Directory Users and Computers utility, and, in the details pane, double-click the Enterprise Admins group to display its properties.

10. Switch to the Members tab, and click Add to display the Select Users, Contacts, Computers, Or Groups dialog box.

11. Under Look In, select CA.BlueSky-inc-10.com, select the Administrator from the list of accounts and groups, click Add, and then click OK.

12. In the Enterprise Admins Properties dialog box, click OK.

At this point, you have assigned the administrator from CA.BlueSky-inc-10.com the permissions to manage the entire Active Directory forest (see Figure 4.10). This was outlined for demonstrative purposes. The privileges of an enterprise administrator, however, are not required to successfully install Exchange 2000 Server.

13. Start the System Manager from the Microsoft Exchange program group.

14. Right-click on the organization object Blue Sky Airlines (Exchange) and, from the shortcut menu, select Delegate Control to start the Exchange Administration Delegation Wizard.

15. On the wizard Welcome screen, click Next, and then, on the Users Or Groups wizard screen, click Add to add the administrator from the CA.BlueSky-inc-10.com domain (CA\Administrator) to the list of Users And Groups.

16. In the Delegate Control dialog box, under Role, select Exchange Full Administrator, and then click OK.

17. Click Next and, on the next wizard screen, click Finish to complete the delegation process, and then close all applications and log off.

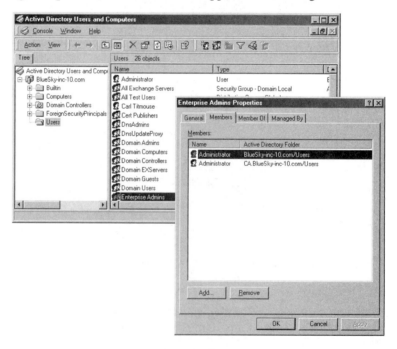

Figure 4.10   Adding the administrator from CA.BlueSky-inc-10.com to the Enterprise Admins

At this point, you have granted the administrator from CA.BlueSky-inc-10.com Exchange Full Administrator permissions, which is required to successfully install an Exchange 2000 server in an existing organization (see Figure 4.11).

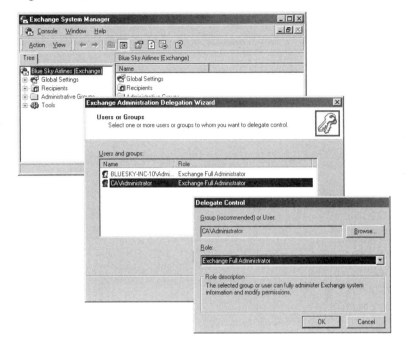

Figure 4.11   Making the administrator from CA.BlueSky-inc-10.com an Exchange Full Administrator

18. On BLUESKY-SRV2, log on as Administrator from the domain BlueSky-inc-10.com (in the Log On To Windows dialog box under Log On To, make sure BLUESKY-INC-10 is selected).

19. Click Start, select Run, and type: **e:\setup\i386\setup.exe /domainprep**, as shown in Figure 4.12.

20. The Welcome To The Microsoft Exchange 2000 Installation Wizard screen appears. Click Next to start the preparation.

21. In the End-User License Agreement dialog box, select I Agree, and then click Next to continue the installation successfully.

22. On the Product Identification wizard screen, under CD Key, enter your CD key, and then click Next.

23. On the Component Selection wizard screen, under Action, in the first row for Microsoft Exchange 2000, make sure DomainPrep is selected, and then click Next.

Figure 4.12   Running DomainPrep in CA.BlueSky-inc-10.com

24. At this point, the Exchange 2000 Setup program is copying required support files to the computer and updates Active Directory using the specified computer account. If a dialog box appears informing you that the domain CA.Bluesky-inc-10.com has been identified as an insecure domain, click OK.

25. On the final wizard screen that informs you about the completion of the preparation, click Finish.

26. Log off and on again as Administrator from CA.BlueSky-inc-10.com (make sure CA is selected in the Log On To list box of the Log On To Windows dialog box).

27. Click Start and select Run to run the command **e:\setup\i386\setup.exe**.

28. On the Welcome To The Microsoft Exchange 2000 Installation Wizard screen, click Next to start the installation.

29. In the End-User License Agreement dialog box, select I Agree, and then click Next.

30. On the Product Identification wizard screen, enter your CD key, and then click Next.

31. Under Action, in the first row for Microsoft Exchange 2000, make sure Typical is selected, and then click Next (see Figure 4.13).

32. On the Licensing Agreement wizard screen, select I Agree That: if you want to successfully install Exchange 2000 Server, and then click Next.

33. In case multiple administrative or routing groups exist in your organization, a Routing Group wizard screen will be displayed prompting you to select the location for the server. Make sure First Administrative Group/First Routing Group is selected, and then click Next. On the Component Summary wizard screen, verify the components included in a typical installation, and then click Next to start the actual installation of Exchange 2000 Server.

34. On the final Microsoft Exchange 2000 Installation Wizard screen, click Finish.

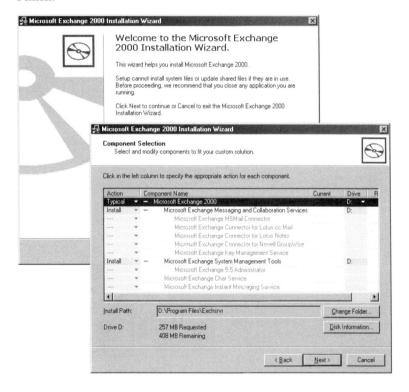

Figure 4.13   Installing Exchange 2000 in a prepared Windows 2000 domain

Exercise Summary

Forest preparation is not necessary if you install Exchange 2000 Server immediately in the domain where the schema master resides. Likewise, you can skip the domain preparation, but domain preparation will be required if you need to support users in domains where you do not plan to install an Exchange 2000 server. The DomainPrep mode creates a global security group named Exchange Domain

Servers and a domain local security group called Exchange Enterprise Servers. Exchange Domain Servers is then added as a member to the Exchange Enterprise Servers group, which grants appropriate rights to the RUS.

Front End/Back End Configurations

Configurations where numerous servers function as front end systems handling incoming client connections and fewer function as back end servers hosting the actual mailboxes are only interesting if you plan to support Internet-based client programs, such as IMAP4 messaging clients or Outlook Web Access. Support of Internet-based clients is the topic of Chapter 11, "Internet-Based Client Access."

Back End Server Configuration

Back end servers are ordinary Exchange 2000 servers hosting mailboxes and public folders. Because these servers are dedicated to handling the actual messaging databases, they are sometimes also called information store servers.

Front End Server Configuration

Front end servers are servers that proxy incoming client connections to the back end systems, which actually contain the users' mailboxes (see Figure 4.14). You configure a front end server by activating the This Is A Front-End Server check box in the server's properties within the Exchange System Manager. No further configuration is required. The information store remains intact on the front end servers, yet Internet-based clients will not access this repository.

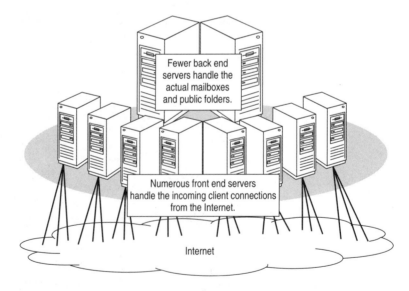

Figure 4.14   Concentration of incoming client connections through front end servers

Advantages of Front End/Back End Architectures

The main advantage of a front end/back end (FE/BE) architecture is the concentration of incoming client connections through front end servers. Every client connection consumes resources on the server and adds traffic to the network. Hence, incoming client connections from millions of potential users would certainly overwhelm a single system. You will need to split the incoming connections across multiple servers, which then concentrate and proxy the connections to the actual back end server where the mailboxes reside.

Front end servers are able to retrieve information about the location of a particular mailbox, or the home server attribute, from Active Directory. This information is available to all of the front end servers, which means that your users can connect to any of the front end servers, which then determine the user's home server and proxy the connection to the correct information store server. Hence, you can use software or hardware load-balancing mechanisms to randomly distribute the load of incoming connections across all of your front end systems. It is also easy to move mailboxes between servers in the back end, for instance, when troubleshooting a particular back end server.

Internet Security Issues

In an FE/BE configuration, you have the option to enforce encrypted connections between front end servers and Internet-based client programs using Secure Sockets Layer (SSL), whereas the servers themselves can communicate nonencrypted over the backbone without any SSL overhead. In this way, processing required for encryption and decryption is only necessary on the front end systems. The workload on the back end servers is not affected.

For maximum security, you can implement advanced firewall configurations between the clients and the front end servers and between the front end and back end systems. Large-scale hosted environments will find this deployment especially appropriate. You can read more about firewall configurations in Chapter 19, "Implementing Advanced Security."

Exercise 5: FE/BE Configuration Options

In this exercise you will configure one computer in your test environment as a front end server and another as the back end system. You will then use Outlook Web Access on the front end server to access your mailbox residing on the back end server running Exchange 2000 Server.

To view a multimedia demonstration that displays how to perform this procedure, run the EX5CH4*.AVI files from the \Exercise_Information\Chapter4 folder on the Supplemental Course Materials CD.

Prerequisites

- You must have successfully completed Exercise 4.
- Log on as Administrator of BlueSky-inc-10.com to BLUESKY-SRV1 running the first Exchange 2000 server in your test environment.
- Log on as Administrator of CA.BlueSky-inc-10.com to BLUESKY-SRV2 running the second Exchange 2000 server in your test environment.

▶ **To configure BLUESKY-SRV2 as a front end Server**

1. On BLUESKY-SRV2, start the System Manager from the Microsoft Exchange program group.
2. Under Administrative Groups, select First Administrative Group, then Servers, and then select BLUESKY-SRV2.
3. Right-click on BLUESKY-SRV2, and then click Properties.
4. Select the This Is A Front-End Server check box and click OK.
5. In the Exchange System Manager dialog box informing you that you need to reboot the server or restart the IIS services, click OK.
6. Close the Exchange System Manager.

   At this point, you have configured BLUESKY-SRV2 as a front end server proxying incoming Internet-client connections to further Exchange 2000 servers in the backbone (see Figure 4.15).

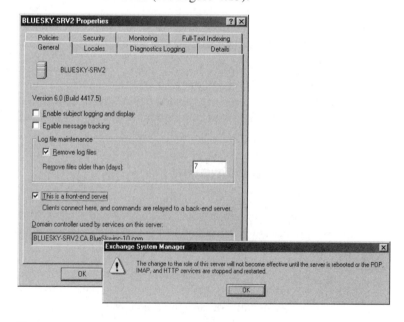

Figure 4.15   Configuring a front end server

7. Click Start, then Run, and, in the Run dialog box, type **iisreset**, and click OK. This will stop and restart all IIS service and put your changes into effect.

8. To create a mailbox for the administrator of CA.BlueSky-inc-10.com, start the Active Directory Users and Computers utility from the Microsoft Exchange program group, select the Users organizational unit from within CA.BlueSky-inc-10.com, right-click on Administrator, and, from the shortcut menu, select Exchange Tasks.

9. On the Welcome page of the Exchange Task Wizard, click Next.

10. On the Available Tasks wizard screen, make sure Create Mailbox is selected, and then click Next.

11. On the Create Mailbox wizard screen, specify the following information:

Alias	AdminCA
Server	Blue Sky Airlines/First Administrative Group/ BLUESKY-SRV1
Mailbox Store	First Storage Group/Mailbox Store (BLUESKY-SRV1)

12. Click Next to create the mailbox on server BLUESKY-SRV1, and, after completion, click Finish in the final wizard screen.

13. On BLUESKY-SRV1, click Start, and then Run again. In the Run dialog box, type **http://bluesky-srv2/exchange/AdminCA**, and click OK to start Outlook Web Access via the front end server BLUESKY-SRV2.

14. If the Internet Connection Wizard appears, select I Want To Set Up My Internet Connection Manually, or I Want To Connect Through A Local Area Network (LAN), and click Next. On the next wizard screen, select I Connect Through A Local Area Network (LAN), and click Next. On the third wizard screen, accept the defaults, and click Next again to reach the next page, where you need to select No to avoid setting up an Internet mail account. Click Next one more time, and then Finish to finally start Internet Explorer.

15. The Enter Network Password dialog box appears because the Administrator account from the BlueSky-inc-10.com domain is not the owner of the mailbox AdminCA (which is the Administrator from the CA.BlueSky-inc-10.com domain). Under User Name, type **CA\Administrator**, and, under Password, type **password**, then click OK.

   At this point, you should be able to verify that you can log on to the AdminCA mailbox using Outlook Web Access. Although it appears as if the resources reside on BLUESKY-SRV2, you are actually working with a mailbox on BLUESKY-SRV1 (see Figure 4.16). If your browser returns an error message, wait several minutes and try again—the Exchange server may still be creating the necessary resources.

16. Close all programs and log off.

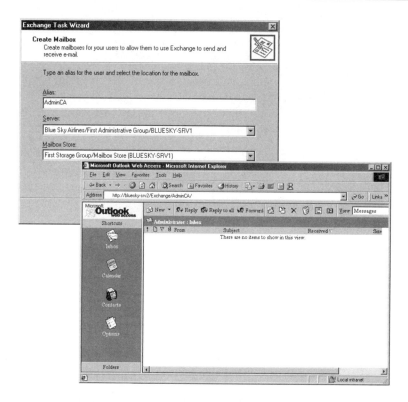

Figure 4.16   FE/BE and Outlook Web Access

Exercise Summary

It is relatively easy to configure a front end server to proxy HTTP, IMAP4, and POP3 traffic to a back end server that actually contains the user's mailbox. The information store on the front end server is not utilized. Instead the front end system accesses the information store server on behalf of the client. The user is not aware that the resources reside on another system somewhere in the provider's network and indeed don't require any direct network connection.

Installing Exchange 2000 Server in a Clustered Environment

The Advanced Server and Datacenter Server editions of Windows 2000 support the cluster technology, which can be used to bind multiple servers so tightly together that they will act as one logical unit. Clustering is a method that provides reliability through complex hardware redundancy. Servers within a cluster interact with each other to provide failover support in emergencies. If a particular process fails on one server, another server takes over, thus continuously providing server-based resources to the network. Clustering can thus significantly improve the reliability of your server-based applications, such as Microsoft SQL Server or Exchange 2000 Server.

Configuration Requirements

The purpose of a cluster is to provide multiple servers to the network as one virtual server. Hence, a cluster requires a LAN-like connection for client access, and the protocol used in the LAN must be TCP/IP. You must bind the nodes of a cluster server using a separate, isolated LAN. The cluster nodes must also share a common central hard disk system, which becomes the storage media for the cluster-aware applications. All nodes can then have access to the cluster resources. In addition, each node requires a local (not shared) hard disk that will host the operating system and the Exchange 2000 Server program files.

Note Use of identical hardware platforms and configurations for all nodes of a particular cluster server is recommended.

The hardware requirements for a cluster server configuration are as follows:

- Central hard disk system, which is shared between the nodes
- Dedicated and isolated LAN link between the nodes
- LAN-like connection and TCP/IP support between cluster and clients
- Local hard disk on each node for the operating system and other program files

The installation of Exchange 2000 Server in a clustered environment is covered in more detail in Chapter 7, "Microsoft Exchange 2000 Server in Clustered Environments."

Chapter Summary

Exchange 2000 is enormously flexible and offers numerous mutually exclusive deployment options. You have to decide between a centralized or decentralized system management. You need to install Exchange 2000 Server in an Active Directory environment on Windows 2000 Server, Windows 2000 Advanced Server, or Windows 2000 Datacenter Server, and you need to be a member of the Domain Admins or Enterprise Admins and Schema Admins groups. For subsequent installations, Schema Admins group membership is not required.

Administrative groups can be used to subdivide the management of resources. It's often applicable to define your administrative topology according to departments or divisions independent of physical resource arrangements. The physical network topology is better reflected through routing groups. Routing groups define message paths across the network. When operating an Exchange 2000 Server environment in mixed mode for backward compatibility with previous Exchange Server versions, a 1:1 relationship between administrative and routing groups and Exchange Server sites is recommended. To gain full system flexibility, you have to switch your organization into native mode.

If your messaging management is separated from Windows 2000 administration, you need to ask the Active Directory administrators to prepare the forest for you by launching ForestPrep prior to installing Exchange 2000 Server. To simplify the deployment of Exchange 2000 Server further, you can run Setup with the option /DomainPrep in each of your domains to add further Exchange-specific configuration information to Active Directory.

You can deploy Exchange 2000 Server in an FE/BE configuration to support large numbers of Internet-based clients. The purpose of an FE/BE configuration is to concentrate incoming client connections through numerous front end servers, thus reducing the processing overhead on the back end systems. You can also install Exchange 2000 Server in a clustered environment to provide reliability through complex hardware redundancy. The purpose of a cluster is to provide multiple servers to the network as one virtual server.

Review

The following review questions can help you determine if you have sufficiently familiarized yourself with the material covered in this chapter. You can find the answers to these questions at the end of this book in Appendix A, "Questions and Answers."

1. Your computer network consists of multiple domains. Most of them are grouped together in a single domain tree, but one domain tree exists in a separate forest for political reasons. You now have to implement an Exchange 2000 organization for all your users. How can you best accomplish this task?

2. Your computer network consists of multiple domains. All domains reside in a single forest. Where do you need to install Exchange 2000 Server first?

3. You are in charge of a complex messaging environment spread across several international locations. You plan to implement decentralized system management, giving all locations Full Administrative permissions over their own resources. How would you structure the Exchange 2000 organization to achieve this goal?

4. What is the purpose of a routing group?

5. What are the restrictions that apply when operating an Exchange 2000 organization in mixed mode?

6. Your messaging management is separated from Windows 2000 administration. Consequently, you need to ask your Windows 2000 administrator to prepare the domain environment for you prior to installing Exchange 2000. What must the Windows 2000 administrator do to prepare the domain environment?

7. What is the difference between Exchange Full Administrator and Exchange Administrator permissions?

8. You are planning to deploy Exchange 2000 Server in a hosted environment that has to support more than 10,000 Internet users accessing their mailboxes primarily through Outlook Web Access. Consequently, you plan to implement an FE/BE configuration. What do you have to do to configure a front end server?

C H A P T E R   5

Installing Microsoft Exchange 2000 Server

About This Chapter

The Setup program of Microsoft Exchange 2000 Server is a highly structured utility that makes the installation task remarkably easy. This program provides a structured user interface in the form of an installation wizard that guides you through the various installation steps. Depending on the options you select, Setup checks whether the prerequisites are met and prevents you from continuing if they are not. Setup records its activities, such as the copying of files, in a specific log file named EXCHANGE SERVER SETUP PROGRESS.LOG, which you can find in the root directory (C:\) after an installation. You can use this file as a diagnostic tool should a setup procedure end unsuccessfully.

For many administrators, an applications setup program makes an important first impression. How you use the setup program, however, depends on whether you want to perform a new installation, add components, or repair an existing system. Most setup programs also support unattended installations using a setup initialization file. Such initialization files inherently are perfect installation documentation.

This chapter deals with the Setup program of Exchange 2000 Server and various postinstallation considerations. Lesson 1 covers in detail the installation types and options that you can select during an installation. In Lesson 2, you can read more about issues you should consider after a setup procedure is completed successfully, such as the delegation of permissions to other Exchange 2000 Server administrators.

Before You Begin

To complete this chapter:

- Reinstall your test environment according to the descriptions given in the "Getting Started" section of "About This Book." Promote your server BLUESKY-SRV1 to a domain controller, but do not install Exchange 2000 Server yet. The setup procedures for Exchange 2000 Server differ from the "Getting Started" section.

- Have a general understanding of Microsoft Windows 2000 networking technologies, the Active Directory directory service, and the delegation of administrative permissions in an Active Directory forest.

Lesson 1: Installation Types

The Setup program of Exchange 2000 Server has a huge job to accomplish, including the installation of files on your server's hard disk, the update of registry entries, possibly the extension of the Active Directory schema, and also the handling of errors (for instance, if the installation media is removed from the CD-ROM drive during the process of copying files). The overall setup process is accomplished in several phases that are different between the first server installation and subsequent installations in a forest.

This lesson introduces all the important installation types you encounter when installing Exchange 2000 Server. You already performed a first server installation and an installation of a subsequent server to accomplish the practical exercises in Chapters 1 through 4. Therefore, these installation types are covered from a more theoretical point of view here. Probably more interesting is the unattended Setup handling installation tasks without any user interaction, which is a valuable installation feature also known as silent setup.

At the end of this lesson, you will be able to:

- List the steps necessary to complete a first server installation.
- Describe the differences between a first server installation and an installation of subsequent servers.
- Explain the process of upgrading a previous version of Exchange Server.
- Perform an unattended installation of Exchange 2000 Server.

Estimated time to complete this lesson: 60 minutes

First Server Installation

As outlined in Chapter 4, you need to make several preparations before running the Setup program. Otherwise, you will be greeted with an unpleasant Microsoft Exchange 2000 Installation Wizard message box. This message box appears, for instance, when you attempt to install Exchange 2000 Server on a computer that is not part of a Windows 2000 domain (see Figure 5.1). The same error message is displayed if Active Directory cannot be accessed. If the Network News Transfer Protocol (NNTP) service was not installed in Windows 2000, on the other hand, the error message is "The NNTP Component of Microsoft Internet Information Services (IIS) Is Not Installed." To correct the former problem, make sure your server is part of a Windows 2000 domain, that a domain controller is available, and that you can access Active Directory with the required permissions. To correct the latter, install the NNTP service via the Add/Remove Programs program from the Control Panel and then repeat the Exchange 2000 Server installation. Setup problems may also be encountered if a \Program Files\Exchsrvr\Mdbdata folder containing old information store database files exists on the partition where you intend to install Exchange 2000 Server. Rename this folder or delete the old database files before starting the Setup program again. You can find more information about the installation preparation in Chapter 4, "Planning the Microsoft Exchange 2000 Server Installation."

Note   If possible, promote your computer to a domain controller before installing Exchange 2000 Server.

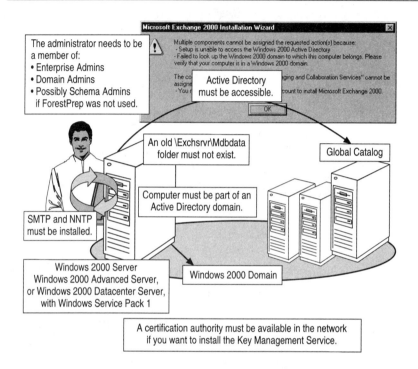

Figure 5.1   Prerequisites for the Exchange 2000 Setup program

Installation Steps

Provided that you did not prepare the Active Directory forest using /ForestPrep beforehand, Setup needs to extend Active Directory during the first server installation. During this process, the directory object for your Exchange 2000 organization is created; hence, Setup prompts you for the organization name. Likewise, the default administrative and routing groups are generated, so you are not prompted to add your server to existing groups. It is important to note that the default names are always First Administrative Group and First Routing Group. It is possible to rename them later. Refer to the "About This Book" section for a description of the steps required to perform a first server installation.

Note   The name of your Exchange 2000 organization cannot be changed after the installation.

Setup Options

When launching the Setup program, you will reach the Components To Install wizard screen after the welcome screen, a second page for the end-user license agreement, which you need to accept to continue the installation, and a third wizard screen where you need to enter your product key. The Components To Install wizard screen lists the Exchange 2000 components that you can install on your server. By default, under Action for Microsoft Exchange 2000, Setup suggests a Typical installation. You can select Custom if you wish to determine the details of the installation manually, such as individual features to be installed and the directories to receive the program files. Experienced administrators usually prefer this option.

Setup offers the following installation options:

- **Custom.**   Allows you to select individual components and to leave out components normally included in a typical installation. For instance, you can use this option to install only the Microsoft Exchange System Management Tools, which are useful for setting up a dedicated management workstation.

- **Minimum.**   Installs Microsoft Exchange 2000 with the minimum number of files needed for Microsoft Exchange Messaging and Collaboration Services. Because administrative utilities are not installed when selecting this option, it is not recommended for a first server installation.

- **Typical.**   Installs Microsoft Exchange 2000 with most common settings (Microsoft Exchange Messaging and Collaboration Services and Microsoft Exchange System Management Tools) and copies the most commonly used files to the computer's hard disk. This is the default option.

Subsequent Server Installations

The installation options (Custom, Minimum, and Typical) are the same for first server and subsequent installations. However, whereas a first server installation asks you whether to join an existing Exchange Server 5.5 organization or to create a new one and then prompts you for the organization name, a subsequent installation has to ask for different information. The most significant difference may be the selection of an administrative group and a routing group for subsequent servers if you have created additional groups in your organization beforehand. A subsequent installation in a prepared domain environment was introduced in Exercise 4 of Chapter 4, "Planning the Microsoft Exchange 2000 Server Installation."

Installation Steps

A subsequent installation may display the following wizard screens:

- **Welcome.**   To introduce you to the installation task
- **End-User License Agreement.**   To accept the End-User License Agreement, which is required to continue the installation

- **Product Key.** To enter the product key of your Exchange 2000 Server copy
- **Components To Install.** To select the list of Exchange 2000 components you want to install
- **Licensing.** To inform you that you need to purchase a Client Access License for every client that will access your Exchange 2000 server
- **Organization Name.** To enter the name of the Exchange 2000 organization this server will join
- **Administrative Group.** To specify the administrative group to which to add this server (this wizard screen only appears if additional administrative groups have been created)
- **Routing Group.** To specify the routing group to which to add this server (this wizard screen only appears if additional routing groups exist in the administrative group that was specified in the Administrative Group wizard screen)
- **Component Summary.** To verify and correct specified options and to start the actual installation

In-Place Upgrade

During an in-place upgrade installation, you upgrade an existing Exchange server to Exchange 2000 Server. This involves different preparation steps depending on the situation. For instance, if you are running Exchange Server on Microsoft Windows NT Server 4.0, you will need to upgrade the operating system to Windows 2000 Server with Service Pack 1 first. If you are using Exchange Server 5.0 (or even 4.0), you will need to update your Exchange Server to version 5.5 with Service Pack 3. The in-place upgrade is only supported over Exchange Server 5.5. Still, you aren't ready for the upgrade yet. You have to configure connection agreements using the Active Directory Connector (ADC) before you can install Exchange 2000 Server.

Windows NT Primary Domain Controllers

It is very likely that you will encounter a Lightweight Directory Access Protocol (LDAP) port conflict when you upgrade a Windows NT primary domain controller (PDC) running Exchange Server 5.5 to Windows 2000. Active Directory claims ownership of the LDAP port and so does the Exchange Server 5.5 directory service. To resolve this port conflict, you need to change the LDAP port number that the Exchange Server 5.5 directory service is using within the Exchange Administrator program. Expand the container that represents your site, then the Configuration container, and then the Protocols container. Double-click the LDAP (Directory) Site Defaults object. Now, you can change the port number to a value other than 389. Don't forget to restart Exchange Server to put the changes into effect.

Note It is advisable, but not required, to change the port number before upgrading the operating system to Windows 2000 Server.

After you have changed the LDAP port number and upgraded the operating system to Windows 2000 Server SP1, you need to set up and configure the ADC connection agreements using the customized port number. The LDAP port in the ADC connection agreement must match the LDAP port of Exchange Server 5.5. As soon as you have verified that the directory replication is working, you are ready to upgrade to Exchange 2000 Server. You can read more about the ADC and connection agreements in Chapter 6, "Coexistence with Previous Microsoft Exchange Server Versions."

Installation Steps

The in-place upgrade is the most inflexible installation type. The only task you need to perform is repeatedly clicking Next to confirm wizard screen after wizard screen. You cannot add or remove components or change the installation directory. If your in-place upgrade is also a first server installation of Exchange 2000 Server in your existing Exchange Server organization, the Active Directory schema must be updated. The ForestPrep phase of the Setup program will generate administrative groups and routing groups that match your Exchange Server 5.5 site topology. It is a good idea to run Setup using the /ForestPrep and /DomainPrep switches prior to an upgrade to Exchange 2000 Server. You can read more about /ForestPrep and /DomainPrep in Chapter 4, "Planning the Microsoft Exchange 2000 Server Installation."

Note Although you cannot change installation options during an in-place upgrade, you can add or remove components later when launching Setup in maintenance mode, as explained in Lesson 2. However, if Exchange 2000 does not support connectors configured on your existing server, such as a Professional Office System (PROFS) connector, those connectors will not be available after the upgrade.

Installations in International Environments

Exchange 2000 Server comes in six different languages—English, French, German, Italian, Japanese, and Spanish. However, it is only possible to install the international versions of Exchange 2000 Server on their corresponding versions of Windows 2000 Server—with the exception of the English version, which is generally supported in any combination. For instance, it is possible to install the French version of Exchange 2000 Server on an English version of Windows 2000 Server, and vice versa. However, you cannot install the French Exchange 2000 Server version on a German Windows 2000 Server. In addition, most Exchange 2000 Server versions support the Windows 2000 Multilanguage Version, which is available only through volume licensing programs. This is a specialized version of Windows 2000 Server that allows changes in the language of the interface without installation of additional software components.

Choosing a Server Platform

In international environments, it still might be advisable to deploy the English versions of Windows 2000 Server and Exchange 2000 Server. The client base is not affected and may use any language version available. If your administrators are able and willing to master the English language, consider the following advantages:

- The English versions of Windows 2000 Server and Exchange 2000 Server are supported in any international environment, which allows you to standardize the Exchange 2000 Server platform across all geographical locations.

- It is easy for your administrators to collaborate, and it is possible to outline and document common maintenance procedures for all deployed server systems.

- English bug fixes and service packs are usually available up to 4 weeks earlier than international versions.

- It is easier to get technical assistance, for instance, through Microsoft Technet, because most discussions and articles deal with the English product versions, and you can search for keywords without the need to translate them back into English first.

- Many advanced Exchange-related solutions of third-party vendors and programming samples are available in English versions only.

To support multilingual MAPI-based clients, you need to install appropriate language support on your Global Catalog servers (Control Panel, Regional Options, General tab, and then Language). You also need to edit the Global Catalog's Registry if you want to support additional sort orders. Add REG_DWORD values to the following Registry key and set them to the desired locale ID values:

```
HKEY_LOCAL_MACHINE

 \Software

 \Microsoft

  \NTDS

   \Language
```

By default, Active Directory supports English sort orders, which correspond to the default value called Language 00000408, which is set to the language ID 0x00000409. If you want to support Russian, for instance, create an additional REG_DWORD value, name it Language 00000419, and set it to the hexadecimal value of 0x00000419.

Table 5.1 details the language codes that you may use with Windows 2000 Server (consult your product documentation if your language is not listed):

Table 5.1 Language Codes for Windows 2000 Server

Language	Language Code
Bulgarian	00000402
Croatian	0000041A
Czech	00000405
Danish	00000406
Dutch (Standard)	00000413
Dutch (Belgian)	00000813
English (United States)	00000409
English (United Kingdom)	00000809
English (Canadian)	00001009
English (NewZealand)	00001409
English (Australian)	00000C09
Finnish	0000040B
French (Standard)	0000040C
French (Belgian)	0000080C
French (Swiss)	0000100C
French (Canadian)	00000C0C
German (Standard)	00000407
German (Swiss)	00000807
German (Austrian)	00000C07
Greek	00000408
Hungarian	0000040E
Icelandic	0000040F
English (Irish)	00001809
Italian (Standard)	00000410
Italian (Swiss)	00000810
Norwegian (Bokmal)	00000414
Norwegian (Nynorsk)	00000814
Polish	00000415
Portuguese (Standard)	00000816
Portuguese (Brazilian)	00000416
Romanian	00000418
Russian	00000419

Table 5.1 Language Codes for Windows 2000 Server *(continued)*

Language	Language Code
Slovak	0000041B
Slovenian	00000424
Spanish (Mexican)	0000080A
Spanish (traditional sort order)	0000040A
Spanish (modern sort order)	00000C0A
Swedish	0000041D
Turkish	0000041F

Unattended Setup Mode

It is possible to customize the setup process by using a predefined initialization file. This file can supply all the information needed for an automatic installation, making it appealing to administrators who need to deploy many Exchange servers. No additional user input is necessary and Setup can run unattended. This is especially useful if you want to delegate the task of installing Exchange 2000 Server to less experienced administrators. As mentioned at the beginning of this chapter, it is also a benefit in documenting the server installation because the initialization file details precisely the installed Exchange 2000 Server components, and it can be used at any time to exactly repeat the server installation (see Figure 5.2).

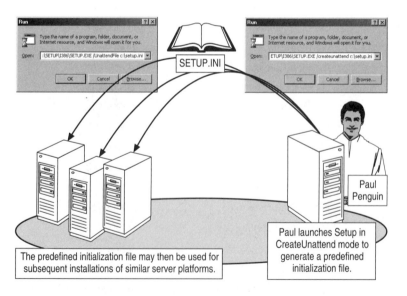

Figure 5.2   Setup in CreateUnattend and UnattendFile mode

Creating an Initialization File

The good news is that you don't need to be familiar with a specific syntax to create a predefined initialization file because Setup can accomplish this job for you. Let's say you want to generate an initialization file named SETUP.INI. Use the e:\Setup\i386\SETUP.EXE /CreateUnattend c:\SETUP.INI (where e:\ stands for your CD-ROM drive) command, which will display the wizard screens according to the given situation (first server or subsequent installation), but will not install the actual components. Instead, Setup creates the initialization file at the specified location, which you may then use for an unattended setup elsewhere. You may even use the /CreateUnattend switch to demonstrate or practice installing Exchange 2000 Server without actually setting up the system. Only the last wizard screen, Completing The Microsoft Exchange 2000 Wizard, indicates that you created an initialization file instead of seriously installing the system.

Note The specified initialization file must not exist prior to launching Setup in CreateUnattend mode.

Encrypting an Initialization File

The Setup initialization file is a standard text file containing numerous entries for individual Exchange 2000 components. This file may contain passwords (such as the Key Management Service password), which may in this way be disclosed to unauthorized administrators. To prevent exposing security-related information, encrypt the initialization file using the /EncryptedMode Setup switch (e:\Setup\i386\SETUP.EXE /EncryptedMode /CreateUnattend c:\SETUP.INI). Setup will run as normal, but creates an encrypted file.

Using an Initialization File

As soon as you have generated an appropriate initialization file for your purposes, running Setup is remarkably easy. Specify the command-line switch /UnattendFile and your predefined initialization file (e:\Setup\i386\SETUP.EXE /UnattendFile c:\SETUP.INI), and Setup will install Exchange 2000 Server without any user interaction. The switch /UnattendFile displays a user interface showing information about the progress of the automated installation.

Exercise 1: Installing Exchange 2000 in Unattended Mode

In this exercise you will examine the available options for an unattended setup of Exchange 2000 Server. You will create an initialization file and use it to set up BLUESKY-SRV1.

To view a multimedia demonstration that displays how to perform this procedure, run the EX1CH5*.AVI files from the \Exercise_Information\Chapter5 folder on the Supplemental Course Materials CD.

Prerequisites

- Log on as Administrator to BLUESKY-SRV1.

- Insert the Exchange 2000 Server installation CD in the CD-ROM drive.

▶ **To perform an unattended install of Exchange**

1. Click Start, select Run, and in the Run dialog box, type
   E:\Setup\i386\SETUP.EXE /? (where E stands for your CD-ROM drive).

2. Click OK to display the Microsoft Exchange 2000 – Usage dialog box, which
   informs you about all the available Setup options.

   At this point, you can examine the individual command-line switches.
   /CreateUnattend and /UnattendFile are particularly important for this exercise
   (see Figure 5.3).

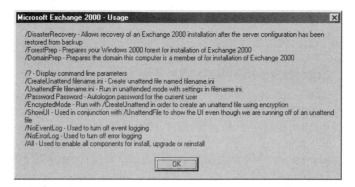

Figure 5.3   The Microsoft Exchange 2000 – Usage dialog box

3. Click OK.

4. Click Start again, select Run, and, in the Run dialog box, type
   E:\Setup\i386\SETUP.EXE /CreateUnattend c:\SETUP.INI, and click OK.

5. On the Welcome wizard screen that appears, click Next.

6. On the End-User License Agreement wizard screen, accept the licensing
   agreement by selecting I Agree, and then click Next.

7. On the Product Identification wizard screen, enter the product key of your
   Exchange 2000 Server installation CD, and then click Next.

8. On the Component Selection wizard screen, under Action for Microsoft
   Exchange 2000, make sure Typical is selected, and then click Next.

9. On the Installation Type wizard screen, make sure Create A New Exchange
   Organization is selected, and then click Next.

10. On the Organization Name wizard screen, under Organization Name, type **Blue Sky Airlines**, and then click Next.

11. On the Licensing Agreement wizard screen, accept the licensing agreement by selecting I Agree That, and then click Next.

12. On the Component Summary wizard screen, review your selections, and then click Next.

    At this point, you have successfully created the initialization file named SETUP.INI, which can be found in the root directory of your C drive (see Figure 5.4). You may open this file in Notepad to examine its contents.

13. On the final wizard screen, click Finish.

Figure 5.4   Creating SETUP.INI

14. Click Start again, select Run, and in the Run dialog box, type **E:\Setup\i386\SETUP.EXE /UnattendFile c:\SETUP.INI**, and click OK.

    At this point, the Microsoft Exchange 2000 Installation Wizard displays the Component Progress wizard screen immediately, informing you about the process of installing Exchange 2000 Server according to the settings specified in the predefined SETUP.INI file (see Figure 5.5).

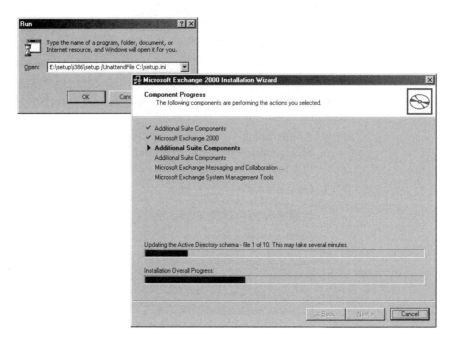

Figure 5.5 Installing Exchange 2000 unattended

Exercise Summary

It is easy to generate a SETUP.INI file using the Microsoft Exchange 2000 Installation Wizard. Launch Setup in /CreateUnattend mode, make your selections, and Setup will generate the file for you. You can then distribute the file to the administrator who is actually supposed to perform the installation. For convenience, place an appropriate Setup shortcut in an e-mail message. This administrator does not need to be familiar with the task of installing Exchange 2000 Server because no user interaction is required to set up the system. The unattended installation procedure is also essential for software deployments using Microsoft Systems Management Server (SMS).

Lesson 2: Postinstallation Considerations

After an installation, you need to perform a number of routine tasks, such as the delegation of administrative permissions and the protection of server resources and share points against unauthorized access. It is also advisable to perform a full system backup, including the system state, using the Windows 2000 Backup program to save the modified Registry and Active Directory information. Because the various Exchange 2000 backup strategies are covered in detail in Chapter 20, "Microsoft Exchange 2000 Server Maintenance and Troubleshooting," this topic is not further discussed in this lesson.

This lesson presents the tasks you should take into consideration once a server has been installed, including the delegation of administrative permissions and various concerns about the security of server files and directories. You are also introduced to a simple method of repairing an Exchange 2000 installation.

At the end of this lesson, you will be able to:

- Install the Exchange 2000 management utilities
- Delegate administrative roles and permissions to other administrators
- Specify default and minimum network access permissions on server share points
- Describe Exchange 2000 service dependencies
- Add Exchange 2000 Server components to an existing installation
- Add server components using Setup in maintenance mode

Estimated time to complete this lesson: 90 minutes

Installing the Exchange 2000 Management Programs

During a typical or custom installation, you can install the Exchange 2000 System Management utilities on any computer running Windows 2000 including Windows 2000 Professional. You just need to install the Microsoft Exchange System Management Tools on a workstation PC for flexible administration of distributed Exchange 2000 servers (see Figure 5.6).

Management Programs on Windows 2000 Professional

Many administrators appreciate the convenience of managing their environment from the desktop. As long as you have administrative access to Active Directory, you can display and change the configuration of most of your resources. Remote procedure call (RPC) communication is also required to use the management tools to their full extent, as illustrated in Chapter 3, "Microsoft Exchange 2000 Server Architecture."

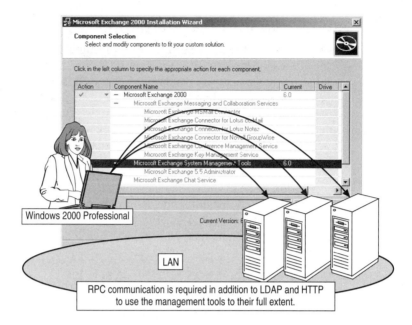

Figure 5.6   Installing the Exchange System
Management Tools on Windows 2000 Professional

It might be necessary to install multiple copies of the Exchange System Manager
on networks with multiple network segments if routers between links filter RPC
communications. You can use the RPCPing utility to test the RPC communication between computers. If RPCPing works fine, the Exchange System Manager
will work as well. RPCPing is discussed in Chapter 10, "MAPI-Based Clients in
a Novell NetWare Environment."

Windows 2000 Tools Extensions

As Setup installs management utilities based on Microsoft Management Console
(MMC), such as the System Manager and related snap-ins, it also extends the
Active Directory Users and Computers tool to provide Exchange-specific features. The original Windows 2000 Backup utility is replaced with an Exchange
2000 version that allows you to perform online backups of the information store
databases, as described in Chapter 20, "Microsoft Exchange 2000 Server Maintenance and Troubleshooting."

Management Programs and Outlook 2000

The Exchange System Management Tools come with a newer version of Messaging Application Protocol Interface (MAPI) components that cause Outlook 2000
to display a warning message because of a version conflict with the MAPI core
files, specifically the MAPI32.DLL. Because Outlook attempts to replace the
newer Exchange 2000 MAPI32.DLL with its older version, it is not advisable to
install Outlook 2000 and the Exchange System Management Tools on the same

workstation. That is also the reason why your test environment requires a dedicated workstation in addition to two servers. However, if you want to use both Outlook 2000 and the Exchange System Manager on the same machine, make sure you install Exchange System Manager first. Otherwise, the version conflict may occur, in which case you need to rename MAPI32.DLL and reinstall Outlook 2000.

Assignment of Administrative Roles and Permissions

The Exchange System Manager includes a feature called Exchange Administration Delegation Wizard that simplifies permission management. Similar to the Delegation Wizard of Windows 2000, you can use this tool to delegate appropriate permissions to other Exchange administrators. You used the Exchange Administration Delegation Wizard during Exercise 4 of Chapter 4, "Planning the Microsoft Exchange 2000 Server Installation."

Assigning Administrative Roles

As discussed in Chapter 4, you can organize your system management based on the Exchange organization and its administrative groups. To test this on BLUESKY-SRV1, launch the Exchange System Manager, right-click on the organization object named Blue Sky Airlines (Exchange), choose Properties, and select the Display Administrative Groups check box. This is required to launch the Exchange Administration Delegation Wizard at the level of the First Administrative Group. After you close the Properties dialog box and restart the Exchange System Manager, right-click on Blue Sky Airlines (Exchange) and, from the shortcut menu, select Delegate Control to launch the Exchange Administration Delegation Wizard. Click Next on the welcome screen to reach the Users Or Groups wizard screen, where you can click Add to specify one or more users to whom to delegate the role of an Exchange administrator (that is, Exchange Full Administrator, Exchange Administrator, and Exchange View Only Administrator). The steps are similar when delegating control for the First Administrative Group. You can read more about permissions management in Chapter 19, "Implementing Advanced Security."

Permission Inheritance

When launching the Exchange Administration Delegation Wizard for an administrative group (for example, by right-clicking on First Administrative Group and choosing Delegate Control), you will notice one or more accounts on the Users Or Group wizard screen. These accounts inherited the role of an Exchange administrator and include the account that was used to install the first Exchange 2000 server. If you select one of these accounts and click Remove, an Exchange System Manager dialog box will appear, informing you that the account cannot be edited or deleted because it was inherited from the organization object. To edit or remove these kinds of Exchange administrators, you need to launch the wizard at the organization level.

Permission inheritance simplifies the task of delegating administrative roles and managing permissions for the following reasons:

- Manual assignment of roles and permissions can be concentrated on a single parent object instead of numerous child objects. Child objects inherit the settings automatically.

- Permission changes can be applied easily via the parent object.

- Roles and permissions attached to the parent object are applied consistently to all child objects.

Disabling the Inheritance Feature

The inheritance feature allows you to quickly configure permissions and roles, but in some situations you may want to customize the inheritance of security-related permissions. For instance, you may want to prevent one administrator specified at the organization level from managing a particular administrative group without affecting other administrative groups. To disable the inheritance feature for a particular directory object, such as the BLUESKY-SRV1 server object within the First Administrative Group, right-click on it, and select Properties to display the corresponding Properties dialog box. Switch to the Security property page, and deselect the Allow Inheritable Permissions From Parent To Propagate To This Object check box. In the Security dialog box that appears, click Copy if you want to copy security-related settings from the parent before adjusting the settings manually. Click Remove to clear all settings, in which case you need to add your accounts and possibly others to the list of accounts with permissions.

Exchange 2000-Related Permissions

When you examine the Security property page of a given Exchange 2000 directory object, there is a large list of Windows 2000 and Exchange 2000-related permissions that you can assign to individual user accounts and groups. The Exchange-related permissions are also called extended permissions because they add extended features to the standard set of Windows 2000 permissions for each Exchange 2000 object.

Note   The configuration of Windows 2000 and Exchange 2000-related permissions gives you total control over the individual access privileges of users and groups. However, such fine-grained configuration is seldom required and introduces the risk of configuration problems. Whenever possible, you should use the Exchange Administration Delegation Wizard to specify security-related settings.

Depending on the selected object, Exchange 2000 allows you to define the following extended permissions:

- **Add PF To Admin Group.**   Specifies whether the account has the permission to add a public folder to an administrative group.

- **Administer Information Store.** Specifies whether the account has the permission to manage the information store service.

- **Create Named Properties In The Information Store.** Specifies whether the account has the permission to create named properties, such as display name, given name, last name deleted item flags, and so forth.

- **Create Public Folder.** Specifies whether the account has the permission to create a public folder under the currently selected folder.

- **Create Top-Level Public Folder.** Specifies whether the account has the permission to create top-level public folders.

- **Full Store Access.** Specifies whether the account has the permission to get full access to the information store databases.

- **Mail-Enable Public Folder.** Specifies whether the account has the permission to mail-enable a public folder.

- **Modify Public Folder ACL.** Specifies whether the account has the permission to modify a public folder's access control list (ACL).

- **Modify Public Folder Admin ACL.** Specifies whether the account has the permission to administer public folder ACLs.

- **Modify Public Folder Deleted Item Retention.** Specifies whether the account has the permission to modify the length of time (in days) that items deleted from the public folder are retained.

- **Modify Public Folder Expiry.** Specifies whether the account has the permission to modify the size limit of the public folder.

- **Modify Public Folder Quotas.** Specifies whether the account has the permission to set public folder quotas.

- **Modify Public Folder Replica List.** Specifies whether the account has the permission to modify the replica list. To successfully configure public folder replication, this permission is required for both the administrative group and the public database to which the replica should be added.

- **Open Mail Send Queue.** Specifies whether the account has the permission to open the Mail Send queue used for queuing messages to and from the information store.

- **Read All Metabase Properties.** Specifies whether the account has the permission to read the Internet Information Services (IIS) metabase, which was covered in Chapter 2, "Integration with Microsoft Windows 2000."

- **Remove PF To Admin Group.** Specifies whether the account has the permission to remove a public folder from an administrative group.

- **View Information Store Status.** Specifies whether the account has the permission to view information store status information, such as information about currently logged on users and allocated resources.

Group Accounts and Exchange Administration

The permissions model of Exchange 2000 is entirely based on the security model for Windows 2000 Active Directory. This implies that you can rely on Windows 2000 security groups for Exchange 2000 administration, which is especially advantageous if you are in charge of configuring roles and permissions for numerous administrators. It is much easier to manage group permissions instead of redundant permissions for individual users. For instance, if you define a global security group for the default First Administrative Group and assign this group the required permissions to manage the Exchange 2000 Server resources, you can activate and deactivate Exchange administrators easily by adding and removing them from this group within the Active Directory Users and Computers utility.

In native mode, Windows 2000 allows you to configure the following security groups:

- **Domain Local.**   This group type can contain user accounts, global groups, and universal groups from any domain as well as domain local groups from the same domain.

- **Global.**   This group type can contain user accounts and global groups from the same domain.

- **Universal.**   This group type is only used in Active Directory forests that contain multiple domains. It can contain user accounts, global groups, and universal groups from any domain.

You can find more information about Windows 2000 groups in Chapter 13, "Creating and Managing Recipients."

Note   During a first server installation, the setup routine automatically creates two default group accounts, Exchange Domain Servers and Exchange Enterprise Servers, in the Users container of the domain tree for your organization. The Exchange Domain Servers group is used to grant the LocalSystem account of computers running Exchange 2000 Server full rights in the Exchange 2000 organization.

Exercise 2: Verifying Incorrect Security Information

In this exercise you will check whether the Exchange Administration Delegation Wizard displays correct and complete security information. You will then set a special Registry key for the Exchange System Manager to view more accurate data.

To view a multimedia demonstration that displays how to perform this procedure, launch the EX2CH5*.AVI files, which you can install on your computer by running the self-extracting executable from the \Exercise_Information\Chapter14 folder on the Supplemental Course Materials CD.

Prerequisites

- Complete Exercise 1, earlier in this chapter.

- Log on as Administrator to BLUESKY-SRV1.

▶ **To check and countercheck security-related information in Exchange System Manager**

1. Start the Exchange System Manager from the Microsoft Exchange program group.

2. Right-click on Blue Sky Airlines (Exchange) and then select Delegate Control.

3. In the welcome screen of the Exchange Administration Delegation Wizard, click Next.

4. In the Users Or Groups wizard screen, verify that BLUESKY-INC-10\Administrator is listed as an Exchange Full Administrator.

5. Select BLUESKY-INC-10\Administrator and then click Edit.

6. In the Delegate Control dialog box, select Exchange View Only Administrator, and then click OK.

7. Verify that BLUESKY-INC-10\Administrator is now listed as an Exchange View Only Administrator in the Users Or Groups wizard screen (see Figure 5.7). Click Next.

8. In the final screen of the Exchange Administration Delegation Wizard, click Finish. Though it seems as if you should lose the ability to change the Exchange 2000 configuration, you will soon discover otherwise.

9. Right-click on Blue Sky Airlines (Exchange) again and select Properties.

10. Click on the Change Mode button. Confirm the Exchange System Manager dialog box informing you that this is an irreversible process by clicking OK. Verify that the change was accomplished successfully, and then click OK.

11. Right-click on Blue Sky Airlines (Exchange) again, select Delegate Control, confirm the welcome screen by clicking on the Next button, and then, in the Users Or Groups wizard screen, verify that BLUESKY-INC-10\Administrator is indeed listed as an Exchange View Only Administrator. Click Cancel.

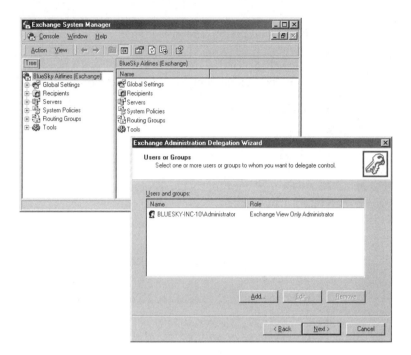

Figure 5.7   Granting the Administrator View Only permissions

Although you are listed as an administrator who does not have the permissions to change the configuration, you are able to switch the organization into native mode or perform any other desired management procedure because your account is a member of the Enterprise Admins group.

12. Click the Start button, point to Programs, then to Administrative Tools, and then select Active Directory Sites and Services.

13. Open the View menu and select the Show Services Node option.

14. In the console tree, expand the Services container, expand the Microsoft Exchange child container, and note that the organization object called Blue Sky Airlines is located underneath.

15. Right-click on the Services container, and then, from the shortcut menu, select Properties.

16. Switch to the Security tab, select Enterprise Admins (BLUESKY-INC-10\ Enterprise Admins), and then, under Permissions, verify that this security group has inherited Full Control for this object (see Figure 5.8). These permissions in turn are further inherited by all child containers including the

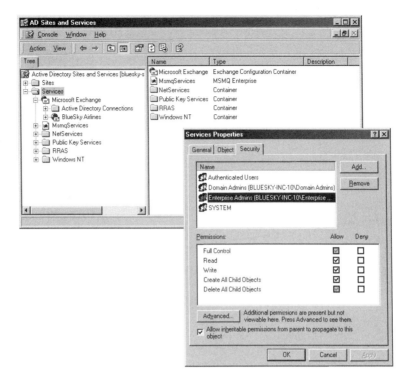

Figure 5.8   Enterprise Admin permissions at the Services container object

Exchange 2000 organization, which is the reason why you are able to manage the environment (although the Exchange Administration Delegation Wizard displays you as a view only administrator).

17. Click OK and close Active Directory Sites and Services.

18. Switch back to the Exchange System Manager, right-click Blue Sky Airlines (Exchange), select Properties, and verify that a Security tab is not provided.

19. Close the Exchange System Manager.

20. Click the Start button, point to Run, and, in the Run dialog box, type **Regedit**, and then click OK.

21. Open the following key in the Registry Editor: HKEY_CURRENT_USER\Software\Microsoft\Exchange\ExAdmin.

22. Open the Edit menu, point to New, and select DWORD Value. Name the new value **ShowSecurityPage**, double-click on it, type **1** under Value Data (see Figure 5.9), and then click OK. Close the Registry Editor.

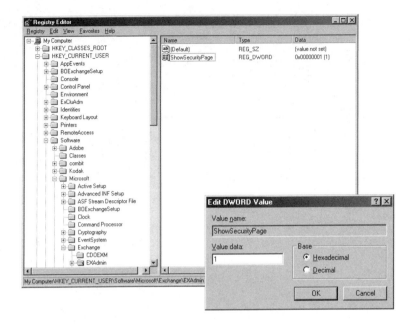

Figure 5.9   Setting the ShowSecurityPage Registry key

Note   The ShowSecurityPage Registry value causes the Exchange System Manager to display the Security tab on all configuration objects. If this value is not present or is set to 0, the Security tab is available only on Address List objects, mailbox and public stores, and top-level public folder hierarchies. According to the HKEY_CURRENT_USER hive, ShowSecurityPage only affects the current user account.

---

23. In the Microsoft Exchange program group, click Exchange System Manager.

24. Right-click on the organization object Blue Sky Airlines (Exchange), and then select Properties.

25. In the Blue Sky Airlines Properties dialog box, click the Security tab.

26. Select the Administrator (BLUESKY-INC-10\Administrator) entry under Name, and, under Permissions, examine the individual permissions granted. These permissions correspond to the set of rights for a view only administrator (see Figure 5.10).

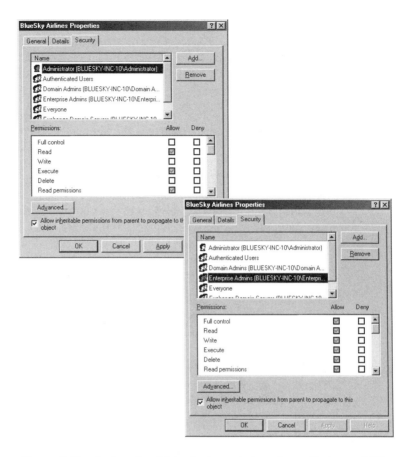

Figure 5.10   Assigned and inherited permissions for an Exchange 2000 organization

27. Select the Enterprise Admins (BLUESKY-INC-10\Enterprise Admins). You will be able to determine that this security group has inherited Full Control for the organization (with the Receive As and Send As rights explicitly denied).

28. Click OK and close the Exchange System Manager without changing the security settings.

Exercise Summary

Exchange 2000 is entirely based on the Windows 2000 security model. Hence, as a member of the Domain Admins or Enterprise Admins group, you inherit management permissions for the Exchange 2000 organization. Keep in mind that settings inherited from higher-level configuration containers in Active Directory are not displayed in the Exchange Administration Delegation Wizard. Nevertheless, this wizard remains your primary tool to delegate administrative permissions because it prevents you from revoking administrators and system processes essential access rights.

The Security property sheet, on the other hand, which you can enable for organization and administrative groups via the ShowSecurityPage Registry key, gives detailed and accurate security information. If possible, refrain from using it to manage access rights and roles because it does not prevent you from setting permissions incorrectly. For instance, if you deny Exchange 2000 services access to configuration information in Active Directory, you will experience serious server problems that may even require you to reinstall the entire system. You can read more about securing your Exchange 2000 resources in Chapter 19, "Implementing Advanced Security."

Default File Locations and Share Point Permissions

During the installation, Setup creates the directory structure to host the files of Exchange 2000 Server. If you accept the default settings, they will be placed under the C:\Program Files\Exchsrvr directory.

Exchange 2000 Directory Structure

Depending on the options selected during the installation, Setup creates the directories listed in Table 5.2 on the server computer (see Figure 5.11).

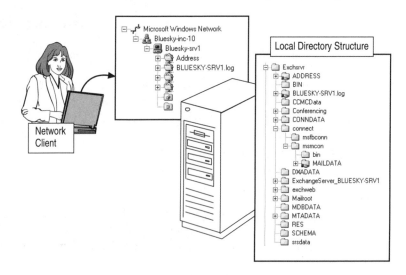

Figure 5.11   Directories and shares created on an Exchange 2000 server

Table 5.2   Directories Created by Setup

Folder Name	This Directory Contains
Address (shared as Address)	E-mail Proxy DLLs that are necessary for address generation in Exchange Server. By default, MS Mail, SMTP, cc:Mail, and X.400 Proxy DLLs can be found.
Bin	Important Exchange 2000 program binaries. For example, the image files of Exchange 2000 services (such as MAD.EXE for the System Attendant (SA)) and the management utilities are copied to this directory.
Ccmcdata	Directory and temporary storage location for the Lotus cc:Mail Connector.
Conferencing	Directory for video conferencing services.
Conndata	Directory and temporary storage location for the Lotus Notes and Novell GroupWise Connectors.
Connect	Exchange Connector components. Default components for the MS Mail Connector and Schedule+ Free/Busy Connector will be copied into this directory.
Connect\Msmcon\ shared as Maildat$)	MS Mail Connector post office also known as MS Mail Interchange Postoffice.
Dxadata	Database for the directory synchronization with MS Mail.
ExchangeServer_ <Server Name>	Contains support index files for the search engine.
Exchweb	Default components for Outlook Web Access will be copied into this directory.
Kmsdata	Key Management database and corresponding log files.
Mailroot	The mail drop directory of the SMTP service, which is moved to this location during the registration of SMTP extensions.
Mdbdata	Mailbox and public stores and associated transaction log files.
Mtadata	The directory for the Message Transfer Agent (MTA). Contains log files and configuration information as well as messages that are currently processed and MTA queues.
Res	Event message DLLs for the Information Store, MTA, and other components.
Schema	Extensible Markup Language (XML) files for schema attributes and classes required for Exchange OLE DB and ActiveX Data Objects (ADO).
Srsdata	Database files for Site Replication Service.
<SERVER NAME> .LOG (shared as <SERVER NAME> .LOG)	Log files for Exchange 2000 services, such as the message tracking center and conferencing services.

Share Points

As indicated in Table 5.2, Setup shares specific directories for network access. It's a good idea to restrict access to these share points to increase the security of the server-based resources. Knowing the share point permissions and the processes that need access to them helps to secure the server appropriately.

The following share points are created automatically on an Exchange 2000 server:

- **Address.**   Corresponds to the \Exchsrvr\Address directory and provides access to proxy address generation DLLs. A proxy address generator is typically responsible for the automatic generation of default e-mail addresses. Each address generator corresponds to a specific e-mail address type. Examples are SMTP, X.400, MS Mail, and Lotus cc:Mail. Addresses of these types will be generated by default for every mailbox, but it is also possible to install additional proxy address generators along with third-party messaging connectors. By default, Administrators and services account have Full Control permissions, and the Everyone account is restricted to Read permission.

- **<SERVER NAME>.LOG.**   Corresponds to the \Exchsrvr\<SERVER NAME>.LOG directory and provides access to log files writing by Exchange 2000 services. By default, Administrators and services account have Full Control permissions, and the Everyone account is restricted to Read permission.

- **Maildat$.**   Corresponds to the \Exchsrvr\Connect\Msmcon\Maildata directory and provides a hidden network share point for the MS Mail Connector. It represents the MS Mail Connector postoffice. By default, Administrators, services account, and Everyone have Full Control permissions.

TCP Ports

The majority of features that Exchange 2000 Server has to offer rely on Internet technologies (such as TCP/IP, DNS, SMTP, NNTP, IMAP4, POP3, HTTP, LDAP, Secure Sockets Layer, Kerberos, and so forth). Consequently, you need to protect your Internet access points, preferably with a firewall. You can read more about Internet-based client access in Chapter 11, "Internet-Based Client Access."

Exercise 3: Checking Active TCP Ports

In this exercise you will check which TCP ports are open on your test machine to handle incoming connections. Knowledge of these TCP ports is especially important when connecting Exchange 2000 Server to the Internet, which requires extra security measures as outlined in Chapter 19, "Implementing Advanced Security."

To view a multimedia demonstration that displays how to perform this procedure, run the EX3CH5.AVI files from the \Exercise_Information\Chapter5 folder on the Supplemental Course Materials CD.

Prerequisites

- Log on as Administrator to BLUESKY-SRV1 running Exchange 2000 Server.
- Insert the Supplemental Course Materials CD in your CD-ROM drive.

▶ **To identify available TCP ports**

1. Copy the files MSWINSCK.OCX and VBPORTSCAN.EXE from the \Exercise_Information\Chapter5\VBPortScan folder on the Supplemental Course Materials CD into your \Winnt\System32 directory.

2. Click Start, and then select Run to display the Run dialog box, where you need to type **regsvr32 mswinsck.ocx**, and then click OK.

3. A RegSvr32 dialog box will appear to confirm that the component was registered successfully. Click OK.

4. Click Start, and then select Run to display the Run dialog box, where you need to type **vbportscan.exe**, and then click OK.

5. The Windows Sockets – Port Tester application is launched. Click Check.

   At this point, you should be able to scroll through the Ports In Use list and verify that all of the important TCP ports for Internet-based client connections are available (see Figure 5.12).

6. Click Exit to close the port tester program.

Exercise Summary

Exchange 2000 Server relies heavily on Internet technologies and consequently prefers a communication based on Windows Sockets (Winsock). Winsock binds an application to a specific port number, which is used to identify network traffic sent to and from the application. You can use a simple TCP port scanner written in Visual Basic to determine which ports are listening. It is a good idea to stop Internet services (and thereby the associated ports) not required in your environment and protect those that are required (such as TCP port 25 for SMTP) with a firewall.

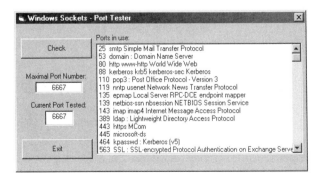

Figure 5.12   Checking available TCP ports

Exchange 2000 Server Service Dependencies

As outlined in Chapter 3, Exchange 2000 Server consists of numerous services that need to communicate with each other to form a functioning messaging and collaboration platform. This communication requires authentication using the Kerberos protocol.

LocalSystem Account

In much the same way you log on to Windows 2000 by providing a user name and password, active Exchange 2000 services need to log on to the system by using a special services account. In previous versions of Exchange Server, this was a normal user account. This left the system vulnerable because it is not feasible to lock a services account after a certain number of failed logon attempts. A locked account would prevent communication between the Exchange Server services. Password-guessing computer criminals prefer to attack services accounts where the account lockout is most likely disabled.

The good news is that you don't need to specify a userlike services account for Exchange 2000 services. Instead, these services are happy with the LocalSystem account of Windows 2000, greatly reducing susceptibility to a successful password-guessing attack against your system. You don't even need to change the password for this services account because Windows 2000 automatically changes it for you every seven days. Even better, the password is very secure because it consists of a random string of characters, putting an effective end to ambitions in password cracking.

Service Account Dependencies for Backward Compatibility

Nevertheless, you need to rely on a userlike services account if you need to connect Exchange 2000 server to Exchange Server 5.5. Within a single site, all Exchange-related services have to use a common Site Services account for authentication.

Note   Exchange 2000 servers use the account name and password set on the administrative group object in the Exchange System snap-in when authenticating against Exchange Server 5.5 services. When communicating with other Exchange 2000 servers, the LocalSystem account is preferred.

Adding or Repairing Components in Maintenance Mode

You can start the Setup program of Exchange 2000 Server at any time. If you run it on a computer that already has Exchange 2000 installed, it will switch into the maintenance mode. Using this mode, you have the ability to add and remove components (Change and Remove action) or to reinstall the entire Exchange 2000 Server (Reinstall action). You will specify the desired action on the Component Selection screen of the Exchange 2000 Installation Wizard.

Setup Registry Key

Setup will detect the presence of any Exchange 2000 Server installation by reading the following Registry key:

```
HKEY_LOCAL_MACHINE

\SOFTWARE

 \Microsoft

  \Exchange

  \Setup
```

The maintenance installation is useful for:

- Adding or removing additional Exchange 2000 components.
- Repeating the entire Exchange 2000 installation without losing directory and configuration information.
- Removing Exchange 2000 Server.

Reinstallation and Service Packs

It might be a good idea to reinstall an Exchange 2000 Server if you suspect important files have been corrupted. The reinstallation can replace these files, thereby repairing any server components. Setup will check the current version of the installed software before it overwrites the server files. Files with newer version numbers than those on the installation CD will not automatically be replaced. To replace those files with files from the appropriate version, you must also reinstall any previously installed service packs. Besides refreshing disk directories and files, Setup also renews Windows NT Registry settings of installed components.

Database files and template information will not be overwritten. This means that the reinstallation is not really risky, but often useful, when Registry entries must be updated or when files are corrupted and finding out what exactly is broken will be an inordinately time-consuming job.

Removing an Exchange 2000 Server Installation

To completely remove the server installation, from the Component Selection wizard screen, under Action, select Remove next to the Microsoft Exchange 2000 entry. You need to reboot the server to complete the process.

Removing Exchange 2000 Server does not remove the Exchange directory structure on the server's hard disk. The \MTAData, and even more important, the \MDBData directories contain files of former message queues and databases. This is important because you will not be able to install Exchange 2000 Server again if an \MDBData directory with an old database file is found on the computer. If you are certain that you don't need to keep the old database files, delete the entire \MDBData directory from the hard disk; otherwise, you should rename it.

It is also important to note that removing an Exchange 2000 Server installation does not affect the configuration objects in Active Directory. In other words, if you have installed a test system in your production environment using the organization name of your future Exchange organization, simply removing the test server doesn't clean the environment. If you install Exchange 2000 Server at a later time on the same server, the old configuration settings will be applied because the organization object in Active Directory will not be overwritten. To start from scratch, use the ADSI Edit utility, and manually delete the CN=Microsoft Exchange node, which you can find in the Configuration container of your domain (CN=Configuration, DC=BlueSky-inc-10, DC=com), under the node labeled CN=Services (see Exercise 2 earlier in this lesson).

Exercise 4: Adding Components to an Exchange 2000 Installation

In this exercise you will add all available components to your existing server installation. To accomplish this task, you will start the Setup program in maintenance mode. However, you will not be able to install the Key Management Service (KMS) yet because this component requires a certification authority. The KMS is covered in detail in Chapter 19, "Implementing Advanced Security."

To view a multimedia demonstration that displays how to perform this procedure, run the EX4CH5.AVI files from the \Exercise_Information\Chapter5 folder on the Supplemental Course Materials CD.

Prerequisites
- Log on as Administrator to BLUESKY-SRV1 running Exchange 2000 Server.
- Insert the Exchange 2000 Enterprise Server CD into the CD-ROM drive (E drive) of BLUESKY-SRV1.

▶ **To launch the Setup program in maintenance mode and add Exchange 2000 Server components**

1. Start the Exchange 2000 Setup program from the \Setup\i386 directory on the installation CD.

2. On the Welcome To The Microsoft Exchange 2000 Installation Wizard screen, click Next.

3. On the Component Selection wizard screen, under Action, in every row that contains a check mark, select Change, and then for all available rows that are not displaying any actions, select Install (with the exception of the Microsoft Exchange Key Management Service).

4. Click Next, and, on the Licensing Agreement wizard screen, select I Agree That, and click Next.

5. On the Component Summary wizard screen, click Next again.

6. When the final wizard screen appears informing you that the installation is complete, click Finish.

   At this point, you have installed Exchange 2000 Server with all possible components excluding the KMS (see Figure 5.13).

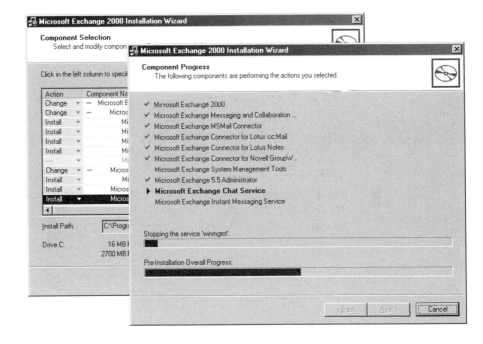

Figure 5.13   Adding additional components to an Exchange 2000 installation

Exercise Summary

It is relatively easy to add or remove Exchange 2000 Server components to an existing installation. Setup detects the installed server automatically and switches into maintenance mode, where you can select the desired components on the Component Selection wizard screen. The component selection might seem a little confusing because you need to set the Action for the parent category (for instance, Microsoft Exchange 2000) to Change first; otherwise, no choice is available for the individual child components. However, this mechanism helps prevent accidental component deletion.

Chapter Summary

The Setup program of Exchange 2000 Server copies the Exchange 2000 Server files on your server's hard disk, updates registry entries, extends the Active Directory schema if necessary, and must react to possible error conditions. The overall Setup process is different between a first server and subsequent installations. During the first server installation, you typically need to specify the name of your (new) messaging organization. Subsequent installations expect to find an organization object in Active Directory and prompt you for different information. Subsequent installations need to know the administrative and routing groups where you want to add the new server.

The Components To Install wizard screen lists the Exchange 2000 components that you can install on your server. Under Action for Microsoft Exchange 2000, Setup suggests a Typical installation, but you can select Custom if you wish to determine the details of the installation manually, or a Minimum installation to set up Exchange 2000 Server with the minimum number of files. It is possible to customize the Setup process by using a predefined initialization file, which is easy to create when launching Setup in /CreateUnattend mode.

When you start the Setup program of Exchange 2000 Server on a computer that already has Exchange 2000 Server installed, it will switch into the maintenance mode. Using this mode, you have the ability to add and remove components or to reinstall Exchange 2000 Server entirely.

Review

The following review questions can help you determine if you have sufficiently familiarized yourself with the material covered in this chapter. You can find the answers to these questions at the end of this book in Appendix A, "Questions and Answers."

1. To save disk space, you have used the Minimum installation option during setup of the first server. Now you want to delegate administrative permissions to a colleague. Why can't you manage the Exchange 2000 Server? What type of installation could you use to install all required components? How can you add the components to the server that was installed with Minimum installation type?

2. You want to designate additional administrators in an administrative group. The additional accounts will be responsible for system configuration only. These administrators should not be able to change security settings. What administrative role do you need to assign these administrators?

3. What administrative role is required to display configuration information?

4. You are using Exchange Server 4.0 in a complex environment. Because of the extended Internet features implemented in Exchange 2000 Server, you decide to upgrade the messaging network. What upgrade strategy should you use?

5. Another administrator has previously installed Outlook 2000 on a server computer, which is an unsupported configuration. To clean up the unsupported configuration, you have decided to remove the client with all its components. You then find that the server no longer works properly because the MAPI32.DLL is missing. How can you fix this problem?

6. You plan to install Exchange 2000 Server unattended to run Setup simultaneously on more than one computer. How would you create the predefined setup initialization file?

7. The messaging network of your company consists of one single location. Five server computers exist within this local area network. You want to administer all these computers from a Windows 2000 workstation in your office. What needs to be installed on the Windows 2000 workstation? How do you install the additional components?

CHAPTER 6

Coexistence with Previous Microsoft Exchange Server Versions

About This Chapter

Because of significant differences in the system architecture, migrating from previous versions of Microsoft Exchange Server to Microsoft Exchange 2000 Server is a complex undertaking. Unlike earlier versions, Exchange 2000 Server does not use its own directory service, but relies on the Active Directory directory service. You therefore need to integrate Exchange Server 5.5 with Active Directory if you wish to bring both Exchange versions together. In fact, Active Directory integration of Exchange Server 5.5 is a very important task during any upgrade project.

It is possible to split the migration process into three general phases: preparation, upgrade, and cleanup. During the preparation phase, you need to integrate Exchange Server 5.5 with Active Directory. This may include updating the operating system to Microsoft Windows 2000 Server Service Pack 1 and the server installation to Exchange Server 5.5 Service Pack 3 first. After that, during the upgrade phase, you need to install Exchange 2000 Server. The upgrade may require a long period of coexistence until you have thoroughly deployed Exchange 2000 Server. The cleanup phase involves deleting Exchange objects from Active Directory, switching the organization into native mode, and removing duplicate user accounts that might have been created during the migration.

This chapter covers, in detail, the important tasks you face when upgrading or migrating an existing Exchange Server 5.5 organization to Exchange 2000 Server. The first lesson illustrates how to integrate Exchange Server 5.5 with Active Directory, an essential prerequisite. The second lesson deals with the actual upgrade procedures and concludes with a discussion of postupgrade tasks.

Before You Begin

To complete this chapter:

- Have a general understanding of Exchange Server administration and the concepts related to synchronizing Active Directory with the Exchange directory service.

- Be familiar with the concepts of upgrading Microsoft Windows NT Server 4.0 to Windows 2000 Server.

- The exercises in this chapter assume that you have installed Windows NT Server 4.0 on two computers operating in a single domain environment. Both computers need to run an installation of Exchange Server 5.5 Service Pack 3, as described in the "Getting Started" section of "About This Book."

Lesson 1: Preparation of Exchange Server Environments

The actual upgrade from Exchange Server 5.5 is relatively easy compared to the various prerequisites that must be met. Directory synchronization between Active Directory and the Exchange directory is important for several reasons. For instance, you need to extend Active Directory with Exchange-specific items and build a common global address list across all platforms.

This lesson focuses on the task of preparing an Exchange Server organization for an upgrade, including installation of Windows 2000 Server and configuration of Active Directory. You will use the Active Directory Connector (ADC) to populate and synchronize user accounts with mailbox information.

At the end of this lesson, you will be able to:

- Identify important aspects of upgrading a primary domain controller (PDC) running Exchange Server 5.5 to Windows 2000 Server and Active Directory.

- Install the ADC and configure user connection agreements for two-way directory synchronization.

Estimated time to complete this lesson: 3 hours

Preparing the Windows Environment

Exchange Server 5.5 is typically used in a Windows NT 4.0 domain environment—Exchange 2000 Server is strictly a Windows 2000 platform. Hence, your preparation requires an upgrade to Windows 2000 Server and Active Directory first. You must deploy Active Directory in your environment if you are planning to install Exchange 2000 Server.

Upgrading the Primary Domain Controller

To avoid the installation of separate Windows 2000 domains, consider upgrading the PDC(s) in your domain environment directly. This is probably the easiest upgrade method because it preserves all account information, including the original security identifiers (SIDs). A SID is a value that uniquely identifies a user account and is used by Windows 2000 to determine access permissions. However, upgrading the PDC involves an additional configuration step if your PDC also runs Exchange Server (see Exercise 1).

Site Services Account Upgrade

Exchange 2000 Server is unable to work with Windows NT 4.0-based security information. This includes the Site Services account used to communicate with previous Exchange Server versions. Because Exchange 2000 Server needs to use the Site Services account, you must first upgrade the PDC of the domain in which this special account exists. During this upgrade, the Site Services account is converted into a Windows 2000 security principal. You can read more about Site Services account dependencies later in this chapter.

Note   You don't need to upgrade your entire Windows NT 4.0 environment to Windows 2000 to upgrade to Exchange 2000 Server. However, it is a good idea to upgrade at least the PDCs of all your user domains.

Active Directory Migration Tool

Apart from upgrading existing domains to Windows 2000 Server, you have the option of installing Windows 2000 in separate domains and using the Active Directory Migration Tool to clone the existing security information. Cloned accounts are specific Windows 2000 accounts for which properties and group memberships have been copied from corresponding Windows NT 4.0 source accounts. Although the account objects have a different primary SID than their source accounts, each source account's SID is copied to the SIDHistory attribute of the corresponding clone. Through the old SID preserved in the SIDHistory attribute, the Windows 2000 user can access all network resources available to the source account—provided that trusts exist between the Windows NT domains and the clone's Active Directory domain.

The Active Directory Migration Tool is appropriate for complex Windows NT environments consisting of multiple Windows NT 4.0 domains because it allows consolidation of the domain environment. You can read more about this tool in *Planning Migration from Microsoft Windows NT to Microsoft Windows 2000*, which is available in the online documentation for Windows 2000 Server.

Avoiding LDAP Port Conflicts

When upgrading PDCs or backup domain controllers (BDCs) running Exchange Server 5.5, you need to change the Lightweight Directory Access Protocol (LDAP) port number for the Exchange directory service. The legacy Exchange directory supports LDAP and so does Active Directory. Hence, both expect incoming LDAP connections on TCP port 389, LDAP's well-known TCP port, by default. On an Active Directory domain controller, such as an upgraded PDC, Active Directory is started automatically and locks TCP port 389 for its own use. When Exchange Server starts, it cannot access the same port and cannot communicate via LDAP until you change the LDAP port for the Exchange directory to a port other than 389 (see Figure 6.1).

Note   Microsoft recommends changing the LDAP port for the Exchange directory service prior to upgrading to Windows 2000 and Active Directory.

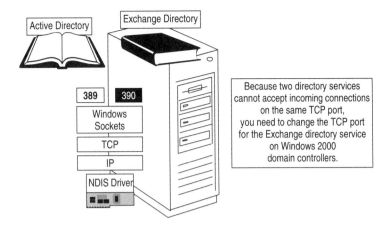

Figure 6.1   Active Directory and Exchange directory on a domain controller

Exercise 1: Changing the LDAP Port for Exchange Server

In this exercise you will change the LDAP port for the Exchange directory service using the Exchange Administrator program. This is a prerequisite for subsequent exercises in this chapter.

To view a multimedia demonstration that displays how to perform this procedure, run the EX1CH6.AVI files from the \Exercise_Information\Chapter6 folder on the Supplemental Course Materials CD.

Prerequisites

- BLUESKY-PDC is configured as the PDC and BLUESKY-BDC functions as a BDC in a single Windows NT 4.0 domain called BLUESKY-OLD-10. Both servers run Exchange Server 5.5 with Service Pack 3.

- Log on as Administrator to BLUESKY-PDC.

▶ **To change the LDAP port for Exchange Server**

1. Start Microsoft Exchange Administrator from the Microsoft Exchange program group.

2. Connect to the server BLUESKY-PDC. If required, select Connect To Server from the File menu to display the Connect To Server dialog box, type **BLUESKY-PDC**, and click OK. The Connect To Server dialog box may also appear automatically when you start the Exchange Administrator program.

3. Expand the site container (BLUESKY-OLD-10), then the Configuration container, and then select the Protocols container to display its contents in the right pane.

4. Double-click the LDAP (Directory) Site Defaults object. In the General tab, change the port number to **390**, and then click OK.

   At this point, you have configured the Exchange directory service to use TCP port 390 (see Figure 6.2).

5. Close Microsoft Exchange Administrator and reboot BLUESKY-PDC to activate the changes.

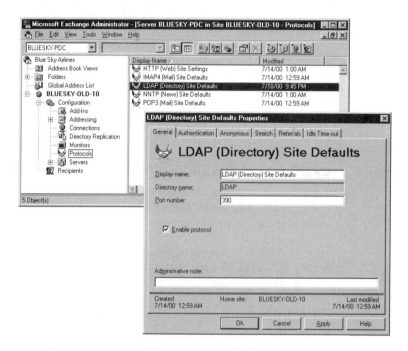

Figure 6.2   Changing the LDAP port number for the Exchange directory

Exercise Summary

To prevent port conflicts when running Exchange 2000 Server on a domain controller, change the TCP port number for the LDAP interface of the Exchange directory service. Be cautious, however, not to specify a TCP port in use by another service. A list of well-known ports can be found in the SERVICES file in the \Winnt\System32\Drivers\Etc directory.

Upgrading the Operating System

Exchange 2000 Server can only be installed on a computer running Windows 2000 Server, Windows Advanced Server, or Windows Datacenter Server updated with Windows 2000 Service Pack 1. Furthermore, the server must be a member of an Active Directory domain. If you are planning to directly upgrade an existing computer from Exchange Server 5.5, you need to upgrade its operating system first.

Mixed Domain Environments

Active Directory supports mixed networks containing computers running Windows NT Server 4.0 and Windows 2000 Server, so you don't need to upgrade all operating systems at once before installing Exchange 2000 Server. Upgrade the PDC first and then the computers running Exchange Server 5.5 one at a time. If the Exchange servers are operating as BDCs, change the LDAP port number for the Exchange directory as previously outlined prior to the upgrade. If your domain also contains member servers running Exchange Server 5.5, upgrade them after the BDCs have been upgraded.

Exercise 2: Upgrading to Windows 2000 Server

In this exercise you will upgrade the PDC of your test environment to Windows 2000 Server. This will preserve all existing accounts, including the Site Services account for Exchange Server.

To view a multimedia demonstration that displays how to perform this procedure, run the EX2CH6*.AVI files from the \Exercise_Information\Chapter6 folder on the Supplemental Course Materials CD.

Prerequisites

- Complete Exercise 1, earlier in this lesson.

- Log on as Administrator to BLUESKY-PDC.

- Insert the Windows 2000 Server or Advanced Server installation CD into the CD drive of BLUESKY-PDC. You will also need the Windows 2000 Service Pack CD to update the installation later on.

▶ **To upgrade to Windows 2000 Server**

1. Launch Setup from the installation CD and, in the Microsoft Windows 2000 Server CD dialog box asking you whether you want to upgrade to Windows 2000, click Yes.

2. The Windows 2000 Setup Wizard will start, showing the Welcome screen. Make sure Upgrade To Windows 2000 (Recommended) is selected before you click Next.

3. On the License Agreement wizard screen, select I Accept This Agreement, and then click Next.

4. On the Your Product Key wizard screen, enter the product key of your Windows 2000 CD, and then click Next.

5. On the Directory Of Applications For Windows 2000 wizard screen, click Next to continue without displaying further information.

   At this point, Setup copies important files to the computer's hard disk and reboots the computer (see Figure 6.3).

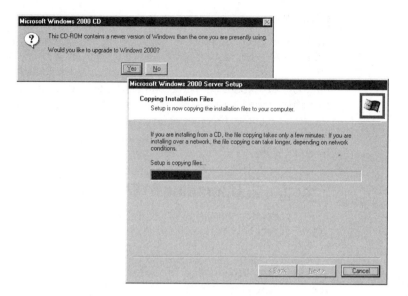

Figure 6.3   Starting the Windows upgrade process

6. BLUESKY-PDC will be rebooted automatically. To continue the upgrade process, make sure Microsoft Windows 2000 Server Setup, on the Boot menu, is the active option.

7. After copying files and saving the current configuration, Setup will reboot the server computer a second time to launch Windows 2000 in graphical mode.

8. Setup now detects and installs devices on your computer; automatically installs network and other software, registers, and components; removes temporary files; and finalizes the upgrade before it reboots the server one more time.

9. Setup will log on to Windows 2000 automatically to launch the Active Directory Installation Wizard. You must install Active Directory because you are upgrading the PDC.

10. On the Welcome wizard screen, click Next.

11. On the Create Tree Or Child Domain wizard screen, select Create A New Domain Tree, then click Next.

12. In the Create Or Join Forest dialog box, make sure Create A New Forest Of Domain Trees is selected, and then click Next.

13. On the New Domain Name wizard screen, type the domain name **BlueSky-Old-10.com**, and then click Next.

14. On the Database And Log Locations wizard screen, accept the defaults, and click Next.

15. On the Shared System Volume wizard screen, accept the defaults, and click Next.

16. An Active Directory Installation Wizard dialog box will appear informing you that a DNS Server could not be contacted. Click OK, and then, on the Configure DNS wizard screen, accept the Yes, Install And Configure DNS On This Computer (Recommended) option by clicking on Next.

17. On the Permissions wizard screen, make sure Permissions Compatible With Pre-Windows 2000 Servers is selected, and then click Next.

18. On the Directory Services Restore Mode Administrator Password wizard screen, under Password and Confirm Password, type **password**, and then click Next.

19. On the Summary wizard screen, verify that the settings are correct, and then click Next to begin the configuration of Active Directory.

    At this point, you have successfully configured the Active Directory environment hosting an Exchange Server 5.5 organization (see Figure 6.4).

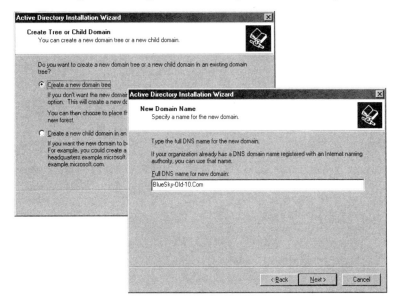

Figure 6.4 Running the Active Directory Installation Wizard

20. On the Completing The Active Directory Installation Wizard screen, click Finish.

21. In the Active Directory Installation Wizard dialog box, click Restart Now.

22. Log on again to BLUESKY-PDC, now running Windows 2000 Server, as Administrator. In the Windows 2000 Configure Your Server window that appears automatically, deselect the Show This Screen At Startup, and then close the window.

23. Insert the Windows 2000 Service Pack 1 CD in the CD-ROM drive, and then click the Start button, point to Run, type **E:\i386\Update\UPDATE.EXE**, and then click OK.

24. In the Windows 2000 Service Pack Setup dialog box, select the Accept The License Agreement (Must Accept Before Installing The Service Pack) check box, and then click Install.

25. In the final Windows 2000 Service Pack Setup dialog box, click Restart to reboot the system and complete the update.

Exercise Summary

As soon as the Active Directory environment is configured, both domain controllers BLUESKY-PDC and BLUESKY-BDC are listed in the domain controllers organizational unit (OU). Because the domain environment operates in mixed mode, BDCs (BLUESKY-BDC) can fully participate and the Exchange Server organization functions as normal. It is only during the upgrade, when Active Directory is not yet configured, that Exchange Server services are unable to start.

Configuring the Active Directory Connector

To ensure a common global address list for all users, whether they still reside on Exchange Server 5.5 or are migrated to Exchange 2000 Server, you need to synchronize the directories with each other. To enable directory synchronization, install the Active Directory Connector (ADC) and configure user connection agreements. Connection agreements can replicate recipient and public folder information between Exchange Server 5.5 and the Global Catalog.

Note   The Active Directory Connector of Exchange 2000 Server requires Exchange Server 5.5 Service Pack 3. Consequently, you need to update at least one server in each site to Exchange Server 5.5 SP3 to achieve complete system integration.

Windows 2000 Versus Exchange 2000 Server

To support Exchange Server 5.5, Windows 2000 provides a basic ADC version. The ADC of Exchange 2000 Server, alternatively, comes with enhanced functionality for replicating configuration and routing information. The Exchange 2000 version updates the Active Directory schema on its first installation. Because this schema extension is a prerequisite for upgrading to Exchange 2000 Server, you must install at least one instance of the Exchange 2000 ADC in your Active Directory forest as part of your upgrade preparation.

Tip   For best performance, upgrade all ADC installations to the version that comes with Exchange 2000 Server.

Synchronizing Directory Information

As soon as the Windows NT user accounts are migrated to Active Directory, you need to synchronize the accounts with their corresponding mailbox information using an ADC connection agreement. Directory synchronization is performed between the Global Catalog and the Exchange directory service (see Figure 6.5). Typically, the Global Catalog is the first server installed in the forest. It is a good idea to assign this role to one server in each Windows 2000 domain. Yet even if you do not plan to deploy ADC in all of your domains, you need to extend the domain where the schema master resides using the ADC Setup program with the /schemaonly switch. As mentioned earlier, the Active Directory schema must be extended to support additional Exchange 2000-related object classes and attributes. As soon as this is accomplished, you can deploy ADC in child domains.

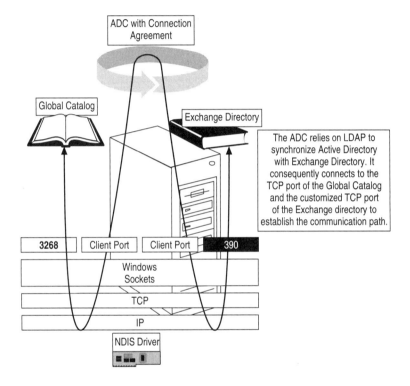

Figure 6.5 Directory synchronization via ADC and a connection agreement

Automatic Account Creation

In Exchange Server 5.5 it is possible to specify one Windows NT account as the primary Windows account for multiple mailboxes. In Exchange 2000 Server, account and mailbox information are part of the same Active Directory object; hence, each Windows 2000 account can have only one mailbox directly associated with it. To synchronize the information from additional mailboxes with Active Directory, additional account objects must be created in Active Directory. The ADC is also able to create Windows accounts for mailbox objects where a corresponding Active Directory object could not be found.

You can control the automatic creation of Active Directory accounts via the Advanced tab of each connection agreement. By default, disabled Windows user accounts are created, but you may change this behavior to create enabled accounts or Windows contacts by selecting the appropriate option from the When Replicating A Mailbox Whose Primary Windows Account Does Not Exist In The Domain check box.

Exercise 3: Installing and Configuring the ADC

In this exercise you will synchronize Active Directory with the Exchange directory using the ADC and a connection agreement. To prepare for an upgrade to Exchange 2000 Server, install and configure the ADC, which can be found on the Exchange 2000 Server installation CD.

To view a multimedia demonstration that displays how to perform this procedure, run the EX3CH6*.AVI files from the \Exercise_Information\Chapter6 folder on the Supplemental Course Materials CD.

Prerequisites

- Complete Exercise 2, earlier in this lesson.
- Log on as Administrator to BLUESKY-PDC.
- Insert the Exchange 2000 Server installation CD into the CD drive of BLUESKY-PDC. You can use the Standard or Enterprise edition to perform the procedure.

▶ **To install and configure the ADC**

1. Click Start, select Run, and, in the Run dialog box, click Browse to display the Browse dialog box.
2. From the Exchange 2000 Server CD, from the directory \ADC\i386, select the Setup executable file, and then click Open.
3. In the Run dialog box, click OK to launch the Microsoft Active Directory Connector Setup Wizard. On the Welcome screen, click Next.
4. On the Component Selection wizard screen, activate the Microsoft Active Directory Connector Service Component and Microsoft Active Directory Connector Management Components check boxes, and then click Next.
5. On the Install Location wizard screen, accept the default folder, which is C:\Program Files\Msadc, and then click Next.
6. On the Service Account wizard screen, specify the services account of your Exchange Server 5.5 services, which should be BLUESKY-OLD-10\Administrator. Enter the corresponding password under Account Password, and then click Next to start the installation process.

   At this point, you have successfully installed the ADC on BLUESKY-PDC and updated the directory schema (see Figure 6.6).

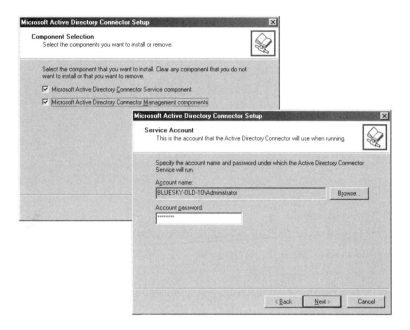

Figure 6.6   Installing the ADC

7. On the Completing The Active Directory Connector Installation wizard screen, click Finish.

8. From the Microsoft Exchange program group, start the Active Directory Connector tool.

9. From the console tree, select Active Directory Connector (BLUESKY-PDC), then right-click on it. In the shortcut menu point to New, and then select Recipient Connection Agreement.

10. In the General tab, under Name, type **CA for Blue Sky Airlines**.

11. Under Replication Direction, select Two-way. In the Microsoft Active Directory Connector Management dialog box informing you that the certification authority (CA) must now write to the Exchange directory, which requires a service account with appropriate permissions, click OK.

12. Switch to the Connections tab, verify that BLUESKY-PDC is listed under Windows Server Information and that the Authentication mechanism is Windows Challenge/Response.

13. Under Connect As, click Modify. In the Connect As (Windows Server) dialog box, under Connect As, click Browse to select the BLUESKY-OLD-10\ Administrator account. Under Password, type **password**, and then click OK.

14. Under Exchange Server Information, in the Server text box, type **BLUESKY-PDC**. Under Port, change the port number to **390**, which is the LDAP port specified earlier for the Exchange directory.

15. Under Connect As, click Modify. In the Connect As (Exchange Server) dialog box, under Connect As, click Browse to select the BLUESKY-OLD-10\ Administrator account. Under Password, type **password**. Verify that the property sheet is now configured as shown in Figure 6.7.

16. Switch to the Schedule tab and select Always for the replication schedule. Select the Replicate The Entire Directory The Next Time The Agreement Is Run check box.

17. Switch to the From Exchange tab, and click Add to choose a recipient container to take updates from.

18. In the Choose A Container dialog box, expand BLUESKY-OLD-10, select Recipients, and then click OK.

19. Under Default Destination, click Modify. In the Choose A Container dialog box, select Users, and then click OK.

20. Switch to the From Windows tab, and click Add to specify an OU to take updates from.

21. In the Choose A Container dialog box, select Users, and then click OK.

22. Under Default Destination, click Modify. In the Choose A Container dialog box, select Recipients, and then click OK.

23. Select the Replicate Secured Active Directory Objects To The Exchange Directory check box.

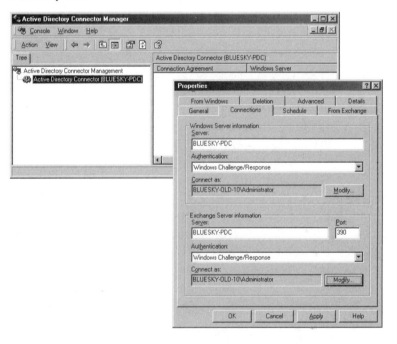

Figure 6.7   Configuring a connection agreement

24. Leave all other settings at their defaults, and click OK.

25. In the Microsoft Active Directory Connector Management dialog box that appears to inform you that this is the first intra-organizational Connection Agreement, click OK.

26. In the Microsoft Active Directory Connector Management dialog box that appears to inform you that your Windows domain operates in mixed mode, click Yes.

27. In the Microsoft Active Directory Connector Management dialog box that appears to inform you that security groups have been created for Exchange 2000 Server, click OK.

28. Close the Active Directory Connector Management console.

Exercise Summary

After you have successfully configured the connection agreement, recipient information is replicated between Active Directory and the Exchange Server organization. According to the default configuration, the ADC creates disabled Windows 2000 accounts for all Exchange Server 5.5 mailboxes that do not have a matching Active Directory object. You can find these disabled accounts in the OU that you have specified in your connection agreement, such as the Users OU.

Lesson 2: Upgrade and Migration Strategies

Now that you have started to deploy Windows 2000 and Active Directory and you have configured at least one connection agreement with ADC to synchronize the Exchange directory with Active Directory, you are ready for upgrading. In a production environment, it is good practice to prepare a full backup of the computer running Exchange Server 5.5 before launching the Setup program of Exchange 2000 Server. You may even restore your system on a test machine and perform a test upgrade there. This helps familiarize you with the entire upgrade task and shows that it can be performed without problems.

This lesson discusses available options for upgrading to Exchange 2000 Server. It introduces two general upgrade strategies that you may find useful. In environments with more than one server, the upgrade is accompanied by a coexistence phase that comes with special requirements, also covered here.

At the end of this lesson, you will be able to:

- Identify the components that allow you to integrate Exchange 2000 Server into an existing Exchange Server 5.5 environment.
- Perform an in-place upgrade to Exchange 2000 Server.
- Perform a migration using the move-mailbox strategy instead of in-place upgrades.
- Clean up Active Directory after the upgrade of an organization is complete.

Estimated time to complete this lesson: 2 hours

Upgrade Strategies

In general, you have to decide between two upgrade strategies. You can either install Exchange 2000 Server directly on a computer running Exchange Server 5.5, performing an in-place upgrade, or join an existing Exchange Server 5.5 site with a new server and move mailboxes and other resources to Exchange 2000 Server manually, which corresponds to a move-mailbox upgrade.

Tip   It is a good idea to review the installation and configuration of connectors, gateways, and any third-party software prior to the upgrade to ensure that they are compatible with Exchange 2000 Server.

In-Place Upgrade

The in-place upgrade is simple and quickly accomplished, but it is only supported over Exchange Server 5.5 Service Pack 3 or later. When you launch the Exchange 2000 Setup program directly on a computer running Exchange Server

5.5 Service Pack 3, the previous version is detected automatically, and Setup switches into upgrade mode, not allowing you to add additional components or change the existing configuration in any way. To make any changes, you will need to launch Setup one more time after the upgrade in maintenance mode, which was introduced in Chapter 5, "Installing Microsoft Exchange 2000 Server."

Database Conversion

During the in-place upgrade, Setup stops the Exchange Server services to convert the information store databases. The upgrade process works with approximately 8 GB per hour, which is extremely fast. However, the actual conversion speed depends on a number of factors, such as the number of mailboxes and public folders.

Note   The database conversion is a resource-intensive task during which the computer or the Setup procedure may appear to hang, for instance, at 85 or at 100 percent completion. This is an expected behavior, especially if the size of the databases being upgraded is large. You will need to be patient; do not terminate the Setup process, and do not restart the server.

Upgrade Prerequisites

The following prerequisites must be met to perform an in-place upgrade:

- The computer running Exchange Server was upgraded to Windows 2000 Server SP1 and is part of an Active Directory domain.

- Internet Information Services (IIS) 5.0 with Simple Mail Transport Protocol (SMTP) and Network News Transfer Protocol (NNTP) service must be installed.

- The server hardware must fulfill the minimum requirements for running Exchange 2000.

- You are running Exchange Server 5.5 Service Pack 3 or later.

- You have the required permissions to install Exchange 2000, as outlined in Chapter 4, "Planning the Microsoft Exchange 2000 Server Installation."

Move-Mailbox Upgrade

A significant disadvantage of the in-place upgrade is server downtime because the Exchange Server services must be stopped during the upgrade process. In-place upgrading also requires installing Windows 2000 Server and possibly updating Exchange Server to version 5.5 with Service Pack 3 first, which also causes the system to be unavailable for a period of time. If your organization is supposed to be up and running 24 hours, 7 days a week, consider a move-mailbox upgrade instead of the in-place approach. During a move-mailbox upgrade, you join an existing site with a machine running Exchange 2000 Server and move all resources from the legacy Exchange server to this computer. As soon as all resources have been moved, the old system may be removed from the site.

Leapfrog Upgrade

You may want to use the upgrade to Exchange 2000 Server as a perfect opportunity to replace outdated server hardware, or you may reuse the old hardware for subsequent Exchange 2000 Server installations after the data has been moved from the old system. This is known as a *leapfrog upgrade* (see Figure 6.8).

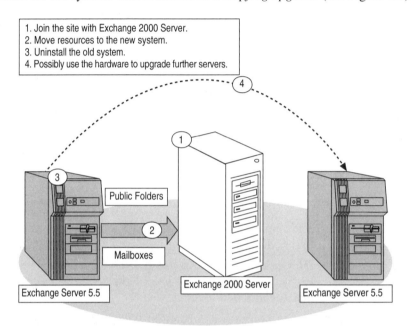

Figure 6.8   The leapfrog upgrade method

Joining an Existing Site

The move-mailbox upgrade involves manual configuration steps, but its most significant advantage is that business processes are not interrupted. Prepare a new computer according to the hardware and software requirements outlined in Chapter 5 and launch the Exchange 2000 Setup program. During Setup, indicate that you will join an existing organization. You need to specify an existing server running Exchange Server 5.5 with Service Pack 3. The name of the existing organization is retrieved from the specified server and replicated to Active Directory. The Exchange 2000 server will then join the selected site. As soon as Exchange 2000 Server is running in the site, you can move mailboxes and replicate public folders to the new system. This doesn't affect the installed client base because clients are redirected to new mailbox and public folder locations automatically, provided that the old home server is still available in the network (see Figure 6.9).

Note   When joining a site you must specify a server running Exchange Server 5.5 with Service Pack 3.

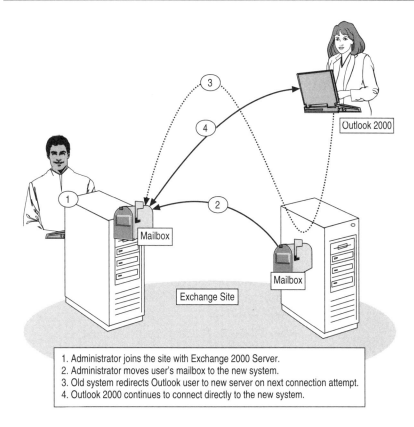

1. Administrator joins the site with Exchange 2000 Server.
2. Administrator moves user's mailbox to the new system.
3. Old system redirects Outlook user to new server on next connection attempt.
4. Outlook 2000 continues to connect directly to the new system.

Figure 6.9   Redirection of Outlook 2000 to Exchange 2000

Dedicated Server Configurations

The move-mailbox migration strategy works best for mailbox and public folder resources. Existing connectors, however, need to be reconfigured on the new server if you plan to remove the old server from the site. This is also true if you have installed Key Management Service (KMS) in your organization. To most conveniently upgrade servers responsible for connectors (bridgehead servers) and KMS, consider the in-place upgrade method.

Note   It is a good idea to check the configuration of messaging connectors after an in-place or leapfrog upgrade. Do not forget to check whether or not the routing information is upgraded properly.

Upgrade Order

You can upgrade to Exchange 2000 Server in any order, which means that you don't need to consider upgrading bridgehead or connector servers first. As a matter of fact, you might want to upgrade these systems last, especially when they are running connector instances not supported by Exchange 2000 Server, such as the Professional Office System (PROFS) connector. It is advisable to upgrade public and mailbox servers first so that your users can benefit from the advanced messaging and collaboration features of Exchange 2000 Server immediately.

Exercise 4: Performing an In-Place Upgrade to Exchange 2000 Server

In this exercise you will perform an in-place upgrade to Exchange 2000 Server. At the end of this exercise, you will be operating an Exchange organization consisting of an Exchange 2000 server and a computer running Exchange Server 5.5.

To view a multimedia demonstration that displays how to perform this procedure, run the EX4CH6*.AVI files from the \Exercise_Information\Chapter6 folder on the Supplemental Course Materials CD.

Prerequisites

- Install the NNTP service of the IIS 4.0 on BLUESKY-PDC according to the installation instructions in "Installation of a Microsoft Windows NT 4.0 and Microsoft Exchange Server 5.5 for Chapter 6, 'Coexistence with Previous Microsoft Exchange Server Versions,'" found in the "Getting Started" section of "About This Book."

- Complete Exercise 3, earlier in this chapter.

- Log on as Administrator to BLUESKY-PDC.

- Insert the Exchange 2000 Server installation CD into the CD drive of BLUESKY-PDC. You can use the Standard or Enterprise edition to upgrade Exchange Server 5.5.

▶ **To perform an in-place upgrade to Exchange 2000 Server**

1. To make sure the in-place upgrade can be performed on BLUESKY-PDC, click the Start button, point to Programs, then Microsoft Exchange, and then select Microsoft Exchange Administrator.

2. Make sure you are connected to BLUESKY-PDC, expand the site container BLUESKY-OLD-10, then select Configuration. In the right window pane, double-click on the DS Site Configuration object.

3. Switch to the Offline Address Book tab, and then, under Offline Address Book Server, select BLUESKY-BDC.

4. Click OK and close the Exchange Administrator program.

5. Click Start, select Run and, in the Run dialog box, click Browse to display the Browse dialog box.

6. From the Exchange 2000 Server installation CD, from the directory \Setup\i386, double-click the Setup executable file, and then click OK.

7. On the Welcome screen of the Microsoft Exchange 2000 Installation Wizard, click Next.

8. In the End-User License Agreement dialog box, select I Agree, and then click Next.

9. On the Product Identification wizard screen, enter the CD key of your Exchange 2000 installation CD, and then click Next.

At this point, you have reached the Component Selection wizard screen, which provides you with information about the individual components that will be updated. It is important to note that you cannot change the Action displayed for any component (see Figure 6.10).

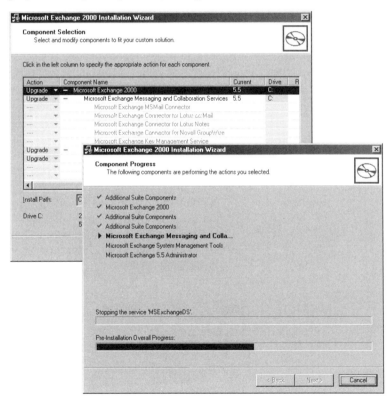

Figure 6.10   The Upgrade action on the Component Selection wizard screen

10. On the Component Selection wizard screen, click Next.

11. On the Service Account wizard screen, make sure Administrator is displayed under User Name and that the Domain is BLUESKY-OLD-10. Under Password, type **password**.

12. Click Next.

13. On the Component Summary wizard screen, click Next to upgrade the server.

14. After Setup has upgraded the server, the final wizard screen is displayed. Click Finish.

15. A Microsoft Exchange 2000 Installation Wizard dialog box will appear, informing you that the system must be restarted. Use the TAB key to set the focus to the OK button, and then press ENTER to confirm the dialog box and restart BLUESKY-PDC.

Exercise Summary

The in-place upgrade method is easy to accomplish if all prerequisites are met. You cannot change any configuration settings during the installation process. During the upgrade, existing configuration information is transferred to Active Directory. To verify that the configuration is now present in Active Directory, start the Exchange System snap-in from the Microsoft Exchange program group. Computers running previous versions of Exchange Server are shown as transparent objects and sites are matched with administrative groups, as explained in Chapter 5, "Installing Microsoft Exchange 2000 Server."

Note   To minimize the risk of permission-related problems during an in-place upgrade of a production system, check the consistency of the server prior to running the Exchange 2000 Server Setup program. Open the Exchange Administrator program, and display the properties of the affected server object. Switch to the Advanced tab, and then click on the Consistency Adjuster button. Select only the Remove Unknown User Accounts From Mailbox Permissions and Remove Unknown User Accounts From Public Folder Permissions check boxes, and then click OK. It is not necessary to synchronize the directory or re-home public folders.

Administering Heterogeneous Exchange Organizations

During the coexistence phase, it is important to coordinate system administration and maintenance carefully. Although Exchange 2000 Server resources are displayed in the directory information tree within the Exchange Administrator, any changes you make to these configuration objects are not replicated to Exchange

2000 Server and don't take effect. When displaying the configuration of the organization in the Exchange System snap-in, resources of previous Exchange versions are shown as transparent objects. The Exchange System snap-in displays
the information as read-only and prevents you from changing settings.

Note   You must administer Exchange Server 5.5 using the Exchange
Administrator program and Exchange 2000 Server using the Exchange System
snap-in and other Microsoft Management Console (MMC) snap-ins.

User Account and Mailbox Management

Use only the Active Directory Users and Computers management tool for mailbox management. Don't use Exchange Administrator for this purpose. After all,
you are migrating away from Exchange Server 5.5, and, therefore, it is a good
idea to create mailboxes for new Windows 2000 accounts on servers running
Exchange 2000 Server only. Avoid the creation of additional mailboxes on the
legacy system.

Directory Replication
with Previous Exchange Server Versions

Whether you join an existing site with a new Exchange 2000 server or perform
an in-place upgrade, thus joining a site automatically, Exchange 2000 Server
must disguise itself on the site to appear as an Exchange 5.5 server. When viewing your organization in Exchange Administrator, note that Exchange 2000 servers are displayed in much the same way as servers running previous versions of
Exchange.

Site Replication Service

The disguising function results from a helper directory service, which the Setup
program of Exchange 2000 Server installs automatically. You can find this service when launching the Services utility from the Administrative Tools program
group. Look for the Microsoft Exchange Site Replication Service (SRS). It will
be activated and its database initialized when you install a first Exchange 2000
server on a site or when you upgrade a directory replication bridgehead server.
On all other Exchange 2000 servers, this component is deactivated by default.
On BLUESKY-PDC, for instance, this service is configured to start automatically
because this is the first Exchange 2000 server on the site.

SRS Directory Integration

You can think of SRS as an Exchange directory service for Exchange 2000
Server. Only the Name Service Provider Interface (NSPI) is disabled to prevent
Microsoft Outlook clients from connecting to SRS and retrieving directory

information from this service. As a matter of fact, SRS contains much of the executable code of the former directory service, which ensures full compatibility with earlier versions.

SRS consists of the following components (see Figure 6.11):

- The Windows 2000 SRS implemented in SRSMAIN.EXE
- A Site Consistency Checker, which runs as part of SRS and performs tasks similar to the Knowledge Consistency Checker of Exchange Server 5.5, such as the creation of replication links
- An SRS database named SRS.EDB and corresponding transaction logs, which hold Exchange Server 5.5 directory information and reside in the \Exchsrvr\Dsadata directory (in-place upgrade) or the \Exchsrvr\Srsdata directory (joining an existing site)

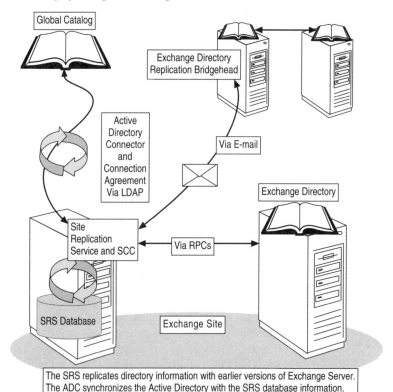

The SRS replicates directory information with earlier versions of Exchange Server. The ADC synchronizes the Active Directory with the SRS database information.

Figure 6.11   Directory replication between Exchange 2000 Server and Exchange Server 5.5

Note When installing or enabling SRS, all existing Exchange 2000 administrators inherit the permissions to manage the SRS environment. Administrators that have been granted permissions in Exchange System Manager at a later time are unable to manage SRS. To grant these administrators SRS permissions, use the Exchange Administrator program and connect to the Exchange 2000 server. Grant the desired user account the appropriate rights, such as Service Account Administrator, as usual at the organization, site, and configuration level. You need the rights of a Permissions Admin.

Intrasite and Intersite Directory Replication

Within a site, SRS automatically replicates directory information using remote procedure calls (RPCs). Between sites, SRS replicates directory information via e-mail messages, just as the Exchange directory service does (see Figure 6.11). SRS automatically disables the directory replication to servers in the site as well as bridgeheads in other sites as soon as they are upgraded to Exchange 2000 Server. This ensures that replication data is not duplicated because the replication between Exchange 2000 systems is handled through Active Directory.

Configuration Connection Agreements

The SRS only replicates data with previous Exchange directories. Connection agreements of the ADC, on the other hand, replicate changes between SRS and Active Directory, as indicated in Figure 6.11. In a manner similar to the Exchange directory service, SRS accepts incoming connections from the ADC via a customized LDAP port if you are running Exchange 2000 Server on a domain controller; otherwise, it accepts them through the well-known LDAP port 389.

During the first installation of Exchange 2000 Server in an existing site, a configuration connection agreement is configured automatically. You can verify its existence when launching the Active Directory Connector tool from the Microsoft Exchange program group. For the ADC of BLUESKY-PDC, for instance, a connection agreement named Config CA_BLUESKY-OLD-10_BLUESKY-PDC was created. As you can see on the Connections property sheet, this connection agreement connects to SRS on BLUESKY-PDC through the customized TCP port 379 to synchronize configuration and routing information from the SRS database with Active Directory.

Note If you are installing a first Exchange 2000 server on a Windows 2000 domain controller not running any previous version of Exchange Server and joining an existing site, SRS automatically uses TCP port 379 to avoid LDAP port conflicts with Active Directory.

Server-to-Server Communication and Message Transfer

As discussed in Chapter 3, "Microsoft Exchange 2000 Server Architecture," the mechanisms for server-to-server communication in Exchange 2000 rely primarily on SMTP and the extended Windows 2000 SMTP service. This is different than previous Exchange Server versions, where directory services performed directory replication and Message Transfer Agents (MTAs) provided the native messaging transport between servers in a site and message transfer to servers in other sites.

Server-to-Server Communication

Within sites, computers running previous versions of Exchange Server communicate with each other using RPCs. When integrating Exchange 2000 Server in a site, the new system must comply with this tradition and use RPCs as well. Specifically, SRS will contact remote Exchange directory services for directory replication, and the MTA of Exchange 2000 Server will transfer messages with legacy MTAs. The MTA of Exchange 2000 Server works similar to the old MTA, with minor enhancements and the exception that the new MTA uses LDAP instead of Directory API (DAPI) to perform directory lookups.

Note If you install two or more Exchange 2000 servers in a site, these servers will detect each other through Active Directory and route messages to one another using the SMTP service rather than the MTA.

RPCs and Authentication Dependencies

All Exchange servers in a site must validate each other using a common Site Services account before server-to-server communication is allowed. Servers not using the correct Site Services account will not be able to communicate. Therefore, Exchange 2000 Server must use the common Site Services account for its communication with previous versions of Exchange Server as well.

When joining an existing site, you will be prompted for the Site Services account information. You can correct or change the Site Services account password within the Exchange System snap-in when displaying the properties of the administrative group that represents your site (such as BLUESKY-OLD-10, which can be found under Administrative Groups). Click Modify on the General property sheet to change the information displayed under Exchange 4.0/5.*x* Service Account For This Site.

Note The Site Services account specified in the properties of an administrative group is only used for communication with legacy Exchange systems. Exchange 2000 servers use the LocalSystem account for their native communication.

Intersite and Gateway Message Transfer

Exchange 2000 Server can utilize any existing connector installed in the site because SRS, in conjunction with the ADC, replicates configuration information, including information about connected sites and gateways, to Active Directory. Likewise, information about existing Exchange 2000 connectors is replicated to all Exchange directories. Earlier versions of Exchange Server can, therefore, also use new connectors for message transfer (see Figure 6.12).

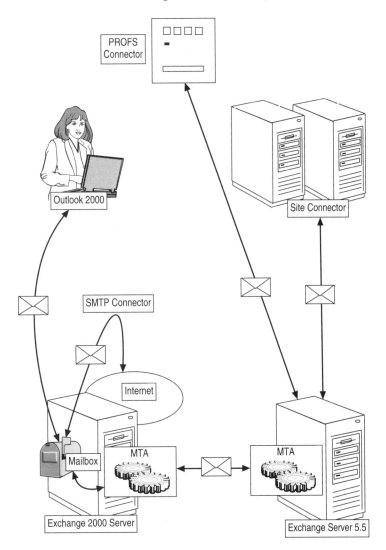

Figure 6.12   Intersite message transfer and gateway connections

---

Note   Through directory replication, routing information from servers running previous Exchange Server versions is placed in the Exchange 2000 Server link state table. This allows Exchange 2000 Servers to include any existing connectors in its routing decisions.

Proxy Addresses

Proxy address definitions must be preserved on Exchange 2000 Server so that all users in a site or administrative group have the same proxy addresses generated. Consequently, when joining an existing site, the proxy address definitions (SMTP, X.400, Lotus cc:Mail, and MS Mail) must be copied to a recipient policy for the administrative group that represents a particular site in Exchange 2000 Server. You can view the definition of the recipient policy in the Exchange System snap-in. In the console tree, open the Recipients container, and then select Recipient Policies. In the details pane, you will find an object with a name that corresponds to your site (such as BLUESKY-OLD-10) that has the highest priority. When you display the properties of this policy object, you will find a Filter Rule in the General property sheet that activates the policy for all objects with a LegacyExchangeDN attribute set to the organization and site name of the site that you joined with the Exchange 2000 server.

Upgrading Outlook Web Access

It is important to note that Outlook Web Access (OWA) will be replaced entirely when upgrading to Exchange 2000 Server. If you have customized the .asp pages of OWA to implement your own Web-based messaging solution, this solution will not work with Exchange 2000 Server, because OWA in Exchange 2000 Server has been entirely redesigned. The rendering process is handled directly by an Internet Server API (ISAPI) component (DAVEX.DLL) and other DLLs, instead of .asp pages. The new architecture is explained in Chapter 22, "Microsoft Outlook Web Access."

To preserve your customized solution, install Exchange 2000 Server on a separate computer running Windows 2000, and then use the move-mailbox approach to migrate mailboxes and public folders. Leave the old server running to front end Exchange 2000 Server with OWA from Exchange Server 5.5. When users connect to their mailboxes via HTTP and the legacy OWA version, the location of the mailbox is determined from the Exchange directory.

Note   You cannot front end a computer running Exchange Server 5.5 with OWA from Exchange 2000 Server.

Switching from Mixed Mode to Native Mode

As outlined in Chapter 5, it is advantageous to switch an Exchange 2000 Server organization into native mode as soon as all earlier versions of Exchange Server are upgraded. This gives you full control over the configuration of administrative and routing groups and eliminates mixed mode limitations. However, as long as computers running previous Exchange Server versions exist in your organization, changing to native mode is impossible. Consequently, the Change Mode button in the General property sheet of the organization (for example, Blue Sky Airlines [Exchange]) is deactivated in the Exchange System snap-in.

Important To switch an organization to native mode, all computers running previous Exchange Server versions must be upgraded or removed. Switching to native mode disables interoperability with previous versions, which is an irreversible process.

Exercise 5: Performing a Move-Mailbox Upgrade and Finalizing the Migration

In this exercise you will complete the migration of the test environment to Exchange 2000 Server by using the move-mailbox approach. As soon as all resources are on BLUESKY-PDC, you will remove the legacy system and switch the organization to native mode.

To view a multimedia demonstration that displays how to perform this procedure, run the EX5CH6*.AVI files from the \Exercise_Information\Chapter6 folder on the Supplemental Course Materials CD.

Prerequisites

- Make sure several mailboxes exist on BLUESKY-BDC, as outlined in the installation description provided in the "Getting Started" section of "About This Book."

- Complete Exercise 4, earlier in this lesson.

- Log on as Administrator to BLUESKY-PDC and BLUESKY-BDC.

▶ **To perform a move-mailbox upgrade and finalize the migration**

1. On BLUESKY-PDC, start the Active Directory Users and Computers management tool and open the Users OU.

2. Right-click Users, point to All Tasks, and then select Find.

3. In the Find Users, Contacts, And Groups dialog box, switch to the Exchange tab, and then select the Show Only Exchange Recipients and Users With Exchange Mailbox check boxes.

4. Click Find Now and then select all accounts listed at the bottom of the dialog box.

5. Right-click the selected accounts, and from the shortcut menu, select Enable Account. You need to enable the user accounts; otherwise, you will experience problems moving the mailboxes.

6. In the Active Directory dialog box informing you that all selected user objects are enabled, click OK.

Note The Active Directory Connector adds a description of Disabled Windows User Account to each disabled object that it creates for an Exchange Server 5.5 mailbox. When enabling these accounts, the description is not changed automatically. In a production environment, you have to update this information manually (or using LDIFDE for batch operation) to avoid confusing account descriptions in Active Directory.

---

7. Right-click the selected accounts again, and from the shortcut menu, select Exchange Tasks.

8. On the Exchange Task Wizard welcome screen, click Next.

9. On the Available Tasks wizard screen, select Move Mailbox, and then click Next.

10. On the Move Mailbox wizard screen, under Server, select Blue Sky Airlines/ BLUESKY-OLD-10/BLUESKY-PDC.

11. Under Mailbox Store, make sure First Storage Group/Private Information Store (BLUESKY-PDC) is displayed, and then click Next.

12. A Task In Progress wizard screen will appear, informing you about the mailbox move. After that a final wizard screen will be displayed summarizing the process. Click Finish and then close Active Directory Users and Computers.

At this point, you have successfully moved all mailbox resources to the new Exchange 2000 server (see Figure 6.13). You would also have to replicate existing public folder instances to the new server, which is not required in the test environment because public folders were not created. Public folder replication is covered in Chapter 18, "Public Folder Replication."

13. On BLUESKY-BDC, insert the Exchange Server 5.5 installation CD into the CD drive, launch Setup in maintenance mode, and remove the Exchange Server installation.

14. On BLUESKY-PDC, start the Exchange System snap-in from the Microsoft Exchange program group.

15. In the console tree, open Administrative Groups, then BLUESKY-OLD-10, then Servers. Verify that the server BLUESKY-BDC still exists in the Active Directory information. Note that you cannot delete the server from within the Exchange System snap-in.

16. From the Microsoft Exchange program group, start the Exchange 5.5 Administrator program.

17. From the File menu, select Connect To Server. In the Connect To Server dialog box, type **BLUESKY-PDC**, and click OK.

18. Expand the directory information tree and, under Servers, select BLUESKY-BDC.

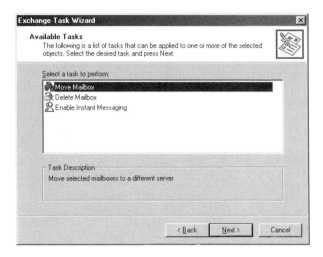

Figure 6.13   Moving mailboxes to Exchange 2000 Server

19. From the Edit menu, select Delete. In the Microsoft Exchange Administrator dialog box asking whether you are sure to delete the server with all its resources, click Yes (see Figure 6.14).

20. In the Microsoft Exchange Administrator dialog box asking whether you are sure to delete all corresponding public folder instances, click Yes.

21. In the final Microsoft Exchange Administrator dialog box informing you that the server was deleted successfully, click OK, and then close the Exchange Administrator program.

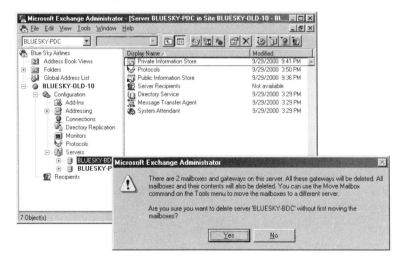

Figure 6.14   An Exchange 2000 organization in native mode

22. Open the Active Directory Connector tool from the Microsoft Exchange program group. Select the configuration connection agreement Config CA_ BLUESKY-OLD-10_BLUESKY-PDC, right-click on it, and, from the shortcut menu, select Replicate Now to immediately transfer the changes from the SRS database to Active Directory. After the replication is complete, close the Active Directory Connector tool.

23. Switch to the Exchange System snap-in, and refresh the view by pressing F5. Notice that the server BLUESKY-BDC disappears.

24. Open the Tools container, then open Site Replication Services. Right-click Microsoft Exchange Site Replication Service (BLUESKY-PDC).

25. From the shortcut menu, select Delete and, in the Exchange System Manager dialog box, click Yes to delete the replication service.

26. Open the Active Directory Connector tool again, and note that the configuration connection agreement was deleted automatically. Delete the user connection agreement CA for Blue Sky Airlines as well. Confirm all warning messages with OK.

27. Switch to the Exchange System snap-in, right-click on the organization object Blue Sky Airlines (Exchange), and, from the shortcut menu, select Properties.

28. In the General property sheet, click on the Change Mode button. In the Exchange System Manager dialog box informing you that this process is irreversible, click Yes, and then click OK.

At this point, you are operating a native mode Exchange 2000 organization that cannot integrate earlier versions of Exchange Server, which is indicated by the missing Site Replication Service container that once was available under Tools in mixed mode.

Exercise Summary

Although the move-mailbox upgrade represents an interesting alternative to the in-place approach, a complete migration requires numerous manual configuration steps. After you have removed a server running an earlier version of Exchange Server from the site, you need to delete its references from Active Directory using the Exchange Administrator program. The last Exchange server must be deleted from the SRS database manually because no other Exchange directory service exists in the site that could accomplish this via directory replication.

Active Directory Cleanups

Upgraded users now working with mailboxes on Exchange 2000 Server will notice subtle changes in the structure of the address book because they now connect to a Global Catalog server for address lookups, as explained in Chapter 2, "Integration with Windows 2000." However, users might sometimes see duplicate accounts in the address book. These duplicate accounts, which might be generated during the migration process, require a dedicated cleanup using the Active Directory Account Cleanup Wizard.

Duplicate Account Generation

The procedures outlined in this chapter rely on a Windows NT and Exchange Server in-place upgrade, which implicitly prevents the generation of duplicate accounts because the user accounts are converted to Windows 2000 accounts first and then synchronized with Exchange Server 5.5 mailbox information. However, depending on the complexity of your Windows NT domain environment, it might be necessary to synchronize Exchange Server 5.5 mailbox information before upgrading Windows NT user accounts, in which case user connection agreements of the ADC create Windows 2000 accounts for all those mailboxes for which user account information was missing in Active Directory. This may happen, for instance, when users work with Exchange Server mailboxes that reside in different domains and all PDCs could not be upgraded to Windows 2000. If ADC user connection agreements generated Windows 2000 accounts for those Windows NT users' mailboxes, and you upgrade these users to Windows 2000 at a later time, you will end up with duplicate accounts (see Figure 6.15).

Tip   To avoid the generation of duplicate accounts in your environment, upgrade all existing PDCs to Windows 2000 before configuring user connections agreements with the ADC.

Using the Active Directory Cleanup Wizard

If you need to remove numerous duplicate accounts from Active Directory, you will find the Active Directory Cleanup Wizard a very helpful tool. It is available in the Microsoft Exchange program group. This utility searches through the Active Directory forest for possible duplicate Windows NT accounts and displays a list of duplicates that were found, giving you the opportunity to review andadjust the cleanup procedure. It is also possible to manually match duplicates that were not found and merge duplicate accounts into a selected destination account. Merging duplicate accounts preserves group and distribution list membership and access permissions to existing resources. You can find more information about the Active Directory Cleanup Wizard in the Microsoft Exchange 2000 Server online documentation.

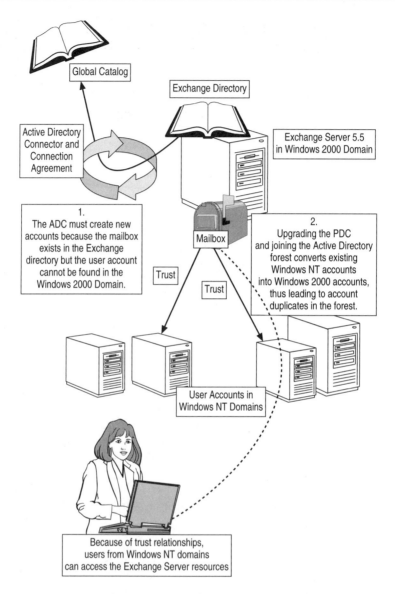

Figure 6.15   Duplicate account creation

Note   It is not possible to perform cleanups or merge operations across multiple Active Directory forests.

Chapter Summary

You must deploy Windows 2000 and Active Directory if you are planning to install Exchange 2000 Server. Because Exchange 2000 Server must use the Site Services account for its communication with previous versions, you must first upgrade the PDC of the domain in which the Exchange Site Services account exists. If you are planning to directly upgrade an existing Exchange Server 5.5 system, you need to upgrade its operating system as well, and possibly change the TCP port number for the LDAP interface of the Exchange directory service.

By upgrading the PDC, you migrate Windows NT user accounts to Active Directory. The corresponding mailbox information, however, still resides in the Exchange directory. Consequently, you need to synchronize both directories via a connection agreement to add the mailbox information to the user account objects.

Whether you join an existing site with a new Exchange 2000 server or perform an in-place upgrade, Exchange 2000 Server must replicate directory information with earlier versions of Exchange Server, which is handled by SRS. A configuration connection agreement transfers the directory information from the SRS database into Active Directory, where previous Exchange Server resources are displayed as transparent objects. In the Exchange Administrator program, Exchange 2000 servers appear similar to servers running previous versions of Exchange Server.

To switch an organization to native mode, all computers running previous Exchange Server versions must be upgraded or removed. Switching to native mode permanently disables interoperability with previous versions.

Review

The following review questions can help you determine if you have sufficiently familiarized yourself with the material covered in this chapter. You can find the answers to these questions at the end of this book in Appendix A, "Questions and Answers."

1. You are planning to integrate Exchange 2000 Server into an existing Exchange Server 5.5 site. Which two strategies can you use?

2. Your Exchange Server organization consists of one site containing a mixed installation of various earlier server versions, such as Exchange Server 5.0 and Exchange Server 5.0 Service Pack 3. You are planning to upgrade with a minimal disruption of business processes. Which upgrade strategy would be best?

3. You have joined an existing site with a new Exchange 2000 server. You now plan to use the Exchange System snap-in to manage the resources of the site. How can you manage Exchange Server 5.5 Service Pack 3 resources via Active Directory?

4. You have joined an existing site of eight servers with one new Exchange 2000 server. Which utility should you use to manage mailbox resources in this site?

5. You have successfully migrated all resources to Exchange 2000 Server using the move-mailbox approach. You now plan to switch the organization into native mode. What do you need to accomplish before you can carry out the change?

C H A P T E R   7

Microsoft Exchange 2000 Server in Clustered Environments

About This Chapter

Digital Equipment Corporation and Microsoft developed their first popular Microsoft Windows NT clustering products in the mid-1990s—Digital Clusters for Windows NT and Microsoft Cluster Server 1.0. The earliest version of Exchange Server offering true clustering support was Microsoft Exchange Server 5.5 Enterprise Edition. With Windows 2000 Advanced Server and Windows 2000 Datacenter Server, clustering is supported in the form of the Cluster service. Of course, Exchange 2000 Enterprise Server also supports clustering, giving you a complete, mission-critical messaging solution. Clustering support is not available with the Exchange 2000 Standard Server.

Clustering is an advanced technology that allows you to design high availability solutions for your enterprise-level applications. It is a complex technology, yet straightforward to handle and worth evaluating. Together with proper hardware and system management, clustering can help you to improve the availability of your systems. Clustering is often brought into play in business-critical services such as messaging in an enterprise environment.

This chapter focuses on the installation of Exchange 2000 Server in a clustered Windows 2000 environment. Lesson 1 provides a brief introduction to the clustering technology. With an eye on Exchange 2000 resources, Lesson 2 then covers important load-balancing concepts, such as active/active clustering and failover procedures. In Lesson 3, you can read about the actual installation of Exchange 2000 Server into clusters that consist of up to four nodes.

Before You Begin

To complete this chapter:

- Prepare your test environment according to the descriptions given in the "Getting Started" section of "About This Book."
- Be familiar with the components of Exchange 2000 Server, as explained in Chapter 3, "Microsoft Exchange 2000 Server Architecture."
- Have a general understanding and practical experience with the Windows 2000 Cluster service.

Lesson 1: Cluster Service Architecture

A cluster is basically a group of servers that appear as a single virtual server. A virtual server corresponds to a generic IP address and a network name, and allows your users to access all the resources in the cluster, including Exchange 2000 services, without having to know the names of the individual nodes. Even if one system fails and a second node must assume the workload, your users can immediately reconnect using the generic cluster name, which hides the complexity of the cluster from the users completely. By grouping two or more computers together in a cluster, you can minimize system downtime caused by software, network, and hardware failures. On one cluster you can configure multiple virtual servers.

This lesson highlights the general characteristics of clustered systems running Windows 2000 Advanced Server or Windows 2000 Datacenter Server. It introduces specific hardware requirements and covers other dependencies that you need to take into consideration when designing a cluster for Exchange 2000 Enterprise Server.

At the end of this lesson, you will be able to:
- Identify important features and issues regarding the clustering technology.
- Describe the architecture of the Windows 2000 Cluster service.

Estimated time to complete this lesson: 75 minutes

Server Clusters in Exchange 2000 Environments

Clustering is a mature technology available for all popular network operating systems, including Solaris and Windows 2000. Nonetheless, it is still a controversial instrumentation. For instance, organizations often utilize clustered Windows 2000 systems to provide continuous, uninterrupted services to their users. Implicitly, it is assumed that clustering provides fault tolerance in all imaginable areas, including information store databases. Despite assumptions and desires, it is impossible to achieve these goals with Windows 2000 Cluster service. Although it is not a 100% perfect solution, clustering does reduce the number of potential single points of failure and thereby improves service availability.

In the case of a system failure, the Cluster service takes the virtual server offline on the first node before it takes it online again on another cluster member; hence, business processes are interrupted, and users need to reconnect to the cluster after the failover. The advantage of clustering, however, is that your users can reconnect almost immediately. The Cluster service is indeed the world's fastest system repair service. Likewise, clusters don't protect and don't repair information store databases, which remain single points of failure no matter how many nodes your cluster contains. Therefore, you still have to develop a sound backup and disaster recovery strategy, as discussed in Chapter 20, "Microsoft Exchange 2000 Server Maintenance and Troubleshooting."

Advantages of Server Clusters

Despite their limitations, clusters can significantly improve system availability in case of hardware or software failures or during planned maintenance. Clusters are an ideal choice if you want to build Exchange 2000 systems that your company depends on for its business. Clusters can also be used to scale to support a very large user base. To give an example, you could group four quad-processor

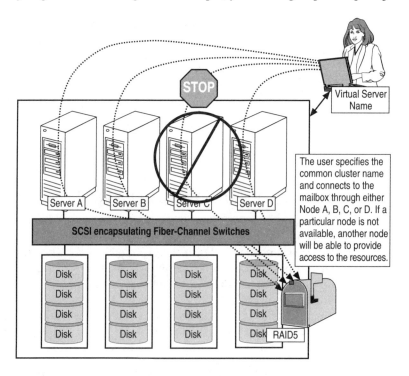

Figure 7.1   A four-node Windows 2000 cluster

systems and four shared redundant arrays of independent disks (RAIDs) together and let this cluster handle four individual storage groups each containing 5000 mailboxes. That's 20,000 users you can support with one clustered system (see Figure 7.1).

Important   To take advantage of four-node clustering and 64 GB memory support, you must install Windows 2000 Datacenter Server.

The advantages of clustered Windows 2000 systems are:

- High availability of system resources
- Improved scalability through grouping of server resources
- Reduced system management costs

Cluster Hardware Configuration

Figure 7.2 illustrates the essential hardware components of a cluster. A shared Small Computer System Interface (SCSI) bus and two network cards are required in addition to typical server equipment, such as a local disk where the operating system must be installed. The shared SCSI bus allows all nodes access to the cluster disks. The public network adapters, again, provide client connectivity and a communication path between the nodes. In intervals of seconds, nodes exchange state information between each other, which is known as a heartbeat. The public network adapters should be configured redundantly on each server to reduce the chance that a failure of a network interface card will result in the failure of the entire cluster. The private network adapter, on the other hand, is optional and should be installed to implement an additional communication channel between the nodes in case the public network fails. The private network adapter is not a requirement, but it is necessary if you want to create a cluster with complete hardware redundancy.

The nodes in a cluster are connected by up to three physical connections:

- **Shared storage bus.**   Connects all nodes to the disks (or RAID storage systems) where all clustered data must reside. A cluster can support more than one shared storage bus if multiple adapters are installed in each node.
- **Public network connection.**   Connects client computers to the nodes in the cluster. The public network is the primary network interface of the cluster. Fast and reliable network cards, such as Fast Ethernet or Fiber Distributed Data Interface (FDDI) cards, should be used for the public interface.
- **Private network connection.**   Connects the nodes in a cluster and ensures that the nodes will be able to communicate with each other in the event of an

outage of the public local area network (LAN). The private LAN is optional but highly recommended. Low-cost Ethernet cards are sufficient to accommodate the minimal traffic of the cluster communication.

It is very important that you check Microsoft's Hardware Compatibility List, specifically, for the Cluster service. Only hardware components, especially host bus adapters and disks that are tested by Microsoft, should be used for clustering. In addition, make sure the host bus adapters are of the same kind and have the same firmware revision. Configure the shared storage carefully. If you are using a traditional SCSI-based cluster, connect only disks and SCSI adapters to it—no tape devices, CDs, scanners, and so forth—and ensure that the bus is terminated properly on both ends. If you choose a critical hardware component or improperly

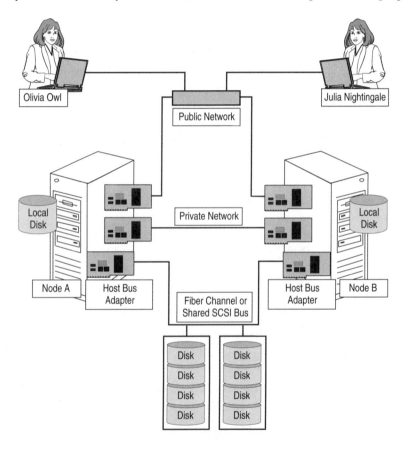

Figure 7.2   Physical connections in a two-node cluster

terminate the shared SCSI bus, you may end up with corruption of the cluster disks instead of a reliable and highly available cluster.

Tip   It is advisable to purchase complete cluster sets from reliable hardware vendors instead of configuring the cluster hardware manually.

Partitioned Data Access

As shown in Figure 7.2, Olivia and Julia are both able to access the shared SCSI disk sets of the cluster through either Node A or Node B. However, it is impossible to access the shared disks through both Node A and Node B at the same time. This is because the Cluster service of Windows 2000 does not support concurrent access to shared disks, also known as the "shared-everything" data access model, which is more common in mainframe-oriented environments.

To avoid the overhead of synchronizing concurrent disk access, the Cluster service of Windows 2000 relies on the partitioned data model, in jargon also called "shared-nothing" model. The shared-nothing model is usually sufficient for PC systems, but its disadvantage is that you cannot achieve dynamic load balancing. For instance, when you configure a resource group for a virtual Exchange 2000 Server in a two-node cluster (as shown in Figure 7.2), only one node at a time can own this resource group and provide access to its resources. In the event of a failure, the Exchange 2000 resource group can be failed over (moved) from the failed node to another node in the cluster, but it is impossible to activate the same virtual server on more than one node in tandem.

Gaining and Defending Physical Control

The fact that the Cluster service relies on the partitioned data model has far-reaching design consequences. For example, it doesn't make much sense to configure a four-node cluster with just one shared physical disk set (see Figure 7.3). As mentioned, this disk set can only be owned by one node. The node owning the resource would request exclusive access to the disk by using the SCSI Reserve command. No other node can then access the physical device unless an SCSI Release command is issued. Hence, the three other nodes must remain idle until the first node fails.

Note   Only one node can gain access to a particular disk at any given time even though the disks on the shared SCSI bus are physically connected to all cluster nodes.

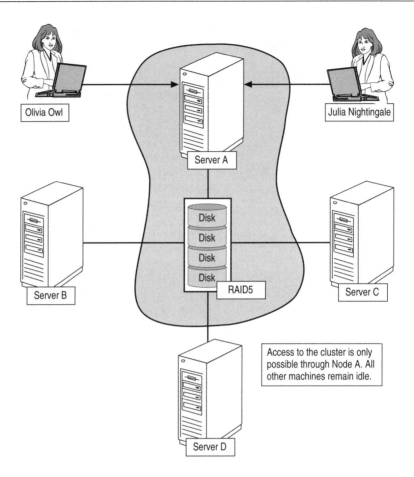

Figure 7.3   A questionable four-node cluster configuration

Windows 2000 Clustering Architecture

To act as one unit, clustered Windows 2000 computers must cooperate with each other closely. The Cluster service consists of several internal elements and relies on additional external components to handle the required tasks. The Node Manager, for instance, is an internal module that maintains a list of nodes that belong to the cluster and monitors their system state. It is this component that periodically sends heartbeat messages to its counterparts running on other nodes in the cluster. The heartbeats allow the node managers to recognize node faults. The Communications Manager, another internal component, manages the communication between all nodes of the cluster through the cluster network driver (see Figure 7.4).

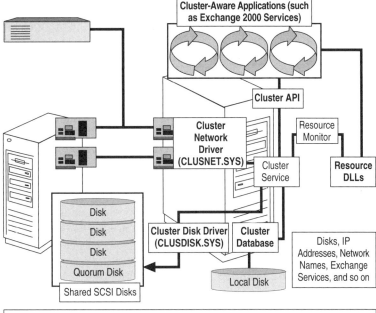

Figure 7.4 Cluster service and its external components

Resource Monitoring and Failover Initiation

The health of each cluster resource is monitored by the Resource Monitor, which is implemented in a separate process communicating with the Cluster service via remote procedure calls (RPCs). Resource Monitor relies on Resource DLLs to manage the resources (see Figure 7.4). Resources are any physical or logical components that the Resource Manager (another internal component of the Cluster service) can manage, such as disks, IP addresses, network names, Exchange 2000 Server services, and so forth. The Resource Manager receives system information from resource monitor and node manager to manage resources and resource groups and initiate actions, such as startup, restart, and failover. To carry out a failover, the Resource Manager works in conjunction with the Failover Manager. The failover procedures are explained in Lesson 2.

Configuration Changes and the Quorum Disk

Other important components are the Configuration Database Manager, which maintains the cluster configuration database, and the Checkpoint Manager, which saves the configuration data in a log file on the quorum disk. The configuration database, also known as the cluster registry, is separate from the local Windows 2000 Registry, although a copy of the cluster registry is kept in the Windows 2000 Registry. The configuration database maintains updates on members, resources, restart parameters, and other configuration information.

The quorum disk, which holds the configuration data log files, is a cluster-specific resource used to communicate configuration changes to all nodes in the cluster. The Global Update Manager provides the update service that transfers configuration changes into the configuration database of each node. The quorum resource also holds the recovery logs written by the internal Log Manager module of the Cluster service. There can only be one quorum disk in a single Windows 2000 cluster.

Joining a Cluster and Event Handling

When you start a server that is part of a cluster, Windows 2000 is booted as usual, mounting and configuring local, noncluster resources. After all, each node in a Windows 2000 cluster is also a Windows 2000 Advanced Server or Datacenter Server in itself. The Cluster service is typically set to automatic startup. When this service starts, the server determines the other nodes in the cluster based on the information from the local copy of the cluster registry. The Cluster service attempts to find an active cluster node (known as the sponsor) that can authenticate the local service. The sponsor then broadcasts information about the authenticated node to other cluster members and sends the authenticated Cluster service an updated registry if the authenticated service's cluster database was found outdated.

From the point of view of other nodes in the cluster, a node may be in one of three states: offline, online, or paused. A node is offline when it is not an active member of the cluster. A node is online when it is fully active, is able to own and manage resource groups, accepts cluster database updates, and contributes votes to the quorum algorithm. The quorum algorithm determines which node can own the quorum disk. A paused node is an online node unable to own or run resource groups. You may pause a node for maintenance reasons, for instance.

The Event Processor, another internal component of the Cluster service, manages the node state information and controls the initialization of the Cluster service. This component transfers event notifications between Cluster service components and between the Cluster service and cluster-aware applications. For example, the Event Processor activates the Node Manager to begin the process of joining or forming a cluster.

Lesson 2: Load Planning and Failover Strategies

As emphasized in Lesson 1, only one node can gain access to a particular disk at any given time. This prevents running a particular virtual Exchange 2000 server on more than one node concurrently. Furthermore, the Windows 2000 Cluster service does not support the moving of running applications between nodes; hence, during a failover, clients will lose their connections and need to reconnect. Nevertheless, Microsoft Outlook 2000 and Exchange 2000 Server are designed to overcome these shortcomings in a smart way. For example, you don't need to restart Outlook 2000 to reconnect. A simple switch to another folder in your mailbox (let's say from Inbox to Contacts) does the job. Exchange 2000 Enterprise Server, again, supports multiple storage groups in the information store, which is the basis of static load balancing in clustered Exchange 2000 systems.

This lesson focuses on the optimal configuration of clustered systems by means of load-balancing mechanisms. Load balancing allows you to run similar services on multiple nodes, thus making better use of the available hardware than suggested in Figure 7.3.

At the end of this lesson, you will be able to:

- Describe how to distribute the workload of Outlook 2000 clients across multiple nodes in a single cluster
- Explain the processes of failover and failback

Estimated time to complete this lesson: 45 minutes

Load-Balancing Clusters

To best utilize the hardware resources available in a cluster, most organizations implement combined application servers that provide more than one kind of client/server services to their users (see Figure 7.5). If one node fails, its application instances (represented as virtual server resource groups) are moved to one of the remaining nodes. This may reduce the performance of this node somewhat, but the cluster quickly continues to provide the complete set of application services, which is probably more important than a temporary performance decrease.

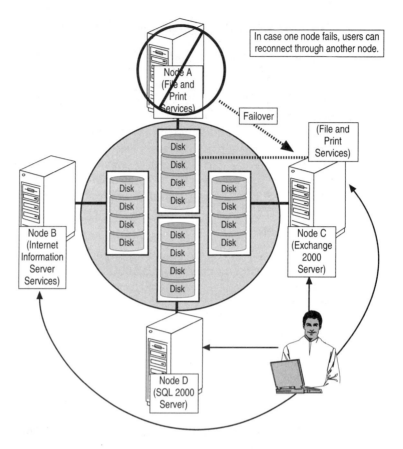

Figure 7.5 An example of a clustered multiapplication server

Active/Active Clustering

It may be desirable to dedicate individual clusters to one application type. For
instance, you might want to configure a two-node cluster for Microsoft SQL
2000 Server and another four-node cluster for Exchange 2000 Server only. In this
case, you need to configure multiple virtual servers of the same type per cluster
and distribute them across the nodes, thus providing static load balancing. This
configuration is often referred to as an active/active configuration. Keep in mind
that each virtual server requires access to its own disk resources, meaning one or
more dedicated sets of physical disks.

Note   Exchange 2000 Enterprise Server supports active/active clustering.

To maximize the use of all available servers in a cluster while maintaining a
failover solution, you can configure multiple virtual servers and distribute them
across your nodes. Virtual servers are resource groups. Resource groups contain

resources, such as an IP address, network name, and a disk. However, only one resource group and therefore one virtual server can own a resource. In other words, if you want to configure four virtual servers in a four-node cluster, you will need four separate physical disks. Because the cluster server requires access to the quorum disk, you can configure $n - 1$ virtual Exchange 2000 servers (see Figure 7.6), where n represents the number of physical disks on the shared storage.

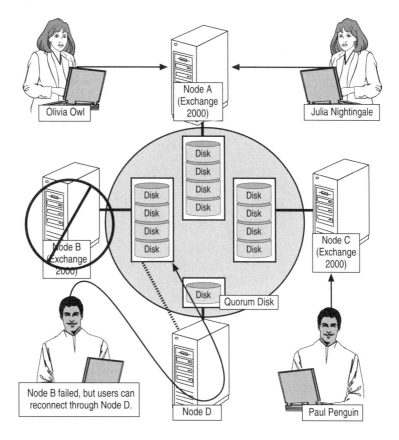

Figure 7.6   A four-node cluster with three virtual Exchange 2000 servers

Tip   Theoretically, you can configure one virtual Exchange 2000 server per physical disk, including the disk containing the quorum resource. However, Microsoft does not recommend adding Exchange 2000 Server services to the virtual server representing the cluster (that is, owning the quorum disk). Defining dedicated virtual servers for Exchange 2000 simplifies service maintenance, such as taking a virtual Exchange 2000 system offline.

Full Load with Hot Spare

The configuration shown in Figure 7.6 corresponds to a fully loaded system with one hot spare node. When all nodes are online, Node D does not own a virtual Exchange 2000 server. This is the hot spare assuming the role of an Exchange 2000 server in case another node in the cluster fails or is unavailable for maintenance reasons. Provided that you don't run other applications on the hot spare, such as SQL 2000 Server, a single node failure will not affect the system performance.

Full-Load Active Nodes

The hot spare configuration bears the disadvantage of an idle server system when every node is operational. If you don't want to invest in this extra server, configure a three-node cluster with four disks, as shown in Figure 7.7 (or add a fifth disk to your four-node cluster). The disadvantage of a full-load cluster is that users might experience performance losses if one node has to take over the load of a failed member. Hence, it is a good idea to operate all nodes in the cluster at less than their maximum capabilities.

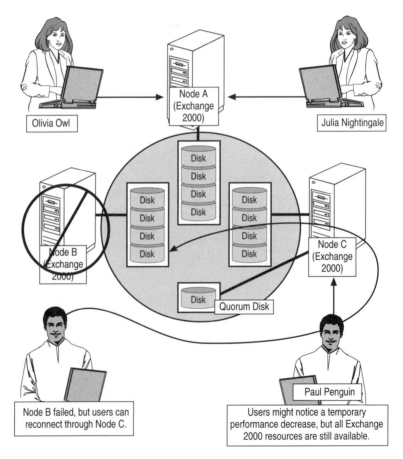

Figure 7.7   A full-load active cluster with three virtual Exchange 2000 servers

To avoid measurable performance losses, you would have to operate the nodes below the following theoretical limits:

- **Two-node clusters.** 50% of the node's power (which is as good as configuring an active/passive cluster and using 100% of the active node's power)
- **Three-node clusters.** 66% of the node's power
- **Four-node clusters.** 75% of the node's power

However, in most cases it will be acceptable to operate the nodes of a full-load cluster at their maximum capabilities because node failures or failovers due to maintenance should seldom occur and temporary performance losses are usually not critical. Note that central processing unit (CPU) utilization is not a perfect measure of the node's power; a node will begin to experience performance degradation if operating above 70% peak CPU utilization for an extended period of time.

Exchange 2000 and Virtual Server Limitations

When designing your clustered Exchange 2000 environment, keep in mind that limitations apply to your virtual servers. Several Exchange 2000 Server components are not supported in a cluster, and others can only run in an active/passive configuration. The Message Transfer Agent (MTA), for instance, cannot run on more than one node in the cluster, implicitly enforcing an active/passive configuration. The same restriction applies to the Chat Service.

The Exchange 2000 components support the following cluster configurations:

- **Chat.** Active/passive
- **Full-text indexing.** Active/active
- **HTTP.** Active/active
- **IMAP.** Active/active
- **Information Store.** Active/active
- **Instant Messaging.** Not supported
- **Key Management Service (KMS).** Not supported
- **MTA.** Active/passive
- **Network News Transfer Protocol (NNTP).** Not supported
- **POP3.** Active/active
- **Simple Mail Transfer Protocol (SMTP).** Active/active
- **System Attendant (SA).** Active/active

Important Exchange 2000 Server supports only one public store in a cluster. When adding an additional virtual server, make sure you delete the public store in the new resource group before bringing the virtual server online.

Failover and Failback Procedures

Failover and failback are cluster-specific procedures to move resource groups (with all their associated resources) between nodes. Failover is transferring resource groups from a decommissioned or failed node to another node in the cluster that is available. Failback describes the process of moving the resource groups back when the node that was offline is online again (see Figure 7.8).

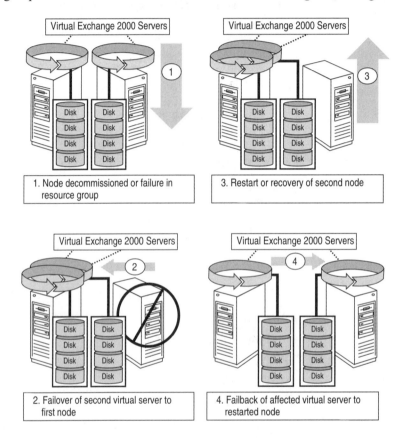

Figure 7.8   Failover and failback of virtual Exchange 2000 servers

Failover

A failover can occur in two situations: Either you trigger it manually for maintenance reasons or the Cluster service initiates it automatically in case of a resource failure on the node owning the resource. If a resource fails, the Resource Manager first attempts a resource restart on the local node. If this does not correct the problem, the Resource Manager will take the resource group offline along with its dependent resources and inform the Failover Manager that the affected group should be moved to another node and restarted there.

The Failover Manager is now responsible for deciding where to move the resource group. It communicates with its counterparts on the remaining active nodes to arbitrate the ownership of the resource group. This arbitration relies on the node preference list that you can specify when creating resources in Cluster Administrator. The arbitration can also take into account other factors such as the capabilities of each node, the current load, and application information. After a new node is determined for the resource group, all nodes update their cluster databases to track which node owns the resource group. At this point, the new owner of the resource group turns control of the resources within the resource group over to its Resource Manager. If multiple resource groups are affected, for instance, because of a total node failure, the process is repeated for all of these groups.

Failback

If you have specified a preferred owner for a resource group, and this node comes back online again, the Failover Manager will fail back the resource group to the recovered or restarted node. Cluster service provides protection against continuous resource failures resulting from repeating failback to nodes that have not been correctly recovered by limiting the number of times the failback is attempted. Likewise, you can configure specific hours of the day during which the failback of a group is prohibited, for instance, at peak business hours.

By default, resource groups are set not to fail back automatically when the original node is recovered. Without manual configuration of a failback policy, groups continue to run on the alternate node after the failed node comes back online.

Lesson 3: Clustering Support in Exchange 2000 Server

Many Exchange 2000 Server components support active/active or at least active/ passive clustering. However, several components, such as the NNTP service, the KMS, or connectors to other mail systems are not supported. Therefore, you should integrate an Exchange 2000 cluster into an environment with nonclustered servers functioning as bridgehead servers to communicate with other systems. This is an acceptable approach because permanent availability is seldom an issue for bridgehead servers that don't host mailboxes or public servers. Likewise, it is not advantageous to install front end servers in systems clustered using the Windows 2000 Cluster service. Because front ends only relay Internet-based clients to back end servers, use Windows 2000 Network Load Balancing or another network load-balancing solution instead.

This lesson discusses the installation of Exchange 2000 Server in a Windows 2000 cluster. It illustrates differences in comparison to an installation in a nonclustered environment and explains how to configure virtual Exchange 2000 servers. This lesson concludes with a brief explanation about how to upgrade Exchange Server 5.5 clusters.

At the end of this lesson, you will be able to:

- Install Exchange 2000 Server in a Windows 2000 cluster
- Identify important resources for virtual Exchange 2000 Server
- Test the failover procedures for virtual servers
- Upgrade clustered Exchange Server 5.5 installations

Estimated time to complete this lesson: 90 minutes

Exchange 2000 Server Clustering Installation

The installation of Exchange 2000 Server in a cluster is a process of four stages. First, you need to install Windows 2000 Advanced Server or Datacenter Server on all nodes in the cluster. In a second step, you have to install the Cluster service on the nodes and configure the cluster environment. Then, you are ready for the Exchange 2000 Server installation. Exchange 2000 Server must be installed on all nodes with exactly the same parameters, and, after that, you can configure and start virtual servers in Cluster Administrator.

Important   You cannot install Exchange 2000 Server on a nonclustered server and integrate this installation into a cluster afterward. Furthermore, it is a good idea to test the installation in a cluster prior to deploying Exchange 2000 Server in the production environment. Exchange 2000 Server may not function properly with your hardware. You need to ensure that a dedicated Physical Disk resource is available for Exchange 2000 Server.

Installing Exchange 2000 in a Cluster

It is easy to install Exchange 2000 Server in a clustered system. When the Setup program detects the Cluster service, it displays the Microsoft Exchange 2000 Installation Wizard, informing you that the cluster-aware version of Exchange 2000 Server will be installed. Setup then copies and configures the Exchange 2000 components and resource DLLs and sets the Exchange 2000 service to start manually. This prevents the services from starting automatically when rebooting the server, which is required at the end of the installation.

Important   Do not start or stop clustered Exchange 2000 services in the Services management tool. You have to use Cluster Administrator to bring clustered services online or offline.

Clustered Installation Features and Dependencies

During the installation of Exchange 2000 Server in a cluster, resource DLLs and other components are added to the configuration of each node. It is important that you install only one node at a time using the same account you used to install the Cluster service. This account must have the required permissions to set up Exchange 2000 Server in a forest as outlined in Chapter 4, "Planning the Microsoft Exchange 2000 Server Installation."

It is also important to specify the same drive letters and directory on all the nodes in the cluster. During installation, you need to place the binary files on the local system drive of each node. The binary files are not shared between the nodes. Don't forget to make sure that drive M is not in use on any node because when you configure virtual servers later on, the Microsoft Web Storage System will use the M drive by default. If this drive is not available, the Web Storage System uses the next drive letter automatically; however, it is important that all nodes use the same drive.

Setup Initialization File

Because you must install the same Exchange 2000 components on all the nodes of the cluster, it is a good idea to create and use a SETUP.INI file. This allows you to run Setup unattended with exactly the same options on all nodes. Keep in mind, however, that you should not start the Setup program on a second node before the first installation is completed and the node rebooted. At minimum, install Microsoft Exchange Messaging and Collaboration and Microsoft Exchange System Management Tools on all nodes.

Exercise 1: Installing Exchange 2000 Server in a Cluster

In this exercise, you will install Exchange 2000 Server in a cluster with two nodes. The configuration of virtual servers, however, is not addressed yet. This will be the objective for Exercise 2 later in this lesson.

To view a multimedia demonstration that displays how to perform this procedure, run the EX1CH7*.AVI files from the \Exercise_Information\Chapter7 folder on the Supplemental Course Materials CD.

Prerequisites

- Prepare the test environment as described in the "About This Book" section.
- Make sure the domain controller BLUESKY-SRV1 running Exchange 2000 Server as a nonclustered system is available in the network.
- Log on as Administrator to BLUESKY-ND1 and BLUESKY-ND2.

▶ **To install Exchange 2000 Server on a clustered system**

1. On BLUESKY-ND1, insert the Exchange 2000 Server CD in the CD drive and launch Setup from the \Setup\i386 directory.

2. The Welcome To The Microsoft Exchange 2000 Installation Wizard screen appears. Click Next to start the installation.

3. In the End-User License Agreement dialog box, select I Agree, and then click Next to continue the installation.

4. On the Product Identification wizard screen, under CD Key, enter your CD key, and then click Next.

5. On the Component Selection wizard screen, under Action, verify that Typical is selected in the first row for Microsoft Exchange 2000. Leave all other settings at their defaults and click Next.

6. On the Licensing Agreement wizard screen, select I Agree That: That I Have Read And Agree To Be Bound By The License Agreements For This Product, and then click Next to continue the installation.

7. On the Component Summary wizard screen, verify that the configuration settings are correct, and then click Next to copy the files to your computer's hard disk.

8. The Microsoft Exchange 2000 Installation Wizard box will appear, informing you that Setup will install the cluster-aware version of Exchange 2000 Server. Click OK.

9. Another Microsoft Exchange 2000 Installation Wizard box will appear, informing you that you need to reboot the server after Setup is completed. Click OK.

10. On the final wizard screen, click Finish and reboot BLUESKY-ND1.

11. After BLUESKY-ND1 is up and running again, repeat the steps on BLUESKY-ND2, and make sure you install Exchange 2000 Server with exactly the same components and directories. At this point, you have installed the Exchange 2000 binary files in the clustered environment (see Figure 7.9).

12. On either node, click Start, point to Programs, then to Administrative Tools, and then click Services.

13. In the Services utility, search for the Exchange 2000 services, and verify that Startup Type is set to Manual.

Figure 7.9   Installing Exchange 2000 in a clustered environment

Exercise Summary

Installation of Exchange 2000 Server is a straightforward process. Setup detects that it is started on a cluster node and configures the Exchange 2000 components and services appropriately. It is important to set up all nodes using the same directories and installation options. The Exchange 2000 services will be configured to start manually. Don't start the services in a cluster in the Services Management tool because this undermines the cluster environment. Clustered services are managed within Cluster Administrator.

Important   Do not configure restart settings in the Services management utility for services that have been installed in a cluster; it would interfere with the cluster management software.

Resource Groups and Virtual Servers

As soon as you have installed Exchange 2000 Server on all cluster nodes, you are ready to configure resource groups. Each virtual server (equivalent to a resource group) requires an IP address and a network name. Your users will specify the network name in the settings of the Exchange transport service to connect to their mailboxes. The configuration of the Exchange transport service is covered in Chapter 8, "Microsoft Outlook 2000 Deployment."

Each virtual Exchange 2000 server requires one or more shared disk resources where the Information Store databases must be placed. You cannot assign a single physical disk to more than one virtual server. As explained in Chapter 3, "Microsoft Exchange 2000 Server Architecture," all Exchange 2000 components depend on the SA, so you also need to assign your virtual server an Exchange SA resource. The remaining Exchange 2000 components are added to the virtual server automatically.

Exercise 2: Configuring Virtual Exchange 2000 Servers

In this exercise you will use Cluster Administrator to configure one virtual server for Exchange 2000 Server in a Windows 2000 cluster. To verify the successful configuration, you will bring the server online.

To view a multimedia demonstration that displays how to perform this procedure, run the EX2CH7.AVI files from the \Exercise_Information\Chapter7 folder on the Supplemental Course Materials CD.

Prerequisites

- You have completed Exercise 1 earlier in this lesson.
- You are logged on as Administrator to BLUESKY-ND1.

▶ **To configure a virtual Exchange Server**

1. From the Administrative Tools program group, start Cluster Administrator.

2. In the Open Connection To Cluster dialog box, type **BLUESKY-CLUST**, and then click Open.

3. In the Cluster Administrator console tree, right-click Groups, point to New, and then select Group.

4. In the New Group wizard screen, under Name, enter **Exchange Cluster**. Under Description, type **Blue Sky Airline's Clustered Exchange 2000 Platform**, and then click Next.

5. For demonstrational purposes, on the Preferred Owners wizard screen, under Available Nodes, select BLUESKY-ND1 and BLUESKY-ND2, click Add, and then click Finish. Configuring preferred nodes allows you to activate the Cluster service's failback capabilities. In the context of Exchange 2000 Server operation, however, this is not required.

6. In the Cluster Administrator dialog box that appears to inform you that you have successfully created the group, click OK. At this point, you have successfully configured a resource group for your virtual Exchange 2000 server (see Figure 7.10).

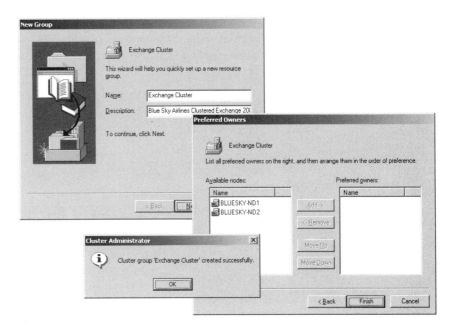

Figure 7.10 Creating a resource group for Exchange 2000 Server

7. In the details pane, right-click on the newly created Exchange Cluster object. In the shortcut menu, point to New, and then select Resource.

8. On the New Resource wizard screen, enter the following information, and then click Next:

Name	**E2K IP**
Description	**Exchange Cluster IP Address**
Resource Type	IP Address
Group	Exchange Cluster

9. On the Possible Owners wizard screen, make sure that under Possible Owners, BLUESKY-ND1 and BLUESKY-ND2 are listed, and then click Next.

10. On the Dependencies wizard screen, click Next.

11. On the TCP/IP Address Parameters wizard screen, enter the following information, and then click Finish:

Address	**192.168.1.76**
Subnet Mask	**255.255.255.0**
Network	Public Connection
Enable NetBIOS For This Address	Enabled

12. In the Cluster Administrator box that appears to inform you that you have successfully created the resource E2K IP, click OK. At this point, you have successfully assigned an IP address to your virtual Exchange 2000 server (see Figure 7.11).

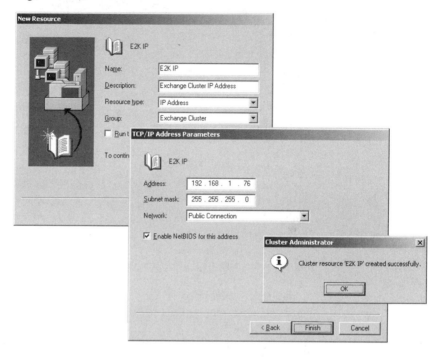

Figure 7.11   Assigning an IP address to a resource group

13. In the details pane, right-click on the Exchange Cluster object again and, in the Shortcut menu, point to New, and then select Resource.

14. On the New Resource wizard screen, enter the following information, and then click Next:

Name	**BLUESKY-E2KS**
Description	**The Name Of The Virtual Exchange 2000 Server**
Resource Type	Network Name
Group	Exchange Cluster

15. On the Possible Owners wizard screen, under Possible Owners, make sure that BLUESKY-ND1 and BLUESKY-ND2 are listed, and then click Next.

16. On the Dependencies wizard screen, from the Available Resources list, select E2K IP, and then click Add. Then click Next.

17. On the Network Name Parameters wizard screen, under Name, type **BLUESKY-E2KS**, and then click Finish.

18. In the Cluster Administrator dialog box that appears to inform you that you have successfully created the resource BLUESKY-E2KS, click OK. At this point, you have successfully created the network name for the virtual Exchange 2000 server, which your users will use later to connect to their mailboxes (see Figure 7.12).

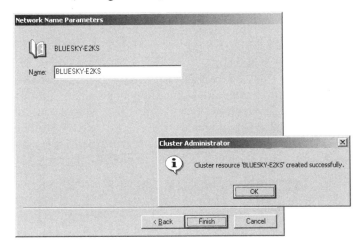

Figure 7.12   Configuring a network name for a virtual Exchange 2000 server

19. In the console tree, open the Resources container, select the disk resource that you want to assign to the Exchange Cluster group (such as Disk T:), and drag and drop it into the Exchange Cluster container.

20. In the Cluster Administrator dialog box asking you whether you are sure you want to move the disk resource, click Yes. In the Move Resources dialog box, click Yes again.

21. Right-click on the Exchange Cluster object again, and, in the shortcut menu, point to New, and then select Resource.

22. In the details pane, right-click on the Exchange Cluster object again, and, in the shortcut menu, point to New, and then select Resource.

23. On the New Resource wizard screen, enter the following information, and then click Next:

Name	**Microsoft Exchange System Attendant**
Description	**The SA Service of the Virtual Exchange 2000 Server**
Resource Type	Microsoft Exchange System Attendant
Group	Exchange Cluster

24. On the Possible Owners wizard screen, under Possible Owners, make sure that BLUESKY-ND1 and BLUESKY-ND2 are listed, and then click Next.

25. On the Dependencies wizard screen, select all of the resources listed under Available Resources, and then click Add and Next.

26. On the Data Directory wizard screen, under Enter Path To The Data Directory, make sure T:\EXCHSRVR is displayed, and then click Finish.

27. In the Cluster Administrator dialog box informing you that you have created the System Attendant resource successfully, click OK.

28. Right-click on the Exchange Cluster container and select Bring Online. At this point, you have successfully configured a full-featured virtual Exchange 2000 server cluster (see Figure 7.13). The state information displayed for the Exchange 2000 services will change from Offline to Online Pending and then to Online. As soon as all services are online, you are ready to work with the clustered Exchange 2000 environment.

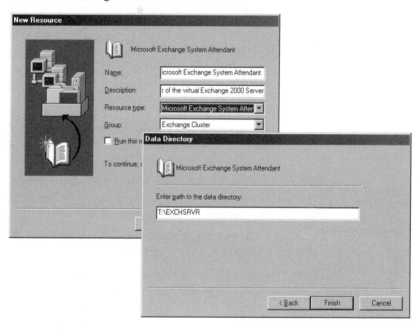

Figure 7.13   Bringing a virtual Exchange 2000 server online

Exercise Summary

You can configure and maintain Exchange 2000 resources in a cluster through Cluster Administrator. Separate physical hard disks are required for each virtual server, as well as a unique IP address and a network name. After that, you are ready to add the Exchange SA resource, which also implicitly adds the remaining cluster-aware Exchange 2000 services to the virtual server. The last step is to bring the server online, which is accomplished quickly via a right mouse click on the virtual server and the Bring Online command.

Important   Each resource group in a cluster running Exchange 2000 Server must contain an IP address, network name, disk, and the Exchange SA resource. Other resources, such as automatically created protocol virtual servers, may be removed. Do not remove the Exchange Message Transfer Instance that you want to connect to Exchange Server 5.5 in a mixed-mode environment from the Exchange virtual server. The MTA is required for intra-site server-to-server communication.

Configuring Additional Virtual Servers

Depending on your load-balancing and failover strategy, you might want to configure multiple virtual Exchange 2000 servers in a cluster. Each virtual server will appear in the network as a separate server. For each, you can specify preferred owner information to distribute the resources equally across the cluster nodes.

Public Information Store Dependencies

When configuring additional virtual servers, keep in mind that you cannot configure more than one public store on the cluster. After adding additional virtual servers, you must delete the public store in new groups before bringing the resource groups online. The configuration of public stores is covered in Chapter 17, "Public Folder Management."

Virtual Protocol Servers

As soon as you have configured a virtual Exchange 2000 server, you can use the Exchange System Manager to configure additional virtual servers for Internet access protocols. However, keep in mind not to use the System Manager to bring a virtual server online. Cluster Administrator is the right utility to complete the configuration of virtual protocol servers.

To complete a virtual server configuration in the test environment of Exercise 2, complete the following steps:

1. Right-click on the Exchange Cluster container, point to New, and then select Resource to add a new resource that corresponds to the Internet virtual protocol server that you created with the Exchange System Manager.

2. On the Possible Owners wizard screen, make sure that the nodes on which you installed Exchange 2000 Server appear in the Possible Owners list. Click Next.

3. On the Dependencies wizard screen, to the Resource Dependencies list, add the Exchange Information Store, and then click Next.

4. On the Virtual Server Instance wizard screen, select your virtual protocol server, and click Finish.

5. Now you can bring the virtual protocol server online by right-clicking on it and selecting the Bring Online command.

You can read more about the configuration of Internet access protocols in Chapter 11, "Internet-Based Client Access."

Note   If you plan to implement separate protocol virtual servers to restrict access to server resources individually per IP address, keep in mind that you should not reject all connections. Otherwise, the affected protocol virtual server cannot accept connections from its local address (such as the Exchange virtual server's IP address), which is necessary to accept IsAlive calls from the Resource Monitor.

Full-Text Indexing and Virtual Servers

Exchange 2000 Server supports full-text indexing in active/active cluster configurations. Consequently, the Exchange MS Search Instance resource is added to your virtual server(s) when you add the Exchange SA resource to your resource group. Even if you don't plan to use the full-text indexing feature of Exchange 2000 Server, do not delete the Exchange MS Search Instance from your virtual server. It is impossible to add it again without deleting and recreating the information store of the virtual server. Keeping the Exchange MS Search Instance in your resource group does not affect the performance of your virtual server, as long as you don't create a full-text index for a mailbox or public store with the Exchange System Manager.

To enable full-text indexing on a cluster with the Exchange System Manager, right-click the desired store, and, from the shortcut menu, select Create Full-Text Index. In the Mailbox Store (Server Name) dialog box, ensure that the catalog is created on the shared disk resource. Storage groups are available in the Storage Group container under your server, which in turn is held in the Servers container.

Exercise 3: Testing Exchange 2000 Failover Procedures

In this exercise you will verify the failover procedure of moving a virtual Exchange 2000 server to another node in a cluster. You will use Cluster Administrator to trigger a manual failover.

To view a multimedia demonstration that displays how to perform this procedure, run the EX3CH7.AVI files from the \Exercise_Information\Chapter7 folder on the Supplemental Course Materials CD.

Prerequisites

- You have completed Exercise 2 earlier in this lesson.
- You are logged on as Administrator to BLUESKY-ND1.

▶ **To manually fail over an Exchange cluster**

1. Launch Cluster Administrator, connect to BLUESKY-CLUST, and make sure the virtual Exchange Cluster server is online.

2. In the console tree, under BLUESKY-ND1 and BLUESKY-ND2, in each node's Active Groups container, verify that the Cluster Group and the Exchange Cluster are active on different nodes.

3. In the console tree, under Groups, open the Exchange Cluster container.

4. In the details pane, right-click the Microsoft Exchange System Attendant– (BLUESKY-CLUST) and, from the console menu, select Initiate Failure.

5. Notice that the state of this resource changes to Failed and all other resources are taken offline.

6. Notice that the state changes several times before all services are online again, now running on the other node as displayed in the Owner column of the details pane.

   At this point, you should be able to verify that the Cluster Group and the Exchange Cluster are now active on the same node (under BLUESKY-ND1 and BLUESKY-ND2, check each one's Active Groups container; see Figure 7.14).

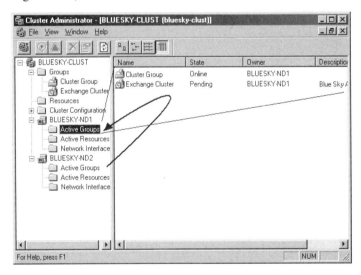

Figure 7.14   Testing the Exchange 2000 failover

Exercise Summary

Using Cluster Administrator, you can test the failover procedures for Exchange 2000 resources easily. Just right-click on an Exchange 2000 resource, and select Initiate Failure. All resources in the cluster group will be taken offline and then brought back online on another available node in the cluster. The process of stopping and starting resource instances is performed automatically and takes only seconds.

Upgrading Exchange Server 5.5 Clusters

A direct update of an Exchange Server 5.5 cluster to Exchange 2000 Server is not possible. However, you can install Exchange 2000 Server in an existing site and use the move-mailbox strategy to move existing mailboxes into a new Exchange 2000 cluster. The move-mailbox approach was introduced in Chapter 6, "Coexistence with Previous Microsoft Exchange Server Versions."

Direct Cluster Upgrades

Another option is to directly upgrade the existing information store database currently used in the Exchange Server 5.5 cluster, provided that the cluster itself is running Windows 2000 with Service Pack 1. The direct approach requires you to backup the existing information store databases and then remove the clustered Exchange Server 5.5 installation from the cluster. For instance, you could take the virtual Exchange Server 5.5 offline, copy the contents of PRIV.EDB and PUB.EDB from the \Program Files\Exchsrvr\MDBData directory to another directory (or simply rename and move this directory elsewhere on the shared drive), and then uninstall Exchange Server 5.5. After that, rename the directory back to \Program Files\Exchsrvr\MDBData. Then, you can install Exchange 2000 Server on all cluster nodes and configure a virtual server. Because of information store database dependencies, it is important to use the same name for the virtual Exchange 2000 resource group (virtual server) that the former virtual Exchange server was using. Do not bring this virtual server online yet. You first need to delete the contents of the new \Program Files\Exchsrvr\MDBData directory, except for PRIV.EDB and PUB.EDB. Rename these files PRIV1.EDB and PUB1.EDB. Now, you are ready to take the virtual Exchange 2000 server online.

Note   Clustered information store databases contain specific structures allowing multiple nodes access to mailbox and public folder data. These structures are not present in nonclustered databases. Hence, you cannot migrate nonclustered information store databases into a cluster using the procedure just outlined. To migrate nonclustered resources (Exchange Server 5.5 or Exchange 2000 Server), use the move-mailbox approach.

Direct Upgrade Limitations

The direct upgrade approach requires you to install Exchange 2000 Server in the site of the former Exchange Server 5.5. If organization and site names are not preserved, the old databases cannot be brought online. Hence, the direct upgrade is only available if you install a nonclustered Exchange 2000 Server version in the existing site first. This procedure requires an Active Directory Connector to populate the Active Directory directory service with the Exchange Server 5.5

mailbox information, as explained in Chapter 6, "Coexistence with Previous Microsoft Exchange Server Versions."

When considering the direct upgrade approach, keep the following facts in mind:

- You cannot use the direct upgrade approach if your Exchange 2000 cluster would be the first Exchange 2000 instance within an Exchange Server 5.5 site. For every site containing clustered Exchange Server 5.5 instances, you must first join a nonclustered Exchange 2000 server to the sites.

- An Exchange 2000 cluster cannot serve as a directory replication bridgehead server to an Exchange Server 5.5 site because Site Replication Service does not support clustering.

Chapter Summary

A cluster is a group of servers that appear as a single virtual server with an IP address, a network name, and disk resources. A virtual server allows users to access all the resources in the cluster, such as Exchange 2000 services, without having to know the names of the individual nodes. If one system fails and a second node assumes the workload, users can immediately reconnect. Cluster technology provides a mechanism for minimizing system downtime. One cluster can contain multiple virtual servers.

Windows 2000 Cluster service relies on the partitioned data model, which does not support concurrent access to physical disks from more than one node. Therefore, each virtual Exchange 2000 server requires its own disk resource. Because resources cannot be assigned to more than one resource group, each virtual server also requires an individual IP address and network name. In the event of a failure, an Exchange 2000 resource group (virtual server) can be failed over from the failed node to another node in the cluster, but it is impossible to activate the same virtual server on more than one node at the same time.

To install Exchange 2000 Server in a clustered environment, the Cluster service must be installed and properly configured first. Then, you need to install Exchange 2000 Server on all nodes, one at a time. Each node must be rebooted to complete the installation of the node. When all nodes are prepared, you can launch Cluster Administrator to configure virtual Exchange 2000 servers. Each virtual Exchange 2000 server requires an IP address, a network name, at least one disk resource, and an Exchange SA resource. Further Exchange services and resources are added to the cluster automatically. As soon as the configuration is complete, you can take the virtual server online with Cluster Administrator. It is important to keep in mind that clustered services must not be started using the Services Management tool or Exchange System Manager. You must control virtual servers from Cluster Administrator.

Review

The following review questions can help you determine if you have sufficiently familiarized yourself with the material covered in this chapter. You can find the answers to these questions at the end of this book in Appendix A, "Questions and Answers."

1. What are the three physical connections that join the nodes of a cluster together?

2. You plan to install Exchange 2000 Server in a Windows 2000 cluster. The cluster consists of two nodes. You want to run Exchange 2000 Server in an active/active configuration. How many disk volumes are required at a minimum if you want to configure dedicated Exchange 2000 resource groups?

3. You have installed and configured a four-node cluster running Windows 2000 Datacenter Server. Now, you want to install Exchange 2000 Server. What are the installation steps you must accomplish?

4. You want to add Exchange 2000 Server to an existing resource group. This resource group is already hosting SQL 2000 Server resources. What resources do you need to add to the existing resource group?

5. You have successfully configured a virtual server for Exchange 2000 and brought it online. Now you want to test the failover behavior of your system. How can you trigger a failover to another node in the cluster?

6. Because of the increased scalability of Exchange 2000 Server in a clustered installation, you plan to consolidate your Exchange resources and replace the existing five nonclustered servers with one Windows 2000 cluster. How can you incorporate the existing information store databases into the cluster installation?

C H A P T E R   8

Microsoft Outlook 2000 Deployment

About This Chapter

Microsoft Outlook is currently the preferred messaging and collaboration client in Microsoft Exchange Server environments. Outlook replaced the former Microsoft Exchange Client and Schedule+ applications, yet these and Internet-based client programs, such as Microsoft Outlook Express or Outlook Web Access, may also be used to access mailboxes and public folders. However, none of the latter provides the vast amount of features or level of integration with Microsoft Exchange 2000 Server that Outlook offers.

It is a good idea to deploy Outlook 2000 to best utilize the capabilities of your messaging and collaboration system. Outlook 2000 is more powerful and more reliable than any of its predecessors, it operates faster, it supports exciting new technologies, and it provides administrators with mighty deployment capabilities.

With Exchange 2000 Server in mind, this chapter focuses on the installation and configuration of Outlook 2000. The first lesson covers the various installation types and valuable setup utilities. The second lesson examines Exchange-specific configuration settings, and the third lesson is dedicated to the configuration of messaging-related Outlook options.

Before You Begin

To complete this chapter:

- Prepare your test environment according to the descriptions given in the "Getting Started" section of "About This Book." Although not necessarily required, it is assumed that you have followed the exercises of Chapter 5, "Installing Microsoft Exchange 2000 Server."

- Be familiar with the general functionality of Outlook 2000 and the interaction of Exchange 2000 Server components with Messaging Application Programming Interface (MAPI)-based clients as explained in Chapter 3, "Microsoft Exchange 2000 Server Architecture."

- You should have a copy of the Custom Installation Wizard, which is included with the Microsoft Office Resource Kit core tool set, available on the Microsoft Office Resource Kit CD as well as the Microsoft Office Resource Kit Web site. To download the tool set, go to the Office Resource Kit home page at *http://www.microsoft.com/office/ork/default.htm*, then click on the link for the Office Resource Kit Toolbox. On the Toolbox page, scroll down to the listing for the Office Resource Kit core tool set, then click the download icon to copy the files to your computer.

Lesson 1: Microsoft Outlook 2000 Installation Types

Microsoft Office 2000 includes Outlook 2000, but this application is also available as a separate product for Exchange 2000 Server, so you are not forced to fully deploy Office to benefit from Outlook's messaging and information management capabilities. Nevertheless, users can benefit from Outlook's tight integration with Microsoft Office, which often leads organizations to the decision to fully deploy Microsoft Office at a later stage. You can deploy Outlook 2000 before, with, or after other Office 2000 applications.

This lesson only covers the installation of Outlook 2000 for Exchange 2000 Server, but the installation strategies and tools remain the same when you are deploying Outlook 2000 as part of Microsoft Office. The Microsoft Office 2000 Resource Kit Tools and Utilities can help facilitate Outlook and Office rollouts. You should also obtain the newest service release for Microsoft Office, currently Service Release 1a, to update your installation with the most updated fixes and patches.

At the end of this lesson, you will be able to:

- List the hardware requirements for the 32-bit version of Outlook 2000.
- Perform a local Outlook installation.
- Install a client using a shared network installation point.
- Use installation tools to configure client parameters prior to setup.

Estimated time to complete this lesson: 90 minutes

Installation Overview

You can install Outlook 2000 with no e-mail support, with only Internet support, or with support for corporate and workgroup environments. No e-mail support is useful for users without a messaging platform who still want to be able to manage personal contacts, tasks, appointments, and documents. Internet support makes sending and receiving mail from an Internet service provider possible. When deploying Outlook in an Exchange 2000 Server organization, however, you should always choose the option for corporate and workgroup environments.

Outlook 2000 Requirements

Outlook 2000 requires at least an Intel Pentium-compliant processor and 8 MB of RAM on Microsoft Windows 95/98, Windows NT, or Windows 2000. To get better performance, however, consider doubling the minimum requirements. Remember that up to 160 MB of disk space is necessary, depending on the selected installation options.

If you are planning to deploy Outlook 2000 on workstations running Windows NT 4.0, make sure at least Service Pack 3 is installed on these computers. You should also take into consideration that Outlook 2000 requires Microsoft Internet Explorer 5.0, which will be installed automatically during setup if it wasn't deployed beforehand. In fact, you cannot install Outlook 2000 without Internet Explorer on the workstation.

Windows Installer

Unlike previous versions of Outlook that required procedural scripts to control the setup process, Outlook 2000 takes full advantage of Windows Installer technology. This new technology relies primarily on .msi package files, which are databases that describe the relationships between the features and components for a given product, such as Outlook 2000. Features are components or groups of components that you can choose to install. Components, in turn, are collections of files, registry keys, and other resources that are handled as an atomic unit, which ensures that mutually dependent files and entries are installed or uninstalled together.

Windows Installer is part of the Windows 2000 operating system, where it runs as a system service using the LocalSystem account. On systems running Microsoft Windows 95/98 and Windows NT Workstation, it will be added to the operating system during the first installation. You can find detailed information about Windows Installer in the Microsoft Office 2000 Resource Kit.

Note   Windows Installer facilitates the deployment and maintenance of Windows-based software and is available to independent software vendors (ISVs) as a universal installation technology.

Setup Command-Line Properties

By specifying command-line options, you can control the way Setup installs Outlook on your computer. You can specify, for instance, whether Setup should run interactively or in quiet mode without user interaction. A complete reference about all the available switches and options, customizable properties, and their formats is available in a spreadsheet called SETUPREF.XLS, which you can find in the Office Information program group (click Start, then point to Programs, Microsoft Office Tools, and then Microsoft Office 2000 Resource Kit Documents) if you have installed the Microsoft Office 2000 Resource Kit.

SETUP.INI

Command-line properties can lead to huge and puzzling commands, such as setup /qn TRANSFORMS="c:\Blue Sky.MST" COMPANYNAME="Blue Sky Airlines", which are difficult to handle. An easier option is to specify the required properties in a SETUP.INI file. A sample SETUP.INI file containing helpful comments is available on Outlook's installation CD in the root directory. Every command-line option has a corresponding .ini setting. Of course, you cannot edit the file on the installation CD directly, but you can save a modified version on your hard disk and specify this file through the /Settings command-line option (for instance, SETUP.EXE /Settings c:\MYSETUP.INI).

Alternatively, you can copy the installation files to a network installation share point and edit SETUP.INI in this location. SETUP.INI is the default initialization file in an installation directory, used when no other file was specified in the command line.

Customizing Installation Packages

You have the option to use the Custom Installation Wizard to further customize the Outlook installation process. As mentioned in the beginning of this chapter, this wizard is part of the Office 2000 Resource Kit. It helps you create .mst transform files, which Windows Installer can apply during the setup process. Transform files allow you to override the settings in the .msi database of Windows Installer. You can read more about the Custom Installation Wizard later in this lesson.

Windows 2000 Group Policies

If you are running Microsoft Windows 2000 Professional on your client computers, deployment of Outlook 2000 becomes remarkably easy. Take advantage of the software installation and maintenance feature provided by Active Directory group policies. You can manage group policies for all or a subset of your Windows 2000 users, which includes central management of software settings. Either assign Outlook 2000 to your users (or computers) or publish the application.

If you assign Outlook 2000, users will be able to launch Outlook from the Programs group in the Start menu without prior installation. Outlook 2000 will then be installed automatically on first use. When you publish the software, on the other hand, you provide users with a dedicated installation option in the Add/Remove Programs applet of the Control Panel. Users then need to install Outlook 2000 themselves before they are able to use it.

Local Installation

A local installation refers to the method of installing all client files on the computer's local hard disk. Outlook offers two different local installation options for this purpose—Install Now and Customize. The Install Now option installs all the components that are required by the average user. However, if you need complete control over the setup process and the selection of Outlook features, choose Customize. The local installation method was used in the "Getting Started" section of "About This Book" to prepare BLUESKY-WKSTA for Chapters 1 through 4.

Starting the Setup Process

To perform a local installation, you need to start SETUP.EXE from the installation CD or from a network share. At startup, Setup checks whether Windows Installer is available on the local computer and installs it if not found.

Note   You need the permissions of a local administrator if you want to install Windows Installer on Windows NT 4.0.

Maintenance Mode

After making sure Windows Installer is available, Setup checks whether Outlook is already installed. If it is, Setup switches into maintenance mode to allow you to add or remove Outlook features. Maintenance mode is signified by the presence of the following Setup options: Repair Outlook, Add Or Remove Features, and Remove Outlook.

Installation Process

To perform the actual Outlook installation, Setup launches MSIEXEC.EXE, a component of Windows Installer. MSIEXEC.EXE utilizes a DLL called MSI.DLL to retrieve information about available components and selections from the .msi database. If you have specified a transform file to customize the installation process, this .mst file is applied on top of the .msi database. Further command-line properties specified for Setup via SETUP.INI or command line are taken in last (see Figure 8.1).

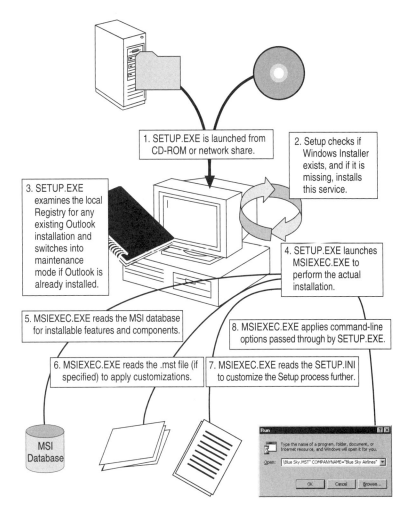

1. SETUP.EXE is launched from CD-ROM or network share.

2. Setup checks if Windows Installer exists, and if it is missing, installs this service.

3. SETUP.EXE examines the local Registry for any existing Outlook installation and switches into maintenance mode if Outlook is already installed.

4. SETUP.EXE launches MSIEXEC.EXE to perform the actual installation.

5. MSIEXEC.EXE reads the MSI database for installable features and components.

8. MSIEXEC.EXE applies command-line options passed through by SETUP.EXE.

6. MSIEXEC.EXE reads the .mst file (if specified) to apply customizations.

7. MSIEXEC.EXE reads the SETUP.INI to customize the Setup process further.

MSI Database

Figure 8.1   Launching the Outlook 2000 setup process

Default Network Installation

A shared client installation refers to a configuration where the majority of the client files are kept on a file server within the network (see Figure 8.2).

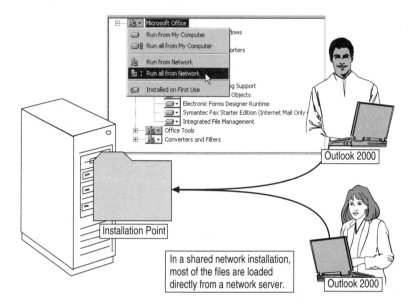

Figure 8.2   Running Outlook from a network share

When running Setup from a network share instead of a local CD, there is a difference in the installation options that are available for individual features. After accepting the licensing agreement, select the Customize option, specify where to install Outlook, and then, on the screen allowing you to select the individual Outlook features, click on the node for Microsoft Outlook For Windows, for example. In the shortcut menu, the Run From CD option changes to Run From Network; Run All From CD becomes Run All From Network (see Figure 8.2). You can specify these options to run the entire client or selected components directly from the installation point. Because the files are not copied from this network share to the local computer, you must keep the network server continuously available to your users.

Note   The advantages of a shared installation, such as saved local disk space, can also become disadvantages. For instance, most of the files must be loaded from the file server during client startup, which increases network traffic and typically slows down the startup process. Likewise, if the network server is temporarily down or not available for any reason, you won't be able to start Outlook at all.

Creating an Administrative Installation Point

The administrative installation point is the shared access point for a customized network installation, which must be created explicitly by running the Setup program with the /A option. Within the installation point, you can edit SETUP.INI or create a transform file and then deploy Outlook over the network. Alternatively, you can burn customized CDs for users who cannot install or run Outlook over the network but want to benefit from a preconfigured installation. Preparing custom Outlook CDs does not infringe the license agreement as long as you make sure these copies are not installed without a client license from Microsoft.

Exercise 1: Preparing an Administrative Installation Point

In this exercise you will prepare an administrative installation point on a computer running Exchange 2000 Server. In subsequent exercises in this chapter, you will use this installation point to deploy Outlook 2000.

To view a multimedia demonstration that displays how to perform this procedure, run the EX1CH8.AVI files from the \Exercise_Information\Chapter8 folder on the Supplemental Course Materials CD.

Prerequisites

- Log on as Administrator to BLUESKY-SRV1.

- Insert the Microsoft Outlook 2000 CD into the CD drive.

▶ **To prepare an administrative installation point**

1. Start Windows Explorer, create a directory called Outlook Installation on drive D (you may have to format drive D with NTFS first), and share this directory for network access under the name Outlook. Assign the Everyone group at least Read permissions to the network share.

2. Click Start button, select Run, and, in the Run dialog box, type **e:\setup.exe / a data1.msi**.

3. Click OK to launch Setup, and, on the Microsoft Outlook 2000 Administrative Mode welcome screen, enter the CD key for your installation CD. Under Company, make sure Blue Sky Airlines is displayed, and then click Next.

4. On the End-User Licensing wizard screen, select the I Accept The Terms In The License Agreement option, and then click Next.

5. On the Location wizard screen, type **D:\Outlook Installation** or click Browse to conveniently select the directory created in Step 1. Then click Install Now.

   At this point, you are creating an administrative installation point on the Exchange 2000 server (see Figure 8.3).

6. In the final Microsoft Outlook 2000 Setup dialog box informing you that Setup was completed successfully, click OK.

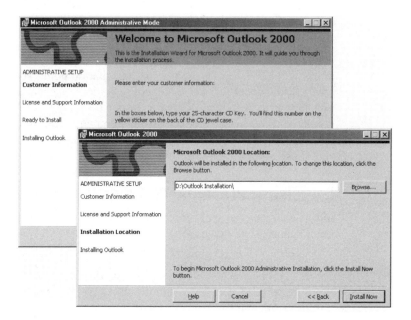

Figure 8.3   Creating an administrative installation point

Exercise Summary

Use the command line SETUP.EXE /A DATA1.MSI to copy the Outlook files to an installation point on a network server. You need to provide the CD key and company name that you want to assign to all Outlook installations from this location and accept the licensing agreement.

Note   Setup /A will modify the package file DATA1.MSI to identify the network share as an administrative installation point.

Preconfiguring the Network Installation

The administrative installation point is an ideal place to preconfigure client settings and specify the components to install. As mentioned earlier in this lesson, you have various options for customizing the setup process.

Important   Do not alter any folders or files in the installation point other than SETUP.INI and transform files to guarantee a properly functioning Setup procedure.

Custom Installation Wizard

The Custom Installation Wizard allows you to modify the setup process extensively, including modifications that you cannot specify in the command line or SETUP.INI. You can specify where to install Outlook and with what features, and you can detail to a large extent the client configuration parameters. You can also add your own files to the installation process, such as advanced business applications or company forms, and set custom registry entries.

Furthermore, it is possible to suppress the display of arbitrary Outlook features by selecting the Hide option for the corresponding item in the Set Feature Installation States screen of the Custom Installation Wizard. Hidden features may still be installed in the background if you have specified the installation state accordingly (Run From Network, Run All From Network, Install On First Use, and so on), but are not displayed when users run Setup interactively.

Note   If you hide a feature in the Custom Installation Wizard, all subordinate features belonging to the feature will be hidden as well.

Conflicting Options

For some options, you can specify a value in SETUP.INI, while a different value may be listed in the transform file, and yet another value could be used in the command line. This clearly leads to a conflict, which Windows Installer handles according to the following rule: The transform file has lowest priority, followed by SETUP.INI, which is superseded by the command-line options.

Unattended Installation

The unattended Setup mode, which is launched using the /Q command-line parameter, is the basis for installing Outlook on numerous workstations automatically. You should prepare an administrative installation point with preconfigured setup files first. You can then deploy the client by running Setup /Q with login scripts via a shortcut in a Web page, through Windows 2000 group policies, or by using Microsoft Systems Management Server (SMS). If you want to use SMS to distribute the client software, you must use SMS package files (.pdf). The Microsoft Office 2000 Resource Kit contains more information about Setup command-line parameters and the deployment of Outlook and other Office programs using SMS.

Exercise 2: Deploying Outlook 2000

In this exercise you will finalize the preparation of the installation point using the Custom Installation Wizard. After that, you will deploy Outlook 2000 using the unattended installation method.

To view a multimedia demonstration that displays how to perform this procedure, run the EX2CH8*.AVI files from the \Exercise_Information\Chapter8 folder on the Supplemental Course Materials CD.

Prerequisites
- Log on as Administrator to BLUESKY-SRV1.

- Obtain the Custom Installation Wizard, as explained at the begging of this chapter. Install it on BLUESKY-SRV1 according to the descriptions in the Microsoft Office Resource Kit. Alternatively, if you cannot obtain or install CIW, run the multimedia demonstration to follow this exercise, and install Outlook 2000 manually with all components on BLUESKY-WKSTA.

▶ **To deploy Outlook 2000**

1. On BLUESKY-SRV1, click Start, point to Programs, then to Microsoft Office Tools, and then to Microsoft Office Resource Kit Tools. Launch the Custom Installation Wizard.

2. On the Welcome To The Custom Installation Wizard screen, click Next.

3. On the Open The MSI File wizard screen, under Name And Path To The MSI File To Open, type **D:\Outlook Installation\Data1.msi**, and then click Next.

4. In the Open The MST File screen, make sure Do Not Open An Existing MST File is selected, and then click Next.

5. On the Select The MST File To Save wizard screen, under Name And Path Of MST File, type **D:\Outlook Installation\BlueSky.mst**, and then click Next.

   At this point, you have specified your installation directory as the location of the transform file (see Figure 8.4). This guarantees that the customization settings are generally available for your Outlook rollout.

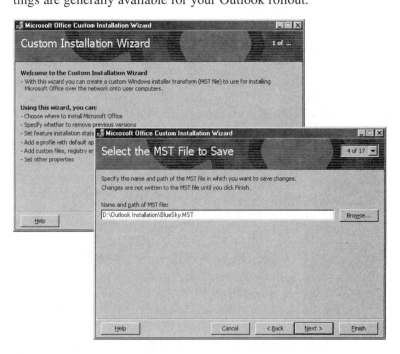

Figure 8.4   Starting the Custom Installation Wizard

6. On the Specify Default Path And Organization wizard screen, under Organization, type **Blue Sky Airlines**, and then click Next.

7. On the Remove Previous Versions wizard screen, notice and accept the defaults, and then click Next.

8. On the Set Feature Installation States wizard screen, click on the Collaboration Data Objects (CDO) node, and select Run From My Computer. It is generally advisable to install CDO on your workstations because many Exchange workgroup solutions rely on this object library.

9. Click on the Electronic Forms Designer Runtime node, and select Run From My Computer to support legacy 16-bit forms of the former Exchange Client.

10. Right-click on the Converters And Filters node, and select Hide, then click Next.

    At this point, you have specified to install Outlook with the most important features and hide the document converters and filters (see Figure 8.5). This feature will still be installed, but users will be unable to change converter settings when running Setup interactively.

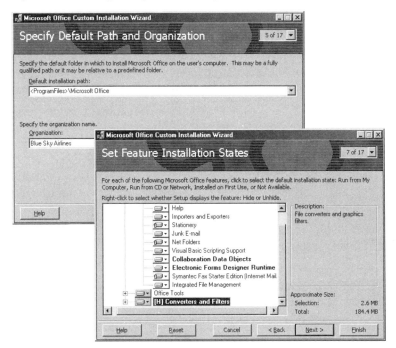

Figure 8.5 Selecting Outlook features

11. On the Customize Default Application Settings wizard screen, do not change any settings, then click Next.

12. On the Add Files To The Installation wizard screen, do not add any files, then click Next.

13. On the Add Registry Entries wizard screen, click Add. In the Add/Modify Registry Entry dialog box, specify the following information (which enables the booking of online conferences via Outlook, as explained in Chapter 25, "Real-Time Collaboration"):

Field	Data
Root	HKEY_CURRENT_USER
Data Type	REG_SZ
Key	Software\Microsoft\Office\9.0\Outlook\ExchangeConferencing
Value Name	(Default)
Value Data	Not Set

14. The actual value is not of interest, but existence of the ExchangeConferencing key enables confirmed reservations of conference resources. Click OK, and then click Next.

15. On the Add, Modify, Or Remove Shortcuts wizard screen, accept the defaults, and click Next.

16. On the Identify Additional Servers wizard screen, do not add additional servers. Additional servers can help to increase the resilience of the deployment, but are not required to successfully implement Outlook in small environments. Click Next.

17. On the Add Installations And Run Programs wizard screen, do not add any programs to the installation, then click Next.

18. On the Customize Outlook Installation Options wizard screen, select Customize Outlook Profile And Account Information, and make sure Corporate Or Workgroup Settings is displayed under Configuration Type.

19. From the list of configuration categories, select General. In the right pane, under Enter Profile Name, type **CIW Generated Profile**. Make sure Microsoft Exchange Server is selected in the Which Service Should Be The Default Store list box. Activate the Overwrite Existing Profile check box.

20. From the Categories list, select Services List. In the right pane, select the following check boxes: Include Microsoft Exchange Server Service and Include Outlook Address Book Service.

21. From the Categories list, select Exchange Settings, and, in the right pane under The Name Of The User's Mailbox, type *%username%*. Underneath, type **BLUESKY-SRV1** as the server running Exchange 2000. Click Next.

    At this point, you have preconfigured the users' default messaging profile (see Figure 8.6).

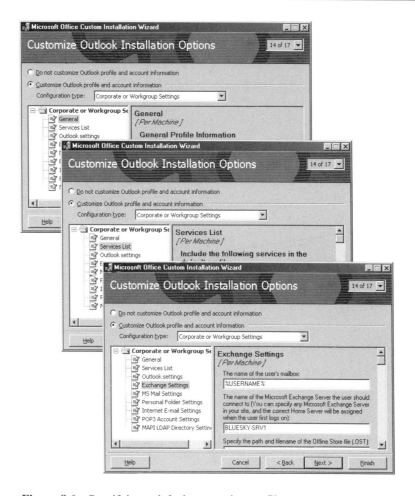

Figure 8.6 Specifying a default messaging profile

22. On the Customize IE 5 Installation Options wizard screen, accept the defaults, and click Next.

23. On the Modify Setup Properties wizard screen, examine the list of options, and then click Next. The options specified here are not written to SETUP.INI; instead, they are kept in the transform file.

24. On the Save Changes wizard screen, click Finish.

    At this point, you have successfully created a transform file, which you can specify in the Setup command line to customize the installation process (see Figure 8.7).

25. On the Custom Installation Wizard screen, note the command line to launch Setup unattended using the transform file, and then click Exit to complete the preparation.

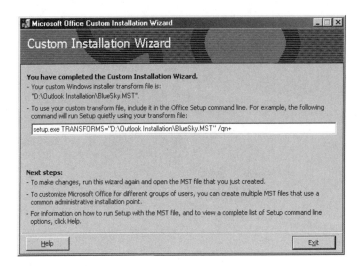

Figure 8.7   Completing the Custom Installation Wizard

26. In Windows Explorer, open the \Outlook Installation directory, and edit the SETUP.INI file, which is a hidden file that is only visible when activating the Show Hidden Files And Folders folder option.

27. Remove the semicolon from the line [MST] and, underneath, add the line **MST1=BlueSky.mst**. Save the changes. In this way, the transform file generated above is always applied when Setup is launched from the \Outlook Installation directory.

28. On BLUESKY-WKSTA, log on as Administrator, click Start, point to Run, and, in the Run dialog box, type **\\bluesky-srv1\outlook\setup /qr**, then click OK.

    At this point, you are installing Outlook 2000 unattended on BLUESKY-WKSTA with the option to display a reduced user interface (see Figure 8.8). Alternatively, you may suppress all progress information and dialogs by specifying the /qn option. Either way, Outlook will take several minutes to install.

Exercise Summary

You can facilitate the deployment of Outlook 2000 when preparing an administrative installation point and configuring the Setup environment using the Custom Installation Wizard. A prepared installation point in the network allows you to run the Outlook 2000 Setup program unattended or via group policy assignments. Windows 2000 group policies, however, require Windows 2000 Professional to be installed on all workstation PCs.

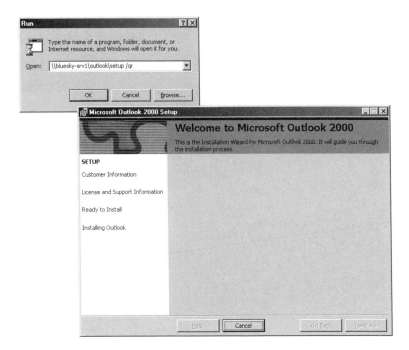

Figure 8.8   Running Setup unattended with a reduced user interface

Default Messaging Profile Generation

A messaging profile, sometimes also called a MAPI profile, describes the set of those information services that should be activated during a particular session. At least one must exist to successfully start Outlook 2000 (see Figure 8.9). You can read more about MAPI profiles in Chapter 9, "MAPI-Based Clients."

Profile Wizard

Immediately after the installation of Outlook on a new computer, no messaging profile exists. However, the client is unable to operate without it, and, therefore, Outlook automatically prompts for all the required information to create a valid messaging profile when you start the client for the very first time. You can read more about Exchange-specific profile settings in Lesson 2.

When you have installed Outlook 2000 without any customization of Setup files, upon startup you need to configure the client with support for corporate and workgroup environments. In the Microsoft Outlook Setup Wizard dialog box, you have to select the Microsoft Exchange Server check box. When you click Next, you must specify the name of your server and ensure the correctness of the mailbox name to successfully start Outlook.

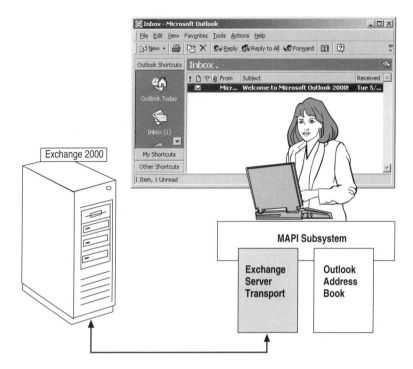

Figure 8.9   A messaging profile for Outlook 2000

OUTLOOK.PRF

The configuration of a messaging profile may overwhelm your end users. Consequently, it is preferable to configure the important settings prior to the client installation. One option is to create a file called OUTLOOK.PRF and place it in the administrative installation point. This file will then be copied to the Windows directory (\Winnt) during the installation. When Outlook starts for the very first time on a new computer, it looks for OUTLOOK.PRF in the Windows directory. If it finds the file, Outlook uses it to generate a default profile. You can read more about the generation of messaging profiles using .prf files in Chapter 9, "MAPI-Based Clients."

Custom Installation Wizard

One significant disadvantage of OUTLOOK.PRF is that you need to edit it using a text editor. A sample OUTLOOK.PRF file will be installed with the Microsoft Office Resource Kit in the \Program Files\Orktools\Toolbox\Docs Lists Samples\Outlook directory.

To conveniently create messaging profiles, most organizations use the Custom Installation Wizard. After launching the Custom Installation Wizard, on the Customize Outlook Installation Options wizard screen, select the Customize Outlook Profile And Account Information option, and then make your choices as required (see Exercise 2). The Custom Installation Wizard saves your changes in the transform file. During Outlook installation, the settings will be transferred into the client's Registry. You will thus not end up with an OUTLOOK.PRF file in the Windows directory through this approach. You have the option of overriding an existing profile, which would be impossible when using OUTLOOK.PRF.

Exercise 3: Verifying the Profile Generation

In this exercise you will verify the automatic generation of messaging profiles when starting Outlook 2000 for the first time on a new workstation.

To view a multimedia demonstration that displays how to perform this procedure, run the EX3CH8.AVI files from the \Exercise_Information\Chapter8 folder on the Supplemental Course Materials CD.

Prerequisites

- Complete Exercise 2, earlier in this lesson.

- Log on as Administrator to BLUESKY-WKSTA.

▶ **To verify the profile generation**

1. On BLUESKY-WKSTA, right-click the Microsoft Outlook icon on the desktop. From the shortcut menu, select Properties.

2. In the Mail dialog box, note that no messaging profile exists on the computer. Click Close, and then start Outlook.

3. Several dialog boxes will appear informing you that Windows installs further components and configures the Outlook settings. After that, Outlook will start and connect to the Administrator's mailbox.

   At this point, Outlook has created the default profile named CIW Generated Profile for you. The environment variable <username>, specified in Exercise 2 for the mailbox name, was substituted with your account information (see Figure 8.10).

4. Repeat Step 1 to verify that the Microsoft Exchange Server transport and Outlook Address Book services have been configured automatically as part of the CIW Generated Profile.

5. Close all dialog boxes and Outlook 2000.

Figure 8.10 An automatically generated default profile

Exercise Summary

The automatic generation of a default messaging profile is a very helpful feature when deploying Outlook 2000 to end users with limited knowledge about MAPI-based information services. Individual default profiles are possible because the user variable <username> is supported in the context of the mailbox name. The user only needs to start Outlook to connect to the correct mailbox that was configured for his or her user account.

Adding or Removing Program Features

Users who are new to Outlook 2000 may be overwhelmed by the set of features that this client application offers. In fact, this is one good reason why many organizations decide to split the deployment into stages, loading only the essential Outlook features first, then the advanced features, and finally the full Microsoft Office 2000 suite. As indicated earlier, you can suppress various features by using the Custom Installation Wizard and a transform file.

Adding Features

To add features to an installation at a later time, you may run the Outlook Setup in maintenance mode, which is launched automatically when an Outlook installation is detected on the local computer. You need use the maintenance mode's Add or Remove Features option. However, this option does not allow you to change the installation state of any features that you suppressed via a transform file in the first place. Uninstalling Outlook and then running Setup again—possibly with a new transform file—is one solution. You could also use the Setup command-line properties ADDLOCAL, ADDSOURCE, ADVERTISE, and REMOVE to change the installation state of any feature including hidden components (but hidden features remain hidden in the Setup windows).

Alternatively, you could also use the Custom Maintenance Wizard to completely reconfigure your Outlook installations. This wizard is downloadable from the Microsoft Office Resource Kit Web site mentioned in the beginning of this chapter. The Custom Maintenance Wizard allows you to create a .cmw file that you can then use to modify an existing installation.

Redeploying Outlook 2000

Files, custom registry keys, and any programs you have added to a transform file to include in your Outlook deployment will not be reinstalled during a repeated installation. This is especially important if you plan to fix a damaged installation by removing and redeploying Outlook 2000 using the transform file. For instance, if you have included an ActiveX control, such as OUTLCTLX.DLL, in your installation and a user deletes this file from his or her computer accidentally, simply reinstalling Outlook in maintenance mode doesn't do the job. Even uninstalling and reinstalling Outlook 2000 does not fix this problem. OUTLCTLX.DLL will not be copied again during subsequent installations using your transform file. Because the content added to a transform file is regarded as permanent, you need to force the reinstallation or removal by editing the Registry on the client computer before running Setup again. First, determine the Product Code of your installation. For this purpose, copy the original transform file that was used for Setup to the local disk drive of your workstation where CIW is installed. Right-click on the file, and, from the shortcut menu, select Properties. In the Properties dialog box, switch to the Statistics tab (you need to copy the file locally to display the Statistics property page). Paste the GUID string displayed under Revision Number into a text file. You will find various GUIDs. Now, open the Registry, and navigate to the following key:

```
HKEY_CURRENT_USER

  \Software

  \Microsoft

   \OfficeCustomizeWizard

     \1.0

      \RegKeyPaths
```

Delete the keys that correspond to the GUIDs from your revision number, and then repeat the installation.

Lesson 2: Configuring the Exchange Transport

The Exchange Server transport is the most important MAPI component that Outlook must use to connect to a server running Exchange 2000 Server. You configure this transport in the context of MAPI independent of the client. The most important configuration parameters, which you can set through the property sheets of the Exchange transport service, are the mailbox and home server names. Only in rare situations might it be necessary to optimize the transport by means of direct manipulation of Registry entries.

This lesson covers the configuration and optimization of the Exchange transport service. This can be accomplished automatically prior to the Outlook installation, as discussed in Lesson 1, or manually, as you will learn in the following.

At the end of this lesson, you will be able to:

- Describe the purpose of the various configuration parameters important for connection to servers running Exchange 2000 Server.

- Optimize the remote procedure call (RPC) communication between Exchange 2000 and Outlook.

Estimated time to complete this section: 30 minutes

Exchange Transport Components

The Exchange transport relies on RPCs for client/server communication. RPCs are used whenever the client interacts with the server, including when setting up the Exchange transport service itself.

RPC Methods

RPCs are a high-level mechanism for interprocess communication (application layer of the Open Systems Interconnection [OSI] network model), as discussed in Chapter 3, "Microsoft Exchange 2000 Server Architecture." Software components that communicate using RPCs can build their connection on a vast variety of network protocols, including local procedure calls (LPCs), Transmission Control Protocol/Internet Protocol (TCP/IP), Internetwork Packet Exchange/Sequenced Packet Exchange (SPX/IPX), Banyan Vines protocol, named pipes, and NetBIOS. Some client computers will have multiple protocols installed and therefore will have multiple ways to establish an RPC connection. Exchange will attempt to communicate over the available protocols in a sequential order until a connection can be established or until all options have been tried without success.

The following are supported RPC communication methods between Outlook and Exchange 2000 Server:

- **Banyan Vines protocol.** For communication with Exchange 2000 Server in Banyan Vines networks

- **LPCs.**   Used when the client and server are installed on the same machine
- **Named pipes.**   Connects to the server using the NetBIOS-based named pipes protocol
- **NetBIOS.**   Connects to the server using NetBIOS over NetBEUI, SPX/IPX, or TCP/IP
- **SPX/IPX.**   Supports native Novell NetWare workstations via SPX/IPX over Windows Sockets (Winsock).
- **TCP/IP.**   Uses Winsock or TCP/IP

The optimization of the RPC client connection order is described later in this lesson. This optimization is particularly important in heterogeneous environments, as you will learn in Chapter 10, "MAPI-Based Clients in a Novell NetWare Environment."

Transport Components

The Exchange transport service is implemented in three DLLs called EMSABP32.DLL, EMSMDB32.DLL, and EMSUI32.DLL. They communicate with the directory to display the server-based address books (EMSABP32.DLL) and with the Information Store service to send and receive messages (EMSMDB32.DLL). As outlined in Chapter 2, "Integration with Microsoft Windows 2000," in Exchange 2000 Server environments, address book information will be retrieved from Global Catalog servers. EMSUI32.DLL, again, is the transport service's configuration library, which is responsible for providing the property sheets and dialog boxes that allow you to configure this service. Only in rare cases must you use the Registry Editor instead of EMSUI32.DLL.

Testing Server Connectivity During Manual Configuration

You can configure the transport through the Mail applet, which will be added to the Control Panel during Outlook 2000 installation. When you launch this applet, it opens the properties of the default messaging profile, which should contain the Microsoft Exchange Server transport. If this information service is missing, you need to include it using the Add button; otherwise, you cannot connect to Exchange 2000 Server. Click Properties to configure the service.

Using the General property sheet of the Microsoft Exchange Server dialog box, enter the name of the home server under Microsoft Exchange Server and the display name of your mailbox under Mailbox. You can then check immediately to see whether the connection to the server is functioning by clicking Check Name. This procedure resolves the mailbox name, while RPCs are working under the surface to accomplish this task. If both server name and mailbox name can be resolved as indicated by an underline, the RPC communication was successful. At this point you can assume that the client/server communication can take place without any problems.

Connection Configuration Settings

Essentially, Microsoft Exchange Server and Mailbox names are required to successfully configure the transport for Exchange 2000 Server. The transport service is able to detect the state of the server connection automatically, and starts offline, for instance, when you work disconnected from the network. To work offline, you need to configure an Offline Folder Store in the Advanced property sheet, which will be explained in Chapter 9, "MAPI-Based Clients." If you connect to your server through a dial-up connection, you may find it useful, under Encrypt Information, to enable the When Using Dial-Up Networking check box, which causes Outlook to encrypt the client/server communication.

The Exchange transport service provides the following property sheets and configuration options:

- **General.** To specify and check the names of server and mailbox and to determine whether the connection state should be detected automatically during startup. You also can set a connection timeout, after which Outlook considers the state disconnected. Some users prefer to specify the connection state manually to avoid startup delays through timeouts.

- **Advanced.** To open additional mailboxes in Outlook, which will be displayed along with the primary mailbox (specified on the General property sheet) in the folders tree. You must delegate access permission to those mailboxes that you select, as explained later in Lesson 3. In addition, you can specify when to encrypt the information you transmit and the method of authentication to be used. To log on to Exchange 2000 Server with your Windows 2000 credentials, make sure NT Password Authentication is selected. Click Offline Folders File Settings to enable the client to work offline, specify offline folder file encryption, and compact the file.

- **Dial-Up Networking.** To select a configured dial-up connection to be used when connecting to Exchange 2000 Server remotely or use an existing connection, and specify an appropriate Windows 2000 account to log on to the remote Windows 2000 domain. The dial-up account can be different from your Exchange 2000 account.

- **Remote Mail.** To specify options regarding the message transfer when using the remote mail options of Outlook 2000, which will be introduced in Chapter 9, "MAPI-Based Clients." You can select to process items you marked for download or deletion or set filter rules and specify criteria for the messages you want to transfer. You can also set a schedule for your connections, which Outlook can use to automatically connect to Exchange 2000 Server and transfer messages that have been marked or filtered.

Client Connection Order

Outlook 2000 will attempt to connect to the server using all available communication methods in a sequential order until it can either connect successfully or until all methods have failed. The default connect order is LPC, TCP/IP, SPX/ IPX, named pipes, NetBIOS, and Banyan Vines protocol.

Modifying the Connection Order

You can modify the client connection order prior to the actual client installation via the Custom Installation Wizard by setting an appropriate custom Registry key. Once Outlook 2000 has been installed, however, you need to use the Registry Editor (REGEDIT) to change the Rpc_Binding_Order value, as shown in Figure 8.11.

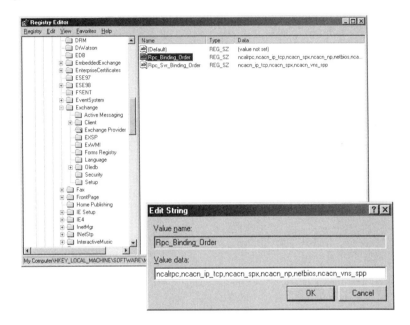

Figure 8.11 Editing the RPC sequence

The Rpc_Binding_Order value can be found under:

```
HKEY_LOCAL_MACHINE

 \SOFTWARE

  \Microsoft

   \Exchange

    \Exchange Provider
```

If you want, you can rearrange or delete entries to speed up the client startup process. For workstations in a Novell NetWare environment, you may want place the *ncacn_spx* synonym in the first position if your network relies primarily on

SPX/IPX. With this modification, the client will try to communicate through RPCs over SPX first. The communication methods in the list must be separated by commas.

The RPC communication methods are:

- LPC: *ncalrpc*
- RPC over TCP/IP: *ncacn_ip_tcp*
- RPC over SPX: *ncacn_spx*
- RPC over named pipes: *ncacn_np*
- RPC over NetBIOS: *netbios*
- RPC over Banyan Vines protocol: *ncacn_vns_spp*

Exercise 4: Testing the Client/Server Communication

In this exercise you will verify the RPC-based client/server communication between Outlook and Exchange 2000. You will edit client connection order to create a situation where RPCs fail and examine the client behavior.

To view a multimedia demonstration that displays how to perform this procedure, run the EX4CH8.AVI files from the \Exercise_Information\Chapter8 folder on the Supplemental Course Materials CD.

Prerequisites

- Complete Exercise 3, earlier in this lesson.
- Log on as Administrator to BLUESKY-WKSTA.

▶ **To test the RPC-based client/server communication**

1. Right-click the Microsoft Outlook icon on the desktop, and, from the shortcut menu, select Properties.

2. Make sure Microsoft Exchange Server is selected from the list of information services, and then click Properties.

3. Under Mailbox, delete the existing entry (Administrator), then type **Admin** in the same field, and click Check Name.

4. Click Start, and then click Run.

5. In the Open dialog box, type **regedit**, and then click OK.

6. Open the HKEY_LOCAL_MACHINE node, then Software, Microsoft, Exchange, and Exchange Provider.

7. Verify that the Rpc_Binding_Order value exists.

   At this point, you are able to notice the default binding order for MAPI-based clients. First is an LPC, followed by TCP/IP (Sockets), followed by SPX (Sockets), named pipes, NetBIOS, and Banyan Vines protocol.

8. Edit the Rpc_Binding_Order value, and remove all entries except the *ncacn_vns_spp* key word, which stands for RPC over Banyan Vines (not supported in the test environment), then click OK.

9. Repeat Step 3, and notice that Outlook cannot resolve the name Admin into Administrator. Two Microsoft Outlook dialog boxes will appear informing you that the name could not be resolved. Click OK. This is an indicator of an RPC communication problem.

10. Switch back to Registry Editor, and restore the default setting of *ncalrpc,ncacn_ip_tcp,ncacn_spx,ncacn_np,netbios,ncacn_vns_spp.*

11. Repeat Step 3, verify that the communication can take place, and then exit Registry Editor (see Figure 8.12).

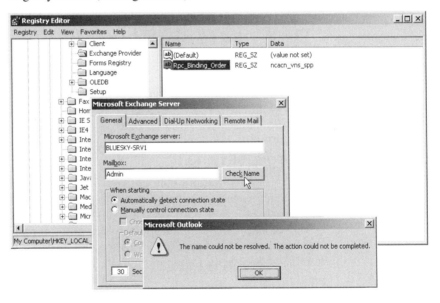

Figure 8.12 Testing RPC Communication

Exercise Summary

It is a good idea to check the mailbox name when configuring a messaging profile. If the name can be resolved, Outlook will most likely connect to the specified server and mailbox. This check can help to avoid unsuccessful client startups.

Lesson 3: Messaging-Related Outlook Options

Outlook is a powerful program that provides much more than the ability to send e-mail messages: It is also a combined calendar, task, contact management, and workgroup application. Exchange 2000 administrators must be familiar with the Outlook features that affect the e-mail functions in particular.

This lesson addresses options that affect new message composition and rules that can manage received items. A brief explanation of client extensions is also presented.

At the end of this lesson, you will be able to:

- Configure basic Outlook settings.
- Define Delegate permissions for your mailbox.
- Describe options to extend the client functionality.

Estimated time to complete this lesson: 60 minutes

E-Mail Options

Outlook offers a wide variety of customization and configuration options. Most of the configuration settings can be reached on the Tools menu through the Options command. When you open the Options dialog box, the Preferences property sheet is displayed by default.

E-Mail Processing

You can configure various options that control how Outlook handles messages on the Preferences property sheet with the E-mail Options button. You can autosave unsent messages, which, by default, temporarily saves the item that you are composing every 3 minutes in the Drafts folder. You can change this setting via Advanced E-mail Options. A copy of sent messages, on the other hand, can be kept in the Sent Items folder. For messages that arrive you might want to display a short notification, such as a sound or a brief change in the cursor, through Advanced E-mail Options. When you click Tracking Options instead, you are able to configure settings that affect the automatic processing of e-mail messages.

Configuring the Startup Mode

When you switch to the Mail Services tab in the Options dialog box, you can specify settings regarding messaging profile and offline folder settings (covered in Chapter 9, "MAPI-Based Clients").

As a default behavior, Outlook starts without asking for a messaging profile to use. However, if multiple profiles have been configured, you might want to select the desired profile when the client starts. To do this, under Startup Settings, select the Prompt For A Profile To Be Used option. A Choose Profile dialog box will appear every time you start the client, offering the available profiles that you have defined for different messaging configurations.

Default Settings for New Messages

On the Mail Format tab, you can set default options for the format of outgoing messages and specify automatic signatures. The defaults can be overwritten again per individual message via the message's Format menu.

Microsoft Word E-Mail Editor

Because Outlook is tightly integrated with Office, you can use the Use Microsoft Word To Edit E-mail Messages option. When this option is selected, Word is used every time you compose a message. This has a number of advantages, such as advanced spell checker and grammar check functionality, but Word is a slow e-mail editor that consumes a lot of computer resources.

HTML Mail

Outlook 2000 is able to format e-mail messages in plain text, in rich text (the default), or in HTML. You can select the appropriate option from the Send In This Message Format list box. Select HTML to format your e-mail with content as rich and attractive as content on the Web. All leading e-mail applications support HTML mail, so it is a perfect choice if you often communicate with recipients over the Internet. You can include pictures rather than references in your e-mail messages when you select the Send Pictures From The Internet check box, which is especially useful if recipients do not have direct access to the graphic files.

Note Outlook 2000 provides basic HTML editing features. Use Microsoft Word as the HTML mail editor instead if you want to author rich HTML mail.

Spell Checker Options

Outlook can check your e-mail messages for typographical errors and other spelling errors. You will be informed if a word has been spelled incorrectly, and you have the opportunity to correct the text before you send your message. This feature is comparable to the spell checker function of Word, but less convenient to use because it does not flag misspelled words directly in the text. The configuration of the Outlook spell checker is set through the Options dialog box on the Spelling tab.

Outlook 2000 Security

With Outlook 2000 you have the option to use Exchange 2000 Server's Advanced Security features or Secure/Multipurpose Internet Mail Extensions (S/MIME) security to exchange secure e-mail messages with others in your organization and over the Internet. Using the Options dialog box, on the Security tab, you can change the current security settings, configure security zones, and import or export your security certificates. Signing and encrypting of e-mail messages will be covered in Chapter 19, "Implementing Advanced Security."

Deleting Items

When you delete messages in Outlook 2000 either manually or automatically (for instance, through an Inbox rule), those messages are moved to the Deleted Items folder first. This helps to easily recover items deleted accidentally. To empty the Deleted Items folder and permanently remove deleted objects, the user has to right-click on the folder and select the Empty "Deleted Items" Folder option. Because end users occasionally fail to perform manual cleanups, you may notice that in some mailboxes the Deleted Items folder contains thousands of messages. This can be critical if you are considering moving mailboxes to another server. Mailbox and resource management is covered in Chapter 13, "Creating and Managing Recipients."

Outlook 2000 can help your users with frequent cleanup tasks. Ask them to launch the Options dialog box, switch to the Other tab, and select the Empty The Deleted Items Folder Upon Exiting check box, prompting Outlook to purge the deleted items every time Outlook is closed. You may also configure Outlook's AutoArchive feature on the same tab, which allows you to keep the number of messages and the size of your messaging folders at a reasonable level. Outlook is able to move outdated items into personal folder files, covered in Chapter 9, "MAPI-Based Clients."

Defining Delegates

Delegate access refers to a configuration where one user is able to read and send messages and modify calendar and task items on behalf of another user. Such a configuration is especially desirable for people in management positions who want to have their assistants handle daily correspondence. On the Delegates tab, you can designate an assistant or configure Delegate permissions for the Outlook folders of your mailbox (see Figure 8.13).

Granting Access Permissions

To assign an assistant the appropriate level of access, on the Delegates tab, click Add to select the assistant from the address book. You are then prompted to specify access permissions for each Outlook system folder (Calendar, Contacts, Inbox, and so forth).

Granting Permissions to Additional Folders

If you want to grant permissions for other private folders, display the appropriate folder's properties by right-clicking on the folder and selecting Properties. Switch to the Permissions tab, where you can specify user permissions. Using this method, it's possible to grant access permissions to all existing message folders of your mailbox and the mailbox object itself.

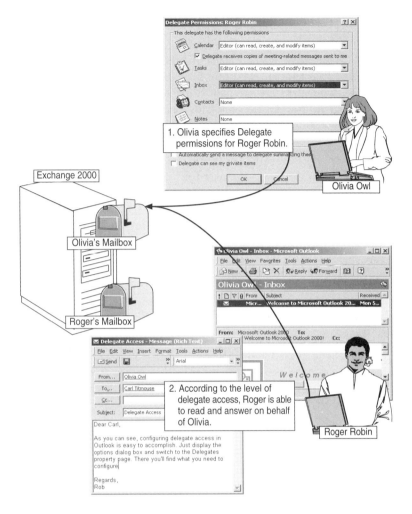

Figure 8.13   Delegate access in Outlook 2000

Opening Another User's Folders

As indicated in Lesson 2, Exchange transport permits a user to work with more than one mailbox in a single session, so a delegate can add your mailbox to his or her profile using the transport service's Advanced tab. The additional mailbox will then appear in the folder list in the client's folder pane. However, the assistant needs at least Read permission for your mailbox and its subfolders, such as the Inbox. Permissions at the mailbox level are not required if your assistant opens your message folders using Outlook's File menu and its Other User's Folder command.

Granting Send On Behalf Of Permissions

Anyone with delegate access to your mailbox is granted Send On Behalf Of permissions, which means that they can use the From button in a message to add your name to the From field. By default, the From button is not displayed, but your delegate can make this button available via the message's View menu and the From Field command. Recipients of the message will see your name under Sent On Behalf Of beside your delegate's name in the From field.

Administrative Permission Assignment

As a mailbox administrator, you also have the option to configure Send On Behalf Of permissions. Open the Active Directory Users and Computers management tool, display the property sheets for the desired account, switch to the Exchange General tab, and then click on Delivery Options. In the Delivery Options dialog box, you will find an Add button that allows you to add user accounts to the list of those with Send On Behalf Of Permissions. You can read more about mailbox management in Chapter 13, "Creating and Managing Recipients."

Send On Behalf Of Only

You might want your assistant to send messages on your behalf without being able to read your messages. In this case, you must not grant Read permission to your mailbox, Inbox, or any other folder. The Send On Behalf Of rights will not be affected by folder privileges. You will typically grant the assistant at least Read permission for your mailbox and Inbox folder, however, to allow him or her to reply to your incoming messages.

Suppressing Send On Behalf Of Information

The assistant's name won't appear in messages sent on your behalf if this person is able to connect to your mailbox using Outlook 2000 and a dedicated MAPI profile (see Exercise 5). If your assistant happens to be an enterprise or domain administrator, you need to grant him or her the Send As permission in addition to the Full Mailbox Access right. Administrators are denied this permission by default to prevent them from opening mailboxes of other users right away. In Active Directory Users Computers, you can overrule this inherited denial through an explicit permission assignment. Because you may designate assistants as administrators in the future, it is advisable to generally grant the Send As permission for Send As delegates. The assistant's name is found on the Exchange Advanced tab with the Mailbox Rights button. In addition, you also need to grant the account Send As permission on the Security property sheet to ensure the information in the Active Directory directory service is correct. The Send As permission does not allow the delegate to open your folders or messages. You must grant the assistant Read permission for your mailbox and Inbox if you want to allow him or her to read your incoming messages.

Note The Mailbox Rights and Security property sheets are only displayed in the Active Directory Users and Computers snap-in when enabling Advanced Features on the View menu.

Storage Group Dependencies

Although Exchange 2000 Server provides you with the ability to configure multiple storage groups on one server to increase fault tolerance and resilience, you need to keep in mind that Outlook 2000 cannot handle delegate access across different mailbox stores. Actually, this is a limitation of the Exchange Server transport, which prevents delegate access between users on different mailbox stores on the same physical server. Delegate access is only supported between users with mailboxes on the same store and across multiple servers. You can read more about the configuration of the Information Store in Chapter 17, "Public Folder Management."

Exercise 5: Assigning Delegate Permissions

In this exercise you will assign another user in the test environment delegate permissions for your mailbox. You will evaluate the two different levels of delegate permissions: the Send On Behalf Of and Send As permissions, which determine whether the delegate's name appears in messages that have been sent on behalf of another user.

To view a multimedia demonstration that displays how to perform this procedure, run the EX5CH8*.AVI files from the \Exercise_Information\Chapter8 folder on the Supplemental Course Materials CD.

Prerequisites

- Complete Exercises 1 and 2, earlier in this chapter.

- Log on as Administrator to BLUESKY-WKSTA.

- You have created a mailbox-enabled user account for Carl Titmouse, as described in the "Getting Started" section of "About This Book."

▶ **To assign delegate permissions and send messages on behalf of another user**

1. Double-click the Microsoft Outlook icon on the desktop.

2. Within Outlook, from the View menu, select the Folder List option.

3. In the Folder List, right-click on the top-level node Outlook Today [Mailbox – Administrator], and then click Properties For "Mailbox – Administrator".

4. The Mailbox – Administrator Properties dialog box appears. Switch to the Permissions tab.

5. Notice that the default permissions prevent anyone else from gaining access to your mailbox. Click Add.

6. In the Add Users dialog box, select Carl Titmouse. Click Add, and then click OK.

7. In the Mailbox – Administrator Properties dialog box, from the Name box, select Carl Titmouse. In the Roles list, select Reviewer. Notice the permissions that are associated with the status of Reviewer.

8. Click OK.

   At this point, you have granted your delegate the permission to open your top-level mailbox object (see Figure 8.14).

Figure 8.14   Granting a delegate Read permission to a mailbox

9. On the Tools menu, select Options to display the Options dialog box, where you need to switch to the Delegates tab.

10. Notice that the Delegates box is empty. Click Add to display the Add Users dialog box. Select Carl Titmouse, click Add, and then click OK.

11. The Delegate Permissions: Carl Titmouse dialog box appears. In the Inbox list box, select Editor (Can Read, Create, And Modify Items). Optionally, you may grant the delegate further permissions for additional Outlook system folders.

12. Select the Automatically Send A Message To Delegate Summarizing These Permissions check box, and then click OK.

13. In the Options dialog box, verify that the delegate is now listed, and then click OK.

At this point, you have assigned Carl Titmouse further permission for your Outlook folders (see Figure 8.15).

14. Close Outlook, and log off from BLUESKY-WKSTA.

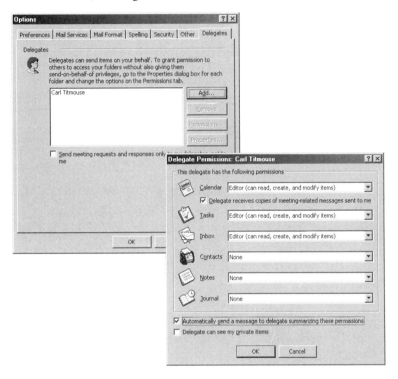

Figure 8.15   Configuring permissions for a delegate

15. Log on as Carl Titmouse to BLUESKY-WKSTA (User Name: **CarlT**, Password: **password**, Log On To: **BLUESKY-INC-10**).

16. Start Microsoft Outlook, and make sure that the default profile automatically generated connects you to the mailbox of CarlT. You will find a message from the Administrator in your Inbox stating You Have Been Designated As A Delegate For. Open the message for a brief overview of the current permissions status.

17. On the File menu, point to Open, and then select Other User's Folder.

18. In the Open Other User's Folder dialog box, click Name to select Administrator from the address book. Under Folder, make sure Inbox is displayed, and

then click OK. You will be able to open the Administrator's Inbox directly in a separate window because the administrator has granted you, among other things, the Read permission to his or her Inbox.

19. Close the Administrator – Inbox – Microsoft Outlook window.

20. From the Tools menu, select Services. In the Services dialog box, make sure Microsoft Exchange Server is selected before you click Properties.

21. In the Microsoft Exchange Server dialog box, click on the Advanced tab.

22. Click Add, and, in the Add Mailbox dialog box, type **Administrator**, then click OK three times to close all dialog boxes.

23. From the View menu, select the Folder List option. In the Folder List, verify that the Mailbox – Administrator object is displayed at the same level as your mailbox and the Public Folders.

At this point, you are able to work with the Administrator's mailbox similar to the mailbox resources of Carl Titmouse. When you expand the Mailbox – Administrator object, you will notice that only those folders for which Carl Titmouse has Read permission are displayed (see Figure 8.16).

Figure 8.16   Two methods to open another user's inbox

24. Make sure you have currently selected Carl Titmouse's Inbox folder. Then open the File menu, and select New Mail Message.

25. In the message window, open the View menu, and click From Field.

26. Click From, and double-click Administrator.

27. Click To, double-click Carl Titmouse, and then click OK.

28. In the Subject line, type **Send On Behalf Permissions**, specify some message text, and then click Send.

    When the new message arrives, open it, and notice that the From field indicates that the message is from Carl Titmouse on behalf of the Administrator (see Figure 8.17).

29. On BLUESKY-SRV1, open the Active Directory Users and Computers tool from the Microsoft Exchange program group.

30. Make sure that, under View, Advanced Features are activated. Double-click the Administrator account from the Users container.

31. Click on the Exchange General tab, and click Deliver Options. Notice that Carl Titmouse is displayed under Send On Behalf, then click OK.

32. Click on the Exchange Advanced tab, and click Mailbox Rights.

33. In the Permissions For Administrator dialog box, click Add, and in the Select Users, Computers, Or Groups dialog box, select Carl Titmouse, click Add, and then click OK.

34. Under Permissions, for Full Mailbox Access, select the Allow check box for Carl Titmouse, then click OK.

35. Click on the Security tab, add Carl Titmouse to the account list (as outlined in step 33), and then, under Permissions, for Send As, select the Allow check box. (Domain users may go without explicit Send As permissions; domain administrators, however, require this setting.)

36. Click OK and close the Active Directory Users and Computers utility.

37. On BLUESKY-WKSTA, in Outlook, open the File menu, and then select Exit And Logoff.

38. Right-click on the Microsoft Outlook icon on the desktop and select Properties.

39. In the CIW Generated Profile Properties dialog box, make sure Microsoft Exchange Server is selected, and then click Properties.

40. Switch to the Advanced tab, verify that Mailbox – Administrator is selected, and then click Remove. In the Microsoft Outlook dialog box asking whether you are sure, click Yes.

41. Switch to the General tab, and, under Mailbox, type **Admin**. Click on the Check Name button and verify that the name can be resolved to Administrator. Then click OK twice to close all dialog boxes.

42. Open Outlook 2000, and, in the Microsoft Outlook dialog box asking you whether you want to recreate the Outlook shortcuts, click No. You are now logged on to the mailbox of Administrator, although, under Windows 2000, you are logged on as Carl Titmouse.

43. In the toolbar click New, type **Carl Titmouse** in the To field, specify **A message from Carl Titmouse as Administrator** in the Subject line, and then enter some message text.

44. Click Send and verify that the message leaves the mailbox, and then select Exit And Logoff Outlook 2000.

45. On the desktop, right-click Microsoft Outlook, select Properties, double-click Microsoft Exchange Server, and then, under Mailbox, type **Carl**, and click Check Names. When the name is resolved successfully, click OK twice to close all dialog boxes.

46. Open Outlook 2000 and check for the new message. Open it and notice that the From field will display Administrator.

47. Double-click Administrator to display the sender properties. There is no hint that Carl Titmouse has sent the message as a delegate (see Figure 8.17). Click OK.

48. Close Outlook 2000 and log off from Windows 2000.

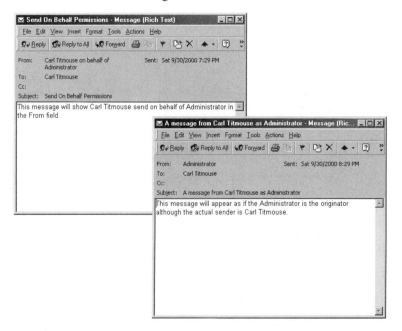

Figure 8.17   Two methods to send a message on behalf of another user

Exercise Summary

Outlook 2000 in conjunction with Exchange 2000 Server can handle two types of delegates: delegates with Send On Behalf Of and delegates with Send As permissions. The difference is that Send On Behalf Of delegates are indicated in the From line when they send messages on behalf of their delegating users, whereas messages from Send As delegates appear as messages from the delegating users directly.

Outlook Client Extensions

Client extensions have existed since the first release of Microsoft Exchange Client 4.0 and Outlook 2000 supports this technology as well. A client extension is a Component Object Model (COM) object that takes advantage of the existing client abilities to extend basic client functionality. The Delegate Access tab discussed in the previous section, for instance, is implemented in the form of a client extension.

Client extensions are enlisted in the Registry under the following key:

```
HKEY_LOCAL_MACHINE

 \Software

  \Microsoft

   \Exchange

    \Client

     \Extensions
```

Add-In Manager

The Add-In Manager allows you to manage registered extensions. To launch the Add-In Manager dialog box, in the Options dialog box, click on the Other tab. Click Advanced Options. In the Advanced Options dialog box, click Add-In Manager.

Out of Office Assistant

The Out of Office Assistant is also a good example of an Outlook extension that extends basic client functionality. The Out of Office Assistant can be used to generate out-of-office notifications that inform the originators of e-mail messages that you are currently unavailable. This assistant is launched through the Tools menu, where you will find the Out Of Office Assistant command.

Try removing the assistant from Outlook to better understand the maintenance of client extensions. Launch the Add-In Manager dialog box by choosing Options from the Tools menu. Click on the Other tab, click Advanced Options, and then click Add-In Manager. Clear the Exchange Extensions Commands check box, and click OK three times to accept the configuration changes, and close the Options dialog box. When you open the Tools menu, you'll find that the Out of Office Assistant command is missing. Outlook is still the same application, but its functionality has been reduced. To restore the assistant, enable the Exchange Extensions Commands check box again.

COM Add-Ins and Visual Basic for Applications

Outlook 2000 supports new technologies based on COM add-ins and Visual Basic for Applications (VBA) that facilitate extending Outlook for developers. COM add-ins can be created using any COM-compliant programming environment including Visual Basic and VBA. COM add-ins are compatible across all Office products, which makes it possible to use a particular add-in in Word and in Outlook, for instance, to control menu items available to the user. You can read more about COM add-ins in the Office 2000 Developer documentation.

VBA in Outlook

VBA has been available since Office 95, but not for Exchange Client or Outlook 97/98. The good news for any VBA programmer is that Outlook 2000 supports macros and VBA and provides access to the Visual Basic Editor, as do all other Office applications. To program macros for Outlook, open the Tools menu, point to Macro, then select Macros or the Visual Basic Editor command. Detailed information about VBA programming is available in the Microsoft Office 2000/Visual Basic Programmer's Guide.

In Outlook, VBA is associated with the running instance of the application. Hence, Outlook only supports a single VBA project, which is stored in a file named VBAPROJECT.OTM. In Windows 2000 Professional, this file can be found in the \Documents and Settings\Administrator\Application Data\Microsoft\Outlook directory.

Chapter Summary

Outlook 2000 is the preferred messaging and collaboration client in Exchange 2000 Server environments, providing numerous features for messaging, collaboration, and information management. The Setup program of Outlook 2000 takes full advantage of Windows Installer technology, which relies primarily on .msi package files. You can customize the installation process via command-line options, SETUP.INI, and transform files. To create transform files, use the Custom Installation Wizard, which gives you far-reaching control over the individual features to be installed. It is a good idea to prepare an administrative installation point in the network, customize the installation files using the Custom Installation Wizard, and then run Setup unattended on the client PCs; or use Windows 2000 group policies for software distribution.

Outlook 2000 is a MAPI-based program that relies on the Exchange transport service to communicate with an Exchange 2000 server over RPCs. You configure this transport in the context of a messaging profile independent of the client. Outlook cannot function without a messaging profile in a workgroup and collaboration environment. The most important configuration parameters are the mailbox and home server names.

Most of the Outlook 2000 configuration options, such as for e-mail preferences, spell checker settings, and client extensions, can be reached on the Tools menu via the Options command. The Options dialog box also allows you to assign other users delegate permissions to your mailbox. However, if you want to grant the Full Mailbox Access and Send As permissions, you need to use the Active Directory Users and Computers snap-in.

Review

The following review questions can help you determine if you have sufficiently familiarized yourself with the material covered in this chapter. You can find the answers to these questions at the end of this book in Appendix A, "Questions and Answers."

1. What are the system requirements for Outlook 2000 on a computer running Windows 2000 Professional?

2. Which three options do you have to customize the Outlook 2000 installation process?

3. You plan to roll out Outlook 2000 to numerous users working on Windows 98, Windows NT 4.0 Workstation, and Windows 2000 Professional. What do you need to accomplish to install the new client platform unattended via a login script?

4. You have created an administrative installation point and customized the installation using SETUP.INI and the Custom Installation Wizard. You are now planning to deploy Outlook through a specific command line, which contains further options. Which settings take precedence over which other settings?

5. Where can you optimize the RPC connection order for Windows 2000-based Outlook 2000 clients?

6. A delegate is sending messages on your behalf, but you don't want the delegate's name to appear on the From line of the message header. What kind of permission must be granted to the assistant to achieve this?

CHAPTER 9

MAPI-Based Clients

About This Chapter

Microsoft Outlook 2000 can work simultaneously with a wide variety of messaging systems because this application relies on the Messaging Application Programming Interface (MAPI) subsystem. MAPI defines several types of information services, such as address book providers, message stores, and transport services, which are configured by means of messaging profiles. A typical messaging profile, for instance, includes the Exchange transport service and the Outlook address book. However, additional information services, such as a personal folder store, can be added. In any case, when connecting to Microsoft Exchange 2000 Server, you must include the Exchange transport service.

The tremendous flexibility of the MAPI subsystem is one of its most remarkable features. Its main limitation is that the configuration resides on the client systems. Fortunately, you can facilitate this task for your users by preconfiguring an administrative Outlook installation point in the network, as discussed in Chapter 8, "Microsoft Outlook 2000 Deployment."

This chapter first introduces the client family of MAPI-based applications. Lessons 2 and 3 then concentrate on the creation and configuration of messaging profiles and the most important MAPI information services. Lesson 4 discusses advanced configuration topics, such as configurations for roaming users and for remote users working disconnected from the network.

Before You Begin

To complete this chapter:

- Prepare your test environment according to the descriptions given in the "Getting Started" section of "About This Book."
- Be familiar with the basic configuration of messaging profiles and the Exchange transport service as briefly explained in Chapter 8, "Microsoft Outlook 2000 Deployment."

Lesson 1: Clients for Exchange 2000 Server

A MAPI-based Exchange client is a messaging application that communicates with an Exchange 2000 Server through MAPI and the Exchange transport, which in turn relies on remote procedure calls (RPCs) to carry out the communication. This type of client provides access to server-based resources in Exchange's native MAPI format—in contrast to Internet-based clients, which retrieve the information in Internet formats, such as Multiple Internet Mail Extensions (MIME; see Chapter 11, "Internet-Based Client Access"). By this definition, when installed in a workgroup and collaboration environment, Outlook is nothing but a MAPI-based client. Another example is the legacy Exchange Client 5.0, which Exchange 2000 Server also supports.

This lesson introduces Microsoft's MAPI-based client applications (Exchange Client and Outlook) according to their operating system requirements. Although MAPI is part of Windows Open Services Architecture (WOSA) and, therefore, strictly speaking, a Microsoft Windows-based interface, MS-DOS and Macintosh clients are covered as well because they provide similar yet reduced functionality.

At the end of this lesson, you will be able to:

- Decide which client to use for MS-DOS, Windows, and Macintosh computers.
- List the features of Outlook for Windows.
- Name the features of Outlook for Macintosh.

Estimated time to complete this lesson: 30 minutes

MS-DOS-Based Clients

It is not really shocking that an MS-DOS-based Outlook client does not exist. If your environment still relies on MS-DOS-based computers, you are forced to either use the legacy Exchange Client or choose another solution, such as Microsoft Terminal Services. Exchange Client is not the best possible choice because it provides only the basic messaging features. For example, scheduling or support for electronic forms is not implemented. You can use TCP/IP, Internetwork Packet Exchange/Sequenced Packet Exchange (IPX/SPX), or NetBEUI to communicate with Exchange 2000 Server via RPC.

The Terminal Services approach is a more robust alternative to deploying the legacy Exchange Client because it allows you to provide users with access to Outlook 2000 and its rich functionality. Just deploy Outlook 2000 on the terminal server and have users connect with the Terminal Server client. You can find more information about the installation of Outlook 2000 in terminal-based environments in the Microsoft Office 2000 Resource Kit.

Windows 3.x–Based Clients

Both Exchange Client and Outlook are available for Microsoft Windows 3.x and Microsoft Windows for Workgroups, and both can communicate with Exchange 2000 Server via RPC over IPX/SPX and NetBEUI, and, if the Windows Sockets (Winsock) interface is installed, via TCP/IP as well. However, the Windows 3.x–based clients do not support Outlook forms, Microsoft Visual Basic Script, and the Component Object Model (COM). Remote mail functionality is implemented in a separate component called ShivaRemote. If this functionality is important to your users, consider upgrading the client systems or using Terminal Services instead of deploying the Windows 3.x–based clients.

Important   Outlook 2000 is not available for Windows 3.x or Windows for Workgroups, so you will have to deploy a previous version of Outlook if you cannot use Terminal Services to provide your users with access to the latest client over the network.

Windows-Based (32-Bit) Clients

Although 32-bit Exchange Clients for Microsoft Windows 95 and Microsoft Windows NT exist, you should not consider deploying them on Windows 95/98, Windows NT, or Microsoft Windows 2000. It is advisable to focus on a deployment of Microsoft Outlook 2000 because no other messaging client provides a comparable set of features for e-mail and information management. Outlook 2000 is easy to use, highly customizable, and remarkably flexible, as discussed in Chapter 8, "Microsoft Outlook 2000 Deployment."

Migration from Exchange Client 4.0/5.0

Microsoft Outlook 97 was designed to completely replace the Exchange Client family. Outlook 2000, representing the third Outlook generation, replaces Exchange Client even better. Upgrading is easy, so if you are still running Exchange Client 4.0 or 5.0, consider a migration to Outlook 2000. After migration, you can continue to use all existing message folders, custom views, electronic forms, and some of the legacy client extensions (see Figure 9.1).

Tip   Former users of Exchange Client may find it useful to display the folder list pane permanently in Outlook (using the Folder List option from the View menu), which gives Outlook a similar user interface to Exchange Client.

Outlook can use the same MAPI profile that might already have been created for Exchange Client, which simplifies the migration process significantly. Only the Outlook address book will be added during setup. This happens automatically, so additional profile configuration is not necessary.

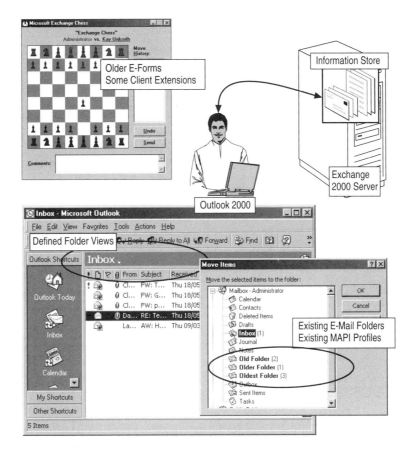

Figure 9.1 Backward-compatible features of Microsoft Outlook

Migration from Schedule+

When migrating from Schedule+ 7.*x* to Outlook 2000, you need to import the existing Schedule+ information into Outlook explicitly if you want to keep it available. Differences exist in the way Outlook stores the items: Whereas Schedule+ uses a hidden folder on the server-based mailbox and a synchronized local calendar file (.scd), Outlook maintains the information using the Calendar, Contacts, Tasks, Journal, and Notes folders in the user's mailbox. Create a local .scd file in Schedule+ first, then synchronize it, and then use this file to import information into Outlook. You'll have three choices regarding how duplicated entries should be treated. You can ignore duplicate entries, replace existing ones, or create a separate entry for each instance of a duplicate item so that both will exist later within Outlook.

Macintosh-Based Clients

Windows 2000 Server systems are accessible for Apple Macintosh computers provided the Services for Macintosh have been installed. Because Exchange 2000 Server integrates tightly with Windows 2000 Server functionality, it benefits from this connectivity and offers Macintosh clients access to server-based resources. Therefore, Exchange Client, Schedule+, and Outlook for Apple Macintosh computers are available. Both Exchange Client and Outlook can communicate with the Exchange Server using the AppleTalk protocol or TCP/IP, so configure Outlook with whichever protocol is supported on your network.

Outlook for Macintosh

Outlook for Macintosh offers a look and feel similar to the Windows-based Outlook version and includes an Outlook bar and a folder banner. The Outlook bar can be customized, and the folder banner allows you to group message items as you want. Likewise, the arrangement of menu and toolbar options is similar to the Windows-based version. Outlook for Macintosh supports calendar and group scheduling features and can replace the Exchange Client for Macintosh family.

Client Limitations

Not all Windows-based client features are supported on the Macintosh platform. For example, electronic forms can't be launched because MAPI doesn't exist. You can't use any of the MAPI information services, and integrated remote mail functionality is not available. Hence, you'll need to ensure that local area network (LAN) connections exist between the Macintosh clients and Exchange 2000 Server. Furthermore, personal folder stores (.pst files), which are used to keep the messages on the client computer, cannot be interchanged with Windows-based .pst files, and Advanced Security features are limited to the local organization. You can read more about Advanced Security in Chapter 19, "Implementing Advanced Security."

Lesson 2: Messaging Application Programming Interface

MAPI is only a specification and not a messaging system in and of itself. It provides only a common way to access messaging backbones. Therefore, you always need to have a MAPI information service available for your existing messaging backbone before you are able to use any MAPI-based client in conjunction with it.

This lesson deals with the architecture and features of the MAPI subsystem. Important information services that come with Outlook are briefly introduced.

At the end of this lesson, you will be able to:

- Describe the general components of the MAPI subsystem.
- Explain the purpose of information services and their three main categories.

Estimated time to complete this lesson: 45 minutes

MAPI Subsystem

MAPI defines standardized interfaces at two layers, which allows the creation of client applications and the development of information services. The client-side specification is called the *client interface,* and the system-side specification is known as the *service provider interface* (see Figure 9.2).

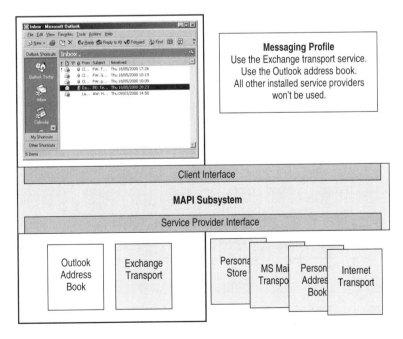

Figure 9.2   Transport provider configuration via messaging profiles

MAPI Advantages

The MAPI subsystem provides many advantages over system-specific interfaces because it frees the developer from learning how to program different messaging systems separately. In other words, no matter which backbone and information services you use, MAPI stays the same.

The following are the advantages of MAPI:

- The client can run MAPI against multiple messaging systems, even simultaneously.
- MAPI is built into Windows.
- MAPI provides separation of messaging backbone and client.
- MAPI is a vendor-independent API.

MAPI Subsets

To simplify messaging programming, the MAPI client interface has been broken down into several subsets. Available subsets are Simple MAPI, Common Messaging Calls (CMC), and Collaboration Data Objects (CDO). (CDO was formerly known as Active Messaging.) The entire client interface is sometimes called Extended MAPI. All programming interfaces are documented in the Microsoft Platform System Development Kit.

Information Services

Information services reside on the lower level of the MAPI subsystem at the level of the service provider interface (see Figure 9.2). They are separated into transport services, address books, and message stores. The MAPI-based client uses them as appropriate whenever it needs to access messaging resources. As discussed earlier, the client uses transport services to access the various backbones, regardless of their data formats or their mechanisms of sending and receiving messages, and it uses address book services to resolve recipient addresses.

Address Books

An address book provider maintains and provides information about recipient objects to the client. The address book provider is an essential component of the MAPI subsystem because without available recipient objects, it would be impossible to send newly composed messages.

For example, you compose a new message and enter the name of the desired recipient in the To box. At this point, the recipient is nothing but a string, which means the recipient name still needs to be resolved to become a unique recipient object. Otherwise, the messaging backbone will not know how to deliver the message. The address will be resolved automatically when the message is sent. If you want, you can also resolve the addresses manually by using the Check Names command on the Tools menu of the New Message window. To resolve the address, the client communicates with the MAPI address book service—for example, the Exchange Server address book. If the address resolution succeeds, the display name of the recipient becomes underlined.

Server-Based Address Books

The server-based address book contains the recipient objects that exist within the Exchange organization, specifically Active Directory directory service. EMSABP32.DLL maintains this service, which is part of the Exchange transport driver. The addresses of all possible recipients in the organization are grouped together within the global address list, which is also used by default for address resolution.

Offline Address Book

The offline address book—also maintained by the Exchange transport service (EMSABP32.DLL)—contains a local copy of the server-based global address list. Once downloaded, it will be used in all situations where the server-based address book is unavailable during offline operation. To download the address information from the server, open the client's Tools menu, point to Synchronize, and then click Download Address Book.

Personal Address Book

The personal address book is maintained within a local .pab file by MSPST32.DLL, which represents the personal address book and the personal folder store service. It is used as the repository for all kinds of personal addresses, especially those that do not exist within the organization.

Outlook Address Book

The Outlook address book implemented in CONTAB32.DLL provides similar functionality to the personal address book, but maintains the address information in Contacts folders rather than a local .pab file. For example, the Contacts folder from your mailbox is added to the Outlook address book by default, so when you create personal contact objects and specify e-mail address information for them, or create distribution lists, these items are available in the client's Outlook address book automatically.

Note It is advisable to use the Contacts folders and the Outlook address book instead of local .pab files to maintain your personal e-mail address information.

Message Repositories

MAPI-based clients generally store e-mail messages, word processing documents, spreadsheets, voice mail files, electronic forms, and other items in folder structures, which can reside on a server or the local computer. Based on their purpose, these folders are named *public*, *private*, *offline*, or *personal folders*. Public folders are used to store collaborative information that is intended to be available to many users in an organization. Private folders refer to those folders that reside on a user's server-based mailbox and are typically available to only one user. They can be synchronized with offline folders, which are nothing more than direct copies of the server-based information placed in a local file with an .ost extension. Offline folders provide access to the information stored in private folders even when the server is unavailable. Messages are also stored locally in personal folders, but personal folders are not synchronized with a server-based mailbox. They are typically used in conjunction with the client's Remote Mail option and reside in local .pst files.

Message Store Providers

Whenever you open a message, save it, copy it to another folder, or delete it, your client communicates with a message store service. EMSMDB32.DLL is involved if you are working with items stored on an Exchange 2000 server. EMSMDB32.DLL is part of the Exchange transport service and provides the services required for accessing public folders and the private folders of your mailbox. EMSMDB32.DLL is also involved if you are working with an offline folder store. When you are working with a personal folder store, on the other hand, you are using the provider that is implemented in MSPST32.DLL.

Transport Providers

A message transport provider is responsible for physical message delivery. This service takes outgoing messages from the MAPI subsystem and transfers them to the underlying messaging backbone to which it corresponds. The message transport provider also hands received messages over to the MAPI subsystem for delivery to the client. Within the Exchange transport service, EMSMDB32.DLL is responsible for message delivery to the Information Store service. Outlook 2000 allows you to install additional transports, including the Internet, fax, Lotus cc:Mail, and the MS Mail transport. Other providers for additional messaging systems such as Lotus Notes are also available and are provided by independent software vendors.

Lesson 3: Creating Messaging Profiles

The installation of a MAPI-based client is usually performed in two stages. In the first stage the Setup program copies the client files to the local hard disk. It also configures relevant Registry settings. When Setup exits, the first stage is completed successfully, but you still can't use the client. The second stage—the creation of a messaging profile—must also be completed.

This lesson introduces the creation of messaging profiles and explains them in respect to Outlook 2000. Options for modifying profiles are outlined and the default services that come with Outlook 2000 are listed.

At the end of this lesson, you will be able to:
- Describe the purpose of messaging profile.
- List available information services.

Estimated time to complete this lesson: 30 minutes

Messaging Profiles

One of the primary goals of the MAPI subsystem is to provide access to various messaging systems, either simultaneously or in separate sessions. To meet this goal, messaging profiles are used. A messaging profile, sometimes also called a MAPI profile, is the set of those information services that should be activated during a particular session. All required configuration settings are stored in the profile.

Setup Wizard

The Microsoft Outlook Setup Wizard guides you through the process of configuring a messaging profile and can be launched in a variety of ways. For example, you can use the Mail applet (it might also be called Mail And Fax) from the Control Panel to display existing messaging profiles and their configurations, or you can right-click on the Microsoft Outlook icon on the desktop and select the Properties command. In the dialog box that appears, click the Show Profiles button, and then click Add to add a new profile, which automatically launches the wizard. The Setup Wizard also appears if no profile exists when you start Outlook. The client is unable to operate without a valid profile, so the wizard prompts for all the required information to create a valid messaging profile before the actual client is launched.

Multiple Profiles

The MAPI subsystem is able to use only one profile at a time; however, more than one profile can be created on the same computer. One profile might connect you to your mailbox on Exchange 2000 Server, and another might connect you to an Internet service provider, but only one profile will be activated at any particular time. You can choose the desired profile at client startup according to its name to connect to the desired messaging system.

MAPI-based clients use a default profile automatically if more than one profile exists. Nevertheless, it is possible to configure Outlook 2000 to prompt you for the profile name at every session startup. To do this, enable the Prompt For A Profile To Be Used option on the Mail Services tab of the client's Options dialog box. The Options dialog box was discussed in Chapter 8, "Microsoft Outlook 2000 Deployment."

Multiple Users

Windows 95, Windows NT, and Windows 2000 provide support for multiple users who share a single computer because these operating systems can maintain messaging profiles on a per-user basis. This means that the profile settings of one user do not affect the configuration of any other. In Windows 2000, profiles for the user currently logged on are stored in the Registry under:

```
HKEY_CURRENT_USER
  \Software
   \Microsoft
    \Windows NT
     \CurrentVersion
      \Windows Messaging Subsystem
       \Profiles
```

Subkeys exist that correspond to every profile a user has created.

Automatic Profile Generator

The Automatic Profile Generator (NEWPROF.EXE) is an installation tool that uses a profile descriptor file (.prf) to create MAPI profiles for users. The Automatic Profile Generator comes with Outlook 2000 and is installed by default in the \Program Files\Common Files\System\Mapi\1033\Nt directory. You can start this tool in login scripts or manually at any time to create additional profiles or to modify existing ones.

You can run NEWPROF.EXE by specifying the following options:

```
NEWPROF [-P <Path to .prf file>] [-S] [-X] [-Z]
```

- **P.**   References the complete path to the .prf descriptor file.
- **S.**   Provides a user interface to select the .prf file and to display status and error messages.
- **Z.**   Displays MAPI status codes in case any errors are encountered. Can only be used in conjunction with the -S switch.

- **X.**   Executes NEWPROF.EXE **-S** automatically without user interaction. Requires the **-P**<Path to the .prf file> switch.

Profile Descriptor File

Let's say that you want to customize an OUTLOOK.PRF file according to Figure 9.3. You want to reflect your given name and surname and point the future profile to your home server. A good starting point could be the OUTLOOK.PRF that comes with the Microsoft Office 2000 Resource Kit. Edit OUTLOOK.PRF to modify the line ProfileName=Microsoft Outlook in the [General] section. For example: ProfileName=Roger Robin. Furthermore, you need to set the HomeServer line, which can be found in the [Service2] section, to BLUESKY-SRV1. It is also a good idea to specify the placeholder %*username*% in an additional line for the mailbox name: MailboxName=%*username*%, which will cause the generated profile to connect you to the mailbox that corresponds to your Windows 2000 account. To ensure that the current profile will be overwritten, you still have to verify that the option OverwriteProfile is set to Yes in the [General] section. Then you can execute the Automatic Profile Generator (NEWPROF.EXE) to specify the modified .prf file. NEWPROF.EXE will create a fresh profile and name it Roger Robin.

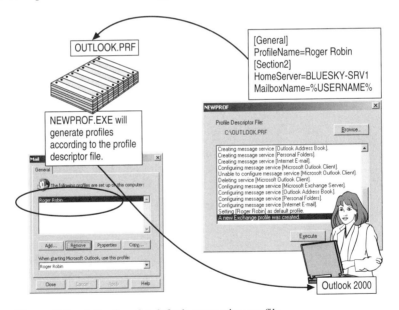

Figure 9.3   Adjusting the default messaging profile

Note   The OUTLOOK.PRF file that comes with the Microsoft Office 2000 Resource Kit contains a description of customizable profile properties in Section 6.

Exercise 1: Creating a New Profile

In this exercise you will create a messaging profile manually using the Profile Wizard. The automatic generation of messaging profiles was already demonstrated in Exercise 3 of Chapter 8, "Microsoft Outlook 2000 Deployment."

To view a multimedia demonstration that displays how to perform this procedure, run the EX1CH9.AVI files from the \Exercise_Information\Chapter9 folder on the Supplemental Course Materials CD.

Prerequisites

- Install Outlook 2000 on BLUESKY-WKSTA, preferably as outlined in Chapter 8, "Microsoft Outlook 2000 Deployment."
- Log on as Administrator to BLUESKY-WKSTA.

▶ **To create a new MAPI profile**

1. Right-click the Microsoft Outlook icon on the desktop, and, from the shortcut menu, select Properties.

2. In case a profile already exists, the <Profile Name> Properties dialog box appears. Click Show Profiles to display the list of available profiles.

3. In the Mail dialog box, click Add.

4. The Microsoft Outlook Setup Wizard is launched, giving you the option to use the Microsoft Exchange Server or Internet E-mail information service. Select the Microsoft Exchange Server check box, and then click Next.

5. On the second wizard screen, under Profile Name, type **Manually Configured Profile,** and then click Next.

6. On the third wizard screen, under Microsoft Exchange Server, type **BLUESKY-SRV1.** Under Mailbox, make sure Administrator is displayed. Click Next.

7. On the fourth wizard screen, make sure that under Do You Travel With This Computer, No is selected, and then click Next.

8. On the final wizard screen, verify that the Microsoft Exchange Server and Outlook Address Book services will be added to the messaging profile, and then click Finish.

9. In the Mail dialog box, under When Starting Microsoft Outlook, Use This Profile, select Manually Configured Profile, and then click Close. At this point, you have configured a messaging profile that connects your Outlook client to the Administrator's mailbox on BLUESKY-SRV1 (see Figure 9.4). Start Outlook to verify that you can successfully log on to the mailbox.

10. Click Start, and select Run to display the Run dialog box. Type **Regedit**, and then click OK.

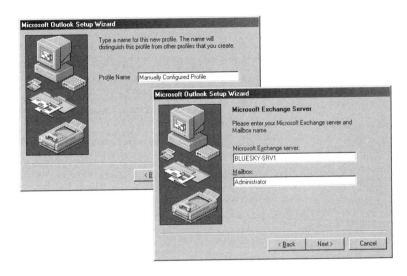

Figure 9.4   Configuring a messaging profile

11. Navigate to and select the following key:

    HKEY_CURRENT_USER\Software\Microsoft\Windows

    NT\CurrentVersion\Windows Messaging Subsystem\Profiles

    At this point, you should be able to verify that the REG_SZ value
    DefaultProfile exists and points to Manually Configured Profile, which is a
    subkey under Profiles holding the settings for the messaging profile (see
    Figure 9.5).

12. Close the Registry Editor.

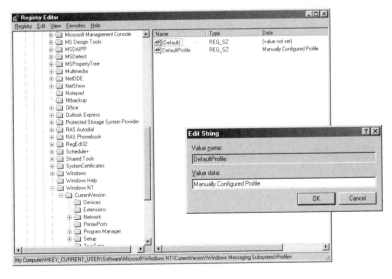

Figure 9.5   Manually configured profile properties

Exercise Summary

You can create messaging profiles using the Outlook Setup Wizard. The wizard can be launched manually or automatically when you start Outlook and you haven't configured a messaging profile. (The exception is starting Outlook for the first time in conjunction with an OUTLOOK.PRF or customized installation point.) The wizard gathers all the required configuration information from you to create a default profile, after which the client can start successfully. Messaging profiles are stored in the Registry under the HKEY_CURRENT_USER hive.

Personal Folder Configuration

The personal folder store allows you to work with personal folders in the same way you work with private or public folders on Exchange 2000 Server. Because the message folders are maintained locally in a .pst file, the personal folder store is an ideal solution for message archiving. In this way, older messages can be copied to a .pst file, archived individually, and deleted from the Exchange 2000 server (see Figure 9.6).

Note A .pst file can contain up to 64,000 entries and can grow to a maximum size of 2 GB.

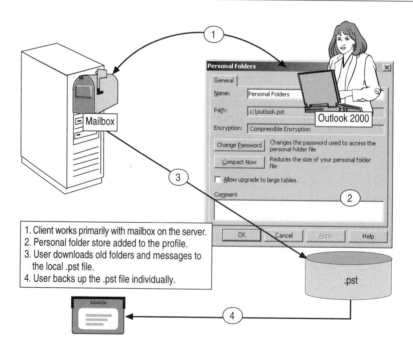

Figure 9.6   Archiving old messages

Personal Folder Security

It is possible to specify an encryption algorithm for personal folder stores. Depending on the security level you need, you can select the options No Encryption, Compressible Encryption, and Best Encryption when creating a .pst file. It is prudent to protect your .pst files using an encryption algorithm and a password, as .pst files contain your personal messages. If you define a password, however, there is one possible catch: The password itself will be stored within the .pst file to protect it from unauthorized access, so you must provide the password on every client startup to open the .pst file. For the sake of convenience, you can save the password in your current messaging profile so the client can read the password from the profile without having to prompt you for it. You will then be able to start your client and access your personal folders immediately.

You might forget your password as time passes and you are not prompted for it. You will still be able to use the .pst file because the password is saved in the messaging profile. You will, however, have a problem if you need to create a new profile that must include the old .pst file. As soon as you try to include the existing .pst file, a dialog box will appear asking you for the password. If you have forgotten the password, there is no way to recover it. If you have deleted the old profile (which stored the password), the data in the .pst file is lost. If you still have access to the old profile, however, you can log on to the personal folder store again—as the password is available in the old profile—to move all messages to a new .pst file.

Assigning a Location for Incoming Mail

When you configure a personal folder store and connect to Exchange 2000 Server via the Exchange transport service at the same time, two mail repositories exist within your messaging profile—the personal folder store and your server-based mailbox. In this situation, the client needs to know where to deliver incoming messages. Using the Services command on the Tools menu, you can configure the message delivery. Click on the Delivery tab to select the primary Inbox under Deliver New Mail To The Following Location. For instance, if you specify the personal folder store, all incoming messages delivered to your mailbox on the server will be downloaded automatically and placed as incoming messages into your personal Inbox folder.

Exercise 2: Creating a Personal Folder Store

In this exercise you will configure a .pst file and include it in your default messaging profile. After that, you will use Outlook's archiving features to archive the contents of all your server-based mailbox folders into yet another personal folder store.

To view a multimedia demonstration that displays how to perform this procedure, run the EX2CH9.AVI files from the \Exercise_Information\Chapter9 folder on the Supplemental Course Materials CD.

Prerequisites

- Complete Exercise 1, earlier in this lesson.
- Log on as Administrator to BLUESKY-WKSTA.

▶ **To create a personal folder store**

1. Start Outlook 2000 using the manually configured profile from Exercise 1.
2. Open the Tools menu, and select Services.
3. Click Add, and, from the Available Information Services list, select Personal Folders, then click OK.
4. In the Create/Open Personal Folders File, under File Name, type **Outlook.pst,** and then click Open.
5. In the Create Microsoft Personal Folders dialog box, in the Password and Verify Password boxes, type **password**.
6. Select Save This Password In Your Password List, and then click OK.
7. In the Services dialog box, click OK.

    At this point, you have successfully added a personal folder store to the default messaging profile (see Figure 9.7). You can also verify the existence of the personal folder store when displaying the Folder List (from the View menu).

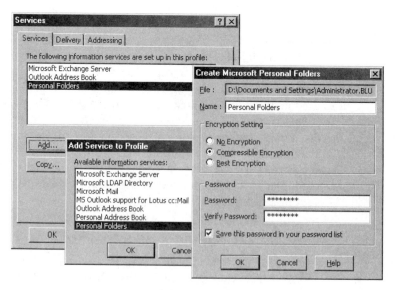

Figure 9.7   Configuring a personal folder store

8. Open the File menu, and select the Archive command.
9. In the Archive dialog box, make sure the Archive This Folder And All Subfolders option is activated, and then select the top-level Mailbox – Administrator object.

10. Under Archive File, click Browse. In the Open Personal Folders dialog box, under File Name, type **Archive.pst**, then click OK.

11. In the Archive dialog box, click OK.

At this point, you are archiving all your mailbox folders into the Outlook ARCHIVE.PST file (see Figure 9.8).

Figure 9.8   Archiving into a personal folder store

Exercise Summary

You can add a personal folders information service to your messaging profile through the Services command on the client's Tools menu, which displays the Services dialog box. The path to the .pst file is the most important configuration parameter. A path to a .pst file is also necessary if you wish to archive your server-based mailbox folders. However, the archive itself is not included automatically in your messaging profile. To open it, you would have to manually include it, for instance, via the Personal Folders File (.pst) command under the Open submenu from the File menu.

Offline Folder Configuration

Offline folders are the basis of a process known as *local replication*. The folders are local copies of server-based message folders. Hence, the offline folder store can be used in conjunction only with the Exchange transport service (see Figure 9.9).

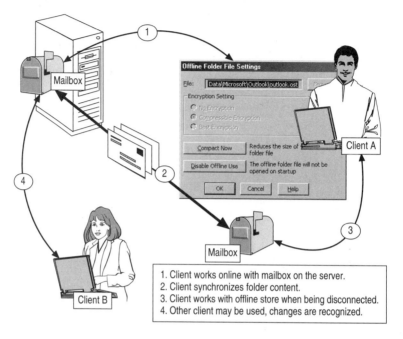

Figure 9.9 Working with offline folders

Note The offline folder store and the offline address book—as implemented in the Exchange transport service—allow you to work while disconnected from the server.

Local Replication Example

Let's say you have configured an offline folder store to synchronize your server-based folders Calendar, Contacts, Deleted Items, Inbox, Journal, Notes, Outbox, Sent Items, and Tasks. While you are working on your notebook computer at home, you can read and delete messages from the Inbox. You can also reply to particular messages. In this situation, you are working with your offline folders. Any messages that you have sent will remain in your local Outbox replica. When you insert your notebook into the docking station the next morning when working in your office, you start the client, and a connection is established with the server. At this point, the new information residing in the offline store will be replicated to your server-based mailbox. Items that you have deleted the evening before while working with your offline Inbox will now be deleted from the server-based Inbox as well. Likewise, the messages in the offline Outbox are replicated to the server-based Outbox, where the Information Store service can retrieve them for delivery.

Configuring Offline Folders

You can configure the offline folder store through the Exchange transport service's property sheets within a messaging profile. You can display these property sheets through the Services command on the client's Tools menu. In the General tab of the Services property sheet, select Microsoft Exchange Server, and then click Properties. Click on the Advanced tab. Here you will find the Offline Folder File Settings button, which launches the Offline Folder File Settings dialog box. This dialog box looks similar to the configuration dialog box for a new .pst file. You must define a name for and a path to the new .ost file. Another important setting determines which encryption algorithm should be used for the storage file.

Important An .ost file (by default, \Winnt\OUTLOOK.OST) might already exist if you answered Yes to the question Do You Travel With This Computer? during the profile creation within the Profile Wizard. An .ost file is associated with a profile. If you create a new profile, you will need to create and synchronize a new .ost file before it can be used with the new profile.

Configuring Message Folders To Be Available Offline

Using Outlook 2000, you can configure the local replication of server-based message folders via the Mail Services property sheet of the Options dialog box. If you have created an .ost file beforehand, you can click on the Offline Folder Settings button to specify the folders for offline use. The system folders Inbox, Outbox, Deleted Items, Sent Items, Calendar, Drafts, Contacts, Journal, Notes, and Tasks are replicated automatically as soon as you enable the offline folders using Outlook. Within the Offline Folder Settings dialog box, the other server-based private and public folders can be configured for local replication as well.

It is likewise possible to synchronize additional folders by explicitly enabling the synchronization using the property sheets of the folder. In this scenario you must right-click the desired folder to select the Properties command. On the Synchronization property sheet, which is available only after you have created offline folders, under This Folder Is Available, you can select When Offline Or Online. The selected folder can be synchronized from then on.

Tip If you want to configure a public folder for local replication, you must first drag the folder to the Favorites container. You can then configure it the same way you configure private folders.

Synchronization Capabilities

You should force the synchronization between the server-based folders and the local replica of folders once they have been included in the local replication. This will ensure that the offline store contains the current data. On the Tools menu, select the Synchronize option. Then you can select either This Folder, which will synchronize the currently highlighted folder only, or All Folders, which will synchronize all folders that are members of the local replication. In addition, Outlook 2000 allows you to set up smaller groups of folders to synchronize to save replication time, especially over slow dial-up connections. To configure smaller groups of folders, click on the Quick Synchronization tab in the Offline Folder Settings dialog box. By default, a Mail And Calendar group exists, synchronizing Calendar, Drafts, Outbox, and Inbox, which you can select accordingly on the Tools menu via the Synchronize option.

Outlook 2000 can also synchronize folders automatically. This will happen whenever Outlook 2000 is started in online mode, and according to the settings that you can specify in the Mail Services tab of the Options dialog box.

If you want information about the current status of the synchronization between the server-based folder and the offline replica, open the Synchronization property sheet of the desired folder again (right-click the folder, and then select the Properties command). You'll be able to determine the date and time of the last synchronization event, along with the current number of items in both the server-based folder and the offline folder.

Filtering Offline Folders

Examining the synchronization capabilities of Outlook 2000 in more detail, there is a wide selection of options to selectively download messages that meet certain criteria. Especially when working on slow dial-up connections, you might want to configure Download Options and Folder Filters in the Offline Folder Settings dialog box to selectively synchronize existing items. Otherwise, it might take a long time to synchronize all new messages that arrive while a user is offline. You can also configure the synchronization filter per folder via the folder's Synchronization property sheet.

Offline Address Book Configurations

When you examine the Offline Folder Settings dialog box, you will see the Download Offline Address Book check box, which allows you to include the download of address book information into the folder synchronization process. This is an important feature because when users are working offline, server-based address books are generally unavailable. Without an address book, however, it is difficult to address new messages to recipients in your organization. Only replies to messages that have been received and synchronized are possible. To keep the address information available while working offline, you must download the offline address book from the server while working online.

Manual Address Book Download

When enabled, the Download Offline Address Book check box allows automatic downloading of the address book as part of the Outlook synchronization cycle. You can also download the address book from the server manually at any time. Access the Download Address Book command from the Synchronize option on the Tools menu. Specify the desired address book under Address Book in the Offline Address Book dialog box, and click OK. By default, your Global Address List (GAL) is available for download, but you may configure additional offline address books in the Exchange System Manager, which is a topic of Chapter 14, "Managing Server Configuration."

Address Book Details

To reduce the size of the address book downloaded to your machine and therefore reduce transmission time, you can choose to download the address book without details that are not required for message creation and addressing. You can also specify that only address book changes that have occurred since the last synchronization be downloaded. To do this, in the Offline Address Book dialog box, select the Download Changes Since Last Synchronization check box. This will reduce the time required to synchronize the offline address book.

Offline Address Book Files

The offline address book (.oab) files are usually stored in the current Windows directory. At a minimum, four .oab files are always downloaded, but a fifth file is available for downloading if you also have specified the retrieval of address details. The ANRDEX.OAB file provides indexes for Ambiguous Name Resolution. The RDNDEX.OAB file helps to manage e-mail addresses. Address book templates are copied to TMPLTS.OAB. Address details are kept in the DETAILS.OAB and BROWSE.OAB files. DETAILS.OAB is usually the largest file because it keeps all the detailed information about the users of your organization. You should not delete this file manually if it becomes too large—use Outlook to remove the DETAILS.OAB file instead. You then need to download the offline address book one more time, this time without detailed information.

Important   The Download Changes Since Last Synchronization option must be deselected if you want to ensure that the DETAILS.OAB file will be deleted. Selecting only the No Details option from the Offline Address Book dialog box is not sufficient.

Lesson 4: Advanced User Configurations

In a typical Exchange 2000 environment, many different kinds of Outlook users cooperate and share information. Typical users work with only one (personal) workstation that is directly connected to the organization's computer network. Remote users, on the other hand, may work primarily offline using a modem or Integrated Services Digital Network (ISDN) card to establish connections for sending and downloading messages. There may exist another category of users in your environment—roving users—who work with multiple computers and multiple messaging clients.

This lesson explains the features that allow you to support roving and remote users using Outlook 2000. It discusses the creation of centralized profiles and the configuration of remote mail features.

At the end of this lesson, you will be able to:

- Support roving user configurations for Outlook 2000 clients.

- Describe the support of remote users by means of the Exchange transport service.

- Identify important configuration issues and dependencies for remote users.

Estimated time to complete this lesson: 60 minutes

Roving User Support

To simplify the task of creating messaging profiles for roving users, you can implement server-based profiles that will be copied to every workstation a roving user logs on to, automatically providing the same messaging environment to the user. Because messaging profile information is stored differently on different client operating systems, you must consider the requirements of each client platform. For example, if a roving user works on machines with Windows 98 and Windows 2000 Professional, you must create one profile for each platform separately. Fortunately, no significant differences exist between Windows 98 and Windows 2000 clients.

Roaming Profiles

Windows 95/98, Windows NT, and Windows 2000 provide built-in support for roving users because MAPI-based clients store their messaging profiles within the user's context in the workstation's Registry. Of course, the user profile can be stored as a server-based profile. A server-based Windows profile can be assigned to each account using the Active Directory Users and Computers management tool. Once the account of the roving user has been associated with a server-based profile, its settings are copied to the local configuration each time the roving user logs on to the domain. The same settings, including the messaging profile, are thus available on every computer running Windows 95/98, Windows NT, or Windows 2000. You can find more information regarding the configuration of roaming profiles in the *Windows 2000 Server Distributed Systems Guide* of the Microsoft Windows 2000 Server Resource Kit.

Personal Folder Store Considerations

Roving users typically want access to all their messages from within any messaging client they are using. If they have stored some of their messages in one or more personal folder stores, precautions must be taken to make sure the associated .pst files are all available over the network. Therefore, .pst files should be placed on a file server that can be accessed by every client machine. If a common file server is not available, a roving user should refrain from using personal folder stores. Instead, roving users should use only the server-based mailbox as a repository for messages.

Outlook Web Access or Terminal Services

The HTTP-based access to server-based mailboxes is an alternative to all other roving user options. By using a regular Web browser that supports JavaScript and frames (such as Microsoft Internet Explorer 5.0), users can gain access to their mailbox through Outlook Web Access (OWA). However, roving users should be aware of security risks when using browser applications. Browser programs view the messaging items in HTML pages, which might be cached temporarily on the workstation. If a roving user does not delete those cached pages after a session, other users can simply open them later to read personal information. More information about OWA is provided in Chapter 22, "Microsoft Outlook Web Access."

Terminal Services allows you to run Outlook 2000 on a server over the network or a dial-up connection from any workstation that is running the Terminal Services client software. Because only display information is sent to the terminal, users may find this approach attractive. From Outlook's point of view, users running Terminal Services client software are not considered roaming users because they are using the same environment on the terminal server every time they connect. It is more like they would work with a single virtual workstation but multiple keyboards and monitors.

Remote User Support

Users who work via modem or ISDN lines usually don't work online continuously. They compose new messages and read downloaded messages while disconnected from the server. In other words, they connect to the server only to send and download new messages, which helps to reduce the amount of time spent dialed in and communications costs. For this reason, downloaded messages are maintained in a local repository, which can be created by means of a personal folder store (see Figure 9.10).

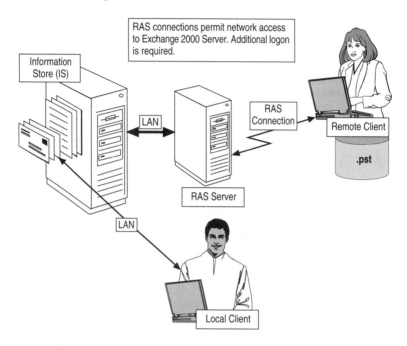

Figure 9.10   Remote client connections

Remote Mail Versus Offline Folders

You cannot use the remote mail features of Outlook 2000 if an offline message store has been configured. In this situation you must disable the offline message store before using remote mail. However, because Outlook 2000 offers far-reaching configuration and filter capabilities for synchronizing server-based folders and because the offline folder approach is usually less complex to handle than the remote mail features, you should consider using offline folders instead of remote mail.

Remote Mail Configurations

Outlook 2000 allows you to configure remote mail connections through the property sheets of the Exchange transport service, which in turn relies completely on the dial-up networking capabilities of the operating system.

Specifying the Dial-Up Connection

The Dial-Up Networking property sheet of the Exchange transport service gives you the option to select a dial-up connection to be used to establish the connection to the server via a Remote Access Service (RAS) server (see Figure 9.10).

The account information used to establish a connection with the RAS server can be specified under User Name, Password, and Domain. This account does not necessarily need to be the same account that you use to connect to your server-based mailbox.

Remote Mail Connections

A connection to your Exchange 2000 server is established when you click Connect under the Remote Mail option on the Tools menu. While this connection is up and running, the headers of messages in your server-based mailbox are downloaded, and the messages composed offline are uploaded. Header information is displayed in Outlook's regular Inbox as an envelope icon with a small telephone. You can then disconnect manually from the server using the Disconnect command, or automatically by using the Disconnect After Connection Is Finished check box, found on the Remote Mail property sheet of the Exchange transport service.

Based on the retrieved header information, you can select which messages to mark for retrieval. This will move the messages to your local store the next time you connect. You can retrieve a copy, which also moves the message to your local store but leaves a copy on the server, or you can mark a message for deletion, which will delete the message from the server without first downloading it the next time you work online. Because you can select each message individually, remote mail is well-suited for downloading only the messages you want over slow dial-up connections.

Scheduled Connections

If you want to automate the processes of establishing a connection and processing marked items, you can configure scheduled connections through the Remote Mail property sheet of the Exchange transport service. During automatically established connections, the client behaves the same way as during manually started remote mail connections. To automate the retrieval of messages, you can configure download filters. So long as no filter criterion has been defined, all messages will be retrieved. Filters can be specified for manual connections under the Remote Mail Connection category and for scheduled connections under Scheduled Connections. The Filter button becomes available if you activate the corresponding Retrieve Items That Meet The Following Conditions option.

Exercise 3: Configuring Remote Mail Support

In this exercise you will configure Outlook 2000 for remote mail support. You will then configure the client to start offline to use Outlook's built-in remote mail features.

To view a multimedia demonstration that displays how to perform this procedure, run the EX3CH9*.AVI files from the \Exercise_Information\Chapter9 folder on the Supplemental Course Materials CD.

Prerequisites

- Complete Exercise 2, earlier in this chapter.
- Log on as Administrator to BLUESKY-WKSTA.

▶ **To configure remote mail support**

1. Right-click on the Microsoft Outlook icon on the desktop, and then select Properties.
2. Make sure Microsoft Exchange Server is selected, and then click Properties.
3. On the General tab, activate the Manually Control Connection State option, and then select the Choose The Connection Type When Starting check box.
4. Click on the Dial-Up Networking tab, and activate the Do Not Dial, Use Existing Connection option.
5. In the Microsoft Exchange Server dialog box, click OK.
6. Click on the Delivery tab (if a Microsoft Exchange Server dialog box appears, click Connect).
7. Under Deliver New Mail To The Following Location, select Personal Folders.
8. Click OK.

   At this point, you have specified the personal folder store created during Exercise 1 as the primary location for incoming messages (see Figure 9.11).

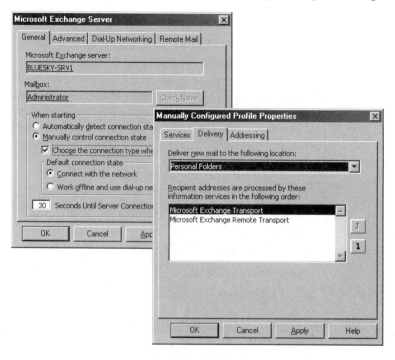

Figure 9.11   Configuring the options for remote mail

9. Start Outlook 2000, and, in the Microsoft Exchange Server dialog box, click Connect.

10. If a Microsoft Outlook dialog box appears informing you that the location messages are delivered to has changed, click Yes to recreate all shortcuts.

11. Your e-mail messages are now downloaded automatically into the Inbox of your .pst file.

12. Close Outlook 2000.

13. Start Outlook 2000 again, and in the Microsoft Exchange Server dialog box, click Work Offline.

14. Compose a new message and, in the Untitled – Message (Rich Text) window, in the To line, type **Administrator@BlueSky-inc-10.com**.

15. In the Subject line, type **A Remote Mail Message**.

16. Type some message text, and then click Send.

17. Open the Tools menu, point to Remote Mail, and then click Connect.

18. On the Remote Connection Wizard screen, make sure Microsoft Exchange Server is selected, and then click Next.

19. On the second Remote Connection Wizard screen, accept the defaults, and click Finish.

At this point, Outlook 2000 is connecting to the Exchange 2000 Server; it then sends the prepared message and downloads the header information from the server (see Figure 9.12).

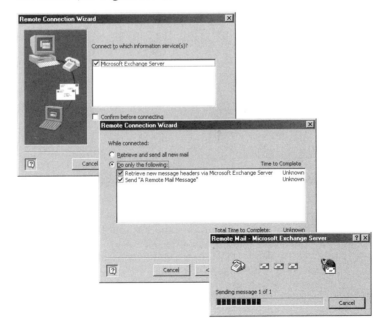

Figure 9.12   Using the remote mail features of Outlook 2000

20. The remote mail message will be displayed in your Inbox with an icon showing an envelope with a small telephone. Select this message, open the Tools menu, point to Remote Mail, and then select Mark To Retrieve.

21. Open the Tools menu again, point to Remote Mail, and then click Connect (or click Connect in the Remote Mail toolbar).

22. On the Remote Connection Wizard screen, make sure Microsoft Exchange Server is selected, and then click Next.

23. On the second Remote Connection Wizard screen, accept the defaults, and click Finish.

24. Outlook 2000 will download the specified message and change the icon correspondingly. The message was downloaded into your .pst file.

Exercise Summary

You can establish remote mail connections through the Remote Mail option on the client's Tools menu, which displays a submenu and allows you to launch the Remote Connection Wizard through the Connect command. You can also select Remote Tools to display an additional toolbar labeled Remote, which gives you convenient access to all remote mail options. It is a good idea to keep address information available while working offline. If you have not downloaded the offline address book from the server, you have to specify recipient information manually or via the Outlook address book when composing new messages. This is not an issue, however, when you reply to existing e-mails. Any messages that you compose can be uploaded when establishing the next dial-up connection. Header information about received messages can be downloaded as well. Through header information, you can specify, in detail, which messages to download, copy, or delete without actually downloading them.

Chapter Summary

Two MAPI-based client platforms are available from Microsoft: the legacy Exchange Client and its current release, Outlook 2000. Consider deploying Outlook 2000 wherever possible to fully benefit from advanced information management capabilities that are unavailable in other clients.

Every MAPI-based client requires a messaging profile, which describes the set of information services, such as address book providers, message stores, and transport services, that should be used in a particular client session. Although multiple profiles can be configured in the Microsoft Outlook Setup Wizard, only one profile can be activated at any given time.

In Windows 2000, MAPI profiles are stored in the Registry under the HKEY_CURRENT_USER hive. Therefore, it is easy to include them in server-based profiles, which is the basis of roaming user support. A user with a server-based profile can use the same messaging profile on any computer running

Windows 2000 because the server-based profile information is downloaded to the workstation automatically when the user logs on to the domain.

When connecting to Exchange 2000 Server, you must include the Exchange transport service. This transport service supports users working online in a LAN environment or offline disconnected from the computer network. The latter can establish connections to Exchange 2000 Server via dial-up networking and a RAS server. To keep messages available offline, you can configure a .pst file and use the remote mail functionality of Outlook 2000 to download messages, or create an .ost file and synchronize this offline repository with your server-based messaging folders. The advantage of the latter approach is that you can work with public folders offline.

Review

The following review questions can help you determine if you have sufficiently familiarized yourself with the material covered in this chapter. You can find the answers to these questions at the end of this book in Appendix A, "Questions and Answers."

1. What is a messaging profile?

2. Which tool assists you in creating messaging profiles?

3. Where are the messaging profiles of a currently logged on user stored in Windows 2000?

4. Which two message stores can be configured to keep messages available offline?

5. You have configured a personal folder store and the Exchange transport service. How can you define the personal folder store as the location for incoming messages?

6. What is the most significant advantage of the offline folder store?

7. How can you assign centralized messaging profiles to roving users that work on computers running Windows 2000?

CHAPTER 10

MAPI-Based Clients in a Novell NetWare Environment

About This Chapter

Microsoft Exchange 2000 Server is tightly integrated into the Microsoft Windows 2000 Server architecture. It is not available on any other platform. As soon as you decide to install Microsoft's most powerful messaging system, you decide to implement Windows 2000 Server and the Active Directory directory service on your computer network as well—even if your network does not contain any Windows 2000 Server computers yet. If you are a Novell NetWare administrator, you will benefit from knowing about the tools that let you integrate Windows 2000 into your NetWare infrastructure.

Native NetWare workstations cannot access Exchange 2000 resources without an additional network component—the Client for Microsoft Networks. This is because neither Microsoft Client Services for NetWare nor Novell NetWare Client software comes with the required remote procedure calls (RPCs) services that Microsoft Outlook 2000 needs for its client-to-server communication. If your NetWare environment supports TCP/IP, you can avoid the installation of the Client for Microsoft Networks by using Internet-based messaging clients or Outlook Web Access (see Chapter 11, "Internet-Based Client Access").

This chapter discusses the main aspects of combining Windows 2000 Server and NetWare in Lesson 1 and introduces tools that simplify your daily work. Lesson 2 then covers the client-side requirements for establishing RPC connections to an Exchange 2000 server and explains how to troubleshoot client connectivity problems.

Before You Begin

To complete this chapter:

- Be familiar with the concepts and administration of Novell NetWare and Novell Directory Services (NDS).

- Be familiar with the concepts and administration of Microsoft Windows 2000 Server and Active Directory.

- Understand the requirements for using Outlook 2000 in an Exchange 2000 environment (see Chapter 3, "Microsoft Exchange 2000 Server Architecture," Chapter 8, "Microsoft Outlook 2000 Deployment," and Chapter 9, "MAPI-Based Clients").

Lesson 1: Integrating Windows 2000 with Novell NetWare

The integration of Windows 2000 Server in a Novell NetWare–based environment introduces several issues. You need to determine a common network protocol for both systems, for instance. You may consider synchronizing the NetWare and Windows 2000 accounts to simplify the environment for your users, who otherwise might have to cope with different account information for NetWare and Windows 2000.

This lesson covers the management and configuration issues that you will encounter when you combine Windows 2000 Server and NetWare in a network. You will learn about configuring networking components such as the NWLink IPX/SPX–Compatible Transport, Gateway Services for NetWare (GSNW), and the Service Advertising Protocol (SAP) Agent. The lesson also discusses additional utilities that can simplify the administration of mixed Windows 2000 Server/NetWare environments.

At the end of this lesson, you will be able to:

- Install the NWLink IPX/SPX–Compatible Transport.
- Use TCP/IP to integrate Windows 2000 with NetWare 5.
- Install and configure GSNW.
- Identify and use additional utilities for NetWare.

Estimated time to complete this lesson: 30 minutes

NWLink-Based Connections

The Internetwork Packet Exchange/Sequenced Packet Exchange (IPX/SPX) protocol is used most often in NetWare networks. The corresponding Windows implementation is known as the NWLink IPX/SPX–Compatible Transport, often simply called IPX/SPX as well. Most of the components for NetWare interoperability supplied by Microsoft require NWLink as the underlying networking protocol. It is a 32-bit transport stack that supports Novell NetBIOS and RPCs (see Figure 10.1).

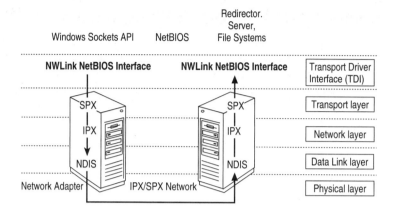

Figure 10.1   The IPX/SPX–compatible implementation

RPC over SPX

SPX, a part of the IPX/SPX protocol, is similar to TCP in that it provides a transport-level communication mechanism between computer systems. One of its tasks is data package sequencing, which ensures that data move in chronological order.

SPX Sockets

Outlook 2000 must contact the Information Store service using RPCs to provide you with access to your server-based mailbox. This means that a communication interface for NetWare workstations that allows use of IPX/SPX for RPC communication must exist. Windows Sockets (Winsock) provides this interface, known as SPX Sockets.

Installation

To support workstations using IPX/SPX, you must install NWLink at the Windows 2000 level on your Exchange 2000 server. You can accomplish this via the Properties of your Local Area Connection. Display the Network And Dial-Up Connections window (right-click My Network Places on the desktop and select Properties from the shortcut menu), right-click Local Area Connection, and then select Properties from the shortcut menu.

By default, only TCP/IP is installed, but you can add the NWLink protocol in the Local Area Connection Properties dialog box by clicking the Install button. In the Select Network Component Type dialog box, select Protocol, click Add, and, from the Network Protocols list, select NWLink IPX/SPX/NetBIOS Compatible Transport Protocol, and then click OK. System files will be copied from the Windows 2000 installation CD-ROM and, after that, you can manually adjust configuration settings if required.

Note   It is not necessary to reboot the server to have the changes take effect.

Frame Types

In the Local Area Connection Properties dialog box, by selecting the NWLink IPX/SPX/NetBIOS Compatible Transport Protocol and clicking the Properties button, you can manually specify frame types for IPX/SPX. By default, frame types are detected automatically; however, if you experience communication problems, disabling automatic frame type detection is a good idea.

The frame type corresponds to the format of data packages sent through the network at the data link layer, which is handled by Ethernet. Frame type is a factor for any network layer protocol, but it is particularly important on NetWare networks because different versions of NetWare support different frame types. You must use the same frame type for all computers in the network; otherwise, communication will fail. Frame types are shown in Table 10.1.

Table 10.1   Frame Types

Frame Type	Network Topology
Ethernet II, 802.3, 802.2, SNAP	Ethernet
Token ring, SNAP	Token ring
802.2, SNAP	FDDI
ArcNet-frames	ArcNet

The default frame type for NetWare 2.0 through 3.11 Ethernet networks is 802.3; later versions use 802.2. For token ring, as you might expect, the default is token ring and for Fiber Distributed Data Interface (FDDI), it is 802.2. If you are not sure which frame type your NetWare servers are using, type **config** at the NetWare server's system console, and check the Frame Type setting for your network adapter.

Setting the Frame Network Number

When manually configuring frame types, you will also need to specify the corresponding external network number with each frame type added. An external network number is an eight-digit number known as the IPX network ID, which identifies every NetWare network. All resources that belong to a particular NetWare network must use the same external network number. Therefore, frame types and their associated network number must match the corresponding configuration on the NetWare servers. You can check the configuration on the NetWare server by typing **config** at the server's system console. It is also possible to determine the network number from the AUTOEXEC.NCF file, where it is specified in the NET= option of the BIND IPX command (for example, BIND IPX 3C90X_1_E82 NET=F47A162C).

Note Windows 2000 typically detects the external network number automatically, but you must adjust it manually if you use multiple frame types or network adapters.

Setting the Internal Network Number

The internal network number identifies every NetWare server and possibly every computer running Windows 2000 Server. This number is frame type independent and must be unique within your NetWare network. It must not be 0 if the Windows 2000 computer is supposed to provide any services to NetWare clients or if it is used to route IPX in the network. In the NWLink IPX/SPX/NetBIOS Compatible Transport Protocol Properties dialog box, use the Internal Network Number box to set this parameter.

NetBIOS over NWLink

As you can see on the Local Area Connection Properties property sheet, NWLink NetBIOS is installed automatically with IPX/SPX. However, any router between your workstation and the server must pass the IPX packet type 0x14; otherwise, the NetBIOS communication cannot take place over IPX, and the connection attempt will fail.

IP-Based Connections

NetWare/IP is available with Novell NetWare 4.0 and later versions. However, NetWare/IP uses a different IP implementation that cannot communicate with Microsoft's TCP/IP stack. Fortunately, Novell's current release, NetWare 5, provides support for native IP and allows you to run your network with IP only, but also with both IP and IPX, or with just IPX.

Advantages of TCP/IP

It is advantageous to configure TCP/IP in your NetWare-based environment because TCP/IP greatly simplifies the integration of Exchange 2000 Server. Exchange 2000 Server requires TCP/IP in any case, and, if NetWare supports TCP/IP as well, you can avoid the installation of NWLink on the Exchange 2000 computer, thus avoiding protocol and configuration overhead.

Installing Gateway (and Client) Services for NetWare

GSNW is an additional service that enables Windows 2000 Server to access resources on NetWare servers. Installing GSNW allows you to access NetWare resources from the Exchange 2000 server.

Using the Local Area Connection Properties dialog box, you can install GSNW from the Windows 2000 Server installation CD-ROM. Click the Install button, and, from the Select Network Component Type dialog box, select Client. Click Add, and, from the Select Network Client dialog box, select Gateway (and

Client) Services for NetWare, then click OK. This time, you must restart the Windows 2000 server. When you log on locally to the server again, you need to provide valid NetWare account information in the Select NetWare Logon dialog box (such as Preferred Server or Default Tree and Context).

Note Gateway (and Client) Services for NetWare requires NWLink and is not supported in TCP/IP-only environments.

Enabling Windows NT Server to Act as a Gateway to NetWare Servers

Communication between Windows 2000 Server (configured as a NetWare client by GSNW) and Novell NetWare servers is accomplished through the NetWare Core Protocol (NCP). Communication between Windows 2000 Server and Microsoft-based workstations relies on Server Message Blocks (SMBs). Consequently, if Windows 2000 Server and GSNW could translate NCP into SMBs, Microsoft-based workstations could access NetWare servers through the Windows 2000 Server.

The good news is Windows 2000 Server can act as a gateway to NetWare— translating incoming Microsoft client requests into the correct NetWare format and thus providing NetWare resources to native Microsoft workstations. The Microsoft workstation is not aware of the translation. To the workstation, it appears that the client is working with resources on the computer running Windows 2000 Server (see Figure 10.2).

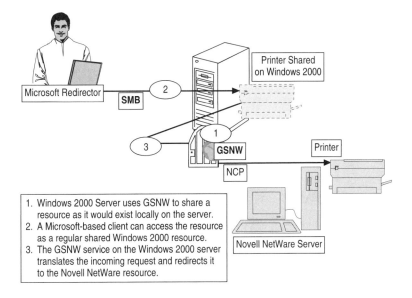

1. Windows 2000 Server uses GSNW to share a resource as it would exist locally on the server.
2. A Microsoft-based client can access the resource as a regular shared Windows 2000 resource.
3. The GSNW service on the Windows 2000 server translates the incoming request and redirects it to the Novell NetWare resource.

Figure 10.2   Accessing Novell NetWare resources via GSNW

Note Windows 2000 Server connects to NetWare servers on behalf of a special NetWare account that must be a member of a special NetWare group called NTGATEWAY. A Novell NetWare administrator must create the account and the group on the NetWare server before you can configure GSNW through the GSNW applet in the Control Panel.

File and Print Services for NetWare

File and Print Services for NetWare (FPNW) allows users on NetWare workstations to access files, printers, and applications on a Windows 2000 server. The machine running Windows 2000 Server acts just like a NetWare server (see Figure 10.3). As a matter of fact, you can use native NetWare utilities to manage—up to a point—a Microsoft Windows NT server if FPNW is installed.

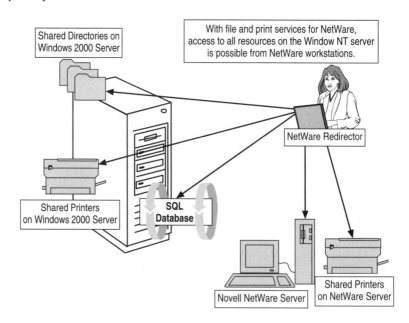

Figure 10.3   File and Print Services for NetWare

Service Advertising Protocol Agent

To ensure that native NetWare workstations can locate a computer running Windows 2000 Server in a NetWare network, you must install the SAP Agent on the server in addition to the GSNW. Support for SAP is required because NetWare clients rely on this protocol to perform name resolution. Native NetWare servers, your Windows 2000 Server computer running FPNW, and all IPX routers must use SAP to periodically broadcast their services, server name, and the IPX internal network address to each other (see Figure 10.4).

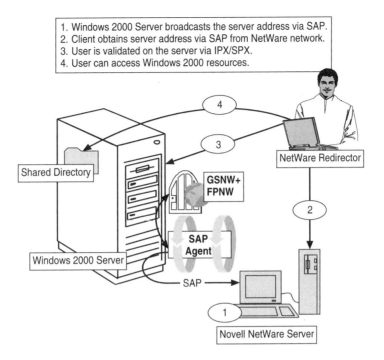

1. Windows 2000 Server broadcasts the server address via SAP.
2. Client obtains server address via SAP from NetWare network.
3. User is validated on the server via IPX/SPX.
4. User can access Windows 2000 resources.

Figure 10.4   Connecting to Windows 2000 with a NetWare workstation over IPX/SPX

To install the SAP Agent on Windows 2000 Server, open the Network And Dial-Up Connections program from the Control Panel and display the properties of the Local Area Connection. Click the Install button to display the Select Network Component Type dialog box, where you need to select Service, and then click Add. In the Select Network Service dialog box, select SAP Agent, and click OK. Because the SAP Agent has no properties to configure, you can close the Local Area Connection Properties dialog box immediately. A server reboot is not necessary.

SAP Broadcast Packet

The SAP Agent itself does not announce a Windows 2000 Server to the NetWare network. This is the task of GSNW. Using both components, the Windows 2000 Server computer advertises itself across the IPX network using a SAP broadcast packet, which contains the server name and the IPX internal network number.

NDS and the Active Directory Directory Service

When integrating Exchange 2000 Server into your NetWare environment, you need to maintain user account and mailbox information in an Active Directory forest in addition to the NetWare directory. Novell NetWare systems rely on NDS or the legacy Bindery for account management. Unfortunately, without additional components, there is no coordination of user accounts and passwords across both platforms. Different policies might force your users to maintain passwords of different length and complexity that might expire at different intervals. Even the account names can differ.

Manual Versus Automatic Logon

Automatic logon allows you seamless access to network resources on the basis of a single authentication when initially accessing the network. If you are working on a native NetWare workstation, you will log on to NetWare first. When you launch Outlook 2000 to connect to your Exchange 2000 mailbox, you need to log on to your Active Directory domain in a separate step. Consequently, the Enter Password dialog box will appear at client startup, prompting you for User Name, Domain Name, and Password.

To support automatic logon, you need to keep the account information in both environments the same. When you log on to your workstation running Windows 2000 Professional, you supply your NetWare account information, which is cached by the operating system. Outlook 2000 can obtain this information and supply it to Exchange 2000 Server automatically—provided that you are using the NT Password Authentication mechanism. Because account name and password are the same, you can get access to your mailbox without being prompted for Windows 2000 account information. The configuration of the Exchange transport service was covered in Chapter 8, "Microsoft Outlook 2000 Deployment."

Directory Synchronization

It is difficult to keep the NetWare and Windows 2000 account information synchronized manually. Fortunately, an automatic synchronization mechanism is available from Microsoft, known as Microsoft Directory Synchronization Services (MSDSS).

MSDSS allows you to synchronize Active Directory accounts with accounts in NDS or Bindery, including password information. However, password synchronization is only supported from Active Directory to NDS (or Bindery) because access to encrypted NetWare passwords is not provided. In other words, when you use MSDSS to create Windows 2000 accounts from your NetWare accounts, you cannot transfer over the users' existing passwords. You will need to specify an initial password value (such as user account name or empty password) in the MSDSS session configuration. If you change your password later on in Active Directory, MSDSS can transfer the password information into the NDS (see Figure 10.5).

Important   MSDSS requires the Novell Client Software to be installed on Windows 2000 Server, which cannot coexist with GSNW. If you are using interoperability solutions that require GSNW, consider installing an additional Windows 2000 domain controller for Novell NetWare Client 5 and MSDSS.

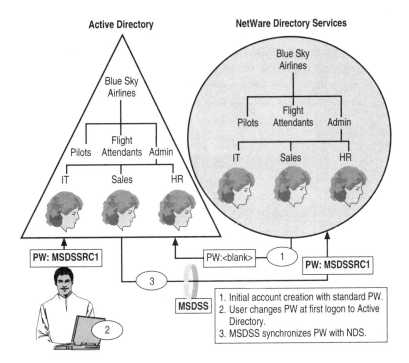

Figure 10.5 NDS and Active Directory synchronization

MSDSS and the Connector to Novell GroupWise

When integrating Exchange 2000 Server in an environment with NetWare and Novell GroupWise, it is important to adjust the MSDSS configuration to avoid the synchronization of GroupWise addresses (that are stored in NDS) with Active Directory. Exchange users cannot use GroupWise addresses replicated through MSDSS. E-mail address information must be synchronized using the Directory Synchronization feature of the Connector for Novell GroupWise, which is introduced in Chapter 29, "Connecting to Novell GroupWise."

To prevent MSDSS from synchronizing GroupWise address information with Active Directory, add the SyncEmailAddress REG_DWORD value to the Registry under the following location:

```
HKEY_LOCAL_MACHINE
  \System
   \CurrentControlSet
    \Services
     \MSDSS
      \Parameters
```

A value of 0 disables the synchronization of GroupWise address information.

Lesson 2: Outlook and NetWare Client Requirements

The integration of Exchange 2000 Server into NetWare networks requires only a few configuration steps on the NetWare workstations. Most of the steps achieve client optimization rather than essential configuration. Exchange 2000 Server comes with an interesting utility that allows you to test client/server communication prior to deploying Outlook 2000.

This lesson discusses the components you must configure on a NetWare workstation to allow access to an Exchange 2000 server. Common troubleshooting tips are also provided.

At the end of this lesson, you will be able to:

- List the NetWare components necessary to access NetWare resources.
- Describe the validation mechanism used by clients to access an Exchange 2000 server.
- Test the client/server communication and troubleshoot communication problems.

Estimated time to complete this lesson: 20 minutes

Network Communication Requirements

One of the most important NetWare communication components is the redirector, which allows the client to communicate with NetWare servers using NCP. On a computer running MS-DOS or Microsoft Windows 3.1 or later, you must load a component called NETX.EXE or a Virtual Loadable Module (VLM) redirector. If you are using Microsoft Windows 95/98, Windows NT Workstation, or Windows 2000 Professional, you can install the Microsoft Client Services for NetWare. Another possible option is to deploy the Novell NetWare Client software, which provides the full set of NetWare functionality including contextless login. This allows you to manage your NetWare environment using NWADMIN.EXE. However, NetWare redirector components are not directly involved when you connect to an Exchange 2000 server.

Communicating with an Exchange 2000 Server Computer

As shown in Figure 10.6, Outlook 2000 can communicate with an Exchange 2000 server in an IPX/SPX-based NetWare network using RPCs over SPX. However, TCP/IP can be used instead if your Novell NetWare 5 environment supports it.

Because NetWare components do not provide any RPC implementations, you need to install the Client for Microsoft Networks on Windows 2000 Professional in addition to your NetWare client software. This enables the Name Service

Provider Interface (NSPI) for the RPC service on your workstation. Installing the Client for Microsoft Networks has advantages because it gives users the ability to access Windows 2000 resources directly. RPC communication was explained in Chapter 3, "Microsoft Exchange 2000 Server Architecture."

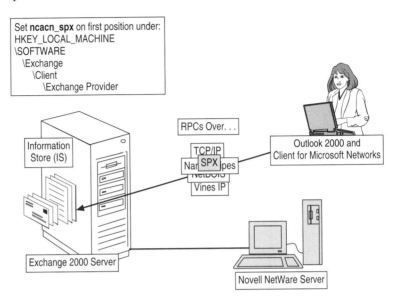

Figure 10.6 RPC communication over IPX/SPX

Note RPC over SPX uses the Winsock interface and does not require a NetWare redirector. You do not have to configure the Exchange 2000 Server computer as a NetWare server using FPNW.

Active Directory Validation

Every user who wants to access a mailbox or any other resource on a computer running Exchange 2000 Server must be validated. As mentioned earlier, Outlook 2000 running on Windows 2000 Professional will automatically use the supplied account information used to log on to NetWare. Only when the NetWare account information does not match the Windows 2000 account are you asked for your account, domain, and password. You can also force an explicit logon using the Advanced property sheet of the Exchange transport service. Under Logon Network Security, select None. More information about configuring the Exchange transport service is provided in Chapter 8, "Microsoft Outlook 2000 Deployment."

Novell NetWare Client

If you have installed the Novell NetWare Client software on your workstation, make sure your computer is a member of your Windows 2000 domain; otherwise the automatic logon to Exchange 2000 will fail. Before you log on to Windows 2000, in the Novell Login dialog box, click the Advanced button. Click on the Windows NT/2000 tab, and then make sure the domain name (such as BLUESKY-INC-10) is displayed in the From list box. The Local Username information should correspond to your Windows 2000 account alias.

Client Connectivity Issues and the RPCPing Utility

Implementing an Exchange 2000 server in a NetWare network means managing two different and complex network operating systems. Hence, it might be a good idea to test the client/server communication to make sure that Outlook can contact Exchange 2000 Server without problems.

Connection Testing with RPCPing

RPCPing is a program family rather than a single utility, which allows examining the RPC-based client/server communication. One part must be launched on the server, and the others will be executed on the workstation (see Figure 10.7). The communication between the server-based and client-based programs will be measured to determine the quality of the client/server RPC connectivity. All parts of RPCPing come with the Exchange 2000 Server installation CD-ROM. The programs can be found in the \Support\Rpcping directory.

The server component has been implemented in a file called RPINGS.EXE. It must be started on the server before any client component can be used to measure the quality of the connectivity. This program maintains the Echo and Stats RPC functions, which are called later by the client component.

You can run RPINGS.EXE without any command-line options, but additional parameters may be used to restrict the RPC test to specific protocol sequences. The following options can be set:

RPINGS [-p Protocol Sequence]

- p ipx/spx
- p namedpipes
- p netbios
- p tcpip
- p vines

To exit the server component, you need to enter the string @q at the RPINGS.EXE command prompt.

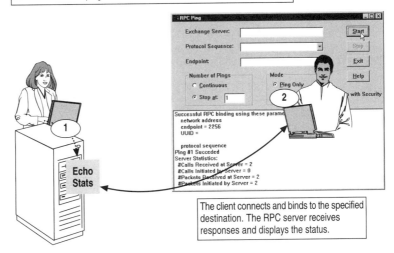

Figure 10.7   Testing the RPC connection

The client component is dependent on the operating system. A separate version exists for MS-DOS, Windows 3.1 and later, and Windows 95/Windows NT/ Windows 2000. The MS-DOS version is called RPINGDOS.EXE. Windows 3.1 and later computers can run RPINGC16.EXE. Windows 95/98, Windows NT, and Windows 2000, in turn, are supported through RPINGC32.EXE.

Typically, you use RPINGC32.EXE to test RPC connectivity. This is a 32-bit Windows program that displays the connection status, available protocol sequences, endpoints, and the quality of the RPC connection as you attempt to check the RPC connection. Before you can start a particular test, you need to set all required communication parameters, such as the destination RPC server and endpoints. Available endpoints are Store, Admin, and Rping. You can select Store within the Endpoint box if you want to simulate the communication with the Information Store.

The following are required RPCPing client parameters:

- The name of the computer running Exchange 2000 Server (or the IP address).

- The protocol sequence, which specifies the RPC mechanism that will be used such as named pipes (default).

- The endpoints, which specify a protocol-specific port, that will be used by the RPCPing client to communicate with the server. This endpoint can be the Information Store (Store), the Directory Service (Admin), or the RPCPing server (Rping).

Improving Client Startup Times

The Exchange transport service tries several RPC communication methods in sequence until it connects. In Windows 2000, the order is determined by the RPC_BINDING_ORDER value in the Registry under the following (see Figure 10.6 and Exercise 4 of Chapter 8, "Microsoft Outlook 2000 Deployment"):

```
HKEY_LOCAL_MACHINE

  \SOFTWARE

    \Microsoft

     \Exchange

     \Exchange Provider
```

By default, the value is:

```
ncalrpc,ncacn_ip_tcp,ncacn_spx,ncacn_np,netbios,ncacn_vns_spp
```

To optimize the client configuration, you should configure RPC over SPX as the preferred communication mechanism if your primary network protocol is IPX/SPX. If *ncacn_spx* is on top of the binding order (the first position), the client uses RPC over SPX first and avoids superfluous attempts.

Chapter Summary

The integration of Exchange 2000 Server into a NetWare-based environment introduces several tasks to provide NetWare users with access to mailboxes in Outlook 2000. On the client machines, this includes the installation of the Client for Microsoft Networks, which is required to support RPC communication. On the server, you need to install NWLink if your NetWare workstations are not configured for TCP/IP.

Several Windows 2000 components are available to provide advanced services to your users. You can install GSNW, for instance, to give native Microsoft workstations the option to work with NetWare resources. You can install FPNW to present the computer running Windows 2000 Server as a NetWare-like server to Novell users. Account synchronization between Active Directory and NDS is possible via MSDSS. Synchronized accounts greatly facilitate the work in a heterogeneous NetWare and Windows 2000 environment through the automatic logon feature.

Review

The following review questions can help you determine if you have sufficiently familiarized yourself with the material covered in this chapter. You can find the answers to these questions at the end of this book in Appendix A, "Questions and Answers."

1. You plan to integrate Exchange 2000 Server into your Novell NetWare network. You install Windows 2000 Server and the NWLink IPX/SPX–compatible Transport. Which two important configuration parameters of the NWLink IPX/SPX–Compatible Transport may need to be configured manually?

2. Because Exchange 2000 Server validates users based on Windows 2000 account information, you need to create a corresponding Windows 2000 account for each existing Novell NetWare user. Which tool can you use to synchronize the account information for both systems?

3. Users on Novell NetWare workstations are complaining about the startup times of Outlook 2000. What should you first check?

4. Your Novell NetWare 5 network relies on TCP/IP only. You have deployed the Novell NetWare 5 Client software on all your workstations running Windows 2000 Professional. Which component do you need to add to the workstation configuration to allow your users to access their Exchange 2000 mailboxes with Outlook 2000?

CHAPTER 11

Internet-Based Client Access

About This Chapter

The Internet holds a huge potential for today's economy. It creates hundreds of billions in revenue per annum and millions of jobs. There is no question that the Internet allows organizations of any size to build closer relationships with customers and business partners. However, the challenge is how to transform the promise of the Internet into business realities. How much does it take to develop an international client base?

With Microsoft Exchange 2000 Server connected to the Internet, people from around the world can share information at ease. Front end/back end (FE/BE) configurations, as introduced in Chapter 4, "Planning the Microsoft Exchange 2000 Server Installation," can enable you to provide messaging and collaboration services to literally thousands of Internet users. Have you ever wanted to quickly check your e-mail during a holiday trip? If you can find a Web browser (for example, at an Internet café), you can check your mail with Exchange 2000 Server's Web messaging.

This chapter deals with popular Internet messaging protocols and their implementation in Exchange 2000 Server. You can learn how to configure virtual servers for access to mailboxes and public folders across the Internet.

Before You Begin

To complete this chapter:

- Prepare your test environment according to the descriptions given in the "Getting Started" section of "About This Book."

- You should have a general understanding of the implementation of Internet Information Services (IIS) in Microsoft Windows 2000 and their communication with the Information Store, as explained in Chapter 3, "Microsoft Exchange 2000 Server Architecture."

Lesson 1: Support for Internet Protocols

From the moment you install Exchange 2000 Server, your messaging environment relies on Internet protocols. Simple Mail Transfer Protocol (SMTP), for instance, is the native e-mail transport protocol for Exchange 2000 Server. Other protocols, such as POP3, IMAP4, Network News Transfer Protocol (NNTP), and HTTP, provide users with a variety of options for accessing their mailboxes and public folders. All of these protocols are part of IIS 5.0. Their implementation and communication with the Information Store was discussed in Chapter 3, "Microsoft Exchange 2000 Server Architecture."

This lesson provides a brief overview of the supported Internet protocols and illustrates their features in the context of accessing Exchange 2000 data. This lesson concludes with a brief introduction of Lightweight Directory Access Protocol (LDAP), which is a component of Windows 2000 rather than Exchange 2000, yet is still important for address book lookups in Internet mail clients, such as Microsoft Outlook Express.

At the end of this lesson, you will be able to:

- Describe the characteristics of supported Internet protocols.
- Access mailbox and public folder resources through Internet protocols.

Estimated time to complete this lesson: 90 minutes

Simple Mail Transfer Protocol

SMTP is an industry standard for the Internet, which rules the transfer of e-mail messages between two messaging hosts. It also defines the message formats. An extension to SMTP is SMTP Service Extensions (ESMTP). ESMTP overcomes several critical limitations of the Internet mail transport. For instance, it allows users to request delivery status notifications on their outgoing messages, and it provides the ability to specify a message size limit for incoming ESMTP connections. Both SMTP and ESMTP require a connection-based transport mechanism; in practice this is the TCP/IP protocol.

Note SMTP is described in RFC 821 (the protocol) and RFC 822 (the format of SMTP messages). ESMTP features are defined in RFC 1869.

Sending Messages Using SMTP

To send a message, an SMTP/ESMTP process first connects to TCP port 25 of the remote host. The remote SMTP system, such as a server running Exchange 2000 Server, then answers the incoming request. The SMTP communication will be established and e-mail messages can be transferred (see Figure 11.1).

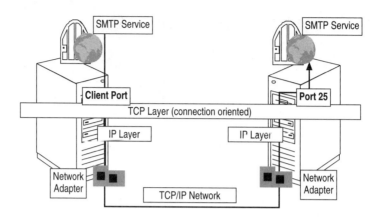

Figure 11.1   An SMTP connection over TCP/IP

SMTP defines the commands and responses at the application layer, which must be used between SMTP systems to transfer messages. These commands are used to begin the message sending while responses acknowledge the reception. The most important elements of every SMTP exchange are the welcome message, which the server returns to the client, the HELO (or EHLO for ESMTP) command to start the session, the MAIL FROM command to indicate an originator address, RCPT TO to specify mail recipients, and DATA to initiate the transfer of the message. The QUIT command ends the current session and initiates the termination of the connection (see Figure 11.2).

SMTP Service Extensions

ESMTP provides a framework for two types of SMTP extensions: registered and unregistered extensions. A good example of a registered extension is the DSN command, which notifies the receiving system that a delivery status notification should be returned to the sending host. Another example is SIZE, which allows restricting the size of incoming messages prior to their transmission. Unregistered commands, also known as local verbs, must start with an X to indicate that they are not standardized. The XEXCH50 command, as it is supported by the SMTP service, represents such a local verb. XEXCH50 is used to allow Exchange-specific content information in messages.

Note   Every ESMTP session begins with the EHLO command, in contrast to HELO, which initiates an ordinary SMTP session.

Name Resolution

To establish a connection, the SMTP service must determine the remote host's IP address. Windows 2000 supports several name resolution mechanisms, including the HOSTS file, DNS, Windows Internet Name Service (WINS), the LMHOSTS file, and Active Directory directory service. Exchange 2000 servers that belong to the same organization are able to locate each other using Active Directory.

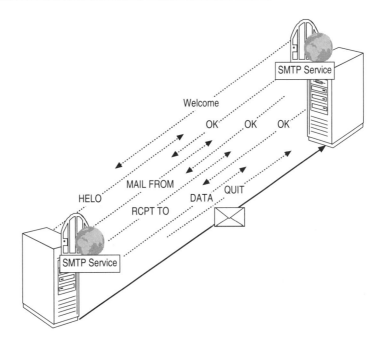

Figure 11.2 Sending SMTP messages

DNS Name Resolution

DNS will most likely be used to accomplish name resolution when communicating with hosts directly on the Internet. To retrieve the IP address of an SMTP host, the SMTP service uses a component of the TCP/IP protocol stack, known as the Resolver, to contact the local DNS server. If the domain name cannot be resolved locally, the local DNS server on behalf of the actual Resolver will query another DNS server. Eventually, the IP address of an SMTP host is finally returned to the Resolver, which in turn passes it to the SMTP service. The SMTP service is then able to establish the connection and transfer the message.

Mail Exchanger Records

DNS mail exchanger (MX) records point to computers that are able to handle SMTP connections. It is common to have multiple SMTP servers within an organization, so more than one MX record may exist per Internet domain. It is possible to identify more important and less important hosts by assigning priorities to MX records. Only in cases where most important hosts (those with lowest preference values) are unavailable will lower priority hosts be contacted. Hosts with the same priority are pooled together, and DNS returns their IP addresses according to the round-robin principle, which determines that the order of the hosts in the list is changed in a cyclic permutation, so the host that was first in the previous list is last in the new list. Multiple mail exchangers can provide load balancing and fault tolerance for incoming messaging connections.

Exercise 1: Examining DNS MX Records

In this exercise you will verify the existence of DNS records for Internet domains. You will use the NSLookup utility on a real-life connection to examine Microsoft's MX entries.

To view a multimedia demonstration that displays how to perform this procedure, run the EX1CH11.AVI files from the \Exercise_Information\Chapter11 folder on the Supplemental Course Materials CD.

Prerequisites

- Your workstation running Windows 2000 is connected to the Internet.
- The interface to the Internet (network card or modem) is manually or automatically configured for a DNS server.

▶ **To use NSLookup for DNS MX queries**

1. Click Start and select Run to display the Run dialog box, where you need to type **cmd** and click OK to open a Windows 2000 command prompt.

2. Type **nslookup** and press ENTER.

3. Type **set type=mx** and press ENTER.

4. Type **microsoft.com** and press ENTER.

   At this point, you should be able to examine the MX entries for the domain microsoft.com (see Figure 11.3).

5. Type **exit** and press ENTER to exit the NSLookup utility.

Figure 11.3   Testing the DNS name resolution

Exercise Summary

The TCP/IP utility NSLookup allows you to check DNS records, which is especially useful if you are experiencing SMTP connection problems on Internet links. One or more MX hosts should be returned per domain. If a domain does not contain mail exchangers, the SMTP service will not be able to resolve the domain name through DNS. You may then associate the IP address with the e-mail domain name in the HOSTS file, which can be found in the \Winnt\ System32\Drivers\Etc directory, or you can configure an SMTP Connector to directly deliver messages to the target domain's SMTP server. The configuration of SMTP Connectors is the topic of Chapter 16, "Message Routing Administration."

Post Office Protocol, Version 3

POP3 is a messaging protocol that defines commands to download messages from a host. In other words, it is a read-only protocol allowing you to download messages from your server-based Inbox only. Access to other server-based message folders is not possible. Examples of POP3 clients are Outlook Express, Eudora, and Netscape Navigator Mail. The POP3 features are described in RFC 1939.

Important   To send messages, POP3 users rely on SMTP. Consequently, you need to provide your users with an SMTP server in addition to a POP3 host for complete messaging functionality. SMTP and POP3 hosts can be the same or different servers.

Commands and Responses

POP3 commands are not case sensitive. They consist of a keyword followed by arguments, if necessary. Each keyword is separated from its arguments by a single space. Only printable ASCII characters are allowed. POP3 responses, on the other hand, are a combination of a status indicator and a keyword. Additional information may follow. Again, only printable ASCII characters can be used. The two existing status indicators are the positive (+OK) and negative (–ERR) response; both appear in uppercase letters. To give an example of a positive indicator, the server's typical response to an incoming connection on port 110 is +OK Microsoft Exchange 2000 POP3 Server Version 6.0.4417.0 (bluesky-srv1.BlueSky-inc-10.com) Ready.

POP3 Session States

A POP3 session progresses through three states, called Authorization, Transaction, and Update. The Authorization state is reached when a server's welcome message is received after the client has opened a connection to TCP port 110. In this state, the user account information can be sent to the server. Once the user has been validated, the session enters the Transaction state. Now, the user can read, download, or delete e-mail messages as desired. The session is released by sending the QUIT command to the server. At this point, the session enters the Update state, in which the POP3 server sends a goodbye message to the client and releases the TCP/IP connection (see Figure 11.4). It is important to note that the POP3 host performs the actual message processing on the server during the Update state once the client connection has been released. In other words, as long as you are connected with a POP3 client, messages are still available in the Inbox even though you might already have downloaded them. When you disconnect, the server purges the messages.

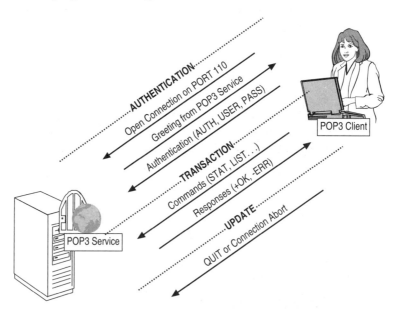

Figure 11.4   POP3 session lifetime

Exercise 2: Examining the POP3 Communication

In this exercise you will examine the POP3 communication. You will use the Telnet utility to manually connect to your server-based mailbox via the Default POP3 Virtual Server of Exchange 2000 Server.

To view a multimedia demonstration that displays how to perform this procedure, run the EX2CH11.AVI files from the \Exercise_Information\Chapter11 folder on the Supplemental Course Materials CD.

Prerequisites

- Make sure BLUESKY-SRV1 is prepared according to the descriptions given in the "Getting Started" section of "About This Book" and running Exchange 2000 Server.

- Log on as Administrator to BLUESKY-SRV1.

▶ **To use Telnet for POP3 tests**

1. Click Start and select Run to display the Run dialog box, where you need to type **cmd** and click OK to display the Windows 2000 command prompt.

2. Type **telnet** and press ENTER.

3. Type **set LOCAL_ECHO** and press ENTER to enable the local echo, or you will not be able to see what you type when you connect to the POP3 host.

4. Type **open localhost 110** and press ENTER. Verify that you are connected to the POP3 virtual server and that the welcome message +OK Microsoft Exchange 2000 POP3 Server Version. 6.0.4417.0 (bluesky-srv1.BlueSky-inc-10.com) Ready is displayed.

5. Type **user administrator** and press ENTER. Verify that the server response is +OK.

6. Type **pass password** and press ENTER. Verify that the server response is +OK User Successfully Logged On.

7. Type **list** and press ENTER. A positive response, together with a list of messages in your Inbox, will be returned.

8. Make sure at least one message exists in your Inbox, then type **retr 1** to retrieve the first message, and press ENTER.

   At this point, the POP3 virtual server should return the message in Multiple Internet Mail Extensions (MIME)-encoded format. Telnet will display bitmaps and other graphical elements as plain text (see Figure 11.5).

9. Type **quit**, press ENTER, and, when the connection is terminated, press any key to continue.

Figure 11.5 Retrieving a message using POP3

10. At the Microsoft Telnet prompt, type **quit**, and press ENTER, then close the command prompt window.

Exercise Summary

POP3 is a simple protocol that you can test manually when using the Telnet utility. Because Telnet has no way to use the integrated Windows 2000 Authentication mechanism, you need to supply a user name and password and rely on the Basic Authentication (clear text). As soon as you are logged on to your mailbox, you can list and download messages from the Inbox. Other folders, however, are not accessible. The authentication mechanisms are covered in more detail in Lesson 2.

Internet Mail Access Protocol Version 4

IMAP4 is a modern Internet protocol that allows you to access all kinds of server-based messaging folders. In other words, using an IMAP4-compliant client, you are not restricted to Inbox access only, as you would be using POP3. This allows you to maintain all messages entirely at the server. However, it is also possible to create a local message store, for instance, if you need to work disconnected from the server and let the IMAP4 client, such as Outlook Express, synchronize the local repository with the data on the server. IMAP4 is described in a series of RFCs, most importantly in RFC 2060.

Note   IMAP4 is defined in RFCs 1731, 1732, 1733, 2060, 2061, 2086, 2087, 2088, 2095, 2177, and 2180.

IMAP4 Session States

IMAP4 defines four subsequent session states, which are the Non-Authenticated, Authenticated, Selected, and Logout states (see Figure 11.6). The Non-Authenticated state will be entered as soon as an IMAP4 client connects to TCP port 143 at the server. In this state, the client must supply authentication credentials. Most commands cannot be used yet. The server's greeting * OK Microsoft Exchange 2000 IMAP4rev1 Server Version 6.0.4417.0 (bluesky-srv1.BlueSky-inc-10.com) Ready is an example of a response allowed in this state.

As soon as the client logs on using the LOGIN command, the session enters the Authenticated state. The important task a client has to accomplish now is selecting a folder from the mailbox. The client will use the SELECT command for this purpose, in this way entering the Selected state. In this state most of the IMAP4 commands are available. STORE and FETCH are good examples of such commands. Users work with their IMAP4 clients typically in Selected state. Once the work is finished, the user will log off. Consequently, the client transmits the LOGOUT command to the server, and the connection enters the Logout state. The connection is being terminated, and the server will close the connection, sending its goodbye notification.

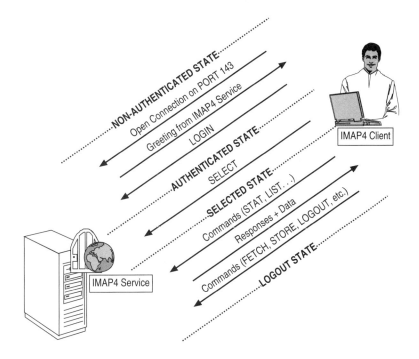

Figure 11.6   IMAP4 session state

Commands and Responses

IMAP4 commands are case-insensitive strings of printable ASCII characters, which consist of a tag followed by a keyword and its arguments, if necessary. Every keyword is separated from its arguments by a single space. An identifier, known as a tag, prefixes each client command. Those tags are necessary because multiple commands may be in progress simultaneously. As the server responds to a command, it will use the tag to identify the command to which the response belongs. Data transmitted by the host and status notifications that are not associated with a client command must be prefixed with the token "*". These constructs are called untagged responses.

Exercise 3: Examining the IMAP4 Communication

In this exercise you will examine the IMAP4 protocol in action. You will use the Telnet utility again to manually connect to your server-based mailbox, this time via the Default IMAP4 Virtual Server of Exchange 2000 Server.

To view a multimedia demonstration that displays how to perform this procedure, run the EX3CH11.AVI files from the \Exercise_Information\Chapter11 folder on the Supplemental Course Materials CD.

Prerequisites

- Make sure BLUESKY-SRV1 is prepared according to the descriptions given in the "Getting Started" section of "About This Book" and running Exchange 2000 Server.

- Log on as Administrator to BLUESKY-SRV1.

▶ **To use Telnet for IMAP4 tests**

1. Click Start and select Run to display the Run dialog box, where you need to type **cmd** and click OK to display the Windows 2000 command prompt.

2. Type **telnet** and press ENTER.

3. Type **set LOCAL_ECHO** and press ENTER to enable the local echo, or you will not be able to see what you type when you connect to the POP3 host.

4. Type **open localhost 143** and press ENTER. Verify that you are connected to the IMAP4 virtual server and that the welcome message * OK Microsoft Exchange 2000 IMAP4rev1 Server Version 6.0.4417.0 (bluesky-srv1.BlueSky-inc-10.com) Ready is returned to you.

5. Type **0000 login administrator password** and press ENTER. Verify that the server response is 0000 OK LOGIN Completed.

6. Type **0001 select "inbox"** and press ENTER. A positive response (0001 OK [READ-WRITE] SELECT Completed.), together with information about the messages in your Inbox, will be returned.

7. Type **0002 fetch 1 all** and press ENTER. Verify that you receive a positive response of 0002 OK FETCH Completed.

   At this point, you should be able to examine the header information, which the IMAP4 virtual server returns to your Telnet client (see Figure 11.7).

8. Type **0003 logout** and press ENTER.

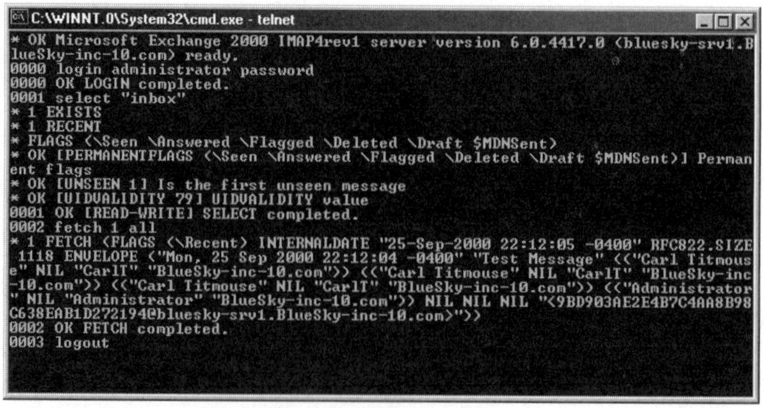

Figure 11.7   Retrieving a message using IMAP4

Exercise Summary

IMAP4 is more powerful than POP3 because it allows you to work with all kinds of messaging folders, including public folders. You need to select the folder you want to access explicitly after you log on. You need to supply a mailbox name and password when examining the IMAP4 protocol in Telnet. The authentication mechanisms are covered in Lesson 2.

Network News Transfer Protocol

USENET is a communication network based on NNTP, which relies on distributed discussion forums known as newsgroups. A vast number of newsgroups exist, but it is not always easy to find the desired information. A good Web site, such as *http://www.usenet.org/*, can simplify use of the USENET network.

Note   NNTP is described in RFC 977. The actual format of USENET articles is defined in RFC 1036; attachments are encoded using either Unix to Unix Encoding (UUENCODE) or MIME.

Newsgroups

Newsgroups can be compared to regular public folders in Exchange 2000 Server. They represent the context of discussions, as do public folders. Articles posted in newsgroups represent bits and pieces of discussions, as do messages in public folders. Last but not least, articles will be replicated to all instances of a particular newsgroup across the USENET, as messages are replicated to all instances of a particular public folder across the organization. Newsgroup replication requires newsfeeds, whereas the public folder replication relies on Information Store replication links. Public folder replication is discussed in Chapter 18, "Public Folder Replication."

Newsreaders

A newsreader application is a client program that can be used to read newsgroup articles. In more technical terms, a newsreader is able to communicate via NNTP. Public folders can be accessed because Exchange 2000 Server supports newsreaders via the extended NNTP service of Windows 2000. In every case, the client needs to establish a connection to TCP port 119 to exchange commands and responses with the server (see Figure 11.8).

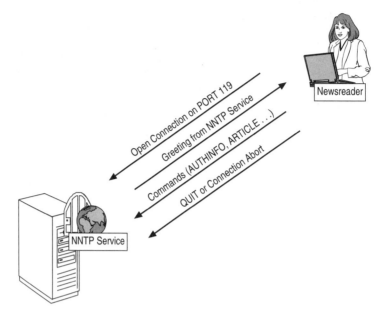

Figure 11.8   Accessing newsgroups over NNTP

Newsfeeds

Multiple instances of one particular newsgroup reside typically on multiple servers. Hence, a mechanism must exist to replicate articles between the instances of the same newsgroup. Processes that accomplish this task are known as newsfeeds. You can think of a newsfeed as a user working with a newsreader. Let's say you want to receive new changes from a remote server. Accordingly, you will connect to the remote server's port 119 first. You can then check the remote server for new articles and request those that you haven't yet received. As you pull new articles, you are acting as a pull feed. On the other hand, you may also have new articles to post. Using your newsreader, you can simply upload them to the remote server. In complicated language, you push your information into the host, acting like a push feed. Through control messages, a newsfeed may even create new newsgroups on the remote host.

Note   In general, two forms of NNTP data transfer exist. They are the pull and the push transfer.

The terms push and pull may also be used to specify which host initiates the communication:

- **Pull feed.**   The local host initiates the connection to the remote server and pulls the information.

- **Push feed.**   The remote server (such as a provider's host) initiates the connection and pushes the information into the local host.

Pull Versus Push

Usage of NTTP differs slightly between pull and push feeds. Whereas pull feeds need a command set for querying remote servers about available articles, push feeds need a command set for newsgroup creation and article posting. Pull feeds are more flexible than push feeds because they allow you to select the newsgroups you want to receive. On the other hand, push feeds provide advantages if the replicated amount of information is large. When configuring push feeds, you typically will need the cooperation of your service provider to specify the newsgroups you want to feed into your organization.

NNTP Communication

NNTP works similar to SMTP, POP3, and IMAP4. Newsreader applications open a connection to TCP port 119 to establish a session. The NNTP server sends its welcome message back to the client, such as 200 NNTP Service 5.00.0984 Version: 5.0.2195.1608 Posting Allowed. After that, client and host can exchange NNTP command and response sequences. NNTP commands are not case sensitive. They are represented as keywords followed by arguments, which are separated by a single space. Only printable ASCII characters are valid.

Exercise 4: Examining the NNTP Communication

In this exercise you will examine the communication with the extended NNTP service of Windows 2000. Similar to Exercises 2 and 3, you will use the Telnet client to establish a session and exchange typical commands and responses.

To view a multimedia demonstration that displays how to perform this procedure, run the EX4CH11.AVI files from the \Exercise_Information\Chapter11 folder on the Supplemental Course Materials CD.

Prerequisites

- Make sure BLUESKY-SRV1 is prepared according to the descriptions given in the "Getting Started" section of "About This Book" and running Exchange 2000 Server.

- Log on as Administrator to BLUESKY-SRV1.

▶ **To use Telnet for NNTP tests**

1. Click Start and select Run to display the Run dialog box, where you need to type **cmd** and click OK to display the Windows 2000 command prompt.

2. Type **telnet** and press ENTER.

3. Type **set LOCAL_ECHO** and press ENTER to enable the local echo, or you will not be able to see what you type when you connect to the POP3 host.

4. Type **open localhost 119** and press ENTER. Verify that you are connected to the IMAP4 virtual server and that the welcome message 200 NNTP Service 5.00.0984 Version: 5.0.2195.1608 Posting Allowed is returned to you.

5. Type **list** and press ENTER to display a list of newsgroups that this server maintains (by default, control.cancel, control.newgroup, and control.rmgroup are listed, which are used to store newsfeed control messages).

6. Type **group control.cancel** and press ENTER. Notice the positive response and the number of e-mails in the newsgroup (most likely there are no messages in this group).

   At this point, you have successfully tested the NNTP connectivity to your Exchange 2000 Server and queried existing newsgroups (see Figure 11.9).

7. Type **quit** and press ENTER.

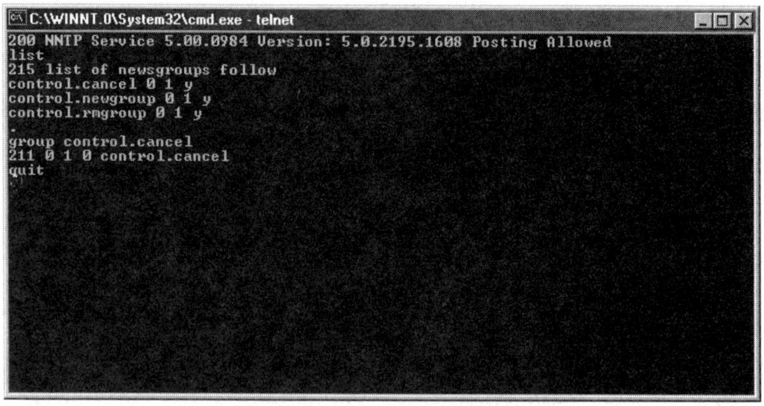

```
C:\WINNT.0\System32\cmd.exe - telnet
200 NNTP Service 5.00.0984 Version: 5.0.2195.1608 Posting Allowed
list
215 list of newsgroups follow
control.cancel 0 1 y
control.newgroup 0 1 y
control.rmgroup 0 1 y
.
group control.cancel
211 0 1 0 control.cancel
quit
```

Figure 11.9   Using Telnet as a newsreader application

Exercise Summary

You can use Telnet to log on to a NNTP newsgroup host. You must provide valid authentication information using the AUTHINFO USER command. The host will return a positive response, 381 Waiting For Password, which indicates that it is now time to enter the password through the AUTHINFO PASS command. A positive response would be 281 Authentication OK. At this point, access to available newsgroups is possible and articles can be retrieved or posted.

Note   The HELP command is useful if you want to explore the set of supported NNTP commands in Telnet.

Hypertext Transfer Protocol

HTTP is the data vehicle of the World Wide Web. Its first version (now referred to as HTTP/0.9) was a simple protocol to transfer data, such as Web pages, across the Internet. In 1996, a revision known as HTTP/1.0 significantly improved and standardized the protocol, which was again superseded by HTTP/1.1 in 1997. The current version of HTTP is defined in RFC 2616.

To transfer data, an HTTP-compliant client, such as Microsoft Internet Explorer or Netscape Navigator, needs to connect to an HTTP (Web) server, such as the World Wide Web Publishing Service of Windows 2000 Server. By default, the Web browser connects to the server's TCP port 80, although you can use custom ports as well.

URIs and URLs

To tell the Web server which document to return, the browser has to provide a Uniform Resource Identifier (URI), most commonly known as a Web address, shortcut, or URL. A URL is actually a specific type of URI that identifies a resource through its location on the network, for instance, *http://www. microsoft.com/exchange/default.htm/*. The other possible type of URI is a Uniform Resource Name (URN), which identifies a resource through its globally unique distinguished name. URI, URL, and URN are described in RFC 2396.

HTTP Extensions for Distributed Authoring

The Distributed Authoring and Versioning Protocol usually referred to as WebDAV is an extension of HTTP/1.1. Unlike HTTP, which is primarily used to request Web pages from a server, WebDAV specifies methods, headers, and content types for the management of resource properties directly on the server, as well as the creation of resource collections, the manipulation of namespaces, and the locking of resources to avoid collisions due to concurrent access from multiple clients. WebDAV can encode data elements either in Extensible Markup Language (XML) or in HTTP headers. The WebDAV protocol is defined in RFC 2518.

IIS 5.0 fully supports WebDAV if Exchange 2000 Server is installed, meaning you can publish a WebDAV directory on your Web server and let your users easily collaborate on documents over the Internet. WebDAV provides methods for resource locking, so other people are blocked from reading a particular document when you are modifying it on the server. When working with Microsoft Office 2000 applications, for instance, you can create, edit, and save documents directly into a WebDAV directory by specifying its URL instead of a Universal Naming Convention (UNC) path. It is likewise possible to connect to a WebDAV directory in Windows 2000 via My Network Places and the Add Network Place Wizard in much the same way you would connect to any ordinary network share.

Microsoft Exchange 2000 Web Storage System

Exercise 4 of Chapter 1, "Introduction to Microsoft Exchange 2000," demonstrated how standard Office 2000 applications could read and write items directly from and to mailboxes and public folders. File system access to Exchange resources is supported by means of the Web Storage System and a component called Exchange Installable File System (ExIFS). Don't get confused: ExIFS relies on the Web Storage System, but they are not the same. The Web Storage System is also involved when accessing Exchange resources via WebDAV, but ExIFS is not.

Every item within in the Web Storage System is accessible via the WebDAV protocol. This means that you are able to publish a public folder, for example, in the form of a WebDAV directory and let your users connect to it using the Add Network Place Wizard and the folder's URL (see Figure 11.10). Every folder and each message or other document in a folder has a URL associated with it.

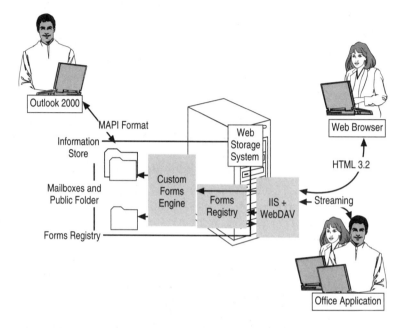

Figure 11.10   Collaborating on documents through WebDAV and the
                  Web Storage System

The Web Storage System associates items accessible through URLs with Web forms, which are comparable to Outlook forms, although they are entirely HTML-based and provide more extensibility capabilities. The Web Storage System relies on content classes to associate particular items with their corresponding forms. Any Web browser that supports HTML 3.2 or later can work with Web forms. Outlook Web Access (OWA) of Exchange 2000 Server, for example, relies on the association of Outlook folders and intrinsic message items with Web views and forms. You can read more about the architecture of the Web Storage System in Chapter 23, "Microsoft Exchange 2000 Web Storage System."

Exercise 5: Working with Published
WebDAV Resources and the Web Storage System

In this exercise you will examine how easy it is to access public folders residing in the Information Store via WebDAV. You will use Windows Explorer to access published folder repositories.

To view a multimedia demonstration that displays how to perform this procedure, run the EX5CH11.AVI files from the \Exercise_Information\Chapter11 folder on the Supplemental Course Materials CD.

Prerequisites

- Reboot BLUESKY-SRV1, start BLUESKY-WKSTA, and log on as Administrator.

▶ **To work with published Exchange-WebDAV directories**

1. On BLUESKY-WKSTA, on the desktop, right-click on My Network Places, and then select Explore.

2. In the right pane of the My Network Places window, double-click on Add Network Place.

3. In the Add Network Place Wizard, under Type The Location Of The Network Place, type **http://bluesky-srv1/public**, and then click Next.

4. In the Completing The Add Network Place wizard screen, under Enter A Name For This Network Place, type **All Public Folders on BLUESKY-SRV1**, and then click Finish.

   At this point, you have successful created a connection to the Web Storage System of BLUESKY-SRV1 (see Figure 11.11).

Figure 11.11   Connecting to public folders via WebDAV

5. The All Public Folders On BLUESKY-SRV1 window will be opened automatically, displaying a subfolder named Internet Newsgroups, which corresponds to the Internet Newsgroups public folder.

6. Open the File menu, point to New, and select Folder. Then press ENTER to accept the default name, New Folder. You now have created a new public folder on BLUESKY-SRV1.

7. Use Windows Explorer to copy a file into the New Folder repository.

8. Click Start, select Run, and, in the Run dialog box, type **http://bluesky-srv1/ exchange**, then click OK to launch a session with Outlook Web Access.

9. If this is the first time you have launched Internet Explorer, the Internet Connection Wizard appears. Select I Want To Set Up My Internet Connection Manually, click Next, select I Connect Through A Local Area Network (LAN), click Next twice, and answer the question, Do You Want To Set Up An Internet Mail Account Now, with No. Click Next, and then click Finish.

10. In Outlook Web Access, in the left frame, click on Folders, and then expand the Public Folders tree.

At this point, you can select the public folder called New Folder and verify that items copied into this public folder are listed (see Figure 11.12).

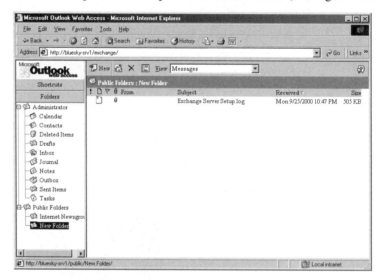

Figure 11.12   Cross-platform collaboration via WebDAV and the Web Storage System

Exercise Summary

By default, every user can access Exchange 2000 Server resources in the context of their access permissions via HTTP and WebDAV. WebDAV relies on the security features offered by Windows 2000, IIS 5.0, and Exchange 2000 Server. For instance, you may use the Add Network Places Wizard to add a connection to the public folder tree, but when you click on a folder for which you don't have the Read permission, the Enter Network Password dialog box will be displayed, prompting you for a different account name and password. If you don't have the Folder Visible permission, the public folder will not be listed in Windows Explorer at all. The management of public folders is the topic of Chapter 17, "Public Folder Management."

Note HTTP and WebDAV are Internet standards supported on all client platforms. Macintosh or UNIX client computers can rely on WebDAV to share information with Windows users directly.

Lightweight Directory Access Protocol

LDAP is a derivation of X.500 Directory Access Protocol . It was originally
developed at the University of Michigan to provide a more efficient way to build
and access a hierarchical directory based on object attributes. This industry standard is described in RFC 1777.

LDAP Features

As designed for the Internet, LDAP uses the TCP/IP transport mechanism for
client-server communication. The server "listens" for incoming requests on TCP
port 389 by default. To provide security, LDAP uses an encoding scheme called
Basic Encoding Rules (BER). The encoding is performed on top of the transport
layer (the layer at which the Transport Control Protocol [TCP] operates).

LDAP implementations assume support for the X.500 naming model for maximum interoperability between client and server. In other words, systems that reference directory objects through distinguished names (for example, a Windows
2000 Global Catalog server) provide an ideal platform for LDAP clients.

Available Versions

Three LDAP versions currently exist, although the third version has not yet been
specified completely. In Exchange 2000 Server organizations, LDAP is available
through Active Directory and Global Catalog servers. Any LDAP application,
such as Outlook Express, can therefore be used to look up the directory and
address information as soon as Active Directory is configured. Active Directory
supports the full set of LDAP features as outlined in the third protocol version.

LDAP and Windows 2000 Active Directory Directory Services

If you plan to use Internet mail clients, such as Outlook Express, to participate in
an Exchange 2000 Server organization, required address information is available
via LDAP and Active Directory. All Exchange 2000 recipient objects are maintained in Active Directory, and their most common attributes are replicated to the
Global Catalog for address name resolution, as explained in Chapter 2, "Integration with Microsoft Windows 2000." The Global Catalog holds the recipient
information for the entire forest. It is therefore advisable to configure an LDAP
connection to a Global Catalog server to be able to search the full set of address
information from your organization. When configuring your LDAP client, make
sure to connect to TCP port 3268 instead of the default port 389 to reach the
Global Catalog.

The following ports allow you to connect to Active Directory via LDAP:

- Port 389 for Active Directory domain controllers
- Port 636 for Active Directory domain controllers over Secure Sockets Layer (SSL)
- Port 3268 for Global Catalog servers
- Port 3269 for Global Catalog servers over SSL

Note   When accessing TCP port 389, only the objects within the home domain of the Active Directory domain controller are searchable. A query to port 3268 gives you the ability to search address information in the entire forest, although only the properties tagged for replication to the Global Catalog will be returned.

The configuration of LDAP searches and the address name resolution are covered in the *Windows 2000 Server Distributed Systems Guide* of the Windows 2000 Server Resource Kit.

Lesson 2: Configuring Virtual Protocol Servers

Exchange 2000 Server facilitates the introduction into messaging and collaboration across the Internet. However, a few questions remain concerning authentication and session security. Especially when connecting to the Internet, it is advisable to restrict access to only those services that are absolutely necessary for authorized users. To give an example, if you plan only to provide access to Exchange resources via HTTP, stop the Microsoft Exchange POP3, Microsoft Exchange IMAP4, and NNTP services in the Services management tool. Then, set their startup type to either manual or disabled.

This lesson broaches important aspects of Internet-based messaging and collaboration, such as the creation of additional virtual protocol servers for better scalability, the tightening of authentication, and the encryption of data channels for higher security. After that, the configuration of newsgroups and newsfeeds will be discussed. The implementation of advanced security features is the topic of Chapter 19, "Implementing Advanced Security," the adjustment of SMTP settings is broached in Chapter 15, "SMTP Transport Configuration," and HTTP-based features are illustrated again in Chapter 22, "Microsoft Outlook Web Access."

At the end of this lesson, you will be able to:

- Create virtual protocol servers for specific purposes.
- Control connections to virtual protocol servers.
- Configure newsgroups and newsfeeds.

Estimated time to complete this lesson: 60 minutes

Protocol Virtual Server Configurations

IIS supports the concept of virtual servers. Through virtual servers, you can enable a single server to appear as several servers. This is particularly interesting for Internet services providers (ISPs) that are hosting numerous independent Web sites for their customers on a small number of servers. You can have multiple virtual servers running on a single computer.

Default Virtual Servers

The Exchange System Manager utility allows you to create additional protocol virtual servers on your Exchange 2000 computer by means of a few mouse clicks. When you expand the nodes in the console tree, you will find a Protocols container underneath each server object. Each Internet protocol is represented as a different container and within each, corresponding virtual protocol servers are grouped together. By default, only one virtual server exists per protocol.

Note With the exception of the default HTTP virtual server, named Exchange Virtual Server, you should manage all IP settings from within the Exchange System Manager utility. To adjust the settings of the Exchange Virtual Server, use the Internet Services Manager.

Adding Virtual Servers

When you right-click on a protocol container (HTTP, IMAP4, NNTP, POP3, or SMTP) and point to New, you can select the <Protocol Type> Virtual Server command, which allows you to add virtual protocol servers to the configuration. You need to define a name for the new virtual server and assign it an IP address. In Windows 2000 Server you can assign a single network card multiple IP addresses or install multiple network adapters and configure each with a separate IP address. If your virtual server is supposed to use all available IP addresses, make sure you specify (All Unassigned) under IP Address.

IP Address and Port Number

During the creation of additional protocol servers, a dialog box might appear informing you that the new virtual server will not start because IP address and port numbers are already in use. It is important to assign each virtual server either a separate IP address or customized TCP port numbers for nonencrypted and SSL-encrypted communication, or both. For instance, the Default IMAP4 Virtual Server awaits incoming connections for all IP addresses on port 143 (nonencrypted) and port 993 (SSL-encrypted). A second virtual server cannot use the same port numbers because only one process can access a particular socket (IP address + port number) at a time. The default port numbers for each protocol type are listed in Table 11.1.

Table 11.1   Well-Known Ports for Internet Access Protocols

Protocol	TCP Port	SSL Port
HTTP	80	433
IMAP4	143	993
NNTP	119	563
POP3	110	995
SMTP	25	Uses Transport Layer Security (TLS) instead of SSL

Adjusting Virtual Server Settings

To adjust the settings of a virtual server, open the corresponding protocol container (such as IMAP4), right-click on the desired virtual server (such as Default IMAP4 Virtual Server), and from the shortcut menu, select Properties. In the General tab, click Advanced, for instance, to display the Advanced dialog box, where you can carry out the required changes to IP address and port mappings.

Table 11.2 summarizes the general configuration settings for protocol virtual servers.

Table 11.2   General Configuration Settings for Protocol Virtual Servers

Property Page	Protocol Type	Configuration Option
General	All types	IP Address and Advanced button; to specify the IP address and port numbers for the virtual server (and a host name if the protocol is HTTP).
		Limit Number Of Connections; to restrict how many users can access the virtual server concurrently.
		Connection Time-Out; to specify a period of time after which idle connections are disconnected from the virtual server.
	HTTP	Exchange Path; to specify whether the HTTP virtual server is used to connect to mailbox (and public folder) resources or public folders only. You can click the Modify button to select a particular sublevel public folder tree.
	IMAP4	Include All Public Folders When A Folder List Is Requested; to allow IMAP4 clients access to public folders.
		Enable Fast Message Retrieval; causes the virtual server to return an estimate of message size to requesting clients, rather than the exact size. Although this option can improve system performance, because an exact calculation of the message size can be avoided, certain IMAP4 clients might display truncated messages when this option is on.
	SMTP	Enable Logging; to maintain a log file about access and message transfer for the virtual server.
Access	All types	Authentication; to enable Anonymous Access, Basic Authentication, and Integrated Windows Authentication, and specify a Default Domain if Basic Authentication is activated for resource access.
	All types except HTTP	Secure Communication; to enable the SSL-based encryption of the communication channel between server and client by installing a server certificate. You can use the Certificate button to request a certificate from a certification authority on the Internet or your private certificate server. *(continued)*

Table 11.2   General Configuration Settings for Protocol Virtual Servers
(continued)

Property Page	Protocol Type	Configuration Option
Access	All types except HTTP	Connection Control; to specify IP addresses or ranges of IP addresses that should be granted or denied access to the virtual server.
	HTTP	Access Control; to restrict the access level for incoming client connections (Read access, Write access, Script Source access, and Directory Browsing).
		Execute Permissions; to specify whether scripts and executable files may be executed from this virtual server.
	SMTP	Relay Restrictions; to specify specific IP addresses or ranges of IP addresses that are allowed or denied the relay of messages through this server.
Message format	IMAP4 and POP3 only	MIME Encoding; to specify whether to format the body of messages in plain text or HTML (the latter supports font formats, and so on).
		Character Set; to specify the character set for the formatting of the message body. By default the Western European (ISO-8859-1) character set is used.
		Use Exchange Rich-Text Format; to send messages to the connecting client in the native Exchange format. This can be useful if your users connect to the virtual server using a client that is capable of handling the Exchange format, such as Outlook 2000 with the POP3 transport service.

Metabase and Active Directory Directory Services

As explained in Chapter 3, "Microsoft Exchange 2000 Server Architecture," IIS maintains its information primarily in its metabase, whereas Exchange 2000 Server stores and retrieves configuration information mainly from Active Directory. When you configure Internet protocols within the Exchange System Manager utility, you manage settings in Active Directory. It is the task of the metabase update service to transfer the changes into the metabase. Because the metabase update may take a few minutes, changes may not take effect immediately.

Authentication Methods

The Access tab provides access to the Authentication button and gives you the ability to enable or disable client authentication methods, such as Anonymous Access, Basic Authentication, and Integrated Windows Authentication). The settings differ slightly between the protocols because some may not apply to a specific protocol type. POP3 and IMAP, for instance, don't support Anonymous Access because this form of access is inappropriate when working with mailbox resources.

Anonymous Access

Exchange 2000 Server supports Anonymous Access to public folders based on HTTP and NNTP. If Anonymous Access has been enabled, users don't need to supply valid user information to connect to the server. Several configuration steps are required to enable this form of access. First, you need to enable Anonymous Access for the corresponding protocol or HTTP virtual directory within the Exchange System Manager. Second, you need to specify an anonymous account at the same location. By default, this is the Internet guest account called IUSR_<SERVERNAME>. Third, within the Exchange System Manager or Outlook 2000, you need to define anonymous access permissions for particular public folders. The configuration of public folders is covered in Chapter 17, "Public Folder Management."

Note   The Internet guest account used to validate anonymous NNTP and HTTP users does not correspond to the Anonymous account displayed in the Client Permissions dialog box. Because it is a valid Windows 2000 account, default permissions apply. To assign anonymous permissions directly, you need to mail-enable IUSR_<SERVERNAME>; otherwise, you are unable to select this account from the Global Address List.

Basic Authentication

If Basic Authentication is enabled (the default), clients are not forced to encrypt the user name or password. Instead, they can directly transmit this information to the server in encoded (and easily decodable) text. To put it plainly, if an intruder can watch the communication between a client and the server, this person can get access to users' account information. Consequently, it is advisable to disable the Basic Authentication method when providing access to Exchange 2000 resources over the Internet. Alternatively, you may enforce the encryption of the communication channel, which also helps to protect users.

For Basic Authentication, it is usually sufficient to supply your user name and password. Your user name will be assumed to be the same as the mailbox alias. However, if you want to access a mailbox other than your own—for instance, if you have configured an additional mailbox where you have been granted Full

Mailbox Access permissions—you need to specify the user name in this format: Domain name/Windows 2000 Account/Mailbox Alias.

Digest Authentication

Digest authentication may be an important authentication mechanism if you want to support Instant Messaging users that connect to their home server via an HTTP proxy. Digest authentication is an Internet Standard that transmits password information in the form of encrypted hash values to the server. Exchange 2000 Server supports this form of authentication without further configuration requirements; however, you need to enable reversible password encryption under Windows 2000 Server to support it. Activate the Store Password Using Reversible Encryption For All Users In The Domain setting in a Group Policy, such as the Default Domain Policy. You can find this setting under Computer Configuration/Windows Settings/Security Settings/Account Policy/Password Policy. You can read more about Group Policies in the Windows 2000 Server product documentation.

Note To verify whether Digest authentication is enabled, launch the Internet Information Services utility. Open the Web site container where the InstMsg virtual directory is located, right-click InstMsg, select Properties, click on the Directory Security tab, and then, under Anonymous Access And Authentication Control, click the Edit button. In the Authentication Methods dialog box, make sure Digest Authentication For Windows Domain Servers is selected.

Integrated Windows Authentication

Integrated Windows Authentication, formerly known as Microsoft Windows NT Challenge/Response authentication, is more complex and secure than the Basic Authentication or the Digest Authentication method because it uses the Windows network security mechanisms. To initiate the authentication, the client sends the AUTH NTLM command to the host. The server returns a positive response code. At this point, the client sends a negotiation message to the server, which contains random information. This random information is important because the server will use it to create a unique string also known as the challenge. The server transmits the challenge to the client. The client must encrypt the challenge using the password of your Windows 2000 account before it sends the encrypted information back to the server. The server, of course, knows the user's password and can decrypt the response to compare the result against the original challenge. If the response and the challenge match one another, the server sends a notification to the client that the user logged on successfully. Otherwise, the client will receive an "access denied" message. If your client happens to be Internet Explorer, the browser will continue to prompt you for a Windows account name and password until a valid user name and password is provided or you cancel the dialog box.

In addition to the Challenge/Response authentication mechanism, Integrated Windows Authentication also supports the Kerberos version 5 authentication protocol. However, your browser, such as Internet Explorer 5.0 running on Windows 2000, also needs to support Kerberos version 5 protocol; otherwise, only the Challenge/Response protocol can be used. Both the client and the server must have a connection to a key distribution center (KDC). The KDC is an integrated part of the security services of Windows 2000 domain controllers. Kerberos uses Active Directory to retrieve security account information.

Setting Security Options

Integrated Windows Authentication works well in environments where users are working with clients that support this authentication method (Internet Explorer and related programs only) and where the network supports the Challenge/ Response and Kerberos protocol. This is usually the case in an intranet. Over the Internet, however, especially over HTTP proxy connections, Windows authentication cannot be used. On a holiday trip, for example, when accessing your mailbox via a Web browser installed on a computer in an Internet café, you are most likely unable to log on to your Windows 2000 domain.

Note Integrated Windows Authentication is best suited for environments where both client and server are members of the same domain and you can ensure that every user is using Microsoft Internet clients and browsers.

Basic Authentication over Encrypted Communication Channels

If you cannot rely on Integrated Windows Authentication, you need to enable the Basic Authentication mechanism to allow your users to log on to the server. As mentioned, this is a critical issue because, without taking further measures, passwords will be transferred over the network in clear text. Hence, it is a good idea to encrypt the communication channel between the Internet clients and the server. An encrypted channel allows you to protect your credentials plus all of the subsequent data. To secure the communication channel, you need to enable and enforce available security features based on SSL.

Secure Sockets Layer

SSL relies on public key cryptography discussed in more detail in Chapter 19, "Implementing Advanced Security." In the Open Systems Interconnection (OSI) reference model, SSL resides between the transport layer and the application layer where the Internet access protocols are located (see Figure 11.13). To encrypt the client data at the SSL, client and server need to agree on the level of security they will use during the session. This information is automatically exchanged in the form of an X.509 certificate during the security handshake, which is carried out as part of the initialization of the TCP/IP connection.

The client receives the server's X.509 certificate, which contains, among other things, the server's public key. Using this public key, the client can encrypt a randomly generated session key (40-bit or 128-bit) and transfer it securely to the server. The server uses its private key to decrypt the data, obtains the session key, and, from this point forward, client and server can use the session key to encrypt the entire communication, including user credentials and messaging data.

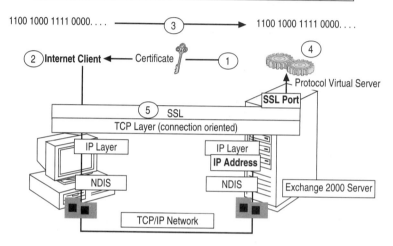

1. The server sends the public encryption key to the client.
2. The client generates session key.
3. The client encrypts the session key using the server's public key and sends the encrypted data to the server.
4. The server decrypts the session key using its private key.
5. Client and server have the session key to encrypt and decrypt their communication.

Figure 11.13   The SSL security handshake

Installing a Security Certificate on the Server

To provide IMAP4-based access to mailbox resources in encrypted form over the Internet, you need to install a security certificate on the server via the Access tab of your IMAP4 virtual server. In this tab, click the Certificate button to launch the Web Server Certificate Wizard. After you've clicked Next in the welcome screen, on the Server Certificate wizard screen, you have the option to Create A New Certificate, Assign An Existing Certificate, or Import A Certificate From A Key Manager Backup File. Make sure the first option is selected, and then click Next. On the Delayed Or Immediate Request wizard screen, you can create the request now and later send it via e-mail to a certification authority on the Internet, or, if you have Windows 2000 Certificate Services installed in your environment, you should choose Send The Request Immediately To An Online Certification Authority. Click Next, and, on the Name And Security Settings wizard screen, you need to specify a name and the bit length of the encryption key. In most cases you can accept the default suggestion (virtual server name and 512 bit) and click Next. On the next three wizard screens, you need to specify organizational information that will be written to the security certificate to identify your host. Make sure you specify correct information for the Organization, Organization Unit, Common Name, Country, State, and City. If you chose to use a certification authority earlier, then you will see the Chose A Certification Authority wizard screen; select your Windows 2000 Certificate Server. Existing certification authorities are retrieved from Active Directory, so you only need to make sure the correct reference is displayed in the Certification Authorities list box, then click Next. Choose a place to store the file on the Certificate Request File Name wizard screen, and click Next. In the Certificate Request Submission dialog box, verify the configuration settings again, then click Next, and subsequently Finish.

Enforcing a Secure Communication

If you have a certification authority already, then the required security certificate is installed after the previous process. You may now enforce the encryption of the client/server communication by clicking the Communication button in the Access tab and selecting the Require Secure Channel check box. If your environment supports strong 128-bit encryption, you may enable the Require 128-Bit Encryption check box as well. This 128-bit session cannot be exported outside the United States and Canada.

Note You will not be able to enforce the encryption without a valid certificate from a certificate authority.

When you click OK, clients will not be able to establish a connection to this server via nonencrypted communication channels. Try this by opening Telnet and connecting to your virtual server's unencrypted port (such as port 143 for the Default IMAP4 Virtual Server). Your welcome message will look like this: *BYE Connection Refused.

Note When enforcing encrypted communication channels, Internet clients need to connect to the SSL port configured for the virtual server instead of the standard TCP port. The default SSL ports are listed in Table 11.1.

Authentication Through Client Certificate Mapping

When you configure the authentication methods for an HTTP virtual server (via the corresponding Web site's Directory Security property sheet in the Internet Services Manager) or an NNTP virtual server (via the Access tab Authentication button), you will notice that you can enable client certificate mappings to Windows user accounts. Client certificates work similar to server certificates in that they represent a digital identification of a user (instead of a host). Each time a user logs on with a client certificate, your protocol virtual server automatically associates that user with the appropriate user account. Hence, your users are authenticated automatically and don't need to rely on any other authentication method. However, the manual mapping of numerous client certificates to Windows 2000 user accounts can be a substantial management task.

Configuring NNTP Virtual Servers

Exchange 2000 Server utilizes event sinks to combine the NNTP functionality of Windows 2000 with public folder resources. After you have installed Exchange 2000 Server on your server, you'll need to use the Exchange System Manager to manage NNTP virtual server settings.

Newsgroup Hierarchies

The implementation of newsgroups based on public folders provides several advantages. The good news is that you don't need to roll out or support newsreader software on your individual client computers. Your users can use Outlook 2000 to fully participate in discussions through newsgroups that you replicate with USENET. You may also implement newsgroup-based discussion forums in your department or organization and let your users share ideas no matter what platform they are working on because newsreaders are available for literally any PC-based operating system.

Making Internet Newsgroups Available to NNTP Clients

The public folder called Internet Newsgroups is the default location for inbound newsgroups replicated to a server running Exchange 2000 Server. This folder represents a hierarchy parent folder. All inbound newsfeeds will maintain their newsgroup folders under this parent folder, and you can create public folders under this parent folder manually as well within Exchange System Manager.

Manually Creating Newsgroups

If you want to create additional discussion forums, you need to manually create the associated public folders under a newsgroup hierarchy also known as a virtual directory. However, you don't create these resources in Outlook 2000. Use Exchange System Manager instead. Expand your NNTP virtual server in the contents pane, right-click Newsgroups, point to New, and select Newsgroup. This will launch the New Newsgroup Wizard. Enter the complete name of the newsgroup (such as discussion.outlook) in the Name box, and click Next. On the second wizard screen, enter a Description and Pretty Name. Some newsreaders are able to display the Description and Pretty Name instead of the newsgroup name and hierarchy. To complete the configuration, click Finish.

Exchange System Manager will automatically create a new public folder structure according to your newsgroup hierarchy under a virtual directory, which defaults to Internet Newsgroups. To complete the preceding example, Outlook 2000 users can participate in discussions about Outlook when opening the public folder All Public Folders\Internet Newsgroups\Discussion\Outlook. Newsreader users can access the same forum when subscribing to the newsgroup discussion.outlook.

Creating Newsgroup Hierarchies

If you want to host your newsgroups in several public folder structures other than Internet Newsgroups, you need to create additional newsgroup hierarchies. Under your NNTP virtual server, right-click Virtual Directories, point to New, and then select Virtual Directory. You will be prompted for a name for your Newsgroup subtree. It is a good idea to specify a name that refers to the overall topic of the hierarchy, such as Flying. Click Next, and, on the second wizard screen, select Exchange Public Folder Database, and then click Next. On the third wizard screen, click the Browse button, and, in the Public Folder Selection, expand the All Public Folder tree, and select the desired public folder. Click OK, and then click Finish.

So far, no newsgroups have been created. You can do so following the procedure just outlined. Avoid the creation of the corresponding public folder under Internet Newsgroups, and instead place it under your custom hierarchy (such as Flying) by including the hierarchical information (such as *flying.*) in the newsgroup name (such as flying.hydroplanes).

Changing Newsgroup Properties

When you right-click a newsgroup folder in Outlook 2000 that was created by means of the Exchange System Manager, let's say under Internet Newsgroups, and you select Properties, you will notice that you cannot manage the newsgroup's properties because of missing client permissions. When you display the properties in Exchange System Manager, only a very limited set of properties, that is, Description, Pretty Name, Read Only, and Moderator, can be set. To manage size limits and other settings, use the property sheets of the NTTP virtual server, particularly the Settings tab. If you want to provide different settings for separate sets of newsgroups, create multiple virtual servers.

In some cases, however, it is desirable to adjust the settings of a particular newsgroup, such as client permissions, without configuring additional protocol virtual servers. The management of public folders can be accomplished in Exchange System Manager. Expand the corresponding public folder store, and select the Public Folder Instances container underneath it. In the contents pane, all public folder instances are listed. Right-click the desired one, and select Folder Properties. To adjust the client permissions, switch to the Permissions tab. If you click the Client Permissions button and add yourself with Owner permissions to the list of accounts, you can fully configure the public folder resource from this point forward in Outlook 2000. The configuration of public folder resources is covered in more detail in Chapter 17, "Public Folder Management."

Moderated Newsgroups

A moderated public folder or moderated newsgroup folder allows a user to forward posted messages to a moderator. The moderator reviews the posted information and allows accepted articles to appear in the newsgroup folder. You have two options to set up a moderated newsgroup—either you set up the newsgroup as a moderated forum in Exchange System Manager or you configure the public folder as a moderated folder in Outlook 2000. With the latter, your users may specify moderators themselves when they configure newsgroups.

Important   You need to have the Owner permissions for a newsgroup's public folder to configure the moderator settings in Outlook 2000.

If you want an NNTP virtual server to forward posted articles to a moderator, you need to specify an SMTP server on the NNTP virtual server's Settings property sheet first (SMTP Server For Moderated Groups). You also need to specify a Default Moderator Domain. After that, you can configure the properties of the desired newsgroups. In the General tab, activate the Moderated settings, and then specify a newsgroup moderator. If you select the Set Default option, new articles are sent to an address that has the format of newsgroup alias@Default Moderator Domain.

Newsgroup Expiration Policies

When you examine the nodes underneath an NNTP virtual server, you will notice a container called Expiration Policies. As its name suggests, you can use it to configure policies that determine how long articles are stored in newsgroups. However, if your newsgroups are referring to public folders, it is advisable to configure the expiration settings in the Information Store, which will be explained in Chapter 17, "Public Folder Management."

Important   Age limits set in the Information Store supersede expiration policies set at the newsgroup level for the NNTP virtual server. If age limits have been configured in the Information Store, NNTP expiration policies are deactivated.

Concurrent Sessions

Every NNTP virtual server provides you with status information regarding current client sessions in the Current Sessions container. All existing sessions are listed as individual objects. In case a connection appears to hang, or you want to terminate it for any other reason, right-click on it, and then select Terminate. Alternatively, you may select Terminate All. However, disconnecting a user this way is only a temporary measure because most newsreader clients reconnect immediately when the user is reading articles.

Creating Newsfeeds

The remaining node under each NNTP virtual server is called Feeds and, as its name implies, it serves to create and maintain newsfeeds. To create a new newsfeed, right-click on it, point to New, and select Feed. On the first New NNTP Feed wizard screen, enter the remote host's name or IP address, and then click Next. On the second wizard screen, make sure Peer is selected for the

remote server role. You may also configure Master and Slave feeds, which correspond to a configuration where clients connect to a slave server to download and
upload articles, while new articles are first forwarded to the master server, which
assigns an ID to them. The typical selection for the USENET is Peer, then click
Next. On the third wizard screen, you need to specify whether your newsfeed is
inbound (pull or accept from push feed) or outbound (push). If you are only
interested in reading articles, then an inbound pull feed is sufficient; otherwise,
you should select the Outbound Feed check box in addition. Click Next, and, on
the fourth wizard screen, specify the age of the articles you want to pull into your
newsgroups (inbound only) upon feed creation, then click Next again. On the last
wizard screen you may specify particular newsgroups to be included or excluded
from the list of groups handled by this feed. If you want to include all available
newsgroups, accept the default (*) for all newsgroups, and click Finish.

Newsfeed Configuration Tasks

You can accomplish newsfeed configuration tasks through the property sheets
that every newsfeed object provides. For instance, you might be required to
enable Basic Authentication to access the remote host. Right-click the desired
newsfeed, and as usual click Properties in the <Newsfeed> Properties dialog box,
switch to the Security tab, and enable Basic (No Encryption). Under User Name
and Password, type the required information, and click OK. The drawbacks of
Basic Authentication were discussed earlier in this lesson.

Controlling Inbound Newsgroups

When you click on the General tab, you can find the Enable Feed check box,
which allows you to temporarily disable a particular newsfeed. This may be especially useful if you discover that a newsfeed replicates too many articles to your
server. Disable the newsfeed, add more hardware, or move other Exchange 2000
resources (such as mailboxes) to another server, compact the affected databases
(see Chapter 20, "Microsoft Exchange 2000 Server Maintenance and Troubleshooting"), and then enable the feed again. Mailbox management is the topic of
Chapter 13, "Creating and Managing Recipients."

Exercise 6: Supporting Internet Messaging Clients

In this exercise you will use Outlook Express as a POP3, IMAP4, NNTP, and LDAP
client to access your mailbox, public folders, newsgroups, and the Global Address
List. First, however, you need to create some newsgroups in Exchange 2000.

To view a multimedia demonstration that displays how to perform this procedure,
run the EX6CH11*.AVI files from the \Exercise_Information\Chapter11 folder
on the Supplemental Course Materials CD.

Prerequisites

- Ensure Exchange 2000 Server is operational and running on BLUESKY-SRV1.

- Log on as Administrator to BLUESKY-SRV1 and BLUESKY-WKSTA.

- If you have completed the exercises of Chapter 9, "MAPI-Based Clients," you need to delete the manually created profile. (Right-click Microsoft Outlook on the desktop, select Properties, click Show Profile, select Manually Configured Profile, click Remove, and then confirm the action by clicking Yes. Make sure that Outlook starts with the CIW Generated Profile.)

▶ **To configure Microsoft Outlook Express as an Internet client for Exchange 2000 Server**

1. On BLUESKY-SRV1, launch Exchange System Manager from the Microsoft Exchange program group.

2. In the console pane, expand Servers, expand BLUESKY-SRV1, expand Protocols, expand NNTP, expand Default NNTP Site, and then select Virtual Directories. Notice that the Default virtual directory points to Public Folders/ Internet Newsgroups.

3. Select Newsgroups, right-click it, point to New, and select Newsgroup.

4. On the first New Newsgroup wizard screen, under Name, type **discussion**, and then click Next.

5. On the second wizard screen, click Finish.

6. Repeat Steps 4 and 5 for the newsgroups **discussion.outlook** and **discussion.exchange**.

   At this point, you have created three additional newsgroups (see Figure 11.14), which you can access from Outlook Express later in this exercise.

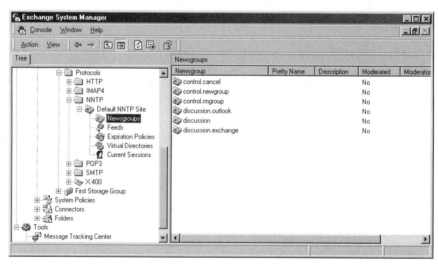

Figure 11.14   Creating newsgroups in Exchange System Manager

7. Close Exchange System Manager, and log off.

8. On BLUESKY-WKSTA, launch Outlook 2000.

9. Open the View menu, and make sure Folder List is selected.

10. Expand Public Folders, then All Public Folders, then Internet Newsgroups, and then verify that the discussion hierarchy was created successfully.

11. Post some items into the Discussion, Exchange, and Outlook folders.

12. Click Start button, point to Programs, and then select Outlook Express.

13. If an Outlook Express dialog box appears informing you that Outlook Express is currently not your default e-mail client, deselect the Always Perform This Check When Starting Outlook Express check box, and then click No.

14. If the Internet Connection Wizard appears, type **Administrator** under Display Name, and then click Next.

15. On the second wizard screen, under I Already Have An E-Mail Address That I'd Like To Use, in the E-Mail Address text box, type **Administrator@Bluesky-inc-10.com**, and then click Next.

16. On the E-Mail Server Names wizard screen, make sure that POP3 is displayed in the list box, and then, under Incoming Mail (POP3, IMAP4 Or HTTP) Server and Outgoing Mail (POP3, IMAP4 Or HTTP) Server, type **BLUESKY-SRV1**, and then click Next.

17. In the Internet Mail Logon dialog box, make sure Administrator is displayed under Account Name, and then, in the Password text box, type **password**. Alternatively, you could activate the logon using Secure Password Authentication (SPA).

18. Click Next and then click Finish.

19. On the Import Messages And Address Book wizard screen, select Do Not Import At This Time, and then click Next.

20. Click Finish.

21. To download all messages from your Inbox, open the Tools menu, point to Send And Receive, and then select BLUESKY-SRV1 (Default).

22. Make sure you can successfully download messages. Switch to Outlook 2000, and verify that your Inbox is now empty.

23. Switch back to Outlook Express, and, in the toolbar, click New Mail.

24. Click the To button, and, in the Select Recipients dialog box, click Find.

25. In the Find People dialog box, select Active Directory from the Look In list box. Under Name, type **Admin**, and click Find Now.

26. Among other directory information, the Administrator account information is retrieved. Select Administrator, and click the To button.

27. Click OK until you return to the new message.

28. In the Subject line, type **Active Directory is easy to search**.

29. In the message body, type **You don't even have to create an LDAP account to access Active Directory manually**.

30. Click Send.

31. Notice that the message leaves your Inbox and appears in your Inbox in Outlook 2000 (see Figure 11.15).

Figure 11.15   Sending messages with POP3 via SMTP

32. Switch back to Outlook Express, open the Tools menu, and select Accounts.

33. Click on the Mail tab, click Add, and select Mail.

34. On the first wizard screen, accept the suggested name Administrator and click Next.

35. On the second wizard screen, accept the E-Mail Address information and click Next.

36. In the E-mail Server Names wizard screen, select IMAP from the list box, and then, under Incoming Mail (POP3, IMAP4 Or HTTP) Server and Outgoing Mail (POP3, IMAP4 Or HTTP) Server, type **BLUESKY-SRV1,** and then click Next.

37. In the Internet Mail Logon dialog box, make sure Administrator is displayed under Account Name, and then, in the Password text box, type **password**. Alternatively, you could activate the logon using SPA.

38. Click Next and then click Finish.

39. In the Internet Accounts dialog box, click Add, and then select News.

40. On the first wizard screen, accept the suggested name Administrator and click Next.

41. On the second wizard screen, accept the E-Mail Address information and click Next.

42. On the Internet News Server Names wizard screen, under News (NNTP) Server, type **BLUESKY-SRV1**. Activate the My News Server Requires Me To Log On check box, and then click Next.

43. In the Internet News Logon dialog box, make sure Administrator is displayed under Account Name, and then, in the Password text box, type **password**. Click Next and then click Finish.

44. In the Internet Accounts dialog box, click Close.

45. An Outlook Express dialog box will appear asking you to download folders from the mail server. Click Yes.

46. In the Show/Hide IMAP Folders dialog box, notice that all available message folders are listed, including public folders. Click OK to close the dialog box.

You are now able to access all message folders directly at the server through Outlook Express and the IMAP4 protocol (see Figure 11.16).

Figure 11.16   Accessing all message folders via IMAP4

47. In the Folders pane, double-click the account node BLUESKY-SRV (2), which corresponds to your newsreader account.

48. If an Outlook Express dialog box appears asking you whether you would like to make Outlook Express your default news client, click Yes.

49. An Outlook Express dialog box will appear asking you whether you would like to download a list of available newsgroups from the server. Click Yes.

50. In the Newsgroup Subscriptions dialog box, select Discussion, and click Subscribe (repeat this step for discussion.exchange and discussion.outlook as well), then click OK.

51. Notice that your newsreader account is now listing three newsgroups. Select the discussion folder, and verify that the items posted with Outlook 2000 earlier are listed as news articles (see Figure 11.17).

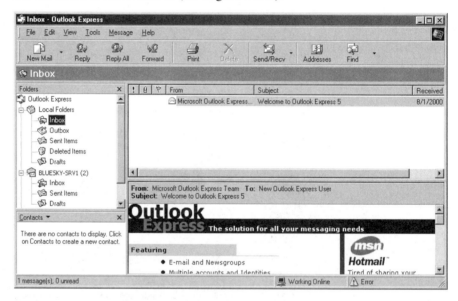

Figure 11.17   Accessing all public folders in the form of newsgroups

Exercise Summary

Exchange 2000 Server and Outlook Express support all the important Internet client protocols. Hence, you can configure and run Outlook Express as a multi-purpose Exchange client application. You can access your Inbox via POP3, all message folders including public folders via IMAP4, and public folders configured as newsgroups via NNTP. The sending of messages is accomplished through SMTP, and directory access is carried out over LDAP. The client configuration parameters required to connect to an Exchange 2000 server do not differ from the settings required to connect to any other Internet host.

Chapter Summary

When you connect your Exchange 2000 Server environment to the Internet, your users will instantly be able to communicate with users from other Internet organizations—provided that MX records exist in DNS for your Internet domain. Your users will also be able to access their mailboxes and public folders via popular Internet mail clients and Web browsers.

The IIS of Windows 2000 manages all Internet client protocol engines. The SMTP and NNTP services are integrated with Exchange 2000 Server. The Exchange 2000 Setup program adds the IMAP4 and POP3 protocol engines to the IIS process in addition. LDAP is supported directly by Windows 2000 Active Directory.

On the server, you manage Internet protocol settings primarily with the Exchange System Manager, with one exception: The default HTTP virtual server must be managed in the Internet Services Manager to remain compatible with existing non-Exchange Web sites. However, the creation of additional virtual servers, the adjustment of virtual server settings, and the configuration of newsgroups and the Web Storage System must be carried out using the Exchange System Manager utility.

On the client, you can work with a variety of Internet-aware programs, such as POP3 and IMAP4 clients, newsreaders, or even Windows Explorer, to access Exchange 2000 resources. The Web Storage System, accessible via HTTP and WebDAV, can provide new avenues for cross-platform collaboration using virtually any application, including Microsoft Office and other Win32 programs.

Review

The following review questions can help you determine if you have sufficiently familiarized yourself with the material covered in this chapter. You can find the answers to these questions at the end of this book in Appendix A, "Questions and Answers."

1. As an Exchange 2000 administrator, you have connected your organization to the Internet. Now you want to support common Internet clients as well. Which Internet protocols does Exchange 2000 Server support?

2. You want to increase the access security for Exchange 2000 resources. How would you limit the group of workstations that are able to access existing servers through IP?

3. Which authentication methods can you use to support all possible POP3/IMAP4 clients?

4. As a management consultant, you want to emphasize the benefits of Exchange 2000 Server in a presentation for your most important customer. Spontaneously, you are asked about this feature called Web Storage System that everybody seems to talk about. How can you demonstrate the Web Storage System ad hoc without any preparation or additional configuration on a computer running Exchange 2000 Server?

5. You have successfully configured a pull feed to replicate newsgroups with the USENET. After three days, you realize that this newsfeed is pulling in several gigabytes of data. You expect to run out of disk space very soon. Which steps should you carry out to avoid a server shutdown due to unavailable disk space?

CHAPTER 12

Management Tools for
Microsoft Exchange 2000 Server

About This Chapter

The management of Microsoft Exchange 2000 Server relies on a set of Microsoft Management Console (MMC) snap-ins. By combining snap-ins, you can create your own customized management tools. Such tools can greatly improve the efficiency of administering the entire Microsoft Windows 2000 and Exchange 2000 environment. To give an example, you may blend the Active Directory Users and Computers snap-in with the Public Folder Management snap-in and assign the new tool to a group of administrators dedicated to maintaining mailboxes and public folder resources.

You may go as far as developing your own snap-ins to extend existing Exchange 2000 management components. The MMC Snap-In Designer for Visual Basic 6.0, for example, can help you get started quickly, provided that you are a Visual Basic programmer. The MMC Snap-In Designer was first introduced with the January 2000 edition of the Platform Software Development Kit (SDK).

This chapter introduces various Windows 2000 and Exchange 2000 snap-ins that are important for managing Exchange 2000 resources. It provides a feature overview. General MMC concepts were discussed in Chapter 2, "Integration with Microsoft Windows 2000."

Before You Begin

To complete this chapter:

- Prepare your test environment according to the descriptions given in the "Getting Started" section of "About This Book."

- Be familiar with the concepts of the MMC and the utilization of MMC snap-ins.

Lesson 1: Windows 2000 Tools and Snap-Ins

More than 100 MMC snap-ins exist for Windows 2000 Server, and Exchange 2000 Server adds additional components to this collection. To be a professional administrator, you don't necessarily need to be familiar with all the available snap-ins, but you do need to know the most important tools and their key features. Typical Windows 2000 management tools that every Exchange administrator should know about are Active Directory Users and Computers, Computer Management, Event Viewer, Internet Services Manager, Performance, Services, Task Manager, and the Backup utility. Depending on the situation, you might need to use additional tools, such as the Registry Editor or the ADSI Edit utility.

This lesson cannot cover all of the Windows 2000 management utilities or all of their features and doesn't intend to. However, it does give a brief summary about important tools that you might find helpful when accomplishing your tasks as an Exchange 2000 administrator.

At the end of this lesson, you will be able to:

- List the important features of typical Windows 2000 management utilities.
- Describe when to use which utility.

Estimated time to complete this lesson: 60 minutes

Active Directory Users and Computers

The Active Directory Users and Computers snap-in is the central tool for user and computer account management in Windows 2000 Server domains. This snap-in allows you to, among other things, create and manage user accounts, contacts, computer accounts, groups and group memberships, organizational units, printers, and shared folders.

When you install the Exchange 2000 management utilities on a computer running Windows 2000, the Active Directory Users and Computers snap-in is extended to support the management of mailbox settings. Typical Exchange-related tasks involve the creation of mailboxes, their transfer to another server, and mailbox deletion. You can read more about mailbox management in Chapter 13, "Creating and Managing Recipients."

Services Snap-In

The Services snap-in, which you can find in the Administrative Tools group, is also an important Exchange 2000 administrative tool. It allows you to control all of the services running on your server (Start, Stop, Pause, and Resume), including the Exchange 2000 services. You can set various configuration parameters, such as the Startup Type and the Log On account. Exchange 2000 Server services typically run in the context of the LocalSystem account, which provides a high security standard under Windows 2000 Server, as explained in Chapter 5, "Installing Microsoft Exchange 2000 Server."

Note   The standard Services utility is designed to manage local resources only. However, you can use the Services snap-in for remote administration when you add it to a custom MMC. In the Services dialog box that appears during the configuration, instruct the snap-in to connect to another computer.

Recovery Options

You can also exclude services from specific hardware profiles (Log On tab) and determine the server's reaction if a service fails (Recovery tab). The operating system performs recovery actions automatically if a critical state has been detected. You can choose Take No Action, Restart The Service, Run A File, or Reboot The Server. These actions can be set for three different levels independently. One escalation level will follow the other if a previous action does not solve the critical state. It is possible to try restarting the critical service twice before the third level will be reached, which may force restarting the entire server.

Rebooting the Server

It is advisable to warn your users to save their work before a server is restarted automatically; otherwise, they may lose data when working with documents stored on this Windows 2000 server. When specifying to reboot the server at any escalation level, the Restart Computer Options button becomes available. Click it, and configure a restart notification and a restart delay. The restart notification will inform all users that are connected to the affected server about the scheduled shutdown. The delay should give them enough time to save their work. The default delay is 1 minute, but it is a good idea to increase it to 2 or 3 minutes.

Note   Reboot The Server may cause the server to reboot repeatedly if the system restart does not solve the problem. Hence, allow for enough time to log on and step in; otherwise, the server may become unmanageable.

Computer Management

Under Microsoft Windows NT, many administrators preferred to place a shortcut to the Services program of the Control Panel on the desktops of their servers. Under Windows 2000, you may do the same for the Services snap-in, but you might find it more advantageous to use the Computer Management utility instead. This tool provides far more capabilities than the Services snap-in.

Using the Computer Management utility, you can conveniently manage services and applications on the local computer as well as remote servers. You also get access to system tools, such as System Information and the Event Viewer, and storage utilities, such as Disk Management and Removable Storage. If you want to manage a remote server instead of the local machine, right-click Computer Management (Local) in the console tree, and select Connect To Another Computer. In the Select Computer dialog box, double-click the computer that you want to administer. The Computer Management utility is covered in more detail in Chapter 14, "Managing Server Configuration."

Performance Utility

You can use either the Computer Management snap-in or the Performance utility to monitor the state of your systems. Both utilities give you access to the Performance Logs and Alerts tool, but the Performance utility also provides the System Monitor, which allows you to display performance data in real-time charts. When you add counters to a chart, you have the option to specify different computers. You can monitor the performance of local and remote computers anywhere in your network and summarize the performance data. Exchange 2000 Server adds numerous counters to the server that let you monitor the health of the system permanently (see Figure 12.1). You can read more about the Performance tool in Chapter 20, "Microsoft Exchange 2000 Maintenance and Troubleshooting."

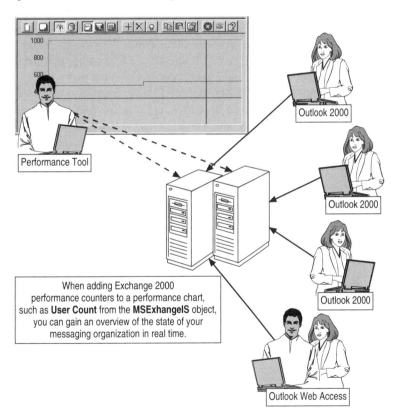

When adding Exchange 2000 performance counters to a performance chart, such as **User Count** from the **MSExhangeIS** object, you can gain an overview of the state of your messaging organization in real time.

Figure 12.1 Monitoring the number of users currently working with Microsoft Exchange 2000 Server

Internet Services Manager

If you have installed Exchange 2000 Server on the computer, you should not configure settings for the Internet protocols in the Internet Services Manager— with the exception of the default Web site, as mentioned in Chapter 11, "Internet-Based Client Access." The Internet Services Manager is available as a stand-alone snap-in from the Administrative Tools program group and as part of the Computer Management tool.

Generally, use the Exchange 2000 management utilities to set the configuration parameters of Internet Information Services (IIS) in the Active Directory directory service. The metabase update service will then transfer the changes into the IIS metabase. This is a one-way replication. If you use the Internet Services Manager to manage the settings of a Web site, these changes are written directly to the metabase and not passed on to Active Directory. You can read more about the Internet Services Manager in the *Internet Information Services Resource Guide* of the Microsoft Windows 2000 Server Resource Kit.

Event Viewer

The Event Viewer snap-in, available as a stand-alone snap-in and as part of the Computer Management utility, enables you to analyze system events, such as application or system errors. It allows you to examine the error information returned by failed services. Events are recorded in event logs (Application, Directory Service, DNS Server, File Replication Service, Security, and System). Exchange 2000 services keep a record of their activities primarily in the application event log. You can read more about Exchange-related application events in Chapter 20, "Microsoft Exchange 2000 Maintenance and Troubleshooting." For more information about the Event Viewer, consult the Windows 2000 Server online help.

Note   After installing Exchange 2000 Server, it is a good idea to check the application event log to make sure that the system is not reporting any problems.

Backup and Restore Utility

All versions of Windows 2000 provide you with a backup utility that enables you to back up your system files, user documents, and network data. When Exchange 2000 Server has been installed on the local machine, you also can save the storage groups of the Information Store online, meaning you don't need to shut down the server services. The backup and restore procedures for Exchange 2000 Server are discussed in detail in Chapter 20, "Microsoft Exchange 2000 Maintenance and Troubleshooting."

The Backup utility allows you to schedule jobs to run automatically, for instance, every night at midnight. Running backups at off-peak hours can ensure that server performance is not degraded during normal business hours. In addition to determining a backup schedule, however, it is important to check how long it takes to complete backup and restore operations. The Windows 2000 Backup utility is optimized for fast backups. Depending on your backup media and system configuration, you may achieve backup rates of up to 40 GB per hour. However, the same is not true for restore procedures, which usually progress at half or even less than half of the backup speed. The overall time it takes to restore a server is an important factor in designing an appropriate disaster recovery plan.

Task Manager

The Task Manager allows you to monitor, control, start, and terminate programs and processes that are running on a Windows 2000 computer. You can launch this tool by right-clicking the clock on the Windows toolbar and selecting Task Manager from the shortcut menu. Alternatively, press CTRL + ALT + DEL, and then click Task Manager in the Windows Security dialog box. In the Task Manager program window, you will find the Processes and Performance tabs. The Processes tab lists all of the active processes on the server and their resource consumption. The Performance tab, on the other hand, provides a graphical overview of central processing unit (CPU) and memory usage.

The End Task button in the Applications tab and the End Process button in the Processes tab enable you to terminate running processes. Terminating a process this way, nevertheless, is not the same as closing an application or stopping a service in the Services utility. The affected process has no chance to notify any attached DLLs that it is terminating. For instance, memory-mapped objects might remain orphaned, consume server resources unnecessarily, and cause problems themselves. Rebooting the server will reset the system state properly after terminating an Exchange 2000 service. You can read more about troubleshooting Exchange 2000 Server in Chapter 20, "Microsoft Exchange 2000 Maintenance and Troubleshooting."

Note You might get the impression that an Exchange 2000 Server service stops responding and hangs for no apparent reason, occupying close to 100 percent of the CPU's capacity. This does not necessarily indicate a critical system state, as the server might be busy with a processor-intensive task, such as the expansion of a very large distribution group. Use the Performance tool to monitor the affected system for a period of time, and don't terminate server processes if you are not absolutely sure that the suspicious component is malfunctioning.

Windows 2000 Registry Editors

The Windows 2000 Registry Editors (REGEDT32.EXE and REGEDIT.EXE) can be used to inspect and modify the startup parameters of Exchange 2000 Server services because their settings are maintained within the Windows 2000 Registry. REGEDIT.EXE is more convenient to use, whereas REGEDT32.EXE provides more functionality (such as the Security menu). With both utilities you need to be very careful when modifying parameters directly because modifications are usually written to the Registry immediately without activating an explicit Save command. In addition, no security mechanism exists to prevent you from entering invalid parameters or values. It is possible to damage an installation seriously, either by accident or on purpose, due to invalid configuration settings.

On the other hand, some configuration parameters cannot be specified using any other administration tool. For example, you have to use Registry Editor if you need to adjust the remote procedure call (RPC) binding order for your Microsoft Outlook client, as illustrated in Exercise 4 of Chapter 8, "Microsoft Outlook 2000 Deployment."

Caution   Using the Registry editors incorrectly can cause serious problems that may require you to reinstall Windows 2000. Use the Registry editors only if no other administrative tool is available.

Active Directory Service Interface Edit

The Active Directory Service Interface (ADSI) Edit snap-in (ADSIEDIT.DLL) is not included in the standard Windows 2000 Server installation for good reasons. Similar to the Registry editors for the Registry database, ADSI Edit enables you directly to access, modify, and delete Active Directory information from the Domain, Configuration, and Schema partitions. This risks seriously damaging the Active Directory environment. However, ADSI Edit is a very powerful utility that displays Active Directory objects in a hierarchical view and allows modifications through a standard properties page. ADSI Edit gives you access to all attributes of a directory object.

Although it isn't installed by default, the ADSI Edit snap-in still ships with the Windows 2000 Server CD. You can find it in the Support\Tools folder. To install it, launch the Setup program from the same location. Product documentation is available in the form of an online help file for all Windows 2000 Support Tools. ADSI Edit is also part of the Microsoft Windows 2000 Resource Kit.

Exercise 1: Managing Exchange 2000 Server with Windows 2000 Administrative Utilities

In this exercise you will use several of the management tools discussed in this lesson to manage Exchange 2000 resources. You will use these utilities to manage local and remote server components.

To view a multimedia demonstration that displays how to perform this procedure, run the EX1CH12*.AVI files from the \Exercise_Information\Chapter12 folder on the Supplemental Course Materials CD.

Prerequisites

- Exchange 2000 Server is installed and operational on BLUESKY-SRV1 and BLUESKY-SRV2.

- Log on as Administrator to BLUESKY-SRV1 and BLUESKY-SRV2.

▶ **To manage Exchange 2000 Server resources with standard admin utilities**

1. On BLUESKY-SRV1, click Start, point to Programs, point to Administrative Tools, and then click Active Directory Users and Computers.

2. In the console tree, expand the Bluesky-inc-10.com container, and then click View, and select Advanced Features. Notice that additional containers are now displayed underneath the domain, such as Microsoft Exchange System Objects, which provides access to recipient objects for system mailboxes and public folders.

3. Click View, and select Filter Options. In the Filter Options dialog box, activate Create Custom Filter, and then click Customize.

4. In the Find Custom Search dialog box, click Field, point to User, and then select Exchange Home Server.

5. From the Condition list box, select Not Present.

6. Click Add, and then click OK twice.

   At this point, you have successfully created a filter to display only those user accounts that don't own a mailbox (see Figure 12.2). Select the Users container and verify the results.

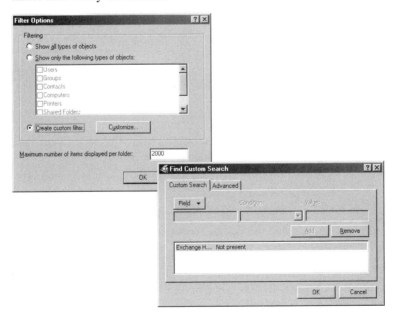

Figure 12.2   Filtering objects based on account attributes in the Active Directory Users and Computers snap-in

7. Click View again, select Filter Options, and, in the Filter Options dialog box, activate Show All Types Of Objects, then click OK. Notice all users now appear under the Users folder. Close the Active Directory Users and Computers snap-in.

8. Launch the Services utility from the Administrative Tools program group.

9. In the console tree, right-click on Services (Local), point to All Tasks, and select Send Console Message.

10. In the Send Console Message dialog box, under Message, type **The server will shut down in approximately 1 minute.**

11. Under Recipients, click Add, and, in the Add Recipients dialog box, type **BLUESKY-SRV2**, then click OK.

12. In the Send Console Message dialog box, click Send.

13. Verify that a Messenger Service dialog box pops up on BLUESKY-SRV2, then click OK (see Figure 12.3).

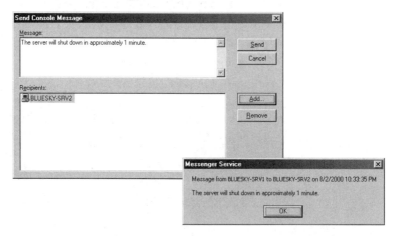

Figure 12.3   Sending console notifications with the Services utility

14. In the contents pane, right-click Microsoft Exchange System Attendant, and, from the shortcut menu, select Stop.

15. In the Stop Other Servicesdialog box, verify that all Exchange 2000 services will be stopped as well. Click Yes to continue and shut down Exchange 2000 Server on the local computer.

16. Launch the Event Viewer from the Administrative Tools program group.

17. In the console tree, select Application Log.

18. Verify that numerous Exchange-related events are displayed in the contents pane. Double-click on the last event where the source is MSExchangeSA.

19. In the Event Properties Description, you can verify that the service was stopped cleanly (see Figure 12.4). Click OK.

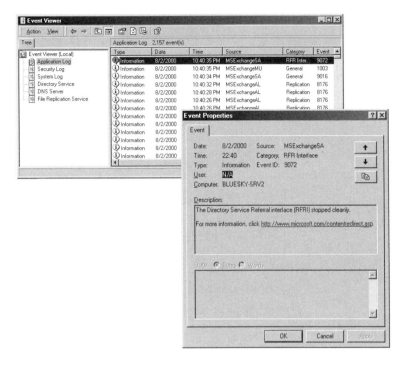

Figure 12.4   Examining Exchange 2000-related events in the Event Viewer

20. Click View and then select Filter to display the Application Log Properties dialog box.

21. Under Event Source, select MSExchangeSA, and then click OK. Notice that at this point only the events of the Exchange System Attendant are displayed in the contents pane.

22. To display all events again, click View and select All Records.

23. In the console tree, right-click Application Log, and, from the shortcut menu, select Properties.

24. In the Application Log Properties dialog box, under Log Size, enter a Maximum Log Size of **2048**, and activate the Overwrite Events As Needed option.

25. Click OK and then close the Event Viewer.

26. Launch the Performance tool from the Administrative Tools program group.

27. In the console tree, make sure System Monitor is selected, and then, in the chart, click the plus sign (+) to display the Add Counters dialog box.

28. By default, the counter % Processor Time is selected from the Processor object. Click Add.

29. In the Add Counters dialog box, under Performance Object, select MSExchangeIS.

30. From the Select Counters From List list box, select User Count, which displays the number of users connected to this Information Store, and then click Add.

31. In the Select Counters From Computer list box, type **\\BLUESKY-SRV2**. Select the User Count counter for this server's MSExchangeIS, and click Add. If a System Monitor Control dialog box appears informing you that the data collection takes longer than expected, click OK.

32. Click Close.

33. Switch to the Service utility, make sure that the Performance tool is still visible on your screen, then right-click Microsoft Exchange Information Store, and select Start.

    At this point, you can notice some processor activities on the local machine because several important Exchange 2000 services are starting (see Figure 12.5). The number of users, however, remains null because no users are currently working with the test environment.

34. Close the Services utility and the Performance tool.

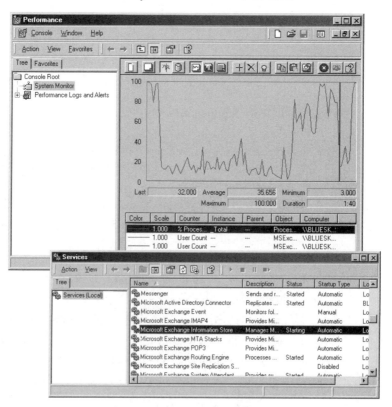

Figure 12.5   Checking the system performance with the Performance utility

35. Click Start, point to Run, and, in the Run dialog box, type **ntbackup**. Click OK.

36. In the Backup utility, click on the Backup tab.

37. In the left pane, expand all nodes under Microsoft Exchange Server.

38. Notice that you are able to back up the existing storage groups of all servers over the network (see Figure 12.6).

39. Select the Microsoft Information Store under BLUESKY-SRV1 and BLUESKY-SRV2.

40. Under Backup Destination, make sure File is selected (this exercise assumes that no tape drives are installed on your test computer; otherwise, you may select your backup media instead and skip Step 41).

41. Click Browse, and, in the Open dialog box, under File Name, type **C:\Exchange Backup\Online Backup**, then click Open.

42. Click Start Backup, and, in the Backup Job Information dialog box, click Start Backup again.

43. If a Folder Does Not Exist dialog box appears, click Yes to create the folder (C:\Exchange Backup).

44. When the backup operation is complete, click Report in the Backup Progress dialog box to verify the success of the backup and the performance.

45. Close all applications and log off from Windows 2000.

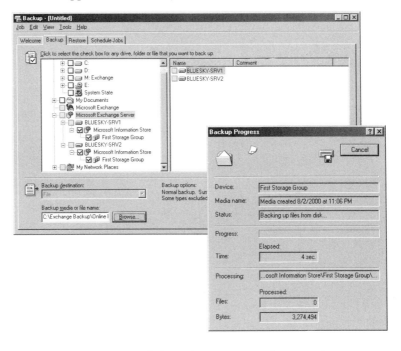

Figure 12.6 Backing up information stores over the network

Exercise Summary

Most of the standard Windows 2000 utilities are extended when Exchange 2000 Server is installed. Others, such as the Services tool, don't require extensions. The Active Directory Users and Computers snap-in is one of the most important standard management utilities because it allows you to manage user accounts in your Windows 2000 environment. The Exchange 2000 Setup program extends this tool to enable the administrator to manage mailbox resources. The filter capabilities of the Active Directory Users and Computers snap-in are very powerful and can help you facilitate the maintenance of recipient objects. You could, for instance, select all user accounts without an Exchange Home Server conveniently and create mailboxes for all of them at once. The management of mailboxes is covered in Chapter 13, "Creating and Managing Recipients."

Lesson 2: Exchange 2000 Tools and Snap-Ins

Dedicated management tools for Exchange 2000 Server are installed during a typical server or custom installation when you select the Microsoft Exchange System Management Tools on the Component Selection page of the Setup Wizard. You don't need to set up an entire server to install the management utilities. For flexible administration of distributed Exchange 2000 servers, put the Exchange System Manager on your workstation PC. In fact, many administrators appreciate the convenience of managing their environment from the desktop. However, your workstation must run under Windows 2000 because other operating systems are not supported. You can read more about the installation of Exchange 2000 components in Chapter 5, "Installing Microsoft Exchange 2000 Server."

This lesson briefly lists the Exchange System Management Tools and focuses on the most important Exchange 2000 management utility—the Exchange System Manager. Among other things, you will learn how the System Manager provides the administrator with management capabilities. The features of the Exchange System Manager are illustrated throughout this book.

At the end of this lesson, you will be able to:

- List the Exchange System Management Tools and describe their purpose.
- Explain how the stand-alone Exchange System snap-in is extended to provide the full set of Exchange 2000 administration features.
- Use the Exchange System Manager to configure server policies.

Estimated time to complete this lesson: 45 minutes

Exchange System Management Tools

In a typical installation, four shortcuts to management tools are created in the Microsoft Exchange program group: Active Directory Cleanup Wizard, Active Directory Users and Computers, Migration Wizard, and System Manager. The Active Directory Cleanup Wizard allows you to merge duplicate user accounts that might have been created during a phase of coexistence with Exchange Server 5.5, as explained in Chapter 6, "Coexistence with Previous Microsoft Exchange Server Versions." The Migration Wizard enables you to migrate user data and address information from foreign mail systems. The Active Directory Users and Computers shortcut points to the USERS AND COMPUTERS.MSC file, which launches the Active Directory Users and Computers snap-in that was introduced earlier in this chapter. By default, the USERS AND COMPUTERS.MSC file resides in the \Program Files\Exchsrvr\Bin directory. The System Manager utility, to complete the list, is the universal administration tool that enables you basically to manage all aspects of your Exchange 2000 Server platform.

Management Tools and Outlook 2000

The Exchange System Management Tools come with a new version of Messaging Application Programming Interface (MAPI) that causes Outlook 2000 to display warning messages. Because those conflicts cannot be resolved, it is not advisable to install Outlook 2000 and the Exchange System Management Tools on the same computer. Windows 2000 Terminal Services, for instance, enables you to manage Exchange 2000 resources remotely without directly deploying the management utilities for Exchange 2000 Server on the workstation. Terminal Services also gives you the option to manage the whole organization remotely from a computer running Microsoft Windows 98, Windows NT Workstation, or any other supported operating system.

Exchange 2000 Snap-Ins

The management tools in the Microsoft Exchange program group are only the tip of the iceberg. To check out the components that actually perform the work, click Start, select Run, and type **mmc** in the Run dialog box. Click OK to launch the MMC. Click Console and select Add/Remove Snap-In. In the Add/Remove Snap-In dialog box, click Add, and, from the Available Standalone Snap-Ins list, select Exchange System. Click Add, examine the options in the Change Domain Controller dialog box, accept the defaults by clicking OK, and then click Close. In the Add/Remove Snap-In dialog box, click on the Extensions tab. From the Snap-Ins That Can Be Extended list box, select Exchange System. In the Available Extensions list box, notice that the Exchange System Manager relies on 19 extension snap-ins to unfold its capabilities.

Let's go ahead and experiment a little. Deselect the Add All Extensions check box, clear all the check boxes from the Available Extensions list, then click OK to return to the management console. Without extensions, the Exchange System snap-in gives a rather lean impression. You can configure global settings, such as Internet Message Formats, and define parameters for outgoing and incoming messages via the Message Delivery object. However, apart from that, the server properties, and the Connectors container, which allows you to add messaging connectors to the configuration, not much of the original Exchange System Manager's functionality remains.

Extensions of Extensions

Extension snap-ins can also extend the functionality of other extensions. For illustration, let's continue the previous example. Click Console again and select the Add/Remove Snap-In command. In the Add/Remove Snap-In dialog box, double-click Blue Sky Airlines (Exchange), and then click on the Extensions tab. Select the Add All Extensions check box, and then, from the Snap-Ins That Can Be Extended list box, select Exchange Protocols. Notice that this extension snap-in relies in turn on eight other extensions. Click OK and then close the MMC without saving the results of the experiment.

Snap-In Registration

With stand-alone snap-ins relying on extensions, which in turn rely on other extension snap-ins, how many MMC components does the Exchange 2000 Setup program register on the local computer when installing the Microsoft Exchange System Management Tools? To count the registered Exchange snap-ins, launch the Registry Editor (REGEDIT.EXE), and open the following key:

```
HKEY_LOCAL_MACHINE

 \SOFTWARE

  \Microsoft

   \MMC

    \SnapIns
```

All MMC snap-ins must be registered in this location. From the Edit menu, select Find, and, in the Find dialog box under Find What, type **Exchange**, then click OK. The Exchange Schedule+ FreeBusy Connector snap-in will be found first. Press F3 to continue the search and advance through the entries. The Setup program of Exchange 2000 has registered 29 snap-ins in the Windows 2000 MMC.

Note   Most of the management components for Exchange 2000 Server are implemented in a single DLL called EXADMIN.DLL, which resides in the \Program Files\Exchsrvr\Bin directory.

Exchange System Manager and Active Directory Directory Service

Exchange System Manager must communicate with a Windows 2000 domain controller to maintain configuration information. Changes are first written to the domain controller that is selected by default and then replicated to the other domain controllers in the forest. The Active Directory replication process performs this job.

As explained earlier, you can specify the domain and domain controller in the Change Domain Controller dialog box when adding the Exchange System snap-in to a custom management console. In a single forest environment, it is usually sufficient to accept the default settings and allow the System Manager to connect to any writeable domain controller. However, you have the option of changing the domain and selecting a specific computer. Because configuration changes are replicated to all domain controllers in a forest, it is typically not required that you connect to a particular machine explicitly (see Figure 12.7).

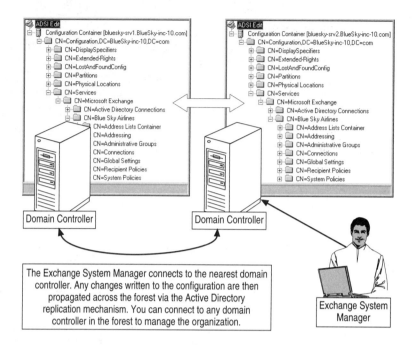

Figure 12.7   Changing the Exchange 2000 Server configuration

The Exchange System Manager Window

When you launch Exchange System Manager, a window with two panes is displayed as a child window of the MMC. This is the Exchange System Manager window, which shows the directory information of the Exchange 2000 organization from the selected domain controller.

Note   Exchange 2000 configuration information is stored in the Microsoft Exchange container under Services in the Configuration partition of Active Directory. You can use Active Directory Sites and Services or the ADSI Edit utility to view the complete directory tree.

New Window From Here

The MMC is capable of displaying multiple Exchange System Manager windows at the same time. Just right-click the desired node and, from the shortcut menu, select New Window From Here, which opens a new Exchange System Manager window with the right-clicked object as the root of the console tree. This feature allows you to focus on the tasks you want to accomplish during a particular session. For instance, if you only want to manage public folders, right-click the Folders object, and select New Window From Here. A new window is displayed, providing access to public folders only. The management of public folders is the topic of Chapter 17, "Public Folder Management."

Hidden Directory Objects

Unlike the ADSI Edit utility, which generally displays the complete set of directory objects, Exchange System Manager suppresses several structures by default to simplify the console tree. To give an example, in an organization with only one administrative and one routing group, these containers are not displayed. To work with these structures, right-click the organization object, such as Blue Sky Airlines (Exchange) on the top of the console tree, and select the Properties command. In the General tab, activate the Display Routing Groups and Display Administrative Groups check boxes. An Exchange System Manager dialog box will appear, informing you that you need to restart the program. Click OK.

Notwithstanding the Exchange System Manager notification, the containers called Administrative Groups, underneath First Administrative Group, Routing Groups, and again underneath First Routing Group are displayed in the console tree immediately. However, it is a good idea to follow Exchange System Manager's advice; otherwise, you might be confronted with unnecessary error messages when continuing the administration. The configuration of administrative and routing groups is covered in Chapter 14, "Managing the Server Configuration."

System Policies

Administrative groups within Exchange System Manager allow you to configure multiple Exchange 2000 servers from a central point of view by creating a single or multiple system policies. A particular system policy applies to all those servers that are associated with it. System policies can simplify the work, especially if you have to manage numerous servers in an administrative group. Instead of applying the same or similar settings multiple times, create one policy, configure the settings once, and then apply the policy to those computers to which it is relevant (see Figure 12.8).

Note The property sheets for mailbox and public store policies correspond to those displayed for each individual mailbox or public store when right-clicking on the store and selecting the Properties command. Some settings, such as database locations, however, can only be applied to individual stores and are deactivated in the store policies.

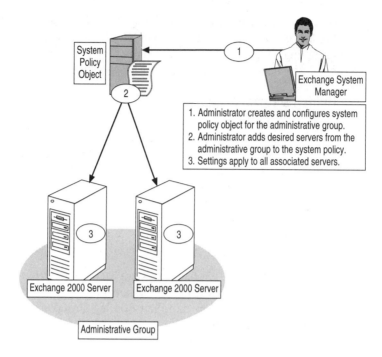

Figure 12.8   Configuring system policies for multiple Exchange 2000 servers

Creating the System Policies Container

System policies are maintained in the System Policies container. By default, however, this container does not exist. You need to add it explicitly to your administrative group by right-clicking the group, pointing to New, and then selecting System Policies Container. Right-clicking the System Policies Container and pointing to New, you can create new server, public store, and mailbox store policies.

Server Policies

Server policies serve the purpose of maintaining message tracking options for multiple servers. Message tracking is a feature that logs information about message transfers in a tracking log file. When enabled, tracking logs are written to the \Program Files\Exchsrvr\<SERVER NAME>.LOG directory (for example, \Program Files\Exchsrvr\BLUESKY-SRV1.LOG) that is shared as <SERVER NAME>.LOG for network access. Every day a new log file is created, named according to the format YYYYMMDD.LOG. You can use the Message Tracking Center to access the <SERVER NAME>.LOG share on all Exchange 2000 servers over the network and track the flow of messages across your organization. The Message Tracking Center is covered in Chapter 20, "Microsoft Exchange 2000 Maintenance and Troubleshooting."

Mailbox Store Policies

Mailbox store policies give you the ability to schedule database maintenance cycles, define storage limits, and configure full-text indexing, among other things. The management of mailbox resources is the topic of Chapter 13, "Creating and Managing Recipients."

You can configure the following tabs for mailbox store policies:

- **General.**   To specify a default public store (see Chapter 17, "Public Folder Management") and an offline address list (see Chapter 14, "Managing Server Configuration"), and to archive all messages sent by users that fall under this policy. Message archiving allows you to keep a history of all the e-mail communication in an organization. You can save the messages in an archival mailbox or public folder. In addition you can specify whether your users' messaging clients support Secure/Multipurpose Internet Mail Extensions (S/MIME) signatures (which is usually the case) and whether to display plain text messages in a fixed-size font.

- **Database.**   To specify the maintenance interval during which the system attendant will defragment the databases online of the servers placed under this policy. (All other settings are deactivated because they are specific to the individual servers.)

- **Limits.**   To set storage quotas (for storage warnings, prohibit send, and prohibit send and receive) and set the warning message interval. You also have the option of defining retention times for deleted items (see Chapter 20, "Microsoft Exchange 2000 Server Maintenance and Troubleshooting").

- **Full-Text Indexing.**   To specify an update interval and a rebuild interval during which the Indexing service refreshes its indexes for the data in mailboxes on the servers placed under this policy.

Public Store Policies

Public store policies enable you to configure similar settings to mailbox store policies. You can configure database maintenance cycles, storage limits, retention times, and full-text indexing. In addition, you can configure a public folder replication interval and replication limits. Public store administration is covered in Chapter 17, "Public Folder Management."

You can configure the following tabs for public store policies:

- **General.**   To specify that messaging clients support S/MIME signatures and whether to display plain text messages in a fixed-size font.

- **Database.**   To specify the maintenance interval during which the system attendant will defragment the databases online.

- **Replication.**   To set a replication interval during which new, modified, and deleted items are replicated to other instances of the same public folders across the organization, and to specify replication limits for the interval and the message sizes. Public folder replication is covered in detail in Chapter 18, "Public Folder Replication."

- **Limits.**   To set storage quotas (for storage warnings to public folder contacts, prohibit post, and maximum item size) and set the warning interval. You also have the option of defining retention times and age limits for deleted items.

- **Full-Text Indexing.**   To specify an update interval and a rebuild interval during which the Indexing service refreshes its indexes for the data in public folders on the servers placed under this policy.

Policy Conflicts

When configuring multiple policies for different configuration scenarios, specific settings in two policies might exclude each other. For example, you may specify to archive messages in one policy and not in another. Exchange System Manager protects you from assigning a single server to multiple conflicting policies. When you add the object to a conflicting policy, a warning message will be displayed. You have the choice of removing the object from all other conflicting policies or refusing the removal and not adding the server to the current policy.

Exercise 2: Defining a Server Policy for Message Tracking

In this exercise you will define a server policy for message tracking across multiple Exchange 2000 servers. You will use Exchange System Manager to manage settings for an entire administrative group.

To view a multimedia demonstration that displays how to perform this procedure, run the EX2CH12.AVI files from the \Exercise_Information\Chapter12 folder on the Supplemental Course Materials CD.

Prerequisites

- Exchange 2000 Server is installed and operational on BLUESKY-SRV1 and you are logged on as Administrator.

- It is assumed that the Administrative Groups container is not displayed in the console tree of the Exchange System Manager (otherwise, skip Steps 1 through 5).

 To configure server policies for the first administrative group

1. Click the Start button, point to Programs, point to Microsoft Exchange, and then click System Manager.

2. In the Exchange System Manager, right-click Blue Sky Airlines (Exchange), and then select Properties.

3. Select the Display Administrative Groups check box, and then click OK.

4. In the Exchange System Manager dialog box that is informing you that you need to restart the Microsoft Exchange System Manager, click OK.

5. Close and restart the Exchange System Manager.

6. In Exchange System Manager, expand Administrative Groups, and then right-click on First Administrative Group.

7. In the shortcut menu, point to New, and then select System Policy Container.

8. A new container object called System Policies is added to the First Administrative Group. Right-click it, point to New, and then select Server Policy.

9. In the New Policy dialog box, select the General check box, and then click OK.

10. In the General tab, type **Message Tracking Policy**, and then click on the General (Policy) tab.

11. Enable the Enable Subject Logging And Display, Enable Message Tracking, and Remove Log Files check boxes, and then, under Remove Files Older Than (Messages), type **7**.

12. Click OK and verify that a new policy object has been created in the System Policy container (see Figure 12.9).

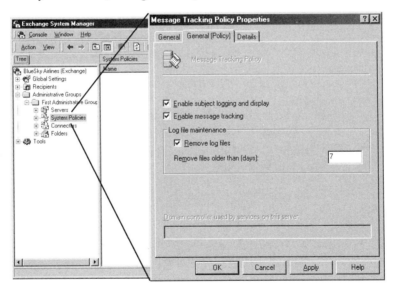

Figure 12.9   Creating a system policy for message tracking

13. Right-click Message Tracking Policy, and, from the shortcut menu, select Add Server.

14. In the Select The Items To Place Under The Control Of This Policy dialog box, from the upper list, select all server objects, and then click Add.

15. Verify that all existing servers are listed in the lower list, and then click OK.

At this point, you have configured a policy for message tracking, which causes all servers in the First Administrative Group to keep a history of messages that pass through the local system (see Figure 12.10).

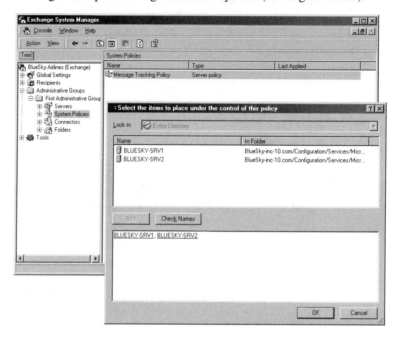

Figure 12.10   Placing servers under the control of a policy

16. In the Exchange System Manager dialog box asking you whether you are sure you want to add the times to this policy, click Yes.

17. Right-click Message Tracking Policy again, and, from the shortcut menu, select Apply Now.

18. In the console tree, open the System Policies container, and select Message Tracking Policy. Notice that all the Exchange 2000 servers from the First Administrative Group are listed in the contents pane.

19. In the console tree, right-click the System Policies container, point to New, and select Server Policy again.

20. In the New Policy dialog box, select General, and then click OK.

21. In the General tab, type **Conflict Policy**. Do not specify any other settings, and click OK.

22. Right-click Conflict Policy and then select Add Server.

23. Select BLUESKY-SRV1, click Add, and then click OK.

24. In the Exchange System Manager dialog box asking you whether you want to add items to this policy, click Yes.

25. Notice the Exchange System Manager conflict warning that the object BLUESKY-SRV1 is already under the control of another policy. The message tracking policy is listed (see Figure 12.11). Click No to leave BLUESKY-SRV1 under the control of the message tracking policy.

26. In the Exchange System Manager dialog box informing you that the object BLUESKY-SRV1 could not be associated with the conflict policy because you refused to remove the object from the control of conflicting policies, click OK.

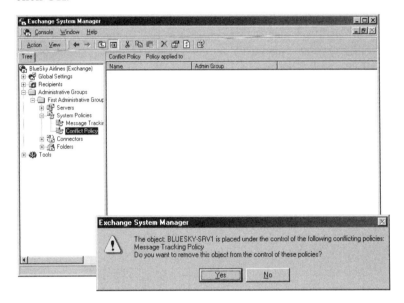

Figure 12.11   Resolving a policy conflict

Exercise Summary

Administrative groups assemble Exchange 2000 servers for easier administration. One way to achieve simplified system management is to configure system policies and apply them to multiple servers. Server policies, for instance, serve the purpose of enabling message tracking to trace the path a message has taken through the organization. Exchange System Manager will protect you from assigning a single server object to multiple conflicting policies.

Chapter Summary

Exchange 2000 administrators are Windows 2000 administrators. Consequently, they need to be familiar with the common management tools for Windows 2000 and the utilities specific to Exchange 2000 Server. A typical tool set includes Active Directory Users and Computers, Computer Management, Event Viewer, Performance, Services, Task Manager, and the Backup utility. For advanced administration tasks, Registry editors and the ADSI Edit utility are available.

The Setup program of Exchange 2000 extends the administrative environment through numerous stand-alone and extension snap-ins. Extended Windows 2000 utilities, such as Active Directory Users and Computers and the Computer Management tool, will allow you to manage a subset of Exchange 2000 resources. Exchange System Manager, on the other hand, loads most of the Exchange-related snap-ins and enables you to manage all aspects of your messaging organization. This utility supports system policies, which can streamline your work as an Exchange 2000 administrator.

Review

The following review questions can help you determine if you have sufficiently familiarized yourself with the material covered in this chapter. You can find the answers to these questions at the end of this book in Appendix A, "Questions and Answers."

1. You want to configure an entire Exchange 2000 Server organization using Exchange System Manager on your Windows NT Workstation computer. How do you install this program and which of the existing servers in your organization can be configured?

2. You add new memory (RAM) to a computer running Exchange 2000 Server. The server performance has not been improved, so you are wondering which component might create the actual bottleneck. Which utility can you use to determine the critical component?

3. You want to manage the available disk space across all of the servers in your administrative group. Therefore, you want to define storage limits. How can you define storage limits for all these servers with minimal effort?

4. A supervisor in the marketing department calls and wants to know whether Fred Pumpkin is working online. You will need to view information about currently logged-on users. Which object provides the fastest access to the desired information?

C H A P T E R   1 3

Creating and Managing Recipients

About This Chapter

Recipient objects are an integral part of any messaging system. They form the address lists from which users can pick message recipients, against which client programs can resolve recipient addresses, and through which message transfer processes learn where to deliver messages. Microsoft Exchange 2000 Server maintains its recipient information entirely in the Active Directory directory service. This allows you, among other things, to add mailbox information to a newly created user account in the Active Directory Users and Computers snap-in.

Windows 2000 Enterprise and Domain Admins are Exchange 2000 administrators by default. In other words, every domain administrator can create, move, and delete user accounts plus mailboxes in his or her home domain. Every enterprise administrator can perform the same actions across the whole forest, including all associated domains. The delegation of Exchange 2000-related permissions was covered in Chapter 4, "Planning the Microsoft Exchange 2000 Server Installation."

This chapter concentrates on the management of recipient objects in Active Directory. Available recipient objects and their characteristics are introduced and resource management tasks are discussed.

Before You Begin

To complete this chapter:

- Prepare your test environment according to the descriptions given in the "Getting Started" section of "About This Book."

- You need a general understanding of how Microsoft Outlook 2000 accesses address information from Global Catalog servers, and you need to be familiar with the concepts of Active Directory and Global Catalog replication (see Chapter 3, "Microsoft Exchange 2000 Server Architecture").

Lesson 1: Configuring Recipient Objects

Sometimes, professionals use slightly incorrect statements to avoid painfully precise and lengthy explanations. For example, when working with Active Directory Users and Computers, you will come across an option to create a mailbox for each selected user. You may believe that you are creating mailboxes; in reality, it's all a little different. Otherwise, how can you create a mailbox when the specified home server is shut down? (See Exercise 1 of this chapter.)

This lesson focuses on the management of recipient objects in Active Directory. You can read about how to add mailbox information and e-mail addresses to user accounts, contacts, and groups.

At the end of this lesson, you will be able to:

- Configure mailbox-enabled user accounts.
- Configure mail-enabled user accounts, contacts, and groups.

Estimated time to complete this lesson: 60 minutes

Overview of Recipient Objects

Potential recipient objects in Active Directory are user accounts, contacts, and groups. They become recipient objects when you add e-mail address information to them. A fourth type of recipient object exists when Exchange 2000 Server is installed, the public folder. Typically, public folders reside in a hidden organizational unit (OU) called Microsoft Exchange System Objects. Public folders do not necessarily own an e-mail address, but if they do, they are hidden from the address lists by default. They are usually not managed in Active Directory Users and Computers. You can read about public folder management in Chapter 17, "Public Folder Management."

Mailbox-Enabled Recipient Objects

Generally, mailbox-enabled objects are user-account objects with associated mailbox information. It is not possible to assign Exchange mailbox resources to any other object type. Mailbox-enabled accounts possess corresponding e-mail addresses and can be used to send and receive messages in an Exchange organization.

Mail-Enabled Recipient Objects

A mail-enabled object is in possession of an e-mail address but isn't associated with an Exchange mailbox. You can assign e-mail addresses to user account objects, contacts, and groups. When connecting to a third-party messaging system, such as Lotus Notes, installed in your Windows 2000 environment, you typically assign e-mail addresses to the Windows 2000 accounts of those users that work with mailboxes in the foreign system (see Figure 13.1). Exchange users can then pick the corresponding recipient information from the Global Address List (GAL) to send them messages. Directory synchronization can help facilitate the task of adding e-mail addresses to Active Directory accounts, explained in Chapters 26 through 29.

Unlike mail-enabled user accounts, mail-enabled contacts are not referring to users working in your Windows 2000 environment. They are usually a representation for recipients that exist outside the organization's own messaging network, such as partners, customers, and other users (on the Internet, for example). In fact, it is impossible to create a mail-enabled contact that references a mailbox- or mail-enabled user account within the same organization because a single e-mail address cannot be associated with multiple recipient objects.

Mail-enabled Windows 2000 groups, on the other hand, provide a convenient way to address multiple recipients at one time. Active Directory supports security and distribution groups with a domain-local, global, or universal scope. You can add e-mail address information to all types of groups. The difference is that security groups can be used to delegate access permissions to members, while distribution groups do not represent security principals and don't support permission assignments. Groups provide a way to reflect, to some degree, the structure of a company in terms of its departments and project teams.

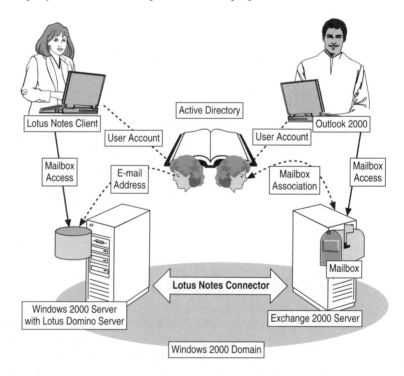

Figure 13.1 Differences between mailbox-enabled and mail-enabled user accounts

Creating Mailbox- and Mail-Enabled Recipient Objects

The creation of mailbox- and mail-enabled recipient objects is parallel to the creation of user accounts, contacts, and groups. However, especially for mail-enabled recipients, some thought needs to be given to the type of directory object to create.

Creating Mailbox-Enabled Recipients

For mailbox-enabled objects, the only answer is user accounts. Launch Active Directory Users and Computers, expand the console tree, right-click the desired container, such as Users, point to New, and select the User command. In the first and second dialog boxes, enter the Windows 2000 account information as usual. After that, if you have installed the Microsoft Exchange System Management Tools on the computer, a third dialog box will appear, asking you whether and where to create a mailbox for the new user. Ensure that the Create An Exchange Mailbox check box is selected and that the displayed information is correct, and then click Next, and click Finish. The new Windows 2000 user can participate in your Exchange organization immediately.

To add mailbox information to an existing user account, on the other hand, right-click the corresponding directory object and, from the shortcut menu, select Exchange Tasks. This will launch the Exchange Task Wizard. Click Next on the welcome screen (if it appears), and, on the Available Tasks wizard screen, select the Create Mailbox option, and click Next. Make sure the settings are correct, and then click Next, and click Finish.

Mailbox-Enabled Recipients and Mailbox Resources

As mentioned earlier, when adding mailbox information to a user account, you are not really creating the actual mailbox resource. Recipient objects reside in Active Directory, whereas mailboxes are repositories in the Information Store. However, by mailbox-enabling a user account, you identify, among other things, the particular mailbox store to hold the mailbox. When the user launches his or her client program, such as Outlook 2000, and logs on, the client retrieves the mailbox information from Active Directory, then contacts the correct Information Store and requests the generation of the actual mailbox. The client will initialize the mailbox folders according to the client language (Inbox, Outbox, Contacts, and so on, for an English client).

Note The first client that accesses a mailbox creates and names the system folders according to its language. They will retain their names until you rename them manually. For instance, if you initialized your mailbox using a French client, your system folders will show French names, even if you work with an English client subsequently. Microsoft Exchange Client 5.0 allows you to rename the system folders (Outlook 2000 doesn't).

Creating Mail-Enabled Recipients

To create a mail-enabled user account, make sure you deselect the Create An Exchange Mailbox check box during account creation. This results in a new account object without associated mailbox information. Right-click the object, select Exchange Tasks, and confirm the welcome screen (if it appears) by clicking Next. On the Available Tasks wizard screen, double-click Establish E-Mail Addresses. On the Establish E-Mail Addresses wizard screen, click Modify, and, in the New E-Mail Address dialog box, double-click the correct type entry (such as Lotus Notes Address), and specify the correct address (such as a user name and Lotus Notes domain). Click OK, then click Next, and then click Finish. The creation of a mail-enabled user account requires slightly more attention than the configuration of a mailbox-enabled account because you need to enter the address information manually. It may be better to migrate the users to Exchange 2000 Server first and then create mailbox-enabled accounts.

The procedure to assign e-mail addresses to security or distribution groups differs from the course of action for mail-enabled user accounts. Right-click the desired group, select Exchange Tasks, and confirm the welcome screen (select the Do Not Show This Welcome Page Again check box if you like). Double-click Establish An E-Mail Address, and, on the Establish An E-Mail Address wizard screen, specify the desired alias. If you are mail-enabling a global or local group (such as Domain Users or Users), read the following note on the Establish An E-Mail Address wizard screen carefully: Usage Of Mail-Enabled Universal Groups Is Strongly Recommended To Ensure Correct Mail Delivery. Later in this lesson, under "Working with Distribution Lists," you can find a discussion about the advantages and disadvantages of mail-enabled universal, global, and local groups.

Managing and Maintaining Mailbox-Enabled Recipients

When you display the properties of a mailbox-enabled user account, you can find three Exchange-related tabs: Exchange General, E-Mail Addresses, and Exchange Features. A fourth tab exists, but it is hidden by default—Exchange Advanced. To display all Exchange tabs, select Advanced Features, available under the Microsoft Management Console (MMC) View button, before displaying the account properties.

For mailbox-enabled user accounts, the following tabs are provided:

- **E-Mail Addresses.** To view, add, and manage e-mail addresses for the account object, such as Simple Mail Transfer Protocol (SMTP) and X.400 addresses.

- **Exchange Advanced.**   To specify a simple display name, hide the account from Exchange address lists, downgrade high priority mail bound for X.400, and to define custom attributes, protocol settings, Internet Locator Service (ILS) settings, and mailbox rights.

- **Exchange Features.**   To enable or disable specific advanced features, such as Instant Messaging (see Chapter 25, "Real-Time Collaboration").

- **Exchange General.**   To change the mailbox alias and to set delivery restrictions, delivery options, and storage limits.

Exercise 1: Managing and Maintaining Mailboxes

In this exercise you will use the Active Directory Users and Computers snap-in to add mailbox information to a new user account. You will create a mailbox on a server that is currently unavailable.

To view a multimedia demonstration that displays how to perform this procedure, run the EX1CH13.AVI files from the \Exercise_Information\Chapter13 folder on the Supplemental Course Materials CD.

Prerequisites

- Exchange 2000 Server is installed and operational on BLUESKY-SRV1 and BLUESKY-SRV2.

- Log on as Administrator to BLUESKY-SRV1.

- Make sure BLUESKY-SRV2 is NOT running.

▶ **To create and manage mailbox resources**

1. Launch the Active Directory Users and Computers snap-in from the Microsoft Exchange program group.

2. In the console tree, expand BlueSky-inc-10.com, and then select Users.

3. Right-click the Users container, point to New, and then select User.

4. In the New Object – User dialog box, enter the following information:

First Name	**Olivia**
Last Name	**Owl**
Full Name	**Olivia Owl**
User Logon Name	**OliviaO**

5. Click Next.

6. On the next wizard screen, under Password and Confirm Password, type **password**, and then click Next.

7. On the next wizard screen, make sure that Create An Exchange Mailbox is selected. From the Server list box, select Blue Sky Airlines/First Administrative Group/BLUESKY-SRV2. Notice that the Mailbox Store information is updated automatically, and then click Next.

8. On the last wizard screen, click Finish.

   At this point, you have created a new Windows 2000 user account for Olivia Owl and associated this account with a mailbox in the Information Store on server BLUESKY-SRV2, although BLUESKY-SRV2 is not running at this point (see Figure 13.2).

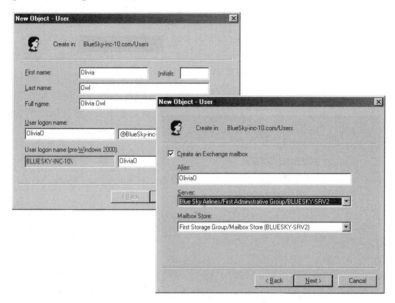

Figure 13.2   Creating user accounts and associated mailboxes

9. Start the computer BLUESKY-SRV2 and wait until it is operational.

10. In the Active Directory Users and Computers utility, make sure the contents of the Users container are displayed in the contents pane, right-click Olivia Owl, and then select Exchange Tasks.

11. On the welcome screen, click Next.

12. On the Available Tasks wizard screen, make sure that Move Mailbox is selected, and then click Next.

13. On the Move Mailbox wizard screen, accept the suggestions to move the mailbox to BLUESKY-SRV1, and then click Next (see Figure 13.3).

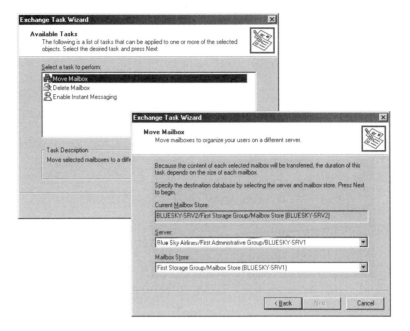

Figure 13.3   Using the Exchange Task Wizard to move mailboxes

14. When The Task In Progress wizard screen appears, follow the progress of the mailbox transfer, and then, on the Completing The Exchange Task wizard screen, click Finish.

15. In the Active Directory Users and Computers snap-in, click View, and select Advanced Features.

16. Open the Users container again and double-click the Olivia Owl user account.

17. Notice the four Exchange tabs called Exchange General, E-Mail Addresses, Exchange Features, and Exchange Advanced.

18. Click on the Exchange Advanced tab, and then click Protocol Settings.

19. In the Protocols dialog box, select the HTTP protocol entry (see Figure 13.4), and then click Settings.

20. In the HTTP Protocol Details dialog box, deselect the Enable For Mailbox check box, and then click OK. Repeat this step for the IMAP4 and POP3 protocol entries as well.

21. Click OK twice. From this point forward, the user Olivia Owl will only be able to access her mailbox using Outlook 2000 or any other Messaging Application Programming Interface (MAPI)-based client.

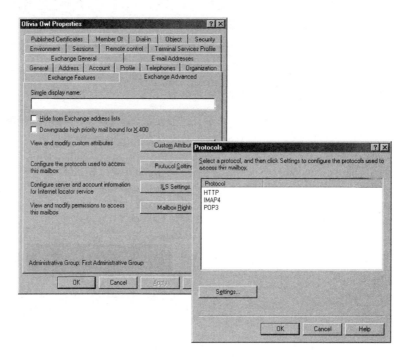

Figure 13.4   Configuring Internet Protocol settings for mailboxes

Exercise Summary

You can create mailbox resources at the same time you create user accounts. The Exchange 2000 server does not even have to be available to associate a user account with a mailbox. The Exchange Task Wizard greatly facilitates mailbox maintenance tasks. You can move one or many mailboxes between servers quickly and conveniently. To adjust mailbox settings, use the Exchange-specific tabs of the mailbox-enabled user account object.

Managing and Maintaining Mail-Enabled Recipients

With minimal differences, the management of mail-enabled recipient objects is performed similar to the administration of mailbox-enabled user accounts.

Managing Mail-Enabled User Accounts and Contacts

Mail-enabled user accounts are very similar to mailbox-enabled objects; they just don't have an Exchange mailbox—yet. However, they can participate in Instant Messaging because this feature is not bound to a particular Exchange mailbox. You can activate this function in the Exchange Features tab if Instant Messaging is installed.

For mail-enabled user accounts, you can configure the following settings:

- **E-Mail Addresses.** To view, add, and manage e-mail addresses for the account object (such as SMTP and X.400 addresses).

- **Exchange Advanced.** To specify a simple display name, hide the account from Exchange address lists, specify whether the user's client program is able to use MAPI rich text format, and to define custom attributes and ILS settings.

- **Exchange Features.** To enable or disable specific features such as Instant Messaging.

- **Exchange General.** To change the alias, to set incoming message size restrictions, and to specify from whom to accept messages.

Note With the exception of the Exchange Features tab, which doesn't apply to users outside the organization, mail-enabled contact objects provide access to the same configuration settings as mail-enabled user accounts.

Managing Mail-Enabled Groups

Mail-enabled groups don't provide access to the Exchange Features tab because Instant Messaging applies to users, not to groups. The Exchange Advanced tab also shows a slightly different layout. The Exchange General and E-Mail Addresses tabs, however, are identical with the property sheets of the other mail-enabled object types.

The Exchange Advanced tab of a mail-enabled group allows you to configure the following settings:

- **Simple Display Name.** To specify a simple display name for systems that cannot understand special characters set in the regular display name.

- **Expansion Server.** To designate a computer in the organization running Exchange 2000 Server as responsible for distribution list expansion.

- **Hide Group From Exchange Address Lists.** To prevent the members of the group from being displayed in the server-based address lists. It is also advisable to activate the Do Not Send Delivery Reports option.

- **Send Out-Of-Office Messages To Originator.** To send out-of-office notifications to the originator of a message even if the recipient, who is currently out of the office, received the message only because he or she is a member of a distribution list.

- **Send Delivery Reports To Group Owner.** To allow the owner of a mail-enabled group to receive detailed delivery reports and nondelivery reports.

- **Send Delivery Reports To Message Originator.**   To allow the originator of a message to receive delivery reports and nondelivery reports directly from the members of the distribution list rather than from the distribution list itself.

- **Do Not Send Delivery Reports.**   To suppress requested delivery reports and nondelivery reports. This setting is especially important if you want to hide distribution list membership and don't want to disclose the information through delivery reports either.

- **Custom Attributes.**   To add more information to the group than provided through default attributes.

Working with Mail-Enabled Groups

Microsoft recommends mail-enabling universal groups. The most obvious disadvantage of global groups in a multidomain environment is that this type of group cannot contain any recipients from other domains. Groups with a local scope, on the other hand, may contain accounts from other domains but cannot be used in other domains to grant permissions on public folders and other resources. Furthermore, the membership lists of local and global groups are not replicated to the Global Catalog, which restricts their functionality. Outlook users in other domains are unable to retrieve full membership information.

Note   In a single domain environment, no restrictions apply because all Global Catalog servers are domain controllers that contain a full replica of the local domain information.

Membership Information and Group Expansion

Universal security and distribution groups can replicate information about group members to the Global Catalog. This information is then available across the entire forest. The SMTP service can expand these mail-enabled groups to determine the delivery path for each individual recipient. If your users are sending messages to mail-enabled local or global groups, on the other hand, the SMTP service may not be able to retrieve the required information.

If a mail-enabled local or global group from another domain needs to be expanded, the SMTP service must establish a direct connection to a domain controller in that domain. Elsewhere, the required information is not available. The communication takes place via LDAP. Hence, direct IP connectivity is required. Because network communication is involved, group expansion is not performed as fast as if the membership data were available locally. Especially if the group contains numerous members, message delivery may be delayed.

To circumvent the disadvantages of remote expansion over the network, specify an expansion server in the Exchange Advanced tab for local and global groups. Make sure the expansion server exists in the group's home domain. All other

SMTP services in the organization will then forward messages addressed to this mail-enabled group to its expansion server first, which can communicate with a local-domain controller and populate the message header with group membership information. It also makes sense to move the expansion of the larger groups—those with thousands of members—from less powerful to more powerful servers.

Note The Expansion Server Any Server In The Organization setting implies that the home server of the sender performs the expansion.

Considerations About Universal Groups

The advantage of universal groups is that their membership information is replicated to the Global Catalog. This is also a disadvantage, especially if the group is large. For large groups, membership changes can result in excessive replication traffic. The membership information for a group is held in a multivalued property of the group object in Active Directory (see Figure 13.5). When members are added or removed, this attribute changes and the property-level Active Directory replication must transfer the entire list to the Global Catalog again. Consequently, it is not advisable to create gigantic mail-enabled universal groups.

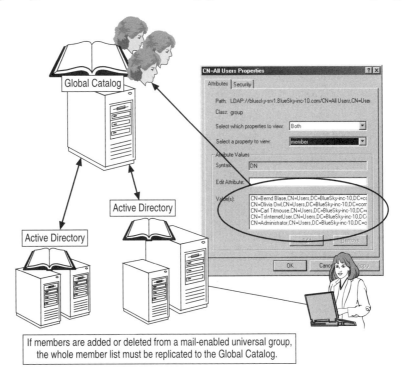

If members are added or deleted from a mail-enabled universal group, the whole member list must be replicated to the Global Catalog.

Figure 13.5 Property-level replication of group membership information

> **Tip**   Microsoft recommends restricting the number of members in mail-enabled groups to less than 5000 to mitigate the risk of excessive network traffic. If more than 5000 members must be included, consider using nested groups.

Nested groups allow you to partition the replication traffic to the Global Catalog. Instead of a single group with 10,000 members, create 10 groups with 1000 members, and then include all of these in an overlay group. When new users are added to one of these groups, only a subset of the membership needs to be replicated while Outlook users can still examine the full membership. Implement global mail-enabled groups instead of universal groups if you need to eliminate the replication traffic. If you change your mind later, you can convert global into universal groups, provided that your domain operates in native mode and that the groups are not members of any other global group.

Security Versus Distribution Groups

Whenever possible, give security groups preference over distribution groups. This allows you to keep the number of groups in your environment at a reasonable level because mail-enabled security groups can serve the purpose of permission assignment as well as message addressing. If you use mail-enabled distribution groups to build your address lists, however, you will have to create separate security groups to manage permissions on resources and public folders. Universal security groups can only be created in native-mode domains.

Exercise 2: Managing and Maintaining Contacts and Groups

In this exercise, you will create contact objects and universal distribution groups and adjust their settings afterward. This exercise suggests the creation of a distribution group to accommodate mixed-mode and native-mode domains.

To view a multimedia demonstration that displays how to perform this procedure, run the EX2CH13*.AVI files from the \Exercise_Information\Chapter13 folder on the Supplemental Course Materials CD.

Prerequisites

- Make sure Exchange 2000 Server is running on BLUESKY-SRV1.
- Log on as Administrator to BLUESKY-SRV1 and BLUESKY-WKSTA.

▶ **To mail-enable contact objects and work with universal distribution groups**

1. On BLUESKY-SRV1, launch the Active Directory Users and Computers snap-in from the Microsoft Exchange program group.

2. Click View and select Advanced Features.

3. Expand the console tree, right-click the Users container, point to New, and select Contact.

4. In the New Object – Contact dialog box, enter the following information:

First Name   **Josephine**

Last Name   **Hummingbird**

Full Name   **Josephine Hummingbird**

Display Name   **JosiH**

5. Click Next, and, in the next dialog box, verify that the Create An Exchange E-Mail Address check box is selected.

6. Click Modify. In the New E-Mail Address dialog box, double-click SMTP Address. In the E-Mail Address box, type **JosiH@External-inc-20.edu**, and then click OK, click Next, and click Finish.

   At this point, you have created a mail-enabled contact object in your Users container (see Figure 13.6). When users address messages to Josephine, these will be delivered to JosiH@External-inc-20.edu outside the local organization.

7. Right-click the Users container again, point to New, and select Group.

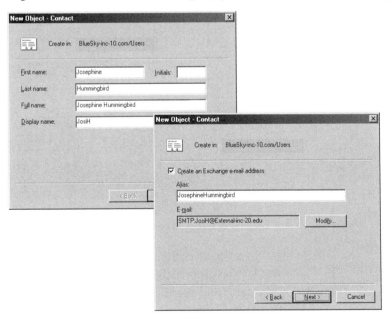

Figure 13.6   Creating a mail-enabled contact

8. In the New Object – Group dialog box, enter the following information:

Group Name	**All Users**
Group Name (pre-Windows 2000)	**All Users**
Group Scope	**Universal**
Group Type	**Distribution**

9. Click Next, and, in the next dialog box, verify that the Create An Exchange E-Mail Address check box is selected, accept the default Alias, click Next, and then click Finish.

   At this point, you have created a mail-enabled universal group (see Figure 13.7). However, this group has no members yet.

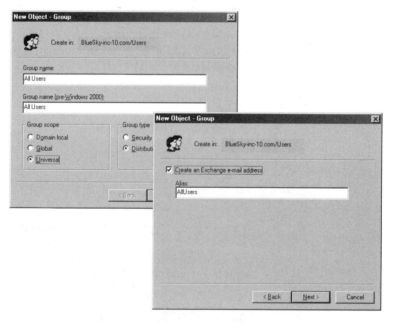

Figure 13.7   Creating a mail-enabled distribution group

10. In the contents pane of the Users container, double-click All Users, and then click on the Managed By tab.

11. Click Change, and select the Administrator account from the domain BlueSky-inc-10.com.

12. Click on the Exchange Advanced tab, and select the Send Out-Of-Office Messages To Originator check box. Click OK.

13. On BLUESKY-WKSTA, launch Outlook 2000, and connect to the Administrator mailbox. If a message box appears asking you whether you would like to use Outlook for Newsgroups, click Yes.

14. From the Tools menu, select Address Book.

15. Double-click All Users to display the All Users Properties dialog box. Notice that the Members list is still empty.

16. Click Modify Members, and, in the Distribution List Membership dialog box, click Add to add the Administrator and JosiH as members to the distribution group.

17. Click OK three times, and close the address book.

   At this point, you are able to add members to the group because you are designated as the group owner (see Figure 13.8).

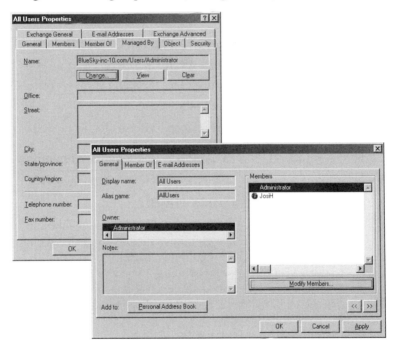

Figure 13.8   Configuring group membership in Outlook 2000

Exercise Summary

The creation of mail-enabled contacts and groups is as easy as the creation of mailbox-enabled user accounts. For groups, don't forget to specify a group owner. This is a useful feature that enables you to delegate the responsibilities of group management to team or department heads. Your valuable time doesn't have to be consumed by the task of keeping track of individual group members. After all, the individual team managers know best who belongs to their group.

Lesson 2: Mailbox and Resource Management

You can manage mailbox resources at different levels in Active Directory Users and Computers and Exchange System Manager. The former gives you the finest granularity. You can use this tool to configure individual mailbox properties. The latter enables you to define default settings for mailbox stores as well as recipient and system policies. Further utilities are available, such as the LDIFDE and CSVDE utilities, which allow you to deal with numerous recipient objects in bulk.

This lesson covers several important aspects that you will come across when managing mailbox resources, including the assignment of permissions to additional user accounts, the definition of storage limits, and the management of default e-mail addresses. The import and export of recipient information are also addressed.

At the end of this lesson, you will be able to:

- Grant user accounts specific permissions on mailbox resources.
- Manage mailbox resources through mailbox store settings and policies.
- Configure the Recipient Update Service.
- Import and export recipient information from Active Directory.

Estimated time to complete this lesson: 75 minutes

Assigning Mailbox Rights

It is advantageous to have the ability to add mailbox information to user accounts upon their creation and remove mailboxes again when their associated accounts are deleted. Yet, the direct mapping of user accounts to Exchange mailboxes has side effects. The overwhelming number of user account property pages, for instance, is not easily comprehensible. Another issue is that it is not trivial to assign a particular account two or more mailboxes.

Configuring a Postmaster Mailbox

It is a good idea to mailbox-enable the general Administrator account and assign it the SMTP service's postmaster address (for example, Postmaster@Bluesky-inc-10.com). As a matter of fact, this is accomplished by default when installing Exchange 2000 Server as Administrator. However, if you have installed your first Exchange 2000 server in the forest using a different account, then this account is currently the postmaster. The postmaster address is used, for instance, in nondelivery reports to indicate delivery problems to the message originator. The originator may then reply to the postmaster address to seek assistance.

It would be inconvenient to use the Administrator mailbox as a personal e-mail account. When working with your own account, though, it is likewise not optimal to have it receiving messages sent to the postmaster. These system messages are not personal. You may even want to share them with other administrators. Therefore, remove the postmaster address from your personal account if you own it currently, and assign it to the Administrator via the E-Mail Addresses tab. After that, grant your account and those of other relevant administrators Full Mailbox Access permissions to the Administrator mailbox, and include it as an additional mailbox into your MAPI profile, as illustrated in Exercise 5 of Chapter 8, "Microsoft Outlook 2000 Deployment."

To successfully open the Administrator mailbox, launch Active Directory Users and Computers, activate Advanced Features, and display the properties of the Administrator. Click on the Exchange Advanced tab, click Mailbox Rights, add your personal account to the list of accounts with Mailbox Rights, and grant yourself the specific Full Mailbox Access right. If you are a Windows 2000 enterprise or domain administrator, you also need to grant your account Send As and Read As permissions on the Security property sheet.

Creating Dedicated, Disabled Mailbox Accounts

You may create disabled user accounts for specific purposes and mailbox-enable them. Then assign your own account the Full Mailbox Access and Read As rights. Although you will not be able to log on using a disabled account, you will be able to open its mailbox and read messages. If you want to send messages on behalf of the disabled account, configure its Delivery Options in the Exchange General tab to grant yourself Send On Behalf permissions (see Chapter 8, "Microsoft Outlook 2000 Deployment").

Management of Server-Based Mailbox Resources

The number of mailboxes that you can put on a single Exchange 2000 Server greatly depends on the available hard disk space. Nevertheless, it is difficult to find out how much hard disk space your users' mailboxes will eventually consume.

Tip The Mailbox Statistics Tool from the BackOffice Resource Kit, which is also included on the companion CD to this book, enables you to gather information about mail-use patterns from your users. This information can help you to size your hardware more precisely.

Single Instance Storage Feature

If you send a particular message to multiple users on the same server, only one copy of the message is initially stored in the database and all local addressees receive a pointer to this particular object. This feature, known as single instance storage, can greatly help improve delivery performance. Instead of delivering a message addressed to 1000 recipients into 1000 mailboxes, the message is delivered once, saving 999 instances of delivery time. Users can access this single message instance and read it just as if it belonged exclusively to them. When they delete the message, only their reference is removed from the single message instance.

However, when calculating the required disk space for your users' mailboxes, ignore the single instance storage feature, and assume that every user receives individual copies of messages. This simplifies the calculation, and actually, the single instance storage feature does not really reduce the requirements for disk space. This may sound astonishing at first, but practice shows that over time the single instance storage ratio is reduced to two or just one recipient per message. Most messages are sent just to one recipient, but consider the following scenario. You send a message to 2000 recipients on a particular Exchange 2000 server informing them that the server will be unavailable due to maintenance next Friday. It is very likely that almost all recipients will delete this message right away, with the exception of those users that never delete a message at all (you will take care of them a little later with storage quotas). After a month, maybe one or at most a few recipients still hold this outdated message in their mailbox. Hence, your single instance storage ratio dropped from 2000 recipients to one or, at most, a few recipients per message. You should not consider the initial ratio of 2000:1 a serious disk space savings.

Tip   The MSExchangeIS Mailbox performance object provides a counter named Single Instance Ratio, which you can use to monitor the single instance storage ratio of your server with the Performance tool that was discussed in Chapter 12, "Management Tools for Microsoft Exchange 2000 Server."

Storage Limits

If your server's disk space is limited, consider applying storage limits. Storage limits allow you to warn your users if their mailbox size exceeds a certain maximum (Issue Warning At [KB]), to prevent them from sending messages (Prohibit Send At [KB]), and to prevent message reception (Prohibit Send And Receive At [KB]). To set these values, display the properties of the desired mailbox store in the Exchange System Manager, and click on the Limits tab. Alternatively, you can define default settings for your servers through system policies (see Chapter 12, "Management Tools for Microsoft Exchange 2000 Server").

Note   You can overrule storage limits assigned to the mailbox store per user account (using the Exchange General tab, Storage Limits button). Users that exceed the limits need to delete messages from the server and may download them into a personal folder store. The configuration of the personal folder store was covered in Chapter 9, "MAPI-Based Clients."

Exercise 3: Configuring Mailbox Storage Limits and Deletion Settings

In this exercise you will define default storage limits for a mailbox store and set deletion settings for items and mailboxes. To test the parameters you will delete items and mailboxes and recover them.

To view a multimedia demonstration that displays how to perform this procedure, run the EX3CH13*.AVI files from the \Exercise_Information\Chapter13 folder on the Supplemental Course Materials CD.

Prerequisites

- Complete Exercise 1, earlier in this chapter.

- Log on as Administrator to BLUESKY-SRV1 and BLUESKY-WKSTA.

▶ **To configure mailbox storage limits and deletion settings**

1. On BLUESKY-SRV1, launch the Exchange System Manager.

2. In the console tree, expand the node for BLUESKY-SRV1 (under Servers in the First Administrative Group), expand First Storage Group, and then right-click Mailbox Store (BLUESKY-SRV1).

3. From the shortcut menu, select Properties, and click on the Limits tab.

4. Select the Issue Warning At (KB) check box and type **10240**.

5. Select the Prohibit Send At (KB) check box and type **20480**.

6. Select the Prohibit Send And Receive At (KB) check box and type **40960**.

7. Notice that the Warning Message Interval will cause the generation of a warning message for users exceeding the mailbox quota at midnight.

8. Under Deletion Settings, in the Keep Deleted Items For (Days) text box, type **7**.

9. In the Keep Deleted Mailboxes for (Days) text box, type **30**.

10. Select the Do Not Permanently Delete Mailboxes And Items Until The Store Has Been Backed Up check box, and then click OK (see Figure 13.9).

11. On BLUESKY-WKSTA, launch Outlook 2000, connect to the Administrator mailbox, and make sure that there is at least one message in the Inbox.

12. Delete the message, open the Deleted Items folder, and notice that the message has not been deleted yet (the user can easily move the message into another Outlook folder).

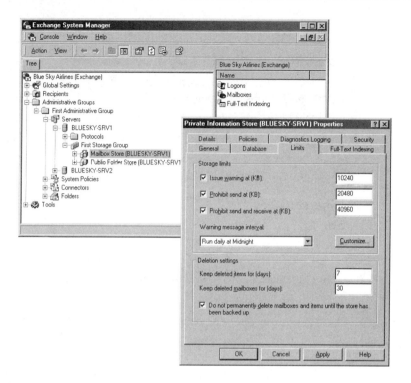

Figure 13.9   Defining storage limits and deletion settings for a mailbox store

13. Right-click Deleted Items, and select Empty "Deleted Items" Folder. In the Microsoft Outlook dialog box asking whether you are sure, click Yes.

14. Notice that the messages are purged from your mailbox.

15. Open the Tools menu, and select the Recover Deleted Items command.

16. In the Recover Deleted Items From – Deleted Items dialog box, notice that the messages deleted in Step 13 are listed.

17. Select the first item, and click the Recover Selected Items button. Notice that the message is placed back in the Deleted Items folder (see Figure 13.10).

18. Close Outlook 2000.

19. On BLUESKY-SRV1, launch the Active Directory Users and Computers snap-in, open the Users container, and right-click the Administrator account.

20. From the shortcut menu, select Exchange Tasks. Click Next on the welcome screen (if it appears), select Delete Mailbox on the Available Tasks screen, and then click Next. Click Next on the Delete Mailbox screen, and click Finish.

21. On BLUESKY-WKSTA, try to start Outlook 2000, and notice that you are unable to open the default e-mail folders, which is an indicator that the

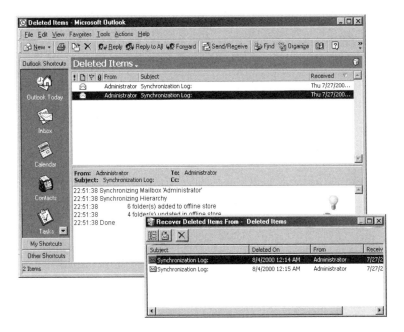

Figure 13.10   Recovering deleted message items in Outlook 2000

mailbox could not be accessed (because it was deleted). In the corresponding Microsoft Outlook dialog box, click OK. When asked whether to open the default file system folder, click No.

22. On BLUESKY-SRV1, switch to the Exchange System Manager, open the Mailbox Store (BLUESKY-SRV1) node in the console tree, and then select Mailboxes. Notice that the Administrator mailbox is still listed as a full mailbox resource.

23. Right-click Mailboxes, and select Run Cleanup Agent. Notice that the Administrator mailbox is now marked as deleted (see Figure 13.11).

24. Right-click the Administrator mailbox, and select Reconnect. (If you select Purge, the mailbox is deleted permanently.)

25. In the Select A New User For This Mailbox dialog box, double-click Administrator. In the Reconnect dialog box informing you that the operation completed successfully, click OK.

26. If an Exchange System Manager dialog box appears informing you that the object has not been replicated to the destination server yet, click OK.

27. Give the Recipient Update Service a few minutes to assign the Administrator account new e-mail addresses, then right-click Mailboxes again, and select Run Cleanup Agent. Verify that the mailbox is now marked as available.

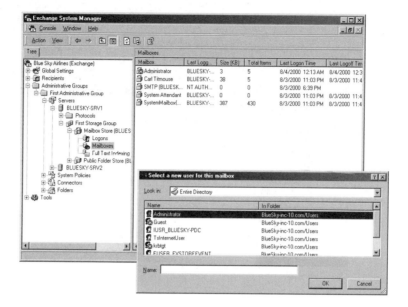

Figure 13.11   Recovering deleted mailboxes

Exercise Summary

The Limits tab of the mailbox store allows you to define default quotas for all mailboxes located in the mailbox store. In addition, you can configure item and mailbox retention times. Within the specified intervals, users can easily undelete purged message items in Outlook 2000 without administrative intervention. Administrators, in turn, can recover deleted mailboxes quickly from within the Exchange System Manager. Once retention time is exceeded, however, accidentally deleted items and mailboxes must be restored from backups.

Management of Recipient Policies

Policies offer many benefits. A default policy in Exchange 2000 Server, for instance, determines the format of e-mail addresses that recipient objects receive when they are mailbox- or mail-enabled. The SMTP address, for instance, defaults to <User Logon Name>@<Domain Name>. Let's say you want your users to have an e-mail address in the form of <First Name>.<LastName@ <Domain Name>, for example, Roger.Robin@Bluesky-inc-10.com. You may adjust the e-mail addresses manually in Active Directory Users and Computers, but this could become a puzzling task in a large organization. The system can take care of this job when you adjust the default policy or create a new one with higher priority.

Adjusting Default Policy Settings

You can configure default policy settings in the Exchange System Manager by expanding the Recipients container and then selecting Recipients Policies. In the contents pane, the Default Policy object is listed. When you double-click it to display its properties, notice that this policy applies to all recipients (mailnickname=* in the General tab). Click on the E-Mail Addresses tab, select the SMTP entry, click Edit, and, under Address, add **%g.%s** to the beginning of the address definition, for example, *%g.%s@Bluesky-inc-10.com*. (Table 13.1 lists the available placeholders.) Click OK, verify that the new rule is displayed in the Generation Rules list, and then click OK again. An Exchange System Manager dialog box will appear asking you whether you want to update all existing recipients. Click Yes if you think this is a good idea. Existing SMTP addresses are preserved, and new addresses are added to the recipient objects.

Note The update process may take a few minutes; give the process sufficient time. You will be able to verify the results in Active Directory Users and Computers when displaying the E-Mail Addresses tab of a mailbox- or mail-enabled object.

Table 13.1   Placeholders in Address Generation Rules

Placeholder	Description
%d	Display name
%g	First name
%i	Initials
%m	Alias
%s	Last name

Note In addition, you may specify how many characters to use (for instance, %1g.%s@Bluesky-inc-10.com would result in R.Robin@Bluesky-inc-10.com).

Adding Recipient Policies

Blue Sky Airlines is an international enterprise with offices around the world. Employees in London, for example, are supposed to have an SMTP address of %g.%1s@Bluesky-inc-10.co.uk. In this scenario, it is advantageous to configure an additional policy and apply it to those recipients who work in London, while the default policy may still apply to users in other locations.

In the Exchange System Manager, right-click Recipient Policies, point to New, and select Recipient Policy. Under Name, type **Users in London**, and then click

Modify. In the Find Exchange Recipients dialog box, click on the Advanced tab, click Field, point to User, and, from the list of attributes, select City. From the Condition list box, select Is (Exactly). Under Value, type **London**, and then click Add. It is a good idea to verify the results of your filter by clicking the Find Now button. If everything is fine, click OK, and then, in the Exchange System Manager dialog box informing you that existing recipient addresses don't change when a filter changes, click OK. Now click on the E-Mail Addresses tab, and adjust the SMTP address (that is, %g.%1s@Bluesky-inc-10.co.uk). Click OK, and update the existing addresses by clicking Yes in the subsequent Exchange System Manager dialog box.

As you will see, the Users In London policy is added to the list of policies with a higher priority than the Default Policy object. If you create further policies, those can be arranged in the contents pane by right-clicking them and selecting the Move Up or Move Down commands. The order in the list determines the policy's priority.

Recipient Update Service

When creating new mailbox- or mail-enabled recipient objects or when updating existing e-mail addresses, there may be a delay before the addresses are displayed correctly. The Recipient Update Service, an internal process of the System Attendant, handles the process of updating in the background. The Recipient Update Service is also responsible for updating address lists in Active Directory.

In the Exchange System Manager, open the Recipients container, and then select Recipient Update Services. At least two update service objects exist. One is for updating information in the naming context (NC) of the domain and the other for the configuration NC of Active Directory. For global administration, Exchange 2000 Server stores the majority of its information in the configuration NC, but recipient objects are maintained in the domain. You can adjust the settings of a particular update service object when right-clicking it and selecting Properties. The domain cannot be changed, but different Exchange Server and Windows 2000 Domain Controller settings may be applied. In addition, you can customize the update interval. For fastest updates, ensure that Always Run is selected.

Note   To immediately update recipient addresses or rebuild the address list memberships and e-mail addresses after a recipient policy is changed, right-click the corresponding update service object, and, from the shortcut menu, select either Update Now or the Rebuild command.

Recipient Updates in Multiple Domain Environments

Because a particular Recipient Update Service keeps only a particular domain posted, you need to configure an individual update service object for each domain in your organization that holds recipient objects. If you install at least one Exchange 2000 server in all of your domains, the required objects are created automatically. If domains without an Exchange 2000 server exist, you need to perform this task manually.

Note If mailbox- or mail-enabled recipient objects exist in a domain where the Recipient Update Service is not configured, corresponding e-mail addresses will not be generated. Recipient objects without e-mail addresses are not displayed in the address book.

To manually create a Recipient Update Service reference, run the Exchange 2000 Setup program in the target domain with the DomainPrep option (see Chapter 4, "Planning the Microsoft Exchange 2000 Server Installation"). After that, in Exchange System Manager, right-click Recipient Update Services, point to New, and select the Recipient Update Service command. In the New Object - Recipient Update Service dialog box, click Browse to conveniently select the desired domain, then click OK, and then click Next to continue. In the second dialog box, click Browse to select an appropriate Exchange 2000 server. This will be the server that runs the Recipient Update Service. The domain controller that will update the recipients in the domain is chosen automatically in the next dialog box. Click Finish.

Tip If you want to update a particular domain through a customized recipient policy, create a filter that checks the ending of the user's logon name. To give an example, if the domain you want to update is Bluesky-inc-10.co.uk, create a filter that checks a condition that ends with co.uk. The configuration of recipient policies was explained earlier in this lesson.

Export and Import Features

Beyond the simple feature of exporting the currently displayed contents pane, the Active Directory Users and Computers snap-in does not provide the functionality of exporting or importing recipient information.

Directory Export and Import Using LDIFDE

Windows 2000 Server provides you with a very powerful console application (LDIFDE.EXE) that supports batch operations based on LDAP Directory Interface Format (LDIF) files. LDIF is a file-format standard for batch operations against LDAP-conforming directories. Exchange 2000 Server, for instance, comes with a large number of LDIF files that are imported into Active Directory during the first server installation.

Although LDIFDE.EXE is not included in Windows 2000 Professional, you can copy it from the server (\Winnt\System32 directory) to your workstation and use it remotely to export or import data in Active Directory. To view the general parameters of LDIFDE.EXE, open the command prompt, type **ldifde**, and press ENTER. The output on the screen explains available options and gives sample command lines. To export directory information from a domain controller, use the command **ldifde -f c:\Export.ldf -s <Domain Controller>** (such as in, ldifde -f export.ldf -s bluesky-srv1 -d "CN=Carl Titmouse,CN=Users,DC=BlueSky-inc-10,DC=com").

After exporting a reference object, it is possible to adjust the settings carefully and use the resulting document as an import file. The following example creates an active and mailbox-enabled user account named Fred Pheasant that owns two different SMTP addresses and one X.400 proxy address. The import command is ldifde -i -f import.ldf -s bluesky-srv1.

```
dn: CN=Fred Pheasant,CN=Users,DC=BlueSky-inc-10,DC=com

changetype: add

displayName: Fred Pheasant

objectClass: user

sAMAccountName: FredP

userPrincipalName: FredP@BlueSky-inc-10.com

msExchHomeServerName:/o=Blue Sky Airlines/ou=First Administrative
Group/cn=Configuration/cn=Servers/cn=BLUESKY-SRV1

mailNickname: FredP

proxyAddresses: SMTP:Fred.Pheasant@BlueSky-inc-10.com

proxyAddresses: smtp:FredP@BlueSky-inc-10.com

proxyAddresses: X400:c=us;a= ;p=Blue Sky
Airline;o=Exchange;s=Pheasant;g=Fred;

userAccountControl: 512
```

Directory Export and Import Using CSVDE

If you are an Exchange Server 5.5 administrator, you are probably familiar with the comma separated values (CSV)-based export/import files as used in the Exchange Administrator program. As a matter of fact, many large networks that operate a heterogeneous messaging environment exchange address book files in .csv format to import the address information into Exchange directories conveniently. With Exchange 2000 Server, you can continue to use .csv files for this purpose.

As its name implies, you can use the CSVDE tool of Windows 2000 Server to export and import CSV-structured Active Directory information. The command syntax is the same as for the LDIFDE utility. Both tools have many features in common, only the resulting files are different. Column-oriented files are better suited for semiautomated processing in Microsoft Excel 2000.

To export Carl Titmouse, for example, type the following command: **csvde -f export.csv -s bluesky-srv1 -d "CN=Carl Titmouse,CN=Users,DC=BlueSky-inc-10,DC=com**. You can use the resulting file as a basis for a bulk import of address information. Edit the file in Excel 2000, eliminate those columns that you don't want to use, populate the table with the desired information, and then use the command **csvde -i -f import.csv -s bluesky-srv1** to create mailbox-enabled user accounts in bulk. The following is a sample header that allows you to create mailbox-enabled recipient objects: *DN, cn, displayName, mail, givenName, objectClass, proxyAddresses, name, sAMAccountName, userAccountControl, userPrincipalName, msExchHomeServerName, mailNickname*.

Tip Using LDIFDE and CSVDE, you can create mailbox-enabled as well as mail-enabled recipient objects. It is advantageous to use the CSVDE utility if you are familiar with the processing of table data through Excel macros (see Figure 13.12). You can read more about these utilities in the *Windows 2000 Server Distributed Systems Guide* of the Windows 2000 Server Resource Kit.

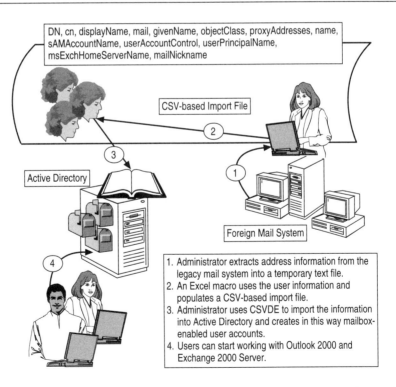

DN, cn, displayName, mail, givenName, objectClass, proxyAddresses, name, sAMAccountName, userAccountControl, userPrincipalName, msExchHomeServerName, mailNickname

CSV-based Import File

Active Directory

Foreign Mail System

1. Administrator extracts address information from the legacy mail system into a temporary text file.
2. An Excel macro uses the user information and populates a CSV-based import file.
3. Administrator uses CSVDE to import the information into Active Directory and creates in this way mailbox-enabled user accounts.
4. Users can start working with Outlook 2000 and Exchange 2000 Server.

Figure 13.12 A high-speed migration scenario based on directory import features

Chapter Summary

The creation of mailbox- and mail-enabled recipient objects is to a large extent the creation of user accounts, contacts, and groups. User accounts can be mailbox- or mail-enabled. Some thought should be given to what type of recipient object to create for mail-enabled resources, such as user accounts, contacts, or groups. Mail-enabled user accounts refer to persons in the organization that are working with a third-party messaging system. Contacts, in turn, are not users in the local enterprise and may work with Exchange 2000 or any other messaging system. Groups, to complete the list, provide a convenient way to address multiple recipients at one time. They can contain other groups, contacts, and user accounts. To avoid excessive Global Catalog replication, if the number of members in a group is large, create nested groups to subdivide the membership information. If possible, assign universal security groups e-mail addresses. Mail-enabled security groups can be used for permission assignments and to address e-mail messages.

The Recipient Update Service of Exchange 2000 Server assigns each recipient object several default e-mail addresses according to the settings defined in recipient policies. Objects without e-mail information are not displayed in the client address book, for instance. Therefore, if any domain in your environment does not host an Exchange 2000 server, you need to configure an update service object in Exchange System Manager manually. If you need to create or modify a large number of recipient objects, consider using LDIFDE or CSVDE.

Review

The following review questions can help you determine if you have sufficiently familiarized yourself with the material covered in this chapter. You can find the answers to these questions at the end of this book in Appendix A, "Questions and Answers."

1. When would you configure mail-enabled contact objects in Active Directory?

2. How do you hide a particular mailbox from the address book?

3. How can you accomplish the transfer of group management responsibilities to a regular user?

4. Your Exchange 2000 server is a very busy machine. Another server in the same administrative group has less work to perform so you decide to designate this computer as an expansion server. How can you accomplish this configuration?

5. Although your Windows 2000 environment consists of multiple domains, you have deployed Exchange 2000 Server only in the top-level domain. What do you need to configure on the Exchange 2000 server to support all users in your organization?

C H A P T E R   1 4

Managing Server Configuration

About This Chapter

Managing a large Microsoft Exchange 2000 Server implementation can be an overwhelming task. To make this task more manageable, you can split complex configuration objects into smaller units.

At the lowest level of the hierarchy, you deal with individual storage groups and other server-based resources (such as Internet protocols). Servers are consolidated by means of administrative and routing groups to manage multiple servers centrally. The organization object resides at the top of the hierarchy. It allows you to delegate permissions for the entire organization, and it holds global configuration objects, such as address list definitions. You will use Exchange System Manager to maintain your Exchange 2000 resources at all available levels.

This chapter focuses on the management of Exchange 2000 resources using Exchange System Manager. It covers important configuration issues at the server, administrative group, and organization levels.

Before You Begin

To complete this chapter:

- Prepare your test environment according to the descriptions given in the "Getting Started" section of "About This Book." If you have successfully completed the exercises in previous chapters, you do not need to reinstall your test environment.

- You need to be familiar with the delegation of administrative permissions, as explained in Chapter 5, "Installing Microsoft Exchange 2000 Server," and the utilization of system policies, as covered in Chapter 12, "Management Tools for Microsoft Exchange 2000 Server," and Chapter 13, "Creating and Managing Recipients."

Lesson 1: Management of Server Resources

When you examine the content of the Servers container in Exchange System Manager, you will notice one or many server objects each representing one server within the selected administrative group. In an organization with only one administrative group, the Servers container appears directly underneath the organization until you change the View settings in the General tab of the organization object (Display Administrative Groups check box).

This lesson concentrates on the administration of Exchange 2000 Server at the server level, which has a higher priority than the administrative group level. You can read about dedicated server configurations and the activation of full-text indexing and diagnostics logging.

At the end of this lesson, you will be able to:

- Manage storage groups as well as mailbox and public stores.
- Activate full-text indexing for mailbox and public stores.
- Enable diagnostics logging for troubleshooting and system analysis.

Estimated time to complete this lesson: 75 minutes

Storage Management in Exchange System Manager

Exchange System Manager can connect to any Microsoft Windows 2000 domain controller for retrieval of Exchange 2000 configuration information from Active Directory directory services. Yet, when adjusting information store settings, you need to communicate directly with the selected Exchange server via remote procedure calls (RPCs). If the server cannot be reached over the network for any reason, Exchange System Manager will display an error message and mark the resources as unavailable.

Important   If you want to manage storage groups and server properties, make sure the selected server is available in the network and its Information Store service is running.

Storage Groups and Information Stores

When you expand the object of an out-of-the-box server in the Exchange System Manager, you can find underneath it one sublevel container called First Storage Group, which provides access to one mailbox and one public store. You can add additional storage groups on a single computer running Exchange 2000 Enterprise Server, as mentioned in Chapter 3, "Microsoft Exchange 2000 Server Architecture." A server is able to handle a maximum of four storage groups, each capable of managing up to five individual stores.

Storage groups define the boundaries for mailbox and public store databases. Within a single storage group, all stores share a common set of transaction log files. Consequently, the transaction log location is a storage group's most important configuration parameter. The purpose of transaction logs is explained in Chapter 20, "Microsoft Exchange 2000 Server Maintenance and Troubleshooting."

For storage groups, the following settings are available:

- **Transaction Log Location.** Specifies the directory where the database transaction log files are located.

- **System Path Location.** Specifies the location of temporary files that may exist during an online backup or normal operation. This is typically the same as the Transaction Log Location.

- **Log File Prefix.** This read-only parameter indicates the name of the active transaction log. For instance, the default First Storage Group uses the prefix E00, which results in a log filename of E00.LOG. Additional storage groups would be assigned the prefixes E01, E02, and so forth.

- **Zero Out Deleted Database Pages.** Helps to increase the security of the server system by clearing deleted data entries from the database file. Activating this option affects the server performance.

- **Enable Circular Logging.** Allows reuse of existing log files for new transactions. This feature helps to save disk space but decreases the system's fault tolerance, as explained in Chapter 20, "Microsoft Exchange 2000 Server Maintenance and Troubleshooting."

Configuring Information Stores

You can manage information stores in storage groups individually or maintain them more conveniently through system policies. With only a few exceptions, system policies provide the same set of properties as information stores. You can read more about the configuration of message stores via mailbox and public folder policies in Chapter 12, "Management Tools for Microsoft Exchange 2000 Server."

Most configuration settings apply to both mailbox and public stores, but a few are store type-specific. Mailbox stores, for instance, allow you to set an Offline Address List in the General tab. Users on this mailbox store will download that address list in Microsoft Outlook 2000 on the Tools menu when you select the Synchronize option and then the Download Address Book command. You can read more about the configuration of Outlook 2000 for offline usage in Chapter 9, "MAPI-Based Clients."

Mailbox stores also give you the option to change the Default Public Store in their General tab, which is the public store that users connect to when browsing through the hierarchy of public folders in Outlook 2000 or when they create top-level folders. Outlook 2000 only supports access to one hierarchy that corresponds to the Public Folders tree, known as the MAPI-based public folder hierarchy. It is not possible to specify a public store in the General tab that does not correspond to the MAPI-based Public Folders. You can read more about public folders in Chapter 17, "Public Folder Management."

Configuring Dedicated Servers

Large organizations might want to distribute their mailbox resources across multiple servers. This increases the overall system scalability because multiple servers can share the workload of mailbox access. The same does not apply to public folders, however. Without public folder replication, which needs to be configured manually, a particular public folder resides on only one server. If all users in an organization need access to a particular public folder, they all have to connect to the same machine. This may slow down the affected server and users with mailboxes on this machine might start complaining about server response times.

The organization shown in Figure 14.1 uses one server where all public folders are located. Several, less powerful computers provide each a subset of users with mailbox access. Even if all users would connect to the public server concurrently, performance of the mailbox servers would not be affected.

To prevent the creation of public folders on the mailbox servers, you might want to delete their public store. This corresponds to a configuration of dedicated mailbox servers. Optionally, you can also remove the mailbox store from the public folder server to avoid the accidental creation of mailboxes on this machine (see Exercise 1).

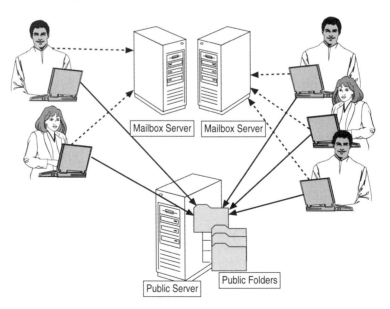

Figure 14.1   Configuring dedicated mailbox and public folder servers

Creating Additional Storage Groups and Information Stores

If you plan to concentrate thousands of mailboxes and public folders on a very large server, consider multiple information stores and storage groups. It would not be advisable to place all resources in a single mailbox or public store because the size of the database files could grow beyond reasonable limits. Huge databases can turn backup and restore procedures and regular maintenance routines into nightmares. It is advisable to avoid extremely time-consuming maintenance jobs.

At a minimum, distribute large numbers of mailboxes across multiple mailbox stores in one storage group. You can mount and dismount individual databases independently; in other words, you can back them up and recover them separately without affecting others. Typically, though, you will include all databases of a single storage group along with their corresponding transaction log files in one backup. If you would like to implement different backup schedules for different repositories, consider the configuration of multiple storage groups. It is necessary to configure multiple storage groups if you want to create more than five information stores on a server.

Multiple information stores can bring you a performance gain, provided that you place their transaction logs and database files on separate physical disk systems, as shown in Figure 14.2. It doesn't give you much of a performance boost to place transaction logs of multiple storage groups on a common physical drive.

Note   The single instance storage feature discussed in Chapter 13, "Creating and Managing Recipients," is not available across multiple databases.

Exercise 1: Creating Dedicated Mailbox and Public Folder Servers

In this exercise you will configure BLUESKY-SRV1 as a dedicated public folder server and BLUESKY-SRV2 as a dedicated mailbox server. You will also create an additional mailbox store on BLUESKY-SRV2.

To view a multimedia demonstration that displays how to perform this procedure, run the EX1CH14.AVI files from the \Exercise_Information\Chapter14 folder on the Supplemental Course Materials CD.

Prerequisites

- Make sure Exchange 2000 Server was first installed on BLUESKY-SRV1; otherwise, trade the server names in the following exercise to avoid the deletion of important system folders.

- You have removed all connector components from BLUESKY-SRV1, installed during Exercise 4 of Chapter 5, "Installing Microsoft Exchange 2000

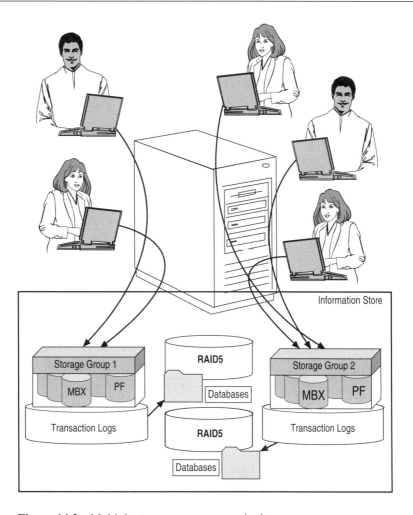

Figure 14.2   Multiple storage groups on a single server

Server." Launch the Setup program in maintenance mode to remove these components.

- Drive D: on BLUESKY-SRV2 is formatted with the NTFS file system.

- Log on as Administrator to BLUESKY-SRV1.

- Use the Active Directory Users and Computers snap-in to move all existing mailboxes from BLUESKY-SRV1 to BLUESKY-SRV2 (moving of mailboxes was demonstrated in Exercise 1 of Chapter 13, "Creating and Managing Recipients").

- Administrative and routing groups are displayed in the Exchange System Manager (Display Routing Groups and Display Administrative Groups check boxes in the properties of the organization object Blue Sky Airlines [Exchange]).

▶   **To configure dedicated servers and add storage groups**

1. Launch the Exchange System Manager, expand Administrative Groups, then First Administrative Group, then Servers, then BLUESKY-SRV1, then First Storage Group, then Mailbox Store (BLUESKY-SRV1), and then select Mailboxes. Make sure no user mailboxes are displayed in the details pane (several system mailboxes may exist). If there are user mailboxes in this store, Exchange System Manager prevents you from removing it.

2. Right-click the Mailbox Store (BLUESKY-SRV1) and select Properties. In the Mailbox Store (BLUESKY-SRV1) Properties dialog box, click on the Database tab, write down the names and paths to the Exchange Database and Exchange Streaming Database, and then click OK. By default, these directories are C:\Program Files\Exchsrvr\Mdbdata\PRIV.EDB and C:\Program Files\ Exchsrvr\Mdbdata\PRIV.STM.

3. Right-click Mailbox Store (BLUESKY-SRV1) and select Delete.

4. In the dialog box informing you that deleting this mailbox store may result in the loss of system messages, click Yes (see Figure 14.3).

5. Another Information Store dialog box will appear asking you if you are sure you want to remove this mailbox store. Click Yes.

6. In the final dialog box informing you that the store has been removed but you must delete the database files manually, click OK. While deleting is not a bad idea, you should keep the files for subsequent exercises.

At this point, you have configured BLUESKY-SRV1 with a public store only, which turns this machine into a dedicated public folder server unable to hold any mailboxes.

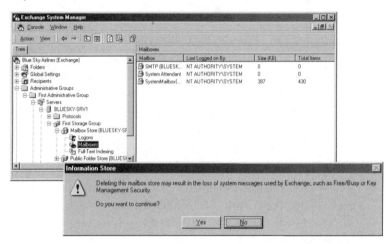

Figure 14.3   Deleting a mailbox store

7. In the console tree, under Servers, expand BLUESKY-SRV2, expand First Storage Group, open Public Folder Store (BLUESKY-SRV2), and then select Public Folder Instances. Make sure no public folders holding user data exist in this store and no system folders other than Globalevents, Internal, and StoreEvents{...} are listed. If there are other public folders, replicate them to BLUESKY-SRV1 (explained in Chapter 18, "Public Folder Replication") before continuing.

8. Right-click Public Folder Store (BLUESKY-SRV2) and select Properties.

9. In the Public Folder Store (BLUESKY-SRV2) Properties dialog box, click on the Database tab, note the names and paths to the databases, and then click OK. By default, these directories are C:\Program Files\Exchsrvr\Mdbdata\PUB1.EDB and C:\Program Files\Exchsrvr\Mdbdata\PUB1.STM.

10. Right-click Public Folder Store (BLUESKY-SRV2) and select Delete.

11. In the dialog box informing you that it is strongly recommended to move any public folder replicas to other servers before removing the public store, click Yes.

12. A Public Folder Store (BLUESKY-SRV2) dialog box will appear, informing you that you need to specify a new default public store for the mailboxes on this server. Click OK.

13. In the Select Public Store dialog box, select the reference to Public Folder Store (BLUESKY-SRV1), and then click OK (see Figure 14.4).

14. Another dialog box might be displayed, prompting you to select a new public store for system folders. In this case, click OK, and select the reference to Public Folder Store (BLUESKY-SRV1) again before clicking OK one more time. This dialog box will not appear in the test environment because BLUESKY-SRV2 does not contain system folders.

15. Another dialog box might appear informing you that this public store holds offline address lists that need to be rebuilt on a new public store. Click OK, select the reference to Public Folder Store (BLUESKY-SRV1), and then click OK again. This dialog box will not appear in the test environment because BLUESKY-SRV2 does not hold the offline address lists.

16. In the final Select Public Store (BLUESKY-SRV2) dialog box asking you whether you want to delete the public store, click Yes.

17. In the final Information Store dialog box informing you that you must remove the database files manually, click OK.

At this point, you have configured BLUESKY-SRV2 as a dedicated mailbox server unable to maintain any public folder data. To work with public folders, users will connect to BLUESKY-SRV1, which holds the default public store.

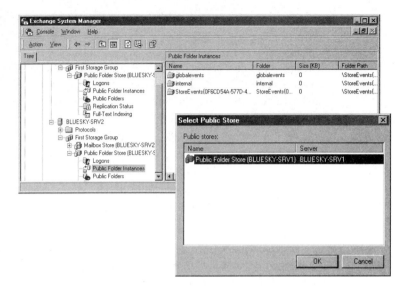

Figure 14.4   Deleting a public store

18. In the console tree, right-click BLUESKY-SRV2, point to New, and then select Storage Group.

19. In the General tab, under Name, type **Management Group**.

20. Under Transaction Log Location and System Path Location, change the drive letter from C to D in both text boxes, and then click OK.

21. If a dialog box appears informing you that the validity of the databases cannot be verified at this point, click Yes to continue.

22. A new, empty container will be created under BLUESKY-SRV2. Right-click Management Group, point to New, and then select Mailbox Store.

23. Under Name type **VIP Mailboxes**.

24. Verify that the Default Public Store resides on BLUESKY-SRV1.

25. Click on the Database tab, and notice that the Exchange Database and Exchange Streaming Database files are placed in the directory of the Management Group by default.

26. Click on the Limits tab, and, under Deletion Settings, in the Keep Deleted Items For (Days) text box, type **21**. Click OK.

27. If a dialog box appears informing you that the validity of the databases cannot be verified at this point, click Yes to continue.

28. In the VIP Mailboxes dialog box informing you that the store was created successfully, click No to not mount the store yet. Give directory replication a few minutes to propagate the changes to BLUESKY-SRV2 first (you are working on BLUESKY-SRV1).

29. Right-click VIP Mailboxes and select Mount Store.

30. In the final VIP Mailboxes dialog box informing you that the store was mounted successfully, click OK.

   At this point, you have created and mounted an additional mailbox store on a separate drive on BLUESKY-SRV2 (see Figure 14.5).

31. Launch Active Directory Users and Computers and open the Users container. Move the mailbox of the Administrator account into the Management Group/ VIP Mailboxes store, as explained in Chapter 13, "Creating and Managing Recipients."

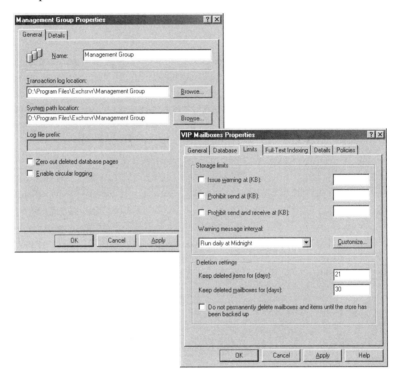

Figure 14.5   Creating an additional mailbox store

Exercise Summary

To avoid the possible loss of user data, mailboxes must be moved to a new home server and public folders must be replicated to another public store before configuring dedicated servers. After a store has been removed successfully, you need to delete the corresponding database files manually. You can determine the path to the databases and their names when displaying the Database property sheet of the affected store prior to its deletion.

The creation of new storage groups and information stores, on the other hand, is uncomplicated. At a minimum, you need to specify a name for new resources. As soon as you have created and mounted a new mailbox store, you can move mail-boxes into it using the Active Directory Users and Computers snap-in.

Full-Text Indexing

By default, Exchange 2000 Server supports attribute-based searches for messages and documents. This corresponds to the search capabilities of earlier versions of Exchange Server, where Outlook users could look up messages and other items based on their attributes. For example, you could search for all messages in your Inbox with the phrase "Full-Text Indexing Was Not Supported" in the subject line. This search would examine every existing object in your Inbox and return the matching items. Depending on the number of messages, this search method might take a very long time.

You could also locate documents by searching for subject, author, keywords, and other document properties. However, full-text searches across documents and attachments in messages were not supported. This reduced the attractiveness of Exchange Server 5.5 as a document management platform.

Microsoft Search Integration

The good news for the knowledge worker is that Exchange 2000 Server supports sophisticated searches for words and phrases contained in documents and mes-sage attachments. This functionality is achieved by integrating the query engine of the Information Store with the Microsoft Search service (see Figure 14.6).

Note Microsoft Search is a Windows 2000 service installed as part of the Exchange 2000 Server setup procedure. It is configured to start automatically. This service operates in the context of the LocalSystem account.

The Microsoft Search service provides support for the following tasks:

- **Indexing.** Maintains full-text catalogs and indexes for mailbox and public stores and populates the full-text indexes.
- **Querying.** Processes full-text searches passed over by the Information Store search engine and returns entries in the index that meet the full-text search criteria. According to this information, the Information Store search engine can construct the query result and return it to the user.

Full-Text Indexing and Catalogs

Full-text indexes provide information about significant words in messages, docu-ments, and attachments for sophisticated word searches. By default, item body, sub-ject, sender, and recipient information are indexed. Because the full-text catalogs are queried instead of the actual message items and documents, searches are performed with increased efficiency, especially if numerous items are involved. However, before the search engine can process a full-text query, the catalog must be populated. Fur-thermore, the query results can only be as accurate as the information in the catalog.

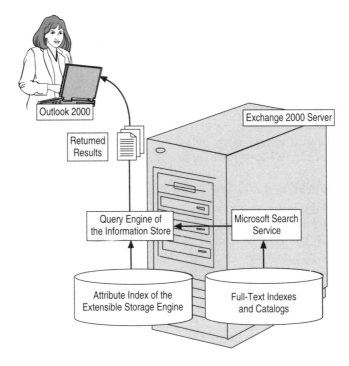

Figure 14.6   Attribute and full-text searches

Note   Full-text indexes and catalogs are not stored in the Information Store. They are located in the Program Files\Exchsrvr\ExchangeServer_<Server Name>\Projects directory and managed by the Microsoft Search service. They consume approximately 20% of disk space of the corresponding store size.

Indexing Information Stores

Full-text indexing can be enabled per individual mailbox and public store. First, you need to create a full-text index for a store. You then need to populate the store's full-text catalog. As soon as this is accomplished, you can make the catalog available for full-text searches by clients. After that, you may define update and rebuild intervals to ensure that search information is always up to date.

Creating a Full-Text Index

Let's assume you want to create a full-text index for the mailbox store added to BLUESKY-SRV2 in Exercise 1 (VIP Mailboxes). Right-click this store and, from the shortcut menu, select Create Full-Text Index. In the Mailbox Store (BLUESKY-SRV2) dialog box accept the default directory, which is \Program Files\Exchsrvr\ExchangeServer_BLUESKY-SRV2\Projects, and click OK. As soon as the catalog is created, right-click VIP Mailboxes again and select Start Full Population. In the Mailbox Store (BLUESKY-SRV2) dialog box informing you that this operation may take time and server resources, click Yes. When the population is complete, expand VIP Mailboxes, and select Full-Text Indexing. Verify that the index was created successfully. You might need to refresh the view for latest status information.

You can also click the Start Full Population command if you want to purge and rebuild an existing index. The index is purged at once but one document at a time. While this process is running, searches against the store will not be able to use the full-text index. When the full population is complete, you should reactivate the full-text index for client searches.

Activating a Full-Text Index

At this point, you have created and populated the full-text index, but your users are still unable to use it because it isn't included in full-text searches. Right-click VIP Mailboxes one more time and select Properties. Click on the Full-Text Indexing tab, and select the This Index Is Currently Available For Searching By Clients check box. When you click OK, a dialog box appears, reminding you that you must make sure that the index is not out of date; otherwise, searches might return incomplete or invalid results. Click OK.

Note   It is advisable not to back up or restore an index separately from its information store. This will guarantee that both index and store are always synchronized. Otherwise, searches will return incomplete or invalid results.

Updating and Rebuilding a Full-Text Index

Changes to folder contents within an indexed store trigger a synchronization event, which informs the Microsoft Search service to update the index correspondingly. By default, however, the index is not updated. You will need to specify an explicit update and rebuild interval in the Full-Text Indexing tab. For automatic updates, under Update Interval, select Always Run. During scheduled and automatic updates, incremental populations are performed, where new items are indexed and their references are added to the catalog. Incorrect references, however, may remain in the index until it is entirely rebuilt. Rebuilding takes significantly more resources than updating; therefore, you should schedule a weekly rebuild interval for off-peak hours over the weekend (you may update the indexing information more frequently or automatically).

Note   If you need to refresh the indexing information manually, consider updating the index incrementally. This allows your users to perform searches while the catalog is being refreshed. Only new and modified items will be indexed. Right-click the desired store and select Start Incremental Population.

Controlling System Resource Consumption

It is important to keep the full-text index current, but indexing consumes system resources. Resource consumption is controlled at the server level. Display the properties of the desired server object (for example, BLUESKY-SRV2) and click on the Full-Text Indexing tab. You will find a parameter called System Resource Usage in this tab, which can be set to four levels: Minimum, Low, High, and Maximum. Low is the default. As mentioned, you should schedule rebuild intervals for off-peak times and set System Resource Usage value to High or Maximum. The index information is then refreshed as quickly as possible. If you must index while users are working with their mailboxes, set System Resource Usage to Low. On a system with high memory usage, decrease the value to Minimum.

Supported File Types and Gather Logs

Microsoft Search supports specific file types through document filters. Filters are provided for Microsoft Office documents, and other documents, such as Adobe .pdf files. Supported file types are recognized by their filename extension, such as .doc or .xls. However, the Microsoft Search service may attempt to index a corrupted document, in which case the indexing fails and continues with the next message or document. A corresponding error will be written to the application event log summarizing the number of corrupted documents. In addition, problematic documents will be logged together with other statistical information in gather files, which can be found in the \Program Files\Exchsrvr\ ExchangeServer_ <Server Name>\GatherLogs directory. Gather files are text files with a filename extension of .gthr.

Microsoft Search provides you with GTHRLOG.VBS, which is a useful utility to examine gather files. You can find it in the \Program Files\Common Files\ System\MsSearch\Bin directory. Launch GTHRLOG.VBS with the desired gather log in the command line (for example, gthrlog <path + filename.gthr>). A series of dialog boxes will display the data found in the gather log file, such as statistical information about the last indexing cycle and references to problematic documents, together with an explanation of error codes. For usage information on this utility, use the command gthrlog /?.

Performing a Full-Text Search

As soon as you activate a full-text index, your Outlook users (and users of IMAP4 clients) are able to perform full-text searches. The user doesn't have to use any new utilities or change search habits because the Information Store takes care of the communication with the Microsoft Search service (see Figure 14.6). In Outlook 2000, for instance, open the Tools menu, and select Advanced Find as usual. In the Advanced Find dialog, type the word or phrase you want to search for under Search For The Word(s), and, from the In list box, select Subject Field And Message Body. Click Find Now, and all items containing the specified phrase, including Office documents, will be returned. It is important to note that full-text searches return complete matches only. A search for the phrase "index" will result in a list of documents that actually contain the word "index." The word "indexing" is not considered a match.

> **Note**   With full-text searches enabled, client searches are performed against the index of the Microsoft Search service first and, after that, against the attributes in the information store. Hence, two separate searches are executed to return one list of resulting messages and documents.

Indexing Service

Don't confuse the Microsoft Search service with the Indexing service. The latter is installed under Windows 2000, but it is not started by default. The Indexing service provides functionality similar to the Microsoft Search service but doesn't work in conjunction with the Information Store directly. It is used against files of the operating system and Web resources. You can configure the Indexing service in the Computer Management snap-in.

Nevertheless, the Indexing service allows you to search for items in mailboxes and public folders via the Microsoft Web Storage System. The Web Storage System provides access to resources based on HTTP and Web Distributed Authoring and Versioning (WebDAV), as discussed in Chapter 11, "Internet-Based Clients." Consequently, users of Web browsers can search the Information Store, even though WebDAV clients do not support searches via the Microsoft Search service. When combined with full-text indexing and HTTP client support, Exchange 2000 Server becomes a very attractive document management platform.

Diagnostic Logging

All active components of Exchange 2000 Server are implemented as Windows 2000 services, which has significant advantages. Windows 2000 services can offer their services to local and remote processes or client programs connected over the network, and they can be controlled and administered remotely. The various communication paths between the individual Exchange 2000 Server components were highlighted in Chapter 3, "Microsoft Exchange 2000 Server Architecture."

For system administrators, nevertheless, Windows 2000 services have one considerable disadvantage: They run entirely unattended, presenting absolutely no user interface. The services of Exchange 2000 Server, for example, run in the context of the LocalSystem account. Even if these services did display a user interface, you would not be able to see it because you aren't working with the same user credentials.

Examining System Activities

To inform the administrator about specific activities and error states, Exchange 2000 components write status information in form of events into the application event log. By default, only a minimum of events, or error notifications, are logged, which can be viewed using the Event Viewer utility mentioned in Chapter 12, "Management Tools for Microsoft Exchange 2000 Server."

If you experience server problems or are interested in more details about the activities of a particular Exchange service in general, you should increase the amount of logged events. This can be accomplished using the Diagnostics Logging tab that every server object provides. To give an example, right-click the server object BLUESKY-SRV1, select Properties, and click on the Diagnostics Logging tab. From the Services list, select the desired component, such as MSExchangeTransport. The Categories list will display corresponding internal components, such as the Routing Engine, Categorizer, and so on. Select one or multiple categories, set the desired Logging Level (None, Minimum, Medium, or Maximum), and then click OK. It is not necessary to restart the affected services for the changes to take effect.

Note   Entries in the application event log can become overwhelming if you set the Diagnostics Logging level to Maximum because most detailed status information will then be retrieved.

Diagnostics Logging Settings in the Registry

When you modify the Diagnostics Logging level for a component in Exchange System Manager, the settings are written to the Windows 2000 Registry. Exchange System Manager also informs the corresponding service to update its configuration information. If you change the settings directly in the Registry, however, you should restart the affected service to make sure the changes are applied.

The diagnostics logging information for Exchange 2000 Server components is located under:

```
HKEY_LOCAL_MACHINE

 \SYSTEM

  \CurrentControlSet

   \Services

    \<Exchange 2000 Component>

     \Diagnostics
```

Within this subkey, REG_DWORD values exist for each of the logging categories. Possible values are 0 for a logging level of None, 1 for Minimum, 3 for Medium, and 5 for Maximum logging. For super-detailed diagnostics logging, you may increase the value to 6. This level is only available when directly editing the Registry.

Lesson 2: Management of Administrative Groups

Exchange 2000 Server supports two means of server grouping. Physically, servers can be set in routing groups, which define areas of high network bandwidth where direct message delivery is possible. Chapter 16, "Message Routing Administration," covers routing group aspects in greater detail. Logically, meaning independent of the physical network, you can group servers for purposes of structuring administration. These arrangements are known as administrative groups.

This lesson focuses on issues regarding the configuration of administrative groups, including adding and removing servers. You need to reinstall a server if you want to move it between administrative groups.

At the end of this lesson, you will be able to:
- Describe the purpose of administrative groups.
- Organize server resources in administrative groups.

Estimated time to complete this lesson: 25 minutes

Configuration at the Administrative Group Level

Administrative groups primarily serve the purpose of permission management. When you right-click an administrative group container in Exchange System Manager, you can select the Delegate Control command to launch the Exchange Administration Delegation Wizard, which was covered in Chapter 5, "Installing Microsoft Exchange 2000 Server."

An administrator with appropriate permissions at the administrative group level can configure individual servers, routing groups, common policy settings, and public folder resources for all or a subset of servers. Corresponding configuration containers are located directly underneath each administrative group object (that is, Servers, System Policies, Routing Groups, and Folders). Additional configuration objects for conferencing services and chat networks may exist depending on the components installed.

Implementing Multiple Administrative Groups

Enterprises with a central information technology (IT) department don't need to implement multiple administrative groups. To keep the administrative environment simple, all servers can be placed in the default First Administrative Group regardless of the organization's size. Large national and international organizations with multiple IT groups responsible for distributed resources in different regions or departments, however, might find a decentralized administrative structure more appropriate for their needs. In this scenario, one administrative group can be created per geographical region or per department.

Note   The flexibility of administrative groups is limited in a mixed Exchange organization, as explained in Chapter 6, "Coexistence with Previous Microsoft Exchange Server Versions."

Administrative Groups in Active Directory Directory Service

In Active Directory, each administrative group is implemented as a separate configuration container that you can find under the following location when using the Active Directory Services Interface (ADSI) Edit utility:

```
CN=Configuration,DC=BlueSky-inc-10,DC=com,

 CN=Services,

  CN=Microsoft Exchange,

   CN=<Organization Name, such as Blue Sky Airlines>,

    CN=Administrative Groups,

     CN=First Administrative Group

      CN=<Further Administrative Groups>
```

To grant user permissions, you simply add the desired Windows 2000 account to the list of accounts with permissions for the corresponding administrative group object. Active Directory propagates security settings to all objects within that administrative group.

Note   Use the Exchange Administration Delegation Wizard instead of the ADSI Edit utility to manage permissions for administrative groups. Incorrect permission assignments using ADSI Edit can lead to serious configuration problems and may require you to restore your systems from backup.

Adding Servers to an Administrative Group

You can add servers to an administrative group only during setup. It is not possible to move servers between administrative groups, and it is likewise impossible to move mailboxes conveniently across administrative group boundaries. Consequently, design your administrative group topology carefully before installing Exchange 2000 Server.

Creating Administrative Groups

As long as only one administrative group exists, the Setup program of Exchange 2000 Server will not prompt you for administrative group information. It adds the new server automatically to the default group. To add a server to another group, you need to create the group before launching Setup and then select it during the installation. Creating administrative groups is trivial because new groups are initially empty containers under Administrative Groups. Start Exchange System Manager, right-click the Administrative Groups container, point to New, and then select the Administrative Group command. The only information you have to provide is a name for the new group. Administrative group names can have up to 64 characters.

After a new group has been created, you can add servers and other resources, such as system policies. With the exception of server resources, configuration objects can be moved or copied between administrative groups in Exchange System Manager.

Removing a Server from Active Directory Directory Services

It is possible to rename administrative groups, but it is not possible to move servers. Microsoft may provide special utilities for this purpose, but, without them, the only way to move a server to another administrative group is to remove and reinstall it. Before removing a server, move existing mailboxes to mailbox stores on other servers and replicate existing public folders. This is similar to the preparation of a dedicated server configuration, as explained earlier in this chapter.

Two strategies are available to remove a server from the organization. The best way is to launch the Exchange 2000 Setup program on the server that you want to remove, and, on the Component Selection wizard screen, select the Remove action. The Setup program was covered in detail in Chapter 5, "Installing Microsoft Exchange 2000 Server."

The second method is right-clicking the server object in Exchange System Manager, pointing to All Tasks, and clicking Remove Server. An Exchange System Manager dialog box will appear asking you whether you are sure. Click Yes. At this point, you will receive an error message if your Exchange 2000 server is still available in the network. Only unavailable servers can be removed using this approach. This is typically the case if the server was removed physically from the network or you have reinstalled the operating system without restoring Exchange 2000 Server from a backup.

Lesson 3: Management of Server Address Lists

An address list allows you to arrange mailbox- and mail-enabled user accounts, contacts, and groups, as well as public folders in virtual containers based on attributes they have in common. The actual recipients may reside elsewhere within the organization. Server-based address lists give you the option to provide a detailed view of the structures of your enterprise through the address book of Outlook 2000.

This lesson deals with the configuration of address lists in Active Directory. It discusses the creation of nested structures and their maintenance using the Recipient Update Service.

At the end of this lesson, you will be able to:

- Create a sophisticated address list structure.
- Create offline address lists for remote Outlook 2000 users.
- Use the Recipient Update Service to update address list information.

Estimated time to complete this lesson: 60 minutes

Domain Information and Global Catalogs

Directory attributes are properties of directory items, such as recipient objects. A validated user, using his or her client's address book to examine the address details of a recipient, can retrieve all available attributes replicated to the Global Catalog. You can read more about the mechanisms of accessing Global Catalog information in Chapter 2, "Integration with Microsoft Windows 2000."

Attributes Included in Global Catalog Replication

During the installation of Exchange 2000 Server, many attributes that users normally require are tagged for Global Catalog replication, such as givenName, Name, mailNickname, extensionAttribute1, and many others. An example of an attribute not replicated to the Global Catalog is userPassword. It wouldn't make sense to replicate this encrypted information.

In Exercise 3 of Chapter 2, "Integration with Microsoft Windows 2000," you used the Active Directory Schema snap-in to examine the properties of directory attributes. If you launch this snap-in once again and double-click the userPrincipalName attribute from the Attributes container, for instance, you can determine that the Replicate This Attribute To The Global Catalog and Index This Attribute In The Active Directory options are activated. The first option includes this attribute in the Global Catalog replication; the latter allows for efficient address book searches. A third option, Ambiguous Name Resolution (ANR), is not activated. It allows a user to simply enter the principal name in the To line and let the client perform the name resolution when sending the message.

The proxyAddresses attribute, which holds e-mail addresses, is a good example of an item for which all three options are enabled. Not all attributes are indexed or included in ANR to save resources on the Global Catalog server.

Note   By default, write operations to the schema are prohibited to protect you from damaging Active Directory accidentally. Schema modifications are explained in the *Windows 2000 Server Distributed Systems Guide* of the Microsoft Windows 2000 Resource Kit.

Server-Based Address Lists

Server-based address lists are directory objects that appear as containers in the client address book when working online. In reality, however, address lists are single directory objects with a global scope. You can configure them in Exchange System Manager, under Recipients, where they can be found under All Address Lists, All Global Address Lists, and Offline Address Lists. Offline address lists are covered later in this lesson.

Default Global Address List

The Default Global Address List object doesn't hold any recipient objects. When you display its property sheet, you can determine that the most important configuration parameter is a filter rule in LDAP Search Filter syntax. The other important configuration information is provided in the Security tab, where you can specify the users that are allowed access to this virtual address repository. Authenticated Users, for instance, have the List Contents permission.

Note   You may create multiple Global Address List objects and assign the List Contents permission to separate divisions and departments. Outlook 2000, however, is only able to work with one Global Address List at a time.

Creating Nested Lists Under All Address Lists

When you open the All Address Lists container, you will find several preconfigured address lists that Exchange 2000 Server provides (All Contacts, All Groups, All Users, and Public Folders). These items are meant merely as samples. You might find it more appropriate to create your own address list structure. Within the client address book, this structure is shown under the All Address Lists tree at the same level as the Global Address List.

Let's create a more involved structure that helps the users of Blue Sky Airlines find recipients more efficiently. Right-click the four default address lists one at a time and click Delete. After that, right-click All Address Lists, point to New, and select the Address List command. Under Address List Name, type **Flying Personnel**, and then click Filter Rules. The syntax of LDAP filters is defined in RFC 2254, yet Exchange System Manager can help you define them without learning the syntax beforehand. Click on the Advanced tab, click Field, point to

User, scroll down in the list of attributes, and select Department. Under Condition, select Is (Exactly), and then, under Value, type **Flying Personnel**. Click Add, test the result by clicking Find Now, and then click OK, and click Finish. The procedure to define the filter rule does not differ from the steps outlined for recipient policies, as explained in Chapter 13, "Creating and Managing Recipients."

If you don't find any recipients by clicking Find Now, then your organization most likely doesn't have a Flying Personnel department yet. Launch Active Directory Users and Computers, display the properties of a mailbox-enabled user account, such as Administrator, click on the Organization tab, and, under Department, type **Flying Personnel**. Under Title, type **Pilot** to anticipate the next address list configuration, and then click OK. Repeat the steps for Carl Titmouse, but specify **Flight Attendant** under Title.

At this point, you can continue the configuration with adding nested address lists, such as for Pilots and Flight Attendants. In Exchange System Manager, right-click the Flying Personnel address list, point to New, and click Address List. Under Address List Name, type **Pilots**. After that, click Filter Rules, click on the Advanced tab, click Field, point to User, scroll down in the list of attributes, and select Job Title. Under Condition, select Is (Exactly), and then, under Value, type **Pilot**. Click Add and then click Find Now. You should be able to find the Administrator account at this time. Click OK, click Finish, and then repeat the procedure for Flight Attendants (Job Title = Flight Attendant).

Note   You can use the Copy & Paste function in Exchange System Manager to conveniently create multiple address lists and adjust their settings afterward.

Updating Address List Information

It may be a while before you can examine the results of your efforts in Outlook 2000. If you want to force the update process, open the Recipient Update Services container, right-click on the Recipient Update Service for your domain, and click Rebuild. A Rebuild Address Lists And Recipient Policies dialog box will appear, informing you that the settings for all recipients are recalculated on the next scheduled update interval. Click Yes. Most likely, this interval is set to Always. If it isn't, you may trigger a manual update by right-clicking the object again and selecting the Update Now command. You can find further information about the configuration of Recipient Update Services in Chapter 13, "Creating and Managing Recipients."

Address List Contents

While it appears as if the Recipient Update Service adds recipient objects to address lists, it's actually the other way around (see Figure 14.7). The Recipient Update Service adds address list information to recipient objects. According to the filter rule that you have specified for your address lists, the showInAddressBook attribute of matching objects will be updated. If you

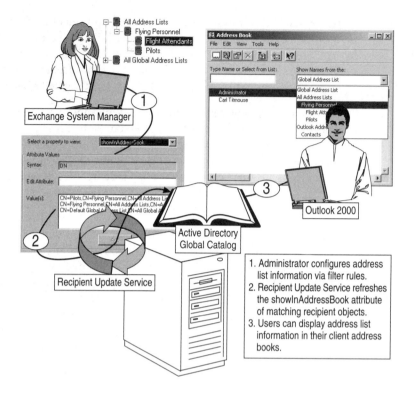

Figure 14.7   Address list information in Active Directory

examine this attribute for the Administrator account using ADSI Edit, for example, you could determine that the Administrator is shown in the Default Global Address List as well as Flying Personnel and Pilots. The showInAddressBook attribute is included in the Global Catalog replication.

Offline Address Lists

The Offline Address Lists container holds a Default Offline Address List object that provides the information from the Default Global Address Lists to remote users. As outlined in Chapter 9, "MAPI-Based Clients," Offline Address Lists can be downloaded from the server using Outlook 2000. This is required if you want to compose new messages during offline operation.

Offline Address Lists must be generated on the server before clients can download them. They correspond to system public folders created on the server during public store maintenance intervals. The Offline Address Lists location can be changed. For this purpose, in the General tab of the address list's configuration object, under Offline Address List Server, click the Browse button. Moving the Offline Address Lists to a new location is necessary, especially if you want to remove the public store from a server, as outlined earlier. If you fail to do so, the

Offline Address Lists will be unavailable until the next store maintenance cycle has recreated the required public folders on the new server.

During the creation of an Offline Address List or later, via the General tab, you can specify which address lists to include. It is possible to have multiple lists. In this scenario, users will be prompted to select the desired Offline Address Lists during address book synchronization in Outlook 2000. However, an Offline Address List must be generated before users can download it. By default, this will happen at 5:00 a.m. each day. If you modify recipients frequently, you may want to generate Offline Address Lists more often. In this case, under Update Interval, you can click the Customize button to specify when to regenerate a particular address list.

Address and Details Templates

Underneath the Recipient Update Services container in the console tree of Exchange System Manager, you can find the Address Templates and Details Templates containers, which are filled with numerous sublevel containers that correspond to supported client languages. These containers, in turn, hold templates to control address dialog boxes, which are actually displayed within the messaging clients.

Customizing Address Templates

Because they are stored on the server but actually used by the messaging client, address and details templates allow you to centrally customize the look of dialog boxes for MS-DOS-based and Windows-based clients. Again, templates are sets of instructions that determine how to display dialog boxes, for instance, within Outlook 2000. When you change the instructions to strip down the complexity of address book dialog boxes for your users or add additional fields required in your organization, Outlook 2000 will change its user interface.

Templates are language dependent, as the number of sublevel containers suggests. Each language version of Outlook 2000 will display its own set of dialog boxes. Hence, if you were the administrator of an international organization in which several language versions were used, you would have to repeat the customization for each version separately. Are you able to speak 30 languages? Fortunately, you don't need to bother with unused versions.

Templates Property Page

To add dialog box controls or to reposition existing ones, you need to select the desired template and display its properties. To give an example, under Details Templates, select English, and, in the details pane, double-click User. You can then click on the Templates tab. When you examine this tab, you will notice the Test button, which allows you to view the resulting dialog box. This is the dialog box that users see when double-clicking on a mailbox-enabled account in the client address book (see Figure 14.8).

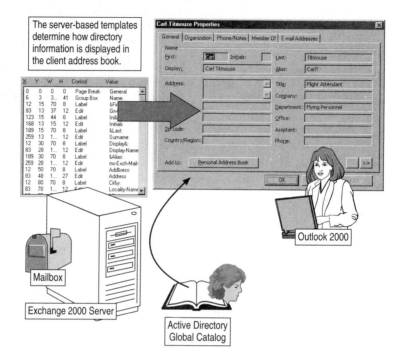

Figure 14.8   Details templates and resulting dialog boxes

You can click Add to insert new items, and you can click Modify if you want to rearrange positioned controls. To trim down a dialog box to let the user focus on the essential address information, click Remove. If you want to undo all template modifications, click Original.

Details Templates

Details templates are used to display detailed recipient information within Outlook 2000. They also describe the Search dialog box, which allows users to search server-based address books for a particular address. You have the ability to modify these templates to create customized dialog boxes.

Address Templates

Address templates determine the client dialog boxes, which prompt the user to enter e-mail address information. A one-off address corresponds to a recipient address that does not exist in the server's Global Address List or in any of the user's personal address books. Typically, the default template format is sufficient since one-off information depends usually on e-mail addresses rather than on any detailed recipient information. If necessary, they can also be modified.

Extension Attributes

Recipient objects provide a variety of predefined properties and attributes that can be specified to provide users of an organization with useful information through their address books. Sometimes it's nice to have additional choices, however. If you need additional attributes, you can specify them per recipient in the Active Directory Users and Computers snap-in. Make sure the advanced features are activated before displaying the properties of a mailbox- or mail-enabled object. Click on the Exchange Advanced tab, and click the Custom Attributes button. Up to 15 additional attributes can be specified.

Exercise 2: Customizing Outlook's Search Capabilities

In this exercise you will modify the Search Dialog Details template to extend the capabilities of address book searches. The modified Search dialog box will allow users to search for addresses based on the extensionAttribute1, which is used in this example to specify the seniority level of Blue Sky Airlines employees.

To view a multimedia demonstration that displays how to perform this procedure, run the EX2CH14*.AVI files from the \Exercise_Information\Chapter14 folder on the Supplemental Course Materials CD.

Prerequisites

- If you have completed Exercise 1, earlier in this chapter, make sure BLUESKY-SRV2 is running, which currently holds the Administrator mailbox.

- Log on as Administrator to BLUESKY-SRV1 and BLUESKY-WKSTA.

▶ **To include a custom attribute in Outlook Address Book searches**

1. On BLUESKY-SRV1, launch Active Directory Users and Computers, click View, and verify that Advanced Features is selected.

2. Open the Users container and double-click Administrator.

3. Click on the Exchange Advanced tab, and then click Custom Attributes.

4. In the Exchange Custom Attributes dialog box, select extensionAttribute1, and click Edit.

5. In the Custom Attributes dialog box, type **5** (which corresponds to the highest seniority level at Blue Sky Airlines), and then click OK three times. Close the Active Directory Users and Computers snap-in.

6. Start Exchange System Manager, expand the Recipients container and the Details Templates container, and then select English.

7. In the details pane, right-click the Search Dialog object, and then select Properties.

8. In the Search Dialog Properties dialog box, click on the Templates tab. (A Loading Schema dialog box appears while the attributes are being loaded.)

9. Click Add to display the Select Control Type dialog box, double-click Label, and, in the Label Control dialog box, type the following information:

X: **183**

Y: **90**

W: **55**

H: **12**

Text: **&Seniority Level:** (There is no space between the "&" and the "S" in Seniority)

10. Click OK.

11. In the Search Dialog Properties box, Value column, select &Seniority Level:, and then click Move Down. The &Seniority Level: label must be listed below the first Page Break entry in the Control column to be displayed on the search page.

12. Click Add to display the Select Control Type dialog box, and then double-click Edit to display the Edit Control dialog box, where you need to type the following:

X: **254**

Y: **90**

W: **25**

H: **12**

13. From the Field list, select ms-Exch-Extension-Attribute-1, and then click OK.

14. Make sure the new Edit control is listed underneath its corresponding Label (use the Move Up and Move Down buttons to arrange the controls), then click Test to display the Search Dialog Template Test dialog box.

15. Verify that the Seniority Level controls are correctly aligned.

16. Click OK twice and close Exchange System Manager.

17. On BLUESKY-WKSTA, launch Outlook, and connect to the Administrator mailbox.

18. On the toolbar, click the Address Book button to display the Address Book dialog box.

19. On the toolbar, click Find Items, and, in the Find dialog box, under Seniority Level, type **5**. Click OK.

20. The Address Book dialog box reappears, displaying the entry for Administrator (see Figure 14.9). This value of 5 was specified as the Administrator's seniority level in the Active Directory Users and Computers snap-in.

21. Close the Address Book and exit Outlook 2000.

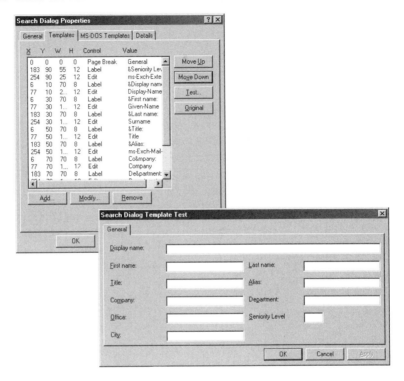

Figure 14.9   Working with a customized search dialog

Exercise Summary

Using the Search Dialog template within the Details Templates container, you can modify the Search dialog box for Outlook 2000. You can associate new controls with additional attributes. If you want to include a new attribute in searches, you must make sure the attribute is replicated to the Global Catalog. Otherwise, users cannot find recipients. Using the Active Directory Schema snap-in, you can verify whether the desired attributes are included in Global Catalog replication. Because the Active Directory schema is flexible, you can add your own set of attributes and use them instead of extensionAttributes1 through 15. It is not possible to rename the Exchange Custom Attributes.

Chapter Summary

Exchange System Manager is the primary tool for managing Exchange 2000 Server configurations. You can manage storage groups and message stores, arrange servers in administrative groups for central management, and define global settings for the entire organization. The organization object and the objects of administrative groups serve the primary purpose of permission delegation to additional administrators. Server objects, on the other hand, enable you to assign computers running Exchange 2000 Server specific tasks. Among other things, you can configure dedicated mailbox and public folder servers.

At the level of individual mailbox and public stores, you can activate Exchange 2000 Server's full-text indexing feature. Full-text indexing allows your Outlook users and users of IMAP4 clients to perform full-text searches of messages, documents, and message attachments. The user doesn't have to use any new utilities or change search habits because Exchange 2000 Server checks available full-text information automatically.

At the global scope of the organization, you can configure server-based address lists, among other things. Address lists allow you to consolidate mailbox- and mail-enabled directory objects based on common attributes. They give you the option of providing a detailed view of the structures of your enterprise through the Outlook 2000 address book.

Review

The following review questions can help you determine if you have sufficiently familiarized yourself with the material covered in this chapter. You can find the answers to these questions at the end of this book in Appendix A, "Questions and Answers."

1. You plan to create multiple storage groups and message stores on an Exchange 2000 server. Which Exchange 2000 Server version do you need to install on this machine, and how many information stores can you configure?

2. Your organization uses various advanced collaboration solutions for account management, sales tracking, and knowledge management. These solutions rely on a specific public folder structure, which is accessed by numerous users from various departments on a daily basis. For best performance, you are considering a dedicated public folder server for these forums. What do you need to accomplish before you can configure a server as a dedicated public folder server?

3. You are planning to implement a document management system and want to activate full-text indexing for the corresponding public store. What are the steps to activate Exchange 2000 Server's full-text indexing feature?

4. How can you move a server between administrative groups?

5. As an administrator for Exchange 2000 Server, you have configured several nested server-based address lists. However, correct address list information is not displayed in the client's address books yet. How can you trigger an immediate address list update?

CHAPTER 15

SMTP Transport Configuration

About This Chapter

The Simple Mail Transfer Protocol (SMTP), introduced in Chapter 11, does not provide a secure method for transporting and delivering electronic messages. As its name implies, it is a *simple* protocol. It was developed in the early 1980s when Internet security issues were still a problem of the future. The vulnerability of SMTP systems was first exploited in a large-scale Internet attack in 1988—the Morris Internet Worm was the first virus flooding the Net with e-mail messages. With Microsoft Exchange 2000 Server, you can effectively put an end to e-mail worms, regardless of the mechanism they abuse, and protect against malicious attempts to swamp your messaging infrastructure.

The core transport engine of Exchange 2000 Server is the SMTP service of Microsoft Windows 2000. SMTP is a very efficient transport protocol; it can transfer messages, for instance, up to 300% faster than X.400. SMTP is very popular, and it is hard to think of a professional messaging system that does not support it. SMTP is easy to configure, but to provide security, you must config-ure your SMTP virtual servers carefully, especially when connected to the Internet.

This chapter deals with the configuration of SMTP virtual servers and the customization of the SMTP service. It does not, however, discuss the administra-tion of the SMTP Connector, which provides fine-grained control over the send-ing of e-mail messages to remote locations. Administration of the SMTP

Connector is covered, together with other connector types, in Chapter 16, "Message Routing Configuration."

Before You Begin

To complete this chapter:

- Prepare your test environment according to the descriptions given in the "Getting Started" section of "About This Book."
- You need to be familiar with the general concepts of creating and configuring protocol virtual servers using Exchange System Manager, as explained in Chapter 11, "Internet-Based Client Access."

Lesson 1: SMTP Configurations and Virtual Servers

By default, every Exchange 2000 server relies on one SMTP virtual server for its communication with other servers in the local routing group. This virtual server can also support users of Internet mail clients for sending messages. The communication is not secured. Users and remote SMTP hosts don't need to authenticate themselves before they can communicate. Anonymous access to the local SMTP service is generally allowed. Nevertheless, you can restrict access through authentication and encrypt the communication, as explained in Chapter 11, "Internet-Based Client Access."

This lesson covers the configuration of SMTP virtual servers in more detail. After that, several topics about Internet connectivity and message transfer are discussed.

At the end of this lesson, you will be able to:
- Configure multiple SMTP virtual servers on a single machine.
- Configure basic connection and delivery settings.
- Describe advanced configurations for Internet connectivity.

Estimated time to complete this lesson: 60 minutes

Configuring Additional SMTP Virtual Servers

One SMTP virtual server is usually sufficient for Exchange 2000 Server, but there are situations in which multiple virtual servers can be helpful. For instance, one virtual server may handle Internet e-mail traffic and another could be responsible for users directly transferring messages to the server with their Internet clients (see Figure 15.1). Separate virtual server entities give you the ability to manage message sizes and other settings separately. Each virtual server must use a unique TCP socket (that is, IP address + TCP port). You can read more about the creation of protocol virtual servers in Chapter 11, "Internet-Based Client Access."

Note Adding additional virtual servers does not increase the server's scalability or performance. Each SMTP virtual server operates with multiple threads being able to handle multiple tasks concurrently.

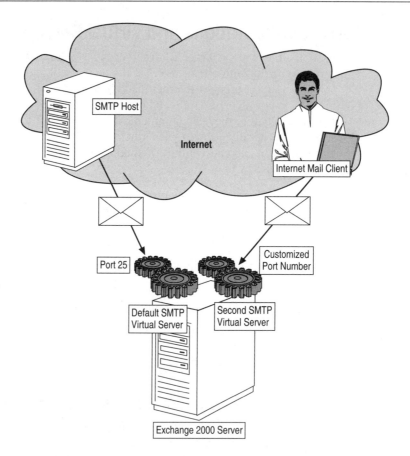

Figure 15.1   Separate virtual servers for public and client communication

Working with Additional Virtual Servers

You can control virtual servers and start, stop, or pause them independently of each other. Pausing a server prevents the establishment of new connections, and existing connections are not terminated. For instance, if you check the number of current connections for a particular virtual server (select the Current Sessions object under the SMTP Virtual Server object in Exchange System Manager) and find an unusually high number of sessions, which could indicate that your host is under a denial-of-service attack from the Internet, you could stop the virtual server without affecting others on the same machine.

Note   Stopping virtual servers in Exchange System Manager leaves the SMTP service running on the computer. Stopping the SMTP service itself, on the other hand, stops all virtual servers. When you restart the SMTP service, only those virtual servers that originally were active when the service was shut down will be activated.

Mailroot Directories of Virtual Servers

Every SMTP virtual server has a separate Mailroot directory. All Mailroot directories are located under \Program Files\Exchsrvr\Mailroot and are named sequentially, for example, Vsi 1, Vsi 2, and so forth. Each of these subdirectories contains three or four folders named Badmail, Pickup, Queue, and possibly Filter. As indicated by its name, Badmail is used to save undeliverable messages. Pickup is the folder where outgoing messages are placed for delivery in the form of text files. A text file must be formatted according to RFC 822. As soon as such a file is present, the SMTP server will pick it up, transfer it into the Queue directory, and attempt its delivery. The Queue directory holds all messages that are currently awaiting delivery. The fourth folder, called Filter, on the other hand, is not present by default. It is created automatically when the first message is filtered after you have enabled message filtering for a particular virtual server, as explained later in this lesson.

If you want to change the location of the Mailroot directory for a particular virtual server, you need to use the MetaEdit utility and change the settings directly in the Internet Information Services (IIS) metabase. MetaEdit was introduced in Exercise 2 of Chapter 3, "Microsoft Exchange 2000 Server Architecture." Exchange System Manager only allows you to change the Badmail directory.

Note The Exchange 2000 Setup program moves the Mailroot directory of the SMTP service from \Inetpub\Mailroot to Program Files\Exchsrvr\Mailroot. The old folder structure will not be deleted, but any messages in the former Pickup and Queue directories are not delivered. To send them, move them to the Pickup directory under the new location.

Managing Incoming Message Traffic

Let's assume the Exchange 2000 server shown in Figure 15.1 is supposed to accept messages from any host on the Internet. How does a remote Internet host find the SMTP virtual server to transfer messages to it? You will need to make sure that the Internet hosts are able to resolve your domain name to your host's public IP address. Typically, DNS provides the required name resolution functionality, as explained in Chapter 11, "Internet-Based Client Access."

Important For other SMTP servers to find your SMTP server on the network, your SMTP domain name must be registered in the Internet DNS (mail exchanger, or MX records).

Controlling Incoming Connections

As soon as your host is connected to the Internet and publicly registered in DNS, all Internet hosts are able to find it, connect to it, and transfer messages. Every connection consumes server resources, so numerous simultaneous connections can decrease system performance. By default, Exchange 2000 Server does not enforce any limits. If your server has to cope with a large number of connections, you should decrease the connection timeout in the SMTP virtual server's General tab to disconnect idle links and free server resources quicker. The default timeout is 10 minutes. You can also specify a limit for the number of inbound connections.

Inbound E-Mail Domains

In addition to routing inbound messages to your SMTP virtual server, the domain names for which your organization is responsible must be identified in Exchange 2000 Server. Otherwise, the messages may reach your server but will be refused.

By default, only the main SMTP domain name of your Exchange 2000 organization is configured as an inbound SMTP domain. If you need to support additional domains, for instance, because some of your users prefer to use a different Internet address, such as User@Bluesky-inc-10.co.uk, you need to configure additional inbound domains. Launch the Exchange System Manager, open the Recipients container, select Recipient Policies, and then, in the details pane, right-click the desired policy, such as Default Policy. From the shortcut menu, select the Properties command. Click on the E-Mail Addresses tab, click New, select SMTP Address, and then click OK. In the SMTP Address Properties dialog box, under Address, enter the Internet domain name, such as @Bluesky-inc-10.co.uk, and make sure the check box called This Exchange Organization Is Responsible For All Mail Delivery To This Address is selected. Click OK.

Note   Configure separate recipient policies and specify filter rules to assign the desired SMTP domain name(s) to the intended recipients. You can read more about recipient policies in Chapter 13, "Creating and Managing Recipients."

Controlling Message Relay

Relaying is the process of accepting a message from a remote SMTP host and forwarding this message to another SMTP host for delivery to the final destination (see Figure 15.2). You can specify the hosts that are allowed to relay in the virtual server's Access tab. Click the Relay button, and then click Add to specify the desired hosts or domains via IP address or domain name. By default, Exchange 2000 Server allows only authenticated computers to relay SMTP messages.

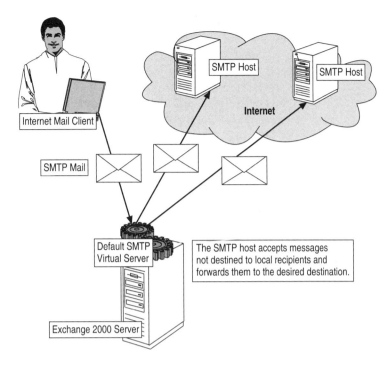

Figure 15.2   Relaying SMTP mail

It is not advisable to loosen relay restrictions for anonymous connections. Doing so may make you a target for those on the Internet that waste precious resources with unsolicited commercial messages. An advertiser might configure his or her Internet mail client to send messages to your SMTP host if it accepts message relaying for anybody. Now, all the advertiser has to do is compose one new message, specify thousands of recipients conveniently from a database, and then send this one message to the relaying host. The client's job is quickly done. It is the host that has to do all the work of sending the unsolicited message to the thousands of users in the Internet. Don't let Internet advertisers abuse your SMTP system.

Configuring Message Filters

Sooner or later, your users will receive unsolicited commercial messages, which can quickly get out of hand. Delivering unnecessary Internet messages is a drain on your system resources; it decreases the productivity of the knowledge worker; and there is always a risk of receiving viruses contained in message attachments.

To prevent the delivery of messages from specific sources, display the properties of the Message Delivery object, which can be found in Exchange System Manager under Global Settings. Click on the Filtering tab, and then use the Add button to specify senders that you want to sort out. As soon as a filter is defined, you can activate the filtering feature on your virtual server. Display its properties, then, in the General tab, click the Advanced button, edit the IP Address – TCP Port mapping, and select the Apply Filter check box. If a message is received with a sender e-mail address that matches a filter entry, the message will be discarded.

To circumvent message filters, senders of unsolicited commercial messages often change their e-mail addresses by inserting altering series of numbers (such as Walt123Lucky456@makeabillioneveryday-times-100.com). Consequently, it is not advisable to specify filter information precisely. You should use wildcards (*) where possible. To filter for entire Internet domains, for instance, use a wildcard as follows: *@makeabillioneveryday-times-100.com. It is also a good idea to filter messages with blank sender information and suppress notifications about the filtering. If you activate the Archive Filtered Messages option in addition, filtered messages are placed in the Filter directory of the SMTP virtual server, where you can check them out to verify that no important messages have been purged.

Reverse DNS Lookups

You can verify the IP address and domain information submitted by a remote SMTP host in the EHLO/HELO command through a reverse domain name lookup. In the Delivery tab, click the Advanced button, then click the Perform Reverse DNS Lookup On Incoming Messages check box. If the verification is unsuccessful, "unverified" appears after the IP address in the SMTP header of messages. However, reverse DNS lookups decrease the server performance, message delivery is not prevented for unverified IP addresses, and most recipients don't check the SMTP header information of Internet messages. Consequently, it is a good idea to activate this feature only for specific security checks.

Configuring Message Delivery Options

Exchange 2000 Server allows you to set message size limits for outbound and inbound messages and to restrict the number of recipients per message (Message Delivery object under Global Settings in the Defaults tab). By default, Exchange 2000 Server accepts messages for delivery to up to 5,000 recipients. Messages with more recipients are returned as undeliverable. However, the settings specified at this location apply only to users with mailboxes in the organization. Limits can be overwritten per user in Active Directory Users and Computers in the user account's Exchange General tab.

Note To forward a copy of nondelivery reports generated by an SMTP virtual server to the Postmaster account, display the SMTP virtual server's property sheets, switch to the Messages tab, and then type **Postmaster@<Your Domain Name>** (for example, **Postmaster@BlueSky-inc-10.com**) in the Send Copy Of Non-Delivery Report To text box.

If you allow anonymous users and SMTP hosts to relay through your Exchange 2000 server, up to 64,000 recipients are accepted per message, because the settings of the SMTP virtual server apply instead of global delivery settings. The number of recipients can be restricted in the virtual server's properties in the Messages tab. You can decrease the value in the Limit Number Of Recipients Per Message To field. Values between 100 and 2000000000 are supported.

Forwarding Messages with Unresolved Recipients

If you examine the Messages tab further, you will discover the Forward All Mail With Unresolved Recipients To Host text box, which allows you to specify the fully qualified domain name (FQDN) of another host for delivery of messages that contain unresolved recipients. Instead of generating nondelivery reports, your SMTP server will forward all nondeliverable messages to the specified host. It is up to this host to deliver the messages or generate nondelivery reports. This is a very useful configuration, especially in migration scenarios (see Figure 15.3).

In the configuration of Figure 15.3, all recipients can keep their existing Internet e-mail addresses. Migrated users with mailboxes on the Exchange 2000 server will receive Internet messages because the SMTP virtual server is able to resolve the recipient information. Messages addressed to nonmigrated users will be forwarded to the legacy system, where they are delivered to their mailboxes as well.

Note To avoid message loops, do not forward messages for unresolved recipients to another virtual server if this server is also configured for forwarding of unresolved messages.

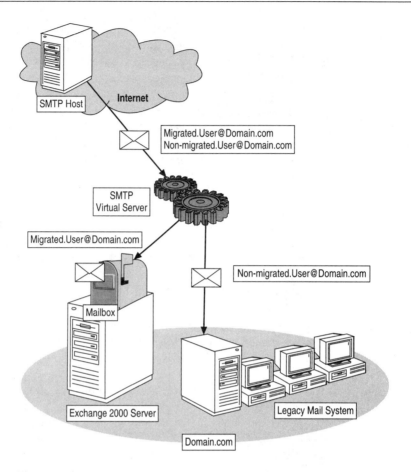

Figure 15.3   Forwarding unresolved recipients to another host

---

Note   The forwarding of nondeliverable messages to another SMTP host affects messages from Internet and MAPI-based clients. If you use this feature to support non-migrated users, keep in mind that nondeliverable messages of MAPI-based clients, such as Outlook 2000, will only contain a WINMAIL.DAT attachment and may not be readable by non-MAPI clients. It is not advisable to use the forwarding of nondeliverable messages for long-term coexistence.

Managing Outgoing Message Traffic

The configuration of outgoing message transfer primarily concerns the notification of local users about the delivery process. In the Delivery tab that every SMTP virtual server provides, you can set retry intervals and determine when to send delay notifications to users and when to cancel delivery. By default, an SMTP virtual server attempts to deliver a message as soon as it arrives. If the remote host is unavailable at that time or if a communication failure occurs, the virtual server queues the message for delivery at later time (or reroutes the message, as explained in Chapter 16, "Message Routing Administration"). The first three retries follow in 10-minute intervals. After that, the virtual server attempts delivery every 15 minutes. If a message cannot be sent for 12 hours, the sender is informed that the message is still awaiting delivery. After two days, the message expires and a nondelivery report is generated and sent back to the originator.

Optimizing Outbound Connections

When you click the Outbound Connections button in the Delivery tab, you can define various connection limits that affect the performance of the SMTP virtual server. Per domain, 100 concurrent connections are allowed by default. If you have a large number of messages to transfer between SMTP hosts, you might increase the number of connections, but the remote host must be able to accept them. In a default configuration, Exchange 2000 Server is able to open up to 1000 concurrent connections to multiple Internet domains and deliver messages to them at the same time.

If messages to multiple domains are awaiting delivery, the SMTP service groups them in memory by their destination domain to send them in a batch over a single connection. To avoid overwhelming a remote SMTP host with numerous messages, the Limit Number Of Messages Per Connection To setting is set to 20 messages by default (Messages tab). This determines that the local SMTP virtual server must establish a new connection when 20 messages have been transferred. The remote host may free allocated resources when the first connection is closed and continue the message transfer in a subsequent connection.

However, the overhead of connection establishment may slow down the mail transfer, especially if your servers have no problems transferring hundreds of messages in a batch. If your server is operating as a central bridgehead in your organization, it may be the case that your SMTP virtual server has to handle a constant stream of messages to downstream servers in other routing groups. In this situation, it could be advantageous to avoid additional handshakes for further connection establishments by not limiting the number of messages per connection. This increases performance because it allows the virtual server to traffic all e-mail over the established link.

Smart Host Message Transfer

In the Outbound Connections dialog box (which you can display via the Delivery tab's Outbound Connections button), you can also find a TCP Port text box, which allows you to change the port number for outbound connections. In most cases, you should not change this setting because it affects all connections. Internet hosts, for instance, generally expect incoming connections on port 25.

However, if you are communicating with a smart host that uses a customized port number, you need to enter the correct value in this box. Don't forget to specify the smart host in the Advanced Delivery dialog box (which you can display via the Delivery tab's Advanced button). A smart host is a server that is able to receive messages from relaying systems and send them to the proper destinations on behalf of the relayers (see Figure 15.4). Internet service providers (ISPs) often provide their customers with access to a central smart host that handles the message transfer.

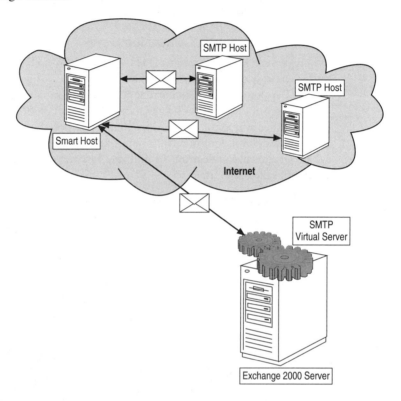

Figure 15.4   Relaying SMTP mail through a smart host

Direct Message Transfer

If you don't use a smart host for message delivery, your SMTP virtual server must be able to resolve e-mail domain names into corresponding IP addresses itself. As mentioned earlier, this is typically accomplished through DNS. However, your internal DNS servers might not be integrated with the public DNS system of the Internet. In this case, querying the internal DNS servers would not bring the desired results and messages would be returned to their originators with nondelivery reports stating that domain or host names could not be resolved.

To add references to external DNS servers to your SMTP virtual server configuration, in the Delivery tab, click the Advanced button. In the Advanced Delivery dialog box that appears, under Configure External DNS Servers, click the Configure button. You can specify one or many DNS servers by their IP address.

Note   By default, Exchange 2000 Server uses DNS to locate remote SMTP hosts.

Automatic Replies to the Internet

Automatic message replies are system messages, such as delivery and nondelivery reports, out-of-office responses, read and nonread receipts, and messages automatically forwarded by means of Inbox rules. By default, these message types can be sent to Internet recipients. This may expose a security breach if your organization requires a very high security standard. Out-of-office notifications, for instance, can inform intruders about how long a user will be out of the office. Delivery and nondelivery reports might inform foes whether specific e-mail addresses are indeed correct. They might use existing addresses in falsified e-mail messages to distribute defamatory or otherwise malicious documents or viruses to damage your organization's reputation. Without advanced security measures it's hard to prove that a message was spoofed. (Advanced security is covered in Chapter 19, "Implementing Advanced Security.")

Therefore, it might be advisable to disable certain automatic replies to the Internet, which can be done through Internet message formats definitions. By default, one definition object, called Default, exists in the Internet Message Formats container under Global Settings. Display the properties of this object, click on the Advanced tab, and deselect the check boxes for those message types that you don't want to allow.

Important   If you deselect the Allow Automatic Forward check box, users cannot forward incoming messages to Internet addresses by means of an Inbox rule. Messages will be generated and sent; however, the SMTP virtual server will discard them silently without generating a nondelivery report. Users might be wondering where their messages got stuck.

Communicating with Other Exchange Organizations over the Internet

Your users will communicate with many Internet domains that actually correspond to other Exchange organizations. After all, Exchange 2000 Server is one of the world's most popular messaging systems. In Exchange organizations, users typically work with MAPI-based clients, such as Outlook 2000, that support advanced rich text information in e-mail messages. The Default message format definition object allows the user to decide whether to send Exchange rich text information in Internet messages.

Sending Exchange Rich Text Information in Outlook 2000

Most users are not aware of the feature that allows them to send Exchange rich text information to recipients in other domains over the Internet, because this feature is rather hidden, especially when manually entering the address information. To try it, compose a new message, type Recipient@Domain.com in the To line, click the Check Names button, double-click the underlined address, and, in the E-mail Properties dialog box, select the Always Send To This Recipient In Microsoft Outlook Rich-Text Format check box. Click OK. It is that simple.

If you maintain address information for recipients in other organizations in the Active Directory directory service, you can specify whether to send the Exchange rich text information in the corresponding contact objects. In Active Directory Users and Computers, activate Advanced Features (under View), display the properties of the desired contact, click on the Exchange Advanced tab, and select the Use MAPI Rich Text Format check box. Exchange rich text information is automatically sent to those recipients if your users select them from a server-based address list. You can read more about the maintenance of recipient objects in Chapter 13, "Creating and Managing Recipients."

Activating Exchange Rich-Text Information for an Internet Domain

If your users are communicating with other domains and know that these rely on Exchange and Outlook for messaging, you can configure Exchange to send rich-text messages. This preserves all message formatting, and recipients are able to view their messages in exactly the form in which they were composed. Even advanced formatting structures and special message types, such as meeting and task requests, are preserved. Furthermore, delivery and read-receipt requests can be requested from recipients in the other organizations (see Figure 15.5).

Note   When sending Exchange rich-text information, the entire message is encapsulated using the transport-neutral encapsulation format (TNEF) and sent as an attachment called WINMAIL.DAT in an SMTP message that contains the message body in plain text.

To ensure Exchange rich-text information is preserved for specific domains, create a new message format definition for each domain separately. In Exchange System Manager, right-click Internet Message Formats, point to New, and click Domain. In the General tab, provide a name, and specify the SMTP domain information. After that, click on the Advanced tab, and, under Exchange Rich-Text Format, select Always Use. Click on the Message Format tab, and, under MIME, select the Provide Message Body As Plain Text option. The body doesn't need to contain any rich text structures itself because this is in the Exchange rich-text information.

In addition, you may want to activate the Apply Content Settings To Non-MAPI Clients check box. This causes Exchange 2000 Server to convert messages from Internet mail clients into MAPI format, which ensures that the remote domain receives consistently formatted e-mail messages from your users regardless of their client applications.

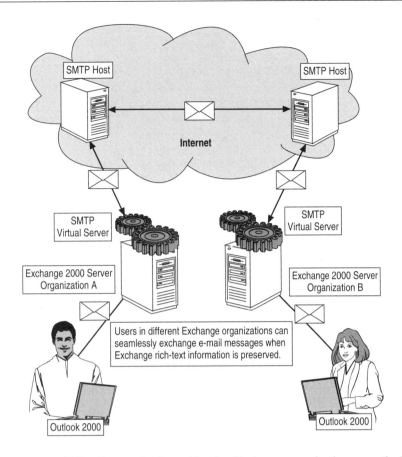

Figure 15.5 Communicating with other Exchange organizations over the Internet

Users of Internet mail clients not working with Exchange mailboxes are unable to interpret the Exchange rich-text information. They will receive a plain text message with a useless WINMAIL.DAT attachment. Any attachments originally included in the message may be encapsulated within the WINMAIL.DAT file and may not be readable. To avoid confusion, don't enforce Exchange rich-text information if you are not sure that the target domain represents an Exchange organization.

Configuring Protocol Logging

SMTP protocol logging is a powerful feature that is useful in many situations. You may keep a history of all SMTP activity in a database, for instance. In this way, you can always prove whether a particular message has left your server. You can also use protocol log information to verify whether the virtual server is performing its work as expected or is experiencing communication problems. Last but not least, SMTP protocol logging can help to identify attacks from the Internet. For troubleshooting purposes, you might find it sufficient to log protocol activities in an ASCII text file instead of an Open Database Connectivity (ODBC)-compliant database.

Display the property sheets of your SMTP virtual server in Exchange System Manager, and activate the Enable Logging check box in the General tab to activate the protocol logging feature. From the Active Log Format list box, select the desired logging format. For maintaining history information in a database, select ODBC Logging, and click the Properties button to specify the required database information. For the most detailed logging in text files, select Microsoft IIS Log File Format. Click the Properties button to specify the desired logging settings and the Log File Directory.

Exercise 1: Relay Restrictions and Junk Mail

In this exercise you will examine the default relay behavior of Exchange 2000 Server. After that, you will configure an SMTP virtual server for filtering of unsolicited commercial e-mail or junk mail.

To view a multimedia demonstration that displays how to perform this procedure, run the EX1CH15.AVI files from the \Exercise_Information\Chapter15 folder on the Supplemental Course Materials CD.

Prerequisites

- Configure BLUESKY-SRV1 as a dedicated public folder server and BLUESKY-SRV2 as a dedicated mailbox server according to the exercises in Chapter 14, "Managing Server Configuration." Make sure both servers are running, as well as BLUESKY-WKSTA.

- Log on as Administrator to BLUESKY-SRV1.

▶ **To examine relay restrictions for anonymous SMTP connections and filter unsolicited e-mail messages**

1. Click Start and then click Run. In the Run dialog box, type **telnet**, and then click OK.

2. At the Microsoft Telnet command prompt, type **set LOCAL_ECHO** and press ENTER.

3. Type **open bluesky-srv1 25** and press ENTER.

4. Verify that you are successfully connected to the ESMTP Mail Service of bluesky-srv1.bluesky-inc-10.com. Type **helo domain.com**, and press ENTER.

5. Type **mail from:<advertiser123@domain.com>** and press ENTER.

6. Type **rcpt to:<recipient@another-domain.com>** and press ENTER. Notice the Unable To Relay For Recipient@Another-Domain.com error message (see Figure 15.6).

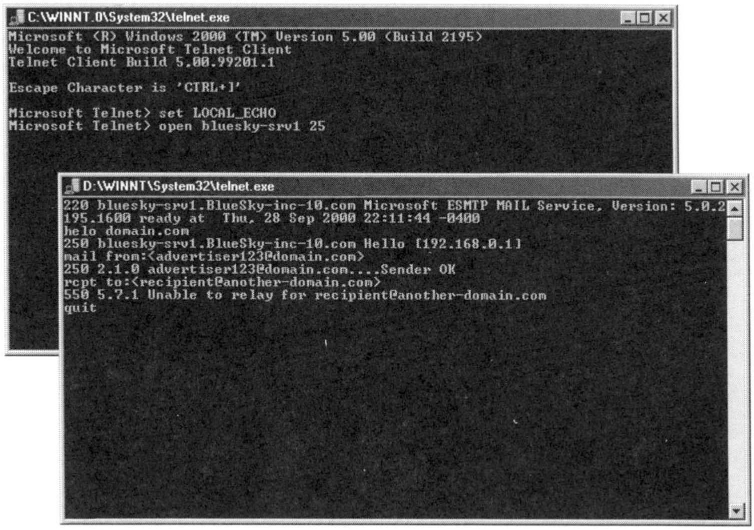

Figure 15.6   Unable to relay anonymously to foreign domains

7. Type **quit** and press ENTER twice to close the connection to BLUESKY-SRV1 and leave Telnet running.

8. Launch Exchange System Manager, right-click Message Delivery under Global Settings, select Properties, click on the Filtering tab, and then click Add.

9. In the Add Sender dialog box, type ***@domain.com**, and then click OK.

10. Activate the Archive Filtered Messages and Filter Messages With Blank Sender check boxes, and then click OK (see Figure 15.7).

11. Right-click the Default SMTP Virtual Server, which you can find under the Protocols container of BLUESKY-SRV1, and select Properties.

12. In the General tab, click the Advanced button, select the existing IP Address – TCP Port mapping, and click Edit.

13. In the Identification dialog box, activate the Apply Filter check box.

14. Click OK three times, and then give the Metabase Update service some time to transfer the configuration changes into the IIS metabase.

15. Switch back to the Microsoft Telnet command prompt, type **open bluesky-srv1 25**, and press ENTER.

16. Type **helo domain.com** and press ENTER.

17. Type **mail from:<sender@unfiltered-domain.com>** and press ENTER.

18. Type **rcpt to:<administrator@bluesky-inc-10.com>** and press ENTER.

19. Type **data** and press ENTER.

20. Type **From: sender@unfiltered-domain.com** and press ENTER.

21. Type **To: administrator@bluesky-inc-10.com** and press ENTER.

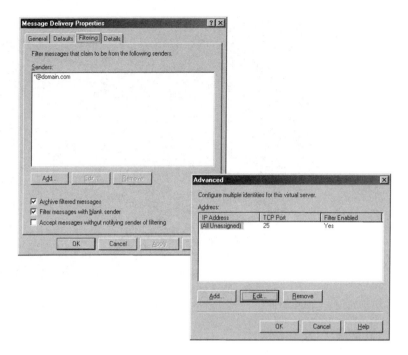

Figure 15.7   Activating a message filter

22. Type **Subject: This is an unfiltered Message** and press ENTER.

23. Press ENTER again, and then type **We are testing message filtering**. Press ENTER.

24. Press ENTER again, type a single period (**.**), and press ENTER again to signal the end of message transfer. Notice the response from the server that the message is queued for delivery.

25. Type **mail from:<advertiser123@domain.com>** and press ENTER. Notice that the server returns the Sender Denied error message and terminates the connection immediately.

26. Press ENTER, type **open bluesky-srv1 25**, and press ENTER again.

27. Type **helo domain.com** and press ENTER.

28. Type **mail from:<sender@unfiltered-domain.com>** and press ENTER.

29. Type **rcpt to:<administrator@bluesky-inc-10.com>** and press ENTER.

30. Type **data** and press ENTER.

31. Type **From: advertiser123@domain.com** and press ENTER.

32. Type **To: administrator@bluesky-inc-10.com** and press ENTER.

33. Type **Subject: This is a filtered Message** and press ENTER.

34. Press ENTER again, and then type **We are testing message filtering**. Press ENTER.

35. Press ENTER again, type a single period (**.**), and press ENTER again to signal the end of message transfer. Notice the response from the server that the sender is denied (see Figure 15.8). You can find this filtered message in form of a .tmp file in the directory \Exchsrvr\Mailroot\Vsi 1\Filter.

36. Close the Telnet client program.

Figure 15.8   Testing a message filter in Telnet

Exercise Summary

Exchange 2000 Server protects your server resources and does not permit anonymous users to relay messages. Only messages to recipients in the local organization are accepted. In addition, you can configure message filters to reject unsolicited messages from the Internet. As soon as the SMTP service detects a match for a filtered sender address, it denies the sender the ability to transfer messages. Unsolicited messages received from users who claim to be nonfiltered senders can still be detected based on the sender information in the message.

Note   SMTP has no mechanism to verify the correctness of e-mail address information. Advertisers and intruders distributing mail viruses can find a way around message filters if they try hard enough.

Lesson 2: Customizing the SMTP Service

The SMTP service of Windows 2000 provides a powerful architecture for enhancements and extensions via synchronous transport and protocol event sinks. Most important, SMTP extensions give you a means by which you can examine messages for critical or unsafe content and block their transmission or delivery. Even if you are not a system programmer, you may find the following lesson interesting because it can give you the information you need to put an end to Internet worms and other malicious codes that spread via e-mail messages. The architecture of the SMTP service was explained in Chapter 3, "Microsoft Exchange 2000 Server Architecture."

This lesson briefly discusses the possibilities of extending the SMTP service using event sinks. You can learn how to check incoming messages using a transport event sink written in Microsoft Visual Basic, Scripting Edition (VBScript), and how to discard critical messages.

At the end of this lesson, you will be able to:

- Explain the purpose of transport and protocol event sinks.
- Describe possible scenarios where transport and protocol event sinks can be useful.
- Enhance the SMTP service using the ISMTPOnArrival interface.

Estimated time to complete this lesson: 30 minutes

SMTP Transport Event Handling

Transport events are an extension mechanism for intercepting messages after the SMTP service has received them, before they are delivered to Exchange mailboxes or relayed to other SMTP hosts. Event sinks rely on Microsoft Collaboration Data Objects 2.0 (CDO 2.0). CDO is Component Object Model (COM)-compliant; hence, you can write transport event sinks in any COM-compliant programming language, including Microsoft Visual C++, Microsoft Visual Basic, and Microsoft Visual J++, as well as in Microsoft VBScript and Microsoft JScript. You can find detailed information about event sinks in the Microsoft Platform Software Development Kit.

As a script programmer, you can intercept only one type of SMTP service event: the OnArrival event that occurs when a message has been successfully received by the SMTP service. Scripts can help achieve a desired solution quickly (see Exercise 2 later), but they don't provide best performance. In addition, you need to take extra measures to protect your scripts through NT file system (NTFS) file permissions. Otherwise, another person might view the source code. For maximum flexibility, best performance, and better security, program your event sinks in Visual C++.

By intercepting the OnArrival event, you can process incoming messages for:

- **Adding standard notifications to message text.**   To add informative text to the message body to inform your users that a message was received from the Internet.

- **Blocking of unsolicited messages.**   In addition to message filters, you can implement sophisticated logic that examines the sender information within messages.

- **Creating mailing list services.**   To answer incoming messages with auto-replies and perform further tasks, such as creating a contact from the sender information and adding this contact to distribution groups.

- **Incoming message logging.**   To maintain a history of all messages received by your SMTP service.

- **Message redirection.**   To replace the recipient list of an incoming message with another set of recipients.

- **Virus checks.**   To cancel delivery of the message, based on message and attachment properties.

Exchange 2000 registers numerous SMTP and Network News Transfer Protocol (NNTP) event sinks to integrate the existing Windows 2000 services with the Information Store. You can read more about the integration of IIS with Exchange 2000 Server in Chapter 3, "Microsoft Exchange 2000 Server Architecture."

Protocol Event Handling

SMTP protocol events allow you to alter the way the SMTP service communicates with other SMTP-based systems. You can implement your own SMTP protocol commands to achieve specific functionality. Exchange 2000 Server, for instance, implements a variety of SMTP protocol event sinks, which propagate, among other things, link state information across the communication infrastructure. You can read more about the purpose of link state information in Chapter 16, "Message Routing Configuration."

There are two types of protocol events that the SMTP service allows you to intercept:

- **Inbound protocol events.**   These occur when a remote SMTP host or client connects to the local SMTP service and establishes a session by sending the HELO or EHLO command.

- **Outbound protocol events.**   These occur when the local SMTP service connects to a remote SMTP host and establishes a session to transfer messages.

Event Binding

For the SMTP service to work with your event sinks, you need to register them in the IIS metabase. A binding associates a particular event, such as OnArrival, with a sink name, such as SMTPMessageCheck (see Exercise 2). Within the metabase a globally unique identifier (GUID) identifies each binding. You can use Server Extension Objects (SEOs) implemented in a DLL called SEO.DLL to manage event sink bindings. To examine them in the IIS metabase, open the MetaEdit utility (from the Windows 2000 Resource Kit), expand the LM node, expand SmtpSvc, expand 1, and then expand the EventManager node. Underneath, you will find the EventTypes container that holds the event bindings.

Note   The Platform Software Development Kit describes a file called SMTPREG.VBS, which allows you to register event sinks conveniently. SMTPREG.VBS relies on SEO.

Virus Protection Using Transport Event Sinks

Transport event sinks are extremely powerful tools for virus protection. A virus scanner, for instance, can use them to check all incoming messages and safely discard those that contain infected file attachments. Sometimes, however, you need to react quicker than vendors can supply updated virus checklists, especially if you need to protect against mail worm viruses that already have affected other networks but haven't reached your organization yet.

Mail worms follow a very simple principle. A recipient opens an infected message attachment, and the virus code is executed. This retrieves the full set of address information from all available address lists or from messages in the Inbox, and a new message addressed to all recipients is generated. The new message contains the infected file attachment again, which subsequent recipients will open, and so the virus spreads in the form of an avalanche. Your organization must immediately cope with a huge amount of messages, which often leads to an overtaxing of the communication infrastructure.

Mail worm messages have certain common characteristics. For instance, the subject line is usually the same in all virus messages. Under virus attack, you probably will receive numerous messages, all with the same subject line. It's easy to identify them. Therefore, if you implement a transport event sink that prevents the reception of these messages, your system will be secure.

Most recent versions of mail worms, however, alter the subject line on every cycle, but you still can handle them easily. Plain e-mail messages cannot contain the virus code: An infected attachment is necessary. Consequently, if you intercept all incoming messages with executable attachments, you can prevent mail worms from penetrating your organization. You could forward suspicious mail to a skilled colleague for careful inspection before forwarding it to the actual recipient in the organization. This measure may be used temporarily or permanently.

Exercise 2: Checking
Incoming Messages for .vbs Attachments

In this exercise you will extend the SMTP service by means of a transport event sink. The VBScript code checks incoming SMTP messages for a subject line containing the word virus, and it checks for attachments with a .vbs extension. In both cases, delivery of suspicious messages is blocked. They are written to the Badmail directory of the SMTP virtual server.

To view a multimedia demonstration that displays how to perform this procedure, run the EX2CH15*.AVI files from the \Exercise_Information\Chapter15 folder on the Supplemental Course Materials CD.

Important   Do not register the event script in a production server without testing it carefully on a reference system beforehand. Incorrect scripts can block the entire incoming SMTP message transfer.

Prerequisites

- Log on as Administrator to BLUESKY-WKSTA and BLUESKY-SRV1.

- Insert the Supplemental Course Materials CD into the CD-ROM drive of BLUESKY-SRV1.

▶ **To register a transport event sink for the SMTP service**

1. On BLUESKY-SRV1, start Windows Explorer and create a new directory called EventSink under the root directory C (C:\EventSink).

2. Copy the file SMTPREG.VBS from the \Exercise_Information\Chapter15\ EventSinks folder on the Supplemental Course Materials CD into the newly created directory.

3. In Windows Explorer, open the C:\EventSink directory, right-click in the left pane, point to New, and select Text Document.

4. Name the new file SMTPMSGCHECK.VBS (if a Rename dialog box appears, click Yes), then right-click on it, and, from the shortcut menu, select Edit. Enter the following VBScript code:

```
<SCRIPT LANGUAGE="VBScript">

Sub IEventIsCacheable_IsCacheable()
'To implement the Interface, and return S_OK implicitly
End Sub


Sub ISMTPOnArrival_OnArrival(ByVal Msg, EventStatus )
```

```
        Dim envFlds
        Dim colAttachs
        Dim iFound
        Set envFlds = Msg.EnvelopeFields


    If Msg.Subject = "" Or Len(Msg.Subject) < 5 Then
       iFound = 0
    Else
     iFound = Instr(1, Msg.Subject, "VIRUS", 1) ' First position of the
    word VIRUS
    End If
    'Check whether the message contains a VBS attachment
    Set colAttachs = Msg.Attachments
    For Each oAttach in colAttachs
       If Instr(1, oAttach.FileName, "vbs", 1) > 0 Then iFound = 1
    Next


    If iFound > 0 Then
       'Do not deliver, place message in the Badmail directory.
       envFlds("http://schemas.microsoft.com/cdo/smtpenvelope/
    messagestatus") = 3
       envFlds.Update        ' Commit the changes of the message status
      'Skip remaining event sinks
      EventStatus = 1
    End If
    End Sub

    </SCRIPT>
```

5. Save the changes and close the editor (Notepad).

6. Create another text file, name it INSTSINK.BAT, then right-click on it, and, from the shortcut menu, select Edit. Enter the following lines:

```
@ECho Off


REM ********** The following 2 lines install the Event Sink to log
SMTP Messages **********


cscript smtpreg.vbs /add 1 onarrival SMTPMessageCheck
CDO.SS_SMTPOnArrivalSink "mail from=*"
```

```
cscript smtpreg.vbs /setprop 1 onarrival SMTPMessageCheck Sink
ScriptName "c:\EventSink\SMTPMsgCheck.vbs"

REM ***** Remove the 'REM' tag from the following line  ******

REM ***** if you want to deinstall the Event Sink again ******

REM cscript smtpreg.vbs /remove     1 onarrival SMTPMessageCheck
```

7. Save the changes and close Notepad.

8. Click Start, select Run, type **cmd**, and click OK to start the Windows 2000 command prompt. Then change into the C:\EventSink directory (type **cd \EventSink**).

9. Type **instsink.bat**, and press ENTER to execute the batch file and register the Event Sink sample to log messages. Verify that the event sink is registered properly, and then type **exit**, and press ENTER to close the command prompt.

10. Launch Exchange System Manager, and restart the Default SMTP Virtual Server under BLUESKY-SRV1.

11. Test the transport event sink using Telnet as demonstrated earlier in Exercise 1 (see Figure 15.9). Alternatively, you can use Outlook Express and send SMTP messages to BLUESKY-SRV1, as demonstrated in Exercise 6 of Chapter 11, "Internet-Based Client Access." If a message contains the word virus in its subject line, or has a .vbs attachment, message delivery is canceled, and the message is placed in the \Program Files\Exchsrvr\Mailroot\Vsi 1\Badmail directory.

Exercise Summary

You can extend the SMTP service with scripts written in Microsoft VBScript or Microsoft JScript. The same is also possible when using Microsoft Visual Basic or Microsoft Visual C++, which generally provides a better performance and more flexibility. However, the principle remains the same: You register your event sinks and process individual messages, which the SMTP service will hand over. You gain full access to the contents of messages passing through your SMTP service. This allows you to log all incoming messages, for instance; add additional text to each of them, such as an official note that this message was received from an insecure network; or perform a basic virus scan. You have the option to block and discard critical messages before they reach the mailboxes of your users or are relayed to other systems.

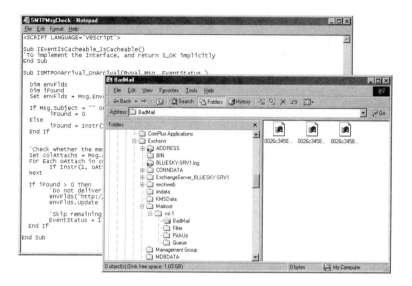

Figure 15.9   Implementing a custom event sink for the SMTP transport

Chapter Summary

Exchange 2000 Server extends the SMTP service of Windows 2000 during installation to implement Exchange-specific functionality through protocol and transport event sinks. In addition, the Mailroot directory is moved to Exchsrvr\Mailroot. Under Mailroot, a structure of one or many subdirectories exists, depending on the number of SMTP virtual servers that have been configured. Typically, one virtual server can handle all SMTP-based message transfer.

If you plan to connect an Exchange 2000 server directly to the Internet, you must make sure that incoming messages are delivered to your server. Your SMTP domain name must be registered in an MX record in the Internet DNS.

As soon as you are publicly known, you might become a target for unsolicited commercial messages, which you can filter to avoid their delivery. Further, relaying of messages from anonymous sources is blocked by default, which helps to protect your system resources. You can also implement advanced logic to check all incoming messages from the Internet for viruses and protect against malicious attempts to swamp your messaging infrastructure.

Review

The following review questions can help you determine if you have sufficiently familiarized yourself with the material covered in this chapter. You can find the answers to these questions at the end of this book in Appendix A, "Questions and Answers."

1. You are the administrator of a small Exchange organization with one Exchange 2000 server. You have successfully connected the server to the Internet. Test messages sent to an Internet address are delivered without problems. Replies to test message, however, end in nondelivery reports. What do you have to accomplish to allow replies to test messages to be delivered to your organization?

2. Your users complain about a large number of unsolicited commercial messages. You check the messages and determine they all come from a domain called Pleasegiveusyourmoney-times-10.com. How can you prevent the delivery of these messages most conveniently?

3. Your server is operating as a central bridgehead server in your organization, which has to handle a constant stream of messages to downstream servers in other routing groups. How can you optimize the throughput of messages?

4. Your internal DNS servers are not integrated with the Internet. How can you enable Exchange 2000 Server to use Internet DNS servers for outbound message transfer?

5. Users complain about lost messages that have been automatically forwarded to an Internet account. What is most likely the cause of this problem?

C H A P T E R   1 6

Message Routing Administration

About This Chapter

Messaging systems are fascinating network applications. You only need to launch Microsoft Outlook 2000, compose a new message, specify a valid e-mail address in the To line, type **I don't care how you get it, but I know you will** in the Subject line, and click Send. Minutes or hours later, the message will have made it into the specified recipient's mailbox. Most likely, the recipient will think, "I don't care either" and delete the message right away. Who cares how messages are delivered?

Microsoft Exchange 2000 Server cares about it. Install as many Exchange 2000 servers in your local area network (LAN) as you like, add all servers to the same routing group, place mailboxes on them, and your users will be able to send each other messages in an instant. Could it be any simpler than that? Sometimes, however, it is not that easy. In those cases, you have to care about the routing of e-mail messages.

This chapter discusses the design of routing topologies in Exchange 2000 organizations. It explains how multiple routing groups are managed to optimize message transfer. It also covers how routing and link state information are propagated between servers.

Before You Begin

To complete this chapter:

- Prepare your test environment according to the descriptions given in the "Getting Started" section of "About This Book." If you have successfully completed the exercises in previous chapters, you do not need to reinstall your test environment.

- Be familiar with the administration of Simple Mail Transfer Protocol (SMTP) virtual servers, as explained in Chapter 15, "SMTP Transport Configuration."

Lesson 1: Routing Group Planning

A routing group is a collection of Exchange 2000 servers that typically share a permanent, reliable, high-bandwidth network connection. In a particular routing group, all servers communicate directly with each other using SMTP. SMTP, in turn, can work efficiently over all types of network connections, including on-demand dial-up links with limited bandwidths and high latencies. This gives you tremendous flexibility when designing the routing topology of your organization.

This lesson covers important aspects of characteristic routing group topologies. The most important reason to engage in routing group planning is minimizing transmission costs by maximizing the efficiency of network communication.

At the end of this lesson, you will be able to:

- Explain the purpose of routing groups.
- Describe the advantages of typical routing group topologies.
- Manage routing groups.

Estimated time to complete this lesson: 75 minutes

Multiple Routing Group Scenarios

The primary reason for multiple routing groups in an Exchange 2000 organization is control and optimization of the flow of messages between servers. Within a routing group, servers communicate directly and immediately with each other by means of SMTP virtual servers. Between routing groups, on the other hand, message transfer relies on messaging connectors. Connector parameters, such as connection times, determine how messages are transferred.

Note   All SMTP virtual servers of a particular Exchange 2000 server must belong to the same routing group.

Single Routing Group Scenario

Organizations operating a homogenous LAN-like network environment will find the deployment of a single routing group sufficient and advantageous. If necessary, servers can be managed in multiple administrative groups, even though they are members of a single routing group. By default, one routing group called First Routing Group exists, and all servers are added to it during their installation (see Figure 16.1).

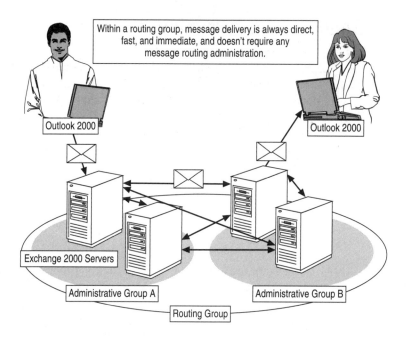

Figure 16.1   A single routing group environment with two administrative groups

In a single routing group environment, connectors are merely used to connect to foreign systems. To give an example, you can use the SMTP Connector to establish an access point to the Internet (see Figure 16.2). The server running the SMTP Connector is called a bridgehead server. All inbound and outbound messages must be transferred to the bridgehead server before they are delivered. With only one bridgehead, you only need to configure one Internet connection with access to external DNS servers. However, it is possible to configure multiple bridgehead servers in a routing group for fault tolerance and load balancing. The configuration of the SMTP Connector is covered in Lesson 2.

The following are some advantages of single routing group organizations:

- **Direct access to public folders.**   Routing groups define the boundaries of direct public folder access. Within a single routing group, all local public folders are available. You can read more about public folder access in Chapter 17, "Public Folder Management."

- **Easiest message routing administration.**   It is not necessary to manage the routing topology manually. Connectors installed on bridgehead servers in the routing group are available to all users in the routing group.

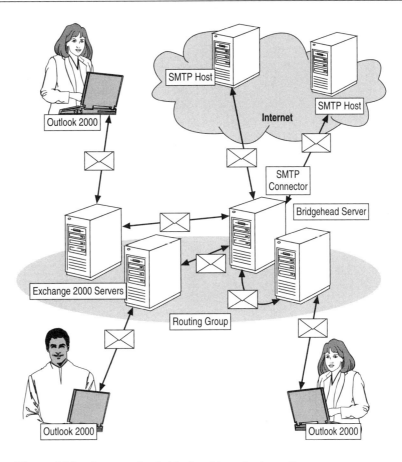

Figure 16.2   A messaging bridgehead in a single routing group

- **Efficient routing of messages.**   Message delivery from server to server is direct and immediate without a necd for intermediate bridgehead servers (single-hop routing).

- **SMTP-based message transfer.**   SMTP is the transport protocol used between Exchange 2000 servers for message transfer in the same routing group.

Reasons for Multiple Routing Groups

If an organization relies on wide area network (WAN) connections, it will be desirable to control network communication. WAN connections may generate transmission costs, may have low bandwidth, may not be permanently available, and may operate unreliably. Here, the implementation of routing groups has advantages. Through the configuration of messaging connectors, you can define dedicated bridgehead servers, which can act as concentrators for message traffic over WAN connections between routing groups (see Figure 16.3).

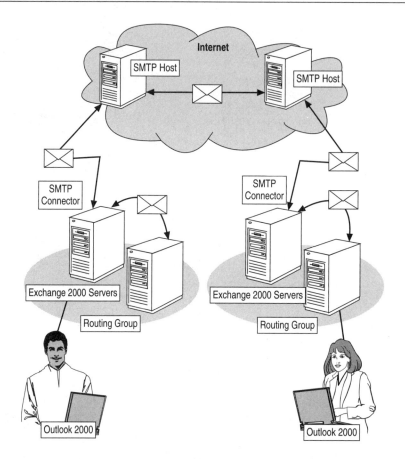

Figure 16.3   Two routing groups separated by WAN

Multiple routing groups enable you to minimize the consumption of network bandwidth. For instance, you can block access to public folders that reside on servers in other routing groups, which is especially desirable over slow network links because it reduces the bandwidth consumed. As explained in Chapter 18, "Public Folder Replication," you can replicate public folder instances to your local routing group if you need to provide them to your users.

Messaging connectors between routing groups can also help minimize transmission costs. You may queue messages and transfer them in batches at specified connection times when transmission charges are minimal (for example, at night). Likewise, it is possible to define a size limit and configure a different connection schedule for oversized messages, which might otherwise delay the transfer of normal messages. Furthermore, data is compressed by an average ratio of 5:1 before it is sent across a connector, which also saves expensive network bandwidth.

Note It is possible to place all servers in one administrative group for global administration but still maintain multiple routing groups for optimized message transfer.

The following are reasons for implementing multiple routing groups:

- Access to public folder resources must be controlled.
- Dedicated bridgehead servers with optimized hardware for message transfer are desired.
- Geographical locations are a consideration.
- Network traffic should be reduced.
- Unstable network links affect message transfer performance.
- WAN transmission generates costs and must be optimized.

Hierarchical Routing Group Arrangement

In a hierarchical arrangement of routing groups, a central group of hub servers controls the entire message transfer between subordinated groups, known as spokes (see Figure 16.4). Especially in large and very large environments, the hierarchical arrangement has proven very reliable, scalable, and resilient. Multiple hub servers share the workload and provide redundancy for well-

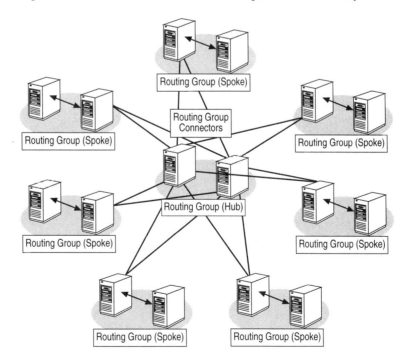

Figure 16.4 A hierarchical backbone architecture

defined message paths between all locations. This design approach prevents uncontrolled rerouting of messages, which was difficult to handle in earlier versions of Exchange Server.

Even though Exchange 2000 Server overcomes certain routing limitations of previous Exchange Server versions, you may avoid using a full-mesh topology. Deploy Exchange 2000 Server in the central location first. As soon as the hub servers are in place and operating reliably, the spoke locations can be deployed or upgraded. Later, you might experiment with Exchange 2000 Server's new and very powerful routing engine by configuring shortcut routes between spokes to speed up and simplify message delivery. Exchange 2000 Server's routing architecture is flexible and allows topology changes at any time.

Note   The new directory architecture and the implementation of the link state algorithm help to overcome many of the deployment issues found in earlier versions of Exchange Server. During the phase of coexistence, however, organize your routing architecture according to the requirements of Exchange Server 5.5.

Full-Mesh Routing Group Arrangement

The hierarchical routing group arrangement has several limitations. Message routing always involves an additional hop, or transfer of a message to a hub server. Hierarchical routing paths may not optimally reflect the physical network infrastructure. Finally, the hub routing group may not be local to the spokes and may require transmission of a large amount of e-mail messages over WAN connections.

By implementing shortcut routes between spokes, you can bypass the hub for more efficient message transfer. In this scenario, you gradually move your routing architecture toward a full-mesh arrangement in which all routing groups can communicate directly with each other, eliminating ping-pong message transfer between bridgehead servers. Based on link state information, Exchange 2000 Server is able to gain a complete overview of connector availability in the organization, which allows for optimal message routing. To give an example, if a central bridgehead server in Rio de Janeiro is shut down, servers in Oslo will be able to recognize this and avoid routing messages to it. You can read more about the propagation of link state information in Lesson 3.

Mixed Routing Group Arrangement

The full-mesh architecture overcomes intermediate hops in message transfer because all bridgeheads communicate directly with each other. However, limited scalability is one significant drawback of the full-mesh topology. Figure 16.5 leaves a confusing impression. As the number of bridgeheads increases, the connector configuration might get out of hand.

As always, an optimal routing architecture depends on a detailed analysis of the underlying network infrastructure. Large organizations might find a hierarchical

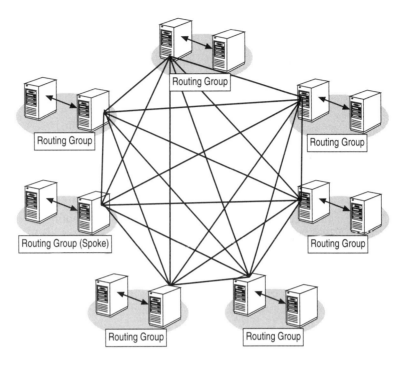

Figure 16.5   A full-mesh backbone architecture

arrangement of fully meshed subbackbones most fitting. Whereas the hierarchical structure corresponds to a global communication infrastructure, local subbackbones can handle the message transfer between geographically close locations directly and efficiently. Users will likely send the majority of their e-mail messages to close recipients.

Managing Routing Groups

The actual management of routing groups is not difficult and requires no special utilities. You can use Exchange System Manager to create routing groups, move servers between them, rename routing groups, or delete them. Moving servers between routing groups is as easy as a simple drag-and-drop operation (see Exercise 1). Connectors associated with a particular server, such as an X.400 Connector, are moved along with the server.

Note   The default First Routing Group is not displayed unless you explicitly enable it via the Display Routing Groups check box (in the General tab of the organization object (for example, Blue Sky Airlines [Exchange]). If you display administrative groups in addition, you will find this routing group under First Administrative Group. All administrators of the First Administrative Group are routing administrators by default.

Dedicated Routing Group Management

If you want to delegate routing group management tasks to a specific group of administrators, you can create a dedicated administrative group to hold all routing groups. Delegate Access permissions for this administrative group to the group of desired routing administrators. Servers from any administrative group can be members of the routing groups. As shown earlier in Figure 16.1, the routing group topology is independent of the administrative group arrangement. You can read more about administrative groups in Chapter 14, "Managing Server Configuration."

Exercise 1: Creating Multiple Routing Groups

In this exercise you will create an additional routing group in your test environment. By means of drag-and-drop, you will move an Exchange 2000 server into the newly created group using Exchange System Manager.

To view a multimedia demonstration that displays how to perform this procedure, run the EX1CH16*.AVI files from the \Exercise_Information\Chapter16 folder on the Supplemental Course Materials CD.

Prerequisites

- If you have completed the exercises of Chapter 14 and configured BLUESKY-SRV1 as a dedicated public folder server, you will need to add a mailbox store to this server, similar to the steps outlined in Exercise 1 of Chapter 14. Name the new mailbox store Mailbox Store (BLUESKY-SRV1) and move the mailbox of Carl Titmouse to BLUESKY-SRV1. The Administrator mailbox should still reside on BLUESKY-SRV2.

- Make sure that administrative and routing groups are displayed in Exchange System Manager—via the Display Routing Groups and Display Administrative Groups check boxes in the properties of the organization object (that is, Blue Sky Airlines [Exchange]).

- Log on as Administrator to BLUESKY-SRV1 and BLUESKY-WKSTA.

▶ **To create an additional routing group and split Exchange 2000 servers**

1. Verify that BLUESKY-SRV2 has been moved into the Members container of the Second Routing Group. Wait a few minutes for Active Directory replication to propagate the changes to BLUESKY-SRV2.

2. Right-click Routing Groups, point to New, and select the Routing Group command.

3. In the Properties dialog box, under Name, type **Second Routing Group**, and then click OK.

4. Expand First Routing Group and Second Routing Group, select the Members container under First Routing Group. Drag BLUESKY-SRV2 from this con-

tainer over the Members container of the Second Routing Group, then let it drop there (see Figure 16.6).

5. Verify that BLUESKY-SRV2 has been moved into the Members container of the Second Routing Group.

6. On BLUESKY-WKSTA, launch Outlook 2000, and send a test message to Carl Titmouse. Notice the nondelivery report stating that the recipient could not be reached.

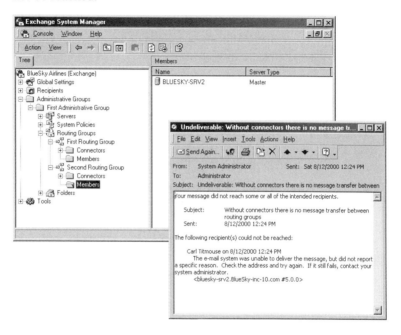

Figure 16.6   Split server resources across multiple routing groups

Exercise Summary

The configuration of routing groups is a simple task. Existing servers can be moved between routing groups easily. However, as soon as servers are separated by means of routing groups, additional configuration is required to provide a message path. Without additional connectors, there can be no e-mail communication between users in different routing groups.

Without additional connectors, there can be no e-mail communication between users in different routing groups. Non-delivery reports (NDRs) are generated for all those messages that cannot reach their recipients. NDRs provide information about delivery problems, suggest possible options to resolve them, and indicate the servers that could not transfer the messages further, such as in the line <bluesky-srv2.bluesky-inc-10.com #5.0.0>.

Lesson 2: Connecting Routing Groups

Exchange 2000 Server provides numerous messaging connectors, but not all can be used to link routing groups together. A connector must be able to handle messages in native Exchange formats and support link state information. Only the Routing Group Connector (RGC), SMTP Connector, and X.400 Connector are able to fulfill the requirements. For load balancing and fault tolerance, configure multiple bridgehead servers between two routing groups.

This lesson introduces the main connectors of Exchange 2000 Server for routing groups. Connections to earlier versions of Exchange Server and connections over dial-up links are also covered.

At the end of this lesson, you will be able to:

- Configure the main connectors of Exchange 2000 Server.
- Explain how to connect to Exchange Server 5.5 sites.
- Use dial-up connections for message transfer.

Estimated time to complete this lesson: 90 minutes

Routing Group Connector

The RGC is the easiest connector to install and more powerful than the others. It provides a high level of fault tolerance because it supports multiple source and destination bridgehead servers. Multiple bridgeheads can guarantee message delivery even if a particular server is shut down. Because it provides many advantages, it is typically the preferred connector. The RGC, as its name implies, can only be used to provide a message path between routing groups in the same organization. In native Exchange 2000 Server environments, the RGC transfers messages in transport-neutral encapsulation format (TNEF) based on SMTP.

Tip   Although messages are transferred in TNEF and not in plain text, messages are not encrypted between bridgehead servers. Experienced intruders will be able to disclose the message content. To encrypt the server-to-server communication, use IP Security (IPSec) tunnels. Microsoft Windows 2000 Server supports IPSec.

Local and Remote Messaging Bridgeheads

It is important to note that the RGC is able to try any SMTP virtual server in the local and remote routing group without message rerouting. Only if all configured remote bridgeheads are unavailable is the RGC is marked as down. Messages are then rerouted to another connector.

You can specify local virtual bridgehead servers in the connector's General tab. By default, the Any Local Server Can Send Mail Over This Connector option is selected and all servers in the local routing group act as outbound bridgehead servers. If you want to implement dedicated bridgehead servers, select the These Servers Can Send Mail Over This Connector option instead, and specify the bridgeheads explicitly. Servers in the local routing group that are not explicitly listed must send their messages to a local bridgehead server first.

Remote bridgehead servers are specified in the Remote Bridgeheads tab. Multiple bridgeheads provide load balancing and fault tolerance, whereas single bridgeheads allow you to implement servers with dedicated purposes in your organization. To resolve a remote bridgehead's host name into an IP address, the local bridgehead relies on the DNS. If DNS cannot provide a valid IP address, NetBIOS name resolution is attempted. Microsoft Windows 2000 Server can automatically register A records when using Windows 2000 dynamic DNS. In this situation, you do not need to manually configure any DNS records for remote bridgehead servers.

Direction of Message Transfer

You should keep in mind that RGCs operate unidirectionally, meaning messages are transferred in only one direction. Hence, for full messaging connectivity, you need to configure RGCs in both connected routing groups. When you create an RGC, Exchange System Manager can retrieve most configuration parameters from the local instance to configure the opposing connector automatically for you.

Configuration Settings

To create a new RGC, expand the desired routing group (for example, First Routing Group), right-click Connectors, point to New, and then select Routing Group Connector. This will display a Properties dialog box with six tabs. At a minimum, you need to specify a name in the General tab, click on the Remote Bridgehead tab, and specify a remote bridgehead server.

The following are the Routing Group Connector Properties dialog box tabs:

- **General.**   Use this tab to define a name for this RGC, define the remote routing group to which this connector is supposed to transfer messages, and specify which SMTP virtual servers in the local routing group are allowed to transfer messages directly to the remote routing group. In addition, you can determine a cost value for the connection, which defines a preference level for this connector if multiple connectors are able to transfer messages to the same destination. Connectors with lower cost values are taken first. You can also select the Do Not Allow Public Folder Referrals check box to prevent Outlook 2000 users from accessing public folder resources in the remote routing group.

- **Remote Bridgehead.**   Use this tab to define SMTP virtual servers in the remote routing group that receive messages directly from this connector. All other servers receive messages indirectly via the bridgeheads. When connecting to an earlier version of Exchange Server, you also can specify the site services account of the remote site under Override Connection Credentials For Exchange 5.*x*.

- **Delivery Restrictions.**   Use this tab to specify who is allowed to send messages over this connector. By default, messages are accepted from everyone.

- **Content Restrictions.**   Use this tab to specify which type of messages can traverse the connector according to priority (High, Normal, or Low), message type (System Messages or Non-System Messages), and message sizes (Allowed Sizes).

- **Delivery Options.**   Use this tab to specify when normal messages are allowed to traverse the connector (Connection Time). It is possible to specify a size limit for oversized messages and configure a separate activation schedule for these messages.

- **Details.**   Use this tab to specify an administrative note for informative purposes.

Exercise 2: Configuring a Routing Group Connector

In this exercise you will connect two routing groups by means of an RGC. You will test the configuration by sending test messages, which will only work in one direction.

To view a multimedia demonstration that displays how to perform this procedure, run the EX2CH16*.AVI files from the \Exercise_Information\Chapter16 folder on the Supplemental Course Materials CD.

Prerequisites

- Complete Exercise 1, earlier in this chapter.

- Make sure BLUESKY-SRV1 and BLUESKY-SRV2 are available in the test environment.

- Log on as Administrator to BLUESKY-SRV1 and BLUESKY-WKSTA.

▶   **To configure an RGC**

1. On BLUESKY-SRV1, launch Exchange System Manager, and, in the console tree, expand all nodes including the container called Second Routing Group.

2. Under Second Routing Group, right-click Connectors, point to New, and select Routing Group Connector.

3. In the General tab, under Name, type **RGC to First Routing Group**.

4. Under Connects This Routing Group With, make sure First Routing Group (First Administrative Group) is displayed (see Figure 16.7).

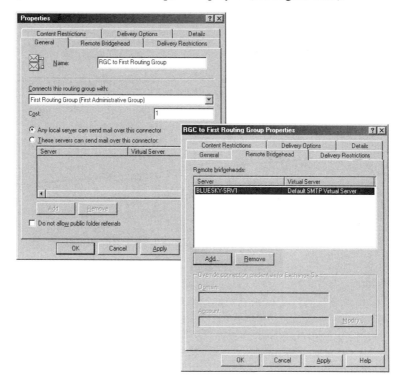

Figure 16.7   Configuring an RGC

5. Click on the Remote Bridgehead tab, and click Add.

6. In the Add Bridgehead dialog box, select BLUESKY-SRV1 – Default SMTP Virtual Server, and then click OK.

7. Click on the Delivery Options tab, and verify that Always Run is displayed in the Connection Time list box.

8. Click OK, and in the Exchange System Manager dialog box that prompts you to create the RGC in the remote routing group as well, click No.

9. Allow some time for Active Directory replication, and then, on BLUESKY-SRV1, send another test message to Carl Titmouse. You should notice that the test message is delivered to Carl; however, he will not be able to reply to this message (see Figure 16.8).

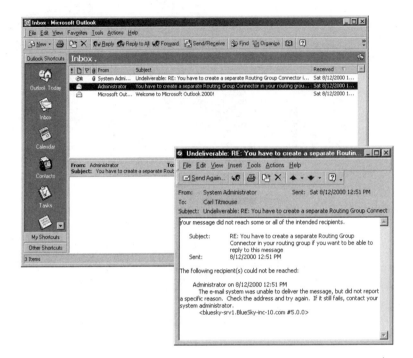

Figure 16.8   Unidirectional message transfer

Exercise Summary

The configuration of an RGC is quickly accomplished. However, because RGCs operate unidirectionally, you have to configure a separate connector in every routing group. Otherwise, users might be able to receive messages, but they will not be able to reply. Exchange System Manager will prompt you to configure an RGC in both routing groups.

SMTP Connector

The primary purpose of the SMTP Connector is to connect an Exchange 2000 organization to foreign SMTP systems, such as SMTP hosts on the Internet or other Exchange 2000 organizations. The SMTP Connector can also be used instead of an RGC to provide messaging connectivity between routing groups in a single Exchange 2000 environment.

Tip   It is advantageous to configure an SMTP Connector to provide Internet connectivity. The connector settings have higher priority than the settings for SMTP virtual servers. You have the ability to define dedicated bridgehead servers.

RGC Versus SMTP Connector

Both the RGC and SMTP Connector use SMTP for message transfer. The RGC is easier to maintain, but the SMTP Connector gives you more control over your routing configuration.

Consider the configuration of an SMTP Connector instead of an RGC in the following situations:

- You need to configure outbound security settings, such as Transport Layer Security (TLS), to encrypt data transferred over the connection without the need for IPSec and to use specific account information for authentication.

- You need to connect to a foreign SMTP host, such as the Internet Mail Service (IMS) of an earlier version of Exchange Server, or to another Exchange 2000 organization.

- You need to issue a TURN, ATRN, or ETRN command to request mail from the queue on a remote SMTP virtual server.

- You want to queue e-mail messages for remote triggered delivery.

DNS and Smart Host Configurations

When connecting to the Internet, the SMTP Connector is able to look up external DNS servers for mail exchanger (MX) records that correspond to Internet domain names specified in recipient addresses. This allows for direct message routing to destination domains. DNS was briefly introduced in Chapter 11, "Internet-Based Client Access," and is covered at length in the *Windows 2000 Server TCP/IP Core Networking Guide* of the Windows 2000 Resource Kit.

Especially over dial-up connections, Internet service providers (ISPs) typically provide their customers with a smart host that relays outgoing messages on behalf of the customer's SMTP host. In this situation, the SMTP Connector should not use DNS, but should forward all outgoing messages to the smart host. You can specify the host name or the smart host's IP address (in square brackets) in the SMTP Connector's General tab under Forward All Mail Through This Connector To The Following Smart Hosts.

If you want to forward messages for a particular domain to a smart host other than the default, configure two individual SMTP Connectors (see Figure 16.9). In the Address Space tab of the connector to the Internet, define an address space of type SMTP with an address of * (for example, SMTP: *). For the connector to the downstream domain, on the other hand, specify the corresponding smart host, and, in the Address Space tab, define a detailed address space, such as SMTP: downstream-domain.com. The most detailed address space match wins. Consequently, for all e-mail addresses of <recipient>@downstream-domain.com, Exchange 2000 Server selects the connector that is forwarding the messages to the correct smart host. You can read more about the configuration of address spaces in Lesson 3.

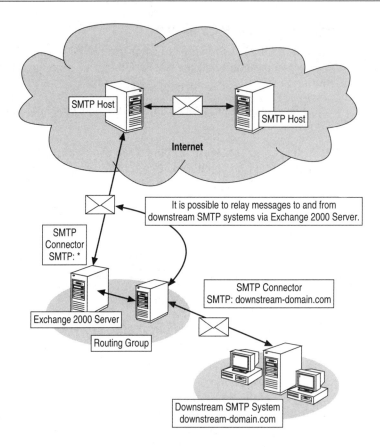

Figure 16.9   Multiple SMTP Connectors for different destinations

As mentioned, parameters of an SMTP Connector have higher priority than the settings of SMTP virtual servers. However, if a recipient address does not match any connector's address spaces, the settings of the SMTP virtual server apply for message delivery. By default, Exchange 2000 Server attempts to locate the remote SMTP host using DNS until you change the delivery options of the SMTP virtual server as explained in Chapter 15, "SMTP Transport Configuration."

SMTP Connectors Between Routing Groups

DNS cannot be used when an SMTP Connector is used to link routing groups together because messages are transferred within the same e-mail domain. Consequently, you need to activate the Forward All Mail Through This Connector To The Following Smart Hosts option and specify the name or IP address (in square brackets) of an existing server in the remote routing group. In the General tab, under Local Bridgeheads, you can specify multiple local bridgehead servers to connect to the remote Exchange 2000 smart host for message delivery.

Retrieving Mail Through ETRN

Modern Extended STMP (ESMTP) systems, including Exchange 2000 Server, support the ETRN command, which is used to signal a remote ESMTP server to send its queued messages to the local host. The remote ESMTP server must be configured to receive and hold messages on behalf of the local destination domain. Messages will be requested based on fully qualified domain names (FQDNs), such as Bluesky-inc-10.com. Defined in RFC 1985, ETRN is commonly accepted across the Internet today.

The SMTP Connector supports the ETRN command completely. That means the SMTP Connector can use ETRN to request data from a remote host and it can answer incoming ETRN requests by sending queued messages to the requesting system. You can read more about recipient policies in Chapter 13, "Creating and Managing Recipients."

Configuration Settings

To create an SMTP Connector, expand the desired routing group (for example, First Routing Group), right-click Connectors, point to New, and then select SMTP Connector. This will display a Properties dialog box with eight tabs. At a minimum, you need to specify a name in the General tab and define a local bridgehead server. If you are connecting routing groups, you also need to specify a remote SMTP virtual server in the form of a smart host, then click on the Connected Routing Groups tab and specify a remote routing group. If you connect to the Internet instead, make sure you define an address space of the type SMTP.

The following are the SMTP Connector Properties dialog box tabs:

- **Address Space.**   Use this tab to identify the SMTP domains that this connector is supposed to transfer messages to. You can also define the scope of the connector as global (available in the entire organization) or local (available in the local routing group only) and select whether to allow messages to be relayed for the specified domains.

- **Advanced.**   Use this tab to configure outbound security, to specify whether to send a HELO instead of a EHLO command to the remote SMTP host (which can be useful if the remote SMTP host does not support ESMTP), and to specify whether to issue an ETRN or TURN command when connecting to remote hosts for message retrieval.

- **Connected Routing Groups.**   Use this tab to specify the names of remote routing groups that can be reached through this SMTP Connector.

- **Content Restrictions.**   Use this tab to specify which type of messages can traverse the connector according to priority (High, Normal, or Low), message type (System Messages or Non-System Messages), and message size (Allowed Sizes).

- **Delivery Options.** Use this tab to specify when normal messages are allowed to traverse the connector (Connection Time). You can also specify a size limit for oversized messages and configure a separate activation schedule for these messages. In addition, the SMTP Connector allows you to queue mail for remotely triggered delivery.

- **Delivery Restrictions.** Use this tab to specify who is allowed to send messages over this connector. By default, messages are accepted from everyone.

- **Details.** Use this tab to specify an administrative note for informative purposes.

- **General.** Use this tab to define a name for the SMTP Connector, to define whether to use DNS and MX records for message delivery or to forward all messages to a smart host, and to specify the SMTP virtual servers in the local routing group that can use this connector to transfer messages to the remote SMTP host. In addition, you can select the Do Not Allow Public Folder Referrals check box to prevent Outlook 2000 users from accessing public folder resources in the remote routing group.

Exercise 3: Configuring an SMTP Connector

In this exercise you will configure an SMTP Connector between two routing groups. You will continue the configuration of the test environment to enable bidirectional message transfer between BLUESKY-SRV1 and BLUESKY-SRV2.

To view a multimedia demonstration that displays how to perform this procedure, run the EX3CH16*.AVI files from the \Exercise_Information\Chapter16 folder on the Supplemental Course Materials CD.

Prerequisites

- Complete Exercise 1, earlier in this chapter.

- Make sure BLUESKY-SRV1 and BLUESKY-SRV2 are available in the test environment.

- Log on as Administrator to BLUESKY-SRV1 and BLUESKY-WKSTA.

▶ **To configure an SMTP connector between two routing groups**

1. On BLUESKY-SRV1, in Exchange System Manager, expand First Routing Group, and, underneath, right-click Connectors, point to New, and select SMTP Connector.

2. In the General tab, under Name, type **SMTP Connector to BLUESKY-SRV2**.

3. Select the Forward All Mail Through This Connector To The Following Smart Hosts option, and, in the corresponding text box, type **bluesky-srv2.bluesky-inc-10.com** (see Figure 16.10).

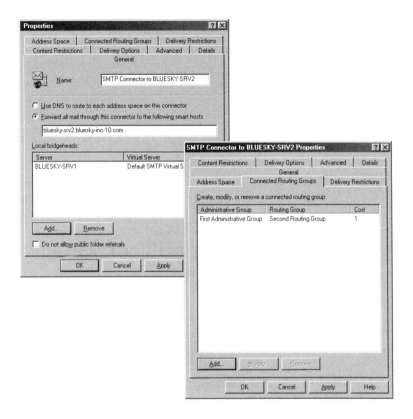

Figure 16.10   Configuring an SMTP Connector

4. Click Add, and, in the Add Bridgehead dialog box, select BLUESKY-SRV1 – Default SMTP Virtual Server, and then click OK.

5. Click on the Connected Routing Groups tab, then click Add. In the Properties dialog box, make sure First Administrative Group/Second Routing Group is displayed under Routing Group, and then click OK.

6. Click on the Delivery Options tab, and make sure Always Run is displayed under Connection Time. Click OK.

   At this point, you should be able to reply as Carl Titmouse to the test message from the Administrator that was sent via the RGC in Exercise 2.

Exercise Summary

The configuration of an SMTP Connector differs from an RGC in that you have to specify the remote bridgehead server in the form of an SMTP host. It is also possible to use DNS MX records to locate the host that accepts messages for a particular Internet domain. Because the SMTP Connector may be used to connect to foreign SMTP systems, you must specify the remote routing group explicitly in the Connected Routing Groups tab.

X.400 Connector

Although Exchange 2000 Server relies on SMTP for native message transfer, deploying an SMTP-based communication infrastructure may not fit your organization's needs. This is particularly the case if your messaging backbone relies on X.400 and connects different e-mail systems together. Using an X.400 Connector, you can connect Exchange 2000 Server to any foreign X.400 system and to earlier versions of Exchange Server and Exchange 2000 Server in different routing groups or organizations.

Tip   Because of simplicity and faster message transport, it is advantageous to use the RGC and SMTP Connector between routing groups. Use X.400 Connectors to connect Exchange 2000 Server with external X.400 systems.

Microsoft Exchange Message Transfer Agent Service

Exchange 2000 Server supports the X.400 standard through its Microsoft Exchange Message Transfer Agent (MTA) Stacks service, which corresponds to an MTA of the 1988 conformance year. This X.400 MTA supports link state information for full X.400 and SMTP interoperability according to RFC 2156, and it uses LDAP for directory lookups. RFC 2156 describes Multipurpose Internet Mail Extensions (MIME) Internet X.400 Enhanced Relay functions.

MTA Transport Stacks

The MTA service of Exchange 2000 Server is able to utilize TCP/IP or X.25 for communication by means of an MTA transport stack, which must be added to the server before you can configure an X.400 Connector. Unfortunately, Exchange 2000 Server does not support the transport protocol class 4 (TP4) protocol because a TP4 protocol stack is not available for Windows 2000.

The TCP/IP transport stack allows you to establish X.400 connections over the Internet and virtual private networks (VPNs). Fortunately, all modern X.400 systems support TCP/IP over LAN connections. To install this stack, launch Exchange System Manager. Expand the desired administrative group, then Servers, then the desired server, and then open the Protocols container. Right-click X.400, point to New, and select TCP/IP X.400 Service Transport Stack. A dialog box will appear, allowing you to define Open Systems Interconnection (OSI) address information. Usually, you don't need to specify any configuration settings because the local protocol configuration is determined by Windows 2000. If desired, however, you can specify a transport service access point (TSAP), session service access point (SSAP), or presentation service access point (PSAP). TSAP, SSAP, and PSAP correspond to the text boxes labeled T Selector, S Selector, and P Selector.

The X.25 protocol, on the other hand, can be used to communicate with remote X.400 systems using a packet switching network. This is usually the case when connecting to a public X.400 provider. The X.25 protocol, also called TP0 (transport protocol class 0), is OSI compliant and designed specifically for WAN connections. A special computer adapter—an X.25 card—and a synchronous modem are required. Before you can install the X.25 X.400 Service Transport Stack, corresponding Windows 2000 protocol drivers need to be configured. The X.121 Address is the most important configuration parameter for X.25, yet all other settings, such as Call User Data and Facilities Data, must be specified precisely as well; otherwise, you will experience communication problems. X.25 configurations are challenging, and it is advisable to have an experienced specialist do the job. As usual, you can define additional service access points using the T Selector, S Selector, and P Selector; however, these options are not necessarily required for proper operation.

Configuring the X.400 Connector

As soon as an MTA transport stack has been installed, X.400 Connectors can be configured. This is a complex task, especially when connecting to a foreign X.400 system. Specify all configuration settings carefully, and make sure they match the configuration of the remote system. To begin the configuration, expand the routing group where you want to add the X.400 Connector, right-click Connectors, point to New, and select either TCP X.400 Connector or X.25 X.400 Connector, according to the configuration of your server. You will be confronted with a dialog box containing 10 tabs. The General tab, for example, is used to define a name for the new X.400 Connector object. You can also determine the desired MTA transport stack.

Connect Request Information

Every X.400 connection is a secured connection. In other words, an X.400 MTA that wants to contact another MTA must identify itself within its connect request. The identification information includes name and password for the local and remote MTA. If this information does not match the configuration of the remote X.400 system, the connection request will be refused and messages cannot be transferred.

The name and password of the local MTA can be determined in the properties of the X.400 object underneath the server's Protocols container. This information must be presented to the remote administrator so that the remote connector or MTA can be configured properly. You also need to retrieve the name and password of the remote MTA from the remote administrator to complete the configuration task yourself. The information must be entered in the Remote Connection Credentials dialog box that you can display by clicking Modify in the connector's General tab.

Important   The MTA password is case-sensitive. If it is misspelled, connections cannot be established.

Transport Stack Configuration

The transport stack configuration, accomplished using the Stack tab, does not refer to the configuration of the local computer. At this location, you need to define the address information for the remote system, such as remote host name or IP address for a TCP/IP X.400 Connector, or the X.121 address for an X.25 X.400 Connector. Via the OSI Address button, you can also specify the SSAP, PSAP, and TSAP configuration of the remote MTA (S Selector, P Selector, and T Selector). The corresponding fields can be left blank if no additional service access points have been defined. You also need to inform the remote administrator about the transport stack configuration of your MTA transport stack.

Overriding Local Information

Especially when connecting to a public X.400 network, you may be forced to override the name and password of the local MTA. The public X.400 carrier provides the required information for you to use. To adjust the configuration on a per-connector basis, use the Override tab. Once specified, the X.400 Connector will use this information to establish connections with the remote system. The local MTA name and password, as defined in the properties of the server's X.400 object, will be ignored. Furthermore, you can adjust the various X.400 protocol parameters, such as Maximum Open Retries and Maximum Transfer Retries, which determine how often a connection or transfer attempt is carried out before messages are returned as undeliverable.

Note   When using an X.400 Connector over an on-demand dial-up connection, it may be advisable to increase the Maximum Transfer Retries to a value of 5. You can read more about the configuration of dial-up connections later in this lesson.

Connecting Routing Groups

Over extremely unreliable, low-bandwidth network links, it might be a good idea to use X.400 Connectors between routing groups. X.400 has the advantage of supporting graceful recovery of transfer associations. In many situations, message transfer can be resumed where it was interrupted. To specify remote routing groups for an X.400 Connector, use the Connected Routing Groups property page.

Keep in mind that the local and remote MTAs represent the only bridgehead servers in each routing group. If multiple bridgeheads are desired, configure additional X.400 Connectors on different computers running Exchange 2000 Server. A single server can support multiple X.400 Connectors, each using the same or different MTA transport stacks.

Advanced Configuration Issues

In the Advanced tab, you can specify X.400 features that should be enabled when connecting the organization to a foreign X.400 system. Important settings are the X.400 conformance year and X.400 body parts. The MTA conformance year, for instance, must match the conformance year of the foreign system because significant differences exist between the 1984 and 1988 X.400 standards. Otherwise, the local MTA overtaxes the remote MTA, and communication problems will occur.

Note Exchange 2000 Server supports the 1988 X.400 standard. As the X.400 standard demands, MTAs of the 1992 conformance year must fall back to the 1988 conformance year for communication with 1988 MTAs.

When connecting to a remote Exchange MTA, make sure the Allow Exchange Contents check box is selected to send messages in native format without the overhead of message conversion. The native Exchange format is not X.400-conforming, but between Exchange MTAs this isn't an issue. Another important setting refers to the global domain identifier (GDI) of the remote system, which prevents message transfer loops.

The following are the X.400 Connector Properties dialog box tabs:

- **Address Space.**   Use this tab to define the type and format of routing addresses. Cost values are associated with address spaces to optimize the routing. In addition, you can specify whether this connector is available to the entire organization or restricted to the local routing group.

- **Advanced.**   Use this tab to specify X.400 message formats and transfer procedures when sending messages to a remote X.400 system or Exchange 2000 server.

- **Connected Routing Groups.**   Use this tab to specify the names of remote routing groups that can be reached through this X.400 Connector.

- **Content Restrictions.**   Use this tab to specify which type of messages can traverse the connector according to priority (High, Normal, or Low), message type (System Messages or Non-System Messages), and message size (Allowed Sizes).

- **Delivery Restrictions.**   Use this tab to specify who is allowed to send messages over this connector. By default, messages are accepted from everyone.

- **Details.**   Use this tab to specify an administrative note for informative purposes.

- **General.**   Use this tab to define a name, the remote X.400 MTA and password, and the transport stack. You can also specify whether remote clients support the Messaging Application Programming Interface (MAPI) and whether to allow public folder referrals.

- **Override.**   Use this tab to override default X.400 attributes of the local MTA.

- **Schedule.**   Use this tab to set the communication schedule. Never, Always (communication occurs constantly), Selected Times (up to 15-minute intervals), and Remote Initiated may be configured.

- **Stack.**   Use this tab to specify required address information, such as remote host name or IP address (or X.121 address), and service access points for the remote system.

Exercise 4: Configuring a TCP/IP-Based X.400 Connector

In this exercise you will configure and test an X.400 Connector between two routing groups. To successfully test the configuration, you should remove the existing connectors from the test environment. Otherwise, test messages may bypass the X.400 Connector.

To view a multimedia demonstration that displays how to perform this procedure, run the EX4CH16*.AVI files from the \Exercise_Information\Chapter16 folder on the Supplemental Course Materials CD.

Prerequisites

- Start BLUESKY-SRV1, BLUESKY-SRV2, and BLUESKY-WKSTA, and make sure they are operational.

- Log on as Administrator to BLUESKY-SRV1 and BLUESKY-WKSTA.

- If you have completed all previous exercises in this chapter, delete the existing connectors between the First Routing Group and the Second Routing Group.

▶   **To configure a TCP/IP-based X.400 Connector between two routing groups**

1. On BLUESKY-SRV1, in Exchange System Manager, expand Servers, expand BLUESKY-SRV1, expand Protocols, right-click the X.400 container, point to New, and select TCP/IP X.400 Service Transport Stack. Accept the default settings and click OK.

2. Right-click the X.400 container and select Properties. Note that the Local X.400 Name is set to BLUESKY-SRV1.

3. Click Modify, delete any entries under Password and Confirm Password, and then click OK twice.

4. Expand BLUESKY-SRV2, expand Protocols, right-click the X.400 container, point to New, and select TCP/IP X.400 Service Transport Stack. Accept the default settings and click OK.

5. Right-click the X.400 container and select Properties. Verify that the Local X.400 Name is set to BLUESKY-SRV2.

6. Click Modify, delete any entries under Password and Confirm Password, and then click OK twice.

7. Expand Routing Groups, expand First Routing Group, and, underneath, right-click Connectors. Point to New and select TCP X.400 Connector.

8. Under Name, type **X.400 to BLUESKY-SRV2**.

9. Under Remote X.400 Name, click Modify, and, in the Remote Connection Credentials dialog box, under Remote X.400 Name, type **BLUESKY-SRV2**. Clear any entries under Password and Confirm Password, and then click OK.

10. Click on the Schedule tab, and verify that the Schedule is set to Always.

11. Click on the Stack tab, make sure the Remote Host Name option is selected, and, under Name, type **BLUESKY-SRV2**.

12. Click on the Connected Routing Groups tab, and click Add.

13. In the Properties dialog box, under Routing Group, make sure First Administrative Group/Second Routing Group is selected, and then click OK.

14. Click on the Advanced tab, and verify that the Allow Exchange Contents check box is selected.

15. Click OK, and, in the Exchange System Manager dialog box informing you that you must configure both sides of this connection before messages can be sent, click OK.

    At this point, you have configured the first part of the X.400 Connector on BLUESKY-SRV1 (see Figure 16.11).

16. Expand Second Routing Group, and, underneath, right-click Connectors, point to New, and select TCP X.400 Connector.

17. Under Name, type **X.400 to BLUESKY-SRV1**.

18. Under Remote X.400 Name, click Modify, and, in the Remote Connection Credentials dialog box, under Remote X.400 Name, type **BLUESKY-SRV1**. Clear any entries under Password and Confirm Password, and then click OK.

19. Click on the Schedule tab, and verify that the Schedule is set to Always.

20. Click on the Stack tab, and make sure the Remote Host Name option is selected. Under Address, type **BLUESKY-SRV1**.

21. Click the Connected Routing Groups tab, click Add, and, in the Properties dialog box, under Routing Group, make sure First Administrative Group/First Routing Group is selected, and then click OK.

22. Click on the Advanced tab, and verify that the Allow Exchange Contents check box is selected.

23. Click OK, and, in the Exchange System Manager dialog box informing you that you must configure both sides of this connection before messages can be sent, click OK.

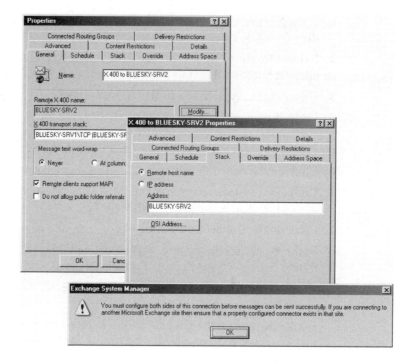

Figure 16.11   Configuring an X.400 Connector on BLUESKY-SRV1

At this point, you have completed the configuration of the X.400 messaging link between the First and the Second Routing Group (see Figure 16.12).

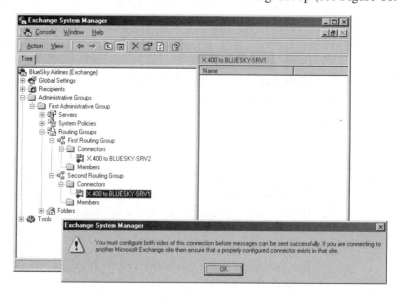

Figure 16.12   Two sides of one X.400 Connector

24. On BLUESKY-WKSTA, log on as Administrator, and send a test message to Carl Titmouse, then log on as the latter, and check whether the test message has been received. Reply to the message, log off, log on as Administrator again, and check that the communication works in both directions.

Exercise Summary

The X.400 Connector is the most complex connector of Exchange 2000 Server. It requires careful configuration of MTAs, X.400 transport stacks, and X.400 Connector components on both ends of the communication link. The configuration must match exactly. Any error, such as a misspelled remote X.400 name, will cause the remote MTA to reject incoming connections, and messages will not be transferred. Message transfer in one direction does not necessarily mean that the other direction is operational as well.

Previous Exchange Connectors

As outlined in Chapter 6, "Coexistence with Previous Microsoft Exchange Server Versions," Exchange 2000 Server can operate in mixed mode to support seamless integration with earlier versions of Exchange Server. This implies that users on the old system can use new Exchange 2000 connectors for message transfer, and vice versa.

Exchange 2000 Server and Earlier Versions in the Same Site or Routing Group

Within the same site or routing group, X.400 over remote procedure call (RPC) is used for server-to-server communication between Exchange 2000 Server and earlier versions of Exchange Server. For native message transfer between computers running Exchange 2000 Server, however, SMTP over TCP/IP is preferred over RPC.

Before you can add Exchange 2000 Server to an existing Exchange Server organization, you need to deploy the Active Directory Connector (ADC). Among other things, ADC, in conjunction with Site Replication Service (SRS), replicates connector and routing information from the existing organization with Active Directory directory service, which allows Exchange 2000 Server to discover and route messages to existing Exchange 5.5 connectors. ADC and SRS are covered in more detail in Chapter 6, "Coexistence with Previous Microsoft Exchange Server Versions."

Note Users with mailboxes on the new system are able to benefit from existing Exchange 5.5 connectors that are not supported in Exchange 2000 Server, such as the Professional Office System (PROFS) Connector.

Gateway Address Routing Table

Earlier versions of Exchange Server use a Gateway Address Routing Table (GWART) for message routing. Exchange 2000 Server relies on connector configurations stored in the configuration naming context of the Active Directory directory service and link state information instead. Nevertheless, a GWART is generated and replicated to Exchange Server 2000. This is an important feature because it allows users with mailboxes on Exchange Server 5.5 to send messages across any connector, including Exchange Server 2000 connectors.

Note Earlier versions of Exchange Server can use Exchange 2000 connectors because ADC and SRS replicate Exchange 2000 routing information to the Exchange Server directory.

Communication Using Messaging Connectors

The RGC of Exchange 2000 Server provides features similar to the Site Connector of Exchange Server 5.5. As a matter of fact, when using the RGC to connect to an Exchange 5.5 server, RPCs are used automatically instead of SMTP. Hence, you can use the RGC to transfer messages to a Site Connector, and vice versa. You need to specify the required Site Services account for the remote Exchange 5.5 server in the Routing Group Connector's Remote Bridgehead tab.

The SMTP Connector is the counterpart of the Internet Mail Service in earlier versions of Exchange Server. Consequently, if you want to transfer messages to a remote site via SMTP, configure a dedicated SMTP Connector as you would to connect to another remote routing group.

Although the X.400 MTA of Exchange 2000 Server provides enhancements over earlier versions, substantial features remained unchanged. Hence, you will find it straightforward to connect Exchange 2000 Server to a remote system running Exchange Server 5.5 via X.400.

Connectors over Dial-Up Connections

When configuring the various main messaging connectors, you will find that direct support for dial-up connections is missing. A Dynamic Remote Access Service (RAS) Connector is not available, nor does any Exchange 2000 connector provide a Dial-Up Connections tab. Nevertheless, all main connectors (RGC, SMTP Connector, and X.400 Connector) support on-demand dial-up connections by means of Windows 2000 Routing and Remote Access Service.

Let's say you want to use an SMTP Connector to connect to a smart host provided by your ISP over a dial-up connection. In a first step, install and configure your modem or Integrated Services Digital Network (ISDN) under Windows 2000. In a second step, enable Routing and Remote Access Service via the Routing and Remote Access utility from the Administrative Tools program group, and configure the server as a network router. Make sure you specify use of demand-dial connections to access remote networks. As soon as Routing and Remote Access Service is active, add a new routing interface to the configuration. Within the Routing and Remote Access utility, open the local server container in the console tree, right-click Routing Interfaces, and select New Demand-Dial Interface. Define the required settings to connect to your ISP in the Demand Dial Interface Wizard, select the desired modem or ISDN adapter, and make sure to route IP packets on this interface. Define the correct dial-in credentials and finish the configuration. After that, right-click the new demand-dial router object in the details pane, and select Set IP Demand-Dial Filters. To prevent any other machines from accessing the dial-up connection, specify the exact IP addresses of the local SMTP Connector and the ISP's smart host by using a subnet mask of 255.255.255.255. After that, you can configure the messaging connector as if it were making a LAN connection. You can read more about the Routing and Remote Access Service in the *Microsoft Windows 2000 Server Resource Kit Deployment Planning Guide*.

Tip To configure specific dial-out hours, make sure the schedule configured for the demand-dial interface in the Routing and Remote Access Service utility matches the configuration of the messaging connector as specified in the Delivery Options or Schedule tab.

Lesson 3: Link Status Information

When you create multiple routing groups and link them together, you establish a system of message pathways across your organization. One or many routes may lead to the same destination. Typically, the most efficient path should be used for message transfer, and additional routes may stand by in case the best path is temporarily unavailable. Exchange 2000 Server features a powerful routing engine that is able to determine the most efficient message routes based on information about the current conditions within the network.

This lesson explains how Exchange 2000 Server determines the best route for a message. It also covers how connector status information is transferred between servers within and between routing groups.

At the end of this lesson, you will be able to:

- Explain how message routing is performed in an Exchange 2000 organization.
- Describe the purpose of link state information.
- Explain how link state information is propagated to guarantee loop-free message routing.

Estimated time to complete this lesson: 75 minutes

Message Routing

Message routing refers to the process of directing messages to their destinations through SMTP virtual server connections, messaging connectors, or gateways. The routing process begins when a message is passed to the SMTP transport engine. For each recipient address of every particular message, the routing engine must determine the correct destination. For this purpose, communication with Active Directory is necessary. The domain naming context contains the actual recipient objects. The configuration naming context, on the other hand, provides access to important connector and routing information.

Note For X.400 Connectors and connectors to foreign messaging systems (gateways), the X.400 MTA performs the message routing. The X.400 MTA of Exchange 2000 Server relies on LDAP to retrieve the required routing information from Active Directory.

If a message is destined for a local recipient, it is transferred to the Information Store service, which delivers the message to the recipient's mailbox. If the recipient does not reside on the local Exchange 2000 server, the message must either be routed to another server in the same routing group by means of an SMTP virtual server, to another server in another routing group, or to a foreign mail system. For all recipients outside the local routing group, the routing engine determines all connectors that are able to transfer the message on a per-recipient basis. The best connector is chosen based on cost values and other criteria, such as connector states. The message is placed into the selected connector's message queue, which in turn transfers the message. If the connector resides on a bridgehead server in the local routing group, the message is transferred to that bridgehead first (see Figure 16.13). You can read more about link state information later in this lesson.

Note The routing information, maintained in the Active Directory configuration naming context, is replicated throughout the Active Directory forest and available to all Exchange 2000 servers.

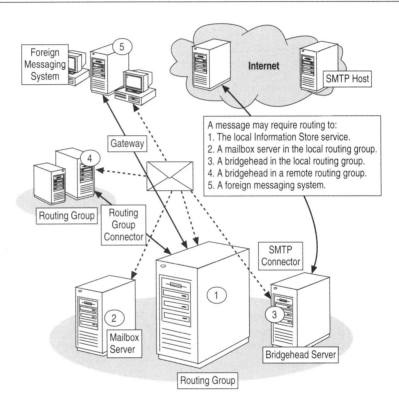

Figure 16.13 Possible message destinations

Address Spaces

Exchange 2000 Server determines possible connectors for a particular message by comparing the recipient's address with available address space information associated with each connector. The result of this comparison is a set of connectors that can be used to transfer the message. If no connector is capable of transferring a particular message, a nondelivery report is generated. This report will indicate the server and the reason for the delivery problem (recipient name could not be resolved).

When connecting routing groups, you associate possible destinations with messaging connectors by means of the Connected Routing Groups tab. The RGC, however, does not provide this tab. Because this connector is used to connect to routing groups only, destination information can be determined implicitly from the connector configuration. By specifying information about connected routing groups, you implicitly configure Exchange address spaces.

You can add explicit address spaces to a connector via the Address Space tab. Each connector requires at least one address space, but multiple address spaces can be defined. Address spaces consist of an address type, such as SMTP, X400, MSMAIL, or CCMAIL, an address portion, and a cost value. You can use wildcards to simplify the address space definition. An address space such as SMTP:* would refer to all possible SMTP addresses. An asterisk (*) represents a multicharacter wildcard, and a question mark (?) can be used as a single-character wildcard. Table 16.1 gives examples of e-mail addresses.

Table 16.1   Examples of E-Mail Addresses

Address Type (Mail System)	Address Example	Address Space
Lotus cc:Mail	user at postoffice	at postoffice
MS Mail (PC)	NETWORK/PO/user	NETWORK/PO
SMTP	Administrator@Bluesky-inc-10.com	Bluesky-inc-10.com
X.400	c=US;a= ;p=BLUESKY; s=Titmouse;g=Carl	c=US;a= ; p=BLUESKY;

Assigning Cost Values to Connectors

Cost values determine which connector is preferred for message transfer. Costs are associated with address spaces and connected routing group information. Address spaces in turn are associated with a particular connector. The cost value can range from 1 to 100, and the connector that owns the address space with the lowest cost value is tried first. If messages cannot pass this connector, the next available connector is tried. If you assign the same cost value to multiple address spaces on different connectors, Exchange 2000 Server selects a random connector to provide a simple form of load balancing.

Connector Selection

If more than one connector is available to deliver a message, the list of all potential connectors must be reduced to one that will be used to transfer the message. To find the best connector, the link state table (LST) is checked. Only connectors on available routes (where all connectors are operational) are included in the message selection process. If multiple routes are available and each has different costs, the connection with the lowest overall cost value will be chosen (see Figure 16.14). If multiple links have the same costs, Exchange 2000 Server chooses connectors

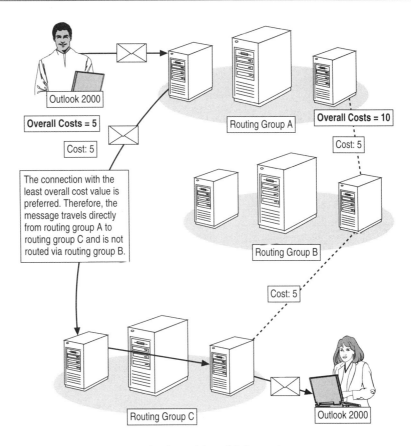

Outlook 2000

Overall Costs = 5

Cost: 5

Routing Group A

Overall Costs = 10

Cost: 5

The connection with the least overall cost value is preferred. Therefore, the message travels directly from routing group A to routing group C and is not routed via routing group B.

Routing Group B

Cost: 5

Routing Group C

Outlook 2000

Figure 16.14   An organization with multiple routing groups

installed on the local computer over connectors installed on remote servers. With more than one potential local connector, random load balancing is performed.

Message Rerouting

If a connector is temporarily unavailable, Exchange 2000 Server will reroute messages over alternative routes (if they exist). For instance, if an RGC has unsuccessfully attempted to transfer a message to its remote bridgehead servers three times, it is marked as unavailable, and other possible connectors may be chosen for message transfer. If all possible connectors are unavailable, the message remains in the local message queue until at least one connector is operational again. If the message expires in the interim (the default wait is 48 hours), Exchange 2000 Server sends a nondelivery report to the originator.

Rerouted messages maintain a retry count for each connector that has been tried. At every rerouting, the retry count is incremented for the current connector. If the maximum number of retries is reached for a particular connector, that connector is excluded from the routing process. If all connectors reach their maximum retry count, the message is returned with a nondelivery report to the originator.

Note   Exchange Development Kit (EDK) gateways and connectors to foreign messaging systems are always considered available. Exchange 2000 Server considers the message delivered when it reaches the connector's message queue. Rerouting is not performed, even if the EDK connector cannot deliver the message.

Rerouting and Activation Schedules

If more than one potential connector is able to deliver a message, Exchange 2000 Server checks activation schedules. If a connector is currently active, its state is known as Active Now. Active connectors are the first choice. If the connector is currently not active but scheduled to connect at a later time, its state is called Will Become Active In The Future. If multiple connectors exist that will become active in the future, Exchange 2000 Server selects the connector that becomes active first. The third state is called Remote Initiated. This means that the connector does not initiate any connection itself. Instead, it waits for a remote server to connect. The fourth state, Never, indicates a disabled connector. For instance, you can set a particular X.400 Connector to Never if you want to accomplish maintenance routines, because in this state the connector does not initiate or receive connections. However, setting an SMTP Connector to Never Run does not bring the connector into Never state. The connector remains available, and messages may be routed to it. Only the message transfer is temporarily disabled. One way to avoid message routing to this connector is to set its maximum message size to 1 KB.

Note   Messages routed to a remote initiated connector will wait in the connector's queue until the remote bridgehead server requests message delivery. Because scheduled connectors are considered available, messages are not rerouted while they are awaiting their retrieval.

Link State Information and Routing Group Masters

Link state information helps to indicate whether a particular connector or routing group is available or unavailable. All link state information is held in an LST, which is used to find the most efficient route for a message based on connector availability.

Note   You can view the LST in Exchange System Manager. In the console tree, expand Tools, and then Monitoring and Status. Select the Status container. In the details pane, all connectors and servers in your organization, together with link state information, are displayed.

Link State Information

Link state information eliminates problems with message looping between servers because each Exchange 2000 server can determine the availability of every connector in the organization. If a downstream connector is currently unavailable, the corresponding link is marked as down. Consequently, messages are not sent to this connector. If no other path exists, messages are held in a queue at the source until the link state information indicates that the downstream connector is available again.

Note   There are only two possible states for any given link (up or down). LSI also includes connector costs for efficient message routing. However, retry counts or activation schedules are not included in link state information.

Link State Table

Every Exchange 2000 server maintains an LST containing information about the current state of each connector. The LST is a small, in-memory database, and each entry (routing group, connector, server) in the database requires approximately 32 bytes of memory. The LST database is not stored on disk. To examine the LST in detail, use the Winroute utility. WINROUTE.EXE is available in the \Support\ Utils\i386 directory on the Exchange 2000 Server CD. This utility is available in the Standard and Enterprise Editions. It connects to TCP port 691 (the Link State Port) on the specified Exchange 2000 server to extract the link state information in raw format. Winroute also interprets the data for easier readability.

Link State Algorithm

The propagation of link state information differs within and between routing groups. To propagate the link state information to all servers in an organization, a link propagation protocol known as link state algorithm (LSA) is used. LSA is based on the Open Shortest Path First (OSPF) protocol.

Within a routing group, a nominated routing group master keeps track of link state information and propagates it to the rest of the servers within the routing group. When a nonmaster server detects that a particular connector is unavailable, it immediately connects to the master's TCP port 691 to provide the new link state information. The master incorporates the changes into the LST and propagates the new information to all remaining servers in the routing group. Again, connections are established to TCP port 691. All servers within a routing group need to communicate with the routing group master through a reliable TCP/IP connection.

Between routing groups, link state information is transferred via main messaging connectors. Typically, the information is transferred using the X-LINK2STATE command over RGC and SMTP Connectors. When you link routing groups together by means of an X.400 Connector, link state information is exchanged between the MTAs as part of the normal message transmission. A binary large object is sent to the receiving MTA before interpersonal messages are transferred.

Note As messages are transferred between two routing groups, link state information is automatically propagated. In addition, a periodic poll updates the link state information.

Changing the Routing Group Master

The master server is normally the first server in a routing group. If this server fails or is taken offline, link state information is no longer propagated within the routing group. Individually, every server still generates and receives link state information, but there is a chance that other servers send messages over a link in which a downstream connection is unavailable. Consequently, if you shut down a routing group master for a significant period of time, nominate a different master using Exchange System Manager to avoid inefficient message routing. Expand the desired routing group and select the Members container. In the details pane, right-click the corresponding server object and select the Set As Master setting.

Message Rerouting Based on Link State Information

Message routing based on link state information is most effective in environments with redundant pathways to destinations. Figure 16.15 shows an organization with four routing groups linked together in ring form using connectors with different cost values.

In the example shown in Figure 16.15, messages from routing group A flow to routing group D as follows:

1. A user sends a message to a recipient with a mailbox in routing group D. Because of the lower overall sum of cost values, the message is transferred to routing group C first.

2. The receiving bridgehead attempts to open a connection to the target bridgehead in routing group D. Because this link is not operational, the connector is marked as unavailable after three unsuccessful connection attempts.

3. The bridgehead connects to the routing group master through TCP port 691 and transmits new link state information. The master incorporates the information into the LST and notifies all other servers in the routing group about the changes.

Note If the connection had been marked unavailable before routing group D began routing the message, it would not have forwarded the message to routing group C.

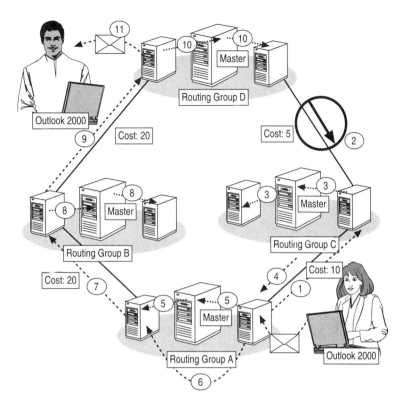

Figure 16.15   Rerouting of messages based on link state information

4. The bridgehead server reroutes the message based on costs and link state information and determines a path via routing groups A and B. Consequently, the message is transferred back to routing group A. However, before the actual message is sent, link state information is propagated using the X-LINK2STATE command verb after issuing an EHLO command to the bridgehead in routing group A.

5. Upon receiving the new link state information, the local bridgehead immediately connects to its master through TCP port 691 and transmits the new information. The master incorporates the data into the LST and notifies all other servers in the routing group about the changes.

6. Using the updated LST, the local bridgehead determines that the message must be routed via routing group B. A connector is available on another bridgehead server in the local routing group. Therefore, the message is transferred to this server directly via SMTP.

7. The second bridgehead routes the message based on the new LST information to routing group B. Yet, before the actual message is transferred, the most recent link state information is propagated using the X-LINK2STATE command.

8. The bridgehead server in routing group B immediately connects to its master through TCP port 691 and transmits the new information. The master incorporates the data into the LST if it hasn't been received through other messages yet and notifies all other servers in the routing group about the changes.

9. The bridgehead in routing group B routes the message to the bridgehead in routing group D and also propagates the new link state information using the X-LINK2STATE command over TCP port 25.

10. The bridgehead server in routing group D informs its master, which updates the LST and notifies all other servers in the routing group about the changes.

11. The message is delivered to the recipient's mailbox.

At this point, all servers in the organization have been informed about the un-availability of the connector between routing groups C and D. Subsequent messages to routing group D are not routed via this path. Messages are routed to routing group B instead. If the connector between routing groups B and D went down for any reason, no message paths to routing group D would be available. Consequently, messages are not rerouted and remain in their queues until the link state information indicates an operational connector on either side.

Note   After a connector is tagged as unavailable, the original bridgehead server continues to retry the connection at 60-second intervals even if no messages are awaiting transfer. As soon as a connection can be established, the connector is considered available again, and the bridgehead notifies the local routing group master about the link state change.

Chapter Summary

A routing group is a collection of Exchange 2000 servers that typically share a permanent, reliable, high-bandwidth network connection. In a particular routing group, all servers communicate directly with each other using SMTP. If your entire network consists of LAN-like connections, you will find the deployment of a single routing group sufficient and advantageous. If you need to control and optimize the flow of messages, on the other hand, you should implement multiple routing groups and connect them using an RGC. It is possible to place all servers in one administrative group for global administration, but they must be in multiple routing groups.

To link separate routing groups of an organization together, you can use RGCs, SMTP Connectors, or X.400 Connectors. Only these connectors support native Exchange message formats, public folder referrals, and link state information. The RGC is the most powerful and easiest to configure, followed by the SMTP Connector. The X.400 Connector configuration, on the other hand, is a complex challenge. It is advisable to rely on X.400 Connectors only for the purpose of building messaging bridges to foreign X.400 systems.

Exchange 2000 Server features a powerful routing engine that is able to determine the most efficient message routes based on link state information. Within each routing group, a master maintains an LST that holds information about the current conditions within the network. The LST is propagated to all servers in the routing group via direct TCP/IP connections. Between routing groups, link state information is transferred by means of RGCs. Message loops and ping-pong effects can be prevented efficiently using link states.

Review

The following review questions can help you determine if you have sufficiently familiarized yourself with the material covered in this chapter. You can find the answers to these questions at the end of this book in Appendix A, "Questions and Answers."

1. When should you separate Exchange 2000 servers by means of routing groups?

2. What are the minimum configuration parameters you need to define for an RGC?

3. What are the minimum configuration parameters you need to define for an SMTP Connector between two routing groups?

4. Your organization consists of numerous routing groups. Within your local routing group 10 servers have been installed. You plan to replace the hardware of the server that was installed in your routing group first. What do you need to accomplish to guarantee efficient message routing while the hardware is replaced?

C H A P T E R   1 7

Public Folder Management

About This Chapter

The information store of Microsoft Exchange 2000 Server is partitioned into two store types—mailbox store and public store. Mailbox stores, as their name implies, contain mailboxes that typically belong to individual users. Public stores, on the other hand, hold public folders, which are available to every user in the organization. Public folders can also be used to share information across organizations and across the Internet. They are an ideal foundation for advanced workgroup and workflow applications, as well as for information and knowledge management solutions.

Using Microsoft Outlook 2000, you can create powerful collaboration systems with minimum effort that provide a tremendous benefit for the organization. A discussion forum, for example, is perhaps the simplest form of a public folder application. A discussion forum is a public folder that contains message items. A document management system is a similar repository. It stores Microsoft Office documents instead of messages. A public folder that holds task elements, on the other hand, could be used as a team management solution. A public journal allows managers to track activities for a team. Public calendars can inform employees about holidays and company events. You also can create public folders that contain contact objects, providing your human resources department with a simple employee tracking system. In Chapter 1, "Introduction to Microsoft Exchange 2000 Server," you used this approach to implement a phone book for external contacts.

This chapter covers the management of public folders that reside on a single Exchange 2000 server. It discusses public folder concepts and the administration of public stores.

Before You Begin

To complete this chapter:

- Prepare your test environment according to the descriptions given in the "Getting Started" section of "About This Book." It is assumed that you have followed the exercises of previous chapters. Otherwise, make sure your Exchange 2000 servers are placed in separate routing groups that are connected using a Routing Group, SMTP, or X.400 Connector, as demonstrated in the exercises of Chapter 16, "Message Routing Administration." Use Active Directory Users and Computers to move the Administrator mailbox to BLUESKY-SRV2 and verify that the mailbox of Carl Titmouse resides on BLUESKY-SRV1.

- You should be familiar with Microsoft Outlook 2000 installed in a workgroup and collaboration environment and configured to connect to Exchange 2000 Server, as explained in Chapter 9, "MAPI-Based Clients."

- You need to have a general understanding of how Internet-based clients can access Exchange 2000 resources, as illustrated in Chapter 11, "Internet-Based Client Access."

Lesson 1: Introduction to Public Folders

Public folders are repositories for all kinds of information. They can contain regular e-mail messages as well as multimedia clips, text documents, spreadsheets, and other data. A variety of messaging applications, including Outlook 2000, Internet mail clients, newsreaders, and Web browsers, can access these folders. You can also use standard Win32 programs, such as Microsoft Windows Explorer or Microsoft Office applications. The Installable File System driver of Exchange 2000 Server (ExIFS) makes public folders as accessible as directories on a hard disk.

This lesson provides a brief overview of public folders, including an introduction to architecture and information on relationships between public folders and directory objects. The advantages of mail-enabled public folders are introduced.

At the end of this lesson, you will be able to:
- Describe the features of public folders.
- List the various parts of a public folder.
- Send messages to and on behalf of a public folder.

Estimated time to complete this lesson: 60 minutes

Public Folder Considerations

Public folders are primarily managed using Exchange System Manager, but users may also use Outlook 2000, Internet clients, Web browsers, or Windows Explorer to create public folders and set permissions and other configuration options. A user who creates a public folder becomes the folder's owner, but additional owners can be defined. The owner can manage permissions and folder rules using Outlook 2000. Other configuration settings, such as public folder replication, can be controlled only using Exchange System Manager. Of course, you need Administrative permissions in your administrative group if you want to control configuration settings.

Public Folder Databases

The actual public folder repositories are maintained in public stores. Each store consists of an Exchange database, which holds items in Messaging Application Programming Interface (MAPI) format, and an Exchange streaming database for items in Internet-based formats. You can check the location of the databases in Exchange System Manager when displaying the desired public store's Database tab. As outlined in Chapter 14, "Managing Server Configuration," one or more storage groups and public stores may be created on a particular server. It is also possible to remove all public stores from a server to create dedicated mailbox servers. However, at least one server holding the default public store for the MAPI-based public folders tree must exist within an administrative group. You can read more about the maintenance of Exchange 2000 Server databases in Chapter 20, "Microsoft Exchange 2000 Server Maintenance and Troubleshooting."

Public Folder Referrals

By default, a newly created top-level public folder is not replicated to any other server. Replication requires an explicit administrative step, but replication is not always necessary because all users in your organization can theoretically have direct access. Within a routing group, users can always work with local public folders, but users from other routing groups cannot if public folder referrals are not allowed. Every Routing Group Connector (RGC) provides a Do Not Allow Public Folder Referrals check box, which you can select to prevent Outlook 2000 users from accessing public folder resources in remote routing groups. Referrals and their purposes are covered in Lesson 3.

Public Folder Replication

Public folder replication gives you the means to distribute multiple instances of a public folder to different Exchange 2000 servers and keep them synchronized. In addition, an InterOrg Replication utility is available, which allows you to replicate public folder instances between Exchange organizations. Multiple public folder instances can share the user load and increase fault tolerance through redundancy. Public folder replication is covered in Chapter 18, "Public Folder Replication."

Internet Publishing

By default, every user can access public folder resources in the context of their access permissions via HTTP and Web Distributed Authoring and Versioning (WebDAV). In Chapter 11, "Internet-Based Client Access," you used the Add Network Places Wizard in Windows Explorer to configure a connection to a public folder tree. HTTP and WebDAV support is a very interesting feature, particularly for Macintosh or UNIX users who want to share information with Windows clients. In addition to the public folder itself, all items within a public folder can be accessed through a URL, which is dynamically generated. URLs are constructed using the path to the folder and the Subject line of the item. This is demonstrated in Exercise 2 of Chapter 22, "Microsoft Outlook Web Access."

You can map public folders to Internet newsgroups and provide access to these forums through Network News Transfer Protocol (NNTP)-based newsreader clients. Likewise, push and pull feeds may be used to replicate public folder content with the USENET. The management of NNTP virtual servers and public folder newsgroups is covered in Chapter 11, "Internet-Based Client Access."

Full-Text Indexing

The Information Store service of Exchange 2000 Server is integrated with the Microsoft Search service of Microsoft Windows 2000 Server. This allows you to index the content of public folders and provide Outlook 2000 users with the ability to locate Microsoft Office documents and message attachments through full-text searches. Exchange 2000 Server is a very attractive document management platform, as explained in Chapter 14, "Managing Server Configuration."

Elements of a Public Folder

Public folder access relies on two elements: the public folder hierarchy and the public folder content (see Figure 17.1). The hierarchy shows a public folder within a public folder tree. The content consists of the actual items (such as messages and attachments, contact objects, or documents) stored in the public folder.

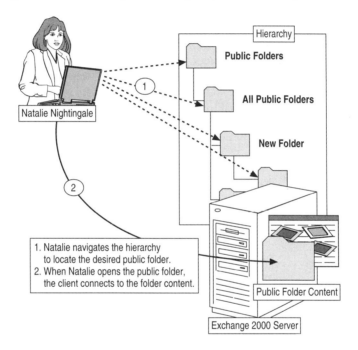

Figure 17.1   The elements of a public folder in the Information Store

Public Folder Hierarchy

A public folder hierarchy develops when multiple folders are created. Top-level folders contain subfolders, and those can contain other subfolders. By navigating through the public folder tree, users can locate discussion forums and other information repositories conveniently. Exchange 2000 Server supports multiple public folder trees, also known as public folder hierarchies, which give you better administrative control and flexibility over workgroup and workflow solutions.

Hierarchy and Public Stores

Per server, each public folder tree must be associated with a separate public store. Public stores on different servers may refer to the same hierarchy, in which case the hierarchy is automatically replicated between them. Dedicated mailbox servers (servers without a public store) do not maintain any public folder tree information.

Exchange System Manager does not provide control over the time interval of the hierarchy replication. By default, hierarchy replication generates an e-mail message 60 seconds after the last modification has occurred. Replication messages are addressed to all those servers that maintain a public store associated with the affected hierarchy.

Public Folder Hierarchies and MAPI-Based Clients

The default MAPI-based hierarchy is created automatically on each server during setup. Because the default public store of each server is associated with the MAPI-based hierarchy, this hierarchy is replicated to all servers across the organization. Therefore, every user can examine the list of existing folders, even though the content might not be accessible (see Figure 17.2). In Outlook 2000 you can display the MAPI-based folder hierarchy (that is, Public Folders\All Public Folders) by selecting the Folder List command, which can be reached from the View menu. Only one MAPI-based hierarchy can exist per server.

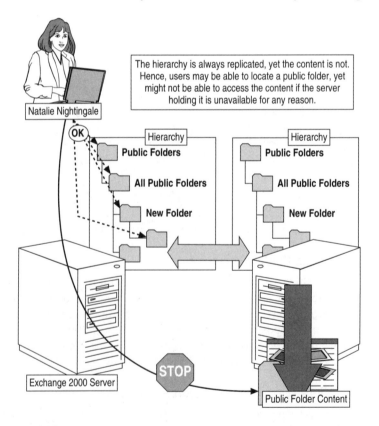

Figure 17.2   Accessing public folder content on a different server

The following are the two types of folder hierarchies supported by Exchange 2000 Server:

- **Default (MAPI clients).**   MAPI-based clients, as well as Web browsers, and Windows applications, such as Microsoft Word, Microsoft Excel, or Windows Explorer, can access this hierarchy.

- **Alternate (general purpose).**   Web browsers and Windows applications, such as Microsoft Word, Microsoft Excel, or Windows Explorer, can access this hierarchy, but MAPI-based clients are unable to display these public folder trees.

Note   Exchange System Manager allows you to create multiple hierarchies. However, Outlook 2000 is only able to access the default MAPI-based public folder tree. Microsoft plans to provide support for alternate public folder trees in future versions of Outlook.

Public Folder Contents

The public folder contents are the actual items in a public folder. To work with the contents, you must open the folder by selecting it in the client's folder pane and displaying the items in the right pane, also called the details pane. When you open a public folder, your client program will send an open request to your home server. If the server has the contents, you will get access. If the home server doesn't have the contents, it returns a referral list to the client. Based on the information from this list, the client will connect to a server within the local routing group or in a remote routing group. If all target servers are inaccessible for some reason, you will receive an error message that the folder content could not be located. You can read more about public folder access in Lesson 3.

It doesn't matter to the user where the data is stored as long as Outlook 2000 has access to the contents. The amount of data that needs to be transferred between networks can be decreased, however, if the content of a public folder is available locally. For this reason, you should consider multiple replicas if public folder usage creates a significant amount of inter-network traffic. There is, however, a trade-off: Replication itself creates network traffic, and the replicated content consumes hard disk space. Public folder replication is covered in depth in Chapter 18, "Public Folder Replication."

Public Folders Within the Active Directory Directory Service

By default, public folders are not mail-enabled, meaning they do not possess e-mail addresses. To mail-enable a public folder, launch Exchange System Manager, expand the corresponding public folder hierarchy, such as the MAPI-based Public Folders, right-click the desired public folder, point to All Tasks, and select the Mail Enable command. To verify the results, display the public folder's properties afterwards. You will find e-mail-related property sheets (Exchange General, E-Mail Addresses, Exchange Advanced, and Member Of) in addition to the standard tabs (General, Replication, Limits, Details, and Permissions). Switch to E-Mail Addresses and check for assigned address information. It may take a little while for the Recipient Update Service to generate the e-mail addresses, but you can accelerate this process, as explained in Chapter 13, "Creating and Managing Recipients."

Note   Mail-enabling a public folder does not affect existing or new sub-folders. These folders do not inherit the mail-enabled state. To mail-enable an entire public folder sub-tree, prepare the top-level folder first, then right-click on it in Exchange System Manager, point to All Tasks, and then select the Propagate Settings command. In the Propagate Folder Settings dialog box, select the Mail Enabled check box, and then click OK.

Mail-Enabled Public Folders and Server-Based Address Lists

Mail-enabled public folders may be hidden from the server-based address lists. If you want to allow your users to select a particular public folder as a message recipient, such as a mail-based discussion forum, you need to make sure that the folder is visible. Launch the Exchange System Manager and display the public folder's properties, switch to the Exchange Advanced tab, and check that the Hide From Exchange Address Lists check box is deselected. This will be the case for all those folders that you have mail-enabled explicitly. However, if you have propagated the mail-enabled configuration from a parent folder to its sub-folders, these sub-folders are hidden by default.

Mail-Enabled Public Folders as Message Archives

It is possible to add a mail-enabled public folder to a distribution group (Member Of property sheet in Exchange System Manager), which allows you to keep track of discussions in teams, workgroups, and so forth. This frees team members from having to maintain personal discussion folders for distribution lists. In addition, you can revoke permissions to delete items from all members and implicitly create an authentic tracking system. Users must have the right to create items in a public folder if they want to send messages to it. Otherwise, a nondelivery report will inform the sender about the missing permissions.

Note   You can forward all messages sent or received by users on a particular mailbox store to a mail-enabled public folder. To achieve this, display the mailbox store's General tab, select the Archive All Messages Sent Or Received By Mailboxes On This Store check box, and select the desired folder. Because the Information Store service performs the archiving in the context of the LocalSystem account, users do not require any permission on the archiving folder.

Public Folders As Mailing List Members

List servers automatically distribute e-mail messages that have been sent to a particular address to all members of the list. The message volume can be large, filling your mailbox unnecessarily. If this situation sounds familiar to you, you might want to subscribe a public folder instead of your personal mailbox to the list. As mentioned earlier, the e-mail addresses of a public folder are listed in the E-Mail Addresses tab in the public folder's properties. Just provide the SMTP address of the desired public folder to the list server, and the list server sends all messages to the corresponding folder. You can view and filter them, and share them with colleagues easily (see Figure 17.3). Old items can also be purged automatically based on age limits. Make sure that the desired public folder is visible in the server-based address lists.

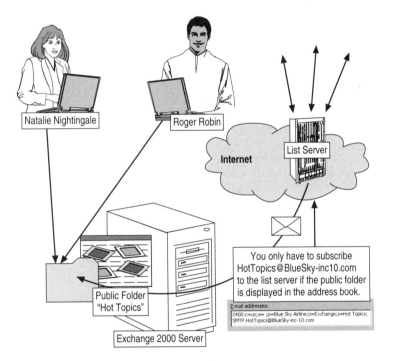

Natalie Nightingale

Roger Robin

Internet

List Server

Public Folder "Hot Topics"

You only have to subscribe HotTopics@BlueSky-inc10.com to the list server if the public folder is displayed in the address book.

E-mail addresses:
(X400:c=us;a= ;p=Blue Sky Airline;o=Exchange;s=Hot Topics;
SMTP:HotTopics@BlueSky-inc-10.com

Exchange 2000 Server

Figure 17.3   Subscribing public folders to list servers

Organizational Units for Mail-Enabled Public Folders

Mail-enabled public folders are associated with recipient objects, which can be displayed in Active Directory Users and Computers. Make sure the Advanced Features option is active, and then, in the console tree, select the container called Microsoft Exchange System Objects. In this location, you can change display names and manage group memberships. You can also move a public folder to another organizational unit, if desired.

Note If you want to move a public folder back into the Microsoft Exchange System Objects container, click View in the toolbar and select the Users, Groups, And Computers As Containers option. Otherwise, the Microsoft Exchange System Objects container is not listed in the Move dialog box.

Directory Names for Public Folders

Active Directory and the Information Store service maintain information about mail-enabled public folders in different ways. The Information Store is responsible for hierarchy and content, whereas Active Directory cares about directory-related issues. Both are synchronized with each other, yet Active Directory does not maintain a hierarchy for public folders as the Information Store does. The missing hierarchical structure does not lead to a conflict when generating directory names, yet users may find it puzzling if public folders with the same display names are listed in their address books.

To give an example, if you create a new top-level public folder in Exchange System Manager, call it DuplicateFolder, and mail-enable it, you can verify that it is only seconds before a corresponding recipient object is listed in Active Directory Users and Computers. Now, create a sub-folder under DuplicateFolder and give it the same name of DuplicateFolder. After that, mail-enable this folder as well, and then check the folder name in Active Directory Users and Computers. You will find that an arbitrary number was appended to the directory name to create a unique second public folder recipient object. The format is DuplicateFolder 12345678. When you check the information in the address book of Outlook 2000, however, you will find two public folders called DuplicateFolder. Because display names do not need to be unique, an arbitrary number is not appended. It is possible to change the display name of a public folder in Active Directory Users and Computers (Folder Display Name setting/General tab).

Replication Latency Issues

Using e-mail messages, the Information Store service replicates public folder hierarchies to all servers with associated public stores. The replication of recipient objects, on the other hand, is the task of Active Directory. Hence, two independent processes replicate information about a single object. Depending on which process is completed first, a mail-enabled public folder may first become visible to all other servers in either the directory or the public folder hierarchy. As time goes by, differences in listed public folders will disappear, but it might create some confusion in the meantime.

Note If you want to compare the hierarchy of a particular public store with other stores, right-click the desired hierarchy object in Exchange System Manager (such as Public Folders), and select Connect To. In the Select A Public Store dialog box, choose the public store that you want to examine.

Mail-Disabling Public Folders

It is possible to delete a public folder recipient object from the Microsoft Exchange System Objects container, in which case you mail-disable the affected folder. However, in Exchange System Manager, the state of the public folder will remain mail-enabled. Therefore, it is not advisable to use Active Directory Users and Computers for this purpose. Exclusively, use Exchange System instead. Right-click the desired mail-enabled public folder, point to All Tasks, and then select the Mail Disable command.

Note   If you have deleted a public folder recipient object in Active Directory Users and Computers, do not forget to complete the process of mail-disabling the folder in Exchange System Manager.

Exercise 1: Creating Public Folder Hierarchies

In this exercise you will create an additional public folder hierarchy using Exchange System Manager. You will associate it with a public store.

To view a multimedia demonstration that displays how to perform this procedure, run the EX1CH17*.AVI files from the \Exercise_Information\Chapter17 folder on the Supplemental Course Materials CD.

Prerequisites

- It is assumed that you have deleted the default public store from BLUESKY-SRV2 as outlined in Exercise 1 of Chapter 14, "Managing Server Configuration." If you did not follow this exercise, skip the steps to recreate the default public store.

- Display administrative and routing groups in Exchange System Manager (Display Routing Groups and Display Administrative Groups in the properties of the organization object).

- Make sure BLUESKY-SRV1and BLUESKY-SRV2 are running.

- Log on as Administrator to BLUESKY-SRV1and BLUESKY-SRV2.

▶ **To create public folder hierarchies and associate them with public stores**

1. On BLUESKY-SRV2, launch Exchange System Manager, expand Administrative Groups, then First Administrative Group, then Servers, then BLUESKY-SRV2, and then right-click First Storage Group. Point to New and select Public Store.

2. In the Properties dialog box, under Name, type **Public Folder Store (BLUESKY-SRV2)**.

3. Under Associated Public Folder Tree, click Browse, and, in the Select Public Folder Trees dialog box, double-click Public Folders (see Figure 17.4).

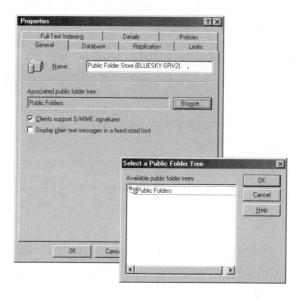

Figure 17.4 Creating a public store for the MAPI-based hierarchy

4. Click OK, and, in the Public Folder Store (BLUESKY-SRV2) dialog box asking you whether you want to mount this store now, click Yes.

5. In the Public Folder Store (BLUESKY-SRV2) dialog box informing you that the store was successfully mounted, click OK.

6. Open the First Storage Group container, verify that the Public Folder Store (BLUESKY-SRV2) exists, right-click Mailbox Store (BLUESKY-SRV2), and select Properties.

7. In the General tab, under Default Public Store, click Browse, and select Public Folder Store (BLUESKY-SRV2) – BLUESKY-SRV2. Click OK twice.

8. If a VIP Mailboxes store exists in the Management Group (created in Exercise 1 of Chapter 14, "Managing Server Configuration"), repeat Steps 6 and 7 to assign this mailbox store the public store on BLUESKY-SRV2 as the default public store.

   At this point, you have recreated the public store on BLUESKY-SRV2 and assigned this store to all existing mailbox stores on this server as the default public store, which corresponds to a default configuration. Close Exchange System Manager.

9. On BLUESKY-SRV1, launch Exchange System Manager, expand Administrative Groups, then First Administrative Group, then Folders, and verify that Public Folders is listed. Public Folders is currently the default MAPI-based hierarchy, which is associated with public stores on BLUESKY-SRV1 and BLUESKY-SRV2.

10. Right-click Folders, point to New, and select Public Folder Tree.

11. In the Properties dialog box, under Name, type **Alternate Tree**. Notice that General Purpose is displayed under Folder Tree Type, and click OK. A new hierarchy is now listed below Public Folders.

12. Expand Servers, then BLUESKY-SRV1, then right-click First Storage Group. Point to New and select Public Store.

13. In the Properties dialog box, under Name, type **Alternate Public Store**, and, under Associated Public Folder Tree, click Browse.

14. Notice that only the new folder hierarchy is listed. The Public Folders tree is already associated with the Public Folder Store (BLUESKY-SRV1) and cannot be associated with a second public store at the same time (see Figure 17.5). Select Alternate Tree and click OK. Click OK again to close the Properties dialog box.

15. An Alternate Public Store dialog box will be displayed, asking you whether you want to mount this store now. Click Yes.

16. In the Alternate Public Store dialog box informing you that the store was mounted successfully, click OK.

17. On BLUESKY-SRV1, launch Windows Explorer, expand drive M, expand Bluesky-inc-10.com, select Alternate Tree, open the File menu, point to New, and click Folder.

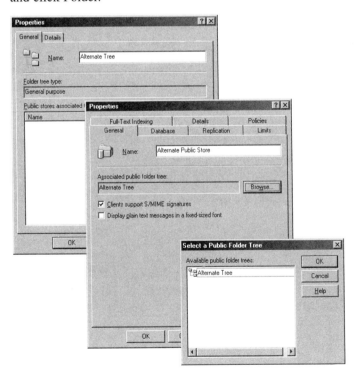

Figure 17.5   Creating an alternate hierarchy and public store

18. Name the new public folder BLUESKY-SRV1 Only, and press ENTER.

19. On BLUESKY-SRV2, launch Windows Explorer, expand drive M, expand Bluesky-inc-10.com, and notice that the Alternate Tree is not displayed because this server does not hold a public store associated with the alternate hierarchy (see Figure 17.6).

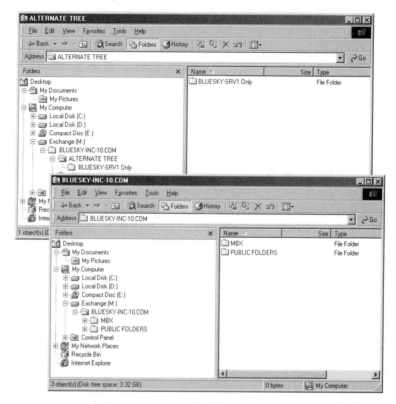

Figure 17.6 Working with different hierarchies on different servers

Exercise Summary

After creating a hierarchy, you need to create a public store to host the tree. Public folder hierarchies can be associated with exactly one public store per server. If multiple servers maintain a public store for the same hierarchy, the hierarchy is automatically replicated. If you create an alternate hierarchy and do not associate it with multiple stores from different servers, no replication takes place. The hierarchy is then available on the local server only.

Lesson 2: Creating and Managing Public Folders

Exchange System Manager provides the required interfaces for public folder administration. Using this utility, you can create and manage public folder hierarchies and stores, as well as create and configure public folder resources. However, Exchange System Manager is not the only program you can use. Outlook 2000, for instance, allows you to administer public folder settings as well, and you can use other programs, such as Windows Explorer or Web browsers, to create public folder resources. You may also work with public folders programmatically using Collaboration Data Objects (CDO).

This lesson focuses on public folder management using Exchange System Manager and Outlook 2000. You will learn about public folder creation and specific configuration settings. Public folder property sheets differ between Exchange System Manager and Outlook 2000.

At the end of this lesson, you will be able to:

- Create and manage public folder resources using Exchange System Manager.

- Create and manage public folder resources using Outlook 2000.

Estimated time to complete this lesson: 75 minutes

Security Settings for Public Folder Hierarchies

Before creating public folders, you should implement essential rules that govern public folder creation across the organization. For instance, the default MAPI-based hierarchy, replicated everywhere, may get out of hand if all users in the organization have permissions to create arbitrary public folder resources at all levels. Top-level folder creation, especially, should be restricted to a small group of administrators because these folders are at the top of the All Public Folders tree. The public folder administrators group can then grant permissions to other groups to manage the creation, content, and permissions of subfolders. By default, all users can create top-level folders.

Centralizing Public Folder Resources

Top-level folders are placed on the user's default public store server. This is typically the user's home server where his or her mailbox store resides—until you change the default public store. Top-level folders, in turn, determine the location of all subfolders regardless of the user who created them (see Figure 17.7). Hence, if you want to centralize the location of all existing public folders, you must ensure that top-level folders are created on only one server. You have two options. The first is to modify the public folder server attribute of all mailbox stores in your administrative group to point to only one common server. The disadvantage of this option is that it relies heavily on a single server, and users cannot browse the public folder hierarchy if the server is unavailable. The second option is to restrict the permissions to create top-level folders to a small group of users, thereby ensuring that top-level folders will be created only on the desired server. If you go with this option, this server must be the default public store server of all those users who can create top-level folders—in other words, it should be their home server. This option has advantages because it achieves the desired result by controlling who can create folders at the top of your public folder hierarchy.

Note   Exchange System Manager allows you to specify the server where new top-level folders should be created. Right-click the desired hierarchy object in Exchange System Manager (such as Public Folders under the Folders branch), and select Connect To to select the desired server.

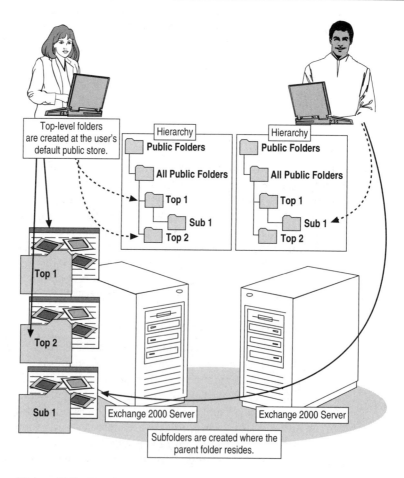

Figure 17.7   Top-level folder and subfolder creation

Configuring Security Settings

To determine who is able to create top-level folders, display the hierarchy's property sheets using Exchange System Manager (for instance, for the Public Folders hierarchy), and click on the Security tab. In the list of permissions, you will find a specific right called Create Top Level Public Folder (see Table 17.1). Make sure only the desired administrators have the right to create folders at the top of the hierarchy.

Note Because Exchange 2000 Server relies on Windows 2000 security features, you can deny the top-level folder creation explicitly. Deny permissions take precedence over granted permissions.

Table 17.1 Important Permissions for Public Folder Hierarchies

Permission	Description
Create Public Folder	Specifies who can create a public folder in this hierarchy.
Create Top Level Public Folder	Specifies who can create top-level folders, which represent the first level in the tree structure.
Modify Public Folder ACL	Specifies who can change client permissions.
Modify Public Folder Admin ACL	Specifies who can change administrative permissions.

Creating a Public Folder

With required permissions, the creation of public folders is a trivial task. In Exchange System Manager, expand the desired Folders hierarchy, right-click the desired parent container, such as Public Folders, point to New, and select Public Folder. The only parameter you need to provide is a value for the Name field. When you click OK, the public folder will be created in the hierarchy, and it is immediately available to users.

In Outlook 2000, several options are available to create a public folder. Perhaps the easiest way is to open the File menu, point to Folder, and select the New Folder command. This command is disabled if required permissions are missing. For example, if you do not have the permission to create top-level folders, but select All Public Folders in the Public Folders tree, the command is grayed out. If you have the permission, on the other hand, clicking this command launches the Create New Folder dialog box, which asks you for a folder name and the folder type (Appointment, Mail, Contact, Journal, Task, or Note Items). You can select the parent folder under Select Where To Place The Folder to finish the job.

Managing Public Folder Properties

Outlook assigns Outlook-specific properties to new public folders, which cannot be created using Exchange System Manager. Exchange System Manager is the right choice, on the other hand, to manage Exchange-specific settings, such as public folder replication, and to manage hierarchies that are not available in Outlook.

Using Exchange System Manager, you can work with the following tabs for mail-enabled folders:

- **Details.** Use this tab to specify an administrative note for informative purposes.

- **E-Mail Addresses.** Use this tab to manage e-mail addresses for a public folder and to specify whether the e-mail addresses should be updated based on recipient policies (see Chapter 13, "Creating and Managing Recipients").

- **Exchange Advanced.** Use this tab to specify a simple display name and to determine whether to show or hide the public folder in Exchange address lists. You can also specify custom attributes.

- **Exchange General.** Use this tab to specify Delegate permissions and forwarding addresses for a public folder and to modify the public folder alias, if desired.

- **General.** Use this tab to specify a description of the public folder, define a name to be displayed in the Global Address List instead of the public folder name, and determine whether read/unread information should be maintained for this folder. Read/unread information gives Outlook 2000 the option to indicate per user which items have been read, similar to messages in the mailbox. This information is maintained and cached on the server, which consumes resources.

- **Limits.** Use this tab to specify storage and age limits and a deleted item retention time. Deleted item retention is explained in Chapter 20, "Microsoft Exchange 2000 Server Maintenance and Troubleshooting."

- **Permissions.** Use this tab to configure client permissions, directory rights, and administrative rights on the public folder.

- **Replication.** Use this tab to specify which servers contain replicas and to set times at which this public folder is replicated to other replicas. Public folder replication is covered in detail in Chapter 18, "Public Folder Replication."

Using Outlook 2000, the following core tabs are available:

- **Administration.** Use this tab to specify a default view for this folder, add it to a personal address book if it isn't included in the Global Address List, determine the folder availability, and configure public folder rules. You also have the option to build moderated public folders (see later).

- **Forms.** Use this tab to manage electronic forms, as explained in Chapter 21, "Microsoft Outlook Forms Environment."

- **General.** Use this tab to specify a name and details for a public folder, define the standard electronic form to be used when posting items to this folder, determine whether to create Exchange Client-compatible views, and check public folder sizes.

- **Home Page.** Use this tab to specify a Web page, such as a Digital Dashboard, to be displayed when the user opens the public folder. Public folder home pages displayed instead of the folder view can display information from various sources, including the public folder content.

- **Permissions.** Use this tab to specify client permissions for this public folder. Users who are not explicitly listed receive the permissions granted to the Default account.

Note Outlook 2000 may display additional tabs, such as Activities for public folders that contain contact items, or Synchronization for folder shortcuts created under the Favorites container. Refer to the Outlook 2000 Online Help and the Office 2000 Resource Kit when working with these tabs.

Configuring Moderated Folders

Using Outlook 2000, you can configure moderated folders, which are the censored version of public folders, allowing you to review posted items before they appear. Exchange 2000 Server forwards all posted messages without modifications to a moderator. The moderator, in turn, reviews and places accepted items in the destination folder. Moderated folders are especially useful when you are setting up discussions across the Internet because they provide control over the tone, style, and topic of communication. In Exercise 3 of Chapter 1, "Introduction to Microsoft Exchange 2000 Server," you configured a public folder repository for contact items as a moderated public folder.

Note Using a public folder's Exchange General tab (Delivery Options button) in Exchange System Manager, you can configure a forwarding address to deliver messages to an alternate address instead of the folder. However, specifying a forwarding address does not result in a moderated folder configuration.

Managing Public Folder Access Permissions

Exchange 2000 Server supports a new security model, which allows you to assign permissions to folders, items, and properties similar to security settings on directories and files on an NT file system (NTFS) volume. Permissions can be inherited from higher level containers, such as the organization, administrative group, public folder hierarchy, and parent folder.

Public Folder Permission Types

Using Exchange System Manager to display the properties of a public folder, there are three buttons in the Permissions tab labeled Client Permissions,

Directory Rights, and Administrative Rights, which allow you to specify who can access and administer a public folder. The Client Permissions button launches a dialog box where you can configure permissions similar to the Permissions tab in Outlook 2000. Client permissions are maintained in conformance with the old legacy security model, which is based on roles, such as Publishing Author, Editor, and Owner, and MAPI address book entries. Exchange 2000 Server configures the corresponding Windows 2000 permissions automatically.

Client permissions correspond to folder and message rights. Folder rights allow you to control folder access, such as Read and Write permissions on a folder. Message rights, conversely, determine on a per-user level what form of access to messages is permitted (that is, edit and delete items). In contrast, when clicking the Directory Rights button, you can determine whether a user is allowed to mail-enable (or disable) a public folder, manage public folder recipient objects, or grant Send As permissions on the folder. Finally, when you click Administrative Rights, you can assign specific rights to administrators, such as the right to add or remove replicas to a public folder.

Note Public folder permissions are divided into four separate categories: folder rights, message rights, directory rights, and administrative rights. Outlook 2000 prevents you from managing public folder permissions if you are not a public folder owner (client permission). In Exchange System Manager, you can administer the same folder if you have the required administrative permissions. Folder ownership is not required in this case.

Working with Client Permissions

When setting client permissions, you are working with security identifiers (SIDs) of Windows 2000 users and groups. Even though you are selecting MAPI address book entries, you are in fact working with mailbox- and mail-enabled Windows 2000 security principals. This is also the reason you cannot assign permissions to mail-enabled distribution groups. Unlike mail-enabled security groups, distribution groups do not represent security principals.

By default, three accounts have access permissions:

- **Anonymous.** Granted the Contributor role
- **Default.** Granted the Author role
- **The user who created the public folder.** Granted the Owner role

The user who created the public folder is listed explicitly because every public folder must have at least one owner. This user is also specified as the folder contact who receives replication conflict notifications, folder design conflict notifications, and quota notifications. You cannot delete any of these three accounts right away, but you can designate an additional owner and contact accounts to remove the original owner entry.

The Anonymous account corresponds to the Anonymous Logon system account of Windows 2000. Default is synonymous for the Everyone group. Users who are not explicitly listed receive the permissions granted to the Default account.

Public Folder Properties Propagation

When you assign permissions to a parent folder, subfolders inherit those permissions when they are created. Changes in permissions to the parent folder are not automatically propagated to existing child folders. Be aware of this because it can lead to a security issue. For example, Outlook 2000 supports shortcuts on the Outlook taskbar and displays a Favorites list next to All Public Folders, which provides an easy way to reach popular public folders. Shortcuts and favorites are links that are similar to shortcuts in Windows 2000; they open the desired public folder without the need to navigate all its parent folders first. They can bypass permissions set on parent folders.

To prevent this way of bypassing permissions, you need to change the permissions for subfolders to those that apply to the parent folder. Exchange System Manager allows you to do this conveniently. Right-click the parent folder in the hierarchy, point to All Tasks, and select Propagate Settings.

The following folder properties can be propagated:

- Administrative and folder rights
- Age and storage limits
- Deleted item retention time
- Keep per user read/unread state
- Mail-enabled and show in address book information
- Replicas, replication message priority, and replication schedule

Note You need to be an owner (client permissions) on the subfolder to successfully propagate configuration changes.

Item-Level Permissions

Item-level permissions refer to security settings applied to individual messages, documents, and other objects in a public folder. Similar to standard file system permissions, you can set these when accessing a public folder through ExIFS. To give an example, place a Microsoft Word document in a public folder using Windows Explorer, then right-click it, select Properties, click on the Security tab, and specify the desired security settings. If you deny a user Read access to items, Outlook will display error messages, such as "Can't open this item, you don't have appropriate permission to perform this operation," or "The custom form could not be opened." Be careful when denying permissions to avoid confusion. It is not possible to hide individual items in a public folder and document properties may be exposed in folder views.

Exercise 2: Creating and Managing Public Folder Resources

In this exercise you will create various public folder resources and manage security settings. You will also use the Exchange System Manager to propagate configuration changes to subfolders.

To view a multimedia demonstration that displays how to perform this procedure, run the EX2CH17*.AVI files from the \Exercise_Information\Chapter17 folder on the Supplemental Course Materials CD.

Prerequisites

- Complete Exercise 1 (BLUESKY-SRV2 holds the Administrator's default public store), and start BLUESKY-WKSTA in addition to BLUESKY-SRV1 and BLUESKY-SRV2.

- Log on as Administrator to BLUESKY-SRV1.

▶ **To create public folders, set permissions, and propagate configuration changes to subfolders**

1. On BLUESKY-SRV1, launch Exchange System Manager, expand First Administrative Group and Folders, right-click Public Folders, point to New, and select Public Folder.

2. Under Name, type **BackDoor,** and click OK. Verify that the new public folder was created successfully.

3. Right-click BackDoor, select Properties, click on the Permissions tab, and click Client Permissions.

4. In the Client Permissions dialog box, click Add, and add Carl Titmouse to the list of users with explicit permissions. Select Carl Titmouse and, under Roles, select Publishing Author. Click OK twice.

5. Log on as Carl Titmouse to BLUESKY-WKSTA, and start Outlook 2000. Open the View menu, and select Folder List to display the list of folders besides the Outlook Bar.

6. Press CTRL+SHIFT+E to launch the Create New Folder dialog box. Under Name, type **Sub-BackDoor**. Under Select Where To Place The Folder, expand Public Folders, then All Public Folders, and then select BackDoor. Click OK.

7. In the Add Shortcut To Outlook Bar dialog box, click Yes. If this dialog box does not appear in your configuration, create a shortcut manually by dragging the folder called Sub-BackDoor from the folder list to My Shortcuts on the Outlook Bar.

8. Verify that a shortcut to Sub-BackDoor has been created under My Shortcuts. Click it to open the folder, and then, in the toolbar, click New, and, in the Untitled – Discussion form, under Subject, type **Changes to parent folder**

settings are not automatically propagated to subfolders. Then click Post and make sure the item is visible in the folder.

9. In Exchange System Manager on BLUESKY-SRV1, right-click Public Folders, and then select Refresh to update the view. Right-click BackDoor and select Properties.

10. Click on the Permissions tab, click Client Permissions, select Carl Titmouse, and, under Roles, select None. Deselect Folder Visible in addition, and click OK twice.

11. On BLUESKY-WKSTA in Outlook 2000, notice that the public folder called BackDoor, together with all subfolders, disappears from the folder list.

12. In the Outlook Bar, under My Shortcuts, click Sub-BackDoor, and notice that you have bypassed the parent folder. The contents of Sub-BackDoor are displayed in the details pane (see Figure 17.8).

Figure 17.8 Bypassing parent folder permissions

13. On BLUESKY-SRV1, in Exchange System Manager, right-click BackDoor, point to All Tasks, and select Propagate Settings.

14. In the Propagate Folder Settings dialog box, select the Folder Rights check box. Click OK and verify that all subfolders are processed.

15. On BLUESKY-WKSTA, in Outlook 2000, click the Sub-BackDoor shortcut again, and notice that Outlook is unable to display the folder contents (see Figure 17.9).

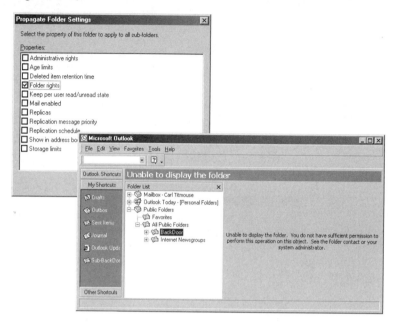

Figure 17.9   Propagating parent folder permissions

Exercise Summary

When creating sublevel public folders, configuration settings, such as client permissions, folder location, and replication settings, are inherited from the parent folder. An owner of a parent folder, for instance, will also become an owner of all sublevel folders by default—in addition to the user who has created the subfolder. When you change permissions for a parent folder either in Exchange System Manager or in Outlook 2000, you need to be aware that those changes are not automatically propagated to subfolders. You need to propagate configuration changes manually, which is only possible in Exchange System Manager.

If you want to revoke permissions for a parent folder but want users to be able to work with subfolders, it is a good idea to move the subfolders to a different location. Using Outlook 2000 or Exchange System Manager, you can move public folders within the same hierarchy via drag-and-drop. However, you cannot move or copy a folder from one public folder tree to another.

Lesson 3: Public Store Configurations

As outlined earlier, public folders consist of a reference in a hierarchy, and the content is hosted in a public store. This relationship is reversibly unambiguous. Each public store contains the contents of exactly one public folder tree and a public folder tree cannot be split across multiple stores. At the public store level, you define default parameters that affect all public folders in the associated hierarchy.

This lesson covers the configuration of important public store parameters. It also discusses the purpose of public folder referrals and how public folder content is accessed across routing group boundaries.

At the end of this lesson, you will be able to:

- Configure public stores.
- Specify public folder affinities.
- Describe how MAPI-based clients locate public folder contents.

Estimated time to complete this lesson: 45 minutes

Managing Public Stores

As outlined in previous chapters, you can maintain public stores for each server individually (see Chapter 14, "Managing Server Configuration") or combined through public store policies (see Chapter 12, "Management Tools for Microsoft Exchange 2000 Server") using Exchange System Manager. Most of the important settings, including replication schedule, age and storage limits, and so on, are available at both levels. Only store-specific parameters, such as for associated public folder trees and database paths, are unavailable in policies. Effective policy settings have higher priority than store settings and cannot be changed at the public store level.

Controlling Public Store Sizes

Public store databases have a size limit of 16 GB (Standard Edition) or no internal size limit (Enterprise Edition), in which case they are restricted only by the capacity of the server's local disk space. They are restricted only by the capacity of the server's local disk space. Storage quotas that you can set in the Limits tab of each individual public store or within a public store policy—Issue Warning At (KB), Prohibit Post At (KB), and Maximum Item Size (KB)—give you control over the amount of disk space a public store might eventually occupy. For instance, Issue Warning At (KB) allows you to specify a size limit for the entire public store. If this limit is exceeded, a warning message is generated indicating that items should be removed. Exchange 2000 Server generates this message at the specified warning message interval. By default, warning messages are generated daily at midnight. The text of the warning message cannot be edited.

Prohibit Post At (KB), on the other hand, allows you to define a definite size limit for the public store. As soon as this limit is reached, new information cannot be contributed until data is deleted from this store. Maximum Item Size (KB), again, defines the maximum size for objects in public folders. Items larger than the limit are rejected. Reasons to restrict item size are given in Chapter 18, "Public Folder Replication."

Note   Size limits at the store or policy level apply to the entire public store. You can also specify storage limits on a per-folder basis using the Limits tab of the corresponding public folder object in the hierarchy. However, it is not advisable to select the Use Public Store Defaults option for a public folder because in this case the public folder is allowed to consume the entire space in the public store. It is advisable to configure size limits for public folders individually.

Specifying Age Limits

Age limits determine how long a public folder retains items before deleting them automatically. This mechanism can ensure that old information in a public folder will not remain there indefinitely. To give an example, if you have subscribed a public folder to a mailing list as explained earlier, or use public folders as newsgroups, as explained in Chapter 11, "Internet-Based Client Access," you may want to define an age limit to ensure that outdated content does not impair the usefulness of your forums.

To set an age limit for all public folders in a public store, use the Limits tab of the public store object. Select the Age Limit For All Folders In This Store (Days) check box to specify the lifetime of items in days. By default, all public folders use the settings defined for their public store. However, you can also specify an individual age limit for a public folder in its Limits tab. Deselect the Use Public Store Defaults check box, and specify the limit under Age Limit For Replicas (Days).

Note   Specifying age limits per public store allows you to maintain different age limits for a public folder on different stores. Setting the age limit at the public folder level defines a common item lifetime for all replicas.

Obtaining Public Folder Status Information

Using the Public Folders object (located under the public store object), you can display status information about the public folder resources in a particular store. Among other things, you can view the disk space used in a given public folder, the total number of items per folder, the last access time, and the path to a folder in its hierarchy. To examine available information and add interesting columns to the details pane of Exchange System Manager, right-click the Public Folders object, point to View, and select Choose Columns. Make your choice in the Modify Columns dialog box.

Next to the Public Folders object, you will find further containers that provide you with information about users who are currently connected (Logons object), allow you to view and configure public folder replicas in the public store (Public Folder Instances object), give a quick overview about the replication status of each public folder (Replication Status object), and allow you to check the current index state (Full-Text Indexing object).

Public Folder Referrals

As long as you navigate through a public folder tree, the client communicates with the associated public store on the local server. Using Outlook 2000 and the MAPI-based hierarchy, this is the default public store, as defined in your mailbox store's properties. Usually, the default public store resides on your home server. When you select a particular public folder in the tree to open it, the client will look for the contents in the associated public store on the local server first, then possibly check other servers in the same routing group or in remote routing groups (see Figure 17.10).

Referrals Across Routing Groups

The routing group defines the boundary in which permanent and reliable network connections are assumed and direct public folder access is allowed. Every RGC provides a Do Not Allow Public Folder Referrals check box, which you can use to control public folder access across routing groups. The cost value of the connector establishes the public folder affinity. The lowest affinity cost determines the most preferred routing group if multiple routing groups exist. In addition, public folder referrals are transitive. If referrals are allowed between routing group A and routing group B, and between routing groups B and C, then referrals are implicitly allowed between A and C as well. All connectors allow referrals by default. Therefore, access to public folders is theoretically possible across the entire organization.

Note You should not allow referrals to routing groups over connections that do not support RPCs, such as routing groups connected through the Internet and firewalls.

Public folder referrals have the following characteristics:

- They can be defined for routing groups, not for single servers.
- If multiple routing groups have the same value, they are pooled and then contacted in a random order.
- Referrals based on routing group connectors are unidirectional; each routing group must maintain its own routing group connectors and its own referrals.
- Routing groups with the lowest public folder referral are tried first.
- Referrals specify the order in which remote routing groups are contacted if the public folder content is not in the local routing group.

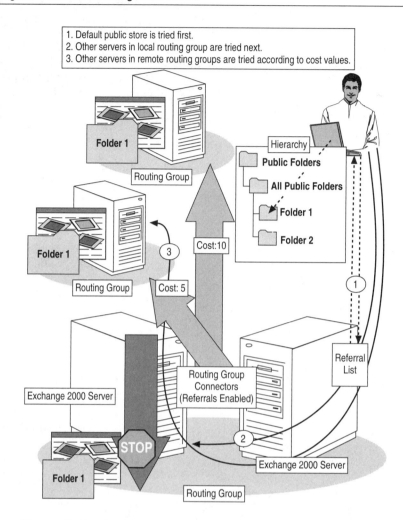

1. Default public store is tried first.
2. Other servers in local routing group are tried next.
3. Other servers in remote routing groups are tried according to cost values.

Figure 17.10   Connecting to public folder content

Public Folder Referral Process

When a client sends an open request to its local public server and this server has a replica, access to the content is possible immediately. Yet, the content may not be available locally. However, the server has complete information about the configuration and can determine where the public folder resides. Consequently, the server will compile a referral list containing all replica servers for the public folder, sort the servers according to affinity costs, and send this list to the client (see Figure 17.10). Based on this list, the client can determine where the folder is located and connect to the nearest server. If a server is unavailable for any reason, the next server in the list is tried.

The order in which a client searches for servers that have the public folder content available is as follows:

1. The client checks the server that holds the default public store of the user's mailbox store. If the content is not available, the client receives a list of replica servers.

2. The client uses a server to which a connection currently exists.

3. If there are no relevant server connections, the client chooses a server within the local routing group of the default public store and establishes a connection to request the content. If multiple servers have the content available, servers are chosen in a random order.

4. If there are no servers in the local routing group that hold a replica, or if these servers cannot be contacted at present, the client selects a server in another routing group based on affinity cost values, beginning with the lowest value.

5. Servers in routing groups with the same affinity value are pooled and contacted in a random order.

6. The client contacts the routing group with the next highest affinity value if it was not able to access the content. This continues until the content is located or until all servers in the list have been checked.

Breaking Through Routing Group Boundaries

The public folder referral process begins in the routing group that is local to the user's default public store. This is not necessarily the local routing group where the mailbox store resides. In other words, it is possible to configure a default public store for a mailbox store that is in a different routing group. In this case, access to hierarchy and content would require communication across routing groups. You need to make sure that a local area network (LAN) connection exists between these routing groups.

Important Access to the default public store cannot be restricted by means of an RGC or the Do Not Allow Public Folder Referrals check box. Clients must always be able to access their default public store, even if it resides in a different routing group.

Exercise 3: Public Folder Access Across Routing Group Boundaries

In this exercise you will block access to public folder contents across routing group boundaries. The task is to prevent access; in Chapter 18, "Public Folder Replication," you will make resources available by means of public folder replication.

To view a multimedia demonstration that displays how to perform this procedure, run the EX3CH17*.AVI files from the \Exercise_Information\Chapter17 folder on the Supplemental Course Materials CD.

Prerequisites

- Make sure your test environment is configured with two routing groups that are connected using an X.400 Connector, according to the exercises in Chapter 16, "Message Routing Administration."

- Complete Exercises 1 and 2, earlier in this chapter.

- Start BLUESKY-SRV1, BLUESKY-SRV2, and BLUESKY-WKSTA.

- Log on as Administrator to all machines (it may be necessary to logoff as Carl Titmouse from BLUESKY-WKSTA).

- Make sure the Administrator mailbox resides in the mailbox store VIP Mailboxes on BLUESKY-SRV2, according to Exercise 1 of Chapter 14, "Managing Server Configuration." Otherwise, move the mailbox to BLUESKY-SRV2 using Active Directory Users and Computers.

▶ **To prevent access to public folder contents across routing group boundaries**

1. On BLUESKY-SRV1, launch Exchange System Manager, expand the Folders object in the First Administrative Group, expand Public Folders, right-click BackDoor, and select Properties.

2. Click on the Replication tab, and verify, under Name, in the Replicate Content To These Public Stores list, that only Public Folder Store (BLUESKY-SRV1) is listed. (This folder exists on BLUESKY-SRV1 and the Administrator mailbox resides on BLUESKY-SRV2. Both servers exist in separate routing groups.)

3. Click on the Permissions tab, click Client Permissions, and make sure that the Administrator account is listed as the owner of the public folder with all permissions.

4. Select Carl Titmouse, and click Remove to grant this account the Default permissions of an Author again. Click OK twice.

5. Right-click BackDoor, point to All Tasks, select Propagate Settings, and, in the Propagate Folder Settings dialog box, select the Folder Rights check box. Then click OK. (Carl Titmouse's mailbox resides on BLUESKY-SRV1.)

6. Under Routing Groups, expand the First Routing Group, and then expand Connectors. Right-click X.400 To BLUESKY-SRV2, and then select the Disallow Public Folder Referrals option (this is the same as selecting the Do Not Allow Public Folder Referrals check box in the connector's General tab).

7. Launch Exchange System Manager on BLUESKY-SRV2, expand the Second Routing Group under Routing Groups in the First Administrative Group, expand Connectors, right-click X.400 To BLUESKY-SRV1, and then select the Disallow Public Folder Referrals option.

8. Wait for the directory replication to propagate the changes to both servers, and then, on BLUESKY-WKSTA, launch Outlook 2000, and make sure you are connected as Administrator.

9. Open the View menu, and make sure the Folder List option is selected to display the list of mailbox and public folders.

10. Expand Public Folders, All Public Folders, and BackDoor. Notice that you can navigate the hierarchy without problems.

11. Select BackDoor, and verify that Outlook 2000 is unable to display the folder content (see Figure 17.11).

12. Log off as Administrator, and log on as Carl Titmouse. Check that Carl is able to work with the public folder content because his default public store has the folder available.

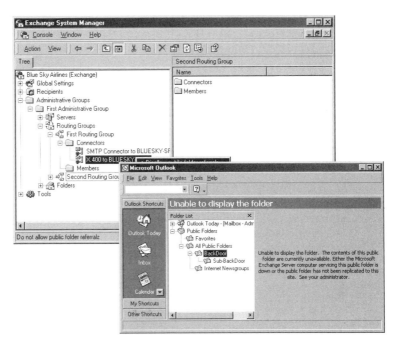

Figure 17.11   Preventing public folder access across routing groups

Exercise Summary

The routing group defines the boundary within which Outlook 2000 can access any server directly via RPCs to request the content of a public folder. Between routing groups, however, access must be granted explicitly by means of routing group connectors (RGC, SMTP Connector, or X.400 Connector). If routing groups are connected via slow and unreliable connections or connections that do not support RPCs, it is advisable to prevent public folder referrals in the routing group connector configuration. Routing groups and connectors are covered in Chapter 16, "Message Routing Administration."

Chapter Summary

Public folders are repositories for all kinds of information, and they are available to all imaginable applications, including standard Win32 programs that can access these repositories via ExIFS. Public folders are primarily managed using Exchange System Manager, but users may also use their client programs for their creation and administration. The actual public folder repositories are maintained in public stores.

Public folder access relies on two elements: the public folder hierarchy and the public folder content. Public folders may also have recipient objects, even though they may be hidden from the Global Address List by default. Exchange 2000 Server supports multiple hierarchies, which gives you better administrative control and flexibility over workgroup and workflow solutions. Public stores on different servers may refer to the same hierarchy, in which case the hierarchy is automatically replicated between them. At least one server holding the default public store for the MAPI-based public folders tree must exist within an administrative group.

When you open a public folder, your client program will send an open request to your home server. If the server has the contents, you will get access. If it doesn't, it returns a referral list to the client. Based on the information from this list, the client will connect to a server within the local or remote routing groups. If all target servers are inaccessible for some reason, you will receive an error message that the folder content could not be located.

Review

The following review questions can help you determine if you have sufficiently familiarized yourself with the material covered in this chapter. You can find the answers to these questions at the end of this book in Appendix A, "Questions and Answers."

1. What is a dedicated public server?

2. Which communication method is used to access the public folder content using Outlook 2000?

3. You have decided to place all public folders on a particular server without configuring dedicated servers. A user works with Outlook 2000 and creates a new top-level folder. Where will the new public folder be located?

4. A user works with the Outlook 2000 and creates a new subfolder directly under a top-level folder. Where will the new public folder be stored?

5. Olivia calls and complains that some other users can't see her new public folder in their public folder trees. Users on the local server are able to work with the new folder. What is most likely the cause of the problem?

6. Users in your routing group need to work with a public folder called Customer Feedback. This folder is not kept in the local routing group, and you don't want to create a local replica of this folder. RPC communication is supported between all servers in your organization. What must be accomplished to allow your users access to the public folder content?

C H A P T E R   1 8

Public Folder Replication

About This Chapter

Organizations that implement advanced workgroup and workflow systems based on public folders will maximize their return on investments in Microsoft Exchange 2000 Server. Public folders open a vast set of tremendous opportunities. However, a single public folder instance is not always suitable. A single instance does not provide fault tolerance. For example, let's say Blue Sky Airlines has implemented a global flight planning system. Flight attendants use this system to plan their monthly flight schedule and to trade unwanted trips with colleagues. If the server holding this system shuts down for any reason, flight schedules would become unavailable and business processes would be interrupted. Of course, this is unacceptable; redundant public folder instances are required to provide fault tolerance for business-critical solutions.

This chapter covers the various aspects of public folder replication, including advantages, granularity, and configuration. It discusses the various methods of collecting and delivering public folder instances from and to other servers and the replication process in detail.

Before You Begin

To complete this chapter:

- Prepare your test environment according to the descriptions given in the "Getting Started" section of "About This Book." It is advantageous to complete the exercises in Chapter 17, "Public Folder Management."

- You should be familiar with the concepts of single public folder instances and their administration, as covered in Chapter 17, "Public Folder Management."

Lesson 1: Public Folder Strategies

Both single and multiple public folder instances have advantages and disadvantages that you need to take into consideration when planning your public folder strategy. Exchange 2000 Server is flexible and allows you to create or eliminate public folder replicas at any time. It is good practice to reassess your approach to public folder replication periodically.

This lesson covers the major aspects of public folder strategies. It points out the various advantages and disadvantages of single and multiple public folder instances and discusses advantages and disadvantages of dedicated server configurations.

At the end of this lesson, you will be able to:
- Describe the advantages and disadvantages of single public folder copies.
- Describe the advantages and disadvantages of one or more replicas.
- Decide whether to configure dedicated public folder and mailbox servers.

Estimated time to complete this lesson: 45 minutes

Stand-Alone Public Folders

Stand-alone public folders are the default configuration, but they may or may not be ideal for your purposes. In other words, public folders are not replicated to other servers without administrative intervention.

Advantages of Stand-Alone Public Folders

A single public folder consumes disk space on one server only; additional disk space for redundant folder copies is not required. Users connect to the central server to work with the public folder. Because there is no replication delay, changes to the contents are seen immediately by users. The single public folder model works best in small environments with local area network (LAN) connections, where redundancy is not critical.

Disadvantages of Stand-Alone Public Folders

As mentioned, stand-alone public folders do not provide fault tolerance. To implement fault tolerance, you must create redundant public folder instances. Furthermore, it is impossible to provide load balancing. All users have to access one particular server to open a public folder, so this server can become a very busy machine. Likewise, users can access public folders only if LAN-like connections exist. If a wide area network (WAN) connection connects routing groups, access to stand-alone public folders in remote routing groups might be slow or impossible (see Exercise 3 of Chapter 17, "Public Folder Management").

The following are notable features of stand-alone public folders:

- Public folder maintenance is centralized because only one public store is affected.

- Underlying network topology determines quality of public folder access.

- No additional disk space on further servers is required.

- There is no overhead or latency due to public folder replication.

- Bottlenecks in public folder access are possible if the public folder server is overtaxed.

- Public folders are not available during server maintenance.

Replicated Public Folders

Public folders are easy to clone. You can have the same public folder on any of your Exchange 2000 servers, but this would consume a lot of disk space. Public folder replication ensures that the content of all instances of the same public folder is kept up to date.

Advantages of One or More Replicas

The main advantage of multiple public folder instances is increased fault tolerance. If one of the servers becomes unavailable, your users can still access the contents. If both servers are available, multiple instances can provide load balancing. Users can work with both replicas at the same time. Through public folder replication, you can address network topology issues. If direct client access is not suitable, create a second replica in an accessible location (see Figure 18.1).

You may want to replicate at least one instance of each public folder to all routing groups, even if direct access over WAN connections is supported, because it can speed up folder access. Furthermore, client traffic over the WAN is eliminated, which benefits other processes, such as message transfer between routing groups. Instead of having multiple users accessing the same information, the information is transferred once using public folder replication messages. You can also schedule the public folder replication and configure other parameters based on routing group connectors, as explained in Chapter 16, "Message Routing Administration."

The following are some features of replicated public folders:

- A replica of a public folder can be kept available in all locations for local access.

- Client access over WAN connections can be eliminated.

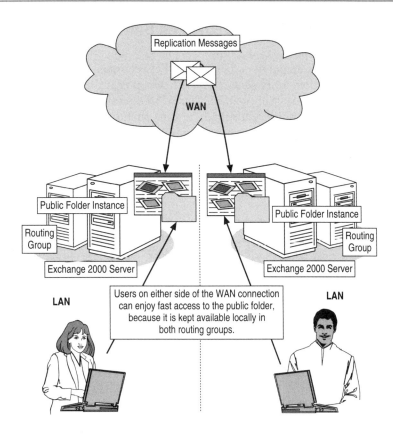

Figure 18.1 Enabling local access to a public folder

- Fault tolerance between multiple servers is available.
- Load balancing between multiple servers is possible.
- Public folder replication can be scheduled.
- New items posted in a public folder instance are not immediately available in all other locations due to public folder replication latency.
- Public folder replication latency increases the chance of conflicts due to concurrent changes of existing items.
- Public folder replication must be configured manually, but new subfolders inherit the settings of their parent folders.
- Public folder replication relies on e-mail messages and increases message traffic.

Public Folder Instances Between Organizations

True public folder replication is only supported within a single organization. To replicate public folder content between separate organizations, the InterOrg Replication utility should be used, which is available on the Exchange 2000 Server CD in the \Support\Exchsync\i386 directory. Network News Transfer Protocol (NNTP) newsfeeds might also be an option for replication. However, NNTP relies on the concept of articles and does not provide the means to replicate other objects directly, such as Microsoft Word documents. The server on the receiving side would end up with message items that contain Word documents as attachments. Support for NNTP was covered in Chapter 11, "Internet-Based Client Access."

The InterOrg Replication utility replicates items in Exchange format. You need to run this utility on a dedicated Microsoft Windows 2000 workstation, which typically belongs to the Windows 2000 domain of the publishing Exchange 2000 server. In essence, this utility behaves like a user connecting to multiple Exchange 2000 servers. In fact, it relies on Microsoft Outlook, and you need to configure mailboxes for it on the servers that you want to connect to. A replication configuration tool (EXSCFG.EXE), which is part of the InterOrg Replication utility, facilitates the configuration task. Another component, the actual replication service (EXSSRV.EXE), is responsible for content replication. You can read more about the InterOrg Replication utility in the Exchange 2000 Server Online Help.

Note   Using the InterOrg Replication utility, it is possible to replicate free/busy information. To map free/busy information to the correct accounts in the destination domain, create corresponding mail-enabled contacts. Make sure that the Simple Mail Transfer Protocol (SMTP) address of the original mailbox-enabled user account matches the underlying e-mail address of the mail-enabled contact object. You can read more about mailbox- and mail-enabled recipient objects in Chapter 13, "Creating and Managing Recipients."

Configuring Dedicated Public Folder Servers

On dedicated public folder servers, mailbox stores have been removed, as demonstrated in Exercise 1 of Chapter 14, "Managing Server Configuration." The separation of server tasks allows you to design hardware resources explicitly and therefore more precisely. All users in the organization can potentially access the public folder server. Therefore, you should optimize the hardware for fast network input/output (I/O). Optimizing storage performance using a redundant array of independent disks (RAID) is the best way to do this.

Because a dedicated public server can take over responsibility of all existing public folders, the response time of the remaining servers will improve with a reduced load. For fault-tolerant implementations and load balancing, you can configure two or more dedicated servers and replicate public folders between them (see Figure 18.2).

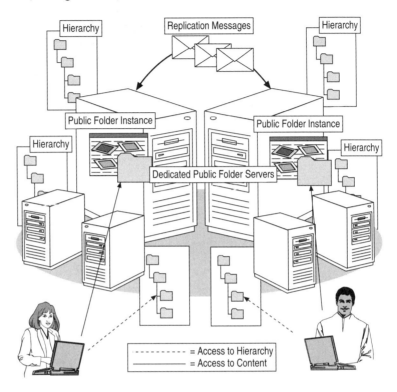

Figure 18.2   Accessing a public folder on a dedicated public folder server

Disadvantages of Dedicated Mailbox Servers

Similar to dedicated public folder servers, you may want to configure dedicated mailbox servers to avoid the accidental creation of top-level public folders on those machines. Although this is possible, you should refrain from it because of significant disadvantages. You would have to delete the public store associated with the default Messaging Application Programming Interface (MAPI)-based hierarchy from the mailbox servers. A default public store on another server must then be specified for all local mailbox stores to provide access to the MAPI-based public folder hierarchy (see Exercise 1 of Chapter 14, "Managing Server Configuration"). Keep in mind that neither fault tolerance nor load balancing is provided for hierarchy access. Hence, if the server that holds the default public store shuts down, users with mailboxes on corresponding mailbox servers will not be able to work with public folders. They can't navigate through the hierarchy any longer, which puts an effective end to public folder access, regardless of the number of public folder servers that have the contents available.

To put it plainly, it is not advisable to delete the public store associated with the MAPI-based hierarchy from any server. Use Exchange System Manager to place all top-level folders on a dedicated public folder server and configure their replication if desired. Revoke permissions to create top-level folders, but grant your users the rights to set up subfolders. Subfolders will be placed where the parent folder is located, and they inherit the parent's configuration, including replication settings. In addition, you always have the option to propagate configuration changes to existing subfolders, as illustrated in Chapter 17, "Public Folder Management."

Lesson 2: Public Folder Replication Configuration

The public folder hierarchy has been separated from the content to distribute information about public folders across the organization without the need to propagate large amounts of data at the same time. The hierarchy is replicated automatically; content replication requires an explicit configuration. Therefore, public folder replication usually refers to the process of replicating public folder contents.

This lesson explains the public folder replication process, beginning with an introduction to replication features. It covers the configuration of the replication process per public folder and per public store.

At the end of this lesson, you will be able to:

- Describe the features of public folder content replication.

- Configure the replication per public folder and per public store.

Estimated time to complete this lesson: 60 minutes

Public Folder Replication Overview

The public folder replication process follows the multimaster model. You can change the public folder hierarchy and the public folder contents from any location. In fact, you can't distinguish a copy from its original. Public folder replication guarantees that changes made on one instance overwrite earlier information in other instances to ensure the uniformity of data.

Note The multimaster model allows you to distribute the workload of public folder servers because users can work on multiple servers, post new information to their local replica, and have the new information replicated to each other.

Network Topology Independence

The replication of both the hierarchy and the contents are always performed using e-mail messages. Even within a single routing group, the Information Store service of the local server does not contact any Information Store running on other servers directly. The e-mail transport simplifies network communications because it abstracts the underlying network topology. If you are able to send a regular e-mail message to a destination server, you can create public folder replicas on that server. In other words, you can create a replica on any Exchange 2000 server in your organization.

> **Note** Public folder replication messages are addressed to the Information Store service, which has an e-mail alias in the form <Server Name>-IS (such as BLUESKY-SRV1-IS). Using Exchange System Manager, you can specify a priority for replication messages per public folder (via the Replication tab).

Public Folder Replication Agent

An internal component of the Information Store service, known as Public Folder Replication Agent (PFRA), is responsible for replicating the public folder content. It tracks changes, generates replication messages for other servers, and receives them from remote servers. The PFRA maintains state information for each item in each folder, which allows identification of the most recent changes as well as replication conflicts, as explained later in Lesson 3.

Public Folder Contents Replication

Too many replicas can increase network traffic and consume disk space unnecessarily, whereas too few copies affect the network bandwidth because users access the content elsewhere across the network.

Granularity of Replication

The granularity of replication refers to the smallest unit that the public folder replication is able to transport, which is the e-mail message or public folder item. As soon as a user modifies an object in one replica, the entire item must be sent to all other replicas. The new object replaces the older version everywhere, accurately updating all copies. Especially when replicating document libraries, it might therefore be advisable to restrict the maximum item size. You can set the corresponding Maximum Item Size (KB) parameter in the Limits tab of the public store as well as for each public folder individually, as explained in Chapter 17, "Public Folder Management."

> **Note** The replication mechanism is not very efficient, and it introduces negative side effects if a replica contains huge documents. Public folders are most suitable if the number of items is large and the item sizes are small. If a public folder contains thousands of documents and you change one, only this document is replicated.

Granularity of Configuration

The granularity of configuration refers to the lowest level of public folder management, which occurs at the public folder level. Public folder configuration affects the entire content, but you cannot apply replication settings directly to single messages in the folder. Configuration changes are propagated to all servers as part of the hierarchy replication.

Replication Configuration per Public Store

Using Exchange System Manager, you can configure public folder replication at the public store level, which can be compared to a situation where you pull public folder instances from other servers into your server. Most important in this scenario is the Public Folder Instances object underneath the container of the public store (see Figure 18.3).

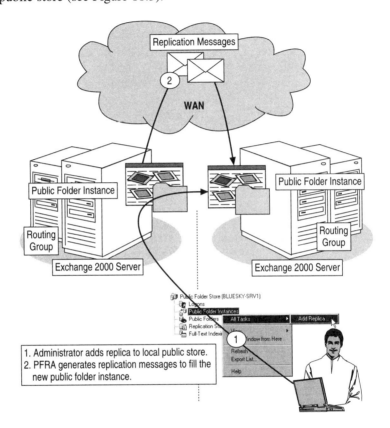

Figure 18.3   Pulling a public folder replica into a public store

Collecting Public Folder Instances

To add a public folder replica from another server to the public store on your server, right-click Public Folder Instances, point to All Tasks, and click Add Replica. This will launch the Public Store dialog box, displaying the associated public folder hierarchy. Expand the public folder hierarchy, select the desired folder, and click OK. If you right-click Public Folder Instances again and select Refresh, the added public folder instance will be listed in the details pane. Keep in mind that configuration changes are not automatically propagated to subfolders. If you want to replicate subfolders together with the parent folder, you need to repeat the configuration or propagate the changes of the parent folder.

Note You can only replicate public folders to a public store that is associated with their hierarchy. It is impossible to add public folder instances from other hierarchies.

Restricting Replica Requests

Pulling replicas into a server potentially allows any administrator to create an instance of any public folder on his or her servers. The administrator does not even need to communicate with the server that holds the public folder, because configuration changes are distributed using the hierarchy replication. If you do not want to allow every neighbor to replicate your public folders, you should restrict administrative access to the public store.

For example, let's say that you want to deny Carl Titmouse the right to configure the replication for the Public Folder Store (BLUESKY-SRV1)—provided that Carl was granted Administrative permissions in the Exchange 2000 organization beforehand. Right-click Public Folder Store (BLUESKY-SRV1), select Properties, click on the Security tab, select Carl Titmouse from the list of administrators, and then, in the list of permissions, select the Deny check box for the Modify Public Folder Replica List permission. It is possible to deny this permission per public store or per public folder (Administrative Rights). Denying this permission per public store is useful if you want to enforce a stand-alone public folder configuration by preventing creation of any replicas from this public store. It also prevents others from pushing public folders into your store, as explained later. Denying this permission per public folder allows you to enforce a global public folder replication strategy for all servers.

Determining Replication Interval and Message Sizes

Every public store provides a Replication tab, where you can configure an interval and a size limit for replication messages. Typically, replication is performed every 15 minutes if changes have occurred. However, you can specify a different replication interval or specific times, which may be useful if your server is connected to the rest of the organization through a slow or dial-up network connection. Configure the replication to occur during off hours to minimize the impact of replication messages on interpersonal message transfer.

Keep in mind that the replication message size limit does not define a maximum limit for replication messages. It is actually the other way around: The replication message size limit determines that items smaller than the specified size should be combined until the replication message reaches the specified size. The default message size limit is 300 KB. It is important to note that the PFRA is unable to split larger items into smaller units; hence, if the PFRA needs to replicate a 10 MB Word document, the document is sent in one single message because it exceeds the specified limit.

Note It is possible to define maximum message size limits per SMTP virtual server and routing group connectors. However, public folder replication messages are system messages, which are unaffected by these size limits. Because large replication messages can disrupt interpersonal message transfer, it is advisable to set appropriate maximum item sizes per replicated public folder or optimize the replication schedule.

Replication Configuration per Public Folder

Using Exchange System Manager, you can also push replicas of a particular public folder into specified servers in your routing group or in other routing groups (see Figure 18.4). Every public folder provides a Replication tab, where you can click Add to launch the Select A Public Store dialog box. Only those public stores that are associated with the public folder's hierarchy but don't hold a replica for the selected folder yet will be listed. As mentioned earlier, you need to have the Modify Public Folder Replica List permission for the public store where you want to add a folder; otherwise, you will receive an error message when you click OK.

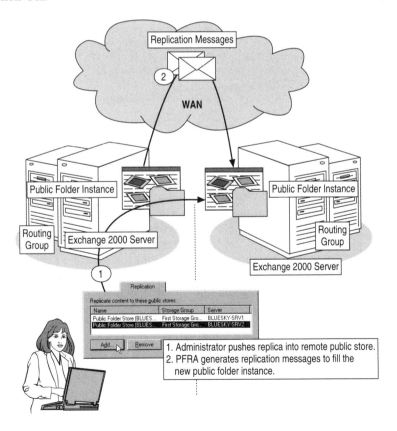

Figure 18.4 Pushing a public folder replica into a public store

Configuring Replication Schedule and Status

When you examine the Replication tab, you will notice the Public Folder Replication Interval check box, which allows you to schedule replication messages independently of the public store schedule. If your public folder contains large items, it might be a good idea to replicate the data during off hours. However, typically you want to set a common schedule for all public folder replicas at the server level through the public store object.

In the Replication tab, the Details button displays the Replication Status dialog box where you can examine the folder's replication status. All servers that hold a replica are listed in the Server Name column together with their Replication Status. In Sync indicates that the local replica has not been modified since changes were last sent. If a user has modified the contents of a replica and the changes have not yet been sent to the other servers, Local Modified is displayed. All servers will be In Sync as soon as the next replication cycle is complete. Another interesting category is Last Received Time, which provides information about the most recently received updates per server. The Avg. Trans. Time (Average Transmission Time) gives you an idea of the average time that it takes to send updates to a selected server.

Tip   It is also possible to examine the replication status for all replicas using the Replication Status container located underneath each public store object. The public store displays the status information in a server-centric way for all instances in the public store.

Configuring Age Limits per Replica

As explained in Chapter 17, "Public Folder Management," you can configure age limits per public store or per public folder. However, neither the public store nor the public folder level allows you to configure age limit exceptions. For example, let's say you want to configure a general item lifetime of 60 days for all instances of a particular public folder but have one server with an age limit of 10 days. To achieve this configuration, in the folder's Limits tab, clear the Use Public Store Defaults check box and, under Age Limit For Replicas (Days), type **60**. Now you need to configure one exception for the replica on the server where you want to apply a limit of 10 days. Expand the corresponding server object's public store, and then select the Public Folder Instances subcontainer. Right-click the desired replica in the details pane, select Replica Properties, activate the Age Limit Of This Folder On This Public Store (Days) check box, and type **10** in the text box. The Effective Age Limit Of This Folder On This Public Store (Days) text box provides a summary about the effective item lifetime.

Replication of System Folders

Every public store holds a number of system folders not visible in the hierarchy. Using Exchange System Manager, you can view a list of all system folders that exist when you right-click the desired hierarchy object under the Folders container and select View System Folders.

The following are important system folders and containers listed in the hierarchy (containers are in uppercase):

- **Events Root.**   Contains subfolders, which in turn hold scripts for the Exchange Server 5.5-compatible Event Service.

- **EFORMS REGISTRY.**   Contains forms (typically send forms) published via the Organization Forms Library, which is explained in Chapter 21, "Microsoft Outlook Forms Environment."

- **OFFLINE ADDRESS BOOK.**   Contains subfolders, which in turn store offline address books, which clients may download, as explained in Chapter 9, "MAPI-Based Clients."

- **SCHEDULE+ FREE/BUSY.**   Contains a subfolder per administrative group for Schedule+ free/busy information. Free/busy information allows Outlook users to view availability information of other users when composing meeting requests.

- **Schema.**   Contains definitions for properties of objects kept in the public store.

- **StoreEvents.**   Contains Exchange 2000 Server-specific global and internal event sinks for a specific server.

Offline Address Books and Schedule+ Free/Busy Information

When you compare the content of the Public Folder Instances subcontainers under Public Folder Store (BLUESKY-SRV1) and Public Folder Store (BLUESKY-SRV2) with each other, you will notice a significant difference in available system folders. BLUESKY-SRV1 holds offline address books and Schedule+ free/busy information and BLUESKY-SRV2 doesn't. By default, only the first server installed in the administrative group holds these system folders. If you shut down this server for maintenance, users will not be able to download offline address books or update free/busy information. Outlook 2000, for instance, may display an error message when working with appointments (see Figure 18.5).

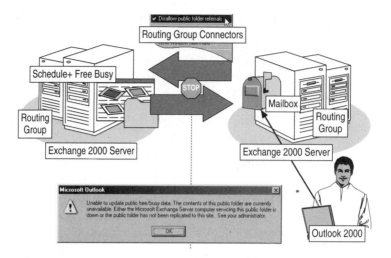

Figure 18.5   Unable to update public free/busy data

Figure 18.5 illustrates a situation where system folders must be replicated between servers in different routing groups. As indicated, public folder referrals are disallowed, which prevents users from accessing the folders on the first installed server across the routing group boundary (see Exercise 3 of Chapter 17, "Public Folder Management"). To avoid frustrating your Outlook users, replicate the offline address books and the Schedule+ free/busy information to a server in each routing group.

Note   To replicate system folders, push the folder into the public store of additional servers, as explained earlier in this lesson. You can right-click system folders in the hierarchy or underneath the Public Folder Store object in the Public Folders subcontainer, select Properties, and then click on the Replication tab.

Moving a Public Folder Between Servers

It is not an easy task to move a public folder between servers, although it might seem simple at first glance. You only need to add a public folder replica to a new server and remove the old instance from the first machine. In the public folder's Replication tab, use the Add and Remove buttons for this purpose. You also could use the Public Folder Instances subcontainer. To remove a public folder via Public Folder Instances, right-click the replicated folder in the details pane, point to All Tasks, and click Remove Replica.

Replication Latency Issues

When moving public folders between servers, you can remove the original replica without waiting for the PFRA to complete its contents replication. The old replica remains on the old server until the replication has taken place and the contents are entirely transferred to the new replica. However, Exchange 2000 Server is a platform for the patient system administrator. Replication, for example, is not an exceptionally fast process, and, if you remove the original replica too quickly, users might end up with an empty folder in Outlook 2000. This effect disappears as the PFRA completes its replication, but, depending on the replication schedule and the importance of the folder, this could cause problems in the interim. You should leave the replica in the original public store and wait until the PFRA has completed the replication. Unfortunately, no feature currently exists to force the PFRA to replicate immediately.

Removing Public Folder Servers

You should move all system folders to a new server in advance if you plan to remove the first server installed in an administrative group. Be very patient if you want to remove a server after its public folders have been moved. Otherwise, you might end up with unpleasant Outlook 2000 problems. Outlook may cache the names of public folder servers, and, if a server has been removed, the client may hang when it is attempting to access the old server. To avoid this problem, wait until all Outlook users have accessed the folders on the new server. Otherwise, affected users may need to create a new MAPI profile for their Outlook clients to fix problems with public folder access.

Note You should not uninstall a public folder server immediately after its resources have been moved. Unplug the server from the network, or stop the Exchange 2000 services and monitor the organization. If users have difficulty accessing public folders, start the old server again. Wait until you feel confident that it is safe to go ahead. Depending on the situation, this may take a week or longer.

Exercise 1: Replicating Public Folder Resources

In this exercise you will replicate public folders and system folders between servers in different routing groups. For better illustration of local public folder access, routing group connectors should disallow public folder referrals between the routing groups.

To view a multimedia demonstration that displays how to perform this procedure, run the EX1CH18*.AVI files from the \Exercise_Information\Chapter18 folder on the Supplemental Course Materials CD.

Prerequisites

- Complete Exercise 3 of Chapter 17, "Public Folder Management."
- Start BLUESKY-SRV1, BLUESKY-SRV2, and BLUESKY-WKSTA.
- Log on as Administrator to all machines.

▶   **To replicate public and system folders between servers in different routing groups**

1. On BLUESKY-SRV2, launch Exchange System Manager, expand Administrative Groups, then First Administrative Group, then Servers, then BLUESKY-SRV2, then First Storage Group, and then Public Folder Store (BLUESKY-SRV2).

2. Right-click Public Folder Instances, point to All Tasks, and click Add Replica.

3. In the Public Store dialog box, expand the public folder tree, and, under Public Folders (BLUESKY-SRV2), select BackDoor. Click OK.

4. Right-click Public Folder Instances again, and select Refresh. Verify that the BackDoor public folder is listed in the details pane (see Figure 18.6).

Figure 18.6   Adding a public folder instance to a public store

5. On BLUESKY-WKSTA, launch Outlook 2000, make sure the folder list is displayed, expand Public Folders, expand All Public Folders, expand BackDoor, and then select the BackDoor folder. Notice that the content is displayed (the folder might be empty, but you are able to post items into it).

6. On the toolbar, click New, and, under Subject, type **Public folder replication settings are not automatically propagated to subfolders**. Click Post. Verify that you are able to work with the public folder.

7. In the folder list, select Sub-BackDoor. Outlook 2000 will be unable to display the folder because it was not replicated to the local routing group.

8. In the Outlook toolbar, click Calendar.

9. In the toolbar, click New. Under Subject, specify **We need to provide access to the Schedule+ Free Busy Folder**, and then click the Save And Close button.

10. Verify that the appointment was created successfully, open the File menu, and select Exit And Log Off.

11. A Microsoft Outlook dialog box will appear, informing you that the client is unable to update public free/busy data (see Figure 18.7). Click OK.

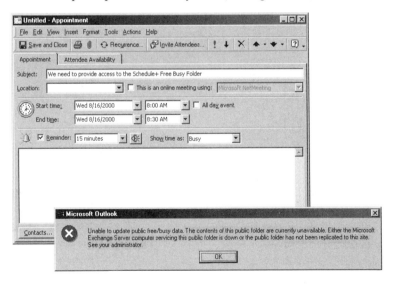

Figure 18.7   Testing the unavailability of system folders

12. On BLUESKY-SRV1, launch Exchange System Manager, expand Administrative Groups, then First Administrative Group, then Folders, and then Public Folders. Right-click BackDoor, point to All Tasks, and select Propagate Settings.

13. In the Propagate Folder Settings dialog box, select the Replicas check box, and click OK.

14. Right-click Public Folders, and select View System Folders.

15. Expand the Offline Address Book container, right-click the first system folder underneath (/o=Blue Sky Airlines/cn=addrlists/cn=oabs/cn=Default Offline Address List), and select Properties. Click on the Replication tab, click Add, and, in the Select A Public Store dialog box, select the available public store from BLUESKY-SRV2 (see Figure 18.8). Click OK twice.

16. Repeat Step 15 for all remaining offline address book folders (such as EX:/o=Blue Sky Airlines/ou=First Administrative Group), for the folder named EX:/o=Blue Sky Airlines/ou=First Administrative Group that is located under Schedule+ Free Busy, and the Schema folder.

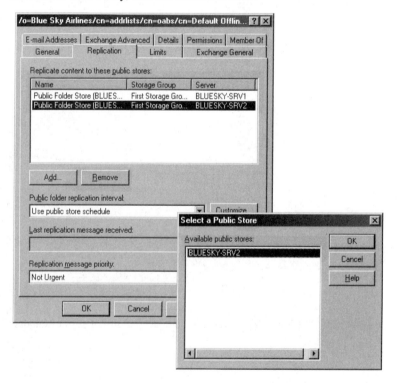

Figure 18.8   Replicating system folders

17. On BLUESKY-WKSTA, launch Outlook 2000, and verify that you can work with the public folder called Sub-BackDoor.

18. In the Outlook toolbar, click Calendar. In the toolbar, click New, and, under Subject, type **Now we have access to the Schedule+ Free Busy Folder**, and then click the Save And Close button.

19. Open the File menu and click Exit And Log Off. Notice that Outlook exists without error messages.

Exercise Summary

Using Exchange System Manager, you can configure public folder replicas in various ways. You can add replicas through the Public Folder Instances object or by means of each individual folder's Replication tab. Another option is to propagate replication settings to subfolders. System folders can be replicated between servers when adding available public stores from other servers to the list of stores with replicas. Public folder replication may require some time, but as soon as replicas are synchronized, all users have seamless access to the resources. For Outlook 2000 users, a public folder is always just a single object in the public folder tree.

Lesson 3: Public Folder Replication Process

Public folder replication is a very complex process. When you add replicas to a public store, the PFRA must fill the new instances. As changes occur on any replica, those changes must be replicated and possible replication conflicts must be detected. If you remove a replica, the PFRA must stop sending replication messages to the affected public store. Likewise, a mechanism is required to handle lost replication messages and outdated servers that have been restored from an old backup.

This lesson explains the public folder replication process in depth and covers how the PFRA monitors replication changes. It also illustrates the backfill process as it is used to resynchronize "out-of-sync" folders, and the resolution of public folder replication conflicts.

At the end of this lesson, you will be able to:

- Describe the public folder replication process.
- Explain the purpose and mechanism of public folder backfilling.
- Determine causes of and solutions to replication conflicts.

Estimated time to complete this lesson: 75 minutes

The Replication Process

Public folder replication is an information distribution mechanism that allows you to synchronize copies of public folders between all servers that maintain a replica.

Public Folder Replication Transport Mechanism

As mentioned many times, content changes are replicated using e-mail messages, but the data must be secured because foreign messaging systems such as SMTP-based hosts on the Internet might be involved in message transfer. The slightest alteration can cause the replication to malfunction. A binary attachment called WINMAIL.DAT containing all of the information in transport-neutral encapsulation format (TNEF) provides the required protection mechanism even in cases where the message must travel through foreign systems. Messaging systems are not supposed to tamper with binary attachments.

PFRA Responsibilities

Per replica, the PFRA is responsible for maintaining a list of servers that is used to address replication messages to the required remote Information Store services. The initiating PFRA must generate replication messages, address them properly, and send them. The Exchange 2000 Server transport has to take care of the delivery. The receiving PFRA has to extract the TNEF attachment and must check if the modified item is more recent than its own to replace the older copy. Thus, replicas are synchronized again. This process is covered in more detail later in this lesson.

Note By addressing more than one remote Information Store within a single replication message, the use of WAN connections and any other e-mail paths is optimized. Similar to an interpersonal message sent to multiple users, the Exchange 2000 Server transfers only one message. Messages are split into multiple instances at the very last point when separate paths must be used.

The following are the responsibilities of the PFRA:

- Addresses replication messages as determined by the public folder replication configuration
- Creates replication messages
- Monitors changes, additions, and deletions as they occur on replicas of public folders
- Receives replication messages and incorporates the changes into local replicas of public folders

Monitoring Message State Information

Message state information describes the collection of change numbers, time stamps, and predecessor change lists, which the PFRA uses to determine most recent items as they are replicated between public folder instances. Every public folder item provides message state information.

The following are the elements of message state information:

- **Change number.** Reflects the sequential modifications for all items of an information store
- **Predecessor change list.** Allows the detection of replication conflicts
- **Time stamp.** Identifies the most recent changes

Change Number

Change numbers identify public folder and content modifications. They are created using the globally unique identifier (GUID) of the information store and a server-specific change counter. The GUID is constant, which allows associating changes of an object with a particular public store. The server-specific change counter, in turn, identifies the most recent alteration, increasing whenever modifications are applied.

Note   The server-specific change counter reflects the sequential changes of all objects within the information store. In other words, whenever users create new public folders, change the design of existing ones, modify the contents of a replica, or perform other actions, the server-specific change counter is increased. The increased value is then assigned to the modified object to mark it as the most recent.

Predecessor Change List

The predecessor change list permits the PFRA to detect folder replication conflicts. It maintains a list of all Information Store services that have ever made changes to an object and their server-specific change counters. Public folder replication conflicts occur whenever multiple users modify the same object on two different locations at the same time. As long as the most recent changes have not been replicated to all other replicas, a chance for a replication conflict exists.

Figure 18.9 illustrates a situation in which the Administrator works with a public folder on BLUESKY-SRV2 while Carl Titmouse does the same using his local replica on BLUESKY-SRV1. Both users work with the same message item x. Item x contains an entry for BLUESKY-SRV1 in its predecessor change list. For simplification, let's say the Information Store ID is 999 (note that a real ID has far more digits), and the server-specific change counter is 2000. Because item x has so far never changed on BLUESKY-SRV2, an entry for BLUESKY-SRV2 is not yet present.

When both users save their changes at the same time, the predecessor change list is modified on both locations. The PRFA running on BLUESKY-SRV1 replaces its own entry with the current server-specific change counter—let's say 3000. Consequently, the predecessor change list of item x on BLUESKY-SRV1 is updated to 999-3000, while item x on BLUESKY-SRV2 still maintains only the entry 999-2000 because replication has not yet occurred. A new entry for BLUESKY-SRV2 is inserted into the predecessor change list—let's say 555-88888.

At this moment, two different copies of one particular message object exist, and both are the most recent copy. The most recent server-specific change number of BLUESKY-SRV1 cannot be found in the predecessor change list of item x on BLUESKY-SRV2. Conversely, the server-specific change number of BLUESKY-SRV2 is not present in the predecessor change list of item x on BLUESKY-SRV1. This is an indicator of a public folder replication conflict. Public folder replication conflicts and resolution are covered later in this lesson.

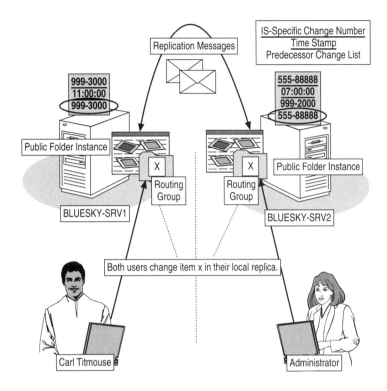

Figure 18.9 Monitoring replicated changes

Time Stamp

The time stamp provides information about when a particular item was last modified. It is used in conjunction with the change number to determine when an object was replicated most recently. Time stamps never decrease but always increase. In other words, if you modify a message within a public folder and the time stamp of the item is more recent than your computer time, the more recent time stamp is kept, meaning that the time stamp will not be changed.

Replicating Created and Deleted Messages

Whenever you create a new item in a particular public folder replica, this object must be created in all other existing replicas. Likewise, whenever you delete an object from a public folder, this object must be removed in all other locations.

Message Creation

New items receive the current change number, time stamp, and predecessor change list at the time of their creation. The PFRA handles the new object just like any other existing item, wrapping it in a replication message and sending it to all other existing instances (see Figure 18.10). The new object appears in all public folder replicas as soon as the replication cycle is completed.

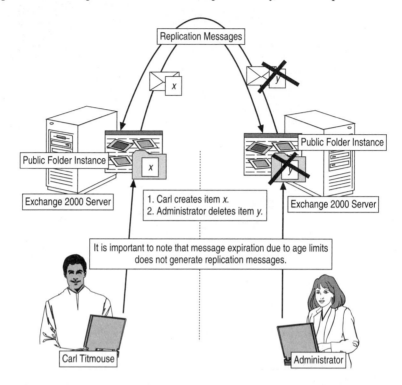

Figure 18.10   Item creation, deletion, and expiration

Message Deletion

Replication of message deletions is performed using PFRA notification messages. The object to be deleted is indicated through its GUID, also known as the MAPI-based PR_ENTRYID property. Exchange 2000 Server assigns a permanent, unique PR_ENTRYID when an object is created. Every PFRA that receives the notification message identifies and deletes the object from its public folder replica.

Message Expiration

Message expiration refers to the automatic deletion of public folder items through defined age limits. In this case, notification messages are not generated or sent to any other replica. This permits the implementation of a different age limit for every public folder instance. In other words, each Information Store service is responsible for managing its own message expirations.

Replicating Item Modifications

All PFRAs exchange modifications directly with each other. It is possible that a particular replica receives old replication information, and, in this case, existing items should not be replaced.

Whenever a user modifies an item in a replicated public folder, a new change number is added to the modified item, its time stamp is updated, the predecessor change list is refreshed, and, finally, public folder replication is initiated. The PFRA places the message state information together with the modified item itself in a replication message, which it addresses to all servers that hold a replica.

As soon as a destination PFRA receives the replication message, message state information and modified item are extracted. The PFRA must double check the state information received with the state information from the local item. An item is replaced only if the change number of the local instance is included in the predecessor change list of the update message. In other words, the most recent changes of the local item are "old news" for the update message (see Figure 18.11).

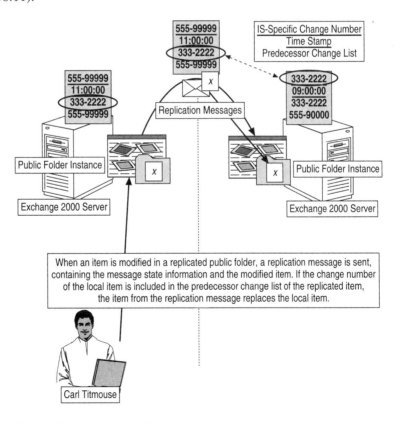

Figure 18.11 Item modification replication

In the reverse order, the local item must not be replaced if its change number cannot be found in the replicated item's predecessor change list. In this case, it's possible that either the local item is more recent than the update message or that a replication conflict has occurred. If the replicated item's current change number is present in the local item's predecessor change list, the local item is more recent and is not replaced. However, if the local item's current change number cannot be found in the replicated item's predecessor change list, a replication conflict must be resolved, as explained later in this lesson.

Out-of-Sync Public Folders and Backfill

It is important to note that delivery confirmations are not exchanged between PFRAs because the e-mail–based transport is not suitable for sequencing and data acknowledgments. A nondelivery report might be the only hint that a replication message has not been transferred, but even that may not be received. The originating PFRA simply cannot determine whether a replication message is received. In fact, as soon as a replication message is sent, the local PRFA assumes that the replicas are synchronized. The local public folder status switches to In Sync right away. Therefore, there is a fair chance that the folders are not synchronized although their status indicates differently.

Status Messages

Status messages allow PFRAs to determine the real status of their replicas by comparing the message state information of the public folder instances themselves. Every public folder maintains a change number, time stamp, and predecessor change list, as do the items of its contents. Even if the contents of a particular replica have not been changed, status notifications are generated frequently to announce the replica's state to all other instances. The folder's message state information is included in these messages, and receiving PRFAs extract this information to check whether the remote change number is present in the local predecessor list. If it is, the replicas are synchronized. If it is not, the remote PRFA must update its replica. In this case, it sends a backfill request back to the other PFRA to receive all the changes that have not yet been incorporated. Backfill responses do not differ from regular replication messages.

Note   Status messages are exchanged periodically, at least once a day. Every replication message carries the status of the affected public folder as well.

Backfill

Backfilling allows PFRAs to resynchronize public folder replicas that are out of sync. When a PFRA determines that the current change number of a remote replica is not included in its own predecessor change list—in other words, if the remote replica contains more modifications than the local instance—a backfill request is returned to the remote PFRA, which includes the old replica-specific change number of the remote PFRA. The remote PFRA then sends all those changes that have a higher change number than indicated in the backfill request. As soon as the local PFRA receives these modifications, all replicas are synchronized again.

The following situations automatically initiate a backfill request:

- A public server has been restored from a backup.
- A public server was down while changes occurred.
- A replication message has been lost.

Accidental Deletion, Backfill, and a Workaround

Imagine that a user has accidentally deleted a replicated public folder. You decide to restore the public folder server from a recent backup. The messages are outdated again, but not for long. The backfill process ensures that all public folder replicas are brought up to date from the restored backup version. The most recent change (in this case, the accidental folder deletion) is replicated back into the restored server, and the folder once again disappears.

To work around this problem, you should restore the backup to a test machine that is not physically connected to the computer network. Then, log on using Outlook 2000, download the folder into a personal folder store (.pst) file, log off, include this .pst file in your actual messaging profile, and copy the folder back into the public folders tree. As you copy it, you create a new public folder containing all items. You will have to reconfigure the public folder replication, but the data was recovered. More information about personal folder store and messaging profiles is provided in Chapter 9, "MAPI-Based Clients."

Adding and Deleting Replicas

Whether you push or pull a new replica into a public store, the new replica will be empty and must be filled. Conversely, when you delete a particular public folder replica, you must ensure that all other servers stop sending update messages for this replica to your server.

Adding Replicas

The PFRA assigns the current change number, time stamp, and a fresh predecessor change list to each new object. It also does this for new public folder replicas. The change number of the new replica, however, does not yet exist on the predecessor change list of any other instance. Therefore, as soon as the first status message is sent to a remote PFRA maintaining a replica, the new out-of-sync replica is detected. The backfill process is launched to bring the new instance to the current state.

Deleting Replicas

You can eliminate public folder replicas by using the Administrator program, but this doesn't mean that you delete the entire public folder from the organization. Only one instance is removed from one server's public store. Other replicas remain, but they must be informed about the deletion to stop sending replication messages to the nonexisting instance.

The deletion of a replica eliminates its reference within the properties of the public folder object. This object is replicated as part of the hierarchy. Consequently, all servers with public stores associated with the hierarchy will be informed about the configuration alteration. Other servers maintaining an instance of the same public folder stop sending their public folder replication messages to the affected server.

Public Folder Conflict Resolution

The PFRA replaces older objects with more recent items, but which item does the PFRA replace in the event of a replication conflict, where two objects are both considered the most recent?

Conflicting Items

A replication conflict is detected if an incoming item does not include the current state of the local item, in other words, if the change number of the local item cannot be found in the predecessor list of the update message (see Figure 18.12).

Recovery

The PFRA cannot resolve replication conflicts; it simply doesn't know which item to prefer. Therefore, manual intervention is necessary. A conflict message, including the conflicting items as attachments, is generated and sent to the users that created the conflict and the public folder owners. This conflict message is also posted into the public folder and replicated to all other instances. You can open this message, check the items, and decide which one to keep to resolve the conflict: the local item, the update, or both items.

Conflicting Design Changes

A replication conflict can also occur when multiple public folder owners have changed the design of a particular public folder in two different locations at the same time. When this occurs, the public folder owners are notified about the design conflict, but no conflict message is posted into the public folder. The conflict message is only a notification that the last design change has been applied, which overwrites all previous changes automatically. It is a good idea to double check which configuration is in effect and readjust the design.

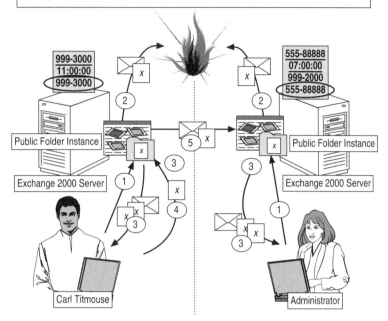

> 1. Both users change item *x* concurrently in different locations.
> 2. Replication conflict occurs.
> 3. Conflict messages are sent to both users to resolve the conflict. The conflict message is also placed in all replicas.
> 4. Carl accepts his local item.
> 5. The item is kept, and the changes are replicated to all other replicas. If the other user accepts her item in the meantime as well, another conflict occurs, which must be resolved

Figure 18.12   Resolving public folder replication conflicts

Exercise 2: Public Folder Conflict Resolution

In this exercise you will modify an item in two locations at the same time to create a public folder replication conflict. You will then use the resulting conflict message to keep both items in the public folder.

To view a multimedia demonstration that displays how to perform this procedure, run the EX2CH18*.AVI files from the \Exercise_Information\Chapter18 folder on the Supplemental Course Materials CD.

Prerequisites

- Complete Exercise 1, earlier in this chapter.

- Start BLUESKY-SRV1, BLUESKY-SRV2, and BLUESKY-WKSTA.

- Log on as Administrator to BLUESKY-SRV2.

- Log on as Carl Titmouse to BLUESKY-WKSTA.

▶   **To create and resolve public folder replication conflicts**

1. On BLUESKY-WKSTA, launch Outlook 2000, make sure you are working with the mailbox of Carl Titmouse, and open the BackDoor public folder.

2. Right-click a free area on the desktop, point to New, and click Text Document.

3. Press ENTER to accept the default name of New Text Document, and then use the mouse to drag this item into the BackDoor public folder.

4. The document will be listed as a new item with a Subject of New Text Document. Wait for the public folder replication to distribute the new document to BLUESKY-SRV2. (Carl Titmouse is working with the default public store on BLUESKY-SRV1.)

5. On BLUESKY-SRV2, right-click My Computer on the desktop, and select Explore.

6. Expand the drive Exchange (M), expand Bluesky-inc-10.com, then Public Folders, and select BackDoor. If the New Text Document is not listed in the details pane, wait a few more minutes for the public folder replication to complete, then right-click the free area in the details pane, and click Refresh.

7. On BLUESKY-SRV2 and BLUESKY-WKSTA, open the New Text Document item at the same time. If Outlook 2000 displays an Opening Mail Attachment dialog box, select Open It, and click OK.

8. On BLUESKY-WKSTA, in Notepad, type **This is a modification on BLUESKY-SRV1**.

9. On BLUESKY-SRV2, in Notepad, type **This is a modification on BLUESKY-SRV2**.

10. On BLUESKY-SRV2 and BLUESKY-WKSTA, at the same time, open the File menu, and select Save. Close Notepad.

11. On BLUESKY-WKSTA, in Outlook 2000, wait until a replication conflict message is received. When the conflict is detected, the icon for the New Text Document item changes in the public folder (see Figure 18.13).

12. In the Outlook toolbar, click Inbox, and check that a new message with a subject of Conflict Message was received.

13. Open the BackDoor public folder again, and double-click the New Text Document item. The Conflict Message is opened, listing both versions of the New Text Document item. (Opening the Conflict Message from the Inbox has the same result.)

14. Double-click both items in the Conflict Message window to compare their content. Close the documents, and then, in the Conflict Message window, click Keep All. Notice that two New Text Document items are now displayed in the public folder.

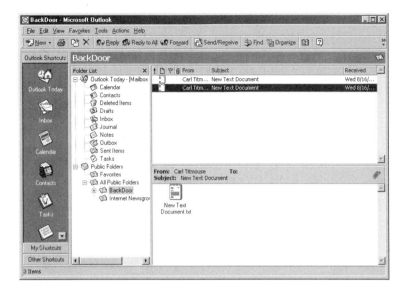

Figure 18.13   Resolving a public folder replication conflict in Outlook 2000

Exercise Summary

Public folder replication conflicts occur if users change the same item in different locations, thus creating two (or more) most recent versions of the item. The PFRA has no means to resolve this conflict and generates a conflict message, which contains the conflicting items. You can decide whether to keep one or all items. If you accept one item, the other objects are deleted from all public folder instances. If you decide to keep all items, two or more items appear in the public folder with the same subject line.

Chapter Summary

Public folder replication provides fault tolerance and load balancing through redundancy, and it can be used to optimize communication over the messaging network. Instead of having all users access a single instance somewhere, you can provide a public folder replica locally for faster and more reliable client access. Public folder replication works within an organization. Between organizations, replication is supported by means of the InterOrg Replication utility. Exchange 2000 Server allows you to create or eliminate public folder replicas at any time.

The public folder replication process follows the multimaster model, which means that you can work with the public folder contents from any location. Public folder replication based on e-mail messages guarantees that changes made on one instance are propagated to all other instances to ensure the uniformity of data. The multimaster model allows you to distribute the workload of public folder servers.

Public folder replication is a very complex process that fills new public folders, keeps all replicas up to date, and detects removed public folder instances. In addition, lost replication messages and outdated servers that have been restored from an old backup must be detected, as well as possible replication conflicts. New public folder replicas and outdated servers are synchronized via backfill. Replicas are kept synchronized through replication messages, which contain updated items and their state information. By checking the state information, the most recent items can be detected. Replication conflicts must be resolved manually. The PFRA will send public folder conflict messages, including the conflicting items as attachments, to the users who created the conflict and the public folder owners. Conflict messages are also posted into the public folder and replicated to all other instances.

Review

The following review questions can help you determine if you have sufficiently familiarized yourself with the material covered in this chapter. You can find the answers to these questions at the end of this book in Appendix A, "Questions and Answers."

1. What are the general advantages of the public folder content replication?

2. Your company has implemented two routing groups because a WAN connec- tion exists that does not support remote procedure calls (RPCs). What needs to be configured to provide all public folders within the organization to all users?

3. You need to create a local replica for a particular public folder, which exists in another routing group, but you don't want to bother the remote administra- tor. However, RPC communication is impossible. How can you achieve the desired configuration?

4. How does the receiving PFRA determine whether a replication conflict has occurred?

5. What does backfill mean?

6. As a public folder contact, you receive a conflict message. Which choices do you have to resolve the public folder replication conflict?

7. At the same time, two public folder owners have modified the design of a public folder on two different instances, generating a design conflict. How can you resolve the conflict?

CHAPTER 19

Implementing Advanced Security

About This Chapter

Modern organizations are increasingly reliant on distributed networking applications for communication and information sharing, to the point that messaging and collaboration solutions have become business critical. You should thus evaluate preventive measures against denial-of-service attacks, eavesdropping, impersonating of users, data tampering, and redirection of information to unauthorized destinations. Network and messaging security, which are important aspects of computer security, address these concerns.

Microsoft Windows 2000 Server includes powerful security technologies that make it possible for you to protect your network efficiently against intruders who intend to snoop around or damage your data. Microsoft Exchange 2000 Server relies on Windows 2000 security features. Using these, you can reliably protect your Exchange 2000 organization and provide cryptography-based security for your communication infrastructure.

This chapter covers in detail how Exchange 2000 Server integrates into the Windows 2000 security architecture and then focuses on advanced security services based on the X.509 industry standard recommended by the Public Key Infrastructure (PKI) working group of the Internet Engineering Task Force (IETF).

Before You Begin

To complete this chapter:

- Prepare your test environment according to the descriptions given in the "Getting Started" section of "About This Book." It is not necessary to rebuild the test environment if you have followed the exercises of previous chapters.
- Be familiar with the concepts of administering Windows 2000 Server and the Active Directory directory service.

Lesson 1: Exchange 2000 Server Security

No computer system is ever completely secure. However, a mail host connected to the Internet has to cope with different threats than a workstation isolated in a private network. Accordingly, you will have to identify a realistic level of security that provides the services your users require. Windows 2000 and Exchange 2000 Server cover the basic security needs and advanced requirements.

This lesson discusses how Exchange 2000 Server integrates with the security architecture of Windows 2000 Server. Fundamental security aspects are covered in the context of working with mailboxes and public folders using Messaging Application Programming Interface (MAPI)-based and Internet-based clients.

At the end of this lesson, you will be able to:

- Control access to resources.

- Separate your internal network from the Internet.

- Describe advanced technologies for signing and sealing of e-mail messages.

Estimated time to complete this lesson: 75 minutes

Controlling Access to Exchange 2000 Resources

All Active Directory objects support a standard set of access rights. Exchange 2000 Server extends Active Directory during the installation of the first server in the forest and implements additional permissions.

Access Control in Windows 2000

Each Active Directory object possesses its own security descriptor, which contains, among other things, information about the object's owner and a discretionary access control list (DACL). The DACL holds a list of access control entries (ACEs), which grant or deny a set of permissions to security principals, such as reading and writing object properties, or creating and deleting child objects. Security principals, in turn, are referenced by security identifiers (SIDs) and typically correspond to user accounts and security groups. Usually, you don't have to work with SIDs directly. If you are interested in a SID example, launch Registry Editor, and open the HKEY_USERS hive. Most likely, you will be able to find a SID that ends with 500, which refers to the built-in Administrator account (for example, S-1-5-21-606747145-152049171-1708537768-500).

When you successfully log on to Windows 2000 Server, the operating system authenticates your user account and password and creates an access token that contains your SID, the SIDs of any groups to which you belong, and information about your user rights (logon rights and other privileges). User rights pertain to the entire computer rather than a particular system object. Objects are protected through their security descriptors, so you can access an object only if its security descriptor grants the necessary access rights to one or a combination of multiple SIDs in your access token. For instance, if you are granted Read permissions for a particular Active Directory object and you are a member of a group, such as Enterprise Admins, that has the Full Control permission for this object, you are allowed Full Control permission. Because the access token is valid for the lifetime of your session, you only need to log on to your domain once to get seamless access to all resources. This also means you have to log off and on again for changes to group memberships for your account to take effect.

Extended Permissions for Exchange 2000 Server

Exchange 2000 configuration objects as well as Information Store service resources must be protected in a way not supported by standard access rights. To give an example, the Exchange-specific Modify Public Folder Replica List permission applies to information store objects and is only relevant in the context of public folder administration (see Chapter 18, "Public Folder Replication"). You can view and set both standard and extended permissions in the Security tab for most of the objects that are displayed in Exchange System Manager. If required, you may add the ShowSecurityPage value to the Registry to enable the Security tab for all objects, as demonstrated in Exercise 2 of Chapter 5, "Installing Microsoft Exchange 2000 Server."

Exchange 2000 Server adds a number of security objects, each representing an extended right, to the Extended Rights container of the Configuration naming context. These extended rights are replicated across the entire forest. Hence, Exchange 2000 Server is always able to perform required access checks. For example, you may grant another user account the mailbox right Full Mailbox Access to your mailbox-enabled user account (via the Exchange Advanced tab's Mailbox Rights button), and Exchange 2000 Server will determine that this user is allowed to work with your mailbox in Microsoft Outlook 2000.

Note   Independent of Windows 2000 auditing settings, the Information Store service will log a security event (Event ID 1016) in the application event log when a user using an account other than the primary account logs on to a mailbox.

Access to the Configuration

Enterprise Admins are automatically administrators for the entire Exchange 2000 organization. Full Control permissions are inherited from the top-level Configuration container to all child objects in the Active Directory Configuration naming context. The organization's configuration information is stored in this location. You can use ADSI Edit to view the entire contents of the Configuration naming context (see Figure 19.1). ADSI stands for Active Directory Services Interface.

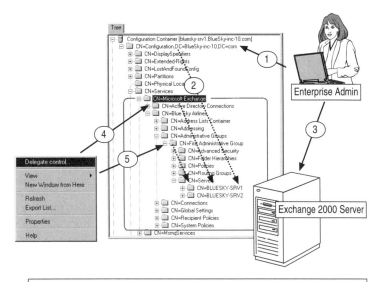

1. Enterprise Admins have Full Control permissions on the Configuration container.
2. Permissions are inherited throughout the hierarchy.
3. Because of inherited permissions, Enterprise Admins can manage all
   Exchange 2000 resources.
4. Administrators defined at the organizational level can manage the entire organization.
5. Administrators defined at the administrative group level can manage the entire
   administrative group.

Figure 19.1 Exchange 2000 Server in the Configuration naming context

Windows 2000 Active Directory relies heavily on the concept of inheritance to simplify the task of permission management. Permissions defined for parent objects are applied consistently to all child objects. Without inheritance, you would have to apply permissions to all child objects manually, which could be a puzzling and error-prone undertaking. However, you have the option to block inheritance, if desired, in an object's Security tab, by deselecting the Allow Inheritable Permissions From Parent To Propagate To This Object check box.

Permissions are required at several different objects to gain the desired level of access. For example, administrators of administrative groups require the Read permission at the organization level as well; otherwise, they are unable to display the organization in Exchange System Manager. Therefore, to assign permissions to administrators at the organization or administrative group level properly, always use the Exchange Administration Delegation Wizard from within Exchange System Manager. Likewise, it is good practice to create security groups, delegate administrative permissions to these groups, and manage Exchange administrators through group memberships.

The following roles apply to organizational administrators at the administrative group level:

- **Exchange View Only Administrator.**   Includes Exchange View Only Administrator permissions at the administrative group level.

- **Exchange Administrator.**   Includes Exchange Administrator and Exchange View Only Administrator permissions at the administrative group level.

- **Exchange Full Administrator.**   Includes Exchange Full Administrator permissions at the administrative group level.

Note   During the installation of Exchange 2000 Server, two groups called Exchange Domain Servers and Exchange Enterprise Servers will be created. All Exchange 2000 server accounts from your domain must be members of the Exchange Domain Servers group, which in turn is a member of Exchange Enterprise Servers. Members of these groups are allowed to perform advanced system tasks, such as mail transfer and directory synchronization.

Access to Mailbox Settings

Security settings for mailbox access are maintained through mailbox-enabled user accounts, which are managed in organizational units (OUs) in the Active Directory Domain naming context. The Information Store handles the corresponding mailbox resources and checks the security settings in Active Directory before allowing a particular user access to a mailbox. Hence, if you want to mailbox-enable user accounts, you need the appropriate permissions in both the OU, where the user accounts are located, and in the mailbox store, where you want to create the mailboxes. The management of mailbox-enabled user accounts was covered in Chapter 13, "Creating and Managing Recipients."

Tip   You should use the Delegation Of Control Wizard in Active Directory Users and Computers to assign administrative permissions to OUs. Use the Exchange Administration Delegation Wizard to grant mailbox administrators the required administrative permissions for organization or administrative groups. For mailbox management, the minimum rights of an Exchange View Only Administrator are required in the Administrative Group where the target Exchange 2000 servers exist.

Access Control Through NTFS Permissions

Access control to file objects on an NT file system (NTFS) partition relies on the same concepts as access control to Active Directory or information store objects. All Exchange 2000–related files should be placed on NTFS partitions, and NTFS permissions should be specified to make sure only authorized administrators and system accounts have access to sensitive data, such as databases and transaction log files. Although somewhat difficult, it is possible to read unencrypted messages within transaction logs of a mailbox store using Notepad. Fortunately, database files are not shared for general network access. You can read more about the maintenance of information store databases in Chapter 20, "Microsoft Exchange 2000 Server Maintenance and Troubleshooting."

Tip   To avoid performance losses, do not compress or encrypt the NTFS directories and database files of Exchange 2000 Server.

Access Control Through File Share Permissions

Only a few directories are shared for network access during the installation of Exchange 2000 Server, as outlined in Chapter 4, "Planning the Microsoft Exchange 2000 Server Installation." Carefully review the accounts with permissions and remove the Everyone group, if possible. Without granted permissions, users cannot access the resource. This is especially important if you have enabled message tracking (covered in detail in Chapter 20, "Microsoft Exchange 2000 Server Maintenance and Troubleshooting"). Message tracking logs are stored in the \Program Files\Exchsrvr\<servername>.log directory (that is, \ProgramFiles\ Exchsrvr\BLUESKY-SRV1.LOG), which is shared on all Exchange 2000 servers as <SERVERNAME>.LOG for everyone in the domain, by default. The logs contain information about message recipients, sizes, senders, delivery times, and possibly message subjects. You may manually restrict access to this share by removing the Everyone group and granting Exchange 2000 administrators explicit permissions. It is not advisable to modify or remove existing system entries.

Denying Permissions

You may want to explicitly deny accounts specific permissions, but you should be very careful, especially if you intend to deny access to special accounts such as the Everyone group. Denied permissions cannot be regranted, but if server services are denied access to their resources, Exchange 2000 Server cannot function properly. In fact, you may irreversibly damage your server installation.

Access to a resource is evaluated until the following occur:

- An ACE in the DACL denies the requested permissions. ACEs that deny permissions are listed first in the DACL and therefore override all other permissions.
- One or many ACEs together grant the requested permissions.
- The end of the DACL is reached with only a subset or no permissions granted.

Exchange Administration Delegation Wizard and Permission Denials

The Exchange Administration Delegation Wizard grants Read and View Information Store permissions to Exchange View-Only Administrators, but this wizard does not deny any rights. In other words, if you delegate View-Only permissions to a member of the Enterprise Admins group, all inherited permissions remain effective and the Enterprise Admin can continue to manage the entire organization without restrictions. To deny individual permissions, you need to use the Security tab provided with most configuration objects.

Note   You can enable the Security tab for all objects by adding a DWORD value called ShowSecurityPage to the following Registry location: HKEY_CURRENT_USER\ Software\Microsoft\ Exchange\ExAdmin. Set this value to 1, as demonstrated in Exercise 2 of Chapter 5, "Installing Microsoft Exchange 2000 Server."

Auditing and Protocol Logging

The Windows 2000 security architecture has two major purposes. It allows you to protect access to system resources, and it enables you to monitor this access. Auditing can be used to track user activities, such as logon attempts, system shutdowns or restarts, how individual users are working with mailboxes, and so on.

System Access Control List

Object security descriptors contain a DACL, and they may also hold a security access control list (SACL). Similar to the DACL, the SACL contains ACEs, which specify auditing directives, not user permissions. ACEs in SACLs reference SIDs and the type of access to be monitored. For example, you may specify that all access to the configuration of the Exchange 2000 organization should be audited for Enterprise Admins, whether or not the access was successful. In this case, when an Enterprise Admin views or changes the configuration, an event is written to the security event log on the server. You can examine events interactively using the Event Viewer that was introduced in Chapter 12, "Management Tools for Microsoft Exchange 2000 Server."

Enabling Security Auditing

Before any security-related events are written to the security event log, auditing must be turned on using Windows 2000 Security Tools, such as Group Policy or Domain Controller Security Policy. You will find various categories for which you can enable success and failure audits under /Computer Configuration/ Windows Settings/Local Policies/Auditing Policies (Group Policy) or Security Settings/Local Policies/Auditing Policies (Domain Controller Security Policy). Failure audits can help to reveal break-in attempts that rely on password-guessing methods (also known as brute-force attacks, in which all possible password combinations are tried until a password is discovered). You can find detailed information about Windows 2000 Security Tools in the Windows 2000 product documentation.

Auditing and System Performance

Auditing degrades the performance of your server. Depending on the number of users and other factors, system components, such as Active Directory and the Information Store service, may write a large number of events into the security event log. Activate security auditing carefully and only in situations when you suspect critical activities in your environment. Security logs are unsuitable for performance reports or statistics. For these purposes, use the Performance utility mentioned in Chapter 12, "Management Tools for Microsoft Exchange 2000 Server."

Internet Protocol Logging

Internet Information Services (IIS) support protocol logging. According to the specified logging level, you can track commands and responses as well as user data sent to or from a virtual server. For each conversation, you can examine the client's IP address, the client's domain name, the date and time, and the message content exchanged between the local and the remote system. This may allow you to detect whether outsiders are attacking your server (for example, denial-of-service attacks). Protocol logging is also an excellent troubleshooting utility.

For Simple Mail Transfer Protocol (SMTP) and Network News Transfer Protocol (NNTP) virtual servers, you can enable protocol logging in the virtual server's General tab in Exchange System Manager (see Chapter 11, "Internet-Based Clients"). For HTTP virtual servers, this is done using Internet Services Manager. However, IMAP4 and POP3 virtual servers do not provide this convenience. You need to use Registry Editor to set the required values under the following subkeys:

```
HKEY_LOCAL_MACHINE

  \System

   \CurrentControlSet

    \Services

     \POP3Svc or \IMAP4Svc

      \Parameters
```

The two important values for POP3 virtual servers are POP3 Protocol Log Path and POP3 Protocol Log Level. Values that refer to the IMAP4 protocol are called IMAP4 Protocol Log Path and IMAP4 Protocol Log Level. The first value points to the directory where the logging files will be created (file names have the format L0000001.LOG). The logging level, in turn, specifies the logged protocol details. Legal values are from 0 for no logging through 5 for most details. Be aware that whenever you modify these settings using the Microsoft Windows NT Registry Editor, you must restart the services for the new parameters to take effect.

Exercise 1: Enabling Security Auditing

In this exercise you will enable and test Windows 2000 security auditing using the Domain Controller Security Policy snap-in. BLUESKY-SRV1 and BLUESKY-SRV2 are configured as domain controllers.

To view a multimedia demonstration that displays how to perform this procedure, run the EX1CH19.AVI files from the \Exercise_Information\Chapter19 folder on the Supplemental Course Materials CD.

Prerequisites

- Restart BLUESKY-SRV1, and log on as Administrator.

▶ **To enable security auditing for unsuccessful attempts to access server resources**

1. Launch Domain Controller Security Policy from the Administrative Tools program group.

2. In the Domain Controller Security Policy window, under Security Settings, expand Local Policies, and then select Audit Policy.

3. In the details pane, double-click Audit Account Logon Events. In the Security Policy Setting dialog box, make sure the Define These Policy Settings check box is selected, select the Success and Failure check boxes, and then click OK. Repeat this step for all other audit categories (see Figure 19.2).

4. Give the system a minute to propagate the changes, then launch Exchange System Manager, expand Administrative Groups and First Administrative Group, then Servers, right-click BLUESKY-SRV1, and select Properties.

5. Click on the Security tab, click Advanced, click on the Auditing tab, select the entry for the Everyone group, and then click View/Edit.

6. Notice that several settings have already been enabled because they are inherited from parent containers. Under Successful and Failed, select the Full Control check boxes. Notice that all other check boxes are automatically selected.

7. Click OK three times to close all dialog boxes.

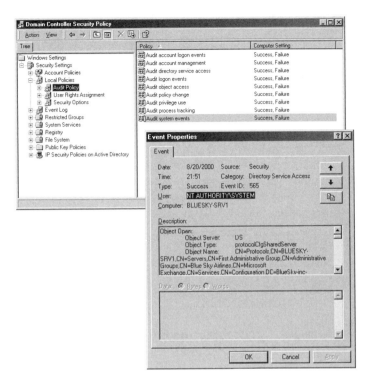

Figure 19.2   Enabling security auditing

8. Right-click BLUESKY-SRV1 again, select Properties, click Details, and, under Administrative Note, type **Security Auditing is fully enabled for domain controllers**, and then click OK (to change the configuration and trigger a security event).

9. From the Administrative Tools program group, start the Event Viewer.

10. In the console tree, select Security Log, and verify that security events have been logged. Display the topmost event with a Category of Directory Service Access. If you do not see any Directory Service Access events, expand several containers within the Exchange System Manager, and then refresh the Event Viewer.

11. Examine the event details, which specify that the Administrator has successfully accessed the configuration object of the server BLUESKY-SRV1.

12. Switch back to the Domain Controller Security Policy, and deactivate all auditing categories again to avoid degrading system performance due to unnecessary event logging.

Exercise Summary

Before any events are logged, you must activate auditing in a group policy. After that, you can enable auditing for Exchange 2000 configuration objects, such as public folder trees, address lists, mailbox stores, and so on, in Exchange System Manager. All security-related events are written to the security event log, where you can view them using the Event Viewer.

Secured Internet Connections

If you are planning to connect your Exchange 2000 organization directly to the Internet, you will have to consider implementing hardware and software that protects your network and blocks unauthorized users while allowing authorized users access. In other words, you need to implement a firewall.

Note   Security breaches often exploit vulnerabilities exposed through software bugs. Microsoft continuously searches for security weaknesses and releases corresponding hot fixes that are incorporated into new Service Packs. You should generally install the newest Service Packs when they become available.

Firewalls, Connectors, and Encryption of Communication Channels

Figure 19.3 shows a minimal firewall architecture that you should consider if your Internet service provider does not provide any security for your network access point. The firewall server is equipped with three network cards, general IP forwarding is disabled, and network communication from either side of the firewall host is only allowed to systems in the demilitarized zone (DMZ), which is also called a perimeter network.

Typically, you do not maintain internal data, such as user mailboxes, on systems in the DMZ. Those servers need to be configured as front end servers relaying client access to back end systems where the actual user mailboxes reside. All incoming connections must pass through the first firewall, which only allows access to specific ports, such as TCP port 80 for HTTP or TCP port 110 for POP3. Any ports that are not required should be blocked. In addition, it is a good idea to enable Secure Sockets Layer (SSL)-based encryption for client connections. For instance, you should require SSL encryption for Outlook Web Access (OWA) to the front end server(s). Open TCP port 443 on the firewall and possibly block TCP port 80. You can read more about the configuration of authentication and SSL in Chapter 11, "Internet-Based Client Access."

Public SMTP connections cannot be encrypted because SMTP hosts of foreign domains will need to communicate with your SMTP relay host in the DMZ in clear text. On the other side, between the DMZ relay server and the servers in the internal network, you may configure an SMTP Connector and require authentication between the servers. This will make it very difficult for intruders to break

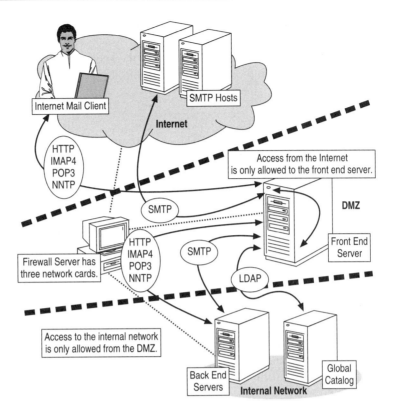

Figure 19.3   Firewall support for Exchange 2000 Server

through to internal servers. Another option is to use X.400 Connectors instead of
SMTP Connectors. In this case, you have to open TCP port 102 to support X.400
over TCP on the second firewall.

Front End Versus Back End Communication

When a client connects to the front end server to access a mailbox server in the
internal network, the front end server has to determine the corresponding back
end mailbox server. For this purpose, communication with Active Directory is
required. To allow access to the Global Catalog, you need to open TCP port 3268
on the second firewall. Be careful to only allow traffic originating from the front
end server; packets from the public Internet with this TCP port number should
not be allowed through. The front end server identifies the appropriate back end
server through LDAP and accesses the mailbox on behalf of the user.

The protocol between the front end and back end systems corresponds to the protocol used on the connection between the client and the front end server. In other
words, if you want to support OWA, you need to open TCP port 80 between the

DMZ and the internal network. For IMAP4 communication, TCP port 143 must be opened, and so forth. You need not enable SSL encryption between the front end and back end systems to avoid the encryption overhead on the back end servers. You should only allow systems in the DMZ to communicate with internal systems over the second firewall.

Note   You may find it useful to configure multiple virtual protocol servers on computers in the DMZ. This allows you to optimize configuration settings in regards to public Internet and internal private connections.

MAPI-Based Clients Through Firewalls

You should carefully evaluate whether to allow MAPI-based clients, such as Outlook 2000, access to Exchange 2000 Server over the Internet. Explicit front end/back end configurations are not supported over MAPI. Hence, direct connectivity to the mailbox server and the Global Catalog is required, exposing a very sensitive data repository. To at least avoid opening access to yet another server, it may be a good idea to configure the Exchange 2000 server that is exposed to the Internet as a Global Catalog server. Furthermore, MAPI relies on remote procedure calls (RPCs) and dynamic TCP port assignments. Consequently, you will have to open TCP port 135 across your firewall system (for the RPC endpoint mapper) and configure static TCP ports for the Active Directory RPC interface and the Information Store service. These ports must be allowed through the firewall system, so you have to break a big hole in your firewall to support MAPI-based clients.

To configure static TCP ports for Information Store and Active Directory, use the Registry Editor to add a DWORD value called TCP/IP Port to the following locations and define desired port numbers in decimal format (for instance, 3501 and 3502):

```
HKEY_LOCAL_MACHINE

 \System

  \CurrentControlSet

   \Services

    \MSExchangeIS

     \ParametersSystem

      and \NTDS

       \Parameters
```

You do not need to reconfigure client computers because MAPI-based clients connect to the RPC endpoint mapper (TCP port 135) to query for the ports they should use. However, you must restart the server for the changes to take effect. You can read more about the communication of MAPI-based clients with Exchange 2000 Server in Chapter 3, "Microsoft Exchange 2000 Server Architecture."

Note Enabling RPC-based communication through firewalls provides an additional avenue for denial-of-service attacks. If you need to support MAPI-based clients from remote locations over the Internet, consider the implementation of virtual private networks (VPNs), which can provide a sufficient level of security without TCP port restrictions.

Private/Public Key Security

Although you have the option to use SSL/Transport Layer Security (TLS), IP Security (IPSec), or VPNs to encrypt the communication between your systems, the messages are still kept in unencrypted form, which makes it possible to intercept them on an unprotected server, redirect them to an unauthorized recipient, or alter them. You need to consider extra encryption technologies if you plan to send sensitive data in e-mail messages over unsecured messaging hosts.

Note Encrypting e-mail messages prevents virus scanners from checking attachments.

Message Signing and Sealing

Security features based on private/public key pairs give you the ability to sign messages digitally, which allows recipients to countercheck if an originator was truly the sender and that the message content has not been changed on its way into recipients' mailboxes. You also can encrypt the message content entirely, known as message sealing, in which case only the intended recipients will be able to decrypt and read the message. If an encrypted message was intercepted and redirected to an unauthorized person, the content is presented in unreadable form.

A sealed message does not necessarily carry a digital signature, and a signed message is not automatically sealed. However, Outlook 2000 encodes messages before signing them to make sure the message contents cannot be tampered with unnoticed. This is known as opaque signing. Clients that do not support Secure/ Multipurpose Internet Mail Extensions (S/MIME) will display opaque signed messages with an empty body and an attachment named SMIME.P7M. In this case, you should send signed messages in clear text, which any Multipurpose Internet Mail Extensions (MIME) client can read. In Outlook 2000, open the Tools menu, select Options, click on the Security tab, and select the Send Clear Text Signed Message check box.

Note E-mail systems may change the content of messages, for instance, when sending them through gateways across foreign systems. Correspondingly, the receiving e-mail client will indicate that a message was tampered with, although not maliciously altered.

Public Key Technology

The X.509 standard describes the handling of private/public key pairs within computer systems. Exchange 2000 Server's advanced security, as a dual key-pair system, relies on two public/private key pairs. Dual key-pair systems provide a higher level of security than single key-pair systems because each key pair has its dedicated purpose and keys are not interchangeable. One key pair is used for verifying and signing and the other for sealing and unsealing messages.

Private keys are available only to the users to whom they belong, and it is very important that these keys are not disclosed. They may be stored in protected format in the Registry database on your hard disk, in which case you can use the keys only with that specific computer (unless you configure server-based user profiles). Depending on the configuration of your computer, it may also be possible to have private keys on smart cards. Outlook 2000 uses a private signing key for signing messages; the private sealing key is used for unsealing (decrypting) encrypted messages you have received.

Because two different private keys exist, there must also be two corresponding public keys, which are available to the entire organization. Generally, all users except the actual key owner use them. A recipient can use the sender's public signing key to verify the digital signature of a received message. You will use the public sealing keys of all recipients during the process of message sending to seal (encrypt) a message for each of them (see Figure 19.4). The process of signing and sealing messages is described in detail later in this chapter.

A secret key, also known as a bulk encryption key, is a security string (password) that is used for both encryption and decryption of information. Outlook 2000, for instance, uses a secret key to encrypt and decrypt your private keys. The secret key cryptography algorithm is also used in conjunction with public sealing keys to encrypt messages. This provides several advantages, as outlined in Lesson 2.

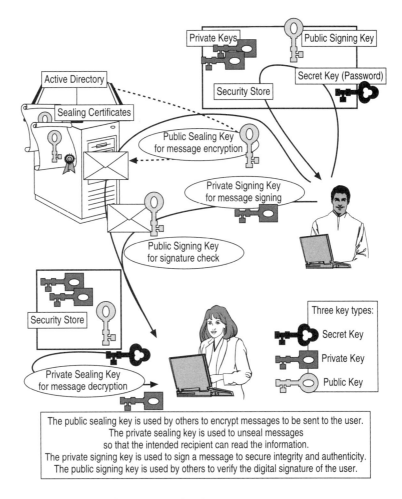

Figure 19.4   Different encryption key types

X.509 Certificate Services

Encryption keys are kept in X.509 certificates, which contain information about the supported encryption methods and ensure the legality of the keys. For instance, mailbox-enabled user accounts enrolled with advanced security hold an X.509 certificate that contains their public sealing key. Every user in the organization can retrieve these public keys from Active Directory. The X.509 certificates bind the public keys to their corresponding users and ensure that nobody has tampered with a sealing key.

To conform to X.509, advanced security certificates must contain the following:

- Unique serial number generated by the certification authority (CA) to identify each user's certificate
- Expiration date for the certificate
- CA's distinguished name
- CA's signature
- Public encryption keys
- User's distinguished name
- Version 3 Extensions, such as key identifiers, certificate policies, alternate names, and so on (only for X.509 version 3)

Certification Authorities

A certification authority (CA) issues certificates to users and computer systems. In Exchange 2000 Server environments, the CA is formed by Windows 2000 Server Certificate Services. Certificate Services deals with X.509 version 3 certificates and allows you to establish a sophisticated public-key infrastructure (PKI). In other words, Certificate Services can operate as a root CA or a subordinate of another CA. You have the option to deploy one or more Enterprise CAs for certificate issuance and revocation. Certificate Services is integrated with Active Directory. All servers running Certificate Services are trusted throughout the forest because they are referenced in a default certificate trust list (CTL) maintained in a group policy object. You can read more about Certificate Services in the Windows 2000 product documentation.

Note   To gain access to the features of X.509 version 3, the Key Management Service (KMS) of Exchange 2000 Server integrates with Certificate Services. Exchange 2000 Server can also issue X.509 version 1 certificates for backward compatibility with Microsoft Outlook 97 and earlier clients.

Exchange Certificate Templates

By default, Certificate Services can issue certificates for SSL-compatible client or server authentication, as well as S/MIME. The latter certificate is also known as a user certificate for secure e-mail communication. It is possible to use those S/MIME certificates with Outlook 2000 and Internet mail clients for message signing and sealing without the need for Key Management Services (KMS). However, these certificates are not integrated with Exchange 2000 Server, which forces each user to maintain certificates individually.

To establish an Exchange 2000 PKI based on the KMS, you need to configure Certificate Services as an Enterprise CA and install additional templates, such as Exchange User and Exchange Signature Only. Templates specify the format and content of certificates. As their names imply, Exchange Signature Only certificates will be issued for message signing, whereas Exchange User allows both message signing and sealing. As mentioned earlier, every Exchange 2000 user enabled with advanced security will work with two private/public key pairs. In addition, you need to install a third certificate template called Enrollment Agent (Computer), which enables KMS to request certificates on behalf of the users.

Note Exchange certificates can be used in Outlook 2000 as well as in Internet mail clients, such as Outlook Express. You should not request additional S/MIME certificates, for instance through the Web interface of Certificate Services. If you are using different certificates and keys in different e-mail clients while working with the same mailbox, you may experience problems with mismatching security keys.

Exercise 2: Installing Windows 2000 Certificate Services

In this exercise you will install Windows 2000 Certificate Services. You will configure an Enterprise CA and add certificate templates required for Exchange 2000 Server's KMS.

To view a multimedia demonstration that displays how to perform this procedure, run the EX2CH19.AVI files from the \Exercise_Information\Chapter19 folder on the Supplemental Course Materials CD.

Prerequisites

- Restart BLUESKY-SRV1, and log on as Administrator.
- Insert the Windows 2000 Server installation CD into the CD-ROM drive.
- The Windows 2000 Service Pack 1 CD is likewise required.

▶ **To install Windows 2000 Certificate Services**

1. Click Start, point to Settings, and click Control Panel.

2. In the Control Panel, launch Add/Remove Programs, and, in the Add/Remove Programs window, click Add/Remove Windows Components.

3. On the Windows Components wizard screen, select the Certificate Services check box. In the dialog box that appears immediately, informing you that this computer cannot be removed from or join another domain when Certificate Services are installed, click Yes, and then click Next.

4. On the Certification Authority Type wizard screen, make sure Enterprise Root CA is selected, and then click Next.

5. On the CA Identifying Information wizard screen, enter the following settings (see Figure 19.5):

CA Name	**Blue Sky Airlines Root CA**
Organization	**Blue Sky Airlines**
Organizational Unit	**Information Technology**

City	**Seattle**
State Or Province	**WA**
Country/Region	**US**
E-Mail	**Administrator@BlueSky-inc-10.com**
CA Description	**The global CA for Blue Sky Airlines.**
Valid For	**2 Years**

Figure 19.5   Installing an Enterprise root CA

6. Click Next.

7. On the Data Storage Location wizard screen, accept the suggested database and database log paths, and click Next.

8. If a Microsoft Certificate Services dialog box appears informing you that you must stop the Internet Information Services, click OK to stop the services. After that, the Windows Components Wizard will begin the installation.

9. An Insert Disk dialog box will appear prompting you to insert the Windows 2000 Service Pack 1 CD. Insert this CD into the CD-ROM drive, and then click OK. If a Files Needed dialog box appears, make sure the path information under Copy Files From is correct, and then click OK again.

10. An Insert Disk dialog box will appear prompting you for the Windows 2000 Service CD. Insert this CD into the CD-ROM drive, and then click OK.

11. On the final Windows Components Wizard screen, click Finish.

12. In the Add/Remove Programs window, click Close, and then close the Control Panel as well.

13. From the Administrative Tools program group, launch the Certification Authority snap-in, expand the Blue Sky Airlines Root CA container, right-click Policy Settings, point to New, and then select Certificate To Issue.

14. In the Select Certificate Template dialog box, select Enrollment Agent (Computer), scroll down to the end of the list, hold down the CTRL key, and select Exchange User and Exchange Signature Only in addition. Then click OK.

15. In the Certification Authority window, select Policy Settings, and make sure the three templates have been added to the server (see Figure 19.6). Close the Certification Authority snap-in.

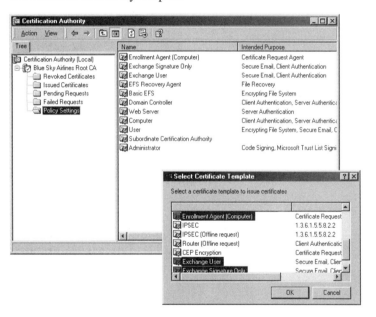

Figure 19.6   Adding Exchange-specific certificate templates

Exercise Summary

Certificate Services can be installed as part of the standard components that come with Windows 2000 Server. During the installation, you need to configure the CA type as well as identification information. A CA for Exchange 2000 Server must be integrated with Active Directory, so it should be an Enterprise Root CA or an Enterprise Subordinate CA, depending on your PKI. Once you have installed Certificate Services, you need to add three Exchange-specific certificate templates to the server to support KMS.

Lesson 2: Advanced Security Features

KMS creates and manages the PKI of your Exchange 2000 organization. It integrates with Windows 2000 Certificate Services, which in turn may be part of a larger PKI that extends beyond the Active Directory forest of your organization. You can install the KMS on one server per administrative group, which turns this machine into a Key Management Server (KM Server). A KM Server is able to service multiple administrative groups or the entire Exchange 2000 organization.

This lesson describes the architecture of the KM Server along with its components, important files, and database. It also explains the role of the KM administrator, covers KMS installation, and details the process of enabling and using advanced security.

At the end of this lesson, you will be able to:

- Install KMS.
- Describe the purpose of KM Server-specific keys and security passwords.
- Enable and maintain advanced security for your users.
- Sign and seal messages.

Estimated time to complete this lesson: 90 minutes

KM Server Architecture

Two main components form a functioning KM Server: Microsoft Exchange KMS and a storage database. Several other components, including the Exchange Advanced Security snap-in (KMSSNAPIN.DLL) and a cryptographic service provider (CSP) for the Microsoft Cryptographic Application Programming Interface (CryptoAPI), are also required to manage and use advanced security features (see Figure 19.7).

Microsoft Exchange Key Management Service

KMS, which runs on the KM Server, is the active component that processes all advanced security requests. The Exchange Advanced Security snap-in, integrated into Exchange System Manager, and the Information Store service are its direct communication partners. This service also forwards certificate requests in Public Key Cryptography Standard (PKCS) #10 format to Certificate Services on behalf of users (see Figure 19.7).

Note   The Exchange Advanced Security tool is available as a stand-alone and an extension snap-in. You may find it useful to combine this tool with the Certification Authority and the Certificates snap-ins to create a customized Microsoft Management Console (MMC) utility for advanced security administration.

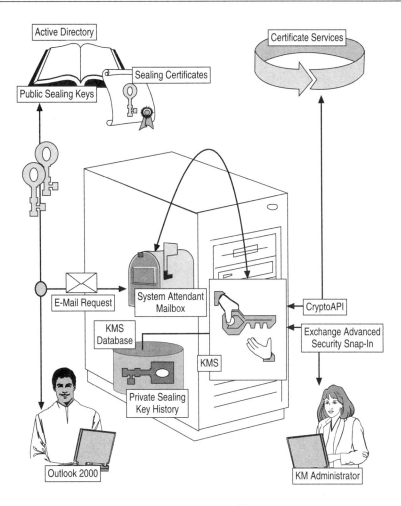

Figure 19.7   Key Management Service architecture

KM Database

The KMS maintains a database, which stores advanced security information for Exchange 2000 users. This database can be found on the KM Server under \Program Files\Exchsrvr\KMSData. Only one KM database can exist in an administrative group. The users' public and private sealing keys are temporarily placed in this database during the process of enabling advanced security. The KM database also permanently contains the private sealing keys for all users that belong to this KM Server. A KM Server must maintain these keys to keep a security key history for all users that have been enabled with advanced security. This history is required for key recovery, key revocation, and other key management tasks.

> **Important**   You must make sure that the KM database is not exposed to unauthorized persons. It is also important to include the KM database in regular server backups to save the security key history of all users who have been enabled with advanced security.

Information Store

During the process of enabling advanced security, the KMS communicates with the Information Store service to handle e-mail communication. The Information Store maintains the System Attendant mailbox through which the KM Server receives request messages from users. This mailbox is also used to send users an enrollment notification and their private and public sealing keys in encrypted messages. The process of enabling advanced security is explained later in this lesson.

Administrator Components

Two configuration objects are important for managing advanced security when using Exchange System Manager: the Encryption Configuration object and the Key Manager object, both of which are located under the Advanced Security container, which is displayed in the corresponding administrative group.

In addition, you can manage security keys and certificates on a per-user basis in Active Directory Users and Computers. Published certificates are displayed in each user account's Published Certificates tab (activate Advanced Features to display this tab), and the Exchange Features tab provides access to the E-Mail Security feature. Selecting E-Mail Security and clicking Properties launches the E-Mail Security dialog box after you enter your KM administrator password. There you can enroll, recover, and revoke advanced security features.

> **Note**   To manage advanced security, make sure RPC communication to the KM Server works.

KM Administrator

A KM administrator is a privileged Exchange 2000 administrator who can enable, revoke, and recover advanced security features. By default, only the person who installed the KM Server is a KM administrator. You can designate additional KM administrators using the Administrators tab of the Key Manager object. Click Add to add additional accounts. You can also revoke KM administrators by clicking Remove. You should use the Administrators tab immediately after KMS installation to change your KM administrator password. The default password is *password*.

> **Note**   The KM administrator password is case sensitive and must contain at least six characters.

Multiple KM Administrator Passwords

By default, every KM administrator is able to perform administrative tasks right away. You can use the Passwords tab of the Key Manager object to enforce a policy that requires two or more administrators to specify their passwords before advanced security administration is allowed. This can help to achieve a higher level of security. When you examine the Key Management Service Login dialog box that repeatedly asks you for your KM administrator password when managing advanced security, you will find information about the total number of administrators required and the total number of administrators that have entered their passwords.

Tip   The most important password policy options, Add/Delete Administrators and Edit Multiple Password Policies, should always require more passwords than the remaining options, Recover A User's Keys, Revoke A User's Keys, Change Certificate Versions, and Import/Export User Records.

Exercise 3: Installing KMS

In this exercise you will install the KMS of Exchange 2000 Server. You will install this service on BLUESKY-SRV2, which turns this server into a KM Server.

To view a multimedia demonstration that displays how to perform this procedure, run the EX3CH19*.AVI files from the \Exercise_Information\Chapter19 folder on the Supplemental Course Materials CD.

Prerequisites

- Completed Exercise 2, earlier in this chapter.
- Make sure BLUESKY-SRV1 and BLUESKY-SRV2 are operational, and log on to both machines as Administrator.
- Insert the Exchange 2000 Server installation CD into the CD-ROM drive of BLUESKY-SRV2.

▶ **To install the Key Management Service of Exchange 2000 Server**

1. On BLUESKY-SRV2, click Start, point to Settings, and click Control Panel.
2. In the Control Panel, launch Add/Remove Programs, and, in the Add/Remove Programs window, select Microsoft Exchange 2000, and click Change/Remove.
3. On the welcome screen of the Microsoft Exchange 2000 Installation Wizard, click Next.
4. On the Component Selection wizard screen, under Action, for both the Microsoft Exchange 2000 and the Microsoft Exchange Messaging And Collaboration Services category, select Change.

5. Under Action for Microsoft Exchange Key Management Service, select Install, and then click Next.

6. On the Key Management Service Information wizard screen, select the Read Password From Disk option, and then click Next (see Figure 19.8).

7. On the second Key Management Service Information wizard screen, under Master Copy Of Startup Password, type **c:**. Under Backup Copy Of Startup Password, type **c:\winnt**, and then click Next.

8. On the Component Summary wizard screen, click Next to begin the installation.

9. On the final wizard screen, click Finish. Close the Add/Remove Programs window and the Control Panel.

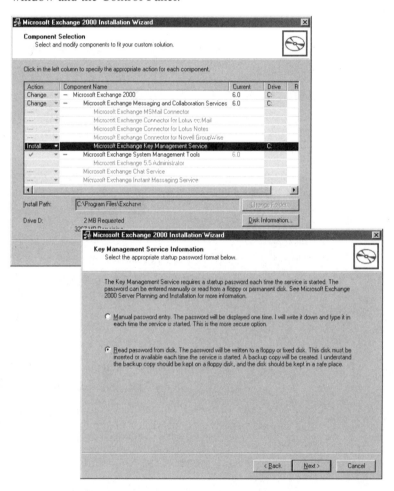

Figure 19.8   Installing the Key Management Service of Exchange 2000 Server

10. On BLUESKY-SRV1, launch the Certification Authority snap-in from the Administrative Tools program group.

11. In the console tree, right-click Blue Sky Airlines Root CA, and then select Properties.

12. Click on the Security tab, click Add, and, in the Select Users, Computers, Or Groups dialog box, select the computer account BLUESKY-SRV2, which is the KMS in the organization of Blue Sky Airlines. Click Add, and then click OK.

13. In the Security tab, make sure BLUESKY-SRV2 is selected, and then select the Allow check box for the Manage permission to grant the server all rights for the CA (see Figure 19.9).

14. Click OK, and close the Certification Authority snap-in.

15. On BLUESKY-SRV2, launch the Services snap-in from the Administrative Tools program group.

16. In the list of services, right-click Microsoft Exchange Key Management Service, then click Start.

17. Verify that the Key Management Service was started successfully, and then close the Services snap-in.

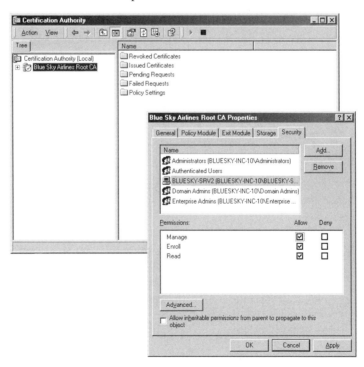

Figure 19.9 Granting Key Management Service Manage permissions

Exercise Summary

KMS can be installed using Exchange 2000 Setup in maintenance mode. A reference to an Enterprise CA must exist in the Active Directory forest. You also need to add the KM Server account to the server running Certificate Services. The KM Server requires Manage permissions to be able to revoke certificates. It must be added to all Certificate Services CAs used to issue certificates for Exchange 2000 Server. During the installation, you need to specify how to maintain the KM Server password. It is ideal not to store this password electronically, but you have the option to do so if this is appropriate. Storing the password in a file allows you to start KMS more conveniently. For convenience, not for maximal security, this exercise suggested storing the KMS password on the server's hard disk. For more reliable security, store the password on floppy disks, and keep these disks in a secure place.

Server Keys and Passwords

Cryptographic keys, stored in the KM database, must be protected from unauthorized access; otherwise, advanced security would be useless. Several security keys and passwords are required for this purpose.

KM Database Master Encryption Key

The KM Database Master Encryption key is used to encrypt and decrypt the KM database. The KMS and every designated KM administrator maintaining advanced security must have access to this key. However, the KM Database Master Encryption key itself is also encrypted to prevent unauthorized access. The number of designated KM administrators determines the number of times (+1 for the KMS itself) that the KM Database Master Encryption key is encrypted. The system uses each of the KM administrator passwords plus the KM Server password for this purpose, creating a lockbox for each password. KM administrators and the KMS use their password to open their corresponding lockbox to retrieve the KM Database Master Encryption key. The KM Database Master Encryption key is accessed when the KMS starts and opens the KM database and when KM administrators need to manage advanced security.

KM Server Password

As illustrated, the KM Server password is generated and possibly written to a text file named KMSERVER.PWD on a floppy or the hard disk during the KM Server installation. You must provide this password each time you start KMS, either through the password file or by typing it in the Startup Parameters box in the service's startup properties (and then click Start in the General tab of the Services tool). Without a valid KM Server password, KMS will not be able to start.

At times you might receive an error message that says Could Not Start The Microsoft Exchange Key Management Service. To get more detailed information, check the application event log. If the application event log contains an event with the Event ID 5057: The Supplied Password Is Not Valid, you should check to see if the KMSERVER.PWD file contains the correct password. If this file is corrupted, you must use the backup copy or specify the password manually using the service's startup parameters. It is important to keep the KMSERVER.PWD file in a secured place.

If you have chosen to save the KM Server password on a floppy or hard disk during installation, two REG_SZ values called MasterPasswordPath and BackupPasswordPath, pointing to the location of their corresponding KMSERVER.PWD files, are written to the Registry under the following location:

```
HKEY_LOCAL_MACHINE

  \Software

  \Microsoft

   \Exchange

   \KMServer
```

If MasterPasswordPath points to a floppy drive (that is, the A drive), you need to insert the disk that contains KMSERVER.PWD into the server's floppy drive during the service startup. This is also the reason KMS is set to manual startup by default. You can also start and stop KMS from a remote computer using Exchange System Manager or the stand-alone Exchange Advanced Security snap-in. Right-click Key Manager, point to All Tasks, and then select Start Service or Stop Service. If the KM Server password was provided in a KMSERVER.PWD file and is available to the KMS locally, the service will start. You can also start the KMS remotely without KMSERVER.PWD. In this case, set the value of MasterPasswordPath to an empty string (""). This will cause Exchange System Manager to display the Service Start Up Password dialog box, where you must type the KM Server password manually.

Note   When using Exchange System Manager locally on the KM Server, it is possible to conveniently change the startup password as well as the password file location. Right-click Key Manager, point to All Tasks, and select Change Startup Password. You will reach the Change Startup Password dialog box, where you can specify settings as during the KMS installation.

Stage 1: Enabling Advanced Security—The Administrator's Side

Installation of a KM Server in an organization does not mean that every user has been enabled with advanced security. In fact, no user can sign or seal messages by default. The KM administrator must first enable advanced security for the users, and each end user must complete this process using Outlook 2000, as explained in the next section.

Steps in the KM Administrator's Process

Although you can use both Active Directory Users and Computers (E-mail Security in the Exchange Features tab) as well as the Exchange Advanced Security snap-in to enable advanced security for individual users, only the Exchange Advanced Security snap-in (stand-alone or in Exchange System Manager) can be used to enroll all users in an administrative group or a subset of users at once. Right-click Key Manager, point to All Tasks, and select Enroll Users. You will be asked for your KM administrator password, and, after that, an Enroll Users Selection dialog box will be displayed, where you can choose between two options. You can either accept the default Display An Alphabetic List Of User Names From The Global Address Book option or activate the Display Mailbox Stores, Exchange Servers, And Administrative Groups Of Eligible Users option. The first option provides you with the ability to select one or more users directly from the global address book, and the latter option allows you to enable users based on mailbox stores and home servers. Only users that have not yet been enrolled can be selected.

Generated Security Information

The most important information generated during Stage 1 is a 12-character security key—a temporary user-specific password. The sealing key pair is also created. The security token is written to a file called ENROLL.LOG in the \Program Files\Exchsrvr\KMSData directory when working with Exchange System Manager or displayed on the screen in a message box when using Active Directory Users and Computers. The sealing key pair is stored temporarily in the KM database until the user downloads this information during Stage 2. You must pass the 12-character security token to the user in a secure manner so he or she can complete the process of enabling advanced security.

Distributing Security Tokens in Enrollment Messages

You may distribute the security token to your users in e-mail messages, which is particularly interesting if you plan to enroll multiple users at once. In this case, in the Key Manager property sheet, click on the Enrollment tab and, under Token Distribution, select the Send Token In An E-Mail check box. However, keep in mind that the enrollment message cannot be encrypted. If an unauthorized person gains access to the security token, this person may decrypt the communication between the KM Server and the client during Stage 2, allowing the intruder to steal the public signing key and the private sealing key. The public signing key is less important, but the private sealing key allows the intruder to decrypt the user's sealed messages. If you want to use advanced security effectively, you must be careful when handling security information.

When you examine the Enrollment tab, you will notice that the Customize Message button is enabled as soon as you select the Send Token In An E-Mail check box, which allows you to customize the enrollment message. Most important in this message is the placeholder %TOKEN%, which will be replaced with the actual security token. You may remove this placeholder to avoid sending this sensitive information to your users in an unencrypted e-mail. However, the enrollment message may still inform the users about the process of enabling advanced security. Without the security token in the enrollment message, the users will have to contact you to get this information. Independent of the enrollment message, the security token is displayed in a message box or written to the ENROLL.LOG file.

Stage 2: Enabling Advanced Security—The Client's Side

In Stage 2, the user sends an e-mail request to the KM Server, which processes the request, forwards it to Certificate Services, and retrieves the approved certificates. If the certificate request is processed successfully, a response is sent back to the user. The user enables advanced security by opening the response, which means that he or she can sign and seal messages.

Note KMS can forward certificate requests to any Enterprise CA in the forest. If all servers running Certificate Services are unavailable, user requests are queued for up to 24 hours, after which time the user will have to reissue the request.

Generated Security Information

To complete Stage 2 of enabling advanced security, users must use Outlook—ideally Outlook 2000—because only MAPI-based clients can generate the required information, such as the user's public and private signing keys and X.509 certificates. The user's public and private sealing keys were created and placed in the KM database during Stage 1. This information will be received from the KM Server at the end of Stage 2.

The following security information is generated:

- Public and private signing keys
- Signing and sealing X.509 certificate requests that identify the individual making the request uniquely.
- User's security password, which is used to encrypt the private keys

Initial Steps on the Client Side

To begin the process of enabling advanced security on the client side in Outlook 2000, open the Tools menu, and click Options to display the Options dialog box. Click on the Security tab, and then click Get A Digital ID. Make sure that you select the Set Up Security For Me On The Exchange Server option because you are requesting certificates from the KMS and not a third-party certification authority. When you click OK, a Setup Advanced Security dialog box will appear, where you need to define a Digital ID Name and type your 12-character security token. After that, you are prompted to define a security password for your new digital ID.

Using Outlook 2000 on Microsoft Windows 2000 Professional, your private keys will be encrypted using the specified security password and stored under the following location in the Registry:

```
HKEY_CURRENT_USER

  \Software

   \Microsoft

    \Cryptography

     \Microsoft Exchange Cryptographic Provider

      \<Digital ID Name>
```

The private signing key is stored in your digital ID right away, but the public signing key must first be sent as part of an X.509 certificate request in an e-mail message to the KM Server. This e-mail message will be encrypted using the 12-character security token, and it is addressed to the System Attendant mailbox. A message box will inform you that the message has been sent successfully.

Note   A single Windows 2000 user can have multiple digital IDs. Multiple digital IDs may be required if you work with different MAPI profiles to access different mailboxes on the same workstation.

Receiving the KM Server Response

The KM Server will retrieve the request message from the System Attendant mailbox, will request the approval of the certificates from an Enterprise CA, and will return the approved certificates together with the public and private sealing keys in another encrypted message to the client. The response message will make its way through the messaging network and will appear in your Inbox like any other e-mail message. The icon will show an envelope locked by a padlock. The originator is the System Attendant, and the subject is Reply From Security Authority. When you double-click this message, you will be asked for your security password. The security information will be retrieved from the message and placed in your security store. Outlook 2000 will also publish your public sealing certificate, which includes your public sealing key, in Active Directory (userCertificate and userSMIMECertificate attributes of your user account). You have to work online to successfully enable advanced security. A message box informs you that you can now send and receive signed and sealed messages.

> **Note** If you have installed Certificate Services to form your own root CA, the self-issued root certificate will be added to the Trusted Root Certification Authorities store on the local computer during the process of enabling advanced security. Only certificates with a valid certification path up to a root certificate that is in the Trusted Root Certification Authorities store are trusted and can be used.

The following information is placed in the KM Server response message:

- The certificate of the approving Enterprise CA
- Private sealing key
- Signing and sealing certificates

Exchanging Signed Messages

With message signing, a message checksum is built, encrypted, and attached to the message. The receiving user builds a checksum and compares it to the decrypted original. If the checksums are identical, the message has not been modified during transmission.

Signing a Message

The client uses a complex mathematical function to derive a unique 128-bit value from the message that you want to sign. This value is called a hash or message digest; the process of building this value is known as hashing. To protect the original digest from unauthorized access, it is encrypted using your private signing key. The encrypted message digest is the digital signature, and a message is considered signed if the digital signature has been attached to it. In addition to the actual digital signature, the client will add your signing certificate, which includes your public signing key, to the message before sending it.

Verifying a Signed Message

When a recipient of a signed message verifies the digital signature, the sender's public signing key is extracted from the certificate enclosed in the message, and then the digital signature is decrypted to retrieve the original message digest. The client then performs the hashing on the original message itself to retrieve the recipient's message digest. The sender and recipient's digests are compared, and if they match, the sender truly sent the message and it was not tampered with on its way to the recipient's mailbox (see Figure 19.10).

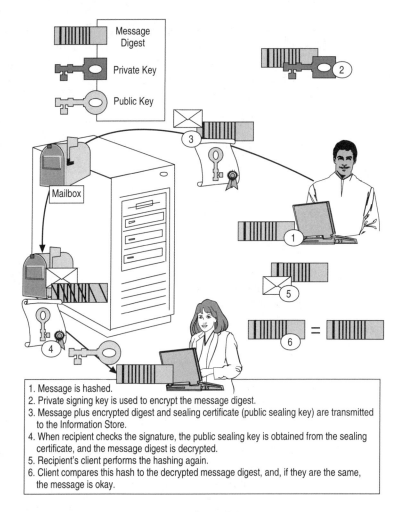

1. Message is hashed.
2. Private signing key is used to encrypt the message digest.
3. Message plus encrypted digest and sealing certificate (public sealing key) are transmitted to the Information Store.
4. When recipient checks the signature, the public sealing key is obtained from the sealing certificate, and the message digest is decrypted.
5. Recipient's client performs the hashing again.
6. Client compares this hash to the decrypted message digest, and, if they are the same, the message is okay.

Figure 19.10 Sending and verifying signed messages

Exchanging Sealed Messages

During the sealing process, the contents of a message and all attachments are encrypted. The sealing process is initiated by clicking the Send button if you have elected to encrypt the message.

Sending a Sealed Message

If you want to send a sealed message, you will compose the message as usual, but, in the Message Options dialog box, you need to select the Encrypt Message Contents And Attachments check box. When you click Send, you will be prompted for your security password so that Outlook can encrypt and send the message.

Outlook will contact Active Directory to obtain a copy of the sealing certificate for each recipient. The sealing certificate contains the public sealing key as well as information about the supported encryption method. The maximum common encryption method for all recipients is determined and is used to encrypt the message. Using the strongest common encryption method, the client generates a bulk encryption key for sealing (and later unsealing) the message. However, before the bulk encryption key can be attached to the message, it must be encrypted using each recipient's public sealing key. In other words, the client creates a bulk encryption lockbox for each recipient. Each lockbox is added to the encrypted message to provide the bulk encryption key (in its encrypted form) to all recipients (see Figure 19.11). The client may also add the sender's sealing certificate to the message so the originator can read the sealed message, as it is stored in the Sent Items folder.

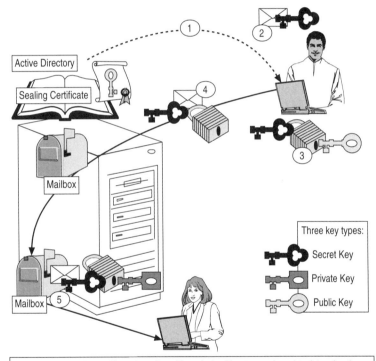

1. Recipient's sealing certificate is retrieved from Active Directory and used to determine the encryption method.
2. A bulk encryption key (secret key) is generated and used to encrypt the message.
3. The bulk encryption key is encrypted using the recipient's public sealing key (creating a lockbox).
4. The encrypted bulk encryption key is added to the message, and the message is transmitted to the Information Store.
5. The user receives the encrypted message and can use her private sealing key to decrypt the bulk encryption key, which in turn is used to decrypt the message.

Figure 19.11   Sending a sealed message

Unsealing a Sealed Message

When you receive a sealed message and open it, the message must be unsealed. Consequently, you will be prompted for your security password to retrieve your private sealing key from the security store. The client uses this key to decrypt (open) your bulk encryption lockbox. This decryption returns the bulk encryption key, which can then be used to decrypt the message.

Exercise 4: Configuring and Using Advanced Security

In this exercise you will set up additional KM administrators and generate security tokens for all users using Exchange System Manager. You will then enable advanced security in Outlook 2000 and send signed and sealed messages.

To view a multimedia demonstration that displays how to perform this procedure, run the EX4CH19*.AVI files from the \Exercise_Information\Chapter19 folder on the Supplemental Course Materials CD.

Prerequisites

- Complete Exercise 3, earlier in this lesson.
- Start KMS on BLUESKY-SRV2.
- Log on as Administrator to BLUESKY-SRV1, BLUESKY-SRV2, and BLUESKY-WKSTA.

▶ **To configure, enable, and use advanced security**

1. On BLUESKY-SRV1, launch Exchange System Manager from the Microsoft Exchange program group.

2. In the console tree, right-click the organization object Blue Sky Airlines (Exchange), and then select Delegate Control.

3. On the welcome wizard screen, click Next.

4. On the Users Or Groups wizard screen, click Add, and, in the Delegate Control dialog box, click Browse to display the Select Users, Computers, Or Groups dialog box, where you need to double-click the user account of Carl Titmouse.

5. In the Delegate Control dialog box, under Role, select Exchange Full Administrator, then click OK.

6. On the Users Or Groups wizard screen, click Next. On the final wizard screen, click Finish.

7. In the console tree, expand Administrative Groups and First Administrative Group, and then select Advanced Security.

8. In the details pane, right-click Key Manager, and select Properties.

9. In the Key Management Service Login dialog box, type **password**, and click OK.

Note The default administrator password is *password.*

10. In the Key Management Properties dialog box, click on the Administrators tab, type **password** again, and then click OK.

11. Click Add, and, in the list of accounts, double-click the account of Carl Titmouse.

12. In the Set Administrator Password dialog box, under New Password and Verify Password, type **password**, and then click OK. This is the initial KMS administrator password for Carl Titmouse (see Figure 19.12).

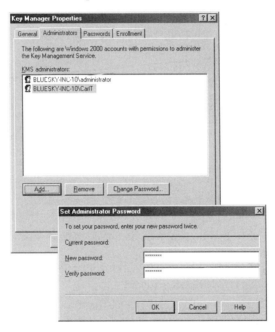

Figure 19.12   Defining additional KMS administrators

13. Click on the Enrollment tab, type **password** again, and click OK. In the Enrollment tab, select the Send Token In An E-Mail check box.

14. Click Customize Message, and delete the last paragraph explaining how to enable Advanced Security using earlier versions of Outlook. Click OK twice, type **password** again, and click OK.

15. Right-click Key Manager, point to All Tasks, and then select Enroll Users.

16. In the Key Management Service Login dialog box, type **password**, and then click OK.

17. In the Enroll Users Selection dialog box, select Display Mailbox Stores, Exchange Servers, And Administrative Groups Of Eligible Users, and then click OK.

18. In the Enroll Users dialog box, expand all containers, select First Administrative Group, and notice that all subcontainers are selected automatically (see Figure 19.13).

19. Click Enroll, and, in the Enroll Users dialog box informing you that the selected users were successfully enrolled, click OK.

20. In the Enroll Users dialog box, click Close.

Figure 19.13   Enrolling all users in an administrative group in bulk

21. On BLUESKY-SRV2, launch Windows Explorer and open the \Program Files\Exchsrvr\KMSData directory.

22. Double-click on the ENROLL.LOG file to display its contents in Notepad. Check for the security token of CarlT and Administrator (you may note down these security tokens to provide them manually during the stage of enabling advanced security in Outlook 2000). Close Notepad and Windows Explorer.

23. To practice key recovery and send an enrollment message, launch Active Directory Users and Computers, select the Users container, and then double-click on the Administrator (or Carl Titmouse) account.

24. Click on the Exchange Features tab, select E-mail Security, and then click Properties. Provide your KMS password and click OK.

25. In the E-mail Security dialog box, click Recover. In the Microsoft Exchange Administrator dialog box, click Send Enrollment Message.

26. In the Microsoft Exchange Administrator dialog box displaying the security token, click OK.

27. Click OK twice to close all dialog boxes. After that, repeat the steps to recover the keys for Carl Titmouse, and then close Active Directory Users and Computers.

28. On BLUESKY-WKSTA, launch Outlook 2000, and make sure you are connected to the mailbox of the Administrator (or CarlT later on).

29. Open the message from the System Attendant with the subject Advanced Security, copy your temporary advanced security key into the clipboard, and then close the message again.

30. On the Tools menu, click Options to display the Options dialog box.

31. Click on the Security tab, click Get A Digital ID, select the Set Up Security For Me On The Exchange Server option, and then click OK (see Figure 19.14).

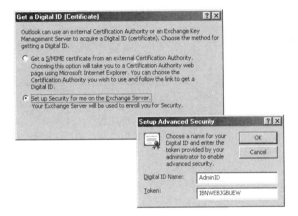

Figure 19.14   Enabling advanced security in Outlook 2000

32. In the Setup Advanced Security dialog box, under Digital ID Name, type **AdminID** (or **CarlID** later on), and, under Token, paste your temporary advanced security key from the clipboard by right-clicking the Token text box and selecting Paste (or type the security key manually), and then click OK.

33. A Microsoft Outlook Security Password dialog box appears, asking you to define a security password for your new digital ID. In the Password and Confirm boxes, type **password**, and then click OK.

34. A Microsoft Outlook dialog box appears, stating that the KM server will notify you when your request has been processed. This is accomplished using an e-mail message. Click OK.

35. The Options dialog box reappears. Click OK, and then wait for an e-mail message with the subject Reply From Security Authority, informing you that you have been enabled for Advanced Security. If it takes more than a minute to get this message, double-check whether the Microsoft Exchange KMS is started on BLUESKY-SRV2. If it is, but the response is still outstanding, reboot BLUESKY-SRV1 and BLUESKY-SRV2.

36. When the message appears in your Inbox, double-click the message. This displays a Microsoft Outlook dialog box requesting your security password. In the Password box, type **password**. Select the Remember Password For 30 Minutes check box, and then click OK.

37. A Root Certificate Store dialog box will appear, asking you whether to add the self-issued certificate of the CA to the root store. Click Yes.

38. The Reply From Security Authority message is opened, indicating that you have been successfully security enabled. Delete this message as well as the message from the System Attendant with the subject Advanced Security.

39. Log off as Administrator, and log on as Carl Titmouse, and then repeat Steps 21 through 32 as Carl Titmouse.

40. Log off as Carl Titmouse and log on as Administrator, launch Outlook 2000, and compose a new message.

41. In the Untitled – Message (Rich Text) window, displaying a blank message form, click To to display the Select Names dialog box. Double-click Carl Titmouse and then click OK.

42. In the Subject box, type **Signed and Sealed Message**.

43. In the message body, type **This signed message allows you to verify its originator and whether it was tampered with on its way to your inbox. Besides, this message was sealed. Therefore, you are the only one who is able to read it.**

44. On the toolbar, click Options. In the Message Options dialog box, enable the Encrypt Message Contents And Attachments and Add Digital Signature To Outgoing Message check boxes (see Figure 19.15). Click Close.

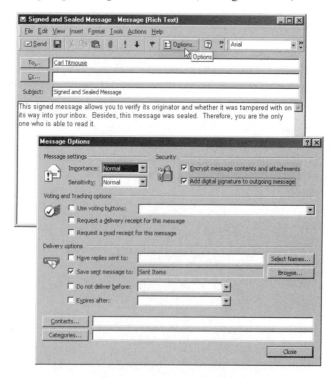

Figure 19.15 Sending signed and sealed messages using Outlook 2000

45. On the toolbar, click Send.

46. The Microsoft Outlook Security Logon dialog box appears. In the Security Password box, type **password**, and then click OK. (If a Non-Secure Recipients dialog box appears, asking you to send the message unencrypted, click Cancel, and wait for the modified directory information of the mailbox Carl Titmouse to be replicated to BLUESKY-SRV2.) You might need to wait for a few minutes.

47. Log off as Administrator and log on as Carl Titmouse, launch Outlook 2000, and check for the Signed And Sealed Message from Administrator. Notice the icon associated with this encrypted message, and then double-click the message.

48. The Microsoft Outlook Security Logon dialog box appears. In the Security Password box, type **password**, and then click OK. If a dialog box appears, informing you that a valid certificate revocation list could not be obtained, click OK.

49. The Signed And Sealed Message – Message (HTML) window is displayed, showing Security information in the header area underneath the Subject. Notice that the S/MIME message was received in HTML format. The Microsoft Outlook Rich Text format is automatically converted into HTML to ensure maximal compatibility with other e-mail clients.

50. Verify that there are two small buttons displayed to the right of the Security information: Verify Encryption Certificate and Verify Digital Signature. Click the Verify Digital Signature button.

51. In the Digital Signature: Valid dialog box displaying the verification results, notice that the signature is valid and that the message was signed by CN=administrator; CN=recipients; OU=first administrative group; O=blue sky airlines.

52. Click View Certificate, and, in the View Certificate dialog box, click on the Certificate Path tab. Notice that the certificate was issued by the Blue Sky Airlines Root CA.

53. Click OK twice, close the message, open Outlook's File menu, and then click Exit And Log Off.

Exercise Summary

At a minimum, administrator rights are required for the administrative group in which the KMS is located to manage the KM Server. The primary task of the KM administrator is to enable users with advanced security. You can enroll mailboxes individually or multiple mailboxes in bulk for entire administrative groups, servers, or individual mailbox stores. In all cases, a 12-character security token is generated for each user. It is convenient to use e-mail messages for the purpose of distributing the security token to the users, but it is more secure to provide these temporary security keys manually. Using the security token, users can complete the process of enabling advanced security in Outlook 2000.

KMS for Multiple Administrative Groups

In environments with multiple administrative groups, you may install a separate KMS in each and grant these servers Manage permissions on the Enterprise CA. In this way, you can distribute advanced security administration. If you want to centralize the management of advanced security, on the other hand, you should only install one KM Server. In this case, you need to create a reference to the central KMS in remote administrative groups. Open the property sheet of the Encryption Configuration object under Advanced Security in each group. In the General tab, click Change to select the location of the KM Server. This option is not available if a local KMS exists in the administrative group.

Country-to-Country Encryption Algorithms

When you examine the properties of the Encryption Configuration object, you will notice the Algorithms tab, which allows you to specify the desired encryption algorithms for your clients. If your users are running Microsoft Outlook 98, Outlook 2000, or Internet mail clients, you should accept the default S/MIME setting under Security Message Format. This guarantees the most flexible interoperability. If you need to support legacy MAPI-based clients, such as Outlook 97, on the other hand, you should activate the Exchange 4.0/5.0 option.

Note   If you enable both version 1 and version 3 certificates for backward compatibility with Outlook 97 and earlier MAPI-based clients (in the Enrollment tab of the Key Manager configuration object), two signing and two sealing key pairs will be issued for each user instead of one. Outlook 98 and Outlook 2000 can use X.509 version 1–based key pairs for compatibility with earlier MAPI-based clients. Internet mail clients support S/MIME encryption only.

Different Versions in One Organization

As a result of export and import restrictions, three different versions of advanced security exist, but all can be used in a single organization. Hence, an organization can use the very safe North American (3DES) version in the United States and Canada, the Other version (RC2-40) in Japan, and a third version called No Advanced Security in France. Of course, it is not desirable to send an encrypted message to a user who cannot decrypt it—for example, a French user. Consequently, your messaging client must check the common security level supported by all recipients of a message to find the best encryption method to use. Messages cannot be encrypted for each recipient separately.

The X.509 sealing certificate, obtained from Active Directory, provides information about the supported encryption methods. Outlook 2000 will contact Active Directory to retrieve the sealing certificates of all recipients. The client uses the highest security level common to the recipients to encrypt the message. For example, if you address a message to recipients in New York (3DES), Tokyo (RC2-40), and Paris (None), you cannot encrypt the message because the maximum common advanced security level is None. In this case, the client displays a warning message asking you whether you want to cancel the send process to remove those recipients that cannot handle encryption from your message or send the message to all recipients unsealed.

Key and Certificate Management

The general tasks of a KM administrator are easy to discover by right-clicking Key Manager and pointing to All Tasks. You'll see three important options: Enroll Users, Revoke Certificates, and Recover Keys.

Key and Certificate Recovery

The recovery of security information is necessary if a user's cryptographic keys are corrupted or accidentally deleted or if the user has forgotten his or her security password. As mentioned, keys and certificates are maintained in security stores, which are part of the user profile in Windows 2000 Professional. This has great advantages. By configuring a server-based (roaming) profile, you can access your cryptographic keys on any workstation in the network. However, if you do not work with roaming profiles and change the computer hardware, your keys are lost if you did not export them in Outlook 2000 beforehand (this can be done via the Options dialog box by clicking on the Security tab and clicking the Import/Export Digital ID button). You will also lose your security keys if another administrator opens the System program from Control Panel on your workstation, clicks the User Profiles tab, and deletes your local user profile. In all these cases, new security information must be created.

From the user's perspective, the process of recovering advanced security is the same as the process of enabling it. You have to send a new request to the KM Server to recreate a valid digital ID for your private keys and place certificates in your security store. Again, a 12-character security token, obtained from the KM administrator, is required to create and encrypt the request message.

The steps the KM administrator has to take to recover security information for a user differ slightly from the steps for enabling it. Either you use the Recover Keys command, as mentioned earlier, or you work directly with the E-Mail Security option in the Exchange Features tab of the troubled user's account object in Active Directory Users and Computers. Click the Recover Key button to launch the recovery routines. During recovery, the KM Server does not create a new sealing key pair. Instead, it restores the original key pair from the KM database. Again, a 12-character security token is returned; you must supply this to the user, as usual.

The public sealing key certificate is still available in Active Directory and doesn't need to be requested again from the Enterprise CA. However, the private signing key is only stored on the user's local machine and was irretrievably lost. Hence, Outlook 2000 must create a new signing key pair as well as a signing certificate request, which is sent to the KM Server in the recovery message. KM Server forwards the request to the Enterprise CA, where a new certificate is issued, and then this certificate, together with the sealing key pair, is returned to the user, who completes the process of recovering advanced security.

Key and Certificate Revocation

Just as you can enable advanced security for a user, you can also disable it via the Revoke Certificates option. This will add the user's private sealing key to an internal revocation list in the KM database. The user's sealing certificate in the Enterprise CA and Active Directory are also invalidated. To do this, the Enterprise CA adds the unique serial number of the user's sealing certificate to its certificate revocation lists (CRLs). Every X.509 version 3 certificate has a CRL Distribution Points attribute that points to the location of the CRL. Clients need to check the CRL to determine whether a recipient's sealing certificate is valid or revoked. CRLs are cached on the local computer for performance improvement.

Certificate Services configured as an Enterprise CA publishes CRLs weekly in the Configuration naming context of Active Directory as well as in the \Winnt\ System32\CertSrv\CertEnroll directory, which is accessible across the network via HTTP through a URL in the following format: http://<server name>/ CertEnroll/<CRL Name>.crl (for example, http://Bluesky-srv1/CertEnroll/Blue Sky Airlines Root CA.crl). You can define additional locations in the properties of your Enterprise CA using the Certification Authority snap-in. Click on the Policy Module tab, then click the Configure button. In the X509 Extensions tab, click the Add CDP button. It is advisable to manually update published CRLs after revoking certificates. In the Certification Authority snap-in, right-click the Revoked Certificates container, point to All Tasks, and select Publish. This immediately prevents users from sending sealed messages to the revoked mailbox.

Revoked Security Keys

The KM Server does not delete revoked security keys. They are stored in the KM database and also in the user's security store because they are needed to decrypt old (and still encrypted) messages. You can re-enable advanced security for a revoked user with a new certificate. In this case, the user will receive the old security keys along with the new security information. The user's old certificate will remain on the CRL until its expiration date is reached.

Key and Certificate Update

The Enterprise CA issues Exchange X.509 certificates with a lifetime of 12 months, but certificates can be renewed as necessary. The client performs the update automatically. When certificates are nearing expiration, the client sends a request to the KM Server asking to update the certificates for an additional period, and the user receives new signing and sealing key pairs. The old private sealing key is not deleted.

Advanced Security Maintenance

The primary task in maintaining advanced security is backing up the KM database, called KMSMDB.EDB (\Program Files\Exchsrvr\KMSData directory), on a regular basis. If this database were somehow corrupted or destroyed, the history of private sealing keys would be lost, and you would not be able to recover security keys. Encrypted messages sent to a user would not be able to be decrypted and would become unreadable at the moment the user loses his or her private sealing key. Using the Windows 2000 Backup utility (NTBACKUP.EXE), it is possible to include the KM database into online backups of Exchange 2000 Server, as explained in Chapter 20, "Microsoft Exchange 2000 Server Maintenance and Troubleshooting."

Moving the KM Server

You can move a KM Server from one server to another server in the administrative group, which may be desirable if you plan to remove the first server completely or dedicate the hardware to other tasks. The relocation of a KM Server to another computer in the same administrative group is basically a backup and restore operation (see Figure 19.16). However, you cannot move a KM Server between administrative groups, but you can move the users, as explained in the following sections.

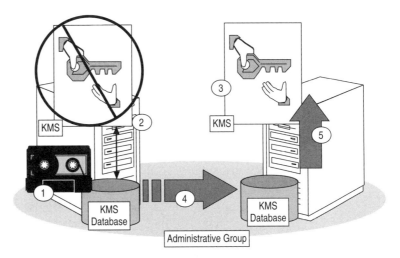

Steps to move a KM Server in an administrative group:
1. Backup the existing KM database.
2. Launch the Exchange 2000 Server Setup program and remove the KMS installation, reboot the server to complete the removal, and wait for Active Directory replication to propagate the configuration changes throughout the forest.
3. Install KMS on the new machine and grant its server account Manager permissions in Certificate Services. It is important to note that you cannot install the KMS if KM database files already exist on the target machine.
4. On the new KMS, delete the existing database files from the \Program Files\Exchsrvr\KMSdata directory, and then restore the old KM Database to the new location. Because the old Kmsdata directory is not removed from the first server, it is possible to move it directly between servers without the need for a backup media.
5. Start the KM Server and provide the KM Server password of the old server, and check the configuration of the new KM Server using the Exchange System Manager.

Figure 19.16   Moving a KM Server

Moving Key Histories Between KM Servers

At times it might be necessary to move users between administrative groups. As outlined in Chapter 13, "Creating and Managing Recipients," this requires you to delete the old mailbox and recreate it on the new Exchange 2000 server using the original e-mail addresses. The user may download existing messages into a local personal folder store prior to the mailbox deletion and upload the messages again after the mailbox creation on the new server. The user's key history, however, will remain on the KM Server in the original administrative group. If the new administrative group uses a different KM Server, the user's private sealing key history must be moved.

Exporting the KM Server Computer Certificate

Before deleting the old mailbox, you need to export the user's key history. After creating the new mailbox, import the history into the new KM Server. Keep in mind that you are working with very sensitive data—the user's private sealing key. Of course, this key must not be exported in unencrypted form. It must be encrypted using the new KM Server's public sealing key, which is available in this KM Server's computer certificate.

Using Exchange System Manager, you can obtain the target KM Server's certificate by right-clicking the Key Manager object under Advanced Security in the target administrative group. Point to All Tasks, and select Save KMS Certificate. Don't forget to write down the first eight characters that are displayed in the Thumbprint box (it is possible to copy this information into the clipboard). Then, specify a path where the certificate will be saved with a .crt extension.

Exporting Cryptographic Key Histories

As soon as the target KM Server's certificate has been obtained, you can export the user from the old KM Server. In the original administrative group, under Advanced Security, right-click Key Manager, point to All Tasks, and then select Export Users. You need to enter your KM administrator password to launch the Exchange KMS Key Export Wizard. Click Next to reach the Encryption Certificate wizard screen, where you have to specify the exported KM Server certificate. Click Next, and type the first eight characters of the thumbprint in the Thumbprint box (or paste them from the clipboard). Click Next, and specify an export file name (such as SEALKEYHIST.SEC). It is not possible to define a file path. The file will be saved in the \Program Files\Exchsrvr\KMSData directory. Click Next to reach the User View Selection wizard screen, where you can make your choice, similar to enrolling users with advanced security. If you are exporting only one user, it is convenient to pick the corresponding account from the global address book. However, it is also possible to bulk export key histories for multiple users per administrative group, mailbox store, or server. The Exchange KMS Key Export Wizard displays a summary on completion of the export process.

Importing Cryptographic Key Histories

At this point, you can safely delete the old mailbox—provided that the user has downloaded his or her messages—and recreate it on the target server. After that, you can import the user's key history. Copy the export file (for example, SEALKEYHIST.SEC) into the target server's \Program Files\Exchsrvr\KMSData directory. After that, right-click the target Key Manager object, point to All Tasks, and select Import Users. Again, you need to enter your KM administrator password to launch the Exchange KMS Key Import Wizard. Click Next, specify the import file (SEALKEYHIST.SEC), and click Next again. You will reach the Unknown Users wizard screen, which lists the user's old account taken from the import file. The wizard is unable to find the corresponding mailbox in the organization because it was deleted. It is not possible to establish an association with the new mailbox automatically. KMS uses the globally unique identifier (GUID) of the mailbox to identify the user in Active Directory. However, the user's new mailbox has a different GUID than the original mailbox. Click the Resolve User button, and select the user's newly mailbox-enabled account from the Select Users dialog box to match the unknown account with the new mailbox. Continue by clicking Next and complete the import.

Re-Enabling Security Keys

At this point, the key history is available in the KM database. However, the new mailbox has not been enabled with advanced security yet, and even if you have not deleted the old mailbox but moved it between KM Servers (KMS installed in remote administrative groups), the user will not be able to use the old certificates any longer. The export of private sealing keys compromises advanced security, and, consequently, affected user certificates are revoked during this process. In any case, you will have to re-enable advanced security for the user to issue a new set of signing and sealing key pairs. The process of enabling advanced security was explained earlier in this lesson.

Note To avoid problems with advanced security, do not revoke certificates or recover keys of affected users during the export and import cycle. Microsoft recommends completing the key recovery within 24 hours of the key history move.

Advanced Security with Other Organizations

S/MIME is an industry standard widely accepted across the Internet. Therefore, you are able to exchange signed and sealed messages with any other e-mail client that supports S/MIME, such as Outlook Express.

S/MIME Interoperability Issues

Both Outlook 2000 and Outlook Express can use the same certificates. You need to use Outlook 2000 to complete the process of enabling advanced security, but as soon as you have received your certificates, you can use them in Outlook Express as well. In Outlook Express, open the Tools menu, select Accounts, click on the Mail tab, and double-click the desired account, such as an account to access your mailbox via IMAP4. Click on the Security tab, and then, under Signing Certificate and Encryption Preferences, click Select to specify the Exchange signing and sealing certificates. Click View Certificate to verify which certificate to use for message signing. In the Details tab, check the attribute called Key Usage. The signing certificate will have the Key Usage attribute set to Digital Signature, while the sealing certificate shows a Key Usage of Digital Signature, Key Encipherment.

Outlook Express supports S/MIME version 2 while Outlook 2000 Service Release 1 supports S/MIME version 3. You may experience problems in Outlook Express when working with sealed messages that were composed in Outlook 2000. Outlook Express does not recognize the content type tag *application/octet-stream* used by Outlook 2000 as an identifier for an S/MIME encrypted message and might display empty messages along with an attachment named SMIME.P7M. To decrypt affected messages, drag them from Outlook Express to the desktop, open them in Notepad, and replace the string *octet-stream* with *pkcs7-mime*. When you save the changes and double-click the item, Outlook Express will be able to recognize and decrypt the SMIME.P7M attachment.

Note   OWA does not support S/MIME and cannot display digital signatures or sealed messages.

Person-to-Person Key Exchange

When you want to send encrypted messages to a particular user, you must use that person's public sealing key. As explained earlier in this lesson, this key is stored in the user's sealing certificate maintained in Active Directory. Active Directory guarantees that sealing certificates are available to all users in the organization.

It might seem impossible to send encrypted messages to users in another organization because the directories of other organizations are typically not accessible. To address this problem, you need to exchange certificates with those users manually. This sounds more complicated than it actually is. By default, the Send These Certificates With Signed Messages option (accessed via the Options dialog box in the Security tab, the Setup Secure E-Mail button) is selected, which causes Outlook to include a copy of your sealing certificate into signed messages. Hence, you should have the person to whom you want to send encrypted messages send you a signed message first. Likewise, you may send the user a signed message yourself. As soon as you have received the digitally signed message, open it, right-click the name in the From field, and then select Add To Contacts. If you have a contact object for this person in your Contacts folder already, you are given the option to update the information.

The sealing certificate will be stored in the contact object. You can double-check its existence on the contact's Certificates property sheet. To send this person sealed messages, you must address them by selecting the contact from the Outlook Address Book. It is important to note that it is not possible to simply reply to the digitally signed message and encrypt the content. You would receive an error message that the message cannot be encrypted because the client is not using the contact object containing the certificate. Delete the recipient from the To line, click To, and select the contact object from the address book to solve this problem.

Note To send a user in another organization sealed messages, your client must trust the recipient's CA that issued the user's certificate. If necessary, import the root certificates of outside organizations into your security store (Trusted Root Certification Authorities), or publish them in your organization's internal CTL using the Certificates snap-in on a domain controller. With the latter approach, all of your users automatically trust the external certificate. This is known as cross-certification. For more information about cross-certification, consult the Windows 2000 documentation on Certificate Services.

Chapter Summary

Exchange 2000 Server relies on Windows 2000 security features, which cover basic security needs as well as advanced requirements. Access to configuration objects, mailboxes, and public folders, for instance, is protected through the Windows 2000 security subsystem based on Active Directory information. Front end/back end configurations allow you to achieve secure connections to the Internet, and encryption technologies give you the ability to encrypt the communication between your mail servers and between your users.

For message security—the signing and sealing of messages—Exchange 2000 Server relies on KMS. KMS integrates with Windows 2000 Certificate Services and establishes an Exchange-specific PKI. Using KMS, you can provide your users with advanced security. Using Outlook 2000, each user must complete this process individually, and after that they can send signed and sealed messages. However, sealed messages can only be sent to other users that have advanced security enabled. Otherwise, the recipient's sealing certificate cannot be obtained from Active Directory. If you want to send encrypted messages to recipients in other organizations, you will need to ask those persons for their sealing certificates and maintain them in contact objects individually. Sealing certificates can be exchanged through signed messages.

Review

The following review questions can help you determine if you have sufficiently familiarized yourself with the material covered in this chapter. You can find the answers to these questions at the end of this book in Appendix A, "Questions and Answers."

1. What are the features of advanced security, and when will you use them?

2. What is the KM Server password used for, and when do you need it?

3. What does a KM administrator need to do to enable a user's advanced security?

4. What does the user need to accomplish to enable advanced security?

5. When does Outlook encrypt a message?

6. How does Outlook sign messages?

7. Which steps must be accomplished to send a sealed message?

8. How can you implement central advanced security management in an organization with two administrative groups?

9. Walter Woodpecker has forgotten the security password for his digital ID. What do you have to accomplish to allow Walter to sign and seal messages again?

C H A P T E R   2 0

Microsoft Exchange 2000 Server Maintenance and Troubleshooting

About This Chapter

For its database repositories, Microsoft Exchange 2000 Server takes advantage of the Extensible Storage Engine (ESE). ESE is a very reliable, tried, and proven transaction-based database technology, which forms the foundation for Exchange 2000 Server's incredible scalability. If you install Exchange 2000 Server on a high-performance system equipped with an uninterruptible power supply (UPS), redundant arrays of independent disks (RAID), duplexed disk controllers, redundant network adapters, and dual processors, you can be confident that your messaging server is ready for thousands of users. In addition, you may consider a clustered environment for maximum system reliability.

Nevertheless, no technical system is perfect. There is no substitute for a correctly implemented disaster prevention and recovery plan. The best disaster prevention tactic is ongoing system maintenance. Exchange 2000 Server gives you a powerful set of features that make it easy to identify and solve most problems and bottlenecks without affecting the work of your users. The foundations of trustworthy disaster recovery policies, on the other hand, are reliable backups and proven restore procedures. It is vital to test recovery procedures periodically. A serious administrator is prepared for even the worst-case scenarios.

This chapter covers important maintenance features that can ease the task of system management. It also addresses backing up and restoring Exchange 2000 Server. This chapter includes in-depth explanations of how to recover information store databases in various situations.

Before You Begin

To complete this chapter:

- Prepare your test environment according to the descriptions given in the "Getting Started" section of "About This Book." If you have completed Chapter 19, "Implementing Advanced Security," there is no need to rebuild your environment.

- Be able to describe the architecture of Exchange 2000 Server and the responsibilities of core components, such as the Information Store service, as explained in Chapter 3, "Microsoft Exchange 2000 Server Architecture."

- Know how to use the Microsoft Windows 2000 Backup utility to back up files and system state information.

- Be familiar with the management of Exchange 2000 Server resources, such as storage groups and information stores, as outlined in Chapter 14, "Managing Server Configuration."

Lesson 1: System Maintenance and Monitoring

Lengthy client response times, delays in message delivery, unnecessary nondelivery reports, and frequent unavailability of the messaging system can frustrate users. Ongoing system monitoring cannot prevent trouble, but it can allow you to discover problems as quickly as possible. If you use the maintenance tools of Exchange 2000 Server extensively, you can most likely resolve most problems before users become aware of them. Even if you cannot solve a problem immediately, it is better to be informed before the first user starts to complain.

This lesson deals with powerful maintenance features of Exchange 2000 Server. It explains how to configure a server for recovery of deleted items without immediate need for a backup. It also explains how to use server monitoring and how to examine pathways that messages have taken across your organization.

At the end of this lesson, you will be able to:

- Configure deleted items retention times.
- Monitor servers and check link and system states.
- Use the Message Tracking Center to verify that messages are delivered properly.
- Force the Active Directory replication to propagate changes as quickly as possible.

Estimated time to complete this lesson: 90 minutes

Deleted Items Retention

Exchange 2000 Server allows you to configure your mailbox and public stores to retain deleted items for a specified period of time. Within that time frame, accidentally deleted items can be recovered quickly without the need for backup. This advantageous feature is known as deleted items retention.

It is a very good idea to specify an appropriate retention time for each store in its Limits tab using the Keep Deleted Items For (Days) and Do Not Permanently Delete Mailboxes And Items Until The Store Has Been Backed Up settings. Seven days is usually an appropriate time frame. Using Microsoft Outlook 2000, users can retrieve deleted items as long as they are still in the store by selecting the Deleted Items folder, opening the Tools menu, and then clicking Recover Deleted Items. This will display the Recover Deleted Items From – Deleted Items window, where desired messages can be selected. Clicking the Recover Selected Items button in the toolbar transfers selected items back into the Deleted Items folder. From there, the messages can be moved into other folders as if the Wastebasket has not been emptied.

A remarkable new feature is the retention of deleted mailboxes. With Exchange 2000 Server, accidental mailbox deletions are a problem of the past. By default, deleted mailboxes are retained for 30 days. Within this interval, you can reconnect mailboxes to the same or different user accounts without difficulty using Exchange System Manager. You can specify a different number of days in the Limits tab for mailbox stores using the Keep Deleted Mailboxes For (Days) setting.

Exercise 1: Recovering a Deleted Mailbox

In this exercise you will recover a mailbox that was (almost) accidentally deleted. You will work with the Exchange 2000 Server Cleanup Agent and the Reconnect feature of Exchange System Manager.

To view a multimedia demonstration that displays how to perform this procedure, run the EX1CH20*.AVI files from the \Exercise_Information\Chapter20 folder on the Supplemental Course Materials CD.

Prerequisites

- Completed Exercise 1 of Chapter 14, "Managing Server Configuration."
- Restart BLUESKY-SRV2 and BLUESKY-WKSTA, and make sure they are operational.
- Log on as Administrator to all machines.

▶ **To reconnect a deleted mailbox to a Windows 2000 user account**

1. On BLUESKY-SRV2, launch Active Directory Users and Computers from the Microsoft Exchange program group.

2. Open the Users container, right-click the Administrator account, and select Exchange Tasks.

3. On the welcome screen of the Exchange Task Wizard, click Next.

4. On the Available Tasks wizard screen, select Delete Mailbox, and then click Next twice to delete the mailbox.

5. On the final wizard screen, verify that the mailbox was successfully deleted, and click Finish.

6. Launch Exchange System Manager, and expand all administrative groups and servers.

7. Under BLUESKY-SRV2, expand Management Group, then VIP Mailboxes, and then select Mailboxes. The Administrator mailbox is displayed as normal.

8. Right-click Mailboxes, and select Run Cleanup Agent. The Administrator mailbox is now displayed as a deleted mailbox (see Figure 20.1).

9. On BLUESKY-WKSTA, launch Outlook 2000. You will not be able to work with your mailbox because it was deleted. In the Microsoft Outlook dialog

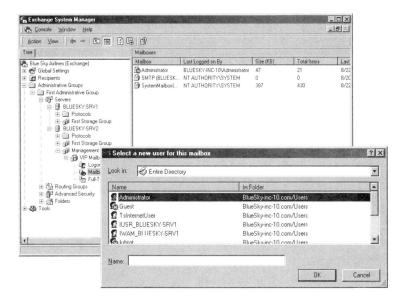

Figure 20.1   Reconnecting a deleted mailbox

box informing you that the default e-mail folders cannot be opened, click OK. In the next Microsoft Outlook dialog box, click No to exit Outlook without opening the default file system folders.

10. In Exchange System Manager on BLUESKY-SRV2, right-click Administrator, and select Reconnect.

11. In the Select A New User For This Mailbox dialog box, select Administrator, and click OK. In the Reconnect dialog box, click OK.

12. If an Exchange System Manager dialog box appears informing you that the object has not been replicated to the destination server yet, click OK.

13. Wait for the Recipient Update Service to assign the Administrator account valid e-mail addresses. Switch to Active Directory Users and Computers, double-click the Administrator account, click on the E-Mail Addresses tab, and verify that e-mail addresses are assigned. Click OK.

14. Switch back to Exchange System Manager, right-click Mailboxes again, and select Run Cleanup Agent. Notice that the mailbox is now reactivated.

15. On BLUESKY-WKSTA, launch Outlook 2000, and verify that you connect to your mailbox as usual and messages have not been lost.

Exercise Summary

The Exchange 2000 Server Cleanup Agent would run typically at database maintenance intervals to check for deleted mailboxes. Deleted mailboxes are not immediately removed but marked as disconnected. By default, the Cleanup Agent purges them after 30 days. For recovery, they are retained as defined by the Keep Deleted Mailboxes For (Days) parameter. Disconnected mailboxes are easy to recover without the need for a backup. Right-click on the mailbox, click Reconnect, then select the desired user account, and your job is done. Users can work with reconnected mailboxes immediately.

System Monitors as Maintenance Tools

A system monitor periodically checks all specified resources. When these are available and operating below a specified threshold, the system is considered active, but as soon as one of the monitored resources is detected as problematic, the system enters a warning or critical state. In this situation, the link state information (LSI) of the affected server is updated, the routing group master is informed, and the new system state is eventually propagated to all servers in the organization. The propagation of LSI was explained in Chapter 16, "Message Routing Administration."

When LSI indicates a serious system state, Exchange 2000 Server can perform specific actions such as launching a process or sending notification messages that you need to define beforehand. In other words, system monitoring can keep you updated about the state of your servers and messaging connectors at all times. System monitoring can also be used in conjunction with the Services snap-in. Notifications inform you about encountered problems, and the Services snap-in allows you to specify immediate actions, such as restarting services or rebooting the server automatically. The Services snap-in was introduced briefly in Chapter 12, "Management Tools for Microsoft Exchange 2000 Server."

Configuring Monitored Services and Resources

Per server, you can specify which resources to monitor. By default, the following services are checked: Microsoft Exchange Information Store, Microsoft Exchange MTA Stacks, Microsoft Exchange Routing Engine, Microsoft Exchange System Attendant, Simple Mail Transfer Protocol (SMTP), and World Wide Web Publishing Service. If any of these services is not running, the server enters the critical state. It is possible to add further services to the list using Exchange System Manager. Display the properties of the desired server object, and click on the Monitoring tab.

Besides services, it is also possible to monitor system resources, such as the available virtual memory, the CPU utilization, free disk space, or the growth of message queues. You can add monitor counters for these categories to your server by clicking on the Monitoring tab and then the Add button. It is advisable to monitor the free disk space on the server, for instance. Exchange 2000 Server shuts down important services if less then 10 MB are available on the drive, but you should not wait until that happens before taking action. Exchange experts prefer to keep half or more of the drives, where mailbox and public store databases have been placed, free. This space can be used for database compaction or offline repair of crashed databases. You can read more about low-level database utilities and offline database maintenance in Lesson 2.

Configuring Notifications

Nothing happens when a server enters the warning or critical state until you configure appropriate notifications. To configure a notification, launch Exchange System Manager, expand Tools in the console tree, and expand Monitoring And Status. Right-click Notifications, point to New, and select E-mail Notification or Script Notification. For both types, you need to specify a monitoring server. You should specify a remote Exchange 2000 server within the same routing group for the purposes of monitoring warning and critical states. If the monitored server goes down, it can no longer send notifications. If the monitoring server resides in a remote routing group, a broken routing group connector may prevent the propagation of LSI and changes of warning, or critical states may not be detected in a timely manner. LSI limitations are discussed later in this section.

For e-mail notifications, you need to enter recipient information, subject, and message text. Standard subject and body consist of a number of Windows Management Instrumentation (WMI) placeholders, which you can modify if desired. More often than not, the standard notification text will be sufficient. You must also identify an e-mail server. This computer should be an internal system because you need to allow anonymous relay through the specified host. Script notifications, on the other hand, expect you to define a command line instead of message parameters to launch the desired program. The security risks of anonymous relay through public SMTP systems were discussed in Chapter 15, "SMTP Transport Configuration."

Note In each server's Monitoring tab (view the properties of the server and click on the Monitoring tab), you will find a Disable All Monitoring Of This Server check box. Select this check box before shutting down services for maintenance. This switches the system state into maintenance mode to prevent the generation of warning and critical state notifications.

Link and System States

If you have been informed that a system has entered a warning or critical state, it is a good idea to get a quick, detailed overview of the situation. First, check the state of connectors and servers using Exchange System Manager. Select the Status container in the console tree, which you can find in the Monitoring And Status container within Tools, to display the LSI of connectors and servers in the details pane. As soon as you have identified a problematic component, check the affected server's application event log—provided that the server is still available. The Event Viewer is able to display event logs from remote computers. Right-click the root object Event Viewer (Local), and select Connect To Another Computer. If you do not find useful hints in the application event log, you may increase the diagnostic logging level of concerned components, as outlined in Chapter 14, "Managing Server Configuration."

Limitations of State Information and System Monitoring

When working with system state information and system monitoring, you need to be aware of several limitations that result from the fact that this feature is based on LSI. System states are logged per server in the corresponding User Data field. You can check this field using the Winroute utility. Launch WINROUTE.EXE from the \Support\Utils\i386 directory on the Exchange 2000 Server CD and connect to your server (such as BLUESKY-SRV1). Under the organization object (for example, Organization Name: Blue Sky Airlines), open the desired routing group (for example, RG: First Routing Group [First Administrative Group]), and expand RG Members, then expand the server object that you are interested in (for example, BLUESKY-SRV1), and then check for User Data. A trouble-free server shows a value that begins with 0701. If the system is in warning state, the value begins with 0702. A critical state is indicated by 0703. In contrast, if you have switched the server into maintenance mode, User Data is set to 0781000000000000. It is perhaps easier to analyze LSI in Exchange System Manager.

The following restrictions apply to system monitoring:

- Clustered servers cannot be monitored because their services do not directly relate to Windows 2000 services. As outlined in Chapter 7, "Microsoft Exchange 2000 Server in Clustered Environments," clustered services must be controlled using Cluster Administrator.

- If you are monitoring servers across routing groups, you need to make sure routing group connectors are functioning to propagate updated LSI. Do not forget to configure notifications for routing group connector states because broken connectors can prevent the propagation of LSI to the monitoring server.

- In Exchange 2000 Server all services start even if databases have been damaged. A running server does not imply that databases are in a consistent state.

- LSI and system monitors rely on the System Attendant service and the Microsoft Exchange Routing Engine and cannot function if these services are not started. In other words, the server status will not be accurate unless System Attendant and Routing Engine are running.

- Only routing group connectors (that is, Routing Group Connectors, SMTP Connectors, and X.400 Connectors) support LSI. The status of gateway connectors, such as the Lotus Notes Connector, will always be marked as Up, whether the corresponding service is started and functioning or not.

- When using Exchange 2000 Server in a mixed organization with earlier versions, do not use Exchange Server 5.5 Server or Link Monitors to check the state of Exchange 2000 servers.

Exercise 2: Configuring System Monitor Notifications

In this exercise you will configure monitored system resources and define a threshold when the server enters the critical state. You will then configure an e-mail notification and test the configuration.

To view a multimedia demonstration that displays how to perform this procedure, run the EX2CH20*.AVI files from the \Exercise_Information\Chapter20 folder on the Supplemental Course Materials CD.

Prerequisites

- Restart BLUESKY-SRV1, BLUESKY-SRV2, and BLUESKY-WKSTA, and make sure they are operational.
- Log on as Administrator to all machines.
- Make sure the Administrator mailbox exists on BLUESKY-SRV2.

▶ **To configure a system monitor e-mail notification**

1. On BLUESKY-SRV1, launch Exchange System Manager, and expand the default administrative group and servers.
2. Under BLUESKY-SRV2, open the Protocols container, expand SMTP, right-click Default SMTP Virtual Server, and select Properties.
3. Click on the Access tab, and then click Relay.
4. Select the All Except The List Below option, make sure the list is empty, and click OK twice to close all dialog boxes. The configuration of SMTP virtual servers was covered in Chapter 15, "SMTP Transport Configuration."
5. Right-click BLUESKY-SRV1 and select Properties.
6. Click on the Monitoring tab, click Add, double-click Free Disk Space, and in the Disk Space Thresholds dialog box, enable the Warning State (MB) check box.
7. In the corresponding text box that is now available, type **1024**, and then click OK.
8. Click the newly created entry, and verify that the Currently Available Drive Space (MB) is below 1024 MB (see Figure 20.2). Otherwise, adjust the settings to specify a value higher than the available disk space to force the monitor to detect a warning state.

Note All resources (that is, Virtual Memory, Free Disk Space, SMTP Queue Growth, X.400 Queue Growth) display current system values in their configured monitors.

---

9. Click OK twice to close the dialog boxes.
10. In the console tree, open Tools, expand Monitoring And Status, and select Status. Verify that BLUESKY-SRV1 has entered the Warning State and that

the Status column indicates that the Disk Space threshold was exceeded (see Figure 20.2). You may need to press F5 to refresh the display.

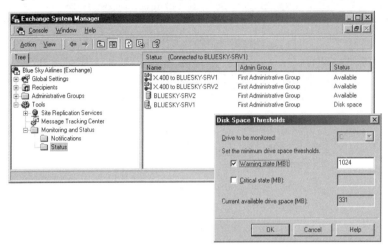

Figure 20.2   Configuring a disk space monitor

11. Right-click Notifications, point to New, and select E-Mail Notification.

12. In the Properties dialog box, click Select, and in the Select Exchange Server dialog box, double-click BLUESKY-SRV2.

13. Under Servers And Connectors To Monitor, select All Servers.

14. Click To, and in the Select Recipient dialog box, double-click Administrator.

15. Leave all other settings at their default (see Figure 20.3), and click OK.

16. Allow time for the Active Directory replication to propagate the newly created components to BLUESKY-SRV2. The replication may take approximately five minutes. On BLUESKY-SRV1, you may load the Exchange System snap-in in a customized management console to connect to BLUESKY-SRV2 explicitly. When the new notification object is visible in the Notifications container on BLUESKY-SRV2, stop the World Wide Web Publishing Service on BLUESKY-SRV1 using the Services snap-in.

17. Switch back to Exchange System Manager, select the Status container, and verify that BLUESKY-SRV1 has entered the critical state.

18. On BLUESKY-WKSTA, launch Outlook 2000, make sure you are connected to the Administrator mailbox, and wait until a notification message arrives. Open the message and check originator and message details.

19. Close the e-mail notification and Outlook 2000.

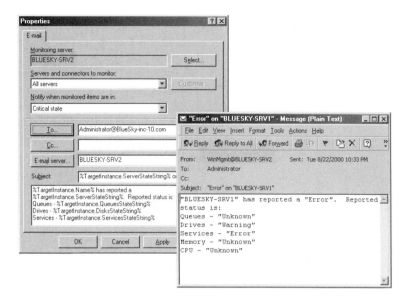

Figure 20.3   Configuring an e-mail notification for critical system states

Exercise Summary

System monitoring is a maintenance utility that should be used extensively. Monitors can warn you before critical states are reached, putting you one step ahead of your users and allowing you to fix many problems before they are noticed. It is a good idea to use multiple machines in each routing group as monitoring servers for warning and critical state notifications.

Using the Message Tracking Center

Message tracking is a feature that allows you to follow the paths of messages as they travel through your organization. All messages routed through the transport engine of a server that is enabled with message tracking are added to the tracking logs. Message tracking is disabled by default. It is possible to activate message tracking per server on the server's General tab or in a server policy. You enabled it for all servers in your test environment in a server policy during Exercise 2 of Chapter 12, "Management Tools for Microsoft Exchange 2000 Server."

Message tracking enables you to do the following:

- Locate specific messages in message queues.
- Verify that a message has been delivered successfully.
- Determine delays on each segment of a route for performance tuning.

Message Tracking Log Files

With message tracking enabled, status information is written to daily log files, which are stored in the \Program Files\Exchsrvr\<servername>.log directory (for example, \Program Files\Exchsrvr\BLUESKY-SRV1.log). Their file name follows the scheme <YYYYMMDD>.LOG (for example, 20001015.LOG). Tracking log files are shared on all Exchange 2000 servers as <SERVERNAME>.LOG for everyone in the domain. You should replace the Everyone group in the access control list with the accounts of those administrators that are supposed to track messages, as mentioned in Chapter 19, "Implementing Advanced Security."

Using Message Tracking

You can analyze tracking information conveniently in the Message Tracking Center. It is also possible to view the information in a text editor. The Exchange Message Tracking Center is available as a stand-alone snap-in and an extension snap-in integrated with Exchange System Manager, where you can find it in the console tree under Tools. The Message Tracking Center reads tracking information from the network shares of each server that has been involved in a particular message transfer. You must specify which server to begin with in the Message Tracking Center dialog box that appears when you right-click the Message Tracking Center container and select Track Message (see Exercise 3, in this chapter).

Message tracking log files are tabulator-separated text files that can also be analyzed in Microsoft Excel. This is useful if you want to quickly check whether a particular message has made its way across the organization to the recipient, but you are currently working on a workstation where the Exchange System Management Tools have not been installed. Table 20.1 lists the header fields in chronological order.

Table 20.1   Header Columns of Tracking Logs

# Date	Time	Client-IP	Client-Hostname
Partner-Name	Server-Hostname	Server-IP	Recipient-Address
Event-ID	MSGID	Priority	Recipient-Report-Status
Total-Bytes	Number-Recipients	Origination-Time	Encryption
Service-Version	Linked-MSGID	Message-Subject	Sender-Address

Note   Message tracking is supported as long as the <SERVERNAME>.LOG shares of the servers are reachable and foreign messaging systems are not involved in the message transfer (see Figure 20.4).

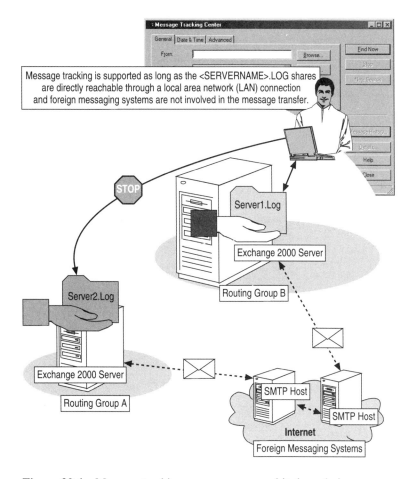

Figure 20.4 Message tracking across servers and its boundaries

Exercise 3: Tracking Messages Across the Organization

In this exercise you will use the Message Tracking Center to examine the path a particular message has taken across your test environment. You will send a message between two Exchange 2000 servers.

To view a multimedia demonstration that displays how to perform this procedure, run the EX3CH20*.AVI files from the \Exercise_Information\Chapter20 folder on the Supplemental Course Materials CD.

Prerequisites

- Restart BLUESKY-SRV1, BLUESKY-SRV2, and BLUESKY-WKSTA, and make sure they are operational.

- Log on as Administrator to all machines.

- Make sure the Administrator mailbox exists on BLUESKY-SRV2.

▶ **To check out the capabilities of the Message Tracking Center**

1. If you have not enabled message tracking in a system policy according to Exercise 2 of Chapter 12, "Management Tools for Microsoft Exchange 2000 Server," launch Exchange System Manager on BLUESKY-SRV2, expand Administrative Groups, expand First Administrative Group, and then expand Servers. Right click BLUESKY-SRV2 and select Properties. In the General tab of the Properties dialog box, select the Enable Message Tracking check box.

2. On BLUESKY-WKSTA, launch Outlook 2000, make sure you are connected to the Administrator mailbox, and send a test message to Carl Titmouse. After that, close Outlook 2000.

3. On BLUESKY-SRV2, launch Exchange System Manager, expand Tools, right-click Message Tracking Center, and then select Track Message.

4. In the Message Tracking Center dialog box, under Server(s), click Browse.

5. Double-click BLUESKY-SRV2 and then click OK.

6. In the Message Tracking Center dialog box, click Find Now. If an Exchange System Manager dialog box appears informing you that some log files cannot be found, click Yes. This is normal because the complete history of tracking logs may not be available if you have just recently enabled message tracking.

7. In the Message Tracking Center dialog box, you will see the message to Carl Titmouse (see Figure 20.5). Click on the last message in the list with Carl Titmouse as Recipient.

8. In the Message History dialog box, examine the message details, and then under Message History, follow the path the message has taken into the mailbox store of Carl Titmouse.

9. In the Message History dialog box, click Save to save the history of this message in a text file. Under File Name, type **Tracked Message,** and click Save.

10. Click Close twice to close the Message History dialog box and the Message Tracking Center.

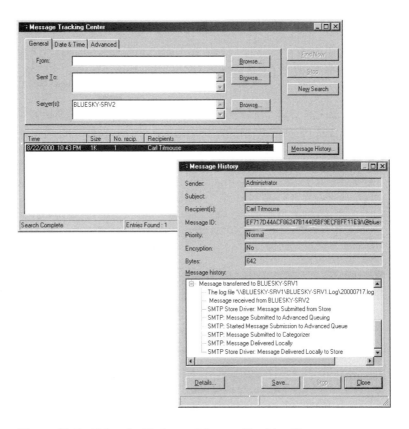

Figure 20.5   Using the Exchange Message Tracking Center

Exercise Summary

Message tracking is a helpful feature if you need to examine the path a message has taken from server to server in your organization. For instance, if a user denies having received a particular message, or if another user complains about apparently lost messages, message tracking can verify where messages have ended up. You can search by originator's e-mail address (From), recipient's e-mail address (Sent To), servers involved in message transfer (Server[s]), specific date information (Date & Time tab), as well as advanced properties, such as the message ID (Advanced tab). You can save message histories to text files for later reference or to preserve this information. Tracking logs are deleted according to the setting specified under Remove Files Older Than (Days) for Log File Maintenance, which you can find in each server's General tab as well as in server policies.

Using Message Queues for Troubleshooting

It is advisable to check the message queues of an Exchange 2000 server frequently to verify that the system is functioning properly. Too many backlogged messages can indicate a configuration or performance problem.

Checking SMTP-Based Message Queues Manually

Every SMTP virtual server provides a subcontainer called Queues that allows access to system and connector queues. While the system queues are always displayed (that is, queues for local delivery, for messages awaiting directory lookup, and messages waiting to be routed), connector queues are displayed only when messages are present. You may want to check these queues when configuring new connectors. To test a new Routing Group Connector, for instance, send test messages to a remote recipient. If these messages remain in the local queues, the connector settings require an adjustment.

Note   The Windows 2000 SMTP service must be running and remote procedure calls (RPCs) between Exchange System Manager and the SMTP service must work; otherwise, you cannot examine SMTP-based message queues.

Deleting and Freezing Messages

If you suspect that a displayed message is blocking a queue, you can delete it by right-clicking on it and selecting Delete (Send NDR) or Delete (No NDR), depending on whether you want to inform the originator about the deletion or not. Similar to the way messages are deleted, you can freeze and unfreeze message items. Selecting the Freeze command keeps a message in the queue until you unfreeze it.

You can delete individual messages, a filtered subset of messages, or an entire queue. To define a filter, right-click the desired queue, and then select Custom Filter. Select the desired action, such as Delete (Send NDR) or Delete (No NDR) from the Action list box. To delete all messages without filtering, on the other hand, right-click on the desired queue, and select Delete All Messages (Send NDR) or Delete All Messages (No NDR) right away. Similarly, you can select Freeze All Messages and Unfreeze All Messages.

Checking SMTP-Based Message Queues Automatically

System Monitor allows ongoing monitoring of SMTP-based messages. Display the properties of your server, click on the Monitoring tab, click Add, and double-click SMTP Queue Growth. You can define a period of time for the warning and the critical state. When the queue grows continuously for the specified interval, Exchange 2000 Server can send you a notification message, as illustrated in Exercise 2. In this way, you will be able to detect performance problems without delay. You might upgrade network connections as required, or configure additional connectors to different bridgeheads, as explained in Chapter 16, "Message Routing Administration."

It is also possible to observe the state of the SMTP service in the Windows 2000 Performance tool. Select the performance object called SMTP Server, and choose from the available counters as appropriate, such as Avg Retries/Msg Sent, which may reflect the quality of your communication link. Using the Performance tool, you can create reports over a longer period of time to gather statistical data about the performance of your system.

Checking X.400-Based Message Queues

It is also possible to work with X.400-based queues. This is required if you have deployed X.400 Connectors to remote routing groups or foreign messaging systems. The Message Transfer Agent (MTA) of Exchange 2000 Server is also responsible for message routing to gateway connectors, such as the Connector to Lotus cc:Mail or Novell GroupWise. Consequently, you will find corresponding X.400-based message queues for these connectors if you have installed them. Gateway connectors are covered in Chapters 25 through 29.

The X.400-based Queues container can be found under the X.400 Protocol container. The Microsoft Exchange MTA Stacks service must be running; otherwise, the queue contents are not displayed. When checking message queues from a remote workstation, RPCs must be supported.

You can monitor the growth of X.400-based message queues as well. In the Monitoring tab of your server, click Add, and double-click X.400 Queue Growth. The parameters are the same as those for SMTP-based message queues. It is also possible to monitor X.400-based message queues using the Performance tool when adding performance counters of the MSExchangeMTA or MSExchangeMTA Connections objects to charts and reports. Gateway connectors will provide additional performance objects for detailed analysis and statistics.

The MTA Check Utility

The MTA is an important component responsible for communication over X.400 Connectors and gateways to foreign messaging systems. This component maintains its message queues in .dat files, which can be found in the \Program Files\Exchsrvr\Mtadata directory. Several of these .dat files are installed during setup and represent important MTA message queues. Others are created during message conversion. Temporary .dat files represent the actual contents of messages that are currently located in an MTA message queue. A few moments later, when the MTA has processed the messages, the related .dat files disappear again.

Fixing MTA Startup Problems

Unfortunately, .dat files can become corrupted just like any other file on a computer's hard disk—during a system crash, for instance. If this happens, you may experience MTA startup difficulties. In this situation, check the application event log for message queue corruption and other MTA-related log entries. If you do find indications of corrupt files, consider using the Mtacheck utility to fix the problems. The Mtacheck utility is a command-line tool that provides several helpful options. Use the command line Mtacheck /? within the \Program Files\Exchsrvr\Bin directory to display a short help file about available parameters. To use the Mtacheck utility, you need to stop the Microsoft Exchange MTA Stacks service.

Forcing Active Directory Replication

Active Directory directory service management is, strictly speaking, not the task of the Exchange 2000 administrator. However, if you have the required administrative Windows 2000 permissions, you can force Active Directory replication using the Active Directory Sites and Services snap-in. This is useful if you want to replicate configuration changes quickly across your forest.

Pulling Configuration Changes

Active Directory replication is a pull process. The server that has configuration changes to propagate informs remote servers about the changes but does not push them into its neighbors. If you plan to initiate this manually, you need to pull changes to target servers instead of pushing the data from the source server. In Active Directory Sites and Services, expand the Sites in the console tree, expand the container that represents the site of the target server (that you want to synchronize), expand the Servers container, then the target server, and then select NTDS Settings. In the details pane, right-click the desired replication connector object, and then select Replicate Now. This initiates the replication of configuration changes from the source server.

Lesson 2: Database Operation and Maintenance

Both Active Directory and Exchange 2000 Server utilize the ESE database engine (ESE.DLL), which in turn manages a variety of database files to ensure data integrity and consistency even in the event of a system crash. In Active Directory, an ESE database holds the configuration information of your organization. In Exchange 2000 Server, ESE databases form information stores and storage groups. Other services, such as Site Replication Service (SRS), Key Management Service (KMS), and the MS Mail directory synchronization also use ESE. It is important to have a thorough understanding of this technology and its maintenance.

This lesson emphasizes the maintenance of Exchange 2000 Server databases. It starts with an explanation of the database characteristics and continues with a discussion of available backup strategies. Low-level database maintenance tools that are at your disposal are introduced.

At the end of this lesson, you will be able to:

- Identify Exchange 2000 databases and corresponding files according to their tasks.

- Use low-level maintenance utilities to compact information store databases.

Estimated time to complete this lesson: 75 minutes

Considerations About Information Stores

Exchange 2000 Server is designed to accommodate a reasonable number of mailboxes and public folders. Its databases can grow beyond all limits up to the capacity of the server's storage system. Several system improvements allow you to consolidate your resources on fewer but larger servers. Benchmark tests prove that Exchange 2000 Server is very scalable. However, extreme limits, such as hundreds of thousands of mailboxes and millions of daily messages per server, do not have a perfect correlation to real-world environments. Server benchmarks are prepared to compare upper limits of competitive platforms with each other, but they do not reflect business requirements or outline deployable scenarios.

Information Store Database Sizes

One important consideration in determining the maximum number of users per server is the resulting size of the information store database files. The more users hold data in their mailboxes and the larger the databases, the longer it will take to back up and restore the system. High-performance backup solutions may be able to save between 25 GB and 50 GB per hour. Again, however, this is a benchmark. It is not realistic to assume a restore rate of 50 GB per hour on a RAID 5 subsystem because checksum recalculation and other factors will slow down the restore. You may be able to achieve a restore rate of 20 GB per hour. Therefore, if you had to recover a server with 10,000 mailboxes, each holding an average of just 20 MB of data, you would have to restore about 200 GB of data. At 20 GB restored per hour, your server would be down for at least 10 hours, not including time to rebuild server hardware and recover the operating system. If 10,000 users cannot work for 10 hours, altogether 100,000 work hours are lost—that's 12,500 workdays or approximately 62 work years (using 200 workdays/year).

Fortunately, it is possible to bring back a crashed Exchange 2000 server very quickly without restoring its databases right away. The server is empty temporarily, but your users could continue their work while you fill the mailboxes with restored data in the background. The high-speed system recovery is explained in Lesson 3.

Multiple Information Store Databases and Storage Groups

If you plan to implement heavyweight servers, you should split mailbox resources across multiple small databases. Exchange 2000 Server supports maintenance operations for individual databases without affecting other stores. Small databases are more quickly restored. It is possible to create up to five stores in a single storage group and a total of four storage groups, which gives you the ability to create up to 20 information store databases.

You may find it useful to create a separate mailbox store for very important persons and configure a different backup schedule for it. As discussed in Chapter 14, "Managing Server Configuration," all databases in a storage group share the same set of transaction log files and should therefore be included in the same backup. For that reason, create multiple storage groups and distribute mailbox stores across them accordingly.

Note   It is not advisable to create a separate database for each individual manager's mailbox. Delegate access to a mailbox (see Exercise 5 of Chapter 8, "Microsoft Outlook 2000 Deployment") does not work between different mailbox stores on the same physical Exchange 2000 server due to a limitation in the client's Exchange transport service. Furthermore, the single-instance storage feature is not available across multiple stores.

Defining the Databases

Exchange 2000 Server databases can be divided into two groups: core databases and additional databases. Core databases maintain user data, and additional databases are required in particular situations. All existing databases should be included in maintenance and backup operations.

Core Databases

The core databases belong to the Information Store service. The databases of the default mailbox store are called PRIV1.EDB and PRIV1.STM, and PUB1.EDB and PUB1.STM for the default public store. These files can be found in the \Program Files\Exchsrvr\Mdbdata directory. As explained in Chapter 14, "Managing Server Configuration," you can create additional databases and place them in arbitrary directories on the server's local disks.

Each store consists of an .edb and an .stm database. The Exchange database (.edb) contains data in standard rich text Messaging Application Programming Interface (MAPI)-based format. The Exchange streaming database (.stm) supports streaming Multipurpose Internet Mail Extensions (MIME) content directly into the store without conversion. For instance, if the Information Store service receives a message from Internet Information Services (IIS), the header information, such as From, To, CC, BCC, Delivery Time, and so on, is converted to MAPI and stored in the .edb file. The message contents, on the other hand, are stored in the .stm file. To give another example, if you save a Microsoft Word document directly into a public folder library using the Microsoft Web Storage System, the document is streamed into the .stm file and document properties are promoted to the .edb file. This is illustrated in Exercise 1 of Chapter 21, "Microsoft Outlook Forms Environment." When you access the same file from within Outlook 2000, the entire file is converted into a MAPI object before it is delivered to the client. Deferred content conversion saves time and system resources because items are only processed when necessary.

Note   You can rename .edb and .stm databases and move them to different directories. Right-click the corresponding information store, select Properties, click on the Database tab, and then click the corresponding Browse buttons to specify the new locations. However, because the .edb and .stm files build a complete store, it is advisable to keep them together and assign them a common name with different extensions (that is, .edb and .stm). Moving databases temporarily dismounts the affected store. You should perform a full backup immediately after moving databases.

Optional Databases

As explained in Chapter 6, "Coexistence with Previous Microsoft Exchange Server Versions," Active Directory Connector (ADC) and SRS coordinate the replication between Active Directory and the legacy Exchange directory if you install Exchange 2000 Server in an existing Exchange Server organization. The SRS emulates an Exchange Server 5.5 directory service and maintains its own database called SRS.EDB, which can be found in the \Program Files\Exchsrvr\ Srsdata directory. SRS.EDB contains configuration information replicated with the Exchange directory service. It is possible to back up the SRS database online using the Exchange 2000 Server–enabled version of the Windows 2000 Backup utility, which is covered in Lesson 3.

The KMS database called KMSMDB.EDB resides in the \Program Files\ Exchsrvr\Kmsdata directory, provided that you have installed KMS on the local computer. This database preserves the history of the encryption keys for all users who have been enabled with advanced security. You can back up the KMS database online using an Exchange 2000 Server–enabled backup utility. Do not forget to secure the KMS database and your KMS administrator password. Likewise, make sure a correct backup of Windows 2000 Certificate Services is performed. At a minimum, back up your certification authority's (CA) certificate in a .p12 file and save the password. KMS was covered in Chapter 19, "Implementing Advanced Security."

The Dirsync database, called XDIR.EDB, is located in the \Program Files\ Exchsrvr\Dxadata directory. It keeps track of MS Mail directory synchronization (Dirsync) transactions. The Dirsync Agent uses this database when directory synchronization with MS Mail has been configured. Losing this database is not a disaster, but you should save the Dirsync database offline using a file-based backup to avoid resetting the Dirsync. You can read more about directory synchronization with MS Mail in Chapter 26, "Connecting to Microsoft Mail and Schedule+."

The Microsoft Search service maintains the database with perhaps the longest name. If you have enabled full-text indexing, a database file called EXCHANGESERVER_<Server Name>.EDB (such as EXCHANGESERVER_BLUESKY-SRV1.EDB) will exist in the \Program Files\Exchsrvr\EXCHANGESERVER_<Server Name> directory. The full-text search database must be backed up offline using a file-based backup. You can read more about full-text indexing in Chapter 14, "Managing Server Configuration."

Main Database Components

If you check out any of the database locations, such as the \Program Files\Exchsrvr\Mdbdata directory, you will find that the .edb and .stm databases are not the only existing items (see Figure 20.6). A number of .log files exist, along with a .chk file and TMP.EDB. TMP.EDB is not important because it contains temporary information that is deleted when all stores in the storage group are dismounted or the Information Store service is stopped. TMP.EDB is not included in backups. However, the .log and .chk files are essential for the fault-tolerant, transaction-based ESE.

Transaction Logs

Transaction log files give ESE the ability to manage data storage efficiently with high speed. ESE stores new transactions, such as the delivery of a message, in a memory cache and in the transaction log concurrently. The data is written sequentially, with new data appended to existing data without the need for complex database operations. At a later time, the transactions are transferred en masse from the memory cache to the actual databases to bring them up to date.

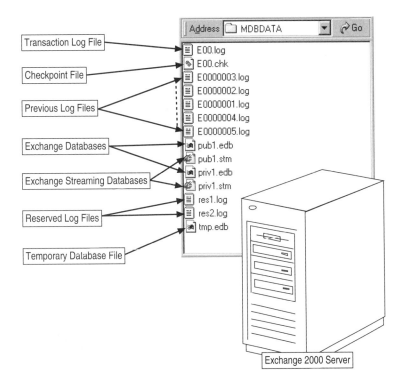

Figure 20.6   Important database files

You can determine the path to a storage group's transaction log file and its name in Exchange System Manager. Right-click the desired storage group, select Properties, and in the General tab, check the Transaction Log Location and the Log File Prefix fields. By default, the First Storage Group maintains its transactions logs in the same directory as the databases and uses the prefix E00, which results in a transaction log file name of E00.LOG. The E00.LOG is used for all mailbox and public stores in this storage group. If you create additional storage groups, the prefix number is incremented to E01, E02, and E03.

Checkpoint Files

The ESE memory cache greatly improves system performance, but this cache may be lost due to a sudden power outage or system failure before the transactions are written to the database. Transaction logs ensure that committed transactions are not lost. When you restart the server, Exchange 2000 Server reads the checkpoint file (for example, E00.CHK), determines the transactions that require processing, and incorporates these into the databases from the log files.

Checkpoint files are updated whenever ESE writes a particular transaction into a database, so the checkpoint file always points to the last transaction that was transferred successfully. This provides a fast recovery mechanism, although checkpoint files are not required to commit transactions to databases. ESE can also process transaction log files directly, determining by itself which transactions have not yet been transferred, but this takes significantly more time. Nevertheless, ESE guarantees that transactions are not written to databases multiple times.

Previous Logs

Transaction log files are always exactly 5.242.880 bytes (5 MB) in size. If a log is completely used, it is renamed to allow the creation of a new, empty file. Renamed transaction logs are called previous log files. The naming format of previous log files is <Log Prefix>XXXXX.LOG (such as E00XXXXX.LOG), where XXXXX represents a five-digit hexadecimal number from 00000 to FFFFF. Previous logs reside in the same directories as the current transaction log file.

Reserved Logs

Reserved logs are an "emergency repository" for transactions. They provide enough disk space to write them from memory to the hard disk even if a server's disk is filled to a point where no new transactions can be added to a log file. Reserved logs are called RES1.LOG and RES2.LOG and can be found in the transaction log directories. They are created automatically when the databases are initialized because—for obvious reasons—they cannot be created later when they are actually needed.

ESE uses RES1.LOG and RES2.LOG only to complete a current transaction process. It then sends an error notification to the store or other service, depending on which database is affected, to shut down the service safely. You will find an entry that indicates the service shutdown along with a description of the reason in the application event log. In this situation, you should create additional free hard disk space (for example, add a new hard disk) before you restart the services. Another possible option is to restart the services immediately and perform a full backup of the databases. This deletes existing transaction logs and frees the server's hard disk resources. The full backup is explained in Lesson 3.

Patch Files

The Exchange 2000 Server version of the NTBACKUP.EXE program allows you to perform backup operations while the server services are running. This means that while you are saving the server databases and transaction log files, users can still send and receive messages. Patch files (such as PRIV1.PAT and PUB1.PAT) catch these current transactions. They are included in the current backup at the end of the operation and incorporated into the databases afterward. Patch files should not exist during regular server operation.

Note   Patch files ensure that the current online backup represents the most recent state.

Log File Maintenance and Circular Logging

Exchange 2000 Server holds each transaction in two file-based repositories: the transaction log and the databases. Consequently, it is possible to restore a database from an uninterrupted sequence of transaction log files since the time the database was created (or last backed up). Because transaction log files are important for data recovery, Exchange 2000 Server does not delete them automatically.

Manual Deletion

Manually deleting transaction log files is not advisable because you run the risk of corrupting the databases. You cannot analyze the checkpoint files to figure out which transactions have already been transferred. Manual deletion will lead to inconsistent databases, which will not be recoverable without a recent backup.

Database Backups

Transaction log files are deleted when you complete a full or an incremental backup. As mentioned earlier, if you need to free hard disk space, perform a full online backup. This is the safest way of deleting transaction logs.

Note   Because all databases within a storage group share the same set of log files, transaction logs are deleted only after all databases have been backed up. This is one reason you should configure backup operations for entire storage groups.

Circular Logging

Circular logging basically means automatically deleting transaction log files and their entries. Circular logging causes the server to discard transactions as soon as they have been committed to the databases. The checkpoint file indicates which log files and transaction entries can be removed. Any existing previous logs are deleted, while transactions within the current transaction log file are marked as obsolete only. New transactions will eventually overwrite the obsolete entries in the current transaction log before a new log file is created as usual.

Circular logging prevents duplicate consumption of disk space, but it is not compatible with sophisticated fault-tolerant configurations and several online backup types, which rely on the existence of transaction logs. You might therefore want to enable this feature only for less important repositories that hold a large amount of data, such as Network News Transport Protocol (NNTP)-based newsgroups implemented in a public store. Right-click the storage group for which you want to enable circular logging, select Properties, and in the General tab, select the Enable Circular Logging check box.

Note   It is not recommended that you enable circular logging for storage groups that hold business-relevant data. With circular logging enabled, you can only recover information included in the last full backup.

Database Partitioning

Each storage group requires a directory for its transaction logs, but this location does not need to be the directory for the databases. If your Exchange 2000 server is equipped with multiple hard disk systems, separating transaction logs from databases can greatly improve your ability to recover the system in the event of a hardware failure.

Transaction Log Location

Disks of transaction log files should not contain any Exchange databases. Furthermore, as ESE maintains separate transaction log files for each storage group, it is advantageous to place the logs of each storage group on separate physical disks, if possible. At first glance, it may seem that this decreases the system reliability because more hard disk systems, which can fail, are added to the server. However, if you kept the transaction log files of all your storage groups on a single dedicated disk system and that system failed, your entire server would be out of order. With transaction logs on separate disks, only a particular storage group will be affected while users with mailboxes in other storage groups can continue to work in Outlook 2000 as if nothing has happened.

It is a Microsoft recommendation to separate transaction log disks per storage group to increase the system resilience. It is a good idea to protect the transaction log disks with RAID, for example, by creating a mirror. If a particular hard disk holding a set of transaction logs breaks, you can split the mirror set and remove the problematic device. Your server will be fully operational again. During a later maintenance cycle, you may add a new disk and reconfigure the mirror set.

Separate transaction log disks may also improve the system performance because ESE threads can then write transactions for separate storage groups to the transaction log files concurrently. Separate disk controllers do not block each other's Input/Output (I/O) operations. However, this configuration does not keep its promises if the majority of activities happen in one particular storage group. A single disk controller would then have to accomplish all the work. Consequently, you achieve better performance by consolidating the disks that would be used for all transaction logs and placing them into a single RAID array (for instance, a mirrored stripe set). Striping the hard disks together improves disk I/O because I/O requests are spread evenly across all disk controllers—even if only a single storage group shows activity.

Note   A problematic storage group or database will not prevent the Information Store service from running. Unaffected databases remain mounted and available.

Database Location

It is not required to place the databases of each storage group on separate hardware-level RAID volumes. A stripe set with parity, or any other advanced

RAID configuration (such as a mirrored or duplexed stripe set), may provide the required level of protection against hardware failures. If one disk breaks, it can be replaced without data losses. Total damage of the RAID system, however, would affect all storage groups of your server. Very cautious administrators may therefore want to implement separate physical disk sets for the databases of each storage group (see Figure 20.7). If one particular disk set indicates problems, affected databases may be moved, dismounted, or restored without affecting stores in other storage groups.

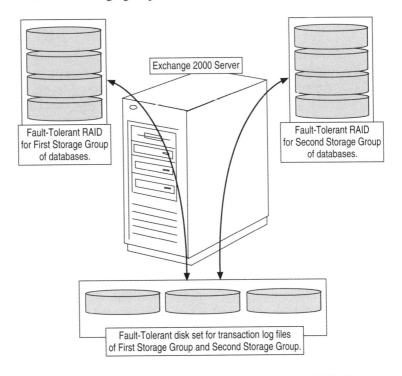

Figure 20.7   An ambitious disk subsystem for Exchange 2000 Server

Even if you do not plan to invest into ambitiously complex hard disk subsystems, it is a good idea to configure multiple storage groups. Using separate backup sessions, it is possible to back up separate storage groups to different tape drives on remote computers in the network concurrently. This saves time and gives you the ability to perform parallel restores as well. To restore multiple storage groups concurrently, launch multiple restore sessions.

Note   It is not possible to backup or restore databases from a particular storage group in multiple restore sessions simultaneously. You may back them up or restore them individually in a series of sessions.

Maintaining Databases

Databases become fragmented over time in a normal process that you can't prevent, just as you can't prevent the fragmentation of a computer's hard disk. However, fragmentation slows down the server, which is not desirable, and significant database fragmentation can lead to database inconsistencies that may cause serious problems. Mailbox and public stores must therefore be maintained (defragmented) regularly.

Database Defragmentation

The Information Store defragments its databases automatically during scheduled maintenance cycles. Database inconsistencies may also be fixed during every startup and shutdown of the server in a process known as soft recovery. For that reason, you don't need to worry about database fragmentation too much. However, you might want to check the maintenance schedule, which can be defined in the Database tab of the corresponding store under Maintenance Interval. Maintenance processes should run at different times from backup operations.

Database Compaction

Online defragmentation does not reduce the size of the databases. Deleted objects are reordered and free space in the database files is marked as available. This is usually sufficient, but it may be desirable to shrink the database size to recover free disk space, for instance, if you have moved a large number of mailboxes away from a particular server. During its online defragmentation cycles, the Information Store will log an event in the application event log (Event ID 1221), which indicates the amount of available free database space. To give an example from the test environment: "The database 'First Storage Group\Mailbox Store (BLUESKY-SRV1)' has 4 megabytes of free space after online defragmentation has terminated."

To reduce the physical size of the database files, you need to use the database compaction tool (ESEUTIL.EXE). ESEUTIL.EXE is a very powerful low-level database utility that allows you to perform database consistency checks, defragmentation, and failure correction at the level of the ESE. If a store is mounted while you try to use ESEUTIL.EXE to compact its databases, the error code -1032 (JET_errFileAccessDenied) will be returned. ESEUTIL.EXE is a command-line utility that can be found in the \Program Files\Exchsrvr\Bin directory. For a complete list of command-line switches, type **eseutil**, and press ENTER. Detailed information is also provided in a file called ESEUTIL.RTF, which can be found in the \Support\Utils directory on the Exchange 2000 Server CD. Do not forget to perform a full backup before compacting databases offline, just to be prepared in case ESEUTIL.EXE acts differently than expected.

Important   Do not leave temporary database files on the Exchange 2000 server and perform an immediate full backup following a successful compaction.

Troubleshooting Database Problems

If you experience Information Store problems, you can use ESEUTIL.EXE with the /g switch to verify database integrity. If you discover a corrupted database, you may attempt to fix the problem. However, you should first reboot the server because soft recovery, which is launched during the server startup, might automatically correct the inconsistency. Likewise, if you have a recent backup available, you should not attempt to fix corruption manually. User data may be lost because the repair works this way: An integrity check is performed to find corrupted pages and their corresponding tables. ESEUTIL.EXE will attempt to repair corrupted tables, but pages (that is, data) that cannot be fixed are purged and can therefore no longer be found in the database.

If all your recent backups cannot be used, you will have to fix corruption using ESEUTIL.EXE with the /p switch. It is important to note that the repair is performed at the level of the ESE, which is below the Information Store. While corrupted pages are fixed and purged, the database is returned to a consistent state, but this does not mean that it still contains all the data that the Information Store needs to operate accurately. Hence, after running ESEUTIL.EXE, you must check the databases at the Information Store level using ISINTEG.EXE.

The Information Store Integrity utility (Isinteg) can find and eliminate database errors and problems in high-level data structures. ISINTEG.EXE can be found in the \Program Files\Exchsrvr\Bin directory. By default, this utility does not correct any corruption; it checks only for table damage, incorrect reference counters, and nonreferenced items. To fix problems, you must specify the -fix option at the command line. ISINTEG.EXE writes details about tests and correction processes to a log file.

Caution   If you have to work with ESEUTIL.EXE and ISINTEG.EXE to fix database corruption, it is advisable to contact Microsoft Product Support Services (MS PSS) for assistance. Before fixing any inconsistencies, always back up all databases. Be aware that you will most likely lose data during the repair. ESEUTIL.EXE and ISINTEG.EXE cannot replace correctly performed backups.

Copying Databases Using the Esefile Utility

It is important to note that low-level database tools, such as ESEUTIL.EXE, work with temporary database files. You need to make sure that you have sufficient free disk space on the machine where you want to perform the operation. As mentioned earlier, it is advantageous to reserve half of your database drives' capacity for maintenance and recovery purposes. If this is not feasible, consider copying the database files to another server with sufficient free disk space before working with ESEUTIL.EXE. It is possible to specify a temporary file on another drive if local disk space is low, but this significantly slows down the entire operation due to the additional copy process.

To copy large database files, use ESEFILE.EXE, which is located in the
\Support\Utils\i386 directory on your Exchange 2000 Server CD. ESEFILE.EXE
with /C <source> <destination> parameter can copy database files larger then
192 GB. ESEFILE.EXE is available in both the Standard and Enterprise Editions
of Exchange 2000 Server. You can find more information about the Esefile in
README.DOC from the \Support\Utils directory.

Exercise 4: Compacting Exchange 2000 Server Databases

In this exercise you will perform an offline compaction of a mailbox store.
You will also check whether the databases are still intact after the compaction
has finished.

To view a multimedia demonstration that displays how to perform this procedure,
run the EX4CH20.AVI files from the \Exercise_Information\Chapter20 folder on
the Supplemental Course Materials CD.

Prerequisites

- Restart BLUESKY-SRV1 and make sure it is operational.

- Log on as Administrator to BLUESKY-SRV1.

▶ **To compact databases and check their integrity**

1. Launch Exchange System Manager from the Microsoft Exchange
   program group.

2. Expand the First Administrative Group, then Servers, then BLUESKY-SRV1,
   then First Storage Group. Right-click Mailbox Store (BLUESKY-SRV1), and
   select Dismount Store.

3. In the Mailbox Store (BLUESKY-SRV1) dialog box informing you that this
   store will no longer be available to the users, click Yes to dismount the store.

4. Click Start, click Run, and in the Run dialog box, type **cmd**, and then
   click OK.

5. At the Windows 2000 command prompt, type **cd \Program
   Files\Exchsrvr\Bin** and press ENTER. If the path to your Exchange directory
   is different, be sure to enter the correct path in this and the following steps.

6. At the command prompt type **eseutil /d "c:\Program Files\Exchsrvr\
   Mdbdata\priv1.edb" /t "c:\mbxstoredfrg.edb" /p** and press ENTER. This
   command line will cause ESEUTIL.EXE to compact the databases in temporary files called MBXSTOREDFRG.EDB and MBXSTOREDFRG.STM,
   which will be created and preserved in the root
   directory (see Figure 20.8).

7. At the command prompt type **eseutil /g "c:\mbxstoredfrg.edb"** and press
   ENTER to launch the database integrity check. Verify that ESEUTIL.EXE does
   not report any errors.

8. At the command prompt type **copy "c:\mbxstoredfrg.edb" "c:\Program Files\Exchsrvr\Mdbdata\priv1.edb" /y** and press ENTER to copy the compacted database over the production database.

9. At the command prompt type **copy "c:\mbxstoredfrg.stm" "c:\Program Files\Exchsrvr\Mdbdata\priv1.stm" /y** and press ENTER to copy the compacted streaming database over the production streaming database.

10. At the command prompt type **del "c:\mbxstoredfrg.*"** and press ENTER to delete the temporary database files.

11. At the command prompt type **isinteg -s bluesky-srv1 -test allfoldertests** and press ENTER to perform a folder group test.

12. ISINTEG.EXE will inform you that only databases marked as offline can be checked. Make sure that the Mailbox Store (BLUESKY-SRV1) is marked as offline, type its corresponding storage number, and then press ENTER.

13. ISINTEG.EXE will inform you that you have selected the databases of First Storage Group / Mailbox Store (BLUESKY-SRV1). Type **y** and press ENTER to launch the check (see Figure 20.8).

14. Verify that ISINTEG.EXE returns no errors or warnings, and then close the command prompt.

15. Switch back to Exchange System Manager, right-click Mailbox Store (BLUESKY-SRV1), and select Mount Store.

16. In the Mailbox Store (BLUESKY-SRV1) dialog box, informing you that the store was mounted successfully, click OK.

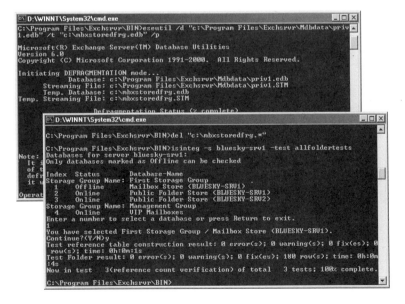

Figure 20.8 Compacting and checking a mailbox store

Exercise Summary

To launch a database compaction, start Eseutil with the /d switch, and specify the complete path to and the name of the desired Exchange database. The corresponding streaming database will be compacted as well (the /i command-line switch excludes the .stm file). ESEUTIL.EXE will read page after page from the original databases and copy them into temporary files. At successful completion, the temporary files are copied over the original databases. You may want to preserve the original databases by specifying the /p command-line switch, which disables the copy process. This allows you to check the compaction results and manually replace the store databases. To perform a high-level database check, use ISINTEG.EXE and specify an appropriate test routine.

Lesson 3: Backup, Restore, and Disaster Recovery

Exchange 2000 Server provides a dedicated API for backing up and restoring databases. This API, implemented in ESEBCLI2.DLL, gives backup applications, such as Microsoft Windows 2000 Backup, the ability to perform backup and restore operations online, without the need to stop database-related services. You can back up and restore mailbox or public stores individually while other stores are mounted. Backup and restore operations can be performed remotely over the network.

This lesson covers backup, restore, and disaster recovery procedures available when using Exchange 2000 Server–enabled backup applications. These procedures are essentially vendor independent because all Exchange 2000 Server–aware backup programs make use of the same backup API.

Caution   Follow the exercises outlined in this lesson in a test environment only. Performing disaster recovery where not needed can cause loss of user data. You should never test disaster recovery procedures in a production environment.

At the end of this lesson, you will be able to:

- Perform live backups that do not interrupt the services of Exchange 2000 Server.

- Restore Exchange 2000 Server from an online backup to recover from various critical situations.

Estimated time to complete this lesson: 5 hours

Backing Up the Databases

You should only use an Exchange 2000 Server–enabled backup program to perform backup and restore operations. The Windows 2000 Backup utility, for example, is made Exchange 2000 Server–aware when you install the Microsoft Exchange System Management Tools using the Exchange 2000 Server Setup program. The actual server services do not need to be installed. This makes it possible to configure a dedicated system for backup operations over the network. To back up system files and databases, you must be an administrator or a backup operator.

Note   In addition to backing up databases, you need to keep a record of the system configuration. It is important to document the installed components, their installation directories and drive letters, service accounts and passwords, and the names of servers, stores, storage groups, administrative groups, and the organization. This information may be required to successfully recover a server.

Offline Backups

An offline backup is a regular file-based backup of the \Program Files\Exchsrvr directory and its subdirectories. It can be performed only when the server services are stopped (offline). Offline backups have an advantage in that they can include the MS Mail Dirsync database, the binary files of Exchange 2000 Server, and message queues of the MTA or gateway connectors. It is a good idea to perform an offline backup immediately after the installation of Exchange 2000 Server and periodically when new components are added to the server (for example, KMS, gateway connectors, or service packs).

Important   If you have placed transaction log files and databases on separate hard disks (highly recommended), you need to include all disk drives in the offline backup to completely save the Exchange 2000 server.

Offline backups have several disadvantages. Most obviously, Exchange 2000 Server is unavailable during backup operations because all services are stopped. Furthermore, you must always perform a complete backup of the entire server, which consumes time and tape space. The offline backup is not aware of databases or transaction log files. It does not detect committed transactions and does not purge transaction log files. However, it is possible to exclude database directories from offline backups and perform an online backup for these files separately. A recent file-based backup that was prepared in addition to online database backups can significantly simplify disaster recovery.

Online Backups

An online backup is performed while the server services are running (online). In fact, the services must be running because the backup application needs to communicate with the services to request the data. Active server services also ensure that users can work with their messaging clients during the backup operation. As mentioned in Lesson 2, patch files guarantee that current transactions are included in the backup. Online backups are aware of the Exchange Server databases and their transaction log files. They guarantee that entire stores are covered even if only transaction log files are written to tape. This can save backup time and tape space. A significant disadvantage of online backups is that they do not include binary files or configuration data.

The following are the four different types of online backups (see Figure 20.9):

- **Full backup.**   Covers the entire information store. It saves databases as well as transaction log entries that have not yet been committed to the databases. In addition, transaction log files whose content is already committed to the actual database files are purged from the system. It enables you to restore the databases from a single backup, but it requires more tape space than any other online backup type. The full backup sets the context for all other backup types.

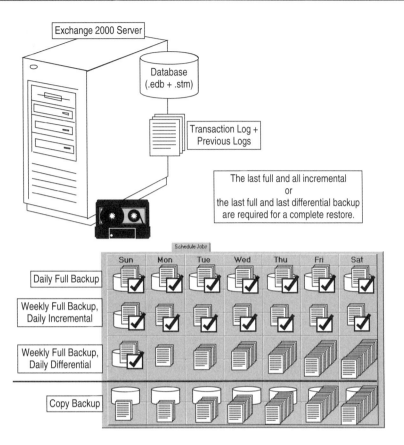

Figure 20.9   Backup strategies for Exchange 2000 Server

- **Incremental backup.**   Saves only new transaction log files, which are purged once they have been backed up, setting the context for the next incremental or differential backup. It is important to understand that the incremental backup does not save any database files, which means that it is useless without a previous full backup. A successful restore requires the last full backup plus all incremental backups since that time. While incremental backups use tape storage media efficiently, they are the most time consuming to restore from. Incremental backups are not supported on storage groups where circular logging is enabled.

- **Differential backup.**   Works similar to the incremental backup, but does not purge transaction log files. Therefore, it does not change the context for the next backup. It is dependent on a previous full backup or incremental backup. A successful restore requires the last full backup plus the last differential backup. This backup type is not supported on servers or storage groups where circular logging is enabled.

- **Copy backup.** Saves databases and transaction logs, but does not purge any files from the system. The copy backup does not change the context for any other backup types. It is useful for archive purposes. It is a good idea to perform a copy backup monthly and whenever you change the configuration or work with offline database utilities.

Note   Using online backups, you can save databases and storage groups separately, but it is impossible to back up individual mailboxes or public folders. You may use the Microsoft Exchange Mailbox Merge Wizard from the \Support\Utils\ i386\Exmerge directory on the Exchange 2000 Server CD (covered later) to perform such operations. Microsoft recommends that you always back up entire storage groups.

Backup Type Dependencies

You should back up your servers at least once every day. Perform full backups, also called normal backups, if the size of your databases and the capacity of your backup media allow it. Full backups do not depend on other backups. The incremental backup, on the other hand, has significant disadvantages because it imposes previous backups. If your backup from yesterday is destroyed, the backup from today is also useless. In this case, only the incremental backups from the days before yesterday can be restored in addition to the last full backup, so the server has effectively lost the most current information. Differential backups overcome this disadvantage, but they require more server disk and tape space than incremental backups because transaction log files are not purged between full backup cycles. If you performed a full backup the day before yesterday and differential backups yesterday and today, only the last full backup and the differential backup from today are required to fully restore the server.

Automating the Backup Process

The Windows 2000 Backup utility provides you with the option to schedule backup jobs (in the Schedule Jobs tab). You should make use of this feature to ensure timely database backups. At a minimum, a full backup should be performed weekly, perhaps over the weekend (see Figure 20.9). Differential or incremental backups may be performed between weekdays if full backups would interfere with normal business hours. Scheduled backup jobs are added to the server's Scheduled Tasks container and executed by the Windows 2000 Task Scheduler service. It is possible to schedule online and offline backups. For more information about scheduling backup jobs and other tasks, see the Windows 2000 product documentation.

Note   Make sure that the maintenance intervals configured for your databases do not conflict with your backup schedule.

Backing Up the Configuration

Backing up the Exchange 2000 Server databases is not sufficient for complete server recovery. The databases do not contain the organization's configuration information, for example. Active Directory maintains this information. Likewise, several service startup parameters are kept in the server's Registry database. The IIS and its associated virtual servers, again, retrieve their configuration information from the IIS metabase. Windows 2000 Server also depends on its boot environment. All of this information and additional data (such as Certificate Services data) must be backed up and can be included when selecting the System State check box in the Windows 2000 Backup utility (in the Backup tab), provided that your Exchange 2000 server is a domain controller.

Note   System state information must be backed up locally and can only be restored on a computer that has the same name as the original server.

Domain Controllers and Exchange 2000 Server

Most computer specialists prefer to install Exchange 2000 Server on member servers. This frees the server from Active Directory replication and other domain controller tasks, such as client authentication. However, member servers have disadvantages because a local copy of the Active Directory database does not exist. You must ensure that your Windows 2000 administrators are backing up Active Directory (which contains the configuration information for your Exchange organization) properly. It is not possible to backup Active Directory information remotely.

The installation of Exchange 2000 Server on member servers has implications of great consequence because the server must establish a connection to an Active Directory domain controller to read and write directory information. Directory information is cached locally (DSAccess) to reduce the impact of Active Directory communication on the network, as explained in Chapter 3, "Microsoft Exchange 2000 Server Architecture." Yet, if domain controllers are unavailable, users cannot get access to Exchange 2000 Server. Consequently, it is vital to provide domain controller redundancy. Small environments should implement a minimum of two
Active Directory domain controllers; medium and large organizations should not go with less than three. It is a very good idea to install Exchange 2000 Server on a domain controller if your Active Directory environment is understaffed.

Note   Exchange 2000 servers that hold user data (mailboxes and public folders) should be installed on domain controllers. Dedicated servers that do not hold user data, such as bridgeheads or front end servers exposed to the Internet, are best installed on member servers.

Verifying Database Backups

Professional backup solutions, including Windows 2000 Backup, are able to verify the successful completion of backup jobs. During the data verification process, Backup compares the data that was written to tape with the data in the databases and detects possible damage. Any errors written to the backup logs or the application event log can indicate that the backup ended in a critical state. Corrupted backups do not allow you to recover the server.

Even if the verification process does not indicate any problems, you should not simply assume that your data is recoverable. Your backup of today may be in perfectly good shape. Yet, you might not be able to restore it. Just imagine a situation where yesterday's incremental backup was lost. As mentioned earlier, your current incremental backup would be lost as well. Thus, it is important to verify backups by restoring the data to a reference computer. If it is not feasible to verify all backups from all servers, rotate the restore process and test backups from various machines. It is not a bad idea to plan a monthly test recovery to check the system, identify potential problems, and practice the worst-case scenarios.

You should have at least one nonproduction reference server available at all times for software and disaster recovery tests. This server must not contain any production data and must not be part of the production Active Directory environment. As explained later, it is vital to use a domain controller from a different Active Directory forest for recovery of Exchange 2000 Server databases. The reference server needs enough disk space for restoring an entire information store. Ideally, the reference server is equipped with hardware similar to the production systems. The tape drives must be compatible.

Exercise 5: Backing Up Exchange 2000 Server

In this exercise you will back up Exchange 2000 Server plus other information required to perform server recoveries, which will be the objective of later exercises. You will use the Windows 2000 Backup utility to carry out a full backup.

To view a multimedia demonstration that displays how to perform this procedure, run the EX5CH20.AVI files from the \Exercise_Information\Chapter20 folder on the Supplemental Course Materials CD.

Prerequisites

- Restart BLUESKY-SRV1 and BLUESKY-SRV2 and make sure they are operational.

- Make sure Drive D on BLUESKY-SRV1 is formatted with NT file system (NTFS) and has enough free space to hold the backup file of BLUESKY-SRV2 (approximately 500 MB).

- Log on as Administrator to BLUESKY-SRV2.

- If you have completed the exercises of Chapter 19, "Implementing Advanced Security," make sure the Microsoft Exchange Key Management Service (KMS) is started.

▶   **To backup Exchange 2000 Server and system state information**

1. On BLUESKY-SRV2, click Start, point to Programs, point to Accessories, point to System Tools, and launch Backup.

2. Click on the Backup tab and select the System State check box.

3. Expand Microsoft Exchange Server (the Microsoft Exchange node is for earlier versions of Exchange Server), expand BLUESKY-SRV2, and select the Microsoft Information Store and Microsoft Key Management Service check boxes (the latter is only available if you have installed and started the KMS as outlined in Chapter 19, "Implementing Advanced Security").

4. Under Backup Destination, make sure File is selected, and then under Backup Media Or File Name type **\\bluesky-srv1\d$\bluesky-srv2.bkf**. (You need to place the backup file on BLUESKY-SRV1 because BLUESKY-SRV2 will be crashed in Exercise 8.)

5. Click Start Backup, and in the Backup Job Information dialog box, click Advanced.

6. Select the Verify Data After Backup (see Figure 20.10) check box, click OK, and then click Start Backup to launch the backup process.

Figure 20.10   Backing up offline data, the system state, and Exchange 2000 Server databases

7. When the backup is finished, click Report in the Backup Progress dialog box. Verify in the backup log that no errors occurred.

8. In the Backup Progress dialog box, click Close.

Exercise Summary

It is easy to back up the entire configuration, including Active Directory, if you have installed Exchange 2000 Server on a domain controller. You only need to include the system state in the backup. Databases can be saved online. If you have a tape drive with sufficient capacity, the server's local drives can be included to perform a file-based backup simultaneously. In this case, exclude the directories of the Exchange 2000 Server databases. Database files are kept open by their respective services and cannot be saved properly using the file-based backup. You would need to stop the services, which in turn would prevent the online backup. To exclude databases from offline backups, open the Tools menu, select Options, click on the Exclude Files tab, and under Files Excluded For All Users, click Add New. In the Add Excluded Files dialog box, under Custom File Mask, type *, and then click Browse to launch the Exclude Path dialog box where you need to specify the database directories, such as \Program Files\Exchsrvr\Mdbdata, \Kmsdata, or \Srsdata.

Designing a Disaster Recovery Plan

It is vital to document your backup and restore procedures, label backup media properly, and store the media in a secure location. Many organizations keep full backups offsite in a separate geographical place for maximum security. The recovery document must provide instructions describing where to obtain the most recent backup media and how to use it to restore data according to various possible scenarios. Responsible contacts and escalation procedures must be defined. Ideal documentation would allow an arbitrary administrator to recover the system. To protect your organization in the event of a natural disaster, a copy of the recovery document and a set of backup tapes should be stored offsite in a secure location. This as well as a dedicated recovery server can help to minimize system downtime.

In addition to policies and procedures, your disaster recovery kit should contain the following items:

- A copy and documentation of any other software, such as service packs or configuration changes applied to the system.

- A copy of the original Windows 2000 Server and Exchange 2000 Server product CDs.

- A file containing exported recipient information in a supported LDIFDE or CSVDE format, as explained in Chapter 13. "Creating and Managing Recipients."

- An emergency repair disk.

- Backups of system state information, which covers Active Directory, Registry, IIS metabase, and data from other system components, such as Certificate Services. System state information must be recent enough to include up-to-date configuration information.

- Descriptions of hard drive partitions and their purposes (system drive, transaction log drives, database drives, and so forth).

- Documentation about the configuration of hardware and the operating system.

- File-based backups of the system and other drives.

- Information about the configuration of Exchange 2000 Server, including installation directories, installed components, configured virtual servers and protocol settings, as well as connector configurations and server passwords.

- Offline backups of Exchange 2000 Server databases (MS Mail Dirsync, MTA message queues, and so on).

- Online backups of Exchange 2000 Server databases (information store, KMS, and SRS).

Restoring to the Same Server

It is straightforward to restore Exchange 2000 Server databases to their original location. You don't even have to stop the server. In fact, you should verify that the services are running, but you have to dismount the problematic store using Exchange System Manager. Other databases can remain mounted to avoid affecting users unnecessarily. Unfortunately, it is not possible to dismount KMS or SRS databases in Exchange System Manager. You will need to stop the service (KMS or SRS), move all existing database files from the work directory (KMSData or SRSData) to a safe location, and then start the corresponding service again. The service will still start in semirunning mode, which allows you to restore the databases using Windows 2000 Backup.

Note   Move old databases to another directory; do not delete them. Your backup sets may turn out to be useless, in which case you may need to fix corrupted databases using ESEUTIL.EXE. It is generally advisable to back up the system before performing any database maintenance.

Restoring a Full Backup with Incremental or Differential Backups

When restoring a full backup with incremental or differential backups, make sure you restore the full backup first. During the restore, you need to specify a temporary location where Backup will place transaction log and patch files. Restoring the full backup will also create a RESTORE.ENV file in this location, which contains, among other things, information about the original and the path to the destination database. RESTORE.ENV controls how old transaction log and patch files are applied to restored databases. This process is generally known as hard recovery, which is triggered when you select the Last Backup Set check box during the last restore cycle.

You should not select the Last Backup Set check box before all incremental or differential backups have been restored. If you forget to activate this option for the last backup set, the databases cannot be mounted. Correspondingly, the Mount Database After Restore check box is only available when the Last Backup Set check box is selected beforehand. If you are restoring a full backup without any incremental backups, do not forget to select the Last Backup Set check box right away.

Performing a Manual Hard Recovery

Nobody is perfect and you may forget to select the Last Backup Set check box. In this situation, Exchange System Manager will not mount restored databases and will report an internal processing error. The error message will suggest that you try restarting Exchange System Manager or the Microsoft Exchange Information Store service, or both. Do not follow this advice. Restarting the Information Store will trigger a soft recovery, but what your databases actually need is a hard recovery. The application event log contains a more precise description of the problem. Check for Event ID 619 where the source is ESE98. The following is a sample error description: "Information Store (1764) Attempted to attach database 'C:\Program Files\Exchsrvr\Management Group\VIP Mailboxes.edb' but it is a database restored from a backup set on which hard recovery was not started or did not complete successfully."

You have two options: You can restore the last backup set again with Last Backup Set activated, or you can run a hard recovery manually. Open the Windows 2000 command prompt, switch to the temporary folder of the transaction log files (where RESTORE.ENV exists), and then type **"c:\Program Files\Exchsrvr\Bin\eseutil"** /cc. The transaction logs, patch files, and RESTORE.ENV are purged during this process. To preserve them, use the /K switch. It is possible to view the contents of RESTORE.ENV using ESEUTIL.EXE with the /CM switch instead of /CC. ESEUTIL.EXE was introduced in Lesson 2.

Important   Do not restore databases from the same storage group sequentially to the same temporary folder without running hard recovery at the last backup set of each restore cycle. Otherwise, subsequent restores will overwrite the RESTORE.ENV from previous rounds, thus preventing all databases recovered earlier from being mountable. If you restore multiple storage groups simultaneously, subfolders will be created in the temporary folder automatically for each group. To avoid conflicts with production databases, never restore transaction log files to the original database locations.

Exercise 6: Restoring a Database to the Same Server

In this exercise you will damage a mailbox store intentionally and restore it using a recent backup. You will not destroy the transaction log files to preserve the most recent information.

To view a multimedia demonstration that displays how to perform this procedure, run the EX6CH20*.AVI files from the \Exercise_Information\Chapter20 folder on the Supplemental Course Materials CD.

Prerequisites

- Complete Exercise 2, earlier in this chapter.
- Start BLUESKY-SRV1, BLUESKY-SRV2, and BLUESKY-WKSTA, and make sure they are operational.
- Log on as Administrator to BLUESKY-SRV1 and BLUESKY-WKSTA.

▶ **To restore a database to the same server and recover the most recent mailbox state**

1. On BLUESKY-WKSTA, launch Outlook 2000, and make sure you are working with the Administrator mailbox.

2. On the toolbar, click New, click To, and select the Administrator account. Click To -> and then click OK to address the message to your own mailbox.

3. In the Subject line, type **Recovery Test Message**.

4. In the Message Body, type **This message was not included in the most recent backup**.

5. Click Send, verify that the test message was received, and then close Outlook 2000.

6. On BLUESKY-SRV2, launch Exchange System Manager from the Microsoft Exchange program group, and expand the administrative groups and server objects.

7. Under BLUESKY-SRV2, expand Management Group, right-click VIP Mailboxes, and select Dismount Store.

8. In the VIP Mailboxes dialog box informing you that this store will be unavailable to any user, click Yes.

9. Right-click VIP Mailboxes again, select Properties, click on the Database tab, and note the directory and names of the databases (C:\Program Files\Exchsrvr\Management Group\VIP MAILBOXES.EDB). Click OK.

10. Launch Windows Explorer, open the directory of the database, and delete the files VIP MAILBOXES.EDB and VIP MAILBOXES.STM. Leave all other files in place.

11. Open the Tools menu, select Folder Options, switch to the View property sheet, and then deselect the Hide File Extensions For Known File Types check box. Click OK, and then create two empty files called VIP MAILBOXES.EDB and VIP MAILBOXES.STM to simulate corrupted databases.

12. Switch back to Exchange System Manager, right-click VIP Mailboxes, and select Mount Store. You will be informed that the database files in this store are corrupted (see Figure 20.11). Click OK.

13. On BLUESKY-SRV1, from the System Tools program group, start Backup. Click on the Restore tab, right-click File, and select Catalog File.

14. In the Backup File Name dialog box, under Catalog Backup File, type **d:\bluesky-srv2.bkf**, and then click OK.

15. Expand the nodes that correspond the to the backup media, and click OK if the Backup File Name dialog box appears.

16. Expand the node BLUESKY-SRV2\Microsoft Information Store\Management Group (click OK in the Backup File Name dialog box), and then select the Log Files and VIP Mailboxes check boxes. Click Start Restore.

17. In the Restoring Database Store dialog box, under Temporary Location For Log And Patch Files, type **c:\winnt\temp**. Select the Last Backup Set and Mount Database After Restore check boxes, and then click OK.

18. In the Enter Backup File Name dialog box, make sure d:\bluesky-srv2.bkf is specified, and then click OK.

19. Verify that the restore operation is performed without problems. In the Restore Progress dialog box informing you that the restore was completed, click Close (see Figure 20.11).

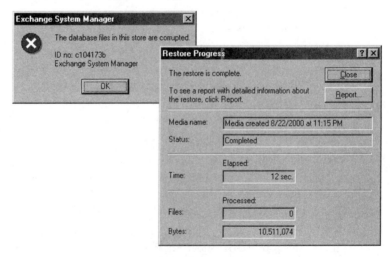

Figure 20.11   Recovering a corrupted database

20. On BLUESKY-WKSTA, launch Outlook 2000 again, and check that the Recovery Test Message is displayed in your mailbox although it was not included in the backup.

Exercise Summary

Before you can restore a database onto an Exchange 2000 server, you need to dismount the affected store—corrupted stores will most likely be dismounted already. The Windows 2000 Backup utility cannot restore over mounted databases and their files would be skipped. An error would be written to the application event log with the Event ID 8012: "The 'Microsoft Information Store' returned 'Database is in use.' from a call to 'HrESERestoreAddDatabase()'..."

When restoring databases and transaction log files, under Temporary Location For Log And Patch File, specify a working directory for the Backup utility. As mentioned, it is important to specify a folder different from the production log file location. A temporary directory, such as \Winnt\Temp is appropriate. During hard recovery, older logs are applied from the temporary directory to the databases before the more recent logs from the production location are replayed. This allows you to recover even those items that have not been included in the backup.

Note To restore Exchange 2000 databases, you need to have the permissions of an Administrator or Backup Operator.

Complete Disaster Recovery

In a complete disaster recovery, you will restore Exchange Server to a different physical computer. This is required if the original server has been fully destroyed. Complete disaster recoveries should also be practiced periodically on a dedicated, nonproduction reference server, just to make sure that the backup media is in good shape and that you are ready to react when disasters strike.

Disaster Recovery Procedure

The desired result of a disaster recovery is a 1:1 copy of the original server. Consequently, the hardware configuration of the recovery server should match the configuration of the original machine. If this is not the case, drivers may be incompatible with the new hardware and may require manual adjustments. The disks must have the same partitioning. They should also have the same capacity (or more).

The following procedure outlines general disaster recovery steps.

1. Reinstall the operating system. Use the same version of Windows 2000 Server that was previously installed, such as Microsoft Windows 2000 Advanced Server. Specify the original system drives, directories, and the old server name during the installation. You also need to reapply any service packs.

It is vital that you install the same Windows 2000 components that were previously installed. The only difference is that the reinstalled server is a member of a workgroup instead of the production domain.

2. When you reboot the newly installed machine and log on as Administrator, you can restore any file-based backups to the drives plus the original system state information. Restoring the system state will turn the new server into a member of the production domain and will bring back the IIS metabase and other information. You need to reboot the server for the changes to take effect.

Note   If you can restore a full offline backup and the system state information, it may not be necessary to continue. The server may be operational already. Therefore, you should prepare full offline backups whenever the software installation changes, for instance when you apply hot fixes or service packs.

3. Without a full offline backup, when the system is rebooted, you will be greeted with an error message that one or more services could not be started, which is understandable because Exchange 2000 Server databases have not been restored yet, while the corresponding services are referenced in the system configuration. At this point, run the Setup program of Exchange 2000 Server in /DisasterRecovery mode. It is important to note that disaster recovery requires that the old server object still exists in the Exchange 2000 Server configuration in Active Directory. This information is required to restore the previous configuration on the server, such as mailbox and public stores. When running Setup /DisasterRecovery, make sure all the components that were previously installed on the server are marked for disaster recovery on the Component Selection wizard screen.

Note   If the Active Directory information was lost (for instance, an administrator has removed the server object from the Exchange organization), you cannot use Setup /DisasterRecovery. However, you can still install Exchange 2000 Server as usual, configure the system manually, and then restore the databases.

4. As soon as Setup completes the disaster recovery, you can restore the databases (including the KMS and SRS databases if necessary) as outlined earlier in this lesson.

5. Reboot the server, and test whether you can log on to your mailbox successfully.

Forklifting Users by Means of a Complete Disaster Recovery

Many organizations use the complete disaster recovery methodology to replace existing server hardware. The idea is simple: You fully restore the server to the new machine including all security and configuration information as well as the databases, and then replace the old hardware with the new system. After a brief period of downtime during the transition, users can use their current account information to log on to their mailboxes as if nothing happened. This procedure is also called forklifting mailboxes to a new server.

Although this strategy sounds promising, you should not use it without careful preparation. For instance, you should not dismantle the old server until you have restored the system to the new machine successfully. Should any of your tapes turn out useless, you may want to switch back to the old server. However, the old server must be disconnected from the production network before you can begin the disaster recovery. The larger your databases (some might be larger then 100 GB), the longer it takes to complete this process. Business processes may be interrupted and you may lose messages if you do not have the most recent transaction logs in your backup.

Replacing Server Hardware with Mailbox Move and Public Folder Replication

There is a better alternative that does not put your data in jeopardy. Move all mailboxes away from the aging server using Active Directory Users and Computers. This has little impact on the client side. Users need to reconnect to Exchange 2000 Server, their MAPI profiles will be updated automatically, and the environment will appear as if nothing happened. You should also move all local public folders, as explained in Chapter 18, "Public Folder Replication."

Server Name Dependencies

Give the old server some time to clear its message queues before replacing the hardware. It is important to note that the automatic redirection of Outlook users to their mailboxes on another server only works as long as a machine with the old server name is running Exchange 2000 Server in the network. A MAPI-based client with outdated profile information will contact this server first. The server will then inform the client about the new location of the mailbox. Hence, try to replace the old system when few users are working, such as over the weekend.

Replacing the Hardware

At this point, when the old server does not contain user data anymore, perform a full backup of the system. Include all drives in a file-based backup, back up the system state information as well, and do not forget KMS or SRS databases, should they exist. Because large databases are not a concern, disaster recovery will not require an extensive amount of time, and the new server will be available quickly. You may then move resources back to the new Exchange 2000 server.

Exercise 7: Performing a Complete Disaster Recovery

In this exercise you will perform a complete disaster recovery for an Exchange 2000 server without a full offline backup. You will reinstall Windows 2000 Server on BLUESKY-SRV2 and format its C drive to simulate a total disaster.

To view a multimedia demonstration that displays how to perform this procedure, run the EX7CH20*.AVI files from the \Exercise_Information\Chapter20 folder on the Supplemental Course Materials CD.

Prerequisites

- Complete Exercise 5 and test the state of the backup file in Exercise 6.
- Install Windows 2000 Server on BLUESKY-SRV2 as outlined in the "Getting Started" section of "About This Book," but do not promote this server to a domain controller, and do not add it to the domain. Install this server in a workgroup called WORKGROUP.

Note   You must not add the newly installed server to the existing Active Directory forest. Otherwise, you would lose the configuration information of BLUESKY-SRV2 that is required to perform a disaster recovery.

- Update the installation of BLUESKY-SRV2 with Windows 2000 Service Pack 1.
- Make sure that all drives are formatted with NTFS.
- You will need the Windows 2000 Server and Exchange 2000 Server, Enterprise Edition, evaluation software installation CD included in the book.
- Log on as Administrator to BLUESKY-SRV1 and BLUESKY-WKSTA.

▶   **To perform a complete disaster recovery for BLUESKY-SRV2**

1. At this point, you have installed the same version of Windows 2000 Server in the same way onto BLUESKY-SRV2 as it was previously installed.
2. Log on as Administrator to BLUESKY-SRV2, and, in the Windows 2000 Configure Your Server application, deselect the Show This Screen At Startup check box. Close this application, and then start the Windows 2000 Backup utility.
3. Click on the Restore tab, right-click File, and select Catalog File.
4. In the Backup File Name dialog box, type **\\bluesky-srv1\d$\bluesky-srv2.bkf**, and then click OK.
5. Open the File and Media nodes, and in the Backup File Name dialog box, click OK.
6. Select the System State check box, and click Start Restore.

Note If you would have backed up the entire server using a file-based backup, you should restore these files before restoring the system state information.

7. In the Warning dialog box, informing you that the current system state will be overwritten, click OK (see Figure 20.12).

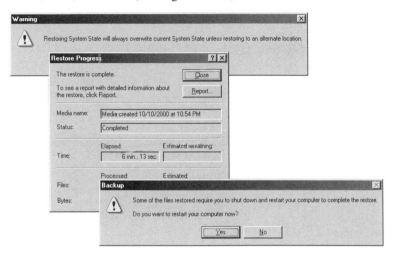

Figure 20.12   Recovering system state information

8. In the Confirm Restore dialog box, click OK, and then in the Enter Backup File Name dialog box, click OK again.

9. If a Windows File Protection dialog box appears prompting you for the Windows 2000 Server CD, insert the CD into the CD-ROM drive and then click Retry. (Close the auto starting Microsoft Windows 2000 CD application by clicking Exit.)

10. At completion of the backup process, in the Restore Progress dialog box, click Close.

11. A Backup dialog box will appear asking you whether you want to restart the server. Click Yes (see Figure 20.12).

12. When the server has been successfully restarted, log on as Administrator again. Notice that the server is now a domain controller in the original domain again because the Active Directory information was restored as part of the system state information.

13. The system state also contains information about Exchange 2000 Server services, which cannot be started because they do not exist yet. In the Service Control Manager dialog box informing you that some services could not be started, click OK.

14. In the Windows 2000 Configure Your Server application, deselect the Show This Screen At Startup check box, and then close this application.

15. Insert the Exchange 2000 Server, Enterprise Edition, evaluation software installation CD into the CD-ROM drive on BLUESKY-SRV2.

16. On the Start menu, point to Run, and in the Run dialog box, type **e:\setup\i386\setup.exe /DisasterRecovery**, and then click OK. You may use the Browse button to conveniently select the Setup executable from the installation CD, but do not forget to add the /DisasterRecovery switch (see Figure 20.13).

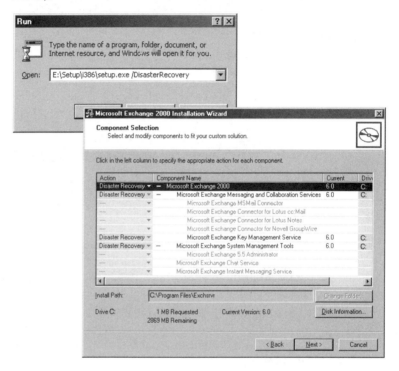

Figure 20.13   Exchange 2000 Server setup in disaster recovery mode

17. On the Microsoft Exchange 2000 Installation Wizard Welcome screen, click Next.

18. On the Component Selection wizard screen, verify that all previously installed components are displayed with an Action column set to Disaster Recovery (see Figure 20.13). Click Next.

19. A Microsoft Exchange 2000 Installation Wizard dialog box appears reminding you that you need to ensure that the original server still exists in Active Directory to complete the disaster recovery successfully. Click OK.

20. A Microsoft Exchange 2000 Installation Wizard dialog box appears informing you that you need to restore the databases after Setup is completed and then reboot the system. Click OK.

21. On the final wizard screen, click Finish.

22. On BLUESKY-SRV1, start Backup, click on the Restore tab, right-click File, and select Catalog File.

23. In the Backup File Name dialog box, under Catalog Backup File, verify that d:\bluesky-srv2.bkf is displayed, and then click OK.

24. Expand the File and Media nodes that correspond to the backup media.

25. Select the BLUESKY-SRV2\Microsoft Information Store\First Storage Group and BLUESKY-SRV2\Microsoft Information Store\Management Group check boxes.

Note   It is assumed that you did not save the password of the Key Management Service. Without this password, you are unable to start the KMS, and therefore you are not able to restore the data under BLUESKY-SRV2\Microsoft Key Management Service\Key Management Service. This demonstrates how vital it is to perform test recoveries. Your backup is perfectly fine, your system is recovered correctly, and still, you are not able to restore all data. Your users' security key histories are lost. Only a test recovery can reveal weaknesses in your recovery procedures. You can find more information about the KMS in Chapter 19, "Implementing Advanced Security."

---

26. Click Start Restore.

27. In the Restoring Database Store dialog box, under Temporary Location For Log And Patch Files, type **c:\winnt\temp**. Select the Last Backup Set check box, and then click OK (see Figure 20.14).

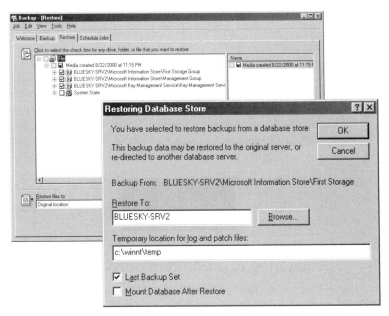

Figure 20.14   Completing the disaster recovery

28. In the Enter Backup File Name dialog box, make sure d:\bluesky-srv2.bkf is specified, and then click OK.

29. Verify that the restore operation is performed without problems. In the Restore Progress dialog box informing you that the restore was completed, click Close.

30. Reboot BLUESKY-SRV2 and, when the server is restarted, launch Exchange System Manager.

31. Expand Administrative Groups, First Administrative Groups, and all server objects, and then, under BLUESKY-SRV2, expand First Storage Group and Management Group.

32. Right-click Mailbox Store (BLUESKY-SRV2) and select Mount Store.

33. In the Mailbox Store (BLUESKY-SRV2) dialog box informing you that the store was mounted successfully, click OK.

34. Repeat steps 32 and 33 for Public Folder Store (BLUESKY-SRV2) and VIP Mailboxes, and then close the Exchange System Manager.

35. On BLUESKY-WKSTA, launch Outlook 2000 to check that you can connect to the Administrator mailbox.

Exercise Summary

Depending on the situation, a complete disaster recover may involve more or less administrative work. At a minimum, you need to configure new hardware according to the former system. You also need to install a minimal version of the operating system. With a full offline backup, you may complete the disaster recovery right away by restoring all data including the system state. Otherwise, you need to recover Exchange 2000 Server using Setup. Fortunately, the majority of the old configuration information will be available in Active Directory on the local computer or a remote domain controller. Based on this configuration information, Setup /DisasterRecovery will reconfigure the local server, including program files, registry settings, and database paths. You need to make sure all previously installed components are selected on the Component Selection wizard screen; otherwise, they will not be restored. After disaster recovery is finished, you can restore databases online.

Note Even small organizations should configure two Active Directory domain controllers in their environment. With domain controller redundancy, Active Directory will always survive a single-server disaster.

Restoring to a Different Server

First, a disclaimer: Restoring mailbox stores to a different production server is not recommended. Restoring to a server with the same name as the original server ensures that users can work with their mailboxes without reconfiguring MAPI profiles. Furthermore, if you need to restore Active Directory information, the server name must always remain the same.

Mailbox Identifiers

When you mailbox-enable a user account in Active Directory, you assign this account a mailbox repository in an information store. A globally unique identifier (GUID) associates the user account with its mailbox. This identifier is called mailbox GUID, and it must be unique within the Active Directory forest. It is important to note that the mailbox GUID is maintained inside the mailbox store, and mailbox-enabled user accounts have an msExchMailboxGuid attribute. For example, if you want to examine the administrator's mailbox GUID in your test environment, use the following command: **ldifde -m -f c:\export.ldf -s bluesky-srv1 -d "CN=Administrator,CN=Users,DC=BlueSky-inc-10,DC=com"**. When you open EXPORT.LDF in Notepad, you can find the GUID in the msExchMailboxGuid line.

Because mailbox GUIDs must be unique in the Active Directory forest, you cannot have two copies of the same database on different servers in the same organization. Exchange 2000 Server does not allow you to reconnect a mailbox from a restored database to the same or another user, so long as the mailbox from the production database is connected to a user account. A particular mailbox GUID can only be assigned to one account at a time. Therefore, to successfully perform a database recovery in the production forest, you would have to delete all user mailboxes from the original database first. This is accomplished implicitly when you remove the destroyed production server from the Exchange organization in Active Directory.

Note If you want to perform database recovery operations while the original production server is available and users are connected to their mailboxes, you must install Exchange 2000 Server in a different forest. It is generally not advisable to perform recovery operations in the production forest. Recovering databases to a different production server is a last resort if you cannot bring back the original server.

Restoring Databases to a Different Server

If the old machine is out of order and a new system is not immediately available, you will be forced to recover the databases onto a different existing production Exchange 2000 server. Restoring to a different server introduces a number of critical issues. For instance, all users will need to update their MAPI profiles manually to connect to their new home server, which may generate many user help desk calls. The configuration of the Exchange transport service was covered in Chapter 8, "Microsoft Outlook 2000 Deployment."

When recovering to a different production server, the following issues are critical:

- Before restoring databases to a different server, original mailbox references of affected users must be deleted. After the restoration, user accounts must be reconnected to the restored mailboxes using Exchange System Manager or the Mailbox Reconnect utility (MBCONN.EXE). You can find MBCONN.EXE on the Exchange 2000 Server CD in the \Support\Utils\i386 directory.

- Client-based MAPI profiles must be updated manually to direct Outlook 2000 to the new home server. You may need to create entirely new profiles to remove cached information that still points to the old server.

- Databases restored to a different server require new database GUIDs. You need to select the This Database Can Be Overwritten By A Restore check box for all those databases that you intend to recover. This causes the Information Store to patch the databases and assign new database GUIDs.

- Public stores are associated with public folder hierarchies. It is not possible to restore a public store to a server that already has a store with a different name for the same hierarchy. Stores with the same storage group and store names would be overwritten, which may lead to lost public folders.

- Stores contain several system mailboxes that are server specific and cannot be reconnected. These mailboxes need to be purged from the databases.

- The target Exchange 2000 server must belong to the same organization and administrative group as the old server.

- The target Exchange 2000 server cannot contain databases with duplicate physical names. Database filenames must be unique across all storage groups. For instance, the default mailbox store databases are always called PRIV1.EDB and PRIV1.STM. Therefore, use different names for the new database files. It is not necessary to keep the original database filenames unless you are restoring offline backups. (In this case you need to rename the existing databases. Renaming database filenames will temporarily dismount the affected store.)

- The target Exchange 2000 server must not contain databases with duplicate logical names (that is, storage group and store name). Otherwise, existing databases will be overwritten. To rename existing storage groups or stores, right-click on the corresponding items in Exchange System Manager, and then choose Rename. (Renaming a storage group or store will not disconnect the users.)

- When removing the first server in the administrative group by manually deleting its reference from the organization and then not restoring public stores, you will lose system folders, such as the offline address book containers and Schedule+ Free/Busy information. You will have to relocate these folders to another server in the administrative group, as discussed in Chapter 18, "Public Folder Replication." Users should start Outlook 2000 with /CleanFreeBusy option (Outlook /CleanFreeBusy) to update the current free and busy information for existing appointments.

- You need to create storage groups and databases on the target server using the same names as on the original server. For instance, to restore the default mailbox store from BLUESKY-SRV2 to BLUESKY-SRV1, you will have to create a database called Mailbox Store (BLUESKY-SRV2) in the First Storage Group on BLUESKY-SRV1.

- You should perform a full backup of the entire system before and after the restoration. Make sure Active Directory information is backed up as well.

Exercise 8: Restoring a Database to a Different Server

In this exercise you will restore a mailbox store to the last remaining Exchange 2000 server in your organization. You will permanently remove BLUESKY-SRV2 from the test environment.

To view a multimedia demonstration that displays how to perform this procedure, run the EX8CH20*.AVI files from the \Exercise_Information\Chapter20 folder on the Supplemental Course Materials CD.

Prerequisites

- Complete at least Exercise 5, earlier in this chapter.

- Reboot BLUESKY-SRV1 and BLUESKY-WKSTA, and then log on to these machines as Administrator.

- Shut down BLUESKY-SRV2 to simulate a destroyed server. This Exchange 2000 server must not be switched on again.

▶ **To restore a database to a different Exchange 2000 server**

1. On BLUESKY-WKSTA, try to launch Outlook 2000, and verify that you cannot connect to your mailbox because the server was destroyed.

2. On BLUESKY-SRV1, launch Exchange System Manager, and expand all administrative groups and servers.

3. Right-click BLUESKY-SRV2, point to All Tasks, and select Remove Server.

4. In the Exchange System Manager dialog box informing you that this step will cause loss of mailbox and public folder data, click Yes.

5. After a few minutes, right-click Servers, and select Refresh. Make sure that BLUESKY-SRV2 was deleted successfully, then right-click BLUESKY-SRV1, point to New, and select Storage Group.

6. In the Name text box, type **Management Group**, and then click OK.

7. Right-click Management Group, point to New, and select Mailbox Store.

8. In the Name text box, type **VIP Mailboxes**, and then click on the Database tab.

9. Select the Do Not Mount This Store At Start-Up and This Database Can Be Overwritten By A Restore check boxes (see Figure 20.15). (Selecting the Do Not Mount This Store At Start-Up check box disables the automatic mounting of the database on service startup.)

10. Click OK, and in the VIP Mailboxes dialog box informing you that the store was created successfully, click No to avoid mounting this store.

11. Launch the Windows 2000 Backup utility, click on the Restore tab, right-click File, and select Catalog File.

12. In the Backup File Name dialog box, under Catalog Backup File, verify that D:\Bluesky-Srv2.bkf is displayed, and then click OK.

13. Expand the nodes that correspond the to the backup media, expand the node BLUESKY-SRV2\Microsoft Information Store\Management Group, click OK in the Backup File Name dialog box, and then select the Log Files and VIP Mailboxes check boxes. Click Start Restore.

14. In the Restoring Database Store dialog box, under Restore To, type **bluesky-srv1**. Under Temporary Location For Log And Patch Files, type **c:\winnt\temp**. Select the Last Backup Set and Mount Database After Restore check boxes, and then click OK (see Figure 20.15).

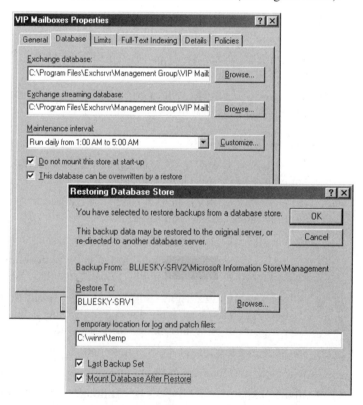

Figure 20.15   Restoring a database to a different server

15. In the Enter Backup File Name dialog box, make sure d:\bluesky-srv2.bkf is specified, and click OK again.

16. After Backup completes, in the Restore Progress dialog box, click Close, and then close the Backup utility.

17. Switch back to Exchange System Manager, expand Management Group, expand VIP Mailboxes (if the store is marked as dismounted, right-click on it, and select Refresh), and then select Mailboxes.

18. Notice that the Administrator mailbox is not marked as deleted. Right-click Mailboxes and select Run Cleanup Agent to update the mailbox information. At this point the Administrator mailbox should be marked with a red cross as deleted.

19. Right-click Administrator and select Reconnect.

20. In the Select A New User For This Mailbox dialog box, double-click Administrator. In the Reconnect dialog box informing you that the operation was performed successfully, click OK.

21. If an Exchange System Manager dialog box appears informing you that the object has not been replicated to the destination server yet, click OK.

22. Wait for the Recipient Update Service to assign the Administrator account valid e-mail addresses. Launch Active Directory Users and Computers, double-click the Administrator account, click on the E-Mail Addresses tab, and verify that e-mail addresses are assigned. Click OK.

23. Switch back to Exchange System Manager, right-click Mailboxes again, and select Run Cleanup Agent. Notice that the mailbox is now reactivated.

24. Right-click the system mailboxes that have been marked as deleted one at a time, select Purge, and in the dialog boxes asking you whether you are sure, click OK to remove these mailboxes.

25. On BLUESKY-WKSTA, on the desktop, right-click Outlook 2000, and then select Properties.

26. In the CIW Generated Profile Properties dialog box, click Show Profiles, and then delete all existing profiles by clicking on the Remove button. In the Microsoft Outlook dialog box asking you whether you are sure, click Yes.

27. Make sure that no profiles are listed and then click Close.

28. On the desktop, double-click Microsoft Outlook.

29. In the Microsoft Outlook Setup Wizard dialog box, select the Microsoft Exchange Server check box, and then click Next.

30. In the second Microsoft Outlook Setup Wizard screen, under Microsoft Exchange Server, type **bluesky-srv1**. Make sure Administrator is displayed under Mailbox, and then click Next.

31. In the next wizard screen, make sure No is selected under Do You Travel With This Computer, and then click Next.

32. In the final Microsoft Outlook Setup Wizard screen, click Finish. Verify that you can successfully connect to the Administrator mailbox.

Exercise Summary

It is possible to restore databases to a different server in the same organization and administrative group. This recovery strategy should only be used as a last resort if the original production server cannot be restored and must be removed from the Exchange organization. You need to create storage groups and databases on the target server that use the same name as the original resources. For all databases that you intend to restore, select the This Database Can Be Overwritten By A Restore check box. Restoring to a different server requires working with the Information Store and Active Directory. You will need to reconnect the users to their restored mailboxes and update MAPI-based client profiles.

High-Speed Recovery with Delayed Restore

Restoring databases directly to the production server implies that users cannot work with their mailboxes during the restoration. The larger the databases, the longer the interruption of business processes. A sophisticated recovery strategy with delayed restore operations can help to minimize system downtime.

The basic idea behind delayed restores is to recover the system very quickly with empty databases first, then restore the databases to another server, and use recovery utilities, such as the Microsoft Exchange Mailbox Merge Wizard, to extract the messages from the recovery server and play them back into the production system. Outlook 2000 initializes new production mailboxes automatically based on mailbox-enabled user account information (see Exercise 1 of Chapter 13, "Creating and Managing Recipients"). Your users will be able to work with their mailboxes right away. Messages and data are restored later.

Note Because Outlook 2000 initializes new mailboxes in new and empty databases, users cannot continue to work with existing offline folder stores. It is required to disable offline folders and reconfigure them using a new .ost file. The configuration of offline folders and the offline folder synchronization are covered in Chapter 9, "MAPI-Based Clients."

Preparing the Recovery Server

Most important, your recovery server must not become part of your production Active Directory forest. As explained earlier, it is impossible to reconnect duplicated mailboxes to user accounts, which effectively prevents access to the restored data. Mailboxes must be unique in the forest. Consequently, it is vital to install the recovery server in a separate forest and reconnect restored mailboxes to recovery accounts.

Consider the following issues when setting up the recovery system:

1. Install Windows 2000 Server and promote the server to a domain controller in the recovery forest. Be sure to use names that are different from those in your production environment. During the domain controller promotion, install and configure the Windows 2000 DNS, but do not configure the Dynamic Host Configuration Protocol (DHCP) to avoid interference with the production environment.

2. Set up Exchange 2000 Server using the organization and administrative group names of the production system. If these names do not match, databases cannot be mounted.

3. Manually create storage groups and stores using the original names. The actual database filenames and log file prefixes, however, do not need to match. The names of storage groups and stores will be listed in your backup sets. You need to dismount the newly created databases and select the This Database Can Be Overwritten By A Restore check box.

4. Ensure that the LegacyExchangeDN information matches its counterpart in the production environment.

Correcting LegacyExchangeDN Values

Most Exchange 2000 Server directory objects have a LegacyExchangeDN attribute, which is used to identify items in a way that is compatible with Exchange Server 5.5. As its name implies, this attribute refers to the legacy distinguished name (DN) in the form of /O=<organization>/OU=<site>/ CN=<container>/CN=<sub-container>/CN=<object>.

When you upgrade to Exchange 2000 Server, the LegacyExchangeDN will be derived from the existing organization and site names. Installing Exchange 2000 Server without upgrading, on the other hand, results in a LegacyExchangeDN containing the new organization name and administrative group name, such as /O=Blue Sky Airlines/OU=First Administrative Group. Consequently, the LegacyExchangeDN values may not match if the original server was upgraded from Exchange Server 5.5 while the recovery system was directly installed, or the recovery server was installed in an administrative group with a different name.

Unfortunately, it is not possible to specify an administrative group name during the installation of the first server in a forest. The first sever will always be installed in First Administrative Group. Renaming administrative groups in Exchange System Manager does not change the LegacyExchangeDN information. The best idea for solving this naming issue is to install Exchange Server 5.5 using the original organization and site names on the recovery system first, and then upgrade the installation to Exchange 2000 Server. Another option is to install a first Exchange 2000 server in First Administrative Group, create an additional administrative group with the correct name, and then install the actual recovery server into this group.

You can also use LDIFDE to export the Exchange 2000 Server objects from the Configuration naming context in Active Directory, then edit the export file to correct the LegacyExchangeDN values, and then import this file to update the directory objects. The following command line exports all objects with a LegacyExchangeDN value that starts with "/O=Blue Sky Airlines/OU=First Administrative Group": ldifde -f c:\export.ldf -p Subtree -l legacyExchangeDN -s Bluesky-srv1 -r "(legacyExchangeDN= /O=Blue Sky Airlines/OU=First Administrative Group*)" -d "CN=Microsoft Exchange, CN=Services,CN=Configuration,DC=BlueSky-inc-10,DC=com".

An import file that changes "/O=Blue Sky Airlines/OU=First Administrative Group" to "/O=Blue Sky Airlines/OU=Exchange 55 Site Name" would have the following format (changes are in boldface):

```
dn: CN=First Administrative Group,CN=Administrative Groups,CN=Blue Sky
Airlines,CN=Microsoft  Exchange,CN=Services,CN=Configuration,DC=BlueSky-
inc-10,DC=com
```

```
changetype: modify
```

```
replace: legacyExchangeDN
```

```
legacyExchangeDN: /o=Blue Sky Airlines/ou=Exchange 55 Site Name
```

You can read more about LDIFDE in Chapter 13, "Creating and Managing Recipients."

Reconnecting Mailboxes

A properly prepared recovery server allows you to restore and mount databases from the production system. The mailboxes will be disconnected because the original user accounts do not exist. You will have to create new accounts in the recovery forest and reconnect the mailboxes. It is possible to use Active Directory Users and Computers as well as Exchange System Manager for this purpose, but reconnecting numerous users calls for a different approach. Bulk operations in Active Directory are best performed using the LDIFDE utility. You can use this tool to export organizational units (OUs) and user accounts from the production environment, then edit the export file to adjust the domain name information, and then use LDIFDE again to import the information into the recovery forest.

Another, perhaps easier way is to use the Mailbox Reconnect utility (MBCONN.EXE), which allows you to generate an .ldf file based on information from the restored mailbox stores. This .ldf file will contain all it needs to create the required user accounts using LDIFDE. You may want to edit this file to remove accounts for system mailboxes before importing the information into the recovery forest. As soon as the user accounts exist, you can reconnect them to their mailboxes with the Mailbox Reconnect utility. You can find further information in the MBCONN.CHM file, which is on the Exchange 2000 Server CD in the \Support\Utils\i386 directory.

Data Retrieval and Playback

It is not possible to reconnect multiple mailboxes to a single account. You have two options: You can either work with individual accounts to extract the data from each mailbox separately, or you can give your administrator account the permission to open all mailboxes simultaneously. To gain full permissions over all mailboxes in a store, display the store's property sheets in Exchange System Manager, click on the Security tab, and grant your account full mailbox permissions including Receive As and Send As. Administrators have inherited implicit denials for Receive As and Send As (as indicated by grayed checkmarks), but you can override those denials by granting yourself explicit permissions. You need full permissions on the recovery and production stores.

Note Members of the Domain Admins or Enterprise Admins group inherit default denials for Receive As and Send As permissions to prevent automatic access to user mailboxes. You need to grant your administrator account explicit permissions at the store level to override the defaults. Accounts that are not members of these groups can gain access to all mailboxes if you add them to the Exchange Domain Servers group.

With full access permissions including Receive As and Send As, it is easy to extract and play back user data. You may use Outlook 2000 to log on to one mailbox at a time, download the folders and messages in a personal folder store (.pst), and then log on to the production system to restore the data from the .pst file. The configuration of .pst files was covered in Chapter 9, "MAPI-Based Clients."

To retrieve and restore data from numerous mailboxes, use the Microsoft Exchange Mailbox Merge Wizard (EXMERGE.EXE), also known as Exmerge. You can find Exmerge on the Exchange 2000 Server CD in the \Support\Utils\ i386\Exmerge directory. You need to copy the files to the c:\Program Files\ Exchsrvr\Bin directory because Exmerge requires several DLLs that come with Exchange System Manager. For detailed information about Exmerge, read the documentation available in the \Support\Utils\i386\Exmerge directory.

Note Essentially, Exmerge is a MAPI-based client that copies messages from mailboxes into .pst files and then imports the data into target mailboxes. Exmerge supports scheduled batch-mode operations. This allows you to use this utility as a mailbox-level backup agent to save single mailbox data to .pst files.

Exercise 9: Performing a High-Speed Recovery with Delayed Restore

In this exercise you will assume a damaged database on an Exchange 2000 server. You will recover the information store with minimum downtime, restore the database to a recovery server, and then use available recovery tools to play back user data.

This exercise is very time consuming. It may require several hours to complete. If you don't have the time or patience to work through this 83-step procedure, you may skip it and view the multimedia demonstration instead. It is also a good idea to display the demonstration before engaging in the task of completing the exercise yourself. Launch the EX9CH20*.AVI files, which you can install on your computer by running the self-extracting executable from the \Exercise_Information\Chapter20 folder on the Supplemental Course Materials CD-ROM.

Prerequisites

- Install Windows 2000 Server with Service Pack 1 on BLUESKY-SRV2 as outlined in the "Getting Started" section of "About This Book," but do not promote this server to a domain controller, and do not add it to the domain. Install this server in a workgroup called WORKGROUP.

Note Recovery servers must not be added to the production Active Directory forest.

- Complete Exercise 8 (the Administrator mailbox resides on BLUESKY-SRV1 in the Management Group/VIP Mailboxes store).
- Log on as Administrator to BLUESKY-SRV1.
- Log on as Carl Titmouse to BLUESKY-WKSTA.
- You will need the Windows 2000 Server, Windows 2000 Service Pack 1, and Exchange 2000 Server Enterprise Edition installation CDs.

▶ **To recover user data using the Mailbox Reconnect and Mailbox Merge utilities**

1. At this point, you have installed Windows 2000 Server and Service Pack 1 on BLUESKY-SRV2. Log on as Administrator to BLUESKY-SRV2, and close the Windows 2000 Configure Your Server application that is launched automatically.

2. Click Start, then click Run. In the Run dialog box, type **dcpromo**, and then click OK to start the Active Directory Installation Wizard.

3. On the first wizard screen click Next. On the Domain Controller Type wizard screen, accept the default selection Domain Controller For A New Domain, and then click Next again.

4. On the Create Tree Or Child Domain wizard screen, accept the default selection Create A New Domain Tree, and then click Next.

5. On the Create Or Join Forest wizard screen, accept the default selection Create A New Forest Of Domain Trees, and then click Next.

6. On the New Domain Name wizard screen, under Full DNS Name For New Domain, type **BlueSky-Recovery.com** (see Figure 20.16), and then click Next.

7. On the NetBIOS Domain Name wizard screen, under Domain NetBIOS Name, verify that BLUESKY-RECOVER is displayed, and then click Next.

8. On the Database And Log Locations wizard screen, accept the default settings, and then click Next. On the Shared System Volume wizard screen, click Next.

9. A dialog box will be displayed informing you that a DNS server could not be contacted. Click OK.

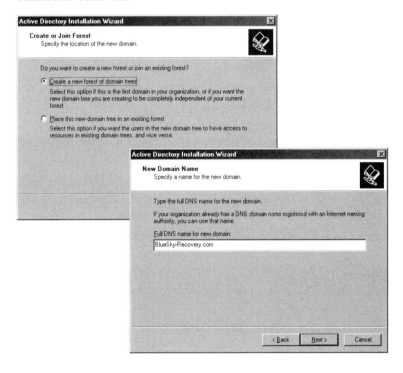

Figure 20.16   Creating a recovery forest in Active Directory

10. On the Configure DNS wizard screen, accept Yes, Install And Configure DNS On This Computer (Recommended), and then click Next. It is not advisable to integrate the recovery system with the product DNS environment.

11. On the Permissions wizard screen, accept the default setting, and click Next.

12. On the Directory Services Restore Mode Administrator Password wizard screen, under Password and Confirm Password, type **password**, and then click Next.

13. On the Summary wizard screen, verify the settings, and then click Next to start the configuration of Active Directory.

14. If an Insert Disk dialog box appears prompting you for the Service Pack 1 CD, insert the CD into the CD-ROM drive, and then click OK.

15. If a Files Needed dialog box is displayed, make sure the E:\i386 directory is selected under Copy Files From, and then click OK.

16. When the Insert Disk dialog box appears again prompting you this time for the Windows 2000 Server CD, insert the CD into the CD-ROM drive, and then click OK.

17. On the final wizard screen, click Finish to complete the configuration procedure. A dialog box will be displayed, prompting you to restart the computer. Click Restart Now.

18. When BLUESKY-SRV2 is rebooted, log on as Administrator again, insert the Exchange 2000 Server, Enterprise Edition installation CD into the CD-ROM drive, and then launch Setup from the \Setup\i386 directory.

19. On the Welcome wizard screen, click Next, accept the license agreement on the End-User License Agreement wizard screen, and click Next. Type your CD Key on the Product Information wizard screen, and click Next.

20. On the Component Selection wizard screen, verify that Typical is displayed under Action for Microsoft Exchange 2000, and then click Next.

21. On the Component Selection wizard screen, accept the default setting Create A New Exchange Organization, and then click Next.

22. On the Organization Name wizard screen, under Organization Name, type **Blue Sky Airlines** (the name must match the configuration of the production organization), and then click Next.

23. On the License Agreement wizard screen, select I Agree That and then click Next.

24. On the Component Summary wizard screen, click Next to start the installation. When a Microsoft Exchange 2000 Installation Wizard dialog box appears, informing you that the domain has been identified as an insecure domain, click OK.

25. On the final wizard screen, click Finish.

26. On BLUESKY-SRV1, perform a full online backup of the entire Microsoft Information Store using Windows 2000 Backup, as illustrated in Exercise 5, earlier in this lesson. Specify D:\BLUESKY-SRV1.BKF as the backup filename.

27. On BLUESKY-WKSTA, launch Outlook 2000, and make sure you are working with the mailbox of Carl Titmouse.

28. On the toolbar, click New, click To, select Carl Titmouse, click To ->, and then click OK to address the message to Carl's mailbox.

29. In the Subject line, type **Exmerge Recovery Test Message**.

30. In the Message Body type **This message was not included in the most recent full backup of BLUESKY-SRV1**.

31. Click Send and verify that the test message was received. Leave Outlook 2000 running.

32. On BLUESKY-SRV1, launch Exchange System Manager, expand the First Administrative Group and the server object BLUESKY-SRV1, then expand First Storage Group, right-click Mailbox Store (BLUESKY-SRV1), and select Dismount Store.

33. In the Mailbox Store (BLUESKY-SRV1) dialog box informing you that the store will be inaccessible, click Yes.

34. Right-click Mailbox Store (BLUESKY-SRV1) again, select Properties, click on the Database tab, and check the path to and the names of the database files (such as, C:\Program Files\Exchsrvr\Mdbdata\MAILBOX STORE (BLUESKY-SRV1).EDB). Click Cancel.

35. At this point it is assumed that the database files have been corrupted—and that it would take an extended period of time to restore them. Launch Windows Explorer, open the \Program Files\Exchsrvr\Mdbdata directory, and move the database files (such as, MAILBOX STORE (BLUESKY-SRV1).EDB and MAILBOX STORE (BLUESKY-SRV1).STM) to the C:\Winnt\Temp directory. (If you are working with a fresh installation of Exchange 2000 Server, your database files are called PRIV1.EDB and PRIV1.STM.)

Note   Do not delete damaged databases before the restore process has been finished successfully. Corrupted backup media will prevent a successful data restoration. In this situation, repairing the damaged databases using ESEUTIL.EXE may be the only rescue.

---

36. Launch Windows 2000 Backup again to perform an incremental backup of the entire Microsoft Information Store. Specify D:\BLUESKY-SRV1-INC.BKF as the backup filename, click Start Backup, then click Advanced, and select Incremental under Backup Type. Click OK, then Start Backup. Backup will

complete without errors because the nonexisting databases of the Mailbox Store (BLUESKY-SRV1) are not included in the backup; however, the current transaction logs are saved.

37. Switch to Exchange System Manager, right-click Mailbox Store (BLUESKY-SRV1), and select Mount Store.

38. A Mailbox Store (BLUESKY-SRV1) dialog box will appear informing you that at least one of this store's database files is missing. Click Yes to force the creation of an empty database (see Figure 20.17).

39. In the Mailbox Store (BLUESKY-SRV1) dialog box informing you that the store was mounted successfully, click OK.

Important   At this point, you should perform another full backup of this information store because you will not be able to restore any former backups successfully without manually deleting all files of this storage group beforehand.

---

40. On BLUESKY-WKSTA, try to work with Outlook 2000. Outlook will not be able to work with Exchange 2000 Server. Restart Outlook 2000; a Microsoft Outlook dialog box will appear, asking you to recreate the shortcuts. Click

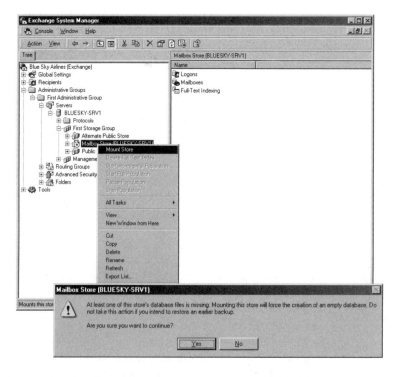

Figure 20.17   Forcing the creation of an empty database

Yes. Notice that the mailbox is empty, but Carl Titmouse can continue to send and receive messages or access public folders.

Important   Outlook users cannot continue to use existing offline folders with newly created mailboxes. The offline folder configuration must be disabled and re-enabled, thus creating a new offline folder store (.ost file). The configuration of .ost files is covered in Chapter 9, "MAPI-Based Clients."

---

41. On BLUESKY-SRV2, launch Exchange System Manager, expand Servers, and then BLUESKY-SRV2. Right-click First Storage Group, and then select Rename. Change the name to Standard Storage Group.

42. Right-click BLUESKY-SRV2, point to New, and select Storage Group.

43. In the Properties dialog box, under Name, type **First Storage Group**, and then click OK.

44. Right-click First Storage Group, point to New, and select Mailbox Store.

45. In the Properties dialog box, under Name, type **Mailbox Store (BLUESKY-SRV1)**.

46. Click on the Database tab and select the This Database Can Be Overwritten By A Restore check box, then click OK.

47. In the Mailbox Store (BLUESKY-SRV1) dialog box asking you whether you want to mount this store now, click No.

48. Launch Windows 2000 Backup and restore the database of the Mailbox Store (BLUESKY-SRV1) and log files from the backup catalog \\BLUESKY-SRV1\D$\BLUESKY-SRV1.BKF to BLUESKY-SRV2, as outlined in Exercise 8. Make sure BLUESKY-SRV2 is displayed (without any backslashes) under Restore To in the Restoring Database Store dialog box and do not yet select the Last Backup Set check box.

49. In a second cycle, restore the log files from the incremental backup (catalog file \\BLUESKY-SRV1\D$\BLUESKY-SRV1-INC.BKF) to BLUESKY-SRV2. This time select both the Last Backup Set and Mount Database After Restore check boxes.

Note   Although BLUESKY-SRV1 and BLUESKY-SRV2 are domain controllers in different Active Directory forests, the Administrator account has the same password in both domains. Therefore, file-based access over the network works without being prompted for user credentials.

---

50. Switch back to Exchange System Manager, open First Storage Group, and verify that the Mailbox Store (BLUESKY-SRV1) is displayed as mounted (you may need to right-click First Storage Group and select Refresh).

51. Expand Mailbox Store (BLUESKY-SRV1), select Mailboxes, and notice the mailbox resources in the details pane.

52. Right-click Mailboxes, and then select Run Cleanup Agent. Notice that most mailboxes are now displayed with a red cross to indicate that they are not connected to user accounts (see Figure 20.18).

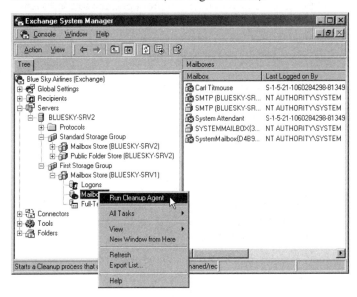

Figure 20.18   A recovered mailbox store with disconnected mailboxes

53. From the \Support\Utils\i386 directory on the Exchange 2000 Server CD, launch the MBCONN.EXE utility. The Mailbox Reconnect utility attempts to write a log file to the local directory; because it's being launched from a CD, this will fail. In the Mailbox Reconnect dialog box, click OK. In the Save As dialog box, click Cancel. In the second Mailbox Reconnect dialog box asking if you are sure that you do not want the log file to be generated, click Yes.

54. Click Next on the Welcome wizard screen.

55. On the Connect To Exchange Server wizard screen, under Exchange Server, type **bluesky-srv2**, and then click Next. Because BLUESKY-SRV2 is a domain controller, you do not need to specify a domain controller explicitly.

56. On the Select Database wizard screen, select Mailbox Store (BLUESKY-SRV1), and then click Finish.

57. A number of disconnected mailboxes will be listed in the Mailbox Reconnect utility (see Figure 20.19). Open the Actions menu and select Export Users.

58. In the Export Users To LDF File dialog box, click on the button that is labeled with '…' (which you can find to the right side of Container), expand BlueSky-Recovery, select the Users container, and then click OK.

59. Under File Name type **c:\import.ldf**, and then click Generate.

60. In the Mailbox Reconnect dialog box informing you that the users have been exported, click OK.

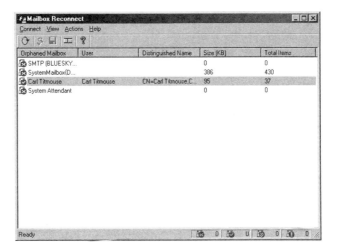

Figure 20.19   Reconnecting restored mailboxes using the Mailbox Reconnect utility

61. Click Start, click Run, and in the Run dialog box, type **cmd**. Click OK.

62. At the command prompt, type **notepad c:\import.ldf**, and then press ENTER.

63. Delete the entries of system mailboxes, save the changes, and then close Notepad. The following is an example IMPORT.LDF file:

```
dn: CN=Carl Titmouse,CN=Users,DC=BlueSky-Recovery,DC=com

changetype: add

UserAccountControl: 66048

displayName: Carl Titmouse

cn: Carl Titmouse

objectclass: user

samAccountName: CarlTitmouse

givenName: Carl

sn: Titmouse
```

64. At the command prompt, type **ldifde -i -f c:\import.ldf -s bluesky-srv2**, and then press ENTER. Verify that the command completes successfully.

65. Switch back to the Mailbox Reconnect utility, open the Actions menu, and select Preview All. In the Browse For Container dialog box, select the Users container, and click OK.

66. Verify that Carl Titmouse is displayed as a mailbox-enabled account (see Figure 20.19). Switch back to the Exchange System Manager, right-click Carl Titmouse, and then select Reconnect.

67. In the Select A New User For This Mailbox dialog box, double-click Carl Titmouse. In the Reconnect dialog box informing you that the operation was completed successfully, click OK again.

68. If an Exchange System Manager dialog box appears informing you that the object has not been replicated to the destination server yet, click OK.

69. Wait for the Recipient Update Service to assign the account of Carl Titmouse valid e-mail addresses. Launch Active Directory Users and Computers, double-click the account of Carl Titmouse, click on the E-Mail Addresses tab, and verify that e-mail addresses are assigned. Click OK.

70. Switch back to Exchange System Manager, right-click Mailboxes again, and select Run Cleanup Agent. Notice that the mailbox is now reactivated.

71. Now that you have reconnected the mailbox of Carl Titmouse to a newly created user account, you need to grant the Administrator additional permissions to open this mailbox. In Exchange System Manager, right-click Mailbox Store (BLUESKY-SRV1). Select Properties, click on the Security tab, and make sure the Administrator account is selected. Under Permissions, select the Receive As and Send As check boxes. Click OK and repeat these steps on BLUESKY-SRV1 because these access rights are required on both servers.

72. On BLUESKY-SRV2, copy all files from the \Support\Utils\i386\Exmerge directory on the Exchange 2000 Server CD to the \Program Files\ Exchsrvr\Bin directory, and then launch EXMERGE.EXE from this location.

73. On the Microsoft Exchange Mailbox Merge Wizard Welcome screen, click Next.

74. On the Procedure Selection wizard screen, select Extract And Import (One Step Procedure), and then click Next.

75. On the Source Server wizard screen, under Microsoft Exchange Server Name, type **bluesky-srv2**, and then click Next. (You may click Options if you want to explore the capabilities of the Mailbox Merge utility.)

76. On the Destination Server wizard screen, under both Microsoft Exchange Server Name and Microsoft Windows 2000 Domain Controller (DC) Name, type **bluesky-srv1**. Under Port Number For LDAP Queries, type **389**, and then click Next.

77. On the Database Selection wizard screen, select the First Storage Group/Mailbox Store (BLUESKY-SRV1) check box, and then click Next (see Figure 20.20).

78. On the Mailbox Selection wizard screen, select the mailbox of Carl Titmouse, and click Next. (If you need to work with numerous mailboxes, you may find the Select All button useful.)

79. On the Locale Selection wizard screen, accept the defaults, and click Next.

80. On the Target Directory wizard screen, make sure the \Exmergedata directory is located on a drive with sufficient capacity, and then click Next.

81. On the Save Settings wizard screen, click Next.

82. The Microsoft Exchange Mailbox Merge Wizard will now move existing messages into Carl Titmouse's mailbox on BLUESKY-SRV1. When this process completes, click Finish.

83. On BLUESKY-WKSTA, verify that all messages have been restored including the Exmerge Recovery Test Message (see Figure 20.20).

Figure 20.20   Performing a delayed restore using the Exchange Mailbox Merge Wizard

Exercise Summary

Following a successful restore of databases to a recovery server outside the production forest, you need to reconnect the mailboxes that you are interested in to newly created user accounts. If the number of mailboxes is small (for instance, if you want to recover only a single mailbox or even just a few messages from a single mailbox), you can work with Active Directory Users and Computers and Exchange System Manager. For numerous mailboxes, on the other hand, use the

Mailbox Reconnect utility to generate an .ldf import file, and then use LDIFDE to create the required user accounts in the recovery forest. After that, it is easy to reconnect the mailboxes. Next, grant your account Receive As and Send As permissions on the production and recovery stores to open all mailboxes using your account, and then use the Exchange Mailbox Merge Wizard to play back the data from the recovery server to the production systems. Outlook users do not need to disconnect from their mailboxes during that time. Their mailboxes can be filled in the background while they continue to send and receive messages.

Chapter Summary

Exchange 2000 Server utilizes the features of the ESE for its database repositories. Transaction logging and other database features turn Exchange 2000 Server into an extremely reliable platform. Even if databases are lost, transaction logs can help to recover all data, including messages not saved in previous backups. With deleted items retention, it might not even be necessary to work with backups to restore accidentally deleted messages or mailboxes. Reconnecting mailboxes to user accounts can be as easy as a few mouse clicks in Exchange System Manager.

Using Exchange System Manager, you can configure system monitors and automatic notifications to keep you constantly informed about the health of your systems. If a server enters a warning or critical state (for instance, because it is running out of disk space), LSI propagates the news to all servers in the organization. A monitoring server may then send you an e-mail message or launch a script to take action.

It is generally advisable to keep sufficient disk space available on database drives for maintenance routines, such as database compaction using ESEUTIL.EXE. By default, transaction log files are not deleted automatically and may fill your drives to capacity. Use full or incremental backups to purge transaction log files. Turn on circular logging only for storage groups that contain less important data, such as newsgroups. Circular logging purges and overwrites previous transactions as soon as they have been committed to the databases, which prevents sophisticated backup and restore procedures.

It is vital to test backup media and restoration methods periodically on a reference system with sufficient disk capacity. The reference server must not be part of your production Active Directory forest. To restore databases online, the corresponding Exchange 2000 Server services must be running, but the databases must be dismounted. Restoring a database does not affect other stores. Unaffected users can continue their work. It is even possible to back up one database while restoring another. You should always include all databases of a single storage group in one backup set. Multiple storage groups may be backed up or restored using multiple sessions simultaneously. To back up Exchange 2000 Server databases, use an Exchange 2000 Server–enabled backup program, such as the extended Windows 2000 Backup utility.

Review

The following review questions can help you determine if you have sufficiently familiarized yourself with the material covered in this chapter. You can find the answers to these questions at the end of this book in Appendix A, "Questions and Answers."

1. A Windows 2000 Server administrator informs you that several user accounts were deleted accidentally from the domain. New accounts have been created, but the users cannot connect to their former mailboxes. How can you provide these users with their messages most quickly?

2. You are the administrator of a complex Exchange 2000 Server organization with multiple administrative and routing groups. You plan to use server monitoring extensively to ensure prompt system maintenance according to service-level agreements. For this purpose, you are configuring system monitors and e-mail notifications. You need to specify a monitoring server. Where should the monitoring server be located?

3. A user informs you that messages must have been lost because they were apparently not delivered to specified recipients. How can you verify that all messages reached their intended addressees?

4. What Exchange 2000 Server databases can be included in online backups?

5. Which files types does ESE utilize in addition to the actual database files?

6. The following event was written to your application event log: "The database 'First Storage Group\Mailbox Store (BLUESKY-SRV1)' has 821 megabytes

of free space after online defragmentation has terminated." How can you recover the disk space unnecessarily consumed by the database?

7. What is the difference between an incremental and a differential backup?

8. You have restored a full and several incremental database backups, but you have forgotten to select the Last Backup Set check box during the last restore operation. How can you complete the database restoration?

9. What is the purpose of the Setup /DisasterRecovery switch?

10. Why do you have to install recovery servers in different Active Directory forests than the production systems?

C H A P T E R   2 1

Microsoft Outlook Forms Environment

About This Chapter

Electronic forms, similar to paper-based forms, are useful for gathering and providing information in a structured way. They contain fields to enter or display data, which are associated with object attributes that hold the actual information in e-mail items. Electronic forms are a key element for rapid deployment of sophisticated and cost-effective workgroup and workflow solutions.

Microsoft Outlook 2000 takes advantage of electronic forms in many ways. Whether you send messages, manage contacts, or handle appointments or tasks, you work with electronic forms. Each item is registered with its corresponding form, which lets Outlook display the information in the correct format. Based on object attributes, you can create views, filters, and rules to structure and process information. You don't need any programming skills to design forms, but you can add Visual Basic Scripting Edition (VBScript) code to implement advanced features.

This chapter covers the development, installation, and use of Outlook forms and related workgroup solutions at a basic level. For detailed information on how to work with Outlook 2000 forms programmatically, see the *Microsoft Office 2000 Visual Basic Programmer's Guide*.

Before You Begin

To complete this chapter:

- Prepare server BLUESKY-SRV1 and workstation BLUESKY-WKSTA according to the descriptions given in the "Getting Started" section of "About This Book."
- Be familiar with the standard modules of Outlook 2000 and the concepts of working with Messaging Application Programming Interface (MAPI)-based clients in a workgroup environment.

Lesson 1: Electronic Forms Applications

It is remarkably easy to implement sophisticated workgroup applications when you start with standard Outlook modules placed in public folders. If you want to achieve special results—for example, if you want to provide unique information—you can customize the standard forms. It is important to note that only Outlook 2000, Microsoft Outlook 98, and Microsoft Outlook 97 users can work with customized Outlook forms.

This lesson briefly introduces the Outlook-based application design environment. After that, it demonstrates how to start designing electronic forms and how to utilize intrinsic features of Outlook 2000.

At the end of this lesson, you will be able to:

- Identify possible elements of Outlook-based workgroup applications.

- Design workgroup solutions based on Outlook forms.

Estimated time to complete this lesson: 45 minutes

Application Design Environment

Outlook-based workgroup applications typically consist of three parts: an electronic form, a folder container (usually a public folder), and the folder design (the view, the filters, and the rules). You use electronic forms to create and display specific items. The folder container stores these objects, and the folder design determines how the contents are presented in Outlook. Folder rules and event sinks help with workflow automation, and public folder replication can distribute the data across the organization, as explained in Chapter 18, "Public Folder Replication."

Views

Outlook 2000 supports a variety of different view types: table, timeline, card, day/week/month, and icon. Table views are the classical view type, consisting only of rows and columns. The items are arranged in rows and the columns determine the attributes to be displayed. A good example is the messages view associated with your Inbox. A timeline view, on the other hand, displays the items in chronological order along with work hour information, which is useful for journaling purposes. The card view shows objects in the form of business cards, as in a card file. Your Contacts folder uses this view type. Day/week/month views, in turn, fit best with calendars and are therefore associated with the Calendar folder. Icon views, finally, present items and files as icons similar to Microsoft Windows Explorer. Consequently, this view type is useful for document libraries.

You can add your own columns to existing views or define new views based on Outlook's standard view types. To define a custom view in Outlook 2000, open the View menu, point to Current View, and then select Define Views. Click New or Copy. When clicking New, you will be prompted for the view type. Furthermore, you can associate your new view with a single folder (This Folder) or with all folders of a particular type (All Mail Folders). When you click OK in the Create A New View dialog box, you will see the View Summary dialog box.

The View Summary dialog box allows you to define the following elements for custom views:

- **Fields.**   To specify the attributes that you want to display in the view.
- **Group By.**   To manage the grouping of items in the view based on object attributes.
- **Sort.**   To sort the items in the view based on object attributes.
- **Filter.**   To display only a subset of all items in the view. For instance, you may configure a filter to display only messages where the originator is the administrator.
- **Other Settings.**   To define the view formatting, enable in-cell editing, activate the AutoPreview feature, and show the Preview Pane.
- **Automatic Formatting.**   To create conditional views that display items that meet certain conditions with specific font formatting.

Folder Home Pages

Folder home pages, also known as Digital Dashboards, allow you to associate Web pages with mailbox or public folders. To define a home page, right-click the desired folder, select Properties, click on the Home Page tab, and specify a URL in the Address text box. It is a good idea to select the Show Home Page By Default For This Folder check box, in addition, to display the Web page automatically when the user selects the folder in Outlook 2000. Otherwise, the user must first open the View menu, and then click the Show Folder Home Page command.

Folder home pages can replace traditional Outlook views. They are far more powerful than folder views because they allow you to display the folder content together with information from other locations, such as databases or Web sites. A folder home page does not even have to display any folder content at all. For instance, it would be possible to create an Exchange Info public folder and associate it with the URL *http://www.microsoft.com/exchange/*. Whenever you select this folder, Microsoft's Web page for Exchange-related product information will be displayed (see Figure 21.1).

Folder home pages are displayed in Microsoft Internet Explorer 5.0, which is shown in the right-hand pane in Outlook. Using Microsoft FrontPage 2000, it is easy to design folder home pages. To view and work with the contents of any mailbox or public folder, add the Microsoft Outlook View Control to your Web page. The Outlook View Control is an ActiveX control that gives your users access to the contents of mailbox and public folders based on standard and custom Outlook views.

Note   Folder home pages can be included in offline folder synchronization to enable offline use. However, home pages based on Active Server Pages (ASP) technology always require interpreting through a Web server.

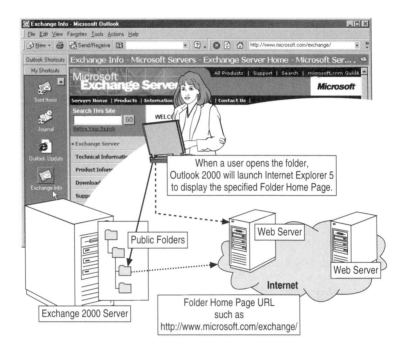

Figure 21.1   A public folder home page displaying information from external sources

Rules

Server-based rules determine the automatic processing of items that meet certain criteria. For public folders, you can define rules without any programming using the Folder Assistant that is available in Outlook 2000. Right-click the desired public folder, select Properties, click on the Administration tab, and then click Folder Assistant. Using folder rules, you can configure message size limits, forward items with specific attributes (such as a specific word in the subject line), or check other information, such as custom properties of Microsoft Office documents. Because Microsoft Exchange 2000 Server is a client/server system, Outlook 2000 is not required to execute folder rules. The client can disconnect completely, but the server still continues to process new items, reply to them, delete them, or perform any other specified actions.

Server-Based Folder Agents

Besides folder rules, Exchange 2000 Server offers far-reaching support for server-side folder processing based on Microsoft Web Storage System events. For backward compatibility, the Exchange Event Service, which is installed during the Exchange 2000 Server setup process and configured for manual startup, is likewise supported. With Exchange 2000 Server, you should give the Web Storage System preference over the Event Service.

Events occur when items are saved or deleted, when a store is mounted or dismounted, or when a specific time interval has elapsed. You can write event sinks for the Web Storage System in scripting languages, such as VBScript or Microsoft JScript, or using any Component Object Model (COM)-compliant development environment, such as Microsoft Visual C++ or Microsoft Visual Basic. The Web Storage System is introduced in Chapter 23, "Microsoft Exchange 2000 Web Storage System."

Exercise 1: Building a Document Management Solution

In this exercise you will use Outlook 2000 to implement a document management application based on a public folder without designing an electronic form. You will configure custom views and folder rules to display and process documents.

To view a multimedia demonstration that displays how to perform this procedure, run the EX1CH21.AVI files from the \Exercise_Information\Chapter21 folder on the Supplemental Course Materials CD.

Prerequisites

- Restart BLUESKY-SRV1 and BLUESKY-WKSTA.
- Log on as Administrator to BLUESKY-WKSTA.

▶ **To implement a basic document management system**

1. On BLUESKY-WKSTA, right-click on the desktop, point to New, and then select WordPad Document (if you have installed Microsoft Word, select Microsoft Word Document instead).

2. Double-click on the newly created NEW WORDPAD DOCUMENT.DOC file to open it in WordPad.

3. Type **Sophisticated document libraries are easily implemented using the standard features of public folders.** Open the File menu, select Save, and then close WordPad.

4. Right-click NEW WORDPAD DOCUMENT.DOC, select Properties, and then click on the Custom tab.

5. Under Name, type **Chapter**, and make sure Text is displayed under Type. Under Value, type **01**, and then click Add.

6. Under Name, type **Section**, and make sure Text is displayed under Type. Under Value, type **A**, click Add, and then click OK to complete the preparation of the document.

7. Start Outlook 2000, open the File menu, point to Folder, and then select New Folder.

8. In the Create New Folder dialog box, under Name, type **User Manual**. Under Folder Contains, make sure Mail Items is selected.

9. Under Select Where To Place The Folder, open the Public Folders tree, then select All Public Folders, and then click OK to close the Create New Folder dialog box.

10. If an Add Shortcut To Outlook Bar dialog box appears, click Yes.

11. On the Outlook toolbar, click My Shortcuts, and then click User Manual to open the folder.

12. Drag NEW WORDPAD DOCUMENT.DOC from the desktop into the User Manual folder. The new item will be displayed in the standard folder view.

13. Open the View menu, point to Current View, and select Define Views to display the Define Views For "User Manual" dialog box.

14. Click New, type **Table of Contents** as the view's name, select Table under Type of View, and then click OK.

15. In the View Summary dialog box, click the Fields button, and remove fields from Show These Fields In This Order until only the Icon, From, and Subject fields appear. Click OK.

16. Click on the Group By button. From the Select Available Fields From list, select User-Defined Fields In Folder. Under Group Items By, select Chapter (see Figure 21.2).

17. Click OK, and then click Sort.

18. Under Select Available Fields From, select User-Defined Fields In Folder. Under Sort Items By, select Section, and then click OK.

19. In the Microsoft Outlook dialog box informing you that the field "Section" is not shown in the view, click No.

20. Click Other Settings and deselect the Show Preview Pane check box.

21. Click OK twice, and then, in the Define Views For "User Manual" dialog box, make sure the newly created Table Of Contents view is selected. Click Copy.

22. In the Copy View dialog box, under Name Of New View, type **Chapter 01 Only**, and then click OK.

23. Click Group By. Under Select Available Fields From, select User-Defined Fields In Folder. Under Group Items By, select Section, and then click OK.

24. Click the Filter button, click on the Advanced tab, click Field, point to User-Defined Fields In Folder, and then select Chapter.

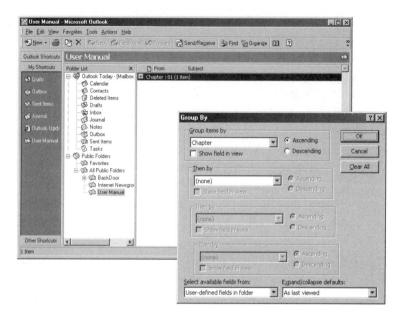

Figure 21.2 Configuring custom views for a document library

25. Under Condition, make sure Contains is displayed, type **01** in the Value box, and then click Add To List.

26. Click OK twice, and then, in the Define Views For "User Manual" dialog box, select the Only Show Views Created For This Folder check box, and then double-click Table Of Contents to apply this view.

27. On the Outlook toolbar, right-click User Manual, select Properties, click on the Administration tab, and, under Initial View On Folder, select Table Of Contents.

28. Click Folder Assistant, click Add Rule, click Advanced, and, under Size (Kilobytes), in the At Least box, type **1024** to specify a maximum document size of 1 MB (see Figure 21.3).

29. Click OK, and, in the Edit Rule dialog box, select the Return To Sender check box. Click OK three times to close all dialog boxes.

30. On the desktop, right-click NEW WORDPAD DOCUMENT.DOC, select Properties, and then click on the Custom tab.

31. In the Properties list, double-click on the Chapter entry, change the value to **02**, and then click Modify.

32. Click OK, drag the document over the User Manual icon on the Outlook toolbar, let it drop there, and notice how Outlook 2000 updates the view automatically.

33. Open the View menu, point to Current View, and then select Chapter01 Only. Notice that only the first copy of the document is displayed—the version with the Chapter value of 01.

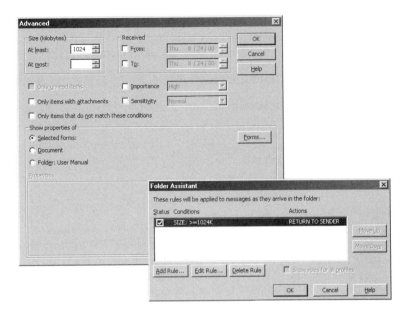

Figure 21.3   Configuring a maximum item size for a document library

34. Optionally, you may configure User Manual as a moderated public folder (see Exercise 3 of Chapter 1, "Introduction to Microsoft Exchange 2000 Server"), create a Web folder shortcut to the public folder using Windows Explorer (as shown in Exercise 5 of Chapter 11, "Internet-Based Client Access"), and enable full-text indexing (as discussed in Chapter 14, "Managing Server Configuration").

Exercise Summary

Exchange 2000 Server is able to determine standard and custom properties of documents stored in mailboxes and public folders automatically. This feature is known as property promotion. You can use these attributes, as well as any standard attributes, to view, sort, and manage shared and personal documents. Likewise, users can use these attributes to configure folder rules, for instance, to define a maximum document size. It is also possible to search across all items in a document library regardless of the document type. With full-text indexing, searches can include the body of documents and message attachments.

Types of Electronic Forms

Electronic forms can be used with two general groups of applications: stand-alone applications and folder applications. Stand-alone solutions, also known as send forms, are used for direct information exchange between users; you would use a stand-alone form to send another person a specially formatted e-mail message. A meeting request form is a good example of a send form. In folder applications, items are posted to a mailbox or public folder directly. These electronic forms are therefore known as post forms. When items are posted to a public folder, multiple users can share the information.

Electronic forms are the right choice if you want to do the following:

- Define the structure of items for workgroup applications and workflow processes.
- Dedicate public folders to discussion forums in which information is posted in a structured way.
- Replace paper forms.

Outlook Forms Designer

The Outlook Forms Designer is a 32-bit design tool that is tightly integrated into Outlook. You can use it to modify all kinds of existing forms, including the standard Mail Message form, Contacts form, and Tasks form, without the need for any programming language. Outlook forms are not compiled but interpreted by Outlook at runtime.

Customizing Standard Forms

To launch the Outlook Forms Designer, open the Tools menu, point to Forms, and then select Design A Form. In the Design Form dialog box, select the form that you want to modify, and then click Open. If you want to create a custom form based on a Microsoft Office document, display the form that you want to modify, and then switch it into design mode. To do this, open the File menu, point to New, and select Office Document. At this point, select the desired document type, such as Microsoft Word Document, in the New Office Document window, and then click OK. You will need to specify whether you want to post or send the form. When you make your choice and click OK, a form will be launched containing the selected Office document. In this window, open the Tools menu, point to Forms, and select Design This Form. The design mode shows (Design) on the title bar.

Note You can customize forms for Office documents by modifying the embedded Office document. However, it is not possible to modify the default pages of the form or add new form elements.

Advanced Design Features

It is possible to extend forms using the Visual Basic Expression Service and VBScript. You can use the Expression Service to validate field input or create formulas and combination fields. A good example is a field that determines an expiration date by adding several days to the current date. VBScript, in turn, can add further intelligence to Outlook forms. VBScript lets you launch dialog boxes, open and close other forms, and perform background calculations while users work with your form in the foreground.

Installing Forms

Outlook forms are published through forms libraries. On the Tools menu of your customized form, point to Forms, and then select the Publish Form As command. Forms libraries and the installation of electronic forms are discussed in Lesson 2.

Developing Outlook Forms

As soon as you have switched a form into design mode, you can delete existing fields and add new fields to achieve the desired functionality. Examples of existing fields are the To, Cc, and Sent lines, which display recipient information and a time stamp. Of course, Outlook provides many other additional fields. They are organized by category, which you can examine using the Field Chooser utility. To display this utility, on the Form menu, select the Field Chooser command. This utility allows you to create custom fields if the standard set of attributes does not meet your needs.

Adding Fields

You can select a field such as the Message Flag Field from a category of the Field Chooser and place it on a form using drag and drop. You can opt to have new controls aligned automatically on the left side of other fields if they are placed below them. Other alignment options are available on the Layout menu. The AutoLayout feature of Outlook Forms Designer, which is enabled by default, automatically aligns the new fields on the form, no matter where you drop them.

Defining New Fields

To create new fields, use the New button in the Field Chooser window. In the New Field dialog box, you need to specify a name and a field type, such as Text, Date/Time, Number, or Currency. Depending on the field type that you select, you might also have to define a specific data format using the Format combo box. When you click OK, the custom field will be added to the User-Defined Fields In <Folder> category of the Field Chooser. You can place the new field on your form just like any other field, using drag and drop, and it can also be included in folder views.

Fields on a Per-Folder Basis

You need Read and Write permissions for the currently selected folder to create new fields. As you add your own fields, they are associated with the current folder. Let's say that you have defined a Yes/No field called Invite For Interview in a folder called Job Applicants. You then can add this field to the folder view of Job Applicants, but you cannot use it to extend a folder view of the Inbox. New fields help to organize items only on a per-folder basis: You must create the same field for other folders if you want to extend their views using user-defined attributes of forms messages.

Field Validation

Field validation is a common programming technique used to ensure that users enter valid information in predefined fields. A check is performed when users close a form during a send or post operation. If a field contains an invalid value, users are informed and are asked for valid input. In this situation, the form is not closed.

For example, you might want to create a user-defined field called Applicant Rating for your Job Applications solution to indicate how well a candidate fits an open job position. Users can only enter values from 0 to 5; other values are not allowed. When you place the field on the form, you can enable the field validation feature. No matter which field you are working with, a right-click on the field displays a shortcut menu that offers the Properties command. Selecting this command displays the Properties dialog box. In the Validation tab, select the Validate Field Before Closing The Form check box, and then define a validation formula and specify a notification. The validation formula will check whether the user has entered a valid value. A notification will inform users about input errors.

Outlook Forms and Custom Controls

Outlook forms support ActiveX controls, which can be used to implement advanced features, such as a date and time picker. To add controls, you need to display the control toolbox. Open the Form menu, and select the Control Toolbox command. When you right-click the free area in the Toolbox dialog box, you can select the Custom Controls command, which allows you to include and use any available ActiveX control in your forms project.

Form Sizes and Forms Cache

You need to keep in mind that the size of your form increases with the number of fields and controls you place on the form. It takes longer to load large forms. If the size of your form was increased dramatically, you may even encounter problems with Outlook's forms cache. To increase performance, Outlook loads custom forms into this cache before displaying them. In Microsoft Windows 2000 Professional, the forms cache is located under \Documents and Settings\<User Name>\Local Settings\Application Data\Microsoft\Forms. The default cache size is 2 MB. To increase the size, in Outlook 2000, open the Tools menu, select Options, and, in the Options dialog box, click on the Other tab. Click Advanced Options, and then click Custom Forms. Increase the value labeled Maximum Space On Hard Disk.

Design-Time Licenses

It is a good idea to avoid adding advanced custom controls to electronic forms. Outlook forms are not compiled. Consequently, custom controls do not become an internal part of your form project. Unlike the actual electronic form, you must deploy your custom controls to all workstations manually. Likewise, because forms are interpreted at runtime and not compiled at design time, it is important to install the design-time licenses on all workstations and not just the runtime versions; otherwise, Outlook 2000 may display a warning that license information could not be found and the custom control will not be loaded. It is vital to test your electronic forms on different workstations when using custom controls.

Disabling the Outlook Forms Designer

You can disable the Outlook Forms Designer by setting a user-specific REG_DWORD value called NoOutlookFormsDesigner in the Registry in the following location:

```
HKEY_CURRENT_USER

  \Software

  \Microsoft

  \Office

  \9.0

  \Outlook
```

If you set this value to 1 and attempt to launch the Outlook Forms Designer, a message box will be displayed informing you that your administrator has made this feature unavailable. Using the Custom Installation Wizard, you can include this Registry value in a customized Outlook installation, which allows you to disable the Outlook Forms Designer for those users that are not supposed to develop custom forms or workgroup applications. The Custom Installation Wizard was introduced in Chapter 8, "Microsoft Outlook 2000 Deployment."

Lesson 2: Managing Outlook Forms

Applications based on Outlook forms are not like typical Windows-based applications because they are available only in Outlook. In other words, they are client application dependent. Workgroup applications are also network dependent because they rely on storage and deployment mechanisms provided by Exchange 2000 Server. You only have to publish a custom form in one step, and it will be available to all users in the organization.

This lesson deals with the management of Outlook forms. It introduces available forms libraries and their specific purposes and covers important management aspects related to send and post forms.

At the end of this lesson, you will be able to:

- Describe the purposes of forms libraries and decide which library to use in a given situation.
- Manage forms libraries available on Exchange 2000 Server.
- Install forms using Outlook 2000.

Estimated time to complete this lesson: 45 minutes

Forms Libraries

Exchange 2000 Server provides three types of libraries where you can store Outlook forms: the folder forms library (FFL), the organizational forms library (OFL), and the personal forms library (PFL). All three let you maintain electronic forms applications centrally on the server (see Figure 21.4).

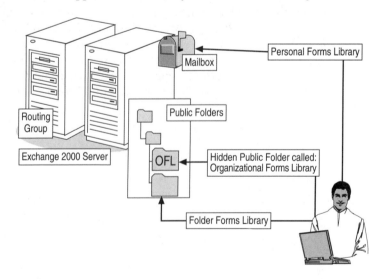

Figure 21.4   Possible server-based repositories for Outlook forms

Folder Forms Library

An FFL associates Outlook forms with message folders, which is the best place for post forms. Whether you install a form in a public, mailbox, or personal folder, the FFL keeps track of the association and provides the form only if the corresponding folder has been opened. For an example, assume that you have installed a Candidates form in a public folder called Job Applicants. Because of the association between the form and the folder, the New Candidates command is available on the Actions menu only if you have already selected the Job Applicants folder.

Public folders are the foundation of workgroup applications because they share their FFLs and all the electronic forms they contain. However, you should not publish workgroup applications during the development phase because they will be replicated between routing groups and made available to users. To test your prototypes, use mailbox and personal folders instead. Alternatively, you may restrict access to the public folder during the forms development phase in the Administration tab by setting the folder's This Folder Is Available Only setting to Owners Only.

Organization Forms Library

An OFL is a system public folder that you can use to maintain send forms, which are not associated with a particular folder. OFLs are commonly available to all users in the organization. To select a form published in an OFL, open the Tools menu, point to Forms, and then select the Choose Form command. In the Choose Form dialog box, under Look In, select Organizational Forms Library, and then double-click the form you want to launch.

By default, no OFL exists. To create an OFL, launch Exchange System Manager. Expand your administrative group, expand Folders, and then right-click Public Folders and select View System Folders. Expand Public Folders, right-click EFORMS REGISTRY, point to New, and then click Organizational Form. You need to define a name for the folder and specify an appropriate language that corresponds to your clients. It is a good idea to include a hint about the OFL language in the name of the OFL folder. Optionally, you may provide a description of the library.

You cannot create more than one OFL per client language. Outlook 2000 will look for an OFL folder that corresponds to the client language before it defaults to the first available library on the server. You must implement separate OFLs for each client language in your organization if you want to provide localized send forms to your users.

OFLs are replicated across the organization through replication of the MAPI-based public folder hierarchy. You may configure content replication to provide access to the organizational forms in all locations. Public folder replication was covered in Chapter 18, "Public Folder Replication."

Personal Forms Library

A PFL maintains the send forms that you don't want to share with other users. This library resides in your mailbox and is not replicated anywhere. An installed form is available only in the Choose Form dialog box of your Outlook client. Other users cannot launch your private form unless they install it manually in their own PFL as well. Certain forms, such as send forms in the development stage, should be installed in a PFL to prevent their distribution across the entire organization.

If you are developing a send form that you are not planning to register in a public forms library (where recipients would have access to it), select the Send Form Definition With Item check box, which you can find in the Properties tab of your form in design mode. Sending the form definition with the message ensures that the recipient will be able to display the custom form when the item is opened. Depending on the size of your forms project, this can significantly increase the size of your messages.

Managing Forms

Forms libraries require minimal administration. It is mainly an issue with OFLs because they do not exist by default. FFLs are created implicitly along with their message folders; they inherit the folders' configurations and user permissions. Only a folder owner can install Outlook forms. PFLs do not require extensive administration either because they are associated with mailboxes. Only the mailbox owner and privileged delegates can install private forms.

OFL Security

By default, only the administrator who created the library can install Outlook forms in an OFL. Consequently, you might have to designate additional privileged OFL owners who can publish send forms in your organization. In Exchange System Manager, right-click the OFL public folder under EFORMS REGISTRY, select Properties, click on the Permissions tab, and click Client Permissions to designate the OFL owners. The configuration of public folders was covered in Chapter 17, "Public Folder Management."

Note   You cannot manage permissions for OFLs using Outlook because OFLs are hidden public folders.

Using Applications Offline

Outlook forms are typically maintained centrally on the server. This can be a problem if users want to open forms messages while working offline. The associated form is not available during offline operation. To work around this problem, you need to configure an offline folder store (.ost), as explained in Chapter 9, "MAPI-Based Clients." Outlook forms are then downloaded implicitly into the local storage file when mailbox and public folders are synchronized. Once the forms are available locally, users can work as if they were online.

Note   You can install post forms in a personal folder (a .pst file) so that they are available for use offline. However, personal folders cannot be shared with other users in your organization.

Installing Outlook Forms

Although you can use Exchange System Manager to create OFLs and manage public folder owners, you cannot use this utility to install Outlook forms in a forms library—you need to use Outlook.

To publish an Outlook form, display the desired form as if you want to create a new item, open the Tools menu, point to Forms, and then select Publish Form As. This command is also available in design mode when working with the Outlook Forms Designer. In the dialog box that appears, specify a Display Name and a Form Name, specify a forms library under Look In, and then click Publish to complete the installation. If you have developed a custom send form, Outlook 2000 will display a message box asking you whether you want to send the form description with the messages. Clicking Yes in this box corresponds to selecting the Send Form Definition With Item check box in the Properties tab.

Managing Installed Outlook Forms

At times you might want to delete installed forms or change a form's properties. For this purpose, use Forms Manager. You can launch this tool in a variety of ways. For instance, you can right-click a public folder, select Properties, click on the Forms tab, and click Manage. Another way is to open the Tools menu, select Options, click on the Others tab, click Advanced Options, click Custom Forms, and then click Manage. Forms Manager allows you to copy forms between forms libraries, update or delete them, or change form properties. You also can use this tool to install legacy 16-bit forms developed with the old Microsoft Exchange Forms Designer. Use the Set button in the upper right corner to select the desired forms library you want to work with.

Working with Outlook Forms

Perhaps the most amazing feature of Outlook forms is their automatic distribution and installation: You simply install the form in a forms library and the system takes care of the rest. For instance, if you have implemented a workgroup solution based on a public folder, associated this folder with a custom form, and used this form to create items in this folder, Outlook will use the correct form automatically when you open these items again. Even if a user has never used your form before, Outlook will determine the form, download it into the user's local forms cache, and use it to display the information. Outlook forms installed in a public forms library are available to all users in your organization who can access the folder contents.

Outlook 2000 associates items with electronic forms based on their message class. Custom forms write message class information into each item's Message

Class field. Custom message classes are derived from the standard forms originally used to create the forms. The form name, defined when publishing a form, is appended to create the new message class. To give an example, a Job Candidate form might have the message class IPM.Contact.Job Candidate.

Outlook checks the item's message class and looks for the associated form in the following locations (see Figure 21.5):

1. **Local forms cache.**   For improved performance, Outlook will load the form from its cache if it was used (and downloaded) previously. However, before the form is launched, Outlook checks for an updated version in the corresponding forms library. The last modified time of the cached form is compared to the last modified time of the form in the forms library. Outlook will update its forms cache if the forms library contains an updated version.

2. **Currently selected folder.**   If the form was not downloaded beforehand but is installed in an FFL, Outlook will find the form in the currently selected folder, download it into the cache, and launch it.

3. **Personal Forms Library.**   If the form is not in the FFL, it might be in the PFL of the current user.

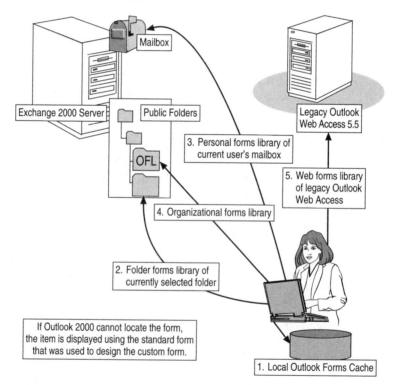

Figure 21.5   Locating an Outlook form

4. **Organizational Forms Library.**   OFLs are checked according to the language of the Outlook client. If the form is available in an OFL, it is downloaded and displayed.

5. **Web Forms Library.**   Outlook can launch HTML forms in your default Internet browser, which can be useful for workgroup applications that rely entirely on HTML forms compatible with earlier versions of Outlook Web Access (OWA). However, OWA of Exchange 2000 Server relies on the Web Storage System, which cannot be used with Outlook 2000 directly. You can read more about the design of Web Storage System solutions in Chapter 23, "Microsoft Exchange 2000 Web Storage System."

If the form cannot be found, the item is displayed using the standard form that was used to create the form, such as IPM.Contact.

Exercise 2: Designing a Custom Outlook Form

In this exercise you will design a Job Applicants solution using the Outlook Contacts form as a template. You will publish your custom form in a public folder.

To view a multimedia demonstration that displays how to perform this procedure, run the EX2CH21.AVI files from the \Exercise_Information\Chapter21 folder on the Supplemental Course Materials CD.

Prerequisites
- Restart BLUESKY-SRV1 and BLUESKY-WKSTA.
- Log on as Administrator to BLUESKY-WKSTA, and make sure Outlook 2000 is started.

▶ **To implement a job applicant's workgroup solution based on a public folder**

1. In Outlook 2000, open the File menu, point to Folder, and then select New Folder.

2. In the Create New Folder dialog box, under Name, type **Job Applicants**.

3. Under Folder Contains, select Contact Items.

4. Under Select Where To Place The Folder, expand the Public Folders tree, select All Public Folders, and then click OK.

5. If a dialog box appears asking you whether you want to create a shortcut on your Outlook toolbar, click Yes.

6. On the Outlook toolbar, click My Shortcuts to display the list of your shortcuts, and then click the Job Applicants icon to open the newly created public folder.

7. Open the Actions menu, and click New Contact.

8. The Untitled – Contact dialog box appears. Open the Tools menu, point to Forms, and click Design This Form.

9. The Untitled – Contact (Design) dialog box appears. Maximize the dialog box, and, in the General tab, delete the Business, Business Fax, Categories, Company, Contacts, Job Title, and Web Page Address fields (and their labels), and arrange all remaining fields as shown in Figure 21.6.

10. In the Field Chooser list box (that is displaying Frequently-Used Fields by default), select Personal Fields from the drop-down list box.

11. From the options that appear, drag the Birthday, Hobbies, and Profession fields to a free area in the General tab (see Figure 21.6).

12. At the bottom of the Field Chooser dialog box, click New.

13. In the Name box, type **Invite for Interview**. From the Type list, select Yes/No. Under Format, select True/False, and then click OK.

14. Click New again. Under Name, type **Applicant Rating**, and then click OK.

15. Drag the Invite For Interview and Applicant Rating fields to the form. Notice that the Yes/No option is translated to a check box.

16. Open the Tools menu, point to Forms, and then click Publish Form As.

17. In the Publish Form As dialog box, under Display Name and Form Name, type **Job Candidate**, and then click Publish.

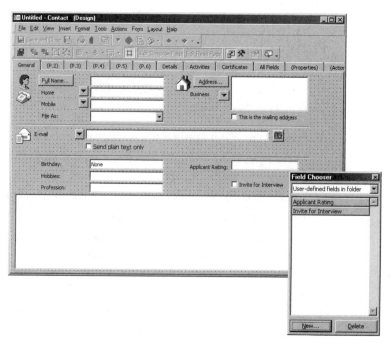

Figure 21.6   Designing an Outlook form

18. On the File menu, click Close, and, in the Microsoft Outlook dialog box asking you whether you want to save the changes, click No.

19. On the Outlook toolbar, right-click Job Applicants, select Properties, and click on the Forms tab. Notice that the Job Candidate form is displayed under Forms Associated With This Folder. Under Allow These Forms In This Folder, select Only Forms Listed Above (see Figure 21.7).

20. Click on the General tab, and, from the When Posting To This Folder, Use list box, select Job Candidate (see Figure 21.7).

21. Click OK, and test the configuration and new form by double-clicking in the empty details pane of the Job Applicants folder, which should launch the Job Candidate form. Alternatively, you may open the Actions menu and select New Job Candidate.

Figure 21.7 Defining a default custom form for a public folder

Exercise Summary

Outlook's standard forms can be customized using the Outlook Forms Designer, which makes it possible to create powerful workgroup solutions in minutes. Instead of their paper equivalents, Outlook forms applications based on public folders can provide a large variety of information to all or specific users. The content of a public folder can be displayed in various ways by means of folder views, and the content of contact-based folders can be made available through the Outlook Address Book, as mentioned in Chapter 9, "MAPI-Based Clients."

Chapter Summary

Electronic forms are templates that allow you to create items of special types. Outlook 2000 provides a set of standard forms that can be customized using Outlook Forms Designer. You can create send forms and post forms. Send forms are used to transmit specially formatted e-mail messages. Post forms allow you to place new items in mailbox and public folders or work with existing articles.

Send forms are typically published across the entire organization by means of an OFL. Post forms, due to their nature, are best published in FFLs—in other words, in public folders. During the development stage, it is a good idea to keep send and post forms in individual forms libraries, such as the PFL (for send forms), the FFL, or a mailbox folder. It is also possible to maintain post forms in personal folders in a .pst file. To install Outlook forms you need to use Outlook.

Review

The following review questions can help you determine if you have sufficiently familiarized yourself with the material covered in this chapter. You can find the answers to these questions at the end of this book in Appendix A, "Questions and Answers."

1. What are the two general types of Outlook forms, and what are their purposes?

2. Which three types of forms libraries can exist on an Exchange 2000 server?

3. You are developing a new send form and want to test your solution. Where would you install the form?

4. You are planning to implement a project management solution for your team of Exchange administrators. You want to use a custom form to manage project tasks. How would you begin the design of your custom form?

C H A P T E R   2 2

Microsoft Outlook Web Access

About This Chapter

Microsoft Outlook Web Access (OWA) has evolved from an Active Server Page (ASP)-based programming sample to a serious messaging and collaboration client based on the Internet Server Application Programming Interface (ISAPI). The new approach uses different technology, gives better performance, and improves scalability, but it is not compatible with the former ASP-based OWA. OWA is an integral part of Microsoft Exchange Messaging and Collaboration Services and will always be installed on your Exchange 2000 server.

The magic of OWA lies in its platform-independent Web browser support. You can gain access to Microsoft Exchange 2000 Server via any browser that supports JavaScript and frames. This might be an ideal solution for everyday UNIX users, and it is certainly an exciting option for avant-garde knowledge workers who need access to information anytime, anywhere, and on any device. With OWA and Microsoft Mobile Explorer, for example, you can turn Internet-enabled smart and feature phones into messaging and collaboration clients.

This chapter focuses on OWA of Exchange 2000 Server. Lesson 1 covers the architecture, and Lesson 2 approaches OWA from a more practical point of view, discussing the various methods of resource access as well as backward compatibility issues.

Before You Begin

To complete this chapter:

- Prepare your test environment according to the descriptions given in the "Getting Started" section of "About This Book. "Although not necessarily required, it is assumed that you have completed the exercises in previous chapters.

- You need to be familiar with the configuration of virtual servers, as introduced in Chapter 11, "Internet-Based Client Access."

- You should have knowledge about the configuration of secured Internet access points for HTTP-based access to Exchange 2000 Server resources, as discussed in Chapter 19, "Implementing Advanced Security."

Lesson 1: Outlook Web Access Overview

OWA supports e-mail, calendar features, and contact management, which represent essential information management features. However, advanced features of Microsoft Outlook 2000, such as tasks or journal items, are unavailable. Microsoft does not intend for OWA to replace Outlook 2000; it is intended to give you a useful cross-platform messaging solution at lower costs.

This chapter covers architecture, features, and limitations of OWA. It also describes the advantages of using Microsoft Internet Explorer 5.0 in an OWA environment.

At the end of this lesson, you will be able to:

- Describe the OWA architecture.
- List the limitations of OWA.
- Identify Internet Explorer–specific features.

Estimated time to complete this lesson: 45 minutes

Outlook Web Access Architecture

OWA requires Microsoft Windows 2000 Server and Internet Information Services (IIS) 5.0. Based on a virtual directory, IIS receives Web browser requests and passes them to the ISAPI component of Exchange 2000 Server (DAVEX.DLL). This ISAPI component uses the Microsoft Web Storage System to access mailbox and public stores on behalf of the user (see Figure 22.1).

Based on information from HTTP request headers, OWA can determine browser version, language, and operating system (HTTP User-Agent Field and HTTP Accept-Language headers). DAVEX.DLL will render the content accordingly before the data is sent to the user. Furthermore, OWA has to find out whether the content should be rendered for a browser or returned to a Web Distributed Authoring and Versioning (WebDAV) application, such as Windows Explorer, without HTML rendering. The HTTP Translate header contains the required information.

The following stages are utilized in accessing Exchange 2000 Server:

1. The World Wide Web Publishing Service receives a browser request for an item in a virtual directory that is mapped to a mailbox or public store.

2. The Web service of IIS determines the user's Microsoft Windows 2000 account and performs an authentication of the user.

3. IIS passes the user's request to the OWA ISAPI component, which obtains information about the mailbox location for the authenticated user from the Active Directory directory service. A query string passed to OWA in the URL

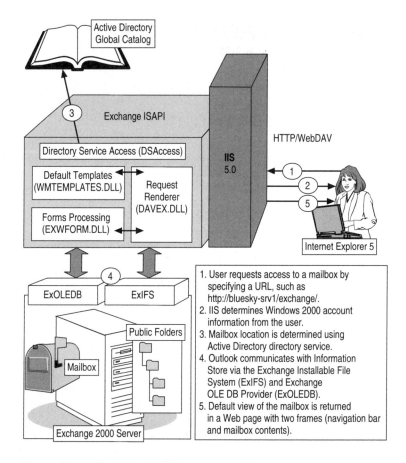

Figure 22.1 The Outlook Web Access architecture

identifies the action that the user wants to perform, such as accessing a mailbox or public folder, or opening a particular message (see Exercise 2 in Lesson 2).

4. If the mailbox resides on another computer and the local server is configured as a front end system, OWA proxies the user request to the user's home server. If the mailbox is on the local server, the OWA ISAPI component communicates with the Microsoft Web Storage System through Exchange Installable File System (ExIFS) and the Exchange Object Linking and Embedding Database (OLE DB) provider (ExOLEDB). ExIFS is used to access the data in the streaming databases (.stm), but ExIFS does not support access to item properties. OWA brings ExOLEDB into play to retrieve the item properties required for forms processing.

5. ExIFS and ExOLEDB communicate with the Information Store service. The high-performance Exchange interprocess communication was introduced in Chapter 3, "Microsoft Exchange 2000 Server Architecture."

6. Based on client permissions, the Information Store permits or denies the user access to the resource, such as a mailbox. If access is permitted, the Information Store returns the information to OWA.

7. OWA determines how to render the item, requests the data from the Information Store, applies language-specific settings, and renders the Web page into HTML and Extensible Markup Language (XML). You can read more about the information retrieval and rendering in Chapter 24, "Workgroup and Workflow Technologies."

8. IIS returns the Web page to the user's Web browser.

Outlook Web Access File Locations

With only a few exceptions, all OWA components are placed in the \Program Files\Exchsrvr\Exchweb directory.

The following directories are important for OWA:

- **\Program Files\Exchsrvr\Bin.**   Contains the server's general executables and DLLs, for instance, WMTEMPLATES.DLL, which defines the default templates used to render HTML forms.

- **\Program Files\Exchsrvr\Exchweb\Bin.**   Holds setup files for Outlook 2000 Multimedia Extensions.

- **\Program Files\Exchsrvr\Exchweb\Controls.**   Contains server-side and client-side script files. IIS uses the server-side Microsoft JScript and the client receives script elements as well to implement the dynamic user interface of OWA.

- **\Program Files\Exchsrvr\Exchweb\Lang.**   Contains localized versions of OWA help files, only created if non-English languages are enabled.

- **\Program Files\Exchsrvr\Exchweb\Img.**   Contains logos and other graphics used by OWA, such as LOGO-IE5.GIF and ICON-DOC-EXCEL.GIF. You may replace the files with customized versions to change the OWA user interface.

Default Virtual Directories

When you start the Internet Services Manager in the Administrative Tools program group, you will notice four virtual directories called Exadmin, Exchange, Exchweb, and Public added to IIS during the installation of Exchange 2000 Server. All four belong to OWA. Exadmin, for instance, points to //./backofficestorage/, which refers to the ExOLEDB provider. Exchange System Manager requires access to Exadmin to retrieve and write public folder properties, so it is an OWA client.

The remaining three virtual directories point to file-system directories. Exchweb is an ordinary virtual directory, which can be used to open graphics and other files that reside in \Program Files\Exchsrvr\Exchweb. Exchange and Public, on the other hand, are associated with the OWA ISAPI component and point to the mailbox root and default public folder hierarchy on ExIFS. The Exchange virtual root (for example, http://bluesky-srv1/exchange/) allows you to access your mailbox and public folders as a validated user. Public (for example, http://bluesky-srv1/public/), on the other hand, provides a way into the default Messaging Application Programming Interface (MAPI)-based public folder hierarchy to access the default set of public folders.

Note   It is not possible to delete the four default virtual directories.

Exercise 1: Publishing a Document Management System Through a Dedicated Outlook Web Access Virtual Directory

In this exercise you will publish a document management system based on a public folder over the Web. You will use OWA to access documents through Internet Explorer 5.0.

To view a multimedia demonstration that displays how to perform this procedure, run the EX1CH22.AVI files from the \Exercise_Information\Chapter22 folder on the Supplemental Course Materials CD.

Prerequisites

- Complete Exercise 1 of Chapter 21, "Microsoft Outlook Forms Environment." (Otherwise, create a simple public folder, name it User Manual, and place some documents in it.)

- Restart BLUESKY-SRV1, and log on as Administrator.

▶ **To assign a document management system a specific URL and access the forum over the World Wide Web**

1. Launch Exchange System Manager from the Microsoft Exchange program group.

2. Expand Administrative Groups, then First Administrative Group, then Servers, then BLUESKY-SRV1. Expand Protocols, HTTP, and Exchange Virtual Server. Notice three of the default OWA virtual directories (Exadmin, Exchange, and Public).

3. Right-click Exchange Virtual Server, point to New, and then select Virtual Directory.

4. In the Properties dialog box, under Name, type **User Manual**.

5. Under Exchange Path, select Public Folder, and then click Modify.

6. In the Public Folder Selection dialog box, expand Public Folders (BLUESKY-SRV1), and then select User Manual. Click OK twice to close all dialog boxes.

7. Give the metabase update service a minute to transfer the information into the IIS metabase. (The metabase update service was covered in Chapter 3, "Microsoft Exchange 2000 Server Architecture.")

8. Right-click on User Manual, and then select Browse (see Figure 22.2).

9. Verify that Internet Explorer 5.0 is launched, displaying the contents of the User Manual forum. From the View list box in the details pane, select Table Of Contents. Expand the chapter groups to check that the documents are listed correctly.

10. Double-click on a document, and, in the File Download dialog box, select Open This File From Its Current Location, then click OK. WordPad will appear, displaying the contents of the document.

11. Close WordPad, Internet Explorer 5.0, and Exchange System Manager.

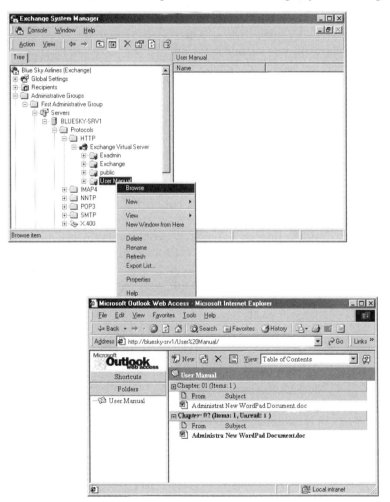

Figure 22.2   Working with a document management system using OWA

Exercise Summary

You can extend the set of standard virtual directories that provide access to Exchange 2000 Server via OWA. Using the HTTP virtual server object in Exchange System Manager, it is easy to create and test virtual directories to alternate public stores or dedicated public folder resources. Keep in mind that new virtual directories must be associated with the OWA ISAPI component. Exchange System Manager does this for you. It doesn't work to create virtual directories using IIS and associating them with resources from the M drive (the ExIFS drive). The OWA ISAPI association would be missing. It is not advisable to use the Internet Services Manager to change the properties of OWA virtual directories.

Outlook Web Access Limitations

Several features, such as delayed message delivery and message expiration, folder rules, offline folders, journaling, printing templates, spell checkers, task management, telephony options and user-defined fields when accessing contacts, and reminders, are not supported. It is likewise impossible to work with Secure/ Multipurpose Internet Mail Extensions (S/MIME) messages. OWA is a thin messaging environment.

Data Security Issues

For security reasons, you should log out after each OWA session, close your Web browser, and log off. This is especially important when working on a public workstation, such as a shared machine in a computer lab. Another user could simply click on the Back button of your browser to read your messages when you are away. In a shared environment, it is crucial to leave the Save Password feature in Internet Explorer 5.0 disabled. Furthermore, ensure that the browser's local caching feature is not activated. With local caching enabled, messages can remain on the local disk and may be disclosed. Although OWA uses a pragma-no-cache HTML metatag in every Web page, as well as no-cache HTTP headers to prevent local caching, whether or not no-cache directives are supported depends on the browser. If you have worked with sensitive information, clear the browser cache manually when you close your session.

Supported Browsers

Internet Explorer 5.0 is the ideal OWA client. It is a WebDAV-enabled browser that allows direct manipulation of data on the server. As demonstrated in Chapter 11, "Internet-Based Client Access," WebDAV can handle any type of data. Internet Explorer 5.0 supports advanced features, such as dynamic HTML (DHTML), shortcut menus, and drag-and-drop operations between folders. Additionally, this Web browser can perform various functions, such as locally rendering mailbox and public folder data instead of sending requests to the server. This minimizes communication between client and server and increases the scalability of the system.

If your computer does not support Internet Explorer 5.0, consider using Netscape Navigator 4.0 or later or any other browser that supports HTML 3.2 and JavaScript. Microsoft has tested OWA with Internet Explorer versions 4 and 5.0, and Netscape Navigator 4.0. You will be able to work with mailbox and public folders, but advanced Internet Explorer 5.0 features will not be available.

The following features are available in Internet Explorer 5.0 only:

- Shortcut menus that are displayed when right-clicking on an item
- Drag-and-drop operations between folders
- XML-based data viewing and manipulation
- Native Kerberos authentication (available on Windows 2000 only)
- Preview pane to view message contents in a preview window without actually opening the item
- Tree control to navigate through the hierarchy of mailbox and public folders

Multimedia Messaging

One of the most exciting features of OWA, if your workstation is equipped with audio and video features, is Multimedia Messaging. This feature is based on Microsoft Exchange Multimedia Control, which allows you to record voice and video directly in an e-mail message and send it as any other message. If you are working on a workstation where Exchange Multimedia Control is not installed, you can download it in OWA by clicking Options in the navigation bar and selecting Download. You can also extend Microsoft Outlook 2000 for Multimedia Messaging. On your workstation, open your browser, enter the URL http://<server name>/Exchweb/Bin/EMSETUP.ASP/ (such as, http://bluesky-srv1/Exchweb/Bin/EMSETUP.ASP/), and then follow the instructions. In addition to Exchange Multimedia Control, the Microsoft Exchange Multimedia Extension for Outlook 2000 will be installed. To remove Multimedia Messaging, use the Add/Remove Programs from the Control Panel. You can read more about Outlook extensions in Chapter 8, "Microsoft Outlook 2000 Deployment."

Lesson 2: Outlook Web Access Environments

By default, every user in an Exchange 2000 Server organization can use OWA to access mailbox and public folders. This allows you to deploy customized, Web-based collaboration systems with minimal effort. Just publish a virtual directory, as illustrated in Exercise 1, and your job is done. If you want to implement Internet-based OWA solutions, however, you need to optimize your environment for both security and performance reasons.

This lesson addresses how to provide access to Exchange 2000 Server via OWA in small-scale and large-scale environments. It demonstrates how to access mailbox and public folder resources and explains how to implement load balancing in front end/back end (FE/BE) arrangements.

At the end of this lesson, you will be able to:

- Access mailbox and public folder resources via OWA.

- Implement load balancing in an FE/BE environment for Internet users.

- Identify backward compatibility issues when working in mixed Exchange organizations.

Estimated time to complete this lesson: 60 minutes

Single-Server Configurations

Single-server environments provide direct access to mailboxes and public servers via the local IIS and the default HTTP virtual server (see Exercise 1). Every user can use a Web browser to connect to his or her home server and access mailbox and public folders via OWA. You can create additional virtual servers and assign them a unique combination of IP address, TCP port, Secure Sockets Layer (SSL) port, and host name to create separate Web server instances for users with different security requirements, as explained in Chapter 11, "Internet-Based Client Access."

Note   When working from outside your home domain, you must add the fully qualified domain name (FQDN) to the host name of the HTTP virtual server that provides access to your mailbox, such as http://bluesky-srv1.bluesky-inc-10.com/ exchange/. Furthermore, your mailbox-enabled user account must have an SMTP address that conforms to the SMTP address definition in the default recipient policy of your organization (for instance, Administrator@Bluesky-inc-10.com where @Bluesky-inc-10.com is defined for SMTP addresses in the default recipient policy).

Front End/Back End Configurations

It is a good idea to deploy Exchange 2000 Server in an FE/BE arrangement if you want to support a large number of users over the Internet. Front end servers concentrate incoming client connections and proxy them to the appropriate back end servers where the mailboxes reside. The front end server looks up the mailbox location using Active Directory. You can move mailboxes between servers without changing the URL that users use to access their mailboxes, because the name of the actual mailbox or public store is not relevant. Make sure the virtual root names match between the front end and back end systems (that is, Exchange, Public, and roots for alternative public folder hierarchies). The configuration of front end servers was covered in Chapter 4, "Planning the Microsoft Exchange 2000 Server Installation" and discussed further in Chapter 19, "Implementing Advanced Security."

Note OWA URLs are based on host or domain names. The URLs are independent of individual information store information.

Front End Load Balancing

In an FE/BE environment, you can group all your front end systems together for load balancing using Microsoft Network Load Balancing or another high-performance hardware load-balancing solution, such as Cisco Local Director. A free alternative is to use a round-robin DNS configuration according to RFC 1794, but there are serious drawbacks. You can read more about Microsoft Network Load Balancing in the Windows 2000 Server product documentation.

Disadvantages of Round-Robin DNS

Round-robin DNS is based on the simple concept of having the same host name mapped to the IP addresses of multiple front end servers, which are supposed to share the workload. To distribute user connections, DNS rotates host records. This also provides some level of fault tolerance because client requests are repeated if a particular front end server is not responding, which eventually will direct the client to an available system. However, Windows 2000 DNS prioritizes multiple host records based on their IP address to return the IP address closest to the client, preventing round-robin DNS from working properly. The behavior depends on the Enable Round Robin setting, found in the DNS snap-in, via the server Properties dialog box in the Advanced tab. You can read more about the configuration of Windows 2000 DNS in the product documentation.

Load Balancing and Secure Sockets Layer

Round-robin DNS should not be used for load balancing across servers if you use SSL to encrypt the communication between the client and the front end server.

The SSL bulk encryption key is maintained on the server and lost if the client is redirected to another host by DNS. In this case, a new session must be established to generate a new bulk encryption key. Microsoft Network Load Balancing carefully manages the connection state and is therefore a more reliable and preferable solution.

Resource Access

You can control access to OWA resources per HTTP virtual server, virtual directory, and user. Unfortunately, when working with the default HTTP virtual server, called Exchange Virtual Server, you have to juggle three different administrative utilities—IIS, Exchange System Manager, and Active Directory Users and Computers. You may find it useful to create a custom Microsoft Management Console (MMC) utility to include all three snap-ins in a single tool for OWA management, as illustrated in Chapter 2, "Integration with Microsoft Windows 2000."

Controlling Access Permissions

IIS is required to manage the properties (including security settings) for the Default Web Site, which provides access to the OWA virtual directories. Exchange System Manager is the right tool to control access to virtual directories. Each virtual directory provides an Access tab, where you can define Access Control settings, Execute Permissions, and Authentication Settings. Last but not least, you can use Active Directory Users and Computers to enable or disable OWA for mailbox-enabled accounts. Make sure Advanced Features is enabled under View, display the account properties, click on the Exchange Advanced tab, and click Protocol Settings. In the Protocols dialog box, select HTTP, and click Settings. In the HTTP Protocol Details dialog box, disable the Enable For Mailbox check box to prevent the user from accessing Exchange 2000 Server through HTTP. Similarly, you can disable POP3 and IMAP4 per user.

Validated Resource Access

Validated users can work with mailbox and public folders and can search the Global Address List. Generally speaking, they have permissions just as if they were logged on directly using Outlook 2000. When using Internet Explorer 4.0 or Internet Explorer 5.0, IIS obtains your Windows 2000 credentials directly from the browser and OWA automatically connects you to your mailbox. With Netscape Navigator and other browsers you will be prompted for an account name and password. Based on the account information, your mailbox will be determined from Active Directory. IIS uses integrated Windows authentication by default. The configuration of authentication mechanisms was covered in Chapter 11, "Internet-Based Client Access."

Because OWA determines mailbox information automatically based on present account information, you only have to specify the URL http://<Server Name>/ Exchange/ to gain access to your personal mailbox. If you want to work with other mailboxes, append the mailbox alias to the URL (such as, http://bluesky-srv1/Exchange/CarlT/). The mailbox alias corresponds to the user-specific portion of the e-mail address, for instance CarlT in CarlT@Bluesky-inc-10.com. It is a good idea to provide your users with an SMTP address that corresponds to the format <Windows 2000 account name>@<domain name>. If you are currently working with an account that does not have the required permissions to access the mailbox, an Enter Network Password dialog box will appear, prompting you for the required account information.

Note You cannot work with two different OWA sessions on the same computer simultaneously.

Anonymous Resource Access

All access to mailbox and public folder resources is validated. Although you have the option to allow anonymous access to public folders, this does not mean that anonymous users are unknown. By default, the system assigns them the guest account of the IIS, such as IUSR_<SERVERNAME>. You can read more about anonymous access to IIS resources in the Windows 2000 Server product documentation.

It is very important to keep in mind that the IIS guest account, IUSR_<SERVERNAME>, is a valid Windows 2000 user account. Therefore, the Default client permissions are applied and not the Anonymous permissions. For this reason, it is not advisable to enable anonymous access to the MAPI-based public folder hierarchy (published as http://<server name>/public). Anonymous Web users would then be able to browse through your public folder resources just as any regular user in your organization. Instead, create additional virtual directories for those public folders that you want to publish and enable anonymous access only for these virtual resources. You can read more about the administration of public folders in Chapter 17, "Public Folder Management."

Note It is a good idea to mail-enable the IIS guest account. This gives you the opportunity to configure explicit access permissions for anonymous users in Exchange System Manager and Outlook 2000.

▶ **To grant anonymous users access to the User Manual virtual directory (created in Exercise 1 of Lesson 1)**

1. In the Internet Information Services tool, right-click the Default Web Site object found under your server (such as Bluesky-srv1), then select Properties. Click on the Directory Security tab, and then, under Anonymous Access And Authentication Control, click Edit. Make sure the Anonymous Access check box is selected, click on the corresponding Edit button, and verify that the IIS guest account (such as IUSR_BLUESKY-SRV1) is displayed under Username. Close all dialog boxes.

2. In Exchange System Manager, expand the Exchange Virtual Server object, found under Blue Sky Airlines (Exchange)\Administrative Groups\First Administrative Group\Servers\BLUESKY-SRV1\Protocols\HTTP. Right-click on the object labeled User Manual, and then select Properties. Click on the Access tab, click Authentication, enable the Anonymous Access check box, and, under Anonymous Account, define a username. Close all dialog boxes.

Note The name you specify under Anonymous Account is used for informational purposes in Exchange System Manager. This account has no meaning for anonymous access over the Web; however, it is a good idea to reference the IUSR_<SERVERNAME> account, such as IUSR_BLUESKY-SRV1.

3. In Exchange System Manager, expand Folders under Blue Sky Airlines (Exchange)\Administrative Groups\First Administrative Group, and then expand Public Folders. Right-click the desired folder , such as User Manual, and select Properties. Click on the Permissions tab, click Client Permissions, and grant the required level of access rights to the Default account. If you have mail-enabled the IUSR_BLUESKY-SRV1 account, you can add the Internet Guest Account to the account list and grant permissions explicitly. You may also use Outlook 2000 to configure client permissions in the folder's Permissions tab.

Note The only difference between an anonymous user and a validated user is that the former does not own a mailbox (although even this is possible) and does not have to specify account information to access Exchange 2000 Server resources. The Information Store will check whether the anonymous account has the permissions to open the requested resource. If the account has sufficient privileges, the access is granted; otherwise, the user is prompted for account information according to defined authentication settings.

Disabling the Exchange Virtual Server

As outlined in Chapter 11, "Internet-Based Client Access," you can stop, start, or pause each virtual server individually. Stopping the HTTP virtual server(s) prevents users from accessing resources via OWA. In Exchange System Manager, select the desired virtual server object, such as Exchange Virtual Server, and then select Stop from the shortcut menu.

Important The default HTTP server provides access to public folder properties through the Exadmin virtual directory. Stopping the virtual server prevents Exchange System Manager from being able to manage public folder settings. You will receive an error notification that access to the public folder has failed.

Exercise 2: Accessing Mailbox and Public Folder Resources with Outlook Web Access

In this exercise you will work with Inbox, calendar, and public folder items by means of OWA. You will examine various URLs that provide access to the resources.

To view a multimedia demonstration that displays how to perform this procedure, run the EX2CH22.AVI files from the \Exercise_Information\Chapter22 folder on the Supplemental Course Materials CD.

Prerequisites

- Complete the exercises of Chapter 21, "Microsoft Outlook Forms Environment." (Otherwise, use Outlook 2000 to create two public folders called Job Applicants and User Manual. For Job Applicants, set the item type to Contact Items. For User Manual, make sure the item type is Mail Items. Register a custom Outlook form in the Job Applicants folder and place some documents in the User Manual.)

- Restart BLUESKY-SRV1, and make sure it is operational.

- Log on as Administrator to BLUESKY-SRV1.

▶ **To send and receive messages and test other OWA features**

1. Click Start, click Run, and, in the Run dialog box, type **http://bluesky-srv1/ exchange/**, and then click OK. Verify that Internet Explorer 5.0 is launched and that the browser shows a Web page that looks similar to Outlook 2000. This can take several minutes to start up.

Note If you receive an HTTP 500 Error when starting OWA, click on the Reload button to open the page successfully. If the HTTP 500 Error occurs repeatedly, restart the Exchange 2000 server to re-initialize the Information Store and IIS.

---

2. Click New, and, in the Untitled — Message window, click To.

Note If you have installed Office 2000 (without HTML Source Edit) and multimedia messaging for OWA, you may be prompted to insert the Office 2000 CD the first time you use Outlook Web Access. The Office 2000 installer program attempts to install HTML Source Edit. If the Office 2000 CD is not at hand, click Cancel in the installer program. This feature is not required for OWA or Office 2000 to work correctly.

---

3. In the Display Name box, type **admin.** Click Find, verify that the Administrator is found, and select this entry. Click To, and then click Close in the upper right corner.

4. In the Subject line, type **Messaging without limits**.

5. In the message text area, type **Normal OWA messages contain rich text formatting and attachments. Delivery and read receipts are also supported. You have to click Options on the toolbar and select the corresponding check boxes. Perhaps even more exciting is Multimedia Messaging. If your computer is equipped with a sound card, you can send audio data with your messages. If you have a video capture board in addition, video may be included as well. The microphone button on the toolbar provides access to multimedia features.**

6. Format the text using a different font, font size, and color (see Figure 22.3), and then click Send.

7. Right-click on the Web page that displays the messages from your Inbox, and then select Refresh. Verify that the newly composed message is displayed.

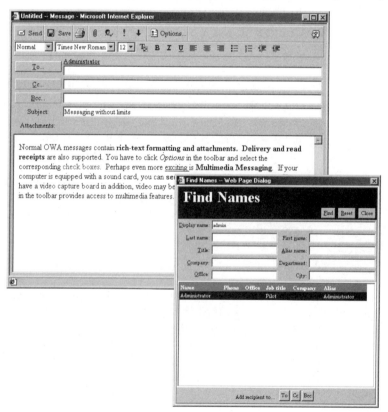

Figure 22.3 Sending a rich text message in OWA

8. In the Outlook Web Access navigation bar, click Contacts.

9. Click New, maximize the Untitled — Contact window, type **Hawk** under Last Name and **Henry** under First Name, and fill in other information as desired.

10. Under E-Mail Address, type **Henry.Hawk@Somewhere-inc-10.com**, and, under Display Name, change the information to **Henry Hawk**.

11. Click Save And Close, and then refresh the view of the Web page to display the newly created contact information (see Figure 22.4).

Figure 22.4   Displaying contacts in OWA

12. In the navigation bar, click Options to examine the settings that you can apply to OWA, such as date and time formats for the Calendar, or an out-of-office notification. Notice the Download button under E-Mail, which allows you to install the latest version of the Exchange Multimedia Control on your workstation.

Note   If you are working on a workstation where the Exchange Multimedia Control is already installed, the Download button will be labeled Re-Install.

13. In the navigation bar, click Folders. Notice that you can access all folders in your mailbox as well as public folders.

14. Expand Public Folders, and then select the Job Applicants folder.

15. Click New to create a new contact and note that the standard OWA contact form is displayed because OWA does not support custom Outlook forms. Close the contact form again.

16. In the navigation bar, right-click on the User Manual public folder, and then select Open In New. Verify that another browser window is opened.

17. From the View list box, select the custom view Table Of Contents that was originally defined in Outlook 2000. Verify that OWA displays the items accordingly. OWA supports custom Outlook views (see Figure 22.5).

Figure 22.5 Displaying items in a custom view

18. In the new browser window, examine the URL. It will have the format http://bluesky-srv1/public/User%20Manual/?Cmd=contents (see Figure 22.6).

19. To experiment with URLs, type **http://bluesky-srv1/Exchange/ Administrator/Inbox/?Cmd=contents** in your browser's Address box, and then press ENTER to display the Inbox folder.

20. Try **http://bluesky-srv1/Exchange/Administrator/Calendar/ ?Cmd=navbar**, and only the OWA navigation bar will be displayed.

21. Type **http://bluesky-srv1/Exchange/Administrator/Inbox/?Cmd=new**, and press ENTER to display an empty message form, which allows you to compose and send a rich text message right away.

22. Try **http://bluesky-srv1/Exchange/Administrator/Inbox/ Messaging%20without%20limits.EML?Cmd=open**, and the message that was composed earlier in this exercise appears ("%20" replaces the spaces in the subject line, but Internet Explorer 5.0 can do this job for you).

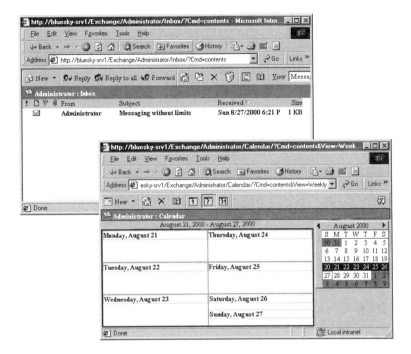

Figure 22.6   Using URLs to access resources directly

23. Use **http://bluesky-srv1/Exchange/Administrator/Calendar/ ?Cmd=contents&View=Weekly** to view your Calendar folder similar to the Day/Week/Month view of Outlook 2000 (see Figure 22.6).

Exercise Summary

With OWA, you have access to all items in your mailbox as well as public folders and the Global Address List. OWA supports exciting new technologies, such as the creation of messages that contain audio or video information using Multimedia Messaging. To access your mailbox, use http://<server name>/Exchange/. To access the MAPI-based public folder hierarchy instead, use http://<server name>/ Public/. It is possible to access individual mailboxes, public folders, and items in folders directly. All items can be referenced in a URL and desired actions may be specified in query strings.

Backward Compatibility Issues

As mentioned at the beginning of this chapter, the new OWA is not compatible with OWA of earlier versions of Exchange Server. Unfortunately, any OWA customizations cannot be retained after upgrading. However, you can use the legacy OWA version to access Exchange 2000 Server resources.

During the upgrading of your organization to Exchange 2000 Server, keep in mind that the new OWA cannot access public folders on earlier versions (see

Figure 22.7). You should replicate all relevant public folders to Exchange 2000 Server to provide access to them. Another option is to directly upgrade the existing public server first. Upgrade strategies are discussed in Chapter 6, "Coexistence with Previous Microsoft Exchange Server Versions."

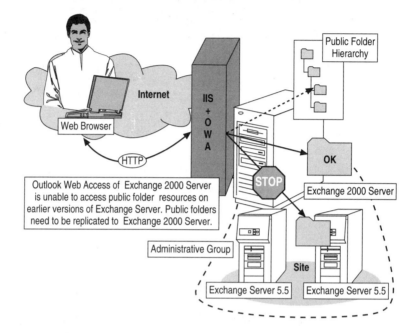

Figure 22.7   Outlook Web Access in a mixed environment

The following issues are important in regards to OWA when upgrading an Exchange organization to Exchange 2000 Server:

- ASP-based customizations of OWA and custom solutions based on collaboration data objects (CDOs) and OWA of earlier versions of Exchange Server are not upgradeable. However, these solutions do not need to be replaced and can be used in a native Exchange 2000 Server organization.

- Only hosts running the same version of OWA can be grouped together for load balancing. Separate URLs should be used for the new and the legacy OWA versions. If you are able to upgrade all servers running legacy OWA simultaneously, adjustments to DNS are not required.

- OWA of Exchange 2000 Server is limited to Exchange 2000 servers. Public folder resources can be replicated to Exchange 2000 Server to fully support OWA users.

- OWA of Exchange Server 5.5 can access mailbox and public folder resources on any server running Exchange Server 5.5 or Exchange 2000 Server.

Chapter Summary

OWA of Exchange 2000 Server is based on the ISAPI of IIS 5.0. It requires Windows 2000 Server and will be installed as an integral part of Microsoft Exchange Messaging and Collaboration Services. Through OWA, users can gain access to Exchange 2000 Server with any browser that supports JavaScript and frames. Ideally, Internet Explorer 5.0 is used.

Based on URLs, IIS determines that Web browser requests must be passed to the ISAPI component of Exchange 2000 Server, and correspondingly OWA will access mailbox and public stores through the Microsoft Web Storage System on behalf of the user. If the Information Store permits access to the resources, the data is retrieved via ExIFS and ExOLEDB, rendered into HTML, interlaced with script elements, and then returned to the browser.

OWA URLs are based on host or domain names. The URLs are independent of individual mailbox or public store locations. In an FE/BE environment, users do not need to know where their mailboxes reside to connect to them. OWA will look up mailboxes in Active Directory to obtain the required information. It is possible to add query strings to OWA URLs to specify a desired action, such as opening a folder or message directly or activating a particular folder view.

Review

The following review questions can help you determine if you have sufficiently familiarized yourself with the material covered in this chapter. You can find the answers to these questions at the end of this book in Appendix A, "Questions and Answers."

1. Why is Exchange 2000 Server OWA incompatible with OWA of earlier versions of Exchange Server?

2. During the installation of Exchange 2000 Server, four OWA-related virtual directories are created. What are their names and purposes?

3. Why is it advantageous to use Internet Explorer 5.0 in conjunction with OWA?

4. You have deployed three front end servers and plan to implement a software solution for load balancing. Which load-balancing solution does Microsoft recommend?

5. Your organization uses OWA to provide access to Exchange 2000 Server over the Internet. Consequently, FE/BE systems have been installed, and SSL was enforced on the front end systems to enforce data security over Internet connections. Why should you refrain from implementing a DNS-based load-balancing solution?

6. You are working under the mailbox-enabled Administrator account. Your mailbox resides on BLUESKY-SRV1. What URL would you have to use to open the Calendar folder of your mailbox in Internet Explorer 5.0 directly?

CHAPTER   23

Microsoft Exchange 2000 Microsoft Web Storage System

About This Chapter

The Microsoft Web Storage System is an innovative approach to integrate the Information Store service of Microsoft Exchange 2000 Server with Web-based technologies, such as HTTP, Extensible Markup Language (XML), Web Distributed Authoring and Versioning (WebDAV), Object Linking and Embedding Database (OLE DB), and ActiveX Data Objects (ADO). The Web Storage System extends the accessibility of the Information Store and provides a means to platform-independent messaging, information management, and high-productivity workgroup and workflow computing. Microsoft Outlook Web Access (OWA), for instance, is based on the Web Storage System.

The Web Storage System supports advanced collaboration technologies, such as electronic forms and store events. Because Exchange 2000 Server is based on semistructured databases (a flexible database schema), the Web Storage System can accommodate all possible data types, such as messages, documents, contacts, appointments, audio, video, HTML files, and Active Server Pages (ASPs). The Software Development Kit (SDK) for Exchange 2000 Server contains a set of development tools that enable you to quickly design powerful Web-based business solutions.

This chapter concentrates on an introduction to the Web Storage System. Lesson 1 covers essential information for administrators. Lesson 2 briefly discusses how to use the features of the Web Storage System to build customized enterprise applications.

Before You Begin

To complete this chapter:

- Prepare your test environment according to the descriptions given in the "Getting Started" section of "About This Book." It is assumed that you have completed the exercises of Chapter 22, "Microsoft Outlook Web Access."

- You need to be familiar with OWA of Exchange 2000 Server, as explained in Chapter 22, "Microsoft Outlook Web Access."

- You should have a general understanding about the essential Exchange 2000 components and their interaction with each other, as covered in Chapter 3, "Microsoft Exchange 2000 Server Architecture."

Lesson 1: The Microsoft Web Storage System

The Web Storage System consolidates file system, database, and collaboration services into a single, comprehensive server system. You can access Web Storage System resources using nearly any application, including Messaging Application Programming Interface (MAPI)-based clients, Web browsers, and standard Win32 programs, such as Microsoft Word. Exercise 5 of Chapter 1, "Introduction to Microsoft Exchange 2000 Server," illustrated how to work with messaging items using WordPad, for instance.

This lesson provides a summary of the Web Storage System. It looks at ways to access system resources, introduces Web Storage System features, and explains the purpose of property promotion.

At the end of this lesson, you will be able to:

- Describe how access to Web Storage System resources is accomplished.
- Use available interfaces to retrieve Web Storage System data.

Estimated time to complete this lesson: 30 minutes

HTTP-Based Interfaces

The Web Storage System relies on Windows 2000 Server and Internet Information Services (IIS) 5.0 to support Web browsers and WebDAV applications by means of HTTP, WebDAV, and XML. You don't need to configure anything extra on the server to provide your users with access to mailbox and public folder resources. As illustrated in Exercise 2 of Chapter 22, "Microsoft Outlook Web Access," every item in the Web Storage System is accessible through a URL.

Note   E-mail messages have an .eml suffix attached to the subject name, which must be provided in the URL. Standard files, such as a Microsoft Office application files, are identified with their file extension (.doc, .ppt, .xls). Contact objects and other special items do not have an extension by default.

Data Rendering

When accessing data through Windows Explorer and Web Folders, you can work with Exchange 2000 Server similar to a file server. When accessing the same information using a Web browser, a different view of the information is generated. The Web Storage System determines the appropriate view based on HTTP Translate header information, which the client sends to the IIS, and the requested item's state. An HTML 3.2 view is rendered and returned to standard Web browsers. The view displays properties promoted from each item in the folder. HTML 4.0 is supported for advanced Web browsers, such as Microsoft Internet Explorer 5.0. The Web Storage System returns Web pages and HTML-based views to browsers only. All other clients must render the data themselves. HTTP/WebDAV provides direct access to folders and items, as discussed in Chapter 11, "Internet-Based Client Access."

Item Properties

XML simplifies querying and modifying of item properties and other information contained in the Web Storage System. Properties are based on various XML namespaces that group similar properties together and ensure their uniqueness. When you access a property, you must specify the desired namespace followed by the actual property name. For instance, the DAV: namespace has a property called displayname that allows you to retrieve the name of an item. Another important DAV property is href, which holds the complete URL for an item. To access properties, programmers need to specify the full property reference, which is commonly known as the schema property name, such as DAV:displayname or DAV:href.

Another interesting namespace is urn:schemas-microsoft-com:xml-data:. This namespace allows you to define your own custom properties. You can also create custom namespaces. Detailed information about namespaces is available in the Exchange 2000 Server SDK.

Important   Property names are case sensitive.

Database Interfaces

The Web Storage System provides an Exchange OLE DB provider (ExOLEDB), which supports record-level access to messaging information. Applications can use OLE DB and ADO 2.5 interfaces to communicate with ExOLEDB. If ADO is used, the ADO run-time DLLs respond to the source application's request to open a record set by communicating with OLE DB. Otherwise, the call is directly passed to OLE DB run-time DLLs, which in both cases send the request to the OLE DB provider (see Figure 23.1). ADO is installed with Windows 2000 Server. ExOLEDB comes with Exchange 2000 Server.

ExOLEDB is a server-side component that is registered automatically during the installation of Exchange 2000 Server. It is important to note that ExOLEDB can only be used directly on the local server. ASP applications, ActiveX DLLs and EXEs, as well as event sinks running on the server, may use this provider to access local resources and return the information to remote clients. To access remote resources, however, HTTP/WebDAV or MAPI need to be used.

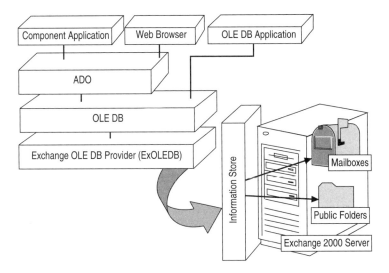

Figure 23.1   Implementation of the ExOLEDB provider

Exchange 2000 Server and Structured Query Language

ADO 2.5 gives you access to the Web Storage System similar to Microsoft Access or Microsoft SQL Server. If you are familiar with developing structured query language (SQL) applications, you can easily write Web Storage System applications using the same development tools. In fact, you can access multiple database management systems (DBMS) similarly from a single application. However, Exchange 2000 Server only supports local transactions because a distributed transaction coordinator (DTC) is not implemented. In plain English, distributed transaction processing, such as between SQL Server and IBM DB2, cannot include Exchange 2000 Server. Separate transactions are necessary.

Note   Database applications can access both Exchange 2000 Server and SQL Server simultaneously.

Exchange 2000 Server supports SQL commands. To open record sets to work with individual items, use the record object. Furthermore, ADO 2.5 supports a fields collection to access item properties and define custom properties. An ADO streams object also exists, which allows you direct access to an item's content.

The following Microsoft Visual Basic Scripting Edition (VBScript) example uses ADO in conjunction with a SQL statement to retrieve the list of top-level public folders from the MAPI-based public folder hierarchy (you can find this script in a file called TopLevelFolders.VBS in the \Sample_Scripts\Chapter23 folder on the Supplemental Course Materials CD):

```
strUrl = "file://./backofficestorage/bluesky-inc-10.com/PUBLIC FOLDERS"


Dim ADOConn
Set ADOConn = CreateObject("ADODB.Connection")
ADOConn.Provider = "ExOLEDB.DataSource"
ADOConn.Open strUrl


Set RecSet = CreateObject("ADODB.Recordset")
Dim SQLStat
SQLStat = "select ""DAV:displayname"", ""DAV:contentclass"""
SQLStat = SQLStat & ", ""DAV:href"" from"
SQLStat = SQLStat & " scope('shallow traversal of """ & strUrl & """')"
SQLStat = SQLStat & " where ""DAV:ishidden"" = False"
SQLStat = SQLStat & " and ""DAV:isfolder"" = True"


RecSet.Open SQLStat, ADOConn
Do While Not (RecSet.EOF)
        strFolderName = RecSet.Fields("DAV:displayname")
        If Trim(strFolderName) = "" Then
            Exit Do
        Else
            MsgBox "Folder Name: " & strFolderName, 64, "Top-level
Folder"
            RecSet.MoveNext
        End If
Loop
```

Note   You can use any Component Object Model (COM)-compliant programming language, such as VBScript, Microsoft Visual Basic, or Microsoft Visual C++, to develop ADO or OLE DB applications. ExOLEDB is a COM+ component.

Constructing OLE DB URLs

The Exchange OLE DB provider supports HTTP and file URL namespaces to identify items in the Web Storage System. The HTTP URL follows the usual format, such as http://bluesky-srv1/Exchange/Administrator/Inbox/. However, you need to keep in mind that the ExOLEDB provider cannot access remote resources. Because ExOLEDB must bind to local items, it is a good idea to use file URLs in your program code, such as file://./backofficestorage/bluesky-inc-10.com/PUBLIC FOLDERS. This URL points explicitly to the local server. Furthermore, file URLs do not require you to configure virtual directories beforehand. For instance, if you have created an alternate public folder hierarchy in your test environment, you can access it right away using a URL similar to the following example: file://./backofficestorage/bluesky-inc-10.com/Alternate Tree.

OLE DB URLs have the following general format:

```
file://./backofficestorage/<domain name>/<MBX for mailboxes or the name
of the public folder hierarchy>/<user alias or name of public folder>/
<name of sub-level folder>
```

Note   The Exchange OLE DB provider registers the namespace file://./backofficestorage with the OLE DB root binder. You do not need to specify ExOLEDB explicitly when using file://./backofficestorage URLs with OLE DB or ADO. However, creating connection objects explicitly increases the readability of your code.

Exchange Installable File System

As mentioned earlier, you can use standard Win32 applications to read and write files directly in the Web Storage System. An Exchange Installable File System (ExIFS) driver allows you to access message streams using functions from Microsoft Win32 file APIs, such as CreateFile, ReadFile, and WriteFile. Item properties are inaccessible, but they can be retrieved using ExOLEDB, HTTP/WebDAV, or MAPI. You can examine a message stream when opening an item via ExIFS in Notepad. Message streams are encoded in Multipurpose Internet Mail Extensions (MIME).

Sharing Exchange 2000 Server Resources

By default, Exchange 2000 Server maps the local M drive to ExIFS. If M is already in use, the next available drive letter is taken. The ExIFS hierarchy starts with a folder that is named according to your Exchange 2000 Server organization, followed by sublevel objects called Public Folders and Mbx. If alternative public folder hierarchies have been created, they will be listed at this level as well.

In the same way that you can share ordinary directories on the server for access over the network, you can share Exchange 2000 Server resources. Unfortunately, these network shares are lost during a server reboot. ExIFS does not preserve the configuration, which requires you to recreate the network shares after each server restart. A batch file can simplify the task of recreating network shares by using net share commands. You may find it more convenient to share Exchange 2000 Server resources via HTTP/WebDAV and use Web Folders to access the repositories, as illustrated in Exercise 5 of Chapter 11, "Internet-Based Client Access."

Application and Data Repository

Direct file access through ExIFS allows you to store Web pages and other elements directly in public folders and then launch them via URLs and HTTP. In this way, you can implement and deploy entire collaboration applications in the Web Storage System (see Figure 23.2). Rather than creating virtual directories on the server's local file system, you can create virtual directories in the Web Storage System. To manage virtual directories, use Exchange System Manager, as explained in Chapter 22, "Microsoft Outlook Web Access."

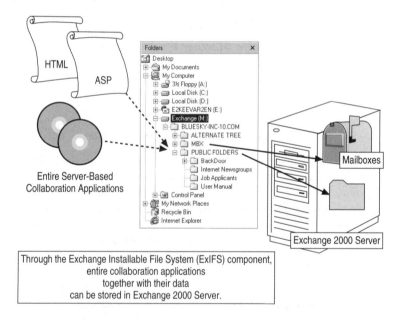

Figure 23.2   Implementing collaboration applications in the Web Storage System

Installing collaboration applications in the Web Storage System provides the following advantages:

- Access to applications can be managed using Exchange System Manager. The Web Storage System is fully integrated with Windows 2000 security and file system infrastructures. Security features are discussed in Chapter 19, "Implementing Advanced Security."

- All application services can be integrated in a single location, making it easier to find, use, and share information.

- Applications installed in public folders can be replicated to other servers for load balancing and increased fault tolerance.

- Backup and restore procedures and ongoing maintenance tasks are centralized. Administrators need to configure, monitor, and back up only one type of server.

- Collaboration applications can benefit from advanced system configurations, such as Windows 2000 active/active clustering.

- The Web Storage System supports transaction logging and ensures data integrity through redundancy.

- Users can employ a wide variety of client applications to access collaboration applications.

Internet and MAPI-Based Messaging Clients

The Web Storage System relies on the Information Store service, and for that reason, most Web Storage System information is accessible for MAPI-based clients as well as Internet mail clients, such as Microsoft Outlook Express. Collaboration solutions implemented in public folders may also be accessed using newsreaders, as explained in Chapter 11, "Internet-Based Client Access."

Important   The Web Storage System is not MAPI dependent. Exchange Interprocess Communication (ExIPC) mechanisms are used to communicate with the Information Store service (see Chapter 3, "Microsoft Exchange 2000 Server Architecture").

Automatic Property Promotion

Information stores consist of an Exchange database (.edb) and an Exchange streaming database (.stm). Data streams from non-MAPI applications are written to the Exchange streaming database in MIME format, as explained in Chapter 20, "Microsoft Exchange 2000 Server Maintenance and Troubleshooting."

The Information Store service parses the item streams for known properties, which are promoted to the .edb database to support MAPI-based applications, such as Microsoft Outlook 2000 (see Figure 23.3). This process is known as property promotion and was illustrated in Exercise 1 of Chapter 21, "Microsoft Outlook Forms Environment."

Automatic property promotion eliminates the need to open and close documents and other items to view and access data. Integrated and custom views, available in Outlook 2000 and OWA, provide an easy and efficient way to display, sort, and manage items. A folder view gives an item summary at a glance and helps to enhance your productivity. Property promotion is supported for MIME-based messages and Microsoft Office documents.

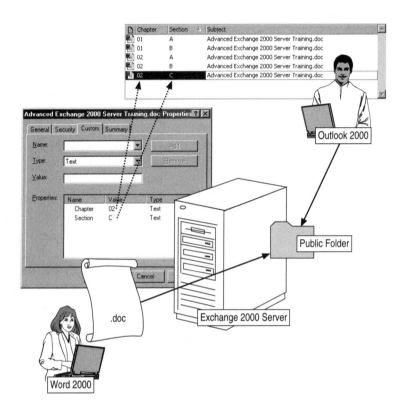

Figure 23.3 Promoted custom properties in a folder view

Lesson 2: Designing a Web Storage System Solution

Exchange 2000 Server supports a powerful set of authoring tools to allow developers to quickly get started with Web Storage System applications. Microsoft Web Storage System Forms for Exchange 2000 Server, for instance, enables you to build HTML-based electronic forms in Microsoft FrontPage 2000 without the need for any programming. Microsoft Visual InterDev can be used to implement advanced collaboration solutions based on ASPs. With Visual Basic and Visual C++, on the other hand, you can develop COM components derived from OLE DB and ADO, which you may then reuse in other applications.

This lesson explains how to utilize the Web Storage System for customized collaboration solutions. It addresses how to extend the user interface of OWA and covers how to process items automatically based on Web Storage System events.

At the end of this lesson, you will be able to:

- Associate Web Storage System items with HTML-based custom forms.
- Describe the various types of Web Storage System events and their purposes.

Estimated time to complete this lesson: 45 minutes

Designing Web Storage System Forms

The Web Storage System is capable of handling electronic forms similar to Outlook 2000. Instead of Outlook forms, HTML- or ASP-based forms are launched when the user opens an item in a Web browser. A DLL called WMTEMPLATES.DLL defines the default templates used by OWA to render standard HTML forms for e-mail messages, contacts, and calendar objects. You can extend OWA by implementing a custom user interface based on Web Storage System forms. Web Storage System forms must be registered in the Web Storage System Forms Registry.

Web Storage System Forms for Exchange 2000 Server SDK

It is a good idea to install the Web Storage System Forms SDK on your Exchange 2000 server and the FrontPage Extensions for Web Storage System Forms on your workstation if you are planning to design Web Storage System forms. The server component integrates a custom forms engine (EXWFORM.DLL) into Exchange 2000 Server, which is used to render HTML forms with information from Web Storage System folders and items (see Figure 23.4).

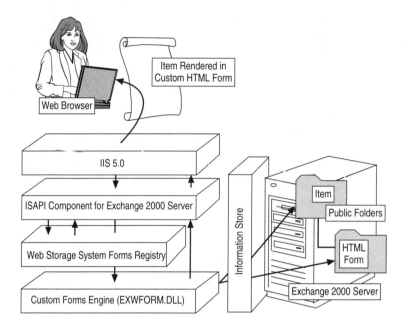

Figure 23.4 Web Storage System forms processing through a custom forms engine

Using FrontPage 2000 with extensions for Web Storage System Forms, you can build Web-based applications directly in the Web Storage System. This has several advantages. For instance, programming know-how is not required, custom properties can be defined conveniently, and HTML forms can be registered in the Web Storage System automatically. Knowledge about Web Storage System internals is not required. Using FrontPage, you can open Web pages directly in the Web Storage System to edit them. The functionality is similar to the FrontPage Extensions Web on a standard file system. Detailed information on how to design HTML-based Web Storage System forms is available in the Web Storage System Forms SDK documentation.

Reusing Outlook Web Access Elements

It is very easy to develop frame-based Web pages using FrontPage. When you set each frame to use a particular Web page, you may specify URLs that point to Web Storage System folders or individual items. OWA will then be used to render the contents in these frames. For instance, you can build a page that displays both the Calendar and the Inbox folder.

Web Storage System Forms Based on Active Server Pages

The Web Storage System is capable of launching ASP-based forms directly and without the need for a custom forms engine. EXWFORM.DLL is not required to fill the Web page because ASPs can retrieve item properties themselves. However, it is convenient to design the forms using FrontPage 2000 first, and then extending the functionality through ASPs developed in Visual InterDev. Visual InterDev does not allow you to manage the forms registry or schema definitions automatically. If you do not want to use FrontPage 2000 for this purpose, you need to create the form registration items and property definitions manually.

Web Storage System Forms Registry

To use custom Web pages in the Web Storage System, you need to reference them in registration items. Every Web Storage System folder provides access to an urn:schemas-microsoft-com:exch-data:schema-collection-ref property, which identifies the default URL of the folder in which to look for schema definition items and forms registries. If this property is not set, the default location is non_ipm_subtree/Schema in the folder's mailbox or public store.

The forms registration is based on items with a DAV:contentclass of urn:schemas-microsoft-com:office:forms#registration. Various properties can be set for this item type to control how the referenced Web page is used. For instance, one Web page may represent the default view for a folder, and another may be launched when an item of a particular content class is opened. Data and forms must reside on the same server. Remote access to forms over the network is not supported.

Based on the information obtained from the browser (that is, requested URL and HTTP header information), the Web Storage System looks for a form definition that matches the requested item, the browser capabilities, and other information. Through a best-fit comparison the appropriate form is determined for the rendering process.

Important information retrieved from forms definitions includes the following:

- **urn:schemas-microsoft-com:office:forms#executeurl.**   Identifies the forms rendering engine (an ASP page or an Internet Server Application Programming Interface [ISAPI] filter, such as EXWFORM.DLL).

- **urn:schemas-microsoft-com:office:forms#formurl.**   Identifies the form that should be used to render the data from the item specified in the data URL.

Note   For ASPs, both executeurl and formurl must be set to the ASP page. ASPs do not require the help of a forms rendering engine to generate Web pages.

Web Storage System Forms Adaptivity

The forms registry has a great influence in the behavior of customized Web Storage System applications. Each registration item maps a certain set of circumstances through its properties to a specific form. For instance, you may implement one form for Internet Explorer 5.0 in English and another form for Microsoft Mobile Explorer in French to render the data in the best way possible according to the user's browser capabilities and language (see Figure 23.5). The user does not need to be concerned about this process. Based on the browser, the requested item, and forms registration information, the Web Storage System determines the appropriate form automatically. You may track message and content states, browser capabilities and version, and parse the browser's language. You can implement different forms for specific URL actions performed on an object (CMD=).

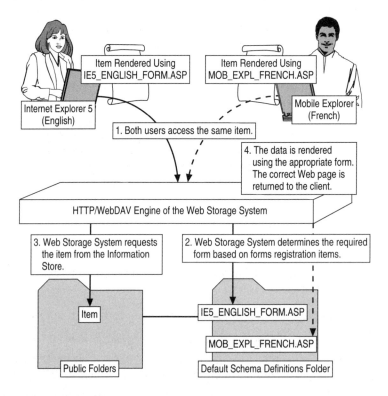

Figure 23.5   Accessing the same item from different Web browsers

To determine which version of a form to use, the Web Storage System checks the following information in subsequent order: HTTP request, URL query string (CMD=), message state, content state, browser capability, browser version, browser platform, major version number, minor version number, and browser language.

Every form registration item must contain the following basic properties:

- Content class of the form registration
- Form's content class
- Form URL
- Execute URL

Exercise 1: Implementing a Custom Web Form for Outlook Web Access

In this exercise you will create a public folder and register a custom ASP page in the Web Storage System. You will use a simple yet very illustrative sample form from the Microsoft Exchange 2000 Server Platform SDK.

To view a multimedia demonstration that displays how to perform this procedure, run the EX1CH23*.AVI files from the \Exercise_Information\Chapter23 folder on the Supplemental Course Materials CD.

Prerequisites

- Restart BLUESKY-SRV1 and BLUESKY-WKSTA.

- Log on as Administrator to both machines.

- Insert the Supplemental Course Materials CD into the CD-ROM drive of BLUESKY-SRV1, which contains the required scripts INSTALLMESSAGE.VBS and CUSTOMMESSAGE.ASP from the Exchange 2000 Server Platform SDK in the \Sample_Scripts\Chapter23 folder.

▶ **To implement a custom Web interface for a contact management solution**

1. On BLUESKY-SRV1, copy the file called INSTALLMESSAGE.VBS from the Supplemental Course Materials CD to the root directory of your system partition (C). The following listing shows the code of INSTALLMESSAGE.VBS (line breaks have been added to handle page formatting):

```
Install

Sub Install

'Get the folder

sFolder = InputBox("Please enter the URL to the folder" _
    & ": example http://serverName/public/foldername" _
    ,"Setup Instructions")

If Trim(sFolder) = "" Then

    Exit Sub

End If

'Create the app folder,
' pointing its SCR to the BIN subfolder

Set oDest = CreateObject("CDO.Folder")

oDest.Fields("urn:schemas-microsoft-com:" _
    & "exch-data:schema-collection-ref") = _
```

```
                         sFolder + "\bin"
        odest.Fields("DAV:contentclass") = "urn:content-classes:folder"
        oDest.Fields.Update
        oDest.DataSource.SaveTo sFolder
        'Create the BIN folder and make it invisible
        Set oDest = CreateObject("CDO.Folder")
        oDest.Fields("DAV:ishidden") = True
        oDest.Fields.Update
        oDest.DataSource.SaveTo sFolder +  "/bin"
        'Fill the BIN folder with form registrations
        Set oCon = CreateObject("ADODB.Connection")
        oCon.ConnectionString = sFolder + "/bin"
        oCon.Provider = "ExOledb.Datasource"
        oCon.Open
        '--------------------------

        'Register the default page for the folder
        Set oRec = CreateObject("ADODB.Record")
        oRec.Open "default.reg", oCon, 3, 0
        oRec.Fields("DAV:contentclass") = _
            "urn:schemas-microsoft-com:office:forms#registration"
        oRec.Fields("urn:schemas-microsoft-com:office:forms#contentclass") = _
            "urn:content-classes:message"
        oRec.Fields("urn:schemas-microsoft-com:office:forms#cmd") = "open"
        oRec.Fields("urn:schemas-microsoft-com:office:forms#formurl") = _
            "CustomMessage.asp"
        oRec.Fields("urn:schemas-microsoft-com:office:forms#executeurl") = _
            "CustomMessage.asp"
        oRec.Fields.Update
        oRec.Close
        'Further instructions
        MsgBox "Copy CustomMessage.ASP into the BIN directory." _
            & " Enable script execution on the directory.", _
            64, "Further Instructions"
        End Sub
```

2. Click Start and point to Run. In the Run dialog box, type **c:\installmessage.vbs**, and then click OK.

3. In the Setup Instructions dialog box, type **http://bluesky-srv1/public/custommsg**, and then click OK (see Figure 23.6).

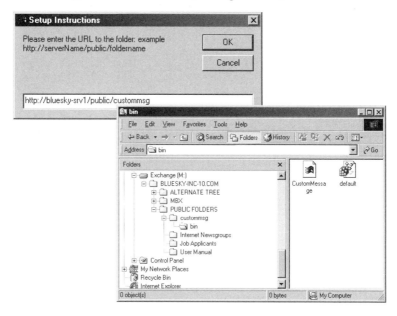

Figure 23.6 Preparing a customized Web Storage System form

4. INSTALLMESSAGE.VBS creates a new public folder called CustomMsg and a subfolder called Bin. It also sets the schema collection reference for CustomMsg to CustomMsg\Bin. When all resources have been created and configured, INSTALLMESSAGE.VBS will display a Further Instructions dialog box to inform you that you need to copy the CUSTOMMESSAGE.ASP file into the Bin directory and that you need to enable script execution for the directory. Click OK.

5. Launch Windows Explorer and copy the CUSTOMMESSAGE.ASP file from the SDK CD into M:\Bluesky-inc-10.com\Public Folders\Custommsg\Bin. Because the Bin directory is hidden, in the Folder Options dialog box, you may have to enable the Show Hidden Files And Folders option. CUSTOMMESSAGE.ASP has the following listing:

```
<%@Language=VBScript%>

<html>

<body>


<%
```

```
dataurl = request.querystring("dataurl")
Set c = Server.CreateObject("ADODB.Connection")
c.ConnectionString = dataurl
c.Provider = "ExOledb.Datasource"
c.Open
Set r = Server.CreateObject("ADODB.Record")
r.Open dataurl, c, 3

%>


<form class="form" method="post"
action="<%=request.querystring("dataurl")%>?Cmd=save">


<h3> Message</h3>
Subject:<input type="text" name="urn:schemas:mailheader:subject"
value="<%=r("urn:schemas:mailheader:subject")%>"


<input type="submit" value="Save">
</form>


<%
r.Close
c.Close
%>
</body>
</html>
```

Important   If anonymous access is enabled for the Public virtual directory, INSTALLMESSAGE.VBS will run in the context of the anonymous IIS account. In this case, you may not have the required permissions to modify items in the CustomMsg or Bin public folder. Use Exchange System Manager to adjust the client permissions and propagate the changes to all subfolders. The configuration of folder permissions was illustrated in Exercise 2 of Chapter 17, "Public Folder Management."

6. Launch Exchange System Manager from the Microsoft Exchange program group, expand Administrative Groups, First Administrative Group, and

Servers. Expand BLUESKY-SRV1, Protocols, HTTP, and then Exchange Virtual Server.

7. Right-click Public, and then select Properties.

8. Click on the Access tab, and select Scripts or Scripts And Executables under Execute Permissions. Click OK.

9. On BLUESKY-WKSTA, launch Outlook 2000, and make sure you are connected to the Administrator mailbox.

10. From the View menu, select the Folder List if it is not already displayed, expand the Public Folders tree, expand All Public Folders, right-click on CustomMsg, and then select Properties.

11. Click on the Home Page tab, and, under Address, type **http://bluesky-srv1/public/custommsg?cmd=contents**. Select the Show Home Page By Default For This Folder check box, and then click OK.

12. Verify that Internet Explorer 5.0 is launched in Outlook 2000 when displaying the details pane of the CustomMsg public folder. In the upper left corner of the Web page, click New.

13. In the Subject line, type The custom form will be launched when an existing item is opened, and then click Post.

14. Right-click the Web page and select Refresh to display the newly created item in the Web page. Double-click it and verify that the item's data is automatically rendered using CUSTOMMESSAGE.ASP (see Figure 23.7).

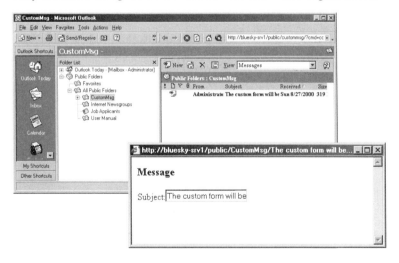

Figure 23.7 Opening items in a custom Web page in Outlook 2000

Exercise Summary

The Web Storage System supports custom HTML forms based on ASP scripts or ISAPI filters. Any form must be registered in a forms registration item. This exercise used an item called DEFAULT.REG to specify the CUSTOMMESSAGE.ASP file for the Open command, oRec.Fields("urn:schemas-microsoft-com:office:forms#cmd") = "open". Based on the registration properties of the DEFAULT.REG item, the Web Storage System is able to locate the desired custom form, retrieve it, and use it to render the data. Custom forms can be stored in the information store along with the actual user items. For ASP pages, you need to ensure that Script and Execute permissions are granted. ISAPI filters, such as EXWFORM.DLL, require Script and Executable permissions for the virtual directory. You do not access the forms renderer, such as an ASP page, directly. Instead, the Web Storage System launches the form automatically when you work with items in the Web Storage System.

Synchronous, Asynchronous, and System Events

The event model of Exchange 2000 Server allows you to work with two general types of events: transport events and Web Storage System events. Both can be asynchronous or synchronous. While transport events allow you to customize the behavior of the Simple Mail Transfer Protocol (SMTP) or Network News Transfer Protocol (NNTP) service, Web Storage System events, based on OLE DB, enable you to implement workflow and process-tracking logic. Web Storage System events are the basis of workflow, which is a topic of Chapter 24, "Workgroup and Workflow Technologies."

Web Storage System events are useful in many scenarios. For example, a vacation planner application could initiate an approval process when a user submits a new vacation request. Through an asynchronous event, you can notify the user's manager that a new request is now awaiting approval in the Web Storage System folder. Likewise, another asynchronous event may inform the user when the manager approves (changes) the request item or denies (deletes) it. Synchronous events, on the other hand, enable you to check data before it is saved. You may use a synchronous event, for instance, to prevent the transmission of incomplete vacation requests (see Figure 23.8).

Synchronous events occur before, and asynchronous events occur after, any changes are committed to the store. Synchronous events are called OnSyncSave and OnSyncDelete. Similarly, asynchronous events are called OnSave and OnDelete. When a user saves an item in the Web Storage System, OnSyncSave is fired before the changes are committed, followed by OnSave. Likewise, OnSyncDelete occurs before an item is deleted, followed by OnDelete when the deletion is committed. In addition, Exchange 2000 Server supports three system events: OnTimer (timer events), OnMDBStartUp (a store is mounted), and OnMDBShutdown (a store is dismounted).

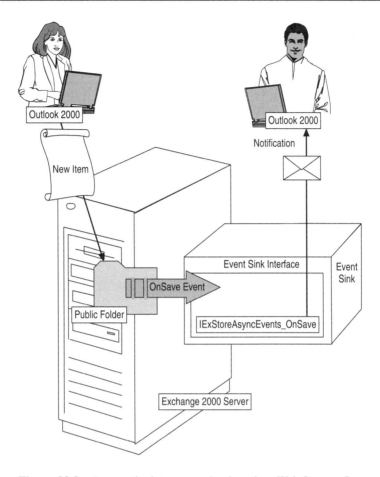

Figure 23.8   Automatic data processing based on Web Storage System events

Synchronous event sinks fire first, followed by folder rules (if defined), and asynchronous event sinks. Synchronous events support priority values, which can be registered for each event sink. Asynchronous events do not support priorities and fire in an arbitrary order. Unlike synchronous events, asynchronous events do not block the event source and cannot obtain exclusive control over the item that triggered the event. An item may be deleted before an asynchronous event is fired.

Event Registrations

Event sinks are the entities that receive and process Web Storage System events. They can be custom COM classes or scripts that the Web Storage System calls according to the properties specified in an event registration. Only when the event meets the event registration criteria is the appropriate event method called in the event sink. To register events, you can use a VBScript file called REGEVENT.VBS, which you can find on the Exchange 2000 Server CD. You can use REGEVENT.VBS to register, enumerate, and delete event registrations. For parameter definitions and examples of how to use REGEVENT.VBS, see the Exchange 2000 Server SDK documentation.

Note   Web Storage System event sinks are registered in the IIS metabase via Server Extension Objects (SEO). The ExOLEDB provider reads the event registration and calls the appropriate bound event sinks.

Chapter Summary

The Web Storage System relies on Microsoft Windows 2000 Server and IIS 5.0. It supports Web browsers and WebDAV applications by means of HTTP, WebDAV, and XML. Other applications, such as Internet mail or MAPI-based clients, can also be used to access information. ADO 2.5 and OLE DB applications work with Exchange 2000 Server resources based on ExOLEDB. Every item in the Web Storage System is accessible through a URL.

When accessing items by means of Windows Explorer and Web Folders, you can work with Exchange 2000 Server similar to a file server. Web browsers receive a different view of the data. The Web Storage System determines the client based on HTTP request header information, checks the requested item and its state, and locates an appropriate form to render the information. Custom Web Storage System forms can be registered per folder in form registration items.

The Web Storage System also supports events based on ExOLEDB. This enables you to implement workflow and process-tracking logic. You can intercept synchronous, asynchronous, and system events. Web Storage System event sinks must be registered in the IIS metabase.

Review

The following review questions can help you determine if you have sufficiently familiarized yourself with the material covered in this chapter. You can find the answers to these questions at the end of this book in Appendix A, "Questions and Answers."

1. Which Exchange 2000 Server component allows applications access to mailbox and public folder resources based on ADO?

2. What is the advantage of the ExIFS driver?

3. You plan to implement a simple Web-based enterprise solution to demonstrate the benefits of Exchange 2000 Server. How can you quickly implement Web-based folder views and custom forms into a demo public folder?

4. What is the purpose of the Web Storage System Forms Registry?

5. You have implemented a Web-based travel expense report application. It is required to route new expense reports to the finance department for approval. Which feature of the Web Storage System would you use to implement the required functionality?

CHAPTER 24

Workgroup and Workflow Technologies

About This Chapter

Collaboration data objects (CDO) is a popular technology to add messaging functionality to business applications. This technology was not always referred to as CDO. In Microsoft Exchange Server 4.0, the name was OLE Messaging, which was changed in Exchange Server 5.0 to Active Messaging. In Exchange Server 5.5, Microsoft decided to change the name again to describe the technology more intuitively. This time the name became Collaboration Data Objects. However, innovation never stops at Microsoft. Although the name hasn't changed, distinct versions of CDO evolved, called CDO for Exchange Server 5.5 (CDO 1.2.1) and CDO for Windows NT Server (CDONTS). Different CDO versions are also available for Microsoft Windows 2000 Server (CDOSYS) and Microsoft Exchange 2000 Server (CDOEX). Furthermore, Exchange 2000 Server introduces CDO for Exchange Management (CDOEXM) and CDO for Workflow (CDOWF). Short, CDO provides a vast spectrum of programmable objects. It is a comprehensive technology to build custom solutions that exactly match the needs of your organization.

CDO for Exchange 2000 Server will install cleanly over CDO for Windows 2000 Server. You do not need to recompile or reprogram any solutions that have been developed with CDOSYS. CDO 1.2.1 and CDOEX, however, are not alike. CDO 1.2.1 is based on the Messaging Application Programming Interface (MAPI).

Because Exchange 2000 Server is fully backward compatible, CDO 1.2.1 remains an important programming technology that comes with Microsoft Outlook 2000 and is also installed as part of Exchange 2000 Server. CDOEX, on the other hand, is based on an entirely new approach that retreats from MAPI and employs the technologies of the Microsoft Web Storage System. It relies on the Exchange Object Linking and Embedding Database (ExOLE DB) provider, which can only be used directly on the server. This is not a disadvantage. CDOEX is a perfect choice for programming Microsoft Active Server Pages (ASPs), ActiveX DLLs, Microsoft Web Storage System event sinks, and Windows 2000 services that run on the server.

This chapter concentrates on the new CDO technologies for Exchange 2000 Server. Lesson 1 introduces CDOEX. Lesson 2 then illustrates how to use CDOEXM to manage an Exchange 2000 server. Lesson 3 discusses CDOWF and related tools to design workflow processes.

Before You Begin

To complete this chapter:

- You need to be familiar with the concepts of ActiveX Data Objects (ADO), ExOLEDB, and the Web Storage System, as explained in Chapter 23, "Microsoft Exchange 2000 Web Storage System."

- You should have a general understanding of the essential Exchange 2000 components and their interaction with each other, as covered in Chapter 3, "Microsoft Exchange 2000 Server Architecture."

- You only need a minimum level of skills for Visual Basic Scripting Edition (VBScript) to follow the code samples in this chapter. All code samples are also available in the form of .vbs files in the Sample_Scripts\Chapter24 folder on the Supplemental Course Materials CD-ROM.

Lesson 1: CDO for Exchange 2000 Server

CDO for Exchange 2000 Server is a fundamental technology for messaging solutions based on the Web Storage System. You can manage folders, messages, and other items. CDOEX supports RFC 822, Multipurpose Internet Mail Extensions (MIME), iCalendar, and vCard formats. The new CDO is closely related to ADO. Their combination is the key to unfolding the full potential of Exchange 2000 Server.

This lesson compares CDO to ADO 2.5 and then introduces typical CDO features. This lesson provides small VBScript code examples that illustrate how to send messages, handle appointments and meeting requests, and deal with contact information.

At the end of this lesson, you will be able to:

- Decide when to use CDO and ADO in a business solution.
- Handle messaging, calendaring, and contact management via CDO.

Estimated time to complete this lesson: 60 minutes

ActiveX Data Objects Versus Collaboration Data Objects

Database developers that need to access Exchange 2000 Server will find ADO very convenient to use. ADO 2.5 works similarly in Exchange 2000 Server, Microsoft Access, or Microsoft SQL Server environments. You can access items in mailbox and public folders similar to discrete rows in database tables. ADO allows you to navigate through record sets, control individual records, save generic items, and so on. As a classic database interface, however, ADO does not provide explicit messaging functionality. You can read more about ADO in Chapter 23, "Microsoft Exchange 2000 Web Storage System."

CDO was designed specifically with messaging and collaboration in mind. It is a set of Component Object Model (COM)-based interfaces that allow you to perform actions such as sending messages, managing contacts, scheduling appointments, handling meeting requests, creating folders, and so on. CDO is the ideal choice to implement workflow and other collaborative applications.

It is advantageous to use both ADO and CDO in your applications where appropriate. CDO objects can be bound to ADO objects directly. Any changes made with CDO can be saved back to ADO. Only one session is required to work with both technologies. This helps minimize resource consumption and increase performance.

Consider using CDO instead of ADO in the following scenarios:

- To encode data using Internet standard transfer formats, such as MIME Base64 (which replaced the legacy Unix–to–Unix encoding method [UUENCODE]), and plain text, quoted-printable (which encodes data similar to US ASCII and results in human readable text).

- To implement business logic that is optimized for messaging and collaboration instead of structured databases.

- To implement calendars, appointments, meeting requests, and contact management.

- To simplify working with the raw data in item streams. CDO formats streams for messages, appointments, and contacts based on Internet standard formats automatically and recreates streams when item properties are changed. ADO does not synchronize message streams with item properties.

Note You can use both CDO and ADO to access Exchange 2000 Server resources. Both technologies rely on ExOLEDB and use the features of the Web Storage System (see Figure 24.1).

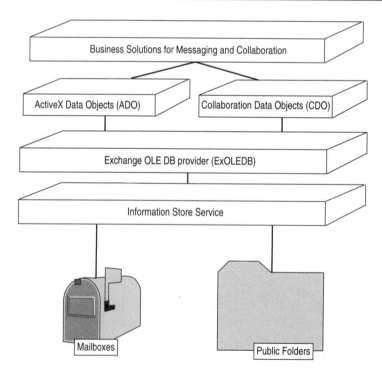

Figure 24.1 Using ADO and CDO for messaging and collaboration

CDO for Exchange 2000 Server Object Model

CDO for Exchange 2000 Server is implemented in CDOEX.DLL, which can be found in the \Program Files\Common Files\Microsoft Shared\Cdo directory. The main interfaces that this component exports are used to form Folder and Message, Appointment, and Person CoClasses (see Figure 24.2). Detailed information about CDO objects is available in the Microsoft Exchange 2000 Server Platform Software Development Kit (SDK).

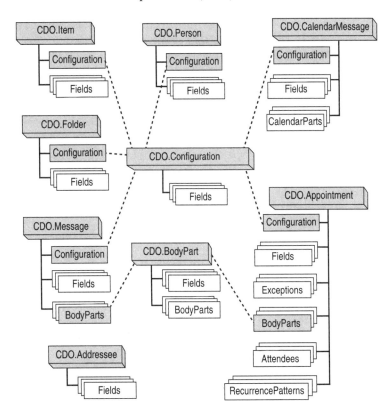

Figure 24.2   The CDO for Exchange 2000 Server Object Model

The Configuration COM Class

A central component in the CDOEX object model is the Configuration CoClass, which allows you to manage configuration settings used with most of the other CDOEX objects. The Configuration object holds specific information in its fields collection, which represents a set of ADO Field objects. The most important configuration fields are defined in the namespace: *http://schemas.microsoft.com/cdo/configuration/*.

Note   Namespaces do not correspond to Web sites.

An important field that you may want to set explicitly corresponds to the http://
schemas.microsoft.com/cdo/configuration/sendusing/ property. It can be set to
cdoSendUsingPickup (1), cdoSendUsingPort (2), or cdoSendUsingExchange (3).
When you set it to cdoSendUsingPickup, new messages are placed in the local
Simple Mail Transfer Protocol (SMTP) service's pickup directory. Specify
cdoSendUsingPort if you want to connect to the SMTP service via TCP port 25
(if you overwrite the port by using the http://schemas.microsoft.com/cdo/con-
figuration/smtpserverport/ property, you also need to identify the target SMTP
host via http://schemas.microsoft.com/cdo/configuration/smtpserver/). The default value, however, is cdoSendUsingExchange, which causes CDO to pass new
messages to the Information Store service.

Note   To send messages to recipients in your Exchange 2000 Server organization, use cdoSendUsingExchange (the default). When sending messages to
Internet recipients, however, you may get better performance by using SMTP
directly (cdoSendUsingPickup or cdoSendUsingPort). Sending messages through
the SMTP service also allows you to specify a nonexisting sender address for
anonymous messages.

When sending messages via Exchange 2000 Server (cdoSendUsingExchange),
the following configuration information may also be important:

- **http://schemas.microsoft.com/cdo/configuration/mailboxurl/.**   Points to
  the URL of the user's mailbox, such as http://bluesky-srv1/Exchange/Admin-
  istrator/. Setting this property explicitly increases performance. If it is not set,
  CDO must query the Active Directory directory service to locate the user's
  mailbox.

- **http://schemas.microsoft.com/cdo/configuration/sendusername/.**   Identifies the mailbox-enabled user account to be used to send messages. The value
  of this property can have the form User@<Domain Name>,
  mailto:User@<Domain Name>, or <NT Domain Name>\User. Among other
  things, the sendusername is used to determine the user's mailbox URL if the
  mailboxurl configuration property was not specified.

- **http://schemas.microsoft.com/cdo/configuration/activeconnection/.**
  Enables you to increase the performance of CDO. You can bind an ADO connection object to the user's mailbox and specify it in the activeconnection
  configuration property. Otherwise, a new connection object must be created
  whenever you send messages, which is automatically destroyed afterward.

- **http://schemas.microsoft.com/cdo/configuration/sendpassword/.**   Allows
  you to specify the user's password for authentication with system services,
  such as Active Directory.

The following code snippet sets the important configuration properties for the Administrator account in the test environment of Blue Sky Airlines (SCRIPT1CH24.VBS):

```
'*-*-* Definition of CDO constants for VBScript *-*-*
const cdoSendUsingMethod = _
   " http://schemas.microsoft.com/cdo/configuration/sendusing"
const cdoSendUserName = _
   "http://schemas.microsoft.com/cdo/configuration/sendusername"
const cdoActiveConnection = _
   "http://schemas.microsoft.com/cdo/configuration/activeconnection"
const cdoSendPassword = _
   "hLtp://schemas.microsoft.com/cdo/configuration/sendpassword"
const cdoMailboxURL = _
   "http://schemas.microsoft.com/cdo/configuration/mailboxurl"
const cdoSendUsingExchange = 3
'*-*-* Creation of an explicit ADO Connection *-*-*
'*-*-* This object must point to the user's mailbox *-*-*
Set oConn = CreateObject("ADODB.Connection")
oConn.Provider = "ExOLEDB.DataSource"
oConn.Open _
"file://./BackOfficeStorage/bluesky-inc-10.com/MBX/Administrator/"


'*-*-* The actual CDO code *-*-*
Set oConf = CreateObject("CDO.Configuration")
Set oFlds = oConf.Fields


oFlds (cdoSendUsingMethod) = cdoSendUsingExchange
oFlds (cdoSendUserName) = "Administrator@bluesky-inc-10.com"
oFlds (cdoActiveConnection) = oConn
oFlds (cdoSendPassword) = "password"
oFlds (cdoMailboxURL) = "http://bluesky-srv1/Exchange/Administrator/"
oFlds.Update
```

Note   CDO for Exchange 2000 Server can determine your current user information automatically when testing program code locally on the server. In this case, you do not have to specify configuration parameters explicitly.

Sending CDO Messages

It is remarkably easy to work with messages using the Message CoClass of CDOEX. The following code example creates and sends an outbound message with an attachment to Carl Titmouse. At a minimum, a recipient address and the originator address must be specified before you can invoke the Send method. Of course, it is also helpful to specify a subject and message text.

The following VBScript example creates and sends a message with an attachment to Carl Titmouse (SCRIPT2CH24.VBS):

```
Set oMsg = CreateObject ("CDO.Message")


oMsg.From = "Administrator@bluesky-inc-10.com"

oMsg.To = "CarlT@bluesky-inc-10.com"

oMsg.Subject = "CDO for Exchange 2000 Server"


oMsg.TextBody = "It is remarkably easy to construct" _
    & " and send messages using CDO for Exchange 2000 Server."


oMsg.AddAttachment("c:\winnt\clock.avi")


oMsg.Send
```

Note   If you want to test this code snippet in a .vbs file, you need to log on as Administrator to BLUESKY-SRV1. Because a CDO Configuration object was not used, sender information will be obtained from the currently logged on user. If you want to test this code in conjunction with the Configuration object created in the previous snippet, insert the following line after Set oMsg = CreateObject ("CDO.Message"): `Set oMsg.Configuration = oConf.`

Sending messages involves the following tasks:

1. CDO creates a message item in the originator's Outbox using ExOLEDB.

2. The message content is streamed into the newly created item.

3. The Information Store is informed to transfer the message.

4. A copy of the message may be saved to the Sent Items folder.

CDO Calendaring

CDO for Exchange 2000 Server provides three objects that allow you to work with calendar information—Appointment, CalendarMessage, and Addressee.

Appointments are discrete items that you can create in private and public calendar folders. CalendarMessage works similar to a normal CDO message, with the exception that it contains a CalendarParts attachment, which provides information about the appointment. A more intuitive name for CalendarMessage would be meeting request. Addressee objects allow you to resolve address information into recipients, which in turn provide access to free/busy information.

It is important to note that CDO sends meeting requests in iCalendar format according to RFC 2445. This provides for highest interoperability between users who have different calendar applications. Exchange 2000 Server is able to convert iCalendar items to meeting requests in MAPI format. In addition, CDO places a plaintext version of the meeting request in the message body. You can overwrite the default text, however, using the TextBody property as demonstrated for a CDO.Message object in the previous code example.

The following VBScript example creates an appointment in the Administrator's Calendar folder and sends a meeting request for this appointment to Carl Titmouse (SCRIPT3CH24.VBS):

```
'*-*-* Definition of CDO constants for VBScript *-*-*
const cdoRequiredParticipant = 0
const cdoSendEmailAddress = _
    "http://schemas.microsoft.com/cdo/configuration/sendemailaddress"


'*-*-* Creating a Configuration object *-*-*
Set oConf = CreateObject ("CDO.Configuration")


oConf.Fields(cdoSendEmailAddress) = "Administrator@bluesky-inc-10.com"
oConf.Fields.Update


'*-*-* Creating the appointment *-*-*
Set oAppt = CreateObject ("CDO.Appointment")
Set oAppt.Configuration = oConf


oAppt.StartTime = #12/31/2000 22:30:00 PM#
oAppt.EndTime = #01/01/2001 2:30:00 AM#
oAppt.Subject = "Happy New Year"


oAppt.TextBody = "Our Annual New Year Party"
```

```
'*-*-* Inviting additional users *-*-*
Set oAttendee = oAppt.Attendees.Add
oAttendee.Address = "CarlT@bluesky-inc-10.com"
oAttendee.Role = cdoRequiredParticipant
'*-*-* Sending a meeting request *-*-*
Set oCalMsg = oAppt.Publish
oCalMsg.Message.To = "CarlT@bluesky-inc-10.com"
oCalMsg.Message.Subject = "New Year Party"
oCalMsg.Message.TextBody = "Come to our annual New Year Party!"
oCalMsg.Message.Send


'*-*-* Saving the appointment in the Calendar folder *-*-*
oAppt.DataSource.SaveToContainer _
"file://./BackOfficeStorage/bluesky-inc-10.com" _
    & "/MBX/Administrator/calendar/"
```

To successfully send meeting requests to attendees, you need to specify the default e-mail address of the message sender (cdoSendEmailAddress) in a Configuration object and add this object to the appointment. You should also ensure that the left half of the sender's SMTP address is specified in the file URL of SaveToContainer. This is not necessarily the user's Windows 2000 account name. For instance, if the Administrator account has an SMTP address of Admin@BlueSky-inc-10.com, you need to specify a URL of "file://./BackOfficeStorage/bluesky-inc-10.com/MBX/Admin/calendar/". Otherwise, SaveToContainer may return CDO error &H80040E19.

Contact Management

The CDO Person object is also interesting. It enables you to create and manage contact information through the Web Storage System. You can also work with contact objects in Active Directory. The only difference is that you need to specify an LDAP URL that points to a directory object instead of a file URL that references an item in a mailbox or public store. Lesson 2 covers management of user-related directory information in greater detail.

The following VBScript example creates a contact object in the Administrator's Contacts folder (SCRIPT4CH24.VBS):

```
'*-*-* Creating a CDO Person object *-*-*
Set oPerson = CreateObject("CDO.Person")
```

```
'*-*-* Specifying Person properties *-*-*
oPerson.FirstName = "Phil"

oPerson.LastName = "Pheasant"

oPerson.WorkCity = "Miami"

oPerson.WorkState = "Florida"

oPerson.WorkPostalCode = "33120"

oPerson.WorkStreet = "23415 SE 19th Street"

oPerson.WorkPhone = "(305) 123456789"

oPerson.WorkFax = "(305) 987654321"

oPerson.Email = "Phil.Pheasant@bluesky-inc-10.com"

oPerson.Fields("objectClass").Value = "contact"

oPerson.Fields.Update


'*-*-* Saving the CDO Person object in the Contacts folder *-*-*
oPerson.DataSource.SaveToContainer _

"   file://./BackOfficeStorage/bluesky-inc-10.com" _

    & "/MBX/Administrator/Contacts/"
```

For compatibility with third-party contact management applications, Person objects provide a GetVCardStream method, which gives you access to the contents in vCard-compliant MIME format.

The following VBScript example retrieves a vCard-compliant stream from the Administrator account and saves it to a file on the server's file system (SCRIPT5CH24.VBS):

```
Set oPerson = CreateObject("CDO.Person")


oPerson.DataSource.Open _

    "LDAP://bluesky-srv1.BlueSky-inc-10.com/" _

    & "CN=Administrator,CN=Users,DC=BlueSky-inc-10,DC=com"


oPerson.GetVcardStream.SaveToFile  "c:\adm_vcard.txt"
```

Lesson 2: CDO for Exchange Management

CDO for Exchange Management offers exciting opportunities for custom management solutions. Similar to Active Directory Services Interface (ADSI), CDOEXM enables you to access and manipulate Active Directory objects. Through Exchange 2000 Server management functionality, collaborative applications can mailbox-enable user accounts, define mailbox properties, create and delete mailbox and public stores, build public folder hierarchies, and configure Exchange 2000 Server as a front end or back end system.

This lesson introduces the main features of CDO for Exchange Management. As in Lesson 1, small VBScript code examples are provided to illustrate the management of Exchange 2000 Server resources via CDOEXM.

At the end of this lesson, you will be able to:

- Decide when to use CDOEXM and ADSI in a business solution.

- Handle the management of mailbox and public stores.

- Mailbox-enable user accounts.

Estimated time to complete this lesson: 35 minutes

Collaboration Data Objects Versus Active Directory Services Interfaces

CDO for Exchange Management is implemented in CDOEXM.DLL, which resides in the \Program Files\Exchsrvr\Bin directory. CDOEXM is based on ADSI to access Exchange 2000 Server–related resources in Active Directory via LDAP. It aggregates the COM interfaces of ADSI to simplify programmatic tasks that are specific to Exchange 2000 Server administration (see Figure 24.3).

CDOEXM extends the ADSI interfaces and simplifies the management of Exchange 2000 Server resources that reside in Active Directory. When working with resources in the Web Storage System, CDOEXM communicates with the Information Store service through the Exadmin virtual directory. The purpose and administration of HTTP virtual directories is discussed in Chapter 22, "Microsoft Outlook Web Access."

You should use CDOEXM, for instance, if you need to create mailboxes for new users, set mailbox properties, or mail-enable contacts or public folders programmatically. ADSI, on the other hand, allows you to develop powerful directory applications that can be used to administer the entire Active Directory environment. However, ADSI is unable to work with Web Storage System resources. You cannot use ADSI to mount or dismount mailbox or public stores, for instance.

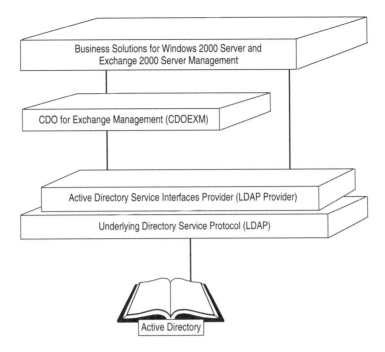

Figure 24.3   Using CDOEXM and ADSI for Exchange 2000 Server management

CDO for Exchange Management Security Issues

Basically, CDOEXM allows you to create management applications similar to Exchange System Manager. You can use CDOEXM remotely to build administrative components and snap-ins that run on separate computers and access Active Directory over the network. However, to manage Exchange 2000 Server, appropriate permissions are required in the organization. There is no difference from Exchange System Manager. You need to have Exchange Administrator permissions if you want to manage an organization, as discussed in Chapter 19, "Implementing Advanced Security."

Note   CDOEXM applications require the same level of permissions as Exchange System Manager.

CDO for Exchange Management Object Model

The CDOEXM object model clearly reflects the structure of Exchange 2000 Server resources in Active Directory (see Figure 24.4). Every Exchange 2000 server can have mailbox and public stores, which are grouped together by means of storage groups. The purpose of storage groups and information stores was discussed in detail in Chapter 20, "Microsoft Exchange 2000 Server Maintenance and Troubleshooting."

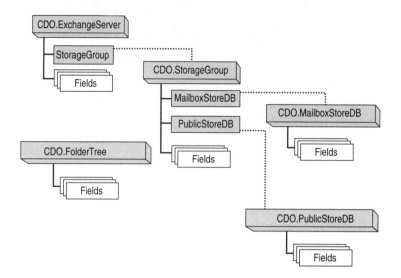

Figure 24.4   The CDO for Exchange Management object model

Working with Information Stores and Public Folder Hierarchies

In addition to interfaces for server, storage group, mailbox, and public stores, CDOEXM also provides a FolderTree object. This object can be used to manage public folder hierarchies, which need to be associated with public stores. Keep in mind that public folder hierarchies can only be associated with one public store on a given Exchange 2000 server. It is also important to note that you cannot create public stores if all existing public folder hierarchies are already associated with existing stores. You can read more about the management of public folder hierarchies in Chapter 17, "Public Folder Management."

The following VBScript example creates a new alternate public folder hierarchy and then associates the hierarchy with a new public store (SCRIPT6CH24.VBS):

```
'*-*-* Creating the required CDOEXM objects *-*-*
Set oHierarchy = CreateObject("CDOEXM.FolderTree")
Set oPubStoreDB = CreateObject("CDOEXM.PublicStoreDB")


'*-*-* Creating the new PF hierarchy *-*-*
strHierarchyURL = "LDAP://bluesky-srv1.BlueSky-inc-10.com/" _
    & "CN=New Hierarchy,CN=Folder Hierarchies," _
    & "CN=First Administrative Group,CN=Administrative Groups," _
    & "CN=Blue Sky Airlines,CN=Microsoft Exchange," _
    & "CN=Services,CN=Configuration,DC=BlueSky-inc-10,DC=com"
```

```
oHierarchy.Name = "New Hierarchy"
oHierarchy.DataSource.SaveTo strHierarchyURL


'*-*-* Creating the new public store *-*-*
oPubStoreDB.Name = "New Hierarchy Store"
oPubStoreDB.FolderTree = strHierarchyURL
oPubStoreDB.DataSource.SaveTo _
    "cn=New Hierarchy Store," _
  & "cn=First Storage Group,cn=InformationStore," _
  & "cn=BLUESKY-SRV1,cn=Servers,cn=First Administrative Group," _
  & "cn=Administrative Groups,cn=Blue Sky Airlines," _
  & "cn=Microsoft Exchange,cn=Services,cn=Configuration," _
  & "dc=BlueSky-inc-10,dc=com"


'*-*-* Mounting the new public store *-*-*
oPubStoreDB.Mount
```

Tip Further samples are available in the Exchange 2000 Server Platform SDK.
They demonstrate how to simplify the creation of LDAP URLs based on the
CDO.Server object.

Mailbox and Public Folder Management

When you examine the CDOEXM object model, you will find that explicit COM
classes for recipient management are not exposed. Instead, the required
CDOEXM interfaces are aggregated into existing CDO and ADSI CoClasses,
such as CDO.Person, CDO.Folder, and ADSI.User. The CDOEXM recipient interfaces are IMailRecipient and IMailboxStore, which you can retrieve from
CDO and ADSI objects by using the GetInterface method.

The following VBScript example demonstrates how to use a CDO.Person object
to create a user account in Active Directory and mailbox-enable it using the
CDOEXM IMailboxStore interface (SCRIPT7CH24.VBS):

```
'*-*-* Creating a new user account *-*-*
Set oPerson = CreateObject("CDO.Person")

oPerson.FirstName = "Geraldine"
oPerson.LastName = "Goose"

oPerson.DataSource.SaveTo "LDAP://bluesky-srv1.BlueSky-inc-10.com/" _
    & "CN=Geraldine Goose,CN=Users,DC=BlueSky-inc-10,DC=com"
```

```
'*-*-* Mailbox-enabling the user account *-*-*
Set oMailbox = oPerson.GetInterface("IMailboxStore")
oMailbox.CreateMailbox _
    "CN=Mailbox Store (BLUESKY-SRV1),cn=First Storage Group," _
  & "cn=InformationStore,cn=BLUESKY-SRV1,cn=Servers," _
  & "cn=First Administrative Group," _
  & "cn=Administrative Groups,cn=Blue Sky Airlines," _
  & "cn=Microsoft Exchange,cn=Services,cn=Configuration," _
  & "dc=BlueSky-inc-10,dc=com"


oPerson.DataSource.Save
```

Of course, you can also mailbox-disable a user account by deleting its mailbox using the CDOEXM IMailboxStore interface (such as oMailbox.DeleteMailbox). It is likewise possible to set mailbox storage limits, set the deleted items retention time, specify additional proxy e-mail addresses, or move mailboxes between information stores programmatically. You can read more about recipient management in Chapter 13, "Creating and Managing Recipients."

To demonstrate the purpose of the IMailRecipient interface, let's show the public folder called Job Applicants in the Global Address List (SCRIPT8CH24.VBS):

```
Set objFolder = CreateObject("CDO.Folder")


objFolder.DataSource.Open _
"file://./BackOfficeStorage/bluesky-inc-10.com" _
  & "/Public Folders/Job Applicants"


Set objPFRecip = objFolder.GetInterface("IMailRecipient")
objPFRecip.HideFromAddressBook = False


objFolder.DataSource.Save
```

Note   Detailed sample code to manage mailboxes and public folders using CDOEXM is available in the Exchange 2000 Server Platform SDK.

Lesson 3: Workflow for Exchange 2000 Server

Workflow applications are very specialized types of collaboration solutions. They automate business processes and are therefore organization specific. Every process that requires a series of actions to accomplish a particular business objective is a good candidate for workflow. At the simplest level, you may add a routing slip to a Microsoft Office document to send it to other users for reviews and resumes (from the File menu, point to Send To, then select Routing Recipient). A moderated public folder, illustrated in Exercise 3 of Chapter 1, "Introduction to Microsoft Exchange 2000 Server," may also be seen as a first workflow approach. However, complex business processes require more than document routing capabilities. The workflow infrastructure must support tracking and audit facilities to measure the process efficiency and resolve exception situations. Central roles are necessary to identify task performers, and advanced business logic should be supported by means of custom script code. CDO for Workflow in Exchange 2000 Server provides a high-end workflow infrastructure based on the Web Storage System.

This lesson introduces typical workflow features of Exchange 2000 Server. It explains the important elements of every Exchange 2000 Server workflow process and illustrates how to quickly get started with a small workflow example.

At the end of this lesson, you will be able to:

- Use the Workflow Designer to install and execute workflow processes.
- Describe important CDO objects for workflow and their purposes.

Estimated time to complete this lesson: 60 minutes

Workflow Basics

Exchange 2000 Server workflow is based on the concept of a central repository that holds the documents to be processed and provides an interface to design workflow solutions in terms of rules, roles, routes, forms, and views. The central repository could be a folder in a mailbox or a public folder (see Figure 24.5). In fact, public folders are ideal workflow repositories because they can be accessed by virtually anybody using any popular messaging client. Forms and views may be implemented in Outlook 2000 and Outlook Web Access (OWA). Public folders can be replicated between Exchange 2000 servers. This increases the fault tolerance and can help to optimize system performance through load balancing. The administration of public folders is the topic of Chapter 17, "Public Folder Management."

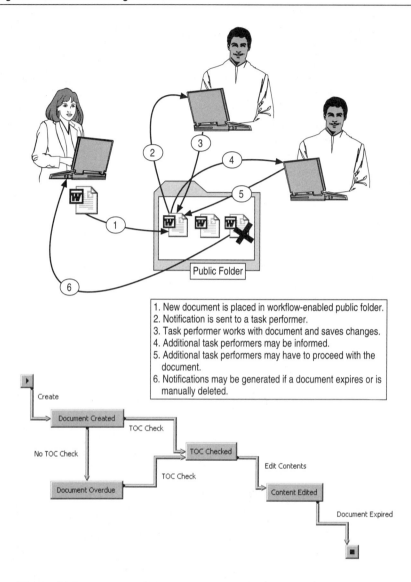

Figure 24.5 Exchange 2000 Server workflow based on public folders

Web Storage System Event Sink and Workflow Engine

Workflow is an event-driven process. During the installation of Exchange 2000 Server, an event sink (CDOWFEVT.DLL) is registered that intercepts the synchronous OnSyncSave and OnSyncDelete Web Storage System events, and the OnTimer system event for workflow-enabled folders. OnSyncSave, for instance, is fired before changes are committed to the store, which enables the workflow system to reliably react to any item or a change to an item. OnSyncDelete gives the system the ability to prevent invalid actions, such as the deletion of documents in the middle of a workflow process. OnTimer allows the detection of expired items that are in a particular state for too long.

To perform the actual workflow after the reception of an OnSyncSave event from the Web Storage System, the workflow event sink calls the IProcessInstance.Advance method for the affected document in the workflow-enabled folder. IProcessInstance represents an interface to the item or document in process. In other words, the item that the user saved in the folder is handled as a ProcessInstance object (see Figure 24.6). The IProcessInstance.Advance invokes the actual workflow engine, implemented in CDOWF.DLL, which evaluates an action table and executes appropriate actions for the item. CDOWF.DLL is in the \Program Files\Exchsrvr\Bin directory. You can implement custom workflow engines if you are an advanced programmer.

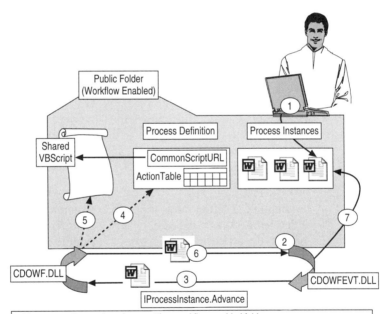

1. User saves changes to a document in a workflow-enabled folder.
2. Web Storage System passes OnSyncSave event to the CDO workflow event sink.
3. Workflow event sink informs CDO workflow engine about the event for the process instance.
4. Workflow engine checks action table to find the appropriate action(s).
5. Workflow engine locates shared script and runs the procedure specified in the action's row of the action table.
6. Based on VBScript procedure, engine may change properties on the process instance, etc., and then writes new state information back into the ProcessInstance object.
7. CDO workflow event sink commits the changes to the object.

Figure 24.6 The CDO for workflow architecture

> **Note**   The workflow event sink is automatically registered as a COM+ applica-
> tion package. To view and manage this component, launch the Component Ser-
> vices utility from the Administrative Tools program group. Navigate through the
> following containers to find the workflow event sink COM+ package: Console
> Root\Component Services\Computers\My Computer\COM+
> Applications\Workflow Event Sink.

Workflow Process Definitions

One of the most important parameters that the event sink passes to the workflow
engine is the event type. Five different event types are known: document created
(cdowfOnCreate), document modified (cdowfOnChange), document deleted
(cdowfOnDelete), document in the current state for too long (cdowfOnExpiry),
and e-mail response received that correlates to the document (cdowfOnReceive).
Based on these five events, you can design your workflow process. To outline a
workflow process, you need to create a ProcessDefinition object. Similar to
forms registration items for custom Web Storage System forms (see Chapter 23,
"Microsoft Exchange 2000 Web Storage System"), workflow process definitions
are stored as items in a public folder.

The ProcessDefinition object implements the IProcessDefinition interface. The
two most important properties of this interface are ActionTable and
CommonScriptURL. The action table is the central part of any CDO-based
workflow application. This table defines the rules that govern the workflow process. You need to define the various item states, such as Document Created,
Document Overdue, TOC Checked, and so on, and the actions that cause transitions between states. The ActionTable property stores this information as an
ADO Recordset.

According to the action table, the workflow engine must determine one or multiple defined actions to execute. Otherwise, an error is returned, thus preventing
changes to the affected item. To give an example, let's say you have defined a
workflow process according to Figure 24.5. If an item is in the Document Created state, users cannot delete this object from the folder even though they might
have full access permissions. Actions have only been implemented for the
cdowfOnChange and cdowfOnExpiry events. However, deleting the object
causes the event sink to pass a cdowfOnDelete event to the CDO workflow
engine. The engine checks the action table, does not find an appropriate action
for the item in this state, and, because no action was defined, an error is returned
to the user and the item is not deleted.

You can implement actions in the form of VBScript code or COM components.
When working with VBScript, actions correspond to procedures implemented in
a single script file, which is known as the shared script. The CommonScriptURL
property of the ProcessDefinition object points to this file. For detailed informa-

tion about the programming interfaces and their usage, refer to the SDK documentation.

Action Tables

The series of actions that you create to move documents from state to state form an action table, which encapsulates the workflow logic; the action table defines the workflow rules. Each row in the table has 14 columns. The entire action table is stored as an ADO recordset in the ActionTable property of the ProcessDefinition object.

A row in the action table has the following columns:

- **ID.** An identifier for the action table row
- **Caption.** Display name for the action
- **State.** The state of the process instance to which the action belongs
- **NewState.** The state to which the process instance changes upon successful completion of the action
- **EventType.** Event type for which the action is executed
- **Condition.** A conditional expression that allows the workflow engine to execute the action when the result is true
- **EvaluationOrder.** Position of the row in the order of all matching rows for an event
- **Action.** The definition of the call to a procedure in the common script or COM object
- **ExpiryInterval.** Duration that the item can remain in the new state before a cdowfOnExpiry event is triggered
- **RowACL.** Reserved for future use
- **TransitionACL.** Defines an access control list (ACL) for the transition
- **DesignToolFields.** Used internally by the Workflow Designer for Exchange 2000 Server and similar tools
- **CompensatingAction.** Call of a procedure in the common script or COM object if the workflow transaction is aborted
- **Flags.** Indicates whether the columns in the action table will contain COM objects or scripts

Preparing the CDO Workflow System Account

CDO for Workflow is installed on your Exchange 2000 server automatically, but this does not imply that you have the required permissions to register workflow processes right away. The preparation of CDO for Workflow involves the creation of a system account, the configuration of its mailbox settings and permissions, and the assignment of workflow authors.

Important   The workflow system account must be mailbox-enabled if you want to send messages via SendWorkflowMessage in restricted workflows (workflows that prohibit the usage of CreateObject in their actions).

System Account Creation

To create the workflow system account, use Active Directory Users and Computers, mailbox-enable the system account, and add it to the Exchange Domain Servers group. Through membership in this group, the workflow system account inherits full Exchange 2000 Server permissions. Permissions management is explained in Chapter 19, "Implementing Advanced Security."

User Rights for the System Account

The workflow system account also requires the Act As Part Of The Operating System user right to support impersonation of actions when running workflow in restricted mode. Launch the Domain Controller Security Policy tool from the Administrative Tools program group, expand Security Settings, then Local Policies, select User Rights Assignment, and, in the details pane, double-click Act As Part Of The Operating System to add the system account.

Configuring the Event Sink Identity

At this point, you can configure the CDO workflow event sink to run under the identity of the system account. Launch the Component Services utility from the Administrative Tools program group. The Workflow Event Sink COM+ package can be found under Console Root\Component Services\Computers\My Computer\COM+ Applications. Right-click Workflow Event Sink, select Properties, and click on the Identity tab. Select This User, click Browse, select your system account, and then, under Password and Confirm Password, provide the correct security information. Click OK.

Restricted and Privileged Workflow Authors

Before you can develop a workflow scenario, you need to grant your Windows 2000 account appropriate permissions for the workflow event sink. In the Component Services utility, expand Workflow Event Sink, expand Roles, then expand Can Register Workflow, and then select Users. Right-click on Users, point to New, and select the User command to add your account to this role. You may also want to check whether this role is activated for the event sink. Under Workflow Event Sink, expand Components, select CdoWfEvt.EventSink.1, and right-click on it. Select Properties, click on the Security tab, and select the Can Register Workflow check box. Make sure the Privileged Workflow Authors check box is selected as well.

To deploy workflow applications, you need to be the owner of the folder that you want to work with, and you need to have the permissions to register workflow process definitions with the Workflow Event Sink COM+ package. The Can Register Workflow role grants your account restricted workflow author rights. If you want to design powerful workflow applications without any restrictions, you need to add your account to the built-in Privileged Workflow Authors role.

The following restrictions apply to the Can Register Workflow role:

- The workflow logic must be written in VBScript (in contrast, privileged mode allows scripts or COM actions).

- The shared VBScript code cannot call CreateObject to instantiate COM classes, such as CDO.Message (for sample code, see Lesson 1).

- Restricted workflow scripts run with guest privileges by default. The VBScript procedures will run in the context of a special account called EUSER_EXSTOREEVENT, which is created automatically in your Windows 2000 domain during the installation of Exchange 2000 Server (in contrast, in privileged mode, scripts run in the context of the system account).

- The workflow system account requires the Windows 2000 Act As Part Of The Operating System permission to allow impersonation of EUSER_EXSTOREEVENT.

Note   When replicating public folders between Exchange 2000 servers, keep in mind that permissions for the workflow event sinks are granted on a per-machine basis. You need to configure the Workflow Event Sink COM+ package on all Exchange 2000 servers where you want to deploy the workflow application.

Exchange 2000 Server Workflow Preparation

It is a good idea to use Microsoft Workflow Designer for Exchange 2000 Server to map out your workflow processes and build a first skeleton of your business solution. This tool has the same user interface and architecture as the Microsoft Workflow Designer for Access and SQL Server. It enables you to create and register action tables and shared scripts quickly and efficiently (see Figure 24.6). The Workflow Designer for Exchange 2000 Server is part of the Platform SDK for Exchange 2000 Server. The Workflow Designer is not provided with this book.

Designing a Basic Workflow

If you have the Exchange 2000 Server Platform SDK CD at hand, you can install the Workflow Designer on your Windows 2000 Professional workstation by double-clicking the EXCHWFD.MSI file found in the \Workflow directory. The installation is straightforward and, with the exception of the licensing agreement and installation directory, it doesn't require much user input. If you have prepared your CDO workflow environment as outlined earlier, you will find the Workflow Designer very convenient to use.

Note   Before launching the Workflow Designer, start Outlook 2000 and create a public folder where you want to implement your workflow solution. If you want to use an existing folder, make sure you have the rights of a folder owner.

Selecting a Public Folder

To begin your workflow project, launch Exchange Workflow Designer from the Microsoft Exchange Workflow program group. An Open Folder dialog box will appear, asking you for server name and public folder. Accordingly, the folder URL will be created for you. For instance, if your server is called BLUESKY-SRV1, type **bluesky-srv1** under Server. If you want to work with a folder called Workflow, type **public/workflow** under Folder, and then click OK.

The Workflow Designer will check whether you have the required permissions; if you do, it will connect to the specified folder. In the General property sheet that is displayed automatically, under Folder Is Enabled For Workflow, select Activated. After that, open the File menu, and then select New Workflow Process. In the New Workflow Process dialog box, type a descriptive name, such as **Workflow Notifications**, and then click OK. The Workflow Designer will open a new process definition for you automatically and ask you for the name of the first item state. Document Created might be a good name. You are free to choose whatever name best suits your purposes. Click OK.

Item States and Actions

In this simple workflow example, you already have two actions. They are Create, which brings the item into Document Created State, and Delete, which deletes the item. You may define additional states using the Insert State button on the toolbar (or open the Edit menu, point to Insert, and then select State). States must be connected through Actions, which you can insert via the Insert Action button on the toolbar or the Action command from the Edit menu under Insert. According to the events supported by the CDO workflow engine, you can define Create, Delete, Change, Receive, and Expiry actions. There are two additional action types that you can select: Enter and Exit. These allow you to invoke workflow logic when an item advances from one state to another. For instance, the Enter action is used to set an expiry timer for items that enter the state. If an item expires, an Expiry action may be triggered.

Shared VBScript Elements

For now, let's work through a very simple example of Create -> Document Created -> Delete. That gives you two actions to work with. You could inform the Administrator, for instance, whenever new items are posted to the workflow public folder, and you may inform the Administrator again if an item is deleted. Only a few lines of VBScript code are necessary to implement this functionality.

In the Workflow Designer, click on the Shared Script tab, and type in the following script code (SCRIPT9CH24.VBS):

```
Sub SendNotification (strRecipient, strSubject, strMsgText, bAddURL)


    Set oMsg = WorkflowSession.GetNewWorkflowMessage


    oMsg.To = strRecipient
    oMsg.Subject = strSubject


    If bAddURL = True Then
        oMsg.TextBody = strMsgText & " " _
            & "<Outlook://Public Folders/All Public Folders/Workflow/" _
            & WorkflowSession.Fields("DAV:displayname") & ">"
    Else
        oMsg.TextBody = strMsgText
    End If


    oMsg.SendWorkflowMessage 0


End Sub
```

Click on the Design tab again, select the Create action, and, under Action Script Procedure, type the following lines to inform the Administrator about new items (SCRIPT10CH24.VBS):

```
SendNotification "Administrator@Bluesky-inc-10.com", _
    "Workflow document Posted", _
    "The following document was posted to the workflow folder", _
    True
```

Select Delete, and then, under Action Script Procedure, type in a slightly different version of the procedure call to inform the owner of the document about its deletion (SCRIPT11CH24.VBS):

```
SendNotification "Administrator@Bluesky-inc-10.com", _
    "Workflow Document Deletion", _
    "The document was deleted from the workflow folder", _
    False
```

Click on the General tab, and then select the Default Workflow Process For This Folder check box. Do not select the Run As Privileged check box unless you have granted yourself unlimited workflow permissions, as explained earlier in this lesson. Open the File menu, and select Save All Changes. To test the workflow, switch to Outlook 2000. When you post a new item, the Administrator will receive a notification, which includes an Outlook URL to the document in the workflow folder (see Figure 24.7). When an item is deleted, a slightly different notification is generated.

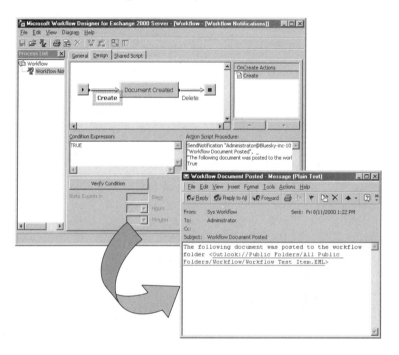

Figure 24.7   Creating a simple workflow example

CDO for Workflow Interfaces

As demonstrated, the Workflow Designer and CDO for Workflow enable you to design workflow solutions without the need for fundamental programming to access the Web Storage System. However, to implement sophisticated workflow logic, advanced script code is required. CDO for Workflow provides you with one important intrinsic object that was already used in the previous example—the WorkflowSession object. This object provides access to the process instance (the workflow item) and to the workflow message object (IWorkflowMessage) without requiring you to use CreateObject for messaging—Set oMsg = CreateObject("CDO.Message") would only be possible in privileged mode.

CDO for Workflow provides the following programmatic interfaces:

- **IAuditTrail.**   To write error entries during a state transition in an audit trail.

- **IProcessDefinition.**   To manage ProcessDefinition objects stored as items in public folders.

- **IProcessInstance.**   To access the workflow items in a workflow-enabled folder. For every new item that is sent or posted to a workflow folder, a ProcessInstance object is created.

- **IWorkflowSession.**   The intrinsic workflow object passed to conditions and actions in a workflow process to communicate with the workflow engine at run time.

- **IWorkflowMessage.**   To support e-mail notifications in restricted workflow and to track responses to a ProcessInstance object. The workflow system account must be mailbox-enabled to support workflow messages.

You can find detailed information about the CDOWF programming interfaces and their purposes along with sample code that demonstrates their usage in the Exchange 2000 Server Platform SDK.

Chapter Summary

CDO is a powerful technology that allows you to add messaging, Exchange 2000 Server management, or workflow functionality to your business applications. CDO for Exchange 2000 Server provides programmable objects for messaging solutions. Similar to ADO, CDOEX is based on the ExOLEDB provider and the Web Storage System and can only be used directly on the server.

If you are planning to develop custom management solutions for Active Directory, you should consider CDO for Exchange Management. This technology deals with Configuration objects of Exchange 2000 Server in Active Directory. You can mailbox-enable user accounts, define mailbox properties, create and delete mailbox and public stores, build public folder hierarchies, and so on. For full-featured Active Directory solutions, you may combine CDOEXM with ADSI.

CDO for Workflow gives you the means to design workflow applications based on the Web Storage System architecture. Similar to CDOEX, CDO for Workflow must run on an Exchange 2000 server. You typically install workflow solutions in public folders, but mailbox folders are also supported. To register a workflow process definition, you need to be the folder owner and have the rights to register workflow with the Workflow Event Sink COM+ package. You can grant restricted or privileged author permissions to your users on a per-server basis.

Review

The following review questions can help you determine if you have sufficiently familiarized yourself with the material covered in this chapter. You can find the answers to these questions at the end of this book in Appendix A, "Questions and Answers."

1. When would you prefer to use CDOEX instead of ADO 2.5 in your custom applications?

2. Which basic CDO CoClass can you use to send e-mail messages?

3. You are developing a CDO-based calendaring application. Which file URL do you need to use to write appointments to a user's Calendar folder?

4. How can you quickly obtain contact information for your Windows 2000 account from Active Directory in vCard format?

5. What level of permissions is required to successfully work with CDO for Exchange Management?

6. You want to develop a workflow solution for your organization. Which tool should you use to implement process definition and business logic?

7. What restrictions apply to the Can Register Workflow role?

C H A P T E R   2 5

Real-Time Collaboration

About This Chapter

Classical e-mail systems transfer data in an asynchronous manner. Using a store and forward mechanism, messages are passed from clients to servers and between servers, until they finally reach their recipients. E-mail is convenient because the communication partners do not need to coordinate their activities. However, e-mail cannot cover the need for interactive communication in real time. A telephone conversation, for instance, is a classic example of real-time communication where all participants have to be on the line to exchange information.

Microsoft Exchange 2000 Server provides a comprehensive set of real-time communication services to give organizations the immediacy of the telephone with the functionality of messaging and collaboration. Instant messaging, for instance, allows users to have a dialogue with other users via small text messages that are posted immediately to the screen. Chat services can be used to support discussions or any other form of group communication. Chat is very popular on the Internet. Furthermore, Microsoft Exchange 2000 Conferencing Server may be deployed to schedule data and videoconferences.

This chapter addresses the features of Exchange 2000 Server for instant communication and real-time collaboration. Lesson 1 covers the architecture and implementation of Instant Messaging. Lesson 2 then illustrates how to use Exchange

2000 Server to create chat communities. Lesson 3 completes this chapter by briefly introducing Exchange 2000 Conferencing Server.

Before You Begin

To complete this chapter:

- Prepare your test environment according to the descriptions given in the "About This Book" section. It is assumed that you have followed the exercises of previous chapters.

- Have the Exchange 2000 Conferencing Server installation CD on hand if you want to provide conferencing capabilities in your organization.

Lesson 1: Instant Messaging

Instant messaging (IM) is an evolving technology that introduces new features that no other messaging technology provides. Through instant messaging, friends may chat with one another on the Internet. Organizations, too, are increasingly noting its advantages. Instant messaging does not only allow you to exchange small messages without the overhead of composing and sending e-mail, but can also provide a backup communication path in case e-mail transfer is interrupted. Furthermore, instant messaging supports the propagation of presence information. You can see when other users are online, idle, or out of the office. You are also able to control who can contact you.

This lesson provides an overview of Instant Messaging as implemented into Exchange 2000 Server. It addresses the various roles that IM servers can assume in an IM domain, and introduces the Microsoft MSN Messenger client, which can be used to participate in an IM environment.

At the end of this lesson, you will be able to:
- Describe the technology and features of Instant Messaging.
- Install Instant Messaging on an Exchange 2000 server.
- Use MSN Messenger for Instant Messaging.

Estimated time to complete this lesson: 75 minutes

The Principle of Instant Messaging

Instant messaging is a client/server technology. Users work with IM client software to exchange text-based messages, and an IM server takes care of message routing and maintenance of presence information. Leading software vendors, including Microsoft and Lotus/IBM, jointly developed an Instant Messaging Presence Protocol (IMPP) specification that allows the exchange of presence information between different systems. Exchange 2000 Server, however, does not use this protocol.

IM Client Logon

When your client starts, it logs you on to Instant Messaging using your current user credentials, and then informs the IM server that you are now online. The server keeps track of this status information and propagates it to all other users that have registered interest in you. In technical language, presence information is propagated to all other users that have subscribed you as a contact. Your IM server also keeps track of your client connection by means of your workstation's IP address to route instant messages to you.

IM Authentication

Of course, your account must be enabled with instant messaging; otherwise, the server will reject your logon attempt (see Exercise 1 in this lesson). Using your current Windows 2000 user account and password, the IM client will log you on implicitly and does not prompt you for user information. Integrated Windows authentication is an easy and very secure method of authenticating users and therefore enabled by default. Only if you are working with an account that is not instant messaging–enabled will you be asked for logon credentials. You can read more about integrated Windows authentication in Chapter 11, "Internet-Based Client Access."

It is recommended to use the integrated Windows authentication, but users that work with instant messaging clients over firewalls or HTTP proxies may then be unable to log on. You can support them via Digest authentication over HTTP. Digest authentication is an Internet Standard that transmits password information in the form of encrypted hash values to the server. In Exchange 2000 Server, Digest authentication is enabled by default, but you also need to allow reversible password encryption under Windows 2000 Server to support this form of authentication. You need to enable the Store Password Using Reversible Encryption For All Users In The Domain setting in a Group Policy that applies to your users. In a Group Policy (for example, the Default Domain Policy object), this option is under Computer Configuration/Windows Settings/Security Settings/Account Policy/Password Policy. You can read more about Group Policies in the Windows 2000 Server product documentation.

Note   To verify whether Digest authentication is enabled, launch the Internet Services Manager utility. Open the Web site container where the InstMsg virtual directory is located, right-click InstMsg, select Properties, click on the Directory Security tab, and then, under Anonymous Access And Authentication Control, click Edit. In the Authentication Methods dialog box, make sure Digest Authentication For Windows Domain Servers is selected.

Obtaining Status Information

If you want to subscribe contacts to receive status information about other users to send them instant messages when they are online, you need to add them to your contact list. The contact list is also referred to as a buddy list. Your IM client will attempt to determine the status of new contacts as soon as you subscribe them by sending a status request to your IM server. If the contact resides on the same IM server, status information is obtained right away. Otherwise, the request is routed to your contact's local server to obtain the status information from there.

Maintaining Subscriber Lists

In addition to the status request, your client also issues a subscription request, which is likewise routed to the contact's home server. Each IM server must maintain subscriber lists for its local users to send notifications to each registered subscriber if the status of a local user changes. Having the server actively send status change notifications ensures that contact lists are always up to date.

However, contact subscriptions are temporary. Your client must periodically renew them to obtain continuous presence information from the server. Each IM client maintains its list of subscribed contacts in the Registry under the following key:

```
HKEY_CURRENT_USER

  \Software

   \Microsoft

    \Exchange

     \Messenger

      \Profiles

\http://<IM domain name>/Instmsg/Aliases/<User Alias>\Contacts
```

Instant Messaging Client Software

The primary IM client is MSN Messenger. This client comes with Exchange 2000 Server and can be installed on Microsoft Windows 95/98, Microsoft Windows NT 4.0, and Microsoft Windows 2000. MSN Messenger requires Microsoft Internet Explorer 5.0. It is a good idea to start the IM client automatically when you log on to your Windows 2000 domain and keep it running for your entire session to be available for instant messages and to provide presence information. As soon as you close this application, your status will change to offline, and other users cannot send further instant messages to you.

Note When you log on to Instant Messaging, MSN Messenger opens a window on the desktop automatically, which displays your subscribed contacts (the Contacts Online and Contacts Offline lists). Closing this window does not close MSN Messenger. The client remains active on your taskbar.

Controlling Presence Information

You can control your IM status in MSN Messenger using the Status button on the toolbar. Seven different status settings are provided: Online, Invisible (your presence information is not propagated), Busy, Be Right Back, Away From Computer, On The Phone, and Out To Lunch. Setting your status appropriately helps other users determine whether it makes sense to send you an instant message at a given moment. E-mail might be a better choice if you are out to lunch, for instance.

There are two further status indicators that the IM client sets for you automatically: Idle and Offline. Idle indicates that you haven't been working with your keyboard for a defined time. Offline is your status when you are logged off (that is, the client is closed).

Note   The MSN Messenger client allows you to block the propagation of presence information via the Privacy command, available on the Tools menu. You may also select the Notify Me When Passport Users Add Me To Their Contact Lists check box to be notified when another user adds you to his or her buddy list. Under Which MSN Messenger Service Users Have Added Me To Their Contact Lists, click View to display a list of users that have subscribed you as a contact.

Instant Messaging Implementation

Instant Messaging is not directly related to other services of Exchange 2000 Server. It is a technology for the World Wide Web. The communication between client and server takes place over the rendezvous protocol (RVP), a proprietary protocol developed by Microsoft as an extension to the Web Distributed Authoring and Versioning (WebDAV) protocol. WebDAV in turn extends HTTP, as discussed in Chapter 11, "Internet-Based Client Access." Instant messages are formatted in Extensible Markup Language (XML).

Note   A significant difference between e-mail and instant messages is that instant messages are not stored on an Exchange 2000 server. Instant messages are dynamic in nature, and they are lost when you close the MSN Messenger window.

Instant Messaging Service Integration

Instant Messaging requires Microsoft Windows 2000 Server and Internet Information Services (IIS) 5.0. It is not necessary to run Exchange 2000 Server on the same computer. However, you must have installed Exchange 2000 Server on at least one server in your organization to prepare the Active Directory forest.

Instant Messaging is implemented in an Internet Server Application Programming Interface (ISAPI)-based DLL called MSIMSRV.DLL, which will be registered for the World Wide Web publishing service in the IIS metabase. MSIMSRV.DLL runs as part of the IIS process (INETINFO.EXE). You can find this DLL in the \Program Files\Exchsrvr\Bin directory.

Components of the Internet Messenger Service

MSIMSRV.DLL represents the server application layer that communicates with other server-side Instant Messaging components, as well as the Active Directory directory service, and IM clients (see Figure 25.1). The server application layer maintains the IM node database (MSIMNODE.EDB) based on the Extensible

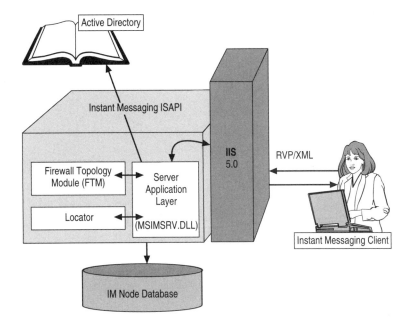

Figure 25.1 Instant Messaging service components

Storage Engine (ESE). This database holds user status information, contact subscriptions, and client IP addresses of active Instant Messaging connections. The remaining Instant Messaging server components are the firewall topology module (FTM) and the locator service. FTM, for instance, provides IP-related data about IM servers that are located behind firewalls. The locator is used to determine home servers to dispatch notifications via an IM router.

FTM and Protected IP Addresses

If you are communicating with external users on the Internet indirectly through a firewall, you need to identify protected IP addresses. To specify firewall and HTTP proxy settings, launch Exchange System Manager, right-click Instant Messaging Settings under Global Settings in the console tree, select Properties, and then click on the Firewall Topology tab. Select This Network Is Protected By A Firewall, and then click Add to define protected IP address ranges. You can also specify a proxy server for outbound requests. The Instant Messaging Settings object will only exist if you have installed the Instant Messaging feature in your organization.

Clients with IP addresses outside the protected ranges communicate indirectly via IM router servers. Clients with IP addresses within the protected address range are allowed direct connections to IM home servers in an Instant Messaging domain. The purpose of IM routers in an IM domain is explained in the following sections.

Instant Messaging Domains

Instant Messaging resources are organized in domains, which have a purpose similar to that of regular Simple Mail Transfer Protocol (SMTP)-based e-mail domains. Instant Messaging domains contain users and IM virtual servers (see Figure 25.2).

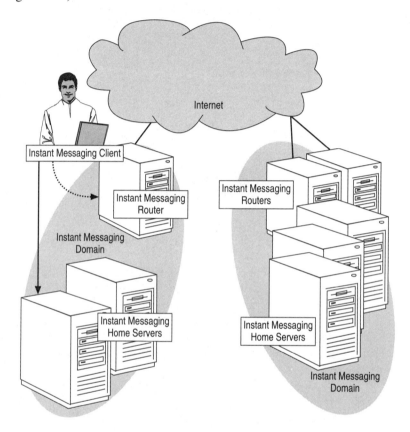

Figure 25.2   Instant Messaging domains with router and home servers

IM Domain Names

Based on the domain name and the user alias, IM clients can locate their home servers. To simplify the messaging environment, you should match the Instant Messaging domain names of your users to their SMTP domain names, as demonstrated in Exercise 1. For instance, users in the SMTP domain bluesky-inc-10.com should have an IM domain name of im.bluesky-inc-10.com, which may be matched to bluesky-inc-10.com by means of a service (SRV) DNS record. The configuration of DNS servers is explained later in this lesson.

Note   Organizations with more than one Active Directory forest must configure separate IM domains, each representing an independent Instant Messaging installation.

IM Home Servers Versus IM Routers

Each Instant Messaging domain contains at least one home server, which hosts the IM accounts of users and maintains their status information. Up to 10,000 online users may be placed on a single IM home server. The home server communicates directly with IM clients via RVP.

Router servers, on the other hand, do not maintain any user accounts. Their purpose is to route instant messages between domains to the correct home servers of IM recipients. IM routers are especially important when exchanging instant messages with Internet users through firewalls. IM routers are supposed to have an upper limit of 20,000 users. If you need to support more users, install additional servers (see Figure 25.2).

Tip   It is recommended to install IM home servers and IM routers on different physical machines.

User Addresses for Instant Messaging

As mentioned earlier, instant messaging is primarily a Web-based technology. Consequently, every IM user must be identified through a unique Instant Messaging URL that points to the user's home server. This URL is known as the home server URL, which has the format http://<FQDN of IM home server>/instmsg/ aliases/<user alias>/ (such as, http://bluesky-srv1.bluesky-inc-10.com/instmsg/ aliases/administrator/). In addition, every IM user must own a second URL that points to the IM domain's router server. This URL is used for external communication. It is therefore called the domain URL or public URL. The public URL has the same format as the home server URL, but it should point to the IM router server instead of the home server. Only in environments with a single IM server are home server and public URLs the same.

Note   You can view the IM address information for your user account in Active Directory Users and Computers. Right-click your account, select Properties, switch to the Exchange Features tab, select Instant Messaging, and then click Properties. In the Instant Messaging dialog box, both the home server and public URL are displayed.

IM User Addresses

Although a Web-based technology, users see Instant Messaging primarily as an e-mail service. To provide users with a consistent address scheme for e-mail and Instant Messaging, IM user addresses have been standardized according to the

SMTP address convention <User Name>@<IM Domain Name> (such as, Administrator@im.bluesky-inc-10.com). Based on this information, the client can construct the required URLs (http://< IM Domain Name>/Instmsg/Aliases/ <User Name>/) internally to carry out the communication via RVP. This process is invisible to the user. However, it is important to note that the IM domain name must be registered in DNS. Otherwise, IM clients will not be able to determine the IP address of the required IM server.

Domain Name Service Dependencies

Instant Messaging domains must be registered in DNS. This is not much different than the registration of SMTP domains in DNS mail exchanger (MX) records. However, specific DNS record types have not been defined for Instant Messaging. Consequently, you need to register your IM domain in a host (A) record and specify the IP address of the IM router server. If you have configured multiple IM routers, you need to create a separate A record for each router using the same "host" (IM domain) name but the appropriate IP address—just as you would match the same host name to different IP addresses in a DNS round-robin configuration.

DNS and Client Logon

To log you on, the MSN Messenger Service needs to resolve the IM domain name that you have specified in your IM address, such as im.bluesky-inc-10.com. Through a DNS lookup, the IP address of your IM domains router server is obtained. The client connects to this server, and the router queries Active Directory to determine your IM home server. Your home server URL will be returned to your client, and based on this URL, the IM client can connect you to your IM home server. As outlined earlier, the home server URL contains the fully qualified domain name (FQDN) of your home server, which is resolved to the corresponding IP address in another DNS lookup. MSN Messenger connects to this server, and your home server validates your Active Directory account and password.

DNS and Message Routing

The routing of instant messages depends on DNS as well. Based on home server URLs, IM clients can send messages to servers of recipients directly if all resources are located within a protected network. Across the boundaries of protected networks, public URLs are used to forward messages to IM router servers first. An IM router can determine correct destinations based on IM domain names and forward the messages to other IM routers or home servers where the users reside.

Note   IM clients outside a protected network only connect to IM routers, which in turn communicate with IM home servers inside the protected network on behalf of the clients.

Service Location Resource Records for Instant Messaging

You have the option to add SRV resource records for IM routers to DNS to map the IM domain name to the service and the TCP port on which the service is provided. SRV records can simplify the IM addressing scheme because they allow you to register a common domain name for SMTP and Instant Messaging, such as Bluesky-inc-10.com.

The following is an example of an SRV record for the IM domain im.bluesky-inc-10.com:

```
_rvp._tcp.bluesky-inc-10.com   SRV 0 0 80 im.bluesky-inc-10.com
```

The symbolic name for IM is _rvp, _tcp refers to the transport protocol, and bluesky-inc-10.com is the domain that replaces the IM domain name (IM.Bluesky-inc-10.com). The two zeroes following SRV represent priority and weight, which can be used for load balancing between multiple servers. The TCP port number follows. It is set to 80 for Instant Messaging over HTTP. The SRV record is completed by the IM domain name, which corresponds to the FQDN of the IM router. In other words, this SRV record allows your users to specify IM user addresses as <User Alias>@Bluesky-inc-10.com instead of <User Alias>@IM.Bluesky-inc-10.com. You can read more about the creation of SRV resource records in the DNS documentation of Windows 2000 Server.

Note   The operating system of your workstation must be able to retrieve symbolic names; otherwise, it is not possible to simplify the IM addressing scheme. Windows 2000, for instance, fully supports SRV records.

System Monitoring of Instant Messaging

As an Instant Messaging administrator, you need to work with three main management utilities: Exchange System Manager to configure Instant Messaging servers and firewall settings; Active Directory Users and Computers to enable, move, or disable instant messaging users; and Internet Services Manager to stop, pause, or restart the virtual IIS server that provides access to the InstMsg virtual directory.

To track Instant Messaging activities, you can use the virtual IIS server's logging capabilities. In Internet Information Services, right-click the Web site under which InstMsg is located, and then, on the Web Site tab, make sure the Enable Logging check box is selected. The virtual IIS server will write information about Instant Messaging activities to the logs in the \Winnt\System32\Logfiles\ W3svc1 directory. You can also check the virtual IIS server's state dynamically using the Performance tool. Important performance objects start with MSExchangeIM. The Performance tool was briefly discussed in Chapter 12, "Management Tools for Microsoft Exchange 2000 Server."

Exercise 1: Deploying Instant Messaging

In this exercise you will configure Instant Messaging on an Exchange 2000 server. You will also install Microsoft MSN Messenger to work with Instant Messaging.

To view a multimedia demonstration that displays how to perform this procedure, run the EX1CH25*.AVI files from the \Exercise_Information\Chapter25 folder on the Supplemental Course Materials CD.

Prerequisites

- Reboot BLUESKY-SRV1 and BLUESKY-WKSTA.

- Log on as Administrator to BLUESKY-SRV1.

- Insert the Exchange 2000 Server, Enterprise Edition, evaluation software installation CD into the CD-ROM drive of BLUESKY-SRV1. It is assumed that the CD-ROM drive is E.

- CarlT has been granted the rights of a local administrator for BLUESKY-WKSTA (on BLUESKY-SRV1, in Active Directory Users and Computers, right-click BLUESKY-WKSTA from the Computers container, select Manage, open the Local Users And Groups container, open Groups, double-click Administrators, and then use the Add button to add the account of Carl Titmouse from the Bluesky-inc-10.com domain to this group).

- For completeness, it is assumed that you have not set up Instant Messaging on BLUESKY-SRV1 yet. However, if you have followed Exercise 4 of Chapter 5, "Installing Microsoft Exchange 2000 Server," Instant Messaging is already installed, in which case you should begin the following procedure with Step 7.

▶ **To implement Instant Messaging in an Exchange 2000 server organization**

1. Click Start, then select Run, and, in the Run dialog box, type **e:\setup\i386\setup.exe**. Click OK.

2. On the welcome screen of the Microsoft Exchange 2000 Installation Wizard, click Next.

3. On the Component Selection wizard screen, under Microsoft Exchange 2000, select Change. For Microsoft Exchange Instant Messaging Services, select Install (see Figure 25.3). Click Next.

4. On the Licensing Agreement wizard screen, select I Agree That, and then click Next.

5. On the Component Summary wizard screen, verify your selection, and then click Next.

6. Setup is now installing the Instant Messaging Services. On the final wizard screen, informing you that you have successfully installed the component, click Finish.

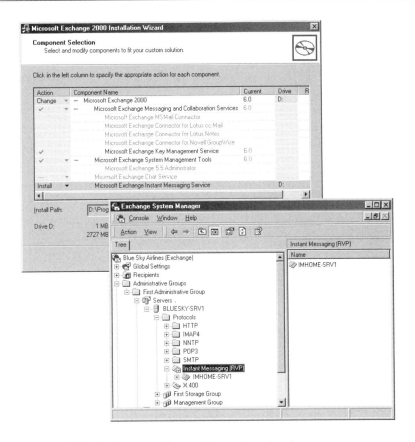

Figure 25.3   Setting up an Instant Messaging virtual server

7. Start Exchange System Manager from the Microsoft Exchange program group.

8. Expand Administrative Groups, then First Administrative Group, then Servers, then expand BLUESKY-SRV1. Open the Protocols container, and then select Instant Messaging (RVP).

9. Right-click Instant Messaging (RVP), and select Properties to examine the location of the IM node database in the General tab. Click OK. If you are prompted to create the directories, click Yes.

10. Right-click Instant Messaging (RVP) again, point to New, and then select Instant Messaging Virtual Server.

11. On the welcome screen of the New Instant Messaging Virtual Server Wizard, click Next.

12. On the Enter Display Name wizard screen, type **IMHOME-SRV1**, and then click Next. IMHOME-SRV1 will be the name of the virtual server displayed in Exchange System Manager.

13. On the Choose IIS Web Site wizard screen, make sure Default Web Site is selected, and then click Next. Every Instant Messaging home server requires a separate IIS virtual server.

14. On the Domain Name wizard screen, type **im.bluesky-inc-10.com**, and then click Next. Because it is assumed that the home server also performs routing functions (a one-machine installation), the default domain name needs to be changed to the Instant Messaging domain name. For home servers that work with a dedicated IM router, you may accept the default domain name obtained from the server's IP configuration.

15. On the Instant Messaging Home Server wizard screen, select the Allow This Server To Host User Accounts check box, and then click Next.

16. On the final wizard screen, informing you that you have successfully created the virtual server, click Finish.

17. Launch the DNS Administration tool from the Administrative Tools program group.

18. Expand BLUESKY-SRV1, then Forward Lookup Zones, and then Bluesky-inc-10.com.

19. Right-click Bluesky-inc-10.com and select New Host.

20. In the New Host dialog box, type **IM** under Name (Uses Parent Domain Name If Blank), and type **192.168.1.22** under IP Address, and then click Add Host. If your server uses a different IP address, you need to change the configuration accordingly. You can obtain your server's configuration information at the command prompt via the IPCONFIG command.

21. In the DNS dialog box, informing you that the host record was successfully created, click OK. In the New Host dialog box, click Done.

22. In the DNS utility, right-click Bluesky-inc-10.com again, and then select Other New Records.

23. In the Resource Record Type dialog box, select Service Location from the list, and then click Create Record.

24. In the New Resource Record dialog box, type **_rvp** under Service, make sure **_tcp** is displayed under Protocol, change Port Number to 80, and then type **im.bluesky-inc-10.com** under Host Offering This Service (see Figure 25.4).

25. Click OK. In the Resource Record Type dialog box, click Done, and then close the DNS administration tool.

26. Start Active Directory Users and Computers from the Administrative Tools program group.

27. Right-click the Administrator account from the Users container, and then select Exchange Tasks.

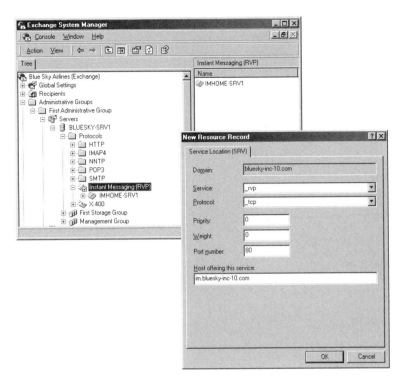

Figure 25.4   Configuring DNS for Instant Messaging

28. On the welcome screen of the Exchange Task Wizard, click Next.

29. On the Available Tasks wizard screen, select Enable Instant Messaging, and then click Next.

30. On the Enable Instant Messaging wizard screen, under Instant Messaging Home Server, click Browse.

31. In the Select Instant Messaging Server dialog box, double-click IMHOME-SRV1.

32. Verify that im.bluesky-inc-10.com is displayed under Instant Messaging Domain Name (see Figure 25.5), and then click Next.

33. On the final wizard screen, review the Instant Messaging User Address, Public URL, and Home Server URL, and then click Finish.

34. Repeat Steps 26 through 33 for the account of Carl Titmouse, and then close the Active Directory Users and Computers utility.

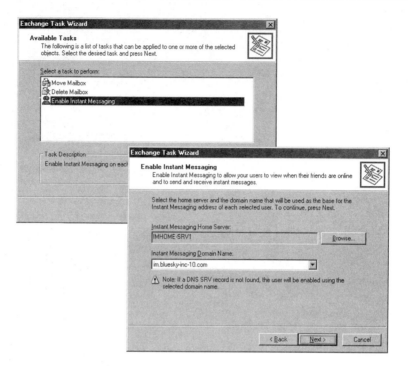

Figure 25.5   Enabling Instant Messaging for Windows 2000 user accounts

35. Click Start, select Run, and, in the Run dialog box, type
    e:\instmsg\i386\client\usa\mmssetup.exe. Click OK.

36. In the Messenger Service 2.2 dialog box displaying the licensing agreement,
    click Yes to begin the client installation.

37. On the welcome screen of the MSN Messenger Service wizard, click Next.

38. On the Provide Microsoft Exchange Instant Messaging Information wizard
    screen, make sure the Use This Program To Talk To My Microsoft Exchange
    Contacts check box is selected, and, under E-mail Address, type
    Administrator@Bluesky-inc-10.com (see Figure 25.6). (For Carl Titmouse,
    type **CarlT@Bluesky-inc-10.com**.)

39. Click Next, and, on the Get A Free Passport wizard screen, select the Use
    Exchange Instant Messaging Only check box, and then click Next.

40. On the final wizard screen, click Finish.

41. The MSN Messenger Service will be launched automatically. Verify that you
    are successfully logged in. The status bar will display Administrator (Online).

Figure 25.6 Installing the MSN Messenger Service

42. On BLUESKY-WKSTA, log on as Carl Titmouse, insert the Exchange 2000 Server installation CD into the CD-ROM drive, and repeat Steps 35 through 40 to set up the MSN Messenger Service.

43. In the MSN Messenger Service application of Carl Titmouse, click Add on the toolbar, accept the default By E-mail Address option on the Add A Contact wizard screen, and then click Next.

44. On the second wizard screen, type **Administrator@Bluesky-inc-10.com**, and then click Next and Finish.

45. Verify that the Administrator is now listed in the MSN Messenger Service application under Contacts Currently Online (see Figure 25.7).

46. On the toolbar, click Send, and then select Administrator.

47. In the Administrator – Instant Message window, type Instant Messaging is a cool technology because it allows you to send and receive immediate messages and supports presence information. Click Send.

48. On BLUESKY-SRV1, verify that the arrival of an instant message is indicated on the taskbar, click on it to open the Carl Titmouse – Instant Message window, type **Goodbye, Carl**, and then click Send.

49. Close the Carl Titmouse – Instant Message window, click Status on the toolbar of the MSN Messenger Service application, and then select Appear Offline.

50. On BLUESKY-WKSTA, verify that Carl Titmouse's MSN Messenger client immediately lists the Administrator under Contacts Not Online.

Figure 25.7   Adding a contact to the MSN Messenger Service

Exercise Summary

To install Instant Messaging, you need to launch the Exchange 2000 Setup program. During the installation, Setup will update the Active Directory schema with IM-related classes and attributes and register an IM management snap-in. You can use this snap-in separately or as part of Exchange System Manager to manage Instant Messaging settings. You need to be an Exchange Administrator to configure IM home servers and routers. To manage IM users, use the Exchange Task Wizard in Active Directory Users and Computers, which allows you to enable or disable Instant Messaging or change the IM home server. Domain Administrator permissions are required for the domain that contains the user accounts. As soon as your account has been enabled with Instant Messaging, you can use the MSN Messenger client to subscribe contacts and exchange instant messages.

Lesson 2: Chat Services

Exchange 2000 Server, Enterprise Edition, supports real-time, text-based communication based on the Internet Relay Chat (IRC) protocol and Internet Relay Chat Extension (IRCX). Jarkko Oikarinen and Darren Reed designed IRC in the late 1980s. The most commonly used version is defined in RFC 1459. IRCX, on the other hand, was developed by Microsoft to support additional functionality, such as additional client and server commands, user modes, and security through Simple Authentication and Security Layer (SASL). Microsoft Chat 2.5 is a popular chat client that supports IRCX.

This lesson introduces Chat Service of Exchange 2000 Server, Enterprise Edition, which allows you to build a group communication network in your organization. You can learn how to install the Chat Service and create chat communities.

At the end of this lesson, you will be able to:

- Describe the chat communication principle.
- Install the Chat Service of Exchange 2000 Server, Enterprise Edition, and create a chat community.

Estimated time to complete this lesson: 25 minutes

Chat Overview

IRC was first developed to allow users of bulletin board systems (BBSs) to communicate with each other. In the 1990s, it became a popular real-time communication method on the Internet. Users log on to a chat server and select a discussion group (a chat channel). They can read the current discussion history and type messages that are displayed to everyone logged into the same channel. Chat channels are often called chat rooms. Chat channels typically focus on a particular topic.

Exchange 2000 Chat Service allows you to create permanent chat channels, called registered channels. You can also allow your users to create new channels themselves for private communication. These manually created chat rooms are also called dynamic channels.

Client/Server Technology

Chat is a client/server technology. Clients connect to a server to obtain the current discussion exchanges and to submit new messages. The server in turn consolidates discussions to pass them to the users. Exchange 2000 chat servers host independent chat communities, which maintain user and channel lists. A single chat server can host several chat communities and up to 20,000 concurrent users. By default, 5000 users are allowed per channel.

By default, chat clients connect to TCP port number 6667, which is automatically assigned to the first chat community on the server. If you plan to create additional communities, you can use additional IP address/port number pairs. Users must specify the name of the chat server to which they want to connect (as well as the port number if the default port 6667 is not used). Microsoft Chat 2.5 is able to connect to TCP ports ranging from 6000 to 7000.

Integration with the Active Directory Directory Service

The Exchange 2000 Chat Service is integrated with Active Directory to maintain configuration information for virtual chat communities, channels, user lists, and other settings, such as bans that prohibit certain users from accessing a channel. The Chat Service relies on Active Directory for authentication and access control to determine the level of access permissions (that is, banned users, allowed users, system operators, or chat administrators). You may create user classes to configure access control for groups of users. Chat administrators can moderate chat communities, and users may be granted permissions to create dynamic chat channels.

Encrypting the Chat Communication

Chat is a clear-text protocol that does not support Secure Sockets Layer (SSL) encryption or Transport Layer Security (TLS). As a result, protocol analyzers such as Microsoft Network Monitor allow users to easily view IRC communications. If you plan to exchange sensitive information in chat forums over public networks, you should consider establishing a virtual private network (VPN) using Point-to-Point Tunneling Protocol (PPTP), Layer 2 Tunneling Protocol (L2TP), or IP Security (IPSec) that is supported in Windows 2000. A VPN encapsulates and encrypts the entire network communication.

Installing the Exchange 2000 Chat Service

You can install the Exchange 2000 Chat Service on an existing Exchange 2000 server or on a standard Windows 2000 server running IIS 5.0. Launch the Setup program from the Exchange 2000 Server, Enterprise Edition, CD. On the Component Selection wizard screen, select Microsoft Exchange Chat Service. Chat does not depend on other Exchange 2000 Server services, but Active Directory and Exchange 2000 Server must be deployed in the domain to support Exchange 2000 Chat Service. Installing the Chat Service on a separate machine allows you to create a server that is dedicated to real-time communication. A single server may provide chat services for the entire organization (see Figure 25.8). It is also possible to deploy Exchange 2000 Chat Service in a distributed environment. However, it is not possible to host a single chat channel on multiple servers.

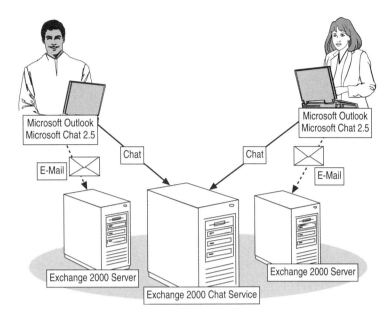

Figure 25.8   Exchange 2000 Chat Service on a dedicated server

Note   To successfully install Exchange 2000 Chat Service, Exchange Administrator permissions are required in the Administrative Group of the chat server.

Managing the Exchange 2000 Chat Service

Using Exchange System Manager, you can manage the Exchange 2000 Chat Service through chat communities. A chat community is composed of a set of channels, bans, and user classes that are assigned to a server on which the Microsoft Exchange Chat service is installed. During the installation, a Default-Chat-Community object is created automatically, which you can find under Chat Communities in your Administrative group. You can rename and configure this object, connect it to a chat server, or use it to create additional chat communities.

Managing Administrative Permissions

When you display the property sheets of a chat community object, you can find a Security tab, which allows you to define the level of permissions for user and group accounts. By default, everyone has user permissions and can participate in chat discussions. You can add additional accounts and grant them User, Sysop, or Administrator rights. A system operator (sysop) is able to monitor and control chat channels using a chat client. An administrator, in turn, can overrule sysop actions, such as excluding a user from a channel. Administrators cannot be denied access to a channel, and they become owners on every channel they join.

Managing User Bans

It is possible to prevent certain users from accessing the channels of a chat community. Open the desired chat community object in Exchange System Manager, right-click the Bans container underneath, point to New, and then select Ban. To identify banned users specify a Nickname or User Name, while the protected chat community is identified by Domain name or IP address. You can also specify an activation interval for the ban. If start and end times match, the ban is always in effect.

Exercise 2: Implementing a Chat Community

In this exercise you will configure the Chat Service on an Exchange 2000 server. You will then use Exchange System Manager to give your users access to a chat community.

To view a multimedia demonstration that displays how to perform this procedure, run the EX2CH25.AVI files from the \Exercise_Information\Chapter25 folder on the Supplemental Course Materials CD.

Prerequisites

- Reboot BLUESKY-SRV1 and BLUESKY-WKSTA.

- Log on as Administrator to BLUESKY-SRV1.

- If you have not followed Exercise 4 of Chapter 5, "Installing Microsoft Exchange 2000 Server," insert the Exchange 2000 Server, Enterprise Edition, installation CD into the CD-ROM drive of BLUESKY-SRV1. It is assumed that the CD-ROM drive is E.

- If you have followed Exercise 4 of Chapter 5, "Installing Microsoft Exchange 2000 Server," the Exchange 2000 Chat service is already installed on BLUESKY-SRV1. In this case, begin the following procedure with Step 6.

▶ **To install the Chat Service and set up a chat community**

1. Click Start, then select Run, and, in the Run dialog box, type **e:\setup\i386\setup.exe**. Click OK.

2. On the welcome screen of the Microsoft Exchange 2000 Installation Wizard, click Next.

3. On the Component Selection wizard screen, under Microsoft Exchange 2000, select Change. For Microsoft Exchange Chat Service, select Install (see Figure 25.9). Click Next.

4. On the Component Summary wizard screen, click Next to begin the installation.

5. On the final wizard screen, verify that the installation was completed successfully, and then click Finish.

Figure 25.9   Setting up the Exchange 2000 Server Chat Service

6. Launch Exchange System Manager from the Microsoft Exchange program group.

7. Expand Administrative Groups, then First Administrative Group, and then select Chat Communities.

8. In the details pane, right-click Default-Chat-Community, and select Properties.

9. In the General tab, under Name, type **Blue-Sky-Airlines-Chat**. Blank spaces are not supported, and the name cannot end in a number.

10. Click on the Channels tab, and make sure the Allow Dynamic Channels check box is selected. You have the option to disallow dynamic channels, which would require you to create permanent chat rooms using the Channels container underneath the chat community object.

11. Click on the Messages property page, and, under Message Of The Day (MOTD), type **Welcome to our internal chat community.**

12. Click on the Authentication tab, deselect the Basic Authentication check box, and then click OK.

13. In the console tree, expand Servers, then BLUESKY-SRV1, and then Protocols. Right-click IRCX and select Properties.

14. In the IRCX Properties dialog box, click Add, and then, in the Add Community dialog box, verify that Blue-Sky-Airlines-Chat (First Administrative Group) is displayed. Click OK.

15. In the Blue-Sky-Airlines-Chat Properties dialog box, select the Enable Server To Host This Chat Community check box, and then click OK.

16. In the IRCX Properties dialog box, click OK.

Exercise Summary

Installation of the Exchange 2000 Chat Service is straightforward. You only need to launch Setup and select Microsoft Exchange Chat Service on the Component Selection wizard screen. A default chat community will be created for you in your administrative group, which you can rename and connect to a server. For a basic chat environment, no further configuration is required. Users can manage dynamic chat channels from their clients. A user who creates a dynamic channel by joining a new channel automatically receives the status of a channel host, also known as a channel operator. You can find more information about the configuration and management of chat services in the Exchange 2000 Server online documentation.

Note Exchange 2000 Chat Service does not support Microsoft Chat version 2.0 and earlier. Microsoft Chat version 2.5 can be downloaded over the Web from *www.microsoft.com/*.

Lesson 3: Online Conferencing

Microsoft Exchange 2000 Conferencing Server is Microsoft's most powerful real-time collaboration platform. It is a separate product that enables you to manage and coordinate virtual meetings and online conferences. Exchange 2000 Conferencing Server is fully compliant with the T.120 recommendation of the International Telecommunications Union (ITU) and supports IP multicast audio and video streams. Clients, such as Microsoft NetMeeting, can use the T.120 protocol to join a data conference. A client for videoconferences is available in the form of an ActiveX control.

This lesson introduces Exchange 2000 Conferencing Server. It covers the basics of data and video conferencing and explains the advantages of client/server in contrast to peer-to-peer conferencing. You can also read about the most important components of Exchange 2000 Conferencing Server and the scheduling of online meetings with Microsoft Outlook 2000.

At the end of this lesson, you will be able to:

- Describe the advantages of Exchange 2000 Conferencing Server for online data and video conferencing.

- Explain how online conferences are scheduled using Outlook 2000.

Estimated time to complete this lesson: 45 minutes

Data and Video Conferencing Overview

Data conferencing allows participants in virtual meetings to share applications, transfer files, exchange information on a whiteboard, collaborate through a shared clipboard, and communicate via text-based chat. Audio and video conferencing, on the other hand, provide participants with the capability to send and receive audio and video streams based on IP multicasting, which is an extension to IP for efficient group communication.

Online conferencing technologies offer the following characteristic features:

- **Application Sharing.**   Users can share programs running on their computers with other participants without any special knowledge of the application capabilities. Only the person who wants to share a program must have the application installed. Participants do not require a local copy of the software to view the information or see how the content is edited or scrolled.

- **Audio and Video Conferencing.**   Participants in a conference can send and receive audio and video streams.

- **Chat.**   Participants in a conference can exchange text-based messages to share common ideas or meeting notes with other participants. Chat may be the basis for communication in the absence of audio support.

- **File Transfer.** Participants in a conference can send files to one or all other participants based on the T.127 standard. Recipients can accept or decline the file transfer.

- **Shared Clipboard.** Participants in a conference can exchange information by means of a shared clipboard, which allows cut, copy, and paste operations between separate computers.

- **Whiteboard.** Participants in a conference can simultaneously use a whiteboard to work with graphic information.

Peer-To-Peer Versus Client/Server Conferencing

Microsoft NetMeeting 3.01 or later is a typical client application for data conferencing. NetMeeting includes a multipoint control unit (MCU), which interconnects conference participants and distributes conference data. However, each client connection to an MCU in a peer-to-peer conference requires NetMeeting to send a separate copy of the data. Hence, if you want to send data to N users, your client must send data through N connections (see Figure 25.10). This can represent a significant drain on the network bandwidth. Slow dial-up connections may not even be suitable for hosts of one-to-many type peer-to-peer conferences. If the link to the computer of the meeting organizer is disconnected, the entire conference is terminated. Furthermore, NetMeeting does not provide a scheduling facility. Without central management of online conferences, it is difficult to join a conference or invite others.

To overcome the limitations and disadvantages of peer-to-peer conferencing, Exchange 2000 Conferencing Server can be used to establish an MCU on a central server. In this client/server conferencing scenario, clients connect to the central server to send and receive data over a single connection, while the server keeps all clients synchronized. Because the conference is now hosted on the server, the meeting organizer can leave the conference without terminating the online meeting.

Server-based MCUs can be placed at the ends of wide area network (WAN) links to minimize the bandwidth consumption on slow connections. Participants can connect to the MCU closest to their physical locations on the network, while the MCUs send single instances of data across the WAN links (see Figure 25.10). Exchange 2000 Conferencing Server automatically directs clients to their closest servers.

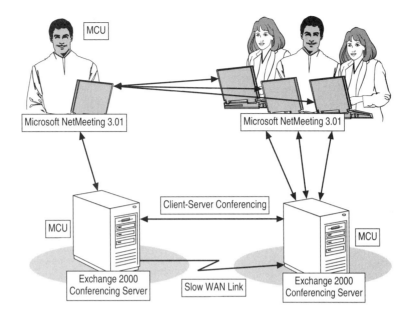

Figure 25.10   Peer-to-peer versus client/server conferencing

Note   Exchange 2000 Conferencing Server supports the full set of T.120 conferencing facilities and allows you to establish a client/server data conferencing environment. In addition, Exchange 2000 Conferencing Server supports audio and video conferencing based on IP multicasts.

Architecture of Exchange 2000 Conferencing Server

Exchange 2000 Conferencing Server provides three key components to overcome the limitations inherent to peer-to-peer conferencing. They are the Conference Management Service, the Data Conference Service, and the Video Conferencing Service (see Figure 25.11). Additional conference technology providers may be available from independent software vendors.

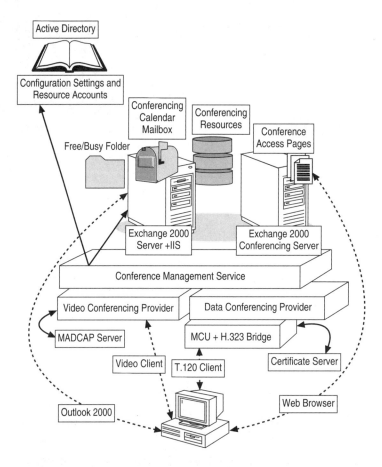

Figure 25.11   The architecture of Exchange 2000 Conferencing Server

Conference Management Service

The Conference Management Service manages conferencing providers and resources. This component contains a resource reservation agent, which provides users with the ability to schedule online meetings based on conference resource accounts with Outlook 2000. The Conference Management Service keeps track of and controls access to online conferences.

The Conference Management Service is responsible for the following tasks:

- **Monitoring of conference resources.**   The Conference Management Service maintains a synchronized meeting definition within a conference calendar mailbox and keeps track of new meetings, changes to existing conferences, and cancellations.

- **Controlling of conferencing providers.**   The Conference Management Service allows providers (such as the Data Conference Service) to host online meetings according to conference schedules and other properties.

- **Redirecting of clients.**   The Conference Management Service redirects clients that want to join an online conference to the server that is hosting the meeting.

Conference Calendar Mailbox

Conferences are started, managed, and closed by the server, but they are scheduled within Outlook 2000. You can do this by creating a meeting request and inviting a conference resource (in addition to meeting participants), as explained later in this lesson. If the conference request is accepted, the Conference Management Service stores the conference details, such as security level and conference participants, in the conference calendar mailbox and updates the conference resource mailbox's free/busy information. Additional information, such as a description of multicast videoconferences for the Video Conferencing Service, may also be associated with online conferences. Before you can schedule an online conference, you need to assign a conference calendar mailbox to the Conference Management Service.

Note   To create the conference calendar mailbox, create and mailbox-enable the desired account in Active Directory Users and Computers. After that, use Exchange System Manager to assign the conference calendar mailbox to the Conference Management Service object.

Data Conference Service

The Data Conference Service gives T.120-compliant clients, such as NetMeeting 3.01, the capability to share applications, clipboards, whiteboards, and chat services in a client/server environment, as explained earlier in this lesson. The MCU unit of the Data Conference Service handles the T.120 communication. The MCU depends on Microsoft Certificate Services for private conferences that use X.509 certificates for authentication and encryption of the conference data. Without a certificate, private conferences are not supported. The MCU automatically retrieves a machine certificate from Certificate Services. Public conferences, on the other hand, are available to any participant who has access to the URL. All public conferences are listed on a general conferencing Web page with a URL in the form of http://<Server Name>/Conferencing/LIST.ASP (such as, http://BLUESKY-SRV1.bluesky-inc-10.com/Conferencing/LIST.ASP/). Conferences are public by default.

H.323 Video Conference Bridge

The MCU of the Data Conference Service also contains an H.323 video conference bridge that allows H.323-compliant client programs that are unable to participate directly in IP multicast conferences, such as NetMeeting, to participate in videoconferences through an H.323 unicast session.

Video Conferencing Service

The Video Conferencing Service supports one-to-many audio and video streams based on Telephony Application Programming Interface (TAPI) version 3.0. Based on multicast groups, data is transferred to all participants via the Real-Time Protocol (RTP) over TCP/IP. Based on RTP, each participant's client receives all other participants' audio and video streams. The data is then mixed locally on the client computer to give the impression of an online conference.

As mentioned, the Video Conferencing Service client is an ActiveX control. This control is automatically downloaded to the client computer via Conferencing Access Pages when a participant joins a videoconference for the first time. The Conferencing Access Pages form the Web site of your conferencing server. To support the ActiveX control, you need to run Windows 2000 on the client computer.

IP Multicasting

The Video Conferencing Service relies on IP multicasting to send audio and video streams to all participants simultaneously. This eliminates the need to transfer the same information multiple times (one time for each participant) over the network. With IP multicasting, only one copy of the information is sent to a group IP address that reaches all participants. IP multicasting results in a greatly reduced load on the network and the sending server. You can read more about IP multicasting in the Windows 2000 Server product documentation.

Note IP multicasting requires a multicast-enabled network. IP routers must be multicast-aware.

Multicast Address Dynamic Client Allocation Protocol

To carry out the multicast communication, the Video Conferencing Service provider must obtain an available Multicast Address Dynamic Client Allocation Protocol (MADCAP) address during the start of the conference. Otherwise, data cannot be sent to the participants, and clients will not be able to join the videoconference. Consequently, you need to configure a MADCAP server to provide the address allocation services for IP multicast videoconferences.

The MADCAP service is installed as part of the Dynamic Host Configuration Protocol (DHCP) service in Microsoft Windows 2000 Server. However, MADCAP and DHCP are independent of each other. For more information regarding MADCAP servers, see the Windows 2000 Server product documentation.

Installing Exchange 2000 Conferencing Server

It is not necessary to install Exchange 2000 Conferencing Server on a server running Exchange 2000 Server. However, Active Directory and Exchange 2000 Server must be deployed in the Windows 2000 domain to successfully complete the setup process. Exchange 2000 Conferencing Server requires Windows 2000 Server and IIS 5.0 on the local server. In addition, your network must be IP multicast-enabled and must provide MADCAP services if you want to support videoconferences. For private conferences, make sure Windows 2000 Certificate Services have been configured in your organization.

The following minimum hardware is recommended:

- 400-MHz Intel Pentium processor (or higher)
- 256 MB of RAM
- 50 MB of available disk space

Note   To install Exchange 2000 Conferencing Server, you need to be logged on as a user with Exchange Full Administrator permissions in the administrative group where you plan to add the conferencing server. Administrative permissions are also required for the Windows 2000 domain. Ideally, you are working with the privileges of an Enterprise Admin.

Installing Individual Conferencing Components

To install a complete version of Exchange 2000 Conferencing Server, launch the Setup program from the installation CD, click Next on the Welcome wizard screen, accept the License Agreement, and enter your 25-digit CD key on the Product Identification wizard screen. On the Setup Type wizard screen, click Complete. When you click Next, you will be prompted for the administrative group of the conferencing server (if there is more than one administrative group in your organization). To begin the actual installation, on the Ready To Install The Program wizard screen, click Install.

On the Setup Type wizard screen, you also have the choice to select the Custom option to display the Custom Setup wizard screen, where four components are available. Most important, you should make sure that the Conference Management Service is selected because this component represents the core service of the conferencing server. The Data Conference Service and Video Conferencing Service will be installed as part of the Conference Management Service. It is likewise a good idea to install the Conferencing Manager, which is a Microsoft Management Console (MMC)–based utility for managing and configuring conferencing services. This snap-in can be used stand-alone or as part of Exchange System Manager. Other significant elements are the Conference Access Pages, which participants use to join online conferences; the T.120 MCU/ H.323 conference bridge, which provides the server-based MCU for T.120-based clients; and a bridge for H.323 clients to participate in audio and videoconferences.

Note   Following the installation of the conferencing server, you need to create the conference calendar mailbox and conference resources in Active Directory Users and Computers to allow your users to schedule online conferences with Outlook 2000. Detailed information about the configuration of conferencing resources is available in the Exchange Conferencing Server online documentation.

Scheduling Online Conferences

After the conferencing environment has been prepared, you can use Outlook 2000 to schedule data and videoconferences. Online meeting requests do not differ much from ordinary meeting requests. You only need to make sure that a conference resource is invited as a resource in addition to desired meeting attendees, and you need to select the This Is An Online Meeting Using check box, and then select Microsoft Exchange Conferencing.

To enable the creation of online meeting requests, you need to add the following Registry key to your workstation running Outlook 2000:

```
HKEY_CURRENT_USER

  \Software

  \Microsoft

   \Office

    \9.0

     \Outlook

      \ExchangeConferencing
```

Joining Online Conferences

You can easily join an online conference from Outlook 2000. Right-click on the desired meeting appointment in your calendar, and then select Join Conference. (Meetings are placed in your calendar automatically when you accept the corresponding requests from the meeting organizers.) A Join Conference button is also available in the Reminder dialog box for online meetings.

If you open an online meeting appointment, you can find the complete conference URL in the Location box. You can copy this URL and paste it into your Web browser to connect to the conference. This will be required if you are not working with Outlook 2000. Your Web browser will connect to the conferencing server and then request participation in the meeting. If you are allowed to join the meeting, a Web page is returned to the browser to add you to the meeting. If you are attempting to join an online meeting that has not started, your browser will display the time and date of the conference.

Note To join a data conference, a T.120 conferencing program, such as Microsoft NetMeeting 3.01, must be installed on the local computer.

Chapter Summary

Microsoft Exchange 2000 Server provides a comprehensive set of real-time communication services, which include Instant Messaging, Chat Service, and Exchange 2000 Conferencing Server. Instant Messaging allows you to exchange small messages without the overhead of composing and sending e-mail, and it provides presence information, so you can see whether other users are online, idle, or away from their desktops. Instant Messaging resources (IM router and home servers) are organized in IM domains. Ideally, IM domain names match their SMTP counterparts. Users can use the Microsoft MSN Messenger client to participate in an IM domain.

Chat, on the other hand, is a popular group communication method on the Internet. Organizations may use Exchange 2000 Chat Service to create chat communities internally or provide them for public discussions. You can create permanent chat channels and allow your users to establish dynamic channels. Chat channels typically focus on a particular discussion topic. You can use Microsoft Chat 2.5 to connect to Exchange 2000 Chat Service.

Exchange 2000 Conferencing Server is a separate product that supports data conferences based on the T.120 standard and videoconferences via IP multicasting. Clients, such as Microsoft NetMeeting, can use the T.120 protocol to join a data conference. A client for videoconferences is available in the form of an ActiveX control. To schedule online meetings, users typically use Outlook 2000. An online meeting request is created, similar to a regular meeting request. The meeting request must include a conference resource account as the resource in addition to the meeting participants.

Review

The following review questions can help you determine if you have sufficiently familiarized yourself with the material covered in this chapter. You can find the answers to these questions at the end of this book in Appendix A, "Questions and Answers."

1. You have successfully deployed Instant Messaging in your organization. You are using MSN Messenger to send and receive instant messages and to propagate your presence information. Using the Status button in MSN Messenger, you change your status to Away From Computer. How does your IM home server propagate this change to other users?

2. How can you block the propagation of presence information?

3. How do IM clients outside a protected network communicate with internal clients that are inside the firewall?

4. You plan to simplify the IM domain naming scheme by matching the IM domain name to the SMTP domain name of your organization (such as bluesky-inc-10.com). How can you achieve the desired configuration?

5. You plan to install Exchange 2000 Chat Service on a computer that is not running Exchange 2000 Server. What level of permissions is required in the Exchange 2000 organization to successfully complete the installation?

6. What are the minimum configuration prerequisites to successfully deploy Exchange 2000 Conferencing Server?

C H A P T E R   2 6

Connecting to Microsoft Mail and Schedule+

About This Chapter

Microsoft Mail for PC Networks (MS Mail) was a popular messaging platform, with several million client licenses sold worldwide in the first half of the 1990s. In 1996, Microsoft Exchange Server 4.0 was released, which was targeted primarily at the installed MS Mail base to replace the former Microsoft messaging system entirely. A careful migration to Exchange Server was essential for the success of the new system. For seamless integration, Exchange Server 4.0 provided powerful MS Mail connectivity components. These components remained basically unchanged in subsequent Exchange Server versions.

Microsoft Exchange 2000 Server continues to support organizations with MS Mail environments. The architectural concepts are still the same although directory synchronization is now performed against the Active Directory directory service. If you are an experienced MS Mail administrator, you will find it straightforward to manage the MS Mail connectivity components of Exchange 2000 Server. The MS Mail Connector turns an Exchange 2000 server virtually into an MS Mail postoffice.

This chapter covers the Microsoft Mail Connector, directory synchronization with MS Mail (Dirsync), and the Microsoft Schedule+ Free/Busy Connector. It describes how to transfer e-mail messages, how to synchronize MS Mail address information with Active Directory recipient objects, and management of free/busy information.

Before You Begin

To complete this chapter:

- Be familiar with the responsibilities of Active Directory and Exchange 2000 Server system components and their interaction, as explained in Chapter 3, "Microsoft Exchange 2000 Server Architecture."

- You should have practical experience in administering and troubleshooting MS Mail postoffices and directory synchronization. For detailed information about MS Mail, read the Microsoft Mail Administrator's Guide.

Lesson 1: The Microsoft Mail Connector

The Microsoft Mail Connector is responsible for message transfer between Exchange 2000 Server and MS Mail postoffices. Theoretically, every Exchange 2000 server can run an instance of the MS Mail Connector. However, you cannot connect a particular MS Mail postoffice to the same Exchange 2000 Server organization multiple times. One connector can service multiple MS Mail postoffices concurrently. You can configure dedicated connector servers to run the MS Mail and other connectors for the entire organization.

This lesson covers the architecture of the MS Mail Connector in depth by explaining its message handling. The lesson also discusses how to configure the MS Mail Connector.

At the end of this lesson, you will be able to:

- Identify the components of the MS Mail Connector for exchanging messages between Exchange 2000 Server and MS Mail.
- Describe the path a message takes through the MS Mail Connector.
- Configure and use the MS Mail Connector.

Estimated time to complete this lesson: 75 minutes

MS Mail Connector Overview

The MS Mail Connector is an additional component that comes with both the Standard and Enterprise Editions of Exchange 2000 Server. One MS Mail Connector is sufficient to connect an entire Exchange 2000 Server organization to an MS Mail network. The MS Mail Connector enables you to connect separate MS Mail networks together or provide MS Mail users with connectivity to foreign messaging systems, such as systems that support the Simple Mail Transfer Protocol (SMTP) or X.400 (see Figure 26.1). Exchange 2000 Server can replace existing MS Mail gateways and legacy MS Mail Message Transfer Agents (MTAs), and it can replace an entire MS Mail infrastructure altogether. Based on the MS Mail Connector, a seamless migration to Exchange 2000 Server is possible.

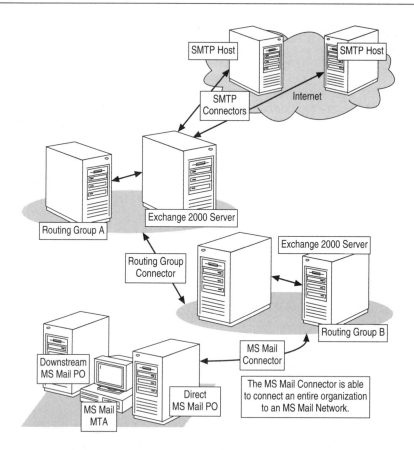

Figure 26.1   Deploying the Microsoft Mail Connector

MS Mail Connector Installation

You can install the MS Mail Connector using the Exchange 2000 Server Setup program. On the Component Selection wizard screen, select Install for the Microsoft Exchange MSMail Connector component. If you want to add the connector to an existing Exchange 2000 Server organization, you must have the permissions of an Exchange Administrator in the administrative group where the target routing group exists. You can read more about the installation of Exchange 2000 Server in Chapter 5, "Installing Microsoft Exchange 2000 Server."

Important Connector Components

The MS Mail Connector comes with a number of components, such as an MS Mail Connector Interchange service, a connector postoffice (Connector PO), a proxy address generator DLL, and address details templates. During the connector installation, connector configuration objects are created in Active Directory. Further elements are added to the installation when you configure the MS Mail

Connector in Exchange System Manager (that is, MS Mail Connector MTA services). Exchange System Manager provides the administrative user interface to manage MS Mail Connector instances.

After the installation of an MS Mail Connector in a routing group, the following separate configuration objects are available in Exchange System Manager:

- **Connector for MS Mail.**   Located under <Organization Name>/Administrative Groups/<Administrative Group Name>/Routing Groups/<Routing Group Name>/Connectors, this configuration object allows you to manage the connector parameters that relate to message routing and transfer.

- **Connector for MS SchedulePlus FreeBusy.**   Located under <Organization Name>/Administrative Groups/<Administrative Group Name>/Routing Groups/<Routing Group Name>/Connectors, this configuration object allows you to specify configuration settings for the Schedule+ Free/Busy Connector.

- **Connectors.**   The Connectors container object itself provides access to the Dirsync Server and Dirsync Requestor commands, which enable you to configure the Microsoft Directory Synchronization Agent (DXA) as an MS Mail Dirsync server or Dirsync requestor.

- **Directory synchronization.**   Located under <Organization Name>/Administrative Groups/<Administrative Group Name>/Servers/<Server Name>, this configuration object allows you to map address details for directory synchronization between MS Mail and Exchange 2000 Server.

MS Mail Dirsync and Schedule+ Free/Busy Connector are explained in subsequent lessons in this chapter.

MS Mail Message Routing in Exchange 2000 Server

As outlined in Chapter 3, "Microsoft Exchange 2000 Server Architecture," the SMTP transport engine works in conjunction with the MTA to handle message transfer to foreign messaging systems, including MS Mail.

Address Spaces

Routing decisions are made based on address spaces that you can add to an MS Mail Connector instance implicitly or explicitly. For every connection to an MS Mail postoffice, configured via the Connections tab of the Connector for MS Mail configuration object, an implicit address space is created. Via the Address Space tab, you may modify existing address spaces or add new entries explicitly. Furthermore, the Address Space tab allows you to restrict the availability of a connector instance to the local routing group. In this case, activate the Routing Group option under Connector Scope. By default, MS Mail Connector instances are available to the entire organization. The purpose and configuration of address spaces is covered in Chapter 16, "Message Routing Administration."

Outbound and Inbound Message Transfer

Address spaces are stored in the routingList attribute on the connector object in Active Directory. On every server startup, this information is incorporated into the link state table (LST) to allow Exchange 2000 Server to route messages to the connector. The MTA receives outbound MS Mail messages from the SMTP routing engine via its message queues in the Information Store and places them in an internal message queue for the MS Mail Connector queue, which is an internal MTA queue not maintained by the Information Store. You can view this queue in Exchange System Manager under <Organization Name>/Administrative Groups/ <Administrative Group Name>/Servers/<Server Name>/Protocols/X.400/ Queues, such as Blue Sky Airlines (Exchange)/Administrative Groups/First Administrative Group/Servers/BLUESKY-SRV1/Protocols/X.400/Queues. Message queues are covered in Chapter 20, "Microsoft Exchange 2000 Server Maintenance and Troubleshooting."

Message Conversion

The MS Mail Connector receives messages from the MTA, converts them into MS Mail format, and sends them to their destination postoffices. For outbound messages, the connector also needs to replace Exchange address information with MS Mail addresses for sender and recipients. When inbound messages must be delivered to an Exchange recipient, the MS Mail Connector gathers them from MS Mail postoffices, converts them, and transfers them to the MTA. The MTA passes them to the SMTP routing engine for further delivery. The interaction of the MTA with the SMTP service was explained in Chapter 3, "Microsoft Exchange 2000 Server Architecture."

MS Mail Connector Architecture

An Exchange 2000 server running the MS Mail Connector is seen as a native MS Mail postoffice to the MS Mail network. Using the MS Mail Administrator program, you must register those Exchange 2000 servers as External Postoffices on each existing MS Mail postoffice. MS Mail users can then send messages to recipients in the Exchange 2000 Server organization.

The MS Mail Connector Interchange

The MS Mail Connector Interchange service works between the MTA and the Connector Postoffice (PO) (see Figure 26.2). It converts messages from Exchange format to MS Mail format and vice versa. The MS Mail Connector Interchange polls the Connector PO to find inbound messages. However, this service is configured to start manually, by default. It is a good idea to set this service to automatic startup via the Services utility in the Administrative Tools program group.

Note   Messages displayed in the Connector for MS Mail (<Server Name>) queue of the MTA have not yet been received by the MS Mail Connector Interchange. A filled queue might indicate MS Mail Connector Interchange problems.

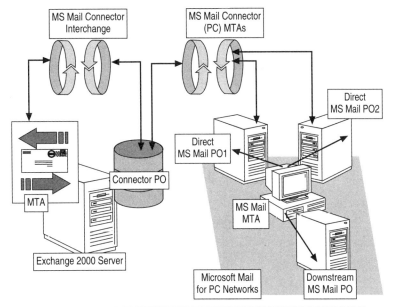

The MS Mail Connector Interchange accepts messages from the MTA, converts them, and writes them to the Connector Postoffice. It also retrieves messages from the Connector Postoffice, converts them, and transfers them to the MTA.
The Connector Postoffice is the intermediate repository for e-mail messages in MS Mail format.It provides the MS Mail interface of Exchange 2000 Server.
The MS Mail Connector MTA transfers messages within the MS Mail network from the Connector PO to MS Mail postoffices and vice versa.

Figure 26.2 Components of the Microsoft Mail Connector

The Connector PO

It is the Connector PO that forms the actual MS Mail interface of Exchange 2000 Server. This postoffice is in the \Program Files\Exchsrvr\Connect\Msmcon\ Maildata directory, which is also shared as Maildat$ for network access. Every Connector PO has a serial number of 22-28798. In fact, the Connector PO is a real MS Mail postoffice that stores messages in MS Mail format. However, it functions solely as an intermediate repository and has no user mailboxes.

Using Exchange System Manager, you can examine the queues in the Connector PO. Display the Connections tab of the MS Mail Connector that you are interested in. Select the desired postoffice under Connections, and then click Queue. If messages remain in the Connector PO, a corresponding MS Mail Connector MTA service may require configuration adjustments.

Note Native MS Mail postoffices see an Exchange 2000 server as an MS Mail postoffice, which you must configure as an external postoffice within MS Mail. All Exchange users, regardless of their home servers, are handled as MS Mail users residing on the Connector PO.

MS Mail Connector MTAs

MS Mail Connector MTAs transfer messages between the Connector PO and the MS Mail network, just as any MS Mail MTA does. MS Mail MTAs are also referred to as MS Mail Externals. An MS Mail Connector MTA is the Exchange 2000 Server equivalent of a regular MS Mail External or the Multitasking MTA provided with MS Mail 3.5. MS Mail Connector MTAs are implemented as Windows 2000 services, which are created during the MS Mail Connector configuration. A particular MS Mail Connector MTA service is not necessarily responsible for all MS Mail postoffices that can be reached through the MS Mail Connector. You can control the list of serviced postoffices using the Connector MTAs property sheet. Up to 10 MS Mail Connector MTA services can run on one Exchange 2000 server.

An MS Mail Connector MTA polls all postoffices for which it is responsible, including the Connector PO. If it detects messages in any outgoing queue, it transfers them to their destinations through the MS Mail network. The message queues in each postoffice determine the MS Mail routing of messages.

Note The MS Mail Connector MTA transfers messages only between the Connector PO and any MS Mail postoffices. Therefore, regular MS Mail MTAs must be used if the Exchange 2000 server is not included in the message path between two MS Mail postoffices (see Figure 26.2).

Supported Communication Mechanisms

The MS Mail Connector MTA supports local area network (LAN) and asynchronous connections. It can transfer messages directly from postoffice to postoffice if a LAN exists using the NetBEUI, Internetwork Packet Exchange/Sequenced Packet Exchange (IPX/SPX), or TCP/IP protocol. With asynchronous connections, a remote MTA must be contacted. The remote communication partner (another MS Mail MTA) answers the incoming call, receives the messages, and places them in the appropriate destination postoffice. To ensure full compatibility with MS Mail MTAs, the MS Mail Connector MTA uses the old-style MS Mail modem scripts to control a modem. The appropriate modem script must be copied in the \Maildata\GLB directory of the Connector PO. Only the four standard ports (COM1-COM4) are supported.

Note The MS Mail Connector MTA is limited to postoffice-to-postoffice communication. Remote MS Mail clients cannot dial into an MS Mail Connector MTA to send or receive messages.

Native MS Mail MTAs and MS Mail Gateways

MS Mail MTAs perform the message interchange between postoffices in a native MS Mail network. They can be used even if an Exchange 2000 server has been integrated because they treat that server as a native MS Mail postoffice. However, the MS Mail Connector is more powerful and should replace MS Mail MTAs, if possible.

The integration of Exchange 2000 Server and MS Mail can be advantageous for both sides. As mentioned earlier, MS Mail users can use existing Exchange connectors. Exchange users, on the other hand, can also benefit from older gateways installed in the MS Mail network, such as an MS Mail Gateway to System Network Architecture Distributed Systems (SNADS). You can even install MS Mail gateways directly on the Connector PO. However, if possible, you should replace all existing MS Mail gateways with corresponding Exchange 2000 Server connector instances. You need to update the gateway access component on the MS Mail postoffices to indicate the Connector PO on the Exchange 2000 server as the gateway postoffice.

Configuring the MS Mail Connector

Exchange System Manager and the Services utility are the primary tools to manage MS Mail Connector instances. First you must configure the connector through its corresponding Connector for MS Mail (<Server Name>) object in Exchange System Manager. You must specify the postoffices you want to connect to, and you must configure MS Mail Connector MTA services. After that, you need to start the MS Mail Connector Interchange service and MS Mail Connector MTA services using the Windows 2000 Services utility. It is a good idea to configure all MS Mail Connector services to start automatically.

Note If you change the MS Mail Connector configuration, you must stop and restart the MS Mail Connector Interchange service or the MS Mail Connector MTA services—depending on which service is affected by your changes—before the changes will take effect.

MS Mail Connector Interchange Settings

When you right-click on the Connector for MS Mail (<Server Name>) object, such as Connector for MS Mail (BLUESKY-SRV1), and then select Properties, you can configure the MS Mail Connector. The Interchange tab is displayed. Here you need to specify an Administrator's Mailbox. In fact, you cannot click on any other tab until you specify a mailbox. This mailbox receives special connector messages, such as notifications about undeliverable items.

Using the Interchange tab, you also can set the code page for the connector under Primary Language For Clients and determine whether to maximize MS Mail 3.x compatibility. If all of your Exchange and MS Mail users are using Outlook as their e-mail client, you may deselect the Maximize MS Mail 3.x Compatibility check box to reduce the size of messages with embedded objects sent from Exchange users to MS Mail recipients. Furthermore, you can enable message tracking, which was covered in Chapter 20, "Microsoft Exchange 2000 Server Maintenance and Troubleshooting."

Connector PO Details and User Addresses

The name of an MS Mail postoffice, such as the Connector PO, consists of a network name and a postoffice name, as in MSMAILNET/MSMAILPO. Both names are used for message routing. A complete MS Mail address also includes the name of a mailbox, as in MSMAILNET/MSMAILPO/MSMAILMBX. For example, the Exchange user named Administrator could possess the proxy MS Mail address BLUESKYAIR/FIRSTADMIN/ADMINISTRA. Network, postoffice, and mailbox names cannot be longer than 10 characters each. You can examine your MS Mail proxy addresses on the E-Mail Addresses property sheet in Active Directory Users and Computers. The address type is MS.

Do not get confused because MS Mail proxy addresses are not assigned automatically to mailbox-enabled Exchange user accounts. As mentioned in Chapter 13, "Creating and Managing Recipients," the Recipient Update Service is responsible for proxy address assignments, yet MS Mail proxy addresses are not enabled by default. To generate and assign them, open the corresponding recipient policy, such as the default policy object under <Organization Name>/ Recipients/Recipient Policies, in Exchange System Administrator. Click on the E-Mail Addresses tab, and select the MS check box to activate the proxy address generation.

It is important to note that the proxy address format is determined using the name of the Connector PO, as displayed in the Local Postoffice tab of the MS Mail Connector object. Here, you can change the postoffice or network name. However, you need to keep in mind that these modifications affect the proxy MS Mail addresses of all users. Messages addressed to the old Connector PO name will not be delivered and result in nondelivery reports. Consequently, you must update the recipient policy to assign your users correct MS Mail proxy addresses.

Note   All Connector POs in the organization must have the same NETWORK/ POSTOFFICE name.

To give an example, let's say you want to change the Connector PO name on BLUESKY-SRV1 from BLUESKYAIR/FIRSTADMIN to BLUESKYAIR/ EXCHANGE. Display the MS Mail Connector properties in Exchange System Manager, switch to the Local Postoffice tab, and change the name under Postoffice to **EXCHANGE**. When you click OK, a Change Local Network/ Postoffice Name dialog box appears, informing you about the tasks that have to be accomplished next. Read the information carefully, and then click Continue to close this dialog box. After that, open the Default Policy from the Recipient Policies container, click on the E-Mail Addresses tab, double-click the MS Mail proxy address entry, and, in the Microsoft Mail Address Properties dialog box, under Address, change the information to **BLUESKYAIR/EXCHANGE**. Click OK twice, and, in the Exchange System Manager dialog box informing you that corresponding e-mail addresses will be updated to match these new addresses, click Yes. The update of address information will take place according to the configuration of the Recipient Update Service.

Note   If you change the name of the Connector PO, you must restart the MS Mail Connector Interchange and all MS Mail Connector MTA services using the Services utility to update their network/postoffice name list. You also need to update the external postoffice information in all MS Mail postoffices using the MS Mail Administrator program.

Specifying MS Mail Postoffices in a LAN

An MS Mail Connector transfers messages only to postoffices specified in the Connections tab. To specify a new postoffice, click Create. This displays the Create Connection dialog box, where you need to click Change and specify the Universal Naming Convention (UNC) path to the postoffice in the Postoffice Path box. The network name and postoffice name are obtained automatically from the specified postoffice.

If additional postoffices can be reached indirectly through the specified MS Mail postoffice, you can have them referenced implicitly by clicking the Upload Routing button. Information about indirectly accessed postoffices is then gathered from MS Mail, thus creating references automatically. You need only select the desired entries and click OK. An associated address space is created for the direct postoffice and all selected indirect postoffices (see Figure 26.3).

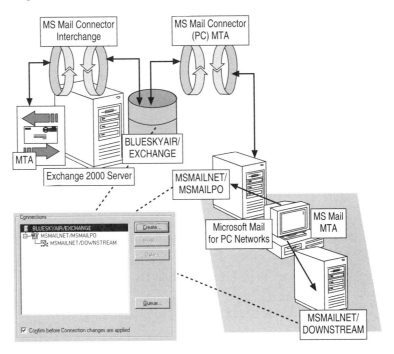

Figure 26.3   Indirect message routing to Microsoft Mail postoffices

Note   You cannot use the Upload Routing feature for connections made through asynchronous connections. The required configuration parameters change if you select the Async option instead of LAN in the Create Connection dialog box. However, you can use the Indirect option to specify a postoffice indirectly through another postoffice.

Creating Connector MTAs

An MS Mail Connector without an MS Mail Connector MTA service is like a car without wheels. It is useless to deliver messages to the Connector PO using the MS Mail Connector Interchange service if there is no service that obtains them and delivers them. As mentioned earlier, MS Mail Connector MTA services must be created explicitly. To create a new Connector MTA instance, in the Connector MTAs tab of the MS Mail Connector object, click New. In the New MS Mail Connector (PC) MTA Service dialog box, specify a descriptive Service Name and other options such as the Polling Frequency. The Service Name is particularly important because it identifies the corresponding Windows 2000 service in the Services utility. Every MS Mail Connector MTA service can be configured to start either automatically or manually. To examine the startup setting, click the Options button. Click OK to create the new Connector MTA instance, which will be displayed in the Connector MTAs tab under MS Mail Connector (PC) MTA Services.

Once you have created an MS Mail Connector MTA service, you must specify the Postoffices Serviced by clicking the List button. Select the desired postoffice, click Add, and then click OK. You must repeat these steps for all direct postoffices. You must start the MS Mail Connector MTA service manually after you complete the configuration.

Configuring the MS Mail Environment

Using the MS Mail Administrator program, you must also configure each MS Mail postoffice; otherwise, MS Mail users will not be able to send messages to Exchange users. As mentioned, you must configure the Connector PO as a regular external postoffice.

▶   **To define the Connector PO in an MS Mail Postoffice**

1. Start the MS Mail Administrator program, and log on using your administrator account. Type **E** for External-Admin, and then **C** for Create.

2. In the Enter Network Name box, type the network name of the Connector PO (such as BLUESKYAIR), and then press ENTER.

3. In the Enter Postoffice Name box, type the postoffice name of the Connector PO (such as EXCHANGE), and then press ENTER.

4. Select Direct under Select Route Type, and then press ENTER.

5. For connections in a LAN, select MS-DOS Drive under Direct Connection Via, and then press ENTER.

6. Press ENTER again to confirm the configuration, and create the External postoffice. Press ESC twice, and then press ENTER to exit the MS Mail Administrator program.

It is a very good idea to check the message transfer from Exchange to MS Mail and vice versa. Successful message transfer in one direction does not imply that messages can also travel in the opposite direction. Keep in mind that it might take several minutes for test messages to arrive in your Inbox. If you want to track the movement of messages in MS Mail, open the MS Mail Administrator program, and check the queue for the external Connector PO. If messages remain in this queue for an extended period, use the Services utility to verify that the MS Mail Connector MTA service has started. In Exchange 2000 Server, messages may remain in the MTA queue for the MS Mail Connector or in the Connector PO if the MS Mail Connector Interchange service is not running.

Lesson 2: Configuring Directory Synchronization

So far, you have configured a connection to an MS Mail network. However, manually addressing MS Mail messages is a rather inconvenient task. Without directory synchronization, you must explicitly enter each MS Mail recipient's Network/Postoffice/Mailbox address (such as MSMAILNET/MSMAILPO/ ADMIN). You cannot simply select a user-friendly address book entry such as Administrator. MS Mail users have the same problem if they want to send messages to Exchange users. To send a test message to the Exchange administrator, for instance, you would need to specify an address similar to BLUESKYAIR/ EXCHANGE/ADMINISTRA. It is very useful to maintain server-based and postoffice-based address lists that let your users address e-mail messages conveniently.

This lesson introduces a way to maintain address information automatically between Exchange 2000 Server and MS Mail. It briefly addresses MS Mail Dirsync and then explains the roles that an Exchange 2000 server can assume in this process. The mapping of Exchange mailbox attributes to MS Mail template information is also covered.

At the end of this lesson, you will be able to:

- Identify the components of Exchange 2000 Server that support the MS Mail Dirsync protocol.
- Configure Exchange 2000 Server as a Dirsync server.
- Configure Exchange 2000 Server as a Dirsync requestor.
- Map the template information of MS Mail recipients to attributes of recipient objects in Active Directory.

Estimated time to complete this lesson: 60 minutes

MS Mail Directory Synchronization Events

The MS Mail Dirsync protocol, which updates MS Mail address lists, was introduced with Microsoft Mail for PC Networks version 3.0. It has not changed since then. Depending on the Dirsync schedule (once a day at most), an active process called Dispatch launches several programs to synchronize the address information of all postoffices in an MS Mail network based on e-mail messages.

Dirsync Server Versus Dirsync Requestors

Dirsync relies on a master postoffice known as the Dirsync server, which maintains global address information, in a file called MSTTRANS.GLB, centrally in the network. Traditionally, only one Dirsync server is supported in a native MS Mail environment. All other postoffices, configured as Dirsync requestors, must send their address changes to the Dirsync server. Once global address information has been updated on the Dirsync server, it is sent back to all Dirsync requestors to update all of their address lists (see Figure 26.4).

The Dirsync Cycle

A complete Dirsync cycle consists of three stages called T1, T2, and T3. During T1, the Dispatch program launches the processes to send address list updates to the Dirsync server. In other words, T1 is the beginning of a Dirsync cycle. Each configured requestor postoffice sends its address changes and a status report. Between T1 and T2, MS Mail MTA processes deliver the system messages to the Dirsync server (see Figure 26.4). During T2, the Dirsync server updates the Global Address List (GAL) and generates an update message for all those requestor postoffices that have transmitted at least a status report. In other words, a requestor that does not send any system messages to the Dirsync server during T1 does not receive any updates after T2. Between T2 and T3, update messages are sent back to the requestor postoffices via MS Mail MTA processes. During T3, requestors commit the address updates to the postoffice address lists.

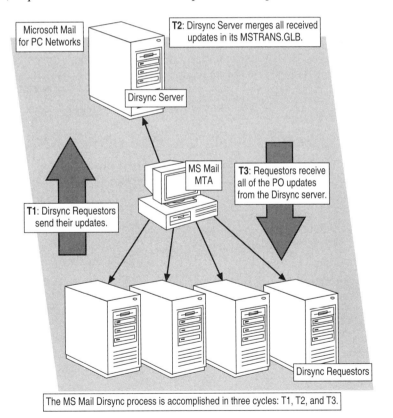

Figure 26.4   A classic Microsoft Mail Dirsync configuration

The following are the Dirsync phases and their descriptions:

- **T1.**   The Dispatch program launches a process called NSDA -RT, which starts the Reqmain -T process to run a T1 cycle according to the Dirsync schedule. Every Dirsync requestor maintains address list changes in a file called REQTRANS.GLB in the \Glb subdirectory of the postoffice. During T1, address changes are placed in an e-mail message that is addressed to the Dirsync server. A second message containing the current status information of the Requestor postoffice is also generated.

- **T2.**   Based on the Dirsync schedule of the Dirsync server, Dispatch launches the NSDA -S process, which starts Srvmain -R and Srvmain -T to perform the necessary processing. Srvmain -R causes the Dirsync server to obtain all changes from its system message queue. It places them in the GAL named MSTTRANS.GLB in the Dirsync server's \Glb subdirectory. It contains all address transactions of all Requestor postoffices. Srvmain -T then generates an update message for each Dirsync requestor containing the global address changes.

- **T3.**   Dispatch launches a process known as NSDA -RT, which starts three independent processes: Reqmain -R, Import, and the optional Rebuild process. Reqmain -R merges received messages in a file called SRVMAIN.GLB, which is in the \Glb subdirectory. After that, the MS Mail Import utility is launched with –Q parameter to commit the Dirsync updates to the postoffice address lists. Depending on the configuration, the start of the Rebuild program might complete the T3 cycle. Rebuild creates the GAL of the postoffice.

Directory Synchronization with Exchange 2000 Server

Exchange 2000 Server can participate in an MS Mail Dirsync as a Dirsync server or Dirsync requestor. A special Exchange 2000 Server component, the DXA, performs the Dirsync processing. It is implemented in a Windows 2000 service called Microsoft Exchange Directory Synchronization, which sends and receives address changes through the MTA and an MS Mail Connector (see Figure 26.5). Via Active Directory Services Interface (ADSI) and LDAP, the address information is committed to Active Directory in the form of recipient objects. When replicating an MS Mail mailbox of a user that does not own a Windows 2000 account, you can create an enabled or disabled account or a mail-enabled contact object. You can find more information about the maintenance of recipient objects in Active Directory in Chapter 13, "Creating and Managing Recipients."

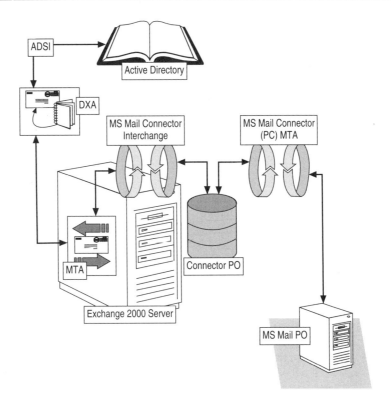

Figure 26.5   The architecture of the Directory Synchronization Agent

Dirsync Database

The DXA maintains a Dirsync database (XDIR.EDB), which resides in the \Program Files\Exchsrvr\Dxadata directory. Based on the information from XDIR.EDB, only new address changes are requested from Active Directory. Sending only updates in a Dirsync cycle helps to reduce the size of Dirsync messages. The DXA places the updates in an e-mail message and sends them to a Dirsync server or to Dirsync requestors depending on the DXA configuration. The DXA also receives updates through MS Mail Connector and MTA and commits them to Active Directory. The XDIR.EDB is continuously updated to keep track of transactions.

Note   Deleting the XDIR.EDB resets the MS Mail DirSync. Complete address list information is then exchanged in the next Dirsync cycle.

DXA as a Dirsync Server

An Exchange 2000 server can act as a Dirsync server in an MS Mail network. This has advantages and disadvantages. As a prerequisite, you must have a functioning MS Mail Connector, which transfers the Dirsync messages between the Exchange 2000 server and the requestor postoffices.

DXA Server Advantages

The DXA server can improve the flexibility of the MS Mail directory synchronization. For instance, the DXA service runs continuously and commits requestor updates to Active Directory as soon as they arrive. There is no delay in the form of a scheduled event. The scheduled T2 time affects only the generation of update messages that are sent back to the requestor postoffices. Using a DXA server, the Dirsync cycle can run more than once a day. In fact, it can theoretically run every 15 minutes if a requestor message was received in the meantime. As mentioned earlier, only requestors that have sent a T1 message since the last cycle will receive an update message. Furthermore, if you have deployed the MS Mail Connector on multiple servers in your organization, you can configure more than one DXA server to bind independent MS Mail networks together. This mechanism relies on Active Directory replication, which distributes address list updates across the entire organization. For instance, a second Exchange 2000 server in another administrative group can act as a DXA server for a different MS Mail network. Both MS Mail networks can perform directory synchronization as usual, and Active Directory will synchronize the DXA servers (in other words, the GALs of both MS Mail networks) in the background.

DXA Server Disadvantages

It is not an easy task to integrate a DXA server into an existing MS Mail Dirsync environment. The problem is not the DXA server itself, but what happens as a result of system reconfiguration. For example, if you have integrated Exchange 2000 Server into an MS Mail network of 10 postoffices containing 5000 mailboxes in all, you may want to refrain from configuring a DXA server. The DXA server would replace the current Dirsync server, which forces you to reset the MS Mail Dirsync configuration on every requestor postoffice. You would have to carry out a time-consuming and complex task using MS Mail low-level utilities, such as DSSCHED.EXE, LISTDS.EXE, and LISTQ.EXE, and all the work would generate a large amount of Dirsync messages, because 5000 mailboxes would have to be synchronized again. Also, postoffices would display incomplete address lists until you had reset every requestor and completed the Dirsync process. For detailed information about resetting the MS Mail Dirsync, see Application Note WA0725 from Microsoft Product Support Services (go to *www.microsoft.com* and search for WA0725).

DXA as a Dirsync Requestor

The DXA can act as either a DXA server or a DXA requestor, but it cannot do both at the same time. If you decide not to configure a DXA server but still want to take advantage of the MS Mail Dirsync, you must configure a Dirsync requestor (see Figure 26.6). A DXA operating as a requestor allows you to integrate an Exchange 2000 Server organization seamlessly into an MS Mail Dirsync environment. You need only configure a new requestor entry on the existing Dirsync server, and the DXA can synchronize address updates with the MS Mail network. Major configuration changes are not required.

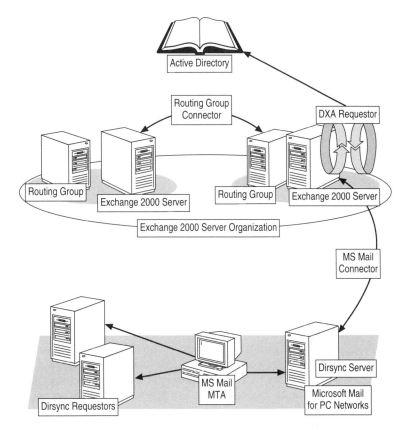

Figure 26.6   Exchange 2000 Server as a Dirsync requestor

DXA Requestor Limitations

The Dirsync server of a DXA requestor must be a regular MS Mail postoffice that processes the address updates of all requestors during T2. That is, you cannot configure the DXA as a requestor that sends address changes to another DXA configured as a DXA server. Hence, you cannot synchronize addresses of two independent Exchange 2000 Server organizations using the MS Mail Dirsync protocol. You cannot even carry out Dirsync between multiple organizations using an MS Mail postoffice acting as a relay DXA server between them.

Note   Because the DXA requestor must send address list changes to an MS Mail Dirsync server, you cannot run the Dirsync cycle more than once a day. As always in MS Mail, the Dirsync server performs the T2 processing of address list changes according to the schedule of the Dispatch program.

Configuring a DXA Server

Before configuring a DXA server, make sure you have configured and successfully tested your MS Mail Connector. To create a DXA server in Exchange System Manager, right-click the connectors object that you can find under <Organization Name>/Administrative Groups/<Administrative Group Name>/ Routing Groups/<Routing Group Name> (such as Blue Sky Airlines (Exchange)/ Administrative Groups/First Administrative Group/Routing Groups/First Routing Group). From the shortcut menu, point to New, and then select Dirsync Server. This displays the General tab of a new DXA server object. To distinguish the new DXA server object from all other configuration objects, you must specify an appropriate DXA server name in the Name box in the General tab. It is good practice to use a name that identifies the MS Mail network.

Tracking Directory Synchronization Messages

The DXA server incorporates address list changes of remote DirSync requestors automatically in Active Directory. MS Mail users are handled as recipient objects. In other words, if recipient objects appear for users of your MS Mail network, you know that Dirsync works. However, in cases of communication problems, you might wait a very long time without success. In this situation, it is useful to trace MS Mail Dirsync messages. You can copy them to an administrative mailbox that you need to specify under DirSync Administrator's Mailbox. Click on the Modify button to select the desired account. After that, you can select the Forward Incoming DirSync Messages To Administrator check box to receive a copy of requestor messages. You can also select the Copy Administrator On Outgoing Messages check box if you want to examine your DXA server's responses.

T2 Schedule

Using its activation schedule, the DXA server generates update messages for each requestor that has sent a T1 message since the last T2 cycle. In the Schedule tab, you can set when and how often the DXA is active. The shortest possible interval is 15 minutes. This does not, however, mean that the DXA server sends a particular MS Mail requestor an update message every 15 minutes (or 96 messages per day). Dirsync messages are processed once when they arrive.

Configuring Remote Dirsync Requestors

To complete the configuration, you must designate existing MS Mail requestor postoffices as remote Dirsync requestors. For this purpose, right-click the newly created DXA server object under Connectors, point to New, and then select the Remote Dirsync Requestor command. This will display the New Requestor dialog box, where you can select a desired MS Mail postoffice and click OK. The DXA server will refuse Dirsync messages from unregistered sources. The MS Mail Dirsync is based on a secured protocol. You can define a requestor password in the General tab of each remote Dirsync requestor object to increase security.

Note A DXA requestor is an Exchange 2000 Server computer. A remote Dirsync requestor is an MS Mail postoffice.

General Remote Dirsync Requestor Properties

For every remote Dirsync requestor, you need to specify a name that refers to the new requestor configuration object. The name that you type in the General tab in the Name box should clearly identify the MS Mail postoffice. Optionally, you may append this name to the display name of imported users. The Export On Next Cycle check box allows you to send complete address information—not only the updates—to the requestor postoffice during the next Dirsync cycle, which is useful if the postoffice address lists appear incomplete.

Importing and Exporting Addresses

In the Import Container tab, you can specify a container that will maintain imported recipient objects for the selected requestor postoffice. You should create a dedicated organizational unit (OU) in Active Directory Users and Computers for this purpose. To select the desired OU for the remote Dirsync requestor, in the Import Container tab, click the Modify button. Exchange System Manager will prompt you to grant the machine account of your Exchange 2000 server (such as BLUESKY-SRV1) required permissions to create and modify recipients in the selected OU. Click Yes to update the permissions on the import container. You also can determine the type of recipient objects to create in Active Directory if replicated mailboxes do not have accounts in the Windows 2000 domain (that is, Create A Disabled Windows User Account, Create A New Windows User Account, and Create A Windows Contact).

In the Export Containers tab, in contrast, you can specify one or more OUs that will be exported to the remote requestor postoffice. The machine account of your Exchange 2000 server requires Read permissions on all OUs that you specify as export containers. Exchange System Manager can grant the required permissions to your server account. Furthermore, if you have decided to create Windows contacts for MS Mail mailboxes, make sure you select the Export Contacts check box if you want to synchronize address information between MS Mail post-offices. You can also include distribution groups in the Dirsync via the Export Groups check box.

Note   If you change the import container for an existing remote Dirsync requestor object later, do not forget to move all affected mailbox accounts from the former import container to the new OU. Recipient objects in the old OU will not be updated any longer.

Configuring a DXA Requestor

Configuring a DXA requestor is less complex than configuring a DXA server. This is not surprising because the DXA requestor is responsible only for itself. You can set several configuration parameters just as you do for a remote Dirsync requestor. For instance, you take the same steps to specify import and export OUs using the Import Container and Export Container tabs.

DXA Requestor Parameters

To create a DXA requestor, right-click the connectors object under <Organization Name>/Administrative Groups/<Administrative Group Name>/Routing Groups/<Routing Group Name>. Point to New, and then select the Dirsync Requestor command. A New Requestor dialog box will appear, asking you for the MS Mail Dirsync server postoffice. Select the correct postoffice, and click OK to launch the Properties dialog box, which asks for further information. In the General tab of the new DXA requestor object, you can set basic configuration parameters such as the name of the DXA requestor object and the requestor language. Several of the settings have the same effect that they do for a remote Dirsync requestor (the Append To Imported User's Display Name option, for example). Other parameters pertain only to a DXA requestor object, so you can specify which address types to accept from the Dirsync server.

Note   You must first configure an MS Mail Connector to connect the Exchange 2000 server to the MS Mail postoffice that represents the Dirsync server; otherwise, you cannot select the correct postoffice reference in the New Requestor window during DXA requestor creation.

T1 Schedule

Two Dirsync times are important for every requestor: T1 and T3. However, you have to schedule only the T1 time because updates are committed to Active Directory as soon as they reach the DXA. In the Schedule tab of the DXA requestor object, you can adjust the T1 time. By default, the DXA requestor sends its changes at midnight.

> **Note** It is sufficient to send one address update message to the MS Mail Dirsync server each day. The Mail Dirsync server incorporates the changes only once at T2 as scheduled for the Dispatch process.

Dirsync Parameters

Several settings of a DXA requestor refer directly to the MS Mail Dirsync protocol. As mentioned earlier for DXA servers, you can secure the communication between the Dirsync server and a requestor by using a password. Once you specify a password at the Dirsync server postoffice, the requestor must provide the password to synchronize addresses. You can enter this password in the Settings tab of the DXA requestor object.

You can also send all of the address information to the Dirsync server during the next Dirsync cycle by selecting the Export On Next Cycle check box. Activating the Import On Next Cycle check box, on the other hand, requests complete address information from the Dirsync server. As a result, all addresses are sent to the requestor during the next cycle. Both options are useful if you discover address inconsistencies between MS Mail and Exchange 2000 Server address information.

If you want to include detailed address information in the MS Mail Dirsync, select the Send Local Template Information and Receive Local Template Information check boxes.

Directory Synchronization Templates

MS Mail users can display detailed address information for recipients from their postoffice address lists. Exchange users can examine the properties and attributes of mailbox- and mail-enabled recipient objects using their address books as well. Therefore, you should map Exchange attributes to MS Mail address information (and vice versa) if MS Mail Dirsync has been configured. This way, Exchange users can examine detailed MS Mail address information, and MS Mail users can display additional information about recipients that seem to reside on the Connector PO address list (which is the MS Mail view of your organization).

MS Mail Address Templates

By default, the MS Mail system provides the alias name, display name, address type, postoffice name, network name, and the name of the mailbox. Using address templates, you can define additional information that is displayed if users examine the details of an address entry. For example, one such template, EXAMPLE.TPL, is in the \Tpl subdirectory of every postoffice installation. It has the following content:

```
Employee Number:~17~6~NP~000001~

Name Title:~17~3~ULP~Mr~
```

```
Initials:~17~2~U~MD~

Surname:~17~15~ULP~Davis~

Division:~17~25~A~Electronic Mail~

Department:~17~15~A~Development~

Phone:~17~15~NP~(303) 555-4345~

FAX:~17~15~NP~(303) 555-1378~

Company:~17~25~LUNP~Microsoft Corp.~

Address 1:~17~50~A~1402 Washington Street~

Address 1:~17~50~A~Hollywood, FL~

Postal Code:~17~7~A~33021~

Phone:~17~15~NP~(303) 555-4345~

Group:~17~15~A~Mail Group~
```

These entries are only suggestions that you can adjust as needed; however, you must rename the EXAMPLE.TPL file as ADMIN.TPL for it to accept additional properties such as Phone, Company, or Address. You will find documentation in the MS Mail Administrator manual.

Mapping of Incoming and Outgoing Template Information

Exchange 2000 Server does not use template information. Detailed information is maintained in the form of recipient object attributes from Active Directory. To synchronize address details, you must map Active Directory attributes for recipient objects to postoffice template labels such as Phone, Company, or Address (see the preceding template listing). You can control the mapping using Exchange System Manager. The directory synchronization object, which can be found under <Organization Name>/Administrative Groups/<Administrative Group Name>/Servers/<Server Name> (such as Blue Sky Airlines (Exchange)/Administrative Groups/First Administrative Group/Servers/BLUESKY-SRV1), provides the required tabs. The most important Incoming Templates and Outgoing Templates. The directory synchronization object lets you configure the template transfer in one or both directions.

You can administer the incoming and outgoing template mappings in a similar way. Click the New button repeatedly to define the desired mappings. For instance, in the Incoming Template Mapping dialog box that appears when you click the New button in the Incoming Templates tab, you must enter the template string (such as Phone) manually. You can select the corresponding mailbox attribute from the Map The Attribute box. When you define mappings, you can rename template labels by assigning them different attributes. You can also suppress labels by leaving them unmapped. However, keep in mind that you must include the template information in the directory synchronization (via the Settings tab of the corresponding DXA requestor object).

Lesson 3: The Schedule+ Free/Busy Connector

Free/busy times are the free and busy times of users as noted in their schedules, marked by start and end dates. This information is shared among users so that they can plan meetings and appointments efficiently. A user who wants to book a meeting can view the free and busy times of all attendees and determine a time when they are all available. Using the Schedule+ Free/Busy Connector in conjunction with the MS Mail Connector, you can synchronize free/busy information between MS Mail and Exchange 2000 Server.

This lesson introduces the Schedule+ Free/Busy Connector and explains its architecture and configuration using Exchange System Manager.

At the end of this lesson, you will be able to:

- Identify the components of the Schedule+ Free/Busy Connector.
- Configure the Schedule+ Free/Busy Connector.

Estimated time to complete this lesson: 45 minutes

Schedule+ Free/Busy Connector Architecture

Free/busy time distribution was introduced with Microsoft Schedule+1.0 in conjunction with MS Mail. Users working with different postoffices can share free/busy information because active processes in the background distribute that information to all postoffices. This feature is also available in Microsoft Schedule+ 7.0, Microsoft Schedule+ 7.5, and Microsoft Outlook and is implemented in Exchange 2000 Server as well.

MS Mail Free/Busy Time Distribution

MS Mail maintains free/busy times on a per-postoffice basis in .pof files, which are in the \Maildata\Cal subdirectory. The file 00000000.POF, for example, contains the free/busy times of users who use the local postoffice. However, the postoffice is a passive file structure. A separate process known as SCHDIST.EXE is required to distribute free/busy information across all postoffices in an MS Mail network.

Three components are very important for free/busy time distribution: SCHDIST.EXE, ADMINSCH.EXE, and a mailbox called Adminsch. As mentioned, SCHDIST.EXE distributes the information across the MS Mail network using e-mail messages, which are sent to the Adminsch mailbox. Once messages are delivered to this mailbox, SCHDIST.EXE can obtain the free/busy information from there to place it in the corresponding .pof files. ADMINSCH.EXE is the Schedule+ Administrator program. You can use it to manage distribution settings, such as the postoffices that receive free/busy information. You should make sure that all target postoffices have an Adminsch account that is included in the MS Mail Dirsync. The MS Mail Dirsync propagates the existence of Adminsch accounts through the MS Mail network.

Schedule+ Free/Busy Information Public Folder

Users with mailboxes on an Exchange 2000 server maintain free/busy information in a hidden system folder in the default public folder hierarchy. You can display this folder in Exchange System Manager. Right-click the default public folder hierarchy (Public Folders), and then select the View System Folders command. A free/busy public folder will exist for each existing administrative group in the Schedule+ Free Busy container. The free/busy public folder is usually on the first server installed in an administrative group. You can replicate it across the organization or move it to a designated free/busy public server. More information about the replication of public folders is provided in Chapter 18, "Public Folder Replication."

Each free/busy public folder contains a single object for each user in its administrative group. These objects store the users' free/busy times. These objects are comparable to regular message items in a visible public folder. If a user stores a free/busy item in this folder, all other users can open it there and read the information. Every user has access to the hidden free/busy public folder when working with Schedule+ 7.0 or later or Outlook.

Schedule+ Free/Busy Connector

The Schedule+ Free/Busy Connector uses the MS Mail distribution protocol to exchange free/busy information between Exchange users and MS Mail users based on e-mail messages. This connector actually accomplishes two tasks. First it creates free/busy messages destined for the MS Mail network. Then it incorporates received information from MS Mail into the free/busy public folder. To access this folder, the connector must communicate with the Information Store service. Once the MS Mail free/busy information is stored on the Exchange 2000 server, users can access it just as any other free/busy information.

The following are the tasks of the Free/Busy Connector:

- Obtains free/busy information from the free/busy public folder.
- Creates and sends free/busy messages to MS Mail SCHDIST.EXE. Messages are addressed to the Adminsch account of each involved postoffice.
- Processes free/busy messages received from MS Mail SCHDIST.EXE. Messages are addressed and delivered to the Adminsch user agent of the Schedule+ Free/Busy Connector.
- Places the received free/busy information in the free/busy public folder.

Adminsch User Agent

The Schedule+ Free/Busy Connector uses a user agent called Adminsch to send and receive Schedule+ free/busy information. A user agent is a special Exchange 2000 Server mailbox that is associated with an active service instead of a regular user. It is created during the Free/Busy Connector installation and is in the Connectors container of the Free/Busy Connector's routing group.

SCHDIST.EXE and Adminsch

SCHDIST.EXE sends its local free/busy information to all other Adminsch mailboxes—in other words, to all other SCHDIST.EXE processes in the MS Mail network. SCHDIST.EXE can also include the Exchange 2000 Server in its information distribution since the Schedule+ Free/Busy Connector maintains an Adminsch user agent (see Figure 26.7).

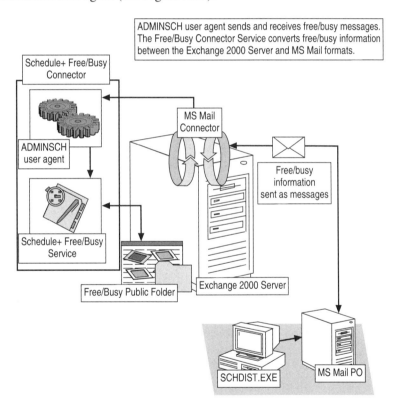

Figure 26.7   The architecture of the Schedule+ Free/Busy Connector

MS Mail Dirsync

For every Exchange and MS Mail user, a recipient object must exist in Active Directory; otherwise, the Schedule+ Free/Busy Connector will not be able to place free/busy information for the user in the free/busy public folder. Consequently, you need to configure the MS Mail Dirsync and synchronize the address lists before configuring the transfer of free/busy data. Among other things, the MS Mail Dirsync will also replicate the Adminsch accounts, which must exist in each postoffice address list as well as Active Directory to address SCHDIST.EXE messages successfully.

Configuring the Schedule+ Free/Busy Connector

The Schedule+ Free/Busy Connector relies on the MS Mail Connector and the MS Mail Dirsync. The MS Mail Connector must guarantee that free/busy messages arrive at the MS Mail postoffices and that SCHDIST.EXE messages reach the Schedule+ Free/Busy Connector. MS Mail Dirsync, in turn, synchronizes the address information, as mentioned earlier.

Connector Configuration

To configure the Schedule+ Free/Busy Connector, launch Exchange System Manager, and display the properties of the Connector for MS SchedulePlus FreeBusy (<Server Name>) object, which is located in the Connectors container of the connector's routing group. This configuration object provides two tabs, General and Details. As for all configuration objects, the Details tab is less important. It provides only an option to specify an informative Administrative Note. The General tab is more important. Among other things, it allows you to define an Administrator's Mailbox, which is used to store corrupted free/busy messages and messages that could not be processed for other reasons.

Note   To have a functioning system, you must configure the MS Mail postoffices using the ADMINSCH.EXE program. The Connector PO must be included in the list of target postoffices.

Sending Free/Busy Information

In the General tab, you will find the Schedule+ Group box, where you need to specify a distribution group that contains the Adminsch accounts of all postoffices you want to include in the free/busy synchronization. Using a distribution list simplifies the task of configuring the connector when several postoffices are included. However, you must create a mail-enabled distribution group for this purpose prior to configuring the connector.

You can select the Send Updates For This Administrative Group Only check box if you want to propagate the free/busy information only of users residing in your administrative group to MS Mail.

Information Updates

By default, the Schedule+ Free/Busy Connector sends changes to free/busy information to the MS Mail network every 15 minutes. This is sufficient for most installations, but you can adjust this in the General tab by using the Update Frequency (Minutes) box. If you discover any inconsistencies between free/busy information in MS Mail and in Exchange, click the Full Export button to send all of the free/busy data to the MS Mail network.

Chapter Summary

The MS Mail Connector is an additional component that comes with both the Standard and Enterprise Editions of Exchange 2000 Server. It allows you to connect one or many MS Mail postoffices to an Exchange 2000 server and is the basis for directory synchronization and exchange of free/busy information. One MS Mail Connector is sufficient to connect an entire Exchange 2000 Server organization to an MS Mail network. Important connector components are the MS Mail Connector Interchange service, the Connector PO, and one or many MS Mail Connector MTA services. The connector is managed using Exchange System Manager.

To participate in MS Mail Dirsync, a DXA was implemented in Exchange 2000 Server. The DXA can function as a Dirsync server or a Dirsync requestor. As a Dirsync server, the DXA consolidates address updates for all those MS Mail postoffices that have been configured as remote Dirsync requestors. Configured as a DXA requestor, on the other hand, Exchange 2000 Server sends update messages to an MS Mail Dirsync server and expects global address updates from this postoffice. It is not possible, however, to let a DXA requestor participate in a Dirsync environment with another Exchange 2000 server functioning as the DXA server. The DXA synchronizes MS Mail address information with Active Directory recipient objects by means of ADSI and LDAP.

The Schedule+ Free/Busy Connector enables you to synchronize free/busy information between MS Mail and Exchange 2000 Server, which allows MS Mail and Exchange users to plan meetings and appointments efficiently. As a prerequisite, you need to configure the MS Mail Connector because free/busy information is transferred in e-mail messages. You also need to configure the directory synchronization because a recipient object in Active Directory must represent each user; otherwise, free/busy information cannot be maintained in the free/busy public folder of Exchange 2000 Server. The MS Mail counterpart of the Schedule+ Free/Busy Connector is SCHDIST.EXE, which propagates free/busy information across the MS Mail network.

Review

The following review questions can help you determine if you have sufficiently familiarized yourself with the material covered in this chapter. You can find the answers to these questions at the end of this book in Appendix A, "Questions and Answers."

1. What are the three most important components of the MS Mail Connector?

2. What is the function of the Connector PO?

3. You have configured an MS Mail Connector between one MS Mail postoffice and an Exchange 2000 server. Exchange users can send messages, but users on the MS Mail postoffice cannot. How can you correct this problem?

4. What are the three stages of a complete Dirsync cycle?

5. You have configured an Exchange 2000 server as a DXA server. MS Mail requestor postoffices are sending their address changes to the Exchange 2000 server through the MS Mail Connector. When will address list changes appear in the specified import container?

6. Which configuration can you use to map MS Mail template information to Exchange mailbox attributes?

7. Why must you configure a distribution group before configuring the Schedule+ Free/Busy Connector?

CHAPTER 27

Connecting to Lotus cc:Mail

About This Chapter

Lotus cc:Mail is a shared-file messaging system similar to Microsoft Mail for PC Networks. Up-to-date environments use Lotus cc:Mail release 8 with database version 8 (DB8), which is the only platform that is fully Year 2000–compliant. For this reason, Microsoft does not provide a connector to earlier releases of cc:Mail, such as Lotus cc:Mail release 6 with database version 6 (DB6). Recently, Lotus Development Corporation announced plans to discontinue their development of Lotus cc:Mail, which can be seen as the end of the shared-file messaging era.

The Connector for Lotus cc:Mail supports the integration of Microsoft Exchange 2000 Server into an existing Lotus cc:Mail network so that it acts as one or many virtual cc:Mail post offices. This is the basis for reliable messaging coexistence and efficient migration to Exchange 2000 Server. The connector configuration is straightforward and does not differ much from its predecessor, included with Microsoft Exchange Server 5.5, although a few features have changed, such as integration with Active Directory directory service. The connector supports the transfer of e-mail messages as well as directory synchronization. It is available in both the Standard and Enterprise editions of Exchange 2000 Server.

This chapter covers the installation and configuration of the Connector for Lotus cc:Mail. It describes the transfer of e-mail messages between both systems and explains the propagation of address information. This chapter focuses on environments with Lotus cc:Mail DB8.

Before You Begin

To complete this chapter:

- Be familiar with the responsibilities of Active Directory and Exchange 2000 Server system components and their interaction, as explained in Chapter 3, "Microsoft Exchange 2000 Server Architecture."

- Have practical experience administering Lotus cc:Mail post offices and Automatic Directory Exchange (ADE). Detailed information is available in the Lotus cc:Mail product documentation.

Lesson 1: The Connector for Lotus cc:Mail

When it comes out of the box, the Connector for Lotus cc:Mail is an incomplete messaging component. In fact, you will not be able to use it without installing additional programs. The missing pieces are IMPORT.EXE and EXPORT.EXE, which you can find in the Lotus cc:Mail installation in the \CCMAIL\Adtools directory or on the Lotus cc:Mail product CD. Microsoft does not provide these essential applications. A license from Lotus Development is required to use them.

This lesson addresses the architecture of the Connector for Lotus cc:Mail. It deals with the internal components and covers its installation and configuration.

At the end of this lesson, you will be able to:

- Describe the features of the Connector for Lotus cc:Mail and identify its components and architecture.
- List issues regarding Lotus cc:Mail IMPORT.EXE and EXPORT.EXE utilities.
- Configure and use the Connector for Lotus cc:Mail.

Estimated time to complete this lesson: 60 minutes

Connector for Lotus cc:Mail Overview

The Connector for Lotus cc:Mail is an optional Exchange 2000 Server component that can be controlled through its own Microsoft Windows 2000 service (CCMC.EXE). It has been developed based on the Microsoft Exchange Development Kit (EDK), and it allows you to connect an Exchange 2000 server to exactly one Lotus cc:Mail post office. Within the Lotus cc:Mail network, e-mail messages can be routed to other post offices further downstream. Ideally, the connector's cc:Mail post office is installed directly on the Exchange 2000 server.

Administrator Programs

You need to work with two separate administrator utilities to establish messaging connectivity to cc:Mail. You will use Exchange System Manager to configure the Connector for Lotus cc:Mail component, and you must manage the Lotus cc:Mail environment using the Lotus cc:Mail Administrator program. Lotus cc:Mail post office release 8 includes a Windows-based Administrator utility (ADMINW.EXE), whereas older versions provide only an MS-DOS program (ADMIN.EXE). Use the Lotus cc:Mail Administrator program primarily to register a remote post office for your Exchange 2000 Server organization.

Connector Installation

The Connector for Lotus cc:Mail can be installed during the initial Exchange 2000 Server setup or later on. To add this connector to an existing installation, permissions of an Exchange Administrator are required in the administrative group where the target routing group exists. Likewise, you need to be a member of the local Administrators group on the target machine. Ideally, you are working with the permissions of an Enterprise Admin.

▶ **To add the connector to an Exchange 2000 server**

1. Launch SETUP.EXE from the \Setup\i386 directory on your Exchange 2000 Server product CD.

2. On the welcome wizard screen, click Next to reach the Component Selection wizard screen, where you need to set the Action for Microsoft Exchange 2000 and Microsoft Exchange Messaging And Collaboration Services to Change.

3. Under Action for the Microsoft Exchange Connector for Lotus cc:Mail, select Install, click Next twice, and then click Finish.

You can find more information regarding the Exchange 2000 Server Setup program in Chapter 5, "Installing Microsoft Exchange 2000 Server."

Multiple Connector Instances

It is not possible to install more than one Connector for Lotus cc:Mail on one Exchange 2000 server. It is also impossible to directly connect to more than one Lotus cc:Mail post office with one connector (see Figure 27.1). However, you can deploy multiple connector instances on several servers in your organization to provide load balancing between large Exchange and Lotus cc:Mail networks.

By default, the entire Exchange 2000 Server organization will act as one huge Lotus cc:Mail proxy post office, which can be connected to a particular Lotus cc:Mail network only once. However, you can split your organization by assigning your Exchange users CCMAIL proxy addresses that appear to be from different proxy post offices (for example, Administrator at FirstAdminGroup and Carl Titmouse at SecondAdminGroup). With multiple proxy post offices, you can spread cc:Mail message routing over multiple connector instances (for example, a connector on BLUESKY-SRV1 for the virtual post office FirstAdminGroup and a connector on BLUESKY-SRV2 for SecondAdminGroup). The configuration of CCMAIL proxy addresses is covered later in this lesson.

Note Carefully plan the directory synchronization topology when connecting a particular organization to the same Lotus cc:Mail network multiple times. Only one connector should be configured for directory synchronization.

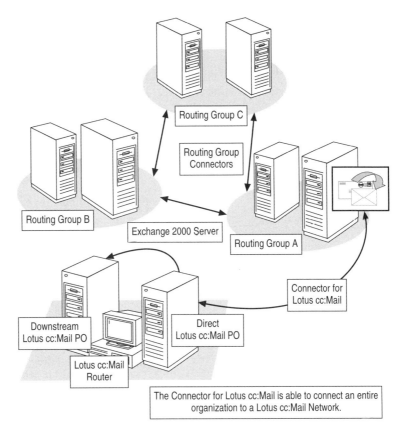

Figure 27.1   Deploying the Connector for Lotus cc:Mail

Message Conversion

The Connector for Lotus cc:Mail is a regular messaging gateway. Therefore, the connector must convert outbound messages into Lotus cc:Mail format. Conversely, the Connector must also convert content and recipient information into Exchange format for inbound messages.

Most message attributes are mapped between both systems. The Connector can convert e-mail addresses, message submission time, sender and recipient display names, subject lines, message bodies, and any attachments, plus their file names. The Connector supports special message flags such as Read Receipt Requested and Last Modified. The connector supports read receipts in addition to nondelivery reports (NDRs). However, some special properties are not supported, such as shortcuts to public folders.

The following features are not supported in Lotus cc:Mail:

- Delivery receipts
- Embedded messages (will be converted to additional text items)
- Embedded OLE objects (will be converted to separate attachments)
- Shortcuts to public folders in Exchange 2000 Server (converted to attachments with names derived from public folder names; Lotus cc:Mail clients are unable to launch these attachments)

Lotus cc:Mail Import/Export

The MS-DOS–based Import and Export programs are used to access the Connector's cc:Mail post office. The Import program places converted outbound messages and address information into the post office. The Export program is responsible for extracting messages and address information from the post office. Both utilities require a local area network (LAN) connection to access the post office successfully. Consequently, the Connector for Lotus cc:Mail is supported only in LAN environments.

It is important to note that your Exchange 2000 server must be connected to Lotus cc:Mail post office using DB8, and the Connector to Lotus cc:Mail must run Import and Export version 8.3 or higher. Otherwise, you may experience problems during message conversion. If you want to use cc:Mail Import and Export version 8.5 with the Connector for Lotus cc:Mail, you need to rename IMPORT32.EXE to IMPORT.EXE and EXPORT32.EXE to EXPORT.EXE. Copy the renamed files together with the files CDMW800.DLL, CFW803.DLL, and CIW803.DLL to a directory that is in the search path on the local Exchange 2000 server, and place the IE.RI and IMPEXP.RI files in the \Program Files\ Exchsrvr\Ccmcdata directory.

Components of the Connector for Lotus cc:Mail

The Connector for Lotus cc:Mail consists of various essential elements, such as message queues in the Information Store, and a Windows 2000 service called Microsoft Exchange Connector for Lotus cc:Mail, plus address generators and templates, and the Lotus cc:Mail Import/Export programs. Another important Connector component is known as the Connector Store. This is the temporary repository for converted messages.

The Microsoft Exchange Connector for Lotus cc:Mail Service

The Connector's Windows 2000 service communicates with the Information Store to transfer messages to and from Exchange 2000 Server. The Connector converts inbound and outbound messages as appropriate using the Connector Store: While the Connector reads inbound mail from the Connector Store, it also writes outbound messages into the Connector Store. The connector service launches the Import and Export programs to place and retrieve messages to and from the connected Lotus cc:Mail post office (see Figure 27.2).

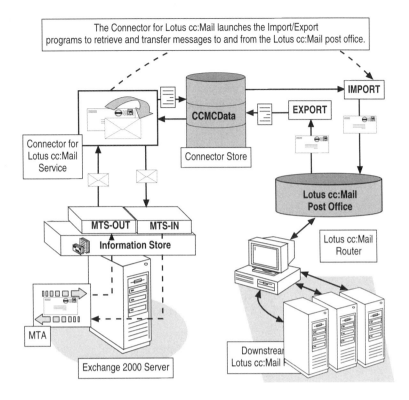

Figure 27.2 Essential Connector for Lotus cc:Mail components

Like every EDK gateway, the Connector for Lotus cc:Mail maintains two important gateway folders in the Information Store, labeled MTS-OUT for outbound messages and MTS-IN for inbound messages. These message queues are not polled. The Information Store notifies the Connector for Lotus cc:Mail if messages have been placed in the MTS-OUT folder. Conversely, the Connector for Lotus cc:Mail service initiates communication with the Information Store if inbound messages are placed in the MTS-IN queue.

Tip   The Connector for Lotus cc:Mail service is set to manual startup by default. It is a good idea to change this to automatic using the Services snap-in from the Administrative Tools program group.

Connector Store

The Connector Store is the intermediate storage location for Lotus cc:Mail messages. The Import program reads the messages from this location to write them into the Lotus cc:Mail post office. The Export program, on the other hand, places messages into this repository once they have been extracted from Lotus cc:Mail.

The messages are stored as scratch files. Scratch files are plain text files in American Standard Code for Information Interchange (ASCII) format that are structured as required by the Import and Export programs. Take care when setting user access to the Connector Store—every user who can open the \Program Files\Exchsrvr\Ccmcdata directory potentially can read Lotus cc:Mail messages. Fortunately, the \Ccmcdata directory is not shared for network access and messages are not stored permanently, by default.

The following subdirectories temporarily contain messages:

- **\Bad.**   Stores messages that could not be converted properly.

- **\Export and \EXPORT.BAK.**   Maintains inbound messages destined for Exchange 2000 Server. The connector keeps copies of exported files in EXPORT.BAK if the Registry parameter Save A Copy Of The Exported Files is set to 1. (The location of Registry parameters is mentioned in the next section.)

- **\Import and \IMPORT.BAK.**   Maintains outbound messages destined for Lotus cc:Mail. The connector keeps copies of import files entering cc:Mail in IMPORT.BAK if the Registry parameter Save A Copy Of The Imported Files is set to 1.

- **\Submit.**   Temporarily stores outbound messages to Lotus cc:Mail during message conversion.

Note   The \Ccmcdata directory does not contain any subdirectories, by default. The Connector for Lotus cc:Mail service creates them when you activate the connector for the first time.

Import and Export of Messages

The Import program checks for scratch files in the \Program Files\Exchsrvr\ Ccmcdata\Import directory, while the Export utility writes scratch files into \Program Files\Exchsrvr\Ccmcdata\Export. The task of the Connector service is to convert outbound messages into scratch files before they are placed in the Connector Store. Likewise, this service must convert scratch files found in the \Export directory into Exchange format before they can be placed in the MTS-IN gateway folder (see Figure 27.2).

The Lotus cc:Mail post office is a passive file structure, which means it requires frequent polling for new messages. Correspondingly, the Connector for Lotus cc:Mail launches the Import and Export programs periodically to poll the Lotus cc:Mail post office. The Import program, however, is launched only when messages need to be transferred into cc:Mail. The default polling interval for Import and Export is 15 seconds.

Configuration Objects in Exchange System Manager

When you install the Connector for Lotus cc:Mail in a routing group, a corresponding configuration object will be created in the Configuration partition of Active Directory. In Exchange System Manager, you can find a corresponding configuration object under <Organization Name>/Administrative Groups/ <Administrative Group Name>/Routing Groups/<Routing Group Name>/ Connectors. Underneath the connector configuration object, you can find the Queues container, which provides access to the MTS-IN and MTS-OUT message queues of the Connector.

The Message Transfer Agent (MTA) receives outbound cc:Mail messages from the Simple Mail Transfer Protocol (SMTP) routing engine and transfers inbound messages to it for further delivery. Consequently, the MTA needs to maintain an internal message queue for the Connector for Lotus cc:Mail. You can view this queue in Exchange System Manager under <Organization Name>/Administrative Groups/<Administrative Group Name>/Servers/<Server Name>/Protocols/ X.400/Queues, such as Blue Sky Airlines (Exchange)/Administrative Groups/ First Administrative Group/Servers/BLUESKY-SRV1/Protocols/X.400/Queues. Message queues are covered in Chapter 20, "Microsoft Exchange 2000 Server Maintenance and Troubleshooting."

Lotus cc:Mail on Windows 2000 Server

If you have installed the Connector's cc:Mail post office directly on the Exchange 2000 server (or another Windows 2000 Server machine), make sure the Registry parameters UseOpportunisticLocking and UseNtCaching are set to 0 on the post office's server; otherwise, post office corruption may occur due to concurrent write operations.

You can add or edit the UseOpportunisticLocking and UseNtCaching values under:

```
HKEY_LOCAL_MACHINE

  \SYSTEM

   \CurrentControlSet

    \Services

     \Lanmanworkstation

      \Parameters
```

Lotus cc:Mail Considerations

The Connector for Lotus cc:Mail uses the interprocess communication mechanisms of Microsoft Windows 2000 Server to start the Import and Export utilities in separate NT Virtual DOS Machines (NTVDM), which is a special Win32-based environment to run MS-DOS–based applications. Both programs are executed in the background. Supplied command-line parameters indicate whether to transfer e-mail messages or address information. For example, the /ITEMSIZE /FORMAT/ FAN /BATCH /FILES/MACBIN2 command-line parameter can be used to initiate an e-mail export cycle from Lotus cc:Mail to Exchange 2000 Server.

The Import and Export programs and the IMPEXP.RI file must be copied to the Exchange 2000 server, and they must be located in a directory that is included in the system search path, such as the \Winnt\System32 directory. The Connector for Lotus cc:Mail will report an error in the application event log if the Import and Export programs cannot be launched. After a number of unsuccessful attempts to start the programs, the service terminates automatically.

Note   Command-line settings can be changed via Registry parameters, such as Export Command Line, Import Command Line, Dir Synch Export Command Line, or Dir Synch Import Command Line.

Lotus cc:Mail Custom Addressing

Lotus cc:Mail uses the address format <user> at <post office> (note that "at" is not a synonym for the @ sign, and <user> @ <post office> would form an invalid address). The address details templates that come with the Connector for Lotus cc:Mail allow Exchange users to address messages to Lotus cc:Mail recipients easily. The corresponding address type CCMAIL identifies addresses of cc:Mail users. Exchange 2000 Server can handle these addresses and make routing decisions. Message routing is covered in Chapter 16, "Message Routing Administration."

However, Lotus cc:Mail users cannot simply specify an Exchange address to reach an Exchange recipient. Rather, Lotus cc:Mail users must handle the Exchange 2000 Server environment as one or many huge remote Lotus cc:Mail post offices, known as proxy post offices. Therefore, it is necessary to assign each Exchange user an appropriate address of the CCMAIL type. The Recipient Update Service generates the proxy CCMAIL addresses for each mailbox- and mail-enabled account automatically, using the proxy address generator CCMPROXY.DLL, which can be found in the \Program Files\Exchsrvr\Address \Ccmail\i386 directory. The default format is <Last, First> at <Organization Name>, but this format can be modified using recipient policies. For example, the proxy CCMAIL address of Carl Titmouse would be Titmouse, Carl at BlueSkyAirlines.

The CCMAIL proxy address generation is deactivated by default. You need to configure and activate the address generation using a recipient policy before the Recipient Update Service can assign mailbox- and mail-enabled accounts for a CCMAIL address. The Recipient Update Service is covered in detail in Chapter 13, "Creating and Managing Recipients."

▶ **To activate the CCMAIL proxy address generation**

1. Launch Exchange System Manager, expand the Recipients container, and open Recipient Policies. Double-click the desired policy, such as the Default Policy object.

2. Click on the E-Mail Addresses tab, and select the CCMAIL check box. (Optionally, double-click the Address entry to customize the proxy address generation.)

3. Click OK, and, in the Exchange System Manager dialog box that appears to inform you that address generation for CCMAIL has been enabled, click Yes to automatically assign this address type to all existing recipient e-mail addresses.

4. Use Active Directory Users and Computers to verify the address assignment according to the schedule of the Recipient Update Service.

Placeholders in Address Generation Rules

To change the default format for proxy CCMAIL addresses, use custom address switches. For instance, the %d switch refers to the display name of a user. If you define %d at BlueSkyAirlines in the default recipient policy, Carl Titmouse will receive the proxy CCMAIL address Carl Titmouse at BlueSkyAirlines. Address generation placeholders are covered in Chapter 13, "Creating and Managing Recipients."

Note   It is important to place the custom address switches before the "at" of the CCMAIL address. It is also important to leave a space before and after "at" to generate valid proxy addresses. Exchange System Manager will warn you if you try to create an invalid addressing scheme before it returns to the cc:Mail Address Properties dialog box.

Lotus cc:Mail and Connector Interfaces

The Connector for Lotus cc:Mail is a translator, but the communication partners must be aware of each other before they begin to "talk." You must manage both Lotus cc:Mail and Exchange 2000 Server to enable the communication.

Configuring the Lotus cc:Mail Post Office

You need to use the Lotus cc:Mail Administrator program to create references to your Exchange 2000 Server organization in form of cc:Mail post offices. A single organization can appear as multiple proxy post offices if you have configured multiple recipient policies that assign different CCMAIL proxy addresses to your users. However, the configuration is simplified if an entire Exchange 2000 Server organization acts as a single proxy post office; that is, all your users have the same post office name, such as BlueSkyAirlines. The default proxy post office corresponds to the entire Exchange 2000 Server organization.

When creating the proxy post office reference in Lotus cc:Mail, set the location code to "P" for a directly connected post office. Do not specify address information for it because the Lotus cc:Mail router is not required for message transfer. It is a good idea to reference the cc:Mail Connector in the Comment field, which should follow the format MSExchangeCCMC <Server Name>, such as MSExchangeCCMC BLUESKY-SRV1. This enables the Connector to determine which post offices it controls in the cc:Mail environment. Based on this information, the Connector can analyze synchronized address information in cc:Mail to only transfer address updates instead of complete address lists during directory synchronization. Directory synchronization is covered in Lesson 2.

Note   The Connector for Lotus cc:Mail can automatically create proxy post office references for Exchange 2000 Server in the Lotus cc:Mail post office if you have enabled directory synchronization, as explained in Lesson 2.

Configuring the Connector for Lotus cc:Mail

Using Exchange System Manager, you can complete the configuration through the Connector for cc:Mail object that resides in the Connectors container. At a minimum, you need to define an Administrator's Mailbox in the Post Office tab, and specify the cc:Mail post office. You also need to provide Exchange 2000 Server with routing information via the Address Space tab.

The Connector for Lotus cc:Mail tabs and their purposes are as follows:

- **Post Office.**   To set information about the Lotus cc:Mail post office, administrator mailbox, ADE, and forwarding history
- **Details.**   To enter an administrative note
- **Advanced.**   To define a maximum message size limit for outgoing messages to Lotus cc:Mail (message size limits are not applied to incoming messages), to select the directory update time, and to run a directory synchronization cycle manually
- **Address Space.**   To define address spaces for messages routing
- **Delivery Restrictions.**   To specify which users can send messages through this connector
- **Import Container.**   To specify the organizational unit (OU) to hold the Lotus cc:Mail recipient objects in Active Directory and to define recipient filtering rules
- **Export Container.**   To set OUs and recipient types (that is, contacts and distribution groups) that will be exported to the Lotus cc:Mail post office
- **Security.** To specify users and groups that are allowed or denied administrative control over this Connector to Lotus cc:Mail. (This property sheet is only available if you have set the ShowSecurityPage Registry key, as outlined in Exercise 2 of Chapter 5, "Installing Microsoft Exchange 2000 Server.")

Referencing the Lotus cc:Mail Post Office

The cc:Mail partner post office of the Connector for cc:Mail must be specified using the Post Office tab. Important parameters are post office name, post office password, and network path to the post office. To enter post office name and password, click the Modify button to the right of the Name box under cc:Mail Post Office. The network path must be specified in Universal Naming Convention (UNC) format (for example, \\BLUESKY-SRV1\CCDATA, as shown in Figure 27.3). Exchange System Manager will display an error notification if no post office can be found at the specified location.

The Import and Export programs use the post office name and password to access the Lotus cc:Mail post office. Because they operate in the context of the Exchange 2000 Server account, it is important to ensure that this account has full access rights at the specified network share. You can use the Connect As field in the Post Office tab to specify an explicit account with access permissions to the network share.

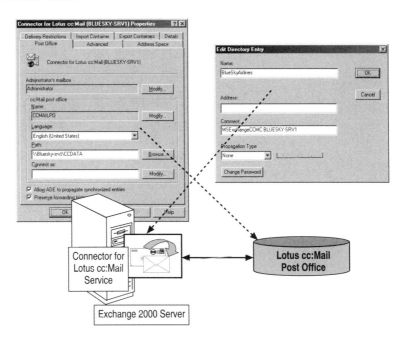

Figure 27.3   Connector for Lotus cc:Mail configuration

Preserving the Forwarding History

Not all properties of a message can be mapped between the Exchange 2000 Server and the cc:Mail format. The forwarding history of a cc:Mail message is the type of property that is usually lost. However, in the Post Office tab, you can select the Preserve Forwarding History check box to generate a FORWARD.TXT attachment for all inbound messages from Lotus cc:Mail. This file is attached to the converted Exchange message and contains the desired forwarding information. The Preserve Forwarding History check box is selected by default.

Post Office Language

The post office language setting refers to the language version of your cc:Mail post office. Make sure you specify the correct version to avoid problems with code page translation.

Assigning CCMAIL Address Spaces

As for every connector, you must assign address spaces using the Address Space tab. Click the Add button to display the Add Address Space dialog box. Select CCMAIL, and then click OK. In the cc:Mail Address Space Properties dialog box, type an asterisk (*) in the Mailbox field, and, under Post Office, specify the post office name where the Lotus cc:Mail users reside. To cover an entire cc:Mail environment at once, type another asterisk (*). An address space of * at * will cause Exchange 2000 Server to route all messages destined for Lotus cc:Mail users to the Connector. Address spaces are stored in the routingList attribute on the connector object in Active Directory and incorporated into the link state table (LST). More information about address spaces is provided in Chapter 16, "Message Routing Administration."

Advanced Connector Maintenance

You should inspect the Connector for Lotus cc:Mail carefully once it has been configured and launched. The Import/Export executables must be located in the system search path. The Connector for Lotus cc:Mail reports delivery problems and critical errors through the application event log if the configuration does not meet the requirements.

Event Logs

Using the Diagnostics Logging tab of the Exchange 2000 server object in the Exchange System Manager (such as BLUESKY-SRV1), you can increase and decrease the level of event logging for the Connector for Lotus cc:Mail. Select the entry MSExchangeCCMC, and then set the desired logging level (None, Minimum, Medium, or Maximum) for the categories General, Outbound, Inbound, NDR, Dir Synch, and MAPI. With a level of None for all categories, only critical events are traced. You can use the Event Viewer to examine the status information, as briefly discussed in Chapter 12, "Management Tools for Exchange 2000 Server."

Generating Nondelivery Reports

The generation of NDRs is a complex process because as soon as a message has been converted into a scratch file and placed in the Connector Store, the job of the connector service is basically done. However, the message has not been delivered yet—the Import program still must complete its task.

If the recipient of a Lotus cc:Mail message is unknown, an NDR must be generated and sent back to the originator on the Exchange server. Import cannot generate such an NDR because it is not aware of the Exchange system. Instead, it places the undeliverable message as a .und file in the Import directory of the Connector Store (for example, NDR904.UND). The Connector for Lotus cc:Mail polls this directory, and if it finds any .und files, it generates the nondelivery notifications using the information it can extract from this file (see Figure 27.4).

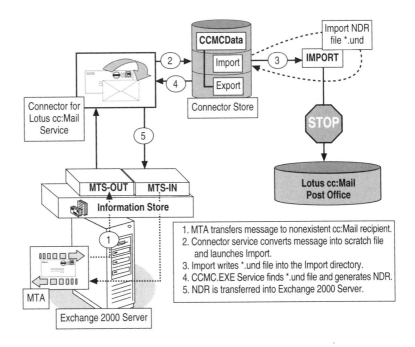

Figure 27.4   Generation of nondelivery reports

Lesson 2: Lotus cc:Mail Directory Synchronization

The main reason to use the Connector for Lotus cc:Mail rather than any other connectivity solution, such as message transfer based on SMTP or X.400, is the automatic exchange of address information between Exchange 2000 Server and Lotus cc:Mail. Only the Connector for Lotus cc:Mail supports directory synchronization, which does not implement a complex protocol and is therefore easy to configure.

This lesson describes the configuration of directory synchronization, as well as the preparation of the Lotus cc:Mail post office and advanced maintenance tasks.

At the end of this lesson, you will be able to:
- Configure the Connector for Lotus cc:Mail for directory synchronization.
- Customize address generation rules based on Registry settings.

Estimated time to complete this lesson: 30 minutes

Configuring the Lotus cc:Mail Post Office

The Connector for Lotus cc:Mail does not use ADE to propagate address information to its cc:Mail partner post office. Instead, it uses the Import/Export programs to accomplish this task (see Figure 27.5). This involves the update of entire address lists, but Exchange 2000 Server avoids this by comparing the current contents of the export and import OUs to the Lotus cc:Mail directory. In this way, the Connector can detect address changes and does not need to update entire directories. As mentioned in Lesson 1, a prerequisite to update-oriented directory synchronization is a properly configured Comment field for the proxy post office in the Lotus cc:Mail environment.

Using the Lotus cc:Mail Administrator program, you must enable the Directory Propagation and Automatic Directory Exchange (ADE) options at the Connector's Lotus cc:Mail post office if you want to synchronize downstream Lotus cc:Mail post offices with Exchange 2000 Server. The Connector's Lotus cc:Mail post office should not be configured as a subordinate or peer post office. Instead, consider a broadcaster or enterprise ADE relationship with the main hub post office in your Lotus cc:Mail environment to let ADE propagate the address information. More information about the configuration of ADE is available in the Lotus cc:Mail product documentation.

Note   To support ADE-based address propagation in the Lotus cc:Mail environment, enable the Allow ADE To Propagate Synchronized Entries check box in the connector's Post Office tab in Exchange System Manager. This setting has no effect when synchronizing address information only with the connector's Lotus cc:Mail post office.

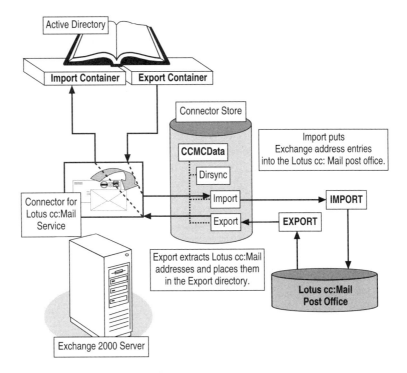

Figure 27.5 Directory synchronization with Lotus cc:Mail

Configuring the Connector for Lotus cc:Mail

The Connector for Lotus cc:Mail configuration object provides several tabs to configure the directory synchronization: Advanced, Import Container, and Export Container. The Advanced tab allows you to schedule the directory synchronization or trigger updates manually.

Importing Address Information

In the Import Container tab, you can specify a container to maintain imported recipient objects for the selected Lotus cc:Mail post office. You should create a dedicated OU in Active Directory Users and Computers for this purpose. To select the desired OU, click the Modify button. Exchange System Manager will prompt you to grant the machine account of your Exchange 2000 server (such as BLUESKY-SRV1) Create and Modify permissions to for the selected OU. Click Yes to update the permissions on the import container. You also can determine the type of recipient objects to create in Active Directory if replicated mailboxes do not have accounts in the Windows 2000 domain (that is, Create A Disabled Windows User Account, Create A New Windows User Account, and Create A Windows Contact).

Furthermore, you can select which Lotus cc:Mail addresses to accept. Generally, three options are at your disposal: Import All Directory Entries, Only Import Directory Entries Of These Formats, and Do Not Import Directory Entries Of These Formats. The default Import All Directory Entries option causes the Connector to import all addresses in the specified Import container. The remaining two options allow you to restrict the address information. In this case, you can define corresponding import filters using the New ?button. For example, you can specify *** at BlueSkyAirlines** under Directory Entry Format in the Import Filter dialog box to prevent the import of CCMAIL proxy addresses that refer to actual Exchange users. In large Lotus cc:Mail environments with multiple cc:Mail connectors, you should filter Exchange address information and exclude it from directory synchronization to avoid the creation of redundant recipient objects in Active Directory.

Note   If you change the Import container at a later time, do not forget to move affected Lotus cc:Mail recipient objects to the new OU to make sure they are updated properly.

Specifying Exported Addresses

As Exchange 2000 Server organizes recipient addresses in OUs in Active Directory, you can specify the appropriate containers that will be exported to the Lotus cc:Mail post office using the Export Container tab. More than one OU can be selected. The machine account of your Exchange 2000 server requires Read permissions on all OUs that you specify as Export containers. Exchange System Manager can grant the required permissions to your server account for you. Furthermore, if you want to synchronize Windows contacts for recipients in other messaging environments, such as an MS Mail network, with Lotus cc:Mail, enable the Export Contacts check box in addition to the Export Groups check box. Export Groups creates address entries for Exchange distribution groups in the cc:Mail post office. Group memberships, however, are not synchronized.

Customizing Address Generation Rules

By default, the Connector for Lotus cc:Mail assumes that Lotus cc:Mail users should appear in Exchange 2000 Server address lists in the format First Name Last Name. It is also assumed that the alias name is built from the first name and one character from the last name. For instance, the user Hawk, Hillary at CCMAILPO would be assigned the first name Hillary, the last name Hawk, the display name Hillary Hawk, and the SMTP address HillaryH@Bluesky-inc-10.com in Active Directory.

You can customize the address generation rules through the Registry by setting the following parameters (under HKEY_LOCAL_MACHINE\SYSTEM\CurrentControlSet\Services\MSExchangeCCMC\Parameters):

- **Dir Synch Alias Name Rule.**   Determines the creation of e-mail aliases for Lotus cc:Mail users.

- **Dir Synch Display Name Rule.**   Determines the creation of display names for Lotus cc:Mail users.

- **Generate Secondary Proxy Address.**   Determines whether Lotus cc:Mail users are assigned two proxy addresses or one in Active Directory. The default value is "0", which causes directory synchronization to create CCMAIL proxy address entries in first name last name at cc:Mail post office format. A value of "1" generates two addresses: a primary proxy address of last name, first name at cc:Mail post office, and a secondary proxy address of first name last name at post office.

You can use placeholders, such as %d, to specify the desired format. Address generation placeholders are outlined in Chapter 13, "Creating and Managing Recipients."

Chapter Summary

The Connector for Lotus cc:Mail supports the transfer of e-mail messages as well as directory synchronization between Exchange 2000 Server and Lotus cc:Mail. It provides reliable messaging connectivity for long-term coexistence, and it supports an efficient migration to Exchange 2000 Server based on automatic synchronization of address information.

Following a connector installation using the Exchange 2000 Server Setup program, the Connector for Lotus cc:Mail can be configured by means of a configuration object in Exchange System Manager. Only a few configuration settings are required, such as parameters regarding the Connector's Lotus cc:Mail partner post office. The Connector is able to register the Exchange 2000 Server organization in the partner post office automatically when directory synchronization is activated. By default, all Exchange users appear in Lotus cc:Mail as recipients on a huge proxy cc:Mail post office that corresponds to the organization name. Lotus cc:Mail users address messages to Exchange recipients just as they do for ordinary cc:Mail recipients.

Review

The following review questions can help you determine if you have sufficiently familiarized yourself with the material covered in this chapter. You can find the answers to these questions at the end of this book in Appendix A, "Questions and Answers."

1. How many direct Lotus cc:Mail post offices does the Connector for Lotus cc:Mail support?

2. What are the main components of the Connector for Lotus cc:Mail?

3. You need to adjust the proxy CCMAIL address format. You are required to assign e-mail aliases in the form of first name immediately followed by first character of the last name. Where and how can you adjust the proxy address format?

4. Which program is used to write messages into the Lotus cc:Mail post office?

5. Which program is used to poll the Lotus cc:Mail post office for address information?

C H A P T E R   2 8

Connecting to Lotus Notes

About This Chapter

Lotus Domino and Lotus Notes together form the high-end messaging and workgroup-computing platform of Lotus Development Corporation. This platform offers features similar to those of earlier versions of Microsoft Exchange Server. Microsoft Exchange 2000 Server opens new horizons, provides new avenues, and impresses with new technologies, but the systems remain basically close competitors. The current major versions of Lotus Domino and Notes are Release 5 or simply R5. This chapter refers to them as Lotus Domino/Notes R5.

As the amount of information in this book reveals, there are many good reasons to deploy Exchange 2000 Server in a Domino/Notes R5 environment. Motivation may stem from technical or strategic considerations; however, this chapter does not compare these platforms. It simply explains how to connect both systems to provide Exchange and Notes users with a chance to work together in an integrated environment. The ease of Exchange 2000 Server administration is highlighted.

This chapter focuses on the architecture and administration of the Connector for Lotus Notes. It explains how to provide messaging connectivity and directory synchronization. The exchange of calendar and free/busy information, however, is not covered because Exchange 2000 Server does not provide a Calendar Connector. Calendar queries must be routed through an Exchange Server 5.5 system, which is supported in mixed-mode organizations.

Before You Begin

To complete this chapter:

- You need to be familiar with the responsibilities of Active Directory directory service and system components of Exchange 2000 Server and their interaction, as explained in Chapter 3, "Microsoft Exchange 2000 Server Architecture."

- You should have practical experience in administering Lotus Domino/Notes environments. Detailed information is available in the Lotus Domino and Notes product documentation.

Lesson 1: The Connector for Lotus Notes

The Connector for Lotus Notes, as its name implies, lets you connect an Exchange organization to a Domino/Notes network. Lotus Notes releases 3 and 4 and Lotus Domino releases 4.5, 4.6, and 5 are supported. The connector is based on the Exchange Development Kit (EDK) and requires a Lotus Notes client, release 4 or 5, to access a Lotus Notes or Domino server. A license from Lotus Development is required to use the client software.

This lesson outlines the basic features of the Connector for Lotus Notes as well as its dependencies. It addresses its components and explains how to configure messaging connectivity between Lotus Domino/Notes and Exchange 2000 Server.

At the end of this lesson, you will be able to:

- Identify the main components of the Connector for Lotus Notes.
- Prepare a Lotus Domino/Notes R5 environment for the Connector for Lotus Notes.
- Configure and use the Connector for Lotus Notes.

Estimated time to complete this lesson: 120 minutes

Connector for Lotus Notes Overview

You can deploy the Connector for Lotus Notes on one or many Exchange 2000 servers to connect your organization to a Domino/Notes network. A particular server can run exactly one Connector instance to directly service one Domino server, which in turn may forward messages from Exchange users to other servers in the Domino/Notes environment. In other words, you can implement dedicated bridgehead servers to support an entire organization (see Figure 28.1). The concept of bridgehead servers is discussed in Chapter 16, "Message Routing Administration."

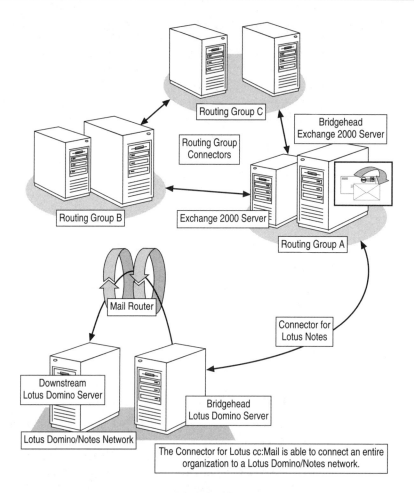

The Connector for Lotus cc:Mail is able to connect an entire organization to a Lotus Domino/Notes network.

Figure 28.1   Deploying the Connector for Lotus Notes

Connector Installation

You can install the Connector for Lotus Notes using Exchange 2000 Server Setup. On the Component Selection wizard screen, under Action for the Microsoft Exchange Connector for Lotus Notes component, make sure you select Install. If you want to add the Connector to an existing Exchange 2000 Server organization, permissions of an Exchange Administrator are required in the administrative group where the target routing group exists. You also need the permissions of a local Administrator on the computer where you want to install the Connector. If possible, log on with an Enterprise Admin account. You can read more about the installation of Exchange 2000 Server in Chapter 5, "Installing Microsoft Exchange 2000 Server."

Application Programming Interfaces

The Connector for Lotus Notes must be able to retrieve and convert messages from Exchange 2000 Server as well as from Lotus Domino/Notes. On the Exchange side, this EDK-based connector relies on the Messaging Application Programming Interface (MAPI), much as the Connector for Lotus cc:Mail does. On the Lotus Domino side, however, a direct server API is not used. Instead, the Connector uses the Notes client API. The disadvantage of this approach is that the Connector requires that a Lotus Notes client be installed on the connector server.

Note For Lotus Domino/Notes R5, you need to install the Lotus Domino Administrator program on the server, which includes the Lotus Notes client.

Lotus Domino/Notes Dependencies

Before you configure the Connector for Lotus Notes, you must configure the Notes client on the connector server to access a Domino server. You must configure a special Notes ID (hereafter called a Connector ID) that has permissions to access Notes databases. Lotus Domino/Notes maintains databases for all kinds of information, including the address book and message queues.

Note Do not include the Connector ID in directory synchronization. If required, edit the connector's Person document, and set the Foreign Directory Sync Allowed option to No, as demonstrated later.

EXCHANGE.BOX and EXCHANGE.BAD

In addition to the Connector ID, you must create and configure several databases. The Connector for Lotus Notes requires a connector database, known as gateway mail file, which should be created before configuring the foreign domain document for your Exchange 2000 Server organization. It is a good idea to name this file EXCHANGE.BOX. The EXCHANGE.BOX database is used to queue outbound messages to Exchange 2000 Server, and the MAIL.BOX database receives messages destined for Lotus Notes. MAIL.BOX is the Domino server's mail router mailbox. The connector also uses an EXCHANGE.BAD database for corrupted messages that cannot be processed.

Although the Connector for Lotus Notes is able to create the EXCHANGE.BOX and EXCHANGE.BAD databases automatically when accessing the Domino server for the first time, it is advisable to create at least the important EXCHANGE.BOX database manually to ensure that the configuration matches the requirements.

Directory Synchronization

For synchronization of address book information between Exchange 2000 Server and Lotus Domino/Notes, the Connector requires access to source and target name and address book files, such as NAMES.NSF, referred to as Domino Directory (see Figure 28.2). The Connector for Lotus Notes provides several ways to synchronize directories, which will be explained in Lesson 2.

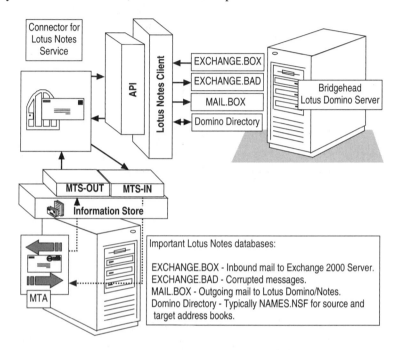

Figure 28.2   Connector for Lotus Notes architecture

The Connector for Lotus Notes requires the following access permissions in Lotus Domino/Notes:

- **Domino Directory.**   The Connector ID requires Editor access with Delete Documents privileges on the target name and address book. For the source address book, Reader access is sufficient.

- **EXCHANGE.BOX and EXCHANGE.BAD.**   The Connector ID requires Manager access with Delete Documents privileges on these databases.

- **MAIL.BOX.**   The Connector ID requires explicit Depositor access. Even though the default access for router mailboxes is Depositor, implicit Depositor access is not sufficient for proper connector operation.

Optionally, you need to add the Connector ID to the Administrators list in the Server document of the Connector's partner Domino server if you want the Connector to handle Notes database compaction. Furthermore, you may want to grant the Connector ID Reader access to the databases in the Domino/Notes environment if you want to support Notes Doclinks, as explained in Tables 28.1 and 28.2.

Message Conversion

The Connector for Lotus Notes must convert outbound messages into Notes format. Conversely, the Connector must convert content and recipient information into Exchange format for inbound messages. Most message attributes are mapped between both systems. The connector supports read receipts, delivery receipts, and nondelivery reports (NDRs), as well as message options, such as importance levels (low, normal, high). Some specific features, however, such as Notes Doclinks, require special treatment because they are not supported in Microsoft Outlook 2000.

Table 28.1 lists the characteristics of message conversion from Exchange 2000 Server to Lotus Domino/Notes, and Table 28.2 provides the same information for message conversion from Lotus Domino/Notes to Exchange 2000 Server.

Table 28.1   Message Conversion from Exchange 2000 Server to Lotus Notes

Object in Exchange Message	Object in Lotus Domino/Notes Message
Regular attachment, position identified by icon	An icon positioned as in an Exchange message.
Object linking and embedding (OLE) Lotus Notes Links	Translated back to Lotus Notes Doclinks if the connector has Reader access to the document associated with the Doclink.
Exchange embedded messages	Converted to a regular attachment in rich text format (RTF), identified by an icon. Embedded messages in embedded messages and attachments in those messages are not supported.
Exchange message links	Converted to OLE attachments and identified by an icon.
OLE object	OLE attachment identified by an icon, as in the original message.

Table 28.2   Message Conversion from Lotus Notes to Exchange 2000 Server

Object in Lotus Domino/Notes Message	Object in Exchange Message
Regular attachment, position identified by icon	An icon positioned as in an Exchange message.
Lotus Notes Doclinks	Depending on connector configuration, Doclinks are converted to:
	■ An attachment in rich text format (RTF), identified by an icon. The Connector must have Reader access to the associated document.
	■ An OLE document link. Connector and recipient must have Reader access to the associated document.
	■ A URL, identified by a URL shortcut. The recipient can launch a Web browser to access the database to which the link points.
OLE object	OLE attachment identified by an icon, as in the original message.

Components of the Connector for Lotus Notes

The Connector for Lotus Notes consists of various essential elements, such as message queues in the Information Store, and a Windows 2000 service called Microsoft Exchange Connector for Lotus Notes, which depends on yet another service called Microsoft Exchange Connectivity Controller. Both services will be installed as part of the Connector setup. As does every gateway connector, the Connector for Lotus Notes comes with address generators and details templates. The Notes client must also be listed as an essential Connector component.

In the Registry, settings for the Connector for Lotus Notes are maintained in the following location:

```
HKEY_LOCAL_MACHINE
    \SYSTEM
            \CurrentControlSet
                \Services
                    \LME-NOTES
```

Tip   The Connector for Lotus Notes service is set to manual startup by default. It is a good idea to change this to automatic using the Services snap-in from the Administrative Tools program group.

Message Queues

The Connector for Lotus Notes uses message queues in the Information Store, just as any EDK-based gateway connector does (see Figure 28.2). As usual, the message queues are labeled MTS-OUT for outbound messages and MTS-IN for inbound messages. Additional queues named BADMAIL, READYIN, and READYOUT also exist for configured connectors. They are required for message processing through the connector's worker processes.

Information Store message queues are not polled. The Information Store notifies the Connector service if messages have been placed in the MTS-OUT folder. Conversely, the Connector initiates communication with the Information Store if inbound messages must be placed in the MTS-IN queue. The Domino server, on the other hand, is polled periodically according to the Connector's polling interval setting. The default polling interval is 15 seconds.

Active Connector Components

The main executable (.exe) of the Connector for Lotus Notes service is called DISPATCH.EXE. However, this executable file does not perform the actual work. As its name implies, it dispatches the various tasks of message transfer and directory synchronization to other processes based on the settings from an EXCHCONN.INI file. EXCHCONN.INI will be created automatically as part of the connector installation and configuration. The actual worker components involved in information handling are MEXNTS, MEXOUT, NTSMEX, MEXIN, DXAMEX, and DXANOTES, which are implemented in separate executables and dynamic-link libraries that reside in the \Program Files\Exchsrvr\Bin directory.

The six active connector processes and their relationships are as follows:

- MEXOUT (LSMEXOUT.EXE) obtains outbound messages from the MTS-OUT queue, looks up Active Directory to replace target recipient information with corresponding Lotus Notes addresses, and places the messages into the READYOUT folder. From there, MEXNTS (LSMEXNTS.EXE) obtains the messages and converts them from Exchange to Notes format before it writes them into MAIL.BOX on the Domino server.

- NTSMEX (LSNTSMEX.EXE) downloads messages from EXCHANGE.BOX, converts them to Exchange format, and places them into the READYIN folder in the Information Store. MEXIN (LSMEXIN.EXE) obtains these converted messages from there, verifies the validity of the recipients, and places the messages into the MTS-IN queue.

- DXANOTES (DXANOTES.DLL) is the process that checks the Domino Directory for address updates. This component also transfers Exchange address information changes into Domino/Notes. DXAMEX (DXAMEX.DLL), on the other hand, is the process that performs the same tasks on Active Directory. The general directory synchronization agent (LSDXA.EXE) controls both DXANOTES and DXAMEX.

Connector Directory

When you examine the \Program Files\Exchsrvr directory on the Connector server, you can find a \Conndata directory with further subdirectories. These subdirectories contain control files used during directory synchronization. Control files are schema definition files and mapping rule files, which determine how attributes in one directory are mapped to the other directory.

The most important control files and their purposes are as follows:

- **AMAP.TBL.**   In the \Dxamex subdirectory, it defines the Exchange mailbox attributes to be synchronized.
- **AMAP.TBL.**   In the \Dxanotes subdirectory, it defines the Lotus Notes attributes to be synchronized.
- **MAPMEX.TBL.**   In the \Dxanotes subdirectory, it determines the attribute mapping from Exchange 2000 Server to Lotus Notes.
- **MAPNOTES.TBL.**   In the \Dxamex subdirectory, it determines the attribute mapping from Lotus Notes to Exchange 2000 Server.

You can customize these control files in Notepad to change the attribute mapping. Stop the connector services before editing these files to ensure that the directory synchronization is not active. More information about directory attribute mappings is available in the Exchange 2000 Server product documentation.

Configuration Objects in Exchange System Manager

When you install the Connector for Lotus Notes, a configuration object will be created in the configuration naming partition of Active Directory. In Exchange System Manager, you can find a corresponding object for the Connector under <Organization Name>/Administrative Groups/<Administrative Group Name>/ Routing Groups/<Routing Group Name>/Connectors. Underneath this Connector object in turn is the Queues container, which provides access to the MTS-IN and MTS-OUT message queues of the Connector.

The Message Transfer Agent (MTA) receives outbound messages to Lotus Notes from the Simple Mail Transfer Protocol (SMTP) routing engine and transfers inbound messages to the routing engine for further delivery. Consequently, the MTA needs to maintain an internal message queue for the Connector for Lotus Notes in addition. You can view this queue in Exchange System Manager, provided that the Connector for Lotus Notes service is started. Open the <Organization Name>/Administrative Groups/<Administrative Group Name>/Servers/ <Server Name>/Protocols/X.400/Queues container, such as Blue Sky Airlines (Exchange)/Administrative Groups/First Administrative Group/Servers/ BLUESKY-SRV1/Protocols/X.400/Queues, and verify that a queue for the

Connector for Lotus Notes exists. Message queues are covered in Chapter 20, "Microsoft Exchange 2000 Server Maintenance and Troubleshooting."

Exchange Connectivity Administrator

The Connector for Lotus Notes comes with an Exchange Connectivity Administrator program (LSADMIN.EXE) that allows you to examine the state of the individual connector processes (that is, MEXNTS, MEXOUT, and so forth). The Connectivity Administrator provides valuable features for tracing connector activities. Make sure that the Microsoft Exchange Connectivity Controller and Microsoft Exchange Connector for Lotus Notes service are started, and then launch this utility directly from the \Program Files\Exchsrvr\Bin directory. You can read more about this utility later in this lesson.

Configuring the Lotus Domino Server

The preparation of the Connector's Domino server is perhaps the most complex task during configuration. If you plan to connect to Domino/Notes R5, make sure you have installed Lotus Domino Administrator on the Exchange 2000 server. As outlined earlier, the Connector requires this software, and you can use it to check the Connector prerequisites outlined earlier.

Creating a Lotus Notes ID for the Connector

To access a Lotus Domino server, the Connector for Lotus Notes requires a certified Notes ID file. In other words, you must create a Person document for the Connector in the Domino Directory. Specifying no password for the Connector simplifies the configuration but introduces a security risk on the Domino/Notes side. Take appropriate steps to secure the Connector ID file to prevent unauthorized access to the Connector's private security keys. If such configuration is inappropriate, you can define a password and specify it later in the Connector's configuration (in the Notes .ini file settings in the General tab). In an isolated test environment, it is certainly safe to go without a password.

Note To create a Connector ID, you must be a Domino/Notes administrator with the UserCreator role or Editor access in the Domino Directory. Keep in mind that each user ID requires a software license.

▶ **To create the Connector ID file (it is assumed that you have installed Lotus Domino/Notes R5 on the Exchange 2000 server)**

1. Launch the Lotus Domino Administrator program from the Lotus Applications program group, and enter your administrator password. If a Welcome To Domino Administrator R5 screen is displayed, click Close This Page. In the Administration window, make sure your Domino/Notes domain's address book is displayed (for example, Bluesky-inc-10's Address Book).

2. In the Administration window, make sure you are in the People & Groups tab. Click the People button to open its shortcut menu, and then select the Register command. Enter the certifier password for your domain, which was created during the initial configuration of Lotus Domino, and then confirm all dialog boxes until you reach the Register Person – New Entry dialog box.

3. In the Register Person – New Entry dialog box, select the Advanced check box, and then click Registration Server to select the Connector's Domino server (if the local server is not the one you want to work with).

4. Under First Name, specify a name (such as LME-NOTES) and define a Last Name for the connector as well (such as BLUESKY-SRV1). Verify that the Password Quality Scale is set to Password Is Optional (0).

5. Click on the Mail icon, and then, from the Mail System list box, select None (see Figure 28.3).

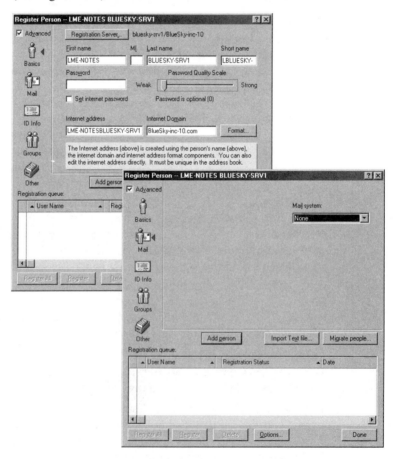

Figure 28.3   Creating the Connector ID

6. Click on the ID Info icon. If needed, you can select a different certifier by clicking the Certifier ID button. The Security Type can be North American (for highest security) or International (for medium security). In the Certificate Expiration Date box, you can change the expiration date of the Connector ID.

Note   A Connector ID file created with the North American security type cannot be used on a computer with international settings.

7. Clear the In Domino Directory check box to prevent the storage of the Connector ID in the public address book. You must select the In File option to save the Connector ID file to disk (for example, A:\EXCHANGE.ID). Although it is possible to save the Connector ID to the hard disk, you should save it to a floppy because the file must be accessible to the server that will run the Notes Connector. If you want to specify a different location or filename, click the Set ID File button under the In File option.

8. Click the Add Person button first, and then click Register to complete the process of creating the Connector ID. In the Domino Administrator dialog box informing you that the person was registered successfully, click OK.

9. In the Register Person dialog box, click Done. Press F9 to refresh the view. Verify that the Connector's Person document is listed (for example, BLUESKY-SRV1, LME-NOTES).

Note   During user ID configuration, when you click on the Other icon, you can create a new Windows 2000 account for each new user ID. This is not required for the Connector for Lotus Notes.

Updating the Connector's Person Document

The Person document identifies the Connector for Lotus Notes as a valid Notes user. It lets the Connector access Domino/Notes databases to perform message transfer and directory synchronization. As mentioned previously, the Connector's Person document must not be replicated to downstream Lotus Domino/Notes domains or synchronized with the Exchange 2000 Server directory because the Connector is not an actual user.

▶   **To update the connector's Person document using Lotus Domino Administrator**

1. In the Administration window, in the People & Groups tab under People, double-click the Connector's Person document to open the LME-NOTES BLUESKY-SRV1/Bluesky-inc-10 document. (The title of this dialog box might be different if you have used different names.)

2. From the Actions menu, select the Edit Person command. After that, in the Person document, click on the Administration tab, and then set the Foreign Directory Sync Allowed option to No (see Figure 28.4).

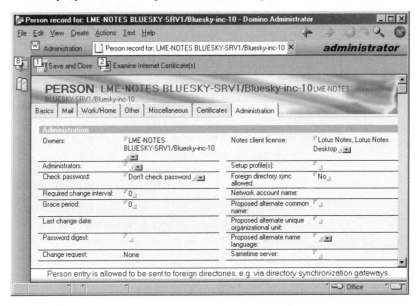

Figure 28.4   Updating the Connector's Person document

3. Click the button next to the Notes Client License field, and then, in the Select Keywords dialog box, check the Lotus Notes Desktop entry. Click OK.

4. Click Save And Close. If prompted, provide your administrator password to complete the operation.

Configuring the Router Mailbox for Connector Access

As mentioned earlier, MAIL.BOX is used to place outgoing messages from Exchange 2000 Server into the Connector's Domino server. Consequently, the Connector for Lotus Notes requires explicit Depositor access to place items in this database, even though the default access for router mailboxes is Depositor. You must have Manager access to administer the access control list (ACL) of MAIL.BOX.

▶   **To assign the Connector Depositor access using Lotus Notes Administrator**

1. Open the File menu, point to Database, and then select the Open command to display the Open Database dialog box.

2. If Local is not the server you want, select the Connector's server under Server (such as Bluesky-srv1/Bluesky-inc-10). Type **MAIL.BOX** in the Filename box, and then click Open (see Figure 28.5).

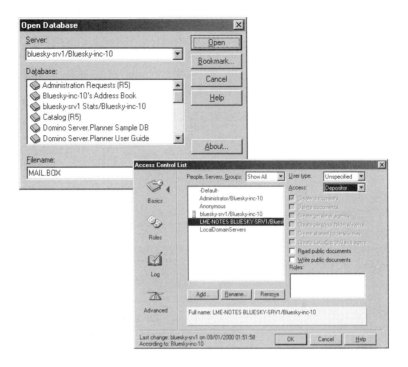

Figure 28.5   Configuring the router mailbox for Connector access

3. Open the File menu one more time, point to Database, and then click Access Control. Click Add, and, in the Add User dialog box, click the button next to Person, Server, Or Group.

4. In the Names dialog box, in the upper left list box, make sure your domain's address book is selected (for example, Bluesky-inc-10's Address Book), then select the Connector ID (for example, BLUESKY-SRV1, LME-NOTES). Click Add, and then click OK.

5. Make sure that the Connector ID is selected in the Access Control List dialog box, and verify that Depositor is listed in the Access box (see Figure 28.5). Click OK.

Creating Connector Databases

It is now time to create the mail database for the Connector using the Lotus Domino Administrator program. It is best to name it EXCHANGE.BOX. If you would like to use a different name, do not forget to configure the Connector in Exchange System Manager accordingly. The purpose of EXCHANGE.BOX was covered earlier in this lesson; the Connector configuration is discussed later.

▶ **To create the EXCHANGE.BOX database in Lotus Notes Administrator**

1. From the File menu, point to Database, and then select the New command. This will display the New Database dialog box.

2. Select the Connector's Lotus Domino server under Server if Local is not the Connector's server, and then type a descriptive name in the Title box (such as **Outgoing Mail to Exchange 2000 Server**).

3. Most important, under File Name, you must change the name of the database file to **EXCHANGE.BOX** (see Figure 28.6).

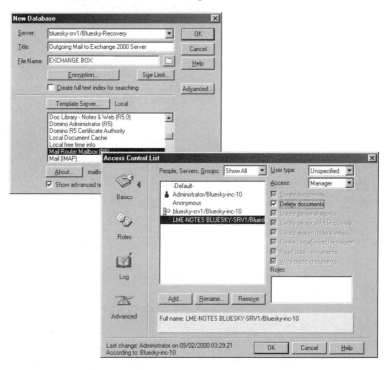

Figure 28.6 Creating an outgoing mail queue to Exchange 2000 Server

4. Select the Show Advanced Templates check box, and then select the Mail Router Mailbox (R5) entry (MAILBOX.NTF) in the list of available templates underneath the Template Server button. Click OK.

5. The About Outgoing Mail to Exchange 2000 Server – Design document appears. At this point, you need to grant the Connector ID Manager with Delete Documents permissions—basically, the Connector needs all available permissions for EXCHANGE.BOX (see Figure 28.6). You can manage the ACL in a way similar to that described for the MAIL.BOX database.

Note In addition to EXCHANGE.BOX, you may create and configure a database called EXCHANGE.BAD to allow the Connector for Lotus Notes to archive corrupted messages that could not be processed. However, the Connector for Lotus Notes is able to create databases automatically.

Registering Exchange 2000 Server as a Foreign Domain

Within Lotus Domino/Notes, an Exchange 2000 Server organization is treated as a foreign domain. This means you must maintain a foreign domain document in the Domino Directory.

▶ **To create the foreign domain document for Exchange 2000 Server using Lotus Notes Administrator**

1. In the toolbar of the Domino Administrator window, click Administration to display the Administration window, then select the Connector's Person document (for example, BLUESKY-SRV1, LME-NOTES) from your domain's address book.

2. Open the Create menu, point to Server, and then select Domain to open a new Domain document.

3. Under Domain Type, make sure Foreign Domain is specified, and then, under Foreign Domain Name, define a name for your Exchange 2000 Server organization (it is best to use the name **Exchange**, as shown in Figure 28.7). Optionally, you can supply a Domain Description to detail the nature of this foreign domain.

4. Click on the Mail Information tab. Type the fully distinguished name of your Lotus Domino/Notes server in the Gateway Server Name box (for example, **Bluesky-srv1/Bluesky-inc-10**), and then, under Gateway Mail File Name, type **EXCHANGE.BOX** (see Figure 28.7).

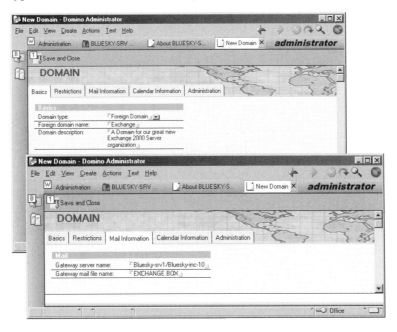

Figure 28.7   Registering Exchange 2000 Server as a foreign domain

5. Click Save And Close to create the foreign domain document.

You can set additional parameters under Administration and Restrictions. Those settings might be important for your Lotus Domino/Notes organization, but they are not essential for the operation of the Connector for Lotus Notes.

Note Incorrect settings in the foreign domain document can prevent Domino/Notes from routing messages to the outgoing Exchange database (EXCHANGE.BOX). For test purposes, use the Notes client to send a test message to testuser@Exchange, and then open the EXCHANGE.BOX database to verify that the message was routed to it correctly. Do not read messages in EXCHANGE.BOX. The connector does not process read messages, which would consequently remain in the message queue.

Granting Access to the Domino Directory

To support directory synchronization, the Connector for Lotus Notes requires special access to the Domino Directory.

▶ **To support directory synchronizations from the Lotus Notes Administrator program**

1. Make sure the Administration window is displayed.
2. Click People, and then open the File menu, point to Database, and select Access Control.
3. Assign the Connector ID an access level of Editor with the right to Delete Documents using steps similar to those outlined earlier for the MAIL.BOX database (see Figure 28.8).

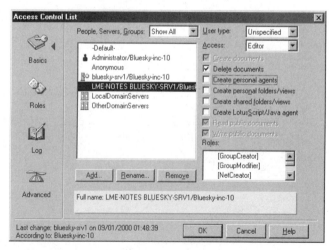

Figure 28.8   Granting access to the Domino Directory

Performing Routine Maintenance

It is advantageous to allow the Connector for Lotus Notes to compact database files because they become fragmented as messages are created and deleted in the EXCHANGE.BOX database. To allow the Connector to run the compaction utility automatically, add the Connector ID to the list of Administrators in the Connector's Server document. You can do this when you display the Administration window in Lotus Domino Administrator.

▶ **To add the Connector ID to the list of Administrators in the Server document**

1. Select the Connector's Person document, open the View menu, point to Server, and then select the Other command to display the Other dialog box, where you can select the Server/Servers entry. Click OK to switch to the list of Lotus Domino servers in your network.

2. Double-click the name of the Connector's server to open the associated server document.

3. Open the Actions menu, and select the Edit Server command to switch the document into edit mode (alternatively, you might just double-click on a document field).

4. Click on the Administration tab, and add the Connector ID to the list of Administrators (see Figure 28.9) by clicking the small button next to the Administrators field, which displays the Names dialog box (where you can double-click the Connector ID and click OK).

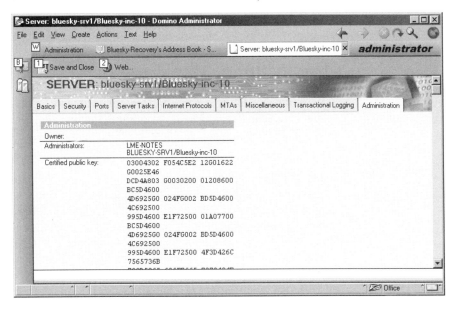

Figure 28.9   Adding the Connector ID to the list of administrators in the server document

5. In the Lotus Domino Administrator program, click Save And Close to save the changes.

Assigning Permissions for Regular Databases

The Lotus Notes environment is now ready for the Connector for Lotus Notes. It might be advantageous to allow the Connector Reader access to Notes databases if the security policy of your organization allows you to do so. Otherwise, the Connector cannot convert Notes Doclinks to .rtf attachments or OLE documents. These kinds of attachments will contain only an error message. The steps for granting the Connector Reader access are the same as those for granting it Depositor permissions for the MAIL.BOX database.

Note   If it is not feasible to grant the Connector ID Reader access to Notes databases, convert Doclinks to URLs instead of .rtf attachments or OLE documents.

Configuring the Lotus Notes Client

Now that you have prepared the Domino/Notes environment, you can finalize the configuration in respect to the Connector's Notes client. It is a very good idea to check whether you can log on to the desired Domino server using the Connector ID file. Provided that you worked with the Lotus Domino Administrator program on the Connector server, close all Notes client applications, and then launch Lotus Notes from the Lotus Applications program group. Enter the administrator password if prompted, and then open the File menu, point to Tools, and select the Switch ID command. In the Choose User ID To Switch To dialog box, select the Connector ID file created earlier, click OK, and verify that you are logged on successfully by opening the address book, for example. Close the Notes client.

Important   The Lotus Notes client uses a NOTES.INI file that must point to the Connector ID file being used (KeyFilename parameter). This file is typically in the \Lotus\Notes directory. To avoid connector problems, do not select another user ID on the Connector server through the Switch ID command.

System Path Configuration

It is vital to include the Notes client directory in the system search path on the Connector server. You can do this using System from the Control Panel. Click on the Advanced tab, click Environment Variables, and then, under System Variables, double-click the Path entry. Append the Notes client directory path to the search path separated by a semicolon (for example, **;C:\Lotus\Notes**), and then click OK three times to close all dialog boxes. Close the Control Panel, and reboot the server to make the system aware of the search path modification. Otherwise, you will not be able to start the Connector for Lotus Notes service successfully using the Services snap-in.

Important   Do not simply copy the NNOTES.DLL from the \Lotus\Notes directory to \Winnt\System32. Although the Connector service will start, the system will not function properly. A glance at the state of the Connector processes in the Exchange Connectivity Administrator will indicate that the LME-NOTES-DXANOTES, LME-NOTES-MEXNTS, and LME-NOTES-NTSMEX processes have problems initializing the Notes interface. Without these processes, there can be no message transfer or directory synchronization. To solve this problem, you must stop the Connector for Lotus Notes one more time, move NNOTES.DLL from the \Winnt\System32 directory back to the \Lotus\Notes directory, add this directory to the system search path, and then reboot the computer.

Configuring the Connector for Lotus Notes

Compared to the preparation of the Lotus Domino/Notes environment, the actual Connector configuration is very straightforward. In Exchange System Manager, right-click the Connector's configuration object under <Organization Name>/Administrative Groups/<Administrative Group Name>/Routing Groups/<Routing Group Name>/Connectors (for example, Blue Sky Airlines/Administrative Groups/First Administrative Group/Routing Groups/First Routing Group/Connectors), and then select Properties. You need only provide the fully qualified name of the connector's Domino server and specify the correct Notes INI File Location (and Password) in the General tab via the Modify button. Click on the Address Space tab to define a NOTES address space in the form of *@* (see Figure 28.10). You also need to activate the NOTES proxy address generation in a recipient policy to assign your Exchange users valid address information. Make sure that the Domino server is available, start the Connector for Lotus Notes service, and you are ready to exchange messages.

The Connector for Lotus Notes tabs and their purposes are as follows:

- **Address Space.**   To define message routing information for this Connector and determine the Connector's scope (that is, Exchange Organization or Routing Group). You can read more about address spaces in Chapter 16, "Message Routing Administration."

- **Advanced.**   To specify the name of the Notes Router Mailbox (if it is not MAIL.BOX), set a Notes Letterhead to format text and graphics at the top of messages that are sent to Notes users, determine the Delivery Order (Priority, FIFO, Size), configure automatic maintenance of Lotus Notes databases, identify Routable Domains in Lotus Domino/Notes that can be reached through this connector, and restrict outbound message sizes. In many cases, organizations will find a delivery order according to priority or FIFO (first in/first out) appropriate.

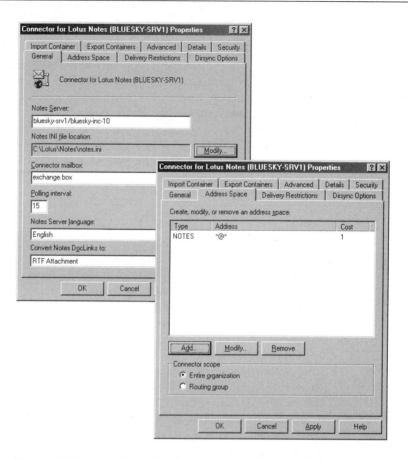

Figure 28.10   A minimal Connector for Lotus Notes configuration

- **Delivery Restrictions.**   To specify users and groups that are allowed or denied message transfer through this connector to Lotus Domino/Notes.

- **Details.**   To provide an Administrative Note for informational purposes.

- **Dirsync Options.**   To set the frequency of directory synchronization, specify source and target address books in Lotus Domino/Notes, and to trigger manual address updates.

- **Export Containers.**   To specify the organizational units (OUs) as recipients containers that you want to export to the Domino Directory, and to determine whether to export contact objects and groups.

- **General.**   To specify the fully qualified name of the Connector's Domino server, identify the Notes INI File Location and Connector Mailbox (default, EXCHANGE.BOX), set the polling interval, determine the Notes Server Language, and define how to handle Notes Doclinks.

- **Import Container.**   To specify an OU in Active Directory where recipient objects should be created for Notes users in the Domino Directory, and to determine the type of recipient objects to create if Notes users do not have Windows 2000 accounts. You can read more about the configuration of export and import OUs in Lesson 2.

- **Security.**   To specify users and groups that are allowed or denied administrative control over this Connector to Lotus Notes. (This property sheet is only available if you have set the ShowSecurityPage Registry key, as outlined in Exercise 2 of Chapter 5, "Installing Microsoft Exchange 2000 Server.")

Examining Connector Processes

You can use the Exchange Connectivity Administrator to verify whether the connector processes are operating properly. Double-click the Process Manager reference in the Overview window. All connector processes should be listed in the Process Manager window in idle state.

For further details, check the application event log using Event Viewer. It may be a good idea to increase the level of event logging for the Connector for Lotus Notes beforehand to obtain the most detailed information. In Exchange System Manager, display the properties of the Exchange 2000 Server object (such as BLUESKY-SRV1), switch to the Diagnostics Logging property sheet, select the LME-NOTES entry, and then set the desired logging level for all categories (None, Minimum, Medium, or Maximum). When you are confident that your Connector operates correctly, decrease the level for all categories to None to avoid unnecessary entries in the event log. With a diagnostics logging level of None, only critical events are traced. The application event log is briefly discussed in Chapter 12, "Management Tools for Microsoft Exchange 2000 Server."

Testing E-Mail Connectivity

Operational Connector processes are a positive indicator that the Connector configuration is okay. To ensure that the message routing really works, send test messages from Lotus Notes to Exchange 2000 Server and vice versa. Use your new NOTES proxy address to specify an Exchange recipient in Lotus Notes, for instance Administrator/First Administrative Group/Blue Sky Airlines@Exchange. To find your proxy address, launch Active Directory Users and Computers, and display the E-Mail Addresses tab for your account.

In the Lotus Notes client, check to see if the message has been delivered to the EXCHANGE.BOX database on the File menu, under the Database option, by selecting the Open command. Once the message is received in Outlook 2000, reply to it, and verify that the reply is received in the Lotus Notes client. It is a golden rule of successful Connector administration that message paths should be tested in both directions.

Lotus Notes Proxy Address Generation

Lotus Notes users see Exchange users as recipients in just another Domino/Notes domain, as identified by the foreign domain created for the Connector. By default, all Exchange users reside in one huge foreign domain called Exchange. As usual, the Recipient Update Service generates the proxy addresses for each mailbox- and mail-enabled account automatically, using a proxy address generator, as soon as the address type is activated in a recipient policy. The Notes proxy address generator is NTSPXGEN.DLL, which can be found in the \Program Files\Exchsrvr\Address\Notes\i386 directory. The recipient policies and the Recipient Update Service are covered in detail in Chapter 13, "Creating and Managing Recipients."

Placeholders in Address Generation Rules

The default format for NOTES proxy addresses is <Display Name>/<Administrative Group Name>/<Organization Name>@Exchange (for example, Carl Titmouse/First Administrative Group/Blue Sky Airlines@Exchange). That is a huge address that is difficult to handle. If possible, customize the NOTES proxy address generation. In Exchange System Manager, open the Recipients container, select Recipients Policies, and then open the desired policy (such as Default Policy). Click on the E-Mail Addresses tab. Double-click the address entry next to NOTES to customize the address generation rule. For instance, remove the reference to the administrative group from the address definition, thus creating addresses in the form <Display Name>/<Organization Name>@Exchange (for example, Carl Titmouse/Blue Sky Airlines@Exchange). Keep in mind that user addresses must be unique in their names space, in this case the organization Blue Sky Airlines, also known as the foreign domain Exchange.

You can use the following placeholders to customize the NOTES address generation (they differ from SMTP, MSMAIL, CCMAIL, and X.400 addresses in that & is used instead of %):

- &d   The user's display name
- &g   The user's given name
- &i   The user's middle initials
- &m   The mailbox alias
- &s   The user's last name (surname)

Note If you enable directory synchronization and then examine e-mail address information in Active Directory Users and Computers, you may find secondary proxy addresses assigned to Notes recipient objects that refer to globally unique identifiers (GUIDs). These GUIDs are used to identify synchronized recipients. You should not delete these secondary NOTES addresses.

Implementing Multiple Connector Instances

You can configure multiple recipient policies to generate NOTES addresses according to different formats. For example, you may assign Carl Titmouse the address Carl Titmouse/Blue Sky Airlines@E2KEastCoast, while the Administrator may have the address Administrator/Blue Sky Airlines@E2KWestCoast. This corresponds to an Exchange 2000 Server organization with two foreign domains. Correspondingly, you need to create two foreign domain documents in Lotus Domino/Notes—one for E2KEastCoast and one for E2KWestCoast. You can point both to the same EXCHANGE.BOX database or to separate databases of different connectors. In this way, multiple connector instances can share the message traffic to Exchange 2000 Server.

Note   When implementing multiple connector instances, carefully design the directory synchronization topology to avoid the creation of duplicate address information.

Configuring Downstream Domains

Just as an Exchange 2000 Server organization can have multiple administrative groups, a Lotus Domino/Notes network can have multiple domains. Those domains may transfer messages indirectly to the Exchange 2000 Server organization through another domain in which the Connector's Domino server resides. These Domino/Notes domains are called downstream domains. A particular connector will allow all users in all domains to communicate with each Exchange user, but additional configuration is required to support message transfer in the opposite direction. You must identify downstream domains in the Advanced tab of the connector object. Click the Add button under Routable Domains, and type the domain in the Add Routable Domains dialog box. You can identify Domino/Notes domains that are referenced in Connection, Foreign Domain, and Nonadjacent Domain documents. Make sure you exclude those foreign domains created for Exchange 2000 Server. Beyond that, correct address space information must be assigned to the Connector for Lotus Notes to allow for proper message routing.

Lesson 2: Directory Synchronization with Lotus Domino/Notes

It is inconvenient to specify NOTES addresses manually, such as Carl Titmouse/ First Administrative Group/Blue Sky Airlines@Exchange. The slightest typo in this lengthy address would render messages undeliverable. Consequently, it is desirable to configure directory synchronization with Lotus Domino/Notes to allow users in both systems to conveniently address their messages by selecting references from their respective address books. A properly functioning directory synchronization process can guarantee that messages are addressed correctly and are therefore deliverable.

This lesson explains in more detail how the components of the Connector for Lotus Notes interact to synchronize directory information between Exchange 2000 Server (Active Directory) and Lotus Domino/Notes. It also describes important configuration tasks.

At the end of this lesson, you will be able to:

- Describe the process of directory synchronization with Lotus Notes.
- Configure the Connector for Lotus Notes for directory synchronization.

Estimated time to complete this lesson: 30 minutes

Directory Synchronization Overview

Directory synchronization with Lotus Domino/Notes is the process of copying recipient information from Active Directory to Domino Directory and vice versa. Either full address information or address updates are processed. Sophisticated directory synchronization is based on address updates to avoid the transfer of redundant data and unnecessary resource consumption.

Directory Synchronization Processes

As mentioned in Lesson 1, the Connector for Lotus Notes uses two processes to synchronize address information between Exchange 2000 Server and Lotus Domino/Notes. The DXAMEX process extracts and imports the information on the Exchange 2000 Server side, and the DXANOTES process accomplishes the same task on the Lotus Domino side (see Figure 28.11).

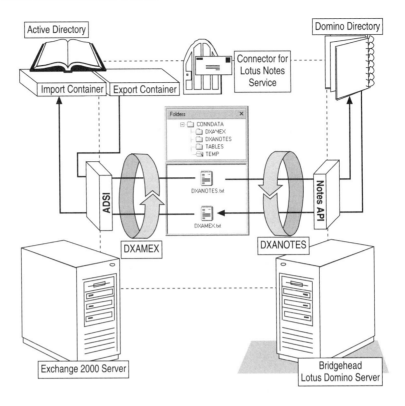

Figure 28.11   Directory synchronization with Lotus Domino/Notes

DXANOTES/DXAMEX Interprocess Communication

Directory synchronization with Lotus Domino/Notes relies on a \Temp subdirectory in the Connector directory \Program Files\Exchsrvr\Conndata to temporarily place address information in message interchange format (MIF) files. As shown in Figure 28.11, these files are called DXANOTES.TXT for address information to Domino Directory and DXAMEX.TXT for address information to Active Directory.

Via Active Directory Services Interface (ADSI), the DXAMEX process extracts address information from export containers in Active Directory, formats the address information in MIF, and then fills the DXANOTES.TXT file with the data. The DXANOTES process reads this file, processes the addresses, and places them in the target name and address books on the Domino server. Address synchronization from Domino/Notes to Exchange 2000 Server simply flows in the opposite direction using the DXAMEX.TXT file.

Configuring Directory Synchronization

It is easy to configure directory synchronization with Lotus Domino/Notes, provided that the Connector configuration was tested and found to be working beforehand. Most important, you need to specify an import container where Notes recipients will be placed. One or many export containers can be selected to transfer address information into the Domino Directory. Optionally, you may customize settings for source and target Notes address books and define the directory synchronization schedule.

Importing Address Information

Using Exchange System Manager, you can specify a container to maintain imported recipient objects when you click on the Import Container tab of the Connector object. To select the desired OU, click the Modify button. You should have created a dedicated OU in Active Directory Users and Computers for this purpose. Exchange System Manager will prompt you to grant your Exchange 2000 server account (such as BLUESKY-SRV1) Create and Modify permissions for the selected OU. Click Yes to update the permissions on the import container automatically. You also can determine the type of recipient objects to create in Active Directory if replicated mailboxes do not have accounts in the Windows 2000 domain (i.e., Create A Disabled Windows User Account, Create A New Windows User Account, and Create A Windows Contact).

Note   If you change the import container at a later time, do not forget to move affected recipient objects to the new OU to make sure they are updated properly.

Specifying Exported Addresses

To export recipient information to Domino/Notes, specify one or many export containers in the Export Container tab. Similar to import containers, export containers are OUs in Active Directory. It is important to keep in mind that the OU that was specified as an import container must not be included as an export container as well to avoid the creation of redundant recipient objects in the Domino Directory. The machine account of your Exchange 2000 server requires Read permissions on all OUs specified as export containers. Exchange System Manager can grant the required permissions to the server account for you.

You can synchronize Windows contacts for recipients in other messaging environments, such as Lotus cc:Mail, using the Connector of Lotus cc:Mail, when you enable the Export Contacts check box. To synchronize distribution group information, make sure the Export Groups check box is selected. Groups appear as user/contact objects in the target directories. Membership information is not synchronized.

Note   The OU, defined as the import container for Notes address information, must not be configured as an export container.

Source and Target Name and Address Books

If your Lotus Domino/Notes network consists of several servers and downstream domains, you should use the Name and Address Book (NAMES.NSF) of the Connector's Lotus Domino server as the source and target name and address book for directory synchronization. This can simplify the configuration because it supports automatic propagation of Exchange-related address information across your Domino/Notes network. However, if you decide to use a different target name and address book, you need to manually ensure that the address information is replicated to all servers and domains. For more information about address book configuration, see the Lotus Domino/Notes R5 product documentation.

To check or define source and target name and address books to be included in directory synchronization, click on the Connector's Dirsync Options tab. Click Address Books Settings to display the Notes Address Books dialog box. In addition to the Default Name And Address Book, you can configure domain-specific address books. In other words, you can split the Exchange address information across multiple Notes address books depending on the foreign domain to which the Exchange user belongs. Users with domain names that are not explicitly specified in the list are still placed in the Default Name And Address Book. Under Source Name And Address Books, you can determine the address books that will be read to retrieve Notes addresses.

Note   Splitting Exchange address information across several name and address books other than NAMES.NSF provides flexibility in determining who has access to foreign addresses in Lotus Domino/Notes.

Testing Directory Synchronization

Because directory synchronization processes operate separately from those that handle message transfer, you must test your configuration explicitly. The required controls are in the Connector's Dirsync Options tab. The most important ones are the Immediate Full Reload buttons under Exchange To Notes Directory Synchronization and Notes To Exchange Directory Synchronization. Click them to force the immediate synchronization of all available address information. If the Connector is working properly, you will find associated addresses in the import container and the target name and address books once the synchronization cycle completes.

> **Note**   It is good practice to examine the processing phases of the directory synchronization agents in the Exchange Connectivity Administrator right after you click the Immediate Full Reload button.

Scheduling Directory Synchronization

When you are confident that everything works, configure the Connector for automatic directory synchronization. This is disabled by default, but you can enable it by clicking Customize to open the Schedule dialog box, where you can set your individual synchronization schedule or select a predefined schedule from the drop-down menu. It is usually sufficient to synchronize address information once every day, such as daily at midnight. Shorter intervals may be necessary during migration from Lotus Domino/Notes to Exchange 2000 Server.

Chapter Summary

The Connector for Lotus Notes supports e-mail transfer and directory synchronization between a Lotus Domino/Notes network and an Exchange 2000 Server organization. This is the basis for reliable messaging connectivity and migration from Lotus Domino/Notes to Exchange 2000 Server. Mixed-mode organizations may also route calendar queries through this connector if they run a Calendar Connector instance on Exchange Server 5.5 machines.

The Connector for Lotus Notes is an EDK-based gateway that requires a Lotus Notes client to access a Lotus Notes or Domino server. This client must be installed locally on the Connector server. You also need to prepare the Domino/Notes environment before you can start the Connector. A Connector ID and special databases are required, as well as a foreign domain document for the Exchange 2000 organization. Beyond this, you also need to grant the Connector ID Access permissions on Notes databases, such as the mail router database MAIL.BOX. For directory synchronization, access is required to source and target name and address books. The Connector ID itself should not be included in directory synchronization.

The connector components involved in message transfer and directory synchronization are: MEXNTS, MEXOUT, NTSMEX, MEXIN, DXAMEX, and DXANOTES. MEXOUT and MEXNTS take care of outbound messages from Exchange 2000 Server to Lotus Domino/Notes. In the other direction, NTSMEX and MEXIN are the team for message transfer and conversion. DXAMEX and DXANOTES handle the directory synchronization jointly.

Review

The following review questions can help you determine if you have sufficiently familiarized yourself with the material covered in this chapter. You can find the answers to these questions at the end of this book in Appendix A, "Questions and Answers."

1. What do you have to configure in Lotus Domino/Notes to support the Connector for Lotus Notes?

2. Which Connector component retrieves messages from the MTS-OUT queue?

3. Which processes perform directory synchronization with Lotus Domino/Notes, and how do they accomplish their tasks?

4. In which tab can you change the name of the Domino server that the Connector for Lotus Notes contacts for message transfer?

CHAPTER 29

Connecting to Novell GroupWise

About This Chapter

Novell GroupWise version 5.5 is the current messaging and collaboration platform of Novell, Inc. This system evolved from a stand-alone desktop library in the 1980s to a shared-file messaging system with client/server support. Previous versions include 4.1, 5.0, and 5.2. Direct connections to earlier versions, such as GroupWise 4.0 or even WordPerfect Office 3.1, are not supported. Novell GroupWise originates from WordPerfect, which is still noticeable in the system architecture. Input and output queues, for instance, are named WPCSIN and WPCSOUT.

A GroupWise Gateway for Microsoft Exchange is available from Novell to integrate GroupWise with earlier versions of Exchange Server. Microsoft also provided a Connector for Novell GroupWise with Microsoft Exchange Server 5.5 Service Pack 3. Both may still be used in mixed-mode organizations when connecting GroupWise to a computer running Exchange Server 5.5. Native-mode organizations, however, require the Connector for Novell GroupWise that comes with Exchange 2000 Server to connect both systems directly.

This chapter introduces the Connector for Novell GroupWise. It explains how to configure messaging connectivity and directory synchronization. The exchange of free/busy information, however, is not covered because Exchange 2000 Server does not provide a Calendar Connector. Calendar queries must be routed through Exchange Server 5.5.

Before You Begin

To complete this chapter:

- You need to be familiar with the responsibilities of the Active Directory directory service, Exchange 2000 Server system components, and their interaction, as explained in Chapter 3, "Microsoft Exchange 2000 Server Architecture."

- You should have practical experience in administering Novell NetWare Directory Services (NDS), and Novell GroupWise post offices and domains. Detailed information is available in the Novell GroupWise product documentation.

Lesson 1: The Connector for Novell GroupWise

Although you can install and run almost all GroupWise components and processes on a Microsoft Windows 2000 server, at least one Novell NetWare 4.1 (or higher) server is required to provide access to configuration and user information in NDS. The Connector for Novell GroupWise, on the other hand, must be installed on an Exchange 2000 server. Consequently, you need to integrate your Exchange 2000 server with NetWare via Gateway and Client Services for NetWare (GSNW) or Novell NetWare Client for Windows 2000. Detailed information regarding this is available in Chapter 10, "MAPI-Based Clients in a Novell NetWare Environment."

This lesson focuses on an integration of Exchange 2000 Server with GroupWise 5.5 in a Novell Netware 5 environment based on GSNW. The preparation of earlier versions of GroupWise differs slightly from GroupWise 5.5, but the connector configuration remains the same. The following explanations address important connector components and the configuration of messaging connectivity.

At the end of this lesson, you will be able to:

- Identify the main components of the Connector for Novell GroupWise.

- Prepare a Novell GroupWise 5.5 environment for connectivity to a foreign messaging system, such as Exchange 2000 Server.

- Configure and use the Connector for Novell GroupWise.

Estimated time to complete this lesson: 75 minutes

Connector for Novell GroupWise Overview

You can deploy the Connector for Novell GroupWise on one or many Exchange 2000 servers to connect your organization to a GroupWise environment. A particular server can run exactly one connector instance to directly service one GroupWise domain. A GroupWise Message Transfer Agent (GroupWise MTA) is required in this domain to route messages to GroupWise post offices, other domains, or external foreign domains.

For best performance, it is a good idea to install the Connector for Novell GroupWise on a dedicated bridgehead server to support an entire organization (see Figure 29.1). Servers with user mailboxes remain unaffected by connector processing and the Connector in turn can enjoy the full availability of system resources on the bridgehead. However, you may find it more cost effective to purchase a single server with greater capacity to improve performance. Often, user services can take advantage of the additional hardware when the demand for client-server communication is high, while connector services may be scheduled to transfer messages during off-peak hours. The concept of bridgehead servers is discussed in Chapter 16, "Message Routing Administration."

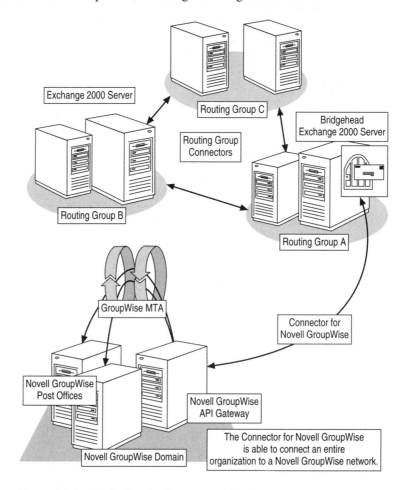

Figure 29.1   Deploying the Connector for Novell GroupWise

Connector Installation

The actual Connector installation is quickly accomplished using Exchange 2000 Server Setup. When you reach the Component Selection wizard screen, select Install under Action for the Microsoft Exchange Connector for Novell

GroupWise. You should not forget to select Install (or Change) for Microsoft Exchange 2000 and Microsoft Exchange Messaging And Collaboration Services beforehand. If you want to add the Connector to an existing Exchange 2000 Server organization, permissions of an Exchange Administrator are required in the administrative group where the target routing group exists. You also need the permissions of a local Administrator on the computer where you want to run the Connector because several settings are written to the local Registry. If possible, log on with Enterprise Admin permissions. You can read more about the installation of Exchange 2000 Server in Chapter 5, "Installing Microsoft Exchange 2000 Server."

Connector Architecture and Application Programming Interfaces

The Connector for Novell GroupWise is a true messaging gateway that communicates with Exchange 2000 Server via Messaging Application Programming Interface (MAPI) to obtain and deliver Exchange messages. To retrieve and map address information, the Connector also must communicate with Active Directory through Active Directory Services Interface (ADSI). On the side of Novell GroupWise, the Connector interacts with Novell GroupWise API Gateway to receive and send messages and to work with recipient information. In short, the Connector is based on the Exchange Development Kit (EDK) on the Exchange side and the Novell Development Kit (NDK) on the side of GroupWise.

Note To support distribution group expansion during message delivery to GroupWise, you must install the Novell GroupWise Patch 2 for API NetWare Loadable Module (NLM) on the Novell NetWare server that is running the Connector's API Gateway. This patch is available from Novell in form of a self-extracting file called GW41API2.EXE.

Novell GroupWise Dependencies

The GroupWise messaging architecture is based on post offices serviced by post office agents (POAs). In a TCP/IP-based client/server environment, POAs are the communication partners of GroupWise MTAs and clients that want to access post office resources. In a traditional, shared-file configuration, post offices are accessed directly. GroupWise MTAs in turn transfer messages between post offices in a domain and between domains (see Figure 29.2). Physically, domains and post offices are file structures on a NetWare or Microsoft Windows NT or Windows 2000 server. Logically, they are configuration objects in NDS.

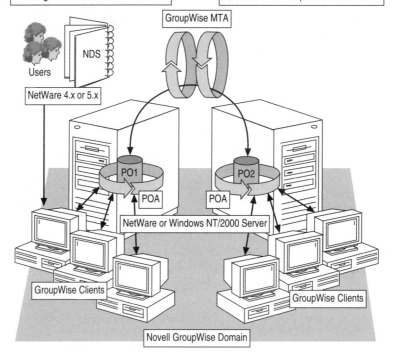

POAs and MTA may run on Novell NetWare or Microsoft Windows NT/2000, yet Novell NDS is required to provide configuration and user information.

In a client/server environment, GroupWise clients and MTA communicate with POAs to access post offices. Only the POA has direct access to its post office structure.

GroupWise MTA

NDS
Users
NetWare 4.x or 5.x
PO1
POA
PO2
POA
NetWare or Windows NT/2000 Server
GroupWise Clients
GroupWise Clients
Novell GroupWise Domain

Figure 29.2   Clients, POAs, and MTAs in a client/server GroupWise domain

Novell GroupWise API Gateway

The GroupWise API Gateway is an extra component that must be added to the GroupWise domain to support the Connector for Novell GroupWise. Novell provides an API Gateway for DOS, OS/2, and NetWare. Use of the Novell NLM version is recommended.

The API Gateway is a universal GroupWise gateway that uses keyword-based text files to communicate with messaging systems that are foreign to GroupWise, such as Exchange 2000 Server. On the GroupWise side, the gateway works in conjunction with the GroupWise MTA (see Figure 29.3). For test purposes, you can use any text editor, such as Notepad, to read and write keyword-based text files in the API Gateway's directory structure, which is demonstrated later in this lesson.

The following API Gateway directories are most important:

- **API_IN.**   Receives incoming message header files from non-GroupWise systems

- **API_OUT.** Holds outgoing message header files to non-GroupWise systems
- **ATT_IN.** Receives incoming message bodies and attachments from non-GroupWise systems
- **ATT_OUT.** Holds outgoing message bodies and attachments to non-GroupWise systems
- **WPCSIN.** The GroupWise MTA inbound queue where incoming messages are placed after their processing through the API Gateway
- **WPCSOUT.** The GroupWise MTA outbound queue where outgoing messages are located before they are converted into keyword-based text files and placed into API_OUT and ATT_OUT through the API Gateway

API Gateway and Connector Account

It is highly recommended to restrict access to the API Gateway directory because the gateway is able to perform management functions similar to a NetWare Administrator. To identify the Connector for Novell GroupWise and grant it permissions to read and write messages in the API input and output directories, a dedicated NetWare account is required. You need to create this account using Novell NetWare Administrator and then use Exchange System Manager to configure the Connector (in the General tab) to use this account for API Gateway access.

Note   The Connector's NetWare account must be a member of a special group called NTGATEWAY, which you need to create using NetWare Administrator. The Connector's NetWare account requires permissions to create, read, write, and delete files in the API Gateway directories.

Directory Synchronization

To perform directory lookups for address conversion and directory synchronization, the Connector for Novell GroupWise interacts with Active Directory based on ADSI. To access the GroupWise directory on the other side, the management functions of the API Gateway are employed. Messages with the keyword MSG-TYPE=Admin are placed in the API input queue to add, delete, modify, and rename references to Exchange users in the GroupWise directory. These types of messages are called administrator messages, which are also used to request user information from GroupWise domains. The process of directory synchronization with Novell GroupWise is explained in detail in Lesson 2.

Note   The API Gateway processes administrator messages and then, in conjunction with the GroupWise agents (POA and MTA), adds Exchange recipient information to GroupWise domains. GroupWise versions earlier than 5.5 use a dedicated administration agent (ADA) for this purpose. In GroupWise 5.5, the ADA is part of the POA.

Message Conversion

Novell GroupWise supports several specific types of messages, such as e-mail messages, appointments, notes, tasks, forms, presentations, or documents, and so forth. MAPI-based message types are mapped to corresponding message types in GroupWise when possible. That is, e-mail messages appear as e-mail messages, meeting requests as appointments, and so on. Message types that are not supported in the other messaging system, such as GroupWise phone messages, will be converted to regular e-mail items. The Connector for Novell GroupWise is able to track delivery confirmation reports, read receipts, and nondelivery reports.

The following features are lost during message conversion:

- **Attachments of embedded messages.** The Connector converts attachments of messages that are embedded in Exchange or GroupWise messages into attachments of the primary message.

- **All-day Exchange meeting request.** The Connector converts all-day meeting requests from Exchange 2000 Server to Notes in GroupWise.

- **Meeting cancellations.** Meeting cancellations can be exported from Exchange 2000 Server to Novell Groupwise, but not vice versa.

- **Meeting reminder times.** The Connector discards this information.

- **Recurring meetings (Exchange).** Not supported in GroupWise and therefore converted to one-day meetings with a description about meeting recurrences in the message text.

- **Reply-to.** Exchange 2000 Server supports the Reply-To Address field, which allows a sender to specify a different address as the recipient for message replies. GroupWise does not support this feature; consequently, replies are delivered to the original sender.

- **Rich text format (RTF) information in Exchange messages.** The Connector discards RTF information in the message body because the API Gateway supports plain text only.

- **Task request.** The Connector converts task requests to e-mail messages.

- **Tentatively accepted meeting requests.** Received as accepted meeting requests.

Note If an Exchange user specifies a GroupWise user multiple times in an e-mail message (if recipient is listed more than once in the To, Cc, or Bcc line or is in more than one specified distribution group), the GroupWise user receives duplicate e-mail messages.

Components of the Connector for Novell GroupWise

The Connector for Novell GroupWise consists of several active components that are implemented as Windows 2000 services. They run on the Exchange 2000 server and use a temporary directory structure (the connector store) for their interprocess communication. All services are installed during Connector setup. Furthermore, a proxy address generator and address details templates are part of the Connector.

Active Connector Services

You can display the various services that form the Connector for Novell GroupWise in the Services snap-in from the Administrative Tools program group. These services are called Microsoft Exchange Connector for Novell GroupWise and Microsoft Exchange Router for Novell GroupWise. The Connector service works with message queues in the Information Store and the router service does the same with the API Gateway (see Figure 29.3).

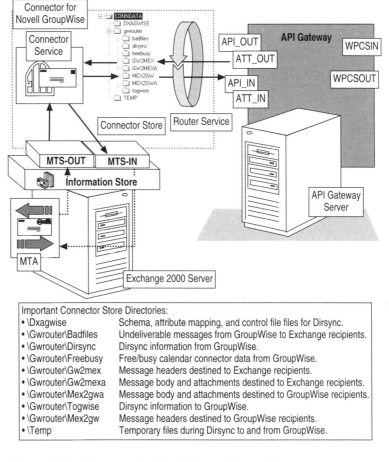

Important Connector Store Directories:
- \Dxagwise — Schema, attribute mapping, and control file files for Dirsync.
- \Gwrouter\Badfiles — Undeliverable messages from GroupWise to Exchange recipients.
- \Gwrouter\Dirsync — Dirsync information from GroupWise.
- \Gwrouter\Freebusy — Free/busy calendar connector data from GroupWise.
- \Gwrouter\Gw2mex — Message headers destined to Exchange recipients.
- \Gwrouter\Gw2mexa — Message body and attachments destined to Exchange recipients.
- \Gwrouter\Mex2gwa — Message body and attachments destined to GroupWise recipients.
- \Gwrouter\Togwise — Dirsync information to GroupWise.
- \Gwrouter\Mex2gw — Message headers destined to GroupWise recipients.
- \Temp — Temporary files during Dirsync to and from GroupWise.

Figure 29.3 Connector for Novell GroupWise architecture

In addition, both services depend on the Microsoft Exchange Connectivity Controller service.

Message Queues

The Connector for Novell GroupWise uses message queues in the Information Store, just as any EDK-based gateway connector does (see Figure 29.3). As usual, the main message queues are named MTS-OUT for outbound messages from and MTS-IN for inbound e-mail to Exchange. Further queues, called BADMAIL, READYIN, and READYOUT, will exist after you start a configured Connector for the first time. BADMAIL is the repository for corrupted messages that cannot be processed. READYIN and READYOUT are explained later.

Tip   The Connector services are set to manual startup by default. For configured Connectors, it is a good idea to change this to automatic using the Services snap-in.

Active Connector Processes

It might be surprising that the Connector for Novell GroupWise relies on the same main executable (.exe) file as the Connector for Lotus Notes. The main executable file is DISPATCH.EXE. This is possible because Dispatch does not perform the actual message processing. Instead, it dispatches the various tasks of message transfer and directory synchronization to other processes based on the settings from the EXCHCONN.INI file. Three of the active processes are the same as for the Connector for Lotus Notes. They are MEXIN, MEXOUT, and DXAMEX. They communicate with the Information Store and Active Directory for message transfer and directory synchronization. Novell GroupWise Connector-specific components are MEX2GW, GW2MEX, and DXAGWISE. The EXCHCONN.INI, .exe files, and .dll files of the worker processes are in the \Program Files\Exchsrvr\Bin directory.

The six active Connector processes and their relationships are as follows:

- MEXOUT (LSMEXOUT.EXE) obtains outbound messages from the MTS-OUT queue, looks up Active Directory to replace target recipient information with corresponding GroupWise addresses, and places the messages into the READYOUT folder. From there, MEX2GW (MEX2GW.EXE) obtains the messages and converts them from Exchange to GroupWise format before it writes them as header and body files into the connector store on the Exchange 2000 server. Converted messages are picked up by the router service (GWROUTER.EXE) and transferred to the API Gateway for further delivery.

- The router service obtains messages in the form of header and body files from the API Gateway and places them in the connector store, where GW2MEX (GW2MEX.EXE) picks them up. GW2MEX converts header and body files to messages in Exchange format and places them into the READYIN folder. MEXIN (LSMEXIN.EXE) obtains these converted messages from there, verifies the validity of the recipients, and places the messages into the MTS-IN queue in the Information Store.

- DXAGWISE (DXAGWISE.DLL) is the agent that processes address updates received from GroupWise by means of router service and connector store. This component also converts Exchange address information into administration messages, which will be placed in the connector store for delivery to the API Gateway. DXAMEX (DXAMEX.DLL), on the other hand, is the process that performs the work on the Active Directory side. The general directory synchronization agent (LSDXA.EXE) controls both DXANOTES and DXAGWISE.

Intermediate Connector Repository

As shown in Figure 29.3, the connector store acts as the communication media between the Connector for Novell GroupWise and the Router for Novell GroupWise. The connector store is the \Program Files\Exchsrvr\Conndata directory with subdirectories, such as \Dxagwise and \Gwrouter. The \Gwrouter directory, for instance, has further subdirectories polled by the Router for Novell GroupWise. The \Dxagwise subdirectory, on the other hand, contains schema definition and attribute mapping files used during directory synchronization with GroupWise.

Note   If you have installed the Connector for Lotus Notes on the same server, you will find a \Dxamex subdirectory under \Conndata. This directory contains the schema definition files and mapping rule files for the directory synchronization with Lotus Domino/Notes. However, DXAMEX uses the files from the \Dxagwise for directory synchronization with Novell GroupWise.

The schema definition and mapping rule files in the \Dxagwise subdirectory have the following purposes:

- **GWAMAP.TBL.**   GroupWise schema attributes to be synchronized
- **MAPMEX.TBL.**   Determines the attribute mapping from Exchange 2000 Server to Novell GroupWise
- **MEXAMAP.TBL.**   Exchange schema attributes to be synchronized
- **MAPGWISE.TBL.**   Determines the attribute mapping from Novell GroupWise to Exchange 2000 Server

You can customize the control files in Notepad to change the attribute mapping. Stop the Connector services before editing these files to ensure that the directory synchronization is not active. In addition, there are control files that allow the Connector to check for address updates that require synchronization (EXTERNAL.TBL, GWPCTA.TBL, MEXPCTA.TBL). Do not edit these files manually. More information about directory attribute mappings is available in the Exchange 2000 Server product documentation.

Configuration Objects in Exchange System Manager

When you install the Connector for Novell GroupWise, a configuration object is created in the configuration naming partition of Active Directory. In Exchange System Manager, you can find a corresponding connector object under <Organization Name>/Administrative Groups/<Administrative Group Name>/Routing Groups/<Routing Group Name>/Connectors. Underneath this connector object in turn is the Queues container, which provides access to BADMAIL, MTS-IN, MTS-OUT, READYIN, and READYOUT. You can check the BADMAIL queue, for instance, to see if there are any corrupted messages.

The MTA receives outbound messages destined for Novell GroupWise from the Simple Mail Transfer Protocol (SMTP) routing engine and transfers inbound messages to the routing engine for further delivery. Consequently, the MTA needs to maintain an internal message queue for the Connector for Novell GroupWise. You can view this queue in Exchange System Manager, provided that the Connector for Novell GroupWise service is started. Open the <Organization Name>/Administrative Groups/<Administrative Group Name>/Servers/ <Server Name>/Protocols/X.400/Queues container, such as Blue Sky Airlines (Exchange)/Administrative Groups/First Administrative Group/Servers/ BLUESKY-SRV1/Protocols/X.400/Queues, and verify that a queue for the Connector for Novell GroupWise exists. Message queues are covered in Chapter 20, "Microsoft Exchange 2000 Server Maintenance and Troubleshooting."

Exchange Connectivity Administrator

The Connector for Novell GroupWise comes with the Exchange Connectivity Administrator program (LSADMIN.EXE) that allows you to examine the state of individual connector processes (that is, GW2MEX, MEXOUT, and so forth). Exchange Connectivity Administrator provides valuable features for checking Connector activities. Make sure that the Microsoft Exchange Connectivity Controller and the other Connector services are started, and then launch this utility directly from the \Program Files\Exchsrvr\Bin directory. You can read more about Exchange Connectivity Administrator later in this lesson.

Configuring the GroupWise Domain and API Gateway

To support the Connector for Novell GroupWise, you need to make sure a dedicated API Gateway is available. This task is accomplished mainly in the NetWare Administrator program. You should work with NetWare Administrator on a workstation where the GroupWise administration files have been installed. The following explanations cover the preparation of a Novell GroupWise 5.5 domain.

Installing the GroupWise API Gateway on a Novell NetWare 5 Server

You should use the NLM version of the API Gateway with the Connector for Novell GroupWise. For installation, copy the corresponding gateway files to a floppy or a directory on your NetWare server. You may also install the API Gateway from CD-ROM or download it from Novell's Web site. Before you start the actual installation, it is a good idea to create a gateway directory in the \Wpgate subdirectory of your GroupWise domain (for example, \API41).

▶ **To install API Gateway and Patch 2 for the API NLM on a NetWare 5 Server called BLUESKY-NW1**

Note The installations of API Gateway and Patch 2 are demonstrated separately; it is assumed that you work with floppy disks.

1. In the System Console, type **NWConfig**, and then press ENTER.

2. Select Product Options and press ENTER. Select Install A Product Not Listed and press ENTER again.

3. Make sure the floppy containing the API Gateway files is inserted in drive A on the NetWare server, and then, in the NetWare Configuration program, press ENTER.

4. The API Gateway Installation screen will be displayed (see Figure 29.4). Change the Domain Path and the Gateway Directory if required, and then select Install, and press ENTER to continue.

5. On the NetWare Configuration screen that appears after the installation is complete, press ESC twice, and then press ENTER to exit the NetWare Configuration program.

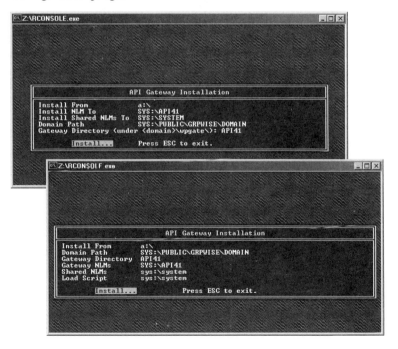

Figure 29.4 Installing the API Gateway on a Novell NetWare 5 server

6. Insert the floppy with the files for Patch 2 for API NLM into drive A, and then, on the NetWare System Console, type **load A:\PINSTALL.NLM**, and press ENTER.

7. On the API Gateway Installation screen, make sure the settings Domain Path, Gateway Directory, Gateway NLMs, Shared NLMs, and Load Script match your API Gateway configuration (see Figure 29.4). Select Install and press ENTER. You will be informed that NGWAPI.PRM already exists and will be moved to the \Save directory. Press ENTER to continue and install the gateway files. The installation will complete automatically.

8. On the System Console, type **Edit**, and press ENTER, and then, in the NetWare Text Editor, specify the path and filename for the gateway's NGWAPI.PRM file (for example, SYS:\API41\NGWAPI.PRM), and then press ENTER again.

9. Scroll down to the line beginning with /Home- and make sure it points to the gateway directory (for example, /Home-SYS:\Public\Grpwise\Domain\ Wpgate\API41). In an installation without Patch 2 for API NLM, you need to correct the default /Home- line manually.

10. Find the line beginning with ;/Group and remove the semicolon in front of it to activate the inbound group expansion.

11. Press ESC. You will be prompted to save the changes. Make sure Yes is selected, and then press ENTER.

12. Press ESC and ENTER to exit the text editor.

Configuring the API Gateway for Exchange 2000 Server

After you have installed the GroupWise API Gateway files, you must start the NetWare Administrator program and create a gateway object in the Novell GroupWise domain.

It is assumed that both domain and post office reside in an organizational unit (OU) called GroupWise, that the domain is called GWDOMAIN, and that the post office is named GWPO.

▶ **To create a gateway object in the Novell GroupWise domain**

1. In NetWare Administrator, select the GroupWise domain object where you want to install the gateway (for example, GWDOMAIN, as shown in Figure 29.5).

2. Right-click the domain object (for example, GWDOMAIN), and then select Create.

3. In the New Object dialog box, double-click GroupWise Gateway/Internet Agent.

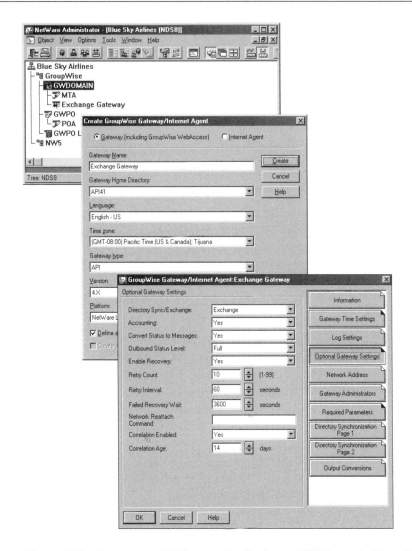

Figure 29.5 Creating an API Gateway for Exchange 2000 Server in GroupWise

4. In the Create GroupWise Gateway/Internet Agent dialog box, specify the following information (leave all others at their defaults, as shown in Figure 29.5), and then click Create:

Gateway Name — A descriptive, unique name within the domain (for example, Exchange Gateway) that identifies the gateway. NetWare Administrator will prevent the creation of gateway objects with duplicate names.

Gateway Home Directory	Select the directory specified during the installation of the API Gateway (for example, API41).
Gateway Type	API
Version	4.x (It is noteworthy that an API Gateway for GroupWise 5.x does not exist.)
Platform	NLM (It is recommended that you use the NLM version of the API Gateway with the Connector for Novell GroupWise.)
Define Additional Properties	Select the corresponding check box to define further settings.

5. The GroupWise Gateway/Internet Agent:Exchange Gateway dialog box is displayed next. Click Optional Gateway Settings, and then, under Directory Sync/Exchange, select Exchange to enable directory synchronization with Exchange 2000 Server. The Connector for Novell GroupWise will control the synchronization process, as explained in Lesson 2.

6. To support delivery reports and other status messages, under Convert Status To Messages, select Yes.

7. From the Outbound Status Level list box, select Full, and then click Required Parameters to switch to the Required Parameters tab.

8. Correct the information displayed under Gateway File Paths to match your API Gateway installation. You need to specify absolute NetWare paths in the form of <Server Name>/<Volume>:\<Path> (for example, BLUESKY-NW1/ SYS:\PUBLIC\GRPWISE\DOMAIN\WPGATE\API41).

9. From the Addressing Format list box, select Component, and then click OK to complete the configuration. The Exchange Gateway configuration object should now be listed in the NetWare Administrator View beneath the GroupWise domain object.

Note   Optionally, you may decrease the value for Idle Sleep Duration to 1 second (Gateway Time Settings) to avoid delays in manual directory synchronization. The API Gateway checks its API_IN directory for inbound messages in intervals according to the Idle Sleep Duration setting. The default value is 30 seconds.

Creating an External Foreign Domain for Exchange 2000 Server

Theoretically, you are now able to start the API Gateway. However, the configuration is not complete. You need to create an external foreign domain for your Exchange 2000 Server organization, and you need to configure the link table of the GroupWise domain to connect the external foreign domain to your GroupWise domain via the API Gateway. Otherwise, GroupWise cannot route messages to Exchange users.

▶ **To create an external domain and link it to the API Gateway using NetWare Administrator**

1. In NetWare Administrator, open the Tools menu, and then select GroupWise View. Expand the GroupWise domain where the API Gateway for Exchange 2000 Server is installed.

2. Right-click the gateway object (for example, Exchange Gateway, as shown in Figure 29.6) and select Create. In the Create External Object dialog box, select External Domain.

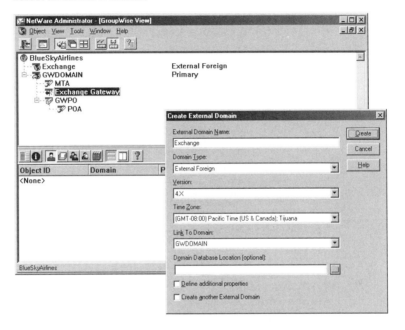

Figure 29.6   External foreign domain for Exchange 2000 Server

3. Type **Exchange** under External Domain Name. This is the default domain name assigned to Exchange users. You need to change the proxy address generation rules if you choose a different name. Proxy address generation is explained later in this lesson.

4. Under Domain Type, select External Foreign.

5. Make sure the Version is set to 4.x (because the API Gateway is version 4.1), and set the Time Zone to the time zone of the Exchange 2000 server that hosts the Connector for Novell GroupWise. Under Link To Domain, the API Gateway's GroupWise domain should be listed (for example, GWDOMAIN).

6. Click Create, and then verify that a foreign domain object is created in the GroupWise tree.

7. Right-click the API Gateway's GroupWise domain (for example, GWDOMAIN), and then select Link Configuration.

8. In the Link Configuration Tool, right-click the newly created external domain (for example, Exchange), and then select Edit.

9. From the Link Type list box, select Gateway.

10. In the Gateway Link list box, make sure the API Gateway is listed (for example, Exchange Gateway) that connects the GroupWise domain to Exchange 2000 Server, and then click OK.

11. Close the Link Configuration Tool. In the Links Have Changed dialog box, click Yes to save the link changes for the GroupWise domain.

Connector Permissions in Novell NetWare

As mentioned earlier in this lesson, you must create a Connector account and assign it permissions to the API Gateway's directories. This NetWare account must be a member of a special group called NTGATEWAY to allow the router service access to the API Gateway directory.

Note   Windows 2000 Server connects to NetWare servers on behalf of a NetWare account that must be a member of the NTGATEWAY group. Otherwise, the Router for Novell GroupWise service will report the following error in the application event log (Event ID 5017): "Error occurred when logging on NetWare server. The system error code is 1317. The specified user does not exist." You can read more about the integration of Exchange 2000 Server into NetWare-based networks in Chapter 10, "MAPI-Based Clients in a Novell NetWare Environment."

▶ **To create a Connector account and the NTGATEWAY group in NetWare Administrator**

1. In the NetWare Administrator View, right-click the desired OU where you want to create the gateway account, and then select the Create command.

2. In the New Object dialog box, double-click User, and then in the Create User dialog box, type **Exchange** under Login Name, type **Server** under Last Name, and select the Define Additional Properties check box.

3. Click Create, and then in the User:Exchange dialog box, click Password Restrictions.

4. Clear the Allow User To Change Password check box, select Require A Password, verify that the displayed Minimum Password Length matches your company's security policies, and then click Change Password.

5. In the Change Password dialog box, under New Password and Retype New Password, type a password (for example, **password**), and then click OK.

6. Click Rights To Files And Directories, and then under Volumes, click Show. Select the NetWare volume where you have installed the API Gateway (for example, BLUESKY-NW1_SYS) in the Select Object dialog box—you

might have to navigate through the NDS tree to find the server—and then click OK.

7. Under Files And Directories, click Add, and then navigate through the directories to select the API Gateway's root directory (for example, BLUESKY-NW1/SYS:\public\grpwise\domain\wpgate\API41). Grant the Exchange account all rights to this directory (except Supervisor and Access Control), and then click OK (see Figure 29.7).

8. To create the NTGATEWAY group, right-click the OU again, and select Create.

9. In the New Object dialog box, double-click Group, and then in the Create Group dialog box, type **NTGATEWAY.**

10. Select the Define Additional Properties check box, and then click Create.

11. Click Members, and then click Add to select the Connector account (for example, Exchange) in the Select Object dialog box, and then click OK.

12. Click OK to close the Group:NTGATEWAY dialog box.

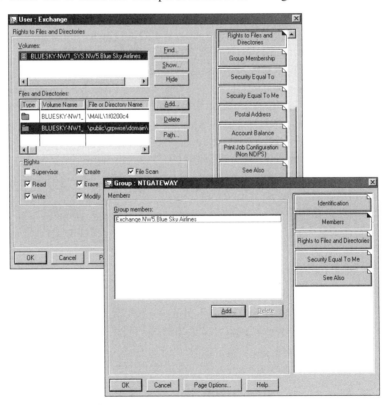

Figure 29.7   Configuring Connector permissions in Novell NetWare

> **Note**   It is a good idea to manually log on to NetWare using the connector's NetWare account to test access to the API Gateway directory. You need to be able to create, read, write, and delete files.

Starting and Testing the API Gateway

At this point, your NetWare and GroupWise environment is ready for Exchange 2000 Server. However, before configuring the Connector for Novell GroupWise, it is a good idea to start and test the API Gateway configuration. Type **API** in the System Console of your NetWare server, and press ENTER to launch the API Gateway's NLM (see Figure 29.8). You may use RCONSOLE.EXE to work remotely.

> **Important**   The API.NCF file is written during the installation of Patch 2 for API NLM. Without the patch, you cannot use the API command to launch the gateway. In this situation, use the following command: load <Volume:\Path> \NGWAPI.NLM(for example, load SYS:\API41\ NGWAPI.NLM).

▶   **To test the GroupWise and API Gateway configuration by simulating the Connector for Novell GroupWise**

1. On your workstation, launch the Novell GroupWise client. Compose a new message, address it to **Exchange.First Administrative Group.Administrator**, and then send it.

2. The API Gateway should place the message body in the form of a .bdy file in the ATT_OUT directory, while the message header should be in an .api file in its API_OUT directory.

3. Copy the .bdy file into the ATT_IN directory (it is important to copy the message body first).

4. Open the .api file in Notepad, and change the mail header information, as shown in the following sample listing (your sender and recipient information may be different):

```
WPC-API= 1.2;
Header-Char= T50;
Msg-Type= MAIL;
From-Text= Exchange Test;
From=
    WPD= Exchange;
    WPPO= First Administrative Group;
    WPU= Administrator;
    LN= admin;
    S= admin; ;
```

```
To=
    WPD= GWDOMAIN;
    WPPO= GWPO;
    WPU= admin;
    WPPONUM= 1;
    WPUNUM= 1;
    CDBA= 0001:0001; ;
All-To=
    WPD= GWDOMAIN;
    WPPO= GWPO;
    WPU= admin;
    WPPONUM= 1;
    WPUNUM= 1; ;
Msg-Id= 39B424B2.CFE6.0001.000;
To-Text= NGWAPI;
Subject= API Gateway Test;
<… further text …>
```

5. Save the .api file in API_IN using the original filename (actually, filename and extension do not need to be retained).

6. Switch to the Novell GroupWise client and verify that you have received the manipulated message (see Figure 29.8). For subsequent tests you need to copy the .bdy file again into the ATT_IN directory before saving the .api file in API_IN.

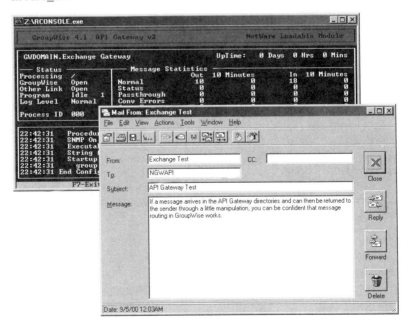

Figure 29.8 Testing the GroupWise API Gateway

7. When you have finished your tests, delete the .bdy and .api files from the API Gateway directory.

Configuring the Connector for Novell GroupWise

It is a complex task to prepare the Novell GroupWise environment, but careful configuration and testing in the first place makes the completion of the Connector configuration easy in Exchange System Manager. Right-click the Connector's configuration object under <Organization Name>/Administrative Groups/ <Administrative Group Name>/Routing Groups/<Routing Group Name>/Connectors (for example, under Blue Sky Airlines/Administrative Groups/First Administrative Group/Routing Groups/First Routing Group/Connectors), and then select Properties.

The Connector for Novell GroupWise tabs and their purposes are as follows:

- **Address Space.** To define message routing information for this Connector and determine the Connector's scope (that is, Exchange Organization or Routing Group). You can read more about address spaces in Chapter 16, "Message Routing Administration."

- **Delivery Restrictions.** To specify users and groups that are allowed or denied message transfer through this Connector to Novell GroupWise.

- **Details.** To provide an Administrative Note for informational purposes.

- **Dirsync Schedule.** To set the frequency of directory synchronization and to trigger manual address updates.

- **Export Containers.** To specify the OUs as recipient containers that you want to export to the GroupWise users, and to determine whether to export contact objects and groups.

- **General.** To specify the Universal Naming Convention (UNC) path to the root directory of the connector's API Gateway, identify the Connector account (member of NTGATEWAY), restrict message sizes, and set the deliver order (by Priority, FIFO, Size). FIFO is short for first in/first out.

- **Import Container.** To specify an OU in Active Directory where recipient objects should be created for GroupWise users, to filter recipients that should be included or excluded, and to determine the type of recipient objects to create if GroupWise users do not have Windows 2000 accounts. You can read more about the configuration of export and import OUs in Lesson 2.

- **Security** To specify users and groups that are allowed or denied administrative control over this Connector to Novell GroupWise. (This property sheet is only available if you have set the ShowSecurityPage Registry key, as outlined in Exercise 2 of Chapter 5, "Installing Microsoft Exchange 2000 Server.")

Minimal Connector Configuration

At minimum, you need only provide the path to the API Gateway's root directory in UNC in the API Gateway Path box in the Connector's General tab, such as \\BLUESKY-NW1\SYS\Public\Grpwise\Domain\Wpgate\API41 (see Figure 29.9). It is a good idea to start Windows Explorer to verify the UNC path. Only connections that support direct access to the API Gateway queues are supported.

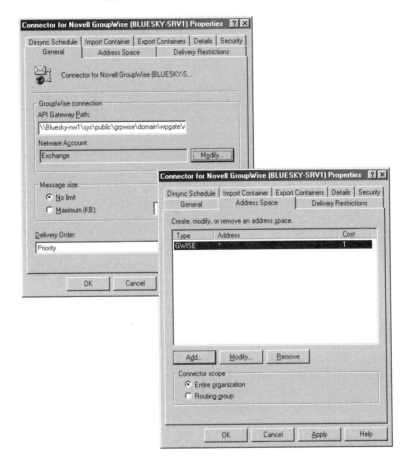

Figure 29.9   A minimal Connector for Novell GroupWise configuration

You also need to provide NetWare account information for the Connector. As mentioned, this account must be a member of the NTGATEWAY group. Use the Modify button to type the account name in the NetWare Account box (for example, Exchange). Under Password and Confirm Password, enter the corresponding password that was defined in NetWare Administrator. Then click on the

Address Space tab to define a GWISE address space for message routing purposes. Click Add, double-click GWISE in the Add Address Space dialog box, then, under Address, type an asterisk (*), and then click OK. Verify that an address space in the form GWISE * is listed (see Figure 29.9). Click OK to close the Connector properties.

Do not forget to activate the GWISE proxy address generation in a recipient policy, such as the default policy object, to assign your Exchange users valid GroupWise addresses. Recipient policies are discussed in Chapter 13, "Creating and Managing Recipients."

Make sure that the API Gateway is running, start the Connector for Novell GroupWise service using the Services snap-in, and you are ready to exchange messages. The Microsoft Exchange Router for Novell GroupWise and the Microsoft Exchange Connectivity Controller services will be started automatically.

Examining Connector Processes

You can use the Exchange Connectivity Administrator to verify whether the Connector processes are operating properly when you double-click the Process Manager reference in the Overview window. All Connector processes should be listed in idle state.

For further details, check the application event log using Event Viewer. For example, if you have misspelled the password of the Connector's NetWare account, the router service will write an error to the application event log (Event ID 5017): "Error occurred when logging on NetWare server. The system error code is 86. The specified network password is not correct." Another useful utility to examine Connector processes is the Performance tool. Windows 2000 management utilities that are useful for Exchange 2000 Server administration are discussed in Chapter 12, "Management Tools for Microsoft Exchange 2000 Server."

Diagnostics Logging

In case of problems, it is a good idea to increase the level of event logging for the Connector for Novell GroupWise to obtain the most detailed information. In Exchange System Manager, display the properties of the Exchange 2000 Server object (such as BLUESKY-SRV1), click on the Diagnostics Logging tab, select the LME-GWISE entry, and then set the desired logging level for all categories (None, Minimum, Medium, or Maximum). When you are confident that your Connector operates correctly, decrease the level for all categories to None to avoid unnecessary entries in the event log. With a diagnostics logging level of None, only critical events are traced. Diagnostics logging is further discussed in Chapter 20, "Microsoft Exchange 2000 Server Maintenance and Troubleshooting."

Testing E-Mail Connectivity

Operational Connector processes displayed in Exchange Connectivity Administrator are a positive indicator that the Connector configuration is okay. To ensure that message routing works, send test messages from Novell GroupWise to Exchange 2000 Server and vice versa. Use your new GWISE proxy address to specify an Exchange recipient in GroupWise, for instance, Exchange.First Administrative Group.Administrator. Once the message is received in Microsoft Outlook 2000, reply to it, and verify that the reply is received in Novell GroupWise. Always test newly created messaging connectors in both directions.

Novell GroupWise Proxy Addresses

If you do not know your GWISE proxy address by heart, launch Active Directory Users and Computers and display the E-Mail Addresses tab for your account. If GWISE address information is missing, you should check the default policy and Recipient Update service configuration in Exchange System Manager.

Note If you enable directory synchronization and then examine e-mail address information in Active Directory Users and Computers, you can find secondary proxy addresses assigned to GWISE recipient objects that refer to globally unique identifiers (GUIDs). These GUIDs are used to identify synchronized recipients. Do not delete them.

Novell GroupWise Proxy Address Generation Rules

By default, Novell GroupWise users see Exchange users as recipients in a huge external foreign domain called Exchange. The post office name corresponds to the administrative group name. As usual, the Recipient Update service generates the proxy addresses for each mailbox- and mail-enabled account automatically using a proxy address generator. The GroupWise proxy address generator is GWXPXGEN.DLL, which can be found in the Program Files\Exchsrvr\Address\Gwise\i386 directory. The Recipient Update service is covered in detail in Chapter 13, "Creating and Managing Recipients."

It is possible to customize GWISE proxy address generation. In Exchange System Manager, open the Recipients container, select Recipients Policies, and then open the desired policy (such as Default Policy). Click on the E-Mail Addresses tab. Make sure that the GWISE check box is selected, and then double-click the address entry next to it to customize the address generation rule. For instance, you might want to shorten or change the reference to the post office name, which by default refers to the administrative group, but you cannot remove it. GroupWise addresses must conform to the GroupWise naming convention of domain.post office.user alias. Do not change the domain name portion until you have created a corresponding external foreign domain in GroupWise. To customize the GWISE address generation, you can use the same placeholders that were already explained for the Connector for Lotus Notes in Chapter 28, "Connecting to Lotus Notes."

Implementing Multiple Connector Instances

You can configure multiple recipient policies to generate GWISE addresses according to different formats. For example, you may assign Carl Titmouse the address E2KEastCoast.First Administrative Group.CarlTitmouse, while the Administrator may have the address E2KWestCoast.First Administrative Group.Administrator. This corresponds to an Exchange 2000 Server organization with two external foreign domains in GroupWise. Correspondingly, you need to create an external foreign domain in GroupWise for E2KEastCoast and one for E2KWestCoast using NetWare Administrator. Either you point both to the same API Gateway or to separate gateways, possibly in different GroupWise domains. In this way, multiple Connector instances can share the message traffic to Exchange 2000 Server.

Note   When implementing multiple Connector instances, carefully design the directory synchronization topology to avoid the creation of duplicate address information through multiple connectors.

Configuring Downstream Domains

One Connector for Novell GroupWise can service multiple GroupWise domains. An address space of GWISE *, for instance, causes Exchange 2000 Server to route messages to all GroupWise users through your Connector. You only need to make sure that the link table configuration of the Connector's GroupWise domain meets your GroupWise routing requirements. The GroupWise MTA must be able to route inbound messages received from the API Gateway to their destinations. To distribute outbound message traffic to GroupWise domains across multiple Connectors for Novell GroupWise, assign detailed GWISE address spaces to each Connector. The most detailed address space wins, as explained in Chapter 16, "Message Routing Administration."

Lesson 2: Directory Synchronization with Novell GroupWise

It is advantageous to configure directory synchronization with Novell GroupWise to allow Exchange and GroupWise users to conveniently address e-mail messages to each other. Nevertheless, it is important to keep in mind that Novell GroupWise utilizes a separate directory from NDS, but GroupWise user information is kept in both directories. NDS may be replicated with Active Directory using Microsoft Directory Synchronization Services (MSDSS), as explained in Chapter 10, "MAPI-Based Clients in a Novell NetWare Environment." This synchronization, however, does not present recipient information in a way that allows Exchange or GroupWise users to address e-mail messages to each other. To achieve this, you need directory synchronization based on the Connector for Novell GroupWise. You may end up with duplicate account objects for NetWare users in your Windows 2000 forest. This behavior is expected and by design because MSDSS and the Connector for Novell GroupWise operate independently of each other. You can use the Active Directory Cleanup Wizard to consolidate duplicate information into one mail-enabled account. The Active Directory Cleanup Wizard was introduced in Chapter 6, "Coexistence with Previous Microsoft Exchange Server Versions."

This lesson concentrates on directory synchronization utilizing the Connector for Novell GroupWise. It explains in detail how Connector components interact with each other to synchronize Active Directory and GroupWise. It also describes important configuration tasks and how to update address information manually.

At the end of this lesson, you will be able to:

- Describe the process of directory synchronization with Novell GroupWise.

- Configure and test directory synchronization.

Estimated time to complete this lesson: 30 minutes

Directory Synchronization Overview

The Connector for Novell GroupWise shares several processes, including DXAMEX, with the Connector for Lotus Notes, as indicated in Lesson 1. The directory synchronization agent (LSDXA.EXE) uses DXAMEX to work with recipient information in Active Directory. LSDXA.EXE is likewise shared between the Connectors for Novell GroupWise and Lotus Notes. Consequently, directory synchronization with Novell GroupWise is similar to the directory synchronization with Lotus Domino/Notes, at least on the side of Exchange 2000 Server. On the Novell GroupWise side, LSDXA.EXE uses the DXAGWISE process to generate administrator messages for directory synchronization, which are then transferred to the API Gateway by means of the Router for Novell GroupWise (see Figure 29.10).

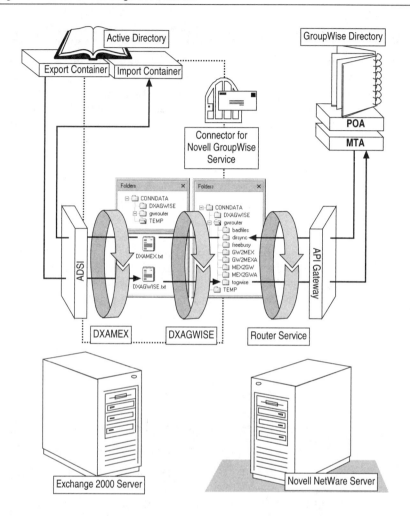

Figure 29.10   Directory synchronization with Novell GroupWise

Directory Synchronization Process and Interprocess Communication

Directory synchronization with Novell GroupWise relies on two directory structures, which are the \Temp and \Gwrouter subdirectories in the connector store \Program Files\Exchsrvr\Conndata. DXAMEX and DXAGWISE use the \Temp directory to transfer address information between each other in the form of message interchange format (MIF) files. These files are temporary and exist only during directory synchronization cycles. They are called DXAGWISE.TXT for address information to GroupWise and DXAMEX.TXT for address information to Active Directory (see Figure 29.10).

The responsibilities of DXAMEX and DXAGWISE are as follows:

- For directory synchronization from Active Directory to GroupWise, DXAMEX extracts recipient information from export containers in Active Directory and saves the data in DXAGWISE.TXT. In the opposite direction, DXAMEX applies the content of DXAMEX.TXT to an import container in Active Directory.

- For directory synchronization from Active Directory to GroupWise, DXAGWISE generates administrator messages to add, modify, or delete users, which are placed in the \Gwrouter\Togwise directory for the router service to transfer them to the API Gateway's API_IN directory. In the opposite direction, DXAGWISE places a request (this time for a list of GroupWise users) in the form of an administrator message in the \Gwrouter\Togwise directory as well. The router service transfers this message into API_IN on the NetWare server. API Gateway, GroupWise MTA, and POA handle the request. The results are returned in as an .api file through the API_OUT directory. The router service picks this file up and places it into \Gwrouter\Dirsync. DXAGWISE receives the recipient information from there and writes updates or the complete list (Full Load) to DXAMEX.TXT.

Note   To examine the content of GroupWise administrator messages, stop the API Gateway, and then perform directory synchronization. Request files are delivered to the API_IN directory. After that, stop the Connector for Novell GroupWise, and start the API Gateway. A response file will be returned through API_OUT.

Configuring Directory Synchronization

Before configuring directory synchronization, make sure that the Connector configuration is tested and performs reliably. Directory synchronization can fill the Connector's message queues with numerous messages if there are transfer problems.

Importing Address Information

You need to specify an import container where recipient objects for GroupWise users will be created. This container is an OU that will receive Active Directory recipient objects for GroupWise users. It is a good idea to create a dedicated OU for this purpose in Active Directory Users and Computers before configuring directory synchronization using Exchange System Manager. You can specify the desired OU in the Import Container tab by clicking Modify. Exchange System Manager will prompt you to grant your Exchange 2000 Server account (such as

BLUESKY-SRV1) Create and Modify permissions for the selected OU. Click Yes to update the permissions on the import container automatically.

Note   If you change the import container at a later time, do not forget to move affected recipient objects to the new OU to make sure they are updated properly.

You also can determine the type of recipient objects to create in Active Directory if replicated mailboxes do not have accounts in the Windows 2000 domain (that is, Create A Disabled Windows User Account, Create A New Windows User Account, and Create A Windows Contact).

Furthermore, you can select which recipients to accept through these options: Import All Directory Entries, Only Import Directory Entries Of These Formats, and Do Not Import Directory Entries Of These Formats. The default Import All Directory Entries option imports all addresses in the specified OU. The remaining two options allow you to restrict the address information. In this case, you can define corresponding import filters using the New ?button. For example, you can specify GWDOMAIN.*.* under Directory Entry Format in the Import Filter dialog box to prevent the import of GroupWise recipient objects that reside in a GroupWise domain called GWDOMAIN.

Specifying Exported Addresses

To export recipient information to GroupWise, specify one or many export containers in the Export Container tab. Similar to the import container, export containers are OUs in Active Directory. The machine account of your Exchange 2000 server requires Read permissions on all OUs specified as export containers. Exchange System Manager can grant the required permissions to the server account for you.

You can synchronize Windows contacts created for recipients in other messaging environments, such as Lotus Notes users synchronized using the Connector for Lotus Notes, when you enable the Export Contacts check box. To synchronize distribution group information, make sure the Export Groups check box is selected. Groups appear as user objects in the target directories. Membership information is not synchronized. For this reason, you need to enable the distribution list expansion feature of the API Gateway, as explained in Lesson 1.

Note   Distribution lists and GroupWise resource accounts are synchronized as user objects.

Testing Directory Synchronization

It is a good idea to test directory synchronization after configuration. It is also advisable to run directory synchronization manually whenever you are under the impression that address lists appear incomplete. The required controls for manual synchronization are in the Connector's Dirsync Schedule tab. The most important ones are the Immediate Full Reload buttons under Exchange To GroupWise Directory Synchronization and GroupWise To Exchange Directory Synchronization. Click them to force the immediate synchronization of all available address information. If the Connector is working properly, you will find associated addresses in the import container and GroupWise once the synchronization cycle completes.

Note   It is good practice to examine the processing phases of the Directory Synchronization agents in the Exchange Connectivity Administrator right after you click the Immediate Full Reload button.

Scheduling Directory Synchronization

When you are confident that everything works, configure the Connector for automatic directory synchronization. This is disabled by default, but you can enable it by clicking Customize to open the Schedule dialog box, where you can set your individual synchronization schedule or select a predefined schedule from the drop-down menu. It is usually sufficient to synchronize address information once every day, such as daily at midnight. Shorter intervals may be necessary during migration from Novell GroupWise to Exchange 2000 Server, when recipient information changes more frequently.

Chapter Summary

You can deploy the Connector for Novell GroupWise on one or many Exchange 2000 servers to connect your organization to a GroupWise environment. A messaging topology with bridgehead servers gives the best performance. The bridgeheads must be integrated with Novell NetWare by means of GSNW or NetWare Client for Windows 2000 to provide access to GroupWise. To install the Connector components, run the Exchange 2000 Server Setup program.

For messaging connectivity, the GroupWise environment and the Connector for Novell GroupWise must be configured. You need to install Patch 2 for API Gateway NLM on a NetWare server. Activate distribution list expansion for the gateway, and then configure a gateway object and an external foreign domain for the Exchange 2000 Server organization in GroupWise. The link table must be updated to connect the GroupWise domain to the external foreign domain via the API Gateway. Do not forget to create a dedicated NetWare account for the Connector and add it to the special NTGATEWAY group. Otherwise, the Connector cannot access the API Gateway directories. To configure the Connector using Exchange System Manager, provide the path to the API Gateway's root directory in UNC format and specify the connector's NetWare account and password. Configure an appropriate address space for message routing and assign your Exchange users GWISE proxy addresses by means of a recipient policy. After that, you are ready to start the Connector's Windows 2000 services and exchange messages with GroupWise users.

To simplify the addressing of e-mail messages, enable directory synchronization. This is quickly accomplished using the Import Container and Export Container tabs of the Connector for Novell GroupWise. In the Dirsync Schedule tab, you should also define a synchronization schedule for automatic address list updates. It is a good idea to trigger the first directory synchronization manually to quickly populate Active Directory and GroupWise with recipient information. Use the Active Directory Cleanup Wizard to consolidate duplicate GroupWise information into single mail-enabled accounts.

Review

The following review questions can help you determine if you have sufficiently familiarized yourself with the material covered in this chapter. You can find the answers to these questions at the end of this book in Appendix A, "Questions and Answers."

1. What needs to be prepared in the GroupWise domain to support the Connector for Lotus Novell GroupWise?

2. Which Connector component retrieves messages from the API Gateway?

3. You have implemented the Connector for Novell GroupWise. Message transfer and directory synchronization work properly; however, an Exchange user calls you and complains that all messages sent to GroupWise users appear in plain text. How can you solve this problem?

4. Based on the Connector for Novell GroupWise, you have configured directory synchronization between Exchange 2000 Server and GroupWise. GroupWise recipients appear in Active Directory, but you want to change the way the GroupWise users appear in the server-based address lists. Where can you find the mapping rule files that you need to edit to achieve the desired results?

5. How does DXAGWISE retrieve GroupWise directory information?

APPENDIX   A

Questions and Answers

Chapter 1

Review Questions

1. Why would you prefer a client/server messaging system to a shared-file messaging system?

   Client/server systems are more scalable than shared-file systems, making client/server messaging systems suitable for the needs of small and large organizations. Clients do not poll the active messaging server, and files will not be opened directly by any messaging client. Furthermore, client/server-based systems are more secure than shared-file systems because the client doesn't need read-write permission in a post office. The server services are the actual components that write messages into and read messages from the server's messaging databases.

2. What is the most significant difference between Exchange Server 5.5 and Exchange 2000 Server?

   Exchange 2000 Server is seamlessly integrated with Windows 2000 Active Directory, which allows single-seat administration because all attributes, including Exchange 2000 Server–related directory information, are maintained in a single repository.

3. Exchange 2000 Server supports a variety of Internet protocols. What clients can be used to access e-mail–related information on the server?

   MAPI-based clients, such as Outlook 2000, can access all messaging-related information stored on the computer running Exchange 2000 Server. IMAP4 clients can access e-mail–related information stored in Exchange 2000 mailboxes and public folders. POP3 clients have the ability to download messages from your inbox. NNTP-based newsreader programs can access public folders as newsgroups. Web browsers are able to work with mailboxes and public folders via Web Store and Outlook Web Access.

4. You are planning to utilize Exchange 2000 Server's powerful collaboration solutions; however, workgroup and workflow applications are new to your

administrators. Which type of collaboration solutions allows you to implement workgroup applications with minimal configuration and development effort?

You should start with instant collaboration solutions because these solutions rely on built-in modules of Outlook 2000 and don't require any programming skills.

5. Your organization is currently using Exchange Server 5.5 for messaging and collaboration. A PROFS connector is installed to provide a messaging path between PROFS and Exchange. You are planning an upgrade to Exchange 2000 Server. How can you provide connectivity to PROFS in the future Exchange 2000 Server environment?

You integrate Exchange 2000 Server into your existing Exchange server environment and continue to use the PROFS connector running on Exchange Server 5.5 for message connectivity. With the exception of the connector server, all computers running Exchange Server 5.5 can be upgraded to Exchange 2000.

Chapter 2

Review Questions

1. After the installation of Exchange 2000 Server, you want to create new mailboxes for your user accounts. Which MMC snap-in would you use?

The Active Directory Users and Computers snap-in.

2. Recently, you have installed Exchange 2000 Server in your organization. Your organization is composed of multiple domain trees arranged in a single forest. You intend to configure your mailbox resources from one of your computers running Exchange 2000. However, when you open the Active Directory Users and Computers snap-in, most of the Exchange-related property pages are not available. What do you have to install on the computer to configure mailboxes successfully?

You have to install the management utilities of Exchange 2000 Server on the server.

3. Your organization has deployed Active Directory and organized its resources in OUs according to the structure of the enterprise. Names of OUs reflect the names of departments. Frequently, users move between departments. Consequently, it is necessary to move user accounts to the appropriate OUs as well. Do you need to delete the old user accounts and create new ones to reflect the organizational changes in Active Directory?

No, using the Active Directory Users and Computers snap-in, it is possible to easily move directory objects, such as user accounts, between OUs. It is not necessary to delete and re-create the user accounts.

4. Active Directory holds all of the address information, such as the Global Address List, of Exchange 2000 Server. How does Exchange 2000 Server support MAPI-based client programs that are expecting to connect to an Exchange-based directory service?

Exchange 2000 Server provides a feature known as DSProxy, which forwards MAPI-based directory lookups without further processing to a Global Catalog server. DSProxy also keeps a reference of connections between clients and servers, ensuring that the response from the Global Catalog is passed back to the correct client.

5. In the past, your organization deployed Outlook 2000 successfully. Now you are installing Exchange 2000 Server. You wish to redirect your Outlook 2000 clients to a Global Catalog server. Outlook 2000 should contact the Global Catalog directly and without proxying. What do you have to configure on the computer running Exchange 2000 to achieve the desired result?

To make DSProxy divert Outlook 2000 and other smart clients, set the registry parameter RFR Target Server on the server machine to the name of the desired Global Catalog server. You need to add the parameter under HKEY_LOCAL_MACHINE\System\CurrentControlSet\ Services\MSExchangeSA\Parameters.

6. You plan to install Exchange 2000 Server in two locations connected to each other via a slow dial-up telephone connection. Do you need to upgrade the existing link to a permanent connection?

No, server-to-server communication in Exchange 2000 environments relies solely on SMTP-based messages. SMTP is an asynchronous transfer protocol that doesn't require permanent network connectivity.

Chapter 3

Review Questions

1. What are the essential Exchange 2000 Server components required to deliver messages in a single-server environment?

The essential components that need to be operational are the System Attendant, the Information Store, the IIS Admin Service, and the SMTP transport. Of course, Active Directory as an essential Windows 2000 service also needs to be available. The System Attendant controls the entire Exchange 2000 server system and is a prerequisite for the Information Store. The Information Store hosts mailboxes and public folders and relies on the SMTP service for message delivery. The SMTP transport, in turn, requires the IIS Admin Service, because this transport is implemented in the form of an IIS.

2. To perform an offline backup, you want to shut down the IIS and the Exchange 2000 Server services without rebooting the entire server. Which of the components must be stopped directly to stop all other server components as well?

You need to stop the System Attendant, which in turn shuts down all Exchange 2000 Server-specific services. You also need to stop the IIS Admin Service, which automatically stops all related IISs, such as the SMTP service and the NNTP service.

3. You have stopped the MTA service. How does this affect the behavior of connected Outlook clients?

The MTA is not required for delivery of messages to recipients on the same computer or on different computers reachable via SMTP. However, messages to X.400 systems and foreign messaging systems are not routed until you restart the Exchange MTA Stacks service.

4. As an administrator you have stopped the Microsoft Exchange Information Store service. How does this affect Outlook clients?

Outlook clients cannot log on to the Exchange 2000 server and will receive an error message indicating that the Exchange Server computer is not available. Outlook users currently logged on will lose their sessions. However, Outlook is able to automatically reconnect the user when you restart the Information Store, so it is not necessary to restart Outlook.

5. To satisfy growing messaging demand, you decide to install a second Exchange 2000 server. Which components communicate directly with each other between servers?

Only the SMTP services communicate directly with each other. All other services rely on e-mail messages and use the SMTP transport as their native communication mechanism.

6. List the two general types of information stores an Exchange 2000 server can maintain.

The two types of information store are the public store, which maintains information stored in public folders, and the mailbox store, which holds all mailboxes and messages sent to individual users.

7. How many storage groups can you configure on a particular Exchange 2000 server, and how many information store databases can each storage group contain?

You can manage up to 16 individual storage groups on a single Exchange 2000 server, and each storage group is capable of holding up to six individual stores. This gives you the capability to create a maximum of 96 physical stores and spread them across your server's hard disk system.

8. As a user using Outlook 2000, you can happily send messages to all other users in your environment. After lunch, however, the situation changes. All of a sudden, your messages don't seem to leave the Outbox anymore. Other users with mailboxes on your server report the same problem. What is most likely the cause of this dilemma?

Another administrator has directly or indirectly stopped the SMTP service on your Exchange 2000 server. The SMTP service hosts the advanced queuing engine, which is the central information controller in Exchange 2000 Server. Without this essential service, Exchange 2000 Server cannot deliver any messages, and all messages must remain in the user's Outbox.

Chapter 4

Review Questions

1. Your computer network consists of multiple domains. Most of them are grouped together in a single domain tree, but one domain tree exists in a separate forest for political reasons. You now have to implement an Exchange 2000 organization for all your users. How can you best accomplish this task?

Exchange 2000 organizations cannot span multiple Active Directory forests. Therefore, the domain in the separate forest must be isolated and integrated into the main forest of the environment before installing Exchange 2000 Server for these users.

2. Your computer network consists of multiple domains. All domains reside in a single forest. Where do you need to install Exchange 2000 Server first?

Because Exchange 2000 Server needs to extend the Active Directory Schema, you need to first install Exchange 2000 Server in the domain where the schema master resides.

3. You are in charge of a complex messaging environment spread across several international locations. You plan to implement decentralized system management, giving all locations Full Administrative permissions over their own resources. How would you structure the Exchange 2000 organization to achieve this goal?

Define an administrative group for each location, and assign the appropriate user accounts Exchange Full Administrator permissions.

4. What is the purpose of a routing group?

Routing groups describe regions of high-speed connections within a network. Messages sent between servers in the same routing group are transferred directly and immediately using the SMTP transport service. You can use a Routing Group Connector, X.400 connector, or an SMTP Connector to provide a message path between Exchange 2000 routing groups.

5. What are the restrictions that apply when operating an Exchange 2000 organization in mixed mode?

Administrative groups are handled similar to Exchange Server 5.5 sites. Therefore, it is impossible to move mailboxes between servers in different administrative groups. It is also impossible to move servers between administrative groups. Finally, routing groups can only contain servers from the same administrative group. Although one administrative group may contain multiple routing groups, routing groups cannot span multiple administrative groups.

6. Your messaging management is separated from Windows 2000 administration. Consequently, you need to ask your Windows 2000 administrator to prepare the domain environment for you prior to installing Exchange 2000. What must the Windows 2000 administrator do to prepare the domain environment?

The Windows 2000 administrator must prepare the forest by launching the Exchange 2000 Setup program in ForestPrep and after that in DomainPrep mode. ForestPrep extends the Active Directory Schema to add Exchange-specific classes and attributes. ForestPrep also creates the directory object for the Exchange 2000 organization and assigns the specified account Exchange Full Administrator permissions. Your Windows 2000 administrator should specify your account at this point. Your account then has the authority to install and manage Exchange 2000 Server throughout the forest and has the authority to assign further administrators Exchange Full Administrative permissions once the first server is installed. DomainPrep, on the other hand, adds further Exchange-specific configuration information to the Active Directory directory service. When Exchange 2000 Server is installed at a later time, Setup can retrieve the configuration information from Active Directory and does not need to prompt the administrator for it.

7. What is the difference between Exchange Full Administrator and Exchange Administrator permissions?

An Exchange Full Administrator can administer the Exchange organization and modify permissions on Exchange configuration objects, whereas an Exchange Administrator can only administer the Exchange organization, but does not have the ability to modify permissions on Exchange configuration objects.

8. You are planning to deploy Exchange 2000 Server in a hosted environment that has to support more than 10,000 Internet users accessing their mailboxes primarily through Outlook Web Access. Consequently, you plan to implement an FE/BE configuration. What do you have to do to configure a front end server?

You configure a front end server by activating the This Is A Front-End Server check box in the server's properties within the Exchange System Manager.

Chapter 5

Review Questions

1. To save disk space, you have used the Minimum installation option during setup of the first server. Now you want to delegate administrative permissions to a colleague. Why can't you manage the Exchange 2000 Server? What type of installation could you use to install all required components? How can you add the components to the server that was installed with Minimum installation type?

   The Minimum installation type installs Exchange 2000 with the minimum number of files needed for messaging and collaboration services. Because administrative utilities are not installed when selecting this option, you cannot manage the first server. Launch the Setup program in maintenance mode to add the management utilities to the server installation, or install these utilities separately on your workstation.

2. You want to designate additional administrators in an administrative group. The additional accounts will be responsible for system configuration only. These administrators should not be able to change security settings. What administrative role do you need to assign these administrators?

   You need to assign these administrators the administrative role Exchange Administrator, which is available at the organization and administrative group level.

3. What administrative role is required to display configuration information?

   Exchange View Only Administrator.

4. You are using Exchange Server 4.0 in a complex environment. Because of the extended Internet features implemented in Exchange 2000 Server, you decide to upgrade the messaging network. What upgrade strategy should you use?

   You need to upgrade the Exchange Server to version 5.5 first because the in-place upgrade to Exchange 2000 is only supported for version 5.5. After that, update the Windows NT Server to Windows 2000, configure connection agreements in the Active Directory Connector, and then launch the Exchange 2000 Server Setup program to accomplish the upgrade.

5. Another administrator has previously installed Outlook 2000 on a server computer, which is an unsupported configuration. To clean up the unsupported configuration, you have decided to remove the client with all its components. You then find that the server no longer works properly because the MAPI32.DLL is missing. How can you fix this problem?

   You need to reinstall Exchange 2000 Server in maintenance mode, which replaces corrupted files and fixes problems with missing components, such as MAPI32.DLL.

6. You plan to install Exchange 2000 Server unattended to run Setup simultaneously on more than one computer. How would you create the predefined setup initialization file?

You need to launch SETUP.EXE in CreateUnattand mode via the command SETUP.EXE /CreateUnattend SETUP.INI. This will launch the Exchange Installation Wizard, where you can make your choices. However, the server will not be installed, but the initialization file is generated at the specified location.

7. The messaging network of your company consists of one single location. Five server computers exist within this local area network. You want to administer all these computers from a Windows 2000 workstation in your office. What needs to be installed on the Windows 2000 workstation? How do you install the additional components?

You need to install the Microsoft Exchange System Management Tools via the Setup program of Exchange 2000 Server. Launch Setup, and under Action in the Microsoft Exchange 2000 category, select Custom.

Chapter 6

Review Questions

1. You are planning to integrate Exchange 2000 Server into an existing Exchange Server 5.5 site. Which two strategies can you use?

The first approach is to upgrade an existing Exchange server directly, thus joining an existing site automatically using the in-place upgrade procedure. The second method involves installing a fresh server and specifying joining an existing site during Setup. Exchange 5.5 resources must then be migrated to the Exchange 2000 server.

2. Your Exchange Server organization consists of one site containing a mixed installation of various earlier server versions, such as Exchange Server 5.0 and Exchange Server 5.0 Service Pack 3. You are planning to upgrade with a minimal disruption of business processes. Which upgrade strategy would be best?

You should rely on the move-mailbox upgrade. Join the existing site with an Exchange 2000 server, specify a server running Exchange Server 5.5 with Service Pack 3 during the installation, and move Exchange resources onto the new system afterward. Outlook clients will be redirected to the new system automatically and users are not noticeably affected. As soon as all resources are on Exchange 2000 Server, you can remove the legacy Exchange Server versions.

3. You have joined an existing site with a new Exchange 2000 server. You now plan to use the Exchange System snap-in to manage the resources of the site. How can you manage Exchange Server 5.5 Service Pack 3 resources via Active Directory?

You cannot manage resources of previous Exchange Server versions via Active Directory. You need to use the Exchange Administrator program to manage Exchange Server 5.5 Service Pack 3 and the Exchange System snap-in to administer Exchange 2000 Server.

4. You have joined an existing site of eight servers with one new Exchange 2000 server. Which utility should you use to manage mailbox resources in this site?

You should use the Active Directory Users and Computers tool to manage the mailbox resources. New mailboxes should be created on the Exchange 2000 server only, which requires the Active Directory Users and Computers tool. Configuration changes on existing mailboxes can also be made using this tool because user connection agreements of an ADC in conjunction with SRS are able to replicate the information from Active Directory to the Exchange directories.

5. You have successfully migrated all resources to Exchange 2000 Server using the move-mailbox approach. You now plan to switch the organization into native mode. What do you need to accomplish before you can carry out the change?

You need to remove the existing installations of earlier Exchange Server versions and their corresponding objects in the SRS database and Active Directory. The switch to native mode is only possible if no previous versions of Exchange Server exist in the organization.

Chapter 7

Review Questions

1. What are the three physical connections that join the nodes of a cluster together?

A shared storage bus and a public and private network connection connect the nodes in a cluster. The shared storage bus connects all nodes to the disks where the clustered data resides. The public network connection connects client computers to the nodes in the cluster and allows the nodes to exchange information as well. The private network connection is optional, connects only the nodes in a cluster, and ensures that the nodes will be able to communicate with each other in the event of an outage of the public network.

2. You plan to install Exchange 2000 Server in a Windows 2000 cluster. The cluster consists of two nodes. You want to run Exchange 2000 Server in an active/active configuration. How many disk volumes are required at a minimum if you want to configure dedicated Exchange 2000 resource groups?

A minimum of three disk volumes must be connected to the Exchange cluster. One disk volume is used as the quorum resource. The remaining two volumes will each be assigned to a separate virtual Exchange 2000 server. Both virtual servers can then run on either node in the cluster.

3. You have installed and configured a four-node cluster running Windows 2000 Datacenter Server. Now, you want to install Exchange 2000 Server. What are the installation steps you must accomplish?

   Install Exchange 2000 Server on one node at a time, and then reboot each node to complete the installation. The Setup program will do the bulk of the work automatically by detecting that it started on a cluster node and configuring the Exchange components accordingly. It is important to set up all nodes using the same directories and installation options. It is advantageous to reserve the M drive on all nodes for the Web Store of Exchange 2000 Server. After you have installed Exchange 2000 Enterprise Server on all nodes, configure the virtual servers.

4. You want to add Exchange 2000 Server to an existing resource group. This resource group is already hosting SQL 2000 Server resources. What resources do you need to add to the existing resource group?

   Because the existing resource group already owns an IP address, network name, and disk, only the Exchange SA needs to be added manually. All other Exchange 2000 resources will be attached automatically.

5. You have successfully configured a virtual server for Exchange 2000 and brought it online. Now you want to test the failover behavior of your system. How can you trigger a failover to another node in the cluster?

   Using Cluster Administrator, you can trigger a failover by right-clicking on an Exchange 2000 resource and selecting Initiate Failure. All resources in the cluster group will be taken offline and then brought back online on another available node in the cluster. The process of stopping and starting resource instances is performed automatically.

6. Because of the increased scalability of Exchange 2000 Server in a clustered installation, you plan to consolidate your Exchange resources and replace the existing five nonclustered servers with one Windows 2000 cluster. How can you incorporate the existing information store databases into the cluster installation?

   You cannot mount nonclustered information store databases in a clustered Exchange 2000 environment. Clustered information store databases contain special structures required to support access from multiple nodes, which aren't present in nonclustered counterparts. To incorporate the existing Exchange resources, install the clustered Exchange 2000 system in the organization, and then move mailboxes and public folders into it. As soon as all resources reside on the cluster, you can remove the nonclustered systems.

Chapter 8

Review Questions

1. What are the system requirements for Outlook 2000 on a computer running Windows 2000 Professional?

   Outlook 2000 requires at least an Intel Pentium-compliant processor and 16 MB of RAM (in addition to Windows 2000's requirements), although it is advisable to double the amount of RAM to get better performance.

2. Which three options do you have to customize the Outlook 2000 installation process?

   You can customize the installation process by using command-line parameters, adjusting SETUP.INI settings, or creating a transform file using the Custom Installation Wizard.

3. You plan to roll out Outlook 2000 to numerous users working on Windows 98, Windows NT 4.0 Workstation, and Windows 2000 Professional. What do you need to accomplish to install the new client platform unattended via a login script?

   You need to launch Setup with the parameter /A to set up an administrative installation point, which you then can customize using the Custom Installation Wizard. At the end of the customization process, a transform file is written, which you will save in the installation point. After that, the Custom Installation Wizard suggests a command line for an unattended installation, which you should copy into the users' login script. You should make sure that the command line is only executed once per user.

4. You have created an administrative installation point and customized the installation using SETUP.INI and the Custom Installation Wizard. You are now planning to deploy Outlook through a specific command line, which contains further options. Which settings take precedence over which other settings?

   The transform file created by the Custom Installation Wizard has lowest priority, followed by SETUP.INI, which is superseded by the command-line options.

5. Where can you optimize the RPC connection order for Windows 2000-based Outlook 2000 clients?

   You can modify the client connection order in the Registry under HKEY_LOCAL_MACHINE\SOFTWARE\Microsoft\Exchange\Exchange Provider. The Rpc_Binding_Order value determines the connection order.

6. A delegate is sending messages on your behalf, but you don't want the delegate's name to appear on the From line of the message header. What kind of permission must be granted to the assistant to achieve this?

The assistant's name won't appear in messages sent on your behalf if the assistant has been granted the Send As for your account, which can be set in the Active Directory Users and Computers management tool.

Chapter 9

Review Questions

1. What is a messaging profile?

A messaging profile contains configuration information about information services that will be used by the Microsoft Exchange Client to establish a session with the underlying messaging backbone. The client cannot start without an existing profile.

2. Which tool assists you in creating messaging profiles?

The Microsoft Outlook Setup Wizard (formerly known as the Microsoft Exchange Setup Wizard).

3. Where are the messaging profiles of a currently logged on user stored in Windows 2000?

The profile of a currently logged on user can be found under: HKEY_CURRENT_USER\Software\Microsoft\Windows NT\CurrentVersion\Windows Messaging Subsystem\Profiles. Subkeys exist corresponding to each configured profile.

4. Which two message stores can be configured to keep messages available offline?

For users to work offline with messages, the messages need to be copied to the computer's hard disk. To do this, you can configure an offline or a personal folder store. The offline store is a replica of the actual server-based content, whereas the personal folder store normally is used to download and remove messages from the server.

5. You have configured a personal folder store and the Exchange transport service. How can you define the personal folder store as the location for incoming messages?

You can configure the message delivery on the Delivery tab of the Services dialog box, which can be displayed using the Services command on the client's Tools menu. In this tab, the primary Inbox can be specified under the Deliver New Mail To The Following Location option.

6. What is the most significant advantage of the offline folder store?

   The offline folder store provides the advantage of synchronizing public folders. In other words, using an offline store, you are able to work with public folders while disconnected from the server.

7. How can you assign centralized messaging profiles to roving users that work on computers running Windows 2000?

   The profiles for Windows 2000–based Outlook Clients will be stored in the user-specific Registry keys (HKEY_CURRENT_USER). These settings can be included in server-based profiles, which will then be activated on any machine as soon as the roving user logs on to the domain.

Chapter 10

Review Questions

1. You plan to integrate Exchange 2000 Server into your Novell NetWare network. You install Windows 2000 Server and the NWLink IPX/SPX–compatible Transport. Which two important configuration parameters of the NWLink IPX/SPX–Compatible Transport may need to be configured manually?

   The frame type and the internal network number.

2. Because Exchange Server validates users based on Windows 2000 account information, you need to create a corresponding Windows 2000 account for each existing Novell NetWare user. Which tool can you use to synchronize the account information for both systems?

   Microsoft Directory Synchronization Services (MSDSS).

3. Users on Novell NetWare workstations are complaining about the startup times of Outlook 2000. What should you first check?

   The RPC Binding Order value in the Registry under: HKEY_LOCAL_MACHINE\SOFTWARE\Microsoft\Exchange\Exchange Provider should be checked first. The RPC over SPX communication method (*ncacn_spx*) should be placed on top.

4. Your Novell NetWare 5 network relies on TCP/IP only. You have deployed the Novell NetWare 5 Client software on all your workstations running Windows 2000 Professional. Which component do you need to add to the workstation configuration to allow your users to access their Exchange 2000 mailboxes with Outlook 2000?

   You need to install the Client for Microsoft Networks to support RPC communication between Outlook 2000 and Exchange 2000 Server.

Chapter 11

Review Questions

1. As an Exchange 2000 administrator, you have connected your organization to the Internet. Now you want to support common Internet clients as well. Which Internet protocols does Exchange 2000 Server support?

    IMAP4, POP3, NNTP, and HTTP, as well as SMTP are supported. LDAP access is available via Active Directory and Global Catalog servers.

2. You want to increase the access security for Exchange 2000 resources. How would you limit the group of workstations that are able to access existing servers through IPs?

    Using Exchange System Manager, display the properties of the desired virtual server, click on the Access tab, and click Connection Control to specify the range of IP addresses that should be granted access to the virtual server.

3. Which authentication methods can you use to support all possible POP3/IMAP4 clients?

    You can use the Basic Authentication or the Integrated Windows Authentication to prompt your users for logon credentials. When using the Basic Authentication method over the Internet, make sure the communication is encrypted using SSL; otherwise, passwords will be exposed because they are transferred in clear text.

4. As a management consultant, you want to emphasize the benefits of Exchange 2000 Server in a presentation for your most important customer. Spontaneously, you are asked about this feature called Web Store that everybody seems to talk about. How can you demonstrate the Web Store ad hoc without any preparation or additional configuration on a computer running Exchange 2000 Server?

    You can open Internet Explorer and connect to the URL *http://localhost/ Exchange/* to demonstrate how to access mailbox and public folder resources from any modern Web browser. You can also launch Windows Explorer and explain how to configure a Web folder connection to access public folder resources via HTTP and WebDAV. The URL *http://localhost/public/* allows you to access the entire public folders tree from within Windows Explorer just as any shared network resource. Finally, you may start an Office or any other application and access mailbox or public folder resources via drive M that corresponds to the ExIFS.

5. You have successfully configured a pull feed to replicate newsgroups with the USENET. After three days, you realize that this newsfeed is pulling in several gigabytes of data. You expect to run out of disk space very soon. Which steps should you carry out to avoid a server shutdown due to unavailable disk space?

A pull feed initiates the connection to a remote USENET host and pulls the information from existing newsgroups. To pause a newsfeed, display its properties, and in the General tab, deselect the Enable Feed check box. Then click OK. This step temporarily disables the newsfeed. Now you can add more disks or move resources to another server to create more disk space, and then enable the feed again.

Chapter 12

Review Questions

1. You want to configure an entire Exchange 2000 Server organization using Exchange System Manager on your Windows NT Workstation computer. How do you install this program, and which of the existing servers in your organization can be configured?

   Exchange System Manager cannot be installed on a computer running Windows NT Workstation. Hence, you will need to use a different approach, such as Terminal Services, in which case you can use an Exchange System Manager instance running on Windows 2000 Server remotely. Theoretically, you can administer all Exchange 2000 servers that are members of administrative groups where you have Administrative permissions. Changes are written to Active Directory and replicated across the entire forest.

2. You add new memory (RAM) to a computer running Exchange 2000 Server. The server performance has not been improved, so you are wondering which component might create the actual bottleneck. Which utility can you use to determine the critical component?

   The Performance tool allows you to monitor performance objects on the local and remote computers. Using this tool, you can create a performance chart for processor utilization, disk and network activities, and Exchange 2000 processes. Performance charts can help to isolate bottlenecks and allow you to precisely allocate hardware upgrades.

3. You want to manage the available disk space across all of the servers in your administrative group. Therefore, you want to define storage limits. How can you define storage limits for all these servers with minimal effort?

   You can define mailbox store policies and set the storage limits according to your preferences on the Limits tab. After that, place all the servers from your administrative group under this policy.

4. A supervisor in the marketing department calls and wants to know whether Fred Pumpkin is working online. You will need to view information about currently logged on users. Which object provides the fastest access to the desired information?

   The Logon object under the Private Information Store object provides the fastest access to the desired information. As soon as you select this

object, status information regarding all logged on users will be displayed in the contents pane of the Administration window.

Chapter 13

Review Questions

1. When would you configure mail-enabled contact objects in Active Directory?

   Mail-enabled contact objects reference recipients outside the organization. They don't possess mailboxes on an Exchange 2000 server. Instead, mail-enabled contacts are wrappers around an underlying e-mail address, which points to the actual recipient somewhere outside.

2. How do you hide a particular mailbox from the address book?

   You need to click on the Exchange Advanced tab of the desired mailbox in Active Directory Users and Computers and select the Hide The Account From Exchange Address Lists check box.

3. How can you accomplish the transfer of group management responsibilities to a regular user?

   By designating the user as the distribution list owner.

4. Your Exchange 2000 server is a very busy machine. Another server in the same administrative group has less work to perform, so you decide to designate this computer as an expansion server. How can you accomplish this configuration?

   You can designate this server for each group separately using the Expansion Server setting in the Exchange Advanced tab. If you have numerous groups to configure, consider updating them in bulk using the LDIFDE or CSVDE utility.

5. Although your Windows 2000 environment consists of multiple domains, you have deployed Exchange 2000 Server only in the top-level domain. What do you need to configure on the Exchange 2000 server to support all users in your organization?

   You need to run the Exchange 2000 Setup program in each domain in DomainPrep mode. After that, an instance of the Recipient Update service must be configured for each domain individually on the server using the Exchange System Manager utility.

Chapter 14

Review Questions

1. You plan to create multiple storage groups and message stores on an Exchange 2000 server. Which Exchange 2000 Server version do you need to install on this machine, and how many information stores can you configure?

You need to install the Exchange 2000 Enterprise Server edition, which is able to handle a maximum of four storage groups, each capable of holding up to five individual stores.

2. Your organization uses various advanced collaboration solutions for account management, sales tracking, and knowledge management. These solutions rely on a specific public folder structure, which is accessed by numerous users from various departments on a daily basis. For best performance, you are considering a dedicated public folder server for these forums. What do you need to accomplish before you can configure a server as a dedicated public folder server?

   Configuring a dedicated public folder server means removing all existing mailbox stores, which cannot be accomplished if the mailbox stores contain user mailboxes. Hence, you need to move all existing user mailboxes from this computer to other servers in the administrative group.

3. You are planning to implement a document management system and want to activate full-text indexing for the corresponding public store. What are the steps to activate Exchange 2000 Server's full-text indexing feature?

   You need to create a full-text index for the public store by right-clicking it and selecting the Create Full-Text Index command. Then, you need to populate the full-text catalog via the Start Full Population command. As soon as this process is complete, you can make the catalog available for full-text searches by clients on the store's Full-Text Indexing tab. You should also define update and rebuild intervals to ensure that search information is always up to date.

4. How can you move a server between administrative groups?

   You cannot move servers between administrative groups. The server must be reinstalled, at which time you can specify the server's new administrative group. The administrative group must be created beforehand in Exchange System Manager.

5. As an administrator for Exchange 2000 Server, you have configured several nested server-based address lists. However, correct address list information is not displayed in the client's address books yet. How can you trigger an immediate address list update?

   Right-click on the Recipient Update service for your domain, and click Rebuild. A Rebuild Address Lists And Recipient Policies dialog box will appear, informing you that the settings for all recipients are recalculated on the next scheduled update interval. To overrule the update interval by triggering an immediate update, right-click the update service object again, and select the Update Now command.

Chapter 15

Review Questions

1. You are the administrator of a small Exchange organization with one Exchange 2000 server. You have successfully connected the server to the Internet. Test messages sent to an Internet address are delivered without problems. Replies to test message, however, end in nondelivery reports. What do you have to accomplish to allow replies to test messages to be delivered to your organization?

   For incoming messages to be delivered to your host, your SMTP domain name must be registered in MX records in the Internet DNS.

2. Your users complain about a large number of unsolicited commercial messages. You check the messages and determine they all come from a domain called Pleasegiveusyourmoney-times-10.com. How can you prevent the delivery of these messages most conveniently?

   You can configure a message filter and activate the filtering for your SMTP virtual server. Under Global Settings, display the properties of the Message Delivery object in Exchange System Manager. Click on the Filtering tab, and use the Add button to specify "*@Pleasegiveusyourmoney.com" as the filtered sender information. As soon as the filter is defined, activate the filtering feature on your virtual server.

3. Your server is operating as a central bridgehead server in your organization which has to handle a constant stream of messages to downstream servers in other routing groups. How can you optimize the throughput of messages?

   It may be advantageous to not limit the number of messages per connection and let the bridgehead handle all e-mail over established links. This increases the performance because it avoids additional handshakes for further connection establishments.

4. Your internal DNS servers are not integrated with the Internet. How can you enable Exchange 2000 Server to use Internet DNS servers for outbound message transfer?

   You can add references to external DNS servers to your SMTP virtual server configuration. In the Delivery tab, click the Advanced button. This will display the Advanced Delivery dialog box. Under Configure External DNS Servers, click the Configure button. You can specify multiple DNS servers.

5. Users complain about lost messages that have been automatically forwarded to an Internet account. What is most likely the cause of this problem?

You have deselected the Allow Automatic Forward check box in the Default message format definition, which is located in the Internet Message Formats container in Exchange System Manager.

Chapter 16

Review Questions

1. When should you separate Exchange 2000 servers by means of routing groups?

   You should configure multiple routing groups if access to public folder resources must be controlled, if dedicated bridgehead servers with optimized hardware for message transfer are desired, if you need to take geographical requirements into consideration, or if you need to optimize or reduce network traffic. Unstable network links affect message transfer performance, which would benefit from the use of multiple routing groups. The same applies to WAN connections that generate costs.

2. What are the minimum configuration parameters you need to define for an RGC?

   At minimum, you need to specify a name in the General tab and a remote bridgehead server in the Remote Bridgehead tab.

3. What are the minimum configuration parameters you need to define for an SMTP Connector between two routing groups?

   At minimum, you need to specify a name in the General tab and define a local bridgehead server. You also need to specify a remote SMTP virtual server in the form of a smart host and a remote routing group in the Connected Routing Groups tab.

4. Your organization consists of numerous routing groups. Within your local routing group, 10 servers have been installed. You plan to replace the hardware of the server that was installed in your routing group first. What do you need to accomplish to guarantee efficient message routing while the hardware is replaced?

   The first server in a routing group typically acts as the routing group master, maintaining the LST for all other servers in the routing group. If you shut down the routing group master for a significant period of time, as you would to replace its hardware, you should designate a different master to avoid inefficient message routing. Launch Exchange System Manager, expand the Local Routing Group, and select the Members container. In the details pane, right-click another server object, and select Set As Master.

Chapter 17

Review Questions

1. What is a dedicated public server?

   A dedicated public server is a server that maintains folders in public stores only. All mailbox stores have been removed.

2. Which communication method is used to access the public folder content using Outlook 2000?

   Outlook 2000 relies on RPCs in any case, whether the content is stored on the user's home server or another public server within the routing group or organization.

3. You have decided to place all public folders on a particular server without configuring dedicated servers. A user works with Outlook 2000 and creates a new top-level folder. Where will the new public folder be located?

   On the user's home server, because this server holds the default public folder store for the user.

4. A user works with the Outlook 2000 and creates a new subfolder directly under a top-level folder. Where will the new public folder be stored?

   All subfolders will be created on the server that maintains the parent folder.

5. Olivia calls and complains that some other users can't see her new public folder in their public folder trees. Users on the local server are able to work with the new folder. What is most likely the cause of the problem?

   The public folder hierarchy replication has not been completed yet. After a short delay, the public folder will appear in the public folder hierarchy.

6. Users in your routing group need to work with a public folder called Customer Feedback. This folder is not kept in the local routing group, and you don't want to create a local replica of this folder. RPC communication is supported between all servers in your organization. What must be accomplished to allow your users access to the public folder content?

   Nothing. Routing group connectors allow public folder referrals by default. If public folder access is prohibited due to manual configuration changes, clear the Do Not Allow Public Folder Referrals check box on the routing group connector's General tab.

Chapter 18

Review Questions

1. What are the general advantages of the public folder content replication?

   Public folder content replication permits maintenance of multiple synchronized copies of a particular public folder. Multiple replicas, in turn, can be used to distribute the workload across multiple servers. This

improves the response time for all users in the organization. Furthermore, multiple replicas provide fault tolerance.

2. Your company has implemented two routing groups because a WAN connection exists that does not support remote procedure calls (RPCs). What needs to be configured to provide all public folders within the organization to all users?

All public folders must be kept locally in all routing groups. The content of each public folder must be replicated to at least one server in each remote routing group to ensure that the content is accessible.

3. You need to create a local replica for a desired public folder, which exists in another routing group, but you don't want to bother the remote administrator. However, RPC communication is impossible. How can you achieve the desired configuration?

To add a public folder replica from another server to the public store on your server, right-click Public Folder Instances under your server's public store, point to All Tasks, and click Add Replica. This will launch the Public Store dialog box, where you can select the desired folder from the associated public folder hierarchy.

4. How does the receiving PFRA determine whether a replication conflict has occurred?

The receiving PRFA checks whether the change number of the local message is included in the predecessor list of the updated message. If it is, the information can be replaced. If the local message change number is not included, a replication conflict will be detected.

5. What does backfill mean?

Backfill is the mechanism used to discover out-of-sync replicas based on message status information, which is included in every replication message. If no changes have to be replicated, status information is exchanged once every day automatically. If a PFRA discovers missing changes, it requests them from any Information Store that maintains a more recent replica.

6. As a public folder contact, you receive a conflict message. Which choices do you have to resolve the public folder replication conflict?

You can accept the local, the updated, or both replicated items.

7. At the same time, two public folder owners have modified the design of a public folder on two different instances, generating a design conflict. How can you resolve the conflict?

Design conflicts do not need to be resolved explicitly because the most recent changes overwrite all others. Public folder contacts and public folder owners are notified because they should check which design was applied.

Chapter 19

Review Questions

1. What are the features of advanced security, and when will you use them?

   Advanced security supports signing and sealing of messages. Signing permits a sender to add a digital signature to a message, which proves the message's origin and authenticity. Sealing is another term for message encryption. Both features can be used individually or simultaneously.

2. What is the KM Server password used for, and when do you need it?

   The KM Server password is used to decrypt the KM Database Master Encryption key to gain access to the KM database. It must be supplied during the KMS startup.

3. What does a KM administrator need to do to enable a user's advanced security?

   The KM administrator has to begin the process of enabling advanced security. During this process, a 12-character security token will be generated, which must be provided to the user. It is possible to enroll multiple users concurrently.

4. What does the user need to accomplish to enable advanced security?

   The user needs to receive the security token from the KM administrator. In the Options dialog box of Outlook 2000, using the Security tab, the user can request a digital ID from the Exchange 2000 server. During this process, the user needs to enter the security token and specify a security password for the digital ID. A request message will be sent to the KM Server, which will forward the request to Certificate Services to obtain approved X.509 version 3 certificates. Finally, a response from the KM Server will be received, which can be opened as usual. At this point, the user will be asked for the security password as recently defined. The user must enter the password to complete the process of enabling advanced security.

5. When does Outlook encrypt a message?

   After the user sends the message.

6. How does Outlook sign messages?

   The original message is hashed, and the user's private signing key is retrieved from the security store. The hash is then encrypted using the private signing key. The encrypted hash will be added to the message as well as the user's signing certificate, which contains the public signing key. The client then sends the message.

7. Which steps must be accomplished to send a sealed message?

First, the client contacts Active Directory to obtain each recipient's sealing certificate, which contains the public sealing key and describes the supported encryption method. Based on this information, the encryption method for the message will be determined. Accordingly, the client generates a bulk encryption key and encrypts the message content. The bulk encryption key will then be encrypted using each recipient's public sealing key, creating a bulk encryption lockbox for each recipient. The lockbox will be attached to the encrypted message. The sender's sealing certificate will also be added to the message before it is sent.

8. How can you implement central advanced security management in an organization with two administrative groups?

Install the KM Server in one administrative group. After that, use the Encryption Configuration object of the second administrative group to specify the KM Server location.

9. Walter Woodpecker has forgotten the security password for his digital ID. What do you have to accomplish to allow Walter to sign and seal messages again?

You need to recover the security keys for this user. The KM Server will generate a new 12-character security token, which must be provided to the user. The user will complete the recovery by repeating the steps of enabling advanced security. A new digital ID will be created for the user.

Chapter 20

Review Questions

1. A Windows 2000 Server administrator informs you that several user accounts were deleted accidentally from the domain. New accounts have been created, but the users cannot connect to their former mailboxes. How can you provide these users with their messages most quickly?

The users' mailboxes were deleted, but deleted mailboxes are retained for 30 days by default. You can reconnect mailboxes to the new user accounts without any difficulty using Exchange System Manager. Right-click on the mailbox, select Reconnect to specify the new user account, and the user will be able to work with the reconnected mailbox immediately.

2. You are the administrator of a complex Exchange 2000 Server organization with multiple administrative and routing groups. You plan to use server monitoring extensively to ensure prompt system maintenance according to service-level agreements. For this purpose, you are configuring system monitors and e-mail notifications. You need to specify a monitoring server. Where should the monitoring server be located?

System monitoring relies on LSI, which is most efficiently propagated between the servers in the local routing group. Consequently, you should specify monitoring servers that reside in the same routing group as the monitored server.

3. A user informs you that messages must have been lost because they were apparently not delivered to specified recipients. How can you verify that all messages reached their intended addressees?

   Message tracking can be used to determine where a message was delivered. You can search for messages by the originator's e-mail address and examine the path the messages have taken from server to server in your organization. The Message Tracking Center reads tracking information from the network shares of each server that has been involved in a particular message transfer. Message tracking must be enabled to write these log files.

4. What Exchange 2000 Server databases can be included in online backups?

   The databases of mailbox and public stores that belong to the Information Store, as well as the databases of the KMS and SRS can be backed up online using an Exchange 2000 Server–enabled backup program.

5. Which files types does ESE utilize in addition to the actual database files?

   Transaction logs, previous logs, reserved logs, checkpoint files, patch files, and a temporary database file.

6. The following event was written to your application event log: "The database 'First Storage Group\Mailbox Store (BLUESKY-SRV1)' has 821 megabytes of free space after online defragmentation has terminated." How can you recover the disk space unnecessarily consumed by the database?

   You can use ESEUTIL.EXE with the /d switch to reduce the physical size of the database files. This operation is known as offline database compaction.

7. What is the difference between an incremental and a differential backup?

   The incremental backup purges transaction log files, setting the context for the next backup. The differential backup does not discard any transactions. It does not change the context for any following incremental or differential backup.

8. You have restored a full and several incremental database backups, but you have forgotten to select the Last Backup Set check box during the last restore operation. How can you complete the database restoration?

   You can restore the last backup one more time with the Last Backup Set check box selected, or you can run hard recovery manually using ESEUTIL.EXE with the /CC switch from the temporary folder of the transaction log files where RESTORE.ENV file exists.

9. What is the purpose of the Setup /DisasterRecovery switch?

   Setup /DisasterRecovery will reconfigure the local server, including program files, registry settings, and database paths based on the

configuration information still available in Active Directory. The old server object must still exist in the Exchange 2000 Server configuration. When running Setup /DisasterRecovery, make sure all the components that were previously installed on the server are marked for disaster recovery on the Component Selection wizard screen. You can restore databases online after the disaster recovery.

10. Why do you have to install recovery servers in different Active Directory forests than the production systems?

Mailbox GUIDs associate user accounts with their mailboxes. These identifiers must be unique within the Active Directory forest. Therefore, you cannot have two copies of the same database on different servers in the same organization. Exchange 2000 Server does not allow you to reconnect a mailbox from a restored database to the same or another user as long as the mailbox from the production database is connected to a user account. To bypass this issue, recovery servers must be installed in different Active Directory forests.

Chapter 21

Review Questions

1. What are the two general types of Outlook forms, and what are their purposes?

It is possible to design send forms or post forms. Send forms are used to send formatted information to other users. The forms definition may be included in the message. Post forms, on the other hand, allow you to share information between users through public folders.

2. Which three types of forms libraries can exist on an Exchange 2000 server?

Organization forms library, folder forms library, and personal forms library.

3. You are developing a new send form and want to test your solution. Where would you install the form?

In the Personal Forms Library.

4. You are planning to implement a project management solution for your team of Exchange administrators. You want to use a custom form to manage project tasks. How would you begin the design of your custom form?

It would be advantageous to create a public folder for tasks items. After that, the standard Outlook task form should be displayed and modified using the Outlook Forms Designer. To load an Outlook form into the designer, you need to launch the form, open the Tools menu, point to Forms, and select the Design This Form command. This will switch the form into design mode, where you can make modifications and add custom functionality. The form also can be published in design mode.

Chapter 22

Review Questions

1. Why is Exchange 2000 Server OWA incompatible with OWA of earlier versions of Exchange Server?

   The new approach is based on ISAPI instead of ASPs, which the former version utilized. (The ASPs were processed by another ISAPI extension called ASP.DLL using a script interpreter.) Because OWA of Exchange 2000 Server does not rely on ASPs, both OWA versions are incompatible. The direct utilization of ISAPI gives better performance and scalability.

2. During the installation of Exchange 2000 Server, four OWA-related virtual directories are created. What are their names and purposes?

   The four virtual directories are called Exadmin, Exchange, Exchweb, and Public. Exadmin allows Exchange System Manager to work with public folder properties. Exchange provides connection to mailboxes. Public can be used to access MAPI-based public folders. Exchweb points to graphics and other files that reside in \Program Files\Exchsrvr\Exchweb.

3. Why is it advantageous to use Internet Explorer 5.0 in conjunction with OWA?

   Internet Explorer 5.0 supports advanced features, such as DHTML and XML, shortcut menus, and drag-and-drop operations between folders. Internet Explorer 5.0 can render mailbox and public folder data locally instead of sending requests to the server. This minimizes network communication and increases the scalability of the system.

4. You have deployed three front end servers and plan to implement a software solution for load balancing. Which load-balancing solution does Microsoft recommend?

   It is recommended to group front end systems using Microsoft Network Load Balancing.

5. Your organization uses OWA to provide access to Exchange 2000 Server over the Internet. Consequently, FE/BE systems have been installed, and SSL was enforced on the front end systems to enforce data security over Internet connections. Why should you refrain from implementing a DNS-based load-balancing solution?

   Round-robin DNS should not be used for load balancing across SSL-enabled hosts. The SSL bulk encryption key is maintained per host and would be lost if the client is redirected to another host by DNS. The client would have to establish a new session to generate a new bulk encryption key.

6. You are working under the mailbox-enabled Administrator account. Your mailbox resides on BLUESKY-SRV1. What URL would you have to use to open the Calendar folder of your mailbox in Internet Explorer 5.0 directly?

http://bluesky-srv1/Exchange/Administrator/Calendar/?Cmd=contents

Chapter 23

Review Questions

1. Which Exchange 2000 Server component allows applications access to mailbox and public folder resources based on ADO?

The Exchange OLE DB provider (ExOLEDB) supports record-level access to messaging information based on OLE DB and ADO 2.5 interfaces.

2. What is the advantage of the ExIFS driver?

ExIFS allows you to access message items using functions from Win32 file APIs. This allows you to access and share mailbox and public folders in much the same way as ordinary directories on the server's file system. Most important, direct file access through ExIFS allows you to store Web pages and other application elements directly in mailbox or public folders.

3. You plan to implement a simple Web-based enterprise solution to demonstrate the benefits of Exchange 2000 Server. How can you quickly implement Web-based folder views and custom forms into a demo public folder?

You should install the Web Storage System Forms SDK on your Exchange 2000 server and the FrontPage Extensions for Web Storage System Forms. Using FrontPage 2000, it is easy to design Web-based folder views and custom forms and register them with the desired public folder.

4. What is the purpose of the Web Storage System Forms Registry?

Web Storage System forms must be registered in registration items. Otherwise, the rendering engine cannot determine the location of the custom form to render the data. Various properties can be set for registration items to control how Web pages are used.

5. You have implemented a Wcb-based travel expense report application. It is required to route new expense reports to the finance department for approval. Which feature of the Web Storage System would you use to implement the required functionality?

You can implement a Web Storage System event sink to intercept the asynchronous OnSave event, which is triggered when new items or item changes are committed. To register your event sink, you can use REGEVENT.VBS.

Chapter 24

Review Questions

1. When would you prefer to use CDOEX instead of ADO 2.5 in your custom applications?

   CDO is the ideal choice to implement workflow and other collaborative applications. It allows you to perform actions such as sending messages, managing contacts, scheduling appointments, handling meeting requests, creating folders, and so on. CDO simplifies working with raw data in item streams. Streams are created automatically based on Internet standard formats. Unlike ADO, CDO recreates streams when item properties are changed.

2. Which basic CDO CoClass can you use to send e-mail messages?

   CDO.Message

3. You are developing a CDO-based calendaring application. Which file URL do you need to use to write appointments to a user's Calendar folder?

   You need to specify a URL of file://./BackOfficeStorage/<domain name/ MBX/<user alias>/calendar/. The user alias corresponds to the left half of the sender's SMTP address, which is not necessarily the user's Windows 2000 account name.

4. How can you quickly obtain contact information for your Windows 2000 account from Active Directory in vCard format?

   You have to create a CDO.Person object, bind it to your account in Active Directory, and then use the GetVCardStream method to write the desired information to a specified file vCard-compliant MIME format.

5. What level of permissions is required to successfully work with CDO for Exchange Management?

   You need to have Exchange Administrator permissions if you want to manage an organization or administrative group. CDOEXM applications require the same level of permissions as Exchange System Manager.

6. You want to develop a workflow solution for your organization. Which tool should you use to implement process definition and business logic?

   Workflow Designer for Exchange 2000 Server.

7. What restrictions apply to the Can Register Workflow role?

   The workflow logic must be written in VBScript, but calls to CreateObject are prohibited. Restricted VBScript code cannot instantiate COM classes. The code runs in the context of a special account called EUSER_EXSTOREEVENT with guest privileges by default. The workflow system account requires the Windows 2000 Act As Part Of The Operating System permission.

Chapter 25

Review Questions

1. You have successfully deployed Instant Messaging in your organization. You are using MSN Messenger to send and receive instant messages and to propagate your presence information. Using the Status button in MSN Messenger, you change your status to Away From Computer. How does your IM home server propagate this change to other users?

   Your IM home server maintains a subscriber list for your account to send notifications to registered subscribers if the status of your account changes. As soon as your state changes to Away From Computer, the server actively sends a status change notification to each subscriber, which ensures that contact lists are always up to date. IM users that have subscribed your account as a contact will see the new status right away.

2. How can you block the propagation of presence information?

   The MSN Messenger client allows you to block the propagation of presence information via the Privacy command, which is available on the Tools menu.

3. How do IM clients outside a protected network communicate with internal clients that are inside the firewall?

   IM clients outside a protected network can only connect to IM routers, which in turn communicate with IM home servers inside the protected network on behalf of the external clients.

4. You plan to simplify the IM domain naming scheme by matching the IM domain name to the SMTP domain name of your organization (such as bluesky-inc-10.com). How can you achieve the desired configuration?

   You have the option to add an SRV resource record for your IM router to DNS and map the common domain name (such as bluesky-inc-10.com) to the Instant Messaging service (_rvp) and the TCP port on which the service is provided.

5. You plan to install Exchange 2000 Chat Service on a computer that is not running Exchange 2000 Server. What level of permissions is required in the Exchange 2000 organization to successfully complete the installation?

   The permissions of an Exchange Administrator are required in the Administrative Group to which you want to add the Chat Service.

6. What are the minimum configuration prerequisites to successfully deploy Exchange 2000 Conferencing Server?

   Exchange 2000 Conferencing Server requires Windows 2000 Server and IIS 5.0. Exchange 2000 Server is not required on the local computer, but Active Directory and Exchange 2000 Server must have been deployed in

the Windows 2000 domain. In addition, the network must be IP multicast-enabled and must provide MADCAP services for videoconferencing. Windows 2000 Certificate Services is required to support private conferences.

Chapter 26

Review Questions

1. What are the three most important components of the MS Mail Connector?

   The MS Mail Connector Interchange, the Connector PO, and one or many MS Mail Connector (PC) MTAs.

2. What is the function of the Connector PO?

   The Connector PO represents the MS Mail interface of Exchange 2000 Server. It is the intermediate repository for MS Mail messages between an Exchange 2000 server and MS Mail postoffices.

3. You have configured an MS Mail Connector between one MS Mail postoffice and an Exchange 2000 server. Exchange users can send messages, but users on the MS Mail postoffice cannot. How can you correct this problem?

   This is an MS Mail-related problem. You need to use the MS Mail Administrator program to check that the Connector PO has been registered as an external postoffice.

4. What are the three stages of a complete Dirsync cycle?

   The three stages are T1, T2, and T3. At T1, requestors generate update messages, which are addressed to the Dirsync server. At T2 time, the Dirsync server incorporates address updates into the master address list. Also, update messages for requestor postoffices will be generated and sent back to the requestors. At T3, received address changes are committed to the postoffice address lists.

5. You have configured an Exchange 2000 server as a DXA server. MS Mail requestor postoffices are sending their address changes to the Exchange 2000 server through the MS Mail Connector. When will address list changes appear in the specified import container?

   Running as a Windows 2000 service, the DXA is permanently active. It will commit address updates to Active Directory immediately as soon as they are received. MS Mail address information is maintained in recipient objects that are placed in an OU that was specified as the import container for the remote Dirsync requestor.

6. Which configuration can you use to map MS Mail template information to Exchange mailbox attributes?

   MS Mail template labels can be mapped to mailbox attributes using the Directory Synchronization configuration object in Exchange System

Manager. A mapping can be defined for both incoming and outgoing information through the Incoming Templates and Outgoing Templates tabs.

7. Why must you configure a distribution group before configuring the Schedule+ Free/Busy Connector?

A distribution group is required to contain the Adminsch accounts of the MS Mail postoffices. The Schedule+ Free/Busy Connector uses this distribution group to address the free/busy update messages.

Chapter 27

Review Questions

1. How many direct Lotus cc:Mail post offices does the Connector for Lotus cc:Mail support?

The Connector for Lotus cc:Mail can only connect to one Lotus cc:Mail post office directly.

2. What are the main components of the Connector for Lotus cc:Mail?

The Information Store maintains the connector message queues (MTS-OUT and MTS-IN). The actual Connector for Lotus cc:Mail service performs the transfer and conversion of messages. The Connector Store acts as the intermediate repository for scratch files. The Lotus cc:Mail programs Import and Export are used to access a Lotus cc:Mail post office. Address and details templates allow specifying Lotus cc:Mail recipients in Microsoft Outlook. The proxy address generator CCMPROXY.DLL allows the Recipient Update service to generate proxy CCMAIL addresses for all recipients in the organization.

3. You need to adjust the proxy CCMAIL address format. You are required to assign e-mail aliases in the form of first name immediately followed by first character of the last name. Where and how can you adjust the proxy address format?

Using Exchange System Manager, you need to customize the proxy address format by means of a recipient policy. Recipient policy objects can be found in the Recipients container, under Recipient Policies. Click on the E-Mail Addresses tab and select the CCMAIL check box. Double-click the Address entry to customize the proxy address generation. Specify the following format: %g%1s at <Organization Name>.

4. Which program is used to write messages into the Lotus cc:Mail post office?

IMPORT.EXE

5. Which program is used to poll the Lotus cc:Mail post office for address information?

EXPORT.EXE

Chapter 28

Review Questions

1. What do you have to configure in Lotus Domino/Notes to support the Connector for Lotus Notes?

   A Connector ID has to be created, which should not be included in directory synchronization. This ID requires Access permissions to the server's router mailbox, called MAIL.BOX, as well as the Connector-specific databases, by default EXCHANGE.BOX and EXCHANGE.BAD. Both can be created using Lotus Notes Administrator. If they are missing, the Connector for Lotus Notes creates them automatically. For directory synchronization, Access permissions for source and target name and address books are required, and it is advisable to add the Connector ID to the list of administrators in the server's Server document if you want the Connector to compact its databases during maintenance cycles. Do not forget to register your Exchange 2000 Server organization in a foreign domain document. To support Doclink conversion, general Reader access to Notes databases is required.

2. Which Connector component retrieves messages from the MTS-OUT queue?

   The MEXOUT process.

3. Which processes perform directory synchronization with Lotus Domino/ Notes, and how do they accomplish their tasks?

   DXANOTES uses the Notes client API to read and write address information in Lotus Domino/Notes and DXAMEX uses ADSI to work with Active Directory. DXANOTES and DXAMEX in turn communicate with each other by means of temporary MIF files called DXANOTES.TXT and DXAMEX.TXT.

4. In which tab can you change the name of the Domino server that the Connector for Lotus Notes contacts for message transfer?

   In the General tab.

Chapter 29

Review Questions

1. What needs to be prepared in the GroupWise domain to support the Connector for Lotus Novell GroupWise?

   You need to install and configure Novell GroupWise Patch 2 for API NLM on a NetWare server and enable it for distribution list expansion. You also need to create a gateway object for it in the GroupWise domain. The Exchange 2000 Server organization must be registered in the form of an external foreign domain, which is connected to GroupWise via API Gateway. The Connector for Novell GroupWise requires a NetWare

account with membership in the NTGATEWAY group to access the API Gateway for message transfer and directory synchronization.

2. Which Connector component retrieves messages from the API Gateway?

The Microsoft Exchange Router for Novell GroupWise, which is implemented in a separate Windows 2000 service running on the Exchange 2000 server.

3. You have implemented the Connector for Novell GroupWise. Message transfer and directory synchronization work properly; however, an Exchange user calls you and complains that all messages sent to GroupWise users appear in plain text. How can you solve this problem?

This happens by design. The API Gateway only supports message bodies in plain text. Consequently, RTF information cannot be preserved in e-mail messages between Exchange and GroupWise users.

4. Based on the Connector for Novell GroupWise, you have configured directory synchronization between Exchange 2000 Server and GroupWise. GroupWise recipients appear in Active Directory, but you want to change the way the GroupWise users appear in the server-based address lists. Where can you find the mapping rule files that you need to edit to achieve the desired results?

The mapping rule file for synchronization from GroupWise to Active Directory is MAPGWISE.TBL, which you can find in the connector store in the \Dxagwise subdirectory.

5. How does DXAGWISE retrieve GroupWise directory information?

DXAGWISE generates an administrator message to request a list of all users in the GroupWise directory. It places this message in the form of an .api file in the \Gwrouter\Togwise directory of the connector store, where the Router for Novell GroupWise picks it up and transfers it into the API Gateway's API_IN directory. GroupWise processes the request and returns a list with all GroupWise users through the API_OUT directory of the API Gateway, which the Router for Novell GroupWise transfers into the \Gwrouter\Dirsync directory.

Glossary

A

access control The process of appropriately authorizing, controlling, and auditing access to a particular object or system resource for a user, group, process, or system that can be identified by a security identifier (SID).

access control entry (ACE) An entry in an access control list (ACL) that associates a security identifier (SID) with a set of permissions to grant or deny access or specify auditing permissions to a particular object or system resource for a user, group, process, or system.

access control list (ACL) A property of every directory object that contains a list of access control entries (ACEs) to grant or deny permission to specific users and groups to access an object or system resource. Only users with Change Permission rights or the owner of an object are allowed to change the entries in an ACL. *See also* discretionary access control list (DACL) and system access control list (SACL).

account An administrative entity associated with a security identifier (SID) that gives identifies a user, group, computer, or process and can be referenced in access to a system access control list (SACL).

ACE *See* access control entry (ACE).

ACL *See* access control list (ACL).

action table A user-defined table of actions used by the Collaboration Data Objects (CDO) workflow engine to evaluate and execute transitions for items in a workflow process. An action table is a map of possible document state transitions.

Active Directory Connector (ADC) A synchronization agent in Microsoft Windows 2000 Server and Microsoft Exchange 2000 Server that keeps information between Active Directory directory service and the directory service of earlier versions of Microsoft Exchange Server consistent. The ADC can synchronize new data and updates in both directory services automatically.

Active Directory directory service The directory service of domain controllers running Microsoft Windows 2000 Server. Active Directory stores information about objects and resources in a hierarchical tree structure and provides a single point of administration for all network resources. Through a single logon process, users can gain access to permitted resources anywhere on the network.

Active Directory forest A distributed database that is made up of many partial databases that can be spread across many domain controllers. Within a single forest, schema, class, and attribute definitions as well as configuration, replication topology, and related metadata are replicated to every domain controller. The Windows 2000 Server domains that belong to the same forest define further directory partitions, which are replicated only to domain controllers in the local domain. *See also* directory partition.

Active Directory Migration Tool (ADMT) A tool to facilitate migration to Active Directory. The ADMT is a task-based wizard used to migrate users and set file permissions. It provides reporting features to assess the impact of the migration, both before and after the move operations. *See also* Active Directory directory service.

Active Directory Schema A partition in an Active Directory forest that contains definitions for the directory schema, its classes, attributes, and syntaxes. The schema is always replicated to every domain controller in the forest. It defines the individual object types that can be stored in the forest. The schema also enforces the rules that govern both the structure and the content of the directory. *See also* Active Directory forest, directory partition.

Active Directory Service Interface (ADSI) A set of application programming interfaces (APIs) that enables client applications to communicate with any directory service for which an ADSI provider is available, such as Active Directory. ADSI is supported on Microsoft Windows 2000, Windows NT, Windows 98, and Windows 95.

Active Directory Users and Computers A Microsoft Management Console (MMC) snap-in that enables you to manage Microsoft Windows 2000 user and computer accounts, security and distribution groups, and other domain resources.

Active Messaging The predecessor of Collaboration Data Objects (CDO) that came with Microsoft Exchange Server 5.0 to provide a library of Component Object Model (COM) objects to interact with the underlying messaging interfaces based on the Messaging Application Programming Interface (MAPI). *See also* Collaboration Data Objects (CDO) and Messaging Application Programming Interface (MAPI).

Active Server Page (ASP) A script-based application that is executed on an Internet Information Services (IIS) or other ASP-capable Web system. An ASP enables you to run scripts and ActiveX components on the server to create dynamic content in Hypertext Markup Language (HTML) for powerful Web-based applications.

active/active A cluster configuration in which an application is concurrently executed on all nodes of the cluster.

active/passive A cluster configuration in which an application is executed only on one node of the cluster at a time.

ActiveX Control A software module based on ActiveX technology that can be implemented as a component in a client/server or Web-based business application. ActiveX controls are often referred to as reusable software components.

ActiveX Data Objects (ADO) A high-level interface to access structured and unstructured data in data sources of any kind, such as structured database management systems (DBMS) or unstructured files systems. ADO provides a single interface for multitier client/server and Web-based business application development.

ADC *See* Active Directory Connector (ADC).

address book Displays recipient information from a directory, such as Active Directory. Users can work with server-based address books maintained centrally or with personal address books. Address books contain one or many address lists. *See also* address list.

address list A logical collection of recipient objects (that is, mailbox-enabled accounts, distribution groups, mail-enabled contacts, and public folders) in the address book, organized by recipient attributes. An example of an address list is the Global Address List (GAL), where all recipient objects of an organization are displayed.

address space A definition of an address mask associated with a cost factor assigned to a messaging connector to identify recipients for which the connector is responsible. The routing engine of Microsoft Exchange 2000 Server relies on address spaces to select the connectors that are candidates for routing a particular message.

address template A set of instructions that determine the controls displayed in address dialog boxes. You can customize the address templates on a server to change the user interface in the client's address book. Address templates are language specific.

ADE *See* Automatic Directory Exchange (ADE).

Administration Delegation Wizard An administrative tool to facilitate the delegation of control for Active Directory objects, such as computers and organizational units (OUs), to a user or group. The Administration Delegation Wizard is often called the Delegation Of Control Wizard.

administrative group A collection of Microsoft Exchange 2000 servers and configuration objects that are grouped together for common administration and system management. An administrative group can contain recipient and system policies, routing groups, public folder hierarchies, servers, virtual server resources, and other administrative elements.

ADMINSCH mailbox A special mailbox in a Microsoft Mail for PC Networks (MS Mail) postoffice used to propagate free/busy information across the messaging environment. Active Microsoft Schedule+ distribution processes (SCHDIST.EXE) receive free/busy updates through messages sent to the ADMINSCH mailbox.

ADMINSCH user agent A component of the Schedule+ Free/Busy Connector that allows Microsoft Exchange 2000 Server to participate in the distribution of free/busy information with Microsoft Mail (MS Mail). The ADMINSCH user agent in Exchange 2000 Server corresponds to an ADMINSCH mailbox in MS Mail.

ADO *See* ActiveX Data Objects (ADO).

ADSI *See* Active Directory Service Interface (ADSI).

ADSI Edit A Microsoft Management Console (MMC) snap-in to directly access and edit directory information based on Active Directory Service Interface (ADSI).

ADSI provider A system component that provides Active Directory Service Interface (ADSI) client applications access to a directory system by providing an ADSI implementation.

Advanced Queuing Engine A central module of the Simple Mail Transfer Protocol (SMTP) service transport in Microsoft Exchange 2000 Server. Every message is routed through this engine for categorization, message routing, and custom processing though event sinks. The Advanced Queuing Engine acts as an information controller that retrieves messages directly from the Information Store service.

alternate hierarchy An additional public folder hierarchy created in Microsoft Exchange 2000 Server to create and organize public folder resources in a separate tree from the default hierarchy. Alternate hierarchies are only available to Internet-based clients and applications that use the Microsoft Web Storage System. Messaging Application Programming Interface (MAPI)-based clients, such as Microsoft Outlook 2000, are unable to display alternate hierarchies. *See also* MAPI-based hierarchy, public folder hierarchy.

Ambiguous Name Resolution (ANR) The process of resolving a string to a full recipient object from an address book based on a set of attributes defined for ANR searches.

American Standard Code for Information Interchange (ASCII) A coding scheme that was developed in 1968 to standardize data transmission between disparate computer systems. ASCII assigns numeric values of seven bits to up to 128 letters, numbers, and special characters.

ANR *See* Ambiguous Name Resolution (ANR).

API *See* application programming interface (API).

API Gateway An optional Novell GroupWise component that serves as a universal gateway to non-GroupWise systems. The Connector for Novell GroupWise uses the API Gateway for message transfer and directory synchronization between Microsoft Exchange 2000 Server and GroupWise.

AppleTalk A suite of protocols that allow Apple Macintosh computers to communicate over a network infrastructure. AppleTalk enables the systems on a network to interact and route data for file sharing, printer access, and other communication. Microsoft Windows 2000 Server can participate in an AppleTalk network through its Services for Macintosh.

application event log A repository maintained by the Windows 2000 Event Log service to write events provided by application-based processes and services running on the computer to a local log file. Events are written to the application event log in the order in which they are received. You can use the Event Viewer to display the history of events.

Application Note WA0725 A document provided by Microsoft Product Support Services (PSS) that outlines the Directory Synchronization Protocol utilized in Microsoft Mail for PC Networks. WA0725 contains low-level utilities to reset directory synchronization processes.

application programming interface (API) A set of methods, properties, and events provided to developers to enable them to use other software components or services from the operating system. An API typically defines how methods should be called, properties accessed, and results obtained.

application sharing A means to share applications, including presentation graphics, word processing, and spreadsheet software, in a real-time data conference with meeting participants. Microsoft NetMeeting supports application sharing.

ASCII *See* American Standard Code for Information Interchange (ASCII).

ASP *See* Active Server Page (ASP).

asynchronous communication A form of electronic communication that allows communication partners to exchange information independently of timing mechanisms.

asynchronous event An event in the transport or Web Storage System of Microsoft Exchange 2000 Server that is fired after a condition has occurred. Asynchronous events do not block the event source and cannot gain exclusive control over the item that triggered the event.

attribute An informational element of an object that describes an object characteristic, such as the display name of a recipient object in Active Directory. Attributes consist of a type identifier and one or more values. For each object class, the directory schema defines mandatory and optional attributes.

attribute mapping file A file containing a set of attributes from one directory that are mapped to a set of attributes in another directory for the purposes of directory synchronization.

audio and video conferencing A technology that enables computer systems to interoperate and exchange audio and video information over a network.

authentication The validation of user credentials during a logon processes. Based on the logon information, the user is associated with an account that allows Microsoft Windows 2000 Server to determine access permissions for the user. When a user logs on to an Active Directory account, a domain controller is used to perform the authentication.

author mode A mode of the Microsoft Management Console (MMC) where all rights are granted to the user that opened the console. Author mode allows you to create custom MMC consoles for delegation of administration. *See also* user mode.

authoritative restore A specific restore operation on a Microsoft Windows 2000 domain controller in which the objects in the restored directory are treated as most recent (authoritative). Through directory replication, all existing replicas of the directory objects will be replaced through the restored information. Authoritative restore is applicable only to replicated system state data such as Active Directory.

Automatic Directory Exchange (ADE) A mechanism to propagate address information across a Lotus cc:Mail network that contains multiple post offices.

Automatic Profile Generator A program (NEWPROF.EXE) that, in conjunction with a profile descriptor file (.prf), automatically creates Messaging Application Programming Interface (MAPI)-based profiles without user intervention.

automatic property promotion A mechanism in Microsoft Exchange 2000 Server where an associated stream content of an item with a particular file extension is automatically parsed for properties, which are promoted to the Messaging Application Programming Interface (MAPI)-based information store.

B

backfill The process of acquiring public folder replication data when a new replica is added to a server, when replication messages are lost, or when a server is restored from backup. When a server determines that it does not contain a complete replica of a public folder, it generates a backfill request to other servers, which indicates the missing information.

backup domain controller (BDC) A computer running Microsoft Windows NT Server that receives a read-only copy of a Windows NT Server domain's directory database to authenticate users. This read-only copy is synchronized periodically and automatically with the master copy that is kept on the primary domain controller. *See also* primary domain controller (PDC).

bandwidth A term used to describe the maximum speed throughput of communication in a network expressed in bits per second (bps). A greater bandwidth indicates greater capacity for bulk data-transfer capabilities between computers in a network.

Banyan Vines An acronym for Banyan Virtual Networking System, which addresses a collection of networking products from Banyan Systems.

Basic (Clear Text) Authentication An authentication method that encodes user name and password in clear text for transmission to an authenticating server system. Because the user credentials are kept in clear text that is nonencrypted, a special decoding utility is not required to access security-related information. Basic (Clear Text) Authentication is less secure then challenge/response or Kerberos authentication. *See also* challenge/response authentication, Kerberos authentication.

Basic Encoding Rules (BER) A set of rules used to encode data into a stream of bits for external storage or transmission. The Lightweight Directory Access Protocol (LDAP) uses a BER encoding method for data transmission over TCP/IP. *See also* Lightweight Directory Access Protocol (LDAP).

BBS *See* bulletin board system (BBS).

BDC *See* backup domain controller (BDC).

BER *See* Basic Encoding Rules (BER).

binary large object (BLOB) A data column in a database table containing binary data such as graphics, sound, or compiled code. Link state information is transferred as a BLOB between routing groups, for instance over X.400.

Bindery A directory database in Novell NetWare 2.*x* and 3.*x* that contains organizational and security information about users and groups. Later versions of Novell NetWare support Bindery in a special mode called Bindery emulation.

binding order The order in which installed network components are linked together to allow the components to communicate with each other. Bindings can be enabled and disabled based on the network components required for communication.

bottleneck A condition that causes an entire system to perform poorly; the resource that limits the performance of a system.

bridgehead server An e-mail system, such as an Exchange 2000 server, that runs connector software and acts as the endpoint of a connection between two routing groups or a connection to a foreign messaging system. In Microsoft Exchange 2000 Server, bridgeheads are responsible for message routing across the routing group boundary.

broadcast A data transmission sent simultaneously to all computers in a network. In practice, broadcasts are only received on local networks, because routers are configured not to forward them. *See also* IP multicast.

brute-force attack A method of obtaining account passwords by trying all possible password combinations until the correct password is disclosed. A specific form of a brute-force attack is a dictionary attack, in which known words in the dictionary and common password combinations are tried.

buddy list Enables Internet users to see presence information for colleagues and friends that use the same Internet service provider (ISP). The buddy list indicates whether friends are online, out of the office, or busy.

bulk encryption key A security string that is used for both encryption and decryption of information. Advanced Security features of Microsoft Exchange 2000 Server use a bulk encryption key

in conjunction with public sealing keys to encrypt messages. *See also* encryption.

bulk encryption lockbox A bulk encryption key that is encrypted with a recipient's public sealing key. The bulk encryption lockbox is sent with the message. Only the correct recipient can decrypt the lockbox using his or her private sealing key to retrieve the bulk encryption key, which is required to decrypt the e-mail message. The lockbox ensures that the bulk encryption key is sent to the recipient in a secure way.

bulletin board system (BBS) A computer system for subscribers to share information and collaborate on. It was a popular forum for chat and online games, but the Internet has increasingly superseded the BBS.

business application A computer program or a group of Active Server Pages (ASP) that perform business-related tasks and incorporate business-specific regulations, policies, and procedures.

C

CA *See* certificate authority (CA)

Calendar Connector A connector component in Microsoft Exchange Server 5.5 that allows Exchange users and Lotus Notes or Novell GroupWise users to query each other's calendars for free/busy information.

categorizer A component that performs directory lookups to check message transfer limits and restrictions in Active Directory. It also handles the expansion of distribution groups for message routing.

CDO *See* Collaboration Data Objects (CDO).

CDO Calendaring A set of functions that allows developers to use Collaboration Data Objects (CDO) to create business applications for creating appointments and accepting and declining meeting requests.

CDO for Exchange 2000 Server (CDOEX) A development technology available with Microsoft Exchange 2000 Server that simplifies writing programs that work with messages, calendars, and contacts. CDOEX is based on the features of the Microsoft Web Storage System and can only be used directly on an Exchange 2000 server.

CDO for Exchange Management (CDOEXM) A development technology available with Microsoft Exchange 2000 Server that allows developers to use Collaboration Data Objects (CDO) instead of Active Directory Service Interface (ADSI) to implement management functionality in business applications. Using CDOEXM, it is possible to create mailbox-enabled user accounts, assign pubic folder hierarchies with information stores, and mount or dismount mailbox and public stores.

CDO for Windows 2000 Server (CDOSYS) A set of programmable objects that enable developers to programmatically access Simple Mail Transfer Protocol (SMTP) and Network News Transfer Protocol (NNTP) stacks on a computer running Microsoft Windows 2000 Server.

CDO for Workflow (CDOWF) A set of programmable objects that simplify the implementation of workflow processes, such as document tracking and approval, into Microsoft Exchange 2000 Server.

CDOEX *See* CDO for Exchange 2000 Server (CDOEX).

CDOEXM *See* CDO for Exchange Management (CDOEXM).

CDOSYS *See* CDO for Windows 2000 Server (CDOSYS).

CDOWF *See* CDO for Workflow (CDOWF).

centralized administration An administration model that enforces centralized control of system management with a hierarchical delegation of control.

certificate authority (CA) An entity or organization that issues, manages, and revokes digital certificates. CAs can be either commercial or organizational and can form the basis for secure communication and authentication.

certificate revocation list (CRL) A document that contains a list of certificates that have been revoked by a certificate authority (CA).

Certificate Service A component of Microsoft Windows 2000 Server, which can act as a certificate authority (CA) in a public-key infrastructure (PKI) to issue and manage X.509 certificates. *See also* X.509 certificate.

certificate trust list (CTL) A set of certificates determined to be trustworthy by an organization. A CTL allows the organization to specify the purpose and validity period of certificates issued by external certificate authorities (CAs).

chat A technology that allows users to take part in online discussions using an Internet Relay Chat (IRC) or Internet Relay Chat Extension (IRCX)-based client. Users can communicate with each other by typing their messages via the keyboard. *See also* Internet Relay Chat (IRC), Internet Relay Chat Extension (IRCX).

chat bans Provide a mechanism to control a chat communication. The creator of a chat channel that acts as the host can exclude (ban) users from a chat channel or restore (unban) a participant.

chat channel Also known as a chat room, a place where chat users meet and enter into private or group conversations on different topics. Microsoft Exchange 2000 Server supports permanent, auditorium-style chat channels that support large audiences and enable users to send questions to a speaker who shares responses with the entire audience. Individual chat users with appropriate privileges can create dynamic channels using an Internet Relay Chat (IRC) or Internet Relay Chat Extension (IRCX) client.

chat community A set of chat users and channels, configured for an instance of a chat service. A chat community is a virtual entity with its own administrative controls.

chat room *See* chat channel.

Checkpoint Manager A cluster service that logs changes to the Registry to the quorum disk for those keys that are registered for checkpointing in a log file maintained by the quorum resource.

child object An object in a hierarchy that is the immediate subordinate of exactly one parent object. A child object can be the parent of other child objects.

Cisco Local Director A system that manages the distribution of network traffic to multiple servers for load balancing and fault tolerance.

client Any computer or program that connects to another computer or program to request services.

Client Access License A special license to allow client computers legal access to server resources. The number of Client Access Licenses purchased from Microsoft determines the maximum number of clients allowed to access a server.

Client for Microsoft Networks A file system driver used to communicate with a server process over the network based on the Server Message Block (SMB) NetBIOS protocol. *See also* Network Basic Input/Output System (NetBIOS), Server Message Block (SMB).

client/server conferencing A data conferencing model in which a server-based multipoint control unit (MCU) assumes the role of central control station. Conference participants can connect to the central server to send and receive data over a single connection, while the server keeps all clients synchronized. *See also* peer-to-peer conferencing.

client/server technology A computer technology by which client applications running on workstations access services on remote servers over a computer network. The client application provides the user interface and the server provides the centralized processing logic for multiple users.

cluster A set of computers that work together to provide services to client applications based on a common virtual server. Clusters enhance the system availability and scalability. *See also* virtual server.

Cluster Administrator An application (CLUADMIN.EXE) that allows an administrator to configure cluster nodes, groups, and resources. *See also* cluster.

cluster-aware application An application or service that can run on a server cluster node, that can be managed as a cluster resource, and that uses the Cluster API to interact with the server cluster environment.

Cluster service The primary executable (CLUSSVC.EXE) of the Windows clustering system that creates a server cluster, controls all aspects of its operation, and manages the cluster resources. The Cluster service is executed on every node in a server cluster.

CoClass An acronym that refers to the globally unique identifier (GUID) and the supported interfaces for a Component Object Model (COM) class. CoClasses, also known as COM Classes, provide public methods, properties, and events to client applications.

Collaboration Data Objects (CDO) A technology designed to simplify the creation of messaging applications based on Component Object Model (COM). CDO version 1.2.1, which comes with Microsoft Exchange Server 5.5 and later, as well as Microsoft Outlook 2000, is a Message Application Programming Interface (MAPI)-based technology. CDO for Microsoft Exchange 2000 Server, on the other hand, is based on the features of the Microsoft Web Storage System. *See also* CDO for Exchange 2000 Server (CDOEX), Web Storage System.

COM *See* Component Object Model (COM).

COM+ The implementation of Component Object Model (COM) in Microsoft Windows 2000 Server. *See* Component Object Model (COM).

COM Class *See* CoClass.

comma-separated value (.csv) import/export file A .csv file that can be used with the Comma Separated Value Directory Exchange (CSVDE) Windows 2000 command-line utility to import or export objects to and from Active Directory. The first row in the .csv file identifies the directory attributes that follow for the objects in subsequent rows. Commas separate the columns in each row. Microsoft Excel CSV can be used to work with .csv files. *See also* Comma Separated Value Directory Exchange (CSVDE).

Comma-Separated Value Directory Exchange (CSVDE) A Microsoft Windows 2000 command-line utility to import or export objects to and from Active Directory in comma-separated value (.csv) file format. *See also* comma-separated value (.csv) import/export file.

Communications Manager A process in a server cluster that manages the communication with all other nodes in the cluster.

Component Object Model (COM) An object-based programming model designed to promote software interoperability. COM allows developers to reuse other software components in their own applications even if these components were written in different programming languages and run on different operating systems. COM is the foundation of ActiveX, Collaboration Data Objects (CDO), and object linking and embedding (OLE) technology.

conference calendar mailbox A special mailbox used by the Conference Management Service to maintain a synchronized meeting definition for conferencing providers and to keep track of new meetings, changes to existing conferences, and cancellations. *See also* conferencing providers.

Conference Management Service The core component of Microsoft Exchange 2000 Conferencing Server, which controls installed conferencing providers, such as the Data Conferencing Provider and Video Conferencing Provider, and manages online meetings.

conferencing providers A component of the Microsoft Exchange 2000 Conferencing Server that supports a particular technology for data or video conferencing. *See also* Conference Management Service.

confidentiality A basic feature of computer security that provides assurance that only authorized users can read or use sensitive information.

Configuration Connection Agreement (ConfigCAs) A special connection agreement supported only by the Active Directory Connector (ADC) of Microsoft Exchange 2000 Server that replicates configuration data from Exchange Server 5.5 sites to administration groups in Active Directory. Directory replication is performed between Exchange Server 5.5 and Site Replication Service (SRS), and then between SRS and Active Directory. *See also* Site Replication Service (SRS).

Configuration Database Manager A process in a server cluster that maintains the cluster configuration database.

configuration naming context Another term for configuration partition. The configuration naming context forms the contiguous subtree of the configuration partition in Active Directory. *See also* naming context.

connection agreement A configuration element within an Active Directory Connector (ADC) that updates information between certain parts of Active Directory and an Exchange Server 5.5 directory. A connection agreement details the direction of directory synchronization and other settings that influence how the directories are synchronized.

connectivity The ability of different computer types to exchange information, such as e-mail messages, with one another.

connectivity controller A component in Microsoft Exchange 2000 Server implemented as a Windows 2000 service that provides information about the internal processes of the Connector for Lotus Notes and Connector for Novell GroupWise.

connector A messaging component that transfers e-mail messages between Microsoft Exchange 2000 servers in different routing groups and to other messaging systems.

Connector for Lotus cc:Mail A connector in Microsoft Exchange 2000 Server that supports the transfer of e-mail messages and the synchronization of address information to and from Lotus cc:Mail.

Connector for Lotus Notes A connector in Microsoft Exchange 2000 Server that supports the transfer of e-mail messages and the synchronization of address information to and from Lotus Notes.

Connector for MS Mail A connector in Microsoft Exchange 2000 Server that supports the transfer of e-mail messages and the synchronization of address information to and from Microsoft Mail for PC Networks.

Connector for Novell GroupWise A connector in Microsoft Exchange 2000 Server that supports the transfer of e-mail messages and the synchro-

nization of address information to and from Novell GroupWise.

Connector ID A specific identifier configured as part of a Person document in a Lotus Domino server to support the Connector for Lotus Notes. This connector uses the Connector ID stored in a user ID file to identify itself as a valid Notes user for message transfer and directory synchronization.

Connector postoffice A special postoffice used by the Connector for MS Mail to provide a native MS Mail interface for the Microsoft Exchange 2000 Server organization to remote MS Mail postoffices for message routing purposes. All Exchange users in an organization appear as MS Mail users on the Connector postoffice, although this postoffice does not contain any mailboxes.

connector store A temporary repository used by various connector components to exchange information. The Connectors for Lotus cc:Mail, Lotus Notes, and Novell GroupWise each rely on a connector store for message transfer and directory synchronization.

console tree The left pane in a Microsoft Management Console (MMC) snap-in that displays items in a hierarchical way. *See also* Microsoft Management Console (MMC).

contact management The maintenance of contact-related information, such as phone numbers, addresses, call histories, and so forth, in a workgroup application for an entire organization or at a personal level.

contact subscription The process of adding a user to the subscriber list of an Instant Messaging (IM) server to receive presence information for the contact in an IM client application, such as Microsoft MSN Messenger. *See also* buddy list.

Control Toolbox A feature of the Microsoft Outlook Forms Designer to add ActiveX and custom controls to an Outlook form. *See also* Outlook Forms Designer.

copy backup A backup that includes all selected files without marking each file as having been backed up. Copy backups are useful if you want to back up files between normal and incremental backups without changing the context for the next scheduled backup. *See also* differential backup, full backup, incremental backup.

CRL *See* certificate revocation list (CRL).

CryptoAPI *See* Cryptographic Application Programming Interface.

Cryptographic Application Programming Interface (CryptoAPI) An application programming interface (API) in Microsoft Windows 2000 that enables applications to encrypt or digitally sign data in a flexible manner while providing protection for private keys. Independent cryptographic service providers (CSPs) perform the actual cryptographic operations. *See also* cryptographic service provider (CSP).

cryptographic service provider (CSP) A software module that contains implementations of cryptographic standards and algorithms to perform cryptography operations such as secret key exchange, digital signing of data, and public key authentication.

cryptography The science of information security that deals with data confidentiality, integrity, authentication, and nonrepudiation. *See also* authentication, confidentiality, integrity, nonrepudiation.

CSVDE *See* Comma-Separated Value Directory Exchange (CSVDE).

CTL *See* certificate trust list (CTL).

custom controls A software component that adheres to the ActiveX programming model to perform tasks not supported by predefined controls.

custom recipient A recipient in a foreign system whose address is in the server-based address book of Microsoft Exchange Server 5.5 and earlier versions. In Microsoft Exchange 2000 Server, mail-enabled contact objects replace custom recipients. *See also* mail-enabled contacts.

D

DACL *See* discretionary access control list (DACL).

DAPI *See* Directory Application Programming Interface (DAPI).

Data Encryption Standard (DES) A specification for encryption of computer data that uses a 56-bit encryption key. DES was originally developed by IBM and adopted by the U.S. government as a standard in 1976.

data source name (DSN) The name assigned to an object linking and embedding (OLE) DB connection. Applications can use DSNs to request a connection to an OLE DB data source. *See also* Exchange OLE DB provider (ExOLEDB).

database A collection of information and objects organized in tables and other structures to facilitate searching, sorting, and recombining data.

database file A file in which a database is stored. Databases in Microsoft Exchange 2000 Server are stored in several files.

database management system (DBMS) A repository for a collection of database files that enables users to perform operations on the data.

datagram An unacknowledged packet of data sent to another computer over a network.

DEC ALL-IN-1 A host system for messaging and collaboration from Digital Equipment Corporation.

decentralized administration An administration model that allows decentralized control of system management according to locations, divisions, business units, or other factors. In a decentralized environment, a number of administrators are responsible for managing the network resources.

default policy object A configuration object in Exchange System Manager that applies e-mail address generation rules to all mailbox- and mail-enabled recipient objects in Active Directory that are not covered by another recipient policy. Recipient policies are used by the Recipient Update Service to generate proxy e-mail addresses for recipient objects. *See also* proxy e-mail address, Recipient Update Service.

defragmentation The process of rewriting parts of a file or sections in a database to contiguous sections to increase system performance.

delegate A person with permission to manage mailbox data for another user. A delegate may be allowed to send mail on behalf of another user, access folders in another user's mailbox, or both.

delegation The process of assigning administrative responsibility to another user or group. In Microsoft Exchange 2000 Server, administration is delegated to other users and groups at the organization and administrative group level using the Delegation of Control Wizard. *See also* Administration Delegation Wizard.

Delegation of Control Wizard *See* Administration Delegation Wizard.

delivery confirmation report A report that confirms delivery of an e-mail message to a recipient's mailbox or a foreign e-mail system where the recipient resides. Delivery confirmation reports can be requested for individual

messages or for all messages, depending on the client configuration.

delivery restrictions A means to accept or reject messages from any sender listed in Active Directory as a recipient object. You can assign delivery restrictions to any Exchange resource that can receive e-mail messages, such as mailboxes and connectors to foreign systems.

demilitarized zone (DMZ) A small computer network placed as a neutral, nontrusted zone between a private network that requires protection and an outside public network. It prevents users in the public network from getting direct access to resources in the private network. The DMZ is also called a perimeter network.

denial-of-service attack An incident in which a system is overloaded with invalid requests to disable a particular network service or all network connectivity and services. This type of attack is typically launched against Web servers or e-mail systems.

design time license A special license for an ActiveX control that allows developers to use the component in a software development project and in script-based business applications. Many ActiveX controls require both a design time and a runtime license. *See also* runtime license.

DHTML *See* Dynamic HTML (DHTML).

diagnostics logging A feature in Microsoft Exchange 2000 Server that determines which events are written to the application event log and other log files for selected services and their internal components. *See also* application event log.

differential backup A backup that includes only those files created or changed since the last normal or incremental backup. The differential backup does not mark files as having been backed up and it does not change the context for the next scheduled backup. *See also* copy backup, full backup, incremental backup.

Digest authentication An authentication method that sends user credentials (account name and password) over the network as a hash value to prevent disclosure of security-related information to unauthorized users. *See also* authentication.

Digital Dashboards A customized solution that displays information from separate data sources in the form of a public folder home page in Microsoft Outlook 2000. A Digital Dashboard pulls together key information sources into a consolidated folder view.

digital signature An advanced security feature that provides assurance that a message originator is indeed the source of a message and verifies that the contents have not been modified during transmission.

directory access cache (DSAccess) Allows the Information Store service and other Microsoft Exchange 2000 Server processes to perform lookups in Active Directory. Results are cached for a period of time to avoid sending the same query to Active Directory again.

Directory Application Programming Interface (DAPI) The legacy application programming interface (API) to perform directory lookups in Exchange Server 5.5 and earlier versions. Microsoft Exchange 2000 Server uses Lightweight Directory Access Protocol (LDAP) instead of DAPI to access information in Active Directory.

directory partition A part of an Active Directory forest that forms a contiguous subtree. Every domain controller has at least three directory partitions: schema, configuration, and domain. The schema and configuration partitions are replicated as single units to every domain controller in the forest. The domain partition is replicated only to the other domain controllers in the local

domain. A read-only copy of the domain partition is replicated to Global Catalog servers. *See* Active Directory forest.

directory service A system service that stores configuration and recipient information about a resources and users, such as administrative groups, recipients, and servers. A directory service enables users and system components to resolve an object based on its attributes to address and route messages. *See also* Active Directory directory service.

Directory Service Manager for NetWare (DSMN) A component that integrates Novell NetWare servers into Microsoft Windows NT and Windows 2000 Server domains. DSMN can synchronize user and group accounts between Windows NT/2000 and NetWare Bindery.

Directory Service Proxy (DSProxy) A process that acts as a facilitator to allow Messaging Application Programming Interface (MAPI)-based clients to access information within Active Directory. It proxies directory requests on behalf of MAPI-based clients to Active Directory and it refers smart MAPI-based clients directly to Active Directory.

directory synchronization The process of synchronizing Active Directory information with directories from foreign messaging systems, such as Microsoft Mail for PC Networks, Lotus cc:Mail, Lotus Notes, and Novell GroupWise.

Directory Synchronization agent (DXA) The active process that performs directory synchronization with a foreign messaging system.

directory synchronization topology The overall arrangement of active processes and connectors to foreign messaging systems that perform directory synchronization.

Dirsync *See* directory synchronization.

Dirsync requestor A Microsoft Mail postoffice that sends address list updates to a Dirsync server for the purposes of updating global address information on all postoffices in a Microsoft Mail network. *See also* Dirsync server.

Dirsync server A special MS Mail postoffice that receives address list updates from Dirsync requestors and incorporates the changes into a master list. The Dirsync server also sends updates to the Dirsync requestors to update their Global Address Lists (GALs). *See also* Dirsync requestor.

disaster recovery A restore operation with the goal of creating a 1:1 copy of the original server.

discontinuous namespace A namespace that does not have a common parent namespace with other namespaces in the Active Directory forest, but shares schema and configuration partitions with other namespaces (for instance, multiple trees in the same forest). *See also* namespace.

discretionary access control list (DACL) An element of every object's security descriptor, which contains the access control entries (ACEs) that grant or deny users, groups, or system accounts permissions to access the object. Only the object owner can change the DACL.

distinguished name (DN) A name that uniquely identifies an object as well as its location in a tree. Distinguished Names are commonly used in directory systems, such as Active Directory. An example of a distinguished name is CN=Administrator,CN=Users,DC=Bluesky-inc-10,DC=Com. *See also* relative distinguished name (RDN).

distributed network A computer network in which individual departments or workgroups set up and maintain their own resources. *See also* decentralized administration.

distributed processing A form of data processing in which separate computer systems share the workload in a computer network.

distributed transaction coordinator (DTC) A process that coordinates transactions across a computer network to reliably update data that resides on two or more database management systems. An example of a DTC is the Microsoft Distributed Transaction Coordinator (MS DTC), which allows transaction processing monitors to control distributed transactions.

distribution group A group of mailbox- or mail-enabled recipient objects that can be addressed as a single recipient. Administrators can create server-based distribution groups that are available in Active Directory.

distribution list In Microsoft Exchange Server 5.5, a term that describes a recipient object in the directory that holds membership information to allow for a group of recipients to be addressed as a single recipient. In Microsoft Exchange 2000 Server, a distribution group is used to emphasize the integration with Active Directory. *See also* distribution group.

DLL *See* dynamic-link library (DLL).

DMZ *See* demilitarized zone (DMZ).

DN *See* distinguished name (DN).

DNS *See* Domain Name System (DNS).

DNS lookup The process of resolving Domain Name System (DNS) names to Internet Protocol (IP) addresses. It is also possible to resolve IP addresses into DNS names, which is known as a reverse DNS lookup.

Doclink A link to a document in a Lotus Notes database that is inserted in a Lotus Notes e-mail message. A Notes doclink provides the user a convenient way to open the document using Lotus Notes client software.

domain A logical arrangement of computers in a network that share a common directory database and security policies.

domain local groups A security group in Active Directory that can contain members from anywhere in the forest, in trusted forests, or in a trusted pre-Windows 2000 domain. Domain local groups are only available in native-mode domains and can only be used to grant permissions to resources within the local domain.

domain mode The configuration of an Active Directory domain in regards to backward compatibility with Microsoft Windows NT Server 4.0. Active Directory domains that operate in mixed mode are fully backward compatible and are therefore restricted to the limitations of the Windows NT 4.0 domain model, such as lack of support for universal security groups. Active Directory domains that operate in native mode are not fully backward compatible, but overcome the limitations of the legacy domain model. In native-mode domains, Windows NT Server 4.0 can only be used on member servers.

Domain Name System (DNS) A collection of distributed databases on domain name servers that provide a means to resolve fully qualified domain and host names into corresponding Internet Protocol (IP) addresses, and vice versa. DNS is used on the Internet and on private TCP/IP networks.

DomainPrep A special mode of the Microsoft Exchange 2000 Server Setup program to prepare a Microsoft Windows 2000 domain for an Exchange 2000 Server organization.

Domino directory The name and address book in a Lotus Domino server.

downstream domains Messaging domains that are reached indirectly through another domain.

DSAccess *See* directory access cache (DSAccess).

DSProxy *See* Directory Service Proxy (DSProxy).

DXA *See* Directory Synchronization agent (DXA).

DXA requestor A Directory Synchronization agent (DXA) configured as a Dirsync requestor in an MS Mail directory synchronization environment. *See also* Dirsync requestor.

DXA server A Directory Synchronization agent (DXA) configured as a Dirsync server in an MS Mail directory synchronization environment. *See also* Dirsync server.

Dynamic DNS (DDNS) A feature of Windows 2000 DNS that enables clients and servers to automatically register their Internet Protocol (IP) addresses in a DNS database, eliminating the need to manually define host records. *See also* Domain Name System (DNS).

Dynamic Host Configuration Protocol (DHCP) A protocol to assign TCP/IP hosts and workstations Internet Protocol (IP) addresses and related configuration information dynamically over the network. It allows for centralized management of IP address allocation, which greatly simplifies the TCP/IP network configuration. DHCP is defined in Request for Comments (RFC) 1541.

Dynamic HTML (DHTML) An extension to Hypertext Markup Language (HTML) that enables developers to create Web pages that dynamically change their content and interact with the user. DHTML is supported by Microsoft Internet Explorer version 4.0 and later.

dynamic-link library (DLL) A file with a .dll extension that contains executable program code, which can be called by a program that requires the features of a specific function or set of functions. Based on the features of the operating system, DLLs can be loaded into memory dynamically, helping to save memory during program execution and enabling code reusability.

E

EDK *See* Exchange Development Kit (EDK).

EDK-based connector A connector component of Microsoft Exchange 2000 Server that was developed based on the Exchange Development Kit (EDK). EDK-based connectors use Messaging Application Programming Interface (MAPI) to access their message queues in the Information Store and they use Active Directory Service Interface (ADSI) to communicate with Active Directory. *See also* Active Directory directory service, Active Directory Service Interface (ADSI),
Exchange Development Kit (EDK).

EHLO A command to begin an Extended Simple Mail Transfer Protocol (ESMTP) session with a Simple Mail Transfer Protocol (SMTP) host. *See also* SMTP service extensions.

e-mail alias An alternative name assigned to a recipient object. The e-mail alias corresponds to the user-specific part of an e-mail address, such as <E-mail Alias>@Bluesky-inc-10.com.

emergency repair disk A disk that contains information about the system configuration of a Microsoft Windows NT or Windows 2000 installation. You can use the Windows 2000 Backup utility to create an emergency repair disk, which can be used to repair the installation if Windows 2000 fails to start because of corrupted system files.

Encrypting File System (EFS) An extension to the NT file system (NTFS) to apply encryption technology to files on a hard disk. With EFS, data in NTFS files can be stored in such a way that users with physical access to the disk media are denied access to the information without the correct security key.

encryption The process of converting a message or data in such a way that unauthorized users cannot gain access to the information. Encryption is necessary to protect sensitive information from disclosure when sending messages over a public network.

Endpoint Mapper A server-based process that listens on TCP port 135. The Endpoint Mapper is used to retrieve port numbers for connection establishment to server-based services that use dynamically assigned ports. *See also* port.

End-User License Agreement (EULA) An individual license agreement that represents a contract between the person who acquires a software package and Microsoft. Upon accepting the EULA, a user is granted the right to use the software.

Enterprise Admins A special Microsoft Windows 2000 group that exists only in the root domain of an Active Directory forest. Members of this group are known as enterprise administrators. They are authorized to accomplish forestwide administration in Active Directory, such as adding an Exchange 2000 Server organization to the forest.

Epoxy *See* Exchange Interprocess Communication (EXIPC).

ESMTP *See* Extended SMTP (ESMTP).

ETRN *See* Extended TURN (ETRN).

event binding The association of a transport, protocol, or Microsoft Web Storage System event with an event sink by registering event sinks in the Internet Information Services (IIS) metabase. *See also* event sink, IIS metabase.

Event Processor A component of the Microsoft Windows 2000 Cluster service that handles common cluster operations and controls Cluster service initialization. *See also* Cluster service.

event sink Executable program code that is invoked when a specified event occurs. Event sinks can be developed in any Component Object Model (COM)-compliant programming language.

Event Viewer An administrative utility that displays the event logs of a computer running Microsoft Windows 2000. *See also* application event log.

Exchange Development Kit (EDK) A part of the Microsoft Platform Software Development Kit (SDK) that contains the files and documentation necessary to build the gateway, mailbox agents, administrative components, and other server-based Exchange solutions.

Exchange Form Designer A design tool that enables developers to design 16-bit electronic forms that may be used with Microsoft Exchange Client and Microsoft Outlook.

Exchange Installable File System (ExIFS) A component that provides file system access to the Microsoft Web Storage System. By default, ExIFS maps to the M drive on the computer running Exchange 2000 Server. If this drive is already in use, the next available drive letter is taken.

Exchange Interprocess Communication (EXIPC) A communication layer between Internet Information Services (IIS) processes and the Information Store service for high-speed data transfer between the protocols and database services on an Exchange 2000 server.

Exchange OLE DB provider (ExOLEDB) A software component that implements OLE DB interfaces and provides access to Exchange 2000 Server resources via the Microsoft Web Storage System.

Exchange Routing Engine A component of Exchange 2000 Server that performs message routing within and across routing group boundaries. The routing engine uses link state information (LSI) to automatically generate an optimized messaging topology. *See also* link state information (LSI).

Exchange System Manager The universal management utility of Microsoft Exchange 2000 Server that allows an administrator with appropriate permissions to manage all aspects of an organization. Exchange System Manager can be launched via the System Manager shortcut from Microsoft Exchange program group.

Exchange Virtual Server (EVS) A virtual instance of an Exchange 2000 server running on a node in a server cluster. Each EVS maintains its own resources as configured using the Cluster Administrator program. An EVS is the unit that can failover to another node. *See also* Cluster service, failover.

ExIFS *See* Exchange Installable File System (ExIFS).

EXIPC *See* Exchange Interprocess Communication (EXIPC).

Exmerge *See* Microsoft Exchange Mailbox Merge Wizard (Exmerge).

ExOLEDB *See* Exchange OLE DB provider (ExOLEDB).

expansion server An Exchange 2000 server designated for distribution group expansion. The expansion server can be defined per mail-enabled group in each group's Exchange Advanced tab.

expiration policy A policy that defines when articles in newsgroups expire and will be purged. When newsgroups are maintained in your in public folders, expiration policies are transferred from the Network News Transfer Protocol (NNTP) virtual server to the public store or individual public folder.

export container An organizational unit (OU) that contains recipient objects included in directory synchronization from Exchange 2000 Server to a foreign messaging system.

Extended MAPI An application programming interface (API) that is used for creating advanced messaging-based applications in C/C++.

Extended SMTP (ESMTP) An extension to Simple Mail Transfer Protocol (SMTP) that allows an SMTP server to inform an SMTP client of the extensions it supports. *See also* Simple Mail Transfer Protocol (SMTP).

Extended TURN (ETRN) An extension to Simple Mail Transfer Protocol (SMTP) that allows an SMTP host to request the message transfer from another SMTP host.

Extensible Markup Language (XML) A metalanguage to create common information formats and to share both the format and the data on the Web.

Extensible Storage Engine (ESE) A universal, transaction-oriented database engine that defines a very low-level application programming interface (API) to underlying database structures. ESE uses log files to ensure that committed transactions are safe. Exchange 2000 Server is based on ESE98. Exchange Server 5.5 and Active Directory use the ESE97 interface.

extension attribute A general attribute of a recipient object in Active Directory to support recipient information not covered by other predefined attributes. Extension attributes are the equivalent of custom attributes in earlier versions of Exchange Server.

external foreign domain An administrative unit in Novell GroupWise, which defines a foreign messaging system that is connected to the local GroupWise domain, typically through a gateway.

F

failback In Windows 2000 Cluster service, the process of moving a failed resource group back to the highest available node in the cluster

according to the resource group's list of preferred owners. *See also* Cluster service.

failover In Windows 2000 Cluster service, the process of taking a resource group offline on a failed cluster node to transfer it to another node in the cluster to bring it back online. *See also* Cluster service.

Failover Manager A component of the Cluster service that works together in conjunction with the Resource Manager to maintain resources and resource groups. The Failover Manager initiates failover operations if a node is detected as nonoperational. *See also* Cluster service, Resource Manager.

Fast Ethernet A data transmission standard that provides a theoretical transfer rate of 100 megabits per second. Fast Ethernet is a local area network (LAN)-based technology also referred to as 100BASE-T.

fault tolerance The assurance of data integrity when system failures occur. A fault-tolerant system has the ability to either to continue the operation without data loss or to shut down safely and recover at next restart.

FDDI *See* Fiber Distributed Data Interface (FDDI).

FFL *See* folder forms library (FFL).

Fiber Distributed Data Interface (FDDI) A low-level protocol standard developed by the American National Standards Institute (ANSI) that is designed to be used with fiber-optic cabling.

Field Chooser A feature of the Outlook Forms Designer that allows a developer to conveniently place message fields on an Outlook form and to create custom fields. *See also* Outlook Forms Designer.

field validation A mechanism to prevent invalid user input in fields of an electronic or Microsoft Outlook form.

File and Print Services for NetWare (FPNW)
Allows users on NetWare workstations to access files, printers, and applications on a Windows 2000 server as if the machine running Microsoft Windows 2000 Server were a NetWare server.

firewall A security system that prevents unauthorized access from a public network (such as the Internet) to the resources in a private network. A firewall can enforce indirect communication by routing data through a proxy server in a demilitarized zone (DMZ). *See also* demilitarized zone (DMZ).

firewall topology modulator (FTM) An Instant Messaging component that maintains Internet Protocol (IP)-related information about Instant Messaging servers that are located behind firewalls.

folder agent A script registered with a public folder to implement sophisticated processing of folder contents based on Microsoft Web Storage System events. *See also* event sinks.

folder forms library (FFL) A location for forms associated with a particular public folder (post forms).

Folder Home Page A feature of Microsoft Outlook 2000 that allows users to associate a folder with a Hypertext Markup Language (HTML) home page. The HTML page replaces the default folder view in the Outlook explorer window, which is the basis for Digital Dashboards and other collaboration solutions. *See also* Digital Dashboards.

folder rule A means to define actions to take if an item matching certain criteria is placed in a folder. Possible actions are forwarding, copying to another folder, generating an automatic response, deleting the item, and so on.

folder views A means to organize and find information in a folder based on defined criteria. Folder views allow the default options to be per-

sonalized and optimized so that the items in a public folder are easier to locate.

foreign domain document A document in a Lotus Domino/Notes server that describes a foreign messaging system.

forest *See* Active Directory forest.

ForestPrep A special mode of the Microsoft Exchange 2000 Server Setup program to prepare an Active Directory forest and its schema for an Exchange 2000 Server organization.

forklifting users The process of moving user mailboxes from a server to a different computer or restoring them to a new computer using a backup of the mailbox store databases.

forms adaptivity A feature of the Microsoft Web Storage System to return different Microsoft Web Storage System forms for the same item to specific Web browsers depending on the information supplied in the Hypertext Transfer Protocol (HTTP) request header. *See also* Web Storage System, Microsoft Web Storage System forms.

forms library A location where electronic forms are stored and made publicly accessible. The four types of forms libraries are organization forms library (OFL), folder forms library (FFL), personal forms library (PFL), and Web forms library (WFL).

FQDN *See* fully qualified domain name (FQDN).

frame type An identifier that specifies the format for data at OSI Layer 2 packets (frames) that NWLink will transmit over the computer network. The frame type must match on different computers for network communications to succeed. Frame types are most important in Novell NetWare environments, where the format must match on all systems for a communication to happen. Different versions default to different frame types.

free/busy information A feature that allows users to see when other users are free or busy and thus to more efficiently schedule meetings.

free/busy information public folder A hidden folder on an Exchange 2000 server that provides free/busy information to all Exchange users in an organization. *See also* free/busy information.

Front end/back end configuration (FE/BE) An arrangement of Exchange 2000 servers in which Internet-based clients access a protocol server (the front end), which in turn communicates on behalf of the client with another server in the backbone (the back end) to retrieve the data. A front-end/back-end configuration allows for a deployment of load-balanced front-end systems, which can act as a single point of contact for all mailbox and public folder data.

FrontPage Extensions Web An extension to Internet Information Services (IIS) that allows a Web designer to create and edit Web sites directly on the server by using Microsoft FrontPage on the client computer.

FTM *See* firewall topology module (FTM).

full backup A backup, also called a normal backup, of all selected files that marks each file as having been backed up. A full online backup of Exchange databases purges previous transaction log files, thus setting the context for the next scheduled backup. *See also* copy backup, differential backup, incremental backup.

full-mesh routing A message routing topology where all mail hosts transfer messages directly to each other.

full-text catalog A collection of full-text indexes maintained by a search engine.

full-text indexing The process of creating an index database of searchable text before searches are executed, which makes fast full-text searches possible. With full-text indexing, every word in a mailbox or public store can be indexed. *See also* full-text search.

full-text search In Microsoft Exchange 2000 Server, a search for one or more items in a mailbox or public store based on the actual message body or document data rather than on an index containing a limited set of keywords.

fully qualified domain name (FQDN) A Domain Name System (DNS) name that consists of a host name and the full domain name to indicate the precise location of the host in the domain namespace.

G

gateway A communication component that connects an Exchange 2000 Server organization to a foreign messaging system. Typical tasks of a gateway include message conversion and translation of recipient information.

Gateway (and Client) Services for NetWare (GSNW) An additional network component that enables Microsoft Windows 2000 Server to access resources on NetWare servers. GSNW also enables Windows 2000 Server to act as a gateway to NetWare servers.

Gateway Address Routing Table (GWART) The primary routing mechanism for the Message Transfer Agent (MTA) in earlier versions of Microsoft Exchange Server. Exchange 2000 Server generates a GWART containing all message routes and their cost factors only for the purposes of backward compatibility. Message routing in Exchange 2000 Server uses a link state table (LST) instead of a GWART. *See also* link state information (LSI), link state table (LST).

gateway mail file A Lotus Notes database where outbound messages to a foreign domain, such as Microsoft Exchange 2000 Server, are delivered by the Lotus Notes Mail Router process. *See also* Lotus Notes Mail Router.

GDI *See* global domain identifier (GDI).

Global Address List (GAL) A virtual container in the address book that lists all recipient objects of an organization that are made visible in the address book.

Global Catalog An Active Directory domain controller that maintains a partial, read-only replica of all domains in the forest in addition to the schema, configuration, and local domain partitions. The Global Catalog can answer Lightweight Directory Access Protocol (LDAP) queries directed to TCP port 3268 with information about all objects in the forest according to the attributes included in Global Catalog replication. A domain controller can be configured as a Global Catalog using the Active Directory Sites and Services snap-in.

global domain identifier (GDI) An identifier that uniquely identifies an X.400 management domain for the purposes of message loop detection. The GDI is added as external trace information to every X.400 message that passes through the management domain. A GDI is typically defined by the country (C), administrative management domain (ADMD), and private management domain (PRMD) portions of the X.400 address space.

global group A group in Active Directory that can be granted rights and permissions to resources in its own domain and in trusting domains, such as other domains in the same forest. A global group can only contain user and group accounts from its own domain.

Global Update Manager A component of the Cluster service that provides a global service used by other components within the server cluster to replicate changes to the cluster database across all nodes. *See also* Cluster service.

globally unique identifier (GUID) A 128-bit identifier that is supposed to be guaranteed unique across all computer systems worldwide.

group policy A feature that allows an administrator to control how programs and network resources can be used. Group policies can be applied to users and computers based on their membership in sites, domains, or organizational units (OUs).

GroupWise administrator message An e-mail message in a Novell GroupWise environment with a special message type of Admin, which contains instructions for GroupWise to accomplish management tasks, such as the creation or deletion of recipient information.

GroupWise domain A management unit in Novell GroupWise that contains one or many post offices and a message transfer agent (GroupWise MTA). *See also* GroupWise Message Transfer Agent.

GroupWise Gateway for Microsoft Exchange A Novell GroupWise component that can be used to connect GroupWise to earlier versions of Microsoft Exchange Server.

GroupWise Message Transfer Agent The active process in a Novell GroupWise domain that performs message routing between GroupWise post offices and GroupWise domains.

GroupWise MTA *See* GroupWise Message Transfer Agent.

GSNW *See* Gateway (and Client) Services for NetWare (GSNW).

GUID *See* globally unique identifier (GUID).

GWART *See* Gateway Address Routing Table (GWART).

H

H.323 A standard of the International Telecommunications Union (ITU) that specifies how multimedia systems can communicate over networks that do not support Internet Protocol (IP) multicasting. H.323 is used for point-to-point audio and video conferencing. *See also* audio and video conferencing.

H.323 Video Conference Bridge A component of Microsoft Exchange 2000 Conferencing Server that allows H.323-compliant client programs that are unable to participate directly in Internet Protocol (IP) multicast conferences, such as NetMeeting, to participate in videoconferences through a H.323 unicast session.

hard recovery The process of applying transaction logs and patch files restored from a backup to a mailbox or public store.

heartbeat A periodic message exchanged between nodes in a server cluster or network load balancing cluster to detect system failures.

home server The Exchange 2000 server that maintains the mailbox store where a user's mailbox is located.

hot fixes Very specific fixes to known problems reported by customers, but not yet regression tested.

hot spare An idle node in a server cluster that is ready to be used whenever a failover occurs. *See also* Cluster service, failover.

HTML *See* Hypertext Markup Language (HTML).

HTTP *See* Hypertext Transfer Protocol (HTTP).

Hypertext Markup Language (HTML) A markup language (set of tags) that Web authors can use to create and design Web pages.

Hypertext Transfer Protocol (HTTP) A protocol to transfer hypertext information (for example, Web pages) to Web browsers over TCP/IP.

I

iCalendar A standard to send and receive meeting requests and responses over the Internet.

IETF *See* Internet Engineering Task Force (IETF).

IIS *See* Internet Information Services (IIS).

IIS metabase The repository of Internet Information Services (IIS) configuration settings. The IIS metabase performs some of the same functions as the system Registry of Microsoft Windows 2000 Server.

IMAP4 *See* Internet Message Access Protocol version 4 (IMAP4).

import container An organizational unit (OU) that receives recipient objects created during directory synchronization with a foreign messaging system. *See also* export container, organizational unit (OU).

importance levels The priority of an e-mail message rated as low, normal, or important.

IMPP *See* Instant Messaging Presence Protocol (IMPP).

incremental backup A backup that includes only those files created or changed since the last normal or incremental backup. The incremental backup marks files as having been backed up. An incremental online backup of Exchange databases purges previous transaction log files, thus setting the context for the next scheduled backup. *See also* copy backup, differential backup, full backup.

independent software vendor (ISV) A software developer or organization that independently provides computer software.

Information Store A core component of Microsoft Exchange 2000 Server that maintains mailbox and public stores and provides other processes and messaging clients with access to the information. *See also* mailbox store, public store.

inheritance The ability of a newly created child object to automatically receive default values for its attributes from its parent object. For example, a newly created child directory can receive access control settings from its parent container. *See also* access control, child object.

in-place upgrade A method of upgrading a server running Microsoft Exchange Server 5.5 SP3 directly to Exchange 2000 Server. The Setup program is executed directly on the server, which performs a direct upgrade of existing resources, such as databases and messaging connectors.

Installable File System (IFS) A storage technology that provides access to resources in the form of a filing system. Standard Win32 processes can access the resources similar to files and folders on a hard disk. *See also* Exchange Installable File System (ExIFS).

instant messages Electronic messages exchanged between Instant Messaging (IM) users in real time. These messages are not stored on disk and are lost when the user closes the IM client application. *See also* Instant Messaging (IM).

Instant Messaging (IM) A service in Microsoft Exchange 2000 Server that supports real-time messaging and presence information. *See also* presence information.

Instant Messaging home server The Instant Messaging server that forwards instant messages to a user and maintains his or her presence information and subscriber list. *See also* Instant Messaging (IM), presence information.

Instant Messaging Presence Protocol (IMPP) A protocol defined by the Internet Engineering Task Force (IETF) to support the exchange of presence information across different computer platforms on the Internet. Instead of IMPP, Microsoft Exchange 2000 Server uses a proprietary published protocol called Rendezvous Protocol (RVP) to communicate with Instant Messaging clients. *See also* presence information, Rendezvous Protocol (RVP).

Instant Messaging router A special virtual server in an Instant Messaging (IM) domain that provides a means for external users to communicate with users in the domain. The IM router must be registered in DNS to receive instant messages from external users, which it forwards to the user's home server. *See also* Instant Messaging home server.

Integrated Services Digital Network (ISDN) A digital telephone and telecommunications network that supports transmission speeds of 64 kilobits per second over a single ISDN channel. ISDN channels can be bundled together to achieve higher transmission rates.

integrity A basic feature of computer security that provides confirmation that the original information has not been altered or corrupted. Hash functions are used to create a cryptographic checksum, which can be checked to verify data integrity.

internal network number An identifier of a virtual Internetwork Packet Exchange (IPX) network inside a computer for addressing and routing purposes. The internal network number is 4 bytes in length and must be unique to the IPX internetwork. *See also* Internetwork Packet Exchange/Sequenced Packet Exchange (IPX/SPX).

International Telecommunications Union (ITU) An organization based in Geneva, Switzerland, that coordinates, develops, and standardizes global telecommunications networks and services.

Internet access protocols Protocols that allow Internet users access to messaging-related information in mailboxes, newsgroups, public folders, and directories. Typical Internet access protocols are HTTP, POP3, IMAP4, NNTP, and LDAP.

Internet Assigned Numbers Authority (IANA) An organization that assigns Internet Protocol (IP) addresses to organizations on the Internet.

Internet Engineering Task Force (IETF) A consortium that issues standards for new technology on the Internet in specifications called Requests for Comments (RFCs). *See also* Request for Comments.

Internet Information Services (IIS) A collection of network and application services integrated into Microsoft Windows 2000 Server that supports multiple Internet access protocols, such as Hypertext Transfer Protocol (HTTP), Simple Mail Transfer Protocol (SMTP), Network News Transfer Protocol (NNTP), and others. Exchange 2000 Server extends the IIS to provide additional functionality.

Internet Message Access Protocol version 4 (IMAP4) A popular Internet access protocol for e-mail messaging. IMAP4 allows an Internet client to access server-based message folders and items without downloading them to the local computer.

Internet Network Information Center (InterNIC) The coordinator of domain names and Internet Protocol (IP) addresses registered in Domain Name System (DNS) on the Internet. *See also* Domain Name System (DNS).

Internet Protocol (IP) The protocol in a TCP/IP-based network that provides a connectionless delivery system. IP routes messages from one host to another, but it does not guarantee that

packets arrive at their destination or that they are received in sequential order.

Internet Protocol Security (IPSec) An industry standard for cryptography-based protection of TCP/IP-based network communication.

Internet Relay Chat (IRC) A protocol that enables a group of people to hold real-time conversations via a chat server. The current version of IRC is defined in Request for Comments (RFC) 1459. *See also* chat, Internet Relay Chat Extension (IRCX).

Internet Relay Chat Extension (IRCX) A protocol originally developed by Microsoft to extend the standard IRC functionality, which added additional client and server commands, user modes, and security. *See also* chat, Internet Relay Chat (IRC).

Internet Server Application Programming Interface (ISAPI) An application programming interface that allows developers to program Internet Information Services (IIS) extensions. Outlook Web Access (OWA) of Microsoft Exchange 2000 Server, for instance, is implemented as an ISAPI component. *See also* Internet Information Services (IIS).

Internet service provider (ISP) An organization that provides access to the Internet through dial-up connections or leased lines. ISPs typically maintain systems that are directly connected to the Internet to provide their services to remote users.

Internetwork Packet Exchange/Sequenced Packet Exchange (IPX/SPX) A network protocol that is typically used in Novell NetWare environments to govern addressing and routing of data packets within and between local area networks (LANs). Newer versions of NetWare support TCP/IP, which can replace IPX/SPX.

interprocess communication (IPC) A mechanism that allows bidirectional communication between programs, services, and multiuser processes running on the local computer or remote computers. IPC is used to support distributed processing. *See also* Exchange Interprocess Communication (EXIPC).

IP multicast A mechanism to send Internet Protocol (IP) traffic to a single destination IP address, while the data is received and processed by multiple IP hosts, regardless of their location on the network. A host can accept traffic for a specific IP multicast address. Intermediary IP routers must be capable of routing IP multicast traffic to subnets with hosts that have registered interest in the data.

IPC *See* interprocess communication (IPC).

IPSec *See* Internet Protocol Security (IPSec).

IPX/SPX *See* Internetwork Packet Exchange/Sequenced Packet Exchange (IPX/SPX).

IRC *See* Internet Relay Chat (IRC).

IRCX *See* Internet Relay Chat Extension (IRCX).

ISAPI *See* Internet Server Application Programming Interface (ISAPI).

ISDN *See* Integrated Services Digital Network (ISDN).

ISP *See* Internet service provider.

ISV *See* independent software vendor (ISV).

ITU *See* International Telecommunications Union (ITU).

J

JavaScript A scripting language that is syntactically similar to Java, which was developed by Netscape Communications to develop dynamic Web pages. JavaScript is standardized by the ECMA 262 language specification.

Joint Engine Technology (JET) A low-level, transaction-oriented database technology used in Exchange Server 5.0 and earlier versions. Later versions of Exchange Server use Extensible Storage Engine (ESE) instead of JET. *See also* Extensible Storage Engine (ESE).

JScript Microsoft's implementation of JavaScript that complies with the ECMA 262 language specification.

K

Kerberos authentication An authentication mechanism used to verify user or server identity for the secure use of distributed software components. Microsoft Windows 2000 Server uses the Kerberos version 5 protocol as its default authentication service. *See also* authentication.

Kerberos protocol An authentication protocol that is defined in Request for Comments (RFC) 1510. *See also* Kerberos authentication.

key distribution center (KDC) A Kerberos service that generates session tickets and temporary session keys for Kerberos authentication. To support Kerberos authentication in Microsoft Windows 2000, the KDC runs on all domain controllers in the Active Directory forest. *See also* Kerberos authentication.

key history A list of expired or revoked security keys associated with a user's mailbox that may be required to decrypt existing sealed messages. *See also* message sealing.

key management The management of security keys for users in an organization to support public key cryptography. *See also* Key Management Service (KMS).

Key Management server (KM server) An Exchange 2000 server that is running the Microsoft Exchange Key Management Service (KMS) to maintain advanced security information. *See also* Key Management Service (KMS).

Key Management Service (KMS) An optional service of Microsoft Exchange 2000 Server that integrates with Microsoft Windows 2000 Certificate Services to issue security certificates for Exchange users. The KMS also maintains a key history for those users for whom it issued certificates. *See also* key history.

key recovery The process of recovering and reissuing lost security keys based on a key history to allow a user to continue working with encrypted messages. *See also* key history.

key revocation The process of canceling a user's security keys by adding the user's X.509 certificate to a revocation list. This is not the same as deleting the security keys. The old keys may still be used to work with existing sealed messages. *See also* key recovery, X.509 certificate.

keyword-based text file An ASCII file that contains keywords describing message properties and contents, which is used by the Novell GroupWise API Gateway for message transfer and directory synchronization. *See also* API Gateway.

KM database master encryption key The password for the Key Management Service (KMS) to decrypt the service's key management database. Without a valid password, the KMS cannot start. *See also* Key Management Service (KMS).

KMS *See* Key Management Service (KMS).

L

LAN *See* local area network (LAN).

latency The delay with which updates are replicated between instances of the same replica. The latency is the gap between the time a given replica is changed and the time the update is applied to other replicas of the same resource.

Layer Two Tunneling Protocol (L2TP) A tunneling protocol at the data-link layer that can be used to establish a virtual private network (VPN) over the Internet. *See also* virtual private network (VPN).

LDAP *See* Lightweight Directory Access Protocol (LDAP).

LDIF Directory Exchange Tool (LDIFDE) A command-line utility that allows an administrator to import, modify, delete, and export objects to and from Active Directory based on an .ldf file according to the LDIF file format standard.

LDIFDE *See* LDIF Directory Exchange Tool (LDIFDE).

leapfrog upgrade A method of upgrading an earlier version of Microsoft Exchange Server to Exchange 2000 Server in which the new platform is installed on a different server. Mailboxes, public folders, and other resources are then moved from the old server to the new server before the earlier version of Exchange Server is uninstalled. The old computer hardware may then be used to install another Exchange 2000 server to continue the upgrade process. The upgrade cycle repeats until all servers running earlier versions are upgraded.

Lightweight Directory Access Protocol (LDAP) An open standard designed to provide access to directory services based on X.500 without the overhead of the Directory Access Protocol (DAP). LDAP is defined in Request for Comments (RFC) 1777.

link state algorithm (LSA) The algorithm used to propagate link state information (LSI) between Exchange 2000 servers in a routing group and between routing groups. Within a routing group, LSI is propagated over TCP port 691. Between routing groups, the X-LINK2STATE command is used to pass the information to the Simple Mail Transfer Protocol (SMTP) service. X.400 connectors propagate LSI in a binary large object

(BLOB) before sending messages. *See also* binary large object (BLOB), link state information (LSI).

link state information (LSI) Information that Microsoft Exchange 2000 Server uses for the purposes of message routing to determine whether connectors are working. Messages are not routed to connectors that are marked as down. *See also* link state algorithm (LSA), link state table (LST).

link state table (LST) The repository of link state information (LSI), which is used for message routing in Microsoft Exchange 2000 Server. The LST replaced the Gateway Address Routing Table (GWART) of earlier versions of Exchange Server. Among other things, the LST provides information about connectors and servers across the entire organization. *See also* link state information (LSI), routing group master (RGM).

load balancing A means to distribute client connections across multiple servers. Sophisticated load-balancing solutions can distribute the workload equally across all hosts or according to a load percentage.

local area network (LAN) A communications network within a geographically close area that uses a protocol that allows any connected device to interact with any other system on the network. A very popular protocol used in LAN environments is TCP/IP.

local replication Offline folder and offline address book synchronization in Microsoft Outlook 2000.

Local Security Authority In Microsoft Windows 2000, a protected subsystem that authenticates and logs users on to the local system. The Local Security Authority also issues security identifiers (SIDs) for local user accounts. The enterprise counterpart of the Local Security Authority is the domain security authority, which generates SIDs

for security principals in a Windows 2000 domain.

localhost A placeholder for the local computer on which a program is running, which is associated with reserved Internet Protocol (IP) address 127.0.0.1 (also known as the loopback IP address).

Log Manager A component of the Cluster service that maintains the recovery log, which is stored on the quorum resource. *See also* Cluster service.

Lotus cc:Mail Directory Propagation A mechanism to propagate recipient information across a Lotus cc:Mail environment. *See also* Automatic Directory Exchange (ADE).

Lotus cc:Mail forwarding history Forwarding information generated by Lotus cc:Mail that can be encapsulated into a FORWARD.TXT file when converting Lotus cc:Mail messages to Exchange format using the Connector for Lotus cc:Mail.

Lotus cc:Mail Import/Export programs Utilities used by the Connector for Lotus cc:Mail to exchange e-mail messages and perform directory synchronization with Lotus cc:Mail.

Lotus Notes Client API An API exposed by the Lotus Notes client and used by the Connector for Lotus Notes for the purposes of message transfer and directory synchronization between Lotus Domino/Notes and Microsoft Exchange 2000 Server.

Lotus Notes Mail Router An active process in a Lotus Domino/Notes environment that routes messages placed into the MAIL.BOX database by the Connector for Lotus Notes to their final destinations.

LSA *See* link state algorithm (LSA).

LST *See* link state table (LST).

M

MADCAP *See* Multicast Address Dynamic Client Allocation Protocol (MADCAP).

mail exchanger A Simple Mail Transfer Protocol (SMTP) host in a Domain Name System (DNS) domain that is registered using an MX record. *See also* MX record.

mailbox A repository of private folders that is associated with a Microsoft Windows 2000 user account and maintained in a mailbox store on an Exchange 2000 server. The mailbox contains, among other folders, the user's Inbox, which is the delivery location for incoming messages addressed to the user.

mailbox identifier A globally unique identifier (GUID) that associates a user account with its mailbox. This identifier is also called a mailbox GUID. *See also* globally unique identifier (GUID).

Mailbox Reconnect Tool (MBCONN) A utility that allows an administrator to generate an .ldf file based on information from restored mailbox stores, which can be used to create user accounts in Active Directory using LDIF Directory Exchange Tool (LDIFDE). As soon as user accounts exist, MBCONN can be used to reconnect the mailboxes in a bulk operation. *See also* LDIF Directory Exchange Tool (LDIFDE).

mailbox store A set of Extensible Storage Engine (ESE) database files that are managed as a unit in Microsoft Exchange 2000 Server to maintain mailboxes of Microsoft Windows 2000 user accounts. A single Exchange 2000 server can have up to 20 separate mailbox stores. *See also* Extensible Storage Engine (ESE), storage group.

mailbox store policy A system policy configured in Exchange System Manager that applies configuration settings to one or many mailbox stores in the administrative group. *See also* public store policy, server policy, system policy.

mailbox-enabled An Active Directory object that is associated with a mailbox in Microsoft Exchange 2000 Server. In Active Directory, only user accounts can be mailbox-enabled. Mailbox-enabled user accounts can send and receive e-mail messages. *See also* mailbox identifier, mail-enabled.

mail-enabled An Active Directory object that has been assigned e-mail addresses and can be selected as a recipient object from the server-based address lists. A mail-enabled recipient object does not have an associated mailbox in Microsoft Exchange 2000 Server. *See also* mailbox-enabled.

mail-enabled contact A mail-enabled object in Active Directory that points to a user outside the local Active Directory forest. *See also* mailbox-enabled, mail-enabled.

mail-enabled user account A mail-enabled object in Active Directory that refers to a user in the local Active Directory forest with a mailbox in a foreign messaging system. *See also* mailbox-enabled, mail-enabled.

MAPI *See* Messaging Application Programming Interface (MAPI).

MAPI-based hierarchy The default public folder hierarchy that is available to all messaging clients supported by Microsoft Exchange 2000 Server. The MAPI-based hierarchy is what the users see when they open the All Public Folders tree in Microsoft Outlook 2000. *See also* alternate hierarchy, public folder hierarchy.

MAPI-based messaging clients A messaging client, such as Microsoft Outlook 2000, that uses the Messaging Application Programming Interface (MAPI) subsystem to communicate with an underlying communication system, such as Microsoft Exchange 2000 Server, by means of a MAPI system provider. *See also* Messaging Application Programming Interface (MAPI).

MAPI-based profile Settings that provide Microsoft Outlook 2000 and other MAPI-based applications with information about the configuration of the Messaging Application Programming Interface (MAPI) subsystem to access a messaging system, such as an Exchange 2000 server.

MBCONN *See* Mailbox Reconnect Tool (MBCONN).

MCU *See* multipoint control unit (MCU).

MDB An acronym for message database, which stands for an instance of a mailbox or public store database implemented in Microsoft Exchange 2000 Server. *See also* mailbox store, public store.

Message Interchange Format (MIF) A file format used by the Connector for Lotus cc:Mail to read and write scratch files during the transfer of e-mail messages and directory information to and from a Lotus cc:Mail post office using the Lotus cc:Mail Import/Export programs. *See also* Lotus cc:Mail Import/Export programs.

message queue A temporary repository for inbound or outbound e-mail messages that require routing, format conversion, or other processing through an active server component, such as the routing engine, Message Transfer Agent (MTA), or a connector to a foreign messaging system.

message sealing The process of encrypting a message using public key technology to prevent the disclosure of its information to nonauthorized recipients. *See also* message signing.

message signing The process of adding a digital signature to an e-mail message, which allows recipients to verify the identity of the originator and the integrity of the message. *See also* digital signature.

message tracking The process of gathering information about message transfer that occurs either on a single Exchange 2000 server or between servers in an organization. Microsoft Exchange 2000 Server writes message tracking information into log files, which can be analyzed using a text editor or the Message Tracking Center. *See also* Message Tracking Center.

Message Tracking Center A management utility that allows an administrator to analyze message tracking logs to examine the path that a message has taken through the entire organization, including its exit points, such as a recipient's mailbox or a connector to a foreign messaging system. *See also* message tracking.

Message Transfer Agent (MTA) A component of Microsoft Exchange 2000 Server that is responsible for messages transfer over X.400 connectors. The MTA is also responsible for message routing to and from connectors to foreign messaging systems.

Messaging Application Programming Interface (MAPI) A standard interface and a Windows subsystem that messaging components can use to communicate with one another. Application programmers can use MAPI to create powerful messaging and workgroup applications. System programmers can create system providers to extend the MAPI subsystem to allow MAPI-based client applications to interact with their messaging platform. Microsoft Outlook 2000 is an example of a MAPI-based client, which uses a MAPI transport service to communicate with Microsoft Exchange 2000 Server.

metabase *See* IIS metabase.

Metabase Editor (MetaEdit) A utility for browsing and modifying configuration settings in the IIS metabase. *See also* IIS metabase.

metabase update service A component of the System Attendant service in Microsoft Exchange 2000 Server that reads configuration data from Active Directory to transfer it into the local IIS metabase. The data transfer is one way.

Microsoft Access Workflow Designer for SQL Server 7.0 A utility for database developers to create and enforce business rules for Microsoft Access 2000 team projects based on SQL Server databases.

Microsoft Chat 2.5 A client program with Internet Relay Chat (IRC) and Internet Relay Chat Extension (IRCX) command support that allows users to participate in chat discussions. *See also* Internet Relay Chat (IRC), Internet Relay Chat Extension (IRCX).

Microsoft Directory Synchronization Services (MSDSS) A solution to synchronize Active Directory accounts with accounts in Novell Directory Services (NDS) or Bindery, including password information. *See also* Bindery, Novell Directory Services (NDS).

Microsoft Exchange Event Service A component of Exchange Server 5.5 that supports customized workflow applications through public folder scripts and asynchronous events. Exchange 2000 Server supports this component for backward compatibility. *See also* asynchronous event.

Microsoft Exchange Mailbox Merge Wizard (EXMERGE) An administrative utility in Exchange 2000 Server that supports the transfer of mailbox contents from a recovery machine to a production server while both systems are online. EXMERGE may also be used as a backup agent to save messages and other items at the mailbox level.

Microsoft Exchange Multimedia Control An ActiveX control that allows users to record voice and video data directly in an e-mail message and send it just as any other message.

Microsoft Mail Connector A component in Exchange 2000 Server that provides connectivity to Microsoft Mail for PC Networks (MS Mail).

Microsoft Mail for PC Networks (MS Mail) A shared-file messaging system from Microsoft.

Microsoft Management Console (MMC) A Windows-based host application that represents a framework for Microsoft Windows 2000 management tools. MMC is part of the Microsoft Platform Software Development Kit (SDK).

Microsoft Mobile Explorer (MME) A modular wireless application platform designed to offer a wide choice of communication services on Internet-enabled mobile phones.

Microsoft MSN Messenger The preferred client for Instant Messaging in Exchange 2000 Server.

Microsoft NetMeeting A conferencing solution from Microsoft that supports the International Telecommunications Union (ITU) standards T.120 and H.323 for multipoint data conferencing and audio and video conferencing.

Microsoft Outlook Express A messaging and collaboration client from Microsoft that supports open Internet standards such as POP3, SMTP, LDAP, MIME, HTML, HTTP, and NNTP. Outlook Express can be used to access resources on an Exchange 2000 server.

Microsoft Platform Software Development Kit (SDK) A resource for software developers that want to develop Windows-based applications and services. The SDK includes header files, import libraries, and code samples, as well as detailed documentation about the technologies supported by Microsoft Windows 2000 and previously released platforms. The Exchange Development Kit (EDK) is part of the Platform SDK. *See also* Exchange Development Kit (EDK).

Microsoft Visual InterDev A development tool from Microsoft for building dynamic Web applications, such as Active Server Pages (ASP). *See also* Active Server Page (ASP).

Microsoft Workflow Designer for Exchange 2000 Server A utility for database developers to map out workflow processes based on the Microsoft Web Storage System and build a first skeleton of the workflow business solution. The workflow designer provides a convenient environment to create and register action tables and shared scripts. *See also* Web Storage System.

MIF *See* Message Interchange Format (MIF).

migration The process of transporting existing applications, user accounts, and data to different computer systems.

MIME *See* Multipurpose Internet Mail Extensions (MIME).

mixed-mode organization An Exchange 2000 Server organization that operates in mixed mode for backward compatibility with earlier versions of Microsoft Exchange Server. *See also* native-mode organization.

MMC *See* Microsoft Management Console (MMC).

moderated public folder A public folder where all postings are forwarded to a designated folder moderator to facilitate discussions in newsgroups or public Internet forums. The moderator must review the items individually and then grant approval by moving them back into the moderated folder.

move-mailbox upgrade *See* leapfrog upgrade.

MS Mail *See* Microsoft Mail for PC Networks (MS Mail).

MS Mail Connector Interchange A component of the MS Mail Connector implemented as a separate Microsoft Windows 2000 service that communicates with the Message Transfer Agent (MTA) to receive messages in Exchange format, converts them into MS Mail format, and places them in the Connector postoffice. The MS Mail Connector Interchange also obtains messages in MS Mail format from the Connector postoffice, converts them into Exchange format, and delivers them to the MTA. *See also* Connector postoffice.

MS Mail Connector MTA Service A Windows 2000 service that transfers messages in MS Mail format between the Connector postoffice and native MS Mail postoffices. See also Connector postoffice.

MS Mail Directory Synchronization events The events that form a complete Dirsync cycle; T1, T2, and T3. At T1, requestor postoffices generate update messages addressed to the Dirsync server. At T2, the Dirsync server incorporates received updates into a global master list and generates a global update message for all requestor postoffices that sent an update. At T3, the requestor postoffices incorporate the global address information into their postoffice address lists.

MS Mail Dirsync database A file called XDIR.EDB that resides in the \Program Files\Exchsrvr\Dxadata directory by default, which is used by the Directory Synchronization agent (DXA) to keep track of address updates received and sent from and to MS Mail postoffices. *See also* Directory Synchronization agent (DXA).

MS Mail external *See* MS Mail MTA.

MS Mail gateways Messaging components implemented as MS-DOS programs that provide MS Mail connectivity to foreign messaging systems, such as a Simple Mail Transfer Protocol (SMTP)-based or X.400-based system.

MS Mail MTA An MS-DOS-based messaging process that transfers messages between MS Mail postoffices.

MS Mail Multitasking MTA A Microsoft Windows NT-based messaging process that transfers messages between MS Mail postoffices.

MSDSS *See* Microsoft Directory Synchronization Services (MSDSS).

MTA *See* Message Transfer Agent (MTA).

MTS-IN The name of an inbound message queue maintained in the Information Store for an Exchange Development Kit (EDK)-based connector to a foreign messaging system. *See also* Exchange Development Kit (EDK), message queue.

MTS-OUT The name of an outbound message queue maintained in the Information Store for an Exchange Development Kit (EDK)-based connector to a foreign messaging system. *See also* Exchange Development Kit (EDK), message queue.

multicast *See* IP multicast.

Multicast Address Dynamic Client Allocation Protocol (MADCAP) An extension to the Dynamic Host Configuration Protocol (DHCP) that can be used to dynamically assign and configure Internet Protocol (IP) multicast addresses to support audio and video conferencing. *See also* audio and video conferencing, Dynamic Host Configuration Protocol (DHCP), IP multicast.

multihomed system A host with multiple network interface cards (NICs) attached to separate physical network segments. *See also* network interface card (NIC).

multimaster clustering A synonym for active/active clustering.

multimedia messaging The recording, transfer, and playback of audio and video data in e-mail messages. *See also* Microsoft Exchange Multimedia Control.

multipoint control unit (MCU) Data conferencing software that interconnects conference participants and distributes conference data based on the T.120 standard. Microsoft Exchange 2000 Conferencing Server provides a server-based MCU that supports client/server-based data conferencing with central management of online conferences.

Multipurpose Internet Mail Extensions (MIME) A standard format for Internet message bodies and attachments that enables the transfer of e-mail messages between different computer systems. MIME is defined in Request for Comments (RFC) 1521.

MX record An entry in a Domain Name System (DNS) database to identify mail exchanger systems (that is, SMTP hosts) for a DNS domain.

N

name and address book A database maintained by a Lotus Domino/Notes server that holds user and recipient information. *See also* Domino directory.

Name Service Provider Interface (NSPI) An interface used by Messaging Application Programming Interface (MAPI)-based clients to access directory information.

namespace A logical grouping of resources or items with the ability to resolve resource names to the actual objects they represent. Within any given namespace, resource names must be unique.

naming context (NC) A contiguous subtree in Active Directory that can be replicated as a unit to other domain controllers. Another term for naming context is directory partition. *See also* directory partition.

NAT *See* network address translation (NAT).

native-mode organization An Exchange 2000 Server organization that consists of only Exchange 2000 servers and provides the most flexible administrative and routing capabilities. Native-mode organizations do not support earlier versions of Exchange Server. *See also* mixed-mode organization.

NC *See* naming context (NC).

NDR *See* nondelivery report (NDR).

NDS *See* Novell Directory Services (NDS).

nesting The process of adding a group to another group with the primary purpose of reducing the replication overhead involved when group membership changes. Nested groups are only supported in native-mode Windows 2000 domains.

NetBEUI *See* NetBIOS Enhanced User Interface.

NetBIOS *See* Network Basic Input/Output System (NetBIOS).

NetBIOS Enhanced User Interface (NetBEUI) The Microsoft implementation of the NetBIOS programming interface that can be used in local area networks (LANs) that do not require the services of a network router.

NetBIOS over TCP/IP (NetBT) The Microsoft implementation of the NetBIOS programming interface over TCP/IP, for instance, to support NetBIOS name resolution in a TCP/IP-based network.

NetWare Core Protocol (NCP) The communication protocol between NetWare client software and a NetWare server on a Novell NetWare network.

NetWare Loadable Module (NLM) A server-based application that can be dynamically loaded and unloaded on a Novell NetWare server version 4.*x* and later.

network address translation (NAT) A feature that allows an administrator to connect a network through a single interface device to the Internet and provide Internet Protocol (IP) address translation between the public and private IP network. With NAT, for example, a small office network can connect to the Internet with a single IP address.

Network Basic Input/Output System (NetBIOS) An application programming interface (API) that can be used to access resources across a network. NetBIOS provides a uniform set of commands to establish sessions between network nodes and to transmit data.

network interface card (NIC) A device used to connect a computer to a local area network (LAN); also known as a network adapter or network card. *See also* local area network (LAN).

network load balancing A clustering feature of Microsoft Windows 2000 Advanced Server that can enhance the availability and scalability of Internet Information Services (IIS) platforms, such as IIS Web servers. Network load balancing supports up 32 hosts per cluster.

Network News Transfer Protocol (NNTP) A protocol used to distribute newsgroup articles to NNTP hosts and to newsreaders on the Usenet and Internet. NNTP is defined in Request for Comments (RFC) 977.

newsfeed control message A specific system message used by newsfeeds on the Usenet to create or delete newsgroups on a remote host.

newsgroup A discussion forum on the Usenet that typically focuses on a particular subject. Users can use newsreader software to participate in newsgroup discussions by contributing new postings or replies in the form of articles, which are replicated through the Usenet based on Network News Transfer Protocol (NNTP). Microsoft Exchange 2000 Server supports newsgroups implemented in public folders. *See also* Network News Transfer Protocol (NNTP).

NLM *See* NetWare Loadable Module (NLM).

NNTP *See* Network News Transfer Protocol (NNTP).

node In hierarchical structures, a location on the tree that can have links to one or more child objects. In computer networks, a device that is connected to the network to communicate with other systems. In the context of a server cluster, a server that is a member of a cluster.

Node Manager A process that runs on every node in a cluster to manage cluster membership and monitor the state of other nodes in the cluster. *See also* cluster.

nondelivery report (NDR) A notice that a message was not delivered to the intended recipient. An NDR typically contains the reason for the delivery problems, such as recipient not found.

nonrepudiation A basic feature of computer security that provides assurance that a participant in a communication cannot falsify another party's identity and that the communication partners cannot deny that part of a communication occurred.

Novell Directory Services (NDS) A directory service that runs on NetWare servers version 4 and later, which enables the centralized management of NetWare resources independent of their location on the network. NDS is a directory service comparable to Active Directory. *See also* Active Directory directory service.

Novell NetWare Client for Windows 2000 A software component from Novell for Microsoft Windows 2000 that can communicate with a Novell NetWare server via NetWare Core Protocol (NCP) in an Internetwork Packet Exchange (IPX)-based or TCP/IP-based environment. *See also* NetWare Core Protocol (NCP).

NSLookup A utility that allows a user to test the Domain Name System (DNS) name resolution. NSLookup also supports reverse DNS lookups and can find a host name from an Internet Protocol (IP) address. *See also* DNS lookup, Domain Name System (DNS).

NSPI *See* Name Service Provider Interface (NSPI).

NT File System (NTFS) A file system for storing and retrieving data in files on a hard disk that was

first introduced with Microsoft Windows NT version 3.1. In Windows 2000, NTFS supports advanced file system services, such as the Encrypting File System (EFS). *See also* Encrypting File System (EFS).

NT Virtual DOS Machine (NTVDM) A special Win32-based environment that translates MS-DOS operating system calls into calls used by the Win32 subsystem. For example, the MS-DOS-based Import/Export programs of Lotus cc:Mail are executed in NTVDMs. *See also* Lotus cc:Mail Import/Export programs.

NTFS *See* NT File System (NTFS).

NTVDM *See* NT Virtual DOS Machine (NTVDM).

NWLink IPX/SPX Compatible Transport (NWLink) The implementation of the Internetwork Packet Exchange/Sequenced Packet Exchange (IPX/SPX) protocol in Microsoft Windows operating systems, which supports communication with NetWare applications over IPX/SPX sockets.

O

object class A definition of supported interfaces and methods that application programs can use to interact with a programmable Component Object Model (COM) object. An object class is essentially a template from which an object of that class can be created.

object model A representation or map of an application's functionality in terms of programmable objects and their hierarchical relationships. For example, Microsoft Outlook provides an object model that allows a developer to create customized Outlook solutions that use the various Outlook objects, including folder and message items and their associated hierarchical dependencies (for instance, a message resides in a folder, but not vice versa).

Offline Address Book A server-based address list that is generated on an Exchange 2000 server and downloaded to a Messaging Application Programming Interface (MAPI)-based messaging client, such as Microsoft Outlook 2000. The Exchange transport service maintains the Offline Address Book in .oab files locally on the client computer.

offline backup A file-based full backup of Exchange database files when all services of Microsoft Exchange 2000 Server are stopped. *See also* online backup.

offline folder store A local message repository that is maintained by the Exchange transport service and automatically synchronized with the information stored on the Exchange 2000 server. Offline folder stores are implemented in .ost files that can contain messages, calendar, and other synchronized information. Users can work with their synchronized folders in the .ost file when not connected to the server. *See also* local replication.

offline folders Synchronized copies of server-based mailbox and public folders that are stored in an offline folder store locally on a client computer. *See also* offline folder store.

OLE DB A collection of Component Object Model (COM) interfaces designed to provide access to relational and nonrelational information sources. *See also* OLE DB provider.

OLE DB provider A software component that implements OLE DB interfaces and can be used to access an information source through the OLE DB subsystem. *See also* Exchange OLE DB provider (ExOLEDB).

OLE Messaging A simple object library (OLEMSG.DLL) provided with Microsoft Exchange Server 4.0 to support the development of interactive Web pages that access messaging-related information. OLE Messaging was replaced by Active Messaging, which in turn was superceded by Collaboration Data Objects (CDO). *See also* Active Messaging, Collaboration Data Objects (CDO).

online backup A backup of Exchange databases when all services of Microsoft Exchange 2000 Server are running. Online backups use the Backup API of Exchange 2000 Server.

Open Shortest Path First (OSPF) A complex routing protocol used in routed computer networks that provides efficient control over the propagation of routing information that allows routers to identify the most efficient path across a network. OSPF is similar to the link state algorithm (LSA) in Microsoft Exchange 2000 Server. *See also* link state algorithm (LSA), link state information (LSI).

Open Systems Interconnection (OSI) A reference model for the transmission of data between nodes in a telecommunication network. The reference model defines seven functional layers with well-defined purposes that represent horizontal end-points of the communication. An OSI-compliant protocol suite is X.400.

organizational forms library (OFL) A hidden system folder for public forms that are not associated with a particular public folder (send forms).

organizational unit (OU) A container object in Active Directory that is used to organize users, groups, computers, and other OUs. An OU is the smallest unit for which administrative permissions can be delegated.

OSI *See* Open Systems Interconnection (OSI).

OSPF *See* Open Shortest Path First (OSPF).

Outlook form An electronic form that is associated with a message class and launched by Microsoft Outlook automatically when an item of that class is opened. Outlook forms are not compiled, but interpreted at runtime. *See also* Outlook Forms Designer.

Outlook forms cache A folder on the local hard disk of the computer running Microsoft Outlook, which is used to download and store electronic forms prior to their execution. Outlook uses the forms cache to increase performance when opening forms. The forms cache eliminates the need to download a form every time an associated item is opened. *See also* Outlook form.

Outlook Forms Designer The development environment available in Microsoft Outlook to design electronic forms based on Outlook standard form types. The Outlook Forms Designer provides the functionality to register custom Outlook forms in an available forms library. *See also* forms library.

Outlook View Control An ActiveX control that can be hosted inside a Web page to gain access to programmable objects exposed by Microsoft Outlook 2000. The Outlook View Control is typically used in Digital Dashboards to provide convenient access to mailbox and public folders. *See also* Digital Dashboards.

Outlook Web Access (OWA) A Web-based messaging and collaboration client used to access message, calendar, and contacts folders using a Web browser. Microsoft Exchange Server 5.5 provides an OWA client that communicates with the Information Store service based on Messaging Application Programming Interface (MAPI). OWA for Microsoft Exchange 2000 Server, in contrast, uses the features of the Web Storage System. *See also* Web Storage System.

P

parent object A container or node that holds other objects and is in relation to these child objects. For example, the inbox folder of a mailbox is a parent object for received messages. An object can be both a parent and a child object; for instance, a subfolder in a public folder.

Patch 2 for API NLM An updated version of the Novell GroupWise API Gateway that is required for proper operation of the Connector for Novell GroupWise. *See also* API Gateway.

PDC *See* primary domain controller (PDC)

peer-to-peer conferencing A data conferencing model in which a client-based multipoint control unit (MCU) must send a separate copy of the data to each conference participant over a separate connection. *See also* client/server conferencing.

Performance snap-in A monitoring tool that is available in Microsoft Windows 2000 Server to monitor the performance of local and remote computers Windows NT or Windows 2000 systems anywhere on a computer network and to log results to a file for later analysis of the performance history.

perimeter network *See* demilitarized zone (DMZ).

permissions inheritance The automatic copying of security information from a parent to a newly created child object. *See also* inheritance.

personal folder store (PST) A folder store that is maintained in a .pst file locally on the client computer by the Messaging Application Programming Interface (MAPI)-based personal folder store provider. The personal folder store may also be located on a file server. It can be used to download messages and other items from a server-based mailbox or public folders.

personal folders A private repository for e-mail messages in a personal folder store (PST). *See also* personal folder store (PST), private folders.

personal forms library (PFL) A location for personal forms that is associated with a particular user's mailbox and not publicly available to other users.

PKCS *See* Public Key Cryptography Standard (PKCS).

PKI *See* public-key infrastructure (PKI).

POA *See* post office agent (POA).

Point-to-Point Tunneling Protocol (PPTP) An open industry standard to establish a virtual private network (VPN) over the Internet. PPTP is often used to replace long-distance dial-up connections with connections to a local Internet service provider (ISP) to reduce costs. *See also* Internet service provider (ISP), virtual private network (VPN).

polling The process of checking whether a resource exists and is available or operating.

POP3 *See* Post Office Protocol version 3 (POP3).

port An endpoint of a Transmission Control Protocol (TCP)- or User Datagram Protocol (UDP)-based connection by which a client can communicate with particular services. A property of TCP and UDP connections that identifies a service on a particular system. TCP and UDP ports range from 0 to 65536. Ports with the numbers 0 to 1024 are well-known ports defined for standard Internet protocols and services, for instance the default port number for Simple Mail Transfer Protocol (SMTP) is 25. *See also* Sockets.

postmaster A special e-mail account used as the originator of system messages, such as nondelivery reports (NDRs). The postmaster account may also receive status messages from active server components, such as messaging connectors. *See also* nondelivery report (NDR).

post office A central repository used in shared-file messaging systems to send and deliver e-mail messages. Clients typically poll the post office at periodic intervals to check for new messages. *See also* polling.

post office agent (POA) An active process in a Novell GroupWise environment that controls and maintains a post office. *See also* post office.

Post Office Protocol version 3 (POP3) A protocol that allows a client application to access a mail repository (Inbox) on a server. Typically, a POP3 client downloads all messages to the local workstation and uses Simple Mail Transfer Protocol (SMTP) to send e-mail messages. POP3 is defined in Request for Comments (RFC 1725). *See also* Simple Mail Transfer Protocol (SMTP).

PPTP *See* Point-to-Point Tunneling Protocol (PPTP).

presence information Information in an Instant Messaging environment that indicates a person's online status. *See also* Instant Messaging (IM).

preview pane A folder view feature in Microsoft Outlook 2000 that divides the Outlook window into two separate panes listing the items of a folder in the upper pane and the contents of the currently selected item in the lower pane without actually opening the item. *See also* folder views.

primary domain controller (PDC) In a Microsoft Windows NT Server domain, the computer that maintains the only writeable copy of the directory database for the domain. The PDC replicates this database to backup domain controlllers (BDCs), authenticates domain logons, and tracks changes made to computer and user accounts. A Windows NT Server domain can only have one PDC. *See also* backup domain controller (BDC).

private folders A private repository in a mailbox that is located on a computer running Microsoft Exchange 2000 Server. Private folders may be replicated to an offline folder store. *See also* offline folder store, personal folders.

private key A secret key that is available only to the user to whom it belongs. The private key is used in conjunction with a public key, which together form a cryptographic key pair. In Microsoft Exchange 2000 Server, private keys are used to digitally sign messages and to decrypt sealed messages. *See also* message sealing, message signing, public key.

Professional Office System (PROFS) IBM office automation software for mainframes that runs under the Virtual Machine (VM) operating system. PROFS provides e-mail messaging, calendaring, and workgroup capabilities.

PROFS *See* Professional Office System (PROFS).

protocol event sink Executable code that is registered with the Simple Mail Transfer Protocol (SMTP) or Network News Transfer Protocol (NNTP) service to extend the service's capabilities though custom verbs or commands. *See also* event sink, transport event sink.

protocol stack The implementation of a specific protocol family into a network driver that can be installed on a computer to serve the needs of network communication.

proxy address generation The process of generating an e-mail address for a foreign messaging system based on Exchange recipient information according to an address generation rule. The Recipient Update Service uses a separate proxy address generator to generate a proxy address of a specific type, for instance an MSMAIL proxy address. *See also* proxy address generator, Recipient Update Service.

proxy address generator A dynamic-link library (DLL) that generates an e-mail address for a foreign messaging system based on information supplied by the Recipient Update Service. *See also* Recipient Update Service.

proxy e-mail address An e-mail address for Exchange users that allows non-Exchange users to send them messages. Proxy addresses areused to represent Exchange user as recipients on a foreign system when sending mail to a non-Exchange recipient.

proxy server A multihomed system that is configured to act on behalf of assigned clients by translating client requests and passing them to another network segment. Proxy servers are often used as firewalls between a private network and the Internet. A proxy server may also cache Web pages for quicker retrieval by clients. *See also* multihomed system.

PTR record (PTR) A record in a Domain Name System (DNS) database that maps an Internet Protocol (IP) address to a host name in the In-addr.arpa domain. PTR records are used to perform reverse DNS lookups. *See also* DNS lookup.

public folder hierarchy A logical arrangement of public folder objects maintained in a tree, where upper nodes may contain zero, one, or many child nodes. Multiple hierarchies can be defined in Microsoft Exchange 2000 Server, but a particular hierarchy can only be associated with a single public store on a server. Each hierarchy is replicated as a unit to all servers that contain a public store associated with it. *See also* alternate hierarchy, MAPI-based hierarchy.

public folder replication The process of keeping public folder replicas on different Exchange 2000 servers synchronized.

public folder store *See* public store.

public key A secret key that is available to all users in an organization, used to verify digital signatures and seal (encrypt) messages for decryption by the owner of the associated private key. *See also* message sealing, message signing, private key.

Public Key Cryptography Standard (PKCS) Standard developed and maintained by RSA Data Security, Inc for defining methods of cryptography in which a public key and a private key are used. Public key cryptography is also called asymmetric cryptography because the encrypting key is different than the decrypting key. *See also* private key, public key.

public-key infrastructure (PKI) A framework of services, technology, protocols, and standards to deploy and manage a security system based on public key technology. A PKI consists of certificate authorities (CAs) and other registration authorities that issue and manage digital certificates. In Microsoft Exchange 2000 Server, PKIs include Certificate Services and a Key Management server. *See also* Key Management Service (KMS).

public store A set of Extensible Storage Engine (ESE) database files (Rich Text .edb database plus streaming .stm database) that are managed as a unit in Microsoft Exchange 2000 Server to maintain information in public folders. *See also* mailbox store.

public store policy A system policy configured in Exchange System Manager that applies configuration settings to one or many public stores in the administrative group. *See also* mailbox store policy, server policy, system policy.

pull feed A newsfeed that initiates connections to a provider host to obtain information and place it in local newsgroups. *See also* push feed.

push feed A newsfeed that initiates connections to a subscriber host to place information in the newsgroups of the remote host. Push feeds are typically used for very large newsfeeds. *See also* pull feed.

Q

quorum algorithm A voting mechanism to arbitrate the ownership of the quorum resource in case the current owner fails. The quorum algorithm guarantees that recovery data is maintained consistently between all cluster members. *See also* quorum resource.

quorum disk A physical disk that acts as the quorum resource and holds the cluster log. *See also* quorum resource.

quorum resource A special resource in a server cluster that provides a physical storage media for the cluster log. Only a single node in the cluster can gain physical control of the cluster resource at a given time and there is only one quorum resource per cluster by default.

R

RAID *See* redundant array of inexpensive disks (also recently referred to as redundant array of independent disks) (RAID).

RCONSOLE A Novell NetWare utility that provides a remote view of the NetWare server's system console to perform management tasks remotely, such as loading an NetWare Loadable Module (NLM).

read receipt (RR) An e-mail confirmation that a recipient has displayed a message. Read receipts can be requested for individual messages or for all messages depending on the client configuration. *See also* delivery confirmation report.

real-time collaboration A set of services that give users the ability to participate in live group discussions, share files and applications, and join online meetings. In Microsoft Exchange 2000 Server, real-time collaboration is supported through online conferencing, Instant Messaging (IM), and Chat.

Real-Time Protocol (RTP) A protocol designed to carry real-time data over a computer network.

recipient object An object in a directory that provides information, such as e-mail addresses, about a destination that can receive e-mail messages. In Active Directory, recipient objects are mailbox-enabled users accounts or mail-enabled user accounts or contacts. Recipient objects are replicated to the Global Catalog to make them available in server-based address books. *See also* Global Catalog.

recipient policy A group of settings that are applied to mailbox- and mail-enabled recipient objects to generate e-mail addresses. *See also* recipient object.

Recipient Update Service A process in Microsoft Exchange 2000 Server that applies settings defined in recipient policies to recipient objects in Active Directory. The primary task is e-mail address generation.

Recipient container In Microsoft Exchange Server 5.5, a container in the Exchange directory that holds recipient objects. Recipient containers can be used to structure server-based address lists, but is not possible to move a mailbox from one Recipient container to another after the mailbox has been created. In Exchange 2000 Server, an organizational unit (OU) that holds mailbox- and mail-enabled accounts, which is not used as a structured address list. It is possible to move accounts and contacts between OUs using Active Directory Users and Computers. *See also* recipient objects.

reconnecting a mailbox The process of reassigning a deleted or otherwise disconnected mailbox to a user account in Active Directory. By default, Exchange Exchange 2000 Server holds disconnected mailboxes in the information store for 30 days to enable administrators to reconnect them to user accounts without the need for a backup.

recovery server A separate computer system that is not part of a production environment to be used to restore information from backup media, such as for disaster recovery purposes.

redundant array of independent disks (RAID) A mechanism of configuring multiple disks as a single logical drive for redundancy, improved performance, and increased resilience.

Registry A system database that stores information about the system, user environments, applications, and hardware devices. An administrator can edit the Registry using standard administrative utilities or a Registry Editor.

relative distinguished name (RDN) That part of an object's distinguished name that refers to the actual object in relation to the container in which the object resides. It is possible for multiple objects in different containers to have the same RDN, but all objects have unique distinguished names (DNs).

remote procedure call (RPC) A client/server protocol for distributed computer systems, which transfers function calls and data between client and server processes.

Rendezvous Protocol (RVP) The protocol used by the Microsoft MSN Messenger client to interact with an Instant Messaging server. See also Instant Messaging Presence Protocol.

Request for Comments (RFC) An industry standard issued by the Internet Engineering Task Force (IETF) that specifies the details for protocols used on the Internet. *See also* Internet Engineering Task Force (IETF).

requestor postoffice A Microsoft Mail for PC Networks postoffice that is configured as a Dirsync requestor. *See also* Dirsync requestor.

Resolver Domain Name System (DNS) process that looks up DNS name information on behalf of TCP/IP-based processes that want to resolve DNS names into Internet Protocol (IP) addresses or vice versa.

Resource Manager A process in a cluster that communicates with the Cluster service to monitor the health of the cluster resources. *See also* Cluster service.

reverse DNS lookup A query in which an Internet Protocol (IP) address is resolved to a Domain Name System (DNS) name. *See also* DNS lookup.

RFC *See* Request for Comments (RFC).

Rich Text Format (RTF) A standard method of encoding formatted text and graphics in documents on MS-DOS, Windows, Windows 95, OS/2, and Apple Macintosh systems.

round-robin DNS A simple Domain Name System (DNS) mechanism to distribute TCP/IP connections over multiple network systems. Round-robin DNS is based on the principle of registering the same DNS domain name with multiple Internet Protocol (IP) addresses to rotate the IP address returned in query answers. *See also* DNS lookup.

Router for Novell GroupWise A component of the Connector for Novell GroupWise that transfers keyword-based text files to and from an API Gateway. *See also* API Gateway, keyword-based text file.

Routing and Remote Access Service (RRAS) A component that provides multiprotocol routing and remote access and services required to establish a virtual private network (VPN). Microsoft Exchange 2000 Server uses RRAS to communicate with remote systems over dial-up connections.

Routing Engine A service in Microsoft Exchange 2000 Server that makes message routing decisions based on link state information (LSI). *See also* link state information (LSI).

routing group A collection of Exchange 2000 servers that typically share a permanent, reliable, high-bandwidth network connection. In a routing group, all servers communicate directly with each other using Simple Mail Transfer Protocol (SMTP).

Routing Group Connector (RGC) A connector that can only be used to provide a message path between routing groups in the same organization. In native-mode organizations, an RGC transfers messages in transport-neutral encapsulation format (TNEF) based on Simple Mail Transfer Protocol (SMTP). In mixed-mode organizations, an RGC communicates via remote procedure call (RPC) when connecting to Microsoft Exchange Server 5.5. *See also* mixed-mode organization, native-mode organization.

routing group master (RGM) An Exchange 2000 server that centrally maintains the link state table (LST) for a routing group and propagates it to all other servers in the routing group. All other servers inform the RGM about any link state information (LSI) changes that they detect. *See also* link state algorithm (LSA), link state information (LSI).

roving user A user who works with multiple computers in different locations, whose profile is stored on a server and downloaded to the current workstation during the logon process to provide the same desktop and user settings on all machines.

RPC *See* remote procedure call (RPC).

RPC Endpoint Mapper A service that allows the remote procedure call (RPC) runtime environment to dynamically resolve and assign Transmission Control Protocol (TCP) ports to applications. *See also* port.

RTP *See* Real-Time Transport Protocol (RTP).

runtime license A special license for an ActiveX control that allows an application that contains the ActiveX controls to load and use it without errors. Runtime licenses are typically distributed with applications that contain ActiveX controls.

RVP *See* Rendezvous Protocol (RVP).

S

SACL *See* system access control list (SACL).

SAP *See* Service Advertising Protocol (SAP).

SASL *See* Simple Authentication and Security Layer (SASL).

Schedule+ Free/Busy Connector A component of the MS Mail Connector to synchronize free/busy information between MS Mail and Microsoft Exchange 2000 Server.

schema The metadata that governs the type of objects that can exist in a database and describes their mandatory and optional attributes. Active Directory supports an extensible schema that allows third parties to create their own object classes. Databases in Microsoft Exchange 2000 Server use a semistructured schema, which provides the required flexibility to support all kinds of information in mailboxes and public folders.

schema administrator A member of the Schema Admins group. *See also* Schema Admins.

Schema Admins A special Windows 2000 group that exists only in the root domain of an Active Directory forest. Members of this group are known as schema administrators. They are authorized to make schema changes in Active Directory.

schema definition file A system file that is used by the Connector for Lotus Notes and Connector for Novell GroupWise to determine the subset of directory attributes that must be synchronized between Active Directory and the foreign system. *See also* directory synchronization.

schema extension An update to the standard Active Directory schema to support additional functionality that is not covered by standard directory object classes and attributes. Microsoft Exchange 2000 Server applies several extensions

to the Active Directory schema to implement Exchange-specific configuration objects and attributes.

scratch file An e-mail message written to a text file in the Connector Store of the Connector for Lotus cc:Mail. *See also* Connector for Lotus cc:Mail.

secret key An encryption key that is used for data encryption and decryption. In an electronic communication, the secret key is shared between the authorized communication partners. It is important to protect the secret key from unauthorized users, for instance by using a public key encryption method.

Secure Password Authentication (SPA) The process of authenticating messaging users using current logon credential information. SPA assumes that the mailbox alias is the same as the user's Windows 2000 account. Internet mail clients can use the Auth NTLM command to initiate an SPA. *See also* authentication.

Secure Sockets Layer (SSL) A communication standard developed by Netscape Communications that resides on top of TCP/IP and provides public key cryptography services to guarantee privacy over public networks. *See also* public key.

Secure/Multipurpose Internet Mail Extensions (S/MIME) An extension of Multipurpose Internet Mail Extensions (MIME) that supports message signing and sealing. *See also* message sealing, message signing.

security descriptor A data structure containing information to secure an object through access control and auditing settings defined for users, groups, and processes. A security descriptor may contain a discretionary access control list (DACL) for access permissions and a system access control list (SACL) for system auditing.

security identifier (SID) A unique name that identifies a security principal, such as an individual user, a group, or a computer. *See also* security principal.

security principal An account that has a security identifier (SID) and can be granted or denied access to objects in Active Directory. In contrast, a nonsecurity principal is an object represented in Active Directory that cannot access resources within the forest (for instance, a mail-enabled contact). *See also* access control.

semistructured database A database, such as Active Directory, with a schema that supports a flexible storage model to provide the ability to store and transport unstructured or semistructured data, such as word processing documents, presentation files, appointment and contact items, or e-mail messages.

SEO *See* Server Extension Objects (SEO).

Server Extension Objects (SEO) A management technology to register event sinks with the Simple Mail Transfer Protocol (SMTP) or Network News Transfer Protocol (NNTP) service, or Microsoft Web Storage System. *See also* event sink.

Server Message Block (SMB) A file-sharing protocol used by NetBIOS for file and printer sharing for communication between all Microsoft networking products. *See also* Network Basic Input/Output System (NetBIOS).

server policy A system policy configured in Exchange System Manager that applies configuration settings to one or many servers in the administrative group. *See also* mailbox store policy, public store policy, system policy.

service account A Windows 2000 user or computer account that is used to run system services. In Microsoft Exchange 2000 Server, services are configured to operate in the context of the local system account. In Exchange Server 5.5, a common user account must be used for all services on all servers in a site, which is therefore also known as site services account.

Service Advertising Protocol (SAP) A protocol used in NetWare environments to advertise server services and to perform name resolution. NetWare servers and all Internetwork Packet Exchange (IPX) routers must use SAP to periodically broadcast their services, server name, and the IPX internal network address.

Service Location Resource Records (SRV) A standard Domain Name System (DNS) resource record to specify the location of a host that provides a specific service over a specific protocol for a defined DNS domain. *See also* Domain Name System (DNS).

Service Provider Interface (SPI) An interface of the Messaging Application Programming Interface (MAPI) subsystem that independent software vendors and third-party developers can use to develop MAPI drivers for messaging systems, such as address book, transport, or message store providers.

ShivaRemote Software included with the Microsoft Exchange client for MS-DOS and Windows 3 or later for full remote connectivity over dial-up connections.

shortcut menu A dynamic menu that is displayed when a user right-clicks a visual element in the user interface to provide object-specific options and commands.

SID *See* security identifier (SID).

SIDHistory An attribute of a user account in Active Directory that is used to maintain former security identifiers (SIDs) so that the user can get access to resources that were made available to a former account. The SIDHistory is particularly important when migrating users from Microsoft Windows NT 4.0 or moving users between domains (because SIDs are domain specific). *See also* security identifier (SID).

Simple Authentication and Security Layer (SASL)
A method for adding authentication support to connection-based protocols. Connecting client must issue the AUTH command to initiate the authentication process with the server. SASL is defined in Request for Comments (RFC) 2222. *See also* authentication.

Simple Mail Transfer Protocol (SMTP) A transport protocol for sending messages from one host to another on a TCP/IP network. SMTP is used on the Internet for e-mail messaging. Microsoft Exchange 2000 Server is based on a powerful SMTP-based routing and transport engine.

single-instance storage A feature to store a message sent to many recipients in a single instance on the server to preserve disk space.

site In Microsoft Windows 2000 Server, an element to organize the physical structure of an Active Directory environment. Sites are collections of Internet Protocol (IP) subnets with high-speed connectivity for direct Active Directory replication. In Exchange Server 5.5, a grouping of servers that communicate directly with each other using remote procedure calls (RPCs).

Site Consistency Checker A component of Site Replication Service (SRS) that creates configuration connection agreements for the Active Directory Connector (ADC) according to the topology of sites, administration groups, and Windows 2000 domains in a mixed-mode organization. An updated version of the Knowledge Consistency Checker of Exchange Server 5.5.

Site Replication Service (SRS) The implementation of the legacy Exchange directory service into Microsoft Exchange 2000 Server to provide an Exchange Server 5.5 interface for directory repli-

cation to earlier versions of Exchange Server. The SRS works in conjunction with the Active Directory Connector (ADC) and is primarily responsible for replicating configuration information. *See also* Active Directory Connector (ADC).

Small Computer System Interface (SCSI) A standard defined by the X3T9.2 committee of the American National Standards Institute (ANSI) to connect peripheral devices, such as hard disks and printers, and other equipment to a computer system.

smart host A system that is located somewhere in the network and can be reached using Simple Mail Transfer Protocol (SMTP) to forward outgoing messages to their destinations on behalf of the sending SMTP system.

SMTP *See* Simple Mail Transfer Protocol (SMTP).

SNA Distributed Systems (SNADS) A message transport protocol for System Network Architecture (SNA)-based systems that communicate in a peer-to-peer network.

snap-in A component of the MMC framework that is used to administer components and services under Microsoft Windows 2000. The Exchange System Manager is an example of a Microsoft Management Console (MMC) snap-in that is used to manage an Exchange 2000 Server organization. *See also* Microsoft Management Console (MMC).

Sockets An implementation of the UC Berkeley Sockets application programming interface (API) that applications use to create TCP/IP connections. A Socket is a combination of an Internet Protocol (IP) address and a port number used to establish a connection between computers in a communication network. *See also* port.

soft recovery The process of applying transaction log files to database files to recover from a failure, such as a power outage. Microsoft Exchange 2000 Server performs a soft recovery automatically when restarting the Information Store service.

SPA *See* Secure Password Authentication (SPA).

spoofing An insidious method of changing data in such a way that it appears to come from another (authorized) user.

SQL *See* structured query language (SQL).

SRS *See* Site Replication Service (SRS).

SRV Records *See* Service Location Resource Records (SRV).

SSL *See* Secure Sockets Layer (SSL).

storage group A collection of mailbox and public stores in Microsoft Exchange 2000 Server that share a common set of transaction log files. The stores in a storage group should be maintained as a unit. A single Exchange 2000 server can have up to four separate storage groups, which can hold each up to five mailbox and public stores. *See also* mailbox store, public store.

storage limits The maximum amount of data as defined by an administrator that can be stored in a mailbox, public folder, or storage group before Microsoft Exchange 2000 Server generates warning messages or prevents message sending or receiving.

store and forward mechanism A mechanism that allows a system to store information until a communication path to the receiver is available. E-mail systems, for instance, operate according to the store and forward mechanism in that a server receives and stores e-mail messages locally to deliver them to the recipient's home server or another intermediary system in the message path when a connection can be established.

streaming database A database of the Information Store service that supports streaming Multipurpose Internet Mail Extensions (MIME) content directly into a mailbox or public store without conversion. File names of the streaming database have an .stm extension, by default. *See also* Multipurpose Internet Mail Extensions (MIME).

structured query language (SQL) A database query and programming language for accessing data, and querying, updating, and managing relational database systems originally developed by IBM.

subnet A separate part of a computer network in which all nodes can communicate directly with each other. A logical grouping of network computers that use IP addresses from a single, contiguous block. A subnet typically connects computers in the same geographical location and the same network segment.

subnet mask A series of 4 bytes that determine which part of an Internet Protocol (IP) address identifies a node's network segment subnet (network ID) and which part refers to the node address.

synchronous event An event that is fired as a condition occurs, which provides event sinks with exclusive control of the item that triggered the event. The event source thread is blocked for the duration of the sink execution.

system access control list (SACL) That part of a security descriptor that controls how the Windows 2000 security subsystem audits attempts to access an object. *See also* security descriptor.

System Attendant (SA) A core service of Microsoft Exchange 2000 Server that performs regular maintenance tasks, such as the monitoring of server services and messaging connectors, starting the defragmentation routines of the

Information Store, and forwarding directory lookups to a Global Catalog.

system policy A configuration object that can be applied to server objects, mailbox stores, or public stores, which defines common configuration parameters that are applied to all objects associated with the policy. *See also* mailbox store policy, public store policy, server policy.

T

T.120 A suite of communications and application protocols for real-time, multipoint data connections and online conferencing.

T.127 A protocol for file transfer based on the T.120 standard.

TCP port *See* port.

TCP/IP *See* Transmission Control Protocol/ Internet Protocol (TCP/IP).

teleconference An online conference that enables more than two participants to communicate in real time. *See also* audio and video conferencing.

Telephony Application Programming Interface (TAPI) A Windows application programming interface (API) to integrate computer and telephone technologies for dial-up access, voice input/output, and other features.

Telnet Utility A terminal emulation program that allows a user to establish a host session to a server using one of several emulation types.

Terminal Services A set of Microsoft Windows 2000 Server services that allows a user to run client applications for data processing and storage directly on the server using a terminal, thin client, or terminal emulator. In a terminal server environment, the server performs all processing. The client sends keyboard and mouse input directly to the server and displays the results on the monitor.

timestamp Information attached to an object in one or more attributes to indicate the time an object was created, changed, or last accessed.

TLS *See* Transport Layer Security (TLS).

TNEF *See* transport-neutral encapsulation format (TNEF).

transaction log file A file that gives the Extensible Storage Engine (ESE) the ability to sequentially append new transactions from the memory cache to existing data in the file without the need for complex database operations. Transaction log files provide fault tolerance in case the content from the memory cache is lost due to a system failure and the data needs to be restored to the databases.

Transmission Control Protocol/Internet Protocol (TCP/IP) A suite of protocols that provide a reliable, routable communication infrastructure for computer systems with different hardware architectures and operating systems. TCP/IP can be used in local area network (LAN) and wide area network (WAN) environments.

transport event An event fired when a message arrives to the Simple Mail Transfer Protocol (SMTP) or Network News Transfer Protocol (NNTP) service. Transport events provide a means to intercept messages and news articles before they are placed in the Microsoft Web Storage System. *See also* event sink.

transport event sink Executable code that is registered with the Simple Mail Transfer Protocol (SMTP) or Network News Transfer Protocol (NNTP) service to process the contents of every message passing through these transports. *See also* event sink, protocol event sink.

Transport Layer Security (TLS) A communication layer similar to Secure Sockets Layer (SSL) that provides privacy, authentication, and data integrity by using a combination of public key and bulk encryption. *See also* Secure Sockets Layer (SSL).

transport-neutral encapsulation format (TNEF) The format of a binary message attachment that is used to package message properties not understood by intermediate messaging systems in the delivery path. In most cases, the binary attachment is named WINMAIL.DAT.

trusted root certification authority A root certificate authority that is trusted by the computer for all purposes defined in its security certificate.

U

UDP *See* User Datagram Protocol (UDP)

unattended setup The process of installing an application without direct user input using a setup initialization file with predefined settings.

UNC *See* Universal Naming Convention (UNC).

unicasting The process of sending data over a computer network to an address that identifies a specific, globally unique host. Unicast addresses are also known as media access control (MAC) addresses.

unified messaging The combination of messaging, fax, voice, and online conferencing technologies to integrate all forms of electronic communication into one infrastructure.

Uniform Resource Identifier (URI) An address string to point to an object of content on the Internet (typically a Web page, but also audio or video, images, or a program). The most common form of URI is the Uniform Resource Locator (URL). *See also* Uniform Resource Locator (URL).

Uniform Resource Locator (URL) An address in the format protocol://serveraddress/path that specifies the location and name of a resource on the Internet or an intranet. *See also* Uniform Resource Identifier (URI).

Uniform Resource Name (URN) A type of Uniform Resource Identifier (URI) that identifies a resource irrespective of its location. *See also* Uniform Resource Identifier (URI).

universal group A specific type of group in Active Directory that is available anywhere in the forest. Universal groups can contain other universal groups, global groups, and accounts from anywhere in the forest. Universal groups are only available in native mode. They are replicated to the Global Catalog.

Universal Naming Convention (UNC) A naming convention to identify computers in a network and their share points. The UNC format defines the server name preceded by two backslashes, followed by other fields that are separated by a single backslash, such as \\servername\sharename\path\filename.

UNIX A portable, multiuser, multitasking operating system written in the C programming language, originally developed at AT&T Bell Laboratories in 1969.

Unix-to-Unix encoding method (uuencode) A method of encoding and decoding files or e-mail attachments into 7-bit ASCII for the purpose of data transfer between systems in a network. *See also* American Standard Code for Information Interchange (ASCII).

Usenet A worldwide communication network of sites and servers that use Network News Transfer Protocol (NNTP) to replicate articles between newsgroup instances. *See also* Network News Transport Protocol (NNTP).

user connection agreement A connection agreement of the Active Directory Connector (ADC) established between Microsoft Exchange Server 5.5 and Active Directory to replicate recipient information between both systems. *See also* Active Directory Connector (ADC).

User Datagram Protocol (UDP) A protocol on top of Internet Protocol (IP) that offers a connectionless datagram service (that is, it does not guarantee delivery or provide packet sequencing). To transfer data over UDP, all information must fit into a single UDP packet. UDP offers improved efficiency over Transmission Control Protocol (TCP) for short messages.

user mode A mode of the Microsoft Management Console (MMC) that provides only a subset of features to the user that opened the console. *See also* author mode.

uuencode *See* Unix-to-Unix encoding method (uuencode).

V

VBScript *See* Visual Basic Scripting Edition (VBScript).

vCard An implementation of an electronic business card to exchange personal information such as address, name, e-mail address, and phone number with other users, regardless of their client programs.

virtual directory A shared Web folder accessible from within Internet Information Services (IIS) that maps to a folder on the file system. *See also* Internet Information Services (IIS).

virtual private network (VPN) A technology that leverages Internet Protocol (IP) connectivity and encryption technology to connect remote clients and remote offices across a public network, such as the Internet, in a manner that emulates the properties of point-to-point private links.

virtual server A collection of services provided to clients as an emulation of a physical server. *See also* virtual server instance (VSI).

virtual server instance (VSI) An instance of a virtual server that consists of a combination of Internet Protocol (IP) address and Transmission Control Protocol (TCP) port number, and individual configuration parameters for a specific protocol service, such as Simple Mail Transfer Protocol (SMTP).

Visual Basic Scripting Edition (VBScript) A subset of Visual Basic that enables developers to create script-based business applications, such as Active Server Pages (ASPs). VBScript can also be used to extend the functionality of Outlook forms or to provide solutions for Microsoft Windows Scripting Host.

VPN *See* virtual private network (VPN).

VSI *See* virtual server instance (VSI).

W

WAN *See* wide area network (WAN).

Web browser A client interface that enables a user to view Hypertext Markup Language (HTML) documents typically transferred to the user's computer via Hypertext Transfer Protocol (HTTP). A good example of a Web browser is Microsoft Internet Explorer 5.0.

Web Distributed Authoring and Versioning (WebDAV) An extension to the Hypertext Transfer Protocol (HTTP) 1.1 standard that allows remote authors to add, search, delete, or change files, directories, and documents and their properties through an HTTP connection.

Web forms library (WFL) A location for Web-based forms for Outlook Web Access (OWA).

Web Storage System A database architecture in Microsoft Exchange 2000 Server that provides access to mailbox and public folder resources through Hypertext Transfer Protocol (HTTP), Extensible Markup Language (XML), Web Distributed Authoring and Versioning (WebDAV), OLE DB, ActiveX Data Objects (ADO), and an installable file system driver.

Web Storage System event Notifications triggered by Exchange OLE DB to activate registered event sinks. Web Storage System events are a means to implement workflow and process-tracking logic for mailbox and public folders. *See also* event sink.

Web Storage System form A Hypertext Markup Language (HTML)-based form that is launched automatically when a user accesses an item in the Web Storage System via HTTP/WebDAV. A custom forms engine is used to render HTML forms.

Web Storage System Forms for Microsoft Exchange 2000 Server Software Development Kit (SDK) A technology for the Web Storage System to enable developers to build Hypertext Markup Language (HTML)-based forms in Microsoft FrontPage 2000 without the need for any programming. *See also* Web Storage System form.

Web Storage System forms registry A forms library in the Web Storage System that is used to register Web Storage System forms. *See also* Web Storage System forms.

Microsoft Web Storage System *See* Web Storage System.

WebDAV See Web Distributed Authoring and Versioning (WebDAV).

wide area network (WAN) A communications network spanning a geographically distributed area, which uses a protocol that allows any connected device to interact with any other system on the network. A very popular protocol used in WAN environments is TCP/IP.

Windows 2000 Service A Win32 executable without a user interface that interacts with the Service Control Manager (SCM) to enable an administrator to control (for example, start, stop, or pause) the service application.

Windows Internet Naming Service (WINS) A name resolution service that resolves Windows networking computer names to Internet Protocol (IP) addresses in a routed environment. A server using this service handles name registrations, queries, and releases.

Windows scripting host (WSH) A scripting host for 32-bit Windows platforms that supports Visual Basic Scripting Edition (VBScript) and JavaScript and is capable of handling other script languages through additional ActiveX scripting engines.

Windows Sockets A term that is typically used to refer to the implementation of the Sockets API on the Microsoft Windows operating system. Sometimes, however, Windows Sockets (or Winsock) is also used to refer to TCP Sliding Windows to differentiate it from a previous version of TCP that did not include sliding Windows. See also Sockets.**WINS** *See* Windows Internet Naming Service (WINS).

Winsock *See* Windows Sockets.

WordPerfect Office A predecessor of Novell GroupWise.

workflow A technology to implement business processes into a communication infrastructure through automated message routing, process tracking, reporting, and exception processing.

workflow author A privileged user that can register a workflow process in the Microsoft Web Storage System.

workflow engine The active process in the workflow environment of Microsoft Exchange 2000 Server that receives notifications from the workflow event sink and processes the workflow logic according to the process definition. *See also* workflow process definition.

Workflow for Exchange 2000 Server A technology in Microsoft Exchange 2000 Server based on Collaboration Data Objects (CDO) for Workflow that provides a high-end workflow infrastructure based on the Web Storage System. *See also* CDO for Workflow (CDOWF).

workflow process definition The outline or set of rules of a workflow process. *See also* workflow.

World Wide Web Publishing Service A service in Microsoft Windows 2000 to build Web severs for publishing information in the form of hypertext and hypermedia using Hypertext Markup Language (HTML) and creating collaboration and workflow solutions based on the Hypertext Transfer Protocol (HTTP).

X

X.400 Connector A connector component in Microsoft Exchange 2000 Server to route messages to foreign X.400 systems and to other Exchange servers running an instance of an X.400 Connector. The X.400 Connector is integrated with the Message Transfer Agent (MTA) and can be used to connect sites or routing groups in an organization.

X.500 An International Telecommunications Union (ITU)-T recommendation that defines the internal structure of electronic directory services.

X.509 An International Telecommunications Union (ITU)-T recommendation that describes the syntax and format of security certificates.

X.509 certificate A document issued by a certificate authority that contains security information used for digital signatures and encryption.

XML *See* Extensible Markup Language (XML).

Index

Note to reader Italicized
page references indicate
illustrations.

Test *your* **readiness** *for the* MCP**exam**

If you took a Microsoft Certified Professional (MCP) exam today, would you pass? With each READINESS REVIEW MCP exam simulation on CD-ROM, you get a low-risk, low-cost way to find out! The next-generation test engine delivers a set of randomly generated, 50-question practice exams covering real MCP objectives. You can test and retest with different question sets each time—and with automated scoring, you get immediate Pass/Fail feedback. Use these READINESS REVIEWS to evaluate your proficiency with the skills and knowledge that you'll be tested on in the real exams.

Microsoft® Resource Kits— powerhouse resources to minimize costs while maximizing performance

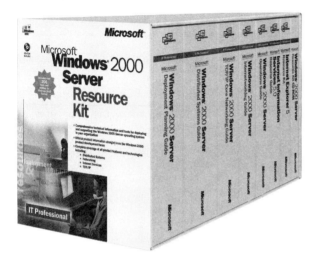

Deploy and support your enterprise business systems using the expertise and tools of those who know the technology best—the Microsoft product groups. Each RESOURCE KIT packs precise technical reference, installation and rollout tactics, planning guides, upgrade strategies, and essential utilities on CD-ROM. They're everything you need to help maximize system performance as you reduce ownership and support costs!

Microsoft® Windows® 2000 Server Resource Kit
ISBN   1-57231-805-8
U.S.A. $299.99
U.K.   £189.99 [V.A.T. included]
Canada $460.99

Microsoft Windows 2000 Professional Resource Kit
ISBN   1-57231-808-2
U.S.A. $69.99
U.K.   £45.99 [V.A.T. included]
Canada $107.99

Microsoft BackOffice® 4.5 Resource Kit
ISBN   0-7356-0583-1
U.S.A. $249.99
U.K.   £161.99 [V.A.T. included]
Canada $374.99

Microsoft Internet Explorer 5 Resource Kit
ISBN   0-7356-0587-4
U.S.A. $59.99
U.K.   £38.99 [V.A.T. included]
Canada $89.99

Microsoft Office 2000 Resource Kit
ISBN   0-7356-0555-6
U.S.A. $59.99
U.K.   £38.99 [V.A.T. included]
Canada $89.99

Microsoft Windows NT® Server 4.0 Resource Kit
ISBN   1-57231-344-7
U.S.A. $149.95
U.K.   £96.99 [V.A.T. included]
Canada $199.95

Microsoft Windows NT Workstation 4.0 Resource Kit
ISBN   1-57231-343-9
U.S.A. $69.95
U.K.   £45.99 [V.A.T. included]
Canada $94.95

mspress.microsoft.com

MICROSOFT LICENSE AGREEMENT

Book Companion CD

IMPORTANT—READ CAREFULLY: This Microsoft End-User License Agreement ("EULA") is a legal agreement between you (either an individual or an entity) and Microsoft Corporation for the Microsoft product identified above, which includes computer software and may include associated media, printed materials, and "online" or electronic documentation ("SOFTWARE PRODUCT"). Any component included within the SOFTWARE PRODUCT that is accompanied by a separate End-User License Agreement shall be governed by such agreement and not the terms set forth below. By installing, copying, or otherwise using the SOFTWARE PRODUCT, you agree to be bound by the terms of this EULA. If you do not agree to the terms of this EULA, you are not authorized to install, copy, or otherwise use the SOFTWARE PRODUCT; you may, however, return the SOFTWARE PRODUCT, along with all printed materials and other items that form a part of the Microsoft product that includes the SOFTWARE PRODUCT, to the place you obtained them for a full refund.

SOFTWARE PRODUCT LICENSE

The SOFTWARE PRODUCT is protected by United States copyright laws and international copyright treaties, as well as other intellectual property laws and treaties. The SOFTWARE PRODUCT is licensed, not sold.

1. **GRANT OF LICENSE.** This EULA grants you the following rights:

    a. **Software Product.** You may install and use one copy of the SOFTWARE PRODUCT on a single computer. The primary user of the computer on which the SOFTWARE PRODUCT is installed may make a second copy for his or her exclusive use on a portable computer.

    b. **Storage/Network Use.** You may also store or install a copy of the SOFTWARE PRODUCT on a storage device, such as a network server, used only to install or run the SOFTWARE PRODUCT on your other computers over an internal network; however, you must acquire and dedicate a license for each separate computer on which the SOFTWARE PRODUCT is installed or run from the storage device. A license for the SOFTWARE PRODUCT may not be shared or used concurrently on different computers.

    c. **License Pak.** If you have acquired this EULA in a Microsoft License Pak, you may make the number of additional copies of the computer software portion of the SOFTWARE PRODUCT authorized on the printed copy of this EULA, and you may use each copy in the manner specified above. You are also entitled to make a corresponding number of secondary copies for portable computer use as specified above.

    d. **Sample Code.** Solely with respect to portions, if any, of the SOFTWARE PRODUCT that are identified within the SOFTWARE PRODUCT as sample code (the "SAMPLE CODE"):

    i. **Use and Modification.** Microsoft grants you the right to use and modify the source code version of the SAMPLE CODE, *provided* you comply with subsection (d)(iii) below. You may not distribute the SAMPLE CODE, or any modified version of the SAMPLE CODE, in source code form.

    ii. **Redistributable Files.** Provided you comply with subsection (d)(iii) below, Microsoft grants you a nonexclusive, royalty-free right to reproduce and distribute the object code version of the SAMPLE CODE and of any modified SAMPLE CODE, other than SAMPLE CODE, or any modified version thereof, designated as not redistributable in the Readme file that forms a part of the SOFTWARE PRODUCT (the "Non-Redistributable Sample Code"). All SAMPLE CODE other than the Non-Redistributable Sample Code is collectively referred to as the "REDISTRIBUTABLES."

    iii. **Redistribution Requirements.** If you redistribute the REDISTRIBUTABLES, you agree to: (i) distribute the REDISTRIBUTABLES in object code form only in conjunction with and as a part of your software application product; (ii) not use Microsoft's name, logo, or trademarks to market your software application product; (iii) include a valid copyright notice on your software application product; (iv) indemnify, hold harmless, and defend Microsoft from and against any claims or lawsuits, including attorney's fees, that arise or result from the use or distribution of your software application product; and (v) not permit further distribution of the REDISTRIBUTABLES by your end user. Contact Microsoft for the applicable royalties due and other licensing terms for all other uses and/or distribution of the REDISTRIBUTABLES.

2. **DESCRIPTION OF OTHER RIGHTS AND LIMITATIONS.**

    - **Limitations on Reverse Engineering, Decompilation, and Disassembly.** You may not reverse engineer, decompile, or disassemble the SOFTWARE PRODUCT, except and only to the extent that such activity is expressly permitted by applicable law notwithstanding this limitation.

    - **Separation of Components.** The SOFTWARE PRODUCT is licensed as a single product. Its component parts may not be separated for use on more than one computer.

    - **Rental.** You may not rent, lease, or lend the SOFTWARE PRODUCT.

- **Support Services.** Microsoft may, but is not obligated to, provide you with support services related to the SOFTWARE PRODUCT ("Support Services"). Use of Support Services is governed by the Microsoft policies and programs described in the user manual, in "online" documentation, and/or in other Microsoft-provided materials. Any supplemental software code provided to you as part of the Support Services shall be considered part of the SOFTWARE PRODUCT and subject to the terms and conditions of this EULA. With respect to technical information you provide to Microsoft as part of the Support Services, Microsoft may use such information for its business purposes, including for product support and development. Microsoft will not utilize such technical information in a form that personally identifies you.

- **Software Transfer.** You may permanently transfer all of your rights under this EULA, provided you retain no copies, you transfer all of the SOFTWARE PRODUCT (including all component parts, the media and printed materials, any upgrades, this EULA, and, if applicable, the Certificate of Authenticity), **and** the recipient agrees to the terms of this EULA.

- **Termination.** Without prejudice to any other rights, Microsoft may terminate this EULA if you fail to comply with the terms and conditions of this EULA. In such event, you must destroy all copies of the SOFTWARE PRODUCT and all of its component parts.

3. **COPYRIGHT.** All title and copyrights in and to the SOFTWARE PRODUCT (including but not limited to any images, photographs, animations, video, audio, music, text, SAMPLE CODE, REDISTRIBUTABLES, and "applets" incorporated into the SOFTWARE PRODUCT) and any copies of the SOFTWARE PRODUCT are owned by Microsoft or its suppliers. The SOFTWARE PRODUCT is protected by copyright laws and international treaty provisions. Therefore, you must treat the SOFTWARE PRODUCT like any other copyrighted material **except** that you may install the SOFTWARE PRODUCT on a single computer provided you keep the original solely for backup or archival purposes. You may not copy the printed materials accompanying the SOFTWARE PRODUCT.

4. **U.S. GOVERNMENT RESTRICTED RIGHTS.** The SOFTWARE PRODUCT and documentation are provided with RESTRICTED RIGHTS. Use, duplication, or disclosure by the Government is subject to restrictions as set forth in subparagraph (c)(1)(ii) of the Rights in Technical Data and Computer Software clause at DFARS 252.227-7013 or subparagraphs (c)(1) and (2) of the Commercial Computer Software—Restricted Rights at 48 CFR 52.227-19, as applicable. Manufacturer is Microsoft Corporation/One Microsoft Way/Redmond, WA 98052-6399.

5. **EXPORT RESTRICTIONS.** You agree that you will not export or re-export the SOFTWARE PRODUCT, any part thereof, or any process or service that is the direct product of the SOFTWARE PRODUCT (the foregoing collectively referred to as the "Restricted Components"), to any country, person, entity, or end user subject to U.S. export restrictions. You specifically agree not to export or re-export any of the Restricted Components (i) to any country to which the U.S. has embargoed or restricted the export of goods or services, which currently include, but are not necessarily limited to, Cuba, Iran, Iraq, Libya, North Korea, Sudan, and Syria, or to any national of any such country, wherever located, who intends to transmit or transport the Restricted Components back to such country; (ii) to any end user who you know or have reason to know will utilize the Restricted Components in the design, development, or production of nuclear, chemical, or biological weapons; or (iii) to any end user who has been prohibited from participating in U.S. export transactions by any federal agency of the U.S. government. You warrant and represent that neither the BXA nor any other U.S. federal agency has suspended, revoked, or denied your export privileges.

DISCLAIMER OF WARRANTY

NO WARRANTIES OR CONDITIONS. MICROSOFT EXPRESSLY DISCLAIMS ANY WARRANTY OR CONDITION FOR THE SOFTWARE PRODUCT. THE SOFTWARE PRODUCT AND ANY RELATED DOCUMENTATION ARE PROVIDED "AS IS" WITHOUT WARRANTY OR CONDITION OF ANY KIND, EITHER EXPRESS OR IMPLIED, INCLUDING, WITHOUT LIMITA-TION, THE IMPLIED WARRANTIES OF MERCHANTABILITY, FITNESS FOR A PARTICULAR PURPOSE, OR NONINFRINGEMENT. THE ENTIRE RISK ARISING OUT OF USE OR PERFORMANCE OF THE SOFTWARE PRODUCT REMAINS WITH YOU.

LIMITATION OF LIABILITY. TO THE MAXIMUM EXTENT PERMITTED BY APPLICABLE LAW, IN NO EVENT SHALL MICROSOFT OR ITS SUPPLIERS BE LIABLE FOR ANY SPECIAL, INCIDENTAL, INDIRECT, OR CONSEQUENTIAL DAM-AGES WHATSOEVER (INCLUDING, WITHOUT LIMITATION, DAMAGES FOR LOSS OF BUSINESS PROFITS, BUSINESS INTERRUPTION, LOSS OF BUSINESS INFORMATION, OR ANY OTHER PECUNIARY LOSS) ARISING OUT OF THE USE OF OR INABILITY TO USE THE SOFTWARE PRODUCT OR THE PROVISION OF OR FAILURE TO PROVIDE SUPPORT SERVICES, EVEN IF MICROSOFT HAS BEEN ADVISED OF THE POSSIBILITY OF SUCH DAMAGES. IN ANY CASE, MICROSOFT'S ENTIRE LIABILITY UNDER ANY PROVISION OF THIS EULA SHALL BE LIMITED TO THE GREATER OF THE AMOUNT ACTUALLY PAID BY YOU FOR THE SOFTWARE PRODUCT OR US$5.00; PROVIDED, HOWEVER, IF YOU HAVE ENTERED INTO A MICROSOFT SUPPORT SERVICES AGREEMENT, MICROSOFT'S ENTIRE LIABILITY REGARDING SUPPORT SERVICES SHALL BE GOVERNED BY THE TERMS OF THAT AGREEMENT. BECAUSE SOME STATES AND JURISDICTIONS DO NOT ALLOW THE EXCLUSION OR LIMITATION OF LIABILITY, THE ABOVE LIMITATION MAY NOT APPLY TO YOU.

MISCELLANEOUS

This EULA is governed by the laws of the State of Washington USA, except and only to the extent that applicable law mandates governing law of a different jurisdiction.

Should you have any questions concerning this EULA, or if you desire to contact Microsoft for any reason, please contact the Microsoft subsidiary serving your country, or write: Microsoft Sales Information Center/One Microsoft Way/Redmond, WA 98052-6399.

System Requirements

To complete the exercises in this book and to use the book's Supplemental Course Materials CD-ROM, you need three networked computers each equipped with the following minimum configuration:

- 128 to 256 megabytes (MB) of RAM

- 2 gigabytes (GB) of available disk space on the drive for Microsoft Exchange 2000 Server

- 500 MB on the system drive

- CD-ROM drive

- Intel Pentium or compatible at 300 megahertz (MHz) or faster

- Microsoft Mouse or compatible pointing device

- Paging file set to twice the amount of RAM or larger

- VGA-compatible display adapter

The following software is required to complete the procedures in this course:

- Microsoft Windows 2000 Server with Service Pack 1

- Microsoft Exchange 2000 Server (120-day Evaluation Edition included on Supplemental Course Materials CD in this kit)

- Microsoft Outlook 2000 (120-day Evaluation Edition included on the Supplemental Course Materials CD in this kit)

- If available, Microsoft Windows NT Server 4.0 with Service Pack 6 and Microsoft Exchange Server 5.5 to follow the optional exercises in Chapter 6

To use the online version of this book from the Supplemental Course Materials CD-ROM, you need a computer additionally equipped with the following:

- 24x CD-ROM drive

- Microsoft Internet Explorer 5.0

Proof of Purchase

0-7356-1028-2

Do not send this card with your registration.
Use this card as proof of purchase if participating in a promotion or
rebate offer on *MCSE Training Kit—Microsoft® Exchange 2000 Server Implementation
and Administration*. Card must be used in conjunction with other proof(s) of payment
such as your dated sales receipt—see offer details.

MCSE Training Kit—Microsoft® Exchange 2000 Server Implementation and Administration

WHERE DID YOU PURCHASE THIS PRODUCT?

CUSTOMER NAME

Microsoft®

mspress.microsoft.com

Microsoft Press, PO Box 97017, Redmond, WA 98073-9830

OWNER REGISTRATION CARD *Register Today!* 0-7356-1028-2

Return the bottom portion of this card to register today.

MCSE Training Kit—Microsoft® Exchange 2000 Server Implementation and Administration

FIRST NAME   **MIDDLE INITIAL**   **LAST NAME**

INSTITUTION OR COMPANY NAME

ADDRESS

CITY   **STATE**   **ZIP**

(   )

E-MAIL ADDRESS   **PHONE NUMBER**

U.S. and Canada addresses only. Fill in information above and mail postage-free.
Please mail only the bottom half of this page.

For information about Microsoft Press®
products, visit our Web site at
mspress.microsoft.com